THE VICTORIA HISTORY
OF THE
COUNTIES OF ENGLAND

———

A HISTORY OF
SHROPSHIRE

VOLUME VIII

THE VICTORIA HISTORY
OF THE
COUNTIES OF ENGLAND

EDITED BY R. B. PUGH

THE UNIVERSITY OF LONDON
INSTITUTE OF
HISTORICAL RESEARCH

Oxford University Press, Ely House, 37 Dover Street, London, W.1

GLASGOW NEW YORK TORONTO MELBOURNE WELLINGTON
BOMBAY CALCUTTA MADRAS KARACHI LAHORE DACCA
CAPE TOWN SALISBURY NAIROBI IBADAN ACCRA
KUALA LUMPUR SINGAPORE HONG KONG TOKYO

© *University of London 1968*

19 722731 7

PRINTED IN GREAT BRITAIN
AT THE UNIVERSITY PRESS, OXFORD
BY VIVIAN RIDLER
PRINTER TO THE UNIVERSITY

INSCRIBED TO THE

MEMORY OF HER LATE MAJESTY

QUEEN VICTORIA

WHO GRACIOUSLY GAVE THE TITLE TO

AND ACCEPTED THE DEDICATION

OF THIS HISTORY

Condover Hall from the North-East

A HISTORY OF
SHROPSHIRE

EDITED BY A. T. GAYDON

VOLUME VIII

PUBLISHED FOR

THE INSTITUTE OF HISTORICAL RESEARCH

BY THE

OXFORD UNIVERSITY PRESS

1968

Distributed by the Oxford University Press until 1 January 1972
thereafter by Dawsons of Pall Mall

CONTENTS OF VOLUME EIGHT

LIST OF ILLUSTRATIONS

Thanks are due to Mr. H. Beaumont and to the Ministry of Defence (Air Force Department) for taking photographs and supplying prints, to Captain R. W. Corbett for allowing the portraits of Sir Richard Corbett and Sir Uvedale Corbett to be photographed in his house, to Mr. T. R. E. Griffiths, Mr. G. A. Lee, and Mr. K. F. Rouse for allowing internal features in their houses to be photographed, and to the Committee for Aerial Photography of the University of Cambridge, Country Life Ltd., Mr. C. R. A. Grant, Mrs. T. Lewis, the National Monuments Record, and Shrewsbury Public Library for permission to reproduce material in their possession and for the loan of prints.

LIST OF ILLUSTRATIONS

LIST OF MAPS

The maps were drawn by K. J. Wass, of the Department of Geography, University College, London, from drafts prepared by A. T. Gaydon; they are based on the Ordnance Survey with the sanction of the Controller of H.M. Stationery Office, Crown Copyright reserved.

EDITORIAL NOTE

VOLUME I of the *Victoria History of Shropshire* was published in 1908. At the time of its publication some progress had been made with compiling two other volumes but they did not come out and the remaining volumes as originally designed were not started. No doubt the First World War put a final stop to all activity on the *History* of Shropshire as of many other counties.

Practical interest was not revived until 1960 when the Shropshire County Council resolved to raise funds to enable a special staff to be appointed to write and organize the completion of the *Shropshire History*. A sub-committee of the County Records Committee was formed in that year to superintend the arrangements. Over this Committee Sir Philip Magnus-Allcroft, Bt., presided until 1967 when he was succeeded by Major General the Viscount Bridgeman, K.B.E., C.B., D.S.O., M.C. Thus was formed another of those partnerships between a group of local patrons and the University of London, of which the prototype is the Wiltshire Victoria County History Committee described in the editorial note to the *Victoria History of Wiltshire*, Volume VII. The essence of such a partnership is that the local patrons undertake to provide money to meet the local expenses of compiling and editing the *History* of their county, and the University agrees to publish what is prepared, provided that it approves the result. The present volume is the first-fruits of this partnership in Shropshire. The generous attitude displayed by the Shropshire County Council is most sincerely appreciated by the University.

In 1960 Mr. A. T. Gaydon was appointed local editor in Shropshire and began work in 1961. Later in the same year he was joined, as assistant editor, by Mr. J. B. Lawson who was succeeded by Mr. M. J. Angold in 1965. In 1967 Mr. D. T. W. Price was appointed Mr. Angold's part-time successor.

Many people have helped in the preparation of this volume. The help of those who were concerned with particular parishes is acknowledged in the footnotes to the accounts of those parishes. Among those whose help has been of a more general kind a special debt of gratitude is due to Mr. H. D. G. Foxall, whose field-name maps, prepared for the use of the Shropshire *History* from tithe apportionments and maps, were an indispensable tool in unravelling the history of the landscape. Thanks are also owed to Miss L. F. Chitty, O.B.E., Miss M. C. Hill, and to Messrs. P. A. Barker, L. C. Lloyd, J. Salmon, and the late Mr. J. L. Hobbs, all of whom read a large part of the text; to the Ven. Archdeacon S. D. Austerberry for making available visitation records of the Archdeaconry of Salop; to the County Education Department for information on primary schools; to the County Surveyor's Department for help with roads and bridges; to Mr. F. W. B. Charles and Mr. J. W. Tonkin for advice on domestic architecture; and to the private householders through whose courtesy it was possible to examine the interiors of numerous smaller houses in the area covered by this volume.

Among the libraries, record offices, and collections public and private whose resources have been drawn upon special mention must be made here of the Shropshire Record Office, the Shropshire County Library, Shrewsbury Public Library, the William Salt Library, Stafford, and the National Library of Wales. The help given by the archivists or librarians of these institutions, and of their respective staffs, is acknowledged with gratitude.

The structure and aims of the *History* as a whole are outlined in an article published in the *Bulletin of the Institute of Historical Research*, Vol. XL (No. 101, May 1967).

LIST OF CLASSES OF DOCUMENTS IN THE PUBLIC RECORD OFFICE

USED IN THIS VOLUME

WITH THEIR CLASS NUMBERS

Chancery

	Proceedings
C 1	Early
C 2	Series I
C 3	Series II
C 47	Miscellanea
C 78	Decree Rolls

	Inquisitions post mortem
C 132	Series I, Hen. III
C 133	Edw. I
C 134	Edw. II
C 135	Edw. III
C 136	Ric. II
C 137	Hen. IV
C 138	Hen. V
C 139	Hen. VI
C 140	Edw. IV & V
C 142	Series II, 2 Hen. VII–Chas. II
C 143	Inquisitions ad quod damnum
C 145	Miscellaneous Inquisitions

Court of Common Pleas

	Feet of Fines
C.P. 25 (1)	Series I
C.P. 25 (2)	Series II
C.P. 40	Plea Rolls
C.P. 43	Recovery Rolls

Ministry of Education

Ed. 7	Public Elementary Schools, Preliminary Statements

Exchequer, Treasury of the Receipt

E 32	Forest Proceedings
E 36	Miscellaneous Books

Exchequer, King's Remembrancer

E 126	Decrees and Orders, Series IV

E 134	Depositions taken by Commission
E 178	Special Commissions of Enquiry
E 179	Subsidy Rolls, &c.

Exchequer, Augmentation Office

E 310	Particulars of Leases
E 315	Miscellaneous Books
E 316	Particulars for Grants of Offices
E 317	Parliamentary Surveys

Exchequer, Lord Treasurer's Remembrancer

E 371	Originalia Rolls

Home Office

H.O. 67	Acreage Returns
H.O. 107	Various, Census Papers, Population Returns
H.O. 129	Various, Census Papers, Ecclesiastical Returns

Justices Itinerant, &c.

J.I. 1	Assize Rolls, Eyre Rolls, &c.

Court of Requests

Req. 2	Proceedings

Special Collections

S.C. 2	Court Rolls
S.C. 6	Ministers' Accounts
S.C. 11	Rentals and Surveys (Rolls)
S.C. 12	Rentals and Surveys (Portfolios)

Court of Star Chamber

	Proceedings
Sta. Cha. 2	Hen. VIII
Sta. Cha. 3	Edw. VI
Sta. Cha. 5	Eliz. I
Sta. Cha. 7	Eliz. I, Addenda
Sta. Cha. 8	Jas. I

SELECT LIST OF COLLECTIONS IN THE
SHROPSHIRE COUNTY RECORD OFFICE
USED IN THIS VOLUME

NOTE ON ABBREVIATIONS

Among the abbreviations and short titles used the following may require elucidation.

All Souls mun.	Muniments of All Souls College, Oxford
Brit. Trans. Rec.	British Transport Historical Records, Paddington
Heref. Dioc. Regy.	Diocesan Registry, Hereford
Heref. City Libr.	Hereford City Library
Lich. Cath. D. & C. mun.	Dean and Chapter muniments, Lichfield Cathedral
Lich. Dioc. Regy.	Diocesan Registry, Lichfield
Longleat MSS.	MSS. at Longleat House, Wiltshire
Loton Hall MSS.	MSS. at Loton Hall, Alberbury
N.L.W.	National Library of Wales, Aberystwyth
N.R.A.	National Register of Archives
S.C.C.	Shropshire County Council
S.P.L.	Shrewsbury Public Library
S.R.O.	Shropshire Record Office
Shrews. Sch.	Shrewsbury School
Staffs. R.O.	Staffordshire Record Office
Visit. Archd. Salop.	Visitations of the Archdeaconry of Salop. penes the Ven. S. D. Austerberry, Great Ness
W.S.L.	William Salt Library, Stafford
Arkwright and Bourne, *Ch. Plate Ludlow Archd.*	Arkwright, D. L., and Bourne, B. W., *The Church Plate of the Archdeaconry of Ludlow. Diocese of Hereford* (Shrewsbury, 1961)
Cranage	Cranage, the Revd. D. H. S., *An Architectural Account of the Churches of Shropshire* (Wellington, 1901–12)
Eyton	Eyton, the Revd. R. W., *Antiquities of Shropshire* (1854–60)
Hearth Tax 1672	Watkins-Pitchford, W. (ed.), *The Shropshire Hearth-Tax Roll of 1672* (Shrewsbury, 1949)
Instit. Dioc. Heref.	Bannister, A.T. (ed.), *Diocese of Hereford. Institutions, etc. (A.D. 1539–1900)*, (Hereford, 1923)
Leland, *Itin.* ed. Toulmin Smith	Toulmin Smith, Lucy (ed.), *Itinerary of John Leland*
Montg. Collect.	*The Montgomeryshire Collections: The Transactions of the Powys-land Club*
Pevsner, *Shropshire*	Pevsner, Nikolaus, *The Buildings of England: Shropshire* (1958)
Plymley, *Agric. Salop.*	Plymley, Joseph, *General View of the Agriculture of Shropshire* (1813)
Salop. N. & Q.	*Shropshire Notes & Queries*
Salop. Char. for Elem. Educ.	*Shropshire Charities for Elementary Education* (Shrewsbury, [1906])
Salop. Mag.	*The Shropshire Magazine*
Salop. Par. Docs.	*Shropshire Parish Documents* (Shrewsbury, n.d.)
Salop. Peace Roll, 1404–14	Kimball, Elisabeth G. (ed.), *The Shropshire Peace Roll, 1404–14* (Shrewsbury, 1959)
S.H.C.	Staffordshire Record Society (formerly William Salt Archaeological Society), *Collections for a History of Staffordshire*
S.P.R. Heref.	*Shropshire Parish Registers, Diocese of Hereford*
S.P.R. Lich.	*Shropshire Parish Registers, Diocese of Lichfield*
S.P.R. (Roman Catholic registers)	*Shropshire Parish Registers, Roman Catholic registers*
T.S.A.S.	*Transactions of the Shropshire Archaeological Society*
Walters, *Ch. Bells Salop.*	Walters, H. B., *The Church Bells of Shropshire* (Oswestry, 1915)

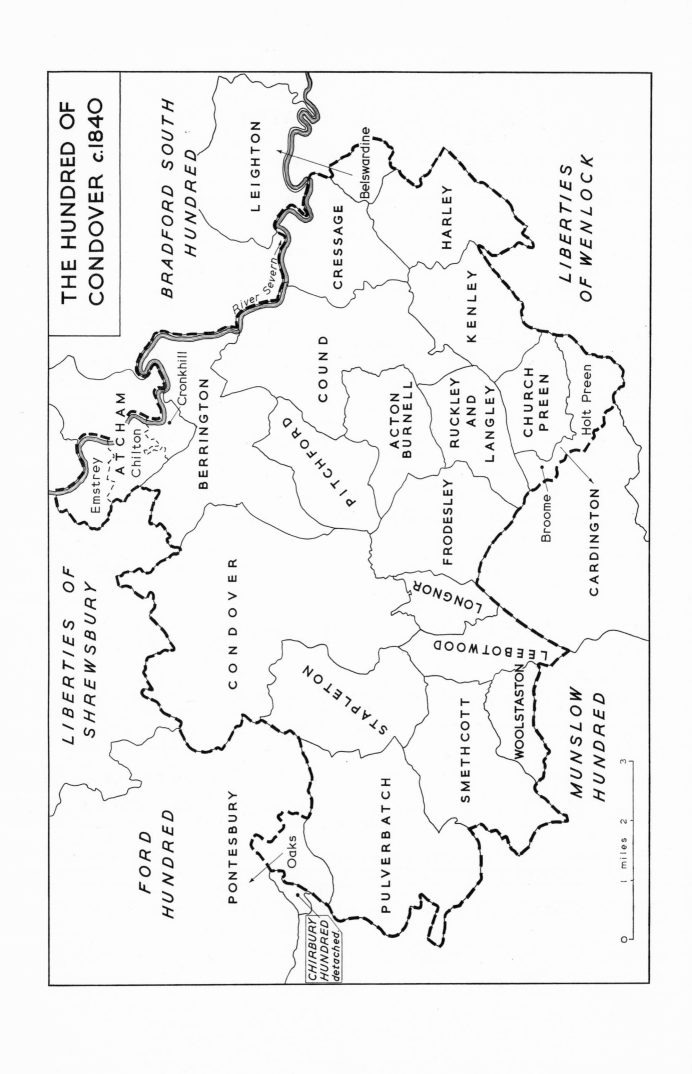

THE HUNDRED OF
CONDOVER c.1840

BRADFORD SOUTH
HUNDRED

LEIGHTON

Belswardine

CRESSAGE

HARLEY

River Severn

LIBERTIES
OF WENLOCK

KENLEY

COUND

Cronkhill

BERRINGTON

PITCHFORD

ACTON
BURNELL

RUCKLEY
AND
LANGLEY

CHURCH
PREEN

Holt Preen

Emstrey

ATCHAM

Chilton

FRODESLEY

Broome

CARDINGTON

LIBERTIES OF
SHREWSBURY

CONDOVER

LONGNOR

LEEBOTWOOD

FORD
HUNDRED

PONTESBURY

Oaks

STAPLETON

SMETHCOTT

WOOLSTASTON

MUNSLOW
HUNDRED

PULVERBATCH

CHIRBURY
HUNDRED
detached

0   1   miles   2   3

CONDOVER HUNDRED

THE Hundred of Condover lies to the south-east of Shrewsbury and is bounded on the north by the River Severn. The northern parishes have an undulating landscape, largely made up of boulder clay and ridges of sand and gravel, but in the south the hundred includes part of Hoar Edge and the northern slopes of the Long Mynd. Settlement has always been most dense along the valley of the River Cound, a tributary of the Severn, which flows northwards through the centre of the hundred. As in other parts of the county, however, the pattern of settlement has been considerably modified since the earlier Middle Ages, chiefly as a consequence of woodland clearance. Of the 61 hamlets which appear to have existed in the hundred at the time of Domesday Book, 8 have since been deserted and 31 have shrunk to one or two farms apiece. The district has always been predominantly agricultural; mixed farming is general in the northern lowlands, but there is rather more emphasis on dairying and stock-rearing on the smaller farms of the hill country to the south. Iron forges and furnaces are recorded from the later 16th century in 5 parishes within the hundred and there is evidence of small-scale coal-mining in parishes to the north and west, but all such industrial activity has long ceased.

The hundred was known by the same name in 1086[1] and was comparatively little affected by the reorganization of the Shropshire hundreds carried out some time before 1158.[2] Ratlinghope manor and the hamlet of Overs in Ratlinghope parish were probably transferred to Purslow Hundred at this time.[3] Womerton, which lay in Condover Hundred in 1086,[4] was subsequently, as a member of Church Stretton manor, accounted part of Munslow Hundred.[5] Four more manors were detached from the hundred later in the 12th century. Lydley in Cardington parish was acquired by the Templars c. 1155–60[6] and after the suppression of that order the manor was accounted, like Cardington, a member of Munslow Hundred.[7] Hughley and Wigwig, held by Wenlock Priory, were annexed to the Liberties of Wenlock when that franchise was established c. 1198.[8] The tenants of Wigwig were, however, still held liable to suit at the sheriff's tourn in the later 13th century.[9] Buildwas, which had been withdrawn by the end of the 12th century when quittance of suit at the hundred court was among the privileges accorded by Richard I to Buildwas Abbey, was annexed to the Hundred of Bradford South after the Dissolution.[10]

Sheinton was a member of Condover Hundred in 1255[11] but its suit had been withdrawn by 1272.[12] The jurors of Condover Hundred alleged in 1273–4 that Richard, Earl of Cornwall, as lord of the barony of Castle Holgate, had been responsible for this change.[13] It is, however, more probable that this manor was detached from the hundred by Roger Mortimer, whose manors of Cleobury Mortimer and Chelmarsh were exempted from suit at hundred courts in 1266 and who seems to have extended this franchise to other parts of his Shropshire estate.[14] Sheinton was later accounted, like

[1] V.C.H. Salop. i. 311.
[2] Eyton, i. 23; ibid. iv. 242.
[3] Ibid. vi. 4–5, 158–62.
[4] V.C.H. Salop. i. 326.
[5] Eyton, vi. 158.
[6] Ibid. 4, 238–9.
[7] Ibid. 4.
[8] Ibid. iii. 237–8; Cal. Chart. R. 1327–41, 129.
[9] Rot. Hund. (Rec. Com.), ii. 91.
[10] Eyton, vi. 330–1.
[11] Rot. Hund. (Rec. Com.), ii. 62.
[12] J.I. 1/736 m. 32.
[13] Rot. Hund. (Rec. Com.), ii. 91.
[14] Eyton, iii. 40; ibid. iv. 221–3; ibid. vi. 5; Cal. Chart. R. 1257–1300, 61.

Cleobury Mortimer, a member of Stottesden Hundred,[15] but it was restored to Condover Hundred in the mid-19th century.[16] Mortimer seems also to have detached Edgbold and one of the two manors of Pulley from the hundred by the same means,[17] but these manors, together with Welbatch and the second manor of Pulley, were accounted part of the Liberties of Shrewsbury by 1515.[18] The hamlets of Betton Strange and Alkmere were said to have been withdrawn from the hundred by John le Strange (III) in the mid-13th century.[19] This franchise was quashed in 1292[20] and Betton Strange was assessed with Condover Hundred to the taxation of 1327,[21] but by the early 16th century it was accounted part of the Liberties of Shrewsbury.[22]

In 1255 nine other manors were said to have withdrawn their suit from the Condover hundred court.[23] Richard, Earl of Cornwall, appears to have annexed the suit of Church Preen, Holt Preen, and Belswardine to his lordship of Castle Holgate c. 1256.[24] Inhabitants of Church Preen owed suit at Castle Holgate until the 19th century,[25] but these three manors were always accounted part of Condover Hundred for taxation purposes.[26] Acton Burnell and Acton Pigott did no suit at the hundred court while they were held by Robert Burnell,[27] but this privilege does not appear to have been claimed by Robert's successors. Chilton, Cronkhill, and Emstrey in Atcham, Broome in Cardington, and Oaks in Pontesbury lay in parishes outside the hundred, but were accounted members of Condover Hundred for taxation purposes until the later 17th century.[28]

Before the Conquest two-thirds of the profits of the hundred were held by King Edward, the 'third penny' presumably being a perquisite of the Earl of Mercia.[29] All the profits were held by Roger, Earl of Shrewsbury, in 1086,[30] but the hundred was retained by the Crown after the forfeiture of Robert of Bellême in 1102[31] and remained a royal hundred until 1672.[32] Hugh de Longslow was hundred bailiff in 1256,[33] William de Munslow in 1272,[34] and Roger de Frodesley in 1292.[35] In 1317 the bailiwick was granted by the Crown to Richard de Ashwell,[36] but no later bailiffs of the hundred are recorded. Ursula, widow of Roger Owen of Condover, may have held the bailiwick in 1618, when the steward of the hundred court was her bailiff Henry Haynes,[37] and in 1653 the office of bailiff was said to have been held time out of mind by 'divers gentlemen of the . . . county'.[38] Richard Salter of Shrewsbury obtained a 31-year lease of the bailiwick in 1661[39] but in 1672 the hundred was granted to Francis, Lord Newport.[40] Its subsequent descent has not been established.

The manor of Condover was said to be no part of the hundred in 1255[41] and throughout the 13th century it exercised its right to make a separate presentment at the eyre.[42] Other franchises within the hundred do not appear to have been of much account. In 1292 the lord of Pulverbatch manor was said to hold pleas of the crown.[43] The lords of Acton Burnell, Cound, and Cressage manors then claimed the assize of bread and ale and there was said to be a manorial gallows in the last-named manor.[44]

[15] Feud. Aids, iv. 232.
[16] Eyton, vi. 5–6.
[17] Ibid. vi. 5–6, 212, 214.
[18] T.S.A.S. 2nd ser. ii. 73.
[19] J.I. 1/739 m. 74d.
[20] Ibid.
[21] T.S.A.S. 2nd ser. xi. 386.
[22] Ibid. ii. 73.
[23] Rot. Hund. (Rec. Com.), ii. 62–63.
[24] Ibid. 91; J.I. 1/736 m. 32d.
[25] S.P.L., Deeds 6232, 10194; A. Sparrow, The History of Church Preen (1898), 32.
[26] See, e.g., T.S.A.S. 2nd ser. xi. 378, 389; Hearth Tax, 1672, 130, 132, 133; E 179/167/204; E 179/167/210.
[27] J.I. 1/736 m. 32; J.I. 1/739 m. 74d.
[28] Hearth Tax, 1672, 131, 132, 133, 135. The history of these townships is reserved for treatment in a later volume.

[29] V.C.H. Salop. i. 315.
[30] Ibid.
[31] Eyton, i. 242; ibid. vi. 6.
[32] Cal. S.P. Dom. 1671–2, 420.
[33] J.I. 1/734 m. 32.
[34] J.I. 1/736 m. 24.
[35] J.I. 1/739 m. 46.
[36] Cal. Fine R. 1307–19, 337.
[37] B.M. Add. Roll 74148.
[38] E 317/Salop./2.
[39] E 134/4 Anne Mich./41.
[40] Cal. S.P. Dom. 1671–2, 420.
[41] Rot. Hund. (Rec. Com.), ii. 64.
[42] J.I. 1/733(a) m. 9d.; J.I. 1/734 mm. 29d., 32; J.I. 1/736 m. 24; J.I. 1/739 mm. 46, 86.
[43] Plac. de Quo Warr. (Rec. Com.), 680.
[44] J.I. 1/739 m. 74d.

In 1255, when dues known as 'stretward' and 'motfee' were paid by 21 manors at a combined rate of 8*d.* a hide, the sheriff was said to receive 12 marks a year from the hundred.[45] Its value had fallen to 7 marks by 1272[46] and it was said to be worth 6 marks a year in 1273–4[47] and 1292.[48] No later evidence for the value of the hundred has been found, but viscontiel rents totalling 3*s.* were due from the townships of Betton Strange and Belswardine in the mid-17th century.[49]

Only one hundred court roll, that of April 1618,[50] has been traced. A wide range of presentments was being dealt with at this time; business before the court included 30 affrays, 28 breaches of the assize of bread and ale, 13 presentments of inclosure of commons, and 14 of failure to repair hedges or gates. A 'parvise', or preliminary meeting held in each parish to discuss presentments to the hundred court, seems to have been normal at this time, for inhabitants of Pitchford and Harley were fined for not attending such meetings.[51] A 'parvise' was still being held in the 18th century at Longnor,[52] whose churchwardens continued to make a charge for summoning it until 1815.[53] A building known as the 'Hundred House' is recorded at Condover in 1609,[54] but the court of 1618 was held at Leebotwood and it is probable that by this date the court had no regular meeting-place.

ACTON BURNELL

Acton Burnell, notable as the meeting-place of the Parliament of 1283, lies 8 miles south of Shrewsbury. The parish contains 1,656 a.[1] and includes the townships of Acton Burnell and Acton Pigott, the squatter settlement of Evenwood, and the site of the deserted hamlet of Allcott. Acton Pigott, originally a chapelry of Cound, was adjudged to be a township of Acton Burnell in 1655.[2] The civil parish of Ruckley and Langley has been a chapelry of Acton Burnell since 1572, but was originally a separate parish. Its history is given in a later article.[3]

Bullhill Brook forms the eastern boundary of the parish and on the south the boundary runs along the crest of Acton Burnell Hill. The northern boundary follows no natural features until it meets a tributary of Bullhill Brook, south of Golding. On the west the boundary follows Lynall Brook[4] for some distance, but to the west of Acton Burnell village it projects westwards, crossing Watling Street. Apart from a small tributary of Bullhill Brook rising in the Park, no other streams run through the parish. Acton Burnell Hill, the most prominent feature of the landscape, is an outlier of Hoar Edge and extends

across the south of the parish, rising to 775 feet. The north of the parish is covered by boulder clay, but Acton Pigott stands on one of several small deposits of sand and gravel.

Woodland has been an enduring feature of the parish landscape, most of it lying on Acton Burnell Hill, part of which was known as 'Cumbes Wood' in 1270.[5] Woodland on its southern slopes, now known as Shadwell Coppice, was regularly cut to supply charcoal for the ironworks of the mid-Severn during the late 17th and early 18th centuries.[6] To the west of the hill a wood called The Shoots adjoined Hobsley Coppice in Frodesley in 1551.[7] Ottley's Hays, on the parish boundary to the west of Watling Street, was woodland in the late 17th century,[8] but had been cleared by 1805.[9] There were only 101 a. of woodland in the parish at this date.[10]

Acton Burnell lay within the Long Forest,[11] but Robert Burnell was granted free warren here in 1281.[12] He imparked 40 a. from 'Cumbes Wood' in 1270,[13] and a further 60 a. was added in 1280.[14] A deer-leap was made in 1283[15] and there were three of them by 1290.[16] The south side of the Park had

45 *Rot. Hund.* (Rec. Com.), ii. 62–64.
46 J.I. 1/736 m. 32.
47 *Rot. Hund.* (Rec. Com.), ii. 91.
48 J.I. 1/739 m. 74d.
49 E 317/Salop./2.
50 B.M. Add. Roll 74148.　　　　　　51 Ibid.
52 S.R.O. 567 uncat., presentment, 1757, and papers *re* Longnor parish boundary, *c.* 1770.
53 Longnor par. rec., churchwardens' accts. 1761–1898.
54 Condover par. rec., churchwardens' accts. 1604–27.

1 O.S. *Area Bk.* (1882). The following topographical description is based, except where otherwise stated, on O.S. Maps 6″ Salop. 49, 50 (1st and later edns.); O.S. Map 1/25,000, SJ 50 (1959); Rocque, *Map of Salop.* (1752); Baugh, *Map of Salop.* (1808); Greenwood, *Map of Salop.* (1827); B.M., O.S. 2″ orig. drawings, sheet 207 (1817); Geol. Survey Map (drift), sheet 152 (1932); Heref. Dioc. Regy., tithe appt. and map, 1845. This article was written

in 1963 and revised in 1965. It makes use of an 18th-century transcript of the muniments of the Smythe family of Acton Burnell (S.P.L., MS.2). The muniments themselves, now S.R.O. 1514, were discovered after the final revision of this article.
2 *Q. Sess. Orders,* i. 22.
3 See p. 141.
4 So named in Lich. Dioc. Regy., glebe terrier, 1612.
5 *Cal. Pat.* 1266–72, 422.
6 E 134/4 Anne East./6.
7 Barnard MSS., Raby Castle, box 2, bdle. 1, no. 1.
8 E 134/4 Anne East./6.
9 S.P.L., MS. 294.
10 Ibid.
11 Eyton, vi. 336–42.
12 *Cal. Close,* 1279–88, 248.
13 *Cal. Pat.* 1266–72, 422.
14 Ibid. 1272–81, 357.
15 Ibid. 1281–92, 108.
16 Ibid. 245.

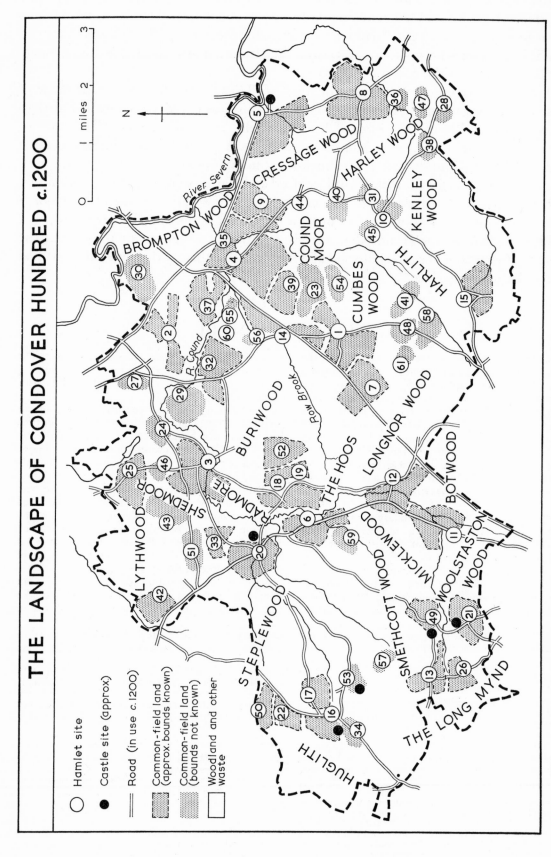

THE LANDSCAPE OF CONDOVER HUNDRED c.1200

Legend:

○ Hamlet site
● Castle site (approx.)
═ Road (in use c.1200)
▨ Common-field land (approx. bounds known)
▧ Common-field land (bounds not known)
□ Woodland and other waste

This map is based on the topographical evidence discussed in the text. The common-field area, where known, is that of the later Middle Ages. It was smaller *c.* 1200, when some hamlets were using the infield-outfield system, and in these and other hamlets the common fields were subsequently enlarged by assarting. For key to hamlets see facing page.

been enclosed with a wall by 1379.[17] In 1805 the Park contained 248 a. and then included the whole of Acton Burnell Hill, except the coppices to the south.[18] After the Hall was enlarged in 1814[19] the Park was extended northwards and in 1845 was bounded by the road to Acton Pigott.[20] Shadwell Pool and Black Dick's Pool, which are not natural formations, are probably the fish-ponds recorded in 1292.[21] In the mid-18th century a grotto, lined with shells and tiles, was constructed on the hill to the south of the Hall.[22] The Lodge, a folly in Gothic style above Black Dick's Pool, dates from the same period.[23] The Gothic exterior of the West Lodge, a timber-framed house near the church, was removed in 1962.

A small common to the east of the Ruckley road, near Hollies Coppice, was inclosed and added to the Park c. 1759.[24] Evenwood Common, a continuation of Cound Moor, lay to the south-east of Acton Pigott, along the eastern boundary of the parish. It contained 38 a. in 1805[25] and was inclosed in 1820, when part was divided into small-holdings.[26]

The former common fields of Acton Burnell were called the Field towards Acton Pigott, the Field towards Frodesley, and The Shoots Field.[27] The latter lay between the Park and Lynall Brook, south of the village. Part of the common fields had been inclosed by 1612[28] and further inclosures were made in 1622.[29] The remainder had been inclosed by 1685.[30] At Acton Pigott the common fields were called the Field towards Acton Burnell, the Field towards Golding (or Cross Field), and Evenwood

Field.[31] Common-field holdings here are last recorded in 1657[32] and the township was wholly inclosed by 1685.[33]

Watling Street ran north-eastwards across the parish, west of Acton Burnell village, crossing Lynall Brook at Radnor bridge, where the abutments of a Roman and a later bridge have been found.[34] The road still followed its ancient course when it was turnpiked in 1764,[35] but had become a country lane by 1808[36] and has long been disused.

There is reason to think that, before the formation of the Park and the building of the Castle in the later 13th century, Acton Burnell village lay to the west of Lynall Brook, nearer to the original line of Watling Street. This would explain the westward projection of the parish boundary at this point. A square moated site near the west bank of the brook, to the south of the Frodesley road,[37] was levelled, 1963–4, when framed timbers forming the base of a bridge and 13th-century pottery were found in the moat.[38] To the west of the moat the road turns southwards, round a field called Townend in 1845.[39] At the north-west corner of Townend Field a small and irregularly shaped field called Little Meadow[40] seems out of place in a part of the parish which was formerly common-field land, and may mark the site of the original hamlet. Additional evidence of early settlement in this area is a D-shaped double-ditched enclosure some 300 yards north-west of Little Meadow, revealed by air photography in 1962.[41] Fields nearby called Old Mills, on Lynall Brook

[17] S.P.L., MS. 2, f. 13.   [18] Ibid. MS. 294.
[19] S.R.O. 1514/2/1222.
[20] Heref. Dioc. Regy., tithe appt.
[21] C 133/63/32.
[22] Pevsner, op. cit. 51.
[23] Print of Castle, 1805, penes Mr. S. Morley Tonkin.
[24] Lich. Dioc. Regy., glebe terrier, 1763.
[25] S.P.L., MS. 294.
[26] Pitchford Hall MSS., Pitchford Hall, accts. of inclosure, 1820.
[27] Lich. Dioc. Regy., glebe terrier, 1612.
[28] Ibid.
[29] N.L.W., Pitchford Hall 2434.

[30] Lich. Dioc. Regy., glebe terrier, 1685.
[31] Ibid. 1612.
[32] N.L.W., Pitchford Hall 1029.
[33] Lich. Dioc. Regy., glebe terrier, 1685.
[34] T.S.A.S. lv. 38–50.
[35] Watling St. road Act, 4 Geo. III, c. 70 (priv. act).
[36] Baugh, Map of Salop. (1808).
[37] O.S. Nat. Grid SJ 528022.
[38] Shropshire Newsletter, Jan. 1964.
[39] Heref. Dioc. Regy., tithe appt.
[40] Ibid.
[41] O.S. Nat. Grid SJ 523024. Air photographs penes Mr. Arnold Baker and Mr. P. A. Barker.

THE LANDSCAPE OF CONDOVER HUNDRED, c. 1200

KEY TO HAMLETS

A. SURVIVING HAMLETS

1. Acton Burnell	7. Frodesley	13. Picklescott	19. Ryton, Little
2. Berrington	8. Harley	14. Pitchford	20. Stapleton
3. Condover	9. Harnage	15. Preen, Church	21. Woolstaston
4. Cound, Upper	10. Kenley	16. Pulverbatch, Castle	22. Wrentnall
5. Cressage	11. Leebotwood	17. Pulverbatch, Church	
6. Dorrington	12. Longnor	18. Ryton, Great	

B. HAMLETS SHRUNKEN AFTER c. 1200

23. Acton Pigott	31. Broomcroft	39. Golding	47. Rowley
24. Allfield	32. Cantlop	40. Harnage Grange	48. Ruckley
25. Bayston	33. Chatford	41. Langley	49. Smethcott
26. Betchcott	34. Cothercott	42. Lyth, Great	50. Walleybourne
27. Betton Abbots	35. Cound, Lower	43. Lyth, Little	51. Westley
28. Blakeway	36. Domas	44. Morton	52. Wheathall
29. Boreton	37. Eaton Mascott	45. Newbold	53. Wilderley
30. Brompton	38. Gippols	46. Norton	

C. HAMLETS DESERTED AFTER c. 1200

54. Allcott	56. Eton, Little	58. Hothales	60. Newton
55. 'La Beche'	57. Hollicot	59. Netley	61. Ramshurst

NOTE. The sites of the former hamlets of Broome and 'Old Town' in Condover parish are not marked.

north-west of Watling Street, record the site of a mill which had ceased to exist by 1612.[42]

In the present village, which stands at the cross-roads east of Lynall Brook, the pattern of settlement appears to have changed little since the 17th century. Apart from 10 Council houses built on the Pitchford road since 1919,[43] the existing houses are nearly all in origin 17th-century timber-framed farm-houses or 18th-century stone cottages. The addition of 'rustic' features in the 19th century has, however, given Acton Burnell the appearance of a model village. In most cases this was achieved by rough-casting and by the application of rectangular hood-moulds above doors and windows. Acton Burnell Farm and Home Farm, the only remaining farm-houses in the village, are timber-framed, but both have been cased in brick.

The ruins of Acton Burnell castle, built in the 1280s,[44] the church, which dates from the same period,[45] and the Hall[46] stand together at the east end of the village. The road running eastwards from the cross-roads now ends at the entrance to the Hall. It formerly continued towards Acton Pigott, but the section running in front of the Hall was closed in 1815, when the Park was extended northwards and a new road to Acton Pigott was laid out to the north of the village.[47] A drive, which in the 19th century ran northwards from the Hall towards Pitchford and passed by a culvert under the present road to Acton Pigott, followed the course of an ancient road from Pitchford to Kenley, which was called Salter's Way in 1625.[48]

The rectory, together with the residence of the lord of the manor and the Village Hall, formerly a Roman Catholic school,[49] are among the houses which stand on the south of the road between the cross-roads and the Hall. With the exception of the Village Hall and the converted outbuildings of the rectory they are all basically timber-framed. Settlement is denser on the road running west from the cross-roads, where the houses stand on both sides. On the north side a brick-cased house at the cross-roads was until the early 19th century the village smithy,[50] but the business had been transferred to the former poor-house, near Lynall Brook, by 1845.[51] The adjoining house, now the village shop, was until the 1870s the Stag's Head Inn.[52] The inn is first so named in 1823,[53] but probably occupies the site of the two alehouses recorded in the early 17th century.[54] A row of cottages opposite incorporates a 17th-century timber-framed house with a central chimney stack. The school, built in 1815,[55] stands on the south of the road at the west end of the village. The mill, which stood on Lynall Brook near the

school, went out of use soon after 1856.[56] Few old houses stand on the roads running north and south of the cross-roads. Home Farm and two 19th-century stone cottages are the only houses on the Ruckley road. On the Pitchford road are three scattered timber-framed houses and two groups of 18th-century stone cottages, but the council estate and a number of other houses have been built here in the past 50 years.

Acton Pigott, one mile north-east of Acton Burnell, now consists of a farm-house and two groups of cottages. Like its near neighbour Golding, it was once a larger hamlet. In the early Middle Ages Acton Pigott was sufficiently populous to have its own chapel, and until the 15th century its own priest.[57] There is no evidence for its size in medieval times. Five houses in Acton Pigott lay in the manorial estate in 1597.[58] There were said to be ten houses here in 1672,[59] but this, like later figures derived from surveys of the manorial estate, includes houses at Evenwood, which lay within the township boundary. There were 3 farms at Acton Pigott in 1717[60] and 1782,[61] together with 5 or 6 cottages, but by 1805 it had shrunk to its present size.[62] Acton Pigott Farm may be in origin a 17th-century timber-framed house, but if so, it was completely encased in brick in the 19th century when the east and west ends were extended. The chapel stood by the roadside to the west of the farm: all traces of it have now disappeared. One group of cottages is of 19th-century date. The other group, formerly Glebe Farm, is a complex timber-framed structure, the oldest part of which probably dates from the 16th century. It stands on the site of the medieval parsonage[63] and was said to be a bawdy-house and an alehouse in 1638.[64]

The hamlet of Allcott lay within the manor of Acton Pigott in the 13th century,[65] but is not later recorded. Its site has not been established, but it may have stood near Evenwood, where a quantity of medieval pottery was found c. 1906.[66]

The squatter settlement at Evenwood, along Bull-hill Brook at the northern end of Evenwood Common, is first recorded in the early 18th century,[67] but some of the cottages are timber-framed and of 17th-century date. There appear to have been 5 families at Evenwood in the first quarter of the 18th century[68] and there were 6 cottages there in 1805.[69] Evenwood Farm, on the east of the Common, was already in existence by 1660,[70] but the present house was built in stone in Gothic style in the mid-19th century.

There were said to be 32 households in the parish in 1603[71] and 144 adults in 1676.[72] The population

[42] Lich. Dioc. Regy., glebe terrier, 1612.
[43] Ex inf. Atcham R.D.C.
[44] See p. 8.
[45] See p. 11.
[46] See p. 8.
[47] Q. Sess. rolls, East. 1815.
[48] N.L.W., Pitchford Hall 1179.
[49] See p. 13.
[50] Q. Sess. rolls, East. 1815.
[51] Heref. Dioc. Regy., tithe appt.
[52] Kelly's Dir. Salop. (1856).
[53] Q. Sess. alehouse reg.   [54] Ibid.
[55] Nat. Soc. Annual rep. 1816.
[56] Kelly's Dir. Salop. (1856).
[57] See p. 12.
[58] S.R.O. 1037 uncat., apportionment of dower of Mary Crompton, 1597.

[59] Hearth Tax, 1672, 133.
[60] Q. Sess., reg. papists' estates, 1717.
[61] Ibid. 1782.
[62] S.P.L., MS. 294.
[63] Lich. Dioc. Regy., glebe terrier, 1612.
[64] Ibid. B/v 1/62.
[65] S.P.L., MS. 2, f. 11; Cal. Chart. R. 1257–1300, 132; Eyton, vi. 95.
[66] T.S.A.S. 3rd ser. vi, pp. xx–xxi; ibid. vii, p. ix.
[67] Q. Sess., reg. papists' estates, 1717; S.P.R. Lich. xix (5), 83.
[68] S.P.R. Lich. xix (5), 83–113.
[69] S.P.L., MS. 294.
[70] Q. Sess., reg. papists' estates, 1717.
[71] B.M. Harl. MS. 594, f. 161.
[72] T.S.A.S. 2nd ser. i. 79.

was 272 in 1801[73] and seems to have increased steadily until 1851, when there were 330 inhabitants.[74] It has since declined, reaching 218, its lowest figure, in 1931.[75] There were 300 inhabitants in 1961.[76]

MANORS. Roger, Earl of Shrewsbury, was overlord of *ACTON BURNELL* manor in 1086.[77] By 1242 the manor was held of the barony of Corbet of Caus,[78] and continued to be held of their heirs until the forfeiture of Francis, Lord Lovell, in 1485.[79] After this date the manor was held of the Crown in chief.[80]

The freeman Godric held the manor before 1066, and in 1086 one Roger was tenant.[81] Thomas Burnell held it in the later 12th century,[82] but between 1189 and 1195 his relative Warin Burnell was awarded a moiety of the manor.[83] On the death of Thomas Burnell in 1195, he was succeeded by his brother William[84] and this moiety of the manor passed from father to son until 1249, the following being lords: William, 1195–*c.* 1220;[85] William, *c.* 1220–47;[86] William, 1247–9.[87] William Burnell was outlawed for murder in 1249 and forfeited his estates to the Crown.[88] The moiety presumably reverted *c.* 1250 to Thomas Corbet as overlord.[89] He seems to have resided at Acton Burnell in 1262,[90] and was sued for disseisin by a tenant there in 1267.[91] Hugh de Beckbury, who was said to hold this moiety in 1255, was probably only his bailiff.[92] The moiety which Warin Burnell had acquired before 1195 had passed to his son Hugh by *c.* 1200.[93] Hugh died before 1238, when he had been succeeded by his son Warin,[94] who held the moiety in 1242.[95] Roger Burnell, possibly the son of Warin, held it in 1249[96] and 1255,[97] and is last recorded in 1259.[98]

Robert Burnell, later Bishop of Bath and Wells, had some interest in the manor by 1265,[99] and by 1269 held the whole manor.[1] He may have been a relative of Roger Burnell, thus acquiring one moiety of the manor by inheritance, and probably purchased the other moiety from Thomas Corbet, with whom he was serving in Wales in 1263.[2] On

Robert Burnell's death in 1292[3] the manor passed to his nephew Philip Burnell, who died in 1294,[4] leaving his estates heavily mortgaged to Italian merchants.[5] Malcoline de Harley was granted custody of the manor in 1295, during the minority of Philip's son Edward,[6] but had been succeeded by Walter de Beauchamp by 1301.[7] Edward Burnell obtained livery of the manor in 1307[8] and at his death in 1315 it was assigned in dower to his widow Aline.[9] In the following year she conveyed her estate to Edward Burnell's sister and heir Maud and the latter's second husband John de Haudlo.[10] The manor was settled on their son Nicholas de Haudlo in 1340, with reversion to the right heirs of Maud.[11] On the death of John de Haudlo in 1346 the manor passed to Nicholas, who had by then taken the name of Burnell.[12] Nicholas Burnell died in 1383[13] and was succeeded by his son Hugh, who held the manor until his death in 1420.[14] It then passed to Katherine, grand-daughter of Hugh Burnell, on whom it had been settled in 1416.[15] She was betrothed to John Talbot, who did fealty for the manor in 1421,[16] but the marriage seems not to have taken place. By 1428 Katherine had married Sir John Radcliffe,[17] who was then holding the manor.[18] He died in 1441[19] and after the death of his widow in 1452[20] the manor reverted to William, Lord Lovell, as right heir of Maud de Haudlo by her first husband John, Lord Lovell of Titchmarsh.[21] It descended from father to son until 1485, the following being lords: William, 1452–5; John, 1455–65; Francis, 1465–85.[22]

On the attainder of Francis, Lord Lovell, in 1485 the manor was forfeited to the Crown,[23] but in the following year was granted to Jasper, Duke of Bedford,[24] who held it until his death in 1495.[25] By 1498 it was among the estates of Henry, Duke of York,[26] on whose accession as Henry VIII it remained in the hands of the Crown until 1514, when it was granted to Thomas Howard, Duke of Norfolk.[27] The latter was succeeded in 1524 by his son Thomas,[28] who sold the manor to Sir John Dudley in 1533.[29] Dudley sold it in 1542 to Fulk Crompton of Cound.[30] The manor remained in the Crompton family[31] until

73 *Census,* 1801.
74 Ibid. 1811–51.
75 Ibid. 1931.
76 Ibid. 1961.
77 *V.C.H. Salop.* i. 324.
78 *Bk. of Fees,* ii. 964.
79 *Close R.* 1268–72, 513; C 133/63/32; C 133/68/10; *Cal. Inq. p.m.* ix, p. 35; *Feud. Aids,* iv. 265.
80 *Cal. Pat.* 1485–94, 64; C 142/177/189.
81 *V.C.H. Salop.* i. 324.
82 Eyton, vi. 122.
83 Ibid. cf. *Pipe R.* 1182 (P.R.S. xxxi), 23; ibid. 1183 (P.R.S. xxxii), 2.
84 *Pipe R.* 1195 (P.R.S. N.S. vi), 246.
85 Eyton, vi. 123.
86 Ibid. 124.
87 *Cal. Inq. Misc.* i, p. 19.
88 Ibid.
89 Eyton, vi. 125–6.
90 Ibid. 126.
91 Ibid.
92 Ibid. 125; *Rot. Hund.* (Rec. Com.), ii. 62.
93 Eyton, vi. 123.
94 Ibid. 124.
95 *Bk. of Fees,* ii. 964.
96 Eyton, vi. 125.
97 *Rot. Hund.* (Rec. Com.), ii. 62.
98 Eyton, vi. 126.
99 *Close R.* 1264–8, 55–56.
1 *Cal. Chart. R.* 1257–1300, 132.
2 Eyton, vi. 127.

3 *Cal. Inq. p.m.* iii, p. 50.
4 Ibid. p. 121.
5 *Cal. Inq. Misc.* i, pp. 469–70.
6 *Cal. Pat.* 1292–1301, 130.
7 *Cal. Inq. p.m.* iii, p. 444.
8 *Complete Peerage,* ii. 434.
9 C 134/48/9; *Cal. Close,* 1313–18, 263–4.
10 *Sir Christopher Hatton's Bk. of Seals,* ed. L. C. Loyd and D. M. Stenton (Oxford, 1950), 245; *Cal. Pat.* 1313–17, 554.
11 *Cal. Inq. p.m.* viii, p. 496.
12 *Cal. Close,* 1346–9, 111.
13 *Complete Peerage,* ii. 435.
14 Ibid.
15 *Cat. Anct. D.* ii, C 2398.
16 *Cal. Close,* 1419–22, 154.
17 *Feud. Aids,* iv. 257.
18 Ibid.
19 *Complete Peerage,* v. 484.
20 Ibid. 485.
21 Ibid. viii. 222 n.
22 Ibid. 222–5.
23 Ibid. 225.
24 *Cal. Pat.* 1485–94, 64.
25 *Complete Peerage,* ii. 73.
26 *Cal. Pat.* 1494–1509, 126.
27 *L. & P. Hen. VIII,* i (2), p. 1170.
28 *Complete Peerage,* ix. 615.
29 C.P. 40/1079 Carte rot. 1.
30 *L. & P. Hen. VIII,* xvii, p. 28.
31 For pedigree see S.P.L., MS. 2794, pp. 591–2. Bracketed entries indicate relationship to preceding lord.

1597, the following being lords: Fulk, 1540–66; Thomas (son), 1566;[32] Thomas (son), 1566;[33] Richard (brother), 1566–87; Richard (son), 1587–97.[34] In 1597 Richard Crompton sold the manor to Richard and George Hopton.[35] The latter sold it in 1609 to Sir George Hayward,[36] whose brother, Sir John Hayward, sold the manor in 1617 to Humphrey Lee of Langley,[37] who was succeeded by his son Richard in 1632.[38] On the death of Richard Lee in 1660[39] the manor passed to his daughter Mary, wife of Edward Smythe.[40] It has subsequently remained in the Smythe family,[41] the following being lords: Edward, 1660–1714; Richard, 1714–36; John (brother), 1736–7; Edward, 1737–84; Edward, 1784–1811; Edward Joseph, 1811–56; Charles Frederick, 1856–97; John Walter (brother), 1897–1919; Edward Walter, 1919–42. On the death of Edward Walter Smythe the estate passed to his sister Mrs. A. D. Bruce, who was succeeded at her death in 1951 by her son Captain R. W. Bruce, who then took the name of Smythe. Captain R. W. Bruce Smythe is the present lord of the manor.

The fortified manor-house, known since the 16th century at least as Acton Burnell Castle,[42] was built between 1283 and 1286 by Robert Burnell, when he was constantly in Wales and the borderland during the Welsh war, and when castle-building operations in Wales were at their height.[43] He received several grants of timber for building the house between these years,[44] and was given licence to crenellate in 1284.[45] Now in ruins, the castle is a rectangular stone building, facing north and south. There are rectangular towers of four storeys at each corner and a central tower in the west wall probably contained Burnell's own apartments. The tower in the north-eastern corner had two bays and housed the chapel on the first floor. The east end of the first floor, which included the hall, had 3 two-light windows, containing geometrical tracery, on the north and south sides, and 2 similar windows on the east. The plan of the castle suggests that there was once a range of buildings attached to the east end.[46] The two stone gable walls of the so-called Parliament Barn, traditionally the meeting-place of the Parliament of 1283,[47] stand some 100 yards to the east of the castle. It is possible that they are the remains of an earlier manor-house. They stand on a level platform, to the east of which is a scarp, parallel to the original side walls of the building. The scarp continues as far as a ploughed field to the south. From

this point the soil-mark of a broad ditch turns and runs westwards to a point a little to the east of the Castle, where it turns northwards and re-enters the field in which the Castle and Parliament Barn stand. The scarp to the east of the barn may thus represent one side of a rectangular ditched enclosure, containing the barn but not the Castle.[48] The ditch cuts through the site of the buildings formerly attached to the east wall of the Castle.

Nicholas Burnell had a large household at the Castle in 1379,[49] and it was still occupied in the 15th century, for the court rolls of Condover manor were kept there until 1485.[50] It may have continued to be the residence of the lords of the manor, since most of the 16th and 17th-century lords lived, intermittently at least, at Acton Burnell.[51] Sir Edward Smythe occupied a 10-hearth house in the parish in 1662,[52] but in 1672 he was living at Langley Hall.[53] The southern half of the castle was converted into a barn between 1731 and 1786, when pyramid roofs were placed on the towers in the south-west corner and in the middle of the west wall.[54]

By 1731 a small stone house had been built on the site of the present Hall.[55] This faced north and south and contained two bays, with sash windows and dormers above. An attenuated wing at the west end had a roof-lantern. The present Hall faces north over the grounds added to the Park at this time. Its main two-storeyed block of 7 bays was in existence at least by 1805,[56] but the central Ionic portico on the north front and other classical embellishments, to designs by John Tasker, were added in 1814.[57] A set of diminishing blocking-courses above the cornice on the south front have been removed since 1842 to enable dormer windows to be inserted in the roof.[58] The three-storeyed west wing may be the building erected in 1810 for the monks of Douai.[59] A chapel at this end of the house was rebuilt in 1846.[60] The interior of the Hall was gutted by fire in 1914.[61] The Sisters of Our Lady of Sion, who have occupied the Hall as a convent boarding school since 1939, purchased it in 1949.[62]

Rainald the sheriff was overlord of *ACTON PIGOTT* manor in 1086[63] and his successors, the FitzAlans, were overlords by 1272, when it was held of the fee of Oswestry,[64] but by 1346 the manor was held of the Crown in chief.[65] Gheri held the manor before 1066 and Odo de Bernières was tenant in 1086.[66] Odo's successors as lords of Kenley were mesne tenants here in the later 12th century.[67] Their

[32] C 142/143/33.
[33] C 142/143/34.
[34] S.P.L., MS. 2, f. 21[v].
[35] Ibid.
[36] Ibid.
[37] S.P.L., MS. 2, f. 17.
[38] C 142/477/189.
[39] S.P.R. Lich. xix (5), 58.
[40] S.P.L., MS. 2793, p. 413.
[41] For pedigree see ibid. pp. 413–14; Burke, *Peerage* (1939).
[42] Sta. Cha. 3/4/80.
[43] The following account is based on *Arch. Jnl.* cv, suppl. 62–64; C. A. Ralegh Radford, 'Acton Burnell Castle' in *Studies in Building History*, ed. E. M. Jope (London, 1961), 94–103. See also plate on facing page.
[44] *Cal. Close*, 1279–88, 202, 211; *Cal. Pat.* 1281–92, 126, 228.
[45] *Cal. Pat.* 1281–92, 110.
[46] *Studies in Building History*, 101.
[47] *Arch. Jnl.* cv, suppl. 62. The name was already current in the early 18th century: Camden, *Britannia*, ed. Gibson (1772), i. 473.

[48] Ex inf. Mr. P. A. Barker.
[49] E 179/242/33.
[50] Sta. Cha. 3/4/80.
[51] *S.P.R. Lich.* xix (5), *passim*.
[52] E 179/255/35 m. 78.
[53] *Hearth Tax, 1672*, 135.
[54] E. and S. Buck, print of Acton Burnell Castle, 1731; S.P.L., MS. 372, vol. i, p. 10.
[55] E. and S. Buck, print of Acton Burnell Castle, 1731.
[56] Print of Castle, 1805, *penes* Mr. S. Morley Tonkin, Ford House.
[57] S.R.O. 1514/2/1222.
[58] Watercolour of Castle by Isaac Shaw, 1842, *penes* Mr. S. Morley Tonkin.
[59] *Downside Rev.* lxi. 67.
[60] Pevsner, *Shropshire*, 51.
[61] *Shrewsbury Chronicle*, 17 Apr. 1914.
[62] Ex inf. Capt. R. W. Bruce Smythe.
[63] *V.C.H. Salop.* i. 320.
[64] *Close R.* 1268–72, 513.
[65] *Cal. Inq. p.m.* viii, p. 496.
[66] *V.C.H. Salop.* i. 320.
[67] Eyton, vi. 93.

The Castle from the south

The Church: interior of the chancel

ACTON BURNELL

CRESSAGE: ST. SAMSON'S CHURCH IN 1785
Demolished in 1840

ACTON PIGOTT CHAPEL IN 1786
Largely destroyed by 1866

tenure is last recorded in 1294,[68] but Robert Burnell appears to have acquired their interest in the manor by 1292.[69]

William Fitz Pain was under-tenant here in the later 12th century.[70] At his death half of the manor passed to his widow Mabel.[71] Her second husband, William Fitz Picot, who was living in 1203,[72] gave the manor its name. The other moiety descended to the three daughters of William Fitz Pain's sister, all of whom were dead by 1203.[73] One of the daughters was then represented by her husband, Roger de Harpcote, another by her son, William de Belswardine, and the third by her three daughters, Maud, wife of Philip de Allcott, Mabel, wife of Richard de Moneford, and Sybil, wife of Robert de Allcott.[74] Ranulph, great-grandson of Roger de Harpcote, and Richard, son of William de Belswardine, held portions of the manor in 1254,[75] but shortly afterwards Richard de Belswardine conveyed his portion to Walter de Golding.[76] Walter's grandson, Robert de Golding, sold it to Roger de Aston in 1344,[77] and this appears to be the small estate in Acton Pigott acquired by the lord of Pitchford manor in 1541.[78] The remaining portion, which had been held by three co-heiresses before 1203, was held by Philip and Gilian de Allcott in 1254.[79] Most of the manor had been acquired by Robert Burnell before 1292.[80] He already held lands in Allcott by 1269, when he had a grant of free warren there,[81] and in Acton Pigott by 1270, when part of the township was imparked.[82] He purchased lands in Allcott in 1283 from Richard de Bouthlers and his wife Maud, probably a descendant of Philip de Allcott.[83] The manor subsequently followed the descent of Acton Burnell.

ECONOMIC HISTORY. Acton Burnell manor was said to be worth 30s. before 1066.[84] Its value afterwards fell to 15s., but had risen to 20s. by 1086, when it was said to contain 3½ hides.[85] It was worth £16 17s. 3d. a year in 1292,[86] and £8 19s. in 1315.[87] There was one plough on the demesne in 1086, when there were 2 serfs here.[88] The demesne comprised 4 carucates in 1292[89] and 180 a. in 1315.[90] The manor of Acton Pigott was worth 20s. before 1066, but its value later fell to 13s.[91] By 1086, when it was assessed at 3 hides, it was worth 13s. 4d.[92] The demesne contained land for one plough in 1086, when there were

3 serfs,[93] and 118 a. in 1294.[94] After the later 13th century the two manors became a single economic unit.[95] In 1845, when the manorial estate comprised 1,479 a., 593 a. were in hand, of which 243 a. lay in the Park and 101 a. consisted of woodland in other parts of the parish.[96] Acton Burnell Farm, Acton Pigott Farm, and smallholdings at Evenwood, some 750 a. in all, were sold in 1921.[97]

Two small freehold estates, held by the Acton and Lee families in the 15th century, were acquired by the lord of Pitchford manor between 1541 and 1545.[98] This estate comprised a little over 100 a. in 1689,[99] but exchanges in 1752[1] and 1799[2] had reduced it to 53 a. by 1845.[3]

In 1086 one villein, 4 bordars, and a radman had 1½ plough-team between them at Acton Burnell,[4] while 4 villeins had one plough-team at Acton Pigott.[5] Robert Burnell granted Acton Burnell a borough charter c. 1268, offering burgage-plots at a rent of 12d. a year.[6] Entry fines were fixed at 12d. on inheritance and 2d. on purchase, but the lord had a right of pre-emption on the sale of a burgage. No rent was to be demanded for three years after a burgage had been taken, or while a house was being built. Burgesses had common of pasture in Acton Burnell outside the lord's woods and Park, and in Acton Pigott and Ruckley and Langley.[7] There were 36 burgage tenants in 1315, whose rents totalled 47s. 8d. a year.[8] Eleven free tenants then paid 30s. a year, and these two classes of tenant must have greatly outnumbered the villeins, whose rents produced only 16s. a year.[9] Although burgages are recorded until 1545,[10] there is no evidence that the terms of the charter were observed in the later Middle Ages.

The three-life lease was in use on the manorial estate in the mid-17th century,[11] but by 1717 there were only 6 leaseholders for lives, whose rents totalled £10 15s. a year, while 17 tenants-at-will paid £207 and 2 tenants on short-term leases paid £68.[12] By 1741 there was only one leaseholder, the remainder being tenants-at-will.[13] Farms were then numerous and presumably small, but their number had been reduced by 1782,[14] and in 1805 806 a. lay in 3 farms of over 200 a.[15] There was then one other holding of 40 a. and 8 smaller than 20 a.[16] The large farms were unchanged in 1845, when there were 10 other

[68] *Cal. Inq. p.m.* iii, p. 121.
[69] Eyton, vi. 95.
[70] Ibid. 93.
[71] Ibid.
[72] Ibid.
[73] Ibid. 93–94.
[74] Ibid.
[75] *Rot. Hund.* (Rec. Com.), ii. 62.
[76] N.L.W., Pitchford Hall 1246, 1385.
[77] Ibid. 1244, 1253.
[78] Ibid. 1152–3.
[79] *Rot. Hund.* (Rec. Com.), ii. 62.
[80] C 133/63/32.
[81] *Cal. Chart. R.* 1257–1300, 132.
[82] *Cal. Pat.* 1266–72, 422.
[83] Eyton, vi. 95.
[84] *V.C.H. Salop.* i. 324.
[85] Ibid.
[86] C 133/63/32.
[87] C 134/48/9.
[88] *V.C.H. Salop.* i. 324.
[89] C 133/63/32.
[90] C 134/48/9.
[91] *V.C.H. Salop.* i. 320.
[92] Ibid.

[93] Ibid.
[94] C 133/68/10.
[95] C 134/48/9; C 135/82/38.
[96] Heref. Dioc. Regy., tithe appt.
[97] S.C.C. title-deeds, SH 35, sale particulars, 1921.
[98] S.P.L., M.S. 2, ff. 10, 10ᵛ, 22; N.L.W., Pitchford Hall 1231, 1382, 1606.
[99] Pitchford Hall MSS., Pitchford Hall, survey, 1689.
[1] N.L.W., Pitchford Hall 1917.
[2] Ibid. 2230.
[3] Heref. Dioc. Regy., tithe appt.
[4] *V.C.H. Salop.* i. 324.
[5] Ibid. 320.
[6] S.P.L., MS. 2, f. 10.
[7] Ibid.
[8] C 134/48/9.
[9] Ibid.
[10] S.P.L., MS. 2, ff. 21ᵛ, 22, 22ᵛ; N.L.W., Pitchford Hall 1231, 1458.
[11] Q. Sess., reg. papists' estates, 1717.
[12] Ibid.
[13] Ibid. 1741.
[14] Ibid. 1782.
[15] S.P.L., MS. 294.
[16] Ibid.

holdings smaller than 20 a.[17] Five of the latter were on the former common at Evenwood, inclosed in 1820.[18]

Land on the estate belonging to Pitchford manor was let on long leases until the early 18th century,[19] when these were replaced by tenancies-at-will or short-term leases.[20] After 1800 the estate was attached to a farm in Pitchford.[21]

There were said to be 279 a. arable in the parish in 1795, when barley was the chief crop.[22] The arable acreage had increased to 491 a. by 1805[23] and to 954 a. by 1845.[24]

A mill is first recorded in 1292, when it was worth 4 marks.[25] There were two mills, worth 26s. 8d. a year, in 1315,[26] but only one mill in 1346.[27] The mill closed soon after 1856.[28]

In 1269 Acton Burnell was granted a weekly market and 2 three-day fairs, at Lady Day and Michaelmas,[29] and in 1272 Robert Burnell obtained letters of protection for merchants trading here and for his men trading elsewhere.[30] The charter of 1269 was confirmed in 1364,[31] but there is no later evidence for the existence of a market in the village.

Apart from the large household of the lord of the manor, the occupations of the inhabitants assessed to the poll tax of 1379 show no higher a proportion of tradesmen than is found in surrounding villages.[32] The 5 tradesmen included, however, a draper as well as a tailor and a smith.[33] There are occasional references to weavers, tilers, and charcoal-burners in the 16th and 17th centuries.[34] In the later 19th century the village contained a blacksmith, a bricklayer, a butcher, a carpenter, a carrier, a grocer, and a wheelwright.[35] A shoemaker was still living at Acton Pigott in 1901.[36] In 1937, when the carrier had been replaced by a haulier, who also ran a local bus, the village had a blacksmith, a builder, a grocer, and a wheelwright.[37]

LOCAL GOVERNMENT. The manor of Acton Burnell was withdrawn from the jurisdiction of Condover hundred court in 1266,[38] and two-thirds of the manor of Acton Pigott were withdrawn from the sheriff's tourn in 1270.[39] The lord of Acton Pigott owed suit every three weeks at the manor court of Kenley in 1294.[40]

There are no manor court rolls or parish records, other than registers, and no records of the borough created c. 1268,[41] apart from a single leaf of a corporation court book, recording the appointment of various local gentlemen as mayor, aldermen, and burgesses, 1681–2.[42] This formality survived until the later 18th century.[43]

Between £8 and £14 was spent annually on poor relief in the 1690s.[44] The poor rates had risen to £54 in 1776[45] and to £190 by 1803.[46] They reached a peak of £280 in 1817,[47] but fell off after 1822,[48] standing at £77 in 1828.[49] A Friendly Society, which had 111 members in 1803[50] and is last recorded in 1843,[51] may in part explain the comparatively low expenditure on poor relief. A poor-house at the village cross-roads, purchased in 1717,[52] was superseded by another house near Lynall Brook c. 1761.[53]

CHURCHES. Acton Burnell church is first recorded between 1268 and 1272,[54] but Robert de Acton, clerk, first mentioned in 1227,[55] may have been rector here. Thomas, the first known rector, was killed in a brawl c. 1288.[56] The church was said c. 1268 to be the mother church of Ruckley chapel,[57] and after 1572 Langley chapel was accounted a chapelry of Acton Burnell.[58] Acton Pigott chapel was served by the rector of Acton Burnell after 1457.[59]

The benefice is a rectory and has been united with Pitchford since 1926.[60] Its advowson followed the descent of the manor until 1542, when it was retained by Sir John Dudley on his sale of the manor.[61] It was forfeited to the Crown in 1553[62] and in 1563 was granted to Thomas Poyner and William Wolryche.[63] They immediately sold it to Thomas Scriven,[64] whose son Edward sold it to Humphrey Lee in 1607.[65] Thereafter it followed the descent of the manor until 1899. The right of next presentation was regularly sold after 1660, when the patrons were Roman Catholics,[66] but in 1899 the advowson was purchased by the incumbent, William Sergeantson, whose family still hold it.[67]

[17] Heref. Dioc. Regy., tithe appt.
[18] Pitchford Hall MSS., Pitchford Hall, inclosure accts. 1820.
[19] N.L.W., Pitchford Hall 676–1569, passim.
[20] Ibid. 2406.
[21] Pitchford Hall MSS., Pitchford Hall, survey, 1800; Heref. Dioc. Regy., tithe appt.
[22] N.L.W., Pitchford Hall uncat., acreage return, 1795.
[23] S.P.L., MS. 294.
[24] Heref. Dioc. Regy., tithe appt.
[25] C 133/63/32.
[26] C 134/48/9.
[27] C 135/82/38.
[28] Kelly's Dir. Salop. (1856).
[29] Cal. Chart. R. 1257–1300, 132.
[30] Cal. Pat. 1266–72, 679.
[31] Cal. Chart R. 1341–1417, 188.
[32] E 179/242/33.
[33] Ibid.
[34] N.L.W., Pitchford Hall 945, 1080, 1516, 1557–8.
[35] Kelly's Dir. Salop. (1856–89).
[36] Ibid. (1901).
[37] Ibid. (1937).
[38] Eyton, vi. 129.
[39] Ibid.
[40] Cal. Inq. p.m. iii, p. 121.
[41] See p. 9.
[42] Bodl. MS. Blakeway 2, f. 391.
[43] Ibid. f. 7.

[44] Ibid. 8, f. 476.
[45] Rep. Cttee. on Overseers' Returns, 1777, p. 441, H.C. (1st ser. ix, reprinted 1803).
[46] Poor Law Abstract, 1803, H.C. 175, pp. 416–17 (1803–4), xiii.
[47] Rep. Cttee. on Poor Rate Returns, 1822, Suppl. App. H.C. 556, p. 141 (1822), v.
[48] Ibid. 1825, H.C. 334, p. 177 (1825), iv.
[49] Acct. of Money Expended on Poor, 1825–9, H.C. 83, p. 390 (1830–1), xi.
[50] Poor Law Abstract, 1803, pp. 416–17.
[51] Q. Sess., index to Friendly Soc. rules.
[52] Char. Com. files.
[53] Ibid.
[54] S.P.L., MS. 2, f. 1.
[55] Eyton, vi. 138.
[56] Ibid.
[57] S.P.L., MS. 2, f. 1.
[58] Ibid. ff. 7, 8. See also p. 145.
[59] Bodl. MS. Blakeway 14, ff. 2ᵛ, 3.
[60] Heref. Dioc. Regy., reg. 1926–38, p. 12.
[61] L. & P. Hen. VIII, xvii, p. 28.
[62] Complete Peerage, ix. 722.
[63] Cal. Pat. 1560–3, 497–8.
[64] S.P.L., MS. 2, f. 3.
[65] Ibid.
[66] S.P.R. Lich. xix (5), p. vii.
[67] Conveyance, 1899, penes the Revd. E. W. Sergeantson, Leebotwood.

The rectory was valued at only £2 a year in 1291,[68] and in 1433 the lord of the manor was paying the rector 26s. 8d. a year because the benefice was of such little value.[69] Its gross annual value rose from £7 in 1535[70] to £30 in 1655.[71] The combined livings of Acton Burnell and Acton Pigott were worth between £200 and £300 in 1799,[72] £450 in 1823,[73] and £350 in 1831[74] and 1843.[75] The tithes of Acton Burnell and Acton Pigott were commuted for a rent charge of £264 in 1845.[76] Nothing is known about the value or method of collection of tithes in Acton Burnell before that date. The glebe of the combined livings amounted to 74 a. in 1698.[77] Land in Acton Burnell Common was added when the common was inclosed in the mid-18th century,[78] but in 1817 that part of the glebe which lay in Acton Burnell was exchanged for lands in Acton Pigott.[79] There were 94 a. of glebe in 1845.[80]

The parsonage house, which contained 5 hearths in 1662[81] and 5 bays of building in 1698,[82] has occupied its present site since at least 1612.[83] It was enlarged and cased in brick in 1714,[84] and further additions at the rear were made between 1823 and 1838.[85]

None of the rectors[86] is known to have been a relative of the lord of the manor. The rector in 1530, and all since 1616, have been graduates. Since 1569 many of them have held the living for long periods—3 for over 40 years, one for 55 years, and one for 60 years. Curates were normally employed only during the old age of incumbents, as in 1756–9[87] and 1799–1811.[88] Robert Hesketh (rector 1813–37) was non-resident[89] and in 1823 his curate was paid £100 a year.[90]

Communion was administered 4 times a year in 1823[91] and 10 times a year in 1843.[92] There were 25 communicants in 1823,[93] and in 1843 their numbers ranged from 34 to 48.[94] Services were held twice on Sundays in the earlier 19th century.[95] In 1851 71 persons attended the morning service and 37 in the evening.[96]

The church of *ST. MARY*, a highly sophisticated building, was built in the late 13th century, probably at the same time as the Castle.[97] Its erection was presumably directed by Robert Burnell and it shows some affinities with contemporary work at his cathedral of Wells. Cruciform in shape, it contains a nave, chancel, and transepts. A low tower, in the angle of the north transept and the chancel, was built in 1887–9, replacing a wooden bell-turret over the nave crossing.

The church is entered through a porch in the north wall of the nave and there is a blocked door in the south wall. Above the west door is a three-light window with bar tracery and there are 3 lancet windows on each side of the nave. High in the wall to the east of the north door is a small quatrefoil window. There is a continuous corbel-table at eaves level, which includes some carved stones.

The transepts and chancel are built in a more elaborate style, using stiff-leaved foliage for capitals, head-stops on hood moulds, and Purbeck marble shafts for some of the windows. The chapel of St. Thomas, mentioned in 1365,[98] was probably in one of the transepts, and the south transept was known as the Ruckley chapel in the early 19th century.[99] The windows in each transept were originally arranged in the same manner—three-light windows with geometrical tracery on the end walls, with pairs of lancets on the east and west walls. The south transept preserves this arrangement, but in the north transept the north window and the two lancets on the east wall had been blocked by 1786, when a large square-headed window had been inserted in the west wall.

The east window of the chancel is of 4 lights and has geometrical tracery and attached Purbeck marble shafts. On the south wall 4 closely set lancets with trefoil heads and attached shafts form a continuous arcade; there are 3 similar lancets in the north wall. To the west of the priest's door in the south wall two simpler lancets resemble those of the nave. Double piscinae in the chancel and both transepts, and an aumbry in the north wall of the chancel, have trefoil heads and are contemporary with the main structure. Near the west end of the north chancel wall is an external arched recess, pierced by a small square opening, possibly the opening from a former anchorite's cell.[1]

Apart from modifications in the north transept and the addition of the tower, there have been no substantial alterations to the church fabric. The north transept has a trussed-rafter roof in medieval style, but other parts of the church have collar-beam roofs, that in the chancel being dated 1571 and that in the nave 1598. All had been covered with plaster ceilings which were removed in 1887.

The octagonal font, a fine example of late-13th-century work, has 8 heavily-moulded trefoil arches supported on attached shafts. The chancel arch, though much restored in 1887, retains slots for a rood-screen, and there are remains of a piscina on

68 *Tax. Eccl.* (Rec. Com.), 244.
69 S.P.L., MS. 2, f. 4ᵛ.
70 *Valor Eccl.* (Rec. Com.), iii. 185.
71 *T.S.A.S.* xlvii. 28.
72 Visit. Archd. Salop. 1799.
73 Ibid. 1823.
74 *Rep. Com. Eccl. Revenues* [67], pp. 458–9, H.C. (1835), xxii.
75 Visit. Archd. Salop. 1843.
76 Heref. Dioc. Regy., tithe appt.
77 Lich. Dioc. Regy., glebe terrier, 1698.
78 Ibid. 1763.
79 Ibid., exchange of glebe, 1817.
80 Heref. Dioc. Regy., tithe appt.
81 E 179/255/35 m. 78.
82 Lich. Dioc. Regy., glebe terrier, 1698.
83 Ibid. 1612.
84 Datestone on western gable.
85 Visit. Archd. Salop. 1823.
86 Except where otherwise stated, this paragraph is based

on Eyton, vi. 138–9; Bodl. MS. Blakeway 14, f. 2; *S.P.R. Lich.* xix (5), pp. vii–viii.
87 Lich. Dioc. Regy., glebe terriers, 1756, 1759.
88 Visit. Archd. Salop. 1799; *S.P.R. Lich.* xix (5), p. viii.
89 Visit. Archd. Salop. 1823.
90 Ibid.   91 Ibid.
92 Ibid. 1843.
93 Ibid. 1823.
94 Ibid. 1843.
95 Ibid. 1823, 1843.
96 H.O. 129/359/1/8.
97 Description of church based, except where otherwise stated, on S.P.L., MS. 372, vol. i, p. 16; S.P.L., J. H. Smith collect. no. 0 (*sic*); Lich. Dioc. Regy., faculty, 1887; Cranage, vi. 452–61; Pevsner, *Shropshire*, 49–51; J. Salmon, *Acton Burnell and its church* (Shrewsbury, n.d.). See also plate facing p. 8.
98 S.P.L., MS. 2, f. 11.
99 Visit. Archd. Salop. 1823.
1 The solution proposed by Mr. Salmon.

the south side. Surviving medieval tiles were relaid in the north transept in 1887, while the rosettes painted on the walls of the south transept are probably medieval. The high-level quatrefoil window in the north wall of the nave is set in a round-headed recess internally; it may have lighted a small wooden gallery in this position. The pulpit and communion table are of early-17th-century date and, although the church was repewed in 1823[2] and 1887, the existing pews retain some 17th-century panelling. A gallery which stood at the west end of the nave was removed in 1887.

There is an early-14th-century tomb-recess in the south wall of the south transept, but most of the notable monuments are in the north transept, where those commemorating lords of the manor were assembled in 1887.

The earliest monument is the tomb-chest and brass effigy of Sir Nicholas Burnell (d. 1382). The sumptuous alabaster monument of Sir Richard Lee (d. 1591) stands against the east wall, and a monument on the west wall commemorating Sir Humphrey Lee (d. 1632) is by Nicholas Stone.[3] There is also a number of memorial tablets to members of the Smythe family, that of William Smythe (d. 1794) being signed by King of Bath.[4]

The church has had 3 bells since at least 1552,[4] but 2 of them were recast in 1651 and 1695 respectively.[5] Of these, only the bell of 1651 now remains. The bell of 1695 and the third bell, which was without an inscription,[6] were cracked by 1843[7] and were recast in 1887.[8] There was a clock in the central bell-turret by 1786.[9] The church possessed a chalice and paten of silver gilt in 1552.[10] The present plate comprises a flagon of 1733, a chalice of 1761, and a paten of 1858.[11] The registers are complete from 1568.[12]

There was a chapel at Acton Pigott in the later 12th century, when Silvester was priest there.[13] It was a chapelry of Cound, to which church one-third of the tithes were paid in 1341.[14] This payment was still being made in the later 17th century,[15] when the inhabitants were also liable to repair a section of Cound churchyard wall,[16] and was commuted for a rent-charge of £19 a year in 1845.[17] The advowson followed the descent of the manor of Acton Pigott, but became merged with that of Acton Burnell after the two manors had been united in the later 13th

century.[18] Two of the 14th-century incumbents were styled rectors.[19] The living was held in plurality with Acton Burnell between 1375 and 1394,[20] and regularly after 1457,[21] until the chapel fell into disuse c. 1730.

The small tithes of Acton Pigott were worth 13s. 4d. in 1341,[22] and all its tithes were valued at £18 in 1655.[23] The glebe, first recorded in the mid-13th century,[24] included in 1612 a house, which may have been the former parsonage.[25] In 1711 the inhabitants of Acton Pigott were said to be entitled to morning prayer in the chapel before service at Acton Burnell on Sundays during the winter, and to communion there on Easter Sunday.[26] Baptisms and marriages could be celebrated there if they wished.[27]

The chapel consisted of a nave and chancel of late-12th-century date, with a western bell-turret.[28] The nave measured 29 feet by 15 feet and the chancel 18 feet by 12 feet. There was a small round-headed window high in the west wall, and single round-headed windows in the north and south walls of the nave. There is no evidence for the appearance of the east end or north wall of the chancel, but there was a small lancet and a round-headed window in its south wall. The hexagonal font, which was still in place in 1786,[29] is now outside the north door of Acton Burnell church. The chapel had two bells, and a chalice and paten of silver in 1552.[30] It had gone out of use by c. 1730, and later in the 18th century the bishop ordered that it should be 'permitted to sink of itself'.[31] It was still substantially intact in 1786,[32] but by 1799 the roof had begun to fall in.[33] The doors and windows were then bricked up to prevent desecration.[34] The west end was still standing c. 1866,[35] but no part now remains.

NONCONFORMITY. Since c. 1650 the lords of Acton Burnell manor have been Roman Catholics.[36] There were said to be 3 recusants in the parish in 1679,[37] but the 10 recusants recorded in 1706[38] were all members of the Smythe household. A chapel in the Hall, served by the Benedictines from 1715,[39] was licensed in 1791.[40] The monks of Dieulouard[41] were given shelter here in 1794,[42] but were replaced in the following year by the monks of Douai, who remained until 1814.[43] During these years they maintained a school at the Hall.[44] A chapel built for the monks in 1799[45] continued to be used as a public

[2] Visit. Archd. Salop. 1823.
[3] Pevsner, *Shropshire*, 50–51.
[4] *T.S.A.S.* 2nd ser. xii. 100.
[5] Birmingham Univ. Libr., Mytton's Ch. Notes, vol. i, f. 9.
[6] Ibid.
[7] Visit. Archd. Salop. 1843.
[8] Walters, *Ch. Bells Salop.* 210.
[9] S.P.L., MS. 372, vol. i, p. 16.
[10] *T.S.A.S.* 2nd ser. xii. 100.
[11] Arkwright and Bourne, *Ch. Plate Ludlow Archd.* 1.
[12] Printed to 1812 in *S.P.R. Lich.* xix (5), 1–168.
[13] Eyton, vi. 93.
[14] *Inq. Non.* (Rec. Com.), 192.
[15] Lich. Dioc. Regy., Cound glebe terriers, 1695, 1698.
[16] Cound par. rec., apportionment for repair of churchyard wall, 1678.
[17] Heref. Dioc. Regy., tithe appt.
[18] See p. 9.
[19] Eyton, vi. 97; cf. Bodl. MS. Blakeway 14, f. 2.
[20] Eyton, vi. 97.
[21] Bodl. MS. Blakeway 2, ff. 2–3.
[22] *Inq. Non.* (Rec. Com.), 192.
[23] *T.S.A.S.* xlvii. 28.
[24] N.L.W., Pitchford Hall 2448.

[25] Lich. Dioc. Regy., glebe terrier, 1612.
[26] Ibid. 1711.
[27] Ibid.
[28] The following description of the church is based on S.P.L., MS. 372, vol. i, p. 4; S.P.L., T. F. Dukes watercolours (churches), no. 4; Visit. Archd. Salop. 1823. See also plate facing p. 9.
[29] B.M. Add. MS. 21236, f. 233.
[30] *T.S.A.S.* 2nd ser. xii. 98.
[31] Visit. Archd. Salop. 1799.
[32] S.P.L., MS. 372, vol. i, p. 4.
[33] Visit. Archd. Salop. 1799.   [34] Ibid.
[35] *Shrewsbury Chronicle*, 13 June 1913.
[36] A. Rimmer, *Hist. of Shrewsbury School, 1551–1888* (1889), 112.
[37] Lich. Dioc. Regy., B/v 1/81.
[38] Ibid. B/a 11.
[39] Ex inf. Mr. D. T. W. Price.
[40] *Q. Sess. Orders*, iii. 53.
[41] Dep. Meurthe et Moselle.
[42] *Downside Rev.* lx. 62.
[43] H. N. Birt, *Hist. of Downside* (1902), 129; *Downside Rev.* lxii. 119.
[44] Ibid.
[45] H. N. Birt, *Hist. of Downside*, 136.

chapel after their departure and was rebuilt to the designs of Charles Hansom in 1846.[46] Already in 1799 the archdeacon advised an increase in the number of services at Langley chapel 'in view of the activities of Roman Catholics in the neighbourhood',[47] and by 1823 two-thirds of the inhabitants of the village were said to be Roman Catholics.[48] This may have been an over-estimate, since the proportion was put at only one-third in 1843.[49] In 1851 an average of 150 persons attended Mass.[50]

Apart from a Quaker, 1668–85,[51] and two dissenters noted in 1676,[52] there is no record of protestant nonconformity in the parish.

SCHOOLS. A rent-charge of 40s. devised by Richard Osbourne of London in 1612 to endow a school[53] was paid to the incumbent until 1664.[54] A schoolmaster is first recorded here in 1614[55] and in the 1670s the school was described as a grammar school.[56] A charity school was maintained by the rector in 1799.[57]

A day school was built by the rector in 1815,[58] with the help of a grant from the National Society,[59] on land given by the lord of the manor.[60] It was enlarged in 1848[61] and 1901[62] and has been a Controlled school since 1948.[63] The school was financed by voluntary subscriptions in 1823,[64] but schoolpence had been introduced by 1833[65] and a graduated scale was in use by 1854.[66] The rector, who paid for the education of 20 of the children in 1823,[67] made up the difference between income and expenditure until at least 1872.[68] School-pence had been abolished by 1892,[69] when about one-third of the school's income was derived from voluntary contributions and the remainder from a government grant.[70] Between 50 and 60 children attended throughout the 19th century.[71] Children from Cound, Frodesley, Kenley, and Pitchford attended in 1843,[72] and by 1872 Frodesley had agreed to pay a proportion of the school's expenses.[73]

A school for Roman Catholic children, endowed by the Smythe family, had been established by 1833,[74] and 58 children attended in 1872.[75] A school, now the Village Hall, was built in 1872,[76] and was attended by 23 children in 1885.[77] The school closed in 1923.[78]

CHARITIES. A total of £20, given during their lifetimes by John Roberts, Thomas Jones, and Richard Reynolds for the provision of bread for the poor, was used by the parish officers in 1717 to purchase a poor-house.[79] This house, which stood at the village cross-roads, became ruinous after a new poor-house was acquired near Lynall Brook and in 1761, when it was again put in repair, the parish officers undertook to allow 20s. a year for distribution in bread, to be paid out of the rent of the house, if occupied, or out of the poor rate if the house were uninhabited. A further 10s. a year was to be set aside to keep the house in repair. Until c. 1810 25s. a year was paid by the tenant of the house to a baker and was distributed in bread, but thereafter the house was occupied rent-free, bread being distributed by the parish officers at irregular intervals. The annual payment of 25s. was restored in 1830, but the endowment was lost c. 1832, when the house was acquired by the agent of the lord of the manor. In 1846 the agent undertook to pay 30s. a year to the parish officers. This payment appears to have been regularly made in the period 1863–1925, but had ceased by 1954.

By will of 1789 Edward Bayley left 10s. a year, arising from lands in Cardington, to be distributed in bread to the poor on New Year's Day and the 9 following Sundays.[80] This charity was still being paid in 1830, but is not later recorded. Humphrey Lee of Langley gave £20 in 1632 to be invested in trust for the poor, and in 1673 Thomas Smyth of Ruckley began to give 5s. a year to be distributed in bread to the poor at Easter, but neither of these charities appears to have continued after the deaths of their founders.

BERRINGTON

THE parish of Berrington now contains 4,374 a. and includes the townships of Berrington, Betton Abbots, Brompton, Cantlop, and Eaton Mascott, and the squatter settlement of Cross Houses, now larger than any of the ancient hamlets.[1] The township of Betton Strange was transferred to Berrington parish

46 Pevsner, *Shropshire*, 51.
47 Visit. Archd. Salop. 1799.
48 Ibid. 1823.
49 Ibid. 1843.
50 H.O. 129/359/1/9.
51 Lich. Dioc. Regy., B/v 1/74; ibid. 1/87.
52 *T.S.A.S.* 2nd ser. i. 79.
53 *S.P.R. Lich.* xix (5), 41–42.
54 N.L.W., Pitchford Hall 2095.
55 Lich. Dioc. Regy., B/v 1/28.
56 Ibid. B/a 4/5.
57 Visit. Archd. Salop. 1799.
58 *Digest of Returns to Cttee. on Educ. of Poor*, H.C. 224, p. 745 (1819), ix (2). See plate facing p. 83.
59 Nat. Soc., *Annual Rep.* 1828.
60 Ed. 7/102/2.
61 *Mins. of Educ. Cttee. of Council, 1849* [1215], p. ccxxvii, H.C. (1850), xliii.
62 *Kelly's Dir. Salop.* (1909).
63 Ex inf. S.C.C. Educ. Dept.
64 Visit. Archd. Salop. 1823.
65 *Educ. Enquiry Abstract*, H.C. 62, p. 768 (1835), xlii.
66 Ed. 7/102/2.
67 Visit. Archd. Salop. 1823.

68 Ed. 7/102/2.
69 *Return of Schs., 1893* [C. 7529], p. 502, H.C. (1894), lxv.
70 Ibid.
71 Nat. Soc. *Annual Rep.* 1816; *Educ. Enquiry Abstract*, p. 768; Visit. Archd. Salop. 1843; Nat. Soc. *Ch. School Returns*, 1846–7; Ed. 7/102/2; *Return of Schs., 1893* [C. 7529], p. 502.
72 Visit. Archd. Salop. 1843.
73 Ed. 7/102/2.
74 *Educ. Enquiry Abstract*, p. 768.
75 Ed. 2/369.
76 *Kelly's Dir. Salop.* (1885).
77 Ibid.
78 Ex inf. Revd. E. M. Abbott.
79 What follows is based on *24th Rep. Com. Char.* H.C. 231, pp. 377–9 (1831), xi, and Char. Com. files.
80 Ibid.
1 O.S. *Area Bk.* (1882). The following topographical description is based, except where otherwise stated, on O.S. Maps 6" Salop. 41, 42 (1st and later edns.); O.S. Map 1/25,000, SJ 50 (1959); Rocque, *Map of Salop.* (1752); Baugh, *Map of Salop.* (1808); B.M. O.S. 2" orig. drawings, sheets 207 (1817), 320 (1827); Geol. Survey Map

from St. Chad's, Shrewsbury, in 1885.[2] Its history is reserved for treatment under the Liberties of Shrewsbury. La Beche, a shrunken hamlet in Pitchford parish, had been part of an estate at Eaton Mascott since the 14th century[3] and paid church and highway rates to Berrington until the mid-18th century.[4] In the 1740s, however, Pitchford successfully challenged Berrington's right to levy poor rates here.[5]

The River Severn forms the northern boundary of the parish; the projecting tongue of land near The Cotons was added to the parish in 1654,[6] when Brompton Heath, acquired by the lord of Brompton manor in 1623,[7] was transferred from Cound parish. The north-eastern boundary probably once followed the alignment of Watling Street south-westwards from Brompton Ford, as it still does for some distance to the north of Cound Brook. The southern boundary follows the Cound as far west as Eaton Mascott Mill. The township of Cantlop, however, lies to the south of the Cound, and the curious southerly projection of the parish boundary at this point is the result of agreements made between the lord of Cantlop manor and those of Pitchford and Condover to determine their respective manorial boundaries in this former woodland area. The eastern boundary was fixed in this way c. 1268,[8] and the boundary with Condover to the west in 1546.[9] That part of the eastern boundary of Cantlop which runs along the valley formed by a tributary of the Cound, known as Dukedale,[10] presumably represents the ancient township boundary and a small part of the western boundary runs along a small stream rising from a spring known as 'Helmwalle' in the 13th century.[11] Elsewhere the boundary here does not make use of natural features. The former western boundary of the parish followed a tributary of the Severn as far as Cross Houses, then ran north-westwards for 1¼ mile along the road to Shrewsbury. It then followed an irregular course through former woodland, touching Shomere Pool in the east and joining the Cound near Boreton Bridge.

Three of the 5 ancient hamlets in the parish stand on or near an undulating ridge of sand and gravel, which runs north-westwards from Venus Bank on the boundary with Cound towards Betton Strange. The ridge rises to 275 feet at Cloud Coppice, near Eaton Mascott, and to 300 feet at various points in the west of the parish. The lower ground in the centre of the parish is boulder clay and includes numerous small pools, notably at Cloud Coppice and to the south and west of Berrington village, most of which are associated with peat deposits. In Brompton township, north of the ridge, the ground

rarely rises above 175 feet. The subsoil here is mostly boulder clay, but a wide belt of alluvial soil flanks the Severn and the hamlet of Brompton itself stands on sand. Impeded drainage to the east and north of the central ridge produced a zone of marshland. Eaton Mascott Pool was formerly known as 'Lechmere',[12] fields called The Bogs adjoin Cound Stank, to the south of Venus Bank, and marshes known as The Moss and The Slough extended along the northern edge of the ridge almost to Cross Houses.[13] Similar conditions occurred to the east of Berrington, where the field-names Alkmoor, Exmore, and Dodmore are found.[14] In Cantlop township the ground rises from 200 feet along Cound Brook to 400 feet in the extreme south of the parish. The subsoil here is boulder clay, capping the Keele Beds sandstone which makes up the Buriwood plateau.

The whole parish once lay within the jurisdiction of the Long Forest, but it had been disafforested by 1300.[15] Considerable progress in forest clearance appears already to have been made by 1086, when the 5 manors in the parish were assessed at a total of 13 hides.[16] The area of cultivated land was relatively small (1 hide) in Cantlop manor, but even here a remarkable increase in value from 20s. to 110s. since before the Conquest[17] may indicate assarting. A wood known as The Cloud lay to the east and south-east of Berrington village, whose inhabitants enjoyed rights of common there in the 13th century.[18] Only isolated coppices remained here by the later 17th century,[19] and there has been little subsequent change. In 1844 some 67 a. lay in 6 coppices, most of them on the escarpment above Cound Brook and to the north of Eaton Mascott,[20] and the greater part of this woodland remained in 1965. The field-name Birch Hill found to the north of the central ridge[21] suggests medieval assarting, but much of the area formerly occupied by woodland here later became common land. Inclosure of the commons at The Cloud was still in progress in the later 17th century.[22]

Scarcely any woodland now remains to the west of Berrington village, but 'assart' field-names like Oaks in Berrington township and Britch, Birch Hill, and Birch Yard in Betton Abbots[23] give some indication of its former distribution. A large wood, now represented by Betton Coppice, once divided Betton Abbots from Betton Strange. Cordwood and pit-props from this wood were used at coal-mines on the Mackworth estate in Sutton in the early 18th century.[24] Only 11 a. of Betton Coppice lay within the parish in 1845.[25]

Brompton Heath lay within Cound parish until the 17th century;[26] the inhabitants of Brompton were paying rent for common rights here to the lord

(drift), sheet 152 (1932); par. rec., tithe appt. 1845, and maps, Betton Abbots, Cantlop, and Eaton Mascott, 1840, Berrington and Brompton, undated, and outline parish map, 1840; Shrews. Sch., MS. James V (survey and map of Berrington township, 1776); S.P.L., Deeds 13462 (survey and map of Cantlop manorial estate, 1768). This article was written in 1962 and revised in 1965.

[2] Census, 1891.
[3] See p. 22.
[4] S.R.O. 112 uncat., letter, Thos. Bell to Thos. Hill, 10 Dec. 1743.
[5] Q. Sess. Orders, ii. 110, 117.
[6] S.P.L., MS. 2, f. 146ᵛ.
[7] S.R.O. 112 uncat., deed, 1623.
[8] Rot. Hund. (Rec. Com.), ii. 93.
[9] S.P.L., Deeds 6694.
[10] S.P.L., Haughmond Cart. f. 59ᵛ.

[11] S.P.L., Deeds 6593.
[12] B.M. Add. MS. 58775.
[13] Par. rec., tithe appt.
[14] Ibid.
[15] Eyton, vi. 342.
[16] V.C.H. Salop. i. 311, 320, 326, 340.
[17] Ibid. 340.
[18] Eyton, vi. 35; S.P.L., Haughmond Cart. ff. 34, 34ᵛ.
[19] S.R.O. 1514 uncat., leases, 1655–98.
[20] Par. rec., tithe appt.
[21] Ibid.
[22] S.R.O. 1514 uncat., lease, 1698.
[23] Par. rec., tithe appt.
[24] E 134/9 Geo. I Mich./1; E 134/13 Geo. I Mich./ 6.
[25] Par. rec., tithe appt.
[26] S.P.L., MS. 2, f. 146ᵛ.

of Cound manor in the 14th century.[27] The 'assart' field-names Bridges and Birch Pits are found on the north-eastern boundary of the parish at this point[28] and inclosure was in progress on the Heath in 1683.[29] Groten Coppice, which contained only 7 a. in 1845,[30] is a remnant of a much larger area of woodland to the north of Brompton, on the banks of the Severn. Holdings described as 'pennyland', recorded here in 1564,[31] were probably assarts. Common meadow land on the banks of the Severn, north-west of Brompton, was shared by the inhabitants of Brompton and Wroxeter.[32] Stints were in use here in the 16th and 17th centuries, when the meadows had been divided into two parts. [33] That to the north was known in the 16th century as Wroxeter Cottons and that to the south as Brompton Cottons.[34]

The most extensive tract of woodland in the parish, that to the south of the hamlet of Cantlop, was part of the forest of Buriwood.[35] Considerable waste was said to have been made in the woods here by 1235,[36] and forest clearance was probably already in progress in the later 11th century. In the early 13th century Hugh Fitz Robert, lord of Cantlop manor and hereditary forester of Shropshire, granted 200 a. of woodland here to his relative Hugh de Longslow,[37] whose successor Hugh de Longslow partitioned the wood with the lord of Pitchford manor c. 1268[38] and appears to have been encouraging assarting by the creation of free tenancies in the later 13th century.[39] Common land called the Heath, on the northern edge of the wood, had been cleared by 1316,[40] and the field known as Magbridge Leasow in 1780[41] is probably another medieval assart. Cantlop Wood was inclosed in 1546,[42] but allotments in lieu of common rights were not made until 1590–5.[43] A substantial part of the wood was preserved in the form of coppices. These contained 110 a. in 1768,[44] and in 1844 Cantlop Wood and Lightgreen Coppice covered 103 a.[45] Part of Cantlop Wood was cleared for an airfield during the Second World War. In 1961 76 a. in Cantlop Wood and Lightgreen Coppice were purchased by the Forestry Commission.[46] The coppices were being managed to supply charcoal to local iron works in the later 17th century,[47] and Richard Reynolds of the Coalbrookdale Company was still obtaining cordwood from Cantlop in 1768.[48]

The common fields of Berrington were known as Atcham Field, Church Field, and Old Field in the early 18th century.[49] Atcham Field lay north of the village, on either side of the road to Cross Houses. Church Field lay alongside a road (now only a field-road) running eastwards from Berrington church towards the main road to Cressage. Old Field, west of the village, lay on either side of the road to Boreton. They had, however, been partially inclosed before 1695,[50] and the remaining common-field lands were inclosed in 1732.[51] The common fields of Betton Abbots and Brompton were still in existence in the 16th century,[52] but had been inclosed by 1698[53] and their names and location cannot be established. The Cantlop common fields were known as Berrington Field, Newton Field, and Wood Field in 1316,[54] but as Low, High, and Barley Fields respectively in 1418.[55] They retained the latter names until inclosure.[56] Berrington or Low Field ran towards Cantlop Mill to the north of the hamlet. Newton or High Field lay to the east and took its earlier name from the former hamlet of Newton in Pitchford parish. Wood or Barley Field lay to the west of the hamlet, north of the road to Condover. Inclosure was under consideration in 1590[57] and appears to have been virtually complete by 1595.[58] A small part of High Field, adjoining Cantlop hamlet, was, however, cultivated in strips until at least 1816.[59]

When first recorded in 1316, the common fields of Eaton Mascott were known as Berrington Field, Brompton Field, and Cound Field.[60] Berrington Field, or Mill Field, lay on the southern slopes of The Cloud and ran north-westwards from Eaton Mascott Mill.[61] Brompton Field was called Lechmere Field in 1556[62] and Pool Field in 1636.[63] It lay north-east of the hamlet, abutting on Eaton Mascott Pool (formerly called Lechmere) to the north and on Watling Street to the east.[64] Cound Field, which occupied the area above Cound Brook, south-east of Eaton Mascott, was probably bounded on the north by a rabbit-warren on The Cloud.[65] The Eaton Mascott common fields were uninclosed in 1556,[66] but some inclosure had taken place in Cound and Berrington Fields by 1636[67] and the process was complete by 1693.[68]

The road from Shrewsbury to Cressage, which is unlikely to have been altered in this part of its course since medieval times, runs through the north of the parish and was turnpiked in 1752.[69] It is now the only major road in the parish, but a number of other roads in Berrington were formerly important cross-country routes. Watling Street enters the parish at

27 Loton Hall MSS., Cound bailiff's acct. 1385–6.
28 Par. rec., tithe appt.
29 S.R.O. 112 uncat., lease, 1683.
30 Par. rec., tithe appt.
31 S.R.O. 1514 uncat., acct. 1564.
32 Ibid.; ibid. 112 uncat., leases, 1556–77.
33 Ibid.
34 Ibid.
35 S.P.L., Deeds 6683.
36 Eyton, vi. 339.
37 Ibid. 289.
38 Rot. Hund. (Rec. Com.), ii. 93.
39 S.P.L., Deeds 6593–4, 6683.
40 B.M. Add. Ch. 47247.
41 S.R.O. 103 uncat., survey of estate of F. Lloyd, 1780.
42 S.P.L., Deeds 6694.
43 S.R.O. 103 uncat., lease, 1590; S.P.L., Deeds 6713, 6714, 7022.
44 S.P.L., Deeds 13642.
45 Par. rec., tithe appt.
46 Ex inf. Forestry Com.
47 N.L.W., Cilybebyll 413, 1291.
48 S.P.L., Deeds 13651.
49 Description of Berrington common fields based on

Lich. Dioc. Regy., glebe terriers, 1612–98; S.R.O. 1514 uncat., inclosure agreement, 1732.
50 Lich. Dioc. Regy., glebe terrier, 1695.
51 S.R.O. 1514 uncat., inclosure agreement, 1732.
52 Ibid. 840 uncat., ct. r. of manor of Hernes, 1548–54.
53 Lich. Dioc. Regy., glebe terrier, 1698.
54 B.M. Add. Ch. 47247.
55 S.P.L., Deeds 6688.
56 Ibid. 9501.
57 S.R.O. 103 uncat., lease, 1590.
58 S.P.L., Deeds 9501.
59 S.R.O. 103 uncat., survey of estate of J. A. Lloyd, 1816.
60 B.M. Add. Ch. 58707.
61 S.P.L., Deeds 1713; S.R.O. 1514 uncat., survey of lands of Sir Humphrey Lee, 1619.
62 N.L.W., Pitchford Hall 1054.
63 S.P.L., Deeds 5135.
64 B.M. Add. Ch. 58775.
65 S.P.L., Deeds 5135.
66 N.L.W., Pitchford Hall 1054.
67 S.P.L., Deeds 5135.   68 Ibid. 1033.
69 Shrewsbury–Wenlock road Act, 25 Geo. II, c. 49 (priv. act).

Brompton Ford, where the remains of a Roman bridge were found in 1927.[70] This Roman road was still in use in the summer, or when the Severn was fordable, when it was turnpiked in 1764,[71] but it was disturnpiked as 'useless' in 1829.[72] The alternative route to the south in 1764 followed the road from Atcham Bridge to Cross Houses, then ran for a short distance along the road to Cressage, rejoining Watling Street north-west of Cound Stank.[73] The road from Condover past Cantlop to Pitchford was described as a portway in 1408.[74] A section of the road from Shrewsbury to Acton Burnell, south of Betton Abbots, is known as King Street. This road was turnpiked in 1797[75] and the elegant cast-iron bridge, replacing a ford across Cound Brook north-west of Cantlop, was built by subscription in 1812 to designs approved by Thomas Telford.[76] The road from Atcham to Condover, turnpiked in 1797,[77] crosses the last-mentioned road at King Street. A toll-house had been erected at this junction by 1808,[78] but it was demolished in the later 19th century. There are two other bridges across the Cound in the parish. The present cast-iron Boreton Bridge was erected by Thomas, Lord Berwick, in 1826,[79] but there has been a bridge at this spot since at least 1659, when it was known as Cliff Bridge.[80] A bridge at Cantlop Mill, whose function is apparent from its 15th-century name, Church Bridge,[81] survived in the form of a plank-bridge for church-goers from Cantlop until the early 18th century.[82] The Severn Valley Railway, which runs across the north of the parish, was opened in 1862.[83]

Air photographs provide abundant evidence of early settlement on the light soils to the north and east of the parish. There are 7 round barrows and an inclosure, all of which probably date from the Bronze Age, on the sandy slope immediately east of Eaton Mascott Pool and close to Watling Street.[84] A circular inclosure in the Severn flood-plain north-east of Brompton[85] and an irregular inclosure to the south of this hamlet[86] are of uncertain date.

Berrington village stands on a small deposit of sand and gravel. Although most of the houses stand on the road from Cross Houses to Boreton, the church and Manor Farm stand at the end of a short lane at right angles and to the east of this road. The lane formerly continued eastwards, joining the main road from Shrewsbury to Cressage to the south-east of Cross Houses, but has been no more than a field-road since the earlier 19th century.[87] The church is a pre-Conquest foundation[88] and has occupied its present site since at least the 13th century, so that the focus of settlement has probably moved since the Middle Ages. Manor Farm is an L-shaped timber-framed house of 2 stories with attics.[89] It was built or enlarged by Richard Blakeway in 1658;[90] the west wing is probably of earlier date. The house retains its original roof of stone slates from Harnage.

There were at least 18 houses in Berrington township as a whole in 1662, 14 of which possessed only one hearth.[91] The village itself appears to have contained 10 houses in 1732[92] and a dozen in 1776.[93] This apparent increase, however, was due to the conversion of 4 farm-houses into cottages, as a result of the reorganization of farms on the manorial estate.[94] Berrington Farm and Grove Farm, the two existing farm-houses on the village street, are both brick-cased timber-framed houses of 17th-century date. A cottage between these two farm-houses was a smithy in 1776[95] and remained in business until c. 1900.[96] An alehouse known as the New Inn is recorded in Berrington in 1589.[97] This is presumably the alehouse which stood opposite Grove Farm,[98] known to have existed in the village between 1616[99] and its closure in 1771.[1] The school, at the junction of the village street and the lane to the church, was built in 1843 on the site of the former parsonage-house.[2] A new parsonage, now known as Berrington Hall, was built a ½ mile north-west of the village in 1804.[3]

Eaton Mascott, which stands on boulder clay, is approached by steep, narrow lanes cut deeply into the sandy slopes of the central ridge. As a result of the divisions of Eaton Mascott manor since the 13th century,[4] the hamlet became a small but prosperous community of freeholders. This is reflected in the Hearth Tax assessment of 1662, when out of 5 houses recorded in the township two contained 4 hearths and one (Eaton Mascott Hall) had nine.[5] There has been little change here since that date. There were two farm-houses and 8 cottages in the hamlet, in addition to the Hall, in the mid-19th century.[6] South Farm, partly stone-built with a timber-framed dairy, probably represents one of the 17th-century freeholds, and the timber-framed building to the east, now converted into cottages, is likely to be another. A smith is recorded here in 1635.[7]

[70] T.S.A.S. 4th ser. xi. 304–6.
[71] Watling Street road Act, 4 Geo. III, c. 70 (priv. act).
[72] Ibid. 10 Geo IV, c. 74 (local and personal act).
[73] Ibid. 4 Geo. III, c. 70 (priv. act).
[74] S.P.L., Deeds 6688.
[75] Atcham–Dorrington road Act, 37 Geo. III, c. 172 (priv. act).
[76] Q. Sess., dep. plans 33; ibid. bridge bk. i. 103; T.S.A.S. lvi. 114.
[77] Atcham–Dorrington road Act, 37 Geo. III, c. 172 (priv. act).
[78] Baugh, Map of Salop. (1808).
[79] Plaque on bridge.
[80] Q. Sess. Orders, i. 65.
[81] S.P.L., Deeds 6688.
[82] S.R.O. 714/9. T.S.A.S. liv. 114 incorrectly assigns this reference to the bridge at Cantlop Ford.
[83] Ex inf. Brit. Trans. Rec.
[84] Air photograph at Shrews. Museum (O.S. Nat. Grid SJ 545066).
[85] S.P.L., air photograph no. 251 (O.S. Nat. Grid SJ 558085).
[86] Ibid. no. 253 (O.S. Nat. Grid SJ 548074).

[87] O.S. 2″ orig. drawings, sheet 207 (1817); par. rec., tithe appt.
[88] See p. 24.
[89] See plate facing p. 132.
[90] Date '1658' and initials 'R.B. M.B.' above north door; S.P.R Lich. xiv (4), 61; E 179/255/35 m. 76.
[91] E 179/255/35 m. 76.
[92] S.R.O. 1514 uncat., inclosure agreement, 1732.
[93] Shrews. Sch., MS. James V.
[94] See p. 23.
[95] Shrews. Sch., MS. James V.
[96] Kelly's Dir. Salop. (1900).
[97] S.R.O. 567 uncat., deed, 1589.
[98] Shrews. Sch., MS. James V.
[99] Q. Sess., alehouse reg.
[1] Ibid.
[2] Ibid.; par. rec., conveyance of site, 1843.
[3] Lich. Dioc. Regy., glebe terrier, 1804.
[4] See pp. 20–21.
[5] E 179/255/35 m. 76. For description of Eaton Mascott Hall see p. 21.
[6] Par. rec., tithe appt.
[7] S.P.L., Deeds 3303.

Betton Abbots, held during the Middle Ages by Shrewsbury Abbey, consisted of a manor-house and 11 other houses in 1553,[8] but had been reduced to 7 houses by 1698.[9] These were described as 'very old' in 1763[10] and were extensively repaired in 1765.[11] In 1782 Noel, Lord Berwick, converted all the farm-houses here into cottages, with the exception of Betton Abbots Farm, and erected new farm-houses on isolated sites.[12] Betton Abbots Farm is a brick-cased timber-framed house. There were 5 cottages here in 1807,[13] but two of these had been demolished by 1845[14] and more timber-framed cottages to the west of the farm-house were demolished c. 1930.[15] Of the 2 cottages remaining by 1965, that to the south of the road was a rough-cast timber-framed house of cruck construction and the other was a modern building. Irregularities in the surface of a field to the west of the cruck cottage presumably represent the site of the former hamlet.

The history of settlement at Brompton closely resembles that at Betton Abbots. Both were owned by Shrewsbury Abbey in the Middle Ages and by the Hills of Attingham since the mid-18th century.[16] There were 13 houses at Brompton in 1553[17] and at least 12 in 1661.[18] Five of the latter were said to contain 2 hearths each and the remainder one hearth in the following year.[19] There were still 7 farms of moderate size and 3 other houses in Brompton in 1755, apart from cottages.[20] Noel, Lord Berwick, reorganized the farms here, apparently between 1790 and 1792,[21] and by 1807 there were 4 farms and 4 cottages in the hamlet.[22] Lower Brompton Farm has been rebuilt on a new site to the north and two other farm-houses have been demolished since 1845. Brompton Farm, a timber-framed house enlarged and cased in brick c. 1800, and two cottages now occupy the site on the ancient hamlet.

Cantlop stands on a short lane which formerly continued across the Cound to Berrington. Like Eaton Mascott it was largely held by freeholders in the later Middle Ages, but their number was reduced in the course of the 16th century.[23] Three of the 7 houses recorded in Cantlop in 1662 contained more than one hearth.[24] The 5-hearth house occupied by the freeholder Richard Calcott in 1672 can be identified with Old Farm.[25] This timber-framed house, now cased in brick, had only one hearth in 1662,[26] but was enlarged in the following year.[27] The earlier

house is probably the house of 3 bays leased to Thomas Farmer in 1590.[28] There were 4 farm-houses and 2 cottages on the site of the hamlet in the later 18th century.[29] Two of the farm-houses, however, were demolished between 1840 and 1845,[30] when their place had been taken by Cantlop Farm, an isolated house to the south-west. The greater part of the township has been a County Council small-holding estate since 1911, and 3 smallholdings have been built here.[31]

Cross Houses appears to have begun as one of the mid-17th-century cross-roads settlements, frequently found elsewhere in the county, which normally consisted of an alehouse and a smithy. Encroachments to the north of the road here are first recorded in 1657[32] and a smithy, established by 1683,[33] can probably be identified with the Fox Inn. This is a timber-framed house, later cased in brick, which is first recorded as an alehouse in 1851, under the name The Golden Cross.[34] It was known by its present name in 1863.[35] Until the 19th century, however, most of the houses here stood to the south of the road, where there were 7 houses by 1776.[36] Two of these had been licensed as alehouses before 1745,[37] but both had been closed by 1790.[38] Nine houses stood to the south of the road by 1805,[39] and the 12 houses there in 1845 included a Wesleyan Methodist Chapel[40] and the Bell Inn. The latter is first recorded in 1828.[41] Tudor Cottage is a small timber-framed house. The Atcham Union Workhouse was built to the north of the road in 1793 to designs by J. H. Hay-cock.[42] There were only 3 other houses on this side of the road in 1807,[43] but 16 houses had been built here by 1845, in addition to the Ebenezer Methodist chapel, built in 1837.[44] The workhouse was enlarged in 1851,[45] and again in 1903, when a nurses' home was built.[46] It is now a geriatric and maternity hospital. Six Council houses were built to the north of the road before 1939, and 63 Council houses and 23 flats have been built since 1945.[47]

A smaller roadside settlement has developed at Cantlop Cross. One of the cottages is timber-framed, but most of them date from the later 19th century. Cantlop Grove and the Oak Inn were built between 1816 and 1845.[48] The latter was first licensed in 1845.[49]

Although all the ancient hamlets have shrunk since the later Middle Ages, there are few isolated

[8] Cal. Pat. 1547–53, 190–1.
[9] Lich. Dioc. Regy., glebe terrier, 1698.
[10] S.R.O. 112 uncat., letter, Thos. Bell to Thos. Hill, 21 Mar. 1763.
[11] Attingham Park estate office, accts. 1755–74.
[12] S.R.O. 112 uncat., estate vouchers, 1782.
[13] Ibid. 1011 uncat., Attingham estate survey, 1807.
[14] Par. rec., tithe appt.
[15] Ex inf. Mrs. V. Bromley, Manor Farm, Berrington.
[16] See p. 19.
[17] S.C. 6/Hen. VIII/3010 m. 58.
[18] S.R.O. 112 uncat., Brompton ct. r. 1657–1824.
[19] E 179/255/35 m. 75.
[20] Attingham Park estate office, accts. 1755–74.
[21] Q. Sess., accts. of Jonathan Scoltock, 1785–92.
[22] S.R.O. 1011 uncat., Attingham estate survey, 1807.
[23] See p. 23.
[24] E 179/255/35 m. 75d.
[25] Hearth Tax, 1672, 131; S.R.O. 103 uncat., survey of estate of F. Lloyd, 1780.
[26] E 179/255/35 m. 75d.   [27] Datestone.
[28] S.R.O. 103 uncat., lease, 1590.
[29] Ibid. survey of estate of F. Lloyd, 1780; S.P.L., Deeds 13642.

[30] Par. rec., tithe appt.
[31] Ex inf. County Land Agent.
[32] S.R.O. 112 uncat., Brompton ct. r. 1657–1824.
[33] Ibid. lease, 1683.
[34] Bagshaw's Dir. Salop. (1851).
[35] Kelly's Dir. Salop. (1863).
[36] Shrews. Sch., MS. James V.
[37] N.L.W., Castle Hill 2244.
[38] Q. Sess., alehouse reg.
[39] S.P.L., MS. 294.
[40] Par. rec., tithe appt.
[41] Ibid.; Q. Sess., alehouse reg.
[42] S.R.O. 83 uncat., Atcham Union minute bk. 1791–4.
[43] Ibid. 1011 uncat., Attingham estate survey, 1807.
[44] W. E. Morris, The History of Methodism in Shrewsbury and District (Shrewsbury, 1960), 42–43.
[45] J. H. Sheldon, Report on Birmingham Hospital Bd. Geriatric Services (Birmingham, 1961), 68.
[46] Ibid.
[47] Ex inf. Atcham R.D.C.
[48] B.M. O.S. 2" orig. drawings, sheet 207 (1817); par. rec., tithe appt.
[49] Q. Sess., alehouse reg.

farms and cottages. In the north of the parish Little Betton Farm and Lower Brompton Farm are the product of reorganization on the Hill estate since the later 18th century,[50] but The Cotons, on the edge of the former Brompton Heath, is first recorded in 1699.[51] The latter is a T-shaped brick-built house. The kitchen to the north dates from *c.* 1800 but the south wing may be timber-framed.

Newman Hall, a brick-cased timber-framed house a ½ mile west of Eaton Mascott, was probably built in the mid-17th century as the farmstead of a newly created freehold belonging to the Blakeway family of Berrington.[52] The Cliff House near Boreton Bridge may have been built for the warrener of the lord of Berrington manor, who had a rabbit-warren here.[53] An isolated farm-house near Lightgreen Coppice in the south of Cantlop township is first recorded in 1595[54] and in 1768 was said to be of cruck construction.[55] Later known as Bendigo, perhaps an allusion to its late-18th-century tenant, Abednego Wellings,[56] it has been demolished since 1845.[57] The group of brick cottages at Cound Stank were built before 1845.[58]

The parish was said to contain 43 households in 1563[59] and 176 adults in 1676.[60] Until 1931 population figures for Berrington in the Census Reports do not normally distinguish inhabitants from the inmates of the workhouse, but the population of the parish appears to have been relatively stationary during the 19th century. There were 528 inhabitants, exclusive of workhouse inmates, in 1841,[61] 537 inhabitants in 1851,[62] and 557 inhabitants in 1931.[63] The population had risen to 623 by 1951 and to 785 by 1961.[64] The Revd. Edward Williams (1762–1833), the Shropshire antiquary, was born at Eaton Mascott.[65]

MANORS. The manor of *BERRINGTON*, held by Thoret before the Conquest, passed shortly after 1066 to Warin the sheriff.[66] On the latter's death in 1086 his widow Amieria married Rainald de Bailleul, who, as Rainald the sheriff, was said to hold the manor of Roger, Earl of Shrewsbury, later in the same year.[67] The overlordship passed to the Fitz-Alans, Earls of Arundel, as heirs of Rainald the sheriff, who are first recorded as overlords in 1165 and held it throughout the Middle Ages.[68]

Azo Bigot, tenant of the manor in 1086,[69] was still living in 1136.[70] Berrington, like the remainder of his estates, appears to have passed to the Le Strange family,[71] for John le Strange granted lands here to Haughmond Abbey before 1172.[72] John appears, however, to have enfeoffed Hamon de St. Remy as under-tenant by 1166.[73] The latter's daughter Helewise granted lands to Haughmond Abbey after 1172.[74] She may have married Hugh le Strange, who was lord of Berrington manor by 1221.[75] He was succeeded before 1242 by co-heirs,[76] who were represented by Richard de Dryton, William Fitz-Alan, John Fitz Phillip, and Phillip de Hungefort in 1255.[77] The estate of the last two is not later recorded; their shares may, however, be represented by the carucate in Berrington granted to John de Lee by John le Strange as mesne lord *c.* 1283.[78]

The portion of the manor held by William Fitz-Alan passed to his sister Parnel, wife of John de la Lee.[79] She was dead by 1276[80] and, although her husband was still alive after 1317,[81] his brother Thomas de la Lee of Stanton-upon-Hine-Heath was lord of the manor in 1311.[82] It was again in the hands of John de la Lee between 1314 and 1317,[83] but John, son of Thomas de la Lee of Stanton, was lord in 1323,[84] probably as the result of an agreement between the two branches of the Lee family *c.* 1319.[85] John, son of John de la Lee of Stanton, was dead by 1370.[86] His son, Robert, who came of age before 1379, married his cousin Parnel, daughter and heir of Roger Lee of Langley, before 1401.[87] After Robert's death the manor was held by his widow, who leased it to her son Ralph Lee in 1439.[88]

The portion of the manor held by Richard de Dryton, who was still alive in 1274,[89] had passed by 1292 to Thomas de Felton.[90] The latter's son Stephen conveyed it in 1323 to John de la Lee,[91] lord of the other moiety of the manor, who granted it for life to his daughter Maud in 1328.[92] Maud de la Lee surrendered her life interest to her nephew Robert de la Lee in 1379, thus reuniting the manor under one ownership.[93] After the death of Ralph Lee in 1479 the manor followed the descent of Langley manor[94] until 1866, when Sir Charles Smythe sold it to Thomas Wells of Eaton Mascott.[95] Berrington has subsequently followed the descent of Eaton Mascott manor.

[50] Little Betton Farm was built *c.* 1782: S.R.O. 112 uncat., estate vouchers, 1782. Lower Brompton Farm was built after 1845: par. rec., tithe appt.
[51] S.R.O. 112 uncat., lease, 1699.
[52] S.P.L., Deeds 1022, 1029, 1030.
[53] E 134/9 Anne East./15.
[54] S.P.L., Deeds 9501.
[55] S.R.O. 665 uncat., survey of Cantlop manorial estate, 1768.
[56] Ibid.
[57] Par. rec., tithe appt.
[58] Ibid.
[59] B.M. Harl. MS. 594, f. 160.
[60] *T.S.A.S.* 2nd ser. i. 80.
[61] *Census*, 1841.
[62] Ibid. 1851.
[63] Ibid. 1931.
[64] Ibid. 1951–61.
[65] *D.N.B.*
[66] *V.C.H. Salop.* i. 320; Eyton, vi. 44; *T.S.A.S.* lvi. 246.
[67] Ibid.
[68] *Red Bk. Exch.* (Rolls Ser.), 272; *Cal. Inq. Misc.* vi, p. 158; *Feud. Aids*, iv. 269; *Visit. Salop. 1623* (Harl. Soc. xxix), ii. 317; C 142/132/17.
[69] *V.C.H. Salop.* i. 320.
[70] Eyton, iv. 127.
[71] Ibid. i. 211.

[72] S.P.L., Haughmond Cart. f. 34; Eyton, vi. 34.
[73] *Red. Bk. Exch.* (Rolls Ser.), 272.
[74] S.P.L., Haughmond Cart. f. 34; Eyton, vi. 35.
[75] Eyton, vi. 35.
[76] Ibid.; *Bk. of Fees*, 973.
[77] *Rot. Hund.* (Rec. Com.), ii. 62.
[78] *Visit. Salop. 1623* (Harl. Soc. xxix), ii. 315; Eyton, vi. 38.
[79] Eyton, vi. 36.
[80] Ibid. v. 125.
[81] Ibid. vi. 39.
[82] *T.S.A.S.* 2nd ser. iv. 347.
[83] Eyton, vi. 38–39; S.P.L., Deeds 3612.
[84] Eyton, vi. 40; S.P.L., Deeds 10782, 10784.
[85] Eyton, vi. 39.
[86] Ibid. ix. 113.
[87] Ibid. vii. 271; *Visit. Salop. 1623* (Harl. Soc. xxix), ii. 316.
[88] *Visit. Salop. 1623* (Harl. Soc. xxix), ii. 316.
[89] *Rot. Hund.* (Rec. Com.), ii. 87.
[90] Eyton, vi. 37.
[91] Ibid. 40.
[92] Ibid.; *Visit. Salop. 1623* (Harl. Soc. xxix), ii. 316.
[93] Eyton, vi. 41.   [94] See p. 143.
[95] Eaton Mascott estate title-deeds, *penes* Messrs. Johnson & Co., solicitors, Birmingham.

A ½ hide in Berrington was held by Thoret of Condover church before the Conquest.[96] This had apparently been merged with the manor of Berrington before 1086, and may have been granted to Warin the sheriff by Shrewsbury Abbey in exchange for the tithes and advowson of Berrington church.[97]

The manor of *BETTON* once included the townships of Betton Abbots and Betton Strange, but the latter was held as a separate manor in the mid-12th century by Hamon le Strange, who granted lands there to Haughmond Abbey *c.* 1160.[98] The Bishop of Chester, who held the manor of Betton before the Conquest, still held it in 1086,[99] but Betton Abbots was granted shortly afterwards to Shrewsbury Abbey.[1] It was leased to Richard de Belmeis, who gave instructions on his deathbed in 1127 that it should be restored to the Abbey.[2] This was contested by Richard's nephew and heir Phillip,[3] but Richard's son Ranulf, who later gained possession of the estate, acknowledged between 1154 and 1160 that his title to it was unsound.[4] Ranulf's heir, Roger de la Zouche, again claimed the manor in 1220, but without success.[5] The manor was known as Little Betton after the later 12th century, to distinguish it from Betton-in-Hales (Great Betton), another possession of Shrewsbury Abbey.[6] It had been absorbed into the composite manor of Hernes by 1333,[7] and was held by Shrewsbury Abbey until the Dissolution.

The manor was granted in 1553 to John Mackworth,[8] and it passed from father to son in this family[9] until 1731, the following being lords: John, 1553–71;[10] Thomas, 1571–87; Richard, 1587–1617; Humphrey, 1617–54; Thomas, 1654–96; Bulkeley, 1696–1731. The last devised it to his nephew Herbert Mackworth[11] who died in 1765. The manor appears to have been mortgaged, during Herbert's lifetime, to Thomas Hill of Tern, who was taking the rents of Betton Abbots by 1755.[12] Hill had probably established his title to the manor by 1776,[13] and it subsequently formed part of the estate of his descendants, the Lords Berwick of Attingham Park.[14] Thomas, Lord Berwick (d. 1947) devised his estate to The National Trust, the present owners.

The manor of *BROMPTON* was held as two manors by the freemen Ernui and Elmer before the Conquest, but they had been united before 1086, when the manor was held of Roger, Earl of Shrewsbury.[15] Picot de Say, its tenant in 1086,[16] granted the manor to Shrewsbury Abbey between 1093 and 1098.[17] This grant appears to have been called into question, for Picot's heir, Henry de Say, obtained the manor of Cheney Longville from the abbey in exchange for Brompton some time before 1130.[18] Like Betton Abbots Brompton formed part of the manor of Hernes by 1333[19] and was held by Shrewsbury Abbey until the Dissolution. It was granted in 1553 to Reynold Corbet,[20] whose son Peter sold it to Edward Bacon in 1588.[21] The last sold Brompton in 1599 to Francis Wolryche,[22] whose descendants held it until 1743, the following being lords:[23] Francis, 1599–1614; Thomas, 1614–68; Francis, 1668–89; Thomas (nephew), 1689–1701; John, 1701–15; Mary (sister), 1715–43.[24] In 1743 Mary Wolryche sold the manor to Thomas Hill[25] and it has since followed the descent of Betton Abbots manor.

The manor of *CANTLOP* was held by Edric before the Conquest and in 1086 by Norman the huntsman of Roger, Earl of Shrewsbury.[26] The Pitchford family, heirs of Norman the huntsman, were its overlords in 1255[27] and 1284,[28] but by 1315 Cantlop was said to be held of the Chetwynd family, the mesne lords of the Pitchfords in Pitchford manor.[29] The Chetwynds were accounted overlords throughout the 14th century,[30] but the manor was said to be held of the Earl of March in 1419.[31] Rents in the manor were held of William, Lord Ferrers of Groby, in 1429,[32] and the moiety of the manor held by William, Lord Lovell, was held of Henry Boston in 1455.[33]

Cantlop manor had been divided by the early 12th century, when one moiety was held by the descendants of Ulger the huntsman and the other by an ancestor of the Arundels of Habberley. Ulger the huntsman, living between 1094 and 1135,[34] is not recorded at Cantlop, but his son William Fitz Ulger granted a moiety of Cantlop Mill to Shrewsbury Abbey in the mid-12th century.[35] Robert Fitz William, to whom this moiety of the manor had passed by 1187,[36] died in 1203.[37] He was succeeded by his son Hugh, who granted it before 1228 to his sister Alice on her marriage to Hugh de Longslow (I).[38] The latter was dead by 1249,[39] when his wife Alice had already granted a portion of the estate to their son Hugh (II).[40] The moiety passed in 1290 to the latter's son Hugh de Longslow (III),[41] who settled it on his daughter Alice at her marriage to Nicholas de Pitchford in 1313.[42] Nicholas, who was lord in 1316[43] and 1343,[44] appears to have died

[96] *V.C.H. Salop.* i. 320.
[97] Ibid.
[98] Eyton, vi. 174.
[99] *V.C.H. Salop.* i. 311.
[1] Eyton, vi. 181–2.
[2] Ibid. 182–3.
[3] Ibid. 183.
[4] Ibid.
[5] Ibid. 184.
[6] Ibid. 185.
[7] S.C. 6/967/16.
[8] *Cal. Pat.* 1547–53, 190–1.
[9] For pedigree see S.P.L., MS. 4080, p. 746.
[10] C 142/159/44.
[11] S.R.O. 112 uncat., will of Bulkeley Mackworth, 1730.
[12] Attingham Park estate office, accts. 1755–74.
[13] Ibid.; S.R.O. 112 uncat., letter, Thos. Bell to Thos. Hill, 21 Mar. 1763.
[14] *Complete Peerage*, ii. 167–8.
[15] *V.C.H. Salop.* i. 335.
[16] Ibid.
[17] Eyton, vi. 169–70.
[18] Ibid. i. 247; ibid. xi. 370.
[19] S.C. 6/967/16.

[20] *Cal. Pat.* 1553, 190–1.
[21] S.R.O. 112 uncat., deed, 1588.
[22] Ibid.
[23] For pedigree see S.P.L., MS. 4080, pp. 2044–5.
[24] S.R.O. 112 uncat., settlement, 1715.
[25] Ibid. deed, 1743.
[26] *V.C.H. Salop.* i. 340.
[27] *Rot. Hund.* (Rec. Com.), ii. 62.
[28] *Cal. Inq. p.m.* ii, p. 337.
[29] Ibid. v, p. 392.
[30] Ibid. viii, p. 496.
[31] C 138/54/116.
[32] C 139/43/12.
[33] C 139/158/28.
[34] Eyton, vii. 265.
[35] N.L.W., MS. 7851D, f. 155ᵛ.
[36] Ibid.; Eyton, vi. 287.
[37] Eyton, viii. 266–7.
[38] Ibid. vi. 288.
[39] S.P.L., Deeds 6592.
[40] B.M. Add. Ch. 66932.
[41] *Cal. Inq. p.m.* ii, p. 462.
[42] S.P.L., Deeds 6595, 6684.
[43] *Feud. Aids*, iv. 230.
[44] C 143/267/10.

without issue, for the manor had reverted by 1363 to William, son of Hugh de Hulle, grandson of Hugh de Longslow (III).[45] Griffin, son of William de Hulle, conveyed this moiety in 1426 to William Cotton,[46] to whom John Stuche, another descendant of Hugh de Longslow (III), released his interest in the manor in 1430.[47] Yet more descendants of Hugh de Longslow had smaller claims on the estate. Elizabeth, wife of Howell ap Gwillym and niece of John Stuche, conveyed her interest to William Cotton in 1434.[48] The descendants of Beatrice, wife of Phillip Maynston, another niece of John Stuche, held rents in Cantlop in 1429[49] and 1449;[50] these were conveyed in 1457 to William Cotton,[51] who had thus extinguished all outstanding claims on this moiety. It was held by Cotton's descendants until 1571, when George Cotton sold it to George Proud and Richard Prince.[52] The latter conveyed it in 1587 to Thomas Owen,[53] who had purchased the other moiety of the manor in the preceding year.[54] The manor subsequently followed the descent of Condover manor.[55]

The other moiety of Cantlop manor was held in 1255 by John de Arundel,[56] who had been succeeded by his son John by 1272.[57] The latter sold it to Robert Burnell, Bishop of Bath and Wells, in 1285,[58] and it followed the descent of Acton Burnell manor[59] until 1548, when Fulk Crompton settled it on his son Thomas.[60] Richard, son of Thomas Crompton, conveyed this moiety to Thomas Owen in 1586.[61]

Like Berrington manor the manor of *EATON MASCOTT* was held by Thoret before the Conquest and by Rainald the sheriff of Roger, Earl of Shrewsbury, in 1086.[62] The overlordship subsequently followed the descent of that of Berrington.[63] Eaton Mascott was held of the lord of Cound manor after 1575,[64] and the lords of the manor still owed suit at the manor court of Cound in 1672.[65] Fulcher, the tenant in 1086,[66] appears to have left no heirs, for between 1135 and 1160, William FitzAlan granted the manor to Marscot,[67] its tenant in 1166.[68] The latter had been succeeded before 1203 by his son Hamon,[69] who was dead by 1242, when the manor was held by William Marscot.[70] William's son William, to whom the manor had passed by 1256,[71] was still living in 1274.[72] He seems to have left no

male heirs, for in 1294 the manor was held by Thomas de Baskerville and William de Preston.[73]

The moiety held by Thomas de Baskerville had passed by 1316 to his son John,[74] who appears to have settled some estate here on his daughter Isabel.[75] In 1326 John and Isabel granted 65 a. at Eaton Mascott to Thomas de la Lee, and 10½ a. to Richard Waters of Betton.[76] The portion of Richard Waters appears to have passed by 1368 to William de Eton, who held another portion of the manor.[77] Thomas de la Lee was probably a cousin of John de la Lee, lord of Berrington manor at this time.[78] His estate at Eaton Mascott was presumably merged with the manor of Berrington, which included lands in Eaton Mascott in 1392.[79] The lord of Berrington was said to be one of the lords of Eaton Mascott manor in 1428.[80] This estate is last recorded in 1636.[81]

One-fifth of the manor, sold in 1359 by William de Aston and his wife Alice to Robert de Thornes of Shrewsbury,[82] may represent a further fragment of the Baskerville moiety. Robert de Thornes had been succeeded before 1388 by his son Robert,[83] whose brother Roger held the estate in 1419[84] and was still alive in 1431.[85] A descendant, John Thornes, held a fifth of Eaton Mascott manor at his death in 1552.[86] He was succeeded by his grandson Nicholas, and the estate then passed from father to son in the Thornes family until 1635, the following being lords: Nicholas, 1552–82;[87] Richard, 1582–1620;[88] Francis, 1620–35.[89] The estate was then purchased by William Dyos, who sold it to Pontesbury Owen in 1639.[90] The latter held it until his death in 1652, being succeeded by his son Pontesbury Owen, 1652–78, and his grandson Edward Owen, 1678–1723.[91] This portion of the manor then passed to Edward's daughter Mary, who married successively Edward Owen of Condover, William Francke (d. 1736), and Edward Rogers.[92] Mary died in 1770 and in the following year Thomas Offley, devisee of Edward Rogers, sold it to Edward Williams.[93]

The other moiety of Eaton Mascott manor was still held by William de Preston, or by a descendant of the same name, in 1346.[94] He appears to be the man more commonly known as William de Eton, who was the most substantial inhabitant of Eaton Mascott in 1327[95] and 1332.[96] The latter's son

45 S.P.L., MS. 2790, p. 140.
46 S.P.L., Deeds 6599.
47 Ibid. 6600.
48 Ibid. 6602.
49 C 139/43/12.
50 C 139/133/10.
51 S.P.L., Deeds 6603.
52 Ibid. 6605.
53 Ibid. 6705.
54 Ibid. 6699–6701.
55 See pp. 38–39.
56 *Rot. Hund.* (Rec. Com.), ii. 62.
57 Eyton, vi. 289.
58 C.P. 25(1)/193/6/12.
59 See p. 7.
60 *Cal. Pat.* 1547–8, 280.
61 S.P.L., Deeds 6699–6761.
62 *V.C.H. Salop.* i. 320.
63 *Red. Bk. Exch.* (Rolls Ser.), 273; *Bk. of Fees*, 962; *Cal. Inq. p.m.* iii, p. 125; *Feud. Aids*, iv. 239.
64 C 142/172/136; S.P.L., MS. 2, f. 156.
65 S.P.L., MS. 2, ff. 148, 148ᵛ.
66 *V.C.H. Salop.* i. 320.
67 Eyton, vi. 102.
68 *Red. Bk. Exch.* (Rolls Ser.), 273.
69 Eyton, vi. 103.
70 *Bk. of Fees*, 971.

71 C.P. 25(1)/196/4/62.
72 Eyton, vi. 104.
73 *Cal. Inq. p.m.* iii, p. 125.
74 S.P.L., Deeds 1713.
75 Eyton, vi. 105–6.
76 Ibid.
77 N.L.W., Pitchford Hall 1356; B.M. Add. Ch. 58308
78 Eyton, vi. 105.
79 S.R.O. 1514 uncat., lease, 1392.
80 *Feud. Aids*, iv. 257.
81 S.R.O. 49/13.
82 C.P. 25(1)/195/16/24.
83 *T.S.A.S.* 4th ser. xii. 150.
84 Ibid. 155; *Cal. Close*, 1419–22, 59.
85 *Feud. Aids*, iv. 239.
86 C 142/97/99.
87 C 142/210/91.
88 C 142/337/93.
89 C.P. 25(2)/477/10 Chas. I Hil.
90 C.P. 25(2)/478/15 Chas. I Mich.
91 *T.S.A.S.* 4th ser. viii. 75.
92 Ibid. 76; Eaton Mascott Hall title-deeds.
93 Eaton Mascott Hall title-deeds.
94 *Feud. Aids*, iv. 236.
95 *T.S.A.S.* 2nd ser. xi. 381.
96 E 179/166/2 m. 5.

William acquired other lands in the township in 1366[97] and 1368,[98] and was said to be lord of the whole manor in 1397.[99] He had been succeeded before 1428 by Roger de Eton,[1] whose daughter and heir carried the estate to her husband William Hopton.[2] A descendant, William Hopton, was said to hold half the manor at his death in 1575.[3] The latter's grandson George sold it in 1611 to John Farmer,[4] whose grandson Richard sold half of the property to James Shepheard of Eaton Mascott in 1669.[5] This moiety was purchased in 1702 by Adam Ottley, Rector of Cound,[6] after whose death in 1723 it was sold to John Hollings.[7] At the death of J. B. Hollings in 1803, this estate, then containing 254 a., passed to his daughter Mabel, whose husband George Best sold it to Richard Williams in 1828.[8] The remainder of the Farmer estate was held by Richard Farmer until 1717, when he sold it to Charles Tayleur of Pulley.[9] After the latter's death in 1741[10] it was held successively by his widow Martha (d. 1751) and his nephew William Tayleur of Buntingsdale (d. 1796),[11] whose grandson John sold it to Richard Williams in 1810.[12]

The whole of Eaton Mascott manor was thus acquired by Edward Williams and his son Richard, and was held by the latter after Edward's death in 1824.[13] Richard was succeeded in 1831 by his son Edward Hosier Williams, who died in 1844. The estate then passed to Edward's brother Richard, who sold it to Thomas Wells, a Staffordshire ironmaster, in 1861. Wells, who purchased Berrington manor in 1866, died in 1876. The estate was then held by his widow Mary (d. 1884) and his sons Charles and Thomas, both of whom died in 1890. In the following year the manors of Berrington and Eaton Mascott were purchased by Charles Holcroft. The estate has since been owned by Sir Charles Holcroft, bt., 1891–1917; Sir George Holcroft, bt. (nephew), 1917–51; Sir Reginald Holcroft, bt., 1952–62; Mr. P. G. C. Holcroft, since 1962.

Eaton Mascott Hall,[14] which is largely brick-built, is an H-shaped house of 2 stories with attics, dating from 1734.[15] Extensive additions were made to the north of the east and west wings in the earlier 19th century.[16] A substantial house stood on the site before 1734—it had 9 hearths in 1662[17]—and part was retained by William Francke when he remodelled the house. The two southern bays of the east wing contain collar-and-tie-beam roof-trusses with straight windbraces, and part of the timber-framed west wall is visible in cupboards on the first floor. The lower part of the south wall of this wing is of sandstone. The central block, which contains a large hall on the ground floor, also has collar-and-tie-beam

roof-trusses. These are without windbraces and the wall-plates are somewhat higher than those of the east wing. The kitchen wing to the west was added in 1734. The south front retains its early-18th-century sash windows, which have stone surrounds, and the central gabled dormer has a pediment and scrolls. Two bay windows were inserted in the east wall in the early 19th century. The principal stair at the east end of the hall has 3 turned balusters to a tread. This, like the simpler stair in the kitchen wing, dates from 1734. To the west of the house is a brick brew-house. A datestone set in a recess in the shallow blind arcading at first-floor-level on its south wall reads 'M.O. 1686 E.O.' (Mary, widow of Pontesbury Owen, and her son Edward).

ECONOMIC HISTORY. The manors of Betton Abbots and Brompton were assessed at 2 hides[18] and 3½ hides[19] respectively in 1086, and there has been no radical change in the constitution of either estate since the 12th century. Both were held by Shrewsbury Abbey until the Dissolution, and have been part of the Attingham Park estate since the mid-18th century.[20] Each manor had demesne sufficient for 1½ plough in 1086, when the Betton tenants included 3 serfs and those of Brompton 3 *bovarii*.[21] The Brompton demesne amounted to 2 carucates in 1291, when it was valued at £2.[22] Since the tithes of Shrewsbury Abbey's former demesne lands were later accounted impropriate to the lords of the two manors,[23] the distribution of demesne can be reconstructed. In both cases the portion of the demesne lying in the common fields had been consolidated before the close of the Middle Ages. The former demesne at Brompton was still known as 'Abbey land' in the 1720s.[24] No other freehold estates are recorded in either manor, and in 1807 the Betton Abbots manorial estate amounted to 594 a. and that of Brompton to 876 a.[25]

The three other manors in Berrington passed into divided ownership in the course of the 13th century. The greater part of Berrington manor was reunited in the 15th century, as was Cantlop manor in 1586, but the manor of Eaton Mascott remained divided until the 19th century. Berrington manor was said to be worth 30s. before the Conquest, but its value had risen to 40s. by 1086, when it was assessed at 2½ hides.[26] Small freeholds were granted to Haughmond Abbey[27] and Brewood Priory (Staffs.)[28] in the 12th century, the former being held on a long lease by the lord of the manor in the later 15th century.[29] The manor was split into 4 parts in the 13th century, but was reunited in the hands of the Lee family in 1323.[30] The Lees appear to have bought in a few

[97] B.M. Add. Ch. 58308.
[98] N.L.W., Pitchford Hall 1356.
[99] *Cal. Inq. Misc.* vi, p. 158.
[1] *Feud. Aids*, iv. 257.
[2] *Visit. Salop. 1623* (Harl. Soc. xxix), ii. 256.
[3] C 142/172/136.   [4] S.P.L., Deeds 5132.
[5] Ibid. 1126.   [6] Ibid. 1038.
[7] N.L.W., Pitchford Hall 1696.
[8] Eaton Mascott Hall title-deeds.
[9] S.P.L., Deeds 5143.
[10] Ibid. 5724; S.P.L., MS. 4080, p. 1775.
[11] Ibid.
[12] S.P.L., Deeds 4296.
[13] What follows is based on Eaton Mascott Hall title-deeds.
[14] For some account of the house, see *T.S.A.S.* 4th ser. viii. 75–77.

[15] Ibid. The datestone there recorded was illegible in 1965.
[16] Particulars of estate, 1861, in Eaton Mascott Hall title-deeds.
[17] E 179/255/35 m. 76.
[18] *V.C.H. Salop.* i. 311.
[19] Ibid. 326.
[20] See p. 19.
[21] *V.C.H. Salop.* i. 311, 326.
[22] *Tax. Eccl.* (Rec. Com.), 260.
[23] Par. rec., tithe appt.
[24] S.R.O. 112 uncat., Brompton ct. r. 1657–1824.
[25] Ibid. 1011 uncat., Attingham estate survey, 1807.
[26] *V.C.H. Salop.* i. 320.
[27] S.P.L., Haughmond Cart. f. 34.
[28] Eyton, vi. 35.
[29] S.P.L., Haughmond Cart. f. 35.
[30] See p. 18.

small freeholds in Berrington in the later Middle Ages,[31] but the Haughmond Abbey freehold was not acquired until 1653.[32] A 30-acre freehold was bought in 1768,[33] and in 1776 the manorial estate amounted to 692 a.[34] The single remaining freehold in the township (90 a.) was acquired in 1798.[35] In 1845 the estate comprised 768 a.[36] The manor had a comparatively large demesne in 1086, with 7 serfs and land sufficient for 2 ploughs.[37] The demesne was leased for 15 marks a year to a single tenant in 1425,[38] and in the later 17th century only Cloud Coppice, Berrington Pool, and Eaton Mascott Pool were kept in hand.[39] Only Cloud Coppice (9 a.) was in hand in 1845.[40]

Cantlop manor was assessed at only one hide in 1086, but its value had risen from 20s. to 110s. since before the Conquest and it then had a demesne almost as large as that of Berrington, with 2 ploughs and 6 serfs.[41] The manor had been divided into two parts by the early 13th century and by the 1290s virtually the whole estate had been alienated to free tenants. The moiety held by the Longslow family included a virgate and 20s. in rents in 1290,[42] and that of Robert Burnell amounted to nothing more than the rents of free tenants, then totalling 48s. 10d.[43] There were 6 such tenants on the Burnell moiety in 1316, when their rents produced 32s.[44] The Longslow moiety was further subdivided at the death of Nicholas de Pitchford after 1343,[45] but was reunited by William Cotton in the earlier 15th century.[46] William Cotton, a descendant of the last-named William, inclosed Cantlop Wood in 1546[47] and in the 1570s the owners of this moiety were establishing their claims over forest encroachments[48] and buying up freeholds in the township.[49] Thomas Owen, who owned both moieties after 1587,[50] inclosed the common fields and made allotments in Cantlop Wood in lieu of common rights between 1590 and 1595.[51] The manorial estate contained 412 a. in 1595,[52] and the freehold of Roger Chirme was added in 1599.[53] No change took place in the size of the manorial estate until the 19th century. It amounted to 443 a. in 1768,[54] but in 1840 113 a. were sold to the lord of Pitchford manor,[55] so that by 1845 the Cantlop estate had been reduced to 319 a.[56]

Eaton Mascott manor, worth 20s. before the Conquest, was of the same value in 1086.[57] It was assessed at 3 hides at the latter date[58] and in 1255.[59] There were 4 serfs here in 1086, when the demesne contained land for one plough,[60] and it seems to have remained of the same size, for it amounted to one carucate in 1294.[61] By this date, however, the manor had been divided into 2 moieties. Of the moiety then held by Thomas de Baskerville,[62] part passed to the lord of Berrington manor[63] and the remainder appears to be the estate held by the Thornes family between 1359[64] and 1635.[65] Both were acquired in the 1630s by Pontesbury Owen,[66] whose descendants probably lived at a house on the site of Eaton Mascott Hall until the early 18th century. The other moiety was held in the earlier 14th century by William de Eton,[67] who enlarged it by the purchase of freeholds in Eaton Mascott[68] and at La Beche in Pitchford.[69] The Farmer family, to whom this property passed in 1611,[70] were resident until 1669.[71] No reliable evidence for the size of either estate is available, but that part of the Farmer estate sold to James Shepheard in 1669 comprised 88 a. in Eaton Mascott and 95 a. in Pitchford.[72] The former Farmer estate was bought in 1777 by Edward Williams,[73] whose grandson acquired the other portion of the manor after 1822[74] and held 446 a. in 1845.[75] With the purchase of Berrington manor by Thomas Wells in 1866 the Eaton Mascott estate became the largest property in the parish. It amounted to 1,346 a. in 1891 and is still of much the same size.[76]

Apart from the fragments of Eaton Mascott manor a number of freehold estates are found in Berrington and Cantlop. In the later 12th century Haughmond Abbey was granted 1½ virgate in Berrington[77] and the mill at Eaton Mascott.[78] A further ½ virgate at Eaton Mascott was granted to the abbey in the 13th century by John de Berrington,[79] their tenant at Eaton Mascott mill.[80] This estate appears to have passed to a member of the Ottley family after the Dissolution.[81] The property at Berrington was purchased in 1614 by Thomas Gardner,[82] who sold it to Richard Meire in 1649.[83] In 1653 Meire sold it to the lord of Berrington manor.[84] Eaton Mascott mill and 25 a. adjoining it[85] remained in the Ottley family

---

[31] S.R.O. 1514 uncat., deeds, n.d., 1439.
[32] Ibid. deed, 1653.
[33] Ibid. 933 (Smythe) uncat., deed, 1768.
[34] Shrews. Sch., MS. James V.
[35] S.R.O. 933 (Smythe) uncat., deed, 1798.
[36] Par. rec., tithe appt.
[37] V.C.H. Salop. i. 320.
[38] S.R.O. 1514 uncat., lease, 1425.
[39] Ibid. leases, 1655–98.
[40] Par. rec., tithe appt.
[41] V.C.H. Salop. i. 340.
[42] Cal. Inq. p.m. ii, p. 462.
[43] Ibid. iii, p. 50.
[44] Ibid. v, p. 392.
[45] C 143/267/10.
[46] S.P.L., Deeds 6599–6603.
[47] Ibid. 6694.
[48] Ibid. 6698.
[49] Ibid. 6696, 6703.
[50] Ibid. 6699, 6705.
[51] S.R.O. 112 uncat., lease, 1590; S.P.L., Deeds 6714, 9501.
[52] S.P.L., Deeds 9501.
[53] Ibid. 6715.
[54] Ibid. 13642.
[55] N.R.A., Pitchford Hall SC/1.
[56] Par. rec., tithe appt.
[57] V.C.H. Salop. i. 320.
[58] Ibid.
[59] Rot. Hund. (Rec. Com.), ii. 62.
[60] V.C.H. Salop. i. 320.
[61] Cal. Inq. p.m. iii, p. 125.
[62] Ibid.
[63] See p. 20.
[64] C.P. 25(1)/195/16/24.
[65] C.P. 25(2)/477/10 Chas. I Hil.
[66] C.P. 25(2)/478/15 Chas. I Mich.
[67] See pp. 20–1.
[68] B.M. Add. Ch. 58308; N.L.W., Pitchford Hall 1356.
[69] S.P.L., Deeds 5192.
[70] Ibid. 5132.
[71] Ibid. 1126.
[72] N.L.W., Pitchford Hall 1640, 1696.
[73] Ibid. 1699.
[74] S.P.L., MS. 1883.
[75] Par. rec., tithe appt.
[76] Eaton Mascott Hall title-deeds.
[77] S.P.L., Haughmond Cart. f. 34.
[78] Ibid. f. 60.
[79] N.L.W., Pitchford Hall 1221.
[80] S.P.L., Haughmond Cart. f. 59.
[81] S.R.O. 1514 uncat., deed, 1588.
[82] Ibid. deed, 1614.
[83] Ibid. deed, 1649.
[84] Ibid.
[85] N.L.W., Pitchford Hall 1285; N.R.A., Pitchford Hall S/1.

until it was sold to Richard Williams in 1777.[86] The small freehold in Berrington acquired before 1221 by Brewood Priory [87] was worth 8s. a year in 1538,[88] but its subsequent history is not known. William Humphreston held some 30 a. in Berrington in 1552.[89] This passed by marriage in 1581 to Vincent Corbet,[90] whose grandson sold it to Richard Lee in 1648.[91] It was purchased by the lord of Berrington manor in 1768,[92] but it was sold in 1805[93] and was again bought into the manorial estate in 1829.[94] Andrew Church, who held 90 a. in Berrington, settled this in 1662 on his niece, Joan, wife of John Farmer.[95] This passed to Henry Staniford in 1748[96] and was purchased by the lord of Berrington manor in 1816.[97]

At least 5 freeholds were created in Cantlop manor in the 13th and early 14th centuries, but only one of them appears to have survived later than the 16th century. Lands in Cantlop were granted by Edward Burnell to his kinsman Thomas de Withington in 1310.[98] The latter seems also to have acquired, through his wife Avelina,[99] the lands held in the early 13th century by Thomas and Henry Mauveysin.[1] John, grandson of Thomas de Withington, held 16s. a year in rents at Cantlop in 1366.[2] The estate was held in 1571 by Humphrey Raven of Withington,[3] who was allotted 17 a. at the inclosure of Cantlop Wood.[4] Humphrey's son Robert sold it in 1621 to William Calcott,[5] and the estate amounted to 113 a. in 1753, when the latter's descendant Rowland Calcott sold it to Edward Lloyd.[6] It passed by exchange to William Jeffreys in 1819[7] and was bought by Richard Laurence in 1820.[8] The latter already held a freehold estate at Cantlop, which had belonged to the Waring family since the later 17th century[9] and was bought by Laurence c. 1780.[10] Laurence's estate (236 a.) was sold to the County Council for small-holdings in 1911.[11]

There is scarcely any evidence for the tenurial history of manors in Berrington between 1086, when 17 villeins and 6 bordars held 11 ploughs between them in the parish as a whole,[12] and the later 16th century. Three-life leases were in general use on all manors from c. 1550 until the end of the 17th century. In Berrington manor, where 3-life leases were last granted in 1713, they were already being super-seded by tenure at will.[13] Four of the 9 larger holdings in Berrington were occupied by tenants-at-will in 1717, when the total rental was £138,[14] and only 2 farms were still held on long leases by 1737.[15] By 1782, when all the farms were set at will, the rental had risen to £526 a year,[16] and it stood at £1,042 a year in 1815.[17] Consolidation of holdings was taking place at the same time. There were 8 farms here in 1741,[18] but by 1776 two large farms accounted for 665 a. of the 692 a. in the manorial estate.[19] The reorganization of farms on the Attingham estate at Betton Abbots and Brompton took place somewhat later in the 18th century. There were 6 tenants at Betton and 10 at Brompton in 1755, whose rents totalled £611 a year,[20] but the Betton estate was consolidated to form 2 large farms c. 1782,[21] and the Brompton estate to form 3 such farms about ten years later.[22] The rents of Betton and Brompton produced £1,042 a year in 1826.[23] By 1845 all the farms in the parish were of over 150 a.; apart from a few outlying portions of farms in other parishes, there were also 3 smallholdings of 10–26 a. and 4 holdings of 1–10 a.[24] Since the 1860s nearly the whole of the Eaton Mascott estate has lain in 3 farms of over 300 a.[25]

The parish was said to contain 1,100 a. arable in 1801, when wheat and barley were the principal crops.[26] The acreage of root crops then reported (94 a.)[27] was probably an under-estimate, for 83 a. roots were grown in Betton and Brompton alone in 1811.[28] There were 1,729 a. arable in the parish in 1845—49 per cent. of the total acreage.[29]

Cantlop mill was worth 10s. in 1086.[30] A moiety of the mill was granted to Shrewsbury Abbey in the mid-12th century,[31] but it appears to have passed to the lord of Berrington manor, who held a mill on Cound Brook in 1323.[32] It was known as Newfordsmill in 1464, when it contained 2 mills under one roof.[33] The mill was conveyed in 1471 to Roger Pontesbury,[34] whose descendants were still in possession in 1510.[35] It had passed by 1564 to John Bailey, who then sold it to Richard Lee, lord of Berrington manor.[36] The mill, which subsequently formed part of the manorial estate, remained in use until c. 1929.[37] Eaton Mascott mill, worth 4s. in 1086,[38] was granted to Haughmond Abbey c. 1230.[39]

[86] N.L.W., Pitchford Hall 1698.
[87] Eyton, vi. 35.
[88] *Valor Eccl.* (Rec. Com.), iii. 193.
[89] S.R.O. 322 uncat., ct. of survey, 1575, in Humphreston ct. r. 1571–8.
[90] C.P. 25(2)/201/23 & 24 Eliz. I Mich.
[91] S.R.O. 933 uncat., deed, 1648.
[92] Ibid. 1768.
[93] Ibid. 1805.
[94] Ibid. 1829.
[95] Ibid. 1662; Shrews. Sch., MS. James V.
[96] S.R.O. 933 uncat., deed, 1816.
[97] Ibid.
[98] Ibid. 103 uncat., deed, 1310.
[99] B.M. Add. Ch. 47247; Eyton, vii. 397.
[1] S.P.L., Deeds 4390, 6681.
[2] C.P. 25(1)/195/17/5.
[3] S.P.L., Deeds 6697.
[4] Ibid. 6714.
[5] S.R.O. 103 uncat., deed, 1621.
[6] Ibid. schedule of deeds, p. 98; ibid. survey of estate of F. Lloyd, 1780.
[7] S.C.C., title-deeds, SH 5.
[8] Ibid.
[9] S.R.O. 714/5.
[10] Ibid.; ibid. 103 uncat., survey of estate of F. Lloyd, 1780.
[11] S.C.C., title-deeds, SH 5.

[12] *V.C.H. Salop.* i. 311, 320, 326, 340.
[13] Q. Sess., reg. papists' estates, 1717–82.
[14] Ibid. 1717.
[15] Ibid. 1737.
[16] Ibid. 1782.
[17] S.R.O. 1514 uncat., tenancy agreements, 1815.
[18] Q. Sess., reg. papists' estates, 1741.
[19] Shrews. Sch., MS. James V.
[20] Attingham Park estate office, accts. 1755–74.
[21] S.R.O. 112 uncat., estate vouchers, 1782.
[22] Ibid.; Q. Sess., accts. of Jonathan Scoltock, 1785–92.
[23] S.R.O. 112 uncat., accts. 1826.
[24] Par. rec., tithe appt.
[25] Eaton Mascott Hall title-deeds.
[26] H.O. 67/14/31.
[27] Ibid.
[28] S.R.O. 1011 uncat., Attingham estate survey, 1807.
[29] Par. rec., tithe appt.
[30] *V.C.H. Salop.* i. 340.
[31] N.L.W., MS. 7851D, f. 279.
[32] C.P. 25(1)/194/10/34.
[33] S.P.L., MS. 2, f. 16.
[34] S.R.O. 1514 uncat., deed, 1471.
[35] Ibid. will of William Pontesbury, 1510.
[36] S.P.L., MS. 2, f. 16.
[37] *Kelly's Dir. Salop.* (1929).
[38] *V.C.H. Salop.* i. 320.
[39] S.P.L., Haughmond Cart. ff. 59, 59ᵛ; Eyton, vi. 106-7.

It was leased to John de Berrington in the later 13th century[40] and to his son Thomas in 1333.[41] In 1545 it was acquired by the lord of Pitchford manor[42] and its later history is given under that parish.[43]

The field-name Cole Hill occurs in Cantlop in 1595,[44] but no reference to coal-mining in the parish has been found. A common brick-kiln is recorded at Betton Abbots in 1737,[45] and bricks were made here[46] and at Brompton[47] for local use in the later 18th century.

Blacksmiths are found at Eaton Mascott in 1635,[48] at Brompton in 1629,[49] at Cross Houses in 1683,[50] and at Berrington in 1737.[51] No later reference has been found to the smithies at Eaton Mascott and Cross Houses, but the Berrington smithy remained in business until c. 1900.[52] A weaver is recorded at Cantlop, 1609–62.[53] In the later 19th century there was a shop and a shoemaker at Cantlop, a shop, a butcher, a tailor, and a shoemaker at Cross Houses, and a shop and a wheelwright at Berrington.[54]

LOCAL GOVERNMENT. There are court rolls for the manor of Hernes (including Betton Abbots and Brompton), 1548–54,[55] for Brompton manor, 1560–64[56] and 1657–1824,[57] and for Cantlop manor, 1571.[58]

The parish records include churchwardens' accounts, 1680–1830,[59] and overseers' accounts, 1793–1837.[60] There are no vestry minutes. The two churchwardens each rendered a separate account and the two overseers each accounted for half their year of office. Expenditure on poor relief was put at £10 a year in 1694,[61] but it seems likely that until the mid-18th century the poor were supported, without recourse to poor rates,[62] by the income from a poor stock of some £5, from Churme's charity, and from the church rates.[63] In 1750 the parish contracted to send its poor to Wellington workhouse for £24 a year,[64] but this experiment was not repeated. Berrington became a member of the Atcham Union in 1792.[65] Poor rates rose from £130 in 1776[66] to £404 by 1799,[67] reaching a peak of £727 in 1817.[68] From 1819 until 1837 the rates averaged £400 a year.[69]

CHURCH. Berrington church is first recorded in 1086.[70] Its advowson had been granted to Shrewsbury Abbey shortly before this date by Warin the sheriff.[71] The abbey held the advowson until the Dissolution. In 1560 it was granted by the Crown to Richard Okeham and Richard Byttenson,[72] who sold it to John Hedley of Shrewsbury in the following year.[73] The advowson was purchased in 1581 by the lord of Berrington manor,[74] whose descendants held it until the later 18th century. Sir Richard Lee (patron 1632–60) and his successors the Smythes of Acton Burnell were recusants[75] and presentations to the living were made by the Crown in 1638[76] and by Timothy Tourneur in 1660.[77] In accordance with the law Cambridge University presented in 1716 and 1746.[78] The advowson was sold c. 1787 to Noel, Lord Berwick,[79] and was held by his descendants until it passed to Radley College (Berks.) under the will of Thomas, Lord Berwick, in 1948.[80]

The living is a rectory and has been united with Betton Strange since 1930.[81] Its gross income rose from £13 6s. 8d. to £20 12s. a year between 1291[82] and 1535,[83] but the net value of the living was about half this amount during the Middle Ages. In addition to pensions paid to Shrewsbury Abbey and Haughmond Abbey in lieu of tithes,[84] 10 marks annually were assigned out of the rectory by Shrewsbury Abbey towards the upkeep of the sacristy of Lichfield Cathedral c. 1240.[85] The annual value of the living was said to be £55 in 1655[86] and about £300 in 1799.[87] It had a net annual value of £400 in 1804[88] and £395 in 1835.[89]

The tithes of Berrington manor passed with the advowson to Shrewsbury Abbey before 1086,[90] but an annual pension of 24s. paid by the rector to the abbey after the early 12th century[91] was probably a payment in lieu of tithes. No reference has been found to the pension after the Dissolution, but the tithes of Berrington were subsequently held by the rector, together with the tithes of Cantlop and such part of the tithes of Betton Abbots, Brompton, and Eaton Mascott as were not impropriate. All the tithes were leased to a Shrewsbury draper for 20 years at

40 S.P.L., Haughmond Cart. f. 59.
41 Ibid. f. 34ᵛ.
42 N.L.W., Pitchford Hall 1285.
43 See p. 121.
44 S.P.L., Deeds 9501.
45 S.R.O. 112 uncat., letter, Thos. Bell to Thos. Hill, 18 Jan. 1738.
46 Attingham Park estate office, accts. 1755–74.
47 Q. Sess., accts. of Jonathan Scoltock, 1785–92.
48 S.P.L., Deeds 3303.
49 S.R.O. 1104 (Gatacre) uncat., accts. 1629–38.
50 S.R.O. 112 uncat., lease, 1683.
51 Q. Sess., reg. papists' estates, 1737.
52 Kelly's Dir. Salop. (1900).
53 S.R.O. 103 uncat., leases, 1609–62.
54 Bagshaw's Dir. Salop. (1851); Kelly's Dir. Salop. (1856–1941).
55 S.R.O. 840 uncat.
56 Ibid. 1514 uncat.
57 Ibid. 112 uncat.
58 S.P.L., Deeds 6697.
59 S.R.O. 714/5.
60 Par. rec.
61 Bodl. MS. Blakeway 8, f. 476.
62 S.R.O. 112 uncat., letter, Thos. Bell to Thos. Hill, 10 Dec. 1743.
63 S.R.O. 714/5.
64 Ibid. 714/10.
65 Atcham Union Act, 32 Geo. III, c. 95 (priv. act).

66 Rep. Cttee. on Overseers' Returns, 1777, p. 441, H.C. (1st ser. ix, reprinted 1803).
67 Par. rec., overseers' accts., 1793–1837.
68 Ibid.
69 Ibid.
70 V.C.H. Salop. i. 320.
71 Eyton, vi. 44.
72 Cal. Pat. 1558–60, 463.
73 S.R.O. 112 uncat., deed, 1561.
74 C.P. 25(2)/201/23 Eliz. I East.
75 See p. 12.
76 T.S.A.S. 4th ser. iii. 360.
77 Ibid. 369.
78 Ibid. v. 191.
79 Ibid. vi. 300.
80 Heref. Dioc. Regy., reg. 1938–53, p. 376.
81 Ibid. reg. 1926–38, p. 246.
82 Tax. Eccl. (Rec. Com.), 247.
83 Valor Eccl. (Rec. Com.), iii. 184.
84 Tax. Eccl. (Rec. Com.), 247.
85 N.L.W., MS. 7851D, f. 338.
86 T.S.A.S. lvii. 27.
87 Visit. Archd. Salop. 1799.
88 Lich. Dioc. Regy., glebe terrier, 1804.
89 Rep. Com. Eccl. Revenues [67], pp. 462–3, H.C. (1835), xxii.
90 Eyton, vi. 44.
91 Ibid.

£24 a year in 1600.[92] The rectorial tithes were commuted for a rent-charge of £526 in 1845.[93]

The demesne tithes of Brompton were granted to Shrewsbury Abbey in the 1090s[94] and those of Betton Abbots to the same abbey before 1182.[95] After the Dissolution the former were deemed to be merged in the freehold of the Brompton manorial estate.[96] John Prince, who obtained a 60-year lease of the demesne tithes of Betton Abbots in 1535,[97] leased them to the tenants of the manor in 1541.[98] The Crown leased the Betton tithes to John Stanley in 1575, but he assigned his interest in the following year to Richard Prince.[99] The demesne tithes were granted by the Crown in 1582 to Edmund Downing and Peter Ashton, who immediately sold them to Thomas Crompton and John Stanley.[1] Richard Wright, who purchased the demesne tithes of Betton in 1590, sold them to Richard Prince in 1593.[2] The demesne tithes of Betton and Brompton subsequently followed the descent of the manor of Longden,[3] but had passed to the lord of the manor by 1845.[4] They were said to be worth £15 a year in 1655.[5]

Two thirds of the tithes of Eaton Mascott were granted to Haughmond Abbey before 1172.[6] After 1291 a modus was paid to the abbey by the Rector of Berrington in lieu of these tithes.[7] This sum was appropriated to the stipend of the prior and subprior in 1459.[8] The abbey's tithes here were leased for life to the rector in 1525 for 40s. a year.[9] In 1555 the Crown leased them for 21 years to Thomas Mynd[10] and in 1568 sold them to Edward Fiennes, Lord Clinton and Saye.[11] Fiennes immediately conveyed them to Simon Kemsey, who sold them to Richard Prince in 1580.[12] The tithes of Eaton Mascott followed the descent of those of Betton Abbots until 1806, when Charles, Earl of Tankerville, conveyed them to Joseph Sparkes.[13] They were later purchased by Sir C. C. C. Jenkinson of Pitchford.[14] The latter and Edward Hosier Williams were owners of the tithes of Eaton Mascott in 1845,[15] when they were commuted for a rent-charge of £73 13s.[16]

The glebe, which was said to be worth 40s. a year in 1341,[17] consisted of a scattered common-field holding of 24½ a. in Berrington township in the early 17th century.[18] Part had already been leased by this date, and by 1683, when the glebe amounted to 29 a., it was leased for £5 10s. a year.[19] A compact glebe, north-west of the village, was assigned to the rector in 1805, following an exchange with the lord of the manor.[20] In 1845 the 31-acre glebe was kept in hand by the rector, who also held 88 a. in Betton Abbots.[21] Apart from land near the school, now used as a playing field, the glebe was sold in 1925.[22]

The former parsonage, a timber-framed house of 4 bays, stood on the site of Berrington school.[23] It was demolished in 1804, when a new parsonage was built for the rector, the Hon. Richard Noel Hill, to designs by Joseph Bromfield of Shrewsbury at an estimated cost of £2,300.[24] This house, now known as Berrington Hall, is brick-built and of 2 stories, with a low-pitched slate roof. It has a west front of 5 bays with a central porch supported by pairs of Tuscan columns. The Hall was sold in 1925[25] and a new parsonage was built to the south of the village in 1927.[26]

Six of 17 rectors, 1574–1920, held the living for more than 25 years, 3 of them for over 40 years, and 10 died in office.[27] Several incumbents held Berrington in plurality with other livings in the 17th and 18th centuries. Samuel Greaves (rector 1619–53) also held Pontesbury third portion,[28] Moses Leigh (rector 1660–76) also held Shrewsbury Holy Cross,[29] and John Lloyd (rector 1716–43) was also Vicar of Shrewsbury St. Mary, where he lived.[30] Rowland Chambre (rector 1787–97) was a friend of the patron's family, and between 1797 and 1885 the living was held by 3 close relatives of the patron— Richard Noel Hill (1799–1846), Thomas Henry Noel Hill (1846–70), and Thomas Noel Hill (1874–85). George Burleton was curate here in 1583.[31] No curate is again recorded until 1795,[32] but they were continuously employed during the earlier 19th century.[33] Notable incumbents include Charles Myddleton, curate c. 1795,[34] who founded a Sunday school in Berrington,[35] Richard Noel Hill, who built Berrington Hall, and Thomas Henry Noel Hill, who supervised the restoration of the church.

A chantry of Our Lady in Berrington church possessed an endowment of a stock of cattle, appraised at £8 14s. 8d. in 1547.[36] Its endowment was, however, said to have consisted of lands in Berrington in 1549, when these were granted to John Peryent and Thomas Reve.[37] Lands in Eaton Mascott, forming the endowment of a light in the church, were granted to Edward Pese and William Wynlove in 1549.[38]

The Berrington 'love-feast', presumably a church-

[92] S.R.O. 1514 uncat., lease, 1600.
[93] Par. rec., tithe appt.
[94] Eyton, vi. 169–70.
[95] Ibid. 185.
[96] T.S.A.S. xlvii. 27; par. rec., tithe appt.
[97] Bodl. MS. Blakeway 2, f. 71.
[98] Ibid.   [99] Ibid.
[1] Ibid.
[2] Ibid.   [3] See pp. 265–6.
[4] Par. rec., tithe appt.
[5] T.S.A.S. xlvii. 27.
[6] S.P.L., Haughmond Cart. f. 59; Eyton, vi. 103.
[7] Tax. Eccl. (Rec. Com.), 247.
[8] S.P.L., Haughmond Cart. f. 84.
[9] S.C. 6/Hen. VIII/3009 m. 38d.
[10] Bodl. MS. Blakeway 2, f. 74.
[11] Ibid.
[12] Ibid.
[13] N.L.W., Pitchford Hall 1023.
[14] Ibid. 1026.
[15] Par. rec., tithe appt.
[16] Ibid.
[17] Inq. Non. (Rec. Com.), 183.

[18] S.R.O. 1514 uncat., glebe terrier, n.d.
[19] Ibid.; Lich. Dioc. Regy., glebe terrier, 1683.
[20] S.P.L., MS. 294.
[21] Par. rec., tithe appt.
[22] Ex inf. the Rector.
[23] Shrews. Sch., MS. James V; Lich. Dioc. Regy., glebe terriers (surveyor's report, 1804).
[24] Lich. Dioc. Regy., glebe terriers (plans and estimates, 1804).
[25] Ex inf. the Rector.
[26] Eaton Mascott Hall title-deeds.
[27] S.P.R. Lich. xiv (4), intro. pp. vii–ix.
[28] Ibid. p. viii.
[29] Ibid.
[30] Ibid.
[31] Lich. Dioc. Regy., B/v 1/15.
[32] S.R.O. 1164/155.
[33] Visit. Archd. Salop. 1799, 1823, 1843.
[34] S.R.O. 1164/155.
[35] See p. 27.
[36] T.S.A.S. 3rd ser. x. 379.
[37] Cal. Pat. 1549–51, 15.
[38] Ibid. 82; T.S.A.S. 3rd ser. x. 374.

ale in origin like that at Condover,[39] is first recorded in 1620.[40] It was held in the church on Easter Day and all parishioners and landowners were bound to attend.[41] Meetings for this purpose inside the church were forbidden in 1639,[42] but the 'love-feast' was still being held in 1713, when it was probably the occasion of the Easter Vestry.[43]

Communion was administered 4 times a year in the 18th century[44] and 5 times a year in the early 19th century, when two services were held on Sundays.[45] Singers are first recorded in 1768[46] and a choir, which had been formed by 1835,[47] was known as the Berrington Philharmonic Society in 1847.[48] A violoncello was bought in 1834.[49] A harmonium, which had been installed before 1859,[50] stood in the gallery in 1878.[51] This was replaced by the present organ in 1913.[52]

The church of *ALL SAINTS*, Berrington, which consists of nave, south aisle, chancel, and western tower, was restored by Edward Haycock of Shrewsbury in 1877.[53] The north wall of the nave dates from the 13th century and is probably the earliest part of the church. It contains a lancet behind the pulpit and formerly had a pointed north door. The latter had been partly blocked to form a window by 1876, but was reused as the outer arch of the south porch in 1877. The other windows in the south wall were inserted in 1877, when a 2-light window to the west of the pulpit, probably of 14th-century date, was removed. The south aisle, added in the early 14th century, has an arcade of 3 pointed arches resting on square chamfered piers. The corbel-shafts to the east and west of the arcade were added in 1877. The 2-light east and west windows of the south aisle are of 14th-century date, but two windows in the Decorated style were inserted in the south wall in 1877, replacing two windows with depressed segmental heads. A piscina with a trefoil head in the south wall presumably served the altar of Our Lady.[54]

The chancel, also of early-14th-century date, has a fine east window with intersecting tracery. There were originally 3 ogee-headed windows on the south wall, but that to the west was replaced by a 2-light window in the Decorated style in 1877. A lean-to annexe against the north wall had been added by 1786, but was probably removed in 1798, when part of the north wall was rebuilt.[55]

The trussed-rafter roofs of the nave and chancel, later concealed by a plaster ceiling, were uncovered in 1877, when the stone roofing slates were replaced with clay tiles. The south aisle has a lean-to roof with a finely moulded wall-plate. The tower, which is of 2 stages, was built in the 15th or early 16th century. It has a traceried west window of 3 lights and its embattled top formerly had 8 pinnacles, but the latter have now been removed. A wooden south porch was replaced between 1786 and 1823 by an embattled stone porch.[56] This in its turn was replaced by the present porch in 1877.

The round font is of 12th-century date and has rudely carved sculpture.[57] Nearly all the remaining fittings have been installed since the 19th century. The church was repewed in 1773–4,[58] but the oak box-pews then installed were replaced by the present open pews in 1877, when the internal walls were stripped of plaster and the brick floor was tiled. A western gallery, erected for the children before 1815,[59] was also removed at this time. The painted wooden altar-screen was made in 1814[60] and the pulpit in 1860.[61] All fittings in the chancel appear to have been renewed in 1877.

The most noteworthy monument is the recumbent oaken effigy of a knight, in armour of the early 14th century, set beneath an arch in the south wall of the aisle. It probably commemorates a member of the Lee family, who may have been responsible for the erection of the south aisle and the endowment of a chantry there.[62] Wall monuments in the chancel include a tablet to Mrs. Adah Greaves (d. 1638), carved with the figure of a kneeling woman below a round arch, set between Ionic pillars and surmounted by a pediment. There is a tablet, signed by John Bacon the younger, to Mrs. Rebekah Williams (d. 1827). The east window contains stained glass by David Evans of Shrewsbury.

A silver chalice and paten, recorded in 1552,[63] were still in the church in 1823, when there was also a pewter flagon.[64] These were replaced by a silver chalice, paten, and flagon in 1865.[65] There is also a chalice and paten of silver plate.[66] The church had 4 bells and a sanctus bell in 1552.[67] There were 5 bells and a sanctus bell in the early 18th century.[68] Two of these were dated 1611, one 1616, and another 1653, but the fifth bell, inscribed 'Fuit homo missus a deo cui nomen erat Iohannes', was probably medieval.[69] The sanctus bell was probably the 'little bell' recast in 1680.[70] Six of the existing bells were cast in 1796 by Thomas Mears of London,[71] whose firm restored them in 1926 and cast 2 additional bells in 1948.[72] The church clock, first recorded in 1680,[73] was renewed in 1796[74] and again in 1888.[75] The sundial on the south side of the churchyard was purcha-

[39] See p. 52.
[40] Lich. Dioc. Regy., B/v 1/39.
[41] *T.S.A.S.* 2nd ser. vii. 203–6.
[42] Ibid.
[43] S.R.O. 714/9.
[44] Ibid. 714/5.
[45] Visit. Archd. Salop. 1799, 1823, 1843.
[46] S.R.O. 714/5.
[47] Par. rec., churchwardens' accts. 1680–1830.
[48] Ibid. voucher, 1847.
[49] Ibid. churchwardens' accts. 1680–1830.
[50] Ibid.
[51] Ibid. faculty, 1876.
[52] Plaque on organ.
[53] Except where otherwise stated, description of church based on S.P.L., MS. 372, vol. i, p. 18; S.P.L., T. F. Duke's watercolours (churches), no. 21; S.P.L., J. H. Smith collect. no. 20; Visit. Archd. Salop. 1823; par. rec., faculty, 1878; Cranage, vi. 463–9.
[54] *T.S.A.S.* 3rd ser. x. 379.
[55] S.R.O. 714/5.

[56] Ibid.
[57] See plate facing p. 55.
[58] S.R.O. 714/5.
[59] Ibid.
[60] Ibid.
[61] *Salop. Shreds & Patches*, ii. 184–5.
[62] *T.S.A.S.* 1st ser. iii. 151–3.
[63] Ibid. 2nd ser. xii. 101.
[64] Visit. Archd. Salop. 1823.
[65] Arkwright and Bourne, *Ch. Plate Ludlow Archd.* 7.
[66] Ibid.
[67] *T.S.A.S.* 2nd ser. xii. 101.
[68] Birmingham Univ. Libr., Mytton's Ch. Notes, vol. i, f. 128a.
[69] Ibid.
[70] S.R.O. 714/5.
[71] Walters, *Ch. Bells Salop.* 211–13; S.R.O. 714/5.
[72] Par. rec., correspondence re bells, 1948.
[73] S.R.O. 714/5.
[74] Ibid.
[75] *Salop. Shreds & Patches*, viii. 202.

sed from Carlines of Shrewsbury in 1814[76] and has a dial by Richard Harper of Shrewsbury. The registers are complete from 1559.[77]

NONCONFORMITY. A single dissenter is recorded in Berrington in 1676.[78] The house of Thomas Nichols at Cross Houses, licensed as a dissenting meeting-house in 1816,[79] was probably used by Methodists, for a congregation of that persuasion existed at Cross Houses by 1823.[80] Thomas Brocas, the son of the prominent Shrewsbury Wesleyan Methodist, Thomas Brocas, built a chapel at Cross Houses in 1836.[81] He conveyed this to the Methodists of the New Connexion in 1849, when it was renamed the Ebenezer chapel.[82] Congregations of 40 at evening services are recorded here in 1851.[83] Another chapel, belonging to the Wesleyan Methodists, existed at Cross Houses in 1845,[84] but this appears to have closed by 1851.[85] A Wesleyan Methodist chapel erected at Eaton Mascott in 1868[86] was closed by 1893.[87]

SCHOOLS. A Sunday school was established by the curate, Charles Myddleton, in 1795.[88] This was supported by subscriptions from the yeomen and tenant farmers, but received no support from the larger landowners.[89] Attendances rose from 57 at the opening of the school[90] to 80 by 1823,[91] and 62 children still attended in 1847.[92] Between 1795 and 1824 some of the children were selected to attend the Berrington day school for one quarter of the year at the expense of the Sunday school.[93]

A school, which is first recorded in 1605,[94] was being held in the church in 1639,[95] but no other day school is recorded in the parish until 1796, when such a school was kept by Thomas Wigley.[96] Forty children attended this school in 1818[97] and 32 in 1833, when 14 children attended two other schools in the parish.[98] Thomas Wigley's school is probably represented by the private school kept by John Wigley in 1851[99] and by Emma Wigley in the 1860s.[1]

A Church school, built in 1843 on the site of the former parsonage, was supported by subscriptions and school pence and was placed under the management of the rector and the owners of Attingham Park and Eaton Mascott Hall.[2] It was affiliated to the National Society in 1871, when the schoolroom was enlarged and a teacher's house was built.[3] The school was in receipt of a government grant after 1874[4] and became a Controlled school in 1954.[5] It was attended by 74 children at its opening[6] and had an average attendance of 58 in 1849.[7] Average attendances rose from 83 in 1893[8] to 102 by 1906.[9]

CHARITIES. In 1629 the sum of £36, including a legacy of £13 by John Churme of Cantlop and London, was converted into an annual rent-charge of 20s., issuing from 5 a. land at Withington.[10] This was later known as Churme's charity and was distributed by the rector and churchwardens to 10 poor persons at Lady Day and Michaelmas. In 1830, when the land had become part of the glebe of Grinshill vicarage, the rent-charge was normally collected at intervals of 3 or 4 years. The Grinshill glebe was sold in the 1920s, but the vicar of that parish continued to pay the rent-charge until 1952. This charity was deemed to be lost in 1957.

Richard Wellings of Brompton gave £20 for the use of the poor in 1723, and at a later date £6 was left by Margaret Thompson to provide bibles for poor children. The funds of both charities had been invested in Shrewsbury Savings Bank by 1830, when a bible or prayer book was given to the Sunday school, or to some other poor parishioner, and the remainder of the income from Thompson's charity was distributed to the poor with Wellings's charity. The annual income of these two charities fell from £1 1s. in 1830 to 15s. 7d. in 1861[11] and to 12s. 8d. in 1945. Distribution took place every 3 years in 1861,[12] but have been made at irregular intervals in the 20th century. A balance of £14 4s. 8d. was in hand in 1945. The parish charities were administered by the Parish Council between 1897 and 1922, since when they have been administered by the Parochial Church Council.

CONDOVER

UNTIL 1934 the parish of Condover contained 7,542 a. and included the townships of Allfield, Bayston, Boreton, Chatford, Condover, Dorrington, Great Lyth, Little Lyth, Norton, Great Ryton, Little Ryton, Westley, and Wheathall, together with the squatter settlement of Annscroft and part of

[76] S.R.O. 714/5.
[77] Printed to 1812 in *S.P.R. Lich.* xiv (4), 1–195.
[78] *T.S.A.S.* 2nd ser. i. 80.
[79] Lich. Dioc. Regy., applications for dissenting meeting-house licenses.
[80] Visit. Archd. Salop. 1823.
[81] W. E. Morris, *The History of Methodism in Shrewsbury and District* (Shrewsbury, 1960), 42–43.
[82] Shrews. Methodist circuit records, trust deed, 1849.
[83] H.O. 129/359/1/13.
[84] Par. rec., tithe appt.
[85] *Bagshaw's Dir. Salop.* (1851).
[86] Eaton Mascott Hall title-deeds.
[87] Ibid.
[88] S.R.O. 1164/154.   [89] Ibid.
[90] Ibid.
[91] Visit. Archd. Salop. 1823.
[92] Ibid. 1847.
[93] S.R.O. 1164/1–138 *passim.*
[94] Lich. Dioc. Regy., B/v 1/24.
[95] Ibid. B/v 1/55.   [96] S.R.O. 1164/13.

[97] *Digest of Returns to Cttee. on Educ. of Poor,* H.C. 224, p. 746 (1819), ix (2).
[98] *Educ. Enquiry Abstract,* H.C. 62, p. 769 (1835), xlii.
[99] *Bagshaw's Dir. Salop.* (1851).
[1] *Kelly's Dir. Salop.* (1863–70).
[2] Par. rec., conveyance of site, 1843; *Mins. of Educ. Cttee. of Council, 1849* [1215], p. ccxvii, H.C. (1850), xliii.
[3] Par. rec., correspondence *re* school, 1871.
[4] Ibid. 1874.
[5] Ex inf. S.C.C. Educ. Dept.
[6] Visit. Archd. Salop. 1843.
[7] *Mins. of Educ. Cttee. of Council, 1849,* p. ccxvii.
[8] *Return of Schs., 1893* [C. 7529], p. 502, H.C. (1894), lxv.
[9] *Voluntary Schs. Returns,* H.C. 178—XXIV, p. 18 (1906), lxxxviii.
[10] Except where otherwise stated, account of charities based on *24th Rep. Com. Char.* H.C. 231, p. 379 (1831), xi; Char. Com. files.
[11] *Digest of Endowed Char. 1862–3,* H.C. 433, pp. 162–3 (1867–8), lii.   [12] Par. rec., benefaction bk.

Bayston Hill.[1] In 1934 a further 1,216 a., comprising the remainder of Bayston Hill and the townships of Hookagate, Pulley, Upper Pulley, Whitley, and Welbatch, were transferred to Condover from Meole Brace parish.[2] The history of Bayston Hill and of these other recent additions to the parish is reserved for treatment under the Liberties of Shrewsbury.

The ancient parish extended nearly 6 miles north and south and some 5 miles from east to west at its widest point. Part of the southern boundary follows Row Brook and the River Cound forms the boundary for short distances near Boreton and Dorrington, but elsewhere the boundary rarely follows marked natural features. Between Great Lyth and Bayston Hill the western boundary corresponded until 1934 with the western boundary of the 'haye' of Lythwood as defined in 1301: it likewise followed the bounds of Lythwood in the north, between Bayston Hill and Sharpstones Hill.[3] The boundary with Cantlop in Berrington on the east was fixed in 1546,[4] but the southern boundary with Longnor seems to have been in doubt at this time.[5] The parochial status of Lythwood remained in doubt until 1665, when its inhabitants were adjudged to be parishioners of Condover and therefore liable to pay church rates.[6]

The parish falls into three main geographical divisions—the Cound valley and related deposits of sand and gravel in the centre and north, the Lythwood plateau to the west, and the Buriwood plateau to the east. The Cound is bordered by a belt of alluvium which is widest to the south of Dorrington. The undulating landscape of the north and centre of the parish is made up of boulder clay and sand and gravel, lying for the most part between 250 and 325 feet. The largest deposit of sand and gravel is the Radmore ridge, which rises abruptly from the Cound valley, west of Condover Green Farm, and runs south-eastwards past the Rytons towards Row Brook. Nine of the 13 former hamlets in the parish stood on or near sand and gravel deposits in this central division of the parish. Lyth Hill, a crescent-shaped outcrop of Longmyndian rocks, runs north-eastwards from Great Lyth to Sharpstones Hill, rising to 550 feet at its highest point. The Lythwood plateau to the west is overlaid with boulder clay and slopes gently westwards towards Welbatch Brook. The narrower belt of boulder clay which surrounds the escarpment on the south and east provided a site for 3 former hamlets. Keele Beds sandstones, which underlie the area south of the Cound and east of the Radmore ridge, are capped with boulder clay to form the 400-foot Buriwood plateau, east of Wheathall. South of the plateau the land falls away sharply

to some 300 feet along Row Brook, while the more gentle northern slopes fall to 300 feet at Condover village.

Much of the parish is drained by the River Cound, which flows north from Longnor and turns eastwards after passing through the gap between Radmore and the Lyth Hill gap, flowing past Condover, Allfield, and Boreton. Its only significant tributary in the parish is Chatbrook, which rises on Longden Common and flows eastwards between Westley and Chatford, joining the Cound near the northern end of the Radmore ridge. Lyth Hill and the Buriwood plateau form watersheds, for the streams of Lythwood flow westwards towards Rea Brook, while the south of the parish is drained by Row Brook. A small stream rising at the foot of Lyth Hill and another flowing from Bomere Pool unite on the northern boundary of the parish, flowing northwards through the gap between Bayston Hill and Sharpstones Hill to join Rea Brook.

The woodland area known as Buriwood lay on the clay-capped sandstone slopes to the south of the Cound, extending into the adjoining parishes of Berrington and Pitchford. It may have derived its name from a tumulus near Pigeondoor which was called The Bury in 1545.[7] Buriwood was accounted a royal forest in 1212,[8] but was said to be common to the tenants of Condover manor at all times by 1292.[9] Clearance was in progress by 1209[10] and in 1265 54½ a. assarts were held by the Condover tenants.[11] In 1308 Richard de Houghton was given licence to clear some 200 a. lying to the east of the road from Condover to Great Ryton, immediately south of Condover village.[12] This property remained a separate freehold estate until acquired by the lord of the manor in 1565[13] and became the principal component of Condover Park, formed c. 1600.[14] Some 335 a. elsewhere in Buriwood were cleared by the tenants of Condover, the Rytons, and Wheathall in the 14th and 15th centuries, of which some 160 a. seem to have been taken into the common fields of those townships and the remainder held in severalty.[15] The steep slopes to the north of Row Brook—known as The Yelds—had been cleared by 1378,[16] the area between the Cound and the road to Cantlop by 1450,[17] and the fields called Cockshutts and Pitwicks to the south of Wheathall by the end of the 15th century.[18] Most of the woodland between Wheathall and the Rytons to the south and Houghton's Fields to the north had been cleared by 1545, when what remained of Buriwood—a little over 400 a.—lay for the most part to the east of the road from Condover to Frodesley.[19] Although a scheme for the inclosure of the remainder of Buriwood was

[1] O.S. *Area Bk.* (1883). Except where otherwise stated, the following topographical description is based on O.S. Maps 1″ sheet lxi (1st edn.); O.S. Maps 6″ Salop. 39, 41, 49 (1st and later edns.); O.S. Maps 1/25,000 SJ 40 (1957), SJ 50 (1956); Rocque, *Map of Salop.* (1752); Baugh, *Map of Salop.* (1808); Greenwood, *Map of Salop.* (1827); B.M. O.S. 2″ orig. drawings, sheets 207 (1817), 320 (1827); Geol. Survey Map (drift), sheet 152 (1932); par. rec., tithe appt. 1841, and map, 1840. This article was written in 1962 and revised in 1966. Among others who have assisted in its preparation, thanks are particularly due to the Revd. B. L. Jones, Vicar of Condover.
[2] County Review Order, 1934.
[3] Eyton, vi. 343–4.
[4] S.P.L., Deeds 6694.
[5] Ibid. MS. 377, f. 148.

[6] Par. rec., churchwardens' accts. 1659–89; S.P.L., MS. 110.
[7] S.P.L., MS. 377, f. 33.
[8] *Bk. of Fees*, i. 145.   [9] C 133/63/32.
[10] E 32/144.
[11] C 145/20/1.
[12] S.P.L., Deeds 6640, 9501.
[13] See p. 43.
[14] S.P.L., Deeds 9509; S.R.O. 665 uncat., accts. 1600–1.
[15] S.P.L., MS. 377, ff. 24ᵛ–38.
[16] S.P.L., Deeds 13477, m. 2.
[17] Ibid. 9136 *passim*.
[18] Ibid. 9136, m. 46; ibid. 9137, m. 19. The Pitwicks probably derived their name from the marl-pits in use there in the 15th century: ibid. 9073.
[19] S.P.L., MS. 377, ff. 31–31ᵛ.

made in 1550,[20] it was not carried out for about 30 years.[21] Most of the remaining timber seems to have been cleared between 1577 and 1586.[22]

Two tracts of ill-drained land to the west of the Radmore ridge were predominantly moorland throughout the Middle Ages. The wide belt of alluvium flanking the Cound to the south of Dorrington and the low-lying boulder clay between the Cound and Row Brook, south of Little Ryton, represent the area then known as The Hoos. Some part of The Hoos was used as common meadowland; Hoo Gates and Welshman's Hill were common meadows in 1427.[23] Water-meadows may have been in use here at this time, for the tenants of Dorrington and Great Ryton performed a service known as 'le watermak'.[24] A further 70 a. in The Hoos were held in severalty by 1545.[25] The site of Radmore, between Radmore Hill and the Cound north-west of Great Ryton, is preserved in 'bog' field-names near Gonsal Farm.[26] This moor was said to contain 47 a. in 1545, when it was 'full of marras and alders'.[27] Radmore was allotted to the lord of the manor in 1550,[28] but fences here were later destroyed by the tenants.[29] It still contained 'many bogs' c. 1768, when the use of the alders growing there to make drainage pipes was recommended.[30]

Waste land was less extensive on the lighter and better drained soils to the north of the Cound and east of Lyth Hill. Shedmoor, which formed the boundary between the townships of Little Lyth to the west and of Norton and Bayston to the east, is a tract of boulder clay and peat now drained only by the small stream flowing northwards towards the Bayston Hill gap. Both Shedmoor and the stream may, however, represent the former course of the Cound.[31] The clays to the north-east of the former hamlet of Bayston, between Bomere Pool and Sharpstones Hill, formed part of the area of rough pasture known as Bulridges during the Middle Ages. The Condover portion of Bulridges was then accounted part of the demesne of Condover manor and was normally leased in the 15th and 16th centuries to Shrewsbury merchants or to the lords of neighbouring manors, possibly for sheep-rearing.[32] Part of Bulridges was formed into a rabbit warren in the 1590s.[33] Fishing rights in Bomere and Shomere Pools were in dispute in the 16th century, when the tenants of Betton Abbots claimed the right to fish one side of Shomere Pool.[34]

Until 1346 Lythwood was a royal 'haye', or inclosed wood, containing some 800 a.[35] Its bounds, described in 1301,[36] followed the ancient parish boundary from Hookagate southwards towards Great Lyth, then ran round the lower slopes of Lyth Hill, where it adjoined the common fields of Great Lyth, Westley, and Little Lyth. Near White House the boundary followed the course of a small stream to the top of Lyth Hill, where it was divided by a trench from Bayston Wood—the later Bayston Common. The north-eastern portion of Lythwood lay for the most part outside the ancient parish. After 1346, when Lythwood passed out of the hands of the Crown,[37] its bounds were more circumscribed. The wooded escarpment of Lyth Hill, under the name 'Lythwoods Held', was accounted part of Pulverbatch manor, together with the adjoining townships of Westley and Little Lyth,[38] and Lyth Bank lay in Great Lyth manor in the 18th century.[39]

Adjoining townships were granted rights of common pasture in Lythwood in 1228.[40] Although they were ejected by the Forest Justice c. 1232,[41] these townships were still held liable for the annual rent of one mark paid for the privilege until it was extinguished in 1280.[42]

Small areas of woodland at Exfordsgreen, Westley, and Great Lyth, on the lower slopes of Lyth Hill, were cleared during the 13th century[43] and between 1232 and 1300 numerous grants of timber in Lythwood were made for fuel or building purposes. Recipients included Shrewsbury Abbey,[44] the churches of Condover,[45] Meole Brace,[46] Shrewsbury St. Chad,[47] and Wenlock,[48] the Dominicans [49] and Franciscans[50] of Shrewsbury, and the castles of Shrewsbury[51] and Bridgnorth.[52]

The first considerable clearance of Lythwood seems to have taken place shortly after it had been granted to Shrewsbury Abbey in 1346.[53] In 1365 it was alleged that half the wood had been devastated and that divers men had been given licence to make assarts there,[54] but receipts from agistment, 1370–5, when Lythwood was again in Crown hands, were not markedly lower than those of the mid-13th century.[55] Most of the Lythwood plateau was still woodland in 1547, for the 10 parcels of land then named in the grant of Lythwood to William Paget were described as coppices or 'hayes'.[56] The lower land to the west was probably the first to be cleared, but there is no evidence for land use here before the

[20] N.L.W., Pitchford Hall 901.
[21] See p. 46.
[22] Ibid.
[23] S.P.L., Deeds 9074; ibid. 9136, mm. 8d., 48. Assarts here are first recorded in 1274; Rot. Hund. (Rec. Com.), ii. 92.
[24] S.P.L., Deeds 13477, mm. 2d., 5d.
[25] S.P.L., MS. 377, ff. 29ᵛ–35ᵛ.
[26] Par. rec., tithe appt.
[27] S.P.L., MS. 377, f. 28ᵛ.
[28] N.L.W., Pitchford Hall 901.
[29] S.P.L., MS. 377, f. 149.
[30] S.R.O. 665 uncat., survey of manorial estate, c. 1768.
[31] R. W. Pocock and others, Geol. Shrews. District (1938), 199–201.
[32] See p. 44.
[33] S.R.O. 665 uncat., letter, Thomas Owen to John Haines, 22 Mar. 1596/7; ibid. lease, 1659.
[34] S.P.L., Deeds 6731, 9139.
[35] The area of Lythwood amounted to 787 a. in 1841: par. rec., tithe appt.
[36] Eyton, vi. 343–4.
[37] See p. 42.

[38] C 138/49/78; C 139/38/20.
[39] S.P.L., MS. 2737.
[40] Eyton, vi. 346; Pipe R. 1230 (P.R.S. n.s. iv), 224; Cal. Inq. Misc. i, p. 351.
[41] Cal. Close, 1279–88, 38; Eyton, vi. 346.
[42] Ibid.
[43] Rot. Hund. (Rec. Com.), ii. 63; E 32/144 mm. 1d, 2; Eyton, vi. 24–25.
[44] Close R. 1231–4, 356; Cal. Close, 1279–88, 158.
[45] Close R. 1231–4, 226.
[46] Ibid. 1237–42, 105.
[47] Ibid. 1231–4, 73; Cal. Close, 1272–9, 297.
[48] Close R. 1231–4, 66, 93, 94.
[49] Ibid. 67, 93.
[50] Ibid. 1264–8, 344.
[51] Ibid. 1231–4, 344; ibid. 1247–51, 336; ibid. 1256–9, 36; Cal. Close, 1279–88, 506, 516; ibid. 1288–96, 22; ibid 1296–1302, 356.
[52] Close R. 1256–9, 36, 169.
[53] Cal. Pat. 1345–8, 73.
[54] E 32/308.
[55] E 32/145; Cal. Inq. Misc. iv, p. 24.
[56] Cal. Pat. 1547–8, 45–47.

early 18th century, when little or no woodland remained in the Lythwood Hall or Lower Lythwood estates.[57] The higher eastern portion of Lythwood, which was described as 'wood grounds' in 1639,[58] contained 70 a. woodland in 1875[59] and is still comparatively well wooded, but there is some evidence of clearance here in the later 16th century. Lythwood Farm, which stands on the site of a former wood called Higgons Hay, was built by William Mall, to whom part of this wood had been leased in 1590 on condition that he cleared it and converted it to tillage.[60] Clearance of Old Coppice, east of Lyth Bank, was taking place in the 1740s.[61]

Bayston Common, the area of which had been considerably reduced by squatter settlement since the early 17th century, contained 53 a. at its inclosure in 1847.[62] It then comprised part of Bayston Hill and a strip of land running south-westwards on either side of Lyth Hill Road.[63] The size and location of Great Lyth Common, inclosed in 1807,[64] are not known, but it appears to have lain near Exfordsgreen and it included lands in the townships of Westley and Chatford as well as Great Lyth.[65]

The common fields of Allfield were inclosed in the earlier 15th century and those of Norton had disappeared by 1504. Orders prohibiting the inclosure of common-field lands were issued by the Condover manor court in 1525[66] and 1565,[67] but the tenant of the demesne was given licence to make such inclosures in 1546[68] and common-field lands bought into the manorial estate later in the 16th century seem to have been inclosed immediately.[69] In other townships inclosure appears to have taken place by means of exchange and consolidation of holdings in the course of the 17th century, but common-field strips were still to be found at Dorrington and Wheathall in the mid-18th century. Evidence for the location of common fields in the 13 townships within the parish is set out below.

Allfield. Thomas Botte, who was said to have inclosed part of the common fields in 1430,[70] was at this time buying up the lands of the remaining copyholders in this township.[71] The whole of Allfield was inclosed by 1595.[72]

Bayston. Wood Field, on the lower slops of Lyth Hill, was divided from the common fields of Little Lyth by a pasture called 'Baillie' in the 15th century and Bald Eye in 1841.[73] The names and location of the remaining common fields are not known, but Clay Furlong is recorded c. 1775[74] and Stoney Furlong lay to the west of the hamlet in 1841.[75]

Boreton. Reference to a 'season field' in 1553[76] indicates that the common fields were still in existence at this time. In 1841 fields called Cross Furlong and Withy Furlong lay on light soil north-west of the hamlet and Moor Furlong and Ten Ridges on the clay to the south.[77]

Chatford. A group of fields called March Field[78] on the higher ground to the west of the hamlet probably represents one of the common fields. Another, which seems to have lain on rising ground between Chatbrook and Hunger Hill, was called Chatford Field in 1592.[79] The third field, probably called Wood Field, lay to the south-east of the township, between the roads to Hereford and Stapleton.[80]

Condover. The common fields[81] lay for the most part on the river gravels to the west and north of the village. West Field, or Radmore Hill Field, which lay south-west of the village, was divided from the former common on Radmore Hill by the 'King's Hedge' in the 16th century.[82] It lay on both sides of the Cound between the former road to Great Ryton and Condover Grange. North Field, or Beslow Hill Field, lay on either side of the present road from Condover to Bayston Hill, running as far west as Shedmoor and adjoining the Norton common fields to the north. East Field, or Allfield Field, lay between Condover and Allfield, on either side of the road from Condover towards Atcham. Open-field strips are last recorded in this township in 1666.[83]

Dorrington.[84] Churchbridge Field lay to the north-west of the present village, bounded by the Cound on the east and the Hereford road on the west. Park Field, or Withen Field, lay to the west of the Hereford road, Cross Brook probably forming its southern boundary. Fields called World's End, on the parish boundary to the south of the road from Dorrington past Netley Old Hall, lay in Park Field in 1377.[85] Moor Field appears to have lain on both sides of the Hereford road, south of Cross Brook. Strips in Ferny Hill and Cockshoot Hill, south of the drive leading to Netley Hall, are recorded in 1558, and Cuckoo Leasow (Cuckoo Brook in 1841) was inclosed from this field c. 1620.[86] Assarts from The Hoos lay to the south-east of Moor Field. Most of the common fields had been inclosed before the early 17th century, but strips in Churchbridge Field are recorded in 1742.[87]

Great Lyth. Such former common-field lands as can be identified from field-names lay on the higher ground to the west of the hamlet.[88] There is no evidence for their names, but inclosure may have taken place here in the later 15th century, for the 55 a. said to have been inclosed by John Gatacre and George Pontesbury in 1517[89] were probably common-field land.

[57] S.P.L., Deeds 6481; S.R.O. 1011 (Harrop) uncat., lease, 1730, in abstract of title of James Beck, c. 1800.
[58] S.P.L., Deeds 3497.
[59] S.R.O. 650/2.
[60] S.P.L., MS. 110.
[61] Ibid. MS. 2737.
[62] Q. Sess., inclosure awards 54.
[63] Ibid.
[64] T.S.A.S. lii. 38; S.R.O. 1011 (Smythe Owen) uncat., trustees' accts. 1808.
[65] Ibid.; par. rec., tithe appt.
[66] S.P.L., Deeds 9138, m. 16.
[67] Ibid. 9074.
[68] Ibid. 9393.
[69] All were inclosed by 1595: ibid. 9501.
[70] Ibid. 9136, m. 16d.
[71] Ibid. mm. 2, 3d., 26d.
[72] Ibid. 9501.
[73] S.R.O. 465/449; par. rec., tithe appt.

[74] S.R.O. 465/475.
[75] Par. rec., tithe appt.
[76] S.R.O. 665 uncat., lease, 1553.
[77] Par. rec., tithe appt.
[78] Ibid.
[79] S.P.L., Deeds 9118.
[80] Par. rec., tithe appt. 'Wodefurlong' occurs in 1421: S.P.L., Deeds 13477, m. 23.
[81] Description based on S.P.L., MS. 377, ff. 24ᵛ–38; S.P.L., Condover ct. r. passim.
[82] S.P.L., MS. 301, vol. ii, p. 2.
[83] S.R.O. 665 uncat., lease, 1666.
[84] Description based on S.P.L., Deeds 7020, 7027A, 9074, 9113, 9118.
[85] Ibid. 13477, m. 1d.
[86] Ibid. MS. 378 (Condover ct. r. 1652); par. rec., tithe appt.
[87] S.P.L., MS. 379.
[88] Par. rec., tithe appt.   [89] C 47/7/2/3 m. 34d.

Little Lyth. Common fields called Wintle Field and Cross Field were in existence in the early 17th century,[90] but 60 pastures in Little Lyth and Westley were said to have been inclosed from the common fields before 1605.[91]

Norton. None known.

Great Ryton. It is difficult to distinguish the former common fields of Great and Little Ryton, but they appear to have lain to the west and east of the Radmore ridge respectively. Those of Great Ryton were known as Heath Field, Mill Field, and Hoo Field. The two former lay on the Radmore ridge and the river gravels to the west of the hamlet. Heath Field is described in some detail in 1545,[92] when it was accounted assarted land. A furlong to the north of Heath Field, adjoining Radmore Hill, was called Manbridges[93]—'the breach [or clearing] of the folk'. Mill Field,[94] to the south of Heath Field, is represented by a line of fields with 'mill' names between the road to Longnor and the Cound.[95] Mill Field included Anno Furlong in 1606:[96] presumably the common field called the Nether Annolde recorded in 1545.[97] Hoo Field lay on clay on either side of the road to Longnor, south of Little Ryton. It was bounded in the east by the lane, formerly known as Cockshoot Lane, running southwards from Ryton Grove towards Little Row.[98] The field called Hoo Gates, near Forge Villa, which was a common meadow in the 16th century,[99] probably lay on the boundary between Hoo Field and The Hoos. The northern part of Heath Field had been inclosed by 1545,[1] but common-field strips are occasionally recorded here until 1652.[2]

Little Ryton. The common fields, which lay to the north and east of the hamlet, seem to have been less extensive than those of Great Ryton. References to them are rare, but they appear to have been called Cross (or Radmore Hill) Field, Lydiat Field, and Little Field.[3] Part of Cross Field was probably incorporated in Condover Park in 1600.[4]

Westley. Common fields were still in use here in the early 17th century.[5] Lampit Field, the only one whose name is known,[6] seems to have lain to the north of the hamlet and was represented by a field called Large Pits in 1841.[7]

Wheathall. Ley Field, or Cockshoot Field, lay to the west of the hamlet and was bounded on the north by Houghton's Fields.[8] Broach Field lay between Cockshoot Lane—the track from Pigeondoor towards Duck Hall[9]—and Row Brook. Over Field, on the clays to the north-east of the hamlet, was bounded on the north by assarts called 'Wythen Greves' (Withy Graves in 1841) and Woodlands in 1545.[10] Inclosure of the Wheathall common fields probably took place in the 17th century. Much of Ley Field was still open in 1600, when the northern part was taken into Condover Park,[11] and in 1841 field boundaries in the area of this former field retained the shape of common field strips, one of them being called Four Butts.[12] Fields to the west of Pigeondoor, called Long Field and The Field in 1841, were still in strips c. 1768.[13]

The only major road in the parish, that from Shrewsbury to Hereford, was described as the road from Wayford to Shrewsbury in 1466,[14] but it is unlikely to be of great antiquity. It was not used as a boundary by any of the townships along its course and to the south of Bayston Hill it runs through the ill-drained area known as Shedmoor. An alternative and probably earlier route was a road running along the crest of the Lyth Hill escarpment, which seems to have descended the hill near Exfordsgreen and to have continued towards Stapleton. The section of this road leading from Bayston Hill to the top of Lyth Hill was turnpiked in 1756,[15] but was disturnpiked as 'useless' in 1821.[16] The present Hereford road, which followed its present course through the parish by 1719,[17] was also turnpiked in 1756.[18] Crossbrook Bridge, south of Dorrington, was built by J. T. Hope in 1834.[19]

A road running across the north of the parish, from Allfield past Hungerhill and Westley to Exfordsgreen is probably a Roman road and was known as Salter's Way during the Middle Ages.[20] The section from Allfield to Hungerhill was turnpiked in 1796.[21]

Before the 18th century the two most used roads in the parish seem to have been that from Pitchford past Cantlop Cross and Condover to Shrewsbury and that from the Rytons through Condover towards Atcham. Both roads crossed the Cound at Condover. The road from Cantlop Cross, which was described as a portway in 1482,[22] crossed the Cound by a horse bridge variously known as Hinfords Bridge, Endsbridge, or Kennel Bridge.[23] This was rebuilt in 1840[24] and again in 1883, when it became a county

[90] B.M. Add. MS. 30312, f. 117.
[91] Ibid. f. 67v; S.P.L., Deeds 9096.
[92] S.P.L., MS. 377, ff. 30–30v.
[93] Ibid. f. 28v. Other forms are 'Monbrugge', 1425 (S.P.L., Deeds 9136, m. 6), and 'Monbrich', 1509 (ibid. 9138, m. 1).
[94] S.P.L., Deeds 9074.
[95] Par. rec., tithe appt.
[96] S.P.L., Deeds 9124.
[97] S.P.L., MS. 377, ff. 30–30v.
[98] Ibid. f. 30v.
[99] S.P.L., Deeds 9074.
[1] S.P.L., MS. 377, f. 30.
[2] Ibid. MS. 378.
[3] S.P.L., Deeds 9094, 9125, 9136 m. 33d.; ibid. 9138 mm. 13, 25.
[4] Ibid. 9509.
[5] B.M Add. MS. 30312; S.P.L., Deeds 9523–4.
[6] Ibid.
[7] Par. rec., tithe appt.
[8] 'Cotecrofte', represented in 1841 by the field known as Cudley Croft in the south-west corner of Condover Park, lay on the southern boundary of Houghton's Fields in 1308 and was there described as 'the field of Wheathall': S.P.L., Deeds 6640.

[9] S.P.L., MS. 377, f. 34.
[10] Ibid. f. 33.
[11] S.P.L., Deeds 9509.
[12] Par. rec., tithe appt.
[13] Ibid.; S.R.O. 665 uncat., draft maps of Condover manorial estate, c. 1768.
[14] S.P.L., Deeds 9137, m. 6d.
[15] Shrewsbury–Church Stretton road Act, 29 Geo. II, c. 61 (priv. act).
[16] Shrewsbury District road Act, 1 & 2 Geo. IV, c. 101 (local and personal act).
[17] T. Gardner, Ludlow–Chester road map (1719); Rocque, Map of Salop. (1752).
[18] Shrewsbury–Church Stretton road Act, 29 Geo. II, c. 61 (priv. act).
[19] Hope–Edwardes MSS., Linley Hall, plan, 1834; Q. Sess., bridge bks.
[20] S.P.L., Deeds 9137, m. 22; ibid. 9138, m. 10d.
[21] Atcham road Act, 37 Geo. III, c. 172 (priv. act).
[22] S.P.L., Deeds 9137, m. 22.
[23] Ibid. 6640, 9501; S.R.O. 1011 (Smythe Owen) uncat., papers re rebuilding bridge, 1840.
[24] Q. Sess., dep. plans, bridges 45; par. rec., vestry minutes, 1758–1894; S.R.O. 1011 (Smythe Owen) uncat., papers re rebuilding bridge, 1840.

bridge.[25] North-west of Condover this road originally passed through Norton and Lower Bayston—a route which was still being used by travellers from Leominster and Ludlow in the early 18th century.[26] It was probably superseded by the present road from Condover village to the Hereford road in 1756, when the latter became a turnpike road.[27]

The road from Condover past Great Ryton towards Longnor runs in part along the Radmore ridge. To the south of Great Ryton this road was known as the Lyde Way during the earlier Middle Ages[28] thus accounting for the field-name Lydiat, (Lyde Gate) found near the road immediately north of that hamlet in 1841.[29] The section to the south of Condover village was formerly known as Houghton's Lane,[30] since it adjoined Houghton's Fields. This road crossed the Cound by a bridge known since the 16th century as the Great Bridge.[31] Between Ryton Fields and Condover the road was diverted about ¼ mile to the west, 1792–5,[32] to enable the lord of the manor to enlarge Condover Park, but the course of the former road is marked by field boundaries in the Park. A new stone bridge, built over the Cound at this time,[33] required constant repairs during the earlier 19th century as a result of damage caused by flood-water.[34] To provide more ample grounds in front of Condover Hall the section of the road towards Atcham which formerly ran due east through the village was diverted northwards beyond the church in 1794.[35] The present road from Dorrington past Condover to Atcham was turnpiked in 1796.[36]

The parish is intersected by a network of other minor roads, the only one of more than local significance being that from Condover to Frodesley. This crossed Row Brook by a ford and footbridge until a road-bridge was built in 1961. A number of lanes went out of use as a result of assarting and inclosure between the 15th and 17th centuries,[37] among them a road from Wheathall to Condover mills, called Church Lane in 1533,[38] which was formally closed in 1586.[39] The existing pattern of minor roads appears to have been unchanged since the 18th century.[40] Three roads were laid out at the inclosure of Bayston Common in 1841, but these followed the course of existing roads.[41] A footbridge by the ford at Boretonbrook, formerly known as Gannow Bridge, is first recorded in 1519,[42] and Church Bridge, north east of Dorrington, first appears in the form 'Schertebrugg' in 1388.[43]

The railway from Shrewsbury to Hereford, which runs from north to south across the parish, was opened in 1852.[44] Stations at Condover and Dorrington, in use by 1853, were closed in 1958.[45]

The parish was said to contain 78 households in 1603[46] and there were said to be 521 adults in 1676.[47] During the earlier 19th century the population rose from 1,289 in 1811 to a peak of 1,871 in 1861, increasing at the rate of about 100 each decade.[48] The 1861 figure, however, included labourers then engaged on the construction of the railway[49] and the population had fallen to 1,650 by 1871.[50] It fluctuated between 1,650 and 1,775 from 1871 until 1921, but had risen to 1,844 by 1931.[51] There were 2,759 inhabitants in 1951, when the parish had been enlarged to include Bayston Hill,[52] and 4,140 inhabitants in 1961.[53]

Friendly Societies had been established at Condover and Dorrington by 1793.[54] The comic actor Richard Tarlton (d. 1588) was said to have been born at Condover.[55]

DEVELOPMENT OF SETTLEMENT. Most of the archaeological evidence for early settlement in the parish so far discovered relates to the northern hills and the light soils of the Radmore ridge. The Burgs, east of Bayston Hill, is a roughly rectangular double-ditched hill-fort, best preserved at its eastern end,[56] and there was another hill-fort on the summit of Lyth Hill.[57] Two cinerary urns, said to date from the Late Bronze or Early Iron Age, were discovered at Little Ryton c. 1905,[58] and a large number of coin-moulds, dating from the early 3rd century, were found when digging sand at Ryton in 1744.[59] Roman coins were found in 1799 in a field called Castle-field,[60] close to Berrywood Lane Farm and to the tumulus, now destroyed, which seems to have given Buriwood its name.[61] The former hamlet of Allfield appears in the form 'Aldefeld' (Old Field) in the later Middle Ages.[62] It stands on the supposed Roman road leading from Uriconium to the lead mines of the Shelve district and may mark the site of a primary settlement, superseded by Condover when the centre of communications moved from Uriconium to Shrewsbury in the Anglo-Saxon period. No archaeological evidence has yet been found to lend support to this possibility.

Condover village stands at the junction of the alluvium of the Cound valley and the northern sands and gravels at a river-crossing which was of importance in the general pattern of communications until the 18th century. Church Street ran parallel to

[25] T.S.A.S. lvi. 118–19.
[26] S.P.L., Deeds 9227.
[27] Shrewsbury–Church Stretton road Act, 29 Geo. II, c. 61 (priv. act).
[28] See p. 108.
[29] Par. rec., tithe appt.
[30] S.P.L., MS. 377, f. 27.
[31] Ibid. f. 28.
[32] Par. rec., surveyors' accts. 1754–99.
[33] Ibid.
[34] Q. Sess., bridge bks.
[35] Q. Sess. rolls, Mich. 1794.
[36] Atcham road Act, 37 Geo. III, c. 172 (priv. act).
[37] In 1567 the lord of Condover manor proposed to lease these to the tenants: S.P.L., MS. 377, f. 150.
[38] S.P.L., Deeds 9138, m. 22; ibid. 13477, m. 6.
[39] C 78/85/no. 15.
[40] Rocque, Map of Salop. (1752); S.R.O. 665 uncat., draft maps of Condover manorial estate, c. 1768.
[41] Q. Sess. order bk. Trin. 1841.
[42] S.P.L., Deeds 9138, m. 11d.

[43] Ibid. 13477, m. 6d.
[44] Ex inf. Brit. Transport Rec.   [45] Ibid.
[46] B.M. Harl. MS. 594, f. 160.
[47] T.S.A.S. 2nd ser. i. 80.
[48] Census, 1811–61.
[49] Ibid. 1871.
[50] Ibid.
[51] Ibid. 1871–1931.
[52] Ibid. 1951.
[53] Ibid. 1961.
[54] Q. Sess. Orders, iii. 66, 185; Q. Sess., index to Friendly Soc. rules.
[55] D.N.B.
[56] V.C.H. Salop. i. 375–6.
[57] Ex inf. Miss L. F. Chitty.
[58] T.S.A.S. 3rd ser. vi, p. xx; ibid. 4th ser. x, pp. xiii–xxv.
[59] V.C.H. Salop. i. 275.
[60] Ibid.; W.S.L. 350/40/3.
[61] S.P.L., Deeds 13477 passim.
[62] S.P.L., MS. 377, f. 33.

the Cound, past the church, until it was diverted northwards in 1794.[63] The green at the eastern end of the street, now very small, seems originally to have extended much further along the street towards the church and southwards towards the Cound. Part of the green was meadow land in 1586,[64] and a cottage recorded there in 1617[65] was still standing c. 1800.[66] A stone cross which formerly stood on the green was demolished in 1586[67] and a timber building called the Buryhall stood nearby in the 15th century.[68] In the 17th century it was customary to erect 'summer poles' on the green.[69]

The Revd. H. M. Auden, apparently basing his opinion on an 18th-century map of the village, now lost, asserted that before its diversion in the 1790s the road from Great Ryton to Condover crossed the Cound between the church and Church House and joined Church Street opposite Butcher Row.[70] This is unlikely, since the Dorrington road is shown entering the village to the east of the green in 1752.[71] The road described by Auden is presumably the drift-way, recorded in 1597 and still in use c. 1800, which led from Church Street, opposite 'Botte's Lane' to a demesne meadow on the Cound.[72] Botte's Lane, now Butcher Row, formerly continued northwards towards Allfield and is probably one of the lanes said to have been inclosed by Thomas Botte of Allfield in 1423.[73]

The church, which is recorded in 1086,[74] has presumably always occupied its present site. The medieval manor-house, replaced in the 1590s by Condover Hall,[75] stood to the west of the church, set back from Church Street behind two chantry houses.[76] It is probably the timber-framed house now known as Church House, the northern wing of which is of cruck construction. Until their demolition in the 1790s several houses stood alongside the former road from Great Ryton, between Church House and the Cound. These included Upper and Lower Mills and a smithy.[77] There is no evidence that any houses stood immediately east of the church before Condover Hall was built, but houses to the north of the churchyard were demolished when the road here was diverted[78] and in the 16th century there were already houses south of the Cound, on the road to Lower Green.[79] Cruciform House, a stone building south-east of Condover Hall, appears to have been originally a service building ancillary to the Hall, probably enlarged and converted into a house in the 19th century. It has a datestone, however, now illegible but said to have read '1559',[80]

and it is locally supposed to have preceded the Hall as manor-house.

The growth of large copyhold estates in the 15th and 16th centuries probably led to a decline in the number of houses in Condover village, as elsewhere in the manor; it was said in 1567 that 47 messuages in the manor had decayed since the time of Henry VI.[81] The unusually large number of houses of cruck construction still to be found in Condover, however, reflects the prosperity of the peasantry in this period. Apart from Church House five houses are known to be of cruck construction. These are the Small House (now called Condover Court), the Old School House, Yew Tree Cottage, and nos. 5 and 7, Church Street. The first three originally comprised a cruck hall and service bay with a two-story solar wing. The Small House, once the home of the Gosnell family,[82] contains 4 bays of cruck construction. Its two-bay hall and solar wing have cusped windbraces. A central fireplace and upper floor were probably inserted in the mid-16th century. The house was extensively restored by the lord of the manor in 1878[83] and contains panelling removed from the church at that time.[84] The Old School House retains only one bay of its cruck hall, but the solar wing has scarcely been altered externally since the house was built.[85] Nos. 5 and 7, Church Street, both cased in brick, stand parallel to the street and no longer possess solar wings. Arbour House, which stood until 1844 on the site of the parsonage at the east end of the green,[86] was probably also of cruck construction.[87]

Comparatively little new building took place in Condover between the 17th century and the Second World War. Daker Cottage is a timber-framed house of two bays with a gable stack, dating from the earlier 17th century, but enlarged in the 19th century. Condover House, the former residence of the Daker family,[88] is brick-built and dates from the earlier 18th century. The Stone House, Church Street, was built in 1777,[89] probably by Joseph Harrington, who seems also to have rebuilt or modified adjoining houses in Butcher Row and Church Street.[90]

Among 3 or 4 alehouses recorded in Condover in the later Middle Ages[91] a house at the Cross to which Sybil Walker 'tranter' was admitted in 1445[92] had a continuous history as an inn until the later 19th century. The oldest portion of the existing building is timber-framed but is not earlier than the 17th century. Its amenities included a cockpit in 1705[93] and it was held by members of the Wood family from 1758 until after 1870.[94] The inn was known as

[63] Q. Sess. rolls, Mich. 1794.
[64] S.P.L., Deeds 9394.
[65] *S.P.R. Lich.* vi (1), 59.
[66] S.R.O. 665 uncat., plan of village, c. 1800.
[67] Par. rec., churchwardens' accts. 1577–97.
[68] S.P.L., Deeds 9136, m. 43; ibid. 9137, m. 27.
[69] S.R.O. 438 uncat., brief in case Daker v. Wood, before 1678.
[70] H. M. Auden, *Notes on Condover* (Shrewsbury, 1932), 24.
[71] Rocque, *Map of Salop.* (1752).
[72] S.P.L., Deeds 9089, 9135; S.R.O. 665 uncat., plan of village, c. 1800.
[73] Ibid.; S.P.L., Deeds 9136, mm. 2, 3d.
[74] *V.C.H. Salop.* i. 315, 320.
[75] See p. 39.
[76] S.P.L., MS. 377, f. 32.
[77] Ibid. ff. 27, 28, 124.
[78] S.R.O. 665 uncat., plan of village, c. 1800.
[79] S.P.L., MS. 377, f. 27ᵛ; S.P.L. Deeds 9501.

[80] Auden, *Condover*, 15.
[81] S.P.L., MS. 377, f. 149.
[82] Auden, *Condover*, 20.
[83] Datestone.
[84] Ex inf. Mrs. F. Cohen, The Small House, Condover.
[85] See plate facing p. 54.
[86] See p. 53.
[87] See description in Visit. Archd. Salop. 1823 and Lich. Dioc. Regy., glebe terrier, 1825.
[88] *Byegones*, 2nd ser. vi. 350–1.
[89] Datestone.
[90] Ibid.; S.R.O. 665 uncat., plan of village, c. 1800. This group of houses was the property of Philip Wilcox in 1841: par. rec., tithe appt.
[91] S.P.L., Deeds 13477, 9136–7 passim.
[92] Ibid. 9136, m. 39.
[93] Ibid. 9304.
[94] N.L.W., Castle Hill 2244; Q. Sess., alehouse reg.; *Kelly's Dir. Salop.* (1870).

The Condover Arms by 1822[95] and was enlarged in stone in 1856, when a magistrates' room was added.[96] It was converted into a village hall in 1928.[97] Another alehouse, said to be lately built in 1768,[98] was held by the Hodges family in the later 18th century[99] and may have been at Church House, which is said to have been an inn in 1794.[1]

Service buildings at the north end of the village— the post office, the wheelwright's shop nearby, and the smithy—were built by the lord of the manor in the earlier 19th century.[2] The school was built in 1880, when a pond known as Piepit was drained to make the playground.[3] Since 1945 houses have been built near Lower Green and there is now a large private housing estate at Grange Close, west of the old village.

Like Condover Dorrington stands on the southern slope of a gravel ridge on the edge of the alluvial soils of the Cound valley. The expansion of the village in the early 19th century has given it the appearance of a roadside settlement, but its original centre probably lay off the Hereford road, on the lane running eastwards opposite the Post Office. This is now merely a service road, which ends at the group of cottages known as Lower Fold, but in the 16th century, when it was known as Hodge Lane, the lane crossed the Cound by a ford.[4] Lower House, at the eastern end of Hodge Lane, appears externally to be no more than a 19th-century brick cottage, but contains a ceiling beam with mid-16th-century mouldings and a fine ashlar fireplace of c. 1600. Most of the remaining houses on the lane are timber-framed and of 17th-century date, but all have been cased in brick. Lower Fold was enlarged and converted into cottages before 1841[5] and Ivy House was enlarged in 1796.[6]

A subsidiary settlement on Bank Lane, to the east of Hereford road and ⅓ mile north of Hodge Lane, had probably been established by the end of the Middle Ages, for there were cottages on the Condover Church Lands here in the later 16th century.[7] The 4 cottages which stood on the Church Lands in 1841[8] have since been rebuilt, but Bank House dates from the 17th century.

Of 7 houses on the Hereford road, known to date from the 17th century, 3 are or have been alehouses. The Cock Inn, now Grove Farm, was first recorded under the name The Black Lion in 1744.[9] 'The Horseshoes', first so named in 1734,[10] was enlarged and extensively altered internally in the 1920s. The

former Greyhound Inn, now no. 20 Main Road, is a timber-framed house of 17th-century date which was probably a farm-house in origin. It is not recorded as an alehouse before 1841.[11] Other houses on the Hereford road built before the mid-18th century are Dinant, nos. 8 and 12 Main Road, Home Farm, and the Old Hall (dated 1679).

The distribution of surviving houses reflects reasonably accurately the pattern of settlement here before the early 19th century. Dorrington seems to have changed little in size between the 14th and later 17th centuries—19 messuages are recorded in 1363,[12] 14 in 1598,[13] and at least 17 in 1662[14]—and most of the houses built in the township during the 18th century lay outside the village. There was an alehouse at Wayford Bridge by 1747[15] and a smithy by 1786.[16] Cottages at Crossbrook had been built by 1784.[17] The Hayward and Oakley families, the principal landowners in late-18th-century Dorrington, also lived outside the village. Wayford House, now Wayford Farm, was built by George Hayward before 1752.[18] Dorrington Grove, a brick house of 2 stories and attics with a stuccoed west front, was built by William Oakley between 1786 and 1802[19] and was known as The Red House in 1817.[20]

Dorrington itself remained a community of small copyholders and tradesmen until the mid-19th century and it was they who were responsible for the expansion of the village northwards along the main road in the period 1800–50. Most of the houses to the north were built by Thomas Southerton of Netley, Philip Heighway (a Dorrington saddler), and James Turner, landlord of 'The Horseshoes'.[21] Dorrington township contained 63 houses and had a population of 328 by 1841;[22] it was described as an 'improving village' in 1851.[23]

The expansion of the Netley estate into Dorrington after 1826 and the construction of the railway in 1852[24] introduced new elements into the life of the village. The Netley estate included 160 a. in Dorrington by 1841[25] and over 300 a. by 1880, when it included most of the houses in the village.[26] The Hope-Edwardes family of Netley were responsible for the building of the church in 1845,[27] the school in 1874,[28] and the Hope-Edwardes Institute in 1906.[29] The Railway Inn was licensed in 1861[30] and regular cattle-sales were held there after 1863.[31] The creamery east of the station had been built by 1926.[32] Three of the 4 alehouses which had been open c. 1850 closed as the Hereford road became less fre-

[95] Q. Sess., alehouse reg.
[96] Auden, *Condover*, 34.
[97] Datestone.
[98] S.R.O. 665 uncat., survey of Condover manorial estate, c. 1768.
[99] Q. Sess., alehouse reg.
[1] Auden, *Condover*, 24.
[2] Ibid. 25.
[3] Ed. 7/102/66; S.R.O. 1011 (Cholmondeley) uncat., plan of proposed school, 1880.
[4] S.P.L., Deeds 9074. Adjoining fields were called Hodgewood in 1841: par. rec., tithe appt.
[5] Par. rec., tithe appt.
[6] Datestone.
[7] Par. rec., churchwardens' accts. 1577–97.
[8] Ibid. tithe appt.
[9] S.P.L., MS. 379.
[10] *S.P.R. Lich.* vi (1), 216.
[11] Par. rec., tithe appt.
[12] *T.S.A.S.* l, 115.
[13] S.P.L., Deeds 7022.
[14] E 179/255/35 mm. 73d.–74.

[15] N.L.W., Castle Hill 2244.
[16] Condover ct. r. 1786, *penes* Messrs. Salt & Sons, solicitors, Shrewsbury.
[17] Ibid. 1784.
[18] S.P.L., MS. 379.
[19] Condover ct. r. 1786–1802 *penes* Messrs. Salt & Sons, solicitors.
[20] B.M. O.S. 2″ orig. drawings, sheet 207 (1817).
[21] Condover ct. r. 1800–50 *penes* Messrs. Salt & Sons, solicitors.
[22] *Census*, 1841.
[23] *Bagshaw's Dir. Salop.* (1851).
[24] See p. 32.
[25] Par. rec., tithe appt.
[26] Ibid. poor rate, 1880.
[27] See p. 55.
[28] See p. 57.
[29] Datestone.
[30] Q. Sess., *Return of Licensed Houses* (1896), 54.
[31] *Cassey's Dir. Salop.* (1863); *Kelly's Dir. Salop.* (1870–1913).
[32] *Kelly's Dir. Salop.* (1926).

quented in the later 19th century—the 'Maltster's Tap' (now Ivy House) by 1856,[33] the 'Cock' by 1870,[34] and the 'Greyhound' by 1885.[35] Apart from 6 Council houses built to the north of the village since 1945[36] very few houses have been built in Dorrington since 1850 and the number of tradesmen remained stationary until the 1920s.[37]

The site of 'Old Town' in Dorrington township, recorded between the 14th and 18th centuries,[38] is not known. It appears to have stood to the south of Crossbrook, for a meadow in the Longnor common field known as Hoo Field, which adjoined the south of Dorrington township, was called 'Aldetones-medewe' in 1323.[39]

With the exception of Great Ryton the remaining hamlets in the parish have shrunk since the Middle Ages. Allfield, Bayston, Boreton, and Norton, on the light soils to the north of the parish, are now represented by single farms, the 4 former hamlets at the foot of Lyth Hill now each consist of two farmhouses, while Wheathall and Little Ryton are still recognizably hamlets.

Six tenants held 8 messuages at Allfield in 1363,[40] but there were only 3 tenants here by 1421[41] and by the end of the 15th century most of the township lay in a single estate, the copyhold 'manor' of Allfield.[42] A moated manor-house, probably built by the Sandford family early in the 16th century, was the only house at Allfield by 1595.[43] This seems to have been L-shaped and to have consisted of a hall, kitchen, and solar wing, for its southern part was described as the 'cross chambers' in 1578.[44] The hall, great parlour, and kitchen were separately occupied by 3 tenants in 1598.[45] The kitchen was demolished c. 1722,[46] but the remainder of the original house appears to be incorporated in the northern part of Allfield Farm. Close-studded timber-framing is visible on the north gable.

The former hamlet of Bayston, now known as Lower Bayston to distinguish it from the squatter settlement of Bayston Hill, stood on the site of Bayston Farm. Six tenants were recorded in the Domesday manor of Bayston[47] and there were at least 6 houses in the township in 1672.[48] The hamlet contained 4 houses in 1770,[49] but there have been only two houses here since 1841.[50] Bayston Farm is a timber-framed house, originally L-shaped and probably dating from the later 16th century. The north wing is jettied but the south wing is a 19th-century addition. The house to the north of Bayston Farm, now two cottages, was formerly a farm-house. It is also timber-framed but has been enlarged and cased in brick.

Norton, now represented by Norton Farm, was the smallest and most short-lived of the northern hamlets. The Domesday manor was assessed at one hide[51] and the township was held to comprise a mere 146 a. in the later 16th century.[52] Four tenants were recorded in 1086[53] and there were said to be 8 freeholders at Norton in 1315.[54] There was, however, probably only one house here by 1504, when its tenant was given exclusive common rights in the township.[55] Norton Farm is a brick house, apparently rebuilt in the earlier 19th century.

The Domesday manor of Boreton had 8 recorded tenants[56] and there were 4 houses at Boreton between 1540 and 1708,[57] but only 2 by 1768.[58] Boreton Farm was rebuilt to designs by John Carline in 1782,[59] and was the only house here in 1841, apart from recently erected labourers' cottages at Boretonbrook.[60] The former hamlet probably stood to the south-east of Boreton Farm, where the sites of former houses were visible in the later 19th century.[61]

The Buriwood hamlets have been less severely affected by shrinkage. Though less than half a mile apart, Great and Little Ryton have always been distinct settlements, being known as Upper and Lower Ryton respectively when first recorded in 1209.[62] Great Ryton stands on the Radmore ridge alongside the road from Condover towards Longnor. There were about 8 messuages in the hamlet in 1421[63] and at least 11 in the township as a whole in 1672.[64] Although the number of houses in the hamlet increased in the earlier 19th century, this was largely due to the conversion of farm-houses into cottages. There were 19 houses here in 1841.[65] Nearly all the existing houses are timber-framed, most of them being rough-cast or cased in brick. No. 2 Grange Cottages contains a 2-bay hall of cruck construction: the brick-cased timber-framed cross-wing to the east is of early-17th-century date but probably replaces an earlier solar. Extended investigation of interiors in this hamlet would reveal more examples of cruck construction. Grange Farm, an early-17th-century house of central-stack plan, contains Jacobean panelling.

Little Ryton, which also contained 8 messuages in 1421,[66] contained 13 houses in 1841.[67] Most of the houses now stand on the Longnor road south of Great Ryton but the site of the medieval hamlet seems to have been on the eastern slopes of the Radmore ridge, where the road to Wheathall meets another road, now a bridle-way, running northwards towards Condover Park. The Old House and Little Ryton Farm, which stand near this junction, are both timber-framed. The former was probably the

33 Ibid. (1856).   34 Ibid. (1870).
35 Ibid. (1885).
36 Ex inf. Atcham R.D.C.
37 Kelly's Dir. Salop. (1856–1926).
38 S.P.L., Deeds 9136, m. 41; ibid. 9138, m. 32d.; ibid. 7027A; S.R.O. 567 uncat., deeds, 1323, 1619: ibid. rentals, 1673, 1753; N.L.W., MS. 18453C.
39 S.R.O. 567 uncat., deed, 1323.
40 T.S.A.S. l, 116.   41 Ibid. 123.
42 See p. 45.
43 S.P.L., Deeds 9501. First recorded in 1547: Sta. Cha. 3/4/8.
44 S.P.L., Deeds 7009.
45 Ibid. 7022.
46 S.R.O. 665 uncat., lease, 1722.
47 V.C.H. Salop. i. 332.
48 Hearth Tax, 1672, 125.
49 S.R.O. 1011 (Cholmondeley) uncat., abstract of title to Bayston manor, 1746–1801.
50 Par. rec., tithe appt.
51 V.C.H. Salop. i. 332.
52 S.P.L., Deeds 9501.
53 V.C.H. Salop. i. 332.
54 C 134/48/9.
55 S.P.L., Deeds 9137, m. 34d.
56 V.C.H. Salop. i. 312.
57 Ibid.; S.R.O., 112 uncat., Boreton title-deeds, 1708.
58 Attingham Park estate office, accts. 1755–74.
59 S.R.O. 112 uncat., vouchers, 1782.
60 Par. rec., tithe appt.
61 Auden, Condover, 35; Salop. N. & Q. viii. 104.
62 E 32/144.
63 T.S.A.S. l. 122.
64 Hearth Tax, 1672, 127.
65 Par. rec., tithe appt.
66 T.S.A.S. l. 121.
67 Par. rec., tithe appt.

home of the Atkis family between the 15th and 18th centuries[68] and contains a fragment of early-17th-century wall-painting. Another timber-framed house formerly stood between the Old House and Ryton Grove.[69] The latter, built before 1795,[70] is a stuccoed brick house of 3 stories. It contains a set of projecting semicircular rooms on the south front. Most of the houses on the Longnor road are of 19th-century date, but part of the Fox Inn is timber-framed. The latter is first recorded in 1841;[71] an earlier alehouse at Little Ryton, licensed by 1747, was suppressed in 1755.[72]

Wheathall, on the western slopes of the Buriwood plateau, was surrounded on 3 sides by woodland during the earlier Middle Ages and was divided from Little Ryton on the west by marshland along the foot of the Radmore ridge called Colemore Slough.[73] 'Assart' elements are common in the names of the Wheathall common fields and of their constituent strips and furlongs. The hamlet formerly stood round a green and is likely to be a comparatively late woodland settlement but it was in existence by 1209.[74] Wheathall was of much the same size as the Rytons during the Middle Ages. Eight messuages are recorded there between 1363 and 1598,[75] but since 1841 there have been only two farm-houses in the hamlet[76] and there were 3 other cottages there in 1962. Wheathall Farm, which has passed by descent since the 15th century in the families of Campion, Daker, and Thornes,[77] contains a single cruck truss to the rear of the brick front added by William Daker in 1720.[78] The farm-house in the centre of the hamlet was built in the early 19th century, but the 3 cottages are all timber-framed.

The 4 hamlets at the foot of Lyth Hill seem to have shrunk to something approaching their present size before the end of the 16th century. Chatford, which stands on the northern slope of a ridge of sand and gravel, south of Chatbrook, contained 7 messuages and 9 tenants in 1363,[79] 6 tenants in 1421,[80] and 4 tenants in 1580.[81] The hamlet seems to have been reduced to 3 houses by 1682.[82] One of the latter was demolished between 1841 and 1881,[83] probably as a result of the reorganization of farms on the Condover manorial estate in the 1870s.[84] Chatford House and Chatford Farm are both timber-framed and of early-17th-century date, but a brick south wing was added to Chatford House in 1776.[85] Two farm cottages have been built here since 1881.[86]

Westley stands on a supposed Roman road at the junction of the Chatbrook river gravels and the clays of the lower slopes of Lyth Hill. The township was formerly divided from Great Lyth by woodland around Exfordsgreen, but on the east, where its common fields adjoined those of Little Lyth, the boundary seems to have been marked by a ditch.[87] There is no evidence for the size of Westley before 1619, when 7 of the 9 recorded inhabitants of the township probably lived in the hamlet itself.[88] The hamlet had shrunk to the two existing farm-houses by 1768.[89]

The two timber-framed houses at Little Lyth may have been the only ones in the hamlet when they were built in the early 17th century. Some of the 6 tenants of Little Lyth recorded in 1619 lived on Lyth Hill[90] and the lease of 5 messuages here to a single tenant in 1564[91] indicates that the hamlet was then in decline.

Unlike the other hamlets bordering Lyth Hill Great Lyth was only briefly a member of the Condover manorial estate.[92] Since the Middle Ages the township has been made up of 3 or 4 modest freeholds. There were said to be 11 tenants here in 1616, but some of these lived outside the hamlet,[93] and there were 4 houses between 1740 and 1841.[94] In 1962, when the manor-house was ruinous and unoccupied, the only other houses on the site of the former hamlet were Great Lyth Farm and Rolleston Grange. The former is timber-framed, but was cased in brick and raised to 3-story height in the later 18th century. The latter, built on the site of two former cottages, is constructed of stone from the old English Bridge, Shrewsbury, and timber from various old houses in the district.[95]

A former hamlet known as 'Brome' lay within Condover manor c. 1265, when its inhabitants were said to owe a plough-share for their pasture rights.[96] A rent of 3d. due from this hamlet is recorded in 1443[97] and 1534.[98] The only evidence for its site occurs in 1566, when two butts at 'Bromes Cross' were said to stand near the highway to Shrewsbury.[99]

Isolated settlement on cleared woodland in Buriwood is first recorded in the 16th century and in its essentials the present pattern of settlement in the south-east of the parish seems to have been established by the mid-17th century. Among the isolated farms to the south of Condover village the houses at Upper Green, Condover Grove, and Ryton Fields are of 19th-century date, but clearly occupy earlier sites. Lower Green, now rough-cast, is a timber-framed house. Berrywood Lane Farm, on the plateau itself, was rebuilt in brick in the 1850s,[1] but the house known to have stood on this site in 1768[2]

[68] 'Mary Atkis 1713' cut in glass above stair. For Atkis family see W.S.L. 29/24, bdle. 3 (title-deeds, 1640–1742) and S.P.L., Condover ct. r. *passim.*
[69] Ex inf. Mrs. T. M. Hazlerigg, The Old House, Little Ryton.
[70] S.R.O. 1056/1.
[71] Par. rec., tithe appt.
[72] N.L.W., Castle Hill 2244.
[73] S.P.L., Deeds 9138, mm. 17, 18, 25d.
[74] E 32/144.
[75] *T.S.A.S.* l. 113, 120; S.P.L., Deeds 7022.
[76] Par. rec., tithe appt.
[77] See p. 47 and S.P.L., Condover ct. r. *passim.*
[78] Datestone.
[79] *T.S.A.S.* l. 114.
[80] Ibid. 123.   [81] Ibid. 129.
[82] Par. rec., overseers' accts. 1682–1708.
[83] Ibid. tithe appt.; O.S. Map 1/2,500 Salop. xli (1st edn.).
[84] S.R.O. 1154/1.   [85] Datestone.

[86] O.S. Map 1/2,500 Salop. xli (1st edn.).
[87] The field-names Upper and Lower Ditches occurred here in 1841: par. rec., tithe appt.
[88] S.P.L., Deeds 9523.
[89] S.R.O. 665 uncat., survey of Condover manorial estate, c. 1768.
[90] S.P.L., Deeds 9523.
[91] Ibid. 6869.
[92] See p. 41.
[93] S.P.L., Deeds 9523.
[94] S.P.L., MS. 2737; S.R.O. 665 uncat., map of Great Lyth, 1793; par. rec., tithe appt.
[95] Ex inf. Mr. R. Oulton, Bayston Hill.
[96] C 145/20/1.
[97] S.P.L., Deeds 7026.
[98] Ibid. 9131.
[99] Ibid. 9074.
[1] Datestone.
[2] S.R.O. 665 uncat., map of Condover manorial estate, c. 1768.

was perhaps the homestead of the small farm in Buriwood occupied by the Cartwright family in 1633.[3] Of the two groups of cottages to the south of this house one dates from the early 19th century[4] and the other from the 1860s.[5] Pigeondoor Farm, on the site of a cottage recorded in 1545,[6] is an early-17th-century house of central-stack plan. Five cottages which stood nearby in 1841[7] have since been demolished. Ten Chimneys, on the top of the steep slope above Row Brook, and Mount Zion (now called The Poplars) to the south were built in local sandstone by the Durnell family in 1771 and 1764 respectively.[8] One or both of these houses probably replaced earlier timber-framed buildings, since 3 families were living in this part of the parish in the early 17th century.[9] Mount Zion derives its name from the assart on which it stands. This was called 'Monkeye' in 1482[10] and Monkeys Patch in the 19th century.[11] The group of cottages known as The Pentre (formerly Ryton View) to the west of Ten Chimneys, has been built since 1841,[12] and Duckhall, on the low ground south of Wheathall, is not recorded before the 19th century.[13]

Although much of the area between the Radmore ridge and the Cound was made up of moorland, the Domesday mill of Condover manor appears to have stood on the site of Old Mills to the west of Radmore Hill,[14] and Gonsal Farm, a modern house, may stand on the site of a former hamlet. The Gosnell family, prominent among the copyholders of Condover manor from the 13th to the 18th centuries,[15] took their name from this place. The small group of houses at Sytch, east of Dorrington, is essentially a 19th-century development. Sytch House, a small, brick, gentleman's residence, was built between 1849 and 1857,[16] but the nearby cottages were formerly a farm-house, built c. 1791,[17] and a wheelwright's house and shop some 250 yards to the north of Sytch House had been built by 1841.[18]

Except at Dorrington and Bayston Hill little settlement took place alongside the main road from Shrewsbury to Hereford, probably because this route was comparatively unimportant before the 18th century. An exception is Hunger Hill, formerly known as Warreytree Hill,[19] probably in reference to a manorial gallows at this cross-roads. A cottage is recorded here in 1592[20] and an alehouse in the early 17th century.[21] Both existing houses at Hunger Hill date from the 17th century: others formerly stood to the east of the main road at this point.[22]

Lythwood Farm, the oldest of the 3 farm-houses

on the Lythwood plateau, was probably built in the last decade of the 16th century.[23] Part of the original timber-framed house forms the central portion of the present house. The external walls are wholly of brick and the north end was raised to 3-story height c. 1800. A dovecote recorded here in 1740[24] is still standing. A house on the site of Lythwood Hall was said to have been standing for a century or more c. 1665;[25] it was described as a capital messuage in 1701.[26] The present Hall was built by George Steuart for Joshua Blakeway c. 1785.[27] This is a large two-story house arranged around three sides of a courtyard. It is built of red brick but part of the north front is faced with stone ashlar: there was formerly a detached portico in the centre of this front.[28] The Hall has been much altered and extended at various times, but the south-east wing may originally have been a stable block. The house was occupied by the Ministry of Supply, 1940–3, and was converted into flats c. 1950.[29] Lower Lythwood Farm is a 19th-century brick house.

Surviving timber-framed houses indicate that squatter settlement on the fringes of Lythwood in the later 16th and early 17th centuries was restricted to three areas. They are found at Bayston Grove and on the adjoining section of Lyth Hill Road at the southern end of the former Bayston Common, to the south of the rope-walk on the summit of Lyth Hill, and at Lyth Bank to the south-west. More is known of the early history of squatter settlement at Exfordsgreen. In that part of Exfordsgreen which lay within the parish about 10 cottages were built between 1607 and 1629, when two alehouses are recorded here.[30] Six of the 11 houses in the Condover portion of Exfordsgreen lay in the Condover manorial estate in 1841, when only one was still owner-occupied,[31] but most of the cottages still possess their original smallholdings.

The roadside settlement at Annscroft, on the parish boundary west of Great Lyth, grew up in the early 19th century, when it seems to have been almost exclusively occupied by miners from the Moat Hall Colliery. No houses stood here in 1802,[32] but there were about 9 in 1827[33] and the settlement had almost reached its present size by 1841.[34]

MANORS. The manor of CONDOVER was a royal manor before the Conquest, but in 1086 it was held by Roger, Earl of Shrewsbury.[35] The manor reverted to the Crown, probably as a result of the rebellion of Robert of Bellême in 1102,[36] and

[3] S.P.L., Deeds 7103; S.R.O. 665 uncat., lease, 1664.
[4] Par. rec., tithe appt.
[5] Datestone.
[6] S.P.L., MS. 377, f. 33.
[7] Par. rec., tithe appt.
[8] Datestones. For Durnell family see pedigree in Condover ct. r. 1833, penes Messrs. Salt & Sons, solicitors.
[9] S.P.R. Lich. vi (1), 34–69 passim.
[10] S.P.L., Deeds 9137, m. 23.
[11] Par. rec., tithe appt.
[12] Ibid.; Auden, Condover, 36.
[13] Par. rec., tithe appt.
[14] See p. 48.
[15] Eyton, vi. 27; S.P.L., Condover ct. r. passim.
[16] Sytch House title-deeds penes Messrs. G. H. Morgan, solicitors, Shrewsbury.
[17] Ibid.
[18] Par. rec., tithe appt.
[19] S.P.L., Deeds 9118; T.S.A.S. l. 129.
[20] S.P.L., Deeds 9118.

[21] Q. Sess., alehouse reg.; S.P.R. Lich. vi (1), 63.
[22] O.S. Map 1/2,500 Salop. xli (1st edn.).
[23] S.P.L., MS. 110.
[24] S.P.L. Deeds 3286.
[25] S.P.L., MS. 110, bill of William Owen v. William Stirchley, c. 1665.
[26] S.R.O. 1011 (Harrop) uncat., abstract of title to Lythwood Hall estate, 1701–1877.
[27] H. M. Colvin, Biog. Dict. of Eng. Arch. 51; Owen and Blakeway, Hist. Shrewsbury, ii. 248.
[28] Pevsner, Shropshire, 71.
[29] Ex inf. Messrs. Clarke & Sons, solicitors, Shrewsbury
[30] B.M. Add. MS. 30312; S.P.L., Deeds 9523–4; Q Sess., alehouse reg. See also plate facing p. 96.
[31] Par. rec., tithe appt.
[32] S.R.O. 665 uncat., sale partics. (with plan), 1802.
[33] B.M. O.S. 2″ orig. drawings, sheet 320 (1827).
[34] Par. rec., tithe appt.
[35] V.C.H. Salop. i. 315.
[36] Eyton, i. 242; ibid. vi. 9.

remained a royal manor until 1226, when it was granted to Henry III's sister Joan, wife of Llewelyn the Great.[37] After a temporary forfeiture in 1228[38] it was restored to her later in the same year,[39] but again reverted to the Crown in 1231.[40]

In 1238 the manor was granted to Henry de Hastings and his wife Ada.[41] This was originally intended as a temporary arrangement, pending the assignment to Ada of a share of the estate of her brother John, Earl of Chester,[42] but the grant was made permanent in 1242.[43] Henry de Hastings died in 1250[44] and the manor was in the custody of Guy de Rochfort from 1252[45] until Henry's son Henry came of age in 1256.[46] The latter held the manor from 1256 until 1266, when his estates were sequestered under the Dictum of Kenilworth.[47] Although he had recovered estates in other counties by 1268,[48] he does not appear to have regained possession of Condover manor before his death in the following year.[49]

Custody of the estates of Henry de Hastings, during the minority of his son John, was granted in 1269 to Richard, Earl of Cornwall,[50] passing to the latter's son Edmund, Earl of Cornwall, in 1272.[51] John de Hastings, who obtained livery of the manor when he came of age in 1283,[52] exchanged it in the following year with Robert Burnell, Bishop of Bath and Wells, for the manor of Wotton (Northants.).[53] Condover followed the descent of Acton Burnell manor[54] until 1315 when, on the death of Edward Burnell, it was assigned in dower to his widow Aline.[55] After her death in 1363[56] the manor passed to Sir Nicholas Burnell, son of John de Haudlo and Maud, sister of Edward Burnell,[57] on whom the reversion had been settled in 1340.[58] It again followed the descent of Acton Burnell manor until the attainder of Francis, Lord Lovell, in 1485.

The manor was granted to Sir Richard Corbet before 1492,[59] but seems to have been once more in the hands of the Crown by 1498, when Sir Thomas Leighton was appointed steward.[60] In 1513 the manor was granted for life to Sir Richard Cornwall.[61] Sir Henry Knyvett, who obtained a grant of the manor in tail in 1533,[62] sold it in 1544 to the

London mercer Robert Longe.[63] After Longe's death in 1552 the manor passed to his widow Cecily.[64] In 1561, when Longe's estates were divided among his 3 daughters, Condover manor was assigned to his daughter Mary and her husband Henry Vynar, a London merchant.[65] On Mary's death in 1565 Vynar converted his life interest in the manor into an estate in tail.[66] Other lands in Condover, acquired by Vynar, were settled on his second wife Anne in 1572, 1577, and 1584.[67] Richard Harford of Bosbury (Herefs.), to whom the manor was leased for 18 years as security for a loan in 1567,[68] assigned the lease in 1578 to Thomas Owen and Stephen Duckett.[69] Vynar died in 1585[70] and in the following year the manor was acquired by Thomas Owen, following a lawsuit with Henry Vynar, son of Henry Vynar by his first wife Mary.[71] At the same time Anne, widow of Henry Vynar the elder, conveyed to Owen her interest in the manor and in other lands settled on her by her husband.[72]

The manor was held until 1728 by the following members of the Owen family:[73] Thomas, 1586–98;[74] Roger (son), 1598–1617:[75] Ursula (widow of Roger), 1617–29;[76] William (brother of Roger Owen) jointly with his son Roger, 1629–62;[77] Thomas (grandson of William Owen), 1662–78;[78] Roger (son), 1678–1718;[79] Edward (son), 1718–28. On the death of Edward Owen in 1728 the manor passed to his sister Letitia, then wife of Richard Mytton.[80] Letitia, who later married Trafford Barnston, died in 1755, having devised the estate to her grand-daughter Anna Maria Leighton.[81] The last-named, who came of age in 1766,[82] married Nicholas Smythe of North Nibley (Glos.). Nicholas died in 1790, when the estate passed to his son Nicholas Owen Smythe, who then assumed the additional surname of Owen.[83] To redeem the heavy debts incurred by the latter's extravagance, the estate was vested in trustees in 1794[84] and again in 1802, when N. O. Smythe Owen fled to Paris to escape his creditors.[85] After the latter's death in the following year[86] trustees continued to administer the estate until 1814, when Edward William Smythe Pemberton, nephew and heir-at-law of N. O. Smythe Owen, came of age.[87]

---

[37] *Rot. Litt. Claus.* (Rec. Com.), ii. 135.
[38] *Close R.* 1227–31, 50, 68–69.   [39] Ibid. 123.
[40] Eyton, vi. 14.
[41] *Cal. Pat.* 1232–47, 224; *Close R.* 1237–42, 60.
[42] Ibid.
[43] *Close R.* 1242–7, 295; *Cal. Lib.* 1240–5, 124; *Pipe R.* 1242 (ed. H. L. Cannon), 4.
[44] *Close R.* 1247–51, 311.
[45] *Cal. Pat.* 1247–58, 134.
[46] *Rot. Hund.* (Rec. Com.), ii. 63; *Close R.* 1254–6, 303–4.
[47] *Complete Peerage*, vi. 346; *Cal. Pat.* 1266–72, 111–12.
[48] *Cal. Pat.* 1266–72, 214.
[49] *Complete Peerage*, vi. 346.
[50] *Cal. Pat.* 1266–72, 360.
[51] Ibid. 657.
[52] *Cal. Close*, 1279–88, 212.
[53] *T.S.A.S.* 4th ser. vii. 108; Eyton, vi. 17.
[54] See p. 7.
[55] *Cal. Close*, 1313–18, 263–4.
[56] *Cal. Inq. p.m.* xi, p. 371.
[57] Ibid. xii, p. 45; *Cal. Close*, 1360–4, 471.
[58] C.P. 25(1)/194/12/54; *Cal. Pat.* 1338–40, 302.
[59] *Cal. Inq. p.m. Hen. VII*, i, p. 476.
[60] *Cal. Pat.* 1494–1509, 157.
[61] *L. & P. Hen. VIII*, i (2), p. 1114.
[62] Ibid. vi. p. 496; ibid. xix (1), p. 626; S.P.L., Deeds 9146; C 142/75/70.
[63] *L. & P. Hen. VIII*, xix (1), p. 195; S.P.L., Deeds 6849, 6853, 9405, 13407.

[64] C 142/97/89; S.P.L., Deeds 9460, 9506.
[65] S.P.L., Deeds 13458; S.R.O. 474/15.
[66] S.P.L., Deeds 6850, 9404; S.R.O. 665 uncat., deeds, 1565.
[67] S.P.L., Deeds 7084; C 142/207/107.
[68] S.R.O. 665 uncat., lease, 1567. Harford was subsequently farmer of the manor: S.P.L., Deeds 7003A/318, 330.
[69] S.R.O. 665 uncat., deed, 1578.
[70] C 142/207/107.
[71] S.P.L., Deeds 6637–7109, 9149, 9404, 13402–69; S.R.O. 475/15; ibid. 665 uncat., legal papers, 1585–6.
[72] S.P.L., Deeds 7065, 9426.
[73] For pedigree see S.P.L., MS. 2792, pp. 378–80.
[74] S.P.L., Deeds 7065.
[75] C 142/374/86; S.P.L., Deeds 9495.
[76] S.P.L., Deeds 7066, 9942.
[77] Ibid. 7043, 7057–8, 9385, 9503.
[78] Ibid. 9388, 9498, 9522.
[79] Ibid. 9955, 13457.
[80] S.P.L., MS. 2792, pp. 378–80; Burke, *Land. Gent.* (1879), p. 1220.
[81] Ibid.   [82] S.P.L., Deeds 17928.
[83] Burke, *Land. Gent.* (1879), p. 1220.
[84] S.P.L., Deeds 10039.
[85] S.R.O. 665 uncat., correspondence of N. O. Smythe Owen, 1800–3.
[86] Burke, *Land. Gent.* (1879), p. 1220.
[87] Ibid.; S.R.O. 1011 (Smythe Owen) uncat., trustees' accts. 1804–14; S.P.L., MS. 2792, p. 380.

The latter, who then assumed the surname Owen,[88] was succeeded in 1863 by his cousin Thomas Cholmondeley, who died in the following year.[89] The manor then passed to Thomas's cousin Reginald Cholmondeley, at whose death in 1896 the Condover estate was sold.[90] The following have since been lords of the manor:[91] E. B. Fielden, 1897–1926; R. Cohen, 1926–8; R. A. L. Cohen, 1928–39; W. H. Abbey, 1939–42; Major J. R. Abbey, 1942–57. Condover Hall, no longer occupied by the owner of the estate after 1939,[92] was sold to the Royal National Institute for the Blind in 1946,[93] and the sale of the remainder of the estate to the tenants had been completed by 1957.[94]

Condover Hall[95] is generally regarded as the finest stone manor-house of the Elizabethan period in Shropshire. Surviving bailiff's accounts[96] throw some light on its construction. Thomas Owen who was a man of wide culture,[97] is likely to have been responsible for its design. He set about assembling building materials as soon as he had acquired the manor in 1586. Between November 1586 and May 1587, 3,935 loads of sandstone from quarries in Buriwood were drawn by hired labour and stone tiles from Harnage were brought to Condover as a boon-work by the tenants of adjoining manors.[98] Grinshill stone was being quarried for use at the Hall by September 1587[99] and John Richmond was preparing window mouldings and quoins at Grinshill during the summer of 1588.[1] A building contract with Richmond was prepared in 1588–9,[2] but was not executed and by November 1591 he had been superseded as master-mason by Walter Hancocks.[3] The building of the Hall was evidently well advanced by this date; the foundations of the north porch were dug in the spring of 1592 and a little later there is a reference to the securing of the 'great cornices' and 'lintels' above the 'court window'.[4] Timber, presumably for the roof and floors of the Hall, was obtained in 1592 from Buriwood, Lythwood, Longnor, Pitchford, and 'Weston'.[5] Lead pipes to bring water from a spring in Botchitt's Meadow were laid in 1592–3.[6] Although Thomas Owen's will of December 1598 contained a bequest of 'provision for building' to his son Roger,[7] it is probable that the Hall was substantially complete by this date. During the autumn of 1598 the carpenter Morris Edmonds was at work on the 'screen' in the hall and on doors in various parts of the house; the 'great walk' in the garden was turfed and a bowling-alley was laid out.[8]

The house has two stories, basement, and attics, and is built of reddish sandstone on an H-shaped plan. The entrance front faces north-east, where the projecting side wings originally enclosed a walled forecourt. The main doorway is in a central three-storied porch which has oriel windows to the upper floors and is crowned by a small decorative gable. There are plain gables flanking the porch and at the sides and ends of the cross-wings. The stone windows are mullioned and transomed, those at the gable-ends being two-storied bays of shallow projection. At first-floor level there is a continuous string-course enriched with panels of carved strapwork. At the centre of each cross-wing a square tower with a pierced parapet rises above the main roof and the sky-line is further elaborated by tall chimneys with multiple brick shafts. On the southwest, or garden, front there is an arcaded loggia of nine bays between the two projecting wings, surmounted by a low mezzanine story. The central windows on this front take the form of a three-storied oriel. Above the mezzanine windows a continuous moulded string is raised to suggest pediments. Stone roundels are placed in the pediments, in the spandrels of the arcade, and on many of the gables of the house. This decorative detail is found on other buildings attributed to Walter Hancocks, including Shrewsbury Market House.[9] The exterior of Condover Hall is basically of traditional Tudor design, the more advanced Renaissance features being the arcaded loggia and the round-headed entrance doorway flanked by Classical columns.

The interior of the house has been considerably altered. In its original form the ground floor of the central block consisted of a parlour and a great hall, the latter having a screens passage entered from the porch across its south-east end. On the garden front, where the ground falls away, the loggia and mezzanine together rise to the same height as the front rooms. Part of the mezzanine was formerly occupied by a long gallery and the principal staircase was below the tower in the centre of the north-west wing. Almost the only original fittings to survive are some oak panelling in the mezzanine and a huge carved stone chimney-piece in the hall. The chimney-piece had been removed to an outhouse, probably in the 18th century, and was later reinstated. It bears the initials of Roger Owen (d. 1617) and was presumably inserted by him after Thomas Owen's death. The somewhat primitively carved figures resemble those on the Owen and Norton monument in Condover church: both may have been the work of Walter Hancocks's successor.[10]

The house was altered in the early 18th century, probably by another Roger Owen (d. 1732). Lead rainwater-heads on the entrance front carry a cipher which is thought to represent his initials.[11] Tall sash windows on the same front, shown in an early-19th-century engraving,[12] may have been inserted at the same time. When the road to the north-east of the house was diverted in 1794[13] the enclosed forecourt was replaced by a straight drive. In 1804 a lead statue of Hercules, which had stood in the court, was

[88] S.P.L., MS. 2792, p. 380.
[89] Auden, *Condover*, 19.
[90] Ibid.; sale partics. 1896, *penes* Mr. J. C. Brookfield, Yew Tree Cottage, Condover.
[91] Ex inf. Mr. J. C. Brookfield (formerly agent for the Condover estate).
[92] Ibid.
[93] Ibid.
[94] Ibid.
[95] See frontispiece.
[96] S.P.L., Deeds 6883–5, 7029.
[97] See his will, ibid. 9938.
[98] Ibid. 6883.

[99] Ibid.
[1] Ibid. 6884.
[2] Ibid. 7081; *Salop. N. & Q.* viii (1899), 7–8.
[3] S.P.L., Deeds 6885.
[4] Ibid.
[5] Ibid.
[6] Ibid. 6863, 6885.
[7] Ibid. 9938.
[8] Ibid. 7029.
[9] Tipping, *English Homes*, iii (1), 165.
[10] Ibid. 166–8; see p. 55.
[11] Tipping, op. cit. 170–1.
[12] Neale's *Views* (1831).   [13] See p. 32.

removed to Shrewsbury and later erected in the Quarry.[14]

The interior of Condover Hall was largely re-modelled between 1864 and 1896 by Reginald Cholmondeley, a lover of the arts and a proficient amateur sculptor.[15] His alterations, mostly in the Jacobean style, included much of his own work. He inserted arcaded stone screens in the hall, carved fireplaces in the long gallery, and a grandiose oak staircase in the former parlour.[16] He also appears to have been responsible for replacing the Georgian sash windows, for reinstating the hall fireplace, for enclosing the loggia, and for erecting the stone arch-way at the end of the drive. Further changes were made by Rex Cohen in 1927, whose work included the replacement of several 18th-century fireplaces by new ones of Tudor design.[17] In his time, or in that of his successor, a side porch and lobby were built against the south-east wing, Cholmondeley's hall screens were removed, and much of the existing oak panelling was introduced. No great changes took place after 1939, when the house ceased to be occu-pied by the owners of the estate.

The manor of *BAYSTON* was among the estates of the Bishopric of Hereford before the Conquest and in 1066 was held on a life-lease by Edric, the bishop's steward.[18] Although the manor had come into the hands of William Pantulf, lord of the neigh-bouring manor of Norton, by 1086,[19] the Bishop of Hereford was accounted overlord until the later 13th century.[20]

The manor was held by Richard Sprenchose in 1255[21] and remained in the possession of his descend-ants, the Sprenchose family of Plaish,[22] until the death of Margaret, widow of Fulk Sprenchose, *c.* 1499, when the estate was divided among Fulk's daughters, Margery, Elizabeth, and Sybil.[23] Mar-gery's husband William Leighton appears to have held Bayston manor in 1502,[24] but Richard Sand-ford, son of Elizabeth Sprenchose, may have held it in 1563, when he purchased lands at Bayston,[25] and his son George was lord of the manor in 1581.[26] The manor was held by the Sandford family of The Isle[27] until 1801, when it was sold to N. O. Smythe Owen,[28] and it was subsequently a member of the Condover manorial estate.

The church of St. Peter, Shrewsbury, held the manor of *BORETON* before 1066[29] and it formed part of the original endowment of Shrewsbury

Abbey *c.* 1094.[30] By 1160, however, the abbey had granted the manor to Gilbert Bozard.[31] On the death of Roger Bozard in 1194 the manor escheated to the Crown[32] and in 1197 the wardship and marriage of Roger's daughters Alice and Isabel were committed to Henry Boscard and Elias de Etting-ham.[33] The manor was subsequently divided be-tween Alice and Isabel. Henry de Boreton, the son of Alice, held a moiety of the manor in 1255,[34] but seems to have surrendered his estate to Shrewsbury Abbey before 1263.[35] Isabel, who married Ralph Marescall (I), was succeeded at her death in 1249 by her son Ralph Marescall (II).[36] On the latter's death in 1263 this moiety of the manor passed to his son Engelard le Marescall *alias* Engelard de Pulley.[37] Engelard, however, held no land in Boreton at his death in 1290[38] and seems to have conveyed his estate here to William Pride of Shrewsbury.[39] The two feoffees who were holding this moiety of the manor in 1343 granted it in the following year to Shrewsbury Abbey to form the endowment of a chantry in the abbey church.[40] In 1345 a rent charge of 100*s.* arising from the manor was granted by the same feoffees to Haughmond Abbey.[41]

The manor was held by Shrewsbury Abbey until the Dissolution,[42] when it was dismembered. Lease-hold cottages and lands in the manor and rents of the free tenants were sold by the Crown in 1557 to Gregory and John Isham,[43] who immediately con-veyed them to Henry Vynar.[44] They subsequently formed part of the Condover manorial estate. The customary lands, which had been sold to Richard and Thomas Lawley in 1545,[45] were held in 1556 by William Crompton, who then had licence to grant them to Fulk Crompton.[46] In 1574 Richard Cromp-ton held the estate,[47] which passed at his death in 1577 to his nephew Richard.[48] In 1585, when the estate was described as the manor of Boreton, Richard Crompton sold it to Thomas Burton,[49] who sold the manor in 1602 to Roger Owen of Condover.[50] On the latter's death in 1617 Boreton manor passed to his infant daughters Alice and Sarah[51] and was granted to their mother Ursula as guardian in 1619.[52] Sarah Owen married Humphrey Davenport, who purchased Alice's moiety of the manor before 1638.[53] Alice and Sarah both died in 1639,[54] when Boreton manor again passed to the lord of Condover manor,[55] but it was sold in 1648 to Robert Betton of Shrews-bury,[56] whose son Wrottesley Betton sold it to

---

[14] Tipping, op. cit. 171, 172–3.
[15] See p. 55.
[16] Tipping, op. cit. 173.
[17] Initials and date on fireplaces.
[18] *V.C.H. Salop.* i. 332. For the identity of Edric, see J. F. A. Mason, 'Edric of Bayston', *T.S.A.S.* lv. 112–18.
[19] *V.C.H. Salop.* i. 332.
[20] *Feud. Aids*, iv. 215.
[21] *Rot. Hund.* (Rec. Com.), ii. 63.
[22] For pedigree see Eyton, vi. 299–300; S.P.L., MS. 2788, pp. 252–3.
[23] S.P.L., Deeds 9137, m. 19.
[24] C.P. 25(1)/195/24/12.
[25] S.R.O. 465/453.
[26] C.P. 25(2)/201/23 Eliz. I East.
[27] For pedigree see *Visit. Salop. 1623* (Harl. Soc. xxix), ii. 432–3; S.P.L., MS. 2788, pp. 240–2.
[28] S.R.O. 1011 (Smythe Owen) uncat., deed, 1801.
[29] *V.C.H. Salop.* i. 312.
[30] Eyton, vi. 171; Dugdale, *Mon.* iii. 519, 521.
[31] Eyton, vi. 174.
[32] Ibid. 175; *Pipe R.* 1194 (P.R.S. N.S. v), 5; ibid. 1195 (P.R.S. N.S. vi), 42.
[33] *Pipe R.* 1197 (P.R.S. N.S. viii), 157; *Bk. of Fees*, 1341.

[34] Eyton, viii. 172.
[35] Ibid. vi. 177–8.
[36] *Cal. Inq. p.m.* i, p. 33.
[37] *Ex. e Rot. Fin.* (Rec. Com.), ii. 404.
[38] *Cal. Inq. p.m.* ii, p. 461.
[39] Eyton, vi. 179.
[40] *Cal. Pat. 1343–5*, 214, 216, 533; *Abbrev. Rot. Orig.* (Rec. Com.), ii. 119.
[41] *Abbrev. Rot. Orig.* (Rec. Com.), ii. 178.
[42] S.C. 6/Hen. VIII/3010 m. 61.
[43] *Cal. Pat. 1555–6*, 286–7.
[44] S.R.O. 474/15.
[45] *L. & P. Hen. VIII*, xx (2), p. 222.
[46] *Cal. Pat. 1555–7*, 64.
[47] C 142/213/149.
[48] Ibid.
[49] C.P. 25(2)/202/27 & 28 Eliz. I Mich.
[50] C.P. 25(2)/262/44 & 45 Eliz. I Mich.
[51] C 142/373/1.
[52] S.P.L., Deeds 7066.
[53] C 142/584/82, 90; C 142/703/64.
[54] Ibid.
[55] S.P.L., Deeds 6929.
[56] S.R.O. 112 uncat., Boreton manor title-deeds, 1648.

Richard Hill of Hawkstone in 1709.[57] Boreton subsequently became part of the Attingham estate, following the descent of the manor of Betton Abbots in Berrington until it was sold in 1949.[58]

The manor of *NORTON*, held by the freeman Ulvric before the Conquest, was held by William Pantulf in 1086.[59] Pantulf's descendant, the baron of Wem, was accounted overlord in 1255,[60] but Thomas Tochet was said to be overlord, 1294–1363,[61] and in 1480, when the overlordship is last recorded, it was said to be vested in the Earl of Arundel.[62] The manor passed in the course of the 12th century to a junior branch of the Pantulf family,[63] but on the death of Adam Pantulf in 1240 his estates were divided among 4 persons, probably the husbands of his 4 daughters.[64] Two of these, Michael de Morton and Richard Irish, were said to be lords of Norton manor in 1255.[65] One or more of the heirs of Adam Pantulf were subsequently accounted mesne lords, being last recorded in 1315,[66] but Norton was said to be a member of Condover manor in 1256[67] and may well have been reduced to this condition before 1240.

In 1462 John, Lord Lovell, granted the manor of Norton to the Shrewsbury merchant Thomas Stone,[68] but Thomas Acton of Longnor, who had bought other lands in Norton in 1475,[69] held the manor at his death in 1480 when it passed to his son Thomas.[70] The latter died in 1514,[71] having devised this and other properties to his wife Joan for life, after which they were to form the endowment of a chantry in Condover church.[72] Joan later married Edmund Acton, to whom the reversion of the estate was leased by the feoffees of Thomas Acton in 1531.[73] He was dead by 1537, when the reversion was assigned to William Cornwall.[74] Joan Acton was living at Norton at her death in 1539,[75] when her residuary legatee Richard Leighton took possession of the property.[76] Joan's heir-at-law, William Acton, who proved his title to the manor in 1540, then leased it to Leighton for 40 years.[77] William Cornwall assigned his interest in Norton to William Acton in 1542.[78] In 1550 Acton sold Norton to Robert Longe, lord of Condover manor.[79] Leighton continued as tenant until his death in 1569, when he was succeeded by his widow Eleanor and his son William,[80] but in 1578 Norton was leased to Richard Owen of Shrewsbury,[81] who assigned it in 1587 to his brother Thomas Owen, lord of Condover

manor.[82] Norton was subsequently part of the Condover manorial estate.

In the early 16th century the property was called indifferently Norton manor or Norton Farm, and in 1566 Richard Leighton asserted that it was no manor.[83] Between 1550 and 1572 several unsuccessful attempts were made by informers to prove that Norton Farm was concealed land, on the grounds that it had formed the endowment of a chantry.[84]

The estate known in the 17th and 18th centuries as the manor of *GREAT LYTH* can be identified with the fief of one hide held by Roger the huntsman within the manor of Condover in 1086.[85] Roger's successors, the lords of Pulverbatch manor, were accounted overlords of Great Lyth until 1368.[86] An unsuccessful attempt was made to reassert this overlordship in 1616.[87]

One Walter Fitz John was probably tenant here in the later 12th century,[88] but the property passed into divided ownership in 1203, when Walter's son, William Fitz Walter, conveyed a half hide at Great Lyth to Robert de Gatacre.[89] The moiety of the estate retained by William Fitz Walter presumably passed to his son Walter Fitz William, who is last recorded in 1227.[90] Its descent during the later Middle Ages is not known but it can probably be identified with the property later known as Great Lyth Farm. This was held by Edward Owen of Eaton Mascott in 1609[91] and in 1721 was sold by Edward's descendant Edward Owen to John Thornton of Shrewsbury.[92] It was acquired *c.* 1752 by Joseph Plymley of Shrewsbury[93] and in 1799, when the latter's descendant Archdeacon Joseph Plymley sold it to N. O. Smythe Owen, it amounted to some 90 a.[94]

The moiety of Great Lyth acquired by Robert de Gatacre in 1203 was retained by the Gatacre family until the 17th century. Geoffrey de Gatacre held it at his death in 1345[95] and Geoffrey's son Thomas was succeeded in 1368 by his widow Alice.[96] The estate was first described as a manor in 1604, when William Gatacre conveyed it to Thomas Harries of Boreatton.[97] The latter's grandson Sir George Harries conveyed it in 1664 to Nicholas Gibbons,[98] who may already have been in possession, since he was resident at Great Lyth in 1662.[99] The Gibbons family[1] held the manor until 1800, when Charles Gibbons sold it to N. O. Smythe Owen.[2] The latter,

57 Ibid. deed, 1709.
58 Ex inf. The National Trust.
59 *V.C.H. Salop.* i. 332.
60 *Rot. Hund.* (Rec. Com.), ii. 62.
61 *Cal. Inq. p.m.* iii, p. 121; ibid. xi, p. 373.
62 C 140/76/55.
63 Eyton, viii. 42–43.
64 Ibid.
65 *Rot. Hund.* (Rec. Com.), ii. 62.
66 *Cal. Inq. p.m.* iii, pp. 50, 121; ibid. v, p. 390.
67 Eyton, vi. 300–1.
68 S.P.L., Deeds 6608–9.
69 Ibid. 6610–11.
70 C 140/76/55.
71 S.P.L., Deeds 6623.
72 Ibid. 6621.
73 Ibid. 6607.
74 Ibid. 13432.
75 C 142/82/115; S.P.L., MS. 377, f. 139.
76 S.P.L., Deeds 6626.
77 Ibid. 6612, 6626.
78 Ibid. 6613.
79 Ibid. 6616.
80 Ibid. 6630.

81 Ibid. 6632.
82 Ibid. 6636.
83 S.P.L., MS. 377, f. 139ᵛ.
84 Ibid. ff. 139ᵛ–143; S.P.L., Deeds 6618–20, 6630, 9148; E 310/23/122 f. 21; C 3/84/11; S.R.O. 474/15; *Cal. Pat.* 1563–6, 63, 307, 419.
85 *V.C.H. Salop.* i. 315; Eyton, vi. 22.
86 Eyton, vi. 22–24; *Cal. Inq. Misc.* iii, p. 258.
87 S.P.L., Deeds 9523.
88 Eyton, vi. 23.
89 Ibid. iii. 88.
90 Ibid. vi. 23, 196.
91 N.L.W., Pitchford Hall 621.
92 S.P.L., Deeds 9966.
93 S.P.L., MS. 2737, f. 307.
94 S.R.O. 1011 (Smythe Owen) uncat., deed, 1799.
95 *Cal. Inq. p.m.* xii, p. 187.
96 *Cal. Inq. Misc.* iii, p. 258; *Cal. Close*, 1369–74, 15.
97 C.P. 25(2)/342/2 Jas. I East.
98 C.P. 25(2)/712/16 Chas. II East.
99 E 179/255/35 m. 74.
1 For pedigree see S.P.L., Deeds 13529.
2 S.R.O. 1011 (Smythe Owen) uncat., deed, 1800.

who had thus reunited the two parts of the estate, retained the manorial rights but sold the lands in 1802 to Thomas Edmunds.[3]

Great Lyth Farm (120 a.)[4] was again separated in 1813, when it was settled on Thomas, son of Thomas Edmunds. The farm was bought in 1863 by J. S. Rutter, whose trustees sold it to Thomas Hockenhull in 1902. The farm was acquired by the County Council for smallholdings in 1920. The remainder of the manorial estate, including the manor-house, amounted to 186 a. in 1841, when it was in the possession of Edward, brother of Thomas Edmunds the elder.[5] It had been acquired before 1880 by L. E. Edwards[6] and passed on the death of H. A. Edwards in 1905 to his 3 daughters, the last of whom died in 1948.[7]

Great Lyth manor-house is a red brick building of two stories and attics, dating from the later 17th century. It consists of a central range, containing hall and parlour, flanked by two side wings. The wings project on the north, or entrance, front, where they terminate in gables with shaped parapets. The brick work is of fine quality, a notable feature being a course of brick modillions at first-floor level. The central doorway on the north front has been blocked, but the modillion course is raised in a semi-circle above its site, suggesting that the door was originally surmounted by a 'shell' or semi-circular hood. Remains of a few original mullioned and transomed windows have survived. The house was said to be in bad condition in 1741, when it was no longer occupied by the owner of the estate.[8] It has been unoccupied since 1948, and by 1966, when almost all the internal fittings including fireplaces and panelling, had been removed and some of the structural timbers had been destroyed by vandals, the house was little more than a shell.[9]

OTHER ESTATES. Lythwood, still accounted a 'haye' within the Long Forest in 1301,[10] was granted to Shrewsbury Abbey in 1346, when the abbey was given licence to impark the 'haye' in return for a fine of £100 and the surrender of a charter from Henry III granting licence to take wood from the Shropshire royal forests.[11] Lythwood was taken into the hands of the Crown in 1370,[12] following allegations that the grant had been fraudulently obtained.[13] It was restored in 1378, at an annual rent of £6,[14] and remained in the possession of Shrewsbury Abbey until the Dissolution.[15]

In 1547 Lythwood was granted to William Paget,[16] whose agent Richard Cupper sold it later in the same year to Robert Longe, lord of Condover manor.[17] The descent of this estate in the later 16th century is obscure, but it appears to have been acquired before 1553 by Thomas and Robert Ireland, who then granted a rent charge arising from Lythwood to endow an almshouse in Shrewsbury.[18] Edward, son of Robert Ireland, held the estate in 1590[19] and Edward's son Richard in 1611.[20] The latter appears to have died without issue soon afterwards, for his father's cousin, George Ireland of Albrighton, held the estate at his death in 1614, when it amounted to 526 a.[21] The greater part of this estate, now represented by Lythwood Farm, passed from father to son in the Ireland family[22] until 1736, when Thomas Ireland sold it to Thomas Powys of Berwick,[23] whose descendants held it until 1875.[24] In the 19th century, when this estate comprised some 400 a., it occupied the south-eastern part of the Lythwood plateau, its western boundary following a footpath from Upper Pulley to Great Lyth.[25]

The later Lythwood Hall estate also derives from the 16th-century Lythwood estate of the Ireland family. It was probably settled on Richard Owen of Whitley at his marriage to Sarah, sister of George Ireland, for in 1625 it was settled on Richard's son, Richard Owen of Pulley.[26] Thomas Owen of Pulley sold the estate to Abraham Giles of Shrewsbury and others c. 1658.[27] Giles was living at a house on the site of Lythwood Hall in 1662[28] and his widow lived there between 1682 and 1698.[29] The estate was settled in 1701 on Abraham Giles, probably son of the above, whose widow Ann devised it to her cousin John Travers in 1727.[30] In 1730, when the Hall was occupied by a tenant, Travers sold the estate to Michael Brickdale of Shrewsbury, and it passed on the latter's death in 1758 to his nephew John Freke Brickdale, who died without issue in 1765.[31] The estate then passed to John's great-nephew Matthew Brickdale, who sold it to Joshua Blakeway in 1776.[32] Later owners of the estate were Mr. Williams of Eaton Mascott and Archibald Campbell.[33] In 1795 Campbell sold Lythwood Hall, then described as a manor, to Charles White.[34] It was held by James Beck, 1801–4, Thomas Parr, 1804–47, Parr's widow Katherine, 1847–52, and the Revd. Robert Hornby, 1852–77.[35] The Lythwood Hall estate was purchased in 1877 by William Harrop of Gatten Lodge,

[3] S.R.O. 1011 (Smythe Owen) uncat., deed, 1802; S.P.L., Deeds 9991; S.C.C. title-deeds, SH 3.
[4] Descent of estate, 1802–1920, based on S.C.C. title-deeds, SH 3.
[5] Par. rec., tithe appt.
[6] Kelly's Dir. Salop. (1880).
[7] Lower Lythwood Farm title-deeds penes Barclay's Bank, Shrewsbury.
[8] S.P.L., MS. 2737, ff. 39, 42.
[9] For a sketch of the house as it was in 1909 see P. H. Ditchfield, The Manor Houses of England (1910), 103.
[10] Eyton, vi. 343–4.
[11] Cal. Pat. 1345–8, 73; ibid. 1377–81, 224; Cal. Close, 1346–9, 214; E 32/308.
[12] Cal. Inq. Misc. vi, p. 24.
[13] E 32/308.
[14] Cal. Pat. 1377–81, 224.
[15] S.C. 6/Hen. VIII/3010 m. 64.
[16] Cal. Pat. 1547–8, 45–47.
[17] S.P.L., MS. 110.
[18] Bodl. MS. Gough Salop. ii, f. 107.

[19] S.P.L., MS. 110.
[20] Ibid.
[21] C 142/345/122.
[22] For pedigree see S.P.L., MS. 2790, pp. 640–3; S.P.L., Deeds 3461, 3497, 3503.
[23] S.P.L., Deeds 3434.
[24] S.R.O. 650/2. For pedigree see S.P.L., MS. 2793, p. 309.
[25] S.R.O. 650/2.
[26] S.P.L., MS. 110; ibid. MS. 2792, p. 382; ibid. MS. 2280, p. 259.
[27] Ibid. MS. 110.
[28] E 179/225/35 m. 73d.
[29] Par. rec., overseers' accts. 1682–1708.
[30] S.R.O. 1011 (Harrop) uncat., abstract of title to Lythwood Hall estate, 1701–1877.
[31] Ibid. For pedigree see S.P.L., MS. 2794, pp. 471–2.
[32] C.P. 25(2)/1394/16 Geo. III Hil.
[33] W.S.L. 350/40/3.
[34] S.R.O. 1011 (Harrop) uncat., abstract of title to Lythwood Hall estate, 1701–1877.
[35] Ibid.

whose descendants retained it until 1921.[36] It was then bought by Mrs. Purcell, who sold the estate to Walter Vaughan in 1937. The Hall was occupied by the Ministry of Supply, 1940–3, and in 1949 was sold to Mr. G. H. Davies of Lythwood Hall Farm, who had by this date acquired most of the land within the estate. The Lythwood Hall estate amounted to 176 a. in 1801,[37] but had been enlarged to 220 a. by 1852 as a result of purchases in Meole Brace and Pulley by Thomas Parr.[38]

A third freehold estate in the south-western part of the Lythwood plateau, now represented by Lower Lythwood Farm and Hookagate Farm, seems to have been sold by Thomas Owen of Pulley to George Llewelyn c. 1658.[39] Llewelyn's grandson owned this property in 1705,[40] but part had been acquired by Thomas Hill of Tern before 1755.[41] The latter's descendant, William, Lord Berwick, held some 50 a. in Lythwood in 1837,[42] probably being that part of Hookagate Farm which lay in Condover parish. Lower Lythwood Farm, which belonged to the Davies family, 1811–65, was later acquired by H. A. Edwards and followed the descent of Great Lyth manor until 1949, when it was purchased by Mr. T. H. Ratcliffe.[43]

The only other substantial medieval freehold in the parish was Houghton's Fields, the portion of Buriwood granted by the lord of the manor to Richard de Houghton in 1308,[44] which was later said to contain some 200 a.[45] The estate was held in 1416 by Thomas Howell in right of his wife Margaret, daughter of Thomas Houghton.[46] John, son of Thomas Howell, on whom Houghton's Fields was settled in 1430,[47] granted it in 1468 to his kinsman and heir Richard Walker, chaplain.[48] On Richard's death in 1502 it passed to his brother Hugh.[49] The latter's widow, Elizabeth, to whom the estate passed in 1504,[50] was still in possession in 1514,[51] but by 1546 it was held by her son-in-law, Thomas Berrington.[52] In 1560 Joan, wife of Thomas Berrington, devised Houghton's Fields to her grandson Thomas Owen,[53] who sold the estate in 1565 to Henry Vynar, lord of Condover manor.[54] A rent of 25s. reserved to the lord of Condover in 1308,[55] was granted with the manor of Norton to Thomas Stone in 1462.[56]

ECONOMIC HISTORY. The manor of Condover included the townships of Allfield, Chatford, Condover, Dorrington, Great Ryton, Little Ryton, and

Wheathall. Bayston, Boreton, and Norton were separate manors in 1086. Norton manor had been merged with that of Condover by 1256, but was again a separate freehold, 1462–1550. Half of Boreton manor was acquired by the lord of Condover in 1557, but the other moiety of the manor has always been a distinct freehold. Bayston remained outside the Condover estate until 1801 and a small freehold here was not brought into the Condover manorial estate until 1836.[57]

Freehold estates were more numerous in the west of the parish. The manor of Great Lyth was apparently divided into two estates in the early 13th century. Lythwood, held by Shrewsbury Abbey from 1346 until the Dissolution, had been split into 3 freeholds by the mid-17th century. Westley and Little Lyth formed part of Pulverbatch manor and some part of these townships was always occupied by tenants, but several small freeholds were created at Westley in the 12th century,[58] apparently to encourage assarting, and there was at least one freeholder in Little Lyth by 1577.[59] The whole of these two townships had, however, been brought into the Condover manorial estate by the mid-18th century.[60]

Although the demesne of Condover manor was assessed at 7 hides in 1086,[61] there were said to be only 120 a. of demesne arable c. 1265[62] and only 60 a. in 1315.[63] When surveyed in 1545 the demesne was found to comprise 92 a. of which 13½ a. lay in small closes adjoining the manor-house to the south-west of Condover village and the remainder was distributed in compact blocks in the 3 common fields.[64]

There were 8 *bovarii* with 4 ploughs on the demesne in 1086[65] and it seems to have been farmed directly while in Crown hands, for it was restocked in 1202 and 1209.[66] Piecemeal leasing of the demesne was evidently of long standing by 1376, when the court rolls begin, and had probably been the practice before 1283, when the heavy labour services exacted from the tenants c. 1265 had been commuted.[67] The demesne meadows, which were let with their mowing services to 4 tenants in 1407[68] and to 2 tenants in 1423,[69] appear to have been held on the same terms in 1443.[70] The whole of the demesne arable was leased in 1439 to John Jones, who was then given licence to inclose it.[71] John Harris was farmer of the manor in 1482.[72] In 1545 the manor-house and demesne were held by Thomas Whitefoot,[73] to whom a 3-life lease was granted in the following

[36] Descent after 1877 based on Lythwood Hall title-deeds *penes* Messrs. Clark & Sons, solicitors, Shrewsbury.
[37] S.R.O. 1011 (Harrop) uncat., abstract of title to Lythwood Hall estate, 1701–1877.
[38] Ibid. sale partics. of Lythwood Hall estate, 1852.
[39] S.P.L., MS. 110.
[40] S.P.L., Deeds 6481.
[41] Attingham Park estate office, accts. 1755–74.
[42] Par. rec., poor rate, 1837.
[43] Lower Lythwood Farm title-deeds *penes* Barclays Bank, Shrewsbury.
[44] S.P.L., Deeds 6640.
[45] Ibid. 9501.
[46] Ibid. 6642; S.R.O. 474/15.
[47] Ibid.; S.P.L., Deeds 9137, m. 13d.
[48] S.R.O. 474/15.
[49] S.P.L., Deeds 9137, m. 31.
[50] Ibid. m. 34.
[51] Ibid. 9138, m. 7d.; C 1/287/88.
[52] S.P.L., Deeds 6615.
[53] Ibid. 9494.
[54] Ibid. 6617, 6624.

[55] Ibid. 6640.
[56] Ibid. 6608.
[57] S.R.O. 1011 (Cholmondeley) uncat., abstract of title, 1746–1836.
[58] *Rot. Hund.* (Rec. Com.), ii. 63.
[59] S.P.L., Deeds 9397.
[60] S.R.O. 665 uncat., survey of Condover manorial estate, c. 1768.
[61] *V.C.H. Salop.* i. 315.
[62] C 145/20/1.
[63] C 134/48/9.
[64] S.P.L., MS. 377, ff. 32–32ᵛ, 36ᵛ–38.
[65] *V.C.H. Salop.* i. 315.
[66] *Pipe R.* 1202 (P.R.S. N.S. xv), 47; ibid. 1209 (P.R.S. N.S. xxiv), 146.
[67] C 145/20/1; *Cal. Inq. Misc.* i, p. 372.
[68] S.P.L., Deeds 13477, m. 16.
[69] Ibid. 9136, mm. 2, 6.
[70] Ibid. 7026.
[71] Ibid. 9136, m. 32.
[72] Ibid. 9137, m. 22.
[73] S.P.L., MS. 377, f. 32.

year.[74] He was still farmer of the demesne in 1580[75] and his son William in 1598.[76]

Bomere and Shomere Pools and the adjoining area of rough pasture known as Bulridges, which were also accounted part of the medieval demesne, comprised 87 a. in 1545.[77] The fishery of Bomere was held on lease by Roger Campion of Condover in 1255, when it was valued at 2s.[78] By the 15th century it was customary to lease Bulridges and the 2 pools to the lords of neighbouring manors. Bulridges was leased to Sir Richard Lacon in 1420[79] and Bomere and Shomere Pools to Fulk Sprenchose of Bayston in 1467.[80] In 1545 the whole area was held by Sir Richard Brereton.[81] Radmore, said to contain 47 a. in 1545,[82] seems to have been leased as a whole to a single tenant from the 15th century.[83]

Enlargement of the manorial estate was begun by Robert Longe and gathered impetus under his successor Henry Vynar. The latter's object was clearly to build up a compact estate centred on Condover village. Norton Farm (147 a.), bought in 1550,[84] Houghton's Fields (202 a.), bought in 1565,[85] and the copyhold 'manor' of Allfield, bought by 1586,[86] all adjoined the medieval demesne. The cottages formerly belonging to Shrewsbury Abbey's manor of Boreton, which were bought in 1557,[87] probably all stood in Condover village. In addition to these freehold estates, some 412 a. copyhold or freehold property had been bought in Condover, Chatford, the Rytons, and Wheathall by 1595, when the manorial estate included 1,419 a. in Condover parish.[88] Partly as a result of these purchases and partly by a stricter supervision of the activities of the copyholders, Vynar increased the annual value of the manor from £29 15s. in 1561[89] to £105 by 1585.[90]

The Owen family added considerably to the manorial estate between 1586 and 1639, their largest purchases being the copyhold lands of the Harris family of Condover in 1615,[91] two farms at Westley in 1596 and in 1619,[92] and the manor of Pulverbatch, which included Westley and Little Lyth, in 1599.[93] The estate was heavily encumbered in the later 17th century and little seems to have been added to it until after 1770. In 1768 the estate amounted to 2,686 a.[94] Additions made by Nicholas Smythe and his son N. O. Smythe Owen between 1772 and 1804 included, besides Bayston[95] and

Great Lyth[96] manors, 21 copyhold properties, most of them in Condover township.[97] Further additions were made to round off the estate in the course of the 19th century. The manorial estate comprised 3,379 a. in 1841,[98] 3,837 a. in 1877,[99] and 3,873 a. at its sale in 1896.[1]

Only some 25 a. adjoining the Hall were kept in hand in 1595,[2] but meadow-land to the south of the Cound had been taken in hand by 1598[3] and Condover Park was probably formed in 1600, when the park wall was under construction.[4] The Park contained 301 a. in 1603,[5] of which 176 a. had been acquired by exchange with the tenants.[6] Some 365 a. were kept in hand in 1768[7] but the principal motive for the late 18th-century additions to the estate seems to have been to provide for the enlargement of the grounds of Condover Hall and the extension of the Park to the north of Condover village. The area kept in hand had risen to 748 a. by 1841.[8]

The manors of Bayston and Boreton were both assessed at one hide in 1086.[9] Bayston manor then had one plough, with 4 serfs, in demesne.[10] Four small freeholds acquired by Thomas Stone, 1448–85,[11] were added to the Bayston manorial estate in 1563[12] and it contained 268 a. at its sale in 1801.[13] The Boreton demesne, also stocked with a single plough in 1086,[14] was assessed at ½ carucate in 1249,[15] but had been leased before 1255.[16] The manorial estate amounted to 350 a. in 1841, when it occupied the greater part of Boreton township.[17]

Three freeholds at Westley, each of ½ virgate, were said to have been established in the time of Henry II.[18] Westley then lay within the Long Forest and the grantees were given hunting rights in the area between Exfordsgreen and Quaking Brook Bridge in All Stretton.[19] In the later 12th century a half virgate at Westley was granted to Elric Sprenchose by the lady of Pulverbatch manor.[20] The descent of these 4 small freeholds in the later Middle Ages has not been established, but they are presumably represented by the 3 freeholds here whose ownership is known from the 15th century onwards. One of these, held by the Poyner family from 1478,[21] was purchased by Thomas Owen in 1596.[22] Another was held in the early 16th century with Houghton's Fields by the Walker and Berrington families.[23] It was purchased by Richard Prince before 1577[24] and

[74] S.P.L., Deeds 9393.
[75] *T.S.A.S.* l. 126.
[76] S.P.L., Deeds 7022.
[77] S.P.L., MS. 377, ff. 28ᵛ–29.
[78] *Rot. Hund.* (Rec. Com.), ii. 63.
[79] S.C. 6/1117/14.
[80] S.P.L., Deeds 9137, m. 8.
[81] S.P.L., MS. 377, ff. 28ᵛ–29.
[82] Ibid. f. 28ᵛ.
[83] Ibid.; S.P.L., Deeds 7026.
[84] S.P.L., Deeds 6616. Acreage from ibid. 9501 (survey, 1595).
[85] Ibid. 6617, 6624, 9501.
[86] See p. 45.
[87] S.R.O. 474/15.
[88] S.P.L., Deeds 9501.
[89] S.P.L., MS. 377, f. 7.
[90] S.P.L., Deeds 9080.
[91] Ibid. 9509. This amounted to some 180 a. in 1595: ibid. 9501.
[92] Ibid. 6674, 6679.
[93] Ibid. 6869.
[94] S.R.O. 665 uncat., survey of Condover manorial estate, c. 1768.
[95] See p. 40.   [96] See p. 41.
[97] S.P.L., Deeds *passim*; S.R.O. 665 uncat. *passim*.

[98] Par. rec., tithe appt.
[99] S.R.O. 1154/1.
[1] Sale partics. 1896, *penes* Mr. J. C. Brookfield, Yew Tree Cottage, Condover.
[2] S.P.L., Deeds 9501.
[3] Ibid. 7022.
[4] Ibid. 9509; S.R.O. 665 uncat., accts. 1600–1.
[5] Ibid. 9509.
[6] Ibid.
[7] S.R.O. 665 uncat., survey of Condover manorial estate, c. 1768.
[8] Par. rec., tithe appt.
[9] *V.C.H. Salop.* i. 312, 332.
[10] Ibid. 332.
[11] S.R.O. 465/446–51.
[12] Ibid. 465/453.
[13] Ibid. 665 uncat., deed, 1801.
[14] *V.C.H. Salop.* i. 312.
[15] *Cal. Inq. p.m.* i, p. 33.
[16] N.L.W., Shrews. Cart. no. 115.
[17] Par. rec., tithe appt.
[18] *Rot. Hund.* (Rec. Com.), ii. 63.
[19] Ibid.
[20] S.P.L., Deeds 9328.
[21] Ibid. 6659, 6661, 6671, 7093.   [22] Ibid. 6674.
[23] Ibid. 6660, 6664, 9494.   [24] Ibid. 9397.

was sold to William Owen of Condover in 1619.[25] The later history of the third freehold, a half virgate belonging to the Jennings family of Walleybourne, 1463–1547,[26] is not known, but it lay within the Condover manorial estate by 1768.[27]

The Reynolds family were freeholders at Little Lyth by 1577[28] and until 1737, when John Reynolds sold a house and 2 cottages here to the lord of Condover manor.[29] Apart from the two portions of Great Lyth manor, a 30-acre freehold in Great Lyth was held by the Adams family in 1728[30] and passed with their Longden estate to the Ashwood and Hawley families.[31]

Apart from the Condover manorial estate and excluding house-properties, there were 47 freehold or copyhold estates in the parish as a whole in 1837.[32] Lord Berwick and H. W. Powys each owned some 400 a. at Boreton and Lythwood and there were two other estates of more than 200 a., but 36 persons then owned fewer than 100 a. A high proportion of these modest proprietors were owner-occupiers: 23 of the 47 estates were wholly, and 11 partly, occupied by their owners, notably the copyholds in Dorrington and the Rytons.

Earl Roger's manor of Condover contained 12 villeins in 1086.[33] On Alward's 4-hide manor, soon afterwards merged with that of Condover, there were then 4 villeins, 2 bordars, and 3 radmen. Domesday Book provides no information on the tenantry of the two other Condover manors, each of one hide, which were occupied at this time by under-tenants.[34] The number of tenants in the manor and the area of cultivated land appear to have increased considerably by the later 13th century. The manor contained 30 virgates, each of 60 a., c. 1265[35] and there were 76 customary tenants in 1315.[36]

Heavy labour services were still due from the tenants c. 1265, when the tenants of each virgate paid rents of 14d. a year, worked for 4 days each week on the demesne, and performed 4 ploughing-services each year.[37] Lighter services were, however, due from the tenants of 17 of the 30 virgates.[38] Labour services were commuted and the legal status of the tenantry improved after the manor passed out of the hands of the Crown. By 1283, when they were described as sokemen, the tenants owed money-rents only,[39] and by 1363 rents from virgated land had been formalized at 8s. per virgate in Condover township and 6s. 8d. elsewhere.[40]

The area of land described in terms of virgates subsequently remained unchanged.[41] From the 14th century such lands were described as 'old hold' and

they descended to the youngest son, who had the right to recover the land if it were alienated.[42] With few exceptions holdings of 'old hold' land tended to be small and to remain in the hands of the same family for long periods. Of 90 tenants recorded in 1363[43] 56 held less than a half virgate of 'old hold' land, while only 2 held one virgate or more. The standard holding in Dorrington was the half virgate; in other townships it was the noke ($\frac{1}{4}$ virgate). Sixteen of the 25 Dorrington tenants held half virgates in 1363, while all the Wheathall tenants and 6 of the 7 Chatford tenants held single nokes. Holdings of more irregular size occurred at Condover and Allfield. The pattern of 'old hold' holdings was very similar in 1421,[44] when there were 6 of one virgate or more.

The most substantial tenant in 1421 was Thomas Botte of Allfield, who held 7 nokes of 'old hold' land.[45] This remained the largest copyhold estate in 15th-century Condover and was said to contain 10$\frac{1}{2}$ nokes in 1547.[46] Thomas Botte died in 1445[47] and in 1453 his widow Alice conveyed the estate to her brother Fulk Sprenchose.[48] On the death of Fulk's widow Margaret c. 1499 her estates were divided among her 4 daughters,[49] Allfield passing to Sybil and her husband William Sandford, who died in 1506.[50] The estate was described for the first time as the 'manor' of Allfield at the admission of William's son Richard in 1507.[51] Repeated but unsuccessful claims on the estate had been made since 1454 by Thomas Botte's nephew Thomas Lake and his descendants.[52] In 1538, however, the manor of Allfield was divided between Thomas Lake and Richard Sandford's son George.[53] Allfield Farm was occupied by the tenants of both owners in 1547 and 1553,[54] but Lake's moiety was sold to Richard Sandford in 1558.[55] Allfield had been bought into the Condover manorial estate by 1586,[56] but the Sandford family retained a rent-charge arising from the estate until 1782.[57] Other large 'old hold' estates in the 15th and 16th centuries were those of the Harris family of Condover and Wheathall and the King and Gascoyne families of Dorrington.[58]

Lands assarted from Buriwood came to play an increasingly important part in the pattern of holdings in the later Middle Ages. These were known as 'purchase land' and could be bought and sold without restriction. It is probable that Edward Burnell's grant of this privilege to the tenants in 1313[59] merely confirmed existing practice. In 1265 the customary tenants were said to hold only 54$\frac{1}{2}$ a. of assarted land, at a rent of 4d. an acre.[60] By 1315, when assized

[25] Ibid. 6679.
[26] Ibid. 9346–7, 12911, 12938–9, 12941.
[27] S.R.O. 665 uncat., survey of Condover manorial estate, c. 1768.
[28] S.P.L., Deeds 9397, 9523–4.
[29] Ibid. 9970.
[30] S.R.O. 165/195.
[31] See p. 270.
[32] Par. rec., poor rate, 1837.
[33] V.C.H. Salop. i. 315.
[34] Ibid.
[35] C 145/20/1.
[36] C 134/48/9.
[37] C 145/20/1.
[38] Ibid.
[39] C 145/42/9.
[40] T.S.A.S. l. 112–16.
[41] Ibid. 132.
[42] Ibid. 135–7.
[43] Ibid. 112–16.

[44] Ibid. 117–24, where the survey is wrongly dated 1430, cf. S.P.L., Deeds 9114.
[45] T.S.A.S. l. 123.
[46] Sta. Cha. 3/4/8.
[47] S.P.L., Deeds 9136, m. 39.
[48] Ibid. m. 46.
[49] Ibid. 9137, m. 29.
[50] Ibid. m. 35; Sta. Cha. 2/30/54.
[51] S.P.L., Deeds 9137, m. 36d.
[52] Ibid. 9136, m. 46; ibid. 9137, m. 19; ibid. 9138, mm. 13, 19.
[53] Ibid. 9138, mm. 17, 24, 24d.; S.R.O. 465/481; Sta. Cha. 2/30/54.
[54] Sta. Cha. 3/4/8; S.P.L., Deeds 9074.
[55] S.P.L., Deeds 6585, 9074, 9087.
[56] Ibid. 6584, 6588, 6883.
[57] Ibid. 9236.
[58] Ibid. 9074/31, 40; ibid. 9137, mm. 14, 26.
[59] Ibid. 6882; S.R.O. 474/15.
[60] C 145/20/1.

rents from 'old hold' land totalled £10 8s. 11d., the assarts, held by 32 of the 76 tenants, produced rents totalling £7 5s. 1d.[61] In 1421, when £10 15s. 9d. rent was paid for 'old hold' lands, some £13 were derived annually from rents of assarts.[62] All but 4 of the 26 tenants in Condover township then held assarts in addition to their 'old hold' lands and assarts also figured prominently in the holdings of tenants in Wheathall and the Rytons. They were less important in Chatford and Dorrington.[63]

By 1545 lands assarted from Buriwood had come into the possession of a relatively small number of tenants. At this date 335 a. in Buriwood were held by 15 tenants, while 6 others held 70 a. in The Hoos. Sybil Campion of Wheathall then had the largest holding of assarted land (72 a.) and 6 other tenants held between 25 a. and 50 a.[64]

During the later Middle Ages the tenants of Condover manor had been able to clear and inclose Buriwood without interference by the non-resident lords of the manor. Licences to hold such assarts in severalty seem to have been granted as a matter of course: 62 of them are recorded on the court rolls, 1377–1500.[65] Assarted lands were normally held at will or by lease, but in a number of cases they were absorbed into 'old hold' holdings. Sir Henry Knyvett seems to have been the first lord to attempt to control the activities of the tenants. In 1535 a memorandum in the court rolls sets out the names of those holding portions of demesne or assarts 'that have nothing to show for them' and for the future tenants were forbidden to hold demesne lands without licence.[66] Fines totalling £105 14s. 1d. were imposed on offending tenants in the following year but only 14s. 1d. was collected.[67] In 1542 the bailiff was instructed to seize Radmore on the ground that it was demesne.[68] An assault made on the lord's receiver in Condover church at this time may have some connexion with these measures.[69]

A more serious attempt to control the tenants was made by Robert Longe, who bought the manor in 1545, and this was continued by his successor Henry Vynar. Numerous lawsuits between the lord and the tenants during the next 30 years were concerned with the interpretation of the customs of the manor and the closely related matter of the inclosure of the remaining portion of Buriwood.[70]

A 'declaration of wastes', which Longe induced the manor court to produce in 1545,[71] served as the basis for a detailed survey of the demesnes (including Buriwood) made later in the same year.[72] In the course of an action in Star Chamber, 1547, the tenants alleged that Longe wished to compel them to surrender their copyholds and hold them for lives by indentures and that he was demanding excessive entry fines.[73] A statement of the customs of the

manor was drawn up in the same year[74] and matters in dispute were settled by a decree of 1550.[75] This fixed rents and entry fines, abolished the payment of 'escheats' which Longe had tried to revive after long disuse, and granted an amnesty (with some exceptions) for past breaches of custom. The decree also provided for the inclosure of Buriwood and Radmore. In Buriwood a total of 300 a. was to be inclosed. Of this 200 a., with their timber, were to be allotted to the tenants in proportion to the size of their 'old hold' holdings and were to be held by copy of court roll. The remaining 100 a. in Buriwood and 28 a. in Radmore were to be leased to the tenants after Longe had disposed of the timber.[76] Longe died shortly afterwards and Vynar did not carry out the provisions of the decree until 1577, when allotments ranging from 1⅛ a. to 20¼ a. were granted to 29 tenants.[77] The tenants chafed at this delay and brought an action against Vynar c. 1567.[78] Their allegation that he was felling an excessive amount of timber[79] is borne out by Vynar's accounts; 225 trees were sold in 1570 and timber sales produced £700, 1572–3.[80]

Some 80 a. of Buriwood remained uninclosed after the apportionment of 1577 and in the following year 4 tenants who had not received allotments asserted their claim to common rights by breaking down the hedges of the new inclosures.[81] In 1580 their claims were satisfied by an allotment of 35¾ a. at Pigeondoor.[82] The status of the Buriwood allotments was finally clarified in 1586, when all the tenants obtained new grants by copy of court roll.[83]

As a result of the inclosure of Buriwood and the expansion of the manorial estate the tenurial structure of Condover manor had become complex by the end of the 16th century.[84] 'Old hold' lands, a few medieval assarts, and the recent allotments in Buriwood were held as copyhold of inheritance. The residue was held at will or by lease. This consisted of the medieval demesne, most of the medieval assarts surveyed in 1545, and a substantial part of the newly created manorial estate. Of the 69 holdings (excluding cottages) recorded in 1598 41 were copyhold and 28 were held at will or by lease, but 19 copyholders also held lands by other tenures. The 18 tenants of Allfield, Norton, and Westley were all leaseholders and elsewhere the proportion of copyhold land varied from township to township. The proportion was smallest in Condover, where only 12 of the 30 tenants were copyholders, 7 of whom held other lands at will or by lease. At Dorrington, however, 11 of the 13 tenants were copyholders and none of them held any part of their holdings by another form of tenure. The approximate size of most holdings at this time can be calculated from the rentals of 1580 and

[61] C 134/48/9.
[62] T.S.A.S. l. 118–24.
[63] Ibid.
[64] S.P.L., MS. 377, ff. 24ᵛ–38.
[65] S.P.L., Deeds 9072, 9136–7, 13477.
[66] Ibid. 9138, m. 24; ibid. 9130.
[67] Ibid. 9130.
[68] Ibid. 9138, m. 30.
[69] Ibid. m. 31.
[70] Ibid. 7003A/318–20, 325–7, 330–1, 333–4, 336–7, 339, 344, 347; ibid. 7021, 9080, 9396; S.P.L., MS. 377, ff. 21–21ᵛ, 156, 168ᵛ; Sta. Cha. 3/4/80; Req. 2/18/65; N.L.W., Pitchford Hall 901.
[71] S.P.L., Deeds 9077.

[72] S.P.L., MS. 377, ff. 24ᵛ–38.
[73] Sta. Cha. 3/4/8; S.P.L., Deeds 7003A/331, 333; ibid. 9080.
[74] T.S.A.S. l. 135–6; S.P.L., MS. 377, ff. 89ᵛ–92.
[75] N.L.W., Pitchford Hall, 901.
[76] Ibid.
[77] S.P.L., Deeds 9075 (ct. r. 1577); ibid. 7003A/327.
[78] Ibid. 7003A/330.   [79] Ibid.
[80] S.P.L., MS. 377, ff. 42ᵛ–43, 161ᵛ–163.
[81] S.P.L., Deeds 7003A/326–7, 336.
[82] Ibid. 7003A/319, 320, 325, 337, 347.
[83] C 78/85 no. 15.
[84] The following is based on S.R.O. 665 uncat., rental, 1580; S.P.L., Deeds 7022.

1598,[85] supplemented by the surveys of 1545[86] and 1595,[87] which provide the acreage of assarted lands rarely given in the rentals. Of the 62 holdings other than cottages recorded in 1580 the size of 15 cannot be established. Of the remainder 16 were smaller than 25 a. and only 5 were larger than 100 a. The largest holdings were the copyholds of Roger Harris of Condover (180 a. in 1595) and Roger Harris of Wheathall (142 a.).

Although much copyhold land was subsequently added to the manorial estate, the copyholders continued to occupy a considerable proportion of the parish, notably in Great Ryton and Wheathall, and in Dorrington until the 19th-century development of the Netley estate. In 1809 the 62 copyholders still held 2,046 a.[88] This was distributed much as it had been in the 16th century. In 1805 the gross rateable value of copyhold land was higher than that of freehold in all townships within the manor except at Little Ryton and was considerably higher in Dorrington and Wheathall.[89] Bound as they still were by the customs of inheritance attached to 'old hold' land, copyholds tended to remain in the same family unless the male line failed and they were divided among heiresses. Of the 31 families of copyholders in 1598[90] 7 still held copyholds in the parish in 1809[91] and two of these (the Dakers and Gosnells) had been copyholders since the 14th century. Copyholds were commonly underlet and in 1809 at least 20 of the 62 copyholders lived outside the parish.[92]

The descent of the Daker estate is typical of other Condover copyholds.[93] Its basis was the ancestral holding of 3 nokes in Condover township,[94] to which 2 nokes and other lands in Wheathall were added at the marriage of William Daker and Margaret, daughter and heir of Thomas Campion, c. 1650. William's younger son Samuel inherited the Condover lands,[95] which followed the male line of this branch of the Daker family until the death of the Revd. Edward Daker in 1820. The Condover estate then passed to Edward's nephew Edward Harley of Bristol and has since remained in the hands of his descendants. It included Condover Green Farm until 1792, when this passed by exchange to the lord of the manor. Edward, elder son of William Daker, succeeded to the Wheathall property, but the male line of this branch failed on the death of his son William in 1744 and the property passed to Edward Thornes in right of his wife Margaret Daker. In

1819, when the Wheathall property amounted to 191 a., it passed to Robert Hayward, whose son George held it in 1841.[96]

Leaseholders and tenants-at-will formed a more numerous class than the copyholders after the later 16th century. Tenure-at-will had disappeared by the mid-17th century and in the 18th century leaseholders formed a class distinct from the copyholders. Of the 31 tenants on the manorial estate in 1841 only 5 owned other freehold or copyhold property.[97] Leases were commonly for 99 years or 3 lives until the 1770s, when they were replaced by 21-year leases.[98] Yearly tenancies, introduced in 1799,[99] were universal during the 19th century.[1]

Leaseholders occupied 2,300 a. in 1768,[2] 2,900 a. in 1837,[3] and 3,500 a. by 1877.[4] Large farms were already an important feature on the estate by 1768, when there were 13 farms of over 100 a. and 19 smaller holdings.[5] Although small leaseholds remained numerous in the earlier 19th century—there were 21 holdings of fewer than 100 a. in 1841[6]—6 of the 14 larger farms were of over 200 a. by 1809.[7] As a result of 'many and great changes . . . in the management of farms' carried out in the 1870s, the farm of over 200 a. was the standard holding here by 1877. There were then 10 farms of over 200 a., 4 of 100–200 a., and only one of fewer than 100 a.[8]

There is little connected evidence for forms of tenure or the size of holdings in the remaining estates within the parish. In Bayston manor, where the 3-life lease was normally employed from 1546 until the end of the 18th century,[9] the Kendrick family were continuously tenants between 1546 and 1837.[10] The manorial estate had been formed into 2 large farms by 1770[11] and continued unchanged after 1801.[12] The moiety of Boreton manor which was merged with Condover manor in 1557 then included the cottages of 6 freeholders and 6 leaseholders.[13] On the remainder of the Boreton estate there were 4 tenants, 1545–1709,[14] 3 tenants by 1755,[15] and 2 tenants, 1768–1880.[16] Three holdings in Boreton were occupied continuously by members of the Wood family, 1545–1682.[17]

At Westley, where leasehold tenure had been introduced by 1310,[18] there were 9 tenants in 1619, in addition to the freeholders.[19] The number of tenants had been reduced to 4 by 1768[20] and to 2 by 1841.[21] Little Lyth contained 4 leaseholders in 1619,[22] the largest holding being the 5 messuages

[85] Ibid.
[86] S.P.L., MS. 377, ff. 24ᵛ–38.
[87] S.P.L., Deeds 9501.
[88] S.R.O. 1011 (Smythe Owen) uncat., rental, 1809.
[89] Par. rec., overseers' accts. 1800–12.
[90] S.P.L., Deeds 7022.
[91] S.R.O. 1011 (Smythe Owen) uncat., rental, 1809.
[92] Ibid.
[93] Except where otherwise stated, this paragraph is based on S.R.O. 867 passim; S.P.L., MS. 379–85; T.S.A.S. 2nd ser. ix. 38–55.
[94] T.S.A.S. l. 126.
[95] S.P.L., MS. 378 (ct. r. 1648).
[96] Par. rec., tithe appt.
[97] Ibid.
[98] S.R.O. 665 uncat., leases, 1535–1730; S.P.L., Deeds 9296, 9971, 9979–80, 9999.
[99] S.R.O. 665 uncat., agreement with tenants, 1799.
[1] Ibid. 1011 (Smythe Owen) uncat., leases, 1797–1864.
[2] Ibid. 665 uncat., survey of Condover manorial estate, c. 1768.
[3] Par. rec., poor rate, 1837.
[4] S.R.O. 1154/1.

[5] Ibid. 665 uncat., survey of Condover manorial estate, c. 1768.
[6] Par. rec., tithe appt.
[7] S.R.O. 1011 (Smythe Owen) uncat., rental, 1809.
[8] Ibid. 1154/1.
[9] Ibid. 465/457–73.
[10] Ibid.; par. rec., tithe appt.
[11] S.R.O. 1011 (Smythe Owen) uncat., survey of Bayston manorial estate, 1770.
[12] Par. rec., tithe appt.; ibid. poor rate, 1880.
[13] S.C. 6/Hen. VIII/3010 mm. 61d.–62.
[14] L. & P. Hen. VIII, xx (2), p. 222; S.R.O. 112 uncat., Boreton title-deeds, 1648–1709.
[15] Attingham Park estate office, accts. 1755–74.
[16] Ibid.; par. rec., tithe appt.; ibid. poor rate, 1880.
[17] L. & P. Hen. VIII, xx (2), p. 222; S.R.O. 112 uncat., Boreton title-deeds, 1648–82.
[18] S.P.L., Deeds 9334, 9341, 12918.
[19] Ibid. 9523.
[20] S.R.O. 665 uncat., survey of Condover manorial estate, c. 1768.
[21] Par. rec., tithe appt.
[22] S.P.L., Deeds 9523.

and 5 'farndels' leased to Thomas Butler in 1564,[23] but, like Westley, the township consisted of 2 farms by 1841.[24]

If the amounts of corn received from Condover township by the impropriator, 1567–1614,[25] accurately represent the proportions of different types of corn then grown in the parish as a whole, rye was by far the most common crop at this time. Modest amounts of barley and oats were grown, but very little wheat. The following quantities of tithe-corn were received in 1603, a typical year; rye 82 bushels, oats 26 bushels, barley 25 bushels, wheat 7 bushels.[26] By 1801, when 2,076 a. were said to be sown with crops, barley had taken first place (788 a.), closely followed by wheat (738 a.).[27] A relatively large acreage was sown with peas, oats, and turnips, but only 5 a. of rye were recorded.[28] On Allfield Farm, on the light soils to the north of the parish, where a 4-course Norfolk rotation of wheat, turnips, barley, and clover was in use in the 1830s, there were 229 a. arable and only 86 a. meadow and pasture in 1835.[29] Excluding the Lythwood plateau, the parish was said to contain 3,474 a. arable and 2,524 a. meadow and pasture in 1838.[30]

There is no evidence of any marked emphasis on livestock husbandry. Sir Roger Owen, who kept a small part of the Condover manorial estate in hand in the early 17th century, bought 186 wethers and ewes, 26 runts, and 7 other cattle in 1604,[31] but it is not known whether these were kept at Condover or on the more extensive demesne pastures at Pontesbury.[32] Of the 44 persons who paid small tithes on a total of 320 cows and 279 calves in 1768 12 had herds of more than 10 cows and 21 owned between 5 and 10 cows.[33] Condover and Westley were the only townships with more than one herd of 10 or more. Sheep seem to have been of little importance at this time. Only 98 sheep, 11 ewes, and 40 lambs were recorded in the parish (excluding Lythwood). They occur in only 4 townships, the largest flock being one of 40 head at Bayston.[34]

The mill recorded in Condover manor in 1086, then worth 8s. 6d.,[35] can probably be identified with the mill known from the later 14th century as Old Mill. This stood on Cound Brook, west of Radmore Hill and about one mile south-west of Condover village. The Domesday mill appears to be that which was granted by Henry II to Elric Sprenchose.[36] Elric's grandson Roger was dispossessed shortly before 1231[37] and the mill was held with Condover

manor until c. 1265, when it was recovered by Roger's son Roger.[38] The latter was still in possession in 1291,[39] but a moiety of the mill had come into the hands of the lord of Condover manor by 1313.[40] The other moiety was acquired by Richard de Eton in 1321,[41] passing to his son Thomas in 1346.[42] The Eton moiety appears to have passed to the Crompton family, who had some interest in Old Mill in the later 16th century,[43] but the mill was wholly in the Condover manorial estate by 1725, when it was leased to Edward Waring.[44] The mill was disused by 1768, when it was held by the tenant of a farm at Great Ryton,[45] and the mill-house was burnt down by sparks from a passing train in 1880.[46]

Two mills appear to have been established by the early 13th century on the banks of the Cound northeast of Condover village. The site of Boreton mill, recorded between 1203 and 1261,[47] is not known. Haughmond Abbey was given licence, c. 1160, to construct a mill-stank in that part of Bulridges which lay in the north bank of the Cound, adjoining the parish boundary with Berrington,[48] but there is no evidence that a mill was built here. Shortly after 1172 the tenant of Boreton manor granted Haughmond Abbey 8 a. on the east bank of the Cound in an area then known as 'Underhelde'[49]—a name preserved in the field-name 'Croggins Yeld' applied in the 19th century to a group of fields on the banks of the Cound south-west of Boreton.[50] A mill which had been constructed here before 1210[51] was known as Allfield Mill later in the Middle Ages. Allfield Mill was leased in 1419 to Richard Gosnell of Condover[52] and was no longer accounted part of the Haughmond Abbey estate at the Dissolution.[53] A fulling mill at Widnall, opposite 'Underhelde' on the west bank of the Cound, was occupied by Gosnell under a lease from the lord of Condover manor in 1443[54] and in 1467 his son Fulk was given licence to erect a mill on his own land.[55] The Gosnell lands in this part of the parish were acquired by Henry Vynar in 1561[56] and the mill subsequently lay within the Condover manorial estate. A leather mill had been built here by 1581, when it was leased to Richard Smythe.[57] Later tenants of the leather mill included Thomas Crompton, 1673,[58] Thomas Bayley, 1730,[59] Samuel Dolphin, c. 1809,[60] and John Tompkins, 1837,[61] but it was kept in hand in 1841[62] and is not later recorded.

Upper Mills (or Lord's Mills) and the Lower Mill stood on the south bank of the Cound, to the west

[23] S.P.L., Deeds 6869.
[24] Par. rec., tithe appt.
[25] S.P.L., MS. 377, ff. 9, 14v, 127v; S.P.L., Deeds 9509.
[26] S.P.L., Deeds 9509.
[27] H.O. 67/14/76.
[28] Ibid.
[29] S.R.O. 1011 (Smythe Owen) uncat., papers re lease of Allfield Farm, 1834–5.
[30] Ibid. tithe commutation agreement, 1838.
[31] S.P.L., Deeds 7025.
[32] See p. 272.
[33] Par. rec., Easter bk. 1768.
[34] Ibid.
[35] V.C.H. Salop. i. 315.
[36] Rot. Hund. (Rec. Com.), i. 91–92.
[37] Ibid.
[38] Ibid.
[39] Plac. de Quo Warr. (Rec. Com.), 676.
[40] Cal. Inq. p.m. v, p. 390.
[41] N.L.W., Pitchford Hall 341.
[42] Ibid. 130, 132, 407.

[43] S.P.L., Deeds 6645; ibid. 9138, m. 26; ibid. 9074; S.P.L., MS. 377, f. 167v.
[44] Ibid. Deeds 9306.
[45] S.R.O. 665 uncat., survey of Condover manorial estate, c. 1768.
[46] Ibid. 1011 (Cholmondeley) uncat., estate correspondence, 1880.
[47] Eyton, vi. 176; E 32/145 m. 1d.
[48] S.P.L., Haughmond Cart. f. 4.
[49] Ibid.
[50] Par. rec., tithe appt.
[51] Eyton, vi. 184.
[52] S.P.L., Haughmond Cart. f. 4v.
[53] Eyton, vi. 181.
[54] S.P.L., Deeds 7026.
[55] Ibid. 9137, mm. 8, 19.
[56] Ibid. 6886, 9074.
[57] Ibid. 9370.
[58] Ibid. 9383.
[59] S.R.O. 665 uncat., lease, 1730.
[60] Ibid. 1011 (Smythe Owen) uncat., rental, 1809.
[61] Par. rec., poor rate, 1837.   [62] Ibid. tithe appt.

and east of the former road from Great Ryton to Condover respectively.[63] Both lay within the Condover manorial estate. There were 2 corn mills and a fulling mill at Upper Mills in 1416, when they were leased to Roger Walker.[64] The mills passed on Roger's death in 1431 to his sons John and William,[65] who were still tenants in 1443.[66] A moiety of the mills was leased to Richard Matthews of Shrewsbury in 1445,[67] but they were all leased in 1461 to Richard and William Walker.[68] Richard Harris was tenant in 1531, when he sublet a moiety to Robert Trustram,[69] the other moiety being leased to Thomas Lake in 1535.[70] Thomas Berrington, owner of Houghton's Fields, had acquired Trustram's moiety by 1540, when the fulling mill had been burnt down,[71] and he occupied the whole mill in 1545.[72] Lake assigned his interest in 1555 to Henry Vynar,[73] to whom the other moiety presumably reverted at the death of Joan Berrington in 1568.[74] Four corn mills recorded at Upper Mills in 1580[75] were rebuilt in 1588.[76] Subsequent tenants included John Vaughan, 1580,[77] John Heynes, c. 1598,[78] Jonathan Rowley, 1647,[79] and John Langford, 1760.[80] Following the construction of the new Ryton road the site of Upper Mills was taken into the grounds of Condover Hall and the buildings were demolished c. 1804.[81] The Lower Mill was probably built by John Harris (d. 1514).[82] It was said to be a malt mill in 1531,[83] but was in decay by 1567[84] and is not again recorded.

A short-lived mill to the east of Dorrington village was erected by two tenants of Condover manor in 1472.[85] One moiety of the mill passed in 1545 to the lord of the manor,[86] who had acquired the remainder by 1567.[87] The mill is last recorded in 1570,[88] but its site was still marked by field-names in the 19th century.[89] There are references to a mill at Westley in 1310[90] and 1618,[91] and at Norton in 1615.[92]

Trials for coal were made by Thomas Owen in Condover township in 1587[93] and Richard Mall was given licence in 1652 to dig for coal wherever he chose in Condover manor.[94] Neither venture appears to have been successful. The stone abutments of a weir and a charcoal spoil-heap on the Cound south-

east of Dorrington Grove[95] mark the site of an iron-forge, probably established, with Longnor Forge, by Richard Holbeck in 1606.[96] This may have been occupied by Adam Harris of Dorrington, who possessed 'tools and implements at the iron work' at his death in 1629.[97] It was known as the Upper Forge in 1650, when it was said to stand on the boundary of Dorrington and Great Ryton townships.[98] Numerous burials of workers at 'the Iron Mills' or 'the Forge' are recorded in the Condover parish registers, 1607–1779,[99] but most of these relate to Longnor Forge. An estate brickyard near Condover Green was established by E. W. Smythe Owen c. 1851.[1]

A windmill and rope-walk at Lyth Hill was set up before 1841, when it lay in the Condover manorial estate and was occupied by John Carter.[2] Rope manufacture was carried on here by the Davies family until c. 1890.[3]

There were 2 or 3 butchers in Condover village in the 15th century and one is recorded at Dorrington in 1424.[4] Condover smithy, on the former road to Great Ryton, is first recorded in the 1560s[5] and continued on the same site until this road was diverted c. 1795.[6] It was rebuilt to the north of the village in the early 19th century and was still open in 1926.[7] A second smithy in the village was purchased by E. W. Smythe Owen in 1824[8] but is not again recorded. A smithy had been built at Wayford Bridge, north of Dorrington, by 1786[9] and the smithy in Dorrington village, not recorded before 1841,[10] was still in business in 1941.[11] There were about 6 other tradesmen in Condover village and about twice that number in Dorrington during the later 19th century.[12] Tradesmen were rare in the remaining hamlets within the parish. At Great Ryton a wheelwright is first recorded in 1841[13] and a shop in 1856.[14] The latter was still open in 1962 but the former had closed by 1941.[15] A smithy set up at Little Ryton before 1841[16] had closed by 1926[17] and there was a wheelwright at Sytch, 1849–c. 1900.[18] A number of tradesmen have settled at Annscroft since the closure of the local coal mines which formerly gave employment

[63] For sites see S.P.L., MS. 377, ff. 27–28.
[64] S.P.L., Deeds 13477, m. 21; *T.S.A.S.* l. 118.
[65] S.P.L., Deeds 9136, m. 16d.
[66] Ibid. 7026.
[67] Ibid. 9436.
[68] Ibid. 6643.
[69] S.R.O. 665 uncat., lease, 1531.
[70] Ibid. 1535.
[71] S.P.L., Deeds 9138, m. 29d.; S.P.L., MS. 377, f. 27.
[72] S.P.L., MS. 377, f. 27.
[73] S.R.O. 665 uncat., deed, 1555.
[74] S.P.L., Deeds 9494.
[75] S.R.O. 665 uncat., lease, 1580.
[76] S.P.L., Deeds 6883.
[77] S.R.O. 665 uncat., lease, 1580.
[78] S.P.L., Deeds 7022.
[79] S.R.O. 665 uncat., lease, 1647.
[80] S.P.L., Deeds 9979.
[81] W.S.L. 350/40/3; S.R.O. 1011 (Smythe Owen) uncat., draft lease, 1797.
[82] S.P.L., Deeds 9138, m. 7d.
[83] S.R.O. 665 uncat., lease, 1531.
[84] S.P.L., MS. 377, f. 148.
[85] Ibid. Deeds 9137, m. 13.
[86] S.P.L., Deeds 9138, mm. 9, 22, 22d., 33; S.P.L., MS. 377, f. 148ᵛ.
[87] S.P.L., MS. 377, f. 148ᵛ.
[88] S.P.L., Deeds 9074.
[89] Par. rec., tithe appt.
[90] S.P.L., Deeds 12918.

[91] Ibid. 9523.
[92] Ibid. 9509.
[93] Ibid. 6883.
[94] S.P.L., MS. 378.
[95] O.S. Nat. Grid SJ 487020.
[96] C 3/390/43. See also p. 112.
[97] Lich. Dioc. Regy., probate inventories, 1629.
[98] S.P.L., MS. 378.
[99] *S.P.R. Lich.* vi (1), 48–294 *passim*.
[1] S.R.O. 1011 (Smythe Owen) uncat., contract, 1851.
[2] Par. rec., tithe appt.
[3] *Kelly's Dir. Salop.* (1856–90).
[4] S.P.L., Deeds 13477, 9137–8 *passim*.
[5] S.P.L., MS. 377, f. 124.
[6] S.P.L., Deeds 9401, 9980.
[7] *Kelly's Dir. Salop.* (1926).
[8] S.R.O. 1011 (Smythe Owen) uncat., abstract of title, 1824–41.
[9] Condover ct. r. 1786, *penes* Messrs. Salt & Sons, solicitors.
[10] Par. rec., tithe appt.
[11] *Kelly's Dir. Salop.* (1941).
[12] Ibid. (1856–1900).
[13] Par. rec., tithe appt.
[14] *Kelly's Dir. Salop.* (1856).
[15] Ibid. (1941).
[16] Par. rec., tithe appt.
[17] *Kelly's Dir. Salop.* (1922–6).
[18] Sytch House title-deeds *penes* Messrs. G. H. Morgan, solicitors, Shrewsbury; *Kelly's Dir. Salop.* (1856–1900).

to most of the inhabitants of this hamlet. A shop is recorded here from 1855, a smithy from 1891, and a baker from 1900.[19]

LOCAL GOVERNMENT. There are court rolls for Condover manor, 1376–1608, 1647–80, and 1713–1877.[20] The jurisdiction of the court included view of frankpledge and the assize of bread and ale. There appears to have been a manorial gallows on Hunger Hill.[21] The court is known to have met in the church on several occasions in the 15th and 16th centuries[22] and the churchwardens had custody of the court rolls from 1485 until 1545.[23] The erection of a court-house was mooted *c.* 1582, but nothing came of this.[24]

Great Courts were held twice a year, normally in spring and summer, while Small Courts, held 5 or 6 times a year in the later 14th century, were meeting every 3 weeks by 1500 and monthly in the 18th century. Until the later 15th century there was little difference between the matters dealt with by each type of court, except that the Great Court included view of frankpledge. By 1500, however, the Great Courts were solely concerned with tenurial matters and the Small Courts with petty civil and criminal business. Although proceedings at Small Courts were entered in the court rolls until 1546,[25] separate registers were in use for Small Court business by 1500.[26] The latest of these (1735–49)[27] records only a very small number of actions.

A reeve was elected annually at the autumn court from the 14th century onwards. A woodward was appointed in 1394 and 1395,[28] but his duties were normally performed by the beadle, who does not appear in the rolls after the early 15th century. Ale-tasters were elected in 1398[29] and annually from 1441.[30] Three constables for the 'liberty' of Condover were appointed in 1399.[31] After 1423 there were normally 2 constables for Condover and 2 for Dorrington,[32] a further 2 constables for Great Ryton being added after 1470.[33] This was the normal arrangement in the later 16th century, when the Condover constables were responsible for Allfield, Chatford, Little Ryton, and Wheathall, as well as Condover township.

No court rolls are known to exist for the manors of Bayston, Boreton, or Great Lyth. Matters relating to Little Lyth and Westley are recorded in the Pulverbatch court rolls.[34]

The parish records include vestry minutes from 1741, churchwardens' accounts, 1577–1689 and from 1740, overseers' accounts, 1654–1708 and 1756–1842, and surveyors' accounts, 1754–1821. In the 16th and 17th centuries parish government was supervised by a body known as The Eight Men. No records of their proceedings have survived but they signed accounts and approved rates until 1706. In the 16th century members of this body served for life and vacancies were filled by co-option,[35] but they appear to have been elected annually by 1610.[36] Although the name occurs occasionally until 1775,[37] The Eight Men were probably superseded by an open vestry in the later 17th century. The change may have occurred in the 1660s, when the parish was involved in heavy expenditure in the rebuilding of the church.[38]

Meetings of The Eight Men and later of the vestry were held in local inns until the end of the 18th century, and in the church in the 19th century. These were held at monthly intervals by 1682[39] and in the 1740s,[40] but became less frequent in the later 18th century. The average number was 4 a year, 1775–95.[41] A resolution of 1803 to establish monthly meetings does not seem to have been acted upon, and after 1815 vestry meetings were held at Easter only.[42] A Committee of Directors was appointed, apparently in 1820, to supervise poor relief.[43] It was rare for more than 6 parishioners, other than the parish officers, to attend vestry meetings at any time. Usually only 3 or 4 were present, but important decisions drew attendances of up to 20.[44] The vicar or his curate did not begin to attend regularly before 1830, but a representative of the lord of the manor was normally present from the later 18th century. A chairman, usually the vicar or curate, first appears in 1840.

Thomas Hasnett and his son Roger, parish clerks in the later 16th and early 17th centuries, combined this office with that of dog-whipper.[45] Members of the Wood family were clerks by 1715 and until *c.* 1810,[46] after which the office was served for a short time by successive superintendents of the workhouse. The clerk received Easter dues and a customary payment known as 'clock corn' until 1802, when an annual salary of £17 was substituted.

The parish was divided for administrative purposes into two unequal parts or 'sides'—the 'Lordship' and the 'Guildable'—representing respectively the areas inside and outside the bounds of Condover manor. This division was in use by 1610, when 6 of The Eight Men were chosen from the Lordship side and 3 from the Guildable. One churchwarden and one overseer acted for each 'side' in the later 18th century, each overseer accounting separately from 1692 and each churchwarden by 1740. There were 5 surveyors of the highways in the 17th[47] and 18th centuries, each representing a township or group of townships. Rates for all parish

[19] *Kelly's Dir. Salop.* (1885–1900).
[20] S.P.L., Deeds 7003–27, 9072–9143, 10236, 13477; S.P.L., MSS. 378–91; ct. r. *penes* Messrs. Salt & Sons, solicitors, Shrewsbury.
[21] *T.S.A.S.* l. 129.
[22] E.g. S.P.L., Deeds 9137, m. 19.
[23] Sta. Cha. 3/4/80; S.P.L., Deeds 7003A/331.
[24] S.P.L., MS. 301, vol. v, p. 134.
[25] S.P.L., Deeds 7027.
[26] S.R.O. 665 uncat., ct. r. 1500–3.
[27] S.P.L., Deeds 9142.
[28] Ibid. 13477, mm. 4, 8.
[29] Ibid. m. 12.
[30] Ibid. 9136, m. 35.
[31] Ibid. 13477, m. 13.
[32] Ibid. 9136, mm. 3, 9.
[33] Ibid. 9137, m. 8d.

[34] See p. 138.
[35] Par. rec., churchwardens' accts. 1577–97.
[36] Ibid. 1604–27. 'The Eight Men chosen annually, which are reputed the body of the parish': S.P.L., MS. 110, deposition of John Smith, *c.* 1664.
[37] Par. rec., vestry minutes, 1758–1894.
[38] See p. 54.
[39] Par. rec., overseers' accts. 1682–1708.
[40] Ibid. vestry minutes, 1741–7.
[41] Ibid. 1758–1894.   [42] Ibid.
[43] Ibid. articles for farming the poor, 1820. The parish records include minutes of this body, 1824–6.
[44] As in 1746, 1769, 1774, and 1781.
[45] Par. rec., churchwardens' accts. 1577–1627.
[46] For their accounts see ibid. Easter bks. 1759–82; S.P.L., Deeds 13197–8.
[47] Par. rec., churchwardens' accts. 1604–27.

purposes were based on 'lewns' until the adoption of a pound rate following the valuation of the parish in 1785.[48]

Annual expenditure on poor relief, about £4 in 1660, had risen to some £50 by 1700 and to £144 by 1760. It rose rapidly after 1780, reaching a peak of £1,745 in 1818, but was rarely more than £800 a year after 1820.[49]

A workhouse[50] is first recorded in 1741, when the existing house was discontinued. After abortive attempts to re-establish a workhouse in 1758 and 1764 a new one was built in 1769 on a site given by the lord of the manor. A governor was appointed in 1770, but the workhouse was farmed in 1772 and had closed by 1774. It was reopened in 1781 and was administered by governors under the direction of the overseers, 1781–4. After being farmed between 1784 and 1794 it was again administered directly by the overseers until 1820. In 1803, when the workhouse contained 14 persons, 122 adults and children were on regular outdoor relief.[51] The workhouse, which probably stood in the present grounds of Condover Hall, was exchanged in 1820[52] for a house on the road to Great Ryton, and from this date until 1837 the poor inside and outside the workhouse were leased to the ropemaker John Barney.[53] The workhouse was sold to the lord of the manor in 1838.[54]

CHURCHES. A priest is recorded at Condover in 1086,[55] when a half hide in Berrington was said to belong to Condover church.[56] It was in origin a 'minster' church and was still served by 3 portioners in the later 12th century,[57] but only two remained by 1315.[58] Betchcott,[59] Frodesley,[60] Leebotwood,[61] Longnor,[62] and Stapleton[63] were originally chapelries of Condover, burials from Frodesley and Longnor still taking place at Condover until the later 18th century.[64] Dorrington and Annscroft were constituted ecclesiastical parishes in 1845[65] and 1872[66] respectively. Part of the ecclesiastical parish of Bayston Hill, formed in 1844,[67] lay within Condover parish, but its history is reserved for treatment under the Liberties of Shrewsbury.

Roger, Earl of Shrewsbury, granted Condover church to Shrewsbury Abbey c. 1094.[68] An annual pension of 18s. from the church was also reserved to the abbey[69] and the latter probably acquired the church lands at Berrington at the same time.[70] Under an instrument of 1315[71] the church was appropriated by Shrewsbury Abbey following the deaths of the two remaining portioners in 1324, when a vicarage was ordained.[72] A pension of 11 marks was then granted to the Dean and Chapter of Lichfield.[73] At the Dissolution the advowson passed to the Crown, who presented to the living in 1552,[74] and was purchased by Henry Vynar in 1557.[75] The rectory, leased by Shrewsbury Abbey to Thomas Glover in 1536,[76] was acquired by Vynar in 1563.[77] Both advowson and rectory subsequently followed the descent of the manor. Major J. R. Abbey was patron of the living in 1966.[78]

The church was said to be worth 30 marks in 1255[79] and £26 6s. 8d. in 1291,[80] but was valued at £53 14s. 8d. at its appropriation in 1324.[81] Until this time one of the portioners had held the great tithes and the other the small tithes, the portions being valued at £33 14s. 8d. and £20 6s. 8d. respectively.[82] The rectory was held on lease for £27 6s. 8d. in 1535.[83] The great tithes, normally leased by the impropriator after the Dissolution, produced £54 10s. 8d. in 1563[84] and £90 in 1585.[85] They were said to be worth about £130 in 1655[86] and were commuted for a rent-charge of £1,092 in 1841.[87]

In 1324 the vicar was assigned the small tithes, mortuaries, and the hay tithes of Dorrington.[88] These remained virtually his only source of income until the 18th century. The value of the vicarage seems to have fallen from £7 in 1341[89] to £5 13s. 4d. by 1535[90] and it was worth only £22 in 1655.[91] By will dated 1700 Edward Owen endowed the vicarage with a reversionary interest in a rent-charge of £69 arising from the Moat Hall estate in Pontesbury and Meole Brace parishes.[92] The vicar became entitled to this after the death of Edward's widow Anne in 1738 and such payments have been made since 1743.[93] The living was said to be worth nearly £200 in 1799[94] and its average annual gross value was put at £277 in 1835.[95] The vicar's net income had fallen from £258 in 1843[96] to £187 by 1891.[97]

A glebe of 1½ a. adjoining the parsonage was

[48] Ibid. overseers' accts. 1774–87.

[49] Ibid. 1654–1842.

[50] Except where otherwise stated, the following is based on par. rec., overseers' accts. 1654–1842; ibid. vestry minutes, 1741–1894.

[51] Poor Law Abstract, 1803, H.C. 175, pp. 416–17 (1803–4), xiii.

[52] For site see Auden, Condover, 34.

[53] Par. rec., articles for farming the poor, 1820, 1835. Richard Wood farmed the poor, 1821–4: ibid. overseers' accts. 1812–42.

[54] S.R.O. 1011 (Smythe Owen) uncat., papers re sale of workhouse, 1838.

[55] V.C.H. Salop. i. 315.

[56] Ibid. 320.

[57] Eyton, vi. 28.

[58] Ibid. 29.

[59] See p. 157.

[60] See p. 83.

[61] See p. 104.

[62] See p. 107.

[63] See p. 167.

[64] S.P.R. Lich. vi (1), passim.

[65] S.R.O. 1037 uncat., trust deed, 1845.

[66] Lond. Gaz. 1872, p. 5846.

[67] Ibid. 1844, p. 3202.

[68] N.L.W., Shrews. Cart. nos. 2, 36.

[69] Ibid. nos. 62, 329; Eyton, vi. 28.

[70] N.L.W., Shrews. Cart. no. 279.

[71] Eyton, vi. 29; Cal. Pat. 1307–13, 497.

[72] Lich. Dioc. Regy., reg. 2, f. 204ᵛ.

[73] Eyton, vi. 29.

[74] Cal. Pat. 1550–3, 277.

[75] Ibid. 1557–8, 159.

[76] S.R.O. 665 uncat., lease, 1536.

[77] Cal. Pat. 1560–3, 559–60.

[78] Crockford (1963–4).

[79] Rot. Hund. (Rec. Com.), ii. 63.

[80] Tax. Eccl. (Rec. Com.), 247.

[81] Lich. Dioc. Regy., reg. 2, f. 204ᵛ.

[82] Ibid.

[83] Valor. Eccl. (Rec. Com.), iii. 189.

[84] S.P.L., MS. 377, f. 9.

[85] S.P.L., Deeds 9080.

[86] T.S.A.S. xlvii. 26.

[87] Par. rec., tithe appt.

[88] Lich. Dioc. Regy., reg. 2, f. 204ᵛ.

[89] Inq. Non. (Rec. Com.), 183.

[90] Valor Eccl. (Rec. Com.), iii. 184.

[91] T.S.A.S. xlvii. 26.

[92] S.P.L., Deeds 9963.

[93] Ibid. 9977; S.R.O. 665 uncat., legal papers, Trafford Barnston v. Corbet Kynaston, 1743.

[94] Visit. Archd. Salop. 1799.

[95] Rep. Com. Eccl. Revenues [67], pp. 470–1, H.C. (1835), xxii.

[96] Visit. Archd. Salop. 1843.

[97] S.R.O. 178/11.

exchanged with the lord of the manor in 1706 for a 4-acre field called Widnall on the road to Allfield.[98] This was said to be worth £7 a year in 1851.[99] Medieval incumbents also held assarts in Buriwood, first recorded in 1265.[1]

The small tithes, which thus made up the greater part of the income of the living before 1743, were due from the whole parish except Lythwood[2] and appear to have been collected in kind until the 18th century.[3] They were commuted for a rent-charge of £211 5s. in 1841.[4] In addition to the customary Easter offerings the vicar profited from a 'drinking' held by ancient custom after evening prayers on Easter Day.[5] This had been abolished before 1577, the churchwardens providing bread and wine for communion in lieu.[6]

Some 7 a. at Dorrington and 8½ a. known as St. Mary Pitwicks at Mount Zion in Wheathall township, given for the repair of the church, are first recorded in the hands of the churchwardens in the mid-15th century.[7] Rents totalling 7s. ½d. arising from lands in Condover, Dorrington, Little Ryton, and Westley were said in 1622 to have been given for the same purpose.[8] Some of these rents were still being paid in the later 17th century, but they are not recorded after 1700.[9] A meadow called Lady Meadow in Woolstaston and 16d. rent arising from Condovers Leys in the same parish had also been given for repairs to Condover church, but the churchwardens were dispossessed by Roger Pope in 1614.[10] Church House, Dorrington, was leased to the overseers for £4 10s. a year in and after 1775,[11] presumably as a poor-house. The Church Lands at Dorrington were then let for £6 a year and rents from the Mount Zion property ranged from £5 to 8 guineas in the later 18th century.[12] Rents from the Church Lands produced £31 a year c. 1830.[13] The Dorrington property was sold for £709 in 1877, when the remaining lands and the proceeds of the sale were vested in the vicar and churchwardens as trustees.[14]

Lands in Condover township had been granted before 1417 to endow a light to the Blessed Virgin Mary.[15] The wardens of this light still held the endowment—a 10-acre field called The Broken—in 1545,[16] but the light is not recorded in 1547.[17] It is probable that some part of the Church Lands had originally been intended as the endowment of a chantry. It was alleged in 1568 that lands producing annual rents of 14s. 6d., then held by the church-

wardens, had formerly been applied towards the stipend of a chantry priest.[18] Lady Meadow, Woolstaston, and a field of the same name in Westley[19] may have formed part of this endowment.

A chantry of Our Lady of Pity was founded by Thomas Acton of Longnor, by will of 1514.[20] He directed that after the death of his wife Joan an annual stipend of £5, derived from the rents of some part of his estate, was to be paid to the chantry priest.[21] The chantry was later said to have been established before Joan's death in 1539, when it was being served by her private chaplain Thomas Turner,[22] but it is not recorded in 1547.[23] At this date, however, a rent of 8s. from Houghtons Fields formed the endowment of an annual obit for Thomas Acton and his wife.[24] The only chantry endowment recorded in 1547 was a stock of cattle valued at £10.[25]

Little is known of the clergy of Condover before 1315. Master John Blund, who received 5 oaks from Lythwood to build a belfry in 1233[26] and was given licence to take materials from the 'King's Hall' in Condover in 1235,[27] was probably one of the portioners at this time.[28] The poverty of the vicarage after 1324 accounts in part for the short incumbencies of such medieval vicars whose dates are known. Only Richard Alcock (vicar c. 1433–83)[29] and John Adderbury, murdered in 1398,[30] are known to have died in the parish. Adderbury lived with his sister and had a servant;[31] his chaplain Richard Cardington sued for arrears of salary in 1398.[32] In the 15th century curates received 10s. from Shrewsbury Abbey and 10s. from the parishioners,[33] but in 1499 the curate was provided with a stipend of £4 10s., the vicar paying 50s. and the abbey the remainder.[34] By 1535 the abbey was paying 73s. 4d. to the curate[35] and this charge passed with the rectory to Henry Vynar in 1563.[36] He was still making this payment to the curate in 1572,[37] but the practice appears to have lapsed by the end of the 16th century.

Post-Reformation vicars remained longer in the parish. Seven of the 12 incumbents, 1540–1797, died in the parish, 5 of them after an incumbency of more than 30 years.[38] All were graduates after 1612. Roger Barnston (vicar 1739–83) and John Smythe (vicar 1787–97) were relatives of the patron. Most vicars also held other livings between 1640 and 1841. Ralph Morhall (vicar 1640–c. 1664) was rector of Pontesbury second portion,[39] his duties at Condover being performed by David Pugh in the 1650s[40] and

[98] Lich. Dioc. Regy., glebe terriers, 1612–1705; S.P.L., Deeds 9964.
[99] H.O. 129/359/1/15.
[1] C 145/20/1; S.P.L., Deeds 13477, m. 9; ibid. 9136, m. 22; ibid. 9073; S.P.L., MS. 377, f. 7.
[2] Lich. Dioc. Regy., glebe terriers, 1705–1832; par. rec., tithe appt.
[3] Par. rec., tithing table, c. 1600, confirmed in 1692 and 1702.
[4] Par. rec., tithe appt.
[5] Ibid. tithing table, c. 1600.
[6] Ibid. churchwardens' accts. 1577–97.
[7] S.P.L., Deeds 9136, m. 42.
[8] S.P.R. Lich. vi (1), 199–205.
[9] Par. rec., churchwardens' accts. 1659–89, 1740–58.
[10] S.P.R. Lich. vi (1), 204–5.
[11] Par. rec., vestry minutes, 1758–1894.
[12] Ibid.
[13] 24th Rep. Com. Char. H.C. 231, p. 383 (1831), xi.
[14] Char. Com. files.
[15] S.P.L., Deeds 13477, mm. 20, 23; ibid. 9136, m. 19; T.S.A.S. l. 119.
[16] S.P.L., MS. 377, f. 31.
[17] T.S.A.S. 3rd ser. x. 374, 381.

[18] S.P.L., MS. 377, f. 42.
[19] S.P.R. Lich. vi (1), 201, 204.
[20] S.P.L., MS. 377, f. 133.
[21] Ibid.
[22] Ibid. ff. 139ᵛ–143.
[23] T.S.A.S. 3rd ser. x. 374, 381.
[24] Ibid. 374.
[25] Ibid. 381.
[26] Close R. 1231–34, 226.
[27] Ibid. 1234–7, 59.
[28] cf. Emden, Biog. Dict. Oxf. Univ. ii. 206.
[29] S.P.L., Deeds 9136, m. 22; ibid. 9073.
[30] Instituted in 1392: Eyton, vi. 32. For his murder see S.P.L., Deeds 13477, m. 10.
[31] S.P.L., Deeds 13477, m. 11.
[32] Ibid. m. 10.
[33] Ibid. 6881.
[34] Ibid.
[35] Valor Eccl. (Rec. Com.), iii. 189.
[36] Cal. Pat. 1560–3, 559–60.
[37] S.P.L., MS. 377, f. 165.
[38] Listed in S.P.R. Lich. vi (1), pp. vi–viii.
[39] Walker Revised (ed. Matthews), 306.
[40] T.S.A.S. xlvii. 26.

by Gilbert Coles in 1662.[41] George Llewelyn (vicar 1705–39) also held Pulverbatch, but lived at Condover and was noted for his interest in music and as a Jacobite.[42] William Pugh was his curate in 1736.[43] Roger Barnston, who was also Rector of St. Michael's, Chester, and a prebendary of Chester Cathedral, seems to have been resident at Condover in 1742 and 1745,[44] but the living was served by his curate Richard Podmore, 1744–83.[45] Forester Leighton (vicar 1798–1806), Lawrence Gardner (vicar 1816–26), and Henry Burton (vicar 1829–41) each held other livings.[46] In 1799 Leighton, who lived in Shrewsbury, performed most of the duties himself, with occasional assistance from the curate of Smethcott.[47] Curates were regularly employed in the later 19th century, but all incumbents have been resident since 1841.[48]

At the ordination of the vicarage in 1324 the parsonage of the former first portioner was assigned as a residence for the vicar.[49] This parsonage, which then comprised a hall and two chambers, with a kitchen, a stable, and a sheepcote,[50] stood at the north-eastern corner of the churchyard.[51] It was said to contain 2 bays c. 1685,[52] but a new 3-story parsonage was built by Llewelyn in 1705.[53] This had a 'great garden' to the south and on the west a smaller garden was taken in from the roadside waste.[54] Part of the great garden was leased in 1769 to Nicholas Smythe,[55] who was then extending the grounds of Condover Hall, and in 1787 the parsonage was demolished, having been exchanged for a house on the site of the present parsonage, called the Arbour House.[56] The latter was described in 1823 as a small old timber house with two low parlours[57] and was replaced by the present stone-built parsonage in 1844.[58] Portraits of Edward Owen (d. 1700) and his executor William Owen, which were given to the vicar of Condover c. 1734 to commemorate the augmentation of the living by Edward Owen,[59] still hang in the parsonage.

Communion was celebrated twice a year in 1584,[60] 4 times a year in the 17th century,[61] and 7 times a year by 1823.[62] In 1843 it was given on the first Sunday of each month and on 4 other occasions.[63] The number of Easter communicants fell from over 100 in 1799 to about 44 in 1847.[64] Services were held at 11 a.m. and 3 p.m. (6 p.m. in summer) between 1799 and 1843[65] and congregations of 400 attended morning services here in 1851,[66] when a further 100 persons attended services at Dorrington church.[67] Attention was paid to church music after the erection of the psalm-singers' gallery at the west end of the nave in 1759[68] and a psalm-singers' dinner was held annually from 1764 until c. 1840.[69] Instrumental accompaniment was provided from 1793[70] and an organ, purchased in 1840,[71] was replaced by the present organ in 1903.[72] A surpliced choir had been introduced before 1889.[73]

The township of Dorrington was constituted an ecclesiastical parish in 1845,[74] when the church was built at his own expense by J. T. Hope of Netley Hall.[75] Hope endowed the benefice with £3,500 stock[76] and in 1849 it obtained a grant of £200 from Queen Anne's Bounty to meet a benefaction of £300 from Lady Edwardes.[77] The advowson, which was vested in J. T. Hope in 1845,[78] has since remained with his descendants. Mrs. Jasper More was patron in 1965.[79] The living has been held in plurality with Stapleton since 1952.[80]

Annscroft, constituted an ecclesiastical parish in 1872,[81] comprised 652 a. in Condover parish (Great Lyth, Exfordsgreen, and part of Lythwood), 18 a. in Meole Brace, and 365 a. (Whitley and Welbatch) in Shrewsbury St. Chad.[82] The advowson was vested in trustees until 1925 when it was transferred to the Bishop of Hereford.[83] Since 1954 the living has been served by the Vicar of Longden.[84]

To provide for those living in distant parts of the parish, services were held at Great Ryton from 1890[85] and a Mission Room was built there in 1896.[86] At this time 'cottage lectures' were given at Westley and Pigeondoor for those too infirm to attend church.[87]

The church of ST. ANDREW AND ST. MARY, Condover,[88] which is built for the most part in pink local sandstone, consists of a nave, chancel, north and south transepts, and western tower. The north transept dates from the later 12th century and the south transept probably from the early 17th century. The nave was rebuilt in the 1660s and the chancel in 1868.

The north transept, which is thus the only sur-

---

[41] Lich. Dioc. Regy., B/v 1/67.
[42] P. A. Scholes, *The Great Doctor Burney* (Oxford, 1948), i. 7.
[43] Lich. Dioc. Regy., glebe terrier, 1736.
[44] Ibid. 1742–5.
[45] *S.P.R. Lich.* vi (1), 230, 300.
[46] Ibid. p. vii.
[47] Visit. Archd. Salop. 1799.
[48] *S.P.R. Lich.* vi (1), p. viii.
[49] Lich. Dioc. Regy., reg. 2, f. 204ᵛ.
[50] Ibid.
[51] S.R.O. 665 uncat., deed of exchange, 1787.
[52] Lich. Dioc. Regy., glebe terrier, c. 1685.
[53] Ibid. 1705.
[54] Ibid.; S.R.O. 665 uncat., deed of exchange, 1787.
[55] *S.P.R. Lich.* vi (1), 349.
[56] S.R.O. 665 uncat., deed of exchange, 1787; par. rec., plan of new parsonage, 1784.
[57] Visit. Archd. Salop. 1823.
[58] Ibid. 1843; Auden, *Condover*, 24–25.
[59] *Salop. N. & Q.* viii. 99–100.
[60] Par. rec., churchwardens' accts. 1577–97.
[61] Ibid. 1634–59.
[62] Visit. Archd. Salop. 1823.
[63] Ibid. 1843.
[64] Ibid. 1799–1843.
[65] Ibid.
[66] H.O. 129/359/1/15.
[67] H.O. 129/359/1/16.
[68] Par. rec., churchwardens' accts. 1759–1819.
[69] Ibid. 1759–1930.
[70] Ibid. 1759–1819.
[71] Ibid. 1819–1930.
[72] Ibid.
[73] Printed rules for choir, in vestry.
[74] S.R.O. 1037 uncat., trust deed, 1845.
[75] Hope-Edwardes MSS., Linley Hall, estimates and bills for building church, 1845; H.O. 129/359/1/16.
[76] C. Hodgson, *Queen Anne's Bounty* (1845), suppl. p. 86.
[77] Ibid. suppl. p. 67.
[78] S.R.O. 1037 uncat., trust deed, 1845.
[79] *Crockford* (1963–4).
[80] Heref. Dioc. Regy., reg. 1938–53, p. 558.
[81] *Lond. Gaz.* 1872, p. 5846.
[82] Ibid.
[83] Ibid.; Heref. Dioc. Regy., reg. 1919–26, p. 379.
[84] Heref. Dioc. Regy., reg. 1953–date, p. 44.
[85] *Condover Par. Mag.* Mar. 1895.
[86] Ibid. 1896–7; S.R.O. 178/12.
[87] *Condover Par. Mag.* Feb. 1894.
[88] Except where otherwise stated, description of church based on S.P.L., MS. 372, vol. i, p. 23; S.P.L., J. H. Smith collect. no. 58; Cranage, vi. 475–81; Pevsner, *Shropshire.* 111–12.

viving portion of the medieval church, has flat pilaster buttresses, a sloping plinth, a round string course, and a corbel-table. In the north wall there are 2 round-headed windows with jamb-shafts externally and wide-splayed rear-arches and there is a single window of a similar design in the west wall. A small quatrefoil window high on the north wall has wide-splayed reveals, the opening becoming circular within the church. The small round-headed door at the north end of the east wall may be a 17th-century insertion. Part of the east wall was demolished in 1868, when a mortuary chapel was built against the north wall of the chancel.[89] This section of wall, however, seems to have been rebuilt in the 1660s, for in 1786 it contained a window similar to those in the nave and the string course did not continue the full length of the wall.[90] A square-headed recess in the north-west corner of the transept is probably the cupboard made in 1667.[91]

The south transept, or 'Frodesley aisle', was so called because it was given c. 1600 to Edward Scriven, lord of Frodesley manor, for the use of his family and their successors on condition that they kept it in repair.[92] Scriven repaired the walls and roof at this time and in 1607 he undertook to repay the churchwardens any money spent by them on repairs to this transept.[93] The timber-framed south gable with its much-restored Jacobean ornament probably dates from this time, as does the window with Perpendicular tracery and door below. Pews in in the south transept remained the property of the Scrivens and their successors until 1787, when they were sold to the lord of Condover manor.[94]

A former central tower collapsed in 1660, after an ill-judged attempt to reduce the dimensions of its supporting piers, and destroyed the nave.[95] The cost of rebuilding, estimated at £2,750 in 1661,[96] was largely met from church rates, which remained very high until 1685.[97] The work seems to have been carried out under the supervision of Edward Owen, to whom the income from rates was paid by the churchwardens.[98] He may also have been responsible for the decision to rebuild in a late Gothic style. The nave, which was rebuilt 1662–4,[99] was no longer aligned on the chancel, since it incorporated the area formerly occupied by a north aisle.[1] It had 4 small square-headed windows on each side and an open timber roof. The latter was concealed in 1776 by a plaster ceiling,[2] but the plaster was removed in 1878, when the present hammer-beam roof appears to have been constructed partly from original timbers.[3]

The nave was entered through a porch in the middle of the north wall until 1800, when a west door in the tower was opened.[4] The present door, at the north-west end of the nave, was inserted in 1878.[5] A vestry projected from the south wall, opposite the north porch, until 1878.[6]

The embattled tower was built 1677–8 by John Orum,[7] whose initials, with the date '1664' are carved on one of the jambs of the tower arch. It is of 3 stages and has diagonal buttresses, with 2-light windows in the belfry, lancets below, and a 3-light pointed window in the west wall.

The chancel, largely undamaged by the fall of the tower in 1660, was for the most part of 13th-century date. In 1786 it had 2 lancets in the north wall, below which was a string course, which did not continue the full length of the north wall.[8] At the west end of the north wall was a square-headed lancet and a blocked door with a segmental head.[9] Both these features probably dated from the 1660s. The east end of the chancel, which had a 5-light window with Perpendicular tracery,[10] appears to have been rebuilt in the 15th century. The present chancel, which has lancets in the north and south walls and a 3-light east window in the Decorated style, was rebuilt in 1868 by Reginald Cholmondeley, who built the mortuary chapel to the north at the same time.[11] The vestry and organ chamber to the south of the chancel were added in 1878.[12]

The fabric of the remainder of the church was extensively restored by Fairfax Wade in 1877–8, Cholmondeley bearing the cost of internal work and the parish the cost of repairs to the exterior.[13] The roof, walls, and gables of the transepts were restored, a north porch was built, the walls of the nave were largely rebuilt, two new windows were inserted, and a parapet was constructed to offset the steep pitch of the nave roof.

A rood-loft is recorded in 1431.[14] Apart from the parish chest, which has 13th-century ironwork,[15] no medieval fittings survive. The interior of the nave and transepts was refitted in the 1660s,[16] 'beautified', 1790–1804,[17] and restored, 1877–8.[18] Box pews, described as 'mean' in 1799,[19] were replaced in oak in 1803.[20] A gallery recorded in 1665[21] probably stood over the north transept and a second gallery was built for the psalm-singers in 1759.[22] The latter seems to have been enlarged for the use of the school-children before 1840, when the organ was installed there.[23] A third gallery, over the south transept, seems to have been constructed in 1855.[24] The

[89] Cranage, vi. 475.
[90] S.P.L., MS. 372, vol. i, p. 23.
[91] Par. rec., churchwardens' accts. 1659–89.
[92] S.P.L., MS. 2791, p. 593.
[93] Ibid.; par. rec., churchwardens' accts. 1604–27.
[94] S.R.O. 665 uncat., conveyance, 1787.
[95] S.P.L., MS. 110, deposition of John Smith, parish clerk, c. 1664.
[96] Q. Sess. Orders, i. 71.
[97] Par. rec., churchwardens' accts. 1659–89.
[98] Ibid.; S.P.L., MS. 110, depositions, c. 1664.
[99] Ibid.
[1] The base of the arcade of the north aisle was uncovered at the restoration of 1877–8: Cranage, vi. 479. cf. S.P.R. Lich. vi (1), 57.
[2] Par. rec., churchwardens' accts. 1759–1819.
[3] Ibid. faculty, 1877; Salop. Shreds & Patches, ii. 206.
[4] Visit. Archd. Salop. 1799, 1823; S.R.O. 665 uncat., letter, R. Pemberton to N. O. Smythe Owen, 1800.
[5] Salop. Shreds & Patches, ii. 206.
[6] Ibid.; par. rec. faculty, 1877.

[7] Par. rec., churchwardens' accts. 1659–89.
[8] S.P.L., MS. 372, vol. 1, p. 23.
[9] Ibid.
[10] S.P.L., T. F. Dukes watercolours (churches), no. 41.
[11] Cranage, vi. 475.
[12] Par. rec., faculty, 1877; Salop. Shreds & Patches, ii. 206; ibid. iii. 91–94.
[13] Ibid.; Pevsner, Shropshire, 111.
[14] S.P.L., Deeds 9136, m. 20d.
[15] The Connoisseur, Oct. 1927.
[16] Par. rec., churchwardens' accts. 1659–89.
[17] Ibid. 1759–1819.
[18] Salop. Shreds & Patches, ii. 206; ibid. iii. 91–94.
[19] Visit. Archd. Salop. 1799.
[20] Par. rec., churchwardens' accts. 1759–1819.
[21] Ibid. 1659–89.
[22] Ibid. 1759–1819.
[23] S.P.L., Watton press cuttings, viii, f. 229ᵛ.
[24] Par. rec., churchwardens' accts. 1819–1930; photograph of interior of church, 1875, in vestry.

CHURCH PULVERBATCH: SHEPPEN FIELDS FARM, *c.* 1918
A 'long house'; the wing on the left was added *c.* 1625 but the rest is of cruck construction

CONDOVER: THE OLD SCHOOL HOUSE
The solar wing and one surviving bay of the open hall of the 15th-century house

MEDIEVAL FARM-HOUSES

BERRINGTON: 12th-century font

PITCHFORD: oak effigy of Sir John de Pitchford (d. 1284)

CONDOVER: monuments in the mortuary chapel

galleries were all removed in 1878, when the box pews were replaced by open pitch-pine pews.[25] The pulpit and font, by Landucci of Shrewsbury, were installed at the same time.[26] A former pulpit, made in 1664,[27] once stood with the reading desk and clerk's desk at the south-east corner of the nave.[28] The font replaced a marble one given by Joseph Pryce of Dorrington before 1823.[29] A scolloped font-bowl, probably that made in 1667,[30] was kept in the base of the tower in 1966.

The mosaic floor of the chancel was laid in 1868.[31] The altar is a plain oak table, given by Joseph Pryce before 1806.[32] This replaced an elaborate marble altar-piece, modelled on that at St. Peter's, Chester, which had been installed under the will of Catherine Owen, 1744.[33] Choir stalls replaced box pews in the chancel in 1878.[34]

The earliest of the notable collection of monuments in the church[35] is that which probably represents Thomas Scriven (d. 1587) and his wife (d. 1612). This large monument, on the south wall of the chancel, includes recumbent alabaster effigies set beneath a four-centred arch flanked by Ionic columns. The figures of their 7 children are carved in relief on the tomb-chest below. The adjoining monument to Martha, wife of Edward Owen (d. 1641)—a bust carved within an oval recess between columns with an infant below—was removed from Old St. Chad's, Shrewsbury.[36] Monuments in the mortuary chapel include that to Thomas Owen, Sir Roger Owen, and Bonham Norton and his wife Jane (sister of Sir Roger Owen). This was carved in 1641 by direction of Jane Norton and consists of 2 pairs of kneeling figures facing each other. The marble monument to Roger Owen (d. 1718) and his daughter Catherine was carved in 1746 by direction of Roger's widow Catherine. It is said to be by Roubiliac, but the contract for the monument was made with Sir Henry Cheere, to whom Roubiliac was then assistant.[37] The kneeling marble figure of Thomas Cholmondeley (d. 1864) is by G. F. Watts, with some assistance from Reginald Cholmondeley.[38] The latter was the sculptor of the recumbent effigies of his wife Alice and their infant daughter (d. 1868).[39] There are plain mural tablets on the north wall of the chancel commemorating other 18th- and 19th-century lords of the manor, and other tablets in the two transepts.

The church had 4 bells until 1591, when another

was cast by John Cleobury of Wellington.[40] Three of these were recast by Thomas Roberts in 1680.[41] A treble bell was given by Edward Owen in 1682[42] and another bell, given by Alice Owen, was recast by Abraham Rudhall of Gloucester in 1701.[43] A sixth bell, recorded in 1752, was of 15th-century date.[44] These were all recast into the existing 8 bells by John Briant of Hertford in 1813.[45] A sanctus bell was in use in 1582,[46] but this was melted down in 1617.[47] Rhyming rules for the ringers, dated 1744, are on a tablet in the tower. There was a clock in the church by 1583;[48] new clocks were bought in 1592, 1633, 1682, and 1878.[49]

The church had a silver chalice and paten in 1613.[50] The present plate includes a silver chalice and paten given by Dorothy Harris in 1629[51] and a silver chalice, a paten, and two flagons left to the church by Edward Owen in 1700, but probably in use before that date.[52] A new set of plate—2 chalices, 2 patens, and a flagon—was bought in 1829 following the theft of the earlier plate.[53] On its recovery in the following year the old plate was deposited at Condover Hall, but was given to Annscroft church in 1872.[54] It was restored to Condover church in 1896 in exchange for the plate of 1829.[55] The registers are complete from 1570.[56]

The church of *ST. EDWARD*, Dorrington,[57] was built of ashlar masonry by J. T. Hope to designs in the Early English style by Edward Haycock in 1845. It consists of a nave, chancel, small north and south transepts, and square western tower. The tower is surmounted by an arcaded parapet, with crocketted angle pinnacles and an octagonal spire. The chancel was raised and extended in 1914, when an organ-chamber and vestry were added in each side.[58] The nave was repewed in 1914,[59] but the church retains its western gallery. The church fittings, most of which were given by members of the Hope-Edwardes family, include an organ (1861), a reredos (c. 1871), a pulpit (1919), a communion table (1925),[60] and a lectern (1946).[61] The monuments include a wall tablet to J. T. Hope (d. 1854). Two bells cast in 1844,[62] were replaced by 6 bells in 1945.[63] The clock, at the third stage of the tower, was installed in 1908. The plate includes a silver chalice, paten, and flagon of 1842 and a silver chalice and paten given by the Hope-Edwardes family in 1895.[64]

CHRISTCHURCH, Annscroft, was built in 1869 to designs by J. L. Randall of Shrewsbury, in

[25] Par. rec., faculty, 1877.
[26] Ibid.; Pevsner, *Shropshire*, 112.
[27] Par. rec., churchwardens' accts. 1659–89.
[28] Ibid. faculty, 1877.
[29] Visit. Archd. Salop. 1823.
[30] Par. rec., churchwardens' accts. 1659–89.
[31] *Salop. Shreds & Patches*, iii. 92.
[32] Visit. Archd. Salop. 1823; table of benefactions in base of tower.
[33] S.P.L., Deeds 9973.
[34] Par. rec., faculty, 1877.
[35] See plate facing p. 55.
[36] Cranage, vi. 476.
[37] S.P.L., Deeds 13408; R. Gunnis, *Dict. Brit. Sculptors*, 329, 331.
[38] Cranage, vi. 475–6.   [39] Ibid.
[40] Par. rec., churchwardens' accts. 1577–97.
[41] Ibid. 1659–89.
[42] Ibid.
[43] Walters, *Ch. Bells Salop.* 214.
[44] Ibid.
[45] Par. rec., churchwardens' accts. 1759–1819.
[46] Ibid. 1577–97.

[47] Ibid. 1604–27.
[48] Ibid. 1577–97.
[49] Ibid. 1577–1930.
[50] Ibid. 1604–27.
[51] Arkwright and Bourne, *Ch. Plate Ludlow Archd.* 24; *S.P.R. Lich.* vi (1), 78.
[52] S.P.L., Deeds 9963; Arkwright and Bourne, op. cit. 24.
[53] Par. rec., memorandum *re* plate, 1897.
[54] Ibid.
[55] Ibid.
[56] Printed to 1812 in *S.P.R. Lich.* vi (1).
[57] Except where otherwise stated, description of church based on Cranage, vi. 489, dated plaques in church, and local inf.
[58] Dorrington par. rec., faculty, 1914.
[59] Ibid.
[60] Heref. Dioc. Regy., reg. 1919–26, p. 369.
[61] Ibid. reg. 1938–53, p. 295.
[62] Walters, *Ch. Bells Salop.* 219.
[63] Heref. Dioc. Regy., reg. 1938–53, p. 260.
[64] Arkwright and Bourne, *Ch. Plate Ludlow Archd.* 27–28.

the Early English style.[65] It is built of sandstone, with dressings of lighter stone, and consists of nave and chancel under one roof, north aisle, southern vestry, and north-western porch, above which is a small spired bell turret. The pulpit was installed c. 1903,[66] the choir stalls c. 1908,[67] and the organ in 1952.[68] In addition to the set of plate made for Condover church in 1829, the plate includes a silver cream jug of 1841, given in 1958.[69]

NONCONFORMITY. A small number of Roman Catholics is recorded in the parish, 1633–98.[70] There were said to be 4 Protestant dissenters here in 1676[71] and the Quaker family of Hodges of Dorrington occurs, 1668–99.[72] There is no evidence of organized nonconformity in the parish before the end of the 18th century and the first dissenting chapel, the Congregational chapel at Lyth Hill, appears to have connexions with the Swan Hill chapel, Shrewsbury.[73] Richard Hodges, whose house was licensed as a dissenting meeting-house in 1787,[74] provided the site for the chapel in 1791.[75] It was built shortly afterwards with some assistance from Sir Richard Hill of Hawkstone.[76] After 1804 Lyth Hill chapel was served by the minister of Dorrington Congregational chapel.[77] Services were held there on Sunday afternoons throughout the 19th century[78] and an average congregation of 40 was recorded in 1851, but there were no church members at this time.[79] The chapel was repaired in 1876[80] and a Sunday School was established there in 1880.[81] The chapel was said to be 'most active' in 1898,[82] but services are last recorded there in 1930.[83] It has since been converted into a private house.

Dorrington Congregational chapel was built in 1808, with assistance from the Revd. William Whitefoot, a native of Dorrington and a minister of the Countess of Huntingdon's Connexion.[84] It was licensed in the following year.[85] Although there were no church members c. 1816, the congregation was re-formed with 7 members in 1819 and by 1851, when morning and evening services were being held, upwards of 120 persons attended evening services.[86] The chapel was repewed in 1822 and enlarged in

1840 and 1868.[87] The vigour of Congregationalism in early-19th-century Dorrington was largely due to the work of the Revd. J. J. Benyon, minister 1816–53.[88] Joseph Pryce of Dorrington left £200 for the support of the chapel by will of 1824[89] and a further £60 was left for the same purpose by Elizabeth Jones of Great Ryton in 1864.[90] Membership was said to have fallen by the 1870s.[91] There were 30–40 church members, 1910–17.[92]

In 1799 many parishioners were said to be attending Methodist meetings at Shrewsbury and Lyth Hill.[93] The latter probably refers to Bayston Hill, where Primitive Methodist house-meetings are recorded c. 1850[94] and a Primitive Methodist chapel was built in 1861.[95] A Primitive Methodist chapel at Great Ryton, built in 1869 as the result of a secession from Dorrington Congregational chapel,[96] had closed by 1906.[97]

SCHOOLS. A school was established at Condover in 1591, when the curate appears to have been master.[98] Thomas Smith of Chatford (d. 1590) and William Mall of Lythwood left a total of 26s. 8d. to support the school[99] and the lord of the manor was paying £2 a year to the schoolmaster in 1591 and 1602.[1] The school may have been closed by 1614, when the above legacies were being misapplied,[2] but it had been revived by 1615, after which date the master's salary was regularly paid by the churchwardens.[3] All the 17th-century masters appear to have been laymen.[4] Richard Cartwright, master 1652–c. 1656,[5] was responsible for the fine penmanship of the churchwardens' accounts, 1654–6. He was still living in Condover c. 1664, but was then employed as a writing-master outside the parish.[6] Jeremiah Bromley, master in 1718, had previously taught at Stapleton.[7] The school had become a private one by 1689, but the fees of 4 foundation scholars were paid by the churchwardens until 1808.[8] The school attended here by Dr. Burney c. 1730[9] was probably an otherwise unrecorded dame school.

In 1799 there were said to be no public or private schools in the parish,[10] but in 1818 60 children at-

[65] Cranage, vi. 462.
[66] Ibid.
[67] Plaque in church.
[68] Ibid.
[69] Arkwright and Bourne, Ch. Plate Ludlow Archd. 3–4.
[70] Lich. Dioc. Regy., B/v 1/53, 1/74, 1/81, 1/87; S.P.R. Lich. vi (1), 156.
[71] T.S.A.S. 2nd ser. i. 80.
[72] Lich. Dioc. Regy., B/v 1/74, 1/81, 1/87; S.P.R. Lich. vi (1), 157, 241, 254.
[73] Dorrington Congregational Chapel, ch. meeting minutes.
[74] Q. Sess. Orders, iii. 24; Q. Sess. rolls, Mich. 1787.
[75] Dorrington Congregational Chapel, ch. meeting minutes.
[76] E. Elliott, A History of Congregationalism in Shropshire (Oswestry, 1898), 176.
[77] Ibid. 171; Dorrington Congregational Chapel, ch. meeting minutes.
[78] Ibid.
[79] H.O. 129/359/1/18.
[80] Dorrington Congregational Chapel, ch. meeting minutes.
[81] Ibid.   [82] Elliott, op. cit. 176.
[83] Dorrington Congregational Chapel, ch. meeting minutes.
[84] Ibid.
[85] Q. Sess. Orders, iii. 156.
[86] Dorrington Congregational Chapel, ch. meeting minutes; H.O. 129/359/1/19.

[87] Dorrington Congregational Chapel, ch. meeting minutes.
[88] Elliott, op. cit. 171–3.
[89] Salop. Char. for Elem. Educ. 29–30.
[90] Dorrington Congregational Chapel, ch. meeting minutes.
[91] Ibid.
[92] Ibid.
[93] Visit. Archd. Salop. 1799.
[94] W. E. Morris, History of Methodism in Shrewsbury and District (Shrewsbury, 1960), 40–41.
[95] Ibid.
[96] Shrews. Methodist Circuit rec., worship licence, 1870; Dorrington Congregational Chapel, ch. meeting minutes.
[97] Shrews. Methodist Circuit rec., resignation of trustees, 1906.
[98] Par. rec., churchwardens' accts. 1577–96.
[99] S.P.R. Lich. vi (1), 198, 203–4.
[1] S.P.L., Deeds 6885; S.R.O. 665 uncat., accts. 1602.
[2] Par. rec., churchwardens' accts. 1604–27.
[3] Ibid. 1604–89.
[4] Ibid.
[5] Ibid.; Lich. Dioc. Regy., B/v 1/53.
[6] S.P.L., MS. 110, depositions, 1664.
[7] Lich. Dioc. Regy., B/v 1/95.
[8] Par. rec., churchwardens' accts. 1689–1819.
[9] P. A. Scholes, The Great Doctor Burney (Oxford, 1948), i. 4–5.
[10] Visit. Archd. Salop. 1799.

tended a school supported by private subscription.[11] A subscription day school attended by 30 girls in 1823[12] may be that supported in 1833 by Mrs. Smythe Owen.[13] Shortly before 1838 the lord of the manor established a school at the former workhouse,[14] which had been transferred by 1841 to the house now known as the Old School House.[15] Attendances at this school rose from 90 in 1838[16] to 180 by 1847,[17] but only 65 children attended in 1871.[18] A new school was built in 1880–1 under the threat of the establishment of a School Board.[19] Until 1953[20] the school remained the property of the lord of the manor, who provided the greater part of its income until 1877, after which date it was in receipt of a government grant.[21] School pence, which were in use in 1877,[22] were levied on a graduated scale after 1881[23] and a voluntary school rate was raised after 1882.[24] The school, which became an Aided school in 1958,[25] provided primary and secondary education until 1963, since which date it has been a primary school.[26]

A school at Dorrington, of which Onesimus Haynes was master in 1759,[27] does not seem to have continued after his death in 1769.[28] In 1823 some 20 children attended a day school here, said to be chiefly in the hands of dissenters.[29] The income from £200, bequeathed by Joseph Pryce by will dated 1824 for the education of children in Dorrington, was being paid to the master of this school in the 1830s for the education of 6 to 8 children who were chosen by the Vicar of Condover.[30] Shortly afterwards separate schools were established for Anglican and Nonconformist children. A dame school supported by Mrs. Hope-Edwardes of Netley Hall, which was attended by 20 girls in 1843,[31] was taking boys also by 1863 and had an attendance of 31 in 1870.[32] This school was still under the management of Mrs. Hope-Edwardes in 1875, when 34 children attended.[33] School pence were then levied and after this date the school also received a government grant.[34] The present Church of England School was built in 1874 on land given in 1872 by Mrs. Hope-Edwardes[35] and was enlarged in 1894.[36] It became an Aided school in 1956.[37]

A day school connected with Dorrington Congregational chapel was probably established in 1839, thus accounting for the enlargement of the chapel in the following year.[38] In 1867 the income from Pryce's charity was divided equally between the Congregational and Anglican schools[39] and in the following year a school was built at the chapel.[40] An average of 23 children attended this school in 1885[41] and 20 in 1891,[42] but it seems to have closed shortly afterwards.[43]

There were several small private schools in the parish in 1818,[44] and 102 children attended the 3 private schools existing in 1833.[45] Sixteen children attended Mrs. Aston's private school in Condover in 1846[46] and Samuel Clouds was running a boarding and day school at Dorrington between 1856 and 1870.[47] Private schools for girls at Ryton Fields and for boys at Park Villa, Wheathall, had been established by 1870, but both had been closed by 1909.[48]

Sunday schools had been established at Condover and at the Dorrington and Lyth Hill Congregational chapels by 1833, when a total of 215 children attended them.[49] The Condover Sunday school, which had been formed before 1823, was providing instruction in reading for adults in 1843[50] and had been affiliated to the National Society by 1846.[51]

CHARITIES. A rent-charge[52] of 53s. arising from lands at Great Ryton was vested in trustees by Thomas Owen in 1598. Out of this 1s. was to be paid weekly to provide bread on Sundays for 12 aged and impotent poor. A further loaf was to be given to the parish clerk 'to the intent and purpose he may be the more mindful and careful to remember or cause the same to be provided'.[53]

William Haynes, who gave 10s. to the poor during his lifetime, added a further 16s. by will c. 1648, both sums being secured as a rent-charge on lands at Cantlop. He directed that the income was to be used to supply 6 pennyworth of bread weekly to the poor.[54]

Henry Haynes gave 26s. a year to the poor during his lifetime and in 1659 this was converted into a rent-charge on lands at Netley. By 1682 this rent-charge was being used to provide bread for the poor on St. Thomas's Day.[55]

By will dated 1700 Henry Brickdale gave £44 to

[11] Digest of Returns to Cttee. on Educ. of Poor, H.C. 224, p. 750 (1819), ix (2).
[12] Visit. Archd. Salop. 1823.
[13] Educ. Enquiry Abstract, H.C. 62, p. 772 (1835), xlii.
[14] Visit. Archd. Salop. 1823.
[15] Par. rec., tithe appt.
[16] Visit. Archd. Salop. 1823.
[17] Ibid. 1843; Nat. Soc. Ch. School Returns, 1846–7.
[18] Returns relating to Elem. Educ. H.C. 201, p. 334 (1871), lv.
[19] Ed. 7/102/66; S.R.O. 1011 (Cholmondeley) uncat., estate correspondence, 1880.
[20] Ed. 7/102/66; par. rec., managers' minutes, 1903–56.
[21] S.R.O. 1011 (Smythe Owen) uncat., executors' accts. of E. W. Smythe Owen, 1863–6; Ed. 7/102/66.
[22] Ed. 7/102/66.
[23] Par. rec., managers' minutes, 1882–1903.
[24] Ibid.
[25] Ex inf. S.C.C. Educ. Dept.
[26] Ibid.
[27] S.P.L., MS. 379 (Condover ct. r. 1759).
[28] S.P.R. Lich. vi (1), 275.
[29] Visit. Archd. Salop. 1823.
[30] 24th Rep. Com. Char. H.C. 231, pp. 382–3 (1831), xi; Educ. Enquiry Abstract, p. 772.
[31] Visit. Archd. Salop. 1843.
[32] Kelly's Dir. Salop. (1863); Returns relating to Elem. Educ. p. 334.
[33] Ed. 7/102/67.

[34] Ibid.
[35] Ibid.; S.R.O. 1037 uncat., conveyance of site, 1872.
[36] Kelly's Dir. Salop. (1900).
[37] Ex inf. S.C.C. Educ. Dept.
[38] Kelly's Dir. Salop (1885); Dorrington Congregational Chapel, ch. meeting minutes.
[39] Salop. Char. for Elem. Educ. 29.
[40] Dorrington Congregational Chapel, ch. meeting minutes.
[41] Kelly's Dir. Salop. (1885).
[42] Ibid. (1891).
[43] Not recorded in Return of Schs., 1893 [C. 7529], H.C. (1894), lxv.
[44] Digest of Returns to Cttee. on Educ. of Poor, p. 750.
[45] Educ. Enquiry Abstract, p. 772.
[46] Nat. Soc. Ch. School Returns, 1846–7.
[47] Kelly's Dir. Salop. (1856–70).
[48] Ibid. (1870–1909); Auden, Condover, 35.
[49] Educ. Enquiry Abstract, p. 772.
[50] Visit. Archd. Salop. 1823, 1843.
[51] Nat. Soc. Ch. School Returns, 1846–7.
[52] Except where otherwise stated, account of charities based on 24th Rep. Com. Char. H.C. 231, pp. 379–83 (1831), xi; Digest of Endowed Char., 1862–3, H.C. 433, pp. 172–5 (1867–8), lii; Char. Com. files.
[53] S.R.O. 665 uncat., trust deed, 1647.
[54] Ibid. 1037 uncat., copy will of William Haynes, c. 1648.
[55] Lich. Dioc. Regy., glebe terrier, 1682.

the poor of Condover and Pulverbatch, to be invested in land to provide bread for 6 poor householders each Sunday. The gift was made conditional upon its amalgamation with two sums of £2 given to provide bread at Whitsun by Richard Lateward and George Hodges before 1682.[56] In 1709 these bequests, with £7 17s. 6d. contributed by Condover parish, were used to purchase a rent-charge of £2 11s. 8d. arising from the tithes of Betton Abbots and Emstrey. In the early 19th century Condover's share of the charity was £1 12s. 6d., most of which was used to provide 6 pennyworth of bread on Sundays.

The charity afterwards known as Vicar's Bread was established by will of Edward Owen, 1700.[57] He directed that from the rent-charge of £69 then devised to the Vicar of Condover, 1s. was to be given weekly in bread to the poor. This charity, which was distributed by the parish clerk in the earlier 18th century,[58] had an annual income of £2 12s. in 1786.

By will dated 1732 Samuel Daker left a rent-charge of 10s. to the poor and a further 10s. was given by his descendant the Revd. Edward Daker (d. 1820). From 1820 these charities were distributed by the Harley family in bread to the poor on the Saturday before St. Andrew's Day. The rent-charges were redeemed for £40 stock in 1937.[59]

By will dated 1797 Benjamin Pryce left £500 to the parish officers to buy bread for the most distressed poor, one-third of which was to be distributed in Dorrington township and the rest over the remainder of the parish. The charity had an annual income of £15 c. 1830, when it was distributed in bread on 2 days each year. The income of the charity had fallen to £13 2s. 9d. by 1862.

By will dated 1811 Richard Plumer left £50,

subsequently deposited in the Salop. Bank, the interest of which was to be distributed by the vicar and churchwardens at Christmas. By 1830, however, the annual income of £2 2s. 6d. was being distributed in bread on St. Thomas's Day, in conjunction with the Henry Haynes charity.

By will dated 1856 George Hayward of Walford House left £50 to provide bread for the poor. This was invested in stock in 1859 and had an annual income of £15 10s. 3d. in 1862.

Except where indicated, the income of all the above charities remained unchanged and they were distributed in accordance with the wishes of their founders. In 1903 a large loaf was given weekly to 25 old people. By a Scheme of 1932 all these charities were consolidated and have since been known as the Condover United Charities. The income, amounting to £27 12s. 8d. in 1951 and to £37 19s. 2d. in 1964, has since been distributed in money or kind among the inhabitants of the ancient parish.

The sum of £50 left to the use of the poor by John Reynolds at an unknown date, was apparently spent on the parish workhouse in 1772. The overseers paid £2 annually as interest to the churchwardens, 1773–1829,[60] but the capital was then used to buy a new set of church plate. Before 1682[61] Edward Owen gave 12d. weekly to the poor. This was paid by his successors as lords of the manor until 1804, but was subsequently lost. Benjamin Hodges gave £10 to provide bread for the poor in January. The capital was held by the churchwardens in 1786, when it yielded an income of 8s. a year, but distributions of bread ceased in 1805.

By will proved in 1948 Ellen Colley left £37 a year for the sick poor of Bayston Hill, Condover, and Ryton.

COUND

THE parish of Cound, which lies some 7 miles south-east of Shrewsbury, contains 3,772 a.[1] and includes the townships of Upper and Lower Cound, Golding, and Harnage. Isolated farms in the south of the parish—Harnage Grange, Moreton Farm, and Bull Farm—stand on the site of deserted hamlets. From the 16th century until 1864 Cressage was accounted a township and chapelry of Cound. It was, however, originally an independent parish and its history is treated in a separate article.[2]

On the north the River Severn forms the parish boundary, which on the south follows an irregular course along the slope of the Kenley ridge. The eastern boundary traverses an area of former moor and woodland and does not follow any natural features. In the south-east its course was fixed at the inclosure of Cressage Wood in the early 17th century.[3] The western boundary follows streams for a great part of its course and the former line of

Watling Street north of Cound Stank. A projection to the west takes in the township of Golding and a similar projection in the south-west corner of the parish, along the upper reaches of Bullhill Brook to the west of Bull Farm, probably represents the bounds of the deserted township of Newbold. This area, later called Little Langley and Highlands, has since the 13th century been associated with the adjoining manor of Langley.

The parish is drained by the River Cound and its tributary, Cound Moor Brook. The latter is fed by a number of small streams rising near the Kenley ridge, which unite to the north of Cound Moor. Apart from the ridge of sand and gravel called Venus Bank,[4] the land to the north of Upper and Lower Cound is flat, at 150–200 feet, but to the south it rises steadily to a little more than 300 feet at Golding and Harnage. Southwards from Cound Moor the land rises gently to 400 feet at Harnage Grange,

[56] Lich. Dioc. Regy., glebe terrier, 1682.
[57] S.P.L., Deeds 9963.
[58] Ibid. 9977.
[59] Char. Com. files.
[60] Par. rec., churchwardens' accts. 1759–1930.
[61] Lich. Dioc. Regy., glebe terrier, 1682.
[1] O.S. Area Bk. 1882. The following topographical description is based, except where otherwise stated, on O.S. Maps 6" Salop. 41, 42, 50 (1st and later edns.); O.S.

Map 1/25,000, SJ 50 (1959); Rocque, Map of Salop. (1752); Baugh, Map of Salop. (1808); B.M. O.S. 2" orig. drawings, sheet 207 (1817); Geol. Survey Map (drift), sheet 152 (1932); par. rec., tithe appt. and map, 1842. This article was written in 1962 and revised in 1964.
[2] See p. 73.   [3] Ibid.
[4] Name first recorded in 1751: Q. Sess. order bk. Jan. 1751. An earlier name may have been Gospel Hill: cf. S.P.L., Deeds 10127.

above which the steep scarp of the Kenley ridge and Grange Hill reaches some 600 feet.

The most significant feature in the landscape of the parish is the ridge of high ground running south-westwards from Harnage towards Evenwood in Acton Burnell. The shales and sandstones of which this is composed are an outcrop of a narrow outlier of the Kenley ridge, which crosses the Severn near Cound Lodge Inn. The greater part of the parish lies on boulder clay. Venus Bank marks the eastern end of the sand and gravel deposits which cover much of Berrington parish, and which extend to the east bank of the River Cound, north of Upper Cound. Golding, Mosterley, and Harnage Grange stand on or near other isolated gravel deposits, but Upper and Lower Cound lie near the edge of a belt of sandstone which divides the alluvial flood-plain of the Severn from the higher ground to the south.

Prominent among many contrasts in the landscape north and south of the Harnage ridge is the former distribution of woodland. To the north there was relatively little woodland in the Middle Ages. In 1086 Cound manor had woodland for only 50 swine,[5] and although the parish was nominally part of the Long Forest, there is a significant absence of references to assarts here in the 12th and early 13th centuries. In 1283 the pasturage of woodland in Cound manor produced 6s. 8d. and the same amount was derived from pannage and a custom known as *wrmtak*.[6] This manorial woodland, of which Long-dole Coppice is a surviving remnant, seems to have lain on the belt of boulder clay which extends northwards from Venus Bank towards the Severn. Cound Park, which in 1752 was depicted as occupy-ing a somewhat improbable site on the adjoining alluvial land to the east of the River Cound,[7] is more likely to have lain in this woodland area. It existed by 1298, when it was stocked with wild swine,[8] and was probably formed soon after 1254, when a grant of free warren was obtained.[9] North of the park lay Cound Heath, in which the tenants of the adjoining manor of Brompton in Berrington parish had common rights.[10] By 1416 the park had been leased and a farm and other assarts had been made on the Heath.[11] Leland, who passed through this part of the parish c. 1540 found 'no great wood in sight'.[12] Elsewhere in the north of the parish the extent of woodland—north-west of Golding and on the banks of Cound Moor Brook near Stevens Hills —has not altered much since the 16th century. Woodland in the present Cound Park[13] and at Harnage Coppice[14] has been planted since the later 18th century.

The Harnage ridge impeded the natural drainage of the clays to the south, thus producing a wide belt of flat and ill-drained land along its south-eastern flank, broken only by the small common fields of the former hamlet of Morton. Cound Moor ran west-wards from Morton towards Evenwood, while Bromley Moor covered land on both sides of the parish boundary and ran north-eastward from Morton towards The Leasowes. Despite its water-logged condition, Cound Moor seems to have sup-ported a growth of timber so extensive that, according to local tradition, 'a squirrel might hop from tree to tree all the way from Evenwood to Morton'.[15] Much of the timber is said to have been sold to make up the purchase price of Cound manor in 1623.[16] Cound Moor comprised 188 a. when it was enclosed in 1830,[17] but in addition to squatter settlement along its western edge its area had been considerably reduced by assarting before the 19th century. The eastern end of the Moor was separated from the former common fields of Morton by a group of small fields, clearly assarts in origin, in-cluding Dinmore, recorded in 1528,[18] and 42 a. which was glebe land by 1612.[19] A stint was imposed on common rights in the moor c. 1750.[20] Bromley Moor seems to have been reclaimed by the end of the 16th century. Assarts at 'Dychefeld' (Ditcher Field in 1842) are recorded in 1528,[21] and at 'Lycheleys Green' (probably The Green, north of Morton) in 1567.[22] Fields called The Criftin and Beach, at the north-western end of the moor, had been inclosed by 1620.[23]

The greater part of the land above the 400-foot contour in the south of the parish seems to have been woodland in the Middle Ages. In 1235 Harnage Wood was said to be well preserved.[24] Its medieval bounds were probably followed by the pale of the former park at Harnage Grange, which coincided closely with the 400-foot contour c. 1750,[25] but by this date woodland was restricted to the south-eastern corner of the estate, where Cressage Wood overlapped the parish boundary.[26] Timber on the Harnage Grange estate was valued at £1,000 in 1791.[27] In 1737 most of Little Langley lay in Lang-ley Park,[28] but by 1805 the park had been leased and most of the woodland cleared.[29]

The acreage of woodland in the parish has in-creased since the early 19th century. There were only 80 a. in 1842,[30] but by 1940 there were some 180 a. in the Cound Hall and Harnage Grange estates alone.[31]

The bounds of the former common fields of Upper Cound, Lower Cound, and Harnage can be determined with some precision.[32] The three fields of Upper Cound were called Sandy Field, Middle

[5] *V.C.H. Salop.* i. 320.
[6] C 133/40/2.
[7] Rocque, *Map of Salop.* (1752).
[8] *Cal. Pat.* 1292–1301, 383.
[9] Ibid. 1247–58, 263. cf. *Cal. Chart. R.* 1257–1300, 403.
[10] Loton Hall MSS., bailiff's acct. 1385–6; S.P.L., MS. 2, ff. 146ᵛ, 148ᵛ 149; S.R.O. 567 uncat., bailiff's accts. 1528, 1567–9, 1572; S.P.L., Deeds 8384, 8403.
[11] Loton Hall MSS., bailiff's acct. 1416–17.
[12] Leland. *Itin.* ed. Toulmin Smith, ii. 84.
[13] See p. 61.
[14] H. F. Jones, *Samuel Butler*, ii. 301.
[15] Bodl. MS. Blakeway 10, f. 329.
[16] Ibid.
[17] Q. Sess., inclosure awards 49.
[18] S.R.O. 567 uncat., bailiff's acct. 1528.
[19] Lich. Dioc. Regy., glebe terrier, 1612; acreage from par. rec., glebe exchange, 1866.

[20] S.R.O. 523/5.
[21] Ibid. 567 uncat., bailiff's acct. 1528.
[22] S.P.L., Deeds 8384.
[23] N.L.W., Wynnstay (1952) Y 52.
[24] Eyton, vi. 339.
[25] Estate map, c. 1750, at Harnage Grange.
[26] Ibid.
[27] S.R.O. 93/345.
[28] Q. Sess., reg. papists' estates, p. 207.
[29] S.P.L., MS. 294.
[30] Par. rec., tithe appt.
[31] Cound estate title-deeds, *penes* Messrs. Travers, Smith, Braithwaite & Co., London; Harnage Grange title-deeds, *penes* Westminster Bank, Shrewsbury.
[32] What follows is based on Lich. Dioc. Regy., glebe terriers, 1612–98; S.P.L., Deeds 10101–74 *passim*; par. rec., tithe appt.

Field, and Kymry Field and ran southwards from the River Cound towards Golding, covering virtually the whole township. They were divided from each other by the two parallel roads from Upper Cound to Golding and Cound Moor. In Lower Cound Ryton Field extended over the sand and gravel between Venus Bank and the River Cound, and Church Field lay south-east of the hamlet, between the former road to Harnage and Cound Moor Brook. The name of the third field in Lower Cound is not known, but it lay to the north of the church and became part of the grounds of Cound Hall in the 18th century.[33] The Harnage fields were Hill Field, on the slopes of the Harnage ridge, south of the hamlet, Broadwell Field (or Epistle Field), and Pool Field (or Vineyard Field), both of which ran north-westwards from Harnage to the former road from Shrewsbury to Cressage.

The lessee of the manor was said to have inclosed 25 a. in Cound in 1513,[34] but the open-field lands of the glebe in 1612[35] and of the Dodd family's estate in Upper Cound in 1616[36] were neither inclosed nor consolidated. There are several references to new inclosures in Upper and Lower Cound in the later 17th century,[37] but strips in Lower Cound field adjoined Cound Hall when it was being built in 1703,[38] and strips and furlongs in the common fields are recorded as late as 1761.[39] The progress of inclosure seems to have been more rapid in Harnage, where in the 17th century the land was in fewer hands. The glebe and the Dodd family lands in Hill Field had been consolidated and presumably inclosed by 1665.[40] Similar changes had taken place in the other two fields by the early 18th century, although the glebe here was still largely uninclosed in the 1680s.[41]

Common meadows lay in the Severn flood-plain, north of Cound Hall, where doles in meadows called Weir Meadow, Oxenhole, and Hurst Meadow were attached to holdings in the 17th century,[42] but much of this area seems always to have lain in the manorial demesne, which included Lord's Meadow and Enchmarsh in 1528.[43]

Little is known of the Golding common fields. They were still in use in the 14th century,[44] but seem to have been inclosed by the 16th century.[45] Field-names suggest that they ran towards the fields of Upper Cound on the higher ground north of Golding Hall.[46] The small common fields of the former townships to the south of the Harnage ridge probably disappeared even earlier than those of Golding.

Of the hamlets in the north of the parish, Upper Cound and Harnage are much the same in size and appearance as they were in the 17th century. Golding had shrunk to its present size by the end of the Middle Ages, and Lower Cound seems to have disintegrated in the 18th century, with the building of Cound Hall and the formation of the Park.

Lower Cound, in the bounds of which lay the church, the manor-house and the medieval demesne, was clearly the primary settlement in the parish. The church, on rising ground to the east of the River Cound, stands in an isolated position which was probably chosen because the underlying sandstone provided a firmer foundation than the alluvial soil to the north. Roads from Upper and Lower Cound and Harnage formerly converged at the church. The road from Upper Cound is now little more than a cart-track and that from Harnage ran to the north of the church until 1841, when it was diverted to its present course.[47] Another road, now a footpath, ran north-eastwards from the church towards Cound Lodge Inn.[48] The old parsonage which stood at the east end of the churchyard, was the only other building here until the 19th century. This was a timber-framed house, containing four hearths in 1662,[49] which was rebuilt or enlarged by James Cresset in 1680.[50] It was largely demolished in 1883, when a new parsonage was built a short distance to the east, but part of its east wall is incorporated in the parish room, known as the Guildhall, then erected on its site[51] and conveyed to the Parish Council in 1922.[52] The school was built opposite the church in 1844,[53] and a few private houses have been built nearby since 1928.

Until the 18th century the main road from Shrewsbury to Cressage ran some distance to the south of its present course between Venus Bank and Cound Lodge Inn,[54] crossing the River Cound by a timber bridge[55] some 100 yards south of the existing bridge.[56] The former manor-house stood to the north of this road.[57] The hamlet of Lower Cound probably lay by the side of the River Cound, along the road leading past the mill towards Upper Cound. Leland, who travelled along the main road c. 1540, came close enough to Lower Cound to describe it as a poor village and added that the Cound passed through it.[58] The hamlet contained three ale-sellers in the later 14th century,[59] and there were at least a dozen houses here in the 17th century.[60] The mill was in use until c. 1930.[61] Its buildings are of 19th-century date, but it probably occupies the same site as it did in 1086.[62] Cound Arbour Farm, opposite

[33] S.P.L., Deeds, 10169.
[34] C 47/7/2/3 m. 34d.
[35] Lich. Dioc. Regy., glebe terrier, 1612.
[36] S.P.L., Deeds 10127.
[37] Ibid. 10080, 10155, 10169.
[38] Ibid. 10159.
[39] Ibid. 10174.
[40] Lich. Dioc. Regy., glebe terrier [1680–9]; S.P.L., Deeds 10126.
[41] Ibid.
[42] Lich. Dioc. Regy., glebe terriers, 1612, 1695; N.L.W., Wynnstay (1952) Y 52.
[43] S.R.O. 567 uncat., bailiff's acct. 1528. cf. Loton Hall MSS., bailiff's accts. 1385–6, 1416–17.
[44] N.L.W., Pitchford Hall 1230, 1244, 1250, 1548.
[45] S.R.O. 567 uncat., bailiff's accts. 1528, 1567; S.P.L., Deeds 8384.
[46] N.L.W., Pitchford Hall uncat., map of Golding, 1736; par. rec., tithe appt.

[47] Q. Sess. rolls Trin. 1841.
[48] Rocque, Map of Salop. (1752); par. rec., tithe appt.
[49] E 179/255/35 m. 76.
[50] Datestone, now in east wall of churchyard. Print of house in P. W. L. Adams, A History of the Jukes Family (Tunstall [1927]), 33.
[51] Kelly's Dir. Salop. (1909).
[52] Char. Com. files.
[53] S.P.L., Watton press-cuttings, v. 166; Cound Par. Mag. Oct. 1904.
[54] Rocque, Map of Salop. (1752).
[55] Leland, Itin. ed. Toulmin Smith, ii. 84.
[56] S.R.O. 227/4.
[57] W.S.L. 350/40/3.
[58] Leland, Itin. ed. Toulmin Smith, ii. 84.
[59] Loton Hall MSS., ct. r. 1366–7.
[60] E 179/255/35 m. 76; Hearth Tax, 1672, 134–5.
[61] Local inf.
[62] V.C.H. Salop. i. 320.

the mill, is first recorded in the early 19th century,[63] and the farm-house, recently demolished, was not much older than this.[64] The only old house is Mill Cottage, which was originally a timber-framed house with a chimney stack on one gable. The field called Forge Yard to the north of the mill is probably the site of the smithy, first recorded in 1567.[65] Nearby stood an alehouse, said to be at the bridge-end in 1670,[66] which is recorded from 1571.[67]

The medieval park and most of the demesne lands lay, like the former manor-house, north of the main road, near the banks of the Severn.[68] The present Park is a creation of the 1740s. Much of the land to the east and south of the hall was brought into the manorial estate by exchange at this time,[69] but its development to the west, along the River Cound, is not recorded. In 1842 there were still a number of small fields to the north of the hall,[70] but by 1902 the whole area between the main road, the Cound on the west, and the Harnage road on the south had been transformed into parkland.[71]

The main road was diverted northwards to its present course shortly after 1748, when the alehouse near the old bridge was last licensed.[72] A Quarter Sessions order of 1751 that the old road should be reopened[73] was evidently not enforced. The bridge erected by the lord of the manor at this time[74] was replaced by a cast iron one in 1795.[75] This proved defective and was rebuilt in 1818.[76] Church Bridge, which crosses the river between Upper and Lower Cound, is also an iron bridge, cast in Coalbrookdale in 1797.[77]

There was no alehouse at Lower Cound after 1748, but the smithy was probably moved at this time to Venus Bank, where it has been since at least 1842.[78] Part of the smithy is stone-built, but it was enlarged in brick in the early 19th century, when windows in Gothic style were inserted. The brick-built blacksmith's house, like no. 38, Venus Bank and Black Barn Cottages, dates from c. 1850,[79] and the only house at Venus Bank earlier in date than 1750 is a timber-framed cottage, now disused, behind the smithy.

Upper Cound stands on rising ground, overlooking the River Cound, at the northern edge of the boulder clay which covers the centre of the parish. The houses lie along a road that leaves Watling Street at Cound Stank and formerly ran south-eastwards to The Green, between Harnage and Morton.[80] Beyond Upper Cound this road crossed Cound Moor Brook by Tillersbridge, last recorded in 1771,[81] but this section had been closed by 1842.[82] Cound Stank Bridge is first so named in 1682.[83] It probably derives its name from the mill-race that passed under Watling Street nearby and served the paper mill, erected on the east bank of the Cound before 1616.[84]

Upper Cound, which was known in the later 14th century as New Street,[85] seems to have been the product of colonization in the later Middle Ages. It was still predominantly a settlement of small free-holders in the 17th century, when it contained at least 15 houses.[86] Most of these houses are still standing. The older ones are timber-framed and in most cases have a ground-plan of two rooms on each side of a central chimney stack. Upper Cound Farm and Glebe Farm are of this type. The former was enlarged in the later 17th century by the addition of service wings on the north and south gables. Glebe Farm belonged to the Dodds of Harnage in the 17th century;[87] additional rooms on the east side were added by William Atkis in 1701.[88] The Post Office, facing the road to Lower Cound, and several adjoining houses were rebuilt in timber-framed style by the lord of the manor, A. C. McCorquodale, between 1906 and 1912.[89] Two alesellers and a smith lived at Upper Cound in the 14th century,[90] and the Phipps family, also tenants of the paper mill in the 18th century,[91] kept an alehouse here, 1619–1755,[92] after which date no alehouse is recorded in the hamlet.

The situation of Harnage, at the northern end of the ridge of shales which effectively divides the parish into two parts, is aptly described by its name.[93] Settlement here conforms to no regular pattern. Although most of the houses lie along the winding road from Lower Cound to Morton, others are scattered on the higher ground to the south, linked by a network of lanes and footpaths. As at Upper Cound, the hamlet has changed little since the 17th century, when there were at least 10 houses.[94] The Rookery and nos. 7–8, Harnage have been virtually unaltered since then. Houses on the sites of Harnage House and Butler's Farm were residences of the Dodd family in the 17th century, under the names of the Lower House and the Upper House respectively.[95] The Lower House seems to have been demolished by 1747[96] and although the present house contains an elaborately carved Jacobean staircase and some evidence of timber-framing in its outside walls, it was probably rebuilt by John Dodd shortly after 1747.[97] Butler's Farm was rebuilt

[63] W.S.L. 350/40/3.
[64] Local inf.
[65] S.P.L., Deeds 8384.
[66] S.R.O. 790/2.
[67] S.P.L., Deeds 9721.
[68] See p. 64.
[69] Lich. Dioc. Regy., glebe exchange, 1748; S.P.L., Deeds 10171–3.
[70] Par. rec., tithe appt.
[71] O.S. Map 6″ Salop. 42 (2nd edn.).
[72] N.L.W., Castle Hill 2244.
[73] Q. Sess. order bk. Hil.–Trin. 1751.
[74] S.R.O. 227/4.
[75] Ibid.; Q. Sess., dep. plans, bridges 48; *T.S.A.S.* lvi. 112–13.
[76] S.R.O. 227/5; *T.S.A.S.* lvi. 114–15.
[77] Plaque on bridge.
[78] Par. rec., tithe appt.
[79] The same brick is used in houses at Upper Cound, dated 1851.
[80] Rocque, *Map of Salop.* (1752).

[81] S.R.O. 790/5.
[82] Par. rec., tithe appt.
[83] S.R.O. 790/2.
[84] S.P.L., Deeds 10127.
[85] Loton Hall MSS., ct. r. 1366–7; ibid. bailiff's acct. 1416–17.
[86] *Hearth Tax, 1672,* 131.
[87] See p. 66.
[88] Datestone.
[89] Datestones.
[90] Loton Hall MSS., ct. r., 1366–7; ibid. bailiff's accts. 1385–6, 1416–17.
[91] See p. 68.
[92] Q. Sess., alehouse reg.; E 179/255/35 m. 76; *Hearth Tax, 1672,* 131; N.L.W., Castle Hill 2244.
[93] Probably derived from 'Haeren-ecg' ('rocky edge'): *Eng. Place-name Elements* (E.P.N.S. xxv), i. 145, 218.
[94] E 179/255/35 m. 75d.; *Hearth Tax, 1672,* 134.
[95] See p. 66.
[96] S.P.L., Deeds 10172.
[97] See p. 66.

in the mid-19th century. Harnage Farm is a small 19th-century house, considerably enlarged by A. C. McCorquodale in 1906.[98]

Two timber-framed cottages north of Harnage Farm lie on the course of a road which formerly ran northwards from Harnage towards the Severn. This road seems to have been in use in 1842[99] and was of some importance when the ferry across the river near Cound Lodge Inn[1] was still working. This route was used by the Newport family to transport corn from their estates south of the river to Eaton Constantine in the 17th century.[2] The road from Shrewsbury to Cressage ran close to the river bank at this point until the construction of the Severn Valley Railway caused it to be diverted to the south of Cound Lodge Inn.[3] A group of houses near the junction of these two roads—Cound Lodge Inn, Punchbowl Cottages, The Leasowes, and Cound Cottage—are of 17th-century date and were originally timber-framed. The Farmer family, who were living at The Leasowes by 1628,[4] seem to have been responsible for developing settlement here. By 1665 a branch of the family was living at what is now Cound Lodge Inn,[5] and one of them had a smithy here in 1680.[6] The Lodge was an alehouse by 1745,[7] and was occupied until at least 1815[8] by the Dodson family, under the name of Cound Lane House. The Punchbowl Inn, now Punchbowl Cottages, which stands on the river bank a short distance from Cound Lodge Inn, probably catered for boatmen rather than travellers on the road. There was a wharf here in 1842.[9] It is first recorded as an alehouse in 1745,[10] and was described as a 'comfortable inn or travellers' house' c. 1830,[11] but it seems to have closed soon after.

Until the Langley family acquired most of the township in 1606, Golding formed an outlying part of the manors of Pitchford and Acton Burnell,[12] and much of the land was attached to farms outside the parish. There were only two houses here by 1662,[13] and probably the same number in 1542.[14] Golding Hall and the timber-framed cottage to the east both date from the early 17th century. The latter was the farm-house of the small estate in Golding which had belonged to Pitchford manor since the 13th century.[15] Golding Hall, probably built soon after 1606,[16] originally had a ground plan of two rooms with a central chimney stack. The stack continues into the cellar, where there is a large fireplace of carved sandstone. The west wing was added by Thomas Langley in 1668[17] and the house was further enlarged in the early 19th century. Four

pairs of crucks, in a barn to the north which lay in the Hall estate in 1736,[18] are re-used and may have come from an earlier house on the site of the Hall. Other cottages at Golding have been built since 1885.[19]

Settlement south of Cound Moor now consists of scattered farms, but three of these—Moreton Farm, Bull Farm, and Harnage Grange—stand on the site of deserted hamlets. Morton stood on boulder clay to the south of Harnage, between Cound Moor and Bromley Moor. Its bounds are referred to in 1232[20] and its open fields probably lay along the tributary of Cound Moor Brook which flows north from Harnage Grange, but under the name of Morton's Field they were in the hands of one tenant by the 16th century.[21] Moreton Farm is stone-built and dates from the 18th century.

Bull Farm stands on a tributary of Bullhill Brook in the valley between Grange Hill and the Kenley ridge. The farm-house is a large and complex structure, mainly timber-framed and of 17th-century date, but with 18th-century additions in stone. It is first mentioned by name in 1740,[22] and although it cannot be certainly identified with the lost hamlet of Newbold, to which there are incidental references between 1236[23] and 1567,[24] it seems likely that they occupy the same site. The absence of any reference to Newbold in the description of the bounds of Harnage Grange in 1232[25] suggests that as a township it had already ceased to exist. By analogy with Morton, its open fields may in part be represented by adjoining fields called Great and Little Bull Field in 1842.[26]

A hamlet existed at Harnage Grange before it became a dependency of Buildwas Abbey in 1232.[27] It was then described as a vill and included tenanted land as well as demesne. Its common fields ran north towards a stream called 'Sciremoresiche', near The Hays Coppice on the Cressage boundary, and an assart made by one Reynold lay on the edge of the estate.[28] A gravel deposit to the east of the Grange, coupled with the natural pools which lie between the house and Grange Hill, provided an attractive site for early settlement. Roads from Harley, Morton, and Bull Farm, which meet at the Grange, followed their present course in 1752,[29] and that from Harley existed in 1232.[30] The course of another road, which in 1752 ran northwards towards Broomcroft in Kenley,[31] is now followed by a footpath.

The Grange[32] consists of west, east, and north wings, forming three sides of a square. The west wing, which is built of stone rubble and has a

[98] Datestone.
[99] Par rec., tithe appt.
[1] Ibid.
[2] Barnard MSS. Raby Castle, box 12, bdle. 1, no. 24; S.P.L., Deeds 10096.
[3] Par. rec., tithe map, 1842, and map of Cound Hall estate, 1862.
[4] S.R.O. 790/1.
[5] S.P.L., Deeds 10126.
[6] The Leasowes title-deeds, penes Barclays Bank, Shrewsbury.
[7] N.L.W., Castle Hill 2244.
[8] Commrs. minutes, 1815–18, in Q. Sess., inclosure awards 49.
[9] Par. rec., tithe appt.
[10] N.L.W., Castle Hill 2244.
[11] W.S.L. 350/40/3.
[12] See pp. 64–5.
[13] E 179/255/35 m. 75d.
[14] E 179/166/173.

[15] N.L.W., Pitchford Hall uncat., map of Golding, 1736.
[16] For some description see T.S.A.S. 4th ser. viii. 81–82.
[17] Datestone.
[18] N.L.W., Pitchford Hall uncat., map, 1736.
[19] Datestone.
[20] Dugdale, Mon. v. 356–7.
[21] S.P.L., Deeds 8384.
[22] Ibid. 12460.
[23] T.S.A.S. 4th ser. iv. 169–70.
[24] C 78/35 no. 19.
[25] Dugdale, Mon. v. 356–7.
[26] Par. rec., tithe appt.
[27] Dugdale, Mon. v. 356–7.
[28] Ibid.
[29] Rocque, Map of Salop. (1752); estate map, c. 1750, at Harnage Grange.
[30] Dugdale, Mon. v. 356–7.
[31] Rocque, Map of Salop. (1752).
[32] For some description see T.S.A.S. xlix. 49–50.

projecting stone chimney stack on the east wall, may incorporate the medieval grange; no recognisable medieval features, however, are visible. In the 15th century the house seems usually to have been occupied by the farmers of the grange,[33] but at least one of the abbots of Buildwas intended to live there in retirement.[34] The south and east wings were added by the Fowler family after 1569. Their outside walls are now brick, but this probably conceals timber-framing. The south wing, which stands at a lower level than the rest of the house, contained service rooms—the south-west end was the dairy until 1933.[35] In the early 18th century a new house was built to the east of the Grange,[36] and by 1747 the Grange itself was occupied by a tenant-farmer.[37] When the new house was demolished in 1878[38] the Grange was enlarged by the addition of a corridor on the inner face of the south and east wings and servants' quarters at the north end of the east wing. Considerable internal alterations have been made since 1933. These include the formation of a large staircase hall open to the roof; extra timbers have been added to the roof trusses to give an appearance of medieval construction. A deer park, which extended over the high ground to the south of the house, is first recorded in 1684[39] and had been disparked by 1774.[40]

The earliest reference to settlement on Cound Moor occurs in 1698,[41] but several of the cottages along the deep valley of Bullhill Brook on the western edge of the moor are of 17th-century date. They are timber-framed or stonebuilt, and are similar in plan to those on Kenley Common. There was an alehouse at Cound Moor, 1745–55[42] but the Fox Inn, which stands on the road constructed across the moor in 1806–7,[43] is first recorded in 1851.[44]

There were 305 adults in the parish in 1676.[45] The population, which stood at 439 in 1801,[46] was subject to short-term fluctuations in the course of the 19th century, reaching 552 in 1861 and a peak of 560 in 1911.[47] It has since declined steadily, there being only 459 inhabitants in 1951 and 408 in 1961.[48] The parish had a Friendly Society with 95 members in 1803.[49] A regular feature in the later 19th century was the annual Harvest Home, instituted c. 1860, which was attended by most of the farmers and their labourers, who were given a day's holiday.[50]

MANORS. The manor of COUND, which had been held by Earl Morcar before 1066, was in 1086 in the hands of Rainald the sheriff, who held it of Roger, Earl of Shrewsbury.[51] With the rest of Rainald's estates it presumably passed shortly after 1102 to Alan fitz Flaad and his descendants the FitzAlans,[52] later earls of Arundel. William FitzAlan (I) held Cound mill and lands at Harnage before his death in 1160.[53] Thomas de Erdington was said to hold the manor c. 1215 as the dower of his daughter Mary, the widow of William FitzAlan (III)[54] but in 1216 it was in the king's hands among the forfeited estates of William's brother and heir John FitzAlan (I).[55] In 1240 the manor was assigned in dower to John's widow Hawise.[56] She died in 1242[57] and the manor remained in the king's hands until her son John FitzAlan (II) came of age in 1244.[58] It was held in dower by John's widow Maud de Verdun from 1267[59] until her death in 1283.[60] John's grandson and heir Richard FitzAlan was then a minor [61] and in 1284 Robert Burnell was his undertenant at Cound.[62] Some time before 1291[63] the manor was settled on Robert's nephew Philip Burnell at his marriage with Maud, sister of Richard FitzAlan.[64] Maud continued to hold the manor after Philip's death in 1294[65] and was still living in 1299,[66] but it had reverted to Edmund FitzAlan, Earl of Arundel, by 1316.[67] A claim to the manor made by John de Haudlo and his wife in 1331, as heirs of Philip Burnell and Maud,[68] was defeated on technical grounds, and was probably a collusive action to assure the FitzAlan title.

Apart from temporary forfeitures in 1326[69] and 1397,[70] the manor was held by the earls of Arundel until 1560, when Henry, Earl of Arundel, sold it to Rowland Hayward.[71] After Hayward's death in 1593[72] it was held in dower by his widow Katherine.[73] She was still living in 1617,[74] but in 1623 her son John Hayward sold the manor to Edward Cresset.[75] It was held until 1792 by the following members of the Cresset family:[76] Edward, 1623–46; Richard, 1646–77; Robert, 1677–1702; Edward, 1702–27; Robert, 1727–8; Edward, 1728–55; Elizabeth, 1755–92.

On the death of Elizabeth Cresset in 1792[77] the manor passed to her cousin Henry Pelham, who had obtained licence to take the name of Cresset in 1753.[78] He died in 1803[79] and was succeeded by his

33 S.C. 6/1117/14.
34 Req. 2/11/40.
35 Ex inf. Mrs. J. H. Scott.
36 Estate map, c. 1750, and watercolour, 1861, at Harnage Grange.
37 S.P.L., Deeds 5371.
38 T.S.A.S. xlix. 50.
39 E 126/28 East. 1761 no. 1.
40 Title-deeds of Mosterley Farm penes Mr. H. P. R. Bland, The Leasowes Farm.
41 Q. Sess. Orders, i. 178.
42 N.L.W., Castle Hill 2244.
43 S.R.O. 790/5.
44 Bagshaw's Dir. Salop. (1851).
45 T.S.A.S. 2nd ser. i. 80.
46 Census, 1801.
47 Ibid. 1801–1911.
48 Ibid. 1911–61.
49 Poor Law Abstract, 1803, H.C. 175, pp. 416–17 (1803–4), xiii.
50 Cound Par. Mag. 1862–1905 passim.
51 V.C.H. Salop. i. 320.
52 Eyton, vii. 209–10, 220–2. For pedigree see ibid. vii. 228–9; Complete Peerage, i. 239–53.
53 Eyton, vi. 70; Cur. Reg. R. i. 308.

54 C 132/42/20.
55 Rot. Litt. Pat. (Rec. Com.), 198.
56 Close R. 1237–42, 197–8.
57 Eyton, vii. 253.
58 Close R. 1242–7, 97; Cal. Pat. 1266–72, 719.
59 Eyton, vii. 256.
60 Cal. Inq. p.m. ii, p. 325.   61 Ibid.
62 Feud. Aids, iv. 215.
63 Cal. Chart. R. 1257–1300, 403.
64 Cal. Inq. p.m. iii. p. 121; Cal. Close, 1288–96, 368.
65 Ibid.
66 Eyton, vi. 79.
67 Feud. Aids, iv. 229.
68 C.P. 40/286 rot. 111d.
69 Cal. Chart. R. 1327–41, 55.
70 C 145/263/12; Cal. Pat. 1396–9, 213, 248, 250.
71 C.P. 25(2)/200/2 Eliz. I East.; Cal. Pat. 1558–60, 368.
72 C 142/241/125.   73 Ibid.
74 C 142/363/194.
75 C.P. 25(2)/344/21 Jas. I Mich.; C.P. 43/163 rot. 84.
76 For pedigree see T.S.A.S. 4th ser. vi. 218–21; S.P.L., MS. 2791, pp. 455–6.
77 Ibid.
78 S.P.L., MS. 2791, p. 460.
79 S.P.R. Lich. ii (4), 263.

son John, an eccentric who died abroad in 1838,[80] when the manor passed to his sister Frances, widow of the Revd. G. A. Thursby. At her death in 1852[81] her son the Revd. Henry Thursby took the name of Thursby Pelham and held the manor until his death in 1878, when it passed to his grandson James A. H. Thursby Pelham.[82] The manor was sold in 1906 to A. C. McCorquodale,[83] after whose death in 1941 it was sold to H. R. Burrows Abbey,[84] who conveyed Cound Hall to J. F. Morris in 1944[85] and the remainder of the estate to Lord Ancaster in 1950.[86] The greater part of the estate has since been sold to the tenants.[87]

A timber-framed manor-house, continuously leased to tenants since at least 1385,[88] stood to the north of the former main road to Shrewsbury in what is now the garden of Cound Hall, where foundations were said still to be visible in 1929.[89] The alluvial soil on which this house stood was unsuitable for a building on the scale of Cound Hall, which was built for Edward Cresset in 1703–4, probably by John Prince of Shrewsbury.[90] The house, of brick with stone dressings, is a rectangular building in the Classical style, consisting of three stories and basement. The principal east and west fronts each have 9 bays, divided into groups of three by tall Corinthian pilasters. It is thought to be the earliest country house of this type in Shropshire and several features, including the use of applied pilasters extending nearly to the full height of the building, do not occur generally until some twenty years later.[91] At Cound the entablature above the pilasters is interrupted to accommodate the second-floor windows, the whole being surmounted by a wide cornice which conceals the roof. Carved stone-work, notably on capitals, window-aprons, frieze, and doorways, is of high quality. The west door originally opened on a large central hall, beyond which a corridor ran the length of the house. The original staircase in the north-west corner of the house was replaced in the early 19th century by a cast iron flying staircase in the hall. Apart from a portion of the south wall, rebuilt c. 1840, the exterior has not been altered since 1704. The panelling in most of the ground-floor rooms had, however, been removed before 1906, and further internal alterations have been made since the house was converted into flats, c. 1944.

The manor of *GOLDING* originally included not only Golding but also the township of Newbold and associated lands in the south-west corner of the parish, now represented by Bull Farm and Highlands Farm.[92] It was held before 1066 by a freeman Suen,[93] possibly the same person as the Suain who then held the adjoining manor of Langley.[94] In 1086 it was held, like Kenley, by Odo de Bernières under Rainald the sheriff.[95] Rainald's successors, the FitzAlans, were overlords of Golding by 1190[96] and their overlordship is last recorded in 1363.[97] The successors of Odo de Bernières as lords of Kenley subsequently appear as mesne lords of Golding.[98] A rent of 1 lb. pepper, assigned to Warner de Willey as mesne lord in 1221,[99] was still due to the lord of Kenley in 1623.[1]

The manor lost its identity in the 12th century, when it was divided into an increasingly complex set of under-tenancies. The earliest of these was associated with the neighbouring manor of Pitchford. Engelard de Stretton, a younger son of the Pitchford family,[2] seems to have acquired lands in Golding with his wife Ermeburga.[3] After Engelard's death his widow and his daughter Felise granted lands in Golding to Haughmond Abbey[4] and Wombridge Priory.[5] The remainder of his estate probably passed to the senior branch of the Pitchford family, since in 1255 part of Golding was held by the guardians of John de Pitchford, then a minor.[6] Ralph de Pitchford leased a messuage and a virgate in Golding to Walter de Golding in 1294.[7] The Golding family, who were small freeholders in Golding before 1221,[8] were still under-tenants here in 1344,[9] but were no longer resident in the parish by 1379,[10] and there is no evidence that the lords of Pitchford manor retained an interest in Golding in the later Middle Ages.

The remainder of the property passed in 1190 to Hugh de Beckbury, as under-tenant of Herbert de Rushbury.[11] Shortly afterwards Hugh increased his holding by acquiring the lands granted to Haughmond and Wombridge abbeys by Ermeburga and Felise de Stretton.[12] The Beckbury under-tenancy was confirmed by Warner de Willey as mesne lord in 1221[13] and by the overlord John FitzAlan in 1236,[14] when it was said to comprise a carucate in Golding and Newbold.[15] It remained in the Beckbury family until 1351,[16] when it was settled on Thomas de la Lowe at his marriage with Parnel, daughter and heir of John de Beckbury.[17] Edmund Lowe held the estate in 1412.[18]

The Golding portion of the Beckbury estate had

[80] S.P.L., MS. 2791, p. 460.
[81] Mon. inscr. Cound church.
[82] *Cound Par. Mag.* Dec. 1898; Burke, *Land. Gent.* (1952).
[83] Cound estate title-deeds.
[84] Ibid.
[85] Ex inf. Mr. J. F. Morris.
[86] Cound estate title-deeds.
[87] Ibid.
[88] Loton Hall MSS., bailiff's acct. 1385–6.
[89] Tipping, *English Homes*, iv (1), 418.
[90] Ibid. 417–23; H. M. Colvin, *Biog. Dict. of Eng. Archit.* 476. See also plate facing p. 82.
[91] Pevsner, *Shropshire*, 35, 114.
[92] *T.S.A.S.* 4th ser. iv. 169–70; Eyton, vi. 101.
[93] *V.C.H. Salop.* i. 320.
[94] Ibid. 342.
[95] Ibid. 320.
[96] Hist. MSS. Com. *10th Rep. App. IV*, 437.
[97] *Cal. Inq. p.m.* xi, p. 373.
[98] Hist. MSS. Com. *10th Rep. App. IV*, 437; *T.S.A.S.* 3rd ser. vi. 172; *Rot. Hund.* (Rec. Com.), ii. 63.
[99] *T.S.A.S.* 3rd ser. vi. 172.

[1] C 142/402/146.
[2] For pedigree see Eyton, vi. 270.   [3] Ibid. 98.
[4] Hist. MSS. Com. *10th Rep. App. IV*, 437–8.
[5] B.M. Eg. MS. 3712, f. 12.
[6] *Rot. Hund.* (Rec. Com.), ii. 62.
[7] N.L.W., Pitchford Hall 1247.
[8] *T.S.A.S.* 3rd ser. vi. 175; Eyton, vi. 100–1. There is no evidence, apart from the garbled statement in *Rot. Hund.* (Rec. Com.), ii. 62–63, for Eyton's assumption that the Golding family were under-tenants of the Beckbury estate here.
[9] N.L.W., Pitchford Hall 1230, 1244, 1250, 1253, 1546, 1548.
[10] E 179/166/23.
[11] Hist. MSS. Com. *10th Rep. App. IV*, 437.
[12] Ibid. 437–8; B.M. Eg. MS. 3712, f. 12.
[13] *T.S.A.S.* 3rd ser. vi. 172.
[14] Ibid. 4th ser. iv. 169–70.   [15] Ibid.
[16] Eyton, ii. 131–2, 134–6; ibid. iv. 136–7; ibid. vi. 100–2; *Cal. Inq. p.m.* v, p. 392.
[17] C.P. 25(1)/195/15/3.
[18] Hist. MSS. Com. *10th Rep. App. IV*, 439.

passed to under-tenants by 1315, when Edward Burnell held a messuage and 30 a. land there of John de Beckbury.[19] This property followed the descent of Acton Burnell manor until the 16th century.[20] Part had passed to the Acton family by 1480,[21] and in 1541 William Acton conveyed this to Adam Ottley, lord of Pitchford.[22] The remainder was conveyed to Robert Hennage in 1599,[23] who sold it in 1606 to George Langley.[24] The latter seems to have been tenant there since 1598[25] and his descendants held the Golding estate until 1820,[26] when it was bought by Sir Charles Jenkinson,[27] thus making the whole township of Golding part of the Pitchford estate.

The descent of the Newbold portion of the estate is obscure. Among the properties in Cound held by Thomas Poyner at his death in 1553[28] were two messuages in Newbold and Golding. Part of this property, probably Bull Farm, must have descended to him from the Beckbury family, since he paid the rent of 1 lb. pepper which had been assigned to the mesne lord of Golding in 1221.[29] The descent of the estate after the death of Thomas Poyner's son Thomas in 1578[30] cannot be traced, but by 1740[31] and until 1957[32] Bull Farm was part of the Harnage Grange estate. Highlands Farm was part of Langley manor in 1628[33] and later passed to the Smythes of Acton Burnell.[34]

The reputed manor of *HARNAGE GRANGE*, first so styled in 1706,[35] but previously accounted a member of the manor of Cound,[36] was in the hands of Hugh de Lacy by 1167.[37] He had probably been enfeoffed before 1155, when he was a vassal of William FitzAlan.[38] The estate seems to have passed to Hugh's brother Amaury, lord of Cressage, whose son Gilbert de Lacy held it in 1200.[39] Gilbert granted the estate, under the name of the vill of Harnage, to Buildwas Abbey in 1232.[40] He was dead by 1233, when his widow Eve claimed a third of the estate in dower.[41] In the course of the resulting lawsuit, which continued until 1236,[42] Gilbert's son Gilbert undertook to warrant his father's grant to the abbey.[43] Buildwas Abbey held the grange until 1536.[44] It was fully stocked in 1291,[45] but seems to have been leased in the later Middle Ages. In 1420 it was held by Hugh Burnell

and occupied by his farmer William Poyner.[46] Richard, Abbot of Buildwas, leased the grange for 51 years to his brother-in-law John Bennett c. 1494.[47] Bennett was ejected by Abbot Richard's successor shortly before 1518,[48] and in 1533 the grange was leased for 60 years to Sir Richard Brereton.[49] In 1537 it was granted by the Crown to Sir Edward Grey, Lord Powys.[50] He was succeeded in 1560 by his illegitimate son Edward Grey,[51] who in 1569 sold the grange to William Fowler.[52] Fowler already occupied the estate, having acquired Brereton's lease before 1565,[53] and it passed from father to son until 1739,[54] the following being owners: William, 1569–98;[55] Richard, 1598–1622;[56] William, 1622–67; Richard, 1667–86; William, 1686–1717; Richard, 1717–31; William, 1731–39.

In 1739 Sir William Fowler sold the grange to John Windsor, a Shrewsbury solicitor,[57] who was succeeded by his son Edward C. Windsor before 1771.[58] The latter sold it in 1792 to John Smytheman of Buildwas,[59] who died in 1809,[60] when it passed to his eldest daughter Catherine, wife of Major Benjamin Edwardes of Belswardine.[61] Their son J. T. Smitheman Edwardes, who died in 1851,[62] devised the estate to his cousin Sir Henry Hope-Edwardes.[63] It has passed through several hands since the death of Lt. Col. H. J. Hope-Edwards in 1919,[64] and was owned by Mr. J. H. Scott in 1963.

OTHER ESTATES. Harnage Grange and the estates deriving from the Domesday manor of Golding between them covered virtually the whole parish south of Cound Moor. In the north there were until the 18th century a number of smaller freehold estates, the most important of which was that built up by the Dodd family in Harnage and Upper Cound in the course of the 17th century.

The Dodds were resident in the parish by 1567,[65] when John Dodd was bailiff of Cound manor and held a substantial leasehold estate. Their earliest purchases were in Upper Cound, where Richard Dodd acquired 2 messuages in 1602.[66] One of these represented the small estate held by the Templars in 1189,[67] which had passed to the Jukes family in 1491.[68] By 1665, however, the greater part of their estate lay in Harnage, where Edward Dodd held some

[19] *Cal. Inq. p.m.* v, p. 392.
[20] See p. 7.
[21] C 140/76/55.
[22] N.L.W., Pitchford Hall 1152.
[23] C 142/364/43.
[24] Ibid.
[25] *T.S.A.S.* 4th ser. viii. 78.
[26] For pedigree see *T.S.A.S.* 4th ser. viii. 78–82; S.P.L., MS. 2793, pp. 115–16; ibid. MS. 4078, pp. 1061, 1058.
[27] N.L.W., Pitchford Hall 1934, 1936.
[28] S.P.L., Deeds 334.
[29] Ibid.; *T.S.A.S.* 3rd ser. vi. 172.
[30] C 142/183/48.
[31] S.P.L., Deeds 12460.
[32] Ex inf. Mr. J. Wild, Bull Farm.
[33] S.R.O. 790/1.
[34] See e.g. Q. Sess., reg. papists' estates, 1737, 1785.
[35] Mosterley Farm title-deeds.
[36] See e.g. C.P. 25(2)/344/21 Jas. I Mich.
[37] *Pipe R.* 1167 (P.R.S. xi), 61.
[38] Eyton, vi. 73–74.
[39] *Cur. Reg. R.* i. 308.
[40] *Cal. Chart. R. 1226–57,* 171; Dugdale, *Mon.* v. 356–7.
[41] Eyton, vi. 75–76.
[42] Ibid.
[43] Ibid.; N.L.W., Pitchford Hall 1417.
[44] S.C. 6/Hen. VIII/3006 mm. 6–7.

[45] *Tax. Eccl.* (Rec. Com.), 260.
[46] S.C. 6/1117/14.
[47] Req. 2/11/40.
[48] Ibid.
[49] C 3/13/30.
[50] *L. & P. Hen. VIII,* xii (2), p. 166; xxi (1), pp. 350–1.
[51] *Cal. Pat. 1558–60,* 366.
[52] C.P. 25(2)/200/2 Eliz. I East.
[53] C 3/25/86.
[54] For pedigree see *T.S.A.S.* xlix. 49–54; S.P.L., MS. 2792, pp. 537–8.
[55] C 142/262/132.
[56] C 142/448/109; N.L.W., Cwrt Mawr 786.
[57] E 126/28 East. 1761, no. 1.
[58] S.P.L., Deeds 1914.
[59] C.P. 25(2)/1395/32 Geo. III East.
[60] S.P.L., MS. 4645, p. 242.
[61] Ibid.
[62] Harnage Grange title-deeds.
[63] Ibid.
[64] Ibid.
[65] S.P.L., Deeds 8384.
[66] Ibid. 10190, f. 69.
[67] *Records of the Templars in England,* ed. B. A. Lees (1935), 39.
[68] C 2/Eliz. I/S 14/26; S.P.L., Deeds 10113–21, 10127, 10190, ff. 67–69.

160 a., including the Lower House (now Harnage House) and Upper House (now Butler's Farm).[69]

The nucleus of this Harnage property seems to have been the estate held by the Poyner family in the 16th century. The Poyners first appear as free tenants in Cound in 1404[70] and by 1420 William Poyner was farmer of Harnage Grange.[71] In 1528 Richard Poyner was lessee of most of the demesne in Cound manor and Thomas Poyner was a free tenant.[72] The latter held 6 messuages in Cound, Harnage, Morton, Golding, and Newbold at his death in 1553.[73] On the death of his son Thomas in 1578[74] the estate passed to two daughters, one of whose moieties was acquired by the Dodd family between 1620 and 1665.[75]

In 1665 the Upper and Lower House estate was settled on Jonas, son of Edward Dodd,[76] while lands purchased from the Yates and Farmer families were settled on his younger brother Samuel.[77] Samuel's estate descended to his grandson John Dodd of Shrewsbury,[78] but on the death of Jonas Dodd in 1680 the ancestral estate passed to his daughters Elizabeth and Christiana.[79] William Atkis, the husband of Christiana, considerably enlarged his share of the estate between 1681 and 1711, his purchases including 5 messuages in Upper Cound and 2 in Harnage,[80] and it was consolidated by exchanges, mainly with the lord of the manor, between 1665 and 1761.[81] In 1747 the Upper and Lower House estate was divided between Atkis's son William, John Dodd, and the Revd. Edward Cresset, lord of Cound manor.[82] Atkis, who then acquired the Upper House with 83 a. land in Harnage, died in 1750, and his estate in Harnage and Upper Cound passed after the death of his son William in 1756 to his daughter Sarah, who died unmarried in 1795.[83] She devised the Upper House to Samuel Drew,[84] shortly after whose death in 1825[85] it passed to Dr. Samuel Butler, headmaster of Shrewsbury School, who is said to have used it to raise meat and vegetables for the boys.[86] It remained with the Butler family until 1919.[87] Samuel Butler, the author, who was owner, 1886–1902, took an interest in the efficient running of the farm.[88] The Atkis estate in Upper Cound, which was not covered by the terms of Sarah Atkis's will,[89] passed to her residuary legatee, Miss M. A. Littlehales, who

owned 130 a. in the parish in 1842,[90] but this seems to have become part of the manorial estate shortly after her death in 1844.[91]

The Lower House, which was assigned to John Dodd in 1747,[92] passed at his death in 1774 to his niece Lucretia, wife of John Wilde.[93] She died in 1833[94] and although her son the Revd. S. D. Wilde seems to have owned the house in 1837,[95] it had been acquired before 1842 by the Revd. H. Thursby, Rector of Cound,[96] and was subsequently part of the manorial estate.[97]

ECONOMIC HISTORY. Cound manor was said to be worth £4 7s. in 1066.[98] By 1086, when it was assessed at 4½ hides, its value had risen to £10.[99] The severance of Harnage Grange from the manor was responsible for a reduction in its size to 3½ hides by 1254.[1] Its annual value was put at £19 7s. 9d. in 1283,[2] and at £35 10s. (inclusive of sales of wool) in 1386,[3] but by 1416 it was valued at only a little above £19.[4] The demesne, on which there were 2 ploughs in 1086,[5] contained 180 a. arable at the end of the 13th century.[6] Though there were 6 male and 4 female serfs in the manor in 1086,[7] by 1287 the only full-time manorial servants were 2 ploughmen, a shepherd, and a carter.[8] The demesne arable had been leased by 1385, but a considerable area of meadowland then remained in hand and the manor carried a stock of over 300 sheep.[9] No sheep remained by 1416, when the hay of the demesne meadows was being sold annually and the remainder of the demesne had been leased for 40s. a year to one Thomas Drayton, who occupied part of the manor-house.[10]

In 1528 the demesne was leased to several tenants for a total rent of £7 7s. 5½d.[11] The greater part of the demesne, later known as Cound Farm, was then held by Richard Poyner.[12] The manor-house and demesne seem to have been continuously leased until the end of the 17th century. Fulk Crompton was tenant in 1567[13] and Henry Crompton in 1572.[14] They were leased in 1591 to Henry Townsend,[15] son-in-law of the lord of the manor, at whose death in 1621[16] they passed to his son Warren Townsend, who was tenant until at least 1655.[17] For some years before 1675 most of the demesne had been held by Edward Granger,[18] who may still have been tenant

69 S.P.L., Deeds 10126. Acreage from ibid. 10172.
70 Bodl. MS. Blakeway 10, f. 333v.
71 S.C. 6/1117/14.
72 S.R.O. 567 uncat., bailiff's acct. 1528.
73 S.P.L., Deeds 334. Hardwicke, citing deeds of the Harnage family, states that the Poyners acquired their Harnage estate by marriage c. 1464: W.S.L. 350/40/3.
74 C 142/183/48.
75 N.L.W., Wynnstay (1952) Y52; S.P.L., Deeds 10126; S.R.O. 438 uncat.
76 S.P.L., Deeds 10126.   77 Ibid. 10144.
78 S.P.L., MS. 2790, p. 119.
79 S.P.L., Deeds 10190, f. 97.
80 Ibid. 10080–10165 passim.
81 Ibid. 10126, 10144, 10169, 10171, 10174.
82 Ibid. 10172.
83 S.P.L., MS. 4077, pp. 397–9.
84 S.P.L., Deeds 10179.   85 Ibid. 10181.
86 H. F. Jones, Samuel Butler, ii. 51–52.
87 Butler's Farm title-deeds, penes National Provincial Bank, Shrewsbury.
88 Jones, op. cit. 51–52.
89 S.P.L., Deeds 10190, ff. 60, 67.
90 Par. rec., tithe appt.
91 S.P.L., MS. 4081, p. 2523; par. rec., map of Cound Hall estate, 1862.
92 S.P.L., Deeds 10172.
93 Ibid. 10185.
94 Mon. inscr. Cound church.
95 S.P.L., Deeds 6113.
96 Par. rec., tithe appt.
97 Ibid., map of Cound Hall estate, 1862.
98 V.C.H. Salop. i. 320.
99 Ibid.
1 Rot. Hund. (Rec. Com.), ii. 62–63.
2 C 133/40/2.
3 Loton Hall MSS., bailiff's acct. 1385–6.
4 Ibid. 1416–17.
5 V.C.H. Salop. i. 320.
6 C 133/40/2; C 133/68/10.
7 V.C.H. Salop. i. 320.
8 S.P.L., MS. 2, f. 148v.
9 Loton Hall MSS., bailiff's acct. 1385–6.
10 Ibid. 1416–17.
11 S.R.O. 567 uncat., bailiff's acct. 1528.
12 Ibid.
13 S.P.L., Deeds 8384.   14 Ibid. 8403.
15 S.P.L., MS. 2, f. 151v.
16 C 142/402/147.
17 S.P.L., MS. 2, f. 151v; Cal. Cttee. for Compounding, 3237.
18 E 134/27 Chas. II Mich./41.

in 1703.[19] In 1675 it was said that the demesne lands were so intermixed that they could not be distinguished from the lands of the tenants.[20]

Two small freeholds were added to the manorial estate *c.* 1660,[21] but there is no evidence of any substantial increase in its size from medieval times until the 18th century. A compact estate in Harnage and Lower Cound was built up in the early 18th century by means of exchanges with neighbouring landowners[22] and this formed the basis for Cound Park, which was developed after the 1740s.[23] A share in the Dodd estate at Harnage passed to Edward Cresset in 1747,[24] and it is probable that a number of small freeholds in Upper and Lower Cound were acquired at about this time. The greater part of Cound Moor was allotted to the lord of the manor in 1830,[25] and by 1842 the manorial estate comprised 1,629 a.[26] A further 150 a. was added in the later 19th century, and some 300 a. were purchased by A. C. McCorquodale between 1908 and 1941.[27]

Of the larger freehold estates in the parish, Golding and the Smythe estate at Little Langley remained little changed in size from medieval times until the early 20th century. In 1086 they were both members of the manor of Golding, assessed at half a hide, with one plough in demesne and 4 recorded tenants.[28] In 1842 there were 402 a. in the Golding estate, the greater part of which was occupied by the owner, the Earl of Liverpool.[29] The Little Langley estate contained 297 a. in 1805[30] and 268 a. in 1842,[31] of which some 160 a. were held by the tenant of Highlands Farm and the remainder belonged to farms in Acton Burnell.

Bull Farm was added to the Harnage Grange estate some time after 1578,[32] but otherwise the boundaries of the Grange, described in 1232,[33] continued unchanged until the Second World War.[34] It comprised 809 a. in 1842.[35] Purchases in the 1940s, including Mosterley Farm, increased it to some 1,150 a. by 1948, but by 1957 it had fallen to 677 a.[36] Until the 1940s, when the owners of the Grange themselves began to farm it, the bulk of the estate was let to tenants. There were 6 farms in 1791, 4 in 1842 and 3 in 1923.[37]

In contrast to the static history of landownership in the south and west of the parish, to the north the acquisitions of the Dodd family and the growth of the manorial estate have wrought considerable

changes since the early 17th century. At least 9 small freeholds disappeared in the course of the 17th century[38] and by 1842 few survived.[39] The manorial estate then included virtually the whole of Lower Cound and all Upper Cound except the scattered fields of the former Dodd estate, then owned by Miss Littlehales.[40] In Harnage the fragmentation of the Dodd estate had created a more complex pattern, but the only other ancient freehold estate in 1842[41] was The Leasowes—a farm which lay partly in Cound and partly in Cressage and which was held by the Farmer family from the early 17th century until 1917.[42] Five small freeholds lay around the eastern edge of Cound Moor.[43] Apart from Moreton Farm (41 a.) these were all of less than 10 a. each[44] and were presumably encroachments on the common.

In 1086 there were 6 villeins and 6 bordars on Cound manor, with 4 ploughs between them.[45] Free tenants, whose rents were 47s. 3d. in 1283,[46] were clearly less numerous than the customary tenants, who paid rents totalling £12 7s. 6½d.[47] Assized rents of some £24 a year were due in 1385 and 1416 from the customary tenants, who also paid 33s. 4d. annually in tallage.[48] Attempts were being made in the 1360s to extract the payment of chevage from tenants living outside the manor,[49] but by 1385 no income was derived from this source.[50] In bailiffs' accounts of 1386 and 1417[51] lengthy lists of lands untenanted or set on lease at lower rents—involving at least 29 houses at the latter date—indicate that a radical change in forms of tenure was taking place here. By 1528, when rents produced £19 6s. 10½d., whatever regularity there may have been in the structure of holdings had already disappeared.[52] Of 31 tenants, the holdings of only 8 are described in terms of virgates. Seventeen tenants held one or more messuages and lands, while 14 held parcels of land only. The largest holdings were those of Thomas Poyner and Thomas Gosnell, who also held freehold land in the parish.[53] Little attempt had been made to increase the value of the estate by 1572, when annual rents totalled £27 9s. 5½d.[54] There were then 24 leasehold and copyhold tenants. Types of tenure are not always distinguished, but most seem to have been copyholders and 19 of the tenants held for terms of one to three lives. About two-thirds of the estate (1,156 a.) lay in 6 farms of over 100 a. in 1842, when there were 20 small-

[19] S.P.L., Deeds 10159.
[20] E 134/27 Chas. II Mich./41.
[21] Ibid.
[22] S.P.L., Deeds 10169, 10171–4; Lich. Dioc. Regy., glebe terriers.
[23] See p. 61.
[24] S.P.L., Deeds 10172.
[25] Q. Sess., inclosure awards 49.
[26] Par. rec., tithe appt.
[27] Ibid. map of Cound Hall estate, 1862; Cound estate title-deeds.
[28] *V.C.H. Salop.* i. 320.
[29] Par. rec., tithe appt.
[30] S.P.L., MS. 294.
[31] Par. rec., tithe appt.
[32] See p. 65.
[33] Dugdale, *Mon.* v. 356–7.
[34] Estate map, *c.* 1750, at Harnage Grange; par. rec., tithe appt.; Harnage Grange title-deeds.
[35] Par. rec., tithe appt.
[36] Harnage Grange title-deeds.
[37] Ibid.; S.R.O. 93/345; par. rec., tithe appt.
[38] Bennett (Harnage): C 142/630/49; S.P.L., Deeds 10157–9; Browne (Upper Cound): S.P.L., Deeds 10095–

10128; Gosnell (Upper Cound): C 142/505/119; S.P.L., Deeds 10150; Jukes (Upper Cound): C 2/Eliz. I/S 14/26; Matthews (Harnage): S.P.L., Deeds 10161–5; Richards: E 134/27 Chas. II Mich./41; Staunton (Upper Cound): C 142/583/22; Walker (Lower Cound): C 142/702/43; S.R.O. 438 uncat.; N.L.W., Wynnstay (1952) Y 62; Yates (Harnage): S.P.L., Deeds 10080–10144.
[39] Par. rec., tithe appt.
[40] Ibid.
[41] Ibid.
[42] S.R.O. 790/1; *T.S.A.S.* 4th ser. v. 303; The Leasowes title-deeds.
[43] Par. rec., tithe appt.
[44] Ibid.
[45] *V.C.H. Salop.* i. 320.
[46] C 133/40/2.
[47] Ibid.
[48] Loton Hall MSS., bailiff's accts. 1385–6, 1416–17.
[49] Ibid. ct. r. 1366–7.
[50] Ibid. bailiff's acct. 1385–6.
[51] Ibid. 1385–6, 1416–17.
[52] S.R.O. 567 uncat., bailiff's acct. 1528.
[53] Ibid.
[54] S.P.L., Deeds 8403.

holdings of 1–25 a.,[55] and the structure of the estate had changed little by the 1940s. There were still 11 holdings of less than 25 a. in 1942, and although about three-quarters (1,558 a.) of the total acreage lay in large farms, this included the former glebe and Butler's Farm, which had been purchased since 1908.[56]

Until the 19th century there was little arable land in the south of the parish, where stock-rearing and dairy-farming seem to have been the chief occupations. In 1756 there were 200 sheep and over 150 head of cattle in the Park at Harnage Grange,[57] and at this time it was said that great numbers of milking cows had always been kept in the parish.[58] Only 745 a. were said to be under the plough in 1801, when wheat and barley were the chief crops.[59] But the inclosure and drainage of Cound Moor, complete by 1830,[60] led to an increase in the arable area, which had already risen to 1,100 a. c. 1825.[61] By 1842 the proportion of arable to pasture was roughly equal at some 1,700 a. and there was slightly more arable than pasture at Harnage Grange.[62]

There were 2 mills in Cound manor in 1086, worth 20s. a year.[63] One of the mills, presumably that at Lower Cound, subsequently remained in the manorial estate. A rent-charge arising from it was granted before 1160 to Shrewsbury Abbey,[64] and in 1385 it was leased for 53s. 4d. a year.[65] Although it was occupied by William Hazledine, the Shrewsbury ironmaster, c. 1830,[66] there is no evidence that it was ever used for anything other than corn-milling. The mill-house was still standing in 1963 and the mill is said to have been in use until c. 1930.[67] The second mill can probably be identified with that held by the free tenant Philip de Presthope in 1323.[68] His widow Constance married Thomas Cresset, on whom the mill was settled in 1335.[69] It was still held by the Cresset family in 1572,[70] but was sold to Sir Henry Townsend, the lessee of the manor, in 1606[71] and was thereafter in the manorial estate. It is likely that this mill stood on the site of the paper-mill at Upper Cound, first recorded in 1616.[72] This was occupied by the Gosnell family, 1624–76,[73] and the Phipps family, c. 1680–1807.[74] The mill closed in 1841[75] and the house was demolished in 1962.[76]

Grange Mill, on Bullhill Brook at the south-west corner of Cound Moor, can probably be identified with Yarford Mill, first recorded before 1292.[77] It was then leased to Buildwas Abbey[78] and was part of the Harnage Grange estate in 1535.[79] Its millers are recorded in 1667 and 1711,[80] and the mill seems to have been in use c. 1750,[81] but it had become a farm-house by 1788.[82]

The mineral resources of the parish have been exploited from an early period. Stone slates from Harnage, which are occasionally found on old houses in the district, were used at Harley manor-house in the 14th century.[83] A limekiln, which seems to have stood near Bull Hill on the borders of the Harnage Grange estate, was already described as old in 1232.[84] Fields called Limekiln Bank south of Harnage House mark the site of kilns belonging in the 18th century to the Atkis family,[85] who also had limeworks in Lime Leasow, north-west of Upper Cound, which were producing lime for sale in 1747.[86] Outcrops of coal occur at various points along the north face of the Harnage ridge.[87] Coal pits were sunk in the manorial estate in 1572[88] and a pit in the field called Coalpit Yard, north of Harnage House, was in use in 1612.[89] Brick Kiln Field, on the Golding road south of Upper Cound, and a field of the same name at Harnage, both lay, like the 18th-century limekilns, in the Atkis estate,[90] but there is no evidence that bricks were made commercially in the parish until the 19th century. In 1842 a brickworks to the north of the Shrewsbury road was occupied by the tenant of the mill[91] and it was still manufacturing bricks in 1891.[92] The sand and gravel pits, which had removed a great part of Venus Bank by 1963, had been opened by 1862.[93]

In the 19th century the number of tradesmen in the parish was small in comparison with its size. In 1870 there were, in addition to the miller and blacksmith, 2 shopkeepers, a tailor, a carpenter, and a wheelwright.[94] Apart from the shop at Upper Cound, these had all gone out of business by 1926.[95] The proportion of tradesfolk was higher in the 14th century than in the nineteenth: the 8 tradesmen in 1379 included a weaver, 2 tailors, and a physician.[96]

LOCAL GOVERNMENT. There are manor court rolls 1366–7,[97] 1571–2,[98] and presentments, 1837–40.[99] Courts were held about 6 times a year in the later 14th century, when sessions of the great court, whose jurisdiction included view of frankpledge and the assize of bread and ale, took place in the spring and autumn. The intermediate little courts then

[55] Par. rec., tithe appt.
[56] Cound estate title-deeds.
[57] S.R.O. 1005/44.
[58] S.P.L., Deeds 12460.
[59] H.O. 67/14/78.
[60] Q. Sess., inclosure awards 49.
[61] Bodl. MS. Blakeway 10, f. 323a.
[62] Par. rec., tithe appt.
[63] V.C.H. Salop. i. 320.
[64] Eyton, vi. 70.
[65] Loton Hall MSS., bailiff's acct. 1385–6.
[66] W.S.L. 350/40/3.
[67] Local inf.
[68] S.P.L., MS. 2, ff. 132, 139ᵛ, 144.
[69] Ibid.
[70] S.P.L., Deeds 8403.
[71] C 142/402/147.
[72] S.P.L., Deeds 10127.
[73] Bodl. MS. Blakeway 10, f. 333; S.R.O. 790/1, 2.
[74] S.R.O. 790/2, 1250/1; T.S.A.S. xlix. 153–5; liii. 147, 151.
[75] T.S.A.S. liii. 151.
[76] Local inf.

[77] S.P.L., MS. 2, f. 12.
[78] Ibid. f. 6.
[79] S.C. 6/Hen. VIII/3006 m. 7.
[80] S.P.R. Lich. ii (4), 178, 202.
[81] Estate map, c. 1750, at Harnage Grange.
[82] S.R.O. 93/2.
[83] S.P.L., MS. 2, f. 438.
[84] Dugdale, Mon. v. 356.
[85] S.P.L., Deeds 10169, 10172.
[86] Ibid. 10170, 10172.
[87] Geol. Survey Map (drift), sheet 152 (1932).
[88] S.P.L., Deeds 8403.
[89] Lich. Dioc. Regy., glebe terrier, 1612.
[90] S.P.L., Deeds 10172, 10174.
[91] Par. rec., tithe appt.
[92] Kelly's Dir. Salop (1891).
[93] Par. rec., map of Cound Hall estate, 1862.
[94] Kelly's Dir. Salop. (1870).
[95] Ibid. (1926).   [96] E 179/166/23.
[97] Loton Hall mun., ct. r. 1366–7.
[98] S.P.L., Deeds 8384, 9721. Extracts from earlier ct. r. are in S.P.L., MS. 2.
[99] S.P.L., Deeds 6113–15.

dealt with a full range of business, but by the 16th century they were concerned only with pleas between party and party.

The parish records include churchwardens' accounts, 1625–1811, overseers' accounts, 1665–1722 and 1751–1841, and a parish book, containing vestry minutes and accounts of parish officers, 1861–1952.[1] Parish government was supervised in the 17th century by a body known as The Six Men, presumably representing each of the 6 townships into which the parish was divided for administrative purposes. They continued to cast rates and examine and sign the accounts of parish officers until the 1670s, but, although they nominally cast church rates until 1756 and poor rates until at least 1722, they were probably of no practical importance by this time. They seem to have been superseded by an open vestry in 1756–7, when a rating system based on 'lewns', or ancient assessments on the team-land, was replaced by a pound rate. An Easter vestry for the election of churchwardens is first recorded in 1763. The latter had previously served in rotation according to the lands which they held and frequently employed deputies. The mode of appointment of overseers is not known, but in 1820 the vestry resolved that the office should be filled by the churchwardens of the preceding year. Vestry meetings, formerly held in the church, took place in the school or the Guildhall after 1887.

Until the mid-17th century routine expenditure on the church was met without recourse to rates. The churchwardens obtained a small income from the smithy, which they leased from the lord of the manor, and rather more from a parish stock, which totalled £10 in 1642. The stock had risen to £136 by 1675, but had by this time been appropriated by the overseers. Communion pence were discontinued in 1633. Rates were occasionally levied for special purposes before the Civil War, as for repairs to the bells in 1628, for a new pulpit in 1633, and for refurnishing the church after a robbery in 1639. They appear to have been levied annually after 1641. In the 17th century the churchwardens were also responsible for the collection of county rates, and these were separately assessed until 1673. The parish clerk received a salary of 8d. per team-land in 1698.[2] For a number of years after 1843 a beadle was appointed to perform the clerk's more menial duties.

The 2 overseers of the poor rendered a combined account for their year of office until 1766; thereafter each overseer normally accounted for six months of the year. Annual expenditure on poor relief, normally ranging from £5 to £15 in the 17th century, and from £10 to £20 in the first quarter of the 18th century, rose rapidly after 1756. It usually exceeded £100 after 1770 and £200 after 1782. Poor rates reached a peak of £545 in 1817.[3] A workhouse is first recorded in 1758. It was managed by a workhouse master or mistress from 1783 until 1795, when it was closed after Cound had effectively become a member of the Atcham Union, established in 1792.[4] The inmates seem to have been employed in cloth manufacture.

Highway surveyors are first recorded in 1633. They appear to have had little power of independent action, since their expenditure was administered by the churchwardens in the 17th century and by the overseers after 1690. There were 4 constables in the 18th century, whose expenses were paid by the overseers.

CHURCH. Cound church is first recorded in 1216,[5] but Heming and Ebrard, the two priests who witnessed a charter of William FitzAlan before 1160,[6] may have been connected with the parish. Kenley and the township of Acton Pigott in Acton Burnell were formerly chapelries of Cound, but Kenley became a parochial chapelry in 1605 and the chapel at Acton Pigott had long been disused in the early 19th century.[7] Cressage, though an independent church in the 12th century, later became a chapelry of Cound and remained subject to it until constituted an ecclesiastical district in 1864.[8] There is no evidence for Eyton's assertion[9] that Acton Burnell, Harley, Pitchford, Ruckley, and Sheinton were originally chapelries of Cound.

The living is a rectory; negotiations to appropriate it to Buildwas Abbey in 1354 were abortive.[10] The advowson followed the descent of the manor until 1951, when it was transferred to the Bishop of Hereford.[11] In 1628 the right of presentation was granted for two turns to Richard Lee and Edward Pytt,[12] and the latter's son James assigned his right to Adam and Thomas Ottley in 1683.[13] Under the terms of the grant of 1628 the right of presentation should have reverted to the lord of the manor as patron, but the Crown presented in 1721[14] and Thomas Pelham in 1737.[15]

The rectory, with its chapelries, was said to be worth £20 in 1291,[16] but was valued at £26 13s. 4d. in 1294.[17] Its gross annual value rose from £33 13s. 4d. in 1535[18] to £75 6s. 8d. in 1655[19] and to £560 in 1799.[20] The living was worth £1,029 gross in 1831,[21] but only £821 gross in 1869,[22] following the separation of Cressage in 1864.

The rector was given 8 oak trees from Cound Wood in 1243 to enlarge his tithe barn.[23] The tithes were worth £16 5s. 10d. in 1341[24] and about £60 in 1655.[25] They were still paid in kind in the 18th

[1] S.R.O. 790/1–6, 1250/1–2; par. rec., par. bk. 1861–1952. Except where otherwise stated, what follows is based on these records.
[2] Lich. Dioc. Regy., glebe terrier, 1698.
[3] Rep. Cttee. on Poor Rate Returns, 1822, Suppl. App. H.C. 556, p. 141 (1822), v.
[4] Atcham Union Act, 32 Geo. III, c. 95 (priv. act).
[5] Rot. Litt. Pat. (Rec. Com.), 198.
[6] Eyton, vi. 70.
[7] See p. 12.
[8] See p. 77.
[9] Eyton, vi. 77.
[10] Cal. Pat. 1354–8, 77; Cal. Papal Regs. iii. 573; Abbrev. Rot. Orig. (Rec. Com.), ii. 234.
[11] Par. rec., par. bk. 1861–1952.
[12] N.L.W., Ottley Papers 1309.
[13] Ibid. 1310.
[14] T.S.A.S. 4th ser. v. 192.
[15] Ibid. 197.
[16] Tax. Eccl. (Rec. Com.), 247.
[17] C 133/68/10.
[18] Valor Eccl. (Rec. Com.), iii. 183.
[19] T.S.A.S. xlvii. 29.
[20] Visit. Archd. Salop. 1799.
[21] Rep. Com. Eccl. Revenues [67], pp. 470–1, H.C. (1835), xxii.
[22] Par. rec., par. bk. 1861–1952.
[23] Close R. 1242–7, 97. Four trees were for crucks and 4 for planks.
[24] Inq. Non. (Rec. Com.), 182.
[25] T.S.A.S. xlvii. 29.

century, apart from the hay tithes on some of the farms,[26] but moduses on milch cows and colts had been introduced by 1842,[27] when tithes were commuted for a rent-charge of £622.[28] One-third of the corn tithes of Acton Pigot chapelry were paid to Cound in the later 17th century;[29] these were commuted in 1845.[30]

The tithes of Harnage Grange were the subject of a number of lawsuits between 1484 and 1537. The rector's right to these tithes was confirmed in 1484, following a dispute with the Abbot of Buildwas, who claimed that his estate was exempt.[31] The abbot later secured the reversal of this decision, but the rector renewed his claim in 1501.[32] The result of this lawsuit is not known, but in 1527 an arrangement was made with the rector, Matthew ap David, whereby the tithes were to be paid to the abbot in return for an annual payment of 20s. to the rector.[33] Matthew ap David's successor evidently did not consider himself bound by this composition, for the abbot brought an action for recovery of tithes against him in 1533.[34] The suit was still in progress when Buildwas Abbey was dissolved in 1536 and in the following year it was decreed that the tithes of Harnage Grange should in future be paid to the rector.[35] In 1757 the rector successfully prosecuted John Windsor for detention of tithes.[36] Depositions in this suit show that the tithes were normally leased to the owners of the Grange, for £11 a year in 1684 and for £30 in 1739.[37]

The glebe was said to be worth about £12 a year in 1655[38] and £110 in 1851.[39] The latter was probably an under-estimate since in 1869 it was valued at £203 10s.[40] The greater part was let in 1842.[41] In 1612, apart from 2 closes adjoining the parsonage, the glebe consisted of scattered strips in the common fields of Cound and Harnage,[42] but these had been inclosed and partly consolidated by 1695.[43] In 1748 isolated parts of the glebe were transferred to the manorial estate and the rector received in exchange lands in Harnage adjoining the existing glebe.[44] In 1842 most of the glebe lay in a compact block on both sides of the road from the church to Harnage.[45] In 1866 some 42 a. in a detached portion near Morton was exchanged for 29 a. and three houses in Upper Cound, including the present Glebe Farm.[46]

The glebe comprised 77 a. in 1698,[47] 96 a. in 1849[48], and 83 a. in 1869.[49] All but 7 a. was sold in 1908.[50]

Corrodies paid to the rector of Cound by Acton Round, Chetton, and Easthope, which are last recorded in 1698,[51] had their origin in an early-13th-century grant by the lord of the manor of a portion of the corn tithes of 2 carucates in each of these parishes.[52] They had been commuted to annual pensions by 1535,[53] which produced £3 6s. 8d. in 1655[54] and £1 2s. 4d. in 1695.[55]

Apart from John de Cheyne, rector 1318–73,[56] no medieval rector of Cound seems to have held the living for more than 20 years.[57] Only one rector before the 17th century is known to have been a relative of the lords of the manor,[58] but at least 2 of the medieval rectors were employed on their affairs. In 1299 Thomas de Acton was given a year's non-residence licence while in the service of Maud Burnell,[59] and John Philip was a member of the lord's council in the early 16th century.[60] Among rectors appointed by the Crown in periods when the manor was in the king's hands, the most notable was the king's clerk, Silvester de Everdon, instituted in 1243,[61] who became Keeper of the Great Seal in the following year.[62] John Pratt, instituted in 1391,[63] was disturbed in 1397 by Joseph Scovill, presented by the Crown after the forfeiture of Richard, Earl of Arundel.[64] Scovill's appointment was confirmed in 1398[65] and in the following year Pratt was given a five-year non-residence licence.[66]

Most post-Reformation rectors have held the living for long periods. Of 13 rectors between 1553 and 1908 only 4 served for less than 20 years. The longest incumbencies were those of Ralph Shaw (1553–1609)[67] and Augustus Thursby Pelham (1864–1908).[68] Edward Cresset (rector 1737–55)[69] and Henry Thursby (rector 1839–64)[70] were also lords of the manor of Cound, while James Cresset (rector 1648–84)[71] and Augustus Thursby Pelham were close relatives of the lord. All rectors have been graduates since 1609[72] and include two bishops— Adam Ottley (rector 1684–1721),[73] Bishop of St. Davids 1713–23[74] and Edward Cresset, Bishop of Llandaff 1749–55.[75] William Adams (rector 1755–89)[76] was Master of Pembroke College, Oxford, and a friend of Dr. Johnson.[77]

[26] Lich. Dioc. Regy., glebe terrier, 1698; S.P.L., Deeds 12460; Salop. N. & Q. n.s. v. 32–33.
[27] Par. rec., tithe appt.   [28] Ibid.
[29] Lich. Dioc. Regy., glebe terriers, 1695, 1698.
[30] See p. 12.
[31] C 1/218/32.
[32] Ibid.
[33] E 126/28/East. 1761 no. 1; Valor. Eccl. (Rec. Com.), iii. 192.
[34] E 315/91 f. 63.
[35] Ibid.; S.C. 6/Hen. VIII/3006 m. 6.
[36] E 126/28/East. 1761 no. 1; S.R.O. 1005/44–60; S.P.L., Deeds 6421, 12460.
[37] Ibid.
[38] T.S.A.S. xlvii. 29.
[39] H.O. 129/359/1/3.
[40] Par. rec., par. bk. 1861–1952.
[41] Ibid., tithe appt.
[42] Lich. Dioc. Regy., glebe terrier, 1612.
[43] Ibid. 1695.
[44] Ibid. exchange, 1748.
[45] Par. rec., tithe appt.
[46] Ibid. exchange, 1866.
[47] Lich. Dioc. Regy., glebe terrier, 1698.
[48] Ibid. 1849.
[49] Par. rec., par. bk. 1861–1952.
[50] Cound estate title-deeds.

[51] Lich. Dioc. Regy., glebe terrier, 1698.
[52] Cal. Pat. 1266–72, 721.
[53] Valor Eccl. (Rec. Com.), iii. 209, 211, 216.
[54] T.S.A.S. xlvii. 29.
[55] Lich. Dioc. Regy., glebe terrier, 1695.
[56] Eyton, vi. 79; S.H.C. n.s. x (2), 204.
[57] Eyton, vi. 79; Bodl. MS. Blakeway 14, f. 68.
[58] John FitzAlan, rector c. 1262: Eyton, vi. 79.
[59] Ibid.
[60] S.R.O. 567 uncat., bailiff's acct. 1528.
[61] Cal. Pat. 1266–72, 719.
[62] Close R. 1242–7, 266.
[63] Eyton, vi. 79.
[64] Cal. Pat. 1396–9, 195, 207.   [65] Ibid. 276.
[66] Eyton, vi. 80.
[67] Lich. Dioc. Regy., B/v 1/15; T.S.A.S. 2nd ser. v. 257.
[68] S.P.R. Lich. ii (4), Cound intro. p. iv; mon. inscr. Cound church.
[69] T.S.A.S. 4th ser. v. 197, 202.
[70] S.P.R. Lich. ii (4), Cound intro. p. iv.
[71] L.J. x. 303b; S.P.R. Lich. ii (4), 185.
[72] Walker Revised, 308.
[73] S.P.R. Lich. ii (4), 185; T.S.A.S. 4th ser. v. 192.
[74] Handbk. of Brit. Chron. 280.
[75] Ibid. 277.
[76] T.S.A.S. 4th ser. v. 202; vi. 300.
[77] Ibid. vii. 99–107; D.N.B.

Until the 19th century the rectors were normally non-resident. In the 14th century 4 rectors received licences for non-residence[78] and one a dispensation to hold Cound in plurality with a distant living.[79] John de Morton, described as parson of Cound in 1341,[80] is the first recorded curate, and Richard Boydor was curate in 1552.[81] Ralph Shaw was non-resident in 1576, when the parsonage was on lease,[82] and his successor Richard Wood was also Vicar of Shawbury.[83] James Cresset, who probably rebuilt or enlarged the parsonage c. 1680,[84] is the only rector known to have lived continuously in the parish.[85] From 1701 until 1816 the living was served by a succession of curates, normally distinct from the curates of Cressage. J. F. Paschoud, curate from 1724[86] until his death in 1757,[87] was the only one to remain at Cound for more than a few years. E. H. Owen, the last of this line of curates, succeeded Thomas Goodinge as rector in 1816.[88] He was continously resident, employing no curates,[89] and by 1823 he had made considerable improvements to the parsonage,[90] which was described as an excellent house c. 1830.[91] Henry Thursby had a curate in 1843,[92] but they do not seem normally to have been employed until 1893, when the appointment of an assistant curate enabled the rector to spend the greater part of his remaining years in foreign travel.[93]

Communion was normally administered twice a year in the 17th century and 3 times a year by the early 18th century.[94] Between 1799 and 1843 it was administered 6 times a year,[95] but by 1889 weekly celebration was said to have been customary for many years.[96] The average number of communicants was 20 in 1823,[97] and from 30 to 40 in 1843.[98]

Two services were held on Sundays between 1799 and 1851.[99] At the latter date 109 adults attended the morning service and 79 in the afternoon.[1] Psalm-singers, first recorded in 1816,[2] were provided with an annual dinner between 1817 and 1839.[3] A small organ was placed in the chancel in 1865;[4] the present organ was installed in 1893.[5] A Mission Room was opened at the Fox Inn on Cound Moor c. 1899,[6] and by 1902 mission services were also held at Harnage.[7]

The church of *ST. PETER*[8] consists of a nave, chancel, south aisle, western tower, and a 19th-century north aisle. The earliest feature in the church is the font, which probably dates from the mid-12th century; the jambs of the tower arch may also be 12th-century work. The nave and chancel were built about a century later and retain a 13th-century chancel arch. A 13th-century priest's door-

way, formerly in the south wall of the chancel, was moved to the east end of the new vestry in 1891. There was formerly a triple-lancet east window in the chancel.[9] The south aisle was probably constructed at the same time as the nave and chancel, since its south door and arcade of 3 bays date from the earlier 13th century. It was remodelled in the 14th century, when the 3-light east window, containing fragments of medieval stained glass, the frame of the adjoining window on the south wall, and the piscina below were inserted. The small single-light west window may have originated as a 13th-century lancet; it is now square-headed, but has wide internal splays and a semicircular rear arch. Additional courses of stonework above the arcade of the south aisle indicate that the nave roof has been raised, probably when the aisle was remodelled. Both the nave and the south aisle have a trussed rafter roof, probably of 14th-century date, though much restored in 1843 and 1891. The Decorated west window suggests that the lower stage of the tower dates from the 14th century, but the upper stage was probably built in the early 16th century. It is supported by diagonal buttresses and is battlemented, with pinnacles and associated gargoyles. The south door, with an original escutcheon plate and handle, dates from the 15th century. The stone-built outer wall of the south porch is medieval and its roof timbers date from the 16th century.

A few minor alterations were made to the church between the 16th and the 19th century. One of the 3 windows in the former north wall of the nave was inserted in 1668,[10] and the south wall of the chancel had been repaired in brick before 1820. A ceiling was inserted below the nave roof in 1695.[11] By 1799 a vestry had been constructed behind the altar at the east end of the chancel.[12]

The north aisle was built at the expense of Frances Thursby in 1842, and the chancel was rebuilt by S. P. Smith in 1862. In 1891 a vestry was built to the north of the chancel and the plaster concealing the roof of the nave was removed. A wall-painting above the chancel arch, depicting the heavenly mansions and the interceding Virgin Mary, was uncovered at this time. Traces of it still remained in 1965.[13]

The church retains some of its ancient fittings. Medieval tiles in front of the communion table and on the floor of the tower escaped the reflooring of 1843, and there is a medieval parish chest. The chancel screen, on which the Decalogue, Creed,

78 Eyton, vi. 79–80.
79 *Cal. Papal Regs.* ii. 99.
80 E 179/166/9.
81 *T.S.A.S.* 2nd ser. xii. 98.
82 Lich. Dioc. Regy., B/v 1/10.
83 *Walker Revised*, 308.
84 Datestone.
85 E 134/27 Chas. II Mich./41.
86 S.R.O. 1250/1.
87 *S.P.R. Lich.* ii (4), 230.
88 *T.S.A.S.* 4th ser. vii. 165.
89 Visit. Archd. Salop. 1823.
90 Ibid.
91 W.S.L. 350/40/3.
92 Visit. Archd. Salop. 1843.
93 *Cound Par. Mag.* 1893–1905.
94 S.R.O. 790/1–2, 1250/1.
95 Visit. Archd. Salop. 1799, 1823, 1843.
96 Par. rec., par. bk. 1861–1952.
97 Visit. Archd. Salop. 1823.
98 Ibid. 1843.

99 Ibid. 1799, 1823, 1843; H.O. 129/359/13.
1 H.O. 129/359/13.
2 S.R.O. 790/6.
3 Ibid.
4 *Cound Par. Mag.* Nov. 1865.
5 Ibid. Nov. 1893.
6 Ibid. Mar., Nov. 1899.
7 Ibid. Mar. 1902.
8 The following description is based, except where otherwise stated, on Cranage, vi. 482–6; *Eng. Topog.* (Gent. Mag.), x. 56; S.P.L., MS. 372, i. 13–14; S.P.L., J. H. Smith collect. no. 60; S.P.L., T. F. Dukes sketches, no. 47; Visit. Archd. Salop. 1799, 1823, 1843; *Cound Par. Mag.* Sept. 1898.
9 Said to be in the churchyard, 1898: *Cound Par. Mag.* Sept. 1898.
10 S.R.O. 790/2.
11 Ibid. 1250/1.
12 Visit. Archd. Salop. 1799.
13 Ex inf. Mr. J. Salmon, Wrekin College.

and Lord's Prayer were painted some time after 1576,[14] stood at the east end of the chancel in 1823, but was removed to its present position at the tower entrance in 1843. The carved oak pulpit was made in 1633.[15] Box pews in the nave were repaired in 1843, but were replaced by the existing pews in 1891. A gallery was erected at the west end of the nave in 1765.[16] There were two galleries *c.* 1830,[17] but both were removed in 1843. Mural tablets in the chancel commemorating members of the Cresset family, 1678–1755 and one in the south aisle to John Dodd (d. 1774) are the only notable monuments. The base of a stone cross stands in the churchyard outside the south porch. The cross was rebuilt or repaired in 1638.[18]

The church had 3 bells in 1552[19] and at least 4 in the 17th century.[20] The bells were recast in 1726[21]; there were 6 of them in 1776, when they were recast by Abraham Rudhall of Gloucester.[22] The church clock is first recorded in 1625.[23] A new one was bought in 1642[24] and a contract for its maintenance was made in 1697.[25] A new clock was bought in 1869.[26] The plate consists of 3 silver chalices and patens, dated 1705, 1870, and 1918–20.[27] There was a silver chalice and a paten in 1552.[28] The registers are complete from 1608[29]; an earlier register, beginning in 1559, was missing by 1831.[30]

NONCONFORMITY

NONCONFORMITY. Lady Townsend, who then lived at the manor house, was presented as a recusant in 1620,[31] and there were 2 Roman Catholics in the parish in 1682.[32]

The Farmer family of The Leasowes were among the first Shropshire Quakers. John Farmer and his son James had become Quakers by 1656,[33] probably under the influence of John's daughter Elizabeth, who had been converted in 1653.[34] There were four Quakers in Cound in 1682.[35] There were no dissenters in the parish in 1799,[36] but there were said to be some Methodists at Cound Moor in 1823.[37]

SCHOOLS

SCHOOLS. Although one George Bennet, schoolmaster, was living in Cound in the early 17th century,[38] there is no evidence that a day school existed in the parish before the 19th century.

Twenty children attended a Sunday school in 1799.[39] This had closed by 1823,[40] but the rector opened another in 1832,[41] attended by 20 children in 1833[42] and 30 in 1843.[43] A parochial library had been formed by 1838.[44]

A private day school existing in 1818[45] had closed by 1823,[46] but there was said to be a day school and a private boarding school here in 1833.[47] A school built by Frances Thursby on glebe land opposite the church was opened in 1844.[48] This remained the property of the rectors of Cound and until 1879 was supported by the Revd. Henry Thursby Pelham.[49] School pence were levied on a graded scale in 1869, when they produced £10 a year,[50] and the school received a government grant from 1870 onwards.[51] School pence were abolished in 1892[52] and in the following year half the school's income was derived from a voluntary school rate,[53] introduced in 1879.[54] Forty children attended on the school's opening day in 1844[55] and there were 59 on the books in 1846,[56] but the average attendance in 1865 ranged from 27 to 44[57] and numbers did not rise markedly until after 1870, reaching a peak of 102 on the books in 1902.[58] In 1889 the infants were transferred to the Guildhall[59] and the school was enlarged in 1912.[60] There were only 16 children on the books when the school was closed in 1963.[61] The children now attend schools at Cressage and Cross Houses.

CHARITIES

CHARITIES. Thomas Langley (d. 1694) devised a rent-charge of £2 10s. a year, arising from Rag Field in Cound, for the provision of 12d. of white bread for the poor on every Sunday in the year except two.[62] Weekly distribution of bread was still being made in 1858, when the land from which the rent-charge was derived had become part of the manorial estate, but by 1862 the bread was distributed annually at Christmas.

By will of 1778 Richard Dutton bequeathed £50 for the benefit of poor householders in the parish, and in 1801 this sum, with a small addition, was invested in £100 stock. In 1830 the income (£3) was being paid equally to the poor widows of Cound and Cressage at Christmas. The Cressage moiety was refused by the incumbent in 1899 and has not since been paid.

[14] Lich. Dioc. Regy., B/v 1/10.
[15] S.R.O. 790/1.
[16] Ibid. 1250/1.
[17] W.S.L. 350/40/3.
[18] S.R.O. 790/1.
[19] *T.S.A.S.* 2nd ser. xii. 98–99, 319.
[20] S.R.O. 790/2.
[21] Birmingham Univ. Libr., Mytton's Ch. Notes, vol. ii, f. 76*b*.
[22] Ibid. 1250/1; Walters, *Ch. Bells Salop.*, 218–19.
[23] S.R.O. 790/1.
[24] Ibid.
[25] Ibid. 1250/1.
[26] *Kelly's Dir. Salop.* (1870).
[27] Arkwright and Bourne, *Ch. Plate Ludlow Archd.* 24–25.
[28] *T.S.A.S.* 2nd ser. xii. 98–99, 319.
[29] Printed to 1812 in *S.P.R. Lich.* ii (4), 149–277.
[30] Ibid. intro. p. iii.
[31] Lich. Dioc. Regy., B/v 1/39, 1/43.
[32] Ibid. 1/87.
[33] *T.S.A.S.* 4th ser. v. 296–7.
[34] For her autobiography see ibid. 303–7.
[35] Lich. Dioc. Regy., B/v 1/87.
[36] Visit. Archd. Salop. 1799.
[37] Ibid. 1823.
[38] *S.P.R. Lich.* ii (4), 155.
[39] Visit. Archd. Salop. 1799.

[40] Ibid. 1823.
[41] *Educ. Enquiry Abstract*, H.C. 62, p. 773 (1835), xlii.
[42] Ibid.
[43] Visit. Archd. Salop. 1843.
[44] Ibid. 1823.
[45] *Digest of Returns to Cttee. on Educ. of Poor*, H.C. 224 p. 750 (1819), ix (2).
[46] Visit. Archd. Salop. 1823.
[47] *Educ. Enquiry Abstract*, p. 773.
[48] S.P.L., Watton press-cuttings, v. 166; *Cound Par. Mag.* Oct. 1904.
[49] Par. rec., par. bk. 1862-1951.
[50] Ed. 7/102/70.
[51] *Cound Par. Mag.* Oct. 1904.
[52] Ibid. Oct. 1891, Oct. 1904.
[53] *Return of Schs.*, 1893 [C. 7529], p. 504, H.C. (1894), lxv.
[54] Par. rec., par. bk. 1862-1951.
[55] *Cound Par. Mag.* Dec. 1904.
[56] Nat. Soc. *Ch. School Returns*, 1846-7.
[57] *Cound Par. Mag.* Jan.–July 1865.
[58] Ibid. Dec. 1904. [59] Ibid.
[60] *Kelly's Dir. Salop.* (1913).
[61] Ex inf. S.C.C. Educ. Dept.
[62] What follows is based, except where otherwise stated, on *24th Rep. Com. Char.* H.C. 231, pp. 384–5 (1831), xi; statement of charities, 1861, in par. rec., par. bk. 1861-1952; Char. Com. files.

By will of 1768 Thomas Bishop left £20 for the purchase of bread for the poor on Sundays, and at some time before 1789 one Sicke left £60 for distribution among the poor. Both sums were invested c. 1789 in £102 stock, and in 1830 15s. was being spent yearly on bread and the rest doled out in cash. John Dodd of Harnage[63] left £20 by will in 1774 to provide bread for the poor. By 1830 the charity was distributed in an annual dole of £1.

Richard Cheese, by will of 1808, left £50, the interest on which was to be distributed in bread on Christmas Day. The capital was invested in 1828 in £66 stock. By 1858 the income was being distributed with that arising from Bishop's, Sicke's, and Dodd's charities.

In 1877 the Bishop, Sicke, and Cheese charities were fused and Dutton's charity fused with them a little later. During the century the stock was augmented by the addition of unspent balances, so that by 1961 the united charities were yielding £15 annually, most of which was doled out to poor widows.

A legacy to the poor left by Anne Eldred by will of 1671, from which the inhabitants of Cressage were said in the following year to be entitled to 20s. a year, had been lost before 1830.

CRESSAGE

CRESSAGE was a separate parish in the 12th century, but in the later Middle Ages its church was served by the rector of Cound. In 1545 it was accounted a chapelry of Cound, which it remained until created an ecclesiastical parish in 1864.[1] It had, however, maintained its own poor since the 17th century.[2]

The parish, which contains 1,823 a.,[3] lies on the south bank of the River Severn, 8 miles south-east of Shrewsbury, and on the main road from Shrewsbury to Much Wenlock. The township of Belswardine, formerly a detached part of Leighton parish, was transferred to Cressage in 1885.[4] The parish boundary, which follows the course of the Severn on the north and runs along one of its tributaries on the east, does not elsewhere make use of any natural features. In the south-east the boundary seems to have been fixed when Cressage and Harley woods were inclosed c. 1519.[5] The boundary with Cound on the south-west was adjusted c. 1527,[6] but was not finally determined until c. 1616.[7]

The greater part of the parish is drained by streams flowing north-eastwards from the Kenley ridge towards the Severn. The principal stream, which flows through the village, was formerly known as Plocks Brook.[8] The village stands at 145 feet on a terrace overlooking the alluvial flood-plain of the Severn, which covers the area north of the Shrewsbury road. Over the remainder of the parish the land rises gently to the 400-foot contour at the foot of the Kenley ridge. There are extensive deposits of sand and gravel alongside the three roads running southwards from the village towards Harley, Kenley, and Harnage Grange, but the greater part of the parish south of the Shrewsbury road is boulder clay.

Cressage lay within the Long Forest until the later 13th century.[9] The manor contained woodland for 200 swine in 1086,[10] and during the Middle Ages woodland seems to have extended over the south-west quarter of the parish, bounded on the north by Plocks Brook.[11] The principal wood was the Hay, along the south-western boundary of the parish, where common rights were granted in 1232 to Buildwas Abbey for its tenants at Harnage Grange.[12] It was inclosed by the lord of the manor in 1527,[13] but the hedges were pulled up by the Abbot of Buildwas in 1530.[14] Woodland here was cleared c. 1616, when allotments in the Hay were granted to the tenants in lieu of common rights.[15] Woodland in the manorial estate was said to have been severely damaged during the Civil War.[16] By 1746 there were 147 a. of woodland in the manorial estate[17] and only 98 a. in the parish by 1849,[18] but Jubilee, Butler's, and Tudor's Plantations were planted in the later 19th century.[19] There were 149 a. of woodland on the manorial estate in 1920.[20] The present Hayes Coppice, with Park Coppice and Lord's Coppice on the southern boundary, are surviving remnants of ancient woodland.

The parish contained several oak-trees with distinctive names, apart from Christ's Oak, which gave the village its name.[21] The Lady Oak, north of the Shrewsbury road, is still standing, but the sites of Gospel Oak and Curst Oak[22] are not known.

The former common fields[23] lay on sand and gravel in the north and east of the parish. Hurst field, also called the West Field or Lady Oak Field, lay to the south of the Shrewsbury road. Hay Field, or the Field towards Morton, ran towards the Hay on the north of the Harnage road. Lee Field, or the Field towards Harley, lay on both sides of the main road south of the village. The common fields, still

[63] For this family see pp. 65–66.

[1] See p. 77. This article was written in 1962 and revised in 1964.
[2] Bodl. MS. Blakeway 8, f. 476.
[3] O.S. *Area Bk.* (1882). The following topographical description is based, except where otherwise stated, on O.S. Maps 6″ Salop. 42, 50 (1st and later edns.); O.S. Maps 1/25,000, SJ 50, SJ 60 (1959); Rocque, *Map of Salop.* (1752); Baugh, *Map of Salop.* (1808); B.M. O.S. 2″ orig. drawings, sheet 207 (1817); Geol. Survey Map (drift), sheet 152 (1932); S.R.O. 1313/127, tithe appt. 1849, and map, 1842.
[4] Local Government Bd. Order 17485.
[5] Sta. Cha. 2/30/51.
[6] Ibid. 2/27/182.
[7] C 142/475/106; C 142/448/109.
[8] Lich. Dioc. Regy., Cound glebe terrier, 1612.

[9] Eyton, vi. 345.
[10] *V.C.H. Salop.* i. 329.
[11] Barnard MSS., Raby Castle, box 4, bdle. 9, nos. 1, 5, 18, 33; *Cal. Chart. R.* 1226–57, 171; S.P.L., Deeds 6303.
[12] *Cal. Chart. R.* 1226–57, 171.
[13] Sta. Cha. 2/27/182.   [14] Ibid.
[15] C 142/475/105; C 142/448/109.
[16] *T.S.A.S.* 2nd ser. xii. 26.
[17] S.R.O. 168/2.
[18] Ibid. 1313/127.
[19] Uppington estate office, terrier, c. 1920.
[20] Ibid.
[21] Eyton, vi. 308–9.
[22] C 139/67/64; *Salop. N. & Q.* v. 306.
[23] Description based on C 139/67/64; Barnard MSS., Raby Castle, box 4, bdle. 9, no. 7; ibid., box 12, bdle. 22; Lich. Dioc. Regy., Cound glebe terrier, 1612.

open in 1612,[24] seem to have been inclosed by the end of the 17th century.[25] In 1746 the only uninclosed lands in the parish were two common meadows and a 30-acre common.[26] The location and date of inclosure of this common are not known.

The Shrewsbury road formerly ran to the north of the present road, roughly on the line of the railway.[27] It was turnpiked in 1752[28] and was diverted to its present course c. 1861, when the Severn Valley Railway was constructed.[29] A toll-house at the west end of the village was sold to the lord of the manor in 1875.[30] On the road to Eaton Constantine a ferry was used to transport passengers across the Severn until 1800[31] when a wooden bridge was built to designs by Thomas Telford.[32] Tolls were introduced in 1799 and abolished in 1912, when the bridge was bought by the County Council.[33] It was rebuilt in ferro-concrete in 1914.[34] The Severn Valley Railway, which runs across the parish, was opened in 1862. Cressage Station, opened in the same year, was closed in 1963.[35]

The small green in the centre of the village is the traditional site of Christ's Oak. A stone cross is said to have stood here in the Middle Ages.[36] By the 18th century this had been replaced by a circular, thatched, wooden structure, known as the Market Cross.[37] This was demolished in the early 19th century,[38] and the War Memorial now stands on its site. The Old Hall, north-east of the green, is a timber-framed house of 17th-century date, which stands on the site of the medieval manor-house.[39] It overlooks a ford across the Severn, and occupies the bailey of an earlier motte-and-bailey castle.[40] The motte was partially destroyed when the railway was constructed.[41] The former church of St. Samson lay some 300 yards west of the green, near the Shrewsbury road.[42]

Until the 17th century the village lay along the main road, north of the present church, and at the northern end of the roads to Harnage and Kenley. Most of the houses here are timber-framed, but many have been enlarged or cased in brick. Among the larger houses are the Old Porch House and the Eagles Inn. Both were originally farm-houses, and the former remained one until the later 19th century,[43] but the 'Eagles' had become an alehouse by 1746,[44] and is first so named in 1823.[45] The Old Crown House, at the head of the Kenley road, was probably also a farm-house in the 17th century, but was a beer-shop by 1849.[46] Oak Tree Farm, now the only farm-house in the village, is a brick house of late-19th-century date, standing on the site of two timber-framed houses.[47] The mill, in use until the mid-18th century,[48] stood on Plocks Brook, near the Kenley road, where the mill-dam remains. One of the isolated cottages on this road, to the south of the mill, is timber-framed and probably dates from the 17th century, but the others are stone-built and are probably the product of squatter settlement in the 18th century.[49]

A row of cottages to the east of the Wenlock road, south of the present church, were built in 1750,[50] probably by the Mullard family, whose smithy stood nearby.[51] Later known as Rotten Row, these cottages were demolished c. 1913.[52] Of the isolated farmsteads to the south of the parish, Cressage House, Park Cottage, and Cressage Farm date from the late 19th century, but New Buildings Farm was already standing in 1849.[53] In the village itself the present church was built in 1841[54] and the former school opposite in 1858.[55] A Methodist chapel was built near Rotten Row in 1854,[56] but has since been converted into a cottage. Apart from two 19th-century cottages, there were no houses on the Sheinton road until after 1919, when a small number of Council houses were built here.[57] This housing estate has grown considerably since 1945, and comprised 59 houses and 8 flats in 1962.[58]

There were said to be 33 households in Cressage in 1603.[59] The population, which numbered 275 in 1801,[60] fluctuated between 250 and 300 during the 19th century, but rose to 356 in 1861 during the construction of the railway.[61] It fell from 328 in 1911 to 264 in 1931,[62] but the erection of Council houses has led to an increase in population since that date. There were 454 inhabitants in 1961.[63]

A Friendly Society, formed in 1791, was affiliated to the Shrewsbury General Provident Society before 1815.[64]

MANOR. Roger, Earl of Shrewsbury, was overlord of *CRESSAGE* manor in 1086.[65] Hugh de Lacy was overlord by 1180,[66] and in 1253 the manor was held of Maud de Lacy, wife of Geoffrey de Geneville,[67] whose grand-daughter Joan had carried it to her husband Roger Mortimer, Earl of March, by

[24] Lich. Dioc. Regy., Cound glebe terrier, 1612.
[25] Ibid. n.d., c. 1680, 1695.
[26] S.R.O. 168/2.
[27] Ibid. 1313/127.
[28] Shrewsbury–Wenlock road Act, 25 Geo. II, c. 49 (priv. act).
[29] Q. Sess., dep. plans 348–9; T. Wright, *Uriconium* (1872), 47.
[30] Barnard MSS., Raby Castle, press 14, no. 87.
[31] S.R.O. 168/2.
[32] Ibid. 571 uncat., Bridge Trustees' accts. 1801–99. See also plate facing p. 83.
[33] Cressage Bridge Act, 39 Geo. III, c. 28 (local and personal act); S.R.O. 571 uncat., contract for sale, 1912.
[34] S.R.O. 571 uncat., specification, 1914.
[35] Ex inf. Brit. Trans. Rec.
[36] Bodl. MS. Blakeway 10, f. 348.
[37] Ibid.
[38] Ibid.
[39] See p. 75.
[40] Described as a moated site, with tumulus, in *V.C.H. Salop.* i. 403, 411, but existing remains clearly indicate a motte-and-bailey.
[41] Wright, *Uriconium*, 47.
[42] Its site is now marked by an inscribed stone.
[43] Barnard MSS., Raby Castle, press 14, no. 103.
[44] S.R.O. 168/2.
[45] Q. Sess., alehouse regs.
[46] S.R.O. 1313/127.
[47] Notes *penes* Miss E. M. Jones, Cressage.
[48] S.R.O. 168/2.
[49] Ibid. 1011 uncat., ct. r. 1786 records a new house in Wood Lane.
[50] Notes and photograph *penes* Miss E. M. Jones.
[51] S.R.O. 1313/127.
[52] Ex inf. Miss E. M. Jones.
[53] S.R.O. 1313/127.
[54] S.P.L., Watton press-cuttings, iv. 63–65.
[55] Ed. 7/102/71.
[56] *Cassey's Dir. Salop.* (1871); photograph *penes* Miss E. M. Jones.
[57] Ex inf. Atcham R.D.C.
[58] Ibid.
[59] B.M. Harl. MS. 594, f. 160.
[60] *Census*, 1801.
[61] Ibid. 1811–1911.
[62] Ibid. 1911–31.
[63] Ibid. 1961.
[64] Q. Sess., Index to Friendly Soc. rules.
[65] *V.C.H. Salop.* i. 329.
[66] Eyton, vi. 311.
[67] Barnard MSS., Raby Castle, box 4, bdle. 9, no. 14a; *Rot. Hund.* (Rec. Com.), ii. 62; *Feud. Aids*, iv. 215.

1306.[68] The manor continued to be held of the Earldom of March,[69] which became Crown land after 1461.[70] The overlordship is last recorded in 1623.[71]

The manor was held by Edric before 1066 and in 1086 by Ralph Peverel.[72] The latter was succeeded by his son, William Peverel of Essex, but the manor had been forfeited to the Crown by 1130.[73] Shortly after 1135 it was held by William Peverel of Nottingham,[74] but was not among his estates when they were forfeited in 1154.[75] By 1180 the manor had passed to Amaury de Lacy, a relative of the overlord.[76] He died before 1186[77] and the manor passed from father to son until 1306, the following being lords: Gilbert de Lacy, c. 1187–1233;[78] Gilbert, 1233–49;[79] Adam, 1249–c. 1292;[80] Amaury, c. 1292–c. 1306.[81] Adam de Lacy was still under age on the death of his father Gilbert in 1249.[82] A third of the manor was held in dower by his mother Agnes[83] and the remainder was leased by the overlord to the Abbot of Buildwas in 1253.[84] Adam was in occupation by 1267[85] and the Abbot surrendered his lease in 1271.[86] Amaury de Lacy, who seems never to have reached full age,[87] was succeeded by his brother John, who died in 1335.[88] The manor then passed to John's son Gilbert,[89] who was still living in 1341.[90] By 1347 it was held by Walter de Baskerville and his wife Elizabeth, daughter of Gilbert de Lacy.[91] Walter was dead by 1360, when Elizabeth had married John de Delves.[92] He held the manor jointly with her, and after her death in 1363[93] remained lord until his death in 1369.[94] Isabel, the second wife of John de Delves, held the manor until 1371,[95] when John de Baskerville, son of Walter de Baskerville and Elizabeth, became lord on coming of age.[96] John de Baskerville died in 1374,[97] and after the death of his son John while still a minor in 1383[98] the manor passed to the latter's cousin Thomas de Foulehurst.[99] It descended from father to son until 1436, the following being lords: Thomas (I), 1383–1402;[1] Thomas (II), 1402

–16;[2] John, 1416–36.[3] On the death of John de Foulehurst in 1436 the manor passed to his brother William, who died in 1439.[4] It then reverted to Richard, Duke of York, as overlord.[5] In 1448 he granted the manor to William Burley of Broncroft,[6] whose sister Isabel, as widow of Thomas de Foulehurst (II), was then holding a third of the manor in dower.[7] William Burley died in 1458[8] and in 1465 his widow Margaret conveyed the manor to her son-in-law Thomas Littleton.[9] It passed from father to son until 1559, the following being lords: Thomas, 1465–81;[10] William, 1481–1508;[11] John, 1508–32;[12] John, 1532–59.[13] In 1559 John Littleton sold it to Sir Richard Newport,[14] whose descendants held it until 1734,[15] the following being lords: Richard, 1559–70;[16] Francis, 1570–1623; Richard, 1623–50; Francis, 1650–1708; Richard, 1708–23; Henry, 1723–34.

On the death of Henry Newport, Earl of Bradford, in 1734,[17] the manor passed to his brother and heir Thomas, an imbecile, who died in 1762.[18] It then passed to John Newport, an illegitimate son of Henry, Earl of Bradford, by his mistress Mrs. Anne Smyth.[19] John Newport, on whom part of the Bradford estates had been settled in 1734,[20] was a lunatic, and the manor was held by his trustees until his death in 1783,[21] when he was succeeded by the trustee, Sir William Pulteney.[22] On the latter's death in 1805 the manor passed to William, Earl of Darlington,[23] and has since been held by his descendants,[24] the following being lords: William, Earl of Darlington, 1805–42; Henry, Duke of Cleveland, 1842–64; William, Duke of Cleveland, 1864; Harry, Duke of Cleveland, 1864–91; Henry, Lord Barnard, 1891–1918; Christopher, Lord Barnard, from 1918.

The Old Hall, formerly the manor-house, stands on the site of a motte-and-bailey castle.[25] The manor-house, which is first mentioned in 1369,[26] included a chapel in 1433.[27] It was continuously let to tenants after 1559,[28] and was sold in 1824.[29] The earlier part of the house, which is timber-framed and

---

[68] *Complete Peerage*, viii. 441.
[69] *Cal. Inq. p.m.* vi, p. 209; ibid. x, p. 255; ibid. xiv, p. 350.
[70] *Complete Peerage*, xii (2), 910.
[71] C 142/402/146.
[72] *V.C.H. Salop.* i. 329.
[73] Eyton, vi. 310.
[74] B.M. Cott. MS. Tib. E. vi, f. 138; Eyton, vi. 310.
[75] Eyton, vi. 310.
[76] Ibid. 311.
[77] *Pipe R.* 1186 (P.R.S. xxxvi), 57.
[78] Eyton, vi. 312.
[79] Ibid.
[80] Ibid. 313.
[81] Barnard MSS., Raby Castle, box 4, bdle. 9, no. 16.
[82] Eyton, vi. 312.
[83] Ibid.
[84] Barnard MSS., Raby Castle, box 4, bdle. 9, no. 14a.
[85] Ibid., no. 13.
[86] S.P.L., Deeds 6302.
[87] Eyton, vi. 314.
[88] *Cal. Inq. p.m.* vi, p. 209.
[89] Ibid.
[90] Ibid. viii, p. 215.
[91] *Cal. Pat.* 1345–8, 326.
[92] *Cal. Inq. p.m.* xiv, p. 350.
[93] *Cal. Fine R.* 1356–69, 253.
[94] C 135/208/15.
[95] *Cal. Fine R.* 1369–77, 20.
[96] *Cal. Close,* 1369–74, 214.
[97] *Cal. Inq. p.m.* xiv, p. 94.
[98] C 136/24/11.
[99] Ibid.
[1] C 137/40/56; *Cal. Pat.* 1401–5, 171.

[2] C 138/25/22.
[3] C 139/68/18.
[4] C 139/100/54.
[5] Ibid.; *Cal. Close,* 1435–41, 401.
[6] I. H. Jeayes, *Charters and Muniments of the Littleton Family* (1893), 89.
[7] C 139/67/64.
[8] *Cal. Fine R.* 1452–61, 211.
[9] Barnard MSS., Raby Castle, box 4, bdle. 9, no. 30.
[10] C 140/81/55.
[11] *Cal. Inq. p.m. Hen. VII,* iii. p. 331.
[12] C 142/54/137.
[13] C.P. 25(2)/200/1 Eliz. I Hil.
[14] Ibid.
[15] For pedigree see S.P.L., MS. 4645, p. 31; *Complete Peerage,* ii. 274–5; ibid. ix. 554–5.
[16] C 142/158/38.
[17] *Complete Peerage,* ii. 275.
[18] Barnard MSS., Raby Castle, receiver's accts. 1768–81.
[19] S. Garbet, *The History of Wem* (Wem, 1818), 107.
[20] *Complete Peerage,* ii. 275.
[21] T. F. Dukes, *Antiquities of Shropshire* (Shrewsbury 1844), 243.
[22] Ibid.
[23] Ibid.
[24] For pedigree see *Complete Peerage,* i. 426–7; ibid. ii. 284–5, 286.
[25] See p. 74.
[26] C 135/208/15.
[27] C 139/67/64.
[28] Barnard MSS., Raby Castle, box 12, bdle. 21; ibid. receiver's accts. 1774–81; E 179/255/35 m. 75d; *Hearth Tax, 1672,* 130; S.R.O. 168/2.
[29] Barnard MSS., Raby Castle, press 13, no. 20.

dates from the mid-17th century, is H-shaped, with projecting wings to the north and south. This retains, to the east, its original roof of stone slates. The interior was considerably altered in the early 19th century. Minor additions were later made to the west front, and a north wing was added by P. G. Baldwin, c. 1923.[30]

ECONOMIC HISTORY. The manor, which was worth £6 in 1066, had increased in value to £10 by 1086, when it was assessed at 1½ hide and had land for 7 ploughs.[31] In 1086 there were 3 ploughs, with 8 serfs, on the demesne,[32] which comprised two carucates in 1369.[33] The demesne seems still to have been in hand in 1649, when it was said to be worth £100 a year.[34]

The growth of the manorial estate can be largely accounted for by the clearance of woodland in the south of the parish.[35] A small freehold belonging to the Castle family was bought in 1586.[36] The manorial estate comprised 1,502 a. in 1746,[37] but was intermixed with the properties of other freeholders until it was consolidated by means of three exchanges between 1808 and 1817.[38] The manor house and 77 a. in the parish were exchanged for lands in other parishes in 1813[39] and 1824,[40] and in 1849 the estate contained 1,414 a.[41] A further 95 a. were added to the estate in the later 19th century,[42] but New Buildings Farm, which contained 228 a. in 1849,[43] had been sold to the Belswardine estate by 1920.[44] By 1945 the manorial estate had been reduced to 1,211 a. and several properties have since been sold.[45]

A few ancient freehold estates survived until the later 19th century. There were 8 freeholders in the parish in 1849, but only 3 of these owned much more than house property.[46] The estate of William Morris, which then contained 151 a.,[47] had belonged to the Pearce family from the 16th century until 1795.[48] The Farmer family of Cound Leasowes Farm owned 88 a. in Cressage in 1849,[49] which had belonged to the Rockes of Shrewsbury by 1701 and until 1773, and was bought by James Farmer in 1806.[50] The only other substantial freehold estate was

an outlying portion of the Belswardine estate in the south-east of the parish, acquired from the manorial estate in 1813,[51] which contained 66 a. in 1849.[52]

The tenantry were already numerous in 1086, when there were 7 villeins, 11 bordars, and 4 cottars, in addition to the 8 serfs on the demesne.[53] Their rents produced £8 a year in 1369[54] and £119 a year c. 1646.[55] Leases for lives, which were already in use here in the early 14th century, had ceased to be the principal form of tenure by 1746.[56] At that date 465 a. were held by 8 leaseholders for lives, 800 a. by 8 tenants-at-will, and 231 a. by 4 other tenants.[57] By 1774 only 165 a. were held by the 3 tenants on long leases and the rest of the estate was held at will.[58] Transition to large farms took place at the same time. In 1746 four farms of over 100 a. occupied 705 a. and there were 16 smaller holdings,[59] but by 1849 1,182 a. of the manorial estate lay in 5 large farms.[60] In 1945 the 3 large farms occupied 931 a. and there were only 4 smaller tenants.[61] An 11-acre field on the Kenley road had been converted into allotments by 1849,[62] but they fell into disuse soon after 1918.[63]

The proportion of arable land seems to have risen in the later 18th century. The manorial estate contained only 450 a. arable in 1746,[64] but there were 838 a. arable in the parish by c. 1829.[65] The estimate of 579 a. arable, given in 1801, is probably unreliable.[66] In 1849 the parish contained 787 a. of arable land and 120 a. of temporary pasture,[67] but by 1945 there were only 460 a. arable on the manorial estate.[68] The principal crops in 1801 were said to be wheat and barley.[69]

Cressage mill is first recorded shortly after 1249, when it was let for 2½ marks a year.[70] It was still working in 1746,[71] but had been burnt down by 1774 and was not rebuilt.[72] A fishery, worth 8s. in 1086,[73] was still in use in 1575, when there was a weir in the Severn.[74]

A smithy, first recorded in 1590,[75] was in 1657 held by John Mullard,[76] whose descendants were still blacksmiths in Cressage in 1937.[77] The village had two smithies, both held by members of the Mullard family, in the later 19th century.[78] In 1851

[30] Datestone on stable.
[31] V.C.H. Salop. i. 329.
[32] Ibid.
[33] C 135/208/15.
[34] T.S.A.S. 2nd ser. xii. 19.
[35] E 32/143–4; Barnard MSS., Raby Castle, box 4, bdle. 9, nos. 18a–b, 33; Sta. Cha. 2/27/182; ibid. 2/30/51; C 142/475/106.
[36] Barnard MSS., Raby Castle, box 1, bdle. 24, no. 9; ibid. bdle. 25b, no. 1.
[37] S.R.O. 168/2.
[38] Barnard MSS., Raby Castle, press 13, nos. 7, 10, 13.
[39] Q. Sess., inclosure awards, 32.
[40] Barnard MSS., Raby Castle, press 13, no. 20.
[41] S.R.O. 1313/127.
[42] Barnard MSS., Raby Castle, press 14, nos. 81, 88, 100. 103.
[43] S.R.O. 1313/127.
[44] Uppington estate office, terrier, c. 1920.
[45] Ibid.
[46] S.R.O. 1313/127.
[47] Ibid.
[48] C 142/475/106; N.L.W., Wynnstay (1952) X 24–8; Barnard MSS., Raby Castle, press 14, no. 81.
[49] S.R.O. 1313/127.
[50] Barnard MSS., Raby Castle, press 13, no. 13.
[51] Q. Sess., inclosure awards, 32.
[52] S.R.O. 1313/127.
[53] V.C.H. Salop. i. 329.

[54] C 135/208/15.
[55] T.S.A.S. 2nd ser. xii. 19.
[56] S.R.O. 168/2.
[57] Ibid.
[58] Ibid.; Barnard MSS., Raby Castle, receiver's accts. 1774–81.
[59] S.R.O. 168/2.
[60] Ibid. 1313/127.
[61] Uppington estate office, terrier, c. 1920.
[62] S.R.O. 1313/127.
[63] Ex inf. Miss E. M. Jones.
[64] S.R.O. 168/2.
[65] Bodl. MS. Blakeway 10, f. 323.
[66] H.O. 67/14/77.
[67] S.R.O. 1313/127.
[68] Uppington estate office, terrier, c. 1920.
[69] H.O. 67/14/77.
[70] Barnard MSS., Raby Castle, box 4, bdle. 9, no. 10.
[71] S.R.O. 168/2.
[72] Ibid.; Barnard MSS., Raby Castle, receiver's accts. 1774–81.
[73] V.C.H. Salop. i. 329.
[74] Hist. MSS. Com. 10th Rep. App. IV, 443–4.
[75] N.L.W., Pitchford Hall uncat., return of alehouses, 1590.
[76] S.P.R. Lich. ii (4), 173.
[77] Kelly's Dir. Salop. (1937).
[78] S.R.O. 1313/127; Bagshaw's Dir. Salop. (1851); Kelly's Dir. Salop. (1885–95).

there were in addition, a tailor, a shoe-maker, a joiner, and a saddler.[79] A wheelwright is recorded in 1856.[80] The blacksmith and wheelwright were still in business in 1941.[81]

LOCAL GOVERNMENT. There are a few draft manor court rolls, 1750–96,[82] and court rolls, 1774–8[83] and 1811–43.[84] Great courts were held twice a year in the 13th[85] and 14th centuries,[86] and the court's jurisdiction included the assize of bread and ale.[87]

The parish records include Easter vestry minutes from 1841. Though a chapelry of Cound, there were two churchwardens in 1552,[88] and Cressage was maintaining its own poor by the later 17th century.[89] In 1694 £6 12s. was spent on poor relief,[90] but poor rates had risen to £63 a year by 1776.[91] Cressage was a member of the Atcham Poor Law Union, formed in 1792.[92] Rates had risen to £118 by 1803[93] and reached a peak of £260 in 1818,[94] but rarely exceeded £130 after this date.[95]

CHURCH. That Christianity came early to Cressage is suggested by the name of the parish—'Cristesac', or Christ's Oak is the earliest known form[96]—and by the dedication of its church to the Celtic saint St. Samson of Dol (c. 485–565).[97] It is unlikely that such a dedication would have been made after the end of the 7th century.

The church is first recorded shortly after 1135, when William Peverel granted it to Hatfield Peverel Priory (Ess.)[98] The prior was alleged to have granted a life-lease of the church to the Rector of Cound in the 15th or early 16th century,[99] and later Rectors of Cound retained it as a chapelry, despite an effort made by a later prior to regain possession.[1] In 1545 the Rector of Cound was ordered to provide a resident curate at Cressage,[2] but the chapel was seized by the Crown as concealed land in 1578,[3] and was granted to John Farnham.[4] It was bought in the following year by William Taylor of Harley,[5] who had sold it to Rowland Lacon by 1585.[6] In 1595 Lacon sold the chapel to Rowland Hayward, lord of

Cound manor and patron of the church.[7] The advowson of Cressage was retained by the lords of Cound manor when it was constituted an ecclesiastical parish in 1864,[8] and was held in 1963 by Mrs. Fitzroy Chapman, the then representative of the Thursby Pelham family.[9]

The tithes and glebe, which had been included in the grant of c. 1135,[10] followed the same course as the advowson in the 16th century and were among the emoluments of the Rector of Cound in 1612,[11] but they retained their separate identity.[12] The tithes, which were worth £44 a year in 1655,[13] were commuted for a rent-charge of £209 in 1849.[14] The glebe was worth £6 a year in 1655.[15] It comprised 15 a. in 1698[16] and 23 a. in 1849.[17] The former parsonage stood to the north of the Shrewsbury road, near the west bank of Plocks Brook. It was not occupied by the curate in 1612[18] and was demolished between 1799 and 1823.[19] The so-called tithe barn, perhaps the barn recorded in 1612,[20] is, however, still standing. The present parsonage was built in 1912.[21]

Apart from a reference to a priest in 1232[22] and a late-16th-century tradition that the living was served by Buildwas Abbey in the later Middle Ages,[23] nothing is known of the medieval clergy of Cressage. After 1545 the curate was always resident and normally distinct from the curates employed by the Rectors of Cound in their own parish.[24] Samuel Smith (curate 1638–55) was an eminent Presbyterian divine,[25] who attracted 'a full congregation of parishioners and others well-affected out of other parishes' to the chapel.[26] The curate received a salary of £35 a year in 1799[27] and £50 in 1823.[28] Frederick Burd, curate from 1853, became Vicar of Cressage in 1864.[29]

In 1545 the curate was instructed to administer the sacraments, but the inhabitants of Cressage were ordered to attend Cound church 'to hear all sermons and preachings'.[30] No pews were reserved for them at Cound in 1655,[31] but they were responsible for the repair of a section of the churchyard wall there in 1678[32] and 1799.[33] Communion was administered

[79] Bagshaw's Dir. Salop. (1851).
[80] Kelly's Dir. Salop. (1856).
[81] Ibid. (1941).
[82] S.R.O. 1011 uncat.   [83] Ibid.
[84] S.R.O. 248/23–26.
[85] Eyton, vi. 313.
[86] S.P.L., Deeds 6303.
[87] Eyton, vi. 313.
[88] T.S.A.S. 2nd ser. xii. 99.
[89] Bodl. MS. Blakeway 8, f. 476.   [90] Ibid.
[91] Rep. Cttee. on Overseers' Returns, 1777, p. 442, H.C. (1st ser. ix, reprinted 1803).
[92] Atcham Union Act, 32 Geo. III, c. 95 (priv. act).
[93] Poor Law Abstract, 1803, H.C. 175, pp. 416–17 (1803–4), xiii.
[94] Rep. Cttee. on Poor Rate Returns, 1822, Suppl. App. H.C. 556, p. 141 (1822), v.
[95] Ibid. 1825, H.C. 334, p. 177 (1825), iv; Acct. of Money Expended on Poor, 1825–9, H.C. 83, p. 390 (1830–1), xi; ibid. 1830–4, H.C. 444, p. 344 (1835), xlvii.
[96] V.C.H. Salop. i. 329.
[97] T.S.A.S. 2nd ser. vi. 120; Welsh D.N.B.
[98] B.M. Cott. MS. Tib. E vi, f. 138.
[99] E 134/20 Eliz. I Hil./6.
[1] C 1/741/31.
[2] S.R.O. 1/66.
[3] E 134/20 Eliz. I Hil./6.
[4] C 66/1157 m. 16.
[5] S.P.L., MS. 2, f. 145.
[6] Ibid. f. 143.   [7] Ibid.
[8] Lond. Gaz. 1864, p. 3050.

[9] Heref. Dioc. Year Bk. (1963).
[10] B.M. Cott. MS. Tib. E vi, f. 138.
[11] Lich. Dioc. Regy., Cound glebe terrier, 1612.
[12] Ibid. 1612–1849.
[13] T.S.A.S. xlvii. 29.
[14] S.R.O. 1313/127.
[15] T.S.A.S. xlvii. 29.
[16] Lich. Dioc. Regy., Cound glebe terrier, 1698.
[17] S.R.O. 1313/127.
[18] Lich. Dioc. Regy., Cound glebe terrier, 1612.
[19] Visit. Archd. Salop. 1799, 1823.
[20] Lich. Dioc. Regy., Cound glebe terrier, 1612. cf. S.R.O. 1313/127.
[21] Kelly's Dir. Salop. (1917); Heref. Dioc. Regy., reg. 1902–19, pp. 481–2.
[22] Cal. Chart. R. 1226–57, 171.
[23] E 134/20 Eliz. I Hil./6.
[24] S.R.O. 1/66; Lich. Dioc. Regy., bishop's transcripts; S.P.R. Lich. ii (2), ii (4) passim; Visit. Archd. Salop. 1799, 1823, 1843.
[25] D.N.B.
[26] T.S.A.S. xlvii. 29.
[27] Visit. Archd. Salop. 1799.
[28] Ibid. 1823. cf. Rep. Com. Eccl. Revenues [67] pp. 470–1, H.C. (1835), xxii.
[29] S.P.R. Lich. ii (2), Cressage intro. p. iii.
[30] S.R.O. 1/66.
[31] T.S.A.S. xlvii. 29.
[32] Cound par. rec., agreement for repair of churchyard wall, 1678.
[33] Visit. Archd. Salop. 1799.

4 times a year in 1799 and 1823[34] and 6 times a year in 1847.[35] There was said to be an average of 10 communicants in 1823[36] and 25 in 1843.[37] Only one service was held on Sundays in 1799 and 1823,[38] but by 1843 two services were normally held.[39] In 1851 110 persons attended morning service and 60 in the evening.[40]

The church of *ST. SAMSON*, demolished in 1840, consisted of a nave and a chancel, with a bell-turret at the west end and a timber-framed porch on the south wall of the nave.[41] The nave had a square-headed two-light west window and a three-light window with Decorated tracery on the south wall. Its pointed south door was probably of 13th-century date. The east window of the chancel, also Decorated, was of 3 lights, with Geometrical tracery above, and there was a single round-headed window in the south wall.

The most striking internal feature was the massive round chancel arch, with square hagioscopes on either side. The rood screen was still in place in the early 19th century,[42] and until 1840 there were open benches with carved finials. The round Norman font was arcaded and decorated above with conventional foliage.[43] A gallery was erected at the west end in 1792,[44] and in 1838 the church was re-roofed and a pointed window was inserted in the south wall of the nave.[45] The porch was rebuilt in brick at about this time.[46] Although expenditure on these alterations had still not been met in 1842,[47] an appeal for subscriptions for building the new church was issued in 1839.[48]

CHRISTCHURCH, Cressage, was built of Grinshill stone in the Early English style to designs by Edward Haycock in 1841.[49] It consists of a nave and shallow altar recess and has a narrow tower at the west end. It has a triple-lancet east window, containing roundels of stained glass in Flemish style by David Evans of Shrewsbury, given by the Revd. Richard Scott. There are 5 lancet windows on each side of the nave and there is an organ gallery, set on cast iron pillars, at the west end. Very few relics of the old church found their way to the new. Carved 17th-century oak wainscot from St. Samson's was used to panel the nave walls, and some medieval tiles were set below the communion rails.

The octagonal pulpit is made up of reused 16th- and 17th-century panelling and the inscription on it, bearing the date 1635, came from a pew in the old church.[50] The font, a copy of the one in St. Samson's, was made in 1842[51] and was moved from the east end to the west end of the nave in 1908.[52]

St. Samson's had 2 bells in 1552[53] and in 1752.[54] The church now has a single bell, dated 1635,[55] and the clock was bought in 1842.[56] The plate comprised a silver chalice and paten in 1552,[57] and a silver chalice, with a pewter paten and flagon, in 1823.[58] The church now possesses a silver tankard, dated 1727, and two silver chalices, with three patens, all of 1843.[59] The registers are complete from 1722.[60] A register beginning in 1581 was missing by 1831.[61] Burials took place at Cound until 1841,[62] but were registered at Cressage before 1710.[63] Marriages were registered at Cound from 1754 until 1841.[64]

NONCONFORMITY. Quakers were meeting at Cressage in 1656,[65] among them members of the Farmer family of Cound Leasowes Farm, but are not later recorded in the parish. There were said to be no dissenters here in 1799,[66] but houses were licensed for nonconformist worship in 1803[67] and 1806.[68] Probably the worshippers were Methodists, of whom there were said to be a few in the parish in 1823.[69] By 1838 the former Methodists were attending the parish church,[70] and there were said to be no nonconformists here in 1843.[71] A Wesleyan Methodist chapel was built on the Harley road in 1854[72] but was disused by *c.* 1900.[73]

SCHOOLS. The curate was teaching children in 1576,[74] and there was a schoolmaster in the village in 1705 and 1726.[75] A small piece of land, yielding an income of £2 10s. a year in the later 19th century,[76] was devised by Edward Pearce, who died in 1795, for the education of poor children in the village.[77] A day school had been established by 1818, when 30 children attended.[78] Attendance had risen to 49 by 1823[79] and 58 by 1833.[80] The school was maintained by subscription for the most part,[81] but school pence had been introduced by 1833.[82] A new school was said to have been opened in 1841,[83] but this

[34] Visit. Arch. Salop. 1799, 1823.
[35] Ibid. 1843.
[36] Ibid. 1823.
[37] Ibid. 1843.
[38] Ibid. 1799, 1823.
[39] Ibid. 1843.
[40] H.O. 129/359/1/4.
[41] The following description, except where otherwise stated, is based on Cranage, vi. 487–8; S.P.L., MS. 372, vol. i, p. 1; Linley Hall, Archd. Owen's sketches. See also plate facing p. 9.
[42] It was given to the curate of St. Mary's, Shrewsbury, who converted it into a bedstead: notes *penes* Miss E. M. Jones.
[43] B.M. Add. MS. 21236, f. 30ᵛ.   [44] Ibid.
[45] Visit. Archd. Salop. 1823.
[46] W.S.L. 350/40/3.
[47] Par. rec., vestry minutes.
[48] S.P.L., Watton press-cuttings, iv. 66.
[49] Ibid. 63–65. See also plate facing p. 253.
[50] B.M. Add. MS. 21236, f. 30ᵛ.
[51] Notes *penes* Miss E. M. Jones.
[52] Ibid.
[53] *T.S.A.S.* 2nd ser. xii. 99.
[54] Walters, *Ch. Bells Salop.* 219.
[55] Ibid.
[56] Par. rec., vestry minutes.
[57] *T.S.A.S.* 2nd ser. xii. 99.

[58] Visit. Archd. Salop. 1823.
[59] Arkwright and Bourne, *Ch. Plate Ludlow Archd.* 25.
[60] Printed to 1812 in *S.P.R. Lich.* ii (2), 61–79.
[61] Ibid. Cressage intro. p. iii.
[62] Ibid.
[63] Lich. Dioc. Regy., bishop's transcripts.
[64] *S.P.R. Lich.* ii (2), Cressage intro. p. iii.
[65] *T.S.A.S.* 4th ser. v. 296–7.
[66] Visit. Archd. Salop. 1799.
[67] Q. Sess. Orders, iii. 118.
[68] Ibid. 131.
[69] Visit. Archd. Salop. 1823.
[70] Ibid.   [71] Ibid. 1843.
[72] *Cassey's Dir. Salop.* (1871).
[73] Ex inf. Miss E. M. Jones.
[74] Lich. Dioc. Regy., B/v 1/10.
[75] Ibid. B/v 1/93; ibid. list of schoolmasters in diocese, 1726.
[76] *Salop. Char. for Elem. Educ.* 31.
[77] Ibid.; Barnard MSS., Raby Castle, press 14, no. 81.
[78] *Digest of Returns to Cttee. on Educ. of Poor,* H.C. 224, p. 750 (1819), ix (2).
[79] Visit. Archd. Salop. 1823.
[80] *Educ. Enquiry Abstract,* H.C. 62, p. 773 (1835), xlii.
[81] *Digest of Returns to Cttee. on Educ. of Poor,* p. 750; Visit. Archd. Salop. 1823; *Educ. Enquiry Abstract,* p. 773.
[82] *Educ. Enquiry Abstract,* p. 773.
[83] Ed. 7/102/71.

was probably no more than a transfer to new premises.

A National School was built in 1857,[84] with the aid of a government grant, on land opposite the church provided by the lord of the manor. The school was managed by the Rector of Cound and the Curate of Cressage until c. 1871,[85] but the former was no longer among the managers by 1886.[86] It became a Controlled school in 1955.[87] Most of the school's income still came from voluntary subscriptions in 1871, when a graduated scale of school pence was in use.[88] School pence had been abolished by 1893, when the school was in receipt of a government grant.[89] From 1846 until 1906 between 45 and

50 children attended.[90] The school was closed in 1957, when a new school was opened on the Sheinton road.[91] There was also a dame school in the village between 1856 and 1870.[92]

CHARITIES. The poor of Cressage were formerly entitled to a portion of the Cound charities of Richard Dutton and Ann Eldred, but appear to have received nothing from this source since 1899.[93] By will proved in 1918 Elizabeth, Lady Harnage, left £100 for the benefit of the poor, to be distributed at the discretion of the vicar.[94] In 1964 the Harnage Charity had an income of some £5 a year, which was distributed by the vicar in money at Christmas.[95]

FRODESLEY

THE parish of Frodesley, which contains 2,262 a.,[1] lies at the foot of the Lawley hill, some 7 miles south of Shrewsbury. The parish boundary follows Row Brook on the north, and on the south runs along the ridge above Causeway Wood; elsewhere it follows in some parts the course of small streams, but in general makes no use of natural features.

The western boundary, which runs through a former woodland area, followed its present course by 1768,[2] but seems to have been in doubt until the 17th century. In 1843 Longnor manor included Longnor Green and Bentley Ford Farms, with other lands, which together covered most of the parish west of Row Brook. Agreements concerning the boundaries of Frodesley and Longnor manors show that this area had been part of Longnor manor since the early 13th century. The boundary between the two estates ran from 'Sullakemor'[3] to the valley of Bentley and along Row Brook ('Kusibroc'), c. 1221.[4] Other landmarks cannot be identified, but at one point the boundary followed the 'haye' of Frodesley.[5] North of Watling Street an assart called 'Bereleye', which was assigned to Longnor manor in 1221, was called The Barley in 1843.[6] In 1603 the boundary between the two manors was marked by ditches and merestones and again touched Bentley Ford at one point.[7]

From Causeway Wood and Lodge Hill in the south of the parish, both of which rise to over 900 feet, there is a steep downward slope, reaching 500 feet north of Park Farm. Over the remainder of the parish the land slopes more gently to 325 feet along

Row Brook. Most of the parish lies between 400 and 500 feet. Causeway Wood and Lodge Hill are made up respectively of Cambrian and Ordovician rocks, and are joined on the west by a ridge of volcanic rock, which is an outlier of the Lawley. The subsoil of the remainder of the parish, below the 500-foot contour, is boulder clay, with isolated small deposits of sand and gravel. The Coal Measures, which underlie the clay to the north and west of the village, have been exploited in the past.[8]

Watling Street, which runs through the centre of the parish, was turnpiked in 1764.[9] In 1817 there was a tollgate at the Acton Burnell boundary, and the toll-house was still standing in 1898.[10] The village street, which has been diverted since 1843, originally led to the Park. Another road to the Park ran southwards from the Hall, parallel to the village street. This is now a cart-track, but is said to have been a broad paved carriage road.[11] A road running to the Park from Longor Green, past Bentley Ford, was only a bridle road in 1831,[12] but was described as a common road to the Park c. 1700.[13] Longnor Green was a 20-acre piece of waste until shortly after 1755, when it was inclosed by Sir Richard Corbett of Longnor, who then set out the present road from the Green to Longnor village.[14]

In 1086 there was sufficient woodland here for 100 swine and three other inclosed woods.[15] It is likely that the area to the west of Row Brook, from Fox Covert to the Lawley, was then woodland. Numerous 'coppice' and 'wood' field-names indicate its former extent. The 'Heypoll' and the

84 Ibid.
85 Ibid.
86 Par. rec., managers' minutes.
87 Ex inf. S.C.C. Educ. Dept.
88 Ed. 7/102/71.
89 *Return of Schs., 1893* [C. 7529], p. 504, H.C. (1894), lxv.
90 Nat. Soc. *Ch. School Returns*, 1846–7; *Returns relating to Elem. Educ.* H.C. 201, p. 334 (1871), lv; *Return of Schs. 1893*, p. 504; *Voluntary Schs. Returns*, H.C. 178–XXIV, p. 20 (1906), lxxxviii.
91 Ex inf. S.C.C. Educ. Dept.
92 *Kelly's Dir. Salop.* (1856, 1870).
93 See p. 72.
94 Char. Com. files.
95 Ex inf. the Vicar.
1 O.S. *Area Bk.* (1883). The following topographical description is based, except where otherwise stated, on O.S. Map 6″ Salop. 49 (1st and later edns.); O.S. Maps 1/25,000 SJ 50, SO 49, 59 (1956); ibid. SJ 40 (1957); Rocque, *Map of Salop.* (1752); Baugh, *Map of Salop.*

(1808); B.M. O.S. 2″ orig. drawings, sheet 207 (1817); Geol. Survey Map (drift), sheet 152 (1932); par. rec., tithe appt. and map, 1843. This article was written in 1961 and revised in 1965.
2 Par. rec., perambulation of bounds, 1768.
3 Perhaps Lake Meadow, north of Watling Street and 200 yards north-east of Lane Farm.
4 S.R.O. 567 uncat.; text in Eyton, vi. 52–53.
5 Ibid.
6 Ibid.; par. rec., tithe appt.
7 S.R.O. 567 uncat., award of Council of the Marches. 1603.
8 See p. 83.
9 Watling St. road Act, 4 Geo. III, c. 70 (priv. act).
10 S.C.C. title-deeds, SH 35.
11 W.S.L. 350/40/3.
12 Par. rec., vestry minutes.
13 S.R.O. 567 uncat., sketch of proposed highway diversion, c. 1700.
14 Ibid., agreement for inclosure, 1755.
15 *V.C.H. Salop.* i. 342.

'Over-heypoll', woods in 1419,[16] can be identified with fields called Hay Pool and Middle Hay Pool to the south of Fox Covert. Parsons Piece, adjoining Middle Hay Pool, is probably the Parsons Leasow, which was woodland in 1607.[17] The 'Rewe', now Row Coppice, is first recorded in 1460, and unidentified woods called 'Shyrmore', 'Barcle', 'Lydehurst', and 'Barunde' are mentioned, 1437–60.[18]

Frodesley lay within the Long Forest, but had been disafforested by 1300.[19] Reference is made to assarts here from 1209 onwards,[20] the most considerable being one at Ramshurst in 1250.[21] In 1235 the tenants were said to have built dwellings in Frodesley Wood and to have wasted the underwood there.[22] Thefts of wood and similar offences bulk large in the court rolls, 1404–60,[23] and Heypoll Wood had been inclosed by the farmer of the manor in 1439,[24] but large-scale clearance of woodland did not take place until the early 17th century, when the timber was used to provide fuel for Longnor Forge.[25] It was said in 1613 that woods worth £200 a year in 1607 had almost all been felled, and that over 12,000 cords of wood had been cut in Frodesley and Longnor between 1605 and 1610.[26] In 1843 there were 127½ a. of woodland in the parish.[27] Row Coppice, Fox Covert, and Hobsley Coppice are still standing. Causeway Wood and Lodge Hill Wood covered 83½ a. in 1843,[28] and 167 a. of woodland here were acquired by the Forestry Commission in 1953–4.[29]

One or more of the three inclosed woods recorded in 1086[30] was kept in hand, c. 1221, by the lord of the manor,[31] who had his own forester by 1248.[32] There was then a lord's wood, a fenced park, and a common wood.[33] Trespasses in the park were presented in 1404.[34] The park appears to have been reformed shortly before 1609[35] and was inclosed with a stone wall c. 1750,[36] but it was disparked after 1787 and divided into fields.[37] The boundary can be seen in field-boundaries, and to the south of Park Farm the stone wall is still standing. Fields called Big and Little Deerhouse Leasow lie within the wall, north-east of Coppice House.[38]

The former common fields seem to have lain in the north-east quarter of the parish. Fields called The Furlong, Middle Furlong, and Lower Furlong lie to the south of Watling Street, east of the village, and between Watling Street and the Condover road are fields called Great, Little, and Far Cross.[39] The Cross Yate was open-field land in the 15th century, when orders to erect summer, winter, and spring hedges indicate that the village then had three common fields.[40] Meadows lay along two tributaries of Row Brook. One of these runs north-westwards from the fish-pond below the Rectory towards Fox Covert, while the other flows northwards through Hobsley Coppice towards Acton Burnell. Lady Meadow lies near the latter and the Great Town Meadow along the former, immediately west of the village.[41] To the north of Watling Street the Town Meadow continued as a narrow belt of meadow-land, where the field lying nearest to the road was a water-meadow called Eight Days Math in 1843.[42] A 17-acre field in the glebe had been recently inclosed in 1635[43] and the Butts Charity lands, on Watling Street, were said to have been inclosed from the waste c. 1755.[44]

There is some evidence of early settlement in the parish. A perforated stone axe was found in the Rectory garden in the 19th century.[45] A barrow which stood in Long Field, south of Hobsley Coppice, was levelled in 1808,[46] and the field-names Near and Far Champions Bury, to the south of Park Farm,[47] suggest that another barrow may once have stood there.

The parish is one of scattered farms and cottages, but this appears to be an 18th-century development. The original settlement lay along the village street, which runs southwards at right angles from Watling Street. Among houses on the east side of the road are Town Farm, built in the early 19th century in Georgian style,[48] Manor Farm, and Hall Farm. Frodesley Hall, which lies off the road, was built in 1882 on the site of the manor-house.[49] Adjoining it is the church, with the parsonage to the south. The parsonage, which contained two bays of building in 1635[50] and had only one hearth in 1662,[51] was rebuilt in 1742[52] and further enlarged in the early 19th century.[53] South of the parsonage the village street formerly ran some 50 yards to the east of the present road to Lodge Farm.[54] Two houses, now demolished, stood on each side of it at this point in 1843.[55] There were then no houses to the west of the street, formerly part of the common meadows, except a cottage near the cross-roads,[56] which is still there. Several houses have since been built here.

One of the cottages on the Condover road north of the village is stone-built and dated 1767[57] and another incorporates a stone cottage of similar date, but most of the houses here were probably built to accommodate workers at the brick-works and coal pits opened nearby in the early 19th century.[58] This would in part account for the increase in the number

[16] B.M. Add. Ch. 54388, m. 2.
[17] E 134/11 Jas. I East/5.
[18] B.M. Add. Ch. 54387–9.
[19] Eyton, vi. 343, 345.
[20] Ibid. vi. 52–53, 137, 292, 294; B.M. Add. Ch. 54387, m. 1d.
[21] Eyton, vi. 345n.; C 47/88/1/15.
[22] Eyton, vi. 293.
[23] B.M. Add. Ch. 54387–9.
[24] S.P.L., Deeds 9136, m. 30.
[25] E 134/11 Jas. I East/5.
[26] Ibid.
[27] Par. rec., tithe appt.
[28] Ibid.
[29] Ex inf. Forestry Com.
[30] V.C.H. Salop. i. 342.
[31] Eyton, vi. 52–53.
[32] B.M. Add. Ch. 54387, m. 1d.
[33] Ibid.
[34] Ibid. m. 1.
[35] C 2/Jas. I/D 7/82.
[36] Salop. N. & Q. n.s. viii. 30–31.
[37] Ibid.
[38] Par. rec., tithe appt.
[39] Ibid.
[40] B.M. Add. Ch. 54387–9.
[41] Par. rec., tithe appt.
[42] Ibid.
[43] S.R.O. 1011 uncat., copy glebe terrier, 1635.
[44] Par. rec., vestry minutes.
[45] V.C.H. Salop. i. 202.
[46] W.S.L. 350/40/3.
[47] Par. rec., tithe appt.
[48] W.S.L. 350/40/3.
[49] T.S.A.S. 4th ser. viii. 82.
[50] S.R.O. 1011 uncat., copy glebe terrier, 1635.
[51] E 179/255/35 m. 74d.
[52] Par. rec., glebe terrier, 1748.
[53] Ibid. 1841.
[54] Par. rec., tithe appt.
[55] Ibid.
[56] Ibid.
[57] Datestone.
[58] See p. 83.

of houses in the parish from 29 in 1801 to 48 in 1861.[59] There were about half a dozen cottages along this road in 1843[60] and at least six more had been built before 1879,[61] but only four remained in 1961. The cottages on Watling Street, on each side of the village cross-roads, date from the early 19th century and include the Swan Inn. An alehouse is first recorded in 1404[62] and again in 1753–72,[63] but none is mentioned thereafter until 1841, when there were two.[64] The Swan Inn, first so named in 1905,[65] has been the only alehouse since 1843.[66]

The remaining farms lie away from the village and, apart from Lodge Farm, are first named in 1805.[67] Lodge Farm[68] is built of stone and occupies a striking site on an outcrop of rock in the former Park on the northern slope of Lodge Hill. Probably intended as a hunting lodge, and built in the first quarter of the 17th century, when the lord of the manor was carrying out improvements in the Park,[69] the house is first mentioned c. 1675, when it was occupied for some years by Sir Richard Corbett of Longnor, during the building of Longnor Hall.[70] The original house is a tower-like gabled building, T-shaped in plan, having four stories and two rooms to each floor. On its north side a semicircular projection contains a stone newel stair, rising the full height of the building and being topped by a flat roof. This presumably provided a vantage point from which to watch hunting in the park. The basement floor, entered from the north side where the ground falls away, consists of a kitchen and, below the east wing, a cellar cut into the rock. The floor above has an entrance from ground level on the south side, where there is a two-storied porch supported on stone piers. A cross passage connects this entrance with the newel stair. There are two external stone chimneys, one on the west wall of the west wing and the other on the north wall of the east wing. The chimneys are surmounted by tall brick shafts, star-shaped in plan. Most of the stone windows, of one or two lights with plain splayed frames, have survived. Other original fittings include two nail-studded entrance doors and some early-17th-century panelling in the upper rooms. A new wing of stone ashlar was added to the west side of the house by Godolphin Edwards c. 1750.[71]

Fields called The Romps, to the east of Lodge Farm,[72] presumably mark the site of the deserted hamlet of Ramshurst. One of the common fields in the adjacent township of Hothales in Ruckley and Langley parish was known as the Field towards Ramshurst in the 13th century.[73] Assarts are recorded here in 1250[74] but the hamlet had probably by that date already shrunk to a single messuage, which is last recorded in 1439.[75]

There were said to be 120 adults in the parish in 1676,[76] and its population was 158 in 1801.[77] After rising steadily to a peak of 261 in 1851, the population fell to 179 in 1891 and, despite a temporary increase to 207 in 1911, it reached its lowest level, 152, in 1931. There were 157 inhabitants in 1961.[78]

MANORS. The manor of *FRODESLEY* was held of Roger, Earl of Shrewsbury, in 1086.[79] Some time after 1165[80] the overlordship came into the possession of the FitzAlans, later Earls of Arundel, who are last recorded as overlords in 1533.[81]

Siward, who had held the manor freely before 1066, was still tenant in 1086,[82] and was probably succeeded by his son Aldred.[83] By 1235 the manor was held by William Hunald,[84] who probably followed Robert Hunald, recorded in 1203[85] but not explicitly associated with Frodesley. William Hunald was lord in 1242,[86] and on his death in 1248[87] wardship of his son Thomas was claimed by John FitzAlan as overlord, whom William's widow Laurencia sued for dower.[88] Thomas, possibly still under age, was holding the manor in 1254[89] and is last mentioned in 1270.[90] He was succeeded by William Hunald, perhaps a brother, who died in 1278[91] and whose widow Joan held lands in Frodesley in dower.[92] William's daughter and heir Philippe, then a minor, was probably a ward of Robert Burnell, to whom custody of Frodesley Wood was granted.[93] On her death in 1290 the wood was delivered to her uncle and heir John Hunald, who presumably succeeded to the manor at the same time[94] and who was certainly lord in 1294.[95] For more than a century thereafter the manor was held by two or more persons called John Hunald, who cannot be distinguished from the existing evidence.[96] Joan, daughter and heir of John Hunald, married John son of Reynold Scriven,[97] to whom the manor had passed in right of his wife by 1406, when he was patron of the living.[98] John Scriven was lord in 1428[99] and 1431,[1] but was probably dead by 1437,

[59] *Census*, 1801–61.
[60] Par. rec., tithe appt.
[61] Smythe deeds, *penes* Messrs. Knapp-Fisher, solicitors, Westminster.
[62] B.M. Add. Ch. 54387, m. 1.
[63] Q. Sess, alehouse reg.
[64] Par. rec., rector's commonplace bk.
[65] *Kelly's Dir. Salop.* (1905).
[66] Ibid. (1856–1900); par. rec., tithe appt.
[67] S.P.L., MS. 294.
[68] See plate facing p. 82.
[69] C 2/Jas. I/D 7/82.
[70] S.R.O. 567 uncat., accts. of Sir Richard Corbett, 1674–82.
[71] *Salop. N. & Q.*, N.S. viii. 30–31.
[72] Par. rec., tithe appt.
[73] S.P.L., MS. 2, f. 13ᵛ.
[74] Eyton, vi. 294–5, 345 n.
[75] B.M. Add. Ch. 54389, m. 3.
[76] *T.S.A.S.* 2nd ser. i. 81.
[77] *Census*, 1801.
[78] Ibid. 1811–1961.
[79] *V.C.H. Salop.* i. 342.
[80] Eyton, vi. 291–2.

[81] C 142/57/14. cf. *Bk. of Fees*, 962, 971; *Rot. Hund.* (Rec. Com.), ii. 62; *Close R.* 1268–72, 505, 514; *Cal. Inq. p.m.* iii, p. 124.
[82] *V.C.H. Salop.* i. 342.
[83] Eyton, vi. 291.
[84] Ibid. 293.
[85] Ibid. 292.
[86] *Bk. of Fees*, 962, 971.
[87] Eyton, vi. 293.
[88] Ibid. cf. *Sir Christopher Hatton's Bk. of Seals*, ed. L. C. Loyd and D. M. Stenton (Oxford, 1950), 237.
[89] *Rot. Hund.* (Rec. Com.), ii. 61–62.
[90] Eyton, vi. 294.
[91] E 371/41 m. 10.
[92] S.P.L., Deeds 3609.
[93] *Cal. Close*, 1288–96, 105.
[94] Ibid.
[95] *Cal. Inq. p.m.* ii, p. 124.
[96] S.P.L., Deeds 428, 3609, 10767; *Feud. Aids*, iv. 239; Eyton, vi. 295–6.
[97] *Visit. Salop. 1623* (Harl. Soc. xxix), ii. 434.
[98] Lich. Dioc. Regy., reg. 7, f. 113.
[99] *Feud. Aids*, iv. 257.
[1] Ibid. 264.

when the manor court was held in the presence of the lady of the manor.[2] His son John had succeeded by 1441[3] and was still living in 1453.[4] The manor had passed to John's son Robert by 1466,[5] and to Robert's son Thomas by 1496.[6] Thomas died in 1533,[7] and the manor then passed from father to son in the Scriven family[8] until 1683, the following being lords: Thomas, 1533–87;[9] Edward, 1587–1631;[10] Thomas, 1631–44;[11] Richard, 1644–83.[12] On Richard's death the manor passed to his eldest daughter Margaret, wife of Roger Whitley of Peover, (Ches.)[13] Their daughter Elizabeth married Richard Lloyd Gwillim,[14] whose son Edward Lloyd Gwillim conveyed the manor to Samuel Edwards in 1712.[15] The latter died in 1738[16] and was succeeded by his son Godolphin, on whose death in 1772[17] the manor passed to his daughter Elizabeth, wife of Lewis Pugh.[18] In 1784 it was sold to Sir Edward Smythe of Acton Burnell to defray the debts of Samuel Edwards.[19] Sir Edward Walter Smythe sold his Frodesley property in 1921, but retained the manorial rights.[20]

The manor-house, demolished in 1882,[21] was built by Edward Scriven in 1594.[22] It faced south and is said to have had 3 projecting wings, of which the one on the west was taken down c. 1680.[23] A 19th-century sketch shows the central wing, comprising the parlour and chamber over, with large projecting mullioned windows, and the east wing, which probably contained the kitchen, dairy, and brewhouse.[24]

The reputed manor of RAMSHURST is first recorded in 1250, when a rent of 15s. 1d. was assessed on its lord for 20 a. of assarted land.[25] This was among other assart-rents which Robert Burnell obtained before 1292[26] and which followed the descent of Acton Burnell manor.[27] A small free-hold estate is recorded here between 1270[28] and 1439,[29] but by 1533 the manor had been consolidated with that of Frodesley.[30]

ECONOMIC HISTORY. The manor, said to have been worth 10s. before 1066 and 8s. in 1086,[31] was valued at £12 in 1294.[32] No indication of the size of the demesne is given before 1787, when 439 a. were in hand.[33] It had been leased to the tenants before 1404.[34] By the later 18th century most of the parish lay in the manorial estate, which contained some 1,800 a. in 1787[35] and 1,791 a. in 1843.[36]

The Frodesley family, who held 32 a. here in 1277[37] and are first recorded c. 1248,[38] were still free tenants in 1404.[39] In 1270 William le Harpur held a small freehold at Ramshurst,[40] which had probably passed by c. 1405 to John Newbold of Shrewsbury,[41] who held a messuage and a noke here at his death in 1439.[42] Richard de Eton held one carucate of land in Frodesley in 1347.[43] In 1843, apart from the 255 a. in the west of the parish which had always been part of Longnor manor and the glebe and charity lands, only 75 a. and a few cottages lay outside the manorial estate.[44]

In 1086 there were in the manor 3 villeins and 3 bordars, with one plough.[45] The only other medieval evidence for the number of tenants and the size of their holdings derives from the court rolls, 1404–60.[46] Rentals of pannage, 1419–20 and 1433, suggest that there were between 14 and 17 tenants, and that the normal holding was a half virgate or one noke (¼ virgate). In 1787 the bulk of the estate lay in large farms and there were few small occupiers; there were then 3 farms of more than 300 a., 3 others of 100–200 a., and only 4 smaller holdings.[47] By 1805 there were 4 farms of over 300 a., but the number of holdings under 100 a. had risen to 7,[48] and by 1843 only one of the farms was over 300 a.; 4 others were of 100–200 a. and there were 10 smaller holdings.[49] Surveys of 1898 and 1921 show that the size of farms subsequently remained virtually unchanged.[50] The Hickmans of Park Farm were said, c. 1833, to have been tenants for many generations,[51] but no other 19th-century tenants remained long in their farms. Seven out of 10 farms had changed hands between 1809 and 1826, and they had all changed hands between 1826 and 1851.[52] Lane Farm was purchased by the County Council in 1928[53] and had been converted into 7 small-holdings by 1937.[54]

[2] B.M. Add. Ch. 54389, m. 2.
[3] Ibid. m. 3.
[4] S.P.L., Deeds 121.
[5] Ibid. 123; Lich. Dioc. Regy., reg. 12, f. 86.
[6] S.P.L., Deeds 188.
[7] C 142/57/14.
[8] For pedigree see Visit. Salop. 1623 (Harl. Soc. xxix), ii. 434–5; S.P.L., MS. 2791, pp. 591–603; ibid., MS. 4645, p. 503.
[9] C 142/57/14; C 142/226/174.
[10] C 142/226/174; S.P.R. Lich. vi (1), 82.
[11] S.P.R. Lich. vi (1), 96. For his activities as a royalist commander in the Civil War see T.S.A.S. 2nd ser. vii. 321; Hist. MSS. Com. 13th Rep. App. I, 143; S.P.L., MS. 2791, pp. 602–3.
[12] Cal. Cttee. for Compounding, iii, p. 1859; W.S.L. 350/40/3; S.P.R. Lich. vi (1), 137.
[13] S.P.R. Lich. iv (1), 118.
[14] S.P.L., MS. 4079, p. 1547.
[15] C.P. 25(2)/960/11 Anne Mich.; C.P. 43/519 m. 7.
[16] T.S.A.S. liii. 201.
[17] Smythe deeds, conveyance of manor, 1787.
[18] Ibid.   [19] Ibid.
[19] S.C.C. title-deeds, SH 35.
[20] T.S.A.S. 4th ser. viii. 82.
[21] Datestone, recorded in W.S.L. 350/40/3, and B.M. Add. MS. 21021, f. 125.
[23] W.S.L. 350/40/3.
[24] Stackhouse Acton, The Castles and Old Mansions of Shropshire (Shrewsbury, 1868), facing p. 44; interior described in W.S.L. 350/40/3.

[25] Eyton, vi. 294–5, 345 n.; C 47/88/1/15.
[26] Cal. Inq. p.m. iii, p. 50.
[27] Ibid. v, p. 393; ibid. viii, p. 495.
[28] Eyton, vi. 294.
[29] B.M. Add. Ch. 54389, m. 3.
[30] C 142/57/14.
[31] V.C.H. Salop. i. 342.
[32] Cal. Inq. p.m. iii, p. 124.
[33] Smythe deeds, conveyance of manor, 1787.
[34] B.M. Add. Ch. 54387, m. 1.
[35] Smythe deeds, conveyance of manor, 1787.
[36] Par. rec., tithe appt.
[37] Eyton, vi. 294–5.
[38] B.M. Add. Ch. 54387, m. 1d.   [39] Ibid. m. 1.
[40] Eyton, vi. 294.
[41] B.M. Add. Ch. 54387, m. 2.
[42] Ibid. 54389, m. 3.
[43] C.P. 25(1)/195/14/14; N.L.W., Pitchford Hall 130,132.
[44] Par. rec., tithe appt.
[45] V.C.H. Salop. i. 342.
[46] B.M. Add. Ch. 54387–9.
[47] Smythe deeds, conveyance of manor, 1787.
[48] S.P.L., MS. 294.
[49] Par. rec., tithe appt.
[50] S.C.C. title-deeds, SH 35.
[51] W.S.L. 350/40/3.
[52] Par. rec., plan of pews, 1809; Bagshaw's Dir. Salop. (1851).
[53] S.C.C. title-deeds, SH 35; ibid., minutes, 1926–8, 310–11; ibid. 1928–9, 119.
[54] Kelly's Dir. Salop. (1937).

Frodesley Lodge from the South-east
Showing semicircular projection containing newel stair

Cound Hall from the South-east

ACTON BURNELL: the School (1815)

CRESSAGE: wooden toll-bridge over the Severn, by Thomas Telford (1800)

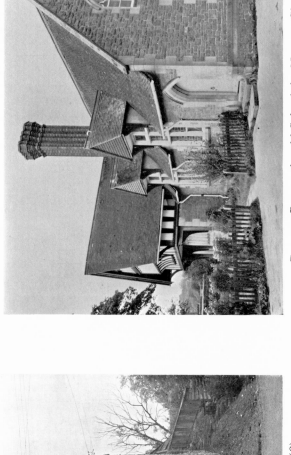

CHURCH PREEN: the old School, by Norman Shaw (1872)

WESTBURY: Minsterley toll-house (c. 1768)

In 1801 there were said to be 499 a. arable, wheat and oats being the chief crops.[55] In 1843 1,289 a. was classed as arable, but this must have included temporary grass.[56] On the eight principal farms there were then 1,001 a. arable, 186 a. meadow, and 474 a. pasture.[57] Hall Farm was said to be a very extensive dairy farm c. 1833[58] and Lane Farm had more meadow than pasture in 1843.[59]

Coal from Frodesley was being supplied to the poor of Condover in the 1740s,[60] and was mined for a few years in the 1830s about a quarter mile south-east of Rowe Farm. It was probably producing about 200 tons of coal a year between 1836 and 1839,[61] but seems to have closed by 1841.[62] One of the two shafts was open in 1961. That coal may have been mined elsewhere in the parish is suggested by the field-names Pit Leasow (a quarter mile south-west of the village cross-roads) and Coalpit Leasow (half a mile south-west of Park Farm).

The former brickworks stand to the east of the Condover road, a quarter mile north of the village. In 1843 the site was leased to William Ison, who combined the manufacture of bricks, tiles, and drainage pipes with farming a small-holding on Watling Street, later West Farm.[63] By 1856 the business had passed to Messrs. Jobson and Hancock[64] and is last recorded in 1870.[65] In 1856 the village had a carpenter, a cooper, two shoemakers, a shopkeeper, and a tailor.[66] There had been a smithy here in 1724.[67] By 1926 only the village shop remained[68] and this closed soon after 1941.[69]

LOCAL GOVERNMENT. The manor court was held twice a year, in spring and autumn, 1404–19, and once yearly, in the winter, 1432–60.[70] It was held before the steward, except in 1437 and 1441 when the lord presided. Its jurisdiction did not include view of frankpledge or the assize of bread and ale, and no officers were appointed.

Apart from vestry minutes, from 1824, there are no civil parish records. Vestry meetings were held irregularly, normally two or three times a year, but at Easter only between 1838 and 1850 and after 1895. The rector was normally chairman and meetings were attended by a few of the farmers, seldom more

than six, who served as parish officers in rotation. Birch Coppice House was in use as a poor-house, or pest-house, in 1825;[71] negotiations to erect a cottage for the use of the poor in 1832 seem to have been abortive. Contracts for medical attendance on the poor were made with Mr. Durnell of Acton Burnell in 1828 and 1835. Poor rates were £27 in 1777,[72] £46 in 1785[73] and £80 in 1803.[74] They rose to a peak of £152 in 1818[75] and thereafter fluctuated between £68 and £123 until 1834.[76]

CHURCH. The church is first recorded in 1272.[77] Thomas of Shrewsbury, mentioned in 1291,[78] is the first incumbent who can be certainly identified, but the Nicholas clericus who witnessed a Frodesley deed before 1248[79] may have been a rector. The church was originally a chapelry of Condover and in 1341 one third of the tithes of wool and lambs belonged to the mother church.[80] It was described as a free chapel in 1358.[81] Burials took place at Condover until the churchyard was consecrated in 1780.[82]

Maud Burnell was patron of the living in 1306,[83] but John Hunald presented in 1320[84] and the advowson then followed the descent of the manor until 1784, when it was conveyed to Sir Thomas Edwardes, Rector of Frodesley, under chancery decree.[85] On his death in 1797 he was succeeded as patron and rector by his son, Sir John Cholmondeley Edwardes Bt.[86] The latter died in 1822 and by 1826 the advowson had passed to T. R. Gleadowe,[87] who in 1836 petitioned the House of Lords for compensation should the value of the advowson be diminished.[88] The Gleadowes held the advowson until 1892, when it was sold to T. G. Northam,[89] whose trustees were still patrons in 1961.[90]

The living was worth £2 in 1291[91] and 1341,[92] and £5 in 1535.[93] Its gross value, said to be £32 in 1655,[94] had risen to c. £130 in 1799[95] and to £392 by 1831.[96] One third of the tithes belonged to Condover in 1341, when Frodeley's share was worth 15s.[97] In 1655, when the tithes were worth £22, a further £2 was derived from herbage dues in Longnor.[98] Between 1833 and 1839 the tithes produced an average of £332 a year,[99] and in 1843 they were commuted for a rent-charge of £405.[1] The glebe,

55 H.O. 67/14/111.
56 Par. rec., tithe appt.
57 Ibid.
58 W.S.L. 350/40/3.
59 Par. rec., tithe appt.
60 Condover par. rec., vestry minutes, 1741–7.
61 Par. rec., rector's commonplace bk. A modus on 18–22 tons of coal was paid annually for tithe, 1836–9.
62 Ibid.
63 Par. rec., tithe appt.
64 Kelly's Dir. Salop. (1856).
65 Ibid. (1870).
66 Ibid. (1856).
67 Smythe deeds, conveyance of manor, 1787.
68 Kelly's Dir. Salop. (1926).
69 Local inf.
70 B.M. Add. Ch. 54387–9.
71 A cottage leased by Sir Edward Smythe, 1787, may have been a poor-house: Smythe deeds.
72 Rep. Cttee. on Overseers' Returns, 1777, p. 442, H.C. (1st ser. ix, reprinted 1803).
73 Rep. Cttee. on State of Poor, 1787, p. 658, H.C. (1st ser. ix, reprinted 1803).
74 Poor Law Abstract, 1803, H.C. 175, pp. 416–17 (1803–4), xiii.
75 Rep. Cttee. on Poor Rate Returns, 1882, Suppl. App. H.C. 556, p. 141 (1822), v.
76 Ibid. 1825, H.C. 334, p. 177 (1825), iv; Acct. of Money

Expended on Poor, 1825–9, H.C. 83, p. 390 (1830–1), xi; ibid. 1830–4, H.C. 444, p. 344 (1835), xlvii.
77 Eyton, vi. 295.
78 Cal. Close, 1288–96, 200.
79 B.M. Add. Ch. 54387, m. 1d.
80 E 179/166/9.
81 Eyton, vi. 295.
82 S.P.R. Lich. iv (1), 137.
83 Eyton, vi. 295.
84 Ibid.
85 W.S.L. 350/40/3.
86 Lich. Dioc. Regy., reg. 27, p. 22.
87 Ibid. reg. 29, pp. 36–37, 72, 99, 100.
88 L.J. lxviii. 737.
89 Lich. Dioc. Regy., reg. 30, p. 275; ibid. reg. 35, p. 280; Smythe deeds.
90 Crockford (1959–60).
91 Tax. Eccl. (Rec. Com.), 244.
92 Inq. Non. (Rec. Com.), 192.
93 Valor Eccl. (Rec. Com.), iii. 183.
94 T.S.A.S. xlvii. 26.
95 Visit. Archd. Salop. 1799.
96 Rep. Com. Eccl. Revenues [67], pp. 478–9, H.C. (1835), xxii.
97 E 179/166/9.
98 T.S.A.S. xlvii. 26.
99 Par. rec., rector's commonplace bk.
1 Ibid., tithe appt.

formerly scattered, was exchanged in 1784 for 2 compact holdings, one adjoining the parsonage and the other to the west of the Condover road.[2] It comprised 23½ a. in 1635[3] and 1843,[4] and 21 a. by 1885.[5]

The original testament of Robert de Longedon (rector 1358–61)[6] is among the parish records.[7] Two of the medieval rectors were relatives of the lord of the manor.[8] Lewis Taylor (rector 1577–1623)[9] was also rector of Moreton Corbet,[10] his duties at Frodesley being performed by curates, one of whom, Thomas Baker, succeeded Taylor as rector.[11] Baker's successor, Thomas Fisher (rector 1633–c. 1646),[12] was probably also non-resident, since Nicholas Keysell was curate in 1636.[13] Fisher, who had been appointed a public preacher in Ludlow in 1630[14] and royalist governor there in 1643,[15] is the first rector known to have been a graduate.[16] John Wilkes (rector 1662–1712)[17] and his successor William Roe (rector 1713–41)[18] held the living in plurality with Pitchford.[19] The living was held successively by 4 members of the Edwardes family 1760–1822,[20] followed by the Gleadowes, 3 of whom were rectors, 1826–92.[21] The rector and his family filled the place of the squire in village life here after 1787. No curates were employed, apart from Benjamin Edwardes, who was licensed in 1815,[22] a year before he succeeded his father as rector.[23]

In 1799 2 services were held every Sunday with a sermon in the morning,[24] and by 1823 a sermon alternated with catechism in the afternoon.[25] At this time communion was given 4 times a year, with an average of 30 communicants.[26] In 1851 there was an average attendance of 70 at morning services and 30 in the afternoon.[27] A gallery had been built by 1809 to accommodate the singers[28] but there was no choir by 1838[29] and the annual payment of one guinea to the singers was discontinued in 1842.[30]

The church of *ST. MARK* consists of a chancel and nave, erected in 1809, and a north aisle added in 1859. Little is known of the appearance of the former church. A sketch of 1789,[31] drawn from the south-west, shows that it was a simple barn-like structure with a small bell-turret at the west end. The south wall was supported by two buttresses. The chancel had a square-headed priest's door and a two-light window, and there were two inserted square windows in the nave. A porch, recorded in 1614,[32] was presumably on the north wall. Stained-glass in the east window and two windows on the south wall depicted the arms of various members of the Scriven family;[33] fragments of this are in the east window of the present church. Carved stones in the parsonage garden are thought to have come from the former church.

In 1808 part of the church had fallen down and most of the remainder was demolished as unsafe.[34] The estimated cost of rebuilding the church was raised with the help of a church brief issued in 1809.[35] The present church is a small Georgian building of stone rubble plastered inside and out, with angle pilasters, a slate roof, and small western bell-turret. It has a round-arched west door and round headed windows at the east end and on the south wall. The chancel walls were panelled at the rector's expense in 1847,[36] but the communion table and reredos is in part constructed from 17th-century oak panelling. The pulpit and reading desk also incorporate 17th- and 18th-century panelling. The north aisle was built in 1859 in a Gothic style to a plan devised by the rector,[37] and the vestry adjoining the north wall of the chancel was in course of erection in 1900.[38]

The box pews in the nave, and the gallery at the west end are in part made from the panelling and roof timbers of the former church.[39] There was no font in 1823, when a basin was borrowed as required,[40] but a slender pedestal font was installed c. 1829.[41] An ancient plain font, formerly in the church-yard, replaced this c. 1939;[42] another is in the parsonage garden. An oak parish chest, of 17th-century date, now forms part of the seat of the rear pew at the west end. The church contains a number of wall-monuments to members of the Edwardes family, 1778–1859. There were 2 bells in 1552,[43] one in 1823[44] and 2 by 1838.[45] Neither of the 2 existing bells have an inscription, but one may be of 13th-century date.[46] The plate consists of a silver chalice and paten, 1589, a silver paten of 1698, a silver caudle cup, 1707, with a cover of 1705, and a silver flagon, 1869.[47] In 1552 there was a silver chalice and pewter paten.[48] The registers are complete from 1547.[49]

[2] Par. rec., glebe terriers, 1748, 1759, 1841.
[3] S.R.O. 1011 uncat., copy glebe terrier, 1635.
[4] Par. rec., tithe appt.
[5] *Kelly's Dir. Salop.* (1885).
[6] Eyton, vi. 295.
[7] Transcript in *S.P.R. Lich.* iv (1), 101.
[8] Thomas Hunald, rector from 1320, and Reginald Scriven, rector from 1406: Eyton, vi. 295–6.
[9] *T.S.A.S.* 2nd ser. i. 260, 263.
[10] Ibid. 260.
[11] Ibid. 3rd ser. i. 263; *S.P.R. Lich.* iv (1), 106.
[12] *T.S.A.S.* 3rd ser. v. 353; ibid. vii. 250.
[13] *S.P.R. Lich.* iv (1), 111.
[14] *T.S.A.S.* 4th ser. ii. 289.
[15] Ibid.; *Cal. Cttee. for Compounding*, ii, p. 1484.
[16] Foster, *Alumni Oxon.*
[17] *T.S.A.S.* 4th ser. iv. 182; ibid. v. 189.
[18] Ibid. v. 189, 198.
[19] Lich. Dioc. Regy., B/v 1/67–96. For Roe see *Salop. Shreds & Patches*, ix. 31.
[20] *T.S.A.S.* 4th ser. v. 204, 206; ibid. vi. 303; Lich. Dioc. Regy., reg. 27, p. 22; ibid. reg. 28, p. 237; ibid. reg. 29, pp. 36–37.
[21] Lich. Dioc. Regy., reg. 29, pp. 99, 100; ibid., reg. 30, p. 275; ibid., reg. 35, p. 280.
[22] Ibid., curates bk. 1813.
[23] Ibid., reg. 28, p. 237.
[24] Visit. Archd. Salop. 1799.
[25] Ibid. 1823.
[26] Ibid.
[27] H.O. 129/359/1/10.
[28] Par. rec., plan of pews, 1809.
[29] Ibid., vestry minutes.
[30] Ibid.
[31] S.P.L., MS. 372, vol. i, p. 118.
[32] Lich. Dioc. Regy., B/v 1/29.
[33] *T.S.A.S.* lii. 205–10.
[34] Q. Sess. order bk. Mich. 1808.
[35] Ibid.; B.M. Ch. briefs, B.L.5.
[36] Par. rec., glebe terrier, 1849.
[37] Ibid., vestry minutes.
[38] Ibid.
[39] W.S.L. 350/40/3.
[40] Visit. Archd. Salop. 1823.
[41] Ibid.
[42] Ex inf. the Rector.
[43] *T.S.A.S.* 2nd ser. xii. 101.
[44] Visit. Archd. Salop. 1823.   [45] Ibid.
[46] Walters, *Ch. Bells Salop.*, 219–20.
[47] Arkwright and Bourne, *Ch. Plate Ludlow Archd.* 30.
[48] *T.S.A.S.* 2nd ser. xii. 101.
[49] Printed to 1812 in *S.P.R. Lich.* iv (1), 101–47.

NONCONFORMITY. There were no dissenters in the parish in 1676,[50] but Stephen Wilcox and his wife Mary were presented for not attending church in 1685.[51] The former was said to be a dissenter, c. 1680[52] and an anabaptist meeting was licensed at his house in 1711.[53] There were no dissenters here in 1799,[54] but a cottage occupied by Sarah Wigley was licensed as a Congregational meeting-house in 1841.[55]

SCHOOLS. There has never been a school in the parish and the children have always attended schools at Acton Burnell or Longnor.[56] In 1870 members of the vestry pledged themselves to raise a fund by voluntary rate to pay for the education of the children at Acton Burnell.[57]

CHARITIES. An acre of waste land by the side of Watling Street, known as The Butts, was given to the poor by Godolphin Edwards some time before his death in 1772. This was occupied, in an un-regulated manner, as garden-ground by 8 poor persons until c. 1830, when formal tenancy agreements were introduced.[58] Two cottages erected here between 1833 and 1850 were then held at a rent of 1d. a year.[59] The property now consists of 3 gardens and 2 cottages, one of which is assigned to the rector for the use of the tenant of the glebe.[60]

A sum of £5, left to the poor by Thomas Scriven, was applied in 1809 to rebuilding the church. In 1830 5s., arising from the church rates, was being paid each year to the rector, who distributed it to two or three poor persons at Easter.[61] This sum may still have been paid in 1851,[62] but the charity has long since been lost.

The Revd. Francis Edwardes (d. 1767) left £20 to the poor. This legacy was apparently never paid over by the executor, but Francis's brother, Sir Thomas Edwardes, paid 16s. a year to the rector, and this payment was increased to 20s. a year, as a voluntary donation, by Sir Thomas's successor J. T. Hope (d. 1854) in the 1820s. It was then distributed by the rector at his discretion.[63] The charity evidently did not continue after Hope's death.

HARLEY

THE parish of Harley, which lies at the foot of Wenlock Edge, contains 1,963 a.[1] Some 110 a. and six houses in the village, formerly a detached part of Much Wenlock parish, were transferred to Harley in 1882.[2] On the south the parish boundary runs along the crest of Wenlock Edge; it follows streams for short distances on the east and west, but other-wise makes no use of natural features. The boundary with Cressage on the north-east seems to have been established following a perambulation of the bounds of Harley and Belswardine manors, carried out in 1237,[3] that between Harley and Cressage on the north-west was determined at the inclosure of Harley and Cressage Woods, c. 1519.[4] A projection of the parish boundary on the slope of Wenlock Edge south-west of Blakeway Farm is probably in origin the assart which the lord of Harley was given licence to make in woodland belonging to Presthope manor in 1331.[5]

The detached part of Much Wenlock, which represented the lands in Harley held by Wenlock Priory in the Middle Ages, consisted of scattered fields in the north and east of the parish. It was not considered part of the parish of Holy Trinity, Wenlock, in the Middle Ages,[6] but tithes arising therefrom were paid to the Priory in 1534[7] and after the Dissolution it seems to have been accounted part of Wenlock parish by virtue of the so-called 'Dictum of St. Milburgh'.[8]

The parish is watered by Harley Brook (formerly called Plash Brook), which runs north-eastwards across its centre and has a number of tributaries. Another stream, formerly called Sandibrook, rises to the north of the village and flows northwards towards the Severn. Harley Brook and its tributaries are bordered by a wide belt of boulder clay. Domas and Rowley, two former hamlets of Harley, lie in this area, to the north and south of Harley Brook respectively. South of the brook the land rises gently from 250 feet to 400 feet near Blakeway Farm. The clay here gives place to Wenlock shales and the escarpment of Wenlock Edge rises sharply to some 850 feet. Harley village stands at about 325 feet on the southern slope of an extensive bed of sand and gravel, which produces the undulating landscape of the north-east quarter of the parish. There are smaller deposits of sand and gravel near Domas and Rowley. On the west the land rises towards the Kenley ridge, reaching 516 feet at the parish boundary.

[50] T.S.A.S. 2nd ser. i. 81. There was one reputed papist in 1706: Lich. Dioc. Regy., B/a 11.
[51] Lich. Dioc. Regy., B/v 1/87.
[52] W.S.L., Hand-Morgan uncat., diocesan survey, c. 1680.
[53] Q. Sess. Orders, ii. 8.
[54] Visit. Archd. Salop. 1799.
[55] Lich. Dioc. Regy., applications for dissenting meeting-house licenses. This cottage, now demolished, stood on the west of the Condover road: par. rec., tithe appt.
[56] Visit. Archd. Salop. 1823; Kelly's Dir. Salop. (1856); local inf.
[57] Par. rec., vestry minutes.
[58] 24th Rep. Com. Char. H.C. 231, p. 385 (1831), xi.
[59] Par. rec., tenancy agreements, 1833, 1850.
[60] Ex inf. the Rector.
[61] 24th Rep. Com. Char. 385.
[62] Bagshaw's Dir. Salop. (1851).
[63] 24th Rep. Com. Char. 385-6.
[1] O.S. Area Bk. (1883). The following topographical description is based, except where otherwise stated, on

O.S. Map 1", sheet lxi (1st edn.); O.S. Map 6" Salop. 50 (1st and later edns.); O.S. Maps 1/25,000, SO 69 (1956), SJ 60 (1958), SJ 50, SO 59 (1959); Rocque, Map of Salop. (1752); Baugh, Map of Salop. (1808); Greenwood, Map of Salop. (1827); B.M. O.S. 2" orig. drawings, sheet 207 (1817); Geol. Survey Map (drift), sheet 152 (1932); par. rec., tithe appt. and map, 1842; S.R.O., 294/5 (Much Wenlock tithe appt. and map (Harley, Wigwig, and Homer), 1846). This article was written in 1962 and revised in 1965.
[2] Census, 1891.
[3] Close R. 1234-7, 571.
[4] Sta. Cha. 2/30/51.
[5] Barnard MSS., Raby Castle, box 1, bdle 29, no. 4.
[6] Not recorded in perambulation of bounds of Much Wenlock, 1331: S.R.O. 1224 uncat.
[7] N.L.W., Wynnstay (1952), box 43, no. 96.
[8] It is described as 'within the precinct of the Holy Trinity of Much Wenlock' in 1541: T.S.A.S. 1st ser. vi. 101. For the Dictum see Eyton, iii. 232-3, 238.

Much of the south and west of the parish was still woodland in the Middle Ages. In 1086 the manor contained sufficient wood for 100 swine,[9] and grants of common rights in Harley Wood are recorded in the 12th and early 13th centuries.[10] Rowley Wood stood in the south-west of the parish, where the tenants of the adjoining manor of Presthope were granted common rights in 1331.[11] That the woodland which still covers much of the escarpment of Wenlock Edge formerly extended northwards towards Harley Brook is indicated by the names Rough Hayes and Hay Field borne by several fields in this area, but it appears to have been cleared by c. 1600.[12] On the west of the parish, running north from Harley Brook, was a belt of woodland which would seem, from the evidence of field-names, to have been about half a mile wide.[13] Some assarting had taken place here by 1537,[14] but the greater part was probably cleared to supply charcoal for an iron forge erected on Harley Brook by 1607.[15] In 1842 there were 206 a. of woodland in the parish, more than half of it on Wenlock Edge,[16] and there has been little subsequent change.

The former common fields of Harley township[17] were called the Field towards Wigwig (or East Field), the Field towards Cressage (or North Field), and the Field towards Blakeway (or West Field). Apart from the southern half of West Field they lay on the gravels to the north and east of the village. The layout of a typical open-field holding was preserved in fossilized form until 1882 in the detached part of Much Wenlock parish. This also shows how far the process of consolidation of strips had progressed here by the early 16th century. The small scattered strips on the gravels of North and East Field stand in contrast to the compact block of land in West Field, where the gravel and boulder clay regions join. There is no evidence of any formal inclosure. The common fields continued to be mentioned until 1734, the last detailed reference to an open-field holding being in 1683.

The road from Wenlock through Harley to Cressage, possibly constructed in this part of its course by Henry I c. 1102,[18] was turnpiked in 1752.[19] A toll-house which stood to the south of Harley Brook in 1808[20] was sold to the lord of the manor in 1875.[21] The stone bridge over the brook was built by Thomas Carline in 1843.[22]

Stone implements found in the parish[23] and the Roman villa site at Yarchester[24] are evidence of early settlement here. The church, standing at the junction of roads from Wigwig, Blakeway, and Kenley with the main road, has always been the central point of the village. The site of the manor-house is not known. The lord was resident in 1327,[25] but it was said to be worth nothing in 1349,[26] and no lord of the manor has subsequently lived in the parish. The materials of the gatehouse and kitchen, the latter roofed with Harnage slates, were sold in 1368.[27] The manorial dovecote, first recorded in the 13th century,[28] stood in a field to the north of the churchyard in the 17th century and was still in use in 1688.[29] This field, then called The Conigree and later First Coney Burrow, was used as a rabbit-warren at this time.[30]

Until the 18th century the houses in the village stood on the roads to Wigwig and Domas and on the west side of the Wenlock road between the church and the mill on Harley Brook. The Old Rectory, to the west of the church, is probably the oldest surviving house. The original house, now the south wing, was a timber-framed building with a central chimney stack and a storied porch on the east side. This had probably been built before 1612.[31] Later in the 17th century[32] a timber-framed wing was added at right angles on the north side, incorporating or replacing the kitchen of the original house. A stone kitchen was built to the west in the 18th century, and a projecting brick wing was added on the north-east between 1805 and 1823.[33] Forge Farm, to the north of the Domas road, appears to be the oldest of the existing farmhouses. It is a brick-cased timber-framed house with a central stack, probably built in the earlier 17th century. No. 3, Harley, opposite the church, is the most striking of several timber-framed houses on the Wenlock road, but is unlikely to have been built before the 17th century.

In the 18th century the farms became larger and less numerous.[34] In the original village houses tended to be more widely spaced and several were then rebuilt in stone, for example, the mill, the cottages on the church lands, and Harley House. At the same time a number of isolated farms and cottages were erected, including Cressage Park Farm,[35] Merrishaw Farm, Domas Farm, 1–2, Domas Cottages, and the cottage called Crow's Nest on the Kenley road. The inclosure of the common fields to the north of the village permitted expansion along the Cressage road. The cottage to the north of the churchyard and the old smithy are both stone houses of 18th-century date. Harley

---

[9] V.C.H. Salop. i. 337.
[10] Eyton, vi. 231; Hist. MSS. Com. Middleton, 51.
[11] Barnard MSS., Raby Castle, box 1, bdle. 29, no. 4.
[12] Ibid. leases.
[13] Between the road to New Hall and Harley Brook it is separated from the former common fields by a number of fields called Stocking.
[14] Sta. Cha. 2/30/32; ibid. 2/30/51.
[15] See p. 89. Charcoal burners' 'rings' have been found in several fields to the north of the forge: ex inf. Mr. L. J. Brookshaw, Forge Farm.
[16] Par. rec., tithe appt.
[17] Description of common fields based on Barnard MSS., Raby Castle, leases; ibid. box 1, bdle. 29, nos. 2, 4, 6, 9; Lich Dioc. Regy., glebe terriers, 1612–1824; par. rec., tithe appt.
[18] Ordericus Vitalis, Historia Ecclesiastica, ed. A. le Prevost (Paris, 1838–55), iv. 176.
[19] Shrewsbury–Wenlock road Act, 25 Geo. II, c. 49 (priv. act).
[20] Baugh, Map of Salop. (1752).

[21] Barnard MSS., Raby Castle, press 14, no. 87.
[22] Q. Sess., dep. plans, 65; Q. Sess. Orders, iv. 32.
[23] T. R. Horton collect., Shrews. Museum.
[24] The site has been partially excavated. See V.C.H. Salop. i. 261; T.S.A.S. lvi. 7; Shropshire Newsletter, Dec. 1957, July 1958. Adjoining fields were called 'Harechester' in the 16th century: Barnard MSS., Raby Castle, leases.
[25] T.S.A.S. 2nd ser. xi. 376.
[26] C 135/96/14.
[27] S.P.L., MS. 2, f. 438.
[28] Barnard MSS., Raby Castle, box 1, bdle 29, no. 1.
[29] Ibid. leases, 1619, 1688.
[30] Ibid. 1598, 1619, 1664, 1688.
[31] Lich. Dioc. Regy., glebe terrier, 1612, where it is described as a house and kitchen under one roof.
[32] Probably before 1662, when the house had 6 hearths: E 179/255/35 m. 75.
[33] Visit. Archd. Salop. 1823.
[34] See p. 89.
[35] Burnt down 1875: notes penes Miss E. M. Jones, Cressage.

Court (formerly Harley Towers), with the windmill and cottages adjoining and the village shop, were built in the early 19th century. Castle Hill House, near Forge Farm on the Domas road, was built *c.* 1840, but stands on the site of an earlier house and derives its name from a crenellated brick tower built by John Corfield in 1791.[36] Only 3 buildings—the school (1859), Grove Farm (*c.* 1923) and the new parsonage—have been erected in the village since 1842, but a few others have been enlarged.

There were two alehouses in Harley in 1616.[37] The 'Unicorn', which adjoined the east of the churchyard and lay partly in Harley and partly in the detached part of Much Wenlock, was closed shortly after 1863.[38] The village had a second alehouse, 1759–72.[39] The 'Feathers', later the 'Plume of Feathers' and now the Feathers Hotel, is first recorded in 1842.[40] It is a stone-built house, probably of 18th-century date, which appears to have been converted into an inn in the early 19th century.

There is reason to believe that the 4 manors which existed in Harley before 1066[41] each represented a distinct hamlet, and that these were Harley itself, Domas, Rowley, and Blakeway. The last three stand on or near a road which formerly ran southwards from Harley to Blakeway, where it was joined by roads from Much Wenlock, Presthope, and Gippols.[42] There is no evidence of common fields at Domas—presumably they were incorporated in Harley's West Field—but 'the Field of Blakeway' is mentioned in 1331[43] and there are traces of ridge-and-furrow in a field to the south-west of Rowley Farm. All 3 hamlets must have shrunk to single farms at an early period. Blakeway Farm and Rowley Farm stood alone when first mentioned in 1536[44] and 1600[45] respectively. Both are brick-cased timber-framed houses, probably built in the early 17th century. At Domas are only the two 18th-century stone houses mentioned above.

The parish contained 100 communicants in 1676.[46] The population rose from 221 in 1801[47] to a peak of 257 in 1831.[48] Thereafter it fell steadily to 178 in 1881[49] and, in spite of the addition of the 25 inhabitants of the detached part of Wenlock in 1882,[50] had fallen to 173 in 1911.[51] Since then the population has remained static: there were 150 inhabitants in 1961.[52]

MANOR. Roger, Earl of Shrewsbury, was overlord of *HARLEY* manor in 1086.[53] It was annexed, probably in 1102, to the honour of Montgomery,[54] with which it was first explicitly associated in 1225, when it was held of Hilary Trusbut.[55] William Cauntelow was overlord in 1242[56] and 1254,[57] and on the death of George Cauntelow in 1273[58] it passed to his sister Millicent, wife of Eudes la Zouche.[59] The substitution of the Earls of March as overlords of Harley, first recorded in 1360,[60] seems to have arisen from confusion with the manor of Meole Brace, where the Mortimers had been overlords by 1086[61] and the Cauntelows mesne lords since 1211.[62] Edmund, Earl of March, was accounted overlord in 1425, when William la Zouche was mesne lord,[63] but the overlordship presumably reverted to the Zouches in 1460, since John, Lord Zouche, was overlord in 1503.[64] The overlordship is last recorded in 1623, when the manor was held of Thomas Edwards as of the manor of Meole Brace.[65]

Before 1066 Harley was held as four manors by the freemen Edric, Ulmar, Elmund, and Edric, and in 1086 Helgot was lord of the single manor here.[66] By 1180 and until *c.* 1209 the manor was held by Malcoline de Harley[67] and it is likely that Edward and Hernulf, who were successively lords of Harley in the early 12th century, were ancestors of his.[68] William de Harley, whose relationship to Malcoline is not clear,[69] was lord by 1221.[70] He died in 1225, when his heir was a minor.[71] This was probably Richard de Harley, who was lord in 1237,[72] 1242,[73] and 1254.[74] He was dead by 1262[75] and his son Robert by 1269.[76] Robert's son Richard was then a minor,[77] but had come of age by 1276[78] and died in 1316.[79] Robert, son of Richard, was lord from 1316[80] until his death in 1349,[81] but his father's widow Burga held one third of the manor in dower and was still living in 1337.[82] The manor then passed to Robert's son Robert,[83] who married Joan Corbet *c.* 1360,[84] when it was settled on their joint heirs.[85] Robert de Harley died intestate in 1370.[86] A con-

[36] Datestone.
[37] Q. Sess., alehouse reg.
[38] Ibid.; N.L.W., Castle Hill 2244; par. rec., tithe appt.
[39] Ibid.
[40] Par. rec., tithe appt.
[41] *V.C.H. Salop.* i. 337.
[42] This road now ends at Rowley Farm and the roads to Presthope and Gippols are disused. The road to Wenlock has been superseded by one following a less precipitous route, constructed in 1859: par. rec., churchwardens' accts. 1793–1837.
[43] Barnard MSS., Raby Castle, box 1, bdle 29, no. 4.
[44] Ibid. no. 27.   [45] Ibid. leases.
[46] *T.S.A.S.* 2nd ser. i. 81.
[47] *Census*, 1801.
[48] Ibid. 1831.
[49] Ibid. 1841–81.
[50] Ibid. 1891.
[51] Ibid. 1911.
[52] Ibid. 1961.
[53] *V.C.H. Salop.* i. 337.
[54] Eyton, vi. 231.
[55] Ibid. xi. 125.
[56] *Bk. of Fees*, 966.
[57] *Rot. Hund.* (Rec. Com.), ii. 62.
[58] *Cal. Inq. p.m.* ii, p. 19.
[59] *Cal. Fine R.* 1272–1307, 18.
[60] *Cal. Inq. p.m.* xiv, p. 350.
[61] *V.C.H. Salop.* i. 347.

[62] Eyton, vi. 354–5.
[63] C 139/19/32.
[64] *Cal. Inq. p.m. Hen. VII*, iii, p. 543.
[65] C 142/402/146.
[66] *V.C.H. Salop.* i. 337.
[67] Eyton, vi. 232; cf. ibid. iii. 294; ibid. iv. 21; ibid. vi. 86, 329.
[68] Ibid. vi. 231–2, citing undated charter to Wenlock Priory. Copy in S.R.O. 1224 uncat., Prior Gosnell's reg.
[69] He was described as son of Robert Malherve in 1221: Eyton, vi. 233. cf. Hist. MSS. Com. *Middleton*, 51.
[70] Eyton, vi. 123–4, 136, 232–3.
[71] Ibid. xi. 125; *Close R.* 1227–31, 249.
[72] *Close R.* 1234–7, 571.
[73] *Bk. of Fees*, 966.
[74] *Rot. Hund.* (Rec. Com.), ii. 62.
[75] Eyton, vi. 234.
[76] Ibid.   [77] Ibid.
[78] *Cal. Pat.* 1272–9, 294; *Abbrev. Plac.* (Rec. Com.), 198.
[79] Eyton, vi. 235.
[80] *Feud. Aids*, iv. 229.
[81] *Cal. Inq. p.m.* ix, p. 186.
[82] Barnard MSS., Raby Castle, box 1, bdle. 29, no. 5.
[83] *Cal. Inq. p.m.* ix, p. 186.
[84] Barnard MSS., Raby Castle, box 1, bdle. 29, nos. 11–14.
[85] Ibid.; C.P. 25(1)/195/16/41.
[86] Barnard MSS., Raby Castle, box 1, bdle. 29, nos. 18–20; *Cal. Pat.* 1374–7, 140, 154.

veyance of the manor to Peter Cornwall in 1370,[87] shortly before Robert's death, was probably no more than a mortgage. Later in the same year the manor was settled jointly on Cornwall and Robert's widow Joan,[88] but by 1375 it was held by Joan alone.[89] She had married John Darras by 1395,[90] but in 1400 her estates were settled on herself for life, with remainder to Henry de Grendon and his wife Elizabeth, Joan's grand-daughter by her first husband.[91] Elizabeth subsequently married Richard Lacon,[92] who was lord of Harley by 1428.[93] The manor passed from father to son in the Lacon family until 1618,[94] the following being lords: Richard, by 1428;[95] William, until 1462;[96] Richard, 1462–1503;[97] Thomas, 1503–36;[98] Richard, 1536–43;[99] Rowland, 1543–1608;[1] Francis, 1608–18.[2] In 1618 Francis Lacon sold the manor to Sir Francis Newport,[3] and it followed the descent of Cressage manor until 1734.[4]

On the death of Henry, Earl of Bradford, in 1734, the manor passed, under the terms of his will, to his mistress Mrs. Anne Smyth in trust for his illegitimate son John Harrison.[5] Mrs. Smyth died in 1742,[6] having devised the reversion to William, Earl of Bath.[7] John Harrison, who later assumed the name of Newport,[8] was a lunatic. His estates were held by William, Earl of Bath, as sole trustee from 1742 until the latter's death in 1764,[9] when the trusteeship and reversion passed to William's brother General Harry Pulteney.[10] Pulteney died in 1767,[11] having devised them to William Pulteney, who obtained possession of the manor on the death of John Newport in 1783.[12] The manor has subsequently followed the descent of Cressage manor.[13]

OTHER ESTATES. An estate of some 110 a.,[14] held by Wenlock Priory, is first recorded in 1379,[15] but was probably acquired in the 12th century. The

Priory obtained a grant of common rights in Harley Wood in the early 12th century,[16] and their Harley estate was subsequently closely associated with the adjoining manor of Wigwig, granted to the Priory in the time of Richard I.[17] In 1379 this property was administered as part of Bradley Grange,[18] but in and after 1390 it was a member of the manor of Marsh.[19] Marsh manor was granted to Stephen Hadnall in 1558[20] and was sold to Sir John Weld in 1619,[21] thereafter following the descent of Willey manor.[22] In 1522 the Harley property consisted of two copyholds held by John and Christopher Taylor.[23] One of these was enfranchised c. 1578[24] and the other probably became freehold at this time, since there is no indication that Hadnall or his successors held anything here apart from manorial rights.[25] The property held by Thomas Taylor in 1578[26] was sold to Sir Richard Newport in 1630,[27] but the other, now Castle Hill, has continued as a small freehold estate until the present time. It was owned by the Corfield family by 1808[28] and had passed by 1830 to John Meire,[29] whose family were the owners until 1922.[30]

Lands at Blakeway were granted to William Gatacre by Richard Lacon in 1536.[31] This estate, first called Blakeway Farm in 1605,[32] was sold to Thomas Lawley in 1612[33] and has since followed the descent of the Wenlock Priory estate.[34]

ECONOMIC HISTORY. The manor, which was worth 21s. before the Conquest, was waste after 1066, but had recovered by 1086, when it was worth 40s.[35] It was then said to contain 4 hides, with land for 4½ ploughs.[36] It was assessed at 3½ hides in 1229[37] and at 3 hides in 1254.[38] In 1349 its annual value had fallen from £7 5s. to £3 13s. 6d. on account of the Black Death.[39] In 1086 land for 1½ plough lay in the demesne,[40] which was said to comprise 2 carucates of arable and 3 a. meadow in

[87] C.P. 25(1)/288/49/707.
[88] Barnard MSS., Raby Castle, box 1, bdle. 29, nos. 18–19.
[89] Ibid. nos. 21–22. Cornwall's interest in the manor had passed to Fulk Corbett by 1382: Cal. Pat. 1374–7, 140, 154; C 136/25/16.
[90] Barnard MSS., Raby Castle, box 1, bdle. 29, no. 23; Visit. Salop. 1623 (Harl. Soc. xxviii), i. 214.
[91] S.R.O. 1224 uncat., deed 1400. cf. S.P.L., Deeds 1715; Visit. Salop. 1623 (Harl. Soc. xxviii), i. 214; ibid. ii. 306.
[92] Visit. Salop. 1623 (Harl. Soc. xxix), ii. 306.
[93] Feud. Aids, iv. 256.
[94] For pedigree see Visit. Salop. 1623 (Harl. Soc. xxix), ii. 302–8.
[95] Ibid.
[96] Barnard MSS., Raby Castle, box 1, bdle. 29, no. 24.
[97] Ibid.; Cal. Inq. p.m. Hen. VII, iii, p. 543.
[98] Cal. Inq. p.m. Hen. VII, iii, p. 543; Barnard MSS., Raby Castle, box 1, bdle. 29, no. 25; C 142/58/60.
[99] C 142/58/60; C 142/68/7.
[1] C 142/68/7; C 142/312/7. In wardship until 1567: L. & P. Hen. VIII, xiii (1), p. 144; Barnard MSS., Raby Castle, box 1, bdle. 29, no. 29a.
[2] C 142/312/147.
[3] Barnard MSS., Raby Castle, box 1, bdle. 29, nos. 38–52.
[4] See p. 75.
[5] Complete Peerage, ii. 275.
[6] Ibid.
[7] S. Garbett, The History of Wem (Wem, 1818), 107; S.P.L., MS. 2791, p. 397.
[8] Complete Peerage, ii. 275.
[9] Q. Sess., gamekeepers' deputations, 1743, 1749; Complete Peerage, ii. 23.
[10] Complete Peerage, ii. 24.
[11] Ibid.

[12] Ibid. 24, 27, 275; S.P.L., MS. 4646, p. 285; Q. Sess., gamekeepers' deputations, 1774, 1799.
[13] See p. 75.
[14] The acreage in 1808: N.L.W., Wynnstay (1952), box 43, no. 8.
[15] Dugdale, Mon. v. 77.
[16] Eyton, vi. 231.
[17] Ibid. 266.
[18] Dugdale, Mon. v. 77.
[19] Eyton, iii. 284.
[20] Cal. Pat. 1557–8, 378–9.
[21] T.S.A.S. 3rd ser. i. 187–8.
[22] S.R.O. 1224 uncat., title-deeds of Willey manor.
[23] N.L.W., Wynnstay (1952), box 56, no. 111.
[24] Barnard MSS., Raby Castle, box 1, bdle. 31, no. 1.
[25] A rental of the manor of Marsh, c. 1600, includes no Harley tenants: S.R.O. 1224 uncat.
[26] Barnard MSS., Raby Castle, box 1, bdle. 31, no. 1.
[27] Ibid. no. 10.
[28] N.L.W., Wynnstay (1952), box 43, no. 8. Edward Corfield, a ratepayer of Harley in 1734, was probably owner of Castle Hill: par. rec., par. bk. 1700–38.
[29] W.S.L. 350/40/3.
[30] Castle Hill title-deeds, penes the late Miss Frances Pitt.
[31] Barnard MSS., Raby Castle, box 1, bdle. 29, no. 27.
[32] Ibid. box 7, bdle. 13, no. 1.
[33] C 3/316/39.
[34] Wenlock Priory title-deeds, penes Barclays Bank, Much Wenlock.
[35] V.C.H. Salop. i. 337.
[36] Ibid.
[37] Close R. 1227–31, 249.
[38] Rot. Hund. (Rec. Com.), ii. 62.
[39] C 135/96/14.
[40] V.C.H. Salop. i. 337.

1349.[41] The growth of the manorial estate, said to contain 1,400 a. by 1609,[42] may be accounted for by the clearance of woodland in the west of the parish, in which the lords seem to have taken the initiative.[43] Comparatively little was added by purchase: two small freeholds were bought in the 14th century[44] and some 48 a. in the detached part of Much Wenlock in 1630,[45] but these were offset by the sale of Blakeway Farm in 1536.[46] In 1842, when the manorial estate totalled 1,552 a., the only other sizeable freehold estates, apart from the glebe (53 a.) and church lands (10 a.), were Blakeway Farm (363 a.) and Castle Hill (51 a.)[47] There were two other freeholds of less than 10 a.[48] The manorial estate comprised 1,515 a. in 1945.[49] last of Rowley Farm (276 a.) was sold in 1957 and the remainder in 1962.[50]

Little is known of the administration of the estate before the 18th century. In 1086 there were 3 serfs on the demesne, with one villein and one bordar.[51] Assized rents of free tenants, normally worth £4, were valued at only 10s. in 1349.[52] There were said to be 20 messuages and 6 cottages in the manor in 1609,[53] and 24 tenants attorned to the new lord in 1618.[54] Rents produced £131 a year c. 1646.[55] Until the mid-18th century a substantial part of the estate was held on three-life leases.[56] The leases, which always included covenants for payment of heriot and for suit of court, contained provisions for military service, 1628–93, and a clause against wearing the livery of strangers, 1638–83.

In 1734 there were 14 leaseholders for lives and 11 tenants-at-will paying rents of £74 and £82 respectively.[57] The structure of the estate was little changed in 1747,[58] when there were 10 leaseholders, 11 tenants-at-will, and 2 holdings under both tenures. Some 1,020 a. leasehold land produced rents of £57 a year, and a little more than 670 a. land held at will, £135 a year. Large farms were already a feature of the estate—there were five holdings of over 100 a.—but 14 of the 23 tenants held farms of 10–100 a. Many leaseholds had been converted to tenure at will by 1768,[59] when there were only 6 leaseholders paying annual rents of £17 and 17 tenants at will paying £276. The transition to large farms was virtually complete by 1842,[60] when some 1,250 a. of the estate lay in five farms of over 100 a. In the parish as a whole there were six farms of over 100 a., five holdings of 10–100 a., and 15 of less than

10 a. Most of the smaller holdings were centred on houses in the village; only two of them may have been in origin forest encroachments. Apart from the glebe and the woodland then kept in hand by the Duke of Cleveland (86 a.) and Sir Watkin Williams Wynn (120 a.), no land in the parish was held by owner-occupiers. In 1945[61] 1,391 a. of the 1,515 a. in the estate lay in the five large farms and there were only two smaller holdings, each of less than 10 a.

An 8-acre field to the north of the Kenley road had been converted into allotments by 1846,[62] when there were 14 tenants. There were still 4 allotments here in 1945,[63] but these have since gone out of use.

There were said to be 524 a. arable in the parish in 1801,[64] but this was probably an under-estimate, and by 1842 there was considerably more arable than pasture.[65] In 1945 most farms on the Barnard estate had slightly more pasture than arable, but Harley House Farm then had more than twice as much arable.[66] The principal crops in 1801 were wheat (223 a.) and oats (161 a.).[67] In 1852 wheat was the main crop on the clay soils, where a three-course rotation of fallow, wheat, and clover was in use; on the gravel soils a four-course rotation was followed.[68]

A water-mill which is recorded in 1086,[69] was in use until c. 1900, but had been closed by 1905[70] and is now a private house. Two water-mills were in operation here in the 17th and 18th centuries and were held by the Carter family by 1619 and until 1734.[71] A windmill which adjoined Harley Court was erected before 1813[72] and in 1842 was held by the tenant of the water-mill.[73] This was a tower windmill, the body of which was demolished in 1960.[74]

An iron forge, presumably managed in conjunction with the furnace at Kenley,[75] had been erected by 1607 on Harley Brook about a mile south-west of the village.[76] In 1638, when it was leased for 10 years to William Boycott and William Fownes,[77] the forge comprised a chafery, an upper and lower finery, and houses for the finer and hammerman.[78] In 1658 it was leased for 12 years to Cornelius Hallen, a Stourbridge copper-worker,[79] but it was described as 'now decayed' in 1664, when two houses on the site were let to a Cardington dyer on condition that he would erect a fulling mill there.[80]

Mineral rights were regularly reserved to the lord

[41] C 135/96/14.
[42] C 142/312/147.
[43] Malcoline de Harley cleared some 60 a. woodland in the later 12th century: Pipe R. 1185 (P.R.S. xxxiv), 128; E 32/143 m. 1; E 32/144 m. 1. For later activity by lords of the manor, see Cal. Chart. R. 1300–26, 29; Barnard MSS., Raby Castle, box 1, bdle. 29, no. 4; Sta. Cha. 2/30/32; ibid. 2/30/51.
[44] C 47/76/2/50; S.P.L., Deeds 1715.
[45] Barnard MSS., Raby Castle, box 1, bdle. 31, no. 10. Acreage from S.R.O. 294/5.
[46] Barnard MSS., Raby Castle, box 1, bdle. 29, no. 27.
[47] Par. rec., tithe appt.; S.R.O. 294/5.
[48] Ibid.
[49] Uppington estate office, terrier, c. 1920.
[50] Ibid.
[51] V.C.H. Salop. i. 337.
[52] C 135/96/14.
[53] C 142/312/147.
[54] Barnard MSS., Raby Castle, box 1, bdle. 29, nos. 50–51.
[55] T.S.A.S. 2nd ser. xii. 21–22.
[56] Ninety Harley leases, 1542–1734, are in Barnard MSS., Raby Castle, wooden box 6, bdle. 19, and wooden box 12, bdles. 13, 16, 21–22, 24–25.

[57] Ibid. receiver's accts. 1734–41.
[58] S.R.O. 168/4.
[59] Barnard MSS., Raby Castle, receiver's accts. 1768–81.
[60] Par. rec., tithe appt.; S.R.O. 294/5.
[61] Uppington estate office, terrier, c. 1920.
[62] S.R.O. 294/5.
[63] Uppington estate office, terrier, c. 1920.
[64] H.O. 67/14/124.
[65] Par. rec., tithe appt.
[66] Uppington estate office, terrier, c. 1920.
[67] H.O. 67/14/124.
[68] Letter, 1852, in Visit. Archd. Salop. 1843.
[69] V.C.H. Salop. i. 337.
[70] Kelly's Dir. Salop. (1900, 1905).
[71] Barnard MSS., Raby Castle, leases.
[72] S.R.O. 1242 uncat., mortgage, 1813.
[73] Par. rec., tithe appt.
[74] Ex inf. Mr. M. P. E. Preece, Harley Court.
[75] See p. 96.
[76] S.R.O. 840 uncat., rental of Lacon estates, 1607.
[77] Barnard MSS., Raby Castle, leases.
[78] Ibid.
[79] Ibid.
[80] Ibid.

in leases after 1638,[81] and in 1657 Sir Francis Newport obtained licence to search for coals in the manor,[82] but no coal is known to have been mined here. Limekilns adjoining the Wenlock road at the foot of Wenlock Edge, were known as the New Works in 1817.[83] They were still in operation in 1842, when a rail-road was used to convey limestone from the top of the Edge.[84] A field a quarter mile south-east of Blakeway Farm, called Limekiln Piece in 1842[85] and Lyme Piece in 1714,[86] was probably the site of the kiln occupied by Thomas Blakeway in 1522.[87] It was part of Blakeway Farm in 1714,[88] but by 1780 was merely producing lime for use on the farm.[89] Bricks were made at some time in a field near Domas called Brick-kiln meadow in 1846[90] and Claypit in 1659.[91]

A smithy is first recorded in 1564, when it stood on Harley Brook to the west of the village,[92] near the site of the iron forge, but it had gone out of use by 1628.[93] Thereafter the smithy was in the village. Harley had its full complement of tradesfolk in 1852, when there were two bricklayers, two carpenters, two tailors, two shoemakers, and a blacksmith.[94] In addition a wheelwright, recorded in 1851,[95] occupied one of the cottages on the Wenlock road to the south of the church.[96] Only a blacksmith remained by 1909,[97] and the smithy closed c. 1944.[98] The village shop, on the Cressage road, occupies the same site as it did in 1842.[99]

LOCAL GOVERNMENT. There are manor court rolls, 1421 and 1436,[1] and suit rolls, 1813–43.[2] The parish records include a parish book, containing accounts of churchwardens and overseers, 1700–38, churchwardens' accounts, 1787–1893, and overseers' accounts, 1793–1837. There are no records of vestry meetings, apart from occasional memoranda in the accounts. Until 1797 there were two churchwardens, who accounted separately, 1735–8 and 1794–7, but between 1797 and 1822 a single churchwarden rendered account, the office being held by the same man for several years. Their routine expenses were covered by rents from the church lands, which produced £6 a year in the early 18th century and £19 6s. in 1841.[3] Additional expenditure was met by loans on the security of the church lands,[4] but resort was had to church rates after 1845. The offices of churchwarden and overseer were occasionally combined in the early 18th century. The two overseers kept a joint account until 1737, but in 1738 and between 1793 and 1816 they each accounted for half their year of office. From 1817 until 1837 their duties were performed and their accounts kept by a salaried assistant overseer. Poor rates, which are entered in the accounts from 1734, were always assessed on a pound rate. A cottage on the church lands was described as the almshouse in 1721, and a poor-house was built in 1724. This was still in use in 1802,[5] but in the 1770s the overseers were renting a poor-house from the lord of the manor,[6] which they probably still held in the early 19th century.[7] Between 1693 and 1738 annual disbursements on poor relief ranged from £3 to £12, but reached £18 in 1734.[8] Expenditure had risen to £48 by 1776[9] and to £150 by 1801.[10] From 1801 to 1822 annual expenses were normally over £150 and reached a peak of some £180 between 1810 and 1815. From 1822 until 1834 they fluctuated between £97 and £154.[11]

CHURCH. Harley church is first recorded in 1291.[12] The benefice is a rectory and from the 16th century at least has normally been held with Kenley, with which it was united in 1939.[13] The advowson has always followed the descent of the manor.

The rectory was valued at £3 6s. 8d. in 1291.[14] Its gross value had risen to £6 by 1535[15] and to £58 by 1655.[16] The annual net income was said to be £200 in 1799[17] and £276 in the 1830s.[18] Tithes were paid in kind until 1842,[19] apart from a modus on the mill, and on milk and calves, which had been introduced by 1698.[20] They were worth £44 in 1655,[21] £107 6s. in 1781,[22] and were commuted for a rent-charge of £270 in 1842.[23] Tithes payable to Wenlock Priory from its Harley estate, which were worth 18s. in 1534,[24] had been leased to Richard Nyld in 1530.[25] They were granted for life in 1554 to Stephen Hadnall,[26] who obtained the reversion in 1558.[27] In 1655, when they were worth £3 a year, they were held by Edward Harnage.[28] By 1846 most of the great tithes arising from the detached part of Much Wenlock were merged in the freehold of the lands concerned, but two landowners paid nominal moduses for small tithes to the vicar of Much Wenlock.[29] The bulk of the scattered glebe, worth £14 a year in 1655,[30] was said to comprise some

[81] Barnard MSS., Raby Castle, leases.
[82] Ibid. box 2, bdle. 5.
[83] B.M. O.S. 2″ orig. drawings, sheet 207 (1817).
[84] Par. rec., tithe appt.
[85] Ibid.
[86] N.L.W., Wynnstay (1952), box E, no. 62.
[87] Ibid. box 56, no. 111.
[88] Ibid. box E, no. 62.
[89] Ibid. box F, no. 8.
[90] S.R.O. 294/5.
[91] Ibid. 1224 uncat., Marsh manor ct. r. 1659.
[92] Barnard MSS., Raby Castle, leases.
[93] Ibid.
[94] Letter, 1852, in Visit. Archd. Salop. 1843.
[95] Bagshaw's Dir. Salop. (1851).
[96] Par. rec., tithe appt.
[97] Kelly's Dir. Salop (1909).
[98] Ex inf. Mr. L. J. Brookshaw, Forge Farm.
[99] Par. rec., tithe appt.
[1] S.R.O. 840 uncat., ct. r. 1421, 1436.
[2] Ibid. 248/27–32.
[3] cf. Lich. Dioc. Regy., glebe terrier, 1841.
[4] As in 1788, 1793, and 1814.
[5] Par. rec., churchwardens' accts. 1787–1893.
[6] Barnard MSS., Raby Castle, receiver's accts. 1768–81.

[7] Par. rec., overseers' accts. 1793–1837.
[8] Bodl. MS. Blakeway 8, f. 476; par. rec., par. bk. 1700–38.
[9] Rep. Cttee. on Overseers' Returns, 1777, p. 442, H.C. (1st ser. ix, reprinted 1803).
[10] Par. rec., overseers' accts. 1793–1837.   [11] Ibid.
[12] Tax. Eccl. (Rec. Com.), 244.
[13] Lond. Gaz. 1939, p. 847.
[14] Tax. Eccl. (Rec. Com.), 244.
[15] Valor Eccl. (Rec. Com.), iii. 184.
[16] T.S.A.S. xlvii. 29.
[17] Visit. Archd. Salop. 1799.
[18] Rep. Com. Eccl. Revenues [67], pp. 480–1, H.C. (1835), xxii.
[19] Lich. Dioc. Regy., glebe terriers; par. rec., tithe appt.
[20] Lich. Dioc. Regy., glebe terrier, 1698.
[21] T.S.A.S. xlvii. 29.
[22] Letter, 1852, in Visit. Archd. Salop. 1843.
[23] Par. rec., tithe appt.
[24] N.L.W., Wynnstay (1952), box 43, no. 96; Valor. Eccl. (Rec. Com.), iii. 216.
[25] S.C. 6/Hen. VIII/3021 m. 8.
[26] Cal. Pat. 1554–5, 21–22.
[27] Ibid. 1557–8, 378–9.   [28] T.S.A.S. xlvii. 29.
[29] S.R.O. 294/5.   [30] T.S.A.S. xlvii. 29.

34 a. in 1679.[31] It was exchanged for a compact holding around the rectory between 1805 and 1823,[32] and in 1842 comprised 52 a. and two cottages.[33] The glebe was leased in the late 18th century,[34] but the rector was farming the greater part of it in 1841.[35] Most of it was sold in 1918.[36]

Lights to Our Lady in Harley church had been endowed with 1½ a. land by 1340[37] and a further 3 a. was granted in 1349.[38] By the 16th century the income was probably being employed, as later, towards the upkeep of the church.[39]

Most of the rectors of Harley have held the living for long periods. Of the 7 rectors before 1563, whose dates are known, 2 served for more than 30 years[40] and 2, as rectors or curates, for over 20 years.[41] Nine out of 11 rectors, 1563–1891, held the living for over 20 years, 2 of them for over 50 years,[42] and 7 died in office. In view of the close connexion between the manor and the church it is surprising that only one of the rectors, Henry son of Richard de Harley (rector 1331–53),[43] was a close relative of the lord of the manor. Benjamin Jenks (rector 1668–1724)[44] was private chaplain to Francis, Earl of Bradford.[45] Only 3 rectors are known to have been consistently non-resident. Henry de Harley obtained licence of absence to study shortly after his institution in 1331.[46] His duties at Harley were being performed by a curate in 1340[47] and he was instituted rector of Berrington in plurality in 1350.[48] Thomas Bent (rector 1588–1633)[49] was living at Kinlet in 1615[50] and employed George Bennet as curate in 1632.[51] Edmund Dana (rector 1781–1805),[52] who was also rector of Eaton Constantine and vicar of Wroxeter,[53] lived in Shrewsbury in 1799[54] and employed a succession of curates at Harley.[55] Four rectors began as curates to their predecessors.[56] The only notable rectors have been Benjamin Jenks, author of a number of theological works,[57] and John Gibbons (rector 1805–59), who consolidated the glebe lands, enlarged the parsonage and was responsible for the rebuilding of the church in 1845.[58]

Communion was administered from 4 to 8 times a year in the early 18th century,[59] 4 times a year in the early 19th century,[60] and monthly from c. 1864 until the end of the 19th century.[61] There were about 15 communicants in 1823[62] and 25 in 1847.[63] In 1799, under a non-resident rector, services were held once on Sundays, alternately at 9 a.m. and 2 p.m.[64] There was still a single Sunday service here in 1823[65] and 1851, when an average of 50 adults attended.[66] A body of psalm-singers, established c. 1792,[67] probably used the gallery, built by 1799.[68] Annual payments to the psalm-singers were made until 1878.[69] A harmonium was bought in 1863[70] and was replaced by another in 1938.

The church of ST. MARY[71] was largely rebuilt in 1845–6. Before 1845 it consisted of a chancel, nave, western tower, and north aisle. The nave and chancel were of 13th-century date. The west door of the nave, the chancel and tower arches, and the triple lancet east window were in Early English style. There were also 2 lancets in the north wall of the chancel and one in the south wall of the nave. On the south wall of the chancel was a priest's door, a small square window of unknown date, and a square-headed mullioned window of 2 lights, probably inserted in the 16th century. The north aisle is said to have been built, probably in the 16th century, by the Harnage family of Belswardine, who attended Harley church, though resident outside the parish,[72] and who had a vault beneath the aisle. It was divided from the nave by four rough wooden piers on stone bases and was lighted by a square-headed mullioned window of 2 lights at the east end, a lancet window at the west end, and a dormer window over the north wall. The nave roof, originally at the same level as that of the chancel, was raised some four feet, probably in the 16th century. The framed timber roof was supported by 2 pilasters on the inner face of the south wall and by 2 buttresses outside. The latter were enlarged until by the 19th century 'each had grown into an enormous ill-shapen mass'.[73] A dormer window like that in the north aisle was inserted above the south wall of the nave in the later 17th century.

The tower, the only part of the old church still remaining, was built in the early 16th century, presumably replacing a smaller tower of 13th-century date. It is of 3 stages, divided by string-

[31] Lich. Dioc. Regy., glebe terrier, 1679.
[32] Visit. Archd. Salop. 1823.
[33] Par. rec., tithe appt. It included 3 a. in the detached part of Much Wenlock: S.R.O. 294/5.
[34] Rates in par. rec., churchwardens' accts. 1787–1893.
[35] Lich. Dioc. Regy., glebe terrier, 1841.
[36] Ex inf. Church Com.
[37] Barnard MSS., Raby Castle, box 1, bdle. 29, no. 1.
[38] Ibid. no. 9.
[39] Not recorded in Chant. Cert: T.S.A.S. 3rd ser. x. 304–83.
[40] William de Stapleford, 1368–1403: Eyton, vi. 237. William Dyson, 1518–63: Bodl. MS. Blakeway 14, f. 101.
[41] Henry de Harley, 1331–53: Eyton, vi. 237. John le Panner, curate by 1340, and rector, 1353–68: Eyton, vi. 237; Barnard MSS., Raby Castle, box 1, bdle. 29, nos. 6, 9.
[42] Benjamin Jenks, 1668–1724: T.S.A.S. 3rd ser. v. 371; ibid. 4th ser. v. 193. John Gibbons, 1805–59: T.S.A.S. 4th ser. vii. 165; Lich. Dioc. Regy., reg. 32, p. 161.
[43] Eyton, vi. 237.
[44] T.S.A.S. 3rd ser. v. 371; ibid. 4th ser. v. 193.
[45] D.N.B.
[46] Eyton, vi. 237.
[47] Barnard MSS., Raby Castle, box 1, bdle. 29, no. 6.
[48] Eyton, vi. 47, 237.
[49] T.S.A.S. 3rd ser. i. 261, 264.
[50] Barnard MSS., Raby Castle, box 1, bdle. 29, no. 37.
[51] Lich. Dioc. Regy, bishop's transcripts.

[52] T.S.A.S. 4th ser. vi. 297; Lich. Dioc. Regy., reg. 28, p. 57.
[53] T.S.A.S. 4th ser. vi. 295, 297.
[54] Visit. Archd. Salop. 1799.
[55] S.P.R. Lich. ii (1), 26.
[56] John le Panner, Michael Ball, Benjamin Jenks, and John Gibbons: Barnard MSS., Raby Castle, box 1, bdle. 29, no. 6; T.S.A.S. 1st ser. vi. 130; D.N.B. sub Jenks; S.P.R. Lich. ii (1), 26.
[57] D.N.B.
[58] S.R.O. 800 uncat., correspondence of John Gibbons.
[59] Par. rec., par. bk. 1700–38.
[60] Visit. Archd. Salop. 1799, 1823, 1843.
[61] Par. rec., churchwarden's accts. 1787–1893.
[62] Visit. Archd. Salop. 1823.
[63] Ibid. 1847.   [64] Ibid. 1799.
[65] Ibid. 1823.
[66] H.O. 129/359/1/1.
[67] Par. rec., churchwardens' accts. 1787–1893.
[68] Visit. Archd. Salop. 1799.
[69] Par. rec., churchwardens' accts. 1787–1893.
[70] Ibid.
[71] Description of church before 1845 based on Eng. Topog. (Gent. Mag.), x. 76–77; T.S.A.S. 1st ser. iv. 329; Cranage, vi. 491–2; S.P.L., MS. 372, vol. 1, p. 60; ibid. vol. iii, p. 103.
[72] Eng. Topog. (Gent. Mag.), x. 77.
[73] S.P.L., Watton press-cuttings, vol. v, p. 226.

courses. In the lowest stage is a late Perpendicular west window of 3 lights. The second stage has round-headed lancet windows on 3 sides, and the belfry 4 cusped round-headed windows of 2 lights. The top of the tower is battlemented and has a pyramidal roof.

The north aisle was not replaced in 1845–6, when the nave and chancel were rebuilt in local stone to designs by S. P. and J. Smith of Shrewsbury.[74] The dimensions of the new church are virtually the same as those of the old. The chancel contains a reproduction of the former east window and chancel arch and has pairs of lancets on the north and south walls. The nave has a stone porch at the west door and windows in the Perpendicular style.

Little is known of the interior of the church before 1845. Part of a medieval chancel screen was still standing in 1827.[75] The existing pews are oak wainscot box-pews of 18th-century date, which were moved to the sides of the nave in 1845 to provide room for free benches in the centre.[76] An oak pulpit and reading desk, both of early-17th-century date, were removed in 1845.[77] There is a plain round font, probably of 12th-century date, which was replaced by a modern one in 1845, but was back in use by 1912.[78] The only notable monument is a brass, formerly on the floor of the north aisle and now in the chancel. This shows a man in armour with his wife and children. Below is a Latin verse inscription. It bears the arms of Lacon and Horde which suggests that it commemorates Sir Richard Lacon (d. 1503).[79] There are tablets to Benjamin Jenks and to various members of the Harnage family, 1677–1918, in the chancel.

The church had a clock by 1701.[80] A new one, bought in 1814,[81] was restored in 1920.[82] The church had 3 bells by 1552,[83] which were recast in 1878.[84] The plate consists of a silver paten of c. 1500, a silver chalice purchased by the churchwardens in 1669, and a silver flagon given in 1865.[85] The registers are complete from 1745,[86] two earlier volumes beginning in 1590 having been lost before 1823.[87]

NONCONFORMITY. There were two Roman Catholics in Harley in 1591,[88] and Margaret, wife of

William Taylor, was presented as a recusant between 1620 and 1639,[89] but there was none in the parish by 1676.[90]

There were no dissenters here in 1799,[91] but in 1823 there was a family of Baptists and a few Methodists.[92] Meeting-houses, presumably Methodist, were licensed in 1821 and 1830,[93] but none was recorded in 1851.[94]

SCHOOLS. A Sunday school had been established at Harley by 1799, when it was kept by John Corfield of Castle Hill,[95] but by 1818 it was supported entirely by the rector.[96] At this date 50 children attended, 20 of them coming from Kenley,[97] but numbers had fallen to 26 by 1846.[98]

Mossenden Carter taught at a school in Harley in 1693.[99] A day school, attended by 12 children at their parents' expense in 1833,[1] was still open in 1843,[2] but had closed by 1846,[3] when children attended schools in Cressage and Much Wenlock.[4] A National School was built in 1859 on a site near the Cressage road provided by the lord of the manor.[5] The school was financed by voluntary contributions and school-pence in 1877,[6] and was in receipt of a government grant by 1892, when school-pence had been abolished.[7] Eighteen children attended in 1871[8] and 40 by 1906,[9] but only 12 children were on the books in 1959.[10] The school was closed in 1961, when the children were transferred to Cressage school.[11]

CHARITIES. Francis, Earl of Bradford (d. 1708), left £14 to the poor of Harley for 99 years, to be distributed by the rector and churchwardens.[12] This charity had come to an end by 1799.[13] By will of 1715 Richard Corfield gave £20 to the poor, the interest of which was to be distributed by the rector and overseers on St. Andrew's Day.[14] The capital was held by his descendants until c. 1818, when it was transferred to one of the churchwardens.[15] It was invested in stock in 1885.[16] In the early 19th century 16s. was distributed annually among the poor at Christmas.[17] In 1964 the charity produced an income of some 2s. a year, which was not regularly distributed.[18]

[74] Par. rec., churchwardens' accts. 1787–1893; Visit. Archd. Salop. 1847; S.P.L., Watton press-cuttings, vol. v, p. 226; Eng. Topog. (Gent. Mag.), x. 78; S.R.O. 800 uncat., draft contract for rebuilding nave and correspondence of John Gibbons.
[75] T.S.A.S. 1st ser. iv. 329.
[76] Visit. Archd. Salop. 1847; par. rec., churchwardens' accts., 1787–1893.
[77] Eng. Topog. (Gent. Mag.), x. 77.
[78] Cranage, vi. 491.
[79] Eng. Topog. (Gent. Mag.), x. 77–78; T.S.A.S. 1st ser. iv. 334–7; Visit. Salop. 1623 (Harl. Soc. xxix), ii. 306; Cal. Inq. p.m. Hen. VII, iii, p. 543.
[80] Par. rec., par. bk. 1700–38.
[81] Ibid. churchwardens' accts. 1787–1893.
[82] Kelly's Dir. Salop. (1926).
[83] T.S.A.S. 2nd ser. xii. 101.
[84] Walters, Ch. Bells Salop. 220.
[85] Arkwright and Bourne, Ch. Plate Ludlow Archd. 32. The chalice was originally given by Thomas Taylor in 1580. It is, however, hall-marked 1669–70 and was purchased in 1669. It is said to have been lost in the Civil War: Kelly's Dir. Salop (1909).
[86] Printed to 1812 in S.P.R. Lich. ii (1), 1–26.
[87] Visit. Archd. Salop. 1823.
[88] T.S.A.S. 3rd ser. i. 412.
[89] Lich. Dioc. Regy. B/v 1/39–65.
[90] T.S.A.S. 2nd ser. i. 81.
[91] Visit. Archd. Salop. 1799.   [92] Ibid. 1823.

[93] Q. Sess. Orders, iii. 266, 280.
[94] H.O. 129/359/1/1.
[95] Visit. Archd. Salop. 1799.
[96] Digest of Returns to Cttee. on Educ. of Poor, H.C. 224, p. 753 (1819), ix (2).   [97] Ibid.
[98] Nat. Soc., Ch. School returns, 1846–7.
[99] Lich. Dioc. Regy., B/v 1/89A; ibid. B/a 4/13.
[1] Educ. Enquiry Abstract, H.C. 62, p. 775 (1835), xlii.
[2] Visit. Archd. Salop. 1843.
[3] Nat. Soc., Ch. School returns, 1846–7.
[4] Visit. Archd. Salop. 1847.
[5] Ed. 7/102/108; par. rec., copy conveyance of school site, 1858.
[6] Ed. 7/102/108.
[7] Return of Schs. 1893 [C. 7529], p. 506, H.C. (1894), lxv.
[8] Returns relating to Elem. Educ. H.C. 201, p. 334 (1871), lv.
[9] Voluntary Schs. Returns, H.C. 178–XXIV, p. 21 (1906), lxxxviii.
[10] S.C.C. Minutes, 1959–60, p. 34.
[11] Ibid. 1961–2, p. 49.
[12] Lich. Dioc. Regy., glebe terrier, 1718.
[13] Visit. Archd. Salop. 1799.
[14] 3rd Rep. Com. Char. H.C. 5, p. 262 (1820), iv.
[15] Ibid.
[16] Char. Com. files.
[17] 3rd Rep. Com. Char. 262.
[18] Ex inf. the Rector.

KENLEY

THE parish of Kenley, which contains 1,914 a.,[1] lies on a slope rising from 300 feet at the southern boundary along Hughley Brook to 625 feet at the crest of the Kenley ridge, where the village itself stands. The northern boundary of the parish runs along the lower slopes of the steep escarpment of the ridge.[2] The western boundary follows a tributary of Hughley Brook, but that on the east does not make use of any natural features. From Hughley Brook a wide belt of boulder clay extends northwards to the 425-foot contour, above which the subsoil consists of grits and shales.

The clay soils to the south of the Kenley ridge were heavily wooded during the Middle Ages—the manor was said to contain woodland for 400 swine in 1086.[3] Assarts had already been made here by the tenants of Hughley before 1203, when they were granted common rights in Kenley Wood.[4] The lord of Kenley, who was then permitted to make assarts in that part of the wood which lay towards Kenley,[5] was said in 1231 to have cleared land outside this area, in the part of the wood lying towards Hughley, where there were two free tenants holding 2 virgates of land.[6] Kenley Wood was said to have been wasted by Robert le Strange, steward of the Long Forest, c. 1265.[7] In 1283 Ralph Sprenchose, a free tenant, was given licence to inclose a 15-acre assart with a ditch and hedge,[8] and in 1302 the lord of the manor obtained a grant of free warren.[9] Kenley Hay, presumably an inclosed wood forming part of the demesne, was leased in 1453, the tenant being allowed to clear trees and underwood there.[10]

There was probably still a large acreage of woodland in the parish at the close of the Middle Ages. Some time in the 16th century an agreement was made between the lords of Kenley and Hughley, setting out the rights of each party to inclose cleared woodland in the south-west of the parish,[11] an area which was then coming to be called Kenley Common. A quarter of the Common was to continue as woodland.[12] This agreement was disregarded by the lord of Kenley manor after 1591, when the erection of an iron-furnace in Kenley and a forge in Harley[13] gave the oak timber in the parish an economic value. By c. 1600 inclosures had been made by 14 tenants in that part of the Common reserved to Hughley and timber was being taken

from the portion of the Common reserved as woodland.[14] In the 1620s charcoal for the furnace was obtained from Holt Preen[15]—an indication that local supplies of timber had been exhausted. Some 120 a. of woodland still remained in 1747,[16] but there were only 18 a. in 1841.[17] Kenley Common, in the south-west of the parish, contained 202 a. in 1747[18] and was inclosed in 1793.[19]

The road from Harley to Church Preen, on which the village stands, is a ridgeway and until the 19th century all other roads in the parish ran from the ridge towards the lower ground to the north and south. Only one of the roads running southwards from the ridge is still in use. This runs past Mapp Farm towards Hughley in the south-west of the parish and was diverted westwards when Kenley Common was inclosed.[20] The course of Furnace Lane, running southwards from the village, can still be followed. A third road formerly ran from the village, past Upper Springs, Gippols, and Blakeway Farm in Harley, towards Much Wenlock, but only short sections of this road were still in use in 1841.[21] The straight road running from east to west across the parish, between Lower Springs and New Hall, was constructed after 1841.[22]

There is no evidence for the names or location of the Kenley common fields. They were still in use in the early 15th century,[23] but appear to have vanished before the close of the Middle Ages and may be represented by the 80 a. arable said to have been inclosed and converted into pasture by the lord of the manor in 1513.[24]

Broomcroft Farm, on the level plateau north-east of Kenley village, and Gippols, near Hughley Brook in the south-east corner of the parish, are first recorded in 1204[25] and 1271[26] respectively. It is likely that both mark the site of former hamlets. Broomcroft, described as a township in 1495,[27] appears to have possessed its own set of common fields in 1204, when a freehold estate here was described in terms of virgates[28] and not in acres, as one would expect in an assarted area. It seems to have been depopulated by 1363, when this freehold was said to be wholly uncultivated for lack of tenants.[29] There are several references to assarts by tenants at Gippols in the 13th century.[30] At least 3 houses stood here in 1600[31] and there were still

[1] O.S. *Area Bk.* (1883). The following topographical description is based, except where otherwise stated, on O.S. Map 1″, sheet lxi (1st edn.); O.S. Map 6″ Salop 50 (1st and later edns.); O.S. Maps 1/25,000, SJ 50, SO 59 (1959); Rocque, *Map of Salop.* (1752); Baugh, *Map of Salop.* (1808); Greenwood, *Map of Salop.* (1827); B.M. O.S. 2″ orig. drawings, sheet 207 (1817); Geol. Survey Map (drift), sheet 152 (1932); Heref. Dioc. Regy., tithe appt. and map, 1841. This article was written in 1962 and revised in 1965.
[2] It followed its present course in 1232: Dugdale, *Mon.* v. 356–7.
[3] *V.C.H. Salop.* i. 320.
[4] *T.S.A.S.* 2nd ser. x. 320–1.   [5] Ibid.
[6] *Cur. Reg. R.* xiv. 247.
[7] E 32/147 m. 8; *Cal. Pat.* 1281–92, 195.
[8] *Cal. Pat.* 1281–92, 82; E 32/147 m. 8.
[9] *Cal. Chart. R.* 1300–26, 29; cf. ibid. 398.
[10] S.R.O. 1224 uncat., ct. r. 1453.
[11] Barnard MSS., Raby Castle, box 12, bdle. 19, plan of common; Wolryche-Whitmore MSS., Dudmaston, memorandum *re* inclosures, c. 1600.

[12] Ibid.   [13] See pp. 89, 96.
[14] Wolryche-Whitmore MSS., Dudmaston, memorandum *re* inclosures, c. 1600.
[15] Ibid., depositions, Thomas Wolryche and others v. Harcourt Leighton and others, 1627.
[16] S.R.O. 168/2.
[17] Heref. Dioc. Regy., tithe appt.
[18] S.R.O. 168/2.
[19] Plymley, *Agric. Salop.* 117.
[20] S.R.O. 283/1.
[21] Heref. Dioc. Regy., tithe appt.   [22] Ibid.
[23] S.R.O. 840 uncat., ct. r. 1421–36; ibid. 1224 uncat., ct. r. 1453–4.
[24] C 47/7/2/3 m. 34d.
[25] *Cur. Reg. R.* iii. 244.
[26] E 32/147 m. 8.
[27] S.R.O. 1037 uncat., lease, 1495.
[28] *Cur. Reg. R.* iii. 244.
[29] C 135/179/10.
[30] E 32/147 m. 8; Eyton, iii. 293.
[31] Barnard MSS., Raby Castle, wooden box 12, bdles. 14, 19, leases, 1580–1609.

two in 1841,[32] but one of these has since been demolished.

Forest clearance permitted the exploitation of the richer clay soils in the south of the parish. By the end of the 16th century the pattern of settlement had become one of isolated farms, sited on or near tributaries of Hughley Brook, and of scattered cottages, whose inhabitants had less need of arable land, on the poorer soils in the north-west of the parish and on the Common on its western boundary. The first reference to an isolated cottage on Kenley Common occurs in 1537,[33] and there were already 12 cottages here by the end of the 16th century.[34] In 1619 5 cottages 'of the better sort' and 9 others were assessed to a poor rate, along with 21 other persons.[35] There were 31 cottages on the Common by 1747.[36]

Surviving houses reflect this contrast between farmers and cottagers. The cottages in the north of the parish[37] are timber-framed or stone-built, some of them in a combination of both materials, and in nearly every case their original ground-plan consisted of a single room with a massive chimney stack on one gable. Scarcely any of them have been rebuilt or substantially enlarged since the 18th century. Of the isolated farms, Broomcroft and Upper Springs were originally of cottage type, but have been considerably enlarged in stone. The remainder were originally timber-framed houses of higher standard, which have since been cased in brick. New Hall, probably built before 1605,[38] was called 'Mr. Lacon's Lower Hall' in 1650.[39] It is a T-shaped house, with a 17th-century newel stair and a roof supported by curved principal rafters, which was enlarged and cased in brick in 1774.[40] The Leasows Farm, first recorded in 1680,[41] consists of an early-17th-century timber-framed house with a central stack, to which a stone kitchen was added in 1761.[42] The most sophisticated house in the parish is Kenley Hall. This was called the Upper Hall in 1605, when it was occupied by a junior branch of the Lacon family.[43] The present house, which was built in 1635,[44] is a rectangular building of stone rubble, with splay-mullioned windows. It is a 3-bay house of 3 stories with attics, the lowest story being a semi-basement kitchen. The latter, the central hall above, and the principal bedroom, were served by a lateral chimney stack on the

north wall, which formerly had 3 octagonal shafts. A stone kitchen was added to the north of the house in 1913.[45]

Kenley probably had two alehouses in 1590.[46] One is recorded in 1616[47] and 1656.[48] In 1745 a farmer was licensed to sell ale[49] and four persons were licensed in 1748.[50] There are no later references to licensed alehouses in the parish, but Park Gate is said to have been an alehouse in the 19th century.[51]

The parish contained at least 40 households in 1656,[52] but there were said to be only 82 communicants in 1676.[53] Since 1801, when there were 300 inhabitants,[54] the population has steadily declined. There were 251 inhabitants in 1851,[55] 182 in 1901,[56] and 104 in 1961.[57] William Farr (1807–83), the pioneer statistician, was born of humble parents at Kenley.[58]

MANOR. Rainald the sheriff was overlord of the manor of *KENLEY* in 1086,[59] and his seignory there descended, as elsewhere, to the FitzAlans.[60] By 1254 half the fee was annexed to Ludlow castle,[61] and in 1272 the other half to Oswestry castle.[62] The overlordship is last recorded in 1623.[63]

Edric was tenant here before 1066 and Odo de Bernières in 1086.[64] On Odo's death, some time after 1121,[65] he was probably succeeded, in Kenley as elsewhere, by Philip Fitz Odo, recorded in 1138 and c. 1145.[66] By 1180, however, the manor seems to have been held by Thomas Fitz Odo, son of Philip's younger son William Fitz Odo.[67] Before 1189 Thomas settled it on Parnel, daughter and heir of Philip Fitz Odo's elder son Roger, and her husband Warner de Willey.[68] Thomas and his brother Roger confirmed this grant in 1194.[69] Warner de Willey died before 1231,[70] the manor having previously been settled on his wife Parnel,[71] who was still living in 1242.[72] On her death the manor passed to her son Nicholas de Willey,[73] who was dead by 1254, when his son Andrew was lord of Kenley.[74] Andrew was killed at the battle of Evesham (1265), leaving as heir his infant daughter Burga,[75] but his estates were forfeited under the Dictum of Kenilworth and Kenley was granted to Robert le Strange.[76] In 1272 the manor was in the custody of his tenant Walter de Pedwardine,[77] but on Robert's death in 1276 it was seized by the Crown,[78] and in

[32] Heref. Dioc. Regy. tithe appt.
[33] Sta. Cha. 2/30/51.
[34] Par. rec., par. bk. 1601–62.
[35] Ibid.
[36] S.R.O. 168/2.
[37] See plate facing p. 96.
[38] Par. rec., par. bk. 1601–62, plan of pews, 1605.
[39] Ibid. poor rate, 1650.
[40] Barnard MSS., Raby Castle, receiver's accts. 1768–81.
[41] Ibid. wooden box 12, bdle. 14, lease, 1680.
[42] Datestone.
[43] Par. rec., par. bk., 1601–62, plan of pews, 1605; Barnard MSS., Raby Castle, wooden box 12, bdle. 14, lease, 1609.
[44] Date on hinges of former south door.
[45] Ex inf. Mr. F. Jarrett, Kenley Hall.
[46] N.L.W., Pitchford Hall uncat., alehouse recognisances, Condover Hundred, 1590.
[47] Q. Sess., alehouse reg.
[48] Q. Sess. Orders, i. 28.
[49] N.L.W., Castle Hill 2244.
[50] Ibid.
[51] Ex inf. Mr. J. Roberts, Broomcroft Farm.
[52] Par. rec., par. bk., 1601–62, highway rate, 1656.
[53] T.S.A.S. 2nd ser. i. 81.
[54] Census, 1801.
[55] Ibid. 1851.
[56] Ibid. 1901.
[57] Ibid. 1961.
[58] D.N.B.
[59] V.C.H. Salop. i. 320.
[60] Eyton, ii. 53; Barnard MSS., Raby Castle, box 1, bdle. 19, no. 1; Bk. of Fees, 962; Feud. Aids, iv. 239, 264; C 142/58/60; C 142/68/7; C 142/402/146.
[61] Rot. Hund. (Rec. Com.), ii. 69.
[62] Cal. Close, 1268–72, 515.
[63] C 142/402/146.
[64] V.C.H. Salop. i. 320.
[65] Eyton, iv. 89.
[66] Ibid. iv. 90; ibid. ii. 205.
[67] Ibid. vi. 81. For pedigree see ibid. 83.
[68] Ibid. ii. 53; ibid. vi. 84; Barnard MSS., Raby Castle, box 1, bdle. 19, no. 1.
[69] Cur. Reg. R. 1194–5 (P.R.S. xiv), 10.
[70] Eyton, ii. 56.
[71] Ibid. 55–56.
[72] Bk. of Fees, 962.
[73] Eyton, ii. 56.
[74] Rot. Hund. (Rec. Com.), ii. 69.
[75] Eyton, ii. 57.
[76] Ibid.; Cal. Pat. 1281–92, 195.

1278 it was granted to Philip de Stapleton,[79] who had married Burga de Willey before 1277.[80] Philip was dead by 1283, when Burga de Willey had married Richard de Harley.[81] On Richard's death in 1316,[82] Burga held the manor in dower and was still living in 1337.[83] It subsequently followed the descent of Harley manor.[84]

ECONOMIC HISTORY. Since the 15th century virtually the whole parish has lain in the manorial estate. The manor, which was worth 30s. before the Conquest, was waste after 1066 and was only worth 4s. in 1086, when it was assessed at one hide.[85] The arable area was then very small—there was woodland for 400 swine and although there was land for five ploughs, only one plough was then in use.[86] Its subsequent expansion by the clearance of woodland was virtually complete by the early 17th century. Although some arable land, as well as meadow, was still kept in hand in the early 15th century,[87] the manor-house had been leased by 1453.[88]

A freehold estate at Broomcroft, which was said to contain 1¼ virgate in 1204,[89] was then claimed by Felise, daughter of Robert Mareschal,[90] but seems to have passed later in the 13th century to the Sprenchose family.[91] Sir Ralph Sprenchose held, in addition, some 15 a. of assarted land in the parish in 1283.[92] John Sprenchose in 1348 conveyed a messuage and lands in Kenley, Broomcroft, and Langley to Sir John de Wottenhull,[93] who was said to hold a carucate of uncultivated land in Kenley at his death in 1363.[94] The estate probably descended to Thomas Charlton of Apley, who held a carucate of land here in 1402,[95] but it had been merged in the manorial estate by 1495.[96]

Common rights on Kenley Common were shared with the tenants of Hughley until its inclosure in 1793, when 52 a. were allotted to the Earl of Bradford as lord of Hughley.[97] Hughley's rights here were defined in 1203, when its lord was granted 60 cart-loads of dead wood a year, freedom from pannage for 60 pigs, and pasture rights for himself and his tenants.[98] In return the tenants of Hughley were obliged to mow King's Meadow.[99] It was alleged in 1231, in the course of one of many disputes over the respective rights of the two parishes, that the lord of Kenley had seized the goats of Hughley tenants and had kept them till they died, then sold their hides and flesh.[1]

An encroachment made by the inhabitants of Langley at Maypole Bank, on the northern boundary of the parish, comprised 19 a. in 1805[2] and 1841,[3] and since at least 1747[4] has been part of the estate of the Smythes of Acton Burnell.

Little is known of the management of the estate before the 18th century. There were 27 tenants in 1453[5] and about the same number in 1618.[6] Their rents produced £76 a year c. 1646.[7] Copyhold was already being replaced by leasehold tenure in the earlier 15th century,[8] and between 1560 and 1750 the greater part of the estate was held on leases for three lives.[9] The leases, which normally contained covenants for heriot and suit of court, included provisions for military service and against wearing the livery of other lords, 1671–1708. Team-service was occasionally required in leases, 1637–1710, and two days team-work continued to be demanded of the tenants until the end of horse transport.[10]

In 1734 the 18 leaseholders paid rents totalling £84 a year, while 7 tenants-at-will paid £98.[11] This pattern was unchanged in 1747, when 18 leaseholders held 1,201 a. and 8 tenants-at-will held 523 a. After 1750 tenancy-at-will rapidly replaced the three-life lease. By 1768 there were 17 tenants-at-will and only 7 leaseholders, whose total annual rents were £304 and £29 respectively. At the same time began a more gradual transition to larger farms. In 1747 there had been only 3 farms of more than 100 a. and 18 others of 30–90 a., but by 1841 1,094 a. lay in 5 farms of over 100 a. and 502 a. in 9 smaller farms. In 1945 there were 9 farms of over 100 a. totalling 1,400 a., with six holdings of 12–100 a., totalling 314 a.

The above figures, however, exclude the cottagers, who have been an important element in the parish since the 16th century. Between 1734 and 1768 there were 31 cottages on the estate with holdings of up to 12 a. attached. Many of these smallholdings were later merged in the larger farms, but they were still numerous in 1841 and 6 holdings of less than 12 a. remained in 1945. On the inclosure of Kenley common in 1793 the 30 a. allotted to the rector of Kenley as glebe were divided by him into ten lots 'to accommodate the poor people of the common who had the largest families'.[12] In 1796 the 'most decent, industrious and well-doing' of the commoners were said to be the four or five families holding 5–10 a., and the poorest and most wretched

77 Eyton, vi. 89–90.
78 Ibid. ii. 58.
79 *Abbrev. Rot. Orig.* (Rec. Com.), i. 27, 30.
80 Eyton, iii. 58.
81 Ibid.
82 Ibid. vi. 235.
83 Barnard MSS., Raby Castle, box 1, bdle. 29, no. 5.
84 See pp. 87–88.
85 *V.C.H. Salop.* i. 320.
86 Ibid.
87 S.R.O. 840 uncat., ct. r. 1421–36; ibid. 1224 uncat., ct. r. 1453–4.
88 Ibid. 1224 uncat., ct. r. 1453–4.
89 *Cur. Reg. R.* iii. 244, 331.
90 Ibid.
91 E 32/147 m. 8.
92 *Cal. Pat.* 1281–92, 82.
93 Barnard MSS., Raby Castle, box 1, bdle. 29, nos. 8, 10.
94 *Cal. Inq. p.m.* xi, p. 410.
95 *Cal. Close*, 1402–5, 22, 23, 25.
96 S.R.O. 1037 uncat., lease, 1495.
97 Plymley, *Agric. Salop.* 117.

98 *T.S.A.S.* 2nd ser. x. 320–1.
99 Ibid.
1 *Cur. Reg. R.* xiv. 247.
2 S.P.L., MS. 294.
3 Heref. Dioc. Regy., tithe appt.
4 S.R.O. 168/2.
5 Ibid. 1224 uncat., ct. r. 1453–4.
6 Barnard MSS., Raby Castle, box 1, bdle. 29, no. 49.
7 *T.S.A.S.* 2nd ser. xii. 21.
8 S.R.O. 840 uncat., ct. r. 1421–36; ibid. 1224 uncat., ct. r. 1453–4.
9 What follows is based on leases, 1561–1729, in Barnard MSS., Raby Castle, wooden box 6, bdle. 11; ibid. wooden box 12, bdles. 14, 19, 21–22.
10 Ex inf. Mr. J. Roberts, Broomcroft Farm.
11 Except where otherwise stated, the following account of the tenurial history of the estate is based on Barnard MSS., Raby Castle, receivers' accts. 1734–41, 1768–81; S.R.O. 168/2; Heref. Dioc. Regy., tithe appt.; Uppington estate office, terrier, c. 1920.
12 Plymley, *Agric. Salop.* 117–18; c.f. A. Alison, *Autobiography* (1883), i. 12.

were those with 20–30 a. 'who are induced to keep something like a team'.[13] The parish was described as 'impoverished and neglected' c. 1830, but the allotment experiment was applauded.[14] Some of the cottagers must always have supplemented their income by non-agricultural pursuits. A weaver was living in Kenley Wood in 1537[15] and a tailor on the Common, c. 1600.[16] Cottage industry is recorded in 1831, when there were 10 manufacturing workers in the parish[17]—probably linen weavers.[18]

Between 1747[19] and 1841 there was as great a change in land-use, and consequently in field sizes, as in the size of farms. Whereas in 1747 fields were rarely larger than 5 a., they were seldom smaller than 5 a. in 1841. In 1747 there were 484 a. arable and 918 a. pasture, although there was up to 60 per cent. arable on some farms. The parish was said to contain only 387 a. arable in 1801, when the chief crops were oats (173 a.) and wheat (162 a.),[20] but this is likely to be an under-estimate. By 1841 the relative importance of arable and pasture had been reversed; there were then 980 a. arable and 723 a. pasture. Some 100 a. of woodland had been cleared since 1747. Pasture again came to predominate in the later 19th century, and by 1945 there were 454 a. arable and 1,209 a. pasture.

In 1203 corn from Kenley seems to have been ground at Hughley mill,[21] but in 1337 mention is made of the new mill of Kenley.[22] There was no mill here by 1637, when tenants owed suit at Harley mill.[23]

An iron furnace was erected near Hughley Brook, south-east of New Hall,[24] by Rowland Lacon shortly before 1591, when it was occupied by Richard Holbeck.[25] Holbeck was still at the furnace in 1606,[26] but must have moved later in the same year to Longnor.[27] John Shaw was lessee in the 1620s,[28] and the furnace may later have been leased to William Fownes, sometimes described as of Kenley,[29] who was a partner at Harley forge in 1638,[30] but it was disused by 1708.[31] Adjoining fields contain large quantities of charcoal and slag.

In 1856 the parish had 2 shopkeepers, 2 tailors, a wheelwright, a blacksmith, a cooper, a shoemaker, and a mason,[32] but only a wheelwright and a blacksmith remained in 1941.[33] In 1962, when the village shop and post office occupied the former school, there were no other tradesmen in the village. Stonemasons, for whom the many cottages must have provided steady employment, are recorded from 1607 until 1922.[34]

LOCAL GOVERNMENT. There are a few manor court rolls, 1422–54,[35] and suit rolls, 1773–82 and 1813–43.[36] The parish records include a parish book, containing accounts of all parish officers, 1601–62. There are occasional memoranda of vestry meetings in this book and in the parish registers.

The parish officers served by rotation in the early 17th century, each substantial tenant owing the duty, which could be performed in person or by deputy. There were then two constables, two overseers, and two churchwardens, and the offices were never served concurrently. A rota for service was drawn up in 1650, when surveyors of the highways were first appointed. Following the Ordinance of 1654 authorizing rates for highway repair, £9 was raised for repairs to the highways in 1655 and £6 in the following year for the erection of a bridge, probably over Hughley Brook.

The overseers' accounts show how the Poor Law Act of 1601 was put into practice in this remote parish. A stock of flax and hemp was raised by assessment, but although a list of 4 impotent poor was drawn up, none came to be set on work when proclamation was made. The stock had been let out at interest by 1628. None but impotent poor was relieved before 1658, when the accounts end. The rate stood at £3 at this time, but it had risen to £12 by 1695[37] and to £30 by 1777.[38] Thereafter it seems to have risen rapidly, and stood at £61 in 1783.[39] Kenley became a member of the Atcham Union in 1792.[40] Poor rates reached a peak of £146 in 1818,[41] but subsequently did not exceed £78.[42] Relative to the population of the parish at this time, and in particular to the large number of cottagers, the expense of poor relief was thus unusually low. Probably this was a result of the allotment experiment of 1793.

CHURCH. Kenley church is first recorded in 1364,[43] but was probably built at least a century earlier. There is no reference to an incumbent before 1552.[44] The benefice was originally a chapelry of Cound,[45] but burials took place at Harley in the 16th century.[46] A burial ground at Kenley was acquired and licensed in 1605[47] and the benefice has thereafter been a parochial chapelry. The incum-

[13] Ibid.
[14] W.S.L. 350/40/3.
[15] Sta. Cha. 2/30/51.
[16] Wolryche-Whitmore MSS., Dudmaston, memorandum re inclosures, c. 1600.
[17] Census, 1831.
[18] Ex inf. Mrs. J. Roberts, Broomcroft Farm, and Mr. H. W. Cook, Upper Springs.
[19] Except where otherwise stated, this paragraph is based on S.R.O. 168/2; Heref. Dioc. Regy., tithe appt.; Uppington estate office, terrier, c. 1920.
[20] H.O. 67/14/149.
[21] T.S.A.S. 2nd ser. x. 320–1.
[22] Barnard MSS., Raby Castle, box 1, bdle. 29, no. 5.
[23] Ibid. wooden box 12, bdle. 14, lease, 1637.
[24] O.S. Nat. Grid SO 574988.
[25] Barnard MSS., Raby Castle, wooden box 12, bdle. 14, lease, 1591.
[26] Par. rec., par. bk. 1601–62, poor rate, 1606.
[27] See p. 112.
[28] Wolrych-Whitmore MSS., Dudmaston, depositions, Thomas Wolryche and others v. Harcourt Leighton and others, 1627.
[29] T.S.A.S. lvi. 189.

[30] See p. 89.
[31] Barnard MSS., Raby Castle, wooden box 12, bdle. 19, lease, 1708.
[32] Kelly's Dir. Salop. (1856).   [33] Ibid. (1941).
[34] Barnard MSS., Raby Castle, wooden box 12, bdle. 14, lease, 1607; Kelly's Dir. Salop. (1922).
[35] S.R.O. 840 uncat., ct. r. 1421–36; ibid. 1224 uncat., ct. r. 1453–4.
[36] S.R.O. 1011 uncat.
[37] Bodl. MS. Blakeway 8, f. 476.
[38] Rep. Cttee. on Overseers' Returns, 1777, p. 442, H.C. (1st ser. ix, reprinted 1803).
[39] Rep. Cttee. on State of Poor, 1787, p. 658, H.C. (1st ser. ix, reprinted 1803).
[40] Atcham Union Act, 32 Geo. III, c. 95 (priv. act).
[41] Rep. Cttee. on Poor Rate Returns, 1822, Suppl. App., H.C. 556, p. 141 (1822), v.
[42] Acct. of Money Expended on Poor, 1830–4, H.C. 444, p. 344 (1835), xlvii.
[43] Barnard MSS., Raby Castle, box 1, bdle. 29, no. 10.
[44] T.S.A.S. 2nd ser. xii. 100.
[45] S.P.L., MS. 2, f. 143.
[46] Barnard MSS., Raby Castle, box 1, bdle. 29, no. 36.
[47] Ibid.

KENLEY: a former squatter's cottage near Park Gate

EXFORDSGREEN: view from the south showing dispersed settlement, dating from the early 17th century, with the Lyth Hill escarpment in the background

SQUATTER SETTLEMENT

LONGNOR: air view from the south-west, 1967. The original village, close to the River Cound, stood alongside the 'Lyde Way' (the road running across the centre of the picture). Dispersed settlement on the semicircular road beyond dates from the 13th century

SMETHCOTT: the church and castle-site in the foreground mark the position of the original hamlet and the houses in the middle distance its later site

CHANGES IN MEDIEVAL SETTLEMENT

bents are technically perpetual curates. The advowson has always followed the descent of the manor, and the living was a donative until c. 1758.[48]

Until the 19th century the tithes of Kenley were held by the impropriator of the living and the perpetual curates received an annual stipend. In 1610 the tithes were leased for £10 a year, the lessee providing a minister.[49] The tithes were worth £32 in 1655,[50] and were leased for £30 a year in the later 17th century.[51] In 1693 the lessee paid the rent of £30 to the perpetual curate.[52] By 1799 the tithes were worth £92 a year[53] and in 1823 the great tithes were said to be part of the endowment of the living.[54] Tithes were commuted for a rent-charge of £143 in 1841.[55] There was no glebe until 1793, when 30 a. in Kenley common were assigned to the minister and divided into allotments,[56] which were being let for £21 a year in 1851.[57] The glebe was still held by the rector in 1964.[58] The living was worth £160 gross in 1823,[59] £119 net in 1843,[60] and £170 gross in 1851.[61] There has never been a parsonage house, but since 1799 any resident minister has always occupied a house on the manorial estate.[62]

Little is known of the perpetual curates of Kenley before the 17th century. George Bennet, who was perpetual curate here by 1620,[63] had been ordained in 1608[64] and held the living until his death at a great age in 1683.[65] Although he lived in Kenley, he seems to have employed the rectors of Harley as his curates,[66] and this practice was normally followed by his successors, who appear to have been uniformly non-resident until the 19th century. Thus James Dewhurst (Rector of Harley 1747–80) was curate here c. 1756–79[67] and John Gibbons (Rector of Harley 1805–59) was curate 1810–39.[68] John Greaves (Perpetual Curate of Kenley 1769–75)[69] was a son-in-law of James Dewhurst[70] and appears to have lived in Harley.[71] The assistant curate received a salary of £53 a year in 1831.[72] Archibald Alison, the most illustrious of the Kenley incumbents, who was responsible for the allotments of 1793,[73] lived in the parish from 1791 until 1800,[74] but later held the living in plurality with High Ercall and Rodington.[75]

From the 17th century until 1847 communion was administered 4 times a year.[76] There were said to be 70 communicants in 1799[77]—a high figure which must reflect the energy of Archibald Alison—but they had fallen to 20 by 1847.[78] Between 1799 and 1851 only one service was held on Sundays.[79] Some 60 people normally attended in 1851.[80]

The church of *ST. JOHN THE BAPTIST*[81] consists of a chancel, nave, and western tower, and was probably built, in coarse local gritstone, in the 13th century. There is no internal or external division between the nave and chancel, apart from a change in the roof timbers. The south door of the nave has a round arch and the blocked north door opposite is of similar type. There is a pointed arch above the entrance from the nave into the tower. The two-light east window was probably inserted in the 14th century, but all other windows in the nave and chancel date from the restoration of the church in 1854, when they replaced a number of narrow square-headed windows. There is a blocked priest's door in the north wall of the chancel. In 1786 the church was lighted by two dormer windows on the south side, one of which had already been taken down by 1854, when the other was removed. The tower, which is lighted by narrow slits, rises no higher than the ridge of the nave roof and is capped by a pyramidal roof. The chancel roof, which is supported by 3 arch-braced collar-beam trusses, has cusped windbraces, forming quatrefoils, and is probably of 14th-century date. The arch-braced collar-beams of the nave roof have all been cased.

The church was refurnished after 1605, when a new communion table was bought and pews were allotted to the parishioners[82]—probably the rough oak forms which survived until 1854,[83] when they were replaced by deal pews. A high box pew of the lord of the manor, which stood in the chancel,[84] was removed at this time. The fine Jacobean pulpit, tester, and reading desk were made in 1634. There was a plain round stone font in 1823,[85] replaced by the existing octagonal one in 1875.[86]

There were two bells in 1552,[87] but the two existing bells are dated 1685.[88] The plate consists of a silver chalice, purchased in 1664, and a silver paten, given in 1884.[89] There was a silver chalice and paten in 1552.[90] The registers are complete from 1682.[91]

48 *T.S.A.S.* xlvii. 28; Lich. Dioc. Regy., reg. 21, p. 67.
49 Barnard MSS., Raby Castle, wooden box 12, bdle. 14, lease, 1610.
50 *T.S.A.S.* xlvii. 28.
51 Barnard MSS., Raby Castle, wooden box 11, bdle. 14, leases, 1665, 1687; Lich. Dioc. Regy., glebe terrier, 1693.
52 Lich. Dioc. Regy., glebe terrier, 1693.
53 Visit. Archd. Salop. 1799.
54 Ibid. 1823.
55 Heref. Dioc. Regy., tithe appt. 1841.
56 Plymley, *Agric. Salop.* 117–18.
57 H.O. 129/359/1/5.
58 Ex inf. the Rector.
59 Visit. Archd. Salop. 1823.
60 *Rep. Com. Eccl. Revenues* [67], pp. 484–5, H.C. (1835), xxii.
61 H.O. 129/359/1/5.
62 Visit. Archd. Salop. 1799.
63 Lich. Dioc. Regy., B/v 1/39.
64 Ibid. B/v 1/62.
65 *S.P.R. Lich.* ii (3), 82.
66 Lich. Dioc. Regy., B/v 1/62; *T.S.A.S.* xlvii. 28.
67 Lich. Dioc. Regy., bishop's transcripts.
68 Ibid.
69 Ibid., reg. 22, p. 9; *S.P.R. Lich.* ii (1), 13.
70 *S.P.R. Lich.* ii (1), 10.
71 Ibid. 11–12.

72 *Rep. Com. Eccl. Revenues*, pp. 484–5.
73 Plymley, *Agric. Salop.* 117–18.
74 Lich. Dioc. Regy., reg. 26, p. 9; A. Alison, *Autobiography* (1883), i. 22.
75 *Rep. Com. Eccl. Revenues*, pp. 484–5.
76 Par. rec., par. bk. 1601–62; Visit. Archd. Salop. 1799, 1823, 1847.
77 Visit. Archd. Salop. 1799. 78 Ibid. 1847.
79 Ibid. 1799, 1823, 1847; H.O. 129/359/1/5.
80 H.O. 129/359/1/5.
81 The following description of the church is based, except where otherwise stated, on par. rec., par. bk. 1601–62; ibid. report on church, 1845, and contract for restoration, 1854; S.P.L., MS. 372, vol. i, p. 7; S.P.L., J. H. Smith collect. no. 111; Cranage, vi. 493–4.
82 Par. rec., par. bk. 1601–62, plan of pews, 1605.
83 Visit. Archd. Salop. 1823; par. rec., report on church, 1845.
84 Par. rec., report on church, 1845.
85 Visit. Archd. Salop. 1823; B.M. Add. MS. 21236, f. 31.
86 Cranage, vi. 494.
87 *T.S.A.S.* 2nd ser. xii. 100.
88 Walters, *Ch. Bells Salop.* 220–1.
89 Arkwright and Bourne, *Ch. Plate Ludlow Archd.* 36.
90 *T.S.A.S.* 2nd ser. xii. 100.
91 Printed to 1812 in *S.P.R. Lich.* ii (3), 81–141.

NONCONFORMITY. There were no dissenters here in 1799,[92] but in 1823[93] and 1843[94] a few Methodists held meetings in their houses. Primitive Methodists continued to meet in farms and out-buildings until the later 19th century, when a disused corrugated iron chapel was bought and erected near Bull Farm, on the northern boundary of the parish. The chapel was moved to Kenley Common in 1936[95] and was still in use in 1965.

SCHOOLS. Thomas Aves kept a school in Kenley in 1576,[96] and a teacher living on Kenley Common was giving instruction to children from Church Preen c. 1788.[97] A Mr. Faed was schoolmaster here c.

1800.[98] His school may have been the day school recorded in 1818,[99] which had closed by 1823.[1] Another day school was opened in 1833[2] and was then attended by 35 children at their parents' expense.[3] This had closed by 1847,[4] and in 1871 children attended schools at Cound and Harley.[5] A National School was built in 1872 on a site opposite the church, provided by the Duke of Cleveland.[6] The school was financed by voluntary contributions, and was in receipt of a government grant by 1893, when no school-pence were paid.[7] The school was closed in 1921.[8]

CHARITIES. None known.

LEEBOTWOOD

THE parish of Leebotwood contains 1,287 a.[1] The village stands on the main road from Shrewsbury to Ludlow and the parish occupies the lower land at the head of the Cound valley, flanked on the west by the foothills of the Long Mynd and on the east by the Lawley escarpment. The parish boundary follows Watling Street on the south-east and runs along Cross Brook in the north. Elsewhere its course was determined by agreement in the late 12th and early 13th centuries. Thus the boundary between Longnor, Stapleton, and Smethcott in the north of the parish follows closely the bounds of Micklewood as defined in 1185 and c. 1221.[2] On the west this followed a road called the Riding Way, now represented by the private road running north-wards from Park Farm.[3] The boundary with Smeth-cott and Stapleton on the west was defined between 1210 and 1227.[4] On the south the boundary with Church Stretton was marked by a trench in 1340,[5] but in 1253 Leebotwood manor extended as far south as All Stretton bridge,[6] and in the 18th century the manorial estate included Brownhill Farm and Lower Wood.[7]

The ground rises gently from about 350 feet in the north of the parish to some 525 feet in the south, and the western boundary runs along the 500-foot contour for much of its course. The River Cound runs north-eastwards across the south of the parish, and Walkmill Brook flows eastwards to join the

Cound north of the village. The latter's course to the east of the Shrewsbury road was diverted northwards after 1817. Both streams are flanked by a belt of alluvium and flood gravels, which is widest at the site of the village. Similar soil conditions obtain in the north, between Micklewood Farm and Netley Brook. Boulder clay covers the rest of the parish, apart from isolated deposits of sand and gravel to the east and north of the village. The Coal Measures which underlie most of the parish were mined in the 18th and 19th centuries.[8]

Its name recalls the origin of the village as a clearing in the forest of Botwood.[9] The whole parish seems to have reverted to forest conditions between 1086 and its grant to Haughmond Abbey c. 1170,[10] but agreements fixing the boundary of the manor and apportioning common rights made between 1185 and 1273,[11] and royal licences for assarts between 1179 and 1283,[12] are evidence of the energy displayed by the abbey in forest clearance during the first century of its tenure of the manor.

Botwood lay on both sides of Watling Street, known as 'Botte Street' in the Middle Ages,[13] and covered much of the land to the east of the River Cound. Field-names indicate that to the south of the village it extended across the parish to join Lower Wood. Woodland at the Riddings, in this area, was converted into charcoal shortly after 1652.[14] In 1674 72 a. of Botwood was still uninclosed,[15]

[92] Visit. Archd. Salop. 1799.
[93] Ibid. 1823.   [94] Ibid. 1843.
[95] W. E. Morris, *The History of Methodism in Shrewsbury and District* (Shrewsbury, 1960), 57–59; ex inf. Mrs. J. Roberts, Broomcroft Farm.
[96] Lich. Dioc. Regy. B/v 1/10.
[97] B.M. Add. MS. 21018, f. 196.
[98] A. Alison, *Autobiography* (1883), i. 20.
[99] *Digest of Returns to Cttee. on Educ. of Poor*, H.C. 224, p. 754 (1819), ix (2).
[1] Visit. Archd. Salop. 1823.
[2] *Educ. Enquiry Abstract*, H.C. 62, p. 776 (1835), xlii.
[3] Ibid.
[4] Nat. Soc. *Ch. School Returns*, 1846–7.
[5] *Returns relating to Elem. Educ.*, H.C. 201, p. 334 (1871), lv.
[6] Par. rec., copy conveyance of site.
[7] *Return of Schs., 1893* [C. 7529], p. 506, H.C. (1894), lxv.
[8] Ex inf. S.C.C. Educ. Dept.
[1] *O.S. Area Bk.* (1883). The following topographical description is based, except where otherwise stated, on O.S. Map 1″, sheet lxi (1st edn.); O.S. Maps 6″ Salop. 49 (1st and later edns.); O.S. Maps 1/25,000, SO 49 (1956), SJ 40 (1957); Rocque, *Map of Salop.* (1752); Baugh, *Map of Salop.* (1808); Greenwood, *Map of Salop.* (1827); B.M.

O.S. 2″ orig. drawings, sheet 207 (1817); Geol. Survey Map (drift), sheet 152 (1932); Heref. Dioc. Regy., tithe appt., 1840, and map, 1839; Apley Park estate office, map, 1777. This article was written in 1963 and revised in 1965.
[2] B.M. Harl. MS. 446, ff. 20ᵛ–21ᵛ.
[3] Ibid.; S.P.L., Haughmond Cart. f. 134; S.R.O. 567 uncat., depositions, Uvedale Corbett v. Roger Pope, 1688.
[4] S.P.L., Haughmond Cart. ff. 134–5.
[5] Ibid. f. 135.
[6] Ibid. f. 132ᵛ. Here called 'le Quakinggebrugge', and known as Quaking Brook Bridge in the 19th century: O.S. Map 1″, sheet lxi (1st edn.).
[7] Apley Park estate office, survey and map, 1777.
[8] See pp. 103–4.
[9] Early forms include 'Lega in foresta de Bottewode', 1172 (B.M. Harl. MS. 3868, f. 11ᵛ); 'Lega apud Botte-wode', 1179 (S.P.L., Haughmond Cart. f. 132); 'Lega Bottewode', c. 1225 (ibid. f. 134ᵛ); 'Lega in Bottewode', 1253 (ibid. f. 132ᵛ).
[10] See p. 102.
[11] Ibid.
[12] Ibid.
[13] B.M. Harl. MS. 446, ff. 20ᵛ–21.
[14] Wolryche-Whitmore MSS., Dudmaston, lease, 1652.
[15] Apley Park estate office, survey, 1674.

presumably represented by the numerous small fields alongside Watling Street, which were amalgamated into larger fields between 1777 and 1840. Inclosure of the common at Botwood was still in progress in the 1720s,[16] but had been completed by 1777. On the west Woolstaston Wood still included a small part of Leebotwood in 1674.[17] Micklewood covered the northern half of the parish in 1185, when it was said to extend as far south as Watling Street,[18] but its southern boundary as described c. 1221 seems to have followed the cart-track running westwards from Newhouse Farm.[19] Half of this area since the 13th century, and the whole since the 16th century, have been part of the Longnor manorial estate,[20] and it has consequently followed a course of development different from that of the rest of the parish. The north-eastern half of Micklewood, allotted to the lord of Longnor c. 1221,[21] was formed into Longnor Park shortly after 1333, when a grant of free warren was obtained.[22] The Park is first named in 1538.[23] Of the remainder, part was assarted by Haughmond Abbey[24] and converted into a grange called 'la Cresse', first recorded c. 1255,[25] but the rest—comprising the south-western part of Micklewood—was still largely woodland in 1538.[26] Longnor Park was extended to include the western part of Micklewood in the 16th century,[27] but its stock of deer was destroyed during the Civil War[28] and it was disparked c. 1686.[29]

The three common fields of Leebotwood[30] lay for the most part on the gravels alongside the River Cound and Walkmill Brook, to the north and north-east of the village. Hill Field derived its name from Hunger Hill, a long narrow gravel ridge running northwards from Home Farm. Its 16th-century name, Alveld Field, was retained by a field on the eastern boundary of the parish near Leasowes Farm, known as Auvill in 1777 and Old Field in 1840. The other common fields lay to the north of Walkmill brook. Lower Field, or Middleyat Field, ran along the Cound to the parish boundary with Longnor and included lands on both sides of the Shrewsbury road. Malliner Field, or Park Field, lay near Padmore, then called Malliner Green. The common fields appear to have survived longer here than in neighbouring parishes. In 1674 there were still 61 a. of common-field land in the manorial estate, held by 16 out of 39 tenants.[31] Part of Lower Field was described as a new inclosure in 1701,[32]

and common-field lands are last recorded c. 1744.[33] No vestiges of the common fields remained in 1777.[34]

The road to Shrewsbury was turnpiked in 1756.[35] It crossed the Cound by a ford in the centre of the village[36] until 1848, when a bridge was erected.[37] At the same time the road, for some 350 yards south of the bridge, was diverted westwards,[38] thus explaining why the houses in this part of the village now stand some distance from the road. All other roads in the parish have remained unchanged since at least 1777.[39] The Shrewsbury and Hereford Railway, which runs from north to south across the parish, was opened in 1852, and Leebotwood station was opened by 1853.[40] The latter was closed in 1958.[41]

Since the early 13th century[42] the church has occupied an unusual position on the western boundary of the parish, about 600 yards distant from the village. As late as 1674 it was surrounded on three sides by Woolstaston Wood.[43] Although a house has stood in or near the churchyard since at least 1539[44] and foundations and pavements are said to have been uncovered nearby,[45] it is unlikely that the village has moved from the vicinity of the church to the main road. The glacial moraine on which the church stands was probably chosen as providing a more secure foundation than the alluvial soil of the village centre. It is possible that manorial buildings stood near the church in the Middle Ages, since nearby fields on either side of Church Lane lay in the medieval demesne.[46] In 1400, however, these buildings were in part surrounded by water,[47] which suggests a site nearer the Cound—perhaps at The Farm, which was leased to a relative or kept in hand by the lord of the manor in the 17th and 18th centuries.[48]

Most of the houses in the village stand to the east of the main road. A timber-framed house, now two cottages, stands at its junction with Church Lane, but the only other buildings to the west of the main road are the Village Hall and one other house, both built since 1920. The mill, first recorded in 1291, also stood to the west of the road, but this had gone out of use by 1796.[49] The Pound Inn—the oldest surviving house in the parish—consists of a two-bay cruck hall with a storied box-framed solar at the south end. The solar wing seems to have been extended westwards towards the main road in the 17th century. Panelling in this part of the house

[16] Wolryche-Whitmore MSS., Dudmaston, ct. r. 1728.
[17] Ibid. map of Woolstaston Wood, 1674.
[18] B.M. Harl. MS. 446, ff. 20ᵛ–21.
[19] Ibid. f. 21.   [20] See p. 111.
[21] B.M. Harl. MS. 446, f. 21.
[22] Cal. Chart. R. 1327–41, 292.
[23] S.R.O. 567 uncat., lease, 1538.
[24] S.P.L., Haughmond Cart. f. 77ᵛ.
[25] Ibid. f. 133ᵛ.
[26] S.R.O. 567 uncat., lease, 1538.
[27] Ibid. lease, 1651.
[28] Ibid. depositions, Uvedale Corbett v. Roger Pope, 1688.
[29] Ibid.
[30] Description of common fields based on Apley Park estate office, survey, 1674; ibid. survey and map, 1777; Heref. Dioc. Regy., tithe appt.; S.C. 6/Hen. VIII/3009 mm. 38d–39d.; S.C. 2/197/112; Wolryche-Whitmore MSS., Dudmaston, leases, 1653–76.
[31] Apley Park estate office, survey, 1674.
[32] Wolryche-Whitmore MSS., Dudmaston, lease, 1710.
[33] Ibid. lease, 1744.
[34] Apley Park estate office, survey and map, 1777.

[35] Shrewsbury–Church Stretton road Act, 29 Geo. II, c. 61 (priv. act). Apley Park estate office, accts. 1750–95, include accounts for work on the road, 1756–61.
[36] Apley Park estate office, map, 1777.
[37] Q. Sess., dep. plans 85. A new bridge was built in 1963.
[38] Wolryche-Whitmore MSS., Dudmaston, plan of proposed diversion, n.d.; Salop. N. & Q., n.s. vi. 33.
[39] Apley Park estate office, map, 1777.
[40] Ex inf. Brit. Trans. Rec.
[41] Ibid.
[42] S.P.L., Haughmond Cart. ff. 134–5, where the churchyard is referred to.
[43] Wolryche-Whitmore MSS., Dudmaston, map of Woolstaston Wood, 1674.
[44] S.C. 6/Hen. VIII/3009 m. 39; S.P.R. Lich. v (2), 376, 388.
[45] Salop. N. & Q., n.s. vi. 31–32.
[46] S.C. 6/Hen. VIII/3009 m. 39.
[47] S.P.L., Haughmond Cart. f. 135.
[48] See p. 102.
[49] Wolryche-Whitmore MSS., Dudmaston, survey, c. 1796.

came from Woolstaston Rectory.[50] It was a farm-house until the early 19th century, when the original inn was burnt down.[51] The latter stood on the site of the 19th-century house known as Broadstead, at the north end of the village, near the stocks and the pound which gave it its name.[52] The smithy, now demolished, stood at the south end of the village, at the junction of the Cardington road with the former course of the main road.[53] Opposite is Horseshoes Farm,[54] originally a timber-framed house of two bays, with a chimney stack on the east gable. A brew-house and other additions in stone to the south suggest that it was converted into an ale-house in the 18th century, but it is first recorded as such in 1840.[55] The two other farms in the village— The Farm and Top Farm—are both timber-framed houses, but the former is now completely cased in brick and the latter has extensive stone additions on the north side. The Farm was originally a two-bay house with a central chimney stack. One room in the north wing, added c. 1700, contains oak panelling removed from Woolstaston Hall c. 1784.[56] Nearly all the remaining houses in the village are of 17th-century date.

The earliest recorded isolated settlements in the parish, outside Micklewood, were the fulling mills on Walkmill Brook. These had probably been established by the early 14th century[57] and two houses still stood by the brook in 1777,[58] but nothing now remains apart from a weir. Botwood attracted few squatters. There were at least 3 cottages there in 1674[59] and 5 in 1690,[60] but most of these, like the more extensive settlement at Lower Wood, were probably in that part of Leebotwood manor that lay in Church Stretton parish. The only surviving house of this type in the parish is Home Farm, on the Cardington road, which was standing in 1777[61] and, like Horseshoes Farm, was orginally a timber-framed house of two bays with a chimney stack on the east gable. Extensive additions in brick to the north were probably built soon after 1821, when the farm was sold to the Corbetts of Longnor.[62] Two cottages on the west side of the main road, north of the village, one of which is timber-framed and the other cased in brick, had been built before 1777.[63]

The small group of cottages at Padmore probably date from the 18th century. This area was known as Malliner Green in the 18th century, and in 1777 there were 9 houses here.[64] No. 22, Padmore incorporates an early-18th-century stone cottage of one bay with a gable chimney stack. Other houses in this area are of brick and were probably built in the early 19th century, when a number of cottages were erected to accommodate workers at Leebot-wood colliery. The latter was opened in 1784[65] and its original workings were only a few yards from the houses on Padmore Lane.[66] After 1804 the pits lay nearer to the main road, east of the line of the rail-way.[67] In 1832 13 cottages in Leebotwood were occupied by colliers.[68] Fields Farm, which stands on the site of the house occupied by the lessee of the colliery in 1784, was rebuilt in brick shortly before 1832.[69] A number of County Council smallholdings, most of them spaced at intervals along the main road, were built in the 1920s,[70] and 6 Council houses at the north end of the village were built 1926–8.[71]

In the area formerly covered by Micklewood, settlement has always taken the form of isolated farms. The earliest of these was Cress Grange established before 1255,[72] which presumably took its name from Cross Brook.[73] There is no evidence that the house was occupied after the dissolution, but the little bank marking its site was still known in 1688, when it was said to have stood on the boundary with Smethcott in the north of Longnor Park[74] probably on the outcrop of shales that runs along the parish boundary north of Park Farm. A house is known to have stood on the site of Micklewood Farm since 1617.[75] This contained one hearth in 1662[76] and 1672,[77] but was replaced shortly before 1689, when the present brick house was built by Waties Corbett.[78] This has stone dressings, brick dentil string courses, and a steeply pitched hipped roof with gabled brick dormers. It faces south and consists of a central block and two projecting wings, each with a lateral chimney. The main doorway has a carved stone surround, which may originally have been surmounted by a semicircular hood. The internal arrangement of the central block, with its asymmetrical hall and chimney-stack, suggests that some features of the earlier plan have survived. The hall contains an elaborate plaster overmantel and a staircase with twisted balusters, both of the later 17th century. A second stair and other alterations, which may have included the insertion of sash windows, date from the earlier 18th century. A back kitchen and a second room in the east wing were built on the north side, probably in the later 18th century, when the farm was occupied by Robert Flint, a relative of the Corbett family.[79] Park Farm, formerly called Lodge Farm and presumably at one time a hunting lodge in Longnor Park, was originally a timber-framed house of two bays with a chimney stack on the south gable. The west wing

[50] Ex inf. Mr. F. A. J. Tissington.
[51] Salop. N. & Q., n.s. vi. 31–33.
[52] Ibid.; Apley Park estate office, map, 1777.
[53] Ibid.
[54] Description based on information from the owner, Mr. J. F. Davies, who has carried out extensive alterations to the interior in the past 10 years.
[55] Heref. Dioc. Regy., tithe appt.
[56] See p. 173.
[57] See p. 103.
[58] Apley Park estate office, map, 1777.
[59] Ibid. survey, 1674.
[60] Wolryche-Whitmore MSS., Dudmaston, ct. r. 1690.
[61] Apley Park estate office, map, 1777.
[62] See p. 102.
[63] Apley Park estate office, map, 1777.
[64] Ibid.
[65] Ibid. accts. 1750–95.
[66] Wolryche-Whitmore MSS., Dudmaston, lease of colliery, 1804.
[67] Ibid.; ibid. valuation of colliery, c. 1832.
[68] Ibid. valuation of colliery, c. 1832.
[69] Ibid. colliery plans and papers, 1796–1833.
[70] S.C.C. Minutes, 1922–3, 76.
[71] Miss A. Evason, 'Leebotwood' (London Inst. Educ. thesis, 1956), 17.
[72] S.P.L., Haughmond, Cart. f. 133ᵛ.
[73] Still known as Cross Brook in the early 17th century: Lich. Dioc. Regy., Stapleton glebe terrier, 1612.
[74] S.R.O. 567 uncat., depositions, Uvedale Corbett v. Roger Pope, 1688.
[75] Ibid.; ibid. marriage settlement of Edward Corbett, 1617.
[76] E 179/255/35 m. 17.   [77] Hearth Tax, 1672, 125.
[78] S.R.O. 567 uncat., lease, 1689.
[79] Ibid. lease, 1763.

was probably added in the later 18th century. Newhouse Farm, erected by 1817,[80] is brick-built and probably dates from the later 18th century.

There were said to be 105 adults in the parish in 1676[81] and 181 inhabitants in 1801.[82] Employment at the colliery was largely responsible for a rise in population in the early 19th century, reaching a peak of 233 in 1841.[83] After the closure of the colliery c. 1875, population fell rapidly to 147 in 1901,[84] but had risen to 189 by 1911.[85] A slow but steady growth of population was maintained until 1951, when there were 211 inhabitants,[86] but it had fallen to 191 by 1961.[87]

MANOR. Eyton's identification of the Domesday manor of Botwood with the later manor of LEE-BOTWOOD[88] is supported only by the coincidence that both were assessed at half a hide.[89] If this is correct, the manor held by the freeman Auti before 1066 and in 1086[90] must have gone out of cultivation soon after this date. Between 1163 and 1170 Henry II granted two landas in Botwood to Haughmond Abbey.[91] They had formerly lain in the royal manor of Condover and were described as assarted land in 1212.[92] Haughmond Abbey held the manor until the Dissolution.[93] Sir Thomas Palmer, to whom the manor had been granted by the Crown in 1552,[94] was attainted for treason in 1554,[95] when it was granted to Rowland Hayward.[96] In 1559 Hayward conveyed the manor to Richard Crompton,[97] who sold it to Richard Harris in 1563.[98] Roger Harris, possibly a brother of Richard,[99] was in possession of the manor by 1568.[1] He died in 1598[2] and was succeeded by his eldest son, Richard Harris, a clergyman.[3] At the latter's death, shortly after 1613,[4] the manor passed to his brother Sir Thomas Harris,[5] who died in 1630.[6] It was held in dower by Sarah, widow of Sir Thomas Harris,[7] until her death in 1641,[8] when it descended to her son Sir Paul Harris. He died in 1644[9] and was succeeded by his son Sir Thomas Harris, at whose death c. 1661[10] the manor passed successively to his brothers George and Paul Harris.[11] Paul Harris died without heirs in 1666,[12] and in 1671 his executors sold the manor

to Roger Pope of Woolstaston.[13] It descended in the Pope family until 1754,[14] the following being lords: Roger, 1671–1710; Bromwich (grandson), 1710–33; Catherine (daughter), 1733–54. Under the will of Catherine Pope, the manor then passed to her cousin Sir Thomas Whitmore of Apley,[15] who in 1771 settled it on his daughter Mary and her husband Major Thomas Whitmore.[16] The latter died in 1795, being succeeded by his brother William Whitmore of Dudmaston,[17] who in 1809 settled the manor on his son William Wolryche-Whitmore.[18] In 1858 it passed to the latter's nephew, the Revd. Francis Laing,[19] who assumed the name of Wolryche-Whitmore in 1864[20] and was succeeded in 1908 by his son Francis Alexander Wolryche-Whitmore.[21] The latter sold his estate in Lee-botwood, Smethcott, and Woolstaston in 1920, when the greater part of the Leebotwood estate was purchased by the County Council for smallholdings.[22]

OTHER ESTATES. When Micklewood was divided, shortly before 1221, the north-eastern part was allotted to Roger Sprenchose, lord of Longnor manor,[23] thus forming the nucleus of the considerable property in the north of the parish which has since been part of the Longnor estate. Lands in Micklewood were included in the moiety of Longnor manor which passed to the Acton family after 1375,[24] but these were acquired by Edward Corbett in 1575.[25]

Haughmond Abbey retained the south-western half of Micklewood, and by 1255 had established Cress Grange on part of this land.[26] The latter was leased to John Herbart in 1304[27] and in 1372 to Edward de Acton of Longnor,[28] whose descendants continued to occupy it until the 16th century.[29] In 1544 the grange was sold to Thomas Corbett.[30] The Actons, however, retained their leasehold interest in the property, which passed to the descendants of John Charlton, to whom the reversion of the lease had been granted in 1536.[31] This is last recorded in 1565, when Thomas Charlton assigned half of the grange to Edward Corbett, who in return

[80] B.M. O.S. 2″ orig. drawings, sheet 207 (1817).
[81] T.S.A.S. 2nd ser. i. 81.
[82] Census, 1801.
[83] Ibid. 1811–41.
[84] Ibid. 1871–1901.
[85] Ibid. 1911.
[86] Ibid. 1921–51.
[87] Ibid. 1961.
[88] Eyton, vi. 244–5.
[89] See p. 102.
[90] V.C.H. Salop. i. 432.
[91] S.P.L., Haughmond Cart. f. 132.
[92] Bk. of Fees, i. 146.
[93] S.C. 6/Hen. VIII/3009 mm. 38ᵛ–39ᵛ.
[94] Cal. Pat. 1550–3, 236.
[95] B.M. Add. Ch. 67031.
[96] Cal. Pat. 1553–4, 478–9.
[97] Ibid. 1558–60, 135; ibid. 1560–3, 140.
[98] C.P. 25(2)/200/5 Eliz. I Trin.
[99] T.S.A.S. 4th ser. vii. 46.
[1] S.P.L., Deeds 17432.
[2] C 142/258/32.
[3] Ibid.
[4] D.N.B.
[5] The lord in 1624: S.R.O. 567 uncat., deed, 1624.
[6] T.S.A.S. 4th ser. vii. 56.
[7] Ibid. 57, 60.
[8] S.P.L., MS. 2792, p. 436.
[9] T.S.A.S. 4th ser. vii. 64–65.

[10] S.P.L., Deeds 17348.
[11] Ibid.; T.S.A.S. 4th ser. vii. 69–70.
[12] T.S.A.S. 4th ser. vii. 70.
[13] Wolryche-Whitmore MSS., Dudmaston, conveyance, 1671.
[14] For pedigree see T.S.A.S. l. 47–48 and Wolryche-Whitmore MSS., Dudmaston, family settlements. Bracketed entries indicate relationship to preceding lord.
[15] Wolryche-Whitmore MSS., Dudmaston, will of Catherine Pope, 1754.
[16] Ibid. settlement, 1771.
[17] Ibid. 1795.
[18] Ibid. 1809; C.P. 43/904 rot. 17, 160.
[19] S.C.C. title-deeds, SH 12 (abstract of title).
[20] Burke, Land. Gent. (1952), p. 2707.
[21] Ibid.
[22] S.C.C. title-deeds, SH 12; S.C.C. Minutes, 1919–20, 202, 268.
[23] B.M. Harl. MS. 446, f. 21; S.P.L., Haughmond Cart. f. 134ᵛ.
[24] S.R.O. 567 uncat., lease, 1540.
[25] Ibid. exchange, 1575.
[26] Ibid.; S.P.L., Haughmond Cart. f. 133ᵛ.
[27] S.P.L., Haughmond Cart. f. 140.
[28] Ibid. f. 51ᵛ.
[29] S.R.O. 567 uncat., lease, 1485.
[30] L. & P. Hen. VIII, xix (2), p. 317; S.R.O. 567 uncat., deeds, 1544.
[31] S.R.O. 567 uncat., deed, 1565.

confirmed Charlton's leasehold estate in the other half.[32] The remainder of Haughmond's estate in Micklewood was leased to Thomas Corbett in 1538[33] and sold to his son Edward in 1544.[34]

Other lands in Leebotwood, outside the bounds of Micklewood, which the Corbetts acquired in the course of the 16th century,[35] were sold to the lord of the manor in 1624.[36] The Corbett estate in Leebotwood comprised 440 a. in 1794,[37] and rose to 676 a. after the purchase of Home Farm in 1821.[38] In 1855 61 a. in Leebotwood and elsewhere were conveyed to T. H. Hope-Edwardes in exchange for lands in Condover.[39] Newhouse Farm was sold in 1960,[40] but Micklewood and Park Farms remain in the Corbett estate.

ECONOMIC HISTORY. The manor of Botwood was assessed at half a hide in 1086, when its value was said to have been 5s. since before 1066. There was then no demesne land and the only tenants were two radmen, who held land for one plough.[41] The estate granted to Haughmond Abbey shortly before 1170 was described as two *landas*, or barren tracts, in the forest of Botwood,[42] and in 1212 the manor was said to consist wholly of assarted lands.[43] This suggests that the Domesday manor had reverted to the forest, but the fact that the Abbey's estate here was assessed at half a hide in 1179,[44] 1212,[45] and 1255[46] is perhaps evidence of continuity.

Whatever was the condition of the manor in 1170, Haughmond quickly set about enlarging the arable area by forest clearance. Royal licences to assart were obtained in 1179,[47] 1232,[48] and 1283,[49] the western boundary of the manor was fixed by agreement with neighbouring lords in the first quarter of the 13th century,[50] and Cress Grange had been established in Micklewood by 1255.[51] By 1291 the demesne comprised one carucate,[52] and manorial buildings are recorded in 1400.[53] The abbey was granted a weekly market on Thursdays at Leebotwood in 1320[54] and by 1327 there were two fulling mills in the parish.[55] Although there is no evidence that the demesne was leased before 1400, when it was demised for life to Thomas de Lee,[56] Cress Grange was continuously leased after 1304.[57] By 1539 the

demesne lands were dispersed among the holdings of several tenants.[58]

Parts of the manorial estate were alienated while the manor was in Crown hands after the Dissolution. Cress Grange, Micklewood, the chapel, and several messuages in the village were granted to Edward Corbett in 1544,[59] and 3 messuages were granted to Edward Basshe and Robert Curtis in 1545.[60] In 1561 the lord of the manor sold a messuage and lands to Richard Harley,[61] probably the holding occupied by the Harley family since 1515.[62] Richard Hopton owned 2 fulling mills, 3 messuages, and 26 a. land here in 1597,[63] but by 1619 these had passed to Francis Jones,[64] and were bought back into the manorial estate in 1624.[65] The Popes of Woolstaston acquired 2 messuages in Leebotwood in 1593,[66] and their estate included 3 messuages here in 1665,[67] but they were reunited with the manorial estate when Roger Pope purchased the manor in 1671. Apart from the estate of the Corbett family, no free-holding created by the 16th-century fragmentation of the manor survived beyond the mid-17th century. The origins of the two freeholders who together owned 37 a. in the parish in 1840[68] are not known.

A farm of 117 a., held on a beneficial lease by Sir Roger Harris between c. 1649 and 1674,[69] seems later to have been kept in hand by the Pope family, and was fully stocked on the death of Catherine Pope in 1754.[70] This was let soon after the Whitmores succeeded to the manor[71] and no land in Leebotwood was kept in hand by 1777.[72]

Rents produced only 10s. 4d. a year in 1291,[73] but had risen to £18 18s. by 1535.[74] Leasehold tenure predominated in 1539, when 14 tenants held on long leases, mostly for 61 years, their rents totalling £12 9s. 8d. a year.[75] There was then only one customary tenant, while tenants-at-will, who cannot have been numerous, paid £4 1s. 10d. a year.[76] Annual rents of £141 were paid by 25 tenants and 7 cottagers c. 1640.[77] The three-life lease was the usual form of tenure here until at least 1729 and, although 21-year leases had been introduced by 1744, these still specified suit of court and mill.[78] The annual rental rose from £303 in 1733 to £406

[32] S.R.O. 567 uncat., deed, 1565.
[33] Ibid. lease, 1538; S.C. 6/Hen. VIII/3009 m. 39.
[34] *L. & P. Hen. VIII*, xix (2), pp. 76, 420; S.R.O. 567 uncat., deeds, 1544.
[35] See below.
[36] S.R.O. 567 uncat., deed, 1624.
[37] N.L.W., MS. 18453C.
[38] Wolryche-Whitmore MSS., Dudmaston, deed, 1821; Heref. Dioc. Regy., tithe appt.
[39] Ex inf. Messrs. Salt & Sons, solicitors, Shrewsbury.
[40] Ibid.
[41] *V.C.H. Salop*. i. 342.
[42] S.P.L., Haughmond Cart. f. 132.
[43] *Bk. of Fees*, i. 146.
[44] S.P.L., Haughmond Cart. f. 132.
[45] *Bk. of Fees*, i. 146.
[46] *Rot. Hund.* (Rec. Com.), ii. 62.
[47] S.P.L., Haughmond Cart. f. 132.
[48] Ibid. f. 77ᵛ.
[49] Ibid.; *Cal. Pat.* 1281–92, 81.
[50] S.P.L., Haughmond Cart. ff. 133ᵛ–5.
[51] Ibid. f. 133ᵛ.
[52] *Tax. Eccl.* (Rec. Com.), 260.
[53] S.P.L., Haughmond Cart. f. 135.
[54] *Cal. Chart. R.* 1300–26, 426.
[55] *T.S.A.S.* 2nd ser. xi. 363.
[56] S.P.L., Haughmond Cart. f. 135.

[57] See p. 101.
[58] S.C. 6/Hen. VIII/3009 m. 39.
[59] *L. & P. Hen. VIII*, xix (2), pp. 76, 317, 420; S.R.O. 567 uncat., deeds, 1544.
[60] *L. & P. Hen. VIII*, xx (2), p. 540.
[61] *Cal. Pat.* 1560–3, 140.
[62] S.C. 6/Hen. VIII/3009 m. 39.
[63] *T.S.A.S.* li. 47, 52.
[64] Wolryche-Whitmore MSS., Dudmaston, bill of complaint, Francis Jones v. Roger Pope, 1619.
[65] S.R.O. 567 uncat., deed, 1624.
[66] Wolryche-Whitmore MSS., Dudmaston, deed, 1593.
[67] Apley Park estate office, accts. 1665–78.
[68] Heref. Dioc. Regy., tithe appt.
[69] *T.S.A.S.* 4th ser. vii. 78–79; Wolryche-Whitmore MSS., Dudmaston, lease, 1658; Apley Park estate office, survey, 1674.
[70] Apley Park estate office, inventory of Catherine Pope, 1754.
[71] Ibid. accts. 1750–95.
[72] Ibid. survey, 1777.
[73] *Tax. Eccl.* (Rec. Com.), 260.
[74] *Valor Eccl.* (Rec. Com.), iii. 192.
[75] S.C. 6/Hen. VIII/3009 m. 39.
[76] Ibid.
[77] *T.S.A.S.* 4th ser. vii. 78–79.
[78] Wolryche-Whitmore MSS., Dudmaston, leases, *passim*.

in 1780, but there were considerable arrears before 1750.[79]

There is no reliable indication of the size of holdings before 1674, when the manor had become part of the Pope estate in Leebotwood, Smethcott, and Woolstaston. The farms of 3 Leebotwood tenants then lay partly in Smethcott parish,[80] and the tendency for farms to extend across parish boundaries became more marked with the growth of larger farms in the 18th century. In 1777 6 out of the 17 farms of over 25 a. lay in more than one parish.[81] In 1675, when the Pope estate in Leebotwood, Smethcott, and Woolstaston comprised 1,741 a., the 98 holdings included only 3 farms of over 100 a. and 72 of less than 25 a.[82] By 1777 the number of tenants on the estate had fallen to 60 and 7 of the farms were of over 100 a.; only 43 were of less than 25 a.[83] During the 19th century the 7 large farms grew at the expense of the holdings of 25–100 a., whose number declined from 10 to 5 between 1777 and 1919.[84] Some 920 a., or a little over one-third of the estate, lay in farms of over 200 a. c. 1796,[85] but by 1917 1,230 a., or two-thirds of the estate, lay in farms of this size.[86] In 1920 the County Council purchased The Farm and Top Farm (407 a.),[87] which were converted into 19 smallholdings in 1922.[88]

Water-meadows had been in use on some Leebotwood farms since the mid-18th century, when the miller at Longnor complained that water was being diverted from the Cound and Walkmill Brook for this purpose.[89] In 1796 the 3 principal farms on the manorial estate contained 198 a. arable, 93 a. clover and leys, and 209 a. meadow and permanent pasture.[90] Wheat was the principal crop,[91] as it was in 1801, when there were some 323 a. arable in the parish and it was said that 'there never was so many acres of all grain in cultivation before'.[92] Arable was more prominent on the clay soils in the north of the parish, where in 1816 Micklewood and Park Farms contained 309 a. arable and only 159 a. pasture.[93] An increasing proportion of the parish came under the plough in the earlier 19th century, and by 1840 it contained 737 a. arable and 514 a. pasture.[94]

The mill recorded in 1291, when it was worth 3s. a year,[95] may be Longnor mill, which also belonged to Haughmond Abbey, but millers were resident in Leebotwood in 1332[96] and 1379.[97] John Sankey, to whom the mill was leased in 1458,[98] was then said to have occupied it for a long time previously[99] and in 1539 it was held by his descendant Hugh Sankey.[1] By 1674 the mill was among the lands occupied by Sir Roger Harris.[2] Millers are recorded in 1730,[3] 1760,[4] and 1777,[5] but the mill had gone out of use by 1796.[6]

Two fullers lived in Leebotwood in 1327[7] and 1332.[8] John Sankey, the miller of 1458, was a fuller by trade and had a fulling mill on the site of the corn mill.[9] Thomas Sankey held the fulling mill at his death in 1533[10] and Hugh Sankey, who held 3 fulling mills in the parish in 1539,[11] was one of the three most wealthy inhabitants of the village in 1544.[12] The subsequent history of these mills is not clear, but they can probably be identified with the 2 fulling mills on the estate of Richard Hopton in 1597.[13] Only one fulling mill remained when this property was reunited with the manorial estate in 1624,[14] and in 1674 it was once more held with the corn mill by Sir Roger Harris.[15] Two fulling mills leased to Peter Botfield in 1539[16] appear to have stood on Walkmill Brook, near the group of fulling mills at Walk Mills in Woolstaston parish. Isaac Sankey held a mill here before 1666,[17] and in 1674 there were two mills on Walkmill Brook, occupied by Richard Kendrick and Richard Davies.[18] The former died in 1689[19] and in 1694 both mills were leased to John Brown,[20] but they had gone out of use by 1757.[21]

Coal was being mined for a short period at the Haines, on Micklewood Farm, c. 1738,[22] but there is no other evidence for coal-mining in the parish before the establishment of Leebotwood Colliery in 1784.[23] The colliery was normally leased, the lord of the manor receiving royalties, and was held by the following tenants until 1808: Mr. Atcherley, 1784–8;[24] C. & J. Carrington, 1788;[25] the Revd. Mr. Atcherley, 1789–95;[26] Richard Boothby of Pontesbury, 1796–1804;[27] John Hazledine of Bridgnorth, 1804–8.[28] It was still said to be leased in 1813,[29] but

[79] Apley Park estate office, accts., 1732–48, 1749–80.
[80] Ibid. survey, 1674.
[81] Ibid. survey, 1777.
[82] Ibid. survey, 1674–5.
[83] Ibid. survey, 1777.
[84] Ibid.; Wolryche-Whitmore MSS., Dudmaston, survey, c. 1796; Heref. Dioc. Regy., tithe appt.; Smethcott and Woolstaston par. rec., tithe appts.; S.C.C. title-deeds, SH 12 (sale partics., 1919).
[85] Wolryche-Whitmore MSS., Dudmaston, survey, c. 1796.
[86] S.C.C. title-deeds, SH 12 (survey, 1917).
[87] Ibid. conveyance, 1920.
[88] S.C.C. Minutes, 1922–3, 76.
[89] S.R.O. 567 uncat., depositions, 1757.
[90] Wolryche-Whitmore MSS., Dudmaston, survey, c. 1796.
[91] Ibid.
[92] H.O. 67/14/157.
[93] S.R.O. 1279/3.
[94] Heref. Dioc. Regy., tithe appt.
[95] Tax. Eccl. (Rec. Com.), 260.
[96] E 179/166/2 m. 5.
[97] E 179/166/23.
[98] S.P.L., Haughmond Cart. f. 135ᵛ.
[99] Ibid.
[1] S.C. 6/Hen. VIII/3009 m. 39ᵛ
[2] Apley Park estate office, survey, 1674.
[3] S.P.R. Lich. v (2), 368.

[4] Ibid. 378.
[5] Apley Park estate office, survey, 1777.
[6] Wolryche-Whitmore MSS., Dudmaston, survey, c. 1796.
[7] T.S.A.S. 2nd ser. xi. 363.
[8] E 179/166/2 m. 5.
[9] S.P.L., Haughmond Cart. f. 135ᵛ.
[10] C 1/812/4.
[11] S.C. 6/Hen. VIII/3009 m. 39ᵛ.
[12] E 179/166/168.
[13] T.S.A.S. li. 47.
[14] S.R.O. 567 uncat., deed, 1624.
[15] Apley Park estate office, survey, 1674.
[16] S.C. 6/Hen. VIII/3009 m. 39.
[17] Wolryche-Whitmore MSS., Dudmaston, lease, 1666.
[18] Apley Park estate office, survey, 1674.
[19] S.P.R. Lich. v (2), 358.
[20] Wolryche-Whitmore MSS., Dudmaston, lease, 1694.
[21] S.R.O. 567 uncat., papers re diversion of streams serving Longnor Mill, 1757.
[22] Ibid. leases, 1689, 1738.
[23] Apley Park estate office, accts. 1750–95.
[24] Ibid.   [25] Ibid.
[26] Ibid.
[27] Wolryche-Whitmore MSS., Dudmaston, leases, 1796, 1804.
[28] Ibid. lease, 1804; ibid. will of John Hazledine, 1808.
[29] Hope-Edwardes MSS., Linley Hall, letter, John Hornblower to J. T. Hope, 1813.

between 1831 and 1834 it was operated by the lord of the manor under a manager.[30] It is not known whether James Smith, who held the colliery in 1840[31] and 1851,[32] and his successor William Ison,[33] were managers or lessees, but Richard Preen, who ran it from c. 1863 until its closure c. 1875[34] seems to have been a lessee. The colliery extended over 7 a. in 1796,[35] 29 a. in 1807,[36] and 41 a. by 1833, when there were 4 pits in operation.[37] Production in 1832 totalled 3,664 tons,[38] but from the outset the bulk of the coal seems to have been used in the manufacture of lime, bricks, and tiles on the site.[39]

The market established in 1320[40] continued to be held weekly on Thursdays until within living memory.[41] An inn, first recorded in 1527,[42] was held in 1539 by Richard Harley under a lease of 1515.[43] In 1544 he was one of the two most prosperous inhabitants,[44] and in 1561 his son Richard acquired the freehold of the property.[45] By 1593, however, when it was called the Talbot, the inn was in the possession of the Pope family,[46] and thus became part of the manorial estate after 1671. It is first called the Pound Inn in 1823, [47] by which date it had probably moved to its present site.[48] Held by the Dodd family, 1806–c. 1913,[49] it had been acquired before 1917 by the People's Refreshment Houses Association.[50] Two ale-sellers were licensed in 1616,[51] but, although 4 persons were fined for selling ale in 1680 and 8 in 1681,[52] there is no other evidence for the existence of more than one ale-house in the village in the 17th and 18th centuries. One of the ale-sellers of 1616 was a blacksmith,[53] and the smith also kept an alehouse—now Horseshoes Farm—between 1840 and 1870.[54] The smithy, first recorded in 1539,[55] and held by the Dickin family, c. 1741–1870,[56] closed in 1941 and was demolished in 1963.[57]

In addition to a butcher,[58] a carpenter,[59] and a tailor,[60] the inhabitants of the parish in the 17th century included a dyer and a cloth-worker.[61] There were two weavers here in the 18th century,[62] when a weaver's shop was attached to the inn.[63] The village shop, adjoining the Pound Inn, is first recorded in 1851.[64] Until c. 1917 it was occupied by the Preen family,[65] who also leased the colliery, c. 1863–75,[66] and were coal-merchants until c. 1905.[67] A carpenter and shoemaker had gone out of business by 1895. With the introduction of smallholdings in the 1920s[68] the number of tradesmen in the village again rose. There were two corn-dealers in 1926,[69] and by 1934 a coal-merchant, a general dealer, a bus proprietor, and a shoemaker.[70]

LOCAL GOVERNMENT. In 1255 the manor was said to be exempt from suit at the hundred court and sheriff's tourn.[71] There are court rolls, 1547–54,[72] and court papers, 1677–1809.[73] The jurisdiction of the court included the assize of bread and ale, but although constables were elected in the 16th century, there is no record of the appointment of manorial officers after 1677. In the later 18th century the court met at the Pound Inn.

There are no parish records other than registers. Poor rates rose from about £11 a year in the later 17th century[74] to £21 a year by 1776.[75] They had risen to £75 by 1803[76] and reached a peak of £123 in 1821,[77] but between 1824 and 1834 never rose above £92 a year.[78] The parish had no work-house in 1803.[79]

CHURCH. There was no church on the estate in Leebotwood granted to Haughmond Abbey c. 1170, but one had been built before 1183, when an unrecorded grant of the chapel of 'Lega' by Henry II to the Abbey was confirmed by the bishop of Coventry and Lichfield.[80] The three portioners of Condover witnessed this grant[81]—an indication that the parish had previously been served by that church. By the same deed the abbey was granted rights of baptism and burial at Leebotwood,[82] which was thus made parochially independent of Condover.

[30] Wolryche-Whitmore MSS., Dudmaston, colliery papers, 1831–4.
[31] Heref. Dioc. Regy., tithe appt.
[32] Bagshaw's Dir. Salop. (1851).
[33] Kelly's Dir. Salop. (1856).
[34] Ibid. (1863, 1870); Longnor par. rec., churchwardens' accts. 1761–1898.
[35] Wolryche-Whitmore MSS., Dudmaston, survey, c. 1796.
[36] Ibid. survey, 1807.
[37] Ibid. colliery papers, 1831–4.
[38] Ibid.
[39] Apley Park estate office, accts. 1750–95; Wolryche-Whitmore MSS., Dudmaston, inventory of colliery, 1833.
[40] Cal. Chart. R. 1300–26, 426.
[41] Miss A. Evason, 'Leebotwood', 17.
[42] Owen and Blakeway, Hist. Shrewsbury, i. 307.
[43] S.C. 6/Hen. VIII/3009 m. 39.
[44] E 179/166/168.
[45] Cal. Pat. 1560–3, 140.
[46] Wolryche-Whitmore MSS., Dudmaston, lease, 1593.
[47] Q. Sess., alehouse reg.
[48] Salop. N. & Q. N.S. vi. 31–33.
[49] Q. Sess., alehouse reg.; Kelly's Dir. Salop. (1856–1913); Salop. N. & Q. N.S. vi. 33.
[50] Kelly's Dir. Salop. (1917).
[51] Q. Sess., alehouse reg.
[52] Wolryche-Whitmore MSS., Dudmaston, ct. r. 1680–1.
[53] Q. Sess., alehouse reg.
[54] Heref. Dioc. Regy., tithe appt.; Bagshaw's Dir. Salop. (1851); Kelly's Dir. Salop. (1856–70).
[55] S.C. 6/Hen. VIII/3009 m. 39v.
[56] Apley Park estate office, accts. 1732–48; Kelly's Dir. Salop. (1870).

[57] Ex inf. the Vicar.
[58] S.R.O. 567 uncat., lease, 1666.
[59] Ibid. deed, 1624.
[60] Wolryche-Whitmore MSS., Dudmaston, lease, 1661.
[61] Ibid. lease, 1676.
[62] S.R.O. 567 uncat., lease, 1666.
[63] S.P.R. Lich. v (2), 376; Wolryche-Whitmore MSS., Dudmaston, lease, 1661; ibid. survey, c. 1796.
[64] Bagshaw's Dir. Salop. (1851).
[65] Kelly's Dir. Salop. (1856–1917).
[66] See above.
[67] Kelly's Dir. Salop. (1863–1905).
[68] Bagshaw's Dir. Salop. (1851); Kelly's Dir. Salop. (1856–95).
[69] Kelly's Dir. Salop. (1926).
[70] Ibid. (1934–41).
[71] Rot. Hund. (Rec. Com.), ii. 62.
[72] S.C. 2/197/112; S.C. 2/197/148.
[73] Wolryche-Whitmore MSS., Dudmaston, ct. r. 1677–1809.
[74] Bodl. MS. Blakeway, 8, f. 476.
[75] Rep. Cttee. on Overseers' Returns, 1777, p. 442, H.C. (1st ser. ix, reprinted 1803).
[76] Poor Law Abstract, 1803, H.C. 175, pp. 416–17 (1803–4), xiii.
[77] Rep. Cttee. on Poor Rate Returns, 1822, Suppl. App., H.C. 556, p. 141 (1822), v.
[78] Ibid. 1825, H.C. 334, p. 177 (1825), iv; Acct. of Money Expended on Poor, 1825–9, H.C. 83, p. 390 (1830–1), xi; ibid. 1830–4, H.C. 444, p. 344 (1835), xlvii.
[79] Poor Law Abstract, 1803, pp. 416–17.
[80] S.P.L., Haughmond Cart. f. 133; B.M. Harl. MS. 3868, f. 10v.
[81] Ibid.
[82] Ibid.

The church remained appropriated to Haughmond Abbey until the Dissolution. In 1544 it was purchased by Edward Corbett[83] and was subsequently, like Longnor, a donative in the hands of the Corbett family. From the 16th century the living was accounted a perpetual curacy and it has normally been held in plurality with Longnor since 1573.[84] The two livings were formally united in 1821.[85] The advowson was vested in the Hereford Diocesan Board of Patronage in 1948.[86]

Initially at least, the chapel was served by one of the canons of Haughmond in person. An ordinance of uncertain date[87] provided him with a daily livery of bread and ale at the abbey. For his maintenance he was to receive an annual pension of half a mark, altar-offerings, and all small tithes except whole fleeces and lambs. In return he was to be responsible for the upkeep of the chapel. In 1532 the chapel and the small tithes were leased to Roger Luter, the curate,[88] who appears to have held them until his death in 1560.[89] Subsequently both great and small tithes were held by the Corbett family as impropriators and the curate received an annual stipend.

The great tithes, said to be worth 26s. 8d. a year in 1341,[90] were normally leased in the later Middle Ages. They were included in a lease of the manor in 1400[91] and the tithes of uncultivated lands in Cress Grange were leased to the tenant in 1485.[92] In 1539 the tithes of Cress Grange and of one other tenement were held by their tenants, while the rest were held by the curate.[93] In 1617 the tithes were said to be worth £20, except those then kept in hand by the Corbetts,[94] and in 1629 they were set, for an entry fine of £160, on a long lease at 20s. a year.[95] In the early 18th century they were leased for £20 a year,[96] and their value had risen to £50 a year by 1772.[97] Apart from a modus for the hay of Broad Meadow (14 a.) they were collected in kind until 1840,[98] when they were commuted for a rent-charge of £105 a year.[99]

The curate was paid no settled salary in 1655,[1] but in 1682 he was receiving an annual stipend of £6 from the impropriator.[2] By 1698 the stipend had been raised to £8 10s. a year,[3] when reckoned as half the annual value of the tithes,[4] and the curate was said to be well satisfied with what he had.[5] He received in addition the surplice fees and Easter dues, said to be worth £2 10s. a year in 1705[6] and £1 10s. in 1722.[7] The annual stipend was still being paid in 1828.[8] By 1764 the curate also received a gratuity of £10 a year,[9] but this was discontinued in 1787.[10] Between 1739 and 1784 four grants of £200 were made to the livings of Leebotwood and Longnor by Queen Anne's Bounty.[11] A further £200 was granted in 1783 to meet a benefaction by Sir Richard Corbett, bringing Leebotwood's share to £800.[12] By 1792 this had been used to purchase 31 a. of glebe land at Plas Bach in Oswestry.[13] In 1833 the glebe of Leebotwood and Longnor at Oswestry was exchanged for 99 a. in Cardington,[14] which was sold in 1920.[15] The gross annual value of the living rose from £45 in 1799[16] to £60 10s. in 1821.[17] In 1835 the average gross annual value of the united benefice was £135.[18]

Despite the low value of the livings of Leebotwood and Longnor, several curates held them for long periods. Of 19 known curates between 1532 and 1935, 9 served for more than 20 years, the longest incumbencies being those of William Penne (curate 1573–c. 1633)[19] and David Rice (curate 1728–84).[20] Until 1784, when Joseph Plymley became curate[21] and was succeeded by 4 members of the Corbett family, who held the living until 1867,[22] none of the curates is known to have been a graduate and none was related to the lord of the manor. Two of them, Roger Luter and Thomas Withington (curate c. 1633–after 1638),[23] seem to have come from local families,[24] and others augmented their income by farming. Thus William Penne was renting a large pasture in Leebotwood from the Corbetts in 1617[25] and 1624,[26] and the accounts of David Rice, 1769–74,[27] witness his farming activities. Rice also held the livings of Smethcott and Church Preen[28] and his 4 immediate successors held two or more other livings.[29] Assistant curates were not normally employed but a succession of them officiated during the old age of David Rice,[30] and Lewis Williams, Rector of Woolstaston, was Plymley's assistant curate at Leebotwood, 1783–1806.[31]

The house which had been leased with the church to Roger Luter in 1532[32] continued to be occupied by the curates until at least 1617.[33] This appears to

83 L. & P. Hen. VIII, xix (2), pp. 76, 420.
84 See p. 113.
85 S.R.O. 567 uncat., decree of union, 1821.
86 Heref. Dioc. Regy., reg. 1938–53, p. 405.
87 S.P.L., Haughmond Cart. f. 133.
88 S.R.O. 567 uncat., lease, 1532.
89 T.S.A.S. 1st ser. vi. 130.
90 Inq. Non. (Rec. Com.), 191.
91 S.P.L., Haughmond Cart. f. 135.
92 S.R.O. 567 uncat., lease, 1485.
93 S.C. 6/Hen. VIII/3009 m. 39.
94 S.R.O. 567 uncat., marriage settlement of Edward Corbett, 1617.
95 Ibid. lease, 1629.
96 Lich. Dioc. Regy., glebe terriers, 1718, 1722.
97 Ibid. 1772.
98 Ibid. 1698–1745; Heref. Dioc. Regy., tithe appt.
99 Heref. Dioc. Regy., tithe appt.
1 T.S.A.S. xlvii. 27.
2 S.R.O. 567 uncat., rental, 1682.
3 Lich. Dioc. Regy., glebe terrier, 1698.
4 Ibid. 1772.   5 Ibid. 1698.
6 Ibid. 1705.   7 Ibid. 1722.
8 Ibid. 1828.   9 Ibid. 1764.
10 S.R.O. 567 uncat., memorandum, c. 1787.
11 C. Hodgson, Queen Anne's Bounty (1845), 294.
12 Ibid. 175, 294; Lich. Dioc. Regy., glebe terrier, 1787.

13 Lich. Dioc. Regy., Longnor glebe terriers, 1792, 1805; ibid. Leebotwood glebe terrier, 1810.
14 Par. rec., plan of glebe, 1832; S.R.O. 567 uncat., deeds, 1832–4.
15 Par. rec., papers re sale of glebe.
16 Visit. Archd. Salop. 1799.
17 S.R.O. 567 uncat., decree of union, 1821.
18 Rep. Com. Eccl. Revenues [67], pp. 484–5, H.C. (1835), xxii.
19 Lich. Dioc. Regy., B/v 1/15, 1/53; S.R.O. 567 uncat., legal papers, c. 1628.
20 S.P.R. Lich. v (2), 432, 440.
21 Ibid. 440.
22 Ibid. Leebotwood intro., p. vi.
23 Lich. Dioc. Regy., B/v 1/53, 1/62.
24 S.P.R. Lich. v (2) passim.
25 S.R.O. 567 uncat., marriage settlement of Edward Corbett, 1617.
26 Ibid. deed, 1624.
27 N.L.W., MS. 18454B.
28 Ibid.
29 S.P.R. Lich. v (2), Leebotwood intro., p. vi.
30 Ibid. 403–4, 439–40, 448–9.
31 Ibid. 392–8, 405–6.
32 S.R.O. 567 uncat., lease, 1532.
33 Ibid. deed, 1597; ibid. marriage settlement of Edward Corbett, 1617.

have been burnt down *c.* 1658,[34] and by 1704 the curate was renting a house at Longnor.[35] David Rice lived at a house there called the Gate House,[36] and in the 19th century curates lived either at the Dower House or at the Roundabout in Longnor.[37] The present vicarage at Leebotwood was built in 1954.[38]

Between 1769 and 1774 services were held once on Sundays, normally at 9 a.m., but were omitted on every third Sunday, when the curate attended at Church Preen.[39] In 1823 and 1843 services were held once on Sundays, alternately with Longnor.[40] Communion was still administered only 4 times a year in 1843, when there were about 25 communicants.[41]

The church of *ST. MARY*[42] is a simple rectangular building, consisting of a nave and chancel under one roof, to which a western tower was added in the early 19th century. Its walls are built of coarse local stone and it contains few clearly original features. On the south wall the pointed arch of the south door and the priest's door, both now blocked, are probably of 13th-century date, as is the segmental rear-arch above the east window. A single lancet above the east window and the two-light window on the north wall cannot be dated, but have been in the church since the 18th century. In 1786 there were 2 two-light windows in the south wall, between the priest's door and the south door, and in the 18th century a window in the Classical style was inserted in the south wall of the chancel. A brick porch was built to the south door, probably in 1774,[43] but this had been removed by 1831.

The church originally had a bell-turret at the west end.[44] This was probably removed when the gallery was erected at the west end of the nave, and in 1823 the bells were hung in the nave roof. The tower, erected in 1829,[45] is of 2 stages, with pointed windows and west door. The latter has since served as the entrance to the church, replacing the south door, which was then blocked and converted into a window. At the same time the triple-lancet east window and the south window of the chancel were inserted.

The whole roof was originally of arch-braced collar-beam type, but only one of the trusses remains. This has chamfered timbers and on its west side are carvings in low relief of dragons with arrows in their mouths.[46] In the bay to the west of this truss are elaborately cusped double windbraces. In the three remaining trusses the collar-beam is supported by queen-posts, but, apart from the 17th-century truss in the chancel, these date from the 19th century. The hollow wooden pillars erected at the entrance to the chancel took the place of a screen, described as 'clumsy' in 1823.

The north and south walls of the nave are said to be decorated with wall-paintings;[47] these are now covered with plaster. Apart from some fragments of 17th-century oak panelling in the pews, there are no fittings of earlier date than the 18th century. The pulpit is of early-18th-century date, and the panelled oak box-pews in the nave were erected in 1776.[48] The reading-desk and clerk's pew probably date from the same year. The date of the gallery is not known. The oak press with side-cupboards, which serves as a communion table, the altar rails, and the simple wainscotting at the east end of the chancel were installed between 1823 and 1843. The font, replacing an ancient plain one, dates from *c.* 1843. A stone reredos, blocking the lower part of the east window, was erected in the later 19th century. The chancel contains numerous monuments to the Corbett family, 1701–1918, the most elaborate being that of Uvedale Corbett (d. 1701) by Henry Powell.[49]

There have been 3 bells in the church since 1552.[50] Those now in use are very small and have no inscriptions, but are not thought to be ancient.[51] The church had a silver chalice in 1552.[52] The existing chalice is dated 1630, but its stem has been inverted and shortened.[53] A silver paten, made in 1717,[54] was acquired after 1823.[55] The plate was stolen in 1955, when a new chalice and paten were purchased, but was recovered in the following year.[56] The registers are complete from 1547, with the exception of the years 1631–58 and 1759–77.[57]

NONCONFORMITY. The parish had one dissenter in 1676,[58] but none in 1799.[59] There were a few Methodists, probably colliers, in the parish in 1823,[60] and a dissenting preacher was living there in 1842,[61] but there were no nonconformists here in the following year.[62]

SCHOOLS. A school, supported by the lord of the manor, had been established by 1818,[63] but had closed before 1823.[64] It had been re-established by 1833, when it was supported by the lord of the manor and the curate and between 20 and 30 children

34 *S.P.R. Lich.* v (2), 347.
35 S.R.O. 567 uncat., rental, 1704–8.
36 Lich. Dioc. Regy., Longnor glebe terriers, 1736–72.
37 *Bagshaw's Dir. Salop.* (1851); *Kelly's Dir. Salop.* (1856–1941).
38 Ex inf. the Vicar.
39 N.L.W., MS. 18454B.
40 Visit. Archd. Salop. 1823, 1843.
41 Ibid. 1843.
42 Description of church based, except where otherwise stated, on S.P.L., MS. 372, vol. i, p. 25; S.P.L., T. F. Dukes watercolours (churches), no. 96; S.P.L., J. H. Smith collect. no. 124; *Gent. Mag.* 1831, p. 393; *Eng. Topog.* (Gent. Mag.), x. 86; Visit. Archd. Salop. 1799, 1823, 1843; Cranage, vi. 498.
43 Apley Park estate office, accts. 1750–95.
44 See, in addition to S.P.L., MS. 372, vol. i, p. 25, sketch of church in Wolryche-Whitmore MSS., Dudmaston, map of Woolstaston Wood, 1674.
45 W.S.L. 350/40/3.
46 See plate facing p. 111.
47 Miss A. Evason, 'Leebotwood', 38.
48 Apley Park estate office, accts. 1750–95.
49 S.R.O. 567 uncat., acct. of burial of Uvedale Corbett, 1701.
50 *T.S.A.S.* 2nd ser. xii. 99, 319, 336.
51 Walters, *Ch. Bells Salop.* 221.
52 *T.S.A.S.* 2nd ser. xii. 99, 319, 336.
53 Arkwright and Bourne, *Ch. Plate Ludlow Archd.* 37.
54 Ibid.
55 Not listed among plate in Visit. Archd. Salop. 1823.
56 Ex inf. the Vicar.
57 Printed to 1812 in *S.P.R. Lich.* v (2), 321–406.
58 *T.S.A.S.* 2nd ser. i. 81.
59 Visit. Archd. Salop. 1799.
60 Ibid. 1823.
61 *Q. Sess. Orders*, iv. 24.
62 Visit. Archd. Salop. 1843.
63 *Digest of Returns to Cttee. on Educ. of Poor*, H.C. 224, p. 754 (1819), ix (2).
64 Visit. Archd. Salop. 1823.

attended.[65] Attendance continued at this level in the 1840s,[66] but the school closed in 1871[67] and children subsequently went to Longnor school.[68]

CHARITIES. The parish was entitled to a share of the charity established by Sir Richard Corbett of Longnor in 1764.[69] No other charities are known.

LONGNOR

LONGNOR was originally a chapelry of Condover[1] and could still be described as a township of Condover in the early 18th century.[2] Its inhabitants were still assessed to Condover church rates in the later 17th century[3] and burials normally took place there until 1821,[4] but the independence of Longnor chapel was established in the 16th century.[5] Longnor was maintaining its own poor by the early 17th century,[6] although an attempt seems to have been made to combine the poor rates of Condover and Longnor c. 1664.[7]

The parish lies some 8 miles south of Shrewsbury and the village stands near the main road from Shrewsbury to Ludlow. The parish was small, containing only 821 a.,[8] until part of Cardington parish was transferred to it in 1934.[9] To the south Watling Street was the ancient parish boundary. Parts of the western boundary follow the River Cound, but it does not elsewhere make use of natural features. In the early Middle Ages the parish was surrounded by woodland on the south, east, and west, but there is no evidence of any adjustment in its boundaries before 1934, except at Longnor Green, in the south-east, where the boundaries of Longnor and Frodesley were fixed c. 1770.[10] The boundaries of the manor have never corresponded with those of the parish.[11]

The River Cound runs through the centre of the parish and the land rises gently from some 325 feet in the north to 425 feet along Watling Street. A wide belt of flood gravels, associated with the River Cound, covers the centre of the parish. The village lies on sand and gravel and there are other isolated deposits of sand and gravel to the west and south-west. The eastern half of the parish is boulder clay.

Longnor lay in the Long Forest, but the area that it covered had been disafforested by 1300.[12] The manor contained woodland for 600 swine in 1086,[13] but much of this lay outside the parish. Most of Longnor Wood was in Frodesley in the 16th century, but it probably once covered land in the south-

east of the parish, near Longnor Green.[14] Longnor Wood and the adjoining Botwood were estimated to contain 300 a. in 1577.[15] Much of the former was converted into charcoal for Longnor Forge shortly after 1605,[16] and appears to have been completely cleared by 1622.[17] Micklewood, in the north of Leebotwood parish, was also part of the manorial estate, but seems never to have extended into Longnor.[18] Any woodland there may once have been in the east of the parish, north of the Moat House, seems to have been cleared by the end of the 13th century.[19]

Until the 18th century Longnor Park lay in Leebotwood. It was probably established shortly after 1333, but is first named in 1538.[20] A waggon-way made from Longnor to the Park was said to have damaged the crops of the tenants in 1540.[21] The present Park, lying alongside the main road to the south of Longnor Hall, seems to have been formed in the 18th century and was described as new in 1794, when it contained 73 a.[22]

The former common fields[23] lay for the most part on flood gravels bordering the River Cound. Rea Field lay to the south and west of the village, in the area now occupied by the Park, running across both the main road and the River Cound. A field variously called Nayles Field, the Field towards Micklewood, or the Field towards the Hoo, ran towards Dorrington and Netley in the north of the parish, and similarly did not make use of the main road or the Cound as a boundary. South-east of the village, abutting on Watling Street, lay Wissybrook Field, also called Kempsall Field or the Field towards Lydley. Small areas of common-field land had been inclosed by the lords of the manor before 1517,[24] and they were wholly inclosed by the end of the 17th century.

The village stands on a road that leaves Watling Street at Longnor Green and runs northwards, parallel to the main road, towards Great Ryton and Condover. This is now a minor road, but appears to have been the main road through the parish in the

[65] *Educ. Enquiry Abstract*, H.C. 62, p. 776 (1835), xlii.
[66] Visit. Archd. Salop. 1843; Nat. Soc. *Ch. School Returns*, 1846–7.
[67] *Returns relating to Elem. Educ.*, H.C. 201, p. 232 (1871), lv.
[68] *Kelly's Dir. Salop.* (1885–1926).
[69] See p. 115.
[1] See p. 113. This article was written in 1963 and revised in 1965.
[2] Lich. Dioc. Regy., glebe terriers, 1730–42.
[3] See p. 113.
[4] Ibid.
[5] Ibid.
[6] S.R.O. 567 uncat., legal papers, c. 1628.
[7] Ibid. will of George Corbett, 1644.
[8] O.S. *Area Bk.* (1883). The following topographical description is based, except where otherwise stated, on O.S. Map 1″, sheet lxi (1st edn.); O.S. Map 6″ Salop. 49 (1st and later edns.); O.S. Maps 1/25,000, SO 49, 59 (1956), SJ 40 (1957); Rocque, *Map of Salop.* (1752); Baugh, *Map of Salop.* (1808); Greenwood, *Map of Salop.* (1827); B.M. O.S. 2″ orig. drawings, sheet 207 (1817);

Geol. Survey Map (drift), sheet 152 (1932); S.R.O. 1279/1.
[9] S.C.C., County Review Order, 1934.
[10] S.R.O. 567 uncat., perambulation of bounds, and case for opinion of counsel, 1771.
[11] See pp. 110–11.
[12] Eyton, vi. 345.
[13] *V.C.H. Salop.* i. 320.
[14] S.R.O. 567 uncat., award *re* boundaries of Longnor and Frodesley manors, 1603.
[15] Ibid. decree, Dickenson v. Crompton, 1577.
[16] See p. 112.
[17] S.R.O. 567 uncat., ct. r. 1622.
[18] See p. 99.
[19] See p. 108.
[20] S.R.O. 567 uncat., lease, 1538.
[21] Ibid. ct. r. 1540.
[22] N.L.W., MS. 18453C.
[23] Description of common fields based on S.R.O. 567 uncat., deeds, c. 1275–1690; ibid. leases, 1564–1667; ibid. ct. r. 1540, 1602; S.R.O. 322, deeds no. 37.
[24] C 47/7/2/3 m. 34d.

Middle Ages. It was known as the Lyde Way and ran from Longnor to Lydley Hays in Cardington.[25] The medieval road to Frodesley[26] is probably represented by a footpath running eastwards from the Moat House, which joins Watling Street near Frodesley Lane Farm. There are no references to the present main road before 1531,[27] but Leland seems to have used it c. 1540.[28] The short road running eastwards from the main road to the village formerly ran directly in front of the Hall but was diverted northwards in 1778.[29] A minor road running north from the Moat House formerly continued towards Little Ryton,[30] and a road which in 1829[31] ran southwards out of the road to Longnor Green was probably in origin a means of access to common-field lands in Rea Field. Both have since gone out of use.

Longnor derives its name—'Longenalra',[32] the long alder[33]—from an alder copse on the banks of the River Cound, near the church. Such a copse was still there in the 13th century[34] and the primary settlement seems to have been by the side of the river along the road from Longnor Green. The church was built in the later 13th century,[35] and a low mound to the south-west marks the site of the medieval manor-house.[36] Longnor Hall, to the west of the river, was built on former common-field land in the later 17th century.[37] The mill closed in 1934,[38] but the mill-house still stands on the road leading from the village to the main road, and the mill-pool, now overgrown, lies between the mill-house and the church. The school, which adjoins the churchyard, was built in 1871,[39] but the schoolmaster's house was used as a charity school in the early 19th century.[40] A number of houses, among them the Malthouse and The Farm, stand on a road running in a half-circle to the north of the village, and probably occupy the sites of houses of free tenants, several of whom were granted assarts in this area in the later 13th century.[41] The most notable of these houses is the Moat House, which stands near the junction of this road with the road to Longnor Green. The large rectangular moat, from which it takes its name, is probably that which in the later 13th century surrounded the homestead of Richard, son of Osbert of Diddlebury, a clerk of the lord of the manor.[42] The present house dates from the later 14th century. It may have been built by Edward de Acton, whose descendants

occupied it as the manor-house of their moiety of Longnor manor, 1377–1610,[43] for in 1370 he was given licence for a private oratory in Longnor.[44] Still externally timber-framed, the house as it now stands is a fragment of a more substantial group of buildings.[45] It comprises a service bay to the north, a screens passage, and 1½ bay of an open hall. The hall originally extended further to the south, but was truncated, probably in the early 17th century, when the stone southern gable wall was built. The roof is of arch-braced collar-beam construction, with tie beams in the main trusses and cusped braces forming quatrefoils at the apex of each truss. There are 3 rows of butt-purlins with cusped single wind-braces. Billet-moulding on the headpieces and the corbel-heads on the east wall of the gallery above the screens passage are original, but the mouldings of the posts themselves date from the early 17th century. Upper floors and a central fireplace were inserted at the same time. The Moat House was a farm-house from c. 1600 until 1865, when it was converted into 2 cottages.[46] It was purchased in 1963 by Mr. K. F. Rouse, who then undertook its restoration.

Apart from a small Council housing estate built since 1945 to the south of the church,[47] nearly all the houses in the village are timber-framed and of 17th-century date. Most of the houses outside the village date from the same period. The small group of timber-framed houses known as Little Longnor, alongside the River Cound on the parish boundary north of the village, were originally associated with the iron forge erected here in 1605.[48] The furnace, erected at the same time, may have stood some 300 yards to the south, where there are remains of a weir and a quantity of slag,[49] but there is another forge or furnace site about the same distance to the north, in Condover parish.[50] In the early 19th century most of the cottages were occupied by colliers from Lee-botwood.[51] The smithy and the house known as the Roundabout stand on the main road to the west of the village. The latter was until c. 1830 an inn called 'The Bowling Green'.[52] Both are timber-framed, the Roundabout being cased in brick, and they are first recorded in the later 17th century.[53]

There were said to be 92 adults in 1676[54] and 177 inhabitants in 1801.[55] By 1811 the population had risen to 231, and continued to rise until 1871, reaching a peak of 278 in 1851.[56] It had fallen to 199

[25] B.M. Harl. MS. 446, f. 20; Eyton, vi. 52; S.R.O. 567 uncat., award re boundary of Longnor and Frodesley manors, 1603.
[26] B.M. Harl. MS. 446, f. 20.
[27] S.R.O. 567 uncat., exchange, 1531.
[28] Leland, Itin. ed. Toulmin Smith, ii. 81.
[29] Q. Sess. rolls, Hil. 1778.
[30] B.M. O.S. 2″ orig. drawings, sheet 207 (1817).
[31] S.R.O. 1279/1.
[32] N.L.W., MS. 7851, f. 34.
[33] Eng. Place-name Elements (E.P.N.S. xxv–xxvi), i. 9, ii. 15.
[34] B.M. Harl. MS. 446, ff. 19ᵛ, 21ᵛ.
[35] See p. 114.
[36] S.R.O. 567 uncat., deed, 1454.
[37] Ibid. lease, 1690. See also p. 107.
[38] Estate papers penes Capt. R. W. Corbett, The Dower House, Longnor.
[39] See p. 114.
[40] Ibid.
[41] Ibid. See also plate facing p. 97.
[42] S.R.O. 567 uncat., grants by Roger Sprenchose to Richard, son of Osbert of Diddlebury, n.d.
[43] Ibid. deeds 1540–98; ibid. leases, 1606–7; ibid.

inspeximus of depositions in Council of Marches, 1576; ibid. marriage settlement of Edward Corbett, 1617.
[44] S.H.C. N.S. viii. 48.
[45] The following description is based on a survey carried out by Mr. F. W. B. Charles of Bromsgrove.
[46] N.L.W., MS. 15154B, 18453C; Lich. Dioc. Regy., glebe terriers, 1730–87; S.R.O. 1279/3; ibid. 1011 uncat., survey, 1853; par. rec., churchwardens' accts. 1761–1898. See also plates facing pp. 111, 216.
[47] Ex inf. Atcham R.D.C.
[48] See p. 112.
[49] Ex inf. Capt. R. W. Corbett.
[50] See p. 49.
[51] Wolryche-Whitmore MSS., Dudmaston, letter, Joseph Corbett to Mr. Bridgeman, 1832.
[52] N.L.W., Castle Hill 2244; Q. Sess., alehouse reg.; par. rec., churchwardens' accts. 1761–1898; W.S.L. 350/40/3.
[53] S.R.O. 567 uncat., particulars of Anne Corbett's jointure lands, 1689.
[54] T.S.A.S. 2nd ser. i. 81.
[55] Census, 1801.
[56] Ibid. 1811–71. cf. par. rec., lists of inhabitants, 1808, 1812–22.

by 1881 and to 164 by 1901.[57] After this date it rose slowly, reaching 199 in 1931.[58] In 1951 the parish, then larger in area, contained 211 inhabitants[59] and there were 257 inhabitants in 1961.[60]

MANOR. The manor of *LONGNOR*, always larger than the parish, was plausibly equated by Eyton with the Domesday manor of 'Lege'.[61] This comprised two estates, both held of Roger, Earl of Shrewsbury.[62] The principal manor was held by Roger the huntsman in 1086, while the other, held by Eldred before 1066, was in 1086 held by Azo of Rainald the sheriff.[63] The descendants of Roger the huntsman were lords of Pulverbatch manor[64] and it is possible that his estate in the manor of 'Lege' was a detached part, later merged with Pulverbatch manor.[65] The tenant of Longnor held lands in the manor of Pulverbatch at the end of the 12th century[66] and Hugh de Kilpeck, baron of Pulverbatch, was said to be overlord of Longnor in 1242,[67] but later lords of Pulverbatch had no connexion with this manor.

The mesne tenure of Raynald the sheriff passed to his successors the FitzAlans,[68] who first appear as overlords of Longnor c. 1221.[69] They continued overlords until last recorded in 1559.[70] Azo's successors were later mesne lords of Longnor. He was still living shortly after 1121, when as Azo Bigot he granted half a hide in Longnor to Shrewsbury Abbey,[71] but his family had become extinct by 1165 and their interest in Longnor seems to have passed shortly afterwards to John le Strange.[72] Members of the le Strange family are recorded as mesne lords between c. 1221 and c. 1272,[73] but by 1312 the manor was said to be held directly of the Earl of Arundel.[74]

Elric Sprenchose, also known as Elric of Longnor, who was living in the time of Henry II, is the first recorded tenant of the manor.[75] He had been succeeded before 1183 by his son Roger Sprenchose,[76] who was lord of Longnor in 1185.[77] Roger was dead by 1221[78] and his two successors, also called Roger, held the manor until shortly after 1300.[79] In 1300 Roger Sprenchose (III) granted the reversion of the manor to Griffin de la Pole,[80] who

was styled lord of Longnor by 1310.[81] In 1312 Griffin sold the manor to his cousin Sir Fulk le Strange, baron of Blakemere.[82] At Fulk's death in 1324[83] the manor was already in the hands of his son Fulk under a settlement of 1322.[84] The latter, who was dead by 1375,[85] left as his coheirs his daughters Margaret, Joan, and Eleanor,[86] but the manor was held in dower by his widow Gillian, who was still alive in 1390.[87] Margaret released her interest in the manor in 1375[88] and after the death of Gillian it was partitioned between the husbands of Margaret's two sisters.[89] Each moiety then followed a separate descent until the 17th century.

Edward de Acton, husband of Eleanor le Strange, was a member of a family which had been steadily building up a freehold estate in Longnor since the early 14th century.[90] Among the Acton purchases seems to have been the Moat House, which later served as the manor-house of this moiety of the manor.[91] The moiety passed from father to son in the Acton family[92] until the death of Thomas Acton in 1480.[93] It was then held in dower by his widow Joan, who survived until 1539,[94] thus outliving her son Thomas (d. 1514)[95] and the latter's nephew Thomas (d. 1524).[96] On Joan's death the moiety passed to her great-grandson William, second son of Thomas Acton.[97] William Acton sold the estate to Fulk Crompton in 1546.[98] Fulk's son Richard, to whom the manor-house and other lands had been leased in 1540,[99] later claimed the manor under the terms of a grant of 1546.[1] This was later alleged to be a forgery and Richard was ordered to confirm Fulk's title to the manor in 1561,[2] but in the following year Richard settled the manor on himself with reversion to his brother Thomas,[3] and held it until his death in 1577.[4] The manor then passed to Richard Crompton, son of Richard's brother Thomas.[5] Richard died in 1587,[6] when his son Richard was still a minor,[7] but he had in the previous year settled the greater part of his Longnor estate on his uncle William Crompton of Meriden (Warws.),[8] who sold the manor to Edward and Reginald Scriven of Frodesley in 1589.[9] Richard Crompton released his rights to the Scrivens in 1598.[10] In 1610 Edward Scriven and others sold

[57] *Census*, 1881–1901.
[58] Ibid. 1911–31.
[59] Ibid. 1951.
[60] Ibid. 1961.
[61] Eyton, vi. 48–49.
[62] *V.C.H. Salop.* i. 320.
[63] Ibid.
[64] See pp. 133–4.
[65] Eyton, vi. 50–51.
[66] Ibid.
[67] *Bk. of Fees*, 973.
[68] Eyton, vii. 209–10, 220–2.
[69] Ibid. vi. 53, 55.
[70] C 142/121/162.
[71] N.L.W., MS. 7851, ff. 30, 34.
[72] Eyton, iv. 128; ibid. vi. 34–35, 49.
[73] Ibid. vi. 53–55, 57; *Bk. of Fees*, 973; *Rot. Hund.* (Rec. Com.), ii. 62. For pedigrees see Eyton, x. 262–3.
[74] Eyton, vi. 62.
[75] Ibid. 49–50, 304.
[76] Ibid. 246.
[77] Ibid. 50.
[78] Ibid. 52.
[79] Ibid. 52–61; *Bk. of Fees*, 973; *Rot. Hund.* (Rec. Com.), ii. 62; S.R.O. 567 uncat., deeds *passim*.
[80] C.P. 25(1)/194/7/34.
[81] Eyton, vi. 62.
[82] S.R.O. 567 uncat., deed, 1312.
[83] *Complete Peerage*, xii (1), 353.

[84] S.R.O. 567 uncat., deed, 1322.
[85] Ibid. deeds, 1360, 1375.
[86] Ibid.
[87] Ibid. deed, 1390; S.P.L., MS. 2790, p. 327.
[88] S.R.O. 567 uncat., deed, 1375.
[89] Ibid.
[90] Ibid. deeds, 1312–31.
[91] See p. 108.
[92] C 145/263/10; S.R.O. 567 uncat., deeds, 1447–54. For pedigree see S.P.L., MS. 2790, p. 327.
[93] C 140/76/55.
[94] C 142/82/115.
[95] C 142/30/75.
[96] C 142/50/119. He attempted to recover the manor from Joan c. 1519: C 1/277/76; C 1/380/1; C 1/462/28.
[97] C 142/82/115.
[98] C.P. 25(2)/35/235; S.R.O. 567 uncat., deed, 1546.
[99] S.R.O. 567 uncat., lease, 1540.
[1] Ibid. copy deed, 1546.
[2] Ibid. decree of Council of Marches, 1561.
[3] Ibid. deed, 1562; C.P. 25(2)/200/5 Eliz. I Trin.
[4] C 142/213/149.
[5] Ibid.
[6] *S.P.R. Lich.* xix (5), 10.
[7] C 142/213/149.
[8] S.R.O. 567 uncat., deed, 1586.
[9] Ibid. deed, 1589; C.P. 25(2)/202/31 Eliz. I East.
[10] S.R.O. 567 uncat., deed, 1598; C.P. 25(2)/203/41 Eliz. I Trin.

the estate, but not the manorial rights, to Thomas Corbett.[11]

The other moiety of the manor passed after 1375 to John Carles in right of his wife Joan, daughter of Fulk le Strange.[12] He was still living in 1397[13] and his widow Joan in 1424.[14] John Corbett, who married the daughter and heir of John Carles,[15] is first recorded as lord of this moiety in 1454,[16] but had probably succeeded by 1433.[17] John's son Edward died in 1517,[18] and the manor descended in the male line of the Corbett family[19] until 1774, the following being lords: Thomas, 1517–59;[20] Edward, 1559–1608;[21] Thomas (brother), 1608–11;[22] Thomas, 1611–45; Edward, 1645–53;[23] Richard (grandson), 1653–83;[24] Uvedale, 1683–1701;[25] Richard, 1701–74.[26] The manor was devised by Richard Corbett to a distant relative, Robert Flint, who then took the name of Corbett.[27] He died in 1804,[28] when the estate passed to Joseph Plymley, son of Robert's sister Diana, who then took the name of Corbett.[29] It has since descended from father to son, the following being lords:[30] Joseph, 1804–38; Panton, 1838–55; Edward, 1855–95; Edward, 1895–1918; Edward Richard Trevor, 1918–48; Richard William, since 1948.

Longnor Hall,[31] begun by Richard Corbett c. 1670,[32] was left unfinished at his death in 1683 and finally completed by his son, Uvedale Corbett, about 1694.[33] It is a rectangular house with a hipped roof, consisting of two stories, basement, and attics. The principal façades, each of 7 bays, face north and south. On the north, or entrance, front the three central bays are carried up to form a gable—a curiously Jacobean feature in an otherwise Classical design. This gable originally had a semicircular parapet,[34] but was rebuilt in a curvilinear form in the 19th century. The walls are of brick, with stone quoins, string courses, doorways, and windows. The central doorways on both fronts are flanked by pilasters and have segmental pediments. Sash windows were not inserted until the 1690s and these were again altered in the 19th century. The ground-plan of the house is a plain rectangle, divided longitudinally by a thick wall, giving two rows of rooms back to back, one facing the front and the other the garden. In the thickness of the dividing wall are three chimneys, two staircases, and a small ante-room connecting the entrance hall with the drawing room behind. This arrangement shows some of the contradications which might be ex-

pected in a provincial design of the period: such features as the disproportionately large hall and unimpressive staircases are legacies from the earlier 17th century, but in its compactness and symmetry the plan is typical of the fully developed Renaissance house. The most striking internal feature, however, is a third staircase, evidently an insertion into what was originally one of the south rooms; as such it is thought to be the work of Uvedale Corbett, although in style it could well be of earlier date. It has elaborately carved strings, newels, and balusters, while there are fine inlaid designs to the treads and half-landings. In general it is difficult to distinguish between Richard Corbett's fittings and those introduced by his son. The latter certainly added his arms, impaling those of his wife, above the north entrance. Monograms, both on the staircase and on the ceiling of the drawing room, have been variously interpreted. Chinese wallpapers, recently discovered in the panelled dining room, may be the earliest examples in the country; they had been covered with velvet and later with 18th-century leather hangings. In 1701 the ground floor was said to comprise a hall, hung with maps and containing a Dutch stove, summer and winter parlours, a drawing room, a smoke room, and a library.[35] The moulded plaster ceiling of the library and its fireplace, both in the 'Adam' style, date from the later 18th century. The house was altered by the architect Edward Haycock in 1842,[36] but had probably already been re-roofed before that time. Haycock's work included new dormer windows as well as alterations to the front gable.[37] A Dutch garden to the north of the Hall was probably destroyed shortly after 1778, when the road to the village was diverted northwards.[38] The Hall was sold in 1949[39] and the garden was newly laid out between 1952 and 1963.[40] The lord of the manor lived in 1965 at the Dower House, a brick-cased timber-framed house in the village. Corbett family portraits, formerly in the Hall, are now at the Dower House.[41]

ECONOMIC HISTORY. The greater part of the woodland which covered much of the large manor of Lege in 1086[42] lay in Frodesley, Cardington, and Leebotwood, where the boundaries of Longnor manor were later more accurately defined. The manorial boundary with Frodesley was fixed c. 1221,[43] but was again in dispute between 1603 and 1619.[44] Woodland in Lydley Hayes, in Cardington

[11] S.R.O. 567 uncat., deed, 1610.
[12] Ibid. deed, 1375.
[13] C 145/263.
[14] S.R.O. 567 uncat., lease, 1424.
[15] S.P.L., MS. 2788, pp. 111–12.
[16] S.R.O. 567 uncat., deed, 1454.
[17] S.P.L., MS. 2788, pp. 111–12.
[18] S.R.O. 567 uncat., inquisition post mortem on Edward Corbett, 1517.
[19] The most reliable pedigree of the family is S.P.L., MS. 2788, pp. 111–17.
[20] C 142/121/162.
[21] S.R.O. 567 uncat., will, 1597; S.P.R. Lich. vi (1), 49.
[22] S.P.R. Lich. v (2), 338.
[23] Ibid. vi (1), 107.
[24] S.R.O. 567 uncat., will, 1681. See plate on facing page.
[25] S.P.R. Lich. v (2), 363. See plate on facing page.
[26] Ibid. 389.
[27] S.P.L., MS. 2788, pp. 114–17, where particulars are given of a lawsuit later brought by Richard Corbett's heir-at-law.
[28] S.P.R. Lich. v (2), 398.

[29] S.P.L., MS. 2788, p. 117; Burke, Land. Gent. (1952), p. 526.
[30] Ibid.
[31] The following account is based, except where otherwise stated, on articles by John Cornforth, Country Life, 13, 20 Feb. 1964. See also plate on facing page.
[32] Initials 'R.C.' and date '1670' are on the soffit of the north doorway.
[33] cf. N.L.W., MS. 15154B, poem, 1692.
[34] Watercolour, 1792, penes Mrs. E. S. Arthur, Woolstaston Rectory.
[35] S.R.O. 567 uncat., inventory, 1701.
[36] Ibid. plans of alterations, 1842.
[37] Ibid.
[38] Q. Sess. rolls, Hil. 1778.
[39] Ex inf. Capt. R. W. Corbett.
[40] Country Life, 20 Feb. 1964, 396.
[41] Ex inf. Capt. R. W. Corbett.
[42] V.C.H. Salop. i. 320.
[43] Eyton, vi. 52–53.
[44] S.R.O. 567 uncat., award re boundaries of Longnor and Frodesley manors, 1603; ibid. deeds, 1616–19.

The Hall from the north in 1792

Sir Uvedale Corbett (d. 1701)

Sir Richard Corbett (d. 1683)

LONGNOR HALL AND ITS BUILDERS

Longnor: The Moat House   Church Pulverbatch: Walleybourne Farm

Leebotwood Church: nave roof showing carved dragon on arch-brace

MEDIEVAL ROOFS

parish, along the western boundary of Frodesley between Watling Street and the Lawley, was assigned to the lord of Longnor in 1222.[45] Agreements between 1185 and c. 1234[46] settled the manorial boundary in Micklewood to the north of Leebotwood parish.

In 1086 the manor which Azo held was said to contain 2 hides, but that of Roger the huntsman, which was 'inland' and thus exempt from geld, was not hidated.[47] The whole estate had been worth £8 before 1066, 20s. when received, and 64s. in 1086.[48] The manor was assessed at one hide in 1254[49] and at 1½ carucate in 1300.[50] The estate of the Corbett family was considerably enlarged by the purchase of the adjoining manor of Lydley and Cardington in 1624,[51] but this was administered separately from Longnor manor. In Leebotwood Thomas Corbett acquired Cress Grange in 1544,[52] and some 300 a. here and in Smethcott were bought from the Wolryche-Whitmore family in 1821.[53] Some 51 a. in Frodesley had been bought by 1794,[54] in addition to the lands in that parish which had always formed part of Longnor manor. In the Hoos in the south of Condover parish, where the lords of Longnor already held assarts in the 13th century,[55] additional land was bought in 1656[56] and 1817.[57] The Corbetts had consolidated their estate by a series of exchanges between 1454 and 1619,[58] but since these exchanges were nearly all made with the lords of the other moiety of the manor they did not affect the overall size of the estate. By 1794 the estate was distributed as follows: Longnor 782 a.; Cardington (excluding the manor of Lydley and Cardington) 34 a.; Condover 17 a.; Frodesley 347 a.; Leebotwood 440 a.; Smethcott 15 a.[59]

There is no medieval evidence for the size of the demesne, other than that given in Domesday Book, which suggests that it was small.[60] In 1086 there was one plough and one serf on Azo's demesne, and 2 ploughs, 3 serfs, and 2 *bovarii* on that of Roger the huntsman.[61] Philip de Medewe was probably farmer of the demesne in 1404,[62] and Thomas Parr was lessee of the Acton moiety in 1540.[63] In addition to the park the lord of the manor held 88 a. in hand in 1794[64] and 66 a. in 1821,[65] but this had been leased by 1853.[66] From 1856 until c. 1917 the Hall was leased with part of the Park, while the Corbetts lived at the Dower House.[67]

Until the 17th century there was a small number of free tenants in the manor. Half a hide in Longnor was granted to Shrewsbury Abbey before 1136.[68] This was later exchanged for a rent-charge of 5s. on the demesne, which was again exchanged for lands at Boreton in Condover parish c. 1279.[69] Several free tenancies were created by Roger Sprenchose (III) at the end of the 13th century, for the most part in assarted lands on the borders of Longnor and Frodesley.[70] The largest of these was that of Sprenchose's clerk, Richard, son of Osbert of Diddlebury, who probably lived on the site of the Moat House.[71] The substantial freehold estate which William de Acton built up between 1312 and 1331[72] was presumably merged with the Acton moiety of the manor after 1375. There were only two free tenants in the manor in the 16th century,[73] whose descendants are last recorded in 1620.[74] Two messuages and a cottage in Longnor, sold by Thomas Corbett in 1610, were subsequently held by the Bowdler family, but were bought back into the manorial estate in 1675.[75] Thereafter the Corbett family were the sole landowners in the parish. The Hall, the Park, and a number of other properties have been sold since 1947.[76]

There were 5 villeins and 9 bordars on the two manors in 1086,[77] but there is little other evidence for the tenurial history of the manor before the later 17th century. In the 16th century there were some 12 messuages in the Crompton moiety of the manor,[78] held by 10 tenants in 1610.[79] There were 26 tenants in the manor in 1617, all of whom held their lands on leases for lives,[80] but by 1689, when 26 tenants were tenants-at-will, there were only 6 leaseholders.[81] Only two farms were held on long leases in the 18th century.[82] Annual rents rose from £318 in 1673[83] to £507 in 1726[84] and to £585 in 1755.[85] The growth of large farms had progressed so far by 1772 that it was virtually impossible for the curate to collect his modus in lieu of small tithes, assessed on the home-closes of 17th-century farmsteads, which were 'so transferred and metamorphosed that few or none know to which they formerly belonged'.[86] In 1794, when 6 farms contained 100–200 a. and one was over 200 a., about two-thirds of the estate lay in large farms.[87] There were then 17 holdings smaller than 50 a.[88] A thorough reorganization of farms was undertaken by Joseph Corbett after 1816.[89] In 1817 there were 3 farms of over 200 a.,[90] and by 1833 he had raised

[45] *T.S.A.S.* 3rd ser. vii. 380.
[46] Eyton, vi. 50–52, 55.
[47] *V.C.H. Salop.* i. 320.
[48] Ibid.
[49] *Rot. Hund.* (Rec. Com.), ii. 62.
[50] C.P. 25(1)/194/7/34.
[51] S.R.O. 567 uncat., deed, 1624.
[52] *L. & P. Hen. VIII*, xix (2), p. 317; S.R.O. 567 uncat., deeds, 1544.
[53] Wolryche-Whitmore MSS., Dudmaston, deed, 1821.
[54] N.L.W., MS. 18453C.
[55] *Rot. Hund.* (Rec. Com.), ii. 63.
[56] S.R.O. 567 uncat., deeds, 1623–62.
[57] Ibid. 1279/3.
[58] Ibid. 567 uncat., deeds, 1454–1619.
[59] N.L.W., MS. 18453C.
[60] *V.C.H. Salop.* i. 320.
[61] Ibid.
[62] *Salop. Peace Roll, 1404–14*, 70.
[63] S.R.O. 567 uncat., lease, 1540.
[64] N.L.W., MS. 18453C.
[65] S.R.O. 1279/3.
[66] Ibid. 1011 uncat., particulars of estate, 1853.
[67] Ibid. leases, 1856–83; *Kelly's Dir. Salop.* (1885–1913).

[68] Eyton, vi. 127; Dugdale, *Mon.* iii. 519.
[69] Eyton, vi. 68–69.
[70] Ibid. 59–61; *T.S.A.S.* 1st ser. xi. 419; S.R.O. 567 uncat., deeds, c. 1275–98; S.R.O. 322, deeds no. 37.
[71] Ibid.
[72] S.R.O. 567 uncat., deeds, 1312–31.
[73] Ibid. ct. r. 1526, 1540, 1592.
[74] Ibid. deed, 1620.
[75] Ibid. deeds, 1610–82.
[76] Map of estate, 1946, *penes* Capt. R. W. Corbett.
[77] *V.C.H. Salop.* i. 320.
[78] S.R.O. 567 uncat., deeds, 1586, 1589.
[79] Ibid. deed, 1610.
[80] Ibid. marriage settlement of Edward Corbett, 1617.
[81] Ibid. rental, 1689.
[82] Ibid. leases, 1759–1805.
[83] Ibid. rental, 1673.
[84] Ibid. 1726.
[85] Ibid. 1755.
[86] Lich. Dioc. Regy., glebe terrier, 1772.
[87] N.L.W., MS. 18453C.
[88] Ibid.
[89] S.R.O. 1279/3.
[90] Ibid.

the annual rental of the Longnor and Leebotwood portions of the estate to £2,589, but only £791 was actually paid in that year.[91] By 1894 there were 6 farms of over 200 a. in the Longnor estate and only 6 holdings smaller than 50 a.[92] There were said to be only 201 a. of arable in the parish in 1801, when the chief crop was wheat,[93] but in 1816 most of the farms on the manorial estate had considerably more arable than pasture.[94]

There was a mill in the manor in 1086.[95] It passed after the death of Roger Sprenchose (I) in 1221 to Haughmond Abbey,[96] and in 1544 was purchased by Edward Corbett.[97] In 1616 three watermills, described as newly built, were sold to Thomas Corbett by Edward Scriven,[98] and there were said to be 6 mills in the manor in 1617.[99] In the later 17th century the mills were held on lease,[1] and Richard Brown, miller in 1794, also held a 21-acre farm,[2] but from 1825[3] until the mill closed in 1934[4] it was kept in hand, the miller receiving a weekly salary.

A fulling mill, held by the Walker family as free tenants in the 14th century,[5] was erected by Stephen le Walker of Shipton in the later 13th century, under a grant from Roger Sprenchose (III).[6] It had been conveyed to John Carles by 1393, when Margery Walker sold him her racks and great vats,[7] and in 1424 it was leased to her son-in-law Richard Walker.[8] In 1614 two fulling mills were leased to William Yate,[9] to whom the water mills had been leased in 1612,[10] but they are not recorded after the lease was surrendered in 1658.[11]

An iron furnace and forge were erected at Longnor by Richard Holbeck in 1605 under a lease from the Scrivens, whose principal motive seems to have been to find a convenient market for their timber in Frodesley and Longnor.[12] The forge had passed into the Corbett estate by 1635, when it was occupied by Roger Blakeway and Francis Walker.[13] The latter was sole lessee in 1663,[14] and had been succeeded before 1689 by Job Walker,[15] who worked the forge until his bankruptcy in 1696.[16] Richard Atkis held it between 1699[17] and 1708.[18] In 1739 it was leased to John Turton of Rowley Regis (Staffs.) and John Webster of Birmingham,[19] who rebuilt it

c. 1742.[20] The forge was producing 150 tons annually in 1717, 100 tons in 1736, and 140 tons in 1750[21] John Webster, who was sole lessee by 1755,[22] renewed his lease in 1767,[23] but by 1761 the forge was occupied by Joseph Webster.[24] The latter took a 31-year lease in 1771,[25] but the operation of the forge was in the hands of William Jones, c. 1783–91,[26] and John Jones, 1792–98.[27] In 1801 it was leased to William Hazledine of Shrewsbury, who then converted it into a paper mill.[28] Subsequent occupiers were William Hazledine, 1800–2, Messrs. Holland & Co., 1803–9, and William Hazledine, 1810–15.[29] The paper mill appears to have been closed after 1815,[30] and Hazledine surrendered his lease in 1821.[31]

Coal pits recorded in the manor in 1763[32] were at the Haines in Leebotwood,[33] and the 26 persons in Longnor employed in coal-mining in 1831 worked at the Leebotwood colliery.[34] The latter, however, had extended its workings into Longnor parish by 1832,[35] and a spoil-heap by the side of the main road, to the south of the Park, marks the site of its latest workings, c. 1864–75.[36]

In 1379 the village had a butcher, a carpenter, a tailor, and a minstrel.[37] A tannery, set up shortly after 1615,[38] belonged to the Bowdler family during the 17th century,[39] but had closed by 1730.[40] The smithy is first recorded in 1640[41] and was held by the Harrison family through the 18th century.[42] Apart from the usual village tradesmen there were in 1863 a builder, two stonemasons, and a bricklayer.[43] There was still a village shop in 1965, when the blacksmith and wheelwright remained in business.

LOCAL GOVERNMENT. There are a few manor court rolls, 1485–1622, and draft court rolls, 1758–70.[44] A single court was held for both moieties of the manor in 1534 and 1540. It met in Longnor Chapel in the early 16th century.[45] The jurisdiction of the court did not include the assize of bread and ale, but two constables were elected annually before 1540.

The parish records include churchwardens' accounts, 1761–1898, and annual lists of inhabitants,

91 S.R.O. 1279/5.
92 Ibid. 1011 uncat., particulars of estate, 1894.
93 H.O. 67/14/166.
94 S.R.O. 1279/3.
95 V.C.H. Salop. i. 320.
96 Eyton, vi. 50, 52, 54; B.M. Harl. MS. 446, ff. 19v–21.
97 L. & P. Hen. VIII, xix (2), pp. 76, 420.
98 S.R.O. 567 uncat., deed, 1616.
99 Ibid. marriage settlement of Edward Corbett, 1617.
1 Ibid. rentals, 1673–1726.
2 N.L.W., MS. 18453C.
3 S.R.O. 567 uncat., mill accts. 1825–7.
4 Estate accts. penes Capt. R. W. Corbett.
5 S.R.O. 567 uncat., deeds, 1338–93.
6 Cited in ibid. deed, 1356.
7 Ibid. deed, 1393.
8 Ibid. lease, 1424.
9 Ibid. 1614.
10 Ibid. 1612.
11 Ibid. 1614.
12 Ibid. 1605; E 134/11 Jas. I East./5.
13 S.R.O. 567 uncat., marriage settlement of Edward Corbett, 1635.
14 Ibid. marriage settlement of Richard Corbett, 1663.
15 N.L.W., Cilybebyll 233.
16 Ibid. 416.
17 S.R.O. 567 uncat., accts. 1699–1701.
18 Ibid. rental, 1704–8.

19 Ibid. lease, 1739.
20 Ibid. constable's presentment, 1757.
21 Trans. Newcomen Soc. ix. 32.
22 S.R.O. 567 uncat. rental, 1755.
23 Ibid. lease, 1767.
24 Par. rec., churchwardens' accts. 1761–1898.
25 S.R.O. 567 uncat., lease, 1771.
26 Par. rec., churchwardens' accts. 1761–1898.
27 Ibid.
28 S.R.O. 567 uncat., lease, 1801, and related papers.
29 Par. rec., churchwardens' accts. 1761–1898.
30 S.R.O. 1279/3.
31 Ibid. 567 uncat., surrender of lease, 1821.
32 Ibid. accts. 1763–6.
33 See p. 103.
34 Census, 1831.
35 Wolryche-Whitmore MSS., Dudmaston, colliery papers, 1831–4.
36 Par. rec., churchwardens' accts. 1761–1898.
37 E 179/242/33.
38 S.R.O. 567 uncat., deeds, 1610–82.
39 Ibid.
40 Lich. Dioc. Regy., glebe terrier, 1730.
41 S.R.O. 567 uncat., lease, 1640.
42 Ibid. rentals, 1689, 1755; N.L.W., MS. 18453C.
43 Kelly's Dir. Salop. (1863).
44 S.R.O. 567 uncat.
45 Ibid. depositions, Dickenson v. Crompton, 1576.

1808, 1812–22. There were two churchwardens in the 18th century, but only one after 1829. Rates were assessed on a pound rate by 1744[46] and church rates were levied annually until 1892. Between £3 and £4 a year was spent on poor relief in the late 17th century.[47] The poor rates, normally about £25 a year in the 1780s,[48] had risen to £51 by 1803,[49] and reached a peak of £104 in 1818.[50]

CHURCH. There is no clear reference to a priest at Longnor before 1547,[51] or to the church before 1514.[52] In the 16th century Longnor chapel was accounted a chapelry of Condover.[53] This was probably its original status, but it seems to have been treated as a private manorial chapel in the later Middle Ages. Lands in Smethcott were devised by Thomas Acton in 1514 as a temporary endowment for a priest here,[54] and in 1547 the chapel was regarded as chantry property.[55] In 1549 it was purchased by Richard Crompton,[56] whose daughter Elizabeth conveyed it to Edward Corbett in 1579.[57] The Chapel has since been held as a donative by the Corbett family.[58]

Vicars of Condover seem to have established some control over the chapel in the time of Richard Crompton when they joined with the inhabitants of Longnor in an attempt to force him to provide adequate service in the chapel.[59] Thomas Fletcher (vicar of Condover, 1569–1612)[60] was often called on to administer the sacraments at Longnor, since the curate there could only read prayers.[61] The great tithes were held by the lords of the manor of Condover as impropriators[62] until 1796, when they were acquired by Robert Corbett,[63] but the vicar of Condover was unsuccessful in an attempt to claim the small tithes c. 1603.[64] The liability of inhabitants of Longnor to contribute to Condover church rates was the subject of lawsuits between the two parishes in 1628, 1640, and 1662, and such rates were paid between 1628 and 1684.[65] In the 18th century Longnor was held liable when the Condover rate was more than 2d. in the pound,[66] but the parish was only once

assessed and then did not pay.[67] Burials normally took place at Condover until 1821,[68] but burials at Leebotwood became common in the 18th century.[69]

Since the 16th century the living has been a perpetual curacy and since 1573[70] has been held in plurality with Leebotwood. The two livings were formally united in 1821[71] and the incumbents have been styled vicars since 1868. The advowson followed the descent of the manor until 1948, when it was vested in the Hereford Diocesan Board of Patronage.[72]

The church had a meagre endowment before 1514, when Thomas Acton devised lands in Picklescott to find a priest at Longnor for 20 years.[73] In 1547 its annual income was £3 5s. 4d. of which 1s. 4d. was derived from church lands in Longnor, 4s. from Picklescott, and 40s. from Cress Grange in Leebotwood.[74] The small tithes and other dues received by the curate were then worth 20s. a year.[75] After 1549 these endowments passed to Richard Crompton, but the churchwardens were still receiving income from the church lands in the later 16th century.[76]

Before 1579 the curate received an annual payment from the inhabitants of Longnor in lieu of small tithes, but when Edward Corbett bought the church he undertook to pay the curate's salary.[77] Easter dues and most of the tithes were thereafter collected by the lord of the manor.[78] The curate received a salary of £2 10s. a year from the lord of the manor for his services at Longnor in 1682,[79] but in the early 18th century his only income seems to have been a modus of £5 in lieu of small tithes of home-closes.[80] This custom, which may have existed in 1655,[81] was said in 1701 to have been in use beyond living memory.[82] Until 1696 the modus was collected by the churchwardens but after that date the curate collected it himself.[83] It became increasingly difficult to determine who was liable for payment and by 1774 the modus was collected by the lord of the manor with his rents and paid by him to the curate.[84]

[46] S.R.O. 567 uncat., church and poor rate, 1744.
[47] Bodl. MS. Blakeway 8, f. 476.
[48] Rep. Cttee. on State of Poor, 1787, p. 658, H.C. (1st ser. ix, reprinted 1803).
[49] Poor Law Abstract, 1803, H.C. 175, pp. 416–17 (1803–4), xiii.
[50] Rep. Cttee. on Poor Rate Returns, 1822, Suppl. App., H.C. 556, p. 141 (1822), v.
[51] T.S.A.S. 3rd ser. x. 353. Richard, son of Osbert of Diddlebury, to whom there are frequent references between 1298 and 1327, was a married clerk, but may have been Roger Sprenchose's chaplain as well as his steward: S.R.O. 567 uncat., deeds, 1298–1326; T.S.A.S. 2nd ser. xi. 356; Eyton, vi. 60. A Nicholas clericus occurs in 1332 (E 179/166/2), and Geoffrey of Longnor, clerk, in 1338 (S.R.O. 567 uncat., deed, 1338).
[52] C 142/30/75.
[53] T.S.A.S. 3rd ser. x. 353; S.R.O. 567 uncat., depositions, Edward Corbett v. Robert Burgess, c. 1603.
[54] C 142/30/75.
[55] T.S.A.S. 3rd ser. x. 353; E 316/67, f. 292.
[56] S.R.O. 567 uncat., deed, 1549.
[57] Ibid. deeds, 1579, 1586.
[58] Lich. Dioc. Regy., glebe terriers, 1730–72.
[59] S.R.O. 567 uncat., depositions, Edward Corbett v. Robert Burgess, c. 1603.
[60] S.P.R. Lich. vi (1), intro. p. vi.
[61] S.R.O. 567 uncat., instructions to proctor, Longnor v. Condover, c. 1628.
[62] Ibid. depositions, Edward Corbett v. Robert Burgess, c. 1603; T.S.A.S. xlvii. 27; Lich. Dioc. Regy., glebe terriers, 1733–92.

[63] S.P.L., Deeds 10054.
[64] S.R.O. 567 uncat., case papers, Edward Corbett v. Robert Burgess, c. 1603–8.
[65] Condover par. rec., churchwardens' accts. 1627–89; Q. Sess. Orders, i. 27.
[66] Lich. Dioc. Regy., glebe terriers, 1730–72.
[67] In 1760: Condover par. rec., churchwardens' accts. 1759–1819.
[68] S.P.R. Lich. vi (1) passim; Lich. Dioc. Regy., glebe terriers, 1730–72.
[69] S.P.R. Lich. v (2), 360–401 passim.
[70] William Penne was said c. 1628 to have been curate of Longnor for 56 years: S.R.O. 567 uncat., instructions to proctor, Longnor v. Condover. He was ordained in 1573: Lich. Dioc. Regy., B/v 1/15.
[71] S.R.O. 567 uncat., decree of union, 1821.
[72] Heref. Dioc. Regy., reg. 1938–53, p. 405.
[73] C 142/30/75.
[74] T.S.A.S. 3rd ser. x. 353; E 315/67 f. 292.
[75] Ibid.
[76] S.R.O. 567 uncat., depositions, Edward Corbett v. Robert Burgess, c. 1603.
[77] Ibid.
[78] Ibid.
[79] S.R.O. 567 uncat., accts. 1682–4.
[80] Lich. Dioc. Regy., glebe terriers, 1697–1828.
[81] T.S.A.S. xlvii. 47.
[82] Lich. Dioc. Regy., glebe terriers, 1701.
[83] Ibid. 1752.
[84] Ibid. 1772, 1824; S.R.O. 567 uncat., rental of small tithes, 1774.

Between 1739 and 1784 four grants of £200 were made to the livings of Longnor and Leebotwood by Queen Anne's Bounty.[85] A further £200, granted in 1787 to meet a benefaction by Sir Richard Corbett, brought Longnor's share to £800, then invested in stocks and producing £16 a year.[86] By 1792 the capital had been used to purchase 30 a. of glebe land at Plas Bach in Oswestry,[87] the rents of which produced £36 16s. in 1792[88] and £52 16s. in 1824.[89] The total value of the living was said to be a little over £40 in 1799[90] and £61 16s. at its union with Leebotwood in 1821.[91] Some account of the post-Reformation clergy is given under Leebotwood.[92] Communion was administered 5 or 6 times a year in the later 18th century[93] and 4 times a year between 1799 and 1860.[94] Services were held once on Sundays, alternately with Leebotwood, between 1769 and 1843.[95] The congregation averaged 130 in 1823,[96] but the number of Easter communicants fell from 80 in 1799[97] to 40 in 1843.[98] Singers are first recorded in 1832.[99] A 'cello and bass viol, in use in the 1840s, had been replaced by a harmonium by 1864.[1]

The church is now dedicated to *ST. MARY*, but its original dedication is not known. It consists of a chancel and nave, with a western bell-turret, and was built in the later 13th century, probably by Roger Sprenchose (III).[2] The tracery of the east and west windows, originally identical in design, consists of three graded lights, with uncusped circles above. Medieval armorial stained glass in the central light of the east window survived until *c.* 1840.[3] Both windows have hood-mouldings externally, that above the west window continuing across the width of the west wall. There are 6 lancet windows on the south wall and 8 on the north. Apart from the pairs at the west end their positions on each wall do not correspond. Each group of lancets is surmounted by continuous hood-moulding. The angles of the west wall are supported by pairs of buttresses.

Only insignificant alterations have since been made to the fabric of the church. The south door was formerly the main entrance to the church and a portico was erected over it in 1775,[4] but it was blocked *c.* 1840 when the west door was inserted. The tracery in the west window was renewed at this time, and the wooden bell-turret above dates from the later 19th century.

With the exception of the 17th-century communion rails and oak reredos all the internal fittings date from the 18th century. The pews, dated 1723, and the pulpit and reading desk are of oak wainscot and were arranged in their present positions *c.* 1840. The west gallery is first recorded in 1793.[5] It is entered through a door made in the window at the south-west end of the nave, to which a flight of stone steps had been erected in 1789. The gallery was enlarged *c.* 1840 thus blocking the north and south doors and making it necessary to cut a new door in the west wall.

Although Richard Crompton was said to have sold the two bells belonging to Longnor chapel shortly after 1549,[6] one of the two existing bells dates from the early 14th century.[7] The other bell is dated 1680.[8] Crompton also sold a gilt chalice.[9] The plate now comprises a silver chalice, dated 1637 and given by George Corbett in 1665, and a paten of 1910.[10] The registers, which begin in 1586, are incomplete for the years 1631–58 and 1759–77.[11]

NONCONFORMITY. There was a small number of recusants in the parish in the early 17th century,[12] and one dissenter in 1676.[13] None is recorded after 1799.[14]

SCHOOLS. The curate of Longnor had a school in 1699;[15] this was described as a grammar school in 1702.[16] A charity school was founded here *c.* 1783,[17] under the will of Sir Richard Corbett, who endowed it with £200, producing an annual income of £10.[18] It was intended that this should serve the poor children of Longnor and the children of tenants on the Corbett estate in Cardington, Frodesley, and Leebotwood.[19] The present schoolmaster's house was used as the school in the early 19th century.[20] The existing school was built in 1871[21] and enlarged in 1894.[22] New classrooms were erected in 1957.[23]

Under the terms of its endowment, management of the school was vested in subsequent owners of Longnor Hall, and until the later 19th century it was financed solely by the Corbett family.[24] By 1885 small annual contributions were made by the

---

[85] C. Hodgson, *Queen Anne's Bounty* (1845), 294.
[86] Ibid. 175, 294; Lich. Dioc. Regy., glebe terriers, 1745–87.
[87] Lich. Dioc. Regy., glebe terriers, 1792, 1805.
[88] Ibid. 1792.
[89] Ibid. 1824.
[90] Visit. Archd. Salop. 1799.
[91] S.R.O. 567 uncat., decree of union, 1821.
[92] See p. 105.
[93] Par. rec., churchwardens' accts. 1761–1898.
[94] Ibid.; Visit. Archd. Salop. 1799, 1823, 1843.
[95] N.L.W., MS. 18454B; Visit. Archd. Salop. 1799, 1823, 1843.
[96] Visit. Archd. Salop. 1823.
[97] Ibid. 1799.
[98] Ibid. 1843.
[99] Par. rec., churchwardens' accts. 1761–1898.
[1] Ibid.
[2] Description of church based, except where otherwise stated, on Cranage, vi. 499–500; Visit. Archd. Salop.1823; S.P.L., MS. 372, vol. i, p. 82; S.P.L., J. H. Smith collect. no. 131.
[3] S.P.L., E. P. Owen etchings, vol. iii, p. 53.
[4] Par. rec., churchwardens' accts. 1761–1898.
[5] Ibid.

[6] S.R.O. 567 uncat., depositions, Edward Corbett *v.* Robert Burgess, *c.* 1603.
[7] Walters, *Ch. Bells Salop.* 221; ibid. plate xv, nos. i–xii. [8] Ibid. 222.
[9] S.R.O. 567 uncat., depositions, Edward Corbett *v.* Robert Burgess, *c.* 1603.
[10] Arkwright and Bourne, *Ch. Plate Ludlow Archd.* 39; S.P.R. Lich. v (2), 421.
[11] Printed to 1812 in *S.P.R. Lich.* v (2), 407–52.
[12] Lich. Dioc. Regy., B/v 1/29, 1/53, 1/60.
[13] *T.S.A.S.* 2nd ser. i. 81.
[14] Visit. Archd. Salop. 1799, 1823, 1843.
[15] Lich. Dioc. Regy., B/v 1/90.
[16] Ibid. B/a 4/13.
[17] When Henry Tyler, schoolmaster in 1787, was first resident in the parish: par. rec., churchwardens' accts. 1761–1898; Lich. Dioc. Regy., glebe terrier, 1787.
[18] *24th Rep. Com. Char.*, H.C. 231, pp. 386–7 (1831), xi.
[19] Ibid.
[20] S.P.L., T. F. Dukes watercolours, vol. ii, no. 22.
[21] Ed. 7/102/138.
[22] *Kelly's Dir. Salop.* (1895).
[23] Ex inf. S.C.C. Educ. Dept.
[24] *24th Rep. Com. Char.* p. 387; Visit. Archd. Salop. 1823; Ed. 7/102/138.

Wolryche-Whitmore family and the Curate of Longnor,[25] and it was in receipt of a government grant by 1892.[26] It has been a Controlled School since 1955.[27]

Some 15 children from Longnor and Cardington attended as foundation scholars in the early 19th century, but other fee-paying pupils also attended.[28] There were said to be 49 children at the school in 1818[29] and between 20 and 30 in the 1830s,[30] but attendances had risen to 46 by 1846[31] and to 87 by 1871.[32] Numbers fell to around 60 later in the 19th century[33] but had risen to 90 by 1913.[34]

A Sunday School, recorded between 1818 and 1846,[35] was being run by 'some young ladies' in 1818, when 65 children attended,[36] but it was taught by the schoolmaster by 1830.[37]

CHARITIES. By will of 1764[38] Sir Richard Corbett directed that the interest on £100 arising from his estate be given to the minister and churchwardens annually on 23 December and distributed to the poor. From the interest on a further £700, £12 a year was to be given to 3 poor tradesmen resident in the county, and the remainder applied to clothing 12 poor children in Longnor, Cardington, Frodesley, and Leebotwood. These legacies were being paid by the lord of the manor c. 1830, when £5 was distributed in money to about 25 poor persons each year, £12 was given to 3 poor tradesmen, and £16 used to clothe 12 poor children. In 1862[39] the charity was being distributed in the same form, but only £8 was then available for clothing.

By will of 1664 George Corbett gave £50, then yielding an annual income of £2, to the parish officers, to be used to clothe 3 poor persons under the supervision of the Corbett family. A further £40, subsequently given by 5 other persons, was added to George Corbett's bequest. The endowment was held c. 1830 by the lord of the manor, who allowed 4 or 5 cottages on his estate, worth £13 10s. a year, to be occupied rent-free. It had been invested in stock by 1862, but was still administered in the same manner.[40] Both the above charities had been lost by the end of the 19th century.[41]

A rent-charge of 10s. a year, arising from lands in Cardington, was given to the poor by Edward Bayley by will of 1789. This was distributed in money on the first 4 Sundays of the year c. 1830, but had been lost by 1862.[42] A legacy of £50, given by a Mr. Cross by will of 1829,[43] produced £2 a year in 1862,[44] when it was being distributed in money, but had been lost by c. 1900.[45]

PITCHFORD

THE parish of Pitchford, which contains 1,684 a., includes the shrunken hamlet of La Beche and the sites of the deserted hamlets of Newton and Little Eton.[1] These three hamlets apparently lay in the parish of St. Chad, Shrewsbury, until the early 12th century, when they were transferred to the newly created parish of Pitchford.[2] They were accounted members of the Liberties of Shrewsbury during the later Middle Ages, and the jurisdiction of the borough court over them was invoked as late as 1501.[3]

The parish boundary follows Cound Brook to the north, Piller Brook to the east, and a tributary of Row Brook to the south. The western boundary follows a valley known as Dukedale[4] for some distance, then runs southwards through the former forest of Buriwood, where its course was determined at the division of Buriwood between the lords of Cantlop and Pitchford manors c. 1272.[5] The parish is drained by Cound Brook and its tributaries; notably by Row Brook, which flows north-westwards, dividing the parish into two parts. Pitchford village and its former common fields lie to the east of the brook, while Eton, Newton, and La Beche lay to the west. Most of the latter area lay in the manorial demesne after the later Middle Ages.[6] East of Row Brook the land rises gently from some 200 feet along Cound Brook in the north to 300 feet at Pitchford village and reaches 350 feet along the southern boundary, near Stockbatch Farm. The western half of the parish is slightly higher. Newton and La Beche stood on a 250-foot plateau to the north and the land rises gently to 400 feet in the south. Apart from isolated deposits of sand and

[25] *Kelly's Dir. Salop.* (1885–1900).

[26] *Return of Schs. 1893* [C. 7529], p. 508, H.C. (1894), lxv.

[27] Ex inf. S.C.C. Educ. Dept.

[28] *24th Rep. Com. Char.* pp. 386–7; *Digest of Returns to Cttee. on Educ. of Poor,* H.C. 224, p. 750 (1819), ix (2); Visit. Archd. Salop. 1823.

[29] *Digest of Returns to Cttee. on Educ. of Poor,* p. 750.

[30] *Educ. Enquiry Abstract,* H.C., 62, p. 777 (1835), xlii.

[31] Nat. Soc. *Ch. School Returns,* 1846–7.

[32] *Returns relating to Elem. Educ.,* H.C. 201, p. 332 (1871), lv.

[33] Ed. 7/102/138; *Return of Schs. 1893,* p. 508; *Kelly's Dir. Salop.* (1885–1909).

[34] *Kelly's Dir. Salop.* (1913).

[35] *Digest of Returns to Cttee. on Educ. of Poor,* p. 750; *Educ. Enquiry Abstract,* p. 777; Visit. Archd. Salop. 1823, 1843; Nat. Soc. *Ch. School Returns,* 1846–7.

[36] *Digest of Returns to Cttee. on Educ. of Poor,* p. 750.

[37] *24th Rep. Com. Char.* p. 387.

[38] Except where otherwise stated, what follows is based on *24th Rep. Com. Char.,* H.C. 231, pp. 386–8 (1831), xi.

[39] *Digest of Endowed Charities, 1862–3,* H.C. 433, pp. 184–5 (1867–8), lii.

[40] Ibid.

[41] Ex inf. Capt. R. W. Corbett.

[42] *Digest, 1862–3,* pp. 184–5.

[43] Ibid.

[44] Ibid.

[45] Ex inf. Capt. R. W. Corbett.

[1] O.S. *Area Bk.* (1882). The following topographical description is based, except where otherwise stated, on O.S. Map 1″, sheet lxi (1st edn.); O.S. Maps 6″ Salop. 41, 42, 49 (1st and later edns.); O.S. Maps 1/25,000, SJ 50 (1959); Rocque, *Map. of Salop* (1752); Baugh, *Map of Salop.* (1808); B.M. O.S. 2″ orig. drawings, sheet 207 (1817); Geol. Survey Map (drift), sheet 152 (1932); Heref. Dioc. Regy., tithe appt. and map, 1843; maps of manorial estate, 1682 and c. 1752, at Pitchford Hall; N.R.A., Pitchford Hall, S/3 (map of manorial estate, 1800). This article was written in 1962 and revised in 1965. Thanks were due to Mr. C. R. A. Grant of Pitchford Hall for permission to use the Pitchford Hall MSS. still in his possession and for helpful criticism. Assistance has also been given by his son, Mr. A. R. C. Grant.

[2] N.L.W., Pitchford Hall 1156; Eyton, vi. 278.

[3] Shrews. Boro. Rec., 'Liber A', f. 1; N.L.W., Pitchford Hall 1155.

[4] S.P.L., Haughmond Cart. f. 59ᵛ.

[5] *Rot. Hund.* (Rec. Com.), ii. 93.

[6] B.M. Eg. Roll 8456.

gravel, the subsoil is largely boulder clay. The Coal Measures which outcrop in valley bottoms to the north and east of the parish were mined in the 17th and early 18th centuries.[7] The pitch well, from which the village takes its name, lies 250 yards north-east of Pitchford Hall.

Pitchford lay within the Long Forest until it was disafforested in the later 13th century.[8] The manor was said to contain woodland sufficient for 100 swine in 1086,[9] and the south-western quarter of the parish —the area now occupied by Pitchford Park Farm and Stockbatch Farm—formed part of Buriwood during the Middle Ages.[10] There were said to be some 300 a. woodland here in 1292.[11] Pitchford Wood was said to be well preserved in 1235,[12] but assarting is recorded from the later 12th century. The lord of the manor had cleared 40 a. by 1199, and a further 22 a. by 1209.[13] Assarting by his tenants is recorded in 1209 and 1273.[14] The field-names 'Bryche' (found near Stockbatch Farm in 1566) and 'Hucklebridge' (found near Radnal Bridge in 1612)[15] are further evidence of assarting in the south of the parish.

That part of Buriwood which lay within the parish seems, however, to have survived the Middle Ages with but little reduction in its area. A deer park formed on the western boundary of the parish before 1596 contained 191 a. in 1682.[16] A further 53 a. was added to the Park in 1729, extending it as far east as the present Park Farm.[17] The area of the park was reduced in 1742[18] and it was probably disparked shortly before 1766.[19] Extensive sales of timber and cordwood are recorded between 1636[20] and 1651,[21] both in the park and in the demesne to the north. In 1637 1,000 cords of wood and 800 tons of timber were sold from the park, the former to the lessee of Longnor Forge, who purchased further cordwood here in 1640 and 1651.[22] In 1682 woodland in the park and demesne was restricted to Big Wood on the banks of Row Brook and some 33 a. near Park Farm.[23] Between 1775 and 1800 46 a. woodland were cleared near Park Farm,[24] and only 100 a. woodland remained in the parish by 1843.[25] Most of the latter lay in Birch Coppice and Big Wood,[26] which were still standing in 1965.

Lower Common, which lay to the west of Pitchford village, north of Park Farm, contained 58 a. in 1682 and Upper Common (or Pools Common), south of the village, then contained 27 a.[27] The former was probably at one time the common of the adjacent settlements of Little Eton, Newton, and La Beche, for tenants at Little Eton and Newton possessed common rights in the 13th century.[28] The Upper and Lower Commons were inclosed c. 1753.[29]

The 3 common fields of Pitchford[30] lay to the east of Row Brook. Stockwell Field ran eastwards from the village towards Watling Street. Standell Field lay north of Stockwell Field between Watling Street and the road to Cound. Quarrell Field, to the south of the village, lay between Watling Street and Row Brook. The two latter fields took their names from adjacent stone-quarries. The common-field holdings of individual tenants were consolidated by agreement in 1586 and 1626, and a general agreement to inclose the common fields and consolidate holdings was reached in 1633.[31] The latter may not have been put into effect, for 118 a. common-field land was inclosed between 1673 and 1682.[32] The common fields of the three other former hamlets in the parish disappeared too early to have left any record.

The Roman alignment of Watling Street, skirting the eastern edge of the parish, was still in use when the road was turnpiked in 1764.[33] In that year the section to the south of Black Pits was diverted westwards to pass through Pitchford village.[34] The section from the Finger Post, south of the village, to Radnal Bridge on the southern boundary was no more than a field-road by 1808, having been replaced by the present road to Acton Burnell.[35] The road from Shrewsbury to Pitchford formerly ran close to Pitchford Hall and the church, crossing Row Brook near the pitch-well and meeting the present village street near Lower Farm.[36] It was diverted eastwards to its present course by the lord of the manor in 1833.[37] The stepped circular base and part of the shaft of a stone cross, known locally as the 'Buttercross', stands near a track leading to Pitchford Hall, to the west of the former Pitchford school.[38] The field-road running south-eastwards from the village to Piller Brook is all that now remains of a road leading to Acton Burnell and Kenley, known as Salter's Way in the 16th century.[39] The straight road from Pitchford to Golding was in existence by 1718,[40] and may have been laid out at the inclosure of the common fields in the later 17th century. The road running north-westwards from Pitchford Hall, past Little Pitchford, which is recorded in 1682,[41] crossed Cound Brook at Eaton Mascott mill by a bridge in 1740.[42] The bridge was rebuilt by William Hazledine shortly after 1797,[43] but is now no more than a footbridge.

[7] See pp. 121–2.
[8] Eyton, vi. 342.
[9] V.C.H. Salop. i. 335.
[10] Rot. Hund. (Rec. Com.), ii. 93.
[11] Eyton, vi. 274.
[12] Ibid. 339.
[13] Pipe R. 1199 (P.R.S. N.S. x), 76; E 32/144 m. 2d.
[14] E 32/144 m. 2d.; N.L.W., Pitchford Hall 1588.
[15] N.L.W., Pitchford Hall 936; Lich. Dioc. Regy., glebe terrier, 1612.
[16] N.L.W., Pitchford Hall 1545; N.R.A., Pitchford Hall S/1.
[17] N.R.A., Pitchford Hall, S/1.
[18] N.L.W., Pitchford Hall uncat., game bks. 1613–1742.
[19] N.L.W., Pitchford Hall 1797.
[20] Ibid. 2043.
[21] Ibid. uncat., contract, 1651.
[22] Ibid. contracts, 1637, 1640, 1651.
[23] N.R.A., Pitchford Hall, S/1.
[24] N.L.W., Pitchford Hall 1796; N.R.A., Pitchford Hall, S/3.

[25] Heref. Dioc. Regy., tithe appt.   [26] Ibid.
[27] N.R.A., Pitchford Hall, S/1.
[28] S.P.L., Deeds 5191; Eyton, vi. 274.
[29] N.L.W., Pitchford Hall 2139.
[30] Description of common fields based on Lich. Dioc. Regy., glebe terriers, 1612, 1673, 1682; N.L.W., Pitchford Hall 825.
[31] N.L.W., Pitchford Hall 905, 1589, 2038.
[32] Ibid. 825.
[33] Watling Street road Act, 4 Geo. III, c. 70 (priv. act).
[34] N.L.W., Pitchford Hall 1920, 1921.
[35] Baugh, Map of Salop. (1808).
[36] N.R.A., Pitchford Hall, no. 122.
[37] Q. Sess. rolls, Trin. 1833.
[38] O.S. Nat. Grid, SJ 529038. Ex inf. Mr. C. R. A. Grant.
[39] N.L.W., Pitchford Hall 1179.
[40] Ibid. 1685.
[41] N.R.A., Pitchford Hall, S/1.
[42] Par. rec., par. bk.
[43] N.L.W., Pitchford Hall uncat., overseers' accts. 1783–1836.

The earliest settlement in the parish was probably on the south bank of Cound Brook, near Eaton Mascott mill. The field-name 'Stanchester', which occurs in this area in the 13th century,[44] may mark the site of a Roman villa. Two of the three pre-Conquest manors in Pitchford[45] can be indentified with the former hamlets of Newton and La Beche. These had been merged in the manor of Pitchford by 1086, when Little Eton was still a separate manor.[46] Newton and La Beche are first recorded by name in the early 12th century.[47] The former stood near Little Pitchford Farm and is last recorded as a hamlet in 1347.[48] The site of La Beche is now occupied by a derelict stone cottage and farm-buildings known as Pitchford Barn, between the Cound and Row Brooks, east of Little Pitchford Farm. This area was known as The Beaches in the 17th century,[49] and the house was called Bishop's Farm in the early 18th century, after its owner Adam Ottley, Bishop of St. David's.[50]

The former hamlet known variously as Eton, Little Eton, and Eton juxta Pitchford,[51] possessed a chapel in the early 12th century.[52] It was held by a free tenant in the 12th and 13th centuries, but had been absorbed into the demesne of Pitchford manor by 1431 and is last named in 1484.[53] Tithes formerly payable to the chapel of Little Eton were later deemed impropriate,[54] and were derived from that part of the parish which lay to the west of Row Brook in 1843.[55] Its names indicate that Little Eton stood near water and near the village of Pitchford, and it is likely that its site was that now occupied by Pitchford Hall and the parish church. These stand by the side of the former main road from Shrewsbury to Pitchford, a ¼ mile north-west of Pitchford village. There is no evidence that the medieval manor-house of Pitchford occupied the site of the 16th-century Pitchford Hall, but the church contains 12th-century features[56] and may originally have been Little Eton chapel.

Most of the houses in Pitchford village have been rebuilt in local sandstone by the lord of the manor since the later 18th century. Only 3 of them are timber-framed—Pitchford Farm, No. 22, Pitchford and the adjoining cottages, and No. 27, Pitchford. Pitchford Farm, to the west of the village street, consists of a two-bay house with a central stack, and a southern cross-wing. The house was originally of 1½ story, but the cross-wing was raised to 2-story height c. 1800, when it was given a stone-built south front of 3 bays and a further stone wing was added to the east. The two other timber-framed houses, now cottages, stand to the east of the street and have been less extensively altered. They are T-shaped, with original chimney-stacks at the junction of house and western cross-wing. No. 27,

Pitchford, set back from the street in the former estate yard, is still externally timber-framed, but the other house is rough-cast. Another timber-framed house to the north of No. 22, Pitchford was demolished in 1962.

Some of the stone houses in the village probably date from the later 18th century, for extensive building is known to have been in progress on the manorial estate in the 1770s.[57] In addition to Rectory Farm (the former parsonage), which was enlarged c. 1803,[58] this earlier phase of stone building included Lower Farm, the former smithy in the estate yard, the cottage to the north of Rectory Farm, and the range of farm buildings formerly attached to No. 22, Pitchford. The last, now the buildings of Rectory Farm, include a hexagonal brick gin-house. A group of derelict cottages to the west of the street, at the north end of the village, are of 1½ story and probably date from this period. The remaining cottages to the west of the street are 'model cottages' of 2 stories, with rectangular hood-moulds, wide eaves, barge-boards, and wooden porches, similar to such cottages at Acton Burnell. They include the former school, built c. 1837,[59] and were all built in the 1830s. Six Council houses at the south end of the village were built before 1939.[60]

An alehouse, first recorded in 1616,[61] was known as 'The Oatsheaf' in the later 18th century.[62] It was at this time a frequent meeting place for the petty sessions of Condover Hundred,[63] but appears to have been closed in 1822.[64]

The former park, on the western boundary of the parish, which was disparked in the 1760s,[65] has left few material remains. The site of a lodge built to the west of the park before 1682[66] is now occupied by a pair of derelict cottages known as Windy Monday. Pitchford manor already included 3 fishponds in the 13th century, one of which was near the mill on Row Brook.[67] The 3 existing pools west of Pitchford Hall—there were 4 of them in 1682[68]—may date from the creation of the park in the 16th century. Another pool, known as Little Heath Pool, was constructed in the park in 1720,[69] and all of these pools were kept stocked with fish between 1630 and the mid-18th century.[70]

Park Farm, which comprises the greater part of the former park, was first leased in 1766.[71] The house is brick-built and was designed by John Gwynn c. 1774.[72] It is a 3-bay house of 2 stories with attics and a large vaulted cellar. The sash windows and central doors in the north and south have plain flat lintels. The gables are raised to form parapets above the low-pitched slate roof. The brick service wing to the west, like the older farm buildings, is of a different bond from the house and is probably of a slightly later date.

[44] S.P.L., Haughmond Cart. f. 59ᵛ; *T.S.A.S.* lvii 13–16.
[45] *V.C.H. Salop.* i. 313, 335.
[46] Ibid.
[47] N.L.W., Pitchford Hall 1156; Eyton, vi. 278.
[48] N.L.W., Pitchford Hall 130; Bodl. MS. Gough Salop. 4, f. 79.
[49] S.P.L., Deeds 5132.
[50] N.L.W., Pitchford Hall 1697.
[51] Ibid. 205, 208; *V.C.H. Salop.* i. 313.
[52] N.L.W., Pitchford Hall 1156.
[53] Ibid. 803; Eyton, vi. 285–6; B.M. Eg. Roll 8456.
[54] Owen and Blakeway, *Hist. Shrewsbury*, ii. 184.
[55] Heref. Dioc. Regy., tithe appt.
[56] See p. 123.
[57] N.L.W., Pitchford Hall uncat., accts. 1770–80.
[58] Visit. Archd. Salop. 1823; Lich. Dioc. Regy., glebe terrier, 1824.
[59] Ed 7/102/189.
[60] Ex inf. Atcham R.D.C.
[61] Q. Sess., alehouse reg.   [62] Ibid.
[63] N.L.W., Castle Hill 2244.
[64] Q. Sess., alehouse reg.
[65] N.L.W., Pitchford Hall 1797.
[66] N.R.A., Pitchford Hall, S/1; ibid. no. 122.
[67] C 133/41/14; C 134/70/7.
[68] N.R.A., Pitchford Hall, S/1.
[69] N.L.W., Pitchford Hall uncat., game bks. 1613–1742.
[70] Ibid.
[71] N.L.W., Pitchford Hall 1797.
[72] Ibid. uncat., acct. of John Gwynn.

A number of timber-framed farm buildings which stood to the south of the Hall in 1714[73] were replaced in the later 18th century by the existing brick buildings immediately south-west of the Hall. The former kennels, also built in the later 18th century, is now Grove Farm. This house, which was presumably built for the huntsman, has a cruciform ground-plan, with a central chimney stack, and is of two stories with a low-pitched hipped roof and wide eaves. The windows, which have peaked hoods, are of 3 lights, the central lights being Yorkshire sashes.

A small park was formed to the east of the Hall shortly after 1833, when the road to Pitchford was diverted eastwards.[74] The two Lodges, in the Tudor style, were presumably built at this time.

Little Pitchford Farm was formed from the Lower Demesne in 1738.[75] The present house is stone-built and is T-shaped, of 2 stories with attics and cellar. Bricks in the cellar floor are dated 1849, but the house has heavily timbered ceilings on the ground floor and probably dates from c. 1800. Stockbatch Farm, adjoining the former Upper Common, had been built by 1800[76] and is an L-shaped stone house of 2 stories. A small squatter settlement at the Knoll, on a tributary of Row Brook south-west of the village, is first recorded in 1638.[77] There were at least 3 houses here in 1688[78] and 6 in 1800,[79] but these were probably demolished in the 1820s.[80]

The medieval mill, on Row Brook immediately east of the Hall, seems to have been demolished shortly before 1795,[81] and a dam on Piller Brook, east of the village, probably marks the site of a fulling mill first recorded in 1284.[82] Another fulling mill had been built near the Hall before 1609.[83] A mill belonging to the manor of Eaton Mascott in 1086[84] stood on the south bank of Cound Brook c. 1236[85] but was still accounted part of Berrington parish in 1545.[86] It was known in the 17th century as Lower Mills and later as Pitchford Forge, since it was used as an iron forge and later as a wire-mill during the 18th century.[87] A pair of brick cottages were built on the site of the mill-house in the earlier 19th century. Their demolition, which was in progress in July 1965, revealed that the northern gable wall contained a cruck truss, sawn off below first-floor level. All other walls were wholly of brick.

The parish contained 15 households in 1563[88] and 100 adults in 1676.[89] The population rose from 220 to 255 between 1801 and 1811, but 11 houses were demolished after 1821, and there were only 197 inhabitants in 1831.[90] Population fluctuated between 170 and 190, 1841–1931,[91] but fell from 175 to 130 between 1951 and 1961.[92]

MANORS. The overlordship of *PITCHFORD* manor, held by Roger, Earl of Shrewsbury, in 1086,[93] presumably passed to the FitzAlans in the 12th century. It had been annexed to their lordship of Oswestry by 1284,[94] and William FitzAlan was overlord in 1346.[95] John, Earl of Arundel, was overlord in 1431, when Pitchford was held as of the manor of Cound,[96] and the overlordship subsequently followed the descent of Cound manor, being last recorded in 1606.[97] The Chetwynd family are recorded as mesne lords here between 1253 and 1428.[98]

Before 1066 Pitchford was held as three manors by the freemen Edric, Leofric, and Ulvric,[99] and in 1086 Turold de Verley was tenant of the single manor here.[1] He probably granted the manor to Ralph de Pitchford before 1102,[2] and it passed from father to son in the Pitchford family until 1301, the following being lords: Ralph, living 1102;[3] Richard, died c. 1157;[4] Richard, c. 1157–c. 1176;[5] Hugh, c. 1176–c. 1212;[6] Ralph, c. 1212–1253;[7] John, 1253–84;[8] Ralph, 1284–1301.[9] In 1301 Ralph de Pitchford sold the manor to Walter de Langton, Bishop of Coventry and Lichfield,[10] on whose death in 1321 it passed to his cousin Edmund Peverel.[11] Edmund died in 1331[12] and was succeeded by his infant son John, who had died without issue before 1353, when his sister Margaret and her husband William de la Pole were in possession.[13] The manor was settled on their daughter Isabel[14] but the reversion was sold in 1358 to Sir Nicholas Burnell.[15] He purchased Isabel's estate there in 1375[16] and was succeeded by his son Sir Hugh Burnell in 1383.[17] At Hugh's death in 1420 the manor was held by feoffees, one of whom was Joan Beauchamp, lady of Bergavenny.[18] In 1421 Pitchford was expressly excluded in a settlement of the Burnell estates,[19] and had probably been settled by Sir Hugh Burnell on Joan Beauchamp, who was his residuary legatee.[20] She was holding the manor in 1431,[21] and at her death in 1435 her lands

[73] Drawing of Hall by J. Bowen, 1714, at Pitchford Hall.
[74] See p. 116.
[75] N.L.W., Pitchford Hall 806.
[76] N.R.A., Pitchford Hall, S/3.
[77] N.L.W., Pitchford Hall 942.
[78] N.R.A., Pitchford Hall, S/1.
[79] Ibid. S/3.
[80] Census, 1831.
[81] N.R.A., Pitchford Hall, P.L./1–2.
[82] C 133/41/14.
[83] N.L.W., Pitchford Hall 707.
[84] V.C.H. Salop. i. 320.
[85] S.P.L., Haughmond Cart. ff. 59, 59ᵛ.
[86] N.L.W., Pitchford Hall 1285.
[87] Ibid. 952, 1554.
[88] B.M. Harl. MS. 594, f. 160.
[89] T.S.A.S. 2nd ser. i. 181.
[90] Census, 1801–31.
[91] Ibid. 1841–1931.
[92] Ibid. 1951–61.
[93] V.C.H. Salop. i, 335.
[94] C 133/41/14.
[95] Feud. Aids, iv. 236.
[96] Ibid. 269.

[97] C 142/292/194.
[98] C 132/51/1; C 133/41/14; C 134/70/7; C 135/27/13; Feud. Aids, iv. 236, 269.
[99] V.C.H. Salop. i. 335.
[1] Ibid.
[2] Eyton, vi. 268.
[3] Ibid.
[4] Ibid. ii. 150.
[5] Ibid. 151.
[6] Ibid. 151–2.
[7] Ibid.; C 132/15/1.
[8] C 132/15/1; C 133/41/14.
[9] C 133/41/14; C.P. 25(1)/194/7/39.
[10] C.P. 25(1)/194/7/39.
[11] C 134/70/7.
[12] C 135/27/13.
[13] C.P. 25(1)/287/44/495.   [14] Ibid.
[15] C.P. 25(1)/195/15/20.
[16] C.P. 25(1)/195/17/57.
[17] C 136/24/19.
[18] C 138/54/116.
[19] Cal. Close, 1419–22, 155.
[20] Reg. H. Chichele (C. & Y.S.), ii. 217–18.
[21] Feud. Aids, iv. 269.

were devised to James de Ormonde,[22] who obtained livery of the manor from the surviving feoffee of Sir Hugh Burnell in 1445.[23] Ormonde's estates were forfeited to the Crown at his execution in 1461,[24] and the manor then passed to John, Lord Lovell,[25] who sold it in 1463 to Thomas Stone, a Shrewsbury merchant.[26] In 1473 Stone's widow Agnes sold the manor to the Shrewsbury merchant Thomas Ottley.[27] It passed from father to son in the Ottley family until 1807,[28] the following being lords: Thomas, 1473–85; William, 1485–1529; Adam, 1529–78; Richard, 1578–1606; Thomas, 1606–22;[29] Francis, 1622–49; Richard, 1649–70; Thomas, 1670–95; Adam, 1695–1752; Thomas, 1752–1807; Adam, 1807.

On the death of Adam Ottley in 1807 the manor passed to his cousin Charles Jenkinson, later Earl of Liverpool. He was succeeded by his daughter, Lady Louisa Cotes, 1851–87, and by her son Col. Charles James Cotes, 1887–1913.[30] It then passed to the latter's sister and heir Victoria, wife of Lt.-Gen. Sir Robert Grant. She was succeeded in 1918 by her son Gen. Sir Charles Grant, whose son Mr. C. R. A. Grant was lord of the manor in 1965.

The manor of *ETON* was held by the church of St. Chad, Shrewsbury, before 1066[31] and in 1086 it was held of St. Chad's by Turold de Verley, the tenant of Pitchford manor.[32] The overlordship of St. Chad's is last recorded in 1253.[33]

There is no evidence for the site of the medieval manor house, recorded between 1284 and 1431.[34] The present Pitchford Hall was probably begun soon after 1549, when John Sandford, a local carpenter, obtained the lease of a tenement in Pitchford 'during the building of a mansion place'.[35] As the house now stands it is considered one of the finest timber-framed manor-houses in the county.[36] It is of two stories and is built on an E-shaped plan, its original entrance front facing south and having a central porch. The side wings are unusually long, enclosing a forecourt about 70 feet square, which, until the 19th century, had a wall across its fourth side. The west wing joins the central range at a slightly oblique angle[37] and is structurally distinct from it; unlike the rest of the building this wing has side walls of close-studded timbering[38] and is not jettied at first-floor level. The central range and the east wing are clearly of one period. The framing here consists of rectangular panels which are subdivided by diagonal struts, giving the effect described as 'lozenges within lozenges'.[39] Some of the wall-posts are carved with cable mouldings, while bressumers

have sunken quatrefoils and vine-trails. These decorative features are all found in timber-framed houses in Shrewsbury dating from the last thirty years of the 16th century. It seems possible, therefore, that the west wing is the only part of John Sandford's building to survive and that it was adapted as the service wing of a slightly later house.

The chimneys throughout have tall brick shafts, but several of these are not original. The two-storied porch in the central range is surmounted by a clock and an ornamental gable; the clock was in existence at least by 1682.[40] This range also has two projecting bays with plain gables, one in each angle of the forecourt. The west bay contains a newel stair and it is possible that a similar stair has been removed from the other; alternatively it may have been a projecting oriel at the upper end of the hall. The hall occupies the eastern half of the central range, divided originally from the service rooms by a screens passage. The passage would have crossed the centre of the building from the front porch to the plainer porch which projects from the north wall. The hall has now been combined with a small parlour further east, but its moulded ceiling beams and massive north chimney appear to be original. The service rooms in the western half of the range have been converted into a dining room. The east wing contains a drawing room with a library beyond it and there is an original chimney in the dividing wall. The fine oak panelling in the drawing room, which has fluted pilasters and a carved frieze, may have been inserted in 1626.[41] The ceiling of this room is divided into panels by moulded plaster ribs, the panels containing emblems which include the wheatsheaf of the Ottley family.

The house was so thoroughly restored in the Elizabethan style in the 19th century that several earlier alterations have been obscured. A continuation of the central range, consisting of a service block which projected beyond the west wing, had been built by 1682;[42] it appears to have been re-modelled in the early 19th century. Probably in the late 18th century a bow window was inserted in the drawing room and the formal terraced garden between the east wing and the stream was altered.[43] It may have been at this period that a timber-framed wing, projecting from the east front near its southern end,[44] was taken down. An unusual garden feature on the high ground to the south of the house is a square timber-framed summer-house, built in the branches of an ancient lime tree. This seems to have been in existence by 1714,[45] but its

---

[22] *Complete Peerage*, i. 26; *Reg. H. Chichele* (C. & Y.S.), ii. 534–9.

[23] N.L.W., Pitchford Hall 1237.

[24] *Complete Peerage*, xii (2), 734.

[25] *Cal. Pat.* 1461–7, 87.

[26] N.L.W., Pitchford Hall 1188.

[27] Ibid. 1190.

[28] Descent of manor after 1473 based on *T.S.A.S.* 2nd ser. vii. 362; *Visit. Salop. 1623* (Harl. Soc. xxix), ii. 381–2; *N.L.W. Jnl.* iv. 61; Burke, *Land. Gent.* (1925), p. 403; ibid. (1965), i. pp. 331–2.

[29] *T.S.A.S.* 2nd ser. vii. 364, 370. The Thomas Ottley whose will was proved in 1647, as noted by Tipping, was the third son of this Thomas Ottley: ibid. 365, 371; Tipping, *English Homes*, iii (1), 5.

[30] G. D. Jones, *The Ottley Papers*, 74 n.

[31] *V.C.H. Salop.* i. 313.

[32] Ibid.

[33] C 132/15/1.

[34] C 133/41/14; B.M. Eg. Roll 8456.

[35] N.L.W., Pitchford Hall 695.

[36] See plate facing p. 132.

[37] Tipping, *English Homes*, iii (1), plan on p. 2. The following description is largely based on Tipping's account.

[38] Photographs at Pitchford Hall and Nat. Mons. Rec. show the west wall before 19th-century additions.

[39] Pevsner, *Shropshire*, 228.

[40] Map of manorial estate (including sketch of Hall), 1682, at Pitchford Hall.

[41] A panel dated 1626 bearing the initials of Thomas Ottley and his wife was found by Col. Cotes and inserted above the library fireplace: Tipping, op. cit. 13. This Thomas Ottley, however, died in 1622: see footnote 29 above.

[42] Map of manorial estate, 1682, at Pitchford Hall.

[43] Tipping, op. cit. 10.

[44] Map of manorial estate, 1682, at Pitchford Hall.

[45] View of Hall and grounds, 1714, at Pitchford Hall.

internal plasterwork, in the 18th-century 'gothick taste', is more likely to be a later insertion. A late-18th-century drawing[46] shows a porch in similar style at the centre of the forecourt wall. By this time single-story brick corridors with lean-to roofs had been built along both sides of the forecourt.[47] In the 18th or early 19th century most of the windows in the house were replaced by sashes.[48]

The Hall was restored by Col. C. J. Cotes and his architect George Devey (d. 1886), the work having started before Cotes succeeded to the estate in 1887.[49] The principal entrance was moved to the north side, enabling the forecourt to be opened up, cleared of additions, and laid out as part of the garden. A bridge over the stream which had given access to it was removed and another was built further north to carry a new drive. In the house itself sashes were replaced by mullioned windows, external timbering was renewed or added, and Tudor fireplaces and panelling were introduced. Additions to the west wing included a new staircase and a small projecting bay. The existing service block was re-roofed, faced with timber-framing, and extended, increasing the length of the many-gabled north front to nearly 200 feet. In general the architectural treatment of the exterior shows so great a respect for the original work that it is not always easy to distinguish old from new. Internal alterations included the rearrangement of rooms in the central range and the introduction of many period features. As the house has not changed hands by sale since it was built it still contains a number of family heirlooms and several notable portraits.

ECONOMIC HISTORY. The manor of Pitchford, formed by the union of three pre-Conquest estates, was assessed at 3 hides in 1086[50] and in 1255.[51] It was worth 8s. before the Conquest and 40s. by 1086.[52] Its value rose from £16 2s. in 1253[53] to £19 8s. in 1284,[54] but it was said to be worth only £7 9s. in 1331.[55] Though held by the lord of Pitchford manor, Little Eton was still accounted a separate manor in 1086.[56] Its value had declined from 8s. to 4s. since before the Conquest.[57] It was assessed at half a hide in 1086[58] but at only one virgate in 1253.[59] It was granted to a free tenant in the course of the 12th century, and was held in the 1190s by Ulger and Oliver de Eton,[60] whose descendants were still in possession in 1347.[61] The estate then comprised a half carucate at Newton and lands at Little Eton and Pitchford,[62] but had been merged with the manorial estate before 1431.[63]

Pitchford manor already had a large demesne in 1086, when it contained land sufficient for 3 ploughs, and 3 serfs and 3 *bovarii* were the only recorded tenants.[64] The demesne arable was assessed at 3 carucates in 1253[65] and at 312 a. in 1284.[66] Although this would suggest that the area of demesne had remained unchanged since 1086, some 62 a. had been added by assarting before 1207.[67] The lord was still concerning himself directly with forest clearance in the early 14th century.[68] There were, however, only 2 carucates of demesne arable in 1331,[69] and the demesne was said to be uncultivated in 1341.[70] By 1431 the whole was in the hands of the tenants.[71] The demesne was taken in hand in the course of the 16th century, when the manorial estate was enlarged by the purchase of the lands of two free tenants.[72] The Upper and Lower Demesne amounted to 664 a. in 1682, of which 191 a. lay in the park or was woodland,[73] and the manorial estate as a whole contained 1,367 a. in 1689.[74] Two further freeholds were purchased in 1721 and 1800,[75] 36 a. was acquired by exchange in 1752,[76] and nearly all the Common (85 a.) was allotted to the lord of the manor at its inclosure c. 1753.[77] In 1800 the manorial estate amounted to 1,520 a.[78] and it was still of the same size in 1843.[79]

The large demesne of the later 17th century did not long remain in hand. The Lower Demesne had been leased, as Little Pitchford Farm, before 1738,[80] and the Upper Demesne (or Park Farm), containing 438 a., was let in 1766.[81] By 1800 only 181 a. remained in hand, of which 81 a. was woodland.[82] There were 415 a. in hand in 1843, when Little Pitchford Farm was untenanted,[83] but the latter was soon afterwards leased with additional lands acquired in Cantlop in Berrington parish.[84]

Free tenants were more numerous than customary tenants during the Middle Ages. In 1284 £5 19s. out of a total rental of £8 18s. were derived from assized rents of free tenants.[85] Apart from the Eton family, whose estate at Little Eton and Newton passed to the lord of the manor after 1348,[86] the family of La Beche held lands at La Beche and Newton. William de la Beche was a free tenant here in 1236,[87] but the family is not recorded after 1327.[88] Another freehold of 35 a. was created at La Beche

[46] At Pitchford Hall.
[47] Ibid. and later drawings at Pitchford Hall. Tipping suggests that the corridors were added after 1807: op. cit. 11.
[48] Nineteenth-century drawings at Pitchford Hall and S.P.L.
[49] Tipping, op. cit. 11–12; D.N.B.
[50] V.C.H. Salop. i. 335.
[51] Rot. Hund. (Rec. Com.), ii. 62.
[52] V.C.H. Salop. i. 335.
[53] C 132/15/1.
[54] C 133/41/14.
[55] C 135/27/13.
[56] V.C.H. Salop. i. 313.
[57] Ibid.
[58] Ibid.
[59] C 132/15/1.
[60] Eyton, vi. 285.
[61] N.L.W., Pitchford Hall 130.
[62] Ibid.
[63] B.M. Eg. Roll 8456.
[64] V.C.H. Salop. i. 335.
[65] C 132/15/1.

[66] C 133/41/14.
[67] Eyton, ii. 151; E 32/144 m. 2d.
[68] Lich. Cath. D. & C. Mun., G. 8.
[69] C 135/27/13.
[70] Inq. Non. (Rec. Com.), 183.
[71] B.M. Eg. Roll 8456.
[72] N.L.W., Pitchford Hall 1158; S.P.L., MS. 2, f. 204.
[73] N.R.A., Pitchford Hall, S/1.
[74] Ibid.
[75] N.L.W., Pitchford Hall 785–6, 3154.
[76] Ibid. 2054.
[77] Ibid. 2139; N.R.A., Pitchford Hall, S/1.
[78] Ibid. S/3.
[79] Heref. Dioc. Regy., tithe appt.
[80] N.L.W., Pitchford Hall 806.
[81] Ibid. 1796–7.
[82] N.R.A., Pitchford Hall, S/1.
[83] Heref. Dioc. Regy., tithe appt.
[84] N.R.A., Pitchford Hall, S.C./1.
[85] C 133/41/14.
[86] N.L.W., Pitchford Hall 13°.
[87] Eyton, vi. 106.
[88] T.S.A.S. 2nd ser. xi. 373.

in 1248,[89] but by the early 17th century, the Hoptons, the successors of the La Beche family, were the only freeholders in this former hamlet.[90] After the later Middle Ages this property was normally held with a larger estate at Eaton Mascott in Berrington parish, where its later history is given.[91] It included 106 a. in Pitchford parish in 1843.[92]

The remaining freeholds were smaller and were based on common-field holdings in Pitchford township. There appear to have been 4 of these in the early 16th century. The estate of the Ruckley family was bought by the lord of the manor in 1515 and 1518[93] and that of the Pearce family in 1576.[94] A 27-acre freehold, held since at least 1586 by the Morrall family of Much Wenlock, was sold to the lord of the manor in 1721.[95] The Parr family, who may have been descendants of the family of Perrour, freeholders in Pitchford in the early 15th century,[96] retained their estate until 1800.[97] Some 60 a. in the south of the parish had been acquired by the lord of Acton Burnell manor before 1272.[98] This amounted to 36 a. in 1752, when it was exchanged with the lord of Pitchford for 31 a. in Acton Burnell.[99]

Labour services of villeins were valued at £1 12s. in 1253[1] and at £2 6s. in 1284.[2] Their rents, which produced £2 19s. in 1284,[3] appear to have fallen to about £2 by 1331.[4] Rents produced £56 a year in the early 17th century.[5] Between 1555 and 1650 leases were normally for 2 lives or for terms of not less than 30 years, but the three-life lease was in general use on the manorial estate in the later 17th century.[6] As these leases fell in from 1723 onwards, they were replaced by 21-year leases,[7] and by 1770 the whole estate was held under this form of tenure.[8] In 1689 the 618 a. of the manorial estate which lay outside the demesne was held by 11 tenants.[9] Five of them held farms of over 50 a. and the remainder had smaller holdings.[10] The transition to large farms probably took place in the later 18th century, and by 1800, when 1,180 a. lay in 5 farms of over 100 a., there were only 4 smaller holdings, totalling 125 a.[11]

The acreage of barley far exceeded that of any other crop sown on the demesne, 1754–75, when considerable quantities of clover were also sown.[12]

The parish contained equal proportions of arable and pasture in 1843.[13]

Pitchford mill, which was granted to Haughmond Abbey c. 1172,[14] was recovered by the lord of the manor between 1176 and 1205.[15] It was said to be worth £2 17s. 2d. a year in 1253,[16] and was leased for 20s. a year in 1431.[17] Its place was probably taken by Eaton Mascott mill in the 16th century, but there was again a water-mill at Pitchford, on Row Brook below the Hall, between 1673 and 1747.[18] This had been demolished before 1795.[19]

A fulling mill worth 10s. a year is recorded in 1284.[20] This probably stood on Piller Brook immediately east of the village. A pool here, where there are remains of a dam, was known as Walkmill Pool in the early 17th century.[21] This was used as a fish-pool until at least 1759,[22] but it had been drained by 1843.[23] A new fulling mill, recorded in 1609, was then said to stand near the corn mill.[24] This may have been on Row Brook, near the Hall, but is more likely to have adjoined Eaton Mascott mill on Cound Brook. The latter, already in existence by 1086,[25] was purchased by the lord of Pitchford manor in 1545,[26] and contained 3 mills under one roof in 1586.[27] It was variously known as Lower Mills or Cooper's Mill in the later 17th century.[28] In 1715 Eaton Mascott mill was converted into an iron forge and was leased to William Corfield of Harley.[29] It was subsequently known as Pitchford Forge and produced 150 tons in 1717 and 70 tons in 1736.[30] Corfield was followed in 1746 by Richard Jordan,[31] and in 1769 the forge was leased to Thomas Gibbons of Wolverhampton and William Gibbons of Kingswinford.[32] At about this time it was converted into a wire-mill.[33] The forge was leased in 1790 to William Hazledine of Shrewsbury,[34] who was still its tenant when it is last recorded in 1800.[35]

Coal was mined in Pitchford in the 17th and early 18th centuries. Trial pits were sunk in 1613,[36] but the first productive pit was that at The Stockbeaches near Stockbatch Farm, recorded in 1656[37] and worked intermittently until c. 1749.[38] Another pit was sunk in Standell Field in 1657,[39] but the principal pit was on the slope to the south of Eaton Mascott mill. Here mining began in 1680[40] and continued

[89] Eyton, vi. 277.
[90] S.P.L., Deeds 5132.
[91] See p. 22.
[92] Heref. Dioc. Regy., tithe appt.
[93] N.L.W., Pitchford Hall 1158, 1160.
[94] S.P.L., MS. 2, f. 204.
[95] N.L.W., Pitchford Hall 785–6, 1589.
[96] B.M. Eg. Roll 8456.
[97] N.L.W., Pitchford Hall 3154.
[98] Eyton, vi. 130.
[99] N.L.W., Pitchford Hall 2054; S.R.O. 1514 uncat., deed, 1752.
[1] C 132/15/1.
[2] C 133/41/14.
[3] Ibid.
[4] C 135/27/13.
[5] N.L.W., Pitchford Hall 1605.
[6] Ibid. 612–2397 (leases), passim.
[7] Ibid. 806, 882, 953, 2419.
[8] Ibid. 1966.
[9] N.R.A., Pitchford Hall, S/1.
[10] Ibid.
[11] Ibid. S/3.
[12] N.L.W, Pitchford Hall uncat., farming accts. 1754–75.
[13] Heref. Dioc. Regy., tithe appt.

[14] N.L.W., Pitchford Hall 1391; Eyton, i. 358.
[15] N.L.W., Pitchford Hall 1414; Eyton, i. 359.
[16] C 132/15/1.
[17] B.M. Eg. Roll 8456.
[18] N.L.W., Pitchford Hall 742, 893.
[19] N.R.A., Pitchford Hall, P.L./1–2.
[20] C 133/41/14.
[21] N.L.W., Pitchford Hall uncat., game bks. 1613–1742.
[22] Ibid.
[23] Heref. Dioc. Regy., tithe appt.
[24] N.L.W., Pitchford Hall 707.
[25] V.C.H. Salop. i. 320.
[26] N.L.W., Pitchford Hall 1285.
[27] Ibid. 653.
[28] Ibid. 821, 887.
[29] Ibid. 952.
[30] Trans. Newcomen Soc. ix. 32.
[31] N.L.W., Pitchford Hall 955.　　[32] Ibid. 2101.
[33] Bodl. MS. Gough Salop. 4, f. 78v.
[34] N.L.W., Pitchford Hall 2104.
[35] N.R.A., Pitchford Hall, S/3.
[36] N.L.W., Pitchford Hall uncat., accts. 1599–1613.
[37] Ibid. lease, 1656.
[38] Ibid. lease, 1672; N.L.W., Pitchford Hall 925.
[39] Ibid. uncat., lease 1657.
[40] N.L.W., Pitchford Hall 951.

until 1725, when the pits were flooded.[41] A salt-spring nearby was leased to Samuel Harrison and William Constantine of Droitwich in 1695,[42] but operations had been suspended by 1715, since water from the coal-pits had spoilt the brine.[43] The pitch-rock occurring in the Coal Measures which outcrop on the banks of Row Brook north-east of Pitchford Hall was leased in 1693 to Martin Eele of Broseley.[44] Experiments carried out at Deptford Yard in 1697 showed that the pitch was inferior to imported supplies.[45] In 1745 the workings were leased to Thomas Betton of Shrewsbury, who manufactured a medical preparation known as 'Betton's British Oil'.[46] Bricks were being made at Pitchford in 1693, at a kiln near Pitchford Grove which was still in use in 1726.[47] The sites of these varied extractive industries were held on lease from the Ottleys, who made considerable profits from royalties. In the decade 1715–25 their net profit on sales of wood, bricks, and coal amounted to over £3,100,[48] and they received £415 on pitch mined in the year 1745.[49]

A smith was among the tenants of Pitchford manor in 1086.[50] The village smithy is known to have been in business from c. 1752[51] until 1941.[52] The village also contained a shop and a tailor in 1851.[53] The former appears to have closed later in the 19th century,[54] but another shop has been open since 1929.[55]

LOCAL GOVERNMENT. There are manor court rolls, 1579–1722.[56]

The parish records include accounts of church-wardens and overseers, 1698–1841, and of highway surveyors and constables, 1698–1740.[57] There are no vestry minutes. The 2 churchwardens served all the other parish offices during their term of office, but accounted separately for each until 1739, when the accounts of overseers, constables, and highway surveyors were combined. After 1739 a single rate was levied for all civil purposes. It is consequently difficult to assess the rising incidence of poor relief. General expenditure, rarely more than £20 a year before 1770, rose to a peak of £212 in 1818, and was normally less than £150 thereafter. A poor-house, built in 1719, was in use until at least 1820.

CHURCH. The present church probably stands on the site of the chapel of Little Eton, a pre-Conquest foundation of St. Chad's, Shrewsbury.[58] It became a parish church as the result of an agreement between St. Chad's and Ralph de Pitchford, lord of the manor, in the earlier 12th century[59] and Engelard, brother of Ralph de Pitchford, was the first parish priest.[60]

The living is a rectory and its advowson has always followed the descent of the manor. It was united with Acton Burnell in 1926.[61] The value of the living rose from £5 in 1291[62] to £6 13s. 4d. by 1535.[63] It was said to be worth £20 in 1635[64] and its gross value was put at £30 in 1655.[65] Its net annual value was £150 in 1799,[66] £226 in 1812,[67] and £206 in 1843.[68] The great tithes of Little Eton, Newton, and La Beche were reserved to St. Chad's at the creation of the parish of Pitchford in the early 12th century.[69] They were let to the lord of the manor in 1544[70] and, after several changes of ownership,[71] were again in his hands in 1594.[72] Subsequent lords of the manor paid an annual chief rent for the tithes to St. Chad's until at least 1798.[73] The small tithes of these 3 hamlets, reserved to the Rector of Pitchford under the terms of the original agreement,[74] were apparently still being paid to him in 1698.[75] By 1726 they seem to have been replaced by a modus of a ewe and a lamb, payable to each rector in his first year of office.[76] All tithes in the 3 hamlets, both great and small, were held by the lord of the manor as impropriator in 1843.[77] Then known as 'demesne tithes' they were derived from 871 a. in the north of the parish, and were commuted for a rent-charge of £168.[78] Small tithes in the parish as a whole were said to be worth 40s. in 1341,[79] but there is no evidence for the value of the rectorial tithes until 1823, when they were worth £150 a year.[80] They were commuted for a rent-charge of £165 in 1843,[81] and appear to have been collected in kind before this date, apart from a modus of 6s. 8d. payable by the tenant of Eaton Mascott mill, recorded between 1612 and 1843.[82]

The glebe, which was still a scattered common-field holding in 1612,[83] was consolidated between 1672 and 1682.[84] Thereafter it lay in the Bradfield, on either side of Watling Street, north-east of the village.[85] It was said to contain 38 a. in 1698;[86] an increase to 42 a. by 1756[87] may have been the result of an allotment at the inclosure of the

41 Bodl. MS. Gough Salop. 4, f. 76.
42 N.L.W., Pitchford Hall 815.
43 Bodl. MS. Gough Salop. 4, f. 76.
44 N.L.W., Pitchford Hall uncat., lease, 1693.
45 Ibid. letter from H. Hosier, 24 Mar. 1713/4.
46 Ibid. lease, 1745; Camden, *Brittania*, ed. Gibson (1772), i. 473.
47 N.L.W., Pitchford Hall uncat., accts. 1715–26; Bodl. MS. Gough Salop. 4, f. 79.
48 N.L.W., Pitchford Hall uncat., accts. 1715–26.
49 Ibid. 1745.
50 *V.C.H. Salop.* i. 335.
51 N.R.A., Pitchford Hall, no. 123; map, 1682, at Pitchford Hall.
52 *Kelly's Dir. Salop.* (1856–1941).
53 *Bagshaw's Dir. Salop* (1851).
54 *Kelly's Dir. Salop.* (1856–80).
55 Ibid. (1929–41).
56 N.R.A., Pitchford Hall, M 1/1–35.
57 Par. rec., par. bk. 1698–1782; ibid. overseers' accts. 1731–82; N.L.W., Pitchford Hall uncat., overseers' accts., 1783–1836.
58 See p. 115.
59 N.L.W., Pitchford Hall 1156; Eyton, vi. 278.
60 Ibid.
61 Heref. Dioc. Regy., reg. 1926–38, p. 12.

62 *Tax. Eccl.* (Rec. Com.), 247.
63 *Valor Eccl.* (Rec. Com.), iii. 185.
64 Lich. Dioc. Regy., B/v 1/65.
65 *T.S.A.S.* xlvii. 28.
66 Visit. Archd. Salop. 1799.
67 N.R.A., Pitchford Hall, Z 5/1.
68 Visit. Archd. Salop. 1843.
69 N.L.W., Pitchford Hall 1156; Eyton, vi. 278.
70 Owen and Blakeway, *Hist. Shrewsbury*, ii. 184.
71 Ibid. 209–10; S.P.L., Deeds 6876, 15759.
72 N.L.W., Pitchford Hall uncat., receipts for chief rents, 1594–1798.
73 Ibid.
74 N.L.W., Pitchford Hall 1156.
75 Lich. Dioc. Regy., glebe terrier, 1698.
76 Ibid. 1726.
77 Heref. Dioc. Regy., tithe appt.
78 Ibid.
79 *Inq. Non.* (Rec. Com.), 183.
80 Visit. Archd. Salop. 1823.
81 Heref. Dioc. Regy., tithe appt.
82 Ibid.; Lich. Dioc. Regy., glebe terrier, 1612.
83 Lich. Dioc. Regy., glebe terrier, 1612.
84 Ibid. 1672, 1682.   85 Ibid. 1682–1756.
86 Ibid. 1698.
87 Ibid. 1756.

Common.[88] There were 46 a. glebe in 1843, when it was kept in hand by the rector.[89]

Two medieval and five post-Reformation rectors are known to have been relatives of the lord of the manor.[90] Roger Tydder (rector 1599–c. 1655)[91] was said to be 'no preacher',[92] but his successor Richard Piper (rector c. 1655–68)[93] was described as 'an able preaching minister' in 1655.[94] John Wilkes (rector 1668–1712)[95] and William Roe (rector 1716–41)[96] held the living in plurality with Frodesley,[97] employing William Hancocks as their curate between c. 1689 and 1727.[98] Curates were rarely employed later in the 18th century, but Charles Walcott (rector 1798–1811)[99] was frequently non-resident and employed them continuously.[1] His last curate, Richard Corfield, succeeded him as rector.[2] The parsonage, now Rectory Farm, contained 3 hearths in 1672.[3] The greater part of the house was rebuilt c. 1803,[4] but a timber-framed wing of 2 bays to the east of the house was not demolished until c. 1960.[5] The present house, which contains no features earlier than 1803, is stone-built and of 2 stories, with a low-pitched, hipped roof and a north front of 3 bays. Rooms on the north side have moulded ceilings and there is a fine Georgian staircase with cast-iron balusters. The parsonage was sold in 1928.[6]

In the later 13th century Thurstan de Pitchford charged a messuage in Pitchford with the payment of 3 lb. wax at the feast of St. John the Baptist and of the same amount on Ascension Day, to provide 2 candles before the altar of St. Michael and one candle before the altar of Our Lady in Pitchford church.[7] The rent-charge was said to be worth 16d. in 1547, when it was still being applied to its original purpose.[8]

Communion was administered 4 times a year in the early 18th century[9] and from 5 to 8 times a year in the early 19th century.[10] An average of 60 communicants was reported in 1823[11] and of 50 in 1847.[12] Two services were held on Sundays between 1799 and 1851, when 73 adults attended morning service and 22 in the afternoon.[13] Although a gallery was erected in 1819, there is no record of singers here.[14] The present organ had been acquired by 1910.[15]

The church of *ST. MICHAEL*[16] consists of a chancel and a nave, and has a wooden bell-turret at the west end. A blocked round-headed window and herring-bone stonework in the north wall of the nave,

as well as the rubble stone at the base of the north wall of the chancel, may have formed part of the former chapel of Eton. There is also a round-headed door, of uncertain date, in the north wall of the chancel. The remainder of the fabric dates for the most part from the 13th century. The blocked north door and the south door of the nave have roll-and-fillet mouldings and pointed arches. The nave also contains two splayed lancets in the north and south walls, one of the former being blocked. A two-light window in the south wall was inserted in the 14th century. Thirteenth-century features in the chancel include a pointed priest's door, the 2 lancets on the north and south walls, and a piscina with a trefoil head. As in the nave, a two-light window was inserted in the south wall of the chancel in the 14th century. The medieval east window was replaced by a tall round-headed window in the Classical style in 1719, when the gable of the east end was rebuilt by the patron.[17] This was in its turn replaced by the present clumsy triple-lancet window in 1819.[18] The roof, which was ceiled and plastered in 1819,[19] is of king-post construction. It was restored in 1910, when the wall-plates were renewed.[20] A vestry was built to the south of the chancel in 1819.[21]

The pulpit, tester, and clerk's reading desk are early-17th-century work, but the communion table and its rails and the pews in the chancel were made in the later 17th century. The reredos was constructed in 1819[22] from 16th-century linenfold panelling and other panelling of 17th-century date. Its fretted top dates from the 15th century and may have come from a former chancel screen, as may the three oak panels, with small traceried lights, now set against the north wall of the nave. The sanctuary is tiled with medieval encaustic tiles. The plain round font, which is probably of 13th-century date, was replaced by another in 1819,[23] but was later restored to the church.

The church is well furnished with monuments to former lords of the manor. The most notable of these is the life-size oaken effigy of Sir John de Pitchford (d. 1284), resting on an arcaded tomb-chest carved with escutcheons.[24] This is now on the south side of the chancel, but it originally stood on the north side with its feet facing eastwards.[25] Four incised alabaster slabs, now set upright against the

88 See p. 116.
89 Heref. Dioc. Regy., tithe appt.
90 Engelard de Pitchford, Robert de Pitchford (1294–1311), Richard Ottley (1509–20), Roger Ottley (c. 1534–63), Adam Ottley (1746–98), John Davies (1741–2), Charles Walcott (1798–1811): Eyton, vi. 280, 282; T.S.A.S. 4th ser. v. 198, 200; ibid. vi. 303; ibid. vii. 166.
91 T.S.A.S. 3rd ser. i. 262; ibid. xlvii. 28.
92 Lich. Dioc. Regy., B/v 1/65.
93 T.S.A.S. 3rd ser. viii. 39; ibid. xlvii. 28.
94 Ibid. xlvii. 28.
95 Ibid. 3rd ser. viii. 39; ibid. 4th ser. v. 189.
96 Ibid. 4th ser. v. 191, 198.
97 S.P.R. Lich. i (1), intro. p. iii; Lich. Dioc. Regy., B/v 1/77.
98 N.L.W., Pitchford Hall 805; S.P.R. Lich. i (1), 75.
99 T.S.A.S. 4th ser. vi. 303; ibid. vii. 66.
1 Visit. Archd. Salop. 1799; S.P.R. Lich. i (1), 101–2, 108.
2 S.P.R. Lich. i (1), 108.
3 Hearth Tax, 1672, 131.
4 Visit. Archd. Salop. 1823; Lich. Dioc. Regy., glebe terrier, 1824.
5 Ex inf. Mrs. M. I. Davies, Rectory Farm.

6 Ex inf. Church Com.
7 S.P.L., MS. 2, f. 226.
8 T.S.A.S. 3rd ser. x. 374.
9 Par. rec., par. bk.
10 Visit. Archd. Salop. 1799, 1823, 1843.
11 Ibid. 1823.
12 Ibid.
13 Ibid. 1799; H.O. 129/359/1/11.
14 S.P.R. Lich. i (1), 103.
15 Par. rec., faculty, 1910.
16 Description of church based, except where otherwise stated, on S.P.L., MS. 372, vol. 1, p. 83; S.P.L., T. F. Dukes watercolours (churches), no. 123; S.P.L., J. H. Smith collect. no. 157; par. rec., faculty, 1910; Cranage, vi. 501–5; Pevsner, Shropshire, 227.
17 S.P.R. Lich. i (1), 73.
18 Ibid. 103.
19 Ibid.
20 Par. rec., faculty, 1910.
21 S.P.R. Lich. i (1), 103.
22 Ibid.   23 Ibid.
24 Detailed account in T.S.A.S. liii 186–97. See also plate facing p. 55.
25 Ibid. 186.

walls of the chancel, lay on the floor until 1819.[26] They commemorate members of the Ottley family, 1529–87, the two latest, signed by John Tarbrook of Bewdley, having been made in 1587. There are hatchments to other members of the Ottley family in the nave.

The church had 2 bells in 1553,[27] but these were replaced by a single bell in 1799.[28] The plate, which comprised a silver chalice and paten in 1553,[29] now includes a silver chalice and paten of 1613 and 2 plated alms dishes.[30] The latter were given in memory of the Revd. Adam Ottley (d. 1798).[31] There was another chalice in the church in 1823 in addition to 2 further patens and a silver flagon.[32] The registers are complete from 1543.[33]

NONCONFORMITY. In 1635 Francis Browne and Mary Ottley were presented for recusancy,[34] but the latter was privileged as one of the Queen's women, and in the following year a certificate to this effect was issued.[35] No Roman Catholics are recorded in 1676[36] or later. There were two nonconformists in the parish in 1676,[37] but none is recorded in or after 1799.[38]

SCHOOLS. William Hancocks, curate of Frodesley, who was schoolmaster at Pitchford in 1699,[39] kept a school here until at least 1718.[40] The school was being maintained by the Ottley family in 1799.[41] Thirty children attended in 1823[42] and in 1833 the school was financed by the parents and by voluntary contributions;[43] school pence were also being raised in 1847.[44] A new school was built c. 1837 by the lord of the manor,[45] whose property it remained throughout its existence.[46] It was in receipt of a government grant by 1893[47] when school pence had been abolished.[48] Attendances of 24 are recorded in 1871,[49] 45 in 1880,[50] and 35 in 1913.[51] The school was closed in 1955, when the ten remaining pupils were transferred to Acton Burnell school.[52]

Between 30 and 40 children attended a Sunday school, 1810–14.[53] This was supported by the rector and the lord of the manor, and reading and writing were taught there.[54]

CHARITIES. Lucy Ottley and Sir Adam Ottley, by wills dated 1687 and 1693 respectively, gave a total of £70 to the poor.[55] In 1786 this sum, together with a parish stock of £20, was vested in the lord of the manor, who paid £5 a year to the parish. Charles Jenkinson, to whom the manor passed in 1807, alleged that the payment was made in lieu of performing parish offices, and ceased to pay it after 1815, when he served as overseer.

CHURCH PREEN

THE parish of Church Preen, which contains 1,174 a.,[1] lies on the southern slope of the Kenley ridge. Its northern boundary runs along the crest of the ridge, while its eastern and part of its southern boundary follow the course of tributaries of Hughley Brook. On the west and south-west an irregular boundary divides Church Preen from the townships of Broome and Holt Preen, in Cardington parish. The latter township seems to have lain in the parish of Church Preen until the 13th century.[2] The parish boundary followed its present course in 1754.[3]

Boulder clay covers the south-eastern half of the parish, where the ground rises gently from 375 feet at Hughley Brook to some 500 feet at Holly Grove. The land then rises sharply to some 900 feet in the west of the parish. The village stands at 700 feet on the steep slope which marks the eastern edge of the Kenley and Caradoc shales which cover the north-west of the parish; a situation similar to that of the adjoining village of Kenley.

The existing roads in the west of the parish are all ancient, but a road running southwards towards Holt Preen has gone out of use since 1817. The straight roads in the flat, eastern, half of the parish followed their present course by 1750,[4] but there were a number of other roads here before the inclosure of the Common.[5]

Surviving traces of ridge-and-furrow indicate that the common fields lay on boulder clay between the village and the Common—the area of the Park—and to the west of the village, near Highlands Farm. The common field in the latter area was called Clawley Field in 1754,[6] but the names of the other fields are not known. As late as 1762 Manor Farm

[26] S.P.R. Lich. i (1), 103.
[27] T.S.A.S. 2nd ser. xii. 319.
[28] Walters, Ch. Bells Salop. 222.
[29] T.S.A.S. 2nd ser. xii. 319.
[30] Arkwright and Bourne, Ch. Plate Ludlow Archd. 49.
[31] Ibid.
[32] Visit. Archd. Salop. 1823.
[33] Printed, 1558–1812, in S.P.R. Lich. i (1), 43–108. A paper register, 1543–87, is now N.R.A., Pitchford Hall, Z 1/1.
[34] Lich. Dioc. Regy., B/v 1/65.
[35] Ibid. 1/60.
[36] T.S.A.S. 2nd ser. i. 81.
[37] Ibid.
[38] Visit. Archd. Salop. 1799 1843.
[39] Lich. Dioc. Regy., B/v 1/90.
[40] Ibid. 1/90, 1/93, 1/95.
[41] Visit. Archd. Salop. 1799.
[42] Ibid. 1823.
[43] Educ. Enquiry Abstract, H.C. 62, p. 780 (1835), xlii.
[44] Nat. Soc. Ch. School Returns, 1846–7.
[45] Ed. 7/102/189.
[46] Ibid.; Voluntary Schs. Returns, H.C. 178–XXIV, p. 24 (1906), lxxxviii.
[47] Return of Schs., 1893 [C. 7529], p. 510, H.C. (1894), lxv.
[48] Ibid.
[49] Returns relating to Elem. Educ., H.C. 201, p. 334 (1871), lv.
[50] Kelly's Dir. Salop. (1880).
[51] Ibid. (1913).
[52] Ex inf. S.C.C. Educ. Dept.
[53] N.R.A., Pitchford Hall, Z 3/1–4.
[54] Ibid.
[55] Account of charities based on 24th Rep. Com. Char., H.C. 231, p. 388 (1831), xi.
[1] O.S. Area Bk. (1883). The following topographical description is based, except where otherwise stated, on O.S. Map 1″, sheet lxi (1st edn.); O.S. Maps 6″ Salop. 49, 50 (1st and later edns.); O.S. Map 1/25,000, SO 59 (1959); Rocque, Map of Salop. (1752); Baugh, Map of Salop. (1808); Greenwood, Map of Salop. (1827); B.M. O.S. 2″ orig. drawings, sheet 207 (1817); Geol. Survey Map (drift), sheet 152 (1932). This article was written in 1963 and revised in 1965.
[2] See p. 127.
[3] S.R.O. 1011 uncat., perambulation of bounds, 1754.
[4] Ibid. 283/1.
[5] S.P.L., Deeds 6232.
[6] S.R.O. 1011 uncat., ct. r. 1754.

included 22 a. of unclosed land in Preen Town Field.[7]

The manor contained woodland for 100 swine in 1086,[8] but some of this lay in Holt Preen. The coppices along the southern boundary, adjoining Holt Preen, and Big Wood, to the north of the Park, are probably ancient woodland and have changed little in extent since 1817. The high ground north of the village was mainly rough pasture until it was brought into cultivation during the Second World War.

Preen Common[9] extended over the relatively flat land in the east of the parish, where natural drainage was poor, and adjoined Kenley Common on the east. It was said to contain 200 a. in 1727[10] and in 1750 its western boundary ran between the North Lodge of the Park, New House, Holly Grove, and Brook House. In addition to a number of small inclosures by cottagers, some 45 a. in the south of the Common was inclosed in the early 18th century by the lord of the manor, who was, however, more interested in exploiting the mineral resources of the Common.[11] The inhabitants of Hughley claimed common rights in Preen Common. In return they ground the corn of the lord of Preen manor at Hughley mill, and allowed Preen tenants to make use of the Hughley town bull and boar. The lady of the manor gave notice of her intention to inclose the Common in 1779, but inclosure does not appear to have taken place until the 1790s. The park is first recorded in 1881, when it contained 110 a.,[12] and was probably laid out by Arthur Sparrow c. 1870, when he rebuilt the manor-house.

As in Kenley the history of settlement in Church Preen is one of dispersal from a hill village to the more fertile boulder clay of the lower ground to the east. The original settlement clustered round the church, bounded on the north and south by two tributaries of Hughley Brook which unite east of the village.

There is now no trace of the Priory, which ran at right angles from the south wall of the church. It appears to have remained unaltered as the manor-house until the later 18th century, when a south wing was added in the same style as the church.[13] The upper part of the Priory was probably pulled down shortly after 1826, when a terrace was formed over the remainder and a new house erected to the west.[14] The whole was demolished in 1870, when a new manor-house was built to designs by Norman Shaw,[15] but much of this was in its turn pulled

down in 1921–2.[16] A smaller house, erected on the site in the 1930s,[17] was being enlarged in 1964. Manor Farm and Preen Cottage, the only remaining large houses in the village, both date from the 19th century. The former was originally timber-framed, but was rebuilt in stone shortly after it was bought by its tenant in 1820.[18] Apart from 6 Council houses built since 1945[19] the few remaining houses in the village are all of stone, and Spout House is the only one likely to have been built before the 18th century. There were 2 alehouses in the parish in 1616,[20] one of them kept by the Mullard family, who kept an alehouse here until 1752.[21]

Settlement on Preen Common is ill-documented until the 18th century, but there were already two cottages in Preen Wood in 1557.[22] By 1750 there were 15 cottages on the Common,[23] but a number of these had ceased to be occupied by 1811, when there were only 13 houses in the whole parish.[24] Several of the houses were originally small stone-built cottages with gable chimney-stacks, like those on Kenley Common, but all have subsequently been enlarged. Pool Farm and New House were rebuilt in brick in the 19th century. The shift in the balance of settlement was recognized in 1872, when the school was built in the centre of the Common.[25]

The population of the parish, 83 in 1793,[26] had fallen to 73 by 1821,[27] but rose in the later 19th century, reaching a peak of 119 in 1871.[28] It declined steadily from 1901 until 1951, when it stood at 71,[29] but had risen to 89 by 1961.[30]

MANOR. Edwin, a free man, held the manor of *CHURCH PREEN* before 1066.[31] In 1086 Helgot held it of Roger, Earl of Shrewsbury.[32] The suzerainty of the Earls of Shrewsbury presumably lapsed after 1102,[33] but Helgot's successors as lords of Castle Holgate[34] retained their overlordship until the 16th century.[35] The manor had been withdrawn from the jurisdiction of the Condover Hundred court by Richard, Earl of Cornwall, c. 1256[36] and its tenants owed suit at Castle Holgate until the 19th century.[37]

The tenant in 1086 was one Richard,[38] probably Richard de Belmeis,[39] but the manor had been granted before 1163 to Wenlock Priory.[40] The monastic cell, later known as the Priory of Preen, which was already in existence at this time,[41] was accounted part of the temporalities of Wenlock Priory in 1291,[42] but later seems to have acquired some degree of independence. The manor is not

[7] Ibid. 93/140.
[8] *V.C.H. Salop.* i. 337.
[9] Account of common based, except where otherwise stated, on S.P.L., Deeds 6232, 12460; S.R.O. 283/1.
[10] A. Sparrow, *The History of Church Preen* (1898), 124.
[11] See p. 127.
[12] *Kelly's Dir. Salop.* (1881).
[13] Sparrow, *Ch. Preen*, 70.
[14] W.S.L. 350/40/3. House illustrated in Sparrow, *Ch. Preen*, facing pp. 24, 40.
[15] Sparrow, *Ch. Preen*, 66–69. Architect's drawing in ibid. facing p. 16.
[16] Ex inf. Lt. Col. A. Hanbury-Sparrow.
[17] *Kelly's Dir. Salop.* (1937).
[18] W.S.L. 350/40/3.
[19] Ex inf. Atcham R.D.C.
[20] Q. Sess., alehouse reg.
[21] N.L.W., Castle Hill 2244.
[22] *Cat. Anct. D.* iii, A 5402.
[23] S.P.L., Deeds 6232.
[24] *Census*, 1811.

[25] See p. 128.
[26] B.M. Add. MS. 21018, f. 196.
[27] *Census*, 1821.
[28] Ibid. 1831–71.
[29] Ibid. 1881–1951.
[30] Ibid. 1961.
[31] *V.C.H. Salop.* i. 337.
[32] Ibid.
[33] Eyton, vii. 290–10, 220–2.
[34] Ibid. iv. 52–69.
[35] *Rot. Hund.* (Rec. Com.), ii. 62; *Cal. Inq. Misc.* i, p. 507; *Cal. Pat.* 1292–1301, 594; *L. & P. Hen. VIII*, xvi, p. 240; C.P. 25(2)/35/234.
[36] *Rot. Hund.* (Rec. Com.), ii. 62.
[37] Sparrow, *Ch. Preen*, 32; S.P.L., Deeds 6232, 10194.
[38] *V.C.H. Salop.* i. 337.
[39] Eyton, i. 149; ibid. vi. 221.
[40] *Ep. Gilbert Foliot*, ed. J. A. Giles (Oxford, 1845), i. 185.
[41] Ibid.
[42] *Tax. Eccl.* (Rec. Com.), 164.

mentioned in later estate records of Wenlock Priory. In 1590 evidence was given to prove that the Prior of Preen had exercised manorial rights, since he had held courts and had granted leases sealed with his own seal. Other witnesses, however, made it clear that he was subordinate to the Prior of Wenlock.[43]

Preen Priory was surrendered by the Prior of Wenlock to the Crown in 1534.[44] The manor was still in Crown hands in 1536,[45] but was shortly afterwards granted to Giles Covert.[46] Covert was succeeded in 1559 by his brother Richard,[47] who sold the manor to Humphrey Dickens in the following year.[48] Members of the Dickens family held the manor until 1749,[49] when it was sold by the mortgagees of John Dickens to Elizabeth Price.[50] The latter was still living in 1779,[51] but had been succeeded before 1784[52] by her sister Sarah, widow of John Windsor of Harnage Grange.[53] On Sarah's death in 1794 the manor passed to her son E. C. Windsor and his two sisters, one of whom, Sarah Windsor, subsequently became sole owner.[54] She died in 1815 and, after her nephew and heir Captain E. C. Windsor was killed at Waterloo, the manor passed to his brother John Windsor.[55] In 1826 the manor was sold to William Webster,[56] whose grandson F. T. Webster sold it to W. H. Sparrow in 1848.[57] It was held by W. H. Sparrow, 1848–67,[58] Arthur Sparrow, 1867–98[59] and Cecil Sparrow, 1898–c. 1904.[60] The estate was sold by the Sparrow trustees to John Todd c. 1919[61] and has since been dispersed by sale.

ECONOMIC HISTORY. The manor was worth 20s. in 1066, but was said to be waste when received by its Norman lord and was worth only 10s. in 1086.[62] It was assessed at 3 hides in 1086[63] and at 2 hides in 1254,[64] when Holt Preen had become a separate manor. It was worth £8 3s. 4d. a year in 1291[65] and £7 3s. 4d. in 1371.[66] The demesne, sufficient for one plough in 1086,[67] seems to have doubled its size by 1291, when it was said to comprise 2 carucates.[68] Hay from the demesne meadows was then valued at 10s. and there was a manorial dovecote, but the small number of livestock (2 cows and 2 sows)[69] suggests that the great part of the demesne had already been leased. By 1371 the area

of demesne land had again fallen to one carucate.[70] Henry Clerk, described as a franklin in 1379,[71] may have been the lessee of the demesne. Before 1534 part of the priory and demesne had been leased to Robert Weaver,[72] who is said to have refused an offer to purchase the manor.[73] Richard Lee seems to have been farmer of the demesne until the manor was purchased by Humphrey Dickens.[74] Until the Park was formed in the later 19th century, none of the manorial estate appears to have been kept in hand. In 1820 Manor Farm (368 a.) presumably representing the former demesne, was held on a 3-life lease by Thomas Minton,[75] to whom it was sold later in the same year.[76] The farm was bought back into the manorial estate in 1873.[77]

Land sufficient for 3 ploughs was held by the tenants in 1086.[78] Since there were then four serfs on the demesne,[79] the labour services of the remaining tenants must have been light. In 1291 their works were worth only 5s., while they paid £5 in rents.[80] In 1371 they were all described as free tenants and paid 10 marks rent a year.[81] Four tenants claimed to be freeholders in 1256, but 2 of them were shown to be leasehold tenants of Wenlock Priory and the only tenant to prove his case later surrendered his lands to the Priory.[82] Three other free tenants are recorded between 1270 and 1296.[83] All but one of these 13th-century freeholds were of a half-virgate or less, and the comparative poverty of those assessed to the taxations of 1327[84] and 1332[85] suggests that their holdings were small. There is no later evidence of other freehold estates in the parish, apart from 70 a., held by the Earl of Bradford in the later 19th century, which was presumably allotted to him as lord of Hughley manor at the inclosure of the Common.[86]

At the dissolution of Preen Priory there were 12 leasehold and copyhold tenants, most of whom held for terms of 61 or 81 years.[87] The right of the Prior of Preen to grant leases was later called into question and at least 7 tenants renewed their leases on counsel's advice between 1578 and 1582.[88] The whole estate was held on 3-life leases until the later 18th century, when it was said to yield not a third of its true annual value.[89] By 1820 only Manor Farm was held on a 3-life lease, the other 3 farms being held by tenants-at-will.[90]

[43] E 134/32 Eliz. I Hil./1; Sparrow, Ch. Preen, 70–104.
[44] Sparrow, Ch. Preen, 30.
[45] Reg. C. Bothe (C. & Y.S.), ii. 369.
[46] Sparrow, Ch. Preen, 76, 79, 89.
[47] Ibid. 41.
[48] C.P. 25(2)/200/2 Eliz. I Hil.
[49] For pedigree see Sparrow, Ch. Preen, 40–46; S.P.L., Deeds 6231; C 78/1325 no. 4.
[50] Sparrow, Ch. Preen, 45.
[51] S.P.L., Deeds 12460.
[52] Instit. Dioc. Heref. 116.
[53] Sparrow, Ch. Preen, 54.
[54] Ibid. 55.
[55] Ibid.
[56] Ibid.
[57] Ibid.
[58] Ibid.
[59] Ibid.
[60] Ex inf. Lt. Col. A. Hanbury-Sparrow.
[61] Ibid.
[62] V.C.H. Salop. i. 337.
[63] Ibid.
[64] Rot. Hund. (Rec. Com.), ii. 62.
[65] Tax. Eccl. (Rec. Com.), 164.

[66] Sparrow, Ch. Preen, 19.
[67] V.C.H. Salop. i. 337.
[68] Tax. Eccl. (Rec. Com.), 164.
[69] Ibid.
[70] Sparrow, Ch. Preen, 19.
[71] E 179/242/33.
[72] Sparrow, Ch. Preen, 77.
[73] Ibid. 79.
[74] T.S.A.S. 2nd ser. xii. 100; Sta. Cha. 4/8/56.
[75] Sparrow, Ch. Preen, 131–2.
[76] Ibid. 55–56.
[77] Ibid.
[78] V.C.H. Salop. i. 337.
[79] Ibid.
[80] Tax. Eccl. (Rec. Com.), 164.
[81] Sparrow, Ch. Preen, 19.
[82] Eyton, vi. 221–3.
[83] Ibid. 223.
[84] T.S.A.S. 2nd ser. xi. 389.
[85] E 179/166/2 m. 5.
[86] Kelly's Dir. Salop. (1856–1900).
[87] Sparrow, Ch. Preen, 77–102 passim.
[88] Ibid.
[89] B.M. Add. MS. 21018, f. 196.
[90] Sparrow, Ch. Preen, 131–2.

Little is known of the economic condition of the cottagers on Preen Common. In the early 18th century they appear to have been benevolently treated by the lord of the manor, and by the other farmers in the parish, who helped the cottagers with their ploughing to keep them off the rates.[91] They were, however, persecuted by the men of Hughley, nicknamed 'the Hughley Lions', who threatened to break open the cottagers' inclosures unless they worked for them at harvest-time.[92] In 1793, when few of the cottagers had cows and they were selling their hay to pay the rent, their diet consisted chiefly of potatoes.[93]

The estate was heavily encumbered when John Dickens succeeded to the manor in the early 18th century. In 1708 he alleged that he had been at great charges in improving his estates at Church Preen and Leaton and had increased their annual value from £90 to £150.[94] The gross rental of the Preen estate was £114 a year in 1712,[95] and the tenants of two farms whose leases were renewed in 1708 paid entry fines totalling £1,000.[96] After his power to renew leases was restricted in 1711,[97] Dickens resorted to other means of increasing the value of the estate. In 1727 he attempted to float a company to exploit the mineral resources of the manor, offering a thousand £100 shares in the form of 21-year leases. He claimed to have discovered salt, coal, and ironstone on the Common and had already collected materials for building an iron furnace.[98] Shortly afterwards he was imprisoned for debt[99] and the scheme was abandoned.

The greater part of the parish is, and seems always to have been, devoted to pasture. There were said to be only 200 a. arable in 1801, when the principal crops were wheat and oats.[1]

The manor contained a mill in 1291[2] and a miller is recorded in 1327.[3] Apart from a wheelwright, who was in business between 1870 and 1905,[4] no other tradesmen are recorded.

LOCAL GOVERNMENT. There are no surviving manorial records, apart from a few suit rolls and presentments, 1749–81,[5] and no parish records other than registers.

CHURCH. The Priory of Church Preen had been founded by 1163, when it was already a cell of

Wenlock Priory.[6] There is no reason to accept Eyton's assertion[7] that Church Preen was originally a chapelry of Cardington. It was described as belonging to the church of Cardington c. 1587,[8] but presumably only because the same incumbent then served both parishes. Both Church Preen and Holt Preen were members of the Domesday manor of Preen[9] and, although Holt Preen manor subsequently followed a separate descent, the lords of both manors shared the advowson until 1244.[10]

Since the dissolution of the priory the living has been a perpetual curacy, but its incumbents have been styled vicars since 1869. It was united in 1927 with Hughley,[11] whose rectors had normally served Church Preen since 1852.[12] The advowson was vested in 1244[13] in Wenlock Priory, whose power to appoint priors was, however, subject to the control of the lords of Castle Holgate as patrons of Preen Priory.[14] After the Dissolution the advowson and rectory followed the descent of the manor until 1926, when the advowson was vested in the Bishop of Hereford.[15]

The curate received an annual stipend of 4 marks c. 1587,[16] and a stipend of £6 was paid him by the lord of the manor between 1655 and the mid-19th century.[17] The value of the living was augmented by grants totalling £1,000 made by Queen Anne's Bounty between 1746 and 1829,[18] and by a Parliamentary grant of £200, made in 1810.[19] Part of these grants was spent on the purchase of 33 a. glebe in Clunton, Clunbury, and Oswestry,[20] and the annual income of the living was said to be £70 in 1831.[21] The glebe was worth £28 a year in 1851, when £22 8s. 6d. a year was derived from other investments.[22] A cottage, called Our Lady House, and lands given to maintain a light in the church were disposed of by the Crown in 1564.[23]

John Corfield, the first recorded perpetual curate,[24] who was a member of a prominent family in the parish,[25] seems to have lived at Church Preen.[26] Henry Willis (curate c. 1685–98)[27] was buried there,[28] and William Webster (curate 1827–43)[29] lived in the manor-house.[30] Since there was no parsonage and the value of the living was so low, most curates held the living in plurality.[31] Fifteen out of 20 curates, 1689–1929, are known to have held other livings for the greater part of their incumbencies. Only 4 curates remained here for

91 S.P.L., Deeds 6232.
92 Ibid.
93 B.M. Add. MS. 21018, f. 196.
94 C 78/1325 no. 4.
95 S.P.L., MS. 4423.
96 S.P.L., Deeds 6231; C 78/1325 no. 4.
97 C 78/1325 no. 4.
98 Prospectus, 1727, in Sparrow, *Ch. Preen*, 123–30. cf. S.P.L., Deeds 6232; S.R.O. 283/1.
99 S.P.L., Deeds 6232.
1 H.O. 67/12/194.
2 *Tax. Eccl.* (Rec. Com.), 164.
3 *T.S.A.S.* 2nd ser. xi. 389.
4 *Kelly's Dir. Salop.* (1870–1905).
5 S.R.O. 1011 uncat.
6 *Ep. Gilbert Foliot*, ed. J. A. Giles (Oxford, 1845), i. 185.
7 Eyton, vi. 223–4.
8 *T.S.A.S.* xlvi. 44.
9 *V.C.H. Salop.* i. 337.
10 *T.S.A.S.* 4th ser. vi. 183–4.
11 Heref. Dioc. Regy., reg. 1926–38, p. 28.
12 Sparrow, *Ch. Preen*, 27–28.
13 *T.S.A.S.* 4th ser. vi. 183–4.

14 *Cal. Inq. Misc.* i, p. 507; *Cal. Pat.* 1292–1301, 595; Sparrow, *Ch. Preen*, 19.
15 Heref. Dioc. Regy., reg. 1919–26, p. 431.
16 *T.S.A.S.* xlvi. 44.
17 Ibid. xlvii. 28; Heref. Dioc. Regy., visitation papers, box 18, churchwardens' presentment, 1663; B.M. Add. MS. 21018, f. 196.
18 C. Hodgson, *Queen Anne's Bounty* (1845), 290.
19 Ibid.
20 *Return of glebe*, H.C. 307, p. 69 (1887), lxiv; B.M. Add. MS. 21018, f. 196.
21 *Rep. Com. Eccl. Revenues* [67], pp. 448–9, H.C. (1835), xxii.   22 H.O. 129/359/1/7.
23 E 178/3075; E 310/23/123 f. 108.
24 *T.S.A.S.* 1st ser. vi. 104.
25 Sparrow, *Ch. Preen*, 47–54.
26 Will, 1548, in ibid. 23–25.
27 *S.P.R. Heref.* xvi (1), 3–8.   28 Ibid. 10.
29 *Instit. Dioc. Heref.* 148, 160.
30 B.M. Add. MS. 21018, f. 197.
31 What follows is based on *Instit. Dioc. Heref., passim*; *S.P.R. Heref.* xvi (1), intro. p. iv; Sparrow, *Ch. Preen*, 25–28; *Kelly's Dir. Salop.* (1917–29); B.M. Add. MS. 21018, ff. 196–7.

A HISTORY OF SHROPSHIRE

more than 20 years in this period, while 13 served for fewer than 9 years. Most of them seem to have served in person, but Joseph Plymley (curate 1784–1815) employed a succession of assistant curates. G. P. Lowther (curate 1822–7) and William Webster were the only curates who were close relatives of the lord of the manor. Services were held once a month in the later 17th century[32] and once a fortnight in the earlier 18th century.[33] In Plymley's time services were held fortnightly in summer, and once a month in winter, when bad roads made the village inaccessible;[34] communion was then celebrated 4 times a year.[35] By 1851 conditions had improved. Robert Armitage (curate, 1843–52),[36] who was also Rector of Easthope,[37] took services at Preen alternately in the morning and afternoon, and an average of 65 persons attended[38] out of a total population of 77.[39]

The church of *ST. JOHN THE BAPTIST*[40] comprises a nave and chancel of roughly equal size. The unusual dimensions of the church, which is 70 feet long and only 13 feet wide, are presumably the result of the adaptation of a small parish church to the needs of a monastic community. A carefully executed sketch of the church made in 1787 shows that the nave wall was then slightly higher than that of the chancel and that there was a distinct break in the north wall at their junction. The nave is the earlier of the two and dates from the 12th century. Its north door formerly had a round arch and its only window on the north wall was a small square-headed one, probably of the same date. The chancel probably dates from the mid-13th century. In the triple-lancet east window all the lancets are of the same size and are united inside beneath a single segmental rear arch. There are 3 lancet windows on the north wall, of which the most westerly, near the junction with the nave, is a low side-window.

The only significant addition to the church between the 13th and 19th centuries was the north porch, probably built in the 17th century. During the restoration of the church in 1866 the west wall and the wooden bell-turret above collapsed. The wall was rebuilt in the style of its predecessor, but the bell turret was replaced by a gabled stone bellcote containing 2 bells. At the same time a vestry was built to the north-west of the nave and the north door and most of the windows were restored. A battlemented chamber, intended as a vault, was built on the south wall of the chancel in the 1930s.

The interior has been considerably altered since 1866, but in the early 19th century a number of

medieval features remained. Traces of the carved rood screen which divided the chancel and nave were standing c. 1830 but had disappeared by 1848, and a simple mural decoration of red and yellow lines could still be seen at the end of the 19th century. There was said to be a well preserved floor of encaustic tiles in 1856.[41] A panelled oak ceiling, then in an advanced state of decay, was removed in 1866, when the present roof was built and new pews were installed.

The existing font is modern, but there is a large square font-bowl in the north porch and a small round one in the chamber to the south of the chancel. The oak pulpit and parish chest are of 17th-century date. The choir stalls contain 17th-century carved oak panelling, presumably from pews, and the reading desk is made up of similar materials, including panels dated 1641 and 1646.

There are now 2 bells, as there were in 1552.[42] One dates from the later 15th century, but the other was recast by Thomas Rudhall in 1779.[43] The plate comprises a silver chalice and paten of c. 1630 and a chalice and 2 patens of 19th-century date.[44] The registers are complete from 1680.[45] The yew tree in the churchyard is one of the largest in England.[46]

NONCONFORMITY. None known.

SCHOOLS. Two unsuccessful attempts were made to start a Sunday school in the parish in the early 19th century,[47] and there was no day school until 1872. Children attended a school on Kenley Common c. 1788[48] and in 1846 were going to Stanton Long.[49] In 1872 a school was built at the cross-roads on Preen Common by the lord of the manor to designs by Norman Shaw.[50] The school remained the property of the Sparrow family until 1919, when it was purchased by the County Council.[51] School-pence were being levied on a graduated scale in 1872, but had been abolished by 1893, when about half of the school's income came from voluntary contributions and half from a government grant.[52] Attendances, which fluctuated between 20 and 40 in the later 19th century,[53] had fallen to 14 by 1926, when the County Council made an unsuccessful attempt to close the school.[54] A new school was built in 1962.[55]

CHARITIES. None known.

---

[32] Heref. Dioc. Regy., visitation papers, box 18, churchwardens' presentment, 1663.
[33] Ibid. box 69, churchwardens' presentment, 1716; ibid. box 68, churchwardens' presentment, 1719.
[34] Sparrow, *Ch. Preen*, 26.
[35] Ibid.
[36] *Instit. Dioc. Heref.* 160, 167.
[37] Ibid. 159, 167.
[38] H.O. 129/359/1/7.
[39] *Census*, 1851.
[40] Description of church based, except where otherwise stated, on Cranage, vi. 470–3; Sparrow, *Ch. Preen*, 107–14: W.S.L. 350/40/3; S.P.L., MS. 372, vol. i, p. 35; S.P.L., J. H. Smith collect. no. 50.
[41] *Kelly's Dir. Salop.* (1856).
[42] *T.S.A.S.* 2nd ser. xii. 100.
[43] Walters, *Ch. Bells Salop.* 87–88.
[44] Arkwright and Bourne, *Ch. Plate Ludlow Archd.* 18.
[45] Printed to 1812 in *S.P.R. Heref.* xvi (1).
[46] For measurements see Sparrow, *Ch. Preen*, 119–22.
[47] B.M. Add. MS. 21018, f. 196.
[48] Ibid.
[49] Nat. Soc. *Ch. School Returns*, 1846–7.
[50] Ed. 7/102/52; *Kelly's Dir. Salop.* (1885). See plate facing p. 83.
[51] *S.C.C. Minutes*, 1919–20, p. 74.
[52] *Return of Schs.* 1893 [C. 7529], p. 504, H.C. (1894), lxv.
[53] Ibid.; Ed. 7/102/52; *Voluntary Schs. Returns*, H.C. 178–XXVI, p. 20 (1906), lxxxviii; *Kelly's Dir. Salop.* (1885–1900).
[54] *S.C.C. Minutes (Educ.)*, 1926–7, pp. 66, 120, 272.
[55] Ex inf. S.C.C. Educ. Dept.

CHURCH PULVERBATCH

THE parish of Church Pulverbatch lies on rising ground in the northern foothills of the Long Mynd. It contains 4,283 a.[1] and comprises the townships of Church Pulverbatch (known locally, since at least the 13th century,[2] as Churton), Castle Pulverbatch, Cothercott, Wilderley, and Wrentnall.

The parish boundary in part follows streams; Habberley Brook on the west, Ipkins[3] (or Walleybourne) Brook on the north, and Wilderley Brook on the south-east. On the east, however, and over Wilderley and Cothercott Hills to the south, it passes through former woodland and does not make use of natural features. The eastern boundary with Stapleton, although determined in 1385,[4] was in dispute in the later 16th century.[5] It was not settled until 1610,[6] when an area known as 'the Challenge Land', between Castle Place and Churton Brook, was transferred to Pulverbatch. To the south of Churton Brook the parish boundary follows the bounds of Wilderley and Stapleton manors, laid out in 1227.[7] The southern boundary was not determined until the inclosure of the Long Mynd, c. 1790.[8] An anomalous projection of the boundary in the south-west corner of the parish, taking in Bank Farm and part of Paulith Bank, was still accounted part of the township of Stitt and Gatten, in Ratlinghope parish, in 1839.[9] This presumably represents the portion of Stiperstones Forest granted to the lord of Pulverbatch manor in 1314.[10]

Besides Ipkins and Wilderley Brooks two other tributaries of the River Cound flow from west to east across the lower, northern, half of the parish. Along them ran most of the internal boundaries between the townships. Wildbach Brook,[11] flowing from Broom Hill towards Moat Farm, Stapleton, was the boundary between Wrentnall and Church Pulverbatch, while Churton Brook divided Church and Castle Pulverbatch on the north from Cothercott and Wilderley on the south. The boundary between Cothercott and Wilderley ran along the road to Sheppen Fields, and that between Church and Castle Pulverbatch was the valley to the east of the road from Shrewsbury to Bishop's Castle.

Over the east and north of the parish the land rises gently from 400 feet in the north-east to some 650 feet near the villages of Church Pulverbatch and Wrentnall and the sites of the former hamlets of Wilderley and Walleybourne. Castle Pulverbatch stands at 700 feet, the only hill village being Cothercott (800 feet) on the north-eastern slopes of Cothercott Hill. The landscape in the west of the parish is dominated by a northward projection of the Long Mynd, comprising Broom Hill (950 feet),

Lawn and Huglith Hills (1,050 feet), and Paulith Bank (1,263 feet), and forming the watershed between Habberley Brook to the west and the Cound tributaries to the east. South of Wilderley and Cothercott rise the steep slopes of Wilderley and Cothercott Hills, the latter reaching 1,450 feet at its summit near the Thresholds.

The parish is ill-endowed with light gravelly soil, which occurs in significant quantities only in the lower reaches of Wildbach Brook and on the low hill between Wrentnall and Walleybourne. Longmyndian shales and grits underlie the thin soils of the high ground to the west and south. Between Wildbach and Churton Brooks in the centre of the parish is an eastward projection of similar character, forming the promontories on which Church and Castle Pulverbatch stand. Cothercott stands on a glacial moraine, which probably accounts for its unusual site. Boulder clay extends over the lower land in the rest of the parish, thus covering the greater part of the townships of Wilderley and Wrentnall and the land to the east of Habberley Brook. The Coal Measures underlying the eastern boulder clay were mined in the 18th and 19th centuries[12] and, with the clearance of the woodland which once covered this part of the parish, the almost unworkable local gritstone became the normal building material here in the 18th and early 19th centuries.

Although the parish contained six ancient townships, the greater part of its area was covered by forest until the later 16th century. Steplewood, on the eastern clays, extended into Stapleton and Pontesbury parishes and Wilderley Wood, its southern continuation, ran southwards from Wilderley Brook into the foothills of the Long Mynd. Woods known as Walleybourne Wood, Broom Hill, and Over and Nether Huglith lay on the clay flanking the range of hills in the west of the parish. Extensive commons on Wilderley and Cothercott Hills were not inclosed until the Second World War.[13]

Steplewood, bounded on the north by Ipkins Brook and on the south by Wilderley Brook,[14] probably ran during the Middle Ages as far west as the main road to Shrewsbury, where the field-name Hayside, north of Black Lion Farm, indicates former woodland.[15] A field called the Broach, south-west of Churton Cottage, suggests that the wood once extended to within a few yards of Church Pulverbatch village.[16] A bailiwick of the Long Forest until withdrawn from its jurisdiction in 1250,[17] Steplewood was said in 1235 to have been much wasted in the past,[18] but few assarts are

---

[1] O.S. *Area Bk.* (1882). The following topographical description is based, except where otherwise stated, on O.S. Map 1″ sheet lxi (1st edn.); O.S. Maps 6″ Salop. 40, 41, 48 (1st and later edns.); O.S. Maps 1/25,000 SO 49 (1956), SO 30, SJ 40 (1957); Rocque, *Map of Salop.* (1752); Baugh, *Map of Salop.* (1808); B.M. O.S. 2″ orig. drawings, sheets 199 (1816), 207 (1817); Geol. Survey Map (drift), sheet 152 (1932); par. rec., Pulverbatch and Wrentnall tithe appt. 1839, and map, 1840; ibid. Cothercott and Wilderley tithe appt. 1839, and map, 1840. This article was written in 1964 and revised in 1965.
[2] S.P.L., Haughmond Cart. f. 169ᵛ.
[3] S.P.L., Deeds 6848B, depositions, c. 1595.
[4] *Cal. Inq. Misc.* iv, p. 177.

[5] C 3/7/22; S.P.L., Deeds, 6848B, depositions, c. 1595.
[6] S.P.L., Deeds 6873.
[7] S.P.L., Haughmond Cart., f. 229.
[8] S.P.L., Deeds 6579.
[9] Par. rec., tithe appts.
[10] S.R.O. 482/6.
[11] S.P.L., Plans 47.
[12] See p. 137.
[13] Ex inf. Mr. J. Shakeshaft, Underhill Hall, Smethcott.
[14] S.P.L., Deeds 6848B.
[15] Par. rec., tithe appts.
[16] Ibid.
[17] Eyton, vi. 340.
[18] Ibid.

recorded there, and its area appears to have changed little between the later 13th century and 1601, when it contained 345 a.[19] In spite of continuous sales of timber and underwood during the later Middle Ages,[20] the wood to the east of Church Pulverbatch was still, in the mid-16th century 'so thick of timber trees and hollies and bushes that one might very hardly find the way'.[21] Butler's, or New, Coppice, along the parish boundary to the north of Castle Place Farm, had been inclosed by 1567[22] and was sold to the Jennings family of Walleybourne in 1578.[23] The remainder of the wood was common to the tenants of Church Pulverbatch and Wrentnall until 1601,[24] common rights in the north of the wood being shared with the tenants of Longden manor after 1283.[25] Steplewood was inclosed c. 1600, when allotments were made to the lord of the manor and the tenants,[26] and in 1611 fences here were broken by the tenants of Stapleton, who claimed rights of common in the wood.[27] The lord of the manor appears to have cleared the remaining timber on his portion of the wood soon after 1619.[28] By 1770 only 6 a. of woodland remained at Starr's Coppice (the former Butler's Coppice).[29] This had been cleared by 1839, when the only surviving areas of woodland within Steplewood were the Gorse (13. a) and small coppices along Wildbach and Churton Brooks.[30]

The field-names Rocking Meadow and the Stocking suggest that the western boundary of Wilderley Wood once lay a little to the east of Wilderley Lane Farm.[31] The wood was said to be sufficient for 100 swine in 1086[32] and to have been recently wasted in 1235,[33] but it had been withdrawn from the jurisdiction of the Long Forest by 1301.[34] Haughmond Abbey, granted free warren here in 1320,[35] seems to have inclosed a portion of the wood, presumably represented by the area known as Abbots Hay,[36] south of Churton Brook on the parish boundary with Stapleton. This was still woodland in 1595,[37] but had been cleared by 1662.[38]

Apart from Huglith the woods in the west of the parish were common to the tenants of Pulverbatch and Wrentnall manors. Walleybourne Wood, the smallest of them, is recorded in the early 13th century.[39] This was probably once the common wood of the former manor of Walleybourne and survived as a 13-acre coppice until 1798.[40] At

Wrentnall, where there was wood for 100 swine in 1086,[41] a common wood called 'Werekwud', recorded between 1235 and 1342,[42] probably lay on Broom Hill. Inclosures had been made on the lower slopes of the hill by 1565, when the wood was said to contain 160 a.[43] Common rights were still enjoyed here c. 1600[44] but the hill had been inclosed by 1615.[45]

Huglith Wood, the greater part of which was held in demesne by the lord of Pulverbatch manor, is first recorded c. 1198[46] and by 1330 it had been divided into two parts,[47] later known as Over and Nether Huglith.[48] The area of the former, which lay on the western slopes of Huglith Hill and Lawn Hill, seems to have been much reduced during the later Middle Ages, for most of it was leased as pasture in the 15th century.[49] Licence was granted to clear underwood on the lower ground and to coppice woodland on the higher ground in 1585.[50] Nether Huglith, in the valley of Habberley Brook, was said to contain 600 a. in the 16th century.[51] It had been leased in 1446 to the tenant of Walleybourne[52] and was probably cleared soon after 1584, when William Jennings of Walleybourne bought all the standing timber.[53] The name Huglith Wood was applied to some 60 a. of woodland on Lawn Hill c. 1780, when the only other surviving portions of the medieval wood were Riddleshill (50 a.) and Brown's Coppice (19 a.).[54] Huglith Wood had been cleared by 1839[55] but the two other woods have survived until the present day.

Common woodland on the eastern slopes of Huglith, bounded on the north by the road from Castle Pulverbatch towards Westcott and on the south by Churton Brook, was inclosed between 1607[56] and 1616.[57] The site of Pulverbatch castle and the Outrack, formerly a drift-way alongside Churton Brook from Castle Pulverbatch to common land on Cothercott Hill, remain common land.[58]

Common rights on Cothercott Hill, enjoyed by the tenants of Church and Castle Pulverbatch since the early 13th century,[59] appear to have been extinguished in 1676, following a dispute with the lord of Wilderley and Cothercott manors.[60] The rights of Cothercott tenants to common on Wilderley and Cothercott Hills were unsuccessfully challenged in 1527 by the inhabitants of Church Stretton, who claimed exclusive rights of common in the whole area outside the common fields of these two town-

[19] S.P.L., Deeds 6848B.
[20] S.R.O. 665 uncat., extracts from ct. r. 1352–1596; ibid. bailiff's accts. 1396–1416.
[21] S.P.L., Deeds 1341B.
[22] S.R.O. 665 uncat., extracts from ct. r. 1352–1596.
[23] Ibid. deed, 1578.
[24] S.P.L., Deeds 6848B.
[25] Cal. Inq. Misc. i, pp. 373–4.
[26] S.P.L., Deeds 9509.
[27] Sta. Cha. 8/182/2.
[28] S.P.L., Deeds 9376.
[29] Hope-Edwardes MSS., Linley Hall, survey, 1770.
[30] Par. rec., tithe appts.
[31] Ibid.
[32] V.C.H. Salop. i. 338.
[33] Eyton, vi. 340.
[34] Ibid. 345.
[35] Cal. Chart. R. 1300–26, 426.
[36] S.P.L., Plans 47; S.P.L., Deeds 6848B, depositions, c. 1595.
[37] Ibid.
[38] S.P.L., MS. 9041/1.
[39] S.P.L., Deeds 6903.
[40] S.R.O. 1011 uncat., sale contract, 1798.
[41] V.C.H. Salop. i. 341.
[42] Eyton, vi. 339; C 135/66/25.
[43] C 3/30/12; C 78/29 no. 23.
[44] S.P.L., Deeds 9509.
[45] S.R.O. 665 uncat., lease, 1615.
[46] S.P.L., MS. 2, f. 421v.
[47] S.R.O. 482/13.
[48] Ibid. 665 uncat., extracts from ct. r. 1352–1596.
[49] S.P.L., Deeds 13381.
[50] Ibid. 9452; S.R.O. 665 uncat., lease, 1585.
[51] C 3/30/12.
[52] S.P.L., Deeds 9451.
[53] Ibid. 13381.
[54] S.R.O. 665 uncat., survey, c. 1780.
[55] Par. rec., tithe appts.
[56] S.R.O. 665 uncat., lease, 1607.
[57] Ibid.; S.P.L., Deeds 994.
[58] S.R.O. 665 uncat., survey, c. 1780; par. rec., tithe appts.
[59] S.P.L., Haughmond Cart. f. 48.
[60] S.P.L., Deeds 3462; S.R.O. 665 uncat., bill of complaint, Ireland v. Owen.

ships.[61] Church Stretton's claims were again raised at the inclosure of the Long Mynd, c. 1790, when the owner of the Wilderley estate was allotted 500 a. on the hills.[62]

Save at Castle Pulverbatch and Walleybourne the names of the common fields of the townships within the parish are not known and their location cannot be satisfactorily reconstructed. At Castle Pulverbatch common fields called Staple Field, Broad Field (or Okeover Field), and Huglith Field,[63] lay on boulder clay to the north and west of the village. The field-names The Furlongs, Near Field, and East Field[64] suggest that the common fields of Church Pulverbatch lay on the relatively level ground to the south of the village, above Churton Brook. At Wrentnall, where the common fields were still in existence in 1629,[65] a field to the west of the village was called Wharstone in 1839.[66] This is clearly a corruption of Horestone and implies that a boundary stone once stood here, presumably marking the boundary between the common fields and woodland on Broom Hill. Another field lay to the east of Wrentnall village, where there were several inclosed common-field strips c. 1780.[67] Though no more than a single farm since the 13th century, the names and location of the former common fields of Walleybourne were still preserved in 1612, when Windmill Field lay to the west, Wall Field to the south, and Coppice Field to the east of Walleybourne Farm.[68] The Cothercott common fields are recorded in the early 13th century[69] and again in 1549.[70] Those of Wilderley had been inclosed by 1651.[71]

A peculiarity of settlement in the parish is that the church and the castle lie in different townships. The church occupies a hill-top site, and stands at the junction of the road from Castle Pulverbatch to Stapleton with roads from Wilderley and Wrentnall. The village of Church Pulverbatch stands along the road to Stapleton on the sheltered east-facing slope of the hill. Of the two farm-houses in the village Lower House Farm was the residence of the Jaundrell family, who were freeholders here from the early 15th century until the early 19th century.[72] The present house was probably built in 1757,[73] although its appearance suggests a date earlier in the 18th century. It is brick-built, with stone dressings and contains two stories with attics, with an interrupted stone cornice and a stone-capped parapet. Early-17th-century oak wainscot has been inserted in the hall, but there is no evidence that the brick exterior cases an earlier timber-framed house. The farm's

timber-framed buildings stand opposite the house, to the south of the road. Churton House Farm (formerly Upper Farm), which adjoins the church, is a rectangular brick house with hipped roof, sash windows, and a projecting Tuscan porch, built by Abraham Jaundrell in the early 19th century.[74] The former parsonage,[75] on the south of the road adjoining the buildings of Lower House Farm, is now ruinous. It is a three-bay timber-framed house of early-17th-century date; and has a ground plan of two rooms on each side of a central chimney-stack, with an unheated room at the east end. The north wall, facing the road, was cased in brick at a later date. After the new rectory was built in the early 19th century, the old rectory was occupied by a smallholder.[76] Churton Lodge, set back from the road to the east of Lower House Farm, was a smithy in the 18th century[77] but had been enlarged and remodelled as a gentleman's residence by 1839.[78] A large room, added to the house between 1845 and 1851,[79] was used as a meeting-place by the Independent Calvinists until c. 1914.[80] The post office was a school-house in the earlier 19th century,[81] being replaced by the present school in 1873.[82] There was an alehouse in the village in 1600,[83] but this was closed in 1776.[84]

Castle Pulverbatch, on the slopes of a rocky promontory overlooking Churton Brook, stands beneath the impressive site of a motte-and-bailey castle,[85] built at the junction of roads running northwards from the Long Mynd and eastwards from Huglith with the main road from Shrewsbury to Bishop's Castle. The castle was still occupied in 1205,[86] but there was said to be no manor-house here in 1292.[87] Although the village is very small, the regularity of its plan suggests that it was deliberately laid out by the lord of the manor in the 12th or 13th century. The grant of a market in 1254[88] shows that the economy of the village was being developed at this time. The White Horse Inn, a farm-house until the 19th century,[89] contains 3 cruck trusses, in positions which suggest that they may be the remains of two houses at right angles to each other. The Gate House, formerly a turnpike house,[90] and Rock Cottage, are cased timber-framed houses, but the two farm-houses—Castle Farm and Home Farm—were built in stone in the 18th century.[91] Fifteen houses, 10 of them Council houses, have been built in the village since 1945.[92] An alehouse is first recorded here in 1599[93] and there may have been two of them since 1616,[94] but the two existing alehouses are not known to have

[61] S.P.L., Deeds 6163–4.
[62] Ibid. 6579; par. rec., tithe appts.
[63] C 135/66/25; S.P.L., Deeds 12923.
[64] Par. rec., tithe appts.
[65] S.R.O. 665 uncat., lease, 1629.
[66] Par. rec., tithe appts.
[67] S.R.O. 665 uncat., survey, c. 1780.
[68] S.P.L., Deeds 9509.
[69] S.P.L., Haughmond Cart. f. 48.
[70] Cal. Pat. 1549–51, 82.
[71] N.L.W., Chirk Castle 6971.
[72] S.R.O. 665 uncat., bailiff's acct. 1421–3; W.S.L. 350/40/3.
[73] Date on gate-posts.
[74] A timber-framed house formerly stood on its site: S.R.O. 665 uncat., farm-house plans, 1794.
[75] W.S.L. 350/40/3.
[76] Par. rec., tithe appts.
[77] S.R.O. 665 uncat., draft sale partics. c. 1800.

[78] Par. rec., tithe appts.
[79] H.O. 129/359/1/21.
[80] Ex inf. Mrs. A. Roberts, Church View, Castle Pulverbatch.
[81] B.M. Add. MS. 21018, ff. 321–2.
[82] See p. 140.
[83] B.M. Add. MS. 30312, f. 17ᵛ.
[84] N.L.W., Castle Hill 2244; Q. Sess., alehouse reg.
[85] V.C.H. Salop. i. 392–3. See also plate facing p. 133.
[86] Rot. Litt. Pat. (Rec. Com.), 50.
[87] C 133/62/5.
[88] Cal. Pat. 1247–58, 274.
[89] S.R.O. 665 uncat., survey, c. 1780; ibid. sale partics. 1801.   [90] Ibid.
[91] Ibid. farm-house plans, 1794; ibid. draft sale partics. c. 1800.
[92] Ex inf. Atcham R.D.C.
[93] B.M. Add. MS. 30312, f. 14.
[94] Q. Sess., alehouse reg.

occupied their present sites before 1839.[95] In 1823 one of the alehouses was known as 'The Letters',[96] while 'The Woodcock' derives its name from its early-19th-century licensee, Samuel Woodcock.[97]

Wrentnall, on the eastern slopes of Broom Hill, contained in the later 17th century a higher proportion of substantial farm-houses than any other township in the parish. In 1662 there were in the village two houses with 3 hearths and one with 2 hearths.[98] The existing houses have been built since the 18th century, with the exception of Farm Cottages—a timber-framed building which was once a farm-house.[99] Wrentnall House was built before 1816[1] by James Freme, who bought most of the township in 1802.[2] He also built Wrentnall Cottage, on the main road, which is dated 1814[3] and was probably intended as a lodge, and Wrentnall Chapel, erected shortly after 1839 for the Baptists,[4] but used as a village hall after Freme's death and as a Methodist Chapel since 1910.[5] Willowburn Cottage, to the north of the chapel, stands on the former outrack leading from Wrentnall towards Broom Hill.[6] An alehouse, recorded in 1613,[7] was closed in 1776.[8]

Walleybourne Farm, below Wrentnall on the northern boundary of the parish and on the edge of one of the few substantial deposits of sand and gravel, was presumably one of the two pre-Conquest manors in Wrentnall[9] and, since it once had its own set of common fields, is undoubtedly the site of a former hamlet. It was held with Wrentnall manor in 1086,[10] and there is no evidence for the existence of a hamlet here when Walleybourne was granted to John *walensis* in the early 13th century.[11] Occupied as a freehold estate by the Walleybourne and Jennings families until 1605,[12] it was subsequently a farmhouse in the manorial estate.[13] The hall and the farm buildings recorded in 1612[14] are still standing, but its gate-house has been demolished and there is now no trace of the moat which seems to have surrounded it.[15] The unimpressive brick exterior of the house conceals a medieval open hall, of 3 or 4 bays, probably built *c.* 1400.[16] The 3 surviving roof trusses are of arch-braced collar-beam construction, two of them being ornamented at their apex with delicate cusping.[17] The spere-truss and one of the door-heads of the screens passage at the east end of the house are still in position. Closely spaced vertical studding visible on the inside of the north wall probably dates from the 16th century, when a fireplace was inserted on the north wall and a two-

storied cross-wing was added at the west end of the hall. The upper floor of the hall itself, however, does not appear to have been inserted until *c.* 1700, perhaps at the same time as the external brick-casing.

Cothercott and Wilderley, the two ancient hamlets in the south of the parish, both appear to have shrunk to their present size in the 18th century. Cothercott, though said to be waste in 1066,[18] was a flourishing hamlet in the 13th century[19] and probably contained 4 farm-houses in 1717,[20] but their number had been reduced to two by 1839.[21] These two houses are now known as Upper and Lower Cothercott Farms but only the former is now a farm. Both are timber-framed and have the common central-stack ground-plan.

Like Castle Pulverbatch the medieval hamlet of Wilderley lay under the shadow of a castle, which was designed to command one of the roads formerly running northwards from the Long Mynd towards the Severn valley. The site of the castle, a motte with two rectangular baileys,[22] lies to the north of Wilderley Hall Farm, sole survivor of the former hamlet. Sources of information about the numbers of houses here in the 17th[23] and 18th[24] centuries do not distinguish houses in the ancient hamlet from isolated farms and squatter cottages, but the general decline in their number in the earlier 18th century suggests that Wilderley was shrinking at this time. Fifteen persons were assessed to poor rates here in 1700[25] and only 10 after 1723.[26] By 1838 the whole township contained only 7 houses, of which only 3 were anything more than small-holdings.[27] Wilderley Hall Farm, enlarged in brick in the 19th century, incorporates a small brick-cased timber-framed house, while timber from former houses nearby seems to have been used in farm buildings to the north of the house.

Isolated settlement in the woodland areas to the east and west of the ancient hamlets is first recorded in the later 16th century. In Steplewood there was a house at Starr's Coppice and a cottage on the site of Castle Place Farm by 1580.[28] The latter derives its name from a large circular depression, apparently natural, which surrounds the house and was formerly known as Toppings Castle.[29] It is a brick house with some Georgian features, built in the early 19th century, while the present house at Starr's Coppice was probably built after 1805.[30] A cottage which stood to the south of Castle Place *c.* 1595[31] has been demolished since 1839.[32] A parish ordinance (*c.* 1617) prohibiting the erection of cottages[33] may

[95] Par. rec., tithe appts.
[96] Q. Sess., alehouse reg.
[97] Par. rec., tithe appts.
[98] E 179/255/35 m. 76.
[99] S.R.O. 665 uncat., farm-house plans, 1794.
[1] B.M. O.S. 2″ orig. drawings, sheet 199 (1816).
[2] S.R.O. 1011 uncat., sale contract, 1802.
[3] Datestone.
[4] W. E. Morris, *History of Methodism in Shrewsbury and District* (Shrewsbury, 1960), 55.
[5] Ibid.
[6] S.R.O. 665 uncat., survey, *c.* 1780.
[7] B.M. Add. MS. 30312, f. 162ᵛ.
[8] N.L.W., Castle Hill 2244; Q. Sess., alehouse reg.
[9] *V.C.H. Salop.* i. 341.   [10] Ibid.
[11] S.P.L., Deeds 6903.
[12] See p. 135.
[13] S.P.L., Deeds 9509.
[14] Ibid.; S.R.O. 665 uncat., lease, 1628; ibid. survey, *c.* 1780.
[15] Ibid.

[16] Description based on a survey by Mr. F. W. B. Charles of Bromsgrove.
[17] See plate facing p. 111.
[18] *V.C.H. Salop.* i. 342.
[19] S.P.L., Haughmond Cart. f. 48.
[20] Q. Sess., reg. papists' estates, 1717.
[21] Par. rec., tithe appts.
[22] *V.C.H. Salop.* i. 392.
[23] N.L.W., Castle Hill 6971.
[24] S.P.L., MS. 9041/1–3.
[25] Ibid. 9041/1.
[26] Ibid. 9041/3.
[27] Par. rec., tithe appts.
[28] S.P.L., Deeds 9509.
[29] *Cal. Pat.* 1385–9, 63–64.
[30] Hope-Edwardes MSS., Linley Hall, survey, 1770 (add. notes).
[31] S.P.L., Deeds 13418; S.R.O. 665 uncat., leases, 1614, 1629.
[32] Par. rec., tithe appts.
[33] S.P.L., MS. 9041/1.

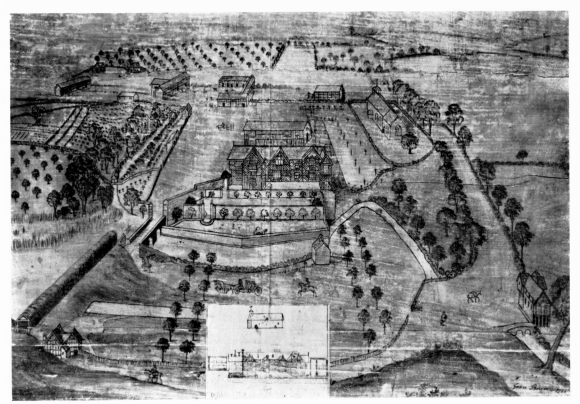

PITCHFORD: VIEW OF THE HALL, CHURCH AND GROUNDS FROM THE EAST IN 1714
The inset shows the south front of the Hall

BERRINGTON: MANOR FARM FROM THE NORTH
The west wing is probably of 16th-century date; the remainder was built in 1658

CHURCH PULVERBATCH: motte and bailey at Castle Pulverbatch from the north-east

ALBERBURY-WITH-CARDESTON: ring motte and bailey at Heath Farm, Amaston, from the west

CASTLE SITES

account for the relatively small number of isolated houses erected in this part of the parish after the inclosure of Steplewood, c. 1600. The only houses here still substantially of early-17th-century date are The Allies, near New House Farm, and Holly Grove Cottages. New House Farm, however, contains a timber-framed wing, and Lower New House Farm, described as a timber-framed house, c. 1780,[34] has since been rebuilt. Holly Grove Farm and Holly Grove House both date from the 19th century.

Wilderley Lane Farm and Cotham Leasowes, the two farms in the area of the former Wilderley Wood, were originally timber-framed. Each had a ground-plan of two rooms with a chimney-stack on the west gable, like the adjacent farm-houses on Shadymoor,[35] but both have been cased in brick and at Wilderley Lane Farm a stone east wing was added, probably in the 18th century. Wilderley Workshop, a cottage south-east of Wilderley Hall, near Wilderley Brook, is partly timber-farmed and, like the two last-mentioned farms, dates from the 17th century. A cottage stood on Churton Brook, north of Cotham Leasowes Farm, in 1601,[36] but had been demolished by 1839.[37]

In the western woodland Huglith Farm and Lawn Farm, first recorded in 1612,[38] were formed after the clearance of Nether Huglith Wood in the later 16th century. The present farm-house at Lawn Farm seems to have been rebuilt in the 18th or 19th century, but Huglith Farm, much enlarged in the 19th century, incorporates one bay of the original house at the south-east end. Prestley Farm, only a few yards from the village of Habberley and in an area occupied by tenants of that manor since the Middle Ages,[39] is a timber-framed house of two bays which dates from the early 17th century. It has been little changed internally, though rough-cast outside, and retains an original staircase alongside a chimney-stack on the east gable.

Few were hardy enough to settle in the windswept hill-country to the south of the parish. The oldest and most impressive of the houses here is the old farm-house at Sheppen Fields, at 925 feet on the northern slopes of Wilderley Hill.[40] A house already stood on this site in the later 13th century, when it was called 'le Shupene'[41] and was the focal point of Haughmond Abbey's sheep-walk on the hill. The present house may have been built shortly after 1464.[42] Now used as a farm building it is a 'long house' in which 3 cruck trusses are still in position. In the early 17th century an ashlar chimney-stack was inserted and a cross-wing added at the east end. Another farm-house, even higher on the hill, known as Upper Sheppen Fields, was standing in the late

17th century[43] and was still occupied in 1717,[44] but had been deserted by 1839.[45] The field-name Pulleys,[46] to the north of Sheppen Fields, marks the site of another medieval homestead, known as the Pool House.[47] Houses still stood here in 1534[48] but no trace of them remained in 1839.[49] Lea Farm, on the road from Castle Pulverbatch to Wilderley and at the foot of the hills, is an early-17th-century timber-framed house, later cased in stone. Cothercott Hill Farm and Cothercott Cottage, standing at 1,000 feet on the northern slopes of Cothercott Hill, are stone-built and date from the 18th century. Both are in origin squatter cottages, and the former has been deserted since c. 1900.[50]

On the high ground west of Castle Pulverbatch, once the site of Over Huglith Wood, an isolated house is recorded in 1613,[51] but the only building now standing here is a ruinous stone cottage known as Pennsylvania, recorded in 1783.[52] The only notable isolated house in this area is Bank Farm, standing at 1,050 feet on Paulith Bank. Built in 1615 by Reece and Mary Bowen,[53] it is a timber-framed house of two bays with a central chimney-stack. A range of timber-framed farm buildings is attached to the east end of the house. Two cottages stand at the foot of Huglith, along the outrack leading from Castle Pulverbatch to Cothercott Hill, one of which is of 17th- and the other of 18th-century date.

The older isolated houses along the main road, between Castle Pulverbatch and Longden Common, are for the most part stone-built and date from the later 18th century. Black Lion Farm, which seems to have been an ale-house until the later 19th century,[54] is first so named c. 1780[55] and is likely to have been the first house on the main road here, but it was rebuilt after 1794.[56]

There were said to be 260 adults in the parish in 1676[57] and 439 inhabitants in 1801.[58] During the earlier 19th century the population rose rapidly to a peak of 574 in 1851, but it declined thereafter, falling to 401 by 1881, 338 by 1931, and 298 by 1951.[59] The erection of new houses has ended this trend and by 1961 the population had increased to 322.[60]

MANORS. The manor of *PULVERBATCH*, held of Roger, Earl of Shrewsbury, in 1086,[61] was by the end of the 12th century the *caput* of the barony of Pulverbatch[62] and was subsequently held of the Crown in chief.[63] Held as three manors by Hunnic and Ulviet before the Conquest, it had been granted by 1086 to Earl Roger's huntsman Roger the huntsman.[64] When next recorded, c. 1135, the tenant was one Roger.[65] He was perhaps the father of Reynold

34 S.R.O. 665 uncat., survey, c. 1780.
35 See pp. 163–4.
36 S.P.L., Plans 47.
37 Par. rec., tithe appts.
38 S.P.L., Deeds 9509.
39 Ibid. 6172; Heref. City Libr. 9133/37, 39.
40 See plate facing p. 54.
41 Eyton, vi. 345; S.P.L., Haughmond Cart. f. 164.
42 S.P.L., Haughmond Cart. f. 38ᵛ.
43 E 134/36 Chas. II Trin./5.
44 Q. Sess., reg. papists' estates, 1717.
45 Par. rec., tithe appts.
46 Ibid.
47 S.P.L., Haughmond Cart. ff. 166, 166ᵛ.
48 S.R.O. 665 uncat., ct. r. manor of Boveria, 1534.
49 Par. rec., tithe appts.
50 Local inf.

51 S.P.L., MS. 9034.
52 S.P.L., Deeds 13647.
53 Date '1615' and initials 'R.B. M.B.' on wainscot on north wall of ground floor. Builder identified from S.R.O. 146/7.
54 Kelly's Dir. Salop. (1863, 1885).
55 S.R.O. 665 uncat., survey, c. 1780.
56 Ibid. farm-house plans, 1794.
57 T.S.A.S. 2nd ser. i. 88.
58 Census, 1801.
59 Ibid. 1801–1951.
60 Ibid. 1961.
61 V.C.H. Salop. i. 341.
62 I. J. Sanders, English Baronies (Oxford, 1960), 73–74.
63 Ibid.; T.S.A.S. 4th ser. v. 124.
64 V.C.H. Salop. i. 341.
65 Cur. Reg. R. xii. 458.

de Pulverbatch, who held the manor after 1154,[66] but had been succeeded before 1189 by his daughter Emma, wife of Herbert de Castello.[67] At her death without issue in 1193,[68] the manor passed to John de Kilpeck, whose relationship to Emma is not known.[69] John did not receive full livery of the manor until 1196,[70] and at his death in 1205 wardship of his son Hugh was granted to William Cauntelow.[71] Hugh de Kilpeck had succeeded to the manor by 1216,[72] and at his death in 1244 he left as his heirs his daughters Isabel, and Joan, wife of Philip Marmion.[73] Marmion did homage for the manor in the same year[74] and in 1258 Isabel, then wife of William Walerand, released to him her rights in the estate.[75] At his death in 1291[76] Philip Marmion's estates passed to three co-heirs, Pulverbatch being assigned in 1292 to his daughter Joan, widow of William de Morteyn.[77] Joan died without issue in 1295,[78] when she was followed by her nephew Ralph le Boteler.[79] The latter, who was lord of Pulverbatch until 1342,[80] had leased the manor by 1327[81] to his son John, who held it until his death in 1339.[82] On Ralph's death in 1342[83] a third of the manor was assigned in dower to his widow Hawise,[84] who survived until 1360.[85] The remainder passed to his grandson Ralph, then a minor.[86] Guy de Brienne, to whom wardship was granted in 1342,[87] also obtained, on Ralph's death while still under age in 1348,[88] the wardship of his brother and heir Edward.[89] The latter had livery of the manor in 1359,[90] but died without issue in 1412,[91] when the manor passed to his cousin, Sir Philip Boteler of Woodhall (Herts.)[92] who died in 1420.[93] The latter's son and heir Edward died under age in the same year,[94] when wardship of Edward's brother and heir Philip was granted to Sir Hugh Willoughby.[95] Philip Boteler came of age in 1435,[96] and the manor passed from father to son until 1599, the following being lords: Philip, 1435–53;[97] John, 1453–1504;[98] John, 1504–15;[99] Philip, 1515–c. 1564;[1] John, c. 1564–c. 1585;[2] Philip, c. 1585–99.[3]

In 1599 Sir Philip Boteler sold the manor to Sir Roger Owen,[4] and it followed the descent of Condover manor until 1802, when the greater part of the manorial estate was sold.[5]

Roger, Earl of Shrewsbury, was overlord of *WRENTNALL* manor in 1086 and, as at Pulverbatch, Roger the huntsman was his tenant.[6] The estate was said to have been held before the Conquest as two manors by Ernui and Chetel,[7] but they may have been merely under-tenants, for it was reported in 1086 that three-quarters of the manor had once belonged to the Church of St. Chad, Shrewsbury.[8] The Church never regained possession and the estate was subsequently merged with the manor of Pulverbatch.[9]

The overlordship of the manors of *COTHERCOTT* and *WILDERLEY*, vested in Roger, Earl of Shrewsbury, by 1086,[10] was annexed in the early 12th century to the Honor of Montgomery,[11] but by 1215 the Abbot of Haughmond, as tenant of the two manors, had been released from all services due to the overlord except scutage.[12] The Cauntelows and their successors as lords of the Honor of Montgomery remained overlords until the Dissolution, when it was vested in the Crown.[13]

The pre-Conquest tenants of these two manors seem also to have held estates in Pulverbatch and Wrentnall, for Hunnic then held Cothercott[14] and Chetel held Wilderley.[15] The two manors were still separate estates in 1086, when Avenel held the former[16] and Hugh fitz Turgis the latter,[17] but they had been united by 1204, when Richard de Wilderley, descendant of Hugh fitz Turgis, sold the manors to Haughmond Abbey to redeem his heavy debts.[18] The abbey only obtained a mesne tenure at Cothercott by this transaction.[19] The under-tenant, John de Cothercott, was succeeded in 1242[20] by his son Baldwin, who conveyed his estate there to the abbey, c. 1265.[21] The estate thereafter formed part of Haughmond Abbey's composite manor of Boveria, which also included lands in Smethcott, Church Stretton, and Ratlinghope.[22] At the Dissolution the manors of Cothercott and Wilderley again passed into divided ownership. Sheppen Fields was granted by the Crown in 1543 to Thomas Ireland,[23] who obtained the remainder of Cothercott manor in 1545.[24] The manor passed from father to son in the Ireland family until 1701,[25] the following being lords: Thomas, 1545–54; George, 1554–1614;

[66] *Cur. Reg. R.* xii. 458.
[67] Eyton, vi. 190.
[68] Ibid.; Sanders, *English Baronies*, 73.
[69] Sanders, *English Baronies*, 73.
[70] *Pipe R.* 1195 (P.R.S. N.S. vi), 42; ibid. 1196 (P.R.S. N.S. vii), 194.
[71] *Rot. Litt. Claus.* (Rec. Com.), i. 17.
[72] Eyton, vi. 195.
[73] *Ex. e Rot. Fin.* (Rec. Com.), i. 412.
[74] Ibid.
[75] C.P. 25(1)/283/350.
[76] C 133/62/5.
[77] *Cal. Fine R.* 1272–1307, 303.
[78] C 133/72/2.
[79] *Cal. Fine R.* 1272–1307, 367.
[80] C 135/66/25.
[81] S.R.O. 482/10.
[82] *Cal. Close*, 1339–41, 178.
[83] Ibid. 1341–3, 675–6.
[84] Ibid.
[85] C 135/149/26.
[86] Ibid.
[87] *Cal. Pat.* 1345–8, 259.
[88] C 135/148/21.
[89] *Cal. Pat.* 1348–50, 205.
[90] *Cal. Close*, 1354–60, 589–90.
[91] C 137/90/16.
[92] Ibid.
[93] C 139/38/78.
[94] C 139/33/30.

[95] S.R.O. 665 uncat., bailiff's acct. 1430–1.
[96] *Cal. Close*, 1435–41, 11.
[97] C 139/149/27.
[98] Ibid.; *Cal. Fine R.* 1485–1509, 356.
[99] *Cal. Fine R.* 1485–1509, 356; P.C.C. 8 Holden.
[1] S.P.L., Deeds 9362.
[2] Ibid. 9452.
[3] Ibid. 9452, 6896.
[4] Ibid. 6869.
[5] S.R.O. 665 uncat., sale partics. 1802.
[6] *V.C.H. Salop.* i. 341.
[7] Ibid.   [8] Ibid.
[9] Eyton, vi. 205.
[10] *V.C.H. Salop.* i. 338, 342.
[11] Eyton, vi. 262.
[12] S.P.L., Haughmond Cart. f. 229.
[13] Eyton, xi. 146; *Bk. of Fees*, 966; *Feud. Aids*, iv. 240; C 142/148/33; C 142/345/122.
[14] *V.C.H. Salop.* i. 342.
[15] Ibid. 338.   [16] Ibid. 342.
[17] Ibid. 338.
[18] S.P.L., Haughmond Cart. f. 228ᵛ; Eyton, vi. 258.
[19] S.P.L., Haughmond Cart. ff. 47ᵛ–48ᵛ.
[20] Eyton, vi. 262.
[21] S.P.L., Haughmond Cart. f. 47ᵛ.
[22] Eyton, vi. 166.
[23] *L. & P. Hen. VIII*, xviii (2), p. 186.
[24] Ibid. xx (1), p. 222.
[25] For pedigree see S.P.L., MS. 2790, pp. 642–3.

Thomas, 1614–50; Robert, 1650–c. 1676,[26] Thomas, c. 1676–1701. On the death of Thomas Ireland in 1701 the manor passed to his widow Elizabeth,[27] who was succeeded at her death in 1720 by her son Thomas.[28] The latter died in 1728[29] and in 1739 his son Thomas sold the manor to Thomas Powys, the lord of Wilderley manor.[30]

The manor of Wilderley was granted in 1551 to Edward Fiennes, Lord Clinton and Saye,[31] who sold it to Richard Goodrich in 1554.[32] Goodrich later sold the manor to Thomas Lodge,[33] from whom Robert Barnfield acquired it in 1557.[34] The manor passed in 1568 to Barnfield's son Richard,[35] who settled it on his second son Robert Barnfield in 1602.[36] The latter sold Wilderley in 1615 to Sir John Egerton,[37] later Earl of Bridgewater,[38] whose son John, Earl of Bridgewater, sold it to Henry Langley in 1674.[39] The manor subsequently passed to the Powys family of Berwick, following the descent of Stapleton manor until 1905,[40] when R. L. Purcell-Llewelyn sold his estate at Cothercott and Wilderley to E. S. L. Walker.[41] The latter conveyed the estate in 1908 to J. B. Walker,[42] on whose death in 1950 it passed to his sister Mary Walker.[43] The estate was broken up after her death in 1957.[44]

OTHER ESTATES. Walleybourne, a member of the Domesday manor of Wrentnall,[45] was the largest of a number of freehold estates created by the lords of Pulverbatch manor in the early 13th century. It was granted, c. 1216–30, to John, son of Roger *walensis*,[46] and may have passed to John *walensis*, who was living in 1272.[47] By 1317 the estate was held by Robert de Walleybourne,[48] who was still alive in 1332.[49] It passed from father to son in this family until 1419,[50] when John de Walleybourne settled it on his daughter Joan at her marriage with John Walker of Lee.[51] Walker, who enlarged the estate by purchases in Wrentnall[52] and acquired the lease of pasture at Nether Huglith,[53] was still living in 1446,[54] but had been succeeded before 1470 by his grandson Thomas Jennings.[55] The estate then passed from father to son and was held by the following members of the Jennings family: Thomas, c. 1470–c. 1499;[56] Rowland, c. 1499–c. 1528;[57] Thomas,

c. 1528–68;[58] William, 1568–87.[59] On the death of William Jennings in 1587 the estate passed to his brother Rowland,[60] who sold it to Sir Roger Owen in 1604.[61]

ECONOMIC HISTORY. No fewer than 5 pre-Conquest estates in Pulverbatch and Wrentnall had by 1086 been united to form a single manor,[62] and from the 12th century the estates of Roger the huntsman in Westley, Great Lyth, and Little Lyth, in Condover parish, were also accounted part of Pulverbatch manor,[63] though separated from it by the forest of Steplewood. Roger the huntsman's estates in Wrentnall and Pulverbatch were assessed at 4 hides in 1086 and were valued at 60s., having been worth £9 before the Conquest and only 45s. when he received them.[64] The manor, including the detached portion in Condover, was assessed at 5 hides in 1255.[65] It was said to be worth £17 8s. 6d. in 1292[66] and only £11 6s. in 1342.[67]

This apparent decline in the value of the manor may be accounted for by the shrinkage of the demesne and by grants to free tenants in the 13th century. Although there were 5 ploughs and 9 serfs on the demesne lands of Pulverbatch and Wrentnall in 1086,[68] there was only one carucate of demesne by 1292,[69] when the manor house was no longer standing.[70] The demesne had been leased by 1342 to 4 tenants, who paid rents of 26s. 8d. a year,[71] and no attempt seems to have been made to enlarge the manorial estate or to increase its value until it was purchased by Sir Roger Owen in 1599.[72] Owen presumably initiated the inclosure of woodland and waste in Steplewood and Broom Hill, and of the common wood of Castle Pulverbatch, shortly after 1600,[73] and he secured an allotment of 158 a. in Steplewood alone.[74] He purchased the Jennings estate at Walleybourne in 1604[75] and acquired 35 a. in 1610,[76] when the eastern boundary with Stapleton was determined. Two small freeholds were purchased in the course of the 18th century[77] and in 1794 lands in Church and Castle Pulverbatch were exchanged to consolidate the manorial estate.[78] The estate contained 1,767 a. c. 1780[79] but 142 a. in Church Pulverbatch were sold in 1794.[80] The

[26] S.P.L., Deeds 3498.
[27] Ibid.
[28] Ibid. 2869.
[29] Ibid. 3460.
[30] Ibid. 3459.
[31] *Cal. Pat.* 1550–3, 206.
[32] S.P.L., Deeds 2840.
[33] C.P. 25(2)/77/655/4 & 5 Philip & Mary Mich.
[34] Ibid.
[35] *T.S.A.S.* 4th ser. iii. 89.
[36] S.P.L., Deeds 3464.
[37] Ibid. 3466.
[38] *Complete Peerage*, ii. 311–12.
[39] S.P.L., Deeds 3467.
[40] See pp. 164–5.
[41] Underhill Hall title-deeds, *penes* Lloyds Bank, Shrewsbury.
[42] Ibid.
[43] Ibid.
[44] Local inf.
[45] *V.C.H. Salop.* i. 341.
[46] S.P.L., Deeds 6903.
[47] Eyton, vi. 201.
[48] S.P.L., Deeds 9331.
[49] E 179/166/2 m. 5.
[50] S.R.O. 482/15–16; *T.S.A.S.* liv. 32.
[51] S.R.O. 482/16.
[52] S.P.L., Deeds 12874–5.

[53] Ibid. 9451.
[54] Ibid.
[55] *T.S.A.S.* liv. 32.
[56] S.P.L., Deeds 6906.
[57] S.R.O. 665 uncat., extracts from ct. r. 1352–1596.
[58] S.P.L., Deeds 6906.
[59] S.R.O. 665 uncat., extracts from ct. r. 1352–1596.
[60] Ibid.
[61] S.P.L., Deeds 6909.
[62] *V.C.H. Salop.* i. 341.
[63] See p. 138.
[64] *V.C.H. Salop.* i. 341.
[65] *Rot. Hund.* (Rec. Com.), ii. 62.
[66] C 133/62/5.
[67] C 135/66/25.
[68] *V.C.H. Salop.* i. 341.
[69] C 133/62/5.
[70] Ibid.
[71] C 135/66/25.
[72] S.P.L., Deeds 6869.
[73] See p. 130.
[74] S.P.L., Deeds 9504.
[75] Ibid. 6909.
[76] Ibid. 6873.
[77] S.R.O. 665 uncat., deed, 1717; S.P.L., Deeds 13647.
[78] S.P.L., Deeds 10046, 10056.
[79] S.R.O. 665 uncat., survey, c. 1780.
[80] Ibid. 1011 uncat., sale partics. 1794.

remainder of the estate was sold, 1801–2,[81] with the exception of New House Farm, which was still owned by the lord of Condover manor in 1895.[82]

By the end of the 13th century there were at least 9 free tenants within the manor,[83] whose rents produced £9 in 1292[84] and £7 18s. 8d. in 1342.[85] There were 11 free tenants here in 1599[86] but, apart from Walleybourne, the only substantial freehold estate was that of the Jaundrell family of Lower Farm, Church Pulverbatch, who had been free tenants here since the early 15th century.[87] This estate, containing some 140 a.,[88] was held by the Jaundrells and their descendants the Corries until the later 19th century.[89] By the end of the 18th century the only other freeholds amounting to anything more than a house or isolated fields were those of Thomas Oswell in Church Pulverbatch (60 a.)[90] and of the Powys family in Wrentnall (62 a.).[91]

Wilderley, the more prosperous of the two manors in the south of the parish, was assessed at 2 hides in 1086, when its value had fallen from 30s. to 20s. since before the Conquest.[92] Cothercott manor, waste in 1066, was assessed at half a hide in 1086, when it was worth only 2s.[93] There was demesne or one plough at Wilderley in 1086,[94] when there were 4 serfs here and 2 at Cothercott.[95] Wholly in the possession of Haughmond Abbey by 1265,[96] Cothercott and Wilderley subsequently formed part of the manor of Boveria.[97] Demesne lands in these townships had probably been leased by 1291, when the demesne of the entire manor of Boveria was worth only 6s. 8d.[98] In 1446 rents of demesne lands in Cothercott and Wilderley, then leased to 6 tenants, produced 37s. a year.[99] The two manors again passed into divided ownership at the Dissolution[1] but were reunited in 1739.[2]

A number of small freehold estates were created at Cothercott in the early 13th century, but these had all been bought in by the abbey before c. 1280.[3] Lea Farm (35 a.) in Wilderley has been a small freehold since it was first recorded in 1656[4] but its origin is unknown. Bank Farm, in the south-west of the parish, has always lain within the Gatten manorial estate,[5] and Prestley Farm likewise was part of Habberley manor[6] until that estate was broken up in 1945.[7]

Of the freehold estates created by the sale of Pulverbatch manor in 1801–2,[8] the largest was the Wrentnall House estate, built up by James Freme in the earlier 19th century, which comprised 430 a. in 1839[9] and 1,080 a. in 1895.[10] With this exception, and in spite of constant minor changes, the overall pattern of landownership in the parish remained little changed throughout the 19th century. In 1839 some 2,750 a. lay in the three large estates of E. W. Smythe Owen, H. W. Powys, and John Freme, and some 1,850 a. in the hands of 28 smaller landowners.[11] Six of the latter owned estates of over 100 a., but 19 owned fewer than 25 a. apiece.[12] Only 11 of these smaller estates were wholly or mainly owner-occupied and 15 of them had non-resident owners.[13] In 1895, when the 3 larger estates accounted for some 2,450 a., the remainder of the parish belonged to 25 smaller landowners.[14] The sizes of their estates and the proportion of resident to non-resident owners was roughly the same as in 1839.[15]

On the manors of Pulverbatch and Wrentnall in 1086 10 villeins and 3 radmen had between them 4 ploughs.[16] Rents of customary tenants were said to be worth 33s. 8d. a year in 1292[17] and 54s. 10d. a year in 1295,[18] but are not separately recorded in 14th-century surveys of the manor.[19] Copyhold tenure survived in Pulverbatch until the 1560s, when most of the land so held was re-granted by the lord of the manor on long leases,[20] and in 1599 the tenants included 11 leaseholders, holding for terms of 19–41 years, and several tenants-at-will.[21] Some tenures-at-will were converted into leaseholds in the early 17th century[22] and the 99-year lease became normal,[23] surviving here until at least 1770.[24] A rapid increase in income from rents in the course of the 18th century—from £239 a year in 1701[25] to £699 in 1784[26]—indicates, however, that conversion to short-term leases was taking place at this time. Farm-sizes also increased during the 18th century. The number of tenants fell from 40 in 1701[27] to 24 by c. 1780, when two-thirds of the estate lay in 8 farms of more than 100 a.[28]

[81] S.R.O. 665 uncat., sale partics. 1801; ibid. 1011 uncat., sale contracts, 1801–2.
[82] Par. rec., rate bk. 1895.
[83] S.P.L., Deeds 6903, 9444; S.P.L., MS. 2, ff. 420v, 421, 423, 423v; S.P.L., Haughmond Cart. f. 169v; Eyton, vi. 205.
[84] C 133/62/5.
[85] C 135/66/25.
[86] B.M. Add. MS. 30312.
[87] S.R.O. 665 uncat., bailiff's acct. 1423–4.
[88] Par. rec., tithe appts.
[89] W.S.L. 350/40/3.
[90] S.R.O. 665 uncat., exchange map, 1794.
[91] Ibid. 731 uncat., sale partics. 1801.
[92] V.C.H. Salop. i. 338.
[93] Ibid. 342.
[94] Ibid. 338.
[95] Ibid. 342.
[96] See p. 134.
[97] Ibid.
[98] Tax. Eccl. (Rec. Com.), 163.
[99] S.C. 6/967/1.
[1] See pp. 134–5.
[2] S.P.L., Deeds 3459.
[3] S.P.L., Haughmond Cart. ff. 48, 48v; Eyton, vi. 261–5.
[4] S.P.L., MS. 9041/1.
[5] S.R.O. 146/7; S.P.L., Deeds 986; par. rec., tithe appts.

[6] S.P.L., Deeds 6172; S.P.L., MS. 2498; Heref. City Libr. 9133–37, 39.
[7] Heighway Jones title-deeds penes Messrs. Sprott, Stokes & Turnbull, solicitors, Shrewsbury.
[8] S.R.O. 665 uncat., sale partics. 1801; ibid. 1011 uncat., sale contracts, 1801–2.
[9] Par. rec., tithe appts.
[10] Ibid. rate bk. 1895.
[11] Ibid. tithe appts.
[12] Ibid.
[13] Ibid.
[14] Ibid. rate bk. 1895.
[15] Ibid.
[16] V.C.H. Salop. i. 341.
[17] C 133/62/5.
[18] C 133/72/2.
[19] C 135/66/25; C 135/76/10.
[20] S.R.O. 665 uncat., extracts from ct. r. 1352–1596; ibid. lease, 1567; S.P.L., Deeds 7031, 9362–3, 13451.
[21] S.P.L., Deeds 13381.
[22] Ibid. 6892, 13456; B.M. Add. MS. 30312; S.R.O. 665 uncat., lease, 1607.
[23] S.P.L., Deeds passim; S.R.O. 665 uncat., leases.
[24] S.P.L., Deeds 13630.
[25] Ibid. 13462.
[26] S.R.O. 665 uncat., rental, 1784.
[27] S.P.L., Deeds 13462.
[28] S.R.O. 665 uncat., survey, n.d.

There were 3 villeins with one plough on Wilder-ley manor in 1086[29] but no tenants are then re-corded at Cothercott.[30] Assized rents from the two townships, which produced £2 6s. 5d. a year in 1291,[31] had risen to £4 8s. 8d. by 1446, when a further 12s. 5d. was derived from rents of assarted lands.[32] Copyhold tenure, still found here in the early 16th century,[33] seems to have disappeared after the Dissolution. Of the 17 tenants in Wilderley in 1651 9 were leaseholders and 8 were tenants-at-will,[34] while at Cothercott in 1717 the six farms were all held on long leases and there were only 2 tenants-at-will, both cottagers.[35] Two of the Wilderley farms were already over 100 a. by 1651, but most of the tenants still had holdings of less than 50 a.[36] The large farm was introduced after the union of the two manors in 1739, and by 1838 the six large farms on the estate accounted for 1,095 a. of the 1,200 a. of inclosed land in the two townships.[37]

Although there is little evidence for the economy of the medieval manor of Boveria, it is clear that its focus, and the chief source of its income, lay on the sheep-walks of Cothercott and Wilderley Hills. Large flocks of sheep still grazed on the common lands there in the later 17th century,[38] and it is likely that the relative affluence of the inhabitants of Wilderley and Cothercott in 1542,[39] compared with those of the 3 northern townships, reflects a higher level of prosperity derived from the sale of wool. Wilderley, on lower ground than Cothercott, may have served for winter pasture. Several meadows are recorded here in 1446[40] and in 1651 the manor was said to be 'a great part meadow'.[41] The cultiva-tion of marginal land on the hills, recorded in 1655[42] and 1684,[43] is perhaps evidence of a shift of emphasis towards arable farming in Wilderley and Cothercott in the later 17th century.

There were said to be 902 a. of arable in the parish in 1801, when roughly equal acreages of wheat, oats, and barley were sown.[44] In 1839 the parish contained 1,086 a. of arable land, of which about half lay in Wilderley and Cothercott.[45]

A corn mill on Churton Brook, first recorded in the early 13th century,[46] was said to be worth 30s. a year in 1292,[47] but it was ruinous in 1345.[48] Still in decay in 1384[49] it had been repaired by 1413[50] and was held by the Gittins family from 1564[51] until last recorded in 1649.[52] The field-name Windmill Field, found at Walleybourne in 1612,[53] suggests that a windmill once stood there.

Coal was mined in the north of the parish in the 18th and 19th centuries, principally near the main road to the east of Wrentnall, where pits are first recorded in 1717.[54] Mines on the glebe to the east of Black Lion Farm were in use for a short period, c. 1734,[55] and were re-opened in 1793,[56] while nearby pits on the manorial estate were leased in 1766[57] and 1792.[58] There were numerous pit-mounds in this area c. 1780.[59] A shaft was sunk at this time near Castle Place Farm,[60] and mining continued there, and at New House Farm, throughout the 19th century.[61] To the south a mine near Cotham Leasowes Farm was in operation c. 1776–82.[62]

Although the local gritstone was the main building material in the parish in the 18th and early 19th centuries, bricks had been made from clays near the Habberley road, west of Castle Pulverbatch, from c. 1780,[63] and along Wilderley Brook, to the west of Cothercott, before 1839.[64] Coal mined on New House Farm was used for brick manufacture after 1832.[65]

Unsuccessful attempts were made to locate deposits of lead and copper on Lawn and Huglith Hills shortly after 1798.[66] Large amounts of barytes, also found in the hills to the south and west of the parish, were extracted between 1890 and 1945 at the following mines: Wrentnall mine, 1890–1925 (recorded output, 1908–18, 10,866 tons); Cothercott mine, 1911–28 (recorded output in this period, 23,000 tons); Huglith mine, 1910–45 (recorded output in this period, 295,108 tons).[67] At Cothercott the ore was processed at the mine but at Huglith mine an aerial rope-way was used to transport the barytes some 3½ miles across the valley of Habberley Brook to Malehurst mill near Minsterley.[68]

A weekly market and an annual three-day fair on the feast of St. Edith (17th September), established at Pulverbatch in 1254,[69] continued to be held until c. 1914,[70] but by 1851 the date of the fair had been changed to 22nd September.[71] Standing on a main road and at the junction of the Severn Valley and the hill country to the south, Castle Pulverbatch was an ideal site for a market, but there is no evidence that the village ever became anything more than a small farming community. In 1379 the only craftsmen in the parish were a carpenter and a wheelwright.[72]

In the later 18th century there were 2 blacksmiths at Castle Pulverbatch and one at Church Pulver-batch,[73] but only one (at Castle Pulverbatch) re-mained in business by 1839.[74] A second smithy was

[29] V.C.H. Salop. i. 338.
[30] Ibid. 342.
[31] Tax. Eccl. (Rec. Com.), 163.
[32] S.C. 6/967/1.
[33] S.R.O. 665 uncat., ct. r. manor of Boveria, 1508–38.
[34] N.L.W., Chirk Castle 6971.
[35] Q. Sess., reg. papists' estates, 1717.
[36] N.L.W., Chirk Castle 6971.
[37] Par. rec., tithe appts.
[38] E 134/36 Chas. II Trin./5.
[39] E 179/166/168.
[40] S.C. 6/967/1.
[41] N.L.W., Chirk Castle 6971.
[42] S.P.L., MS. 9041/1.
[43] E 134/36 Chas. II Trin./5.
[44] H.O. 67/12/195.
[45] Par. rec., tithe appts.
[46] S.P.L., Haughmond Cart. f. 169ᵛ.
[47] C 133/62/5.
[48] C 135/76/10.
[49] S.R.O. 665 uncat., bailiff's acct. 1383–4.
[50] Ibid. 1412–13.
[51] Ibid. extracts from ct. r. 1352–1596.
[52] S.P.L., Deeds 13379.
[53] Ibid. 9509.
[54] S.R.O. 665 uncat., note of deed, 1717.
[55] Ibid. award re coal and timber on glebe, c. 1734.
[56] S.P.L., Deeds 13627.
[57] Ibid. 1277.
[58] Ibid. 2676.
[59] S.R.O. 665 uncat., survey, c. 1780.
[60] Ibid.
[61] Report of Inspectors of Mines, 1873 [C. 1056], pp. 78–79, H.C. (1874), xiii; ibid. 1883 [C. 4058] pp. 140–1, H.C. (1884), xix.
[62] S.R.O. 883/314.
[63] Ibid. 665 uncat., survey, c. 1780.
[64] Par. rec., tithe appts.
[65] S.P.L., Deeds 13629.
[66] Ibid. 13628.
[67] Bull. Geol. Survey, xiv. 38–39.
[68] Ibid.
[69] Cal. Pat. 1247–58, 274.
[70] Local inf.
[71] Bagshaw's Dir. Salop. (1851).
[72] E 179/166/23.
[73] S.R.O. 665 uncat., survey, c. 1780.
[74] Par. rec., tithe appts.

opened, *c.* 1917[75] and both continued until *c.* 1941.[76] In 1856 the two villages also contained 2 shoemakers, a tailor, a butcher, a grocer, 4 carriers, and 2 shops,[77] of which only the shops remained in 1964.

LOCAL GOVERNMENT. The jurisdiction of Pulverbatch manor court, for which there are extracts from court rolls, 1352–1596,[78] court rolls, 1577, 1580, 1599–1629,[79] and presentments, 1777–1840,[80] included view of frankpledge and the assize of bread and ale and extended over the three northern townships, and over Great Lyth, Little Lyth, and Westley in Condover parish. There are court rolls for the manor of Boveria, 1508–38 and 1547,[81] and for Wilderley Manor, 1718–44.[82]

The parish records include two parish books, containing accounts of churchwardens and overseers, 1653–1708, and overseers' accounts, 1708–43.[83] Churchwardens' accounts, 1708–45, vestry minutes from 1850, together with a quantity of overseers' papers, recorded *c.* 1900,[84] were missing in 1964.

The two churchwardens and two overseers were still appointed in rotation in the mid-18th century, the churchwardens of one year serving as overseers in the next. Until 1669 the churchwardens and overseers each rendered a combined account, but the parish was then split, for administrative purposes, into northern and southern divisions, the former comprising Church Pulverbatch, Castle Pulverbatch, and Wrentnall, and the latter, Cothercott and Wilderley. Subsequently each churchwarden and each overseer rendered a separate account for his division. Although there was still a poor stock of £21 in 1662, the income of the parish officers was later derived entirely from rates, which were first assessed on a pound rate in 1692.

Annual expenditure on poor relief ranged from £5 to £18 in the later 17th century and rarely exceeded £30 before 1740. Poor rates, £82 a year in 1776,[85] had risen to £197 by 1803,[86] and reached a peak of £421 a year in 1817.[87] The poor were farmed to contractors, 1734–7, and in 1742, but, although a poor-house on Pulverbatch outrack had been leased by 1784,[88] no workhouse appears ever to have been established.

A vestry resolution of 1655 that the constables of each township should act as highway surveyors was revoked by the county justices, who required the overseers to assume the office. Separate highway surveyors, appointed in the following year, last appear in 1692. Constables for the five townships were being appointed at the manor courts in the mid-17th century.[89]

CHURCH. John the chaplain, recorded before 1193,[90] is the first known priest at Pulverbatch, and Church Pulverbatch was already known, *c.* 1221, by its local name—'Churcheton'[91] now Churton. The status of the church during the Middle Ages was anomalous for it was a benefice without cure of souls.[92] Described as a free chapel it was valued as part of the assets of the manor in 1421.[93] Its incumbents were styled rectors,[94] but the office seems to have been a sinecure and the church was normally served by one of the portioners of Pontesbury.[95] Pulverbatch thus became in some measure dependent on Pontesbury, and its inhabitants were required to repair a section of Pontesbury churchyard wall until 1714.[96]

The advowson followed the descent of Pulverbatch manor until 1794,[97] but Thomas Goch claimed the right to present to the living in 1394,[98] his nominee being confirmed in possession by the Crown in the following year,[99] and Richard Prince presented, *c.* 1579.[1] The advowson was purchased in 1794 by Thomas Noel, Lord Berwick,[2] but had passed before 1806 to George, Lord Kenyon.[3] It remained in the Kenyon family until 1927, when G. L. T. Kenyon granted it to Wrekin College, Wellington.[4] The Church of England and Martyrs' Memorial Trust have subsequently exercised the right of presentation.[5]

The little evidence available about the value of the living suggests that its meagre income in the Middle Ages increased considerably after the church ceased to be dependent on Pontesbury and after the enlargement of the glebe at the inclosure of Steplewood. The church was said to be worth £6 in 1291,[6] £10 10*s.* in 1421,[7] and £10 0*s.* 8*d.* in 1535.[8] In 1655 the rector had a gross annual income of £60,[9] which had risen to £592 by the 1830s.[10] In 1607 the glebe, which amounted to some 27 a., lay in a number of small inclosed pastures in the common fields of the three northern townships.[11] Enlarged soon afterwards by an allotment in Steplewood,[12] the glebe contained 45 a. in 1839,[13] when it still consisted of a number of scattered fields. The

[75] *Kelly's Dir. Salop.* (1917).
[76] Ibid. (1941).
[77] Ibid. (1856).
[78] S.R.O. 665 uncat.
[79] S.P.L., Deeds 9397, 9509, 9523–4; B.M. Add. MS. 30312.
[80] S.R.O. 1011 uncat.
[81] Ibid. 665 uncat., ct. r. 1508–38; S.C. 2/197/52.
[82] Ibid. 883/95.
[83] S.P.L., MS. 9041/1–3.
[84] *Salop. Par. Docs.* 118–19.
[85] *Rep. Cttee. on Overseers' Returns, 1777*, p. 442, H.C. (1st ser. ix, reprinted 1803).
[86] *Poor Law Abstract, 1803*, H.C. 175, pp. 416–17 (1803–4), xiii.
[87] *Rep. Cttee. on Poor Rate Returns, 1822, Suppl. App.*, H.C. 556, p. 141 (1822), v.
[88] S.R.O. 665 uncat., rental, 1784.
[89] Ibid. 883/95.
[90] S.P.L., Haughmond Cart. f. 169.
[91] Ibid. f. 169ᵛ.
[92] *Cal. Pat.* 1358–61, 190; *Reg. J. Trefnant* (C. & Y.S.), 178; *Reg. T. Spofford* (C. & Y.S.), 366.

[93] S.R.O. 665 uncat., bailiff's acct. 1421–2.
[94] *E.H.R.* xlv. 462.
[95] *Reg. J. Trefnant* (C. & Y.S.), 178; *Tax. Eccl.* (Rec. Com.), 167.
[96] *S.P.R. Heref.* xii. 98–99, 257.
[97] B.M. Add. MS. 21018, ff. 321–2.
[98] S.P.L., Deeds 365.
[99] *Cal. Pat.* 1391–6, 601.
[1] S.P.L., Deeds 13381.
[2] B.M. Add. MS. 21018, ff. 321–2.   [3] Ibid.
[4] Heref. Dioc. Regy., reg. 1926–38, p. 38.
[5] Ex inf. The Church of England and Martyrs' Memorial Trust.
[6] *Tax. Eccl.* (Rec. Com.), 167.
[7] S.R.O. 665 uncat., bailiff's acct. 1421–2.
[8] *Valor Eccl.* (Rec. Com.), iii. 213.
[9] *T.S.A.S.* xlvii. 27.
[10] *Rep. Com. Eccl. Revenues* [67], pp. 448–9, H.C. (1835), xxii.
[11] Heref. Dioc. Regy., glebe terrier, 1607.
[12] Part of the glebe lay in this area in 1840: par. rec., tithe appts.
[13] Ibid.

small tithes were valued at 40s. in 1341[14] and £4 14s. 4d. in 1421,[15] when the great tithes were worth £6 14s. 8d.[16] There is no evidence on the method of tithe-collection here, or for the value of the tithes after the Middle Ages, but no moduses are recorded in 1840, when the tithes of Church Pulverbatch, Castle Pulverbatch, and Wrentnall were commuted for a rent-charge of £385 a year.[17] The tithes of Cothercott and Wilderley had been commuted for an annual rent-charge of £140 in the preceding year.[18] A modus of 1s. a year was, however, being paid in 1846 by the tenant of that part of the township of Stitt and Gatten which lay in Pulverbatch parish.[19] Lands in Pulverbatch, worth 14d. a year in 1547, formed the endowment of a light in the church.[20]

Four medieval incumbents bore the same surname as the lord of the manor and were probably related to him,[21] and another was a king's clerk.[22] Thomas Newport (rector, 1394–1413),[23] who was a graduate,[24] also held Pontesbury first portion.[25] He employed a curate at Pulverbatch,[26] but the church seems to have gone out of use in the 15th century—perhaps as a result of the rising of Owen Glendower[27]—and Newport's successor Thomas Cockayne, who was also non-resident, did not appoint a curate here.[28]

Nine of the 13 rectors of Pulverbatch, 1551–1883, held the living for over 20 years.[29] The only one to be a relative of the lord of the manor was William Owen (rector, 1642–6, 1662–72),[30] but between 1664 and 1806 most of them were non-resident and employed curates to serve the living.[31] Evan Evans, curate 1721–45,[32] was also the curate of Longden,[33] where he was succeeded by John Eyton, rector of Pulverbatch, 1744–81.[34] Between 1750 and c. 1787 Eyton and his successor John Pyefinch (rector, 1781–1806), who also held Westbury first portion,[35] employed as their curate here Thomas Mills, who lived at Pulverbatch[36] and was also Vicar of Habberley, 1758–98,[37] and one of the curates of Pontesbury.[38] Rectors have normally been resident since 1806, but William Gilpin (rector 1806–48),[39] for whom the present parsonage was built by the patron,[40] employed a curate in 1823[41] and continuously after 1832.[42]

In 1421 services appear to have been held only at Christmas, Easter, and Whitsun.[43] Communion was administered from 3 to 5 times a year in the later 17th century[44]—there were 159 communicants at Easter, 1658[45]—and 6 times a year c. 1790, when there were 40 Easter communicants.[46] Two services were held on Sundays c. 1790[47] and in 1851, when 122 persons attended morning service and 50 in the evening.[48]

The church of ST. EDITH,[49] which has been completely rebuilt since the 18th century, consists of a chancel and nave under one roof, a north aisle, and a western tower. It was among the churches said to have been destroyed by the Welsh before 1414[50] and was reconsecrated in 1521.[51] A sketch of 1653 shows that this church consisted of a nave and chancel with a south porch and bell-turret at the west end. In the south wall of the chancel was a priest's door and a small window of two round-headed lights. There was a similar window in the south wall of the nave and, at its west end, a dormer window had been inserted to light a gallery within.[52] The dormer window and the priest's door were preserved when the church was remodelled in the Classical style in 1773. A large round-headed window with a plain keystone was then inserted at the east end and two smaller windows of similar design in the south wall. A new south porch was also built, but the only surviving portion of this church is the tower. The latter, which is of three stages, has rusticated quoins and a similar treatment to the windows and west doorway. There are circular windows to the ringing chamber and, at the belfry stage, a round-headed window with forking tracery on each face. The parapet is surmounted by angle vases. An external stone staircase on the south wall gives access to the ringing chamber. The church was entered through the west door, c. 1790, but in 1828, when the south porch was reopened, the west door was blocked and the base of the tower made into a vestry.

In 1854 the nave and chancel were rebuilt in the Decorated style by Edward Haycock, who also built the north aisle, divided from the nave by an arcade of 3 pointed arches.[53] Local gritstone was used throughout, apart from freestone work on windows, but none of the surviving fragments of the

14 *Inq. Non.* (Rec. Com.), 185.
15 S.R.O. 665 uncat., bailiff's acct. 1421–2.
16 Ibid.
17 Par. rec., tithe appts.
18 Ibid.
19 Ibid. Stitt and Gatten tithe appt. 1846.
20 *T.S.A.S.* 3rd ser. x. 373.
21 *Reg. T. Charlton* (C. & Y.S.), 81; *Reg. J. Stanbury* (C. & Y.S.), 190; *Reg. C. Bothe* (C. & Y.S.), 332; *Valor Eccl.* (Rec. Com.), iii. 213.
22 *Cal. Pat.* 1358–61, 191.
23 *Reg. J. Trefnant* (C. & Y.S.), 178; *Reg. R. Mascall* (C. & Y.S.), 178.
24 S.P.L., Deeds 365.
25 *Reg. J. Trefnant* (C. & Y.S.), 179.
26 *E.H.R.* xlv. 462.
27 *Reg. R. Mascall* (C. & Y.S.), 120.
28 S.R.O. 665 uncat., bailiff's acct. 1421–2.
29 *Instit. Dioc. Heref.* 8–196 passim.
30 *T.S.A.S.* 4th ser. xi. 200; S.P.L., MS. 9041/4.
31 S.P.L., MS. 9041/1–3; Heref. Dioc. Regy., visitation papers, box 14, churchwardens' presentment, 1674; ibid. reg. 1755–71, f. 67; ibid. reg. 1772–1802, ff. 121, 165, 185.
32 S.P.L., MS. 9041/3.
33 Ibid.

34 *Instit. Dioc. Heref.* 113.
35 Ibid. 126.
36 B.M. Add. MS. 21018, ff. 321–2.
37 *Instit. Dioc. Heref.* 99, 127.
38 *S.P.R. Heref.* xii. 503–10.
39 *Instit. Dioc. Heref.* 133, 163.
40 W.S.L. 350/40/3.
41 Ibid.
42 Heref. Dioc. Regy., reg. 1822–42, ff. 185, 296, 408, 575.
43 S.R.O. 665 uncat., bailiff's acct. 1421–2.
44 S.P.L., MS. 9041/1–2.
45 Ibid. 9041/1.
46 B.M. Add. MS. 21018, ff. 321–2.
47 Ibid.
48 H.O. 129/359/1/21.
49 Description of church based, except where otherwise stated, on watercolour in nave, 1653; S.P.L., MS. 372, vol. ii, p. 4; S.P.L., T. F. Dukes watercolours (churches) no. 127; S.P.L., J. H. Smith collect. no. 162; B.M. Add. MS. 21013, f. 71; ibid. 21018, ff. 321–2; Cranage, vi. 474.
50 *Reg. R. Mascall* (C. & Y.S.), 120.
51 *Reg. C. Bothe* (C. & Y.S.), 106.
52 Gallery first recorded in 1657: S.P.L., MS. 9041/1.
53 Par. rec., contract for church restoration, 1854.

16th-century church was preserved. The roofs of the nave and north aisle are of arch-braced collar-beam construction.

Within the church few fittings older than 1854 now survive. Panels from the box-pews, made in 1779 with wainscot taken from Woolstaston Hall,[54] were re-used in 1854. The communion table is a late-18th-century side-table; its predecessor, made in 1675,[55] is probably the oak table stored in the gallery in 1964. The pulpit dates from c. 1800. The octagonal font, in the Perpendicular style, is unlikely to be older than 1854, since the church had a small round font with a slender stem in 1823.[56] The choir stalls were inserted in 1896.[57]

The church had a silver chalice in 1552.[58] The existing plate—a chalice, 2 patens, and a flagon—are all of silver plate and are probably of 19th-century date.[59] There were two bells in the church in 1552[60] and in 1740.[61] Five of the present peal of six bells, cast by Thomas Rudhall of Gloucester, were acquired when the church was remodelled in 1773,[62] and the sixth bell was cast by John Rudhall in 1789.[63] The parish registers[64] are complete from 1542.

NONCONFORMITY. The parish was said to contain only one dissenter in 1676[65] and a single family of sectaries c. 1790.[66] The latter were probably Methodists and may have met at a house in Church Pulverbatch, licensed as a dissenting meeting-house in 1816.[67] They still met at a private house in 1851, when they had been affiliated to the Primitive Methodist Association and had an average congregation of 40.[68] A Baptist chapel at Wrentnall, built by James Freme of Wrentnall House c. 1840,[69] had an average congregation of 26 in 1851, when it was served from Pontesbury.[70] The chapel closed c. 1875[71] but since 1910 it has again been used as a chapel by the Methodists recorded above.[72] An Independent Calvinist congregation, established by the Revd. R. Maydwell c. 1845,[73] met at Churton Cottage (now Churton Lodge), Church Pulverbatch. This had an average congregation of 30 in 1851[74] and 168 baptisms are recorded between 1845 and 1898.[75] The meeting had a flourishing Sunday School in the later 19th century and continued until c. 1914.[76]

SCHOOLS. Rectory Cottage, Church Pulverbatch, is the site of a day school built by public subscription on the glebe before 1818,[77] on the initiative of the rector, George Gilpin.[78] The rector also provided a Sunday School, first recorded in 1828.[79] Between 80 and 90 children attended it in 1833, when there were two private schools in the parish.[80] In 1839 the day school was placed under the management of a committee of churchwardens and subscribers.[81] By 1846 the school had been affiliated to the National Society, when the standard of education was said to be improving, but 'little, if at all, above mediocrity'.[82] George Bowen, appointed schoolmaster in 1839,[83] was also the postmaster, and kept a grocer's shop, 1851–79.[84] This school was replaced by the present school, built on the glebe in 1873.[85]

The school was still supported solely by voluntary subscriptions in 1833,[86] but school-pence were introduced in 1839.[87] By 1854 these were assessed on a graduated scale and then produced £18 a year,[88] but they had been abolished by 1893.[89] The school became Controlled in 1951.[90] Sixty children attended in 1818[91] and attendance continued at this level until 1906.[92] The Sunday School is not recorded after 1833, but the Independent Calvinists provided a night school in the later 19th century.[93]

CHARITIES. The poor of Pulverbatch[94] were entitled, with those of Condover, to a share in the charity established by Henry Brickdale by will of 1700.[95] The endowment of £44, with some other Condover charity funds, was used in 1709 to purchase a rent-charge of £2 11s. 6d. arising from the tithes of Betton Abbots and Emstrey.[96] Pulverbatch received £1 a year from this source c. 1830, when it was distributed in bread to 6 widows on alternate Sundays, but as a result of a recommendation by the Charity Commissioners the share paid to Pulverbatch had been increased to £1 5s. 7d. by 1862. The charity was being distributed in the same manner c. 1864, but was lost after 1877, when the agent for the Betton estate refused to pay the rent-charge.

By will of 1777 Ann Jaundrell left £20, to be distributed in bread to the poor. This sum was then

[54] B.M. Add. MS. 21018, ff. 321–2.
[55] S.P.L., MS. 9041/2.
[56] B.M. Add. MS. 21013, f. 72v.
[57] Heref. Dioc. Regy., reg. 1883–1901, pp. 56–57.
[58] T.S.A.S. 2nd ser. xii. 98.
[59] Arkwright and Bourne, Ch. Plate Ludlow Archd. 50–51.
[60] T.S.A.S. 2nd ser. xii. 98.
[61] Walters, Ch. Bells Salop. 206–8.
[62] Ibid.   [63] Ibid.
[64] S.P.L., MSS. 9034–40.
[65] T.S.A.S. 2nd ser. i. 88.
[66] B.M. Add. MS. 21018, f. 321.
[67] Q. Sess. Orders, iii. 200.
[68] H.O. 129/359/1/23.
[69] W. E. Morris, History of Methodism in Shrewsbury and District (Shrewsbury, 1960), 55.
[70] H.O. 129/359/1/24.
[71] Morris, Methodism, 55.   [72] Ibid.
[73] Par. rec., register bk. 1845–98.
[74] H.O. 129/359/1/22.
[75] Par. rec., register bk. 1845–98.
[76] Ex inf. Mrs. A. Roberts, Church View, Castle Pulverbatch.
[77] Digest of Returns to Cttee. on Educ. of Poor, H.C. 224, p. 758 (1819), ix (2).
[78] B.M. Add. MS. 21018, ff. 321–2.   [79] Ibid.

[80] Educ. Enquiry Abstract, H.C. 62, p. 781 (1835), xlii.
[81] Par. rec., school minutes, 1839–45.
[82] Nat. Soc. Ch. School Returns, 1846–7.
[83] Par. rec., school minutes, 1839–45.
[84] Bagshaw's Dir. Salop. (1851); Kelly's Dir. Salop (1856–79).
[85] Voluntary Schs. Returns, H.C. 178–XXIV, p. 20 (1906), lxxxviii.
[86] Educ. Enquiry Abstract, p. 781.
[87] Par. rec., school minutes, 1839–45.
[88] Ed. 7/162/53.
[89] Return of Schs. 1893 [C. 7529], p. 504, H.C. (1894), lxv.
[90] Ex inf. S.C.C. Educ. Dept.
[91] Digest of Returns to Cttee. on Educ. of Poor, p. 758.
[92] Educ. Enquiry Abstract, p. 781; Nat. Soc. Ch. School Returns, 1846–7; Ed. 7/162/53; Returns relating to Elem. Educ., H.C. 201, p. 334 (1871), lv; Return of Schs. 1893, p. 504; Voluntary Schs. Returns, p. 20.
[93] Ex inf. Mrs. A. Roberts, Church View, Castle Pulverbatch.
[94] Account of charities based, except where otherwise stated, on 24th Rep. Com. Char., H.C. 231, pp. 388–9 (1831), xi; Digest of Endowed Char. 1862–3, H.C. 433, pp. 194–5 (1867–8), lii; Char. Com. files.
[95] 24th Rep. Com. Char. 380–1.
[96] Ibid.

put towards the expenses of repewing the church, and £1 was thereafter paid annually by the church-wardens to provide bread for the poor on St. Thomas's Day and New Year's Day. This charity had been lost by 1886. By will of 1790 James Perkins left to the rector an annual rent-charge of £1 6s. arising from a farm at Marton in Chirbury, to be distributed in bread every Sunday to 6 widows. The owner of the estate was paying the rent-charge c. 1830, when it was distributed with Brickdale's charity, but the rent-charge was later held to be void under the Mortmain Act and was no longer being paid in 1862. A similar fate seems to have overtaken the charity of Richard Perkins (d. 1798); who gave a rent-charge of £1 6s. arising from lands at Church Pulverbatch, to be distributed to the poor on New Year's Day. This sum was being paid by his daughter, Margaret Wall, c. 1830, when it was distributed with part of Jaundrell's charity, but the charity is not recorded after 1862.

Margaret Perkins, by will dated 1840, left £400 stock, the interest on which was to be distributed to the poor. Payments began in 1855 and in 1866 were being made to 42 families, when each family received between 4s. and 6s. In 1931, when the charity is last recorded, its annual income of £10 was distributed to 32 persons.

By will proved in 1916 Mary Anne Corrie left £100, the interest on which was to be distributed among the poor at the rector's discretion. Payments began in 1924, and in 1964 its income of £3 1s. 2d. was given to 4 poor persons at Christmas.

RUCKLEY AND LANGLEY

THE parochial status of Ruckley and Langley is confused. It was a parish in the Middle Ages, with its own priest and an advowson distinct from that of Acton Burnell. Since the 16th century, however, when presentations to Langley chapel lapsed, it has been accounted a chapelry of Acton Burnell[1]— a state of dependence the more easily achieved since from 1617 both parishes have been part of the same estate.[2] Notwithstanding this, Ruckley and Langley maintained its own poor by 1718[3] and has since been accounted a civil parish.

The parish, which contains 1,536 a.,[4] lies 8 miles south-east of Shrewsbury, and includes the hamlets of Ruckley, Langley, and Causeway Wood, together with the deserted sites of the manor of Hawksley and the hamlet of Hothales. It is situated in a valley between the Kenley ridge on the south-east and, on the north-west, Lodgehill and Acton Burnell Hill, which mark the northern end of Hoar Edge. It is drained by Bullhill Brook, which runs north-eastwards across the centre of the parish. The northern and southern boundaries follow the crest of the surrounding hills, but the north-eastern boundary runs across the valley bottom through the former Langley Park. In the valley the ground, which is mainly boulder clay, falls gently eastwards from 675 feet at Causeway Wood to 435 feet east of Langley Hall. The hills rise to 900 feet on the north and to 825 feet on the south.

The parish lay in the Long Forest but the area which it covered had been disafforested by 1300.[5] The greater part was probably woodland in 1086, when the manors of Langley and Hawksley together were only assessed at one hide.[6] The western boundary of the parish was still indistinct in the 13th century, for lands in the south-west were then accounted part of the manor of Cardington,[7] while woodland at Chatwall in Cardington lay in Langley manor[8] and still paid tithes to the lord of Langley in the 17th century.[9] Assarts are continuously mentioned from the late 12th[10] until the mid-14th century[11] among them 'Fulewood', near Ruckley, which is first recorded in 1231[12] and was said to be the haunt of wolves in 1283.[13] The woods on the slopes of Causeway Wood and Lodgehill are all that now remains of a large wood, called 'Harlith' in 1274,[14] lying between Bullhill Brook and Hoar Edge. Netherwood Coppice still extends along the scarp of the Kenley ridge. There were 172 a. of woodland in the parish in 1846, since when its area has not been significantly changed. In 1960 60 a. woodland in Causeway Wood were purchased by the Forestry Commission.[15]

The eastern half of the parish, together with some 300 a. in Cound, lay in Langley Park. There was said to be a park here in 1249,[16] but it is not recorded in surveys of the later 13th century.[17] It may have been created afresh after a grant of free warren had been obtained in 1319.[18] There is no reliable evidence for its size and bounds before the later 18th century, when it was restricted to the area east of the road from Langley to Kenley,[19] but it seems earlier to have extended as far west as the road from Ruckley to Acton Burnell.[20] It was still stocked with deer in 1688[21] but was disparked between 1785[22] and 1805.[23]

[1] See p. 145.
[2] See p. 143.
[3] Q. Sess. Orders, ii. 31.
[4] O.S. Area Bk. (1883). The following topographical description is based, except where otherwise stated, on O.S. Map 1″, sheet lxi (1st edn.); O.S. Maps 6″ Salop. 49, 50 (1st and later edns.); O.S. Maps 1/25,000, SJ 50, SO 59 (1959); Rocque, Map of Salop. (1752); Baugh, Map of Salop. (1808); B.M. O.S. 2″ orig. drawings, sheet 207 (1817); Geol. Survey Map (drift), sheet 152 (1932); Tithe Redemption Com., tithe appt. and map, 1846. This article was written in 1963 and revised in 1965. The Smythe family muniments, now S.R.O. 1514, were discovered after the final revision of this article.
[5] Eyton, vi. 345.
[6] V.C.H. Salop. i. 341, 342.
[7] Cal. Inq. Misc. i, pp. 290–1.
[8] C 143/6/10.
[9] C 142/477/189.
[10] E 32/143 m. 1.
[11] S.P.L., MS. 2, f. 22.
[12] Eyton, vi. 124.
[13] C 143/6/10.
[14] Cal. Inq. Misc. i, pp. 290–1.
[15] Ex inf. Forestry Com.
[16] Cal. Inq. Misc. i, p. 19.
[17] Ibid. p. 176; C 134/32/8; C 145/125/20.
[18] Cal. Chart. R. 1300–26, 415.
[19] S.P.L., MS. 294.
[20] Tithe Redemption Com., tithe appt.
[21] Smythe deeds, penes Messrs. Knapp Fisher, solicitors, Westminster.
[22] Q. Sess., reg. papists' estates, 1785.
[23] S.P.L., MS. 294.

The creation of the park seems to have affected the course of roads in the east of the parish. A grant to the lord of Langley of a right of way from Langley to Cressage in 1319 suggests that a road may then have run eastwards through Cound.[24] The present road to Kenley, which leaves the parish at Park Gate, runs through the middle of the former park. It seems originally to have been a private road to Langley Hall and is not recorded before 1817. In the west the roads running from Ruckley to Acton Burnell and Chatwall are ancient. The latter was known as 'Mershall's way' in 1274.[25] At Causeway Wood it uses the exposed surface of a supposed Roman road, locally known as the Devil's Causeway, but the latter, which is thought to have served quarries at Cardington in Roman times,[26] does not seem to have followed the course of the present road. It probably ran round the lower slopes of Lodgehill, joining Watling Street between Acton Burnell and Frodesley.[27]

Ruckley, Langley, and the deserted hamlet of Hothales each had their own common fields in the Middle Ages. Those of Hothales were known in the 13th century as the Field towards Ruckley,[28] the Field towards Harlith,[29] and the Field towards the chapel (of Ruckley).[30] The last seems to have adjoined the common fields of the deserted hamlet of Ramshurst in Frodesley.[31] Two of the Ruckley fields were called the Field towards the chapel[32] and the Field towards Acton Burnell.[33] Those of Langley must have been included in the park at an early date, but one of them adjoined the wall of Acton Burnell Park in 1379.[34] The date at which the common fields of Ruckley and Hothales were inclosed is not known. Line Hill, a tract of waste land in the north-east of the parish below Acton Burnell Hill, was inclosed between 1805[35] and 1846.[36]

The three medieval hamlets all lay on boulder clay near Bullhill Brook. Since no tenants are recorded on the manor of Langley in 1086, other than the serfs on the desmesne,[37] it is possible that Ruckley and Hothales were later settlements. Both were inhabited by free tenants in the 13th century.[38] There were at least 7 houses at Langley in 1662,[39] but by 1805 there were only 3, including Park Gate on the Kenley ridge.[40] Langley Hall, which had become a farm-house by 1717,[41] was demolished in the later 19th century, when the present Langley Hall Farm was built, but the Gatehouse and part

of the outer wall are still standing.[42] Langley chapel, probably built in 1564,[43] occupies an isolated position 100 yards east of the Gatehouse. There was an alehouse at Langley in 1616,[44] but this had been moved to Park Gate by 1747[45] and closed in 1774.[46] Ruckley had probably shrunk to its present size by 1662. There were then said to be at least 7 houses here,[47] but these would include the settlement at Causeway Wood. There were 3 houses in Ruckley in 1805.[48] Ruckley Hall Farm is a stone building of late-19th-century date, but it stands on the site of an earlier house which had 11 hearths in 1662.[49] A ruinous stone cottage on the north of the road, to the west of the hamlet, was formerly the parish poor-house.[50] The deserted hamlet of Hothales, first recorded in 1253,[51] probably lay between Ruckley and Causeway Wood, on a knoll south of the road, overlooking Bullhill Brook and near a field called Whethalls Meadow in 1848.[52] It still existed in 1478,[53] but in 1501[54] there was pasture here and by 1572, when the name last occurs in this form,[55] it had probably disappeared. The Domesday manor of Hawksley, which was waste in 1086,[56] was said to lie between Langley and Ruckley in 1269[57] and in 1535 its site lay within Langley Park.[58]

Among medieval assarts was a small settlement known as Brochouses, which is recorded between 1327[59] and 1377.[60] This may be the origin of the settlement later known as Causeway Wood, first recorded in 1572.[61] There were 4 houses at Causeway Wood in 1805,[62] 3 of which are still standing. The cottages here and at Ruckley are stone-built and are similar in plan to those on Kenley Common. Causeway Wood Farm is the only surviving timber-framed farm-house in the parish.

There were 82 inhabitants in the parish in 1801[63] and 75 in 1821.[64] Its population remained stationary until 1871, when it rose to 107, but thereafter has steadily declined.[65] There were only 56 inhabitants in 1961.[66] John Kirk (1760–1851), the Roman Catholic divine and antiquary, was born at Ruckley.[67]

MANORS. Roger, Earl of Shrewsbury, was overlord of *LANGLEY* manor in 1086,[68] but the suzerainty of the earls of Shrewsbury presumably lapsed after 1102.[69] In 1212 the manor was held of the Crown in serjeanty, for the service of carrying a goshawk from Shrewsbury castle to Stepney

24 S.P.L. MS. 2, f. 12.
25 *Cal. Inq. Misc.* i, pp. 290–1.
26 *T.S.A.S.* lv. 43–44.　　27 Ibid.
28 S.P.L., MS. 2, f. 14.
29 Ibid. f. 13.
30 Ibid. ff. 13ᵛ, 14; S.P.L., Deeds 10768.
31 S.P.L., MS. 2, f. 13ᵛ.
32 Ibid. f. 10.
33 Ibid. f. 14.
34 Ibid. f. 13.
35 Ibid. MS. 294.
36 Tithe Redemption Com., tithe appt.
37 *V.C.H. Salop.* i. 342.
38 *Bk. of Fees*, 1241–2.
39 E 179/255/35 m. 8.
40 S.P.L., MS. 294.
41 Q. Sess., reg. papists' estates, 1717.
42 See p. 143.
43 B.M. Add. MS. 21021, f. 157.
44 Q. Sess., alehouse reg.
45 N.L.W., Castle Hill 2244.
46 Q. Sess., alehouse reg.
47 E 179/255/35 m. 8.
48 S.P.L., MS. 294.
49 E 179/255/35 m. 8.
50 Q. Sess., reg. papists' estates, 1785.
51 *Cal. Inq. Misc.* i, p. 176.
52 O.S. Nat. Grid. SO 529993; Tithe Redemption Com., tithe appt.
53 S.P.L., MS. 2, f. 14.
54 C 142/13/94.
55 S.P.L., MS. 2, f. 8.
56 *V.C.H. Salop.* i. 341.
57 Eyton, vi. 151.
58 *Valor Eccl.* (Rec. Com.), iii. 189
59 *T.S.A.S.* 2nd ser. xi. 374.
60 S.P.L., MS. 2, f. 17ᵛ.
61 Ibid. f. 8.
62 Ibid. MS. 294.
63 *Census*, 1801.
64 Ibid. 1821.
65 Ibid. 1831–1931.
66 Ibid. 1961.
67 *D.N.B.*
68 *V.C.H. Salop.* i. 342.
69 Eyton, i. 245.

(Mdx.) once a year.[70] In 1250 the serjeanty was converted into a tenure by knight service for the service of ⅓ knight's fee.[71] Shortly before 1273 Robert Burnell created a mesne tenure here when he granted the manor to Richard Burnell, to hold for the service of ¼ knight's fee.[72] After Robert Burnell's death in 1292 this transaction was alleged to be illegal, presumably by the retrospective application of Quia Emptores, and the manor was seized by the Crown.[73] It was restored in 1297, when the mesne tenure under the Burnells of Acton Burnell was converted into a tenure-in-chief for the service of ¼ knight's fee.[74]

Before 1066 Langley manor was held by the freeman Suain and in 1086 Toret was tenant.[75] By 1212 the manor was held by William Burnell, a member of the senior branch of the Burnell family of Acton Burnell,[76] whose brother Thomas had been lord of Hawksley manor in 1194.[77] It followed the descent of Acton Burnell manor until 1249,[78] when it was granted to Elias de Ettingham to hold during pleasure.[79] The latter died in 1250,[80] and in 1251 the manor was granted to William de Gardinis,[81] who held it until his death in 1264.[82] By 1266 William's son William had sold the manor to Robert Burnell, Bishop of Bath and Wells,[83] who before 1273 granted it to his relative Richard Burnell.[84] Until 1377 the manor passed from father to son in this branch of the Burnell family, the following being lords: Richard, by 1273–1313,[85] William, 1313–31;[86] Edward, 1331–77.[87] On the death of Edward Burnell in 1377 it passed to his wife Margaret.[88] She died later in the same year,[89] when the manor was divided between her three daughters, Joan, wife of Robert de la Lee, Katherine, wife of John de Stapleton, and Hugelina, wife of Robert le Coyne.[90] On the death of Joan de la Lee in 1400 her portion of the manor passed to her daughter and heir Parnel, wife of Robert Lee of Roden.[91] Parnel died in 1442,[92] being followed by her son Ralph Lee, and this part of the manor descended from father to son until 1660, the following being lords: Ralph, 1442–79;[93] Richard, 1479–1500;[94] Fulk, 1500–16;[95] Thomas, 1516–74;[96] Richard, 1574–91;[97] Humphrey, 1591–1632.[98] After 1617, when Humphrey Lee acquired the manor of Acton Burnell, Langley followed the descent of that manor.[99]

The portion of the manor which Katherine de Stapleton inherited in 1377 descended in her heirs until c. 1458, when it was conveyed to Ralph Lee.[1] That of Hugelina le Coyne also descended in her heirs until c. 1505, when Robert Coyne exchanged it with Fulk Lee for lands in Hunkington in Upton Magna.[2] After this date the whole manor was held by the Lee family and their descendants. Causeway Wood and Ruckley Hall Farm were sold in 1921.[3]

Langley Hall,[4] demolished in the later 19th century, was an L-shaped house, partly of stone and partly timber-framed, surrounded by a moat.[5] In 1672, when it had 16 hearths, the house was still the residence of the lord of the manor,[6] but it had been let to one of the tenants as a farm-house by 1717.[7] It was still standing in 1846.[8] The main building faced north and south and included a timber-framed hall with a porch on the north side. A stone-built wing was added at the east end, probably in the later 16th century. This had mullioned and transomed windows, and a stone bay-window stood in the angle between it and the hall. A timber-framed wing continued at a lower level to the west of the hall. The only part of the Hall still standing is the gatehouse, which was detached from the main building; in 1963 it was in use as a farm store. Most of the structure probably dates, like the two wings of the Hall, from the later 16th century. On its western or outer face it is stone-built and some of the lower masonry, including a pointed archway of two chamfered orders, appears to be of medieval origin. The upper storey, which has mullioned windows and gables, is a later addition. The inner face is timber-framed, with diagonal strutting resembling that on the former west wing. An embattled wall, running northwards from the gatehouse, was slighted in 1961.[9]

Roger, Earl of Shrewsbury, was overlord of HAWKSLEY manor in 1086.[10] Alric was tenant before 1066 and Teodulf in 1086.[11] The manor had been granted before 1194 to Shrewsbury Abbey,[12] who held it until the Dissolution,[13] but after 1194, when Thomas Burnell held it of the abbey,[14] the manor was always leased to the lords of Langley manor.[15] It lost its separate identity after the Dissolution.

ECONOMIC HISTORY. The manor of Langley was said to be worth 5s. before 1066 and again in

[70] Bk. of Fees, 145.　[71] Ibid.
[72] S.P.L., MS. 2, f. 1.
[73] Cal. Pat. 1292–1301, 291; S.P.L., MS. 2, f. 1ᵛ.
[74] Ibid.
[75] V.C.H. Salop. i. 342.
[76] Bk. of Fees, 145.
[77] Eyton, vi. 148.
[78] See p. 7.
[79] Close R. 1247–51, 188.
[80] Ex. e Rot. Fin. (Rec. Com.), ii. 94.
[81] Close R. 1247–51, 407.
[82] Cal. Inq. p.m. i, p. 179.
[83] T.S.A.S. 4th ser. iv. 178.
[84] S.P.L., MS. 2, f. 1.
[85] C 134/32/8.
[86] C 135/25/12.
[87] Cal. Inq. p.m. xiv, pp. 304–5. During the minority of Edward Burnell, 1331–8, the manor was held in dower by Rose, widow of William Burnell: Cal. Close, 1330–3, 210; ibid. 1337–9, 553.
[88] Cal. Close, 1374–7, 483.
[89] Cal. Inq. p.m. xv, pp. 2–3.
[90] Cal. Fine R. 1377–83, 60.
[91] C 137/23/35.
[92] Cal. Fine R. 1437–45, 227.
[93] C 140/72/71.
[94] Ibid.; Cal. Inq. p.m. Hen. VII, ii, pp. 132–3.
[95] C 142/30/8, 63.
[96] C 142/132/17.
[97] C 142/230/64.
[98] C 142/477/189.
[99] See p. 8.
[1] S.P.L., MS. 2, ff. 12, 12ᵛ; Feud. Aids, iv. 256, 264.
[2] C 137/22/25; S.P.L., MS. 2, ff. 11ᵛ, 12, 12ᵛ, 16ᵛ.
[3] S.C.C. title-deeds, SH 35 (sale partics. 1921).
[4] Description of house based on water-colours, 1789, in S.P.L. MS. 372, vol. i, pp. 104, 119. See also plate facing p. 144.
[5] V.C.H. Salop. i. 404.
[6] Hearth Tax, 1672, 135.
[7] Q. Sess., reg. papists' estates, 1717.
[8] Tithe Redemption Com., tithe appt.
[9] T.S.A.S. lvii. 2.
[10] V.C.H. Salop. i. 341.
[11] Ibid.
[12] Eyton, vi. 148.
[13] S.C. 6/Hen. VIII/3010 m. 67.
[14] Eyton, vi. 148.
[15] Ibid. 151; T.S.A.S. 2nd ser. x. 309; S.P.L., MS. 2, f. 13.

1086, when it was assessed at half a hide.[16] Its annual value, which was said to be a little over £8 in 1247,[17] had fallen to £6 18s. by 1313,[18] but had risen to £9 2s. by 1334.[19] Hawksley manor, also assessed at half a hide, was said to be waste in 1066 and in 1086.[20] It was then held at farm for 6d. a year and seems to have been entirely woodland, since no other manorial assets are recorded. Part of the manor had been assarted by 1194, when the rent was 6s. a year.[21]

In 1086 there were 4 serfs and one plough on the Langley desmesne,[22] which seems to have remained unchanged in size until the early 14th century. It comprised one carucate in 1249[23] and 120 a. in 1313,[24] but had increased to 2 carucates by 1334.[25] A substantial acreage seems always to have been kept in hand, even after Langley Hall was leased in the later 17th century. The lord had 310 a. in hand in 1805[26] and 378 a. in 1846,[27] but most of this was woodland.

The decline in the value of the manor during the 13th century seems to have been due to the creation of a number of free tenancies. By 1247 there were 14 free tenants, holding a total of 2 virgates, 7 bovates, and 36½ a. land, said to be worth 66s. a year.[28] Several of these freeholds were bought back into the manorial estate by Rose, wife of William Burnell, between 1319 and 1331,[29] but others survived until the 15th century. The 14 free tenants of 1247 were probably the only tenants in the manor, for in 1313 all the tenants were described as free, and they paid rents totalling £4 0s. 4d. a year.[30] By 1334 there were both free and unfree tenants, paying rents of £5 10s. a year.[31] An attempt seems also to have been made to limit the independence of the remaining freeholders, since a grant made to a free tenant before 1331 required an amercement if he was brought before the king's justices, together with a relief on the marriage or knighthood of the lord's eldest son, and an aid if the lords' hall was burnt.[32]

From 1377 until the mid-15th century each of the three parts into which the manor was divided seems to have been separately administered. By 1439, however, Ralph Lee, who had obtained a life-lease of his mother's estate at Berrington before 1439,[33] had probably secured control of her Langley estate by the same means. He vigorously set about consolidating the manorial estate. He acquired the remaining freeholds in Ruckley and Hothales between 1439 and 1455,[34] and took long leases of the two other portions of the manor.[35] The interests of the other co-parceners had been extinguished by 1506.[36]

The value of the estate showed little change during the 17th and 18th centuries. The demesne lands and rents were worth £274 in 1649,[37] when the demesne may still have been in hand. Rents produced £239 a year in 1717[38] and £295 in 1785.[39] If it had ever been widely used on this estate, the three-life lease had virtually disappeared by 1717.[40] Two small properties were then held on long leases at a rent of £27 a year, while 4 short-term lease-holders paid £155 and 4 tenants-at-will paid £57 a year.[41] Langley Hall and Ruckley Hall were already the homesteads of large farms in 1717[42] and several smaller holdings disappeared in the course of the 18th century.[43] In 1805 Langley Hall and Ruckley Hall Farms were both of over 400 a., and Causeway Wood Farm contained 297 a.[44] There were then 3 holdings smaller than 20 a., while 70 a. were attached to farms in Acton Burnell and Cound.[45] The trend towards larger farms had, however, been reversed by 1846, when there were 5 farms totalling 1,022 a. and 5 holdings of 5–50 a.[46]

There were said to be 210 a. arable in the parish in 1794, when the chief crop was oats,[47] but this was probably an under-estimate, since there were 552 a. arable and some 750 a. pasture in 1805.[48] There were roughly the same quantity of arable and pasture in 1846.[49]

There were mills at Hothales and Langley in the Middle Ages. That at Hothales is first recorded in 1247.[50] It is not named after 1284,[51] but was probably one of the two mills in the manor in 1334.[52] Langley mill, worth 10s. in 1313,[53] is last recorded in 1691.[54]

LOCAL GOVERNMENT. There are no surviving manor court rolls or parish records, but the parish was maintaining its own poor by 1718.[55] There was a single overseer here in 1823.[56] Poor rates rose from £25 in 1776[57] to £70 in 1803,[58] and reached a peak of £92 in 1816.[59] After 1818 they declined steadily and stood at £36 in 1834.[60] A poor-house at Ruckley,

[16] V.C.H. Salop. i. 342.
[17] Cal. Inq. Misc. i, p. 19.
[18] C 134/32/8.
[19] C 145/125/20.
[20] V.C.H. Salop. i. 341.
[21] S.P.L., MS. 2, f. 5.
[22] V.C.H. Salop. i. 342.
[23] Cal. Inq. Misc. i, p. 19.
[24] C 134/32/8.
[25] C 145/125/20.
[26] S.P.L., M.S. 294.
[27] Tithe Redemption Com., tithe apt.
[28] Eyton, vi. 145–6.
[29] S.P.L., Deeds 10767; S.P.L., MS. 2, f. 13ᵛ.
[30] C 134/32/8.
[31] C 145/125/20.
[32] S.P.L., MS. 2, f. 12.
[33] Visit. Salop. 1623 (Harl. Soc. xxix), ii. 316.
[34] S.P.L., MS. 2, ff. 10ᵛ, 11, 13ᵛ, 14, 14ᵛ.
[35] Ibid. ff. 11ᵛ, 12, 16ᵛ.
[36] See p. 143.
[37] S.P.L., MS. 109.
[38] Q. Sess., reg. papists' estates, 1717.
[39] Ibid. 1785.
[40] Ibid. 1717.

[41] Ibid.
[42] Ibid.
[43] Ibid. 1717, 1741, 1785.
[44] S.P.L., MS. 294.
[45] Ibid.
[46] Tithe Redemption Com., tithe appt.
[47] N.L.W., Pitchford Hall uncat., acreage return, 1794.
[48] S.P.L., MS. 294.
[49] Tithe Redemption Com., tithe appt.
[50] Eyton, vi. 146.
[51] S.P.L., MS. 2, f. 14.
[52] C 145/125/20.
[53] C 134/32/8.
[54] N.L.W., Pitchford Hall 821.
[55] Q. Sess. Orders, ii. 31.
[56] Visit. Archd. Salop. 1823.
[57] Rep. Cttee. on Overseers' Returns, 1777, p. 442, H.C. (1st ser. ix, reprinted 1803).
[58] Poor Law Abstract, 1803, H.C. 175, pp. 416–17 (1803–4), xiii.
[59] Rep. Cttee. on Poor Rate Returns, 1822, Suppl. App., H.C. 556, p. 141 (1822), v.
[60] Ibid. 1825, H.C. 334, p. 177 (1825), iv; Acct. of Money Expended on Poor, 1825–9, H.C. 83, p. 390 (1830–1), xi; ibid. 1830–4, H.C. 444, p. 344 (1835), xlvii.

Langley Hall in 1789 with the gatehouse to the right of it

Interior of Langley Chapel from the west

RUCKLEY AND LANGLEY

recorded in 1785,[61] was still held by the overseers in 1846.[62]

CHURCH. There was a hermit at Langley in the later 12th century.[63] Ruckley chapel, which seems to have stood to the west of Ruckley township, is first recorded in 1249,[64] and its first known priest was John de Arderne, living c. 1250.[65] Before 1313 Richard Burnell was said to have obtained licence to erect a chapel at Langley.[66] This probably stood on the site of the present Langley chapel. Priests continued to be presented to Ruckley chapel until 1410.[67] In 1381 the advowsons of Ruckley and Langley were said to be united.[68]

Acton Burnell was said to be the mother-church of Ruckley, c. 1270,[69] but the chapels of Ruckley and Langley seem to have been independent of Acton Burnell until 1572,[70] and their advowson followed the descent of Langley manor. Langley chapel had its own priest in 1552,[71] but in 1570 the Crown claimed the chapel as concealed land.[72] When this claim was defeated in 1572, the benefice was adjudged to be a donative in the hands of the patron of Acton Burnell.[73] Thereafter the living was normally served by the Rectors of Acton Burnell, although Langley had a separate curate between 1655 and 1667.[74] Shortly before 1799 the Rector of Acton Burnell disclaimed responsibility for Langley, saying that it was 'no chapel of his'.[75] The curate of Acton Burnell performed services here in 1823[76] and the Rector of Hughley in 1843.[77]

There was glebe belonging to Ruckley chapel in the 13th century,[78] but no later reference can be found. In 1341 the small tithes of Ruckley were worth 24s.[79] The great tithes had belonged to the lords of Langley manor since the 13th century,[80] and in 1655 were worth £9 10s. a year.[81] In 1717 tithes were paid by the tenants as part of their rent,[82] and in 1846 they were commuted for a rent-charge of £180 a year.[83] During the Middle Ages the priest was said to receive an annual stipend of £4 from the lord of the manor, who also provided him with diet and livery.[84] In 1799 the lord paid the officiating minister £2 10s. a year for his services.[85]

Between 1799 and 1847 services were held at Langley chapel on St. Stephen's Day and on the Tuesday after Easter, when communion was administered.[86] There were 40 communicants in 1799 and 20 in 1847.[87] Registration took place at Acton Burnell from the 16th century,[88] but a baptism

at Langley chapel is recorded in 1711[89] and in 1823 a marriage was said to have been solemnized there within living memory.[90] Parishioners normally attended Acton Burnell church, where the south transept was known as the Ruckley chapel in 1823.[91]

Langley chapel has no known dedication.[92] It is a small rectangular building, consisting of a nave and a chancel, with a wooden bell-turret at the west end. It may have been built in 1564,[93] but the style of some of its architectural features suggests that it may be a reconstruction of an earlier church. The 3-light east window has bar tracery and there is a pointed window at the west end. On the north wall is a 2-light square-headed window, and there is a small round-headed opening on the south wall. The nave and chancel roofs, though uniformly tiled in stone, are of different construction. The former, dated 1601, has 4 arch-braced collar-beam trusses, while the latter is of the trussed rafter type. On the south side the roof and wall of the nave are connected within by a plaster frieze, ornamented with Tudor roses, fleurs-de-lis, and rosettes. A similar frieze on the north wall was accidentally destroyed in 1900.

The chancel, which is floored with medieval tiles, is raised from the nave by a step. The furnishings here and in the nave are all of early-17th-century date and preserve their original arrangement.[94] The communion table stands in the centre of the chancel and is surrounded by seats and kneeling rests on the north, east, and south walls. The rails round the table were erected between 1823 and 1829.[95] The eastern half of the nave is occupied on the south side by two large pews, doubtless occupied by the household of the lord of the manor, and on the north by the pulpit and reading desk. The low benches at the west end of the nave are roughly made, but their bench-ends have poppy-head finials. A high pew in the north-east corner of the nave may have been intended for musicians.

The two bells recorded in 1552[96] were still in the chapel in 1843.[97] By 1915 only one bell remained[98] and this has since been removed. There was no church plate in 1552,[99] and in the early 19th century plate was borrowed from Acton Burnell when required.[1]

Since the early 19th century the chapel has been subject to periodic neglect. In 1823 it was said to be 'in a most filthy state, covered with the ordure of owls, who seem to have taken possession of it',[2] but it was 'very respectable and clean' in 1829[3] and

[61] Q. Sess., reg. papists' estates, 1785.
[62] Tithe Redemption Com., tithe appt.
[63] E 32/143 m. 1.
[64] *Cal. Inq. Misc.* i, p. 176.
[65] S.P.L., MS. 2, f. 11ᵛ.
[66] Ibid. f. 8.
[67] Eyton, vi. 147; Bodl. MS. Blakeway 15, f. 50
[68] S.P.L., MS. 2, f. 2.
[69] Ibid. f. 8.
[70] Ibid.
[71] *T.S.A.S.* 2nd ser. xii. 99.
[72] S.P.L., MS. 2, f. 4.
[73] Ibid. f. 8.
[74] *T.S.A.S.* xlvii, 28; *S.P.R. Lich.* xix (5), 62; Lich. Dioc. Regy., B/a 4/5.
[75] Visit. Archd. Salop. 1799.
[76] Ibid. 1823.
[77] Ibid. 1843.
[78] S.P.L., MS. 2, f. 11.
[79] *Inq. Non.* (Rec. Com.), 192.
[80] *T.S.A.S.* 4th ser. iv. 178; S.P.L., MS. 2, f. 1.
[81] *T.S.A.S.* xlvii. 28.

[82] Q. Sess., reg. papists' estates, 1717.
[83] Tithe Redemption Com., tithe appt.
[84] S.P.L., MS. 2, f. 8.
[85] Visit. Archd. Salop. 1799.
[86] Ibid. 1799, 1847.
[87] Ibid.
[88] *S.P.R. Lich.* xix (5) *passim*.
[89] Ibid. 80.
[90] Visit. Archd. Salop. 1823.
[91] Ibid.
[92] Account of church based, except where otherwise stated, on Cranage, vi. 495–7; S.P.L., MS. 372, vol. i, p. 103; S.P.L., J. H. Smith collect. no. 122.
[93] B.M. Add. MS. 21021, f. 157.
[94] See plate facing p. 144.
[95] Visit. Archd. Salop. 1823.
[96] *T.S.A.S.* 2nd ser. xi. 99.
[97] Visit. Archd. Salop. 1843.
[98] Walters, *Ch. Bells Salop.* 221.
[99] *T.S.A.S.* 2nd ser. xi. 99.
[1] Visit. Archd. Salop. 1799, 1823.
[2] Ibid. 1823.
[3] Ibid.

remained in good order until at least 1843.[4] In 1900 it was repaired by the Society for the Protection of Ancient Buildings,[5] and in 1915 was placed in the guardianship of the Ministry of Works,[6] who restored it in 1962–3.

NONCONFORMITY. None known.

SCHOOLS. The curate was given licence to teach in Langley chapel in 1662 and 1667.[7] No later reference to a school in the parish has been found.

CHARITIES. Inhabitants of Ruckley and Langley formerly benefited from the Acton Burnell charities, all of which had been lost by 1962.[8]

SMETHCOTT

THE parish of Smethcott, on the northern foothills of the Long Mynd, contains 2,742 a.[1] and includes the townships of Smethcott, Picklescott, and Betch- cott. These all lie to the south of the parish, settle- ment in the north taking the form of isolated farms and cottages. Betchcott was a chapelry of Condover until c. 1183, when the chapel was appropriated by Haughmond Abbey.[2] After the Dissolution the parochial status of the township remained confused until the 19th century.[3] It was claimed as a chapelry of Leebotwood in the 18th century[4] and was described as extra-parochial c. 1789.[5]

On the south the parish boundary runs along the valleys of Walkmill Brook and Betchcott Brook. The latter, and the Portway to the west, formed the boundaries of Betchcott township by 1253,[6] while Wilderley Brook, to the north of Pease Lane, was the north-western boundary of Smethcott manor by 1340.[7] The remainder of the western boundary, and the northern and eastern boundaries, do not follow natural features. That with Leebotwood was fixed c. 1217–27,[8] and it is likely that the boundary with Stapleton in the north-east, which followed its present course by 1340,[9] was also determined in the early 13th century, since the adjacent boundary of Stapleton and Wilderley was laid out in 1227.[10] The western boundary, between Picklescott and Pease Lane, seems not to have been defined until the inclosure of the Long Mynd, c. 1790.[11] Some of the boundary stones, erected on the parish boundary to the west of Picklescott at this time, are still standing.[12] Although the upland area around Underhill Hall seems always to have been accounted part of Wilderley manor in Pulverbatch,[13] it lay within Smethcott parish by the early 17th century.[14]

The boundaries of the three townships followed tributaries of Walkmill Brook. That between Pickle- scott and Smethcott was the stream flowing south- eastwards from the Slad towards Branmills,[15] and that between Picklescott and Betchcott the stream

flowing eastwards from Prestley, which joins Walk- mill Brook near Branmills.

Outcrops of rock, glacial moraines, and the deeply cut valleys of streams have given the parish a rough and uneven landscape, but in general the ground rises from east to west. The eastern boundary runs along the 500-foot contour and in the north- east corner of the parish, along Cross Brook, the land falls to 425 feet. After rising gently over the eastern half of the parish to some 800 feet at Smethcott church, the ground rises more steeply. Picklescott and Betchcott both stand at about 900 feet and in the west the contours rise to 1,100 feet at Picklescott Hill, 1,300 feet at Betchcott Hill, and to 1,425 feet in the south-western tip of the parish, under Henley Nap.[16]

The parish is drained by numerous tributaries to the River Cound. Smethcott and Picklescott stand on the watershed between Betchcott Brook and Oakham Brook to the south, which unite to form Walkmill Brook at Branmills, and Wilderley Brook, Hollicot Brook,[17] and other streams to the north, which rise in the former Smethcott Common and run north-eastwards towards Stapleton and Dorrington.

There are extensive deposits of sand and gravel in the south-east quarter of the parish, above Walkmill Brook, and a smaller belt in the north, running eastwards from the boundary with Wilder- ley towards New Hall Farm. A number of small pockets of sand and gravel in the western half of the parish have, except at Betchcott, had little significant effect on settlement. Shales and grits, deriving from the Long Mynd, underlie the thin soil of the ground above the 1,100-foot contour in the south and west. A similar subsoil occurs along Hollicot Brook and Smethcott Dingle, and runs across the north of the parish from Smethcott Bank to Park- head. Glacial moraines occur east of Picklescott village and south of Betchcott, while to the west of

4 Visit. Archd. Salop. 1843.
5 Cranage, vi. 497.
6 Ex inf. Ministry of Public Buildings and Works.
7 Lich. Dioc. Regy., B/a 4/5.
8 See p. 13.
1 O.S. *Area Bk.* (1883). The following topographical description is based, except where otherwise stated, on O.S. Map 1″, sheet lxi (1st edn.); O.S. Maps 6″ Salop. 48, 49 (1st and later edns.); O.S. Maps 1/25,000, SO 49 (1956), SJ 40 (1957); Rocque, *Map of Salop.* (1752); Baugh, *Map of Salop.* (1808); B.M. O.S. 2″ orig. drawings, sheet 207 (1817); Geol. Survey Map (drift), sheet 152 (1932); par. rec., tithe appt. and map, 1844; Apley Park estate office, Bridgnorth, survey and map, 1777; Wolryche- Whitmore MSS., Dudmaston, inclosure award and map, Smethcott Common, 1798. This article was written in 1964 and revised in 1965.
2 S.P.L., Haughmond Cart. f. 153. See also p. 157.
3 See p. 157.
4 Lich. Dioc. Regy., Leebotwood glebe terriers, 1730–87.

5 S.P.L., Deeds 6579.
6 S.P.L., Haughmond Cart. f. 132ᵛ.
7 Wolryche-Whitmore MSS., Dudmaston, partition of woodland, 1340.
8 S.P.L., Haughmond Cart. f. 134.
9 Wolryche-Whitmore MSS., Dudmaston, partition of woodland, 1340.
10 S.P.L., Haughmond Cart. f. 229.
11 S.P.L., Deeds 6579.
12 Ex inf. Mr. J. Shakeshaft, Underhill Hall.
13 S.R.O. 883/95. For bounds of Wilderley manor, see Wolryche-Whitmore MSS., Dudmaston, inclosure award, Smethcott Common, 1798.
14 *S.P.R. Lich.* i (2), 109–15.
15 Wolryche-Whitmore MSS., Dudmaston, partition of woodland, 1340.
16 Par. rec., tithe appt.
17 The former name of the stream running past Pogan Hall and Smethcott Bank: Wolryche-Whitmore MSS., Dudmaston, partition of woodland, 1340.

Picklescott a long ridge of morainic material runs north-westwards towards Underhill Hall. Over the remainder of the parish the subsoil consists of boulder clay.

Until the 16th century landscape and land-use here followed closely the limits imposed by its geology. The village of Smethcott, and the greater part of its common fields, lay on the light soil to the south east. Picklescott and Betchcott stood on or near glacial moraines and their common fields on the surrounding boulder clay. Outcrops of shale and grit to the north of the parish formed the northern, western, and eastern boundaries of Smethcott Common, while woodland covered most of the boulder clay zone. Near Pease Lane, however, was an ancient cultivated area, known as Hollicot.[18]

Although Smethcott manor was said to have woodland for only 50 swine in 1086,[19] there was considerably more woodland in the parish during the Middle Ages than this would suggest. The woodland was divided between the lords of the three portions of Smethcott manor in 1340,[20] and it is possible to reconstruct its area at this time with some accuracy. It was divided, north and south, into three roughly equal shares. The boundary of the central portion began at Hollicot Nether Ford, presumably the point at which the road running eastwards from Coppice Farm crosses Hollicot Brook, and followed the brook downstream to the parish boundary with Stapleton. It ran eastwards along the parish boundary to Smethcott Dingle, and followed the stream, then known as 'Tymbrynkes-bechesbrok', southwards towards Smethcott and returned to the Nether Ford around the northern edge of Smethcott Common. The eastern portion was bounded on the west by Smethcott Dingle, by the parish boundary on the east, and by the common fields of Smethcott on the south-west. A field called Horestone, ½ mile east-north-east of Lawley View,[21] probably marked the boundary between the common fields and the wood at this point. A large boundary stone, which formerly stood in the middle of this field, was demolished within living memory.[22] The third, western, portion of woodland comprised the whole area west of Hollicot Brook, including a wood known as 'Wilardewik', which seems to have lain to the south of Pease Lane.

Smethcott Wood was said to be well stocked with oaks and underwood in 1235, but encroachments had already been made near the village.[23] Assarting seems to have been encouraged by the 13th-century lords of the manor, who granted to free tenants lands on the borders of the wood, as at the Criftin, north-

east of Smethcott Pool,[24] and at Pluntnall, in the south-east of the parish.[25] The central and eastern portions of the wood, as divided in 1340, went under the general name of Smethcott Wood in the 16th and 17th centuries.[26] That part of the western portion which lay to the north of Pease Lane was then known as Trentham's Wood,[27] but 'Wilarde-wik' is not recorded after 1340. Apart from the wooded banks of Smethcott Dingle and Hollicot Brook, the only surviving remnant of ancient woodland in the parish is Birch Coppice, to the west of New Hall Farm, which was so named by 1619.[28] There is no evidence for the clearance of woodland in Smethcott in the later Middle Ages, but in 1578 9 persons were alleged to have inclosed 192 a. in the wood.[29] Although Smethcott Wood was still said to extend from New Hall to the boundary with Lee-botwood in 1583,[30] it is probable that by this date it consisted only of isolated coppices. New Hall and Bank Farms were established on cleared land in the north-east of the parish, but the remainder of the former woodland, apart from assarts around the perimeter of the Smethcott common fields, was later accounted part of Smethcott Common.[31] Old Coppice, containing 20 a. in 1595, adjoined Longnor Park,[32] and Braddock's Coppice, in the same area, is recorded in the early 17th century.[33] Surviving parts of Smethcott Wood within the manorial estate were said to have been inclosed c. 1619[34] and c. 1651[35] and amounted to some 60 a. at Lyes Coppice and Pluntnall in 1675.[36] Both had been cleared by 1777, when the only woodland within the estate lay along the banks of Walkmill Brook.[37] Timber in Trentham's Coppice was sold to John Bradley in 1611[38] and a rabbit-warren had been established here by 1625,[39] but 61 a. of woodland still remained in 1675.[40] The area to the north of Coppice Farm was accounted part of Smethcott Common in 1777.[41]

Like the wood Smethcott Common was divided among the lords of the manor in 1340,[42] when its southern boundary appears to have followed practically the same course as it did on the eve of its inclosure in 1798.[43] The product of impeded drainage, owing to the shales and grits bordering it to the north, its area was little reduced by assarting and it attracted few settlers. Although encroachments on the common bulk large in the business of the manor court in the 17th and 18th centuries—there were 26 cases in 1681[44] and 37 in 1699[45]—these were not in the common proper, but in areas formerly in Smethcott Wood. The common was said to contain 418 a. in 1675,[46] 526 a. in 1777,[47] and 647 a. in

---

[18] See pp. 153-4.
[19] V.C.H. Salop. i. 342.
[20] Wolryche-Whitmore MSS., Dudmaston, partition of woodland, 1340.
[21] Par. rec., tithe appt. So named in 1612: Lich. Dioc. Regy., glebe terrier, 1612.
[22] Ex inf. Mr. L. Manley, Red House Farm.
[23] Eyton, vi. 340.
[24] Wolryche-Whitmore MSS., Dudmaston, grant, n.d.
[25] Ibid.
[26] See e.g. ibid. lease of New Hall, 1583.
[27] Ibid. deeds, 1584-1625.
[28] Ibid. answer, Roger Pope v. Edward More and others, 1619.
[29] C 2/Eliz. I/H 11/56.
[30] Wolryche-Whitmore MSS., Dudmaston, lease, 1583.
[31] Ibid. inclosure award, Smethcott Common, 1798; Apley Park estate office, map, 1777.
[32] S.P.L., Deeds 7085.

[33] Wolryche-Whitmore MSS., Dudmaston, answer, Roger Pope v. Edward More and others, 1619.
[34] Ibid.
[35] S.R.O. 567 uncat., depositions, Uvedale Corbett v. Roger Pope, 1688.
[36] Apley Park estate office, survey, 1675.
[37] Ibid. survey and map, 1777.
[38] Sta. Cha. 8/74/14.
[39] Wolryche-Whitmore MSS., Dudmaston, lease, 1625.
[40] Apley Park estate office, survey, 1675.
[41] Ibid. survey and map, 1777.
[42] Wolryche-Whitmore MSS., Dudmaston, partition of woodland, 1340.
[43] Ibid.; ibid. inclosure award, Smethcott Common, 1798.
[44] Ibid. ct. r. 1681.
[45] Ibid. 1699.
[46] Apley Park estate office, survey, 1675.
[47] Ibid. survey, 1777.

1798,[48] but in the two last the area included parts of the former wood. Inclosure of the common was mooted in the late 17th century[49] and again *c.* 1755,[50] but was not carried out until 1798.[51]

Common rights in Smethcott Common were shared by the tenants of Smethcott and Wilderley manors,[52] the boundaries of their respective portions being marked by boundary stones still standing near Pogan Hall. The commons of Picklescott and Betchcott lay on the slopes of the Long Mynd. Betchcott's rights to common here were confirmed by royal charter in 1253,[53] and Picklescott tenants claimed similar rights in the 17th century.[54] The inhabitants of Church Stretton, however, who alleged in 1656 that their parish boundary ran along the edge of the common fields of these townships,[55] successfully prosecuted the inhabitants of Betchcott for trespass on the Long Mynd in the later 18th century.[56] The tenants of Underhill Hall enjoyed common rights on Cothercott Hill until the Second World War.[57]

It seems likely that the area of common-field land in Smethcott and Picklescott was extended by assarting during the later Middle Ages. At Smethcott[58] Castle Field, which lay to the west of the church, was bounded on the north by marshy land adjoining Smethcott Pool and on the west by the brook which formed the boundary with Picklescott. It was the smallest of the three fields and was known as Old Field in the 13th century.[59] Of the two other fields Stocking Field, otherwise known as Broad Field or Lower Field, lay on both sides of the road running from Smethcott towards Parkhead, its name suggesting that it included assarted land, and Cross Field, or Lynch Field, lay east of the church, to the south of the road to Leebotwood. The glebe was still uninclosed in 1612,[60] but recent inclosures in Cross Field and Stocking Field are recorded in 1636[61] and by 1675 only 10 a. here still lay in openfield strips.[62]

Of the common fields of Picklescott[63] the Field next Betchcott, called Hullegrene Field in the 15th century, ran southwards from the village and was bounded on the west by pastures called Presley and the Sallins. Cross Field, or the Field beneath the town, lay to the east of the village and Cockshut Field to the north, on both sides of the road to Wilderley, where field-names like Ashen Stubs, Thorny Acre, and the Brooches indicate that it included more recently cleared land. Small inclosures in the common fields here are recorded in

the 1520s,[64] but inclosure here was probably delayed owing to the number of small freeholders in the township. Several holdings still consisted of small scattered fields in the mid-19th century,[65] and the process of rationalizing farm boundaries here is still not complete.[66]

The common fields of Betchcott were presumably inclosed during the Middle Ages. Two of them were known as Orrington Field and Upper Field,[67] of which the former survives in the field-name Orration Field, east of Betchcott Hall, while High Furlong, south-east of Upper Betchcott Farm, probably lay in the Upper Field. The names Bone Furlong and Lower Butts, found on the ridge of sand and gravel north-west of Middle Betchcott Farm, indicate that the third common field lay in this part of the township. An outrack, or driftway, to the Long Mynd, running westwards from Middle Betchcott Farm, presumably followed the boundary between Upper Field and this unnamed common field.

During the Middle Ages the principal road in Smethcott was that running from the Long Mynd towards Shrewsbury, which entered the parish at Branmills and ran north-eastwards, past the school, Smethcott Farm, and Parkhead towards Dorrington.[68] This was known as the Portway in the 17th century[69] and is still classed as a public road, but only isolated sections are now maintained. In the 15th century the road from Betchcott to Picklescott was also described as a portway,[70] and that from Picklescott to Smethcott as *via regalis*.[71] The latter followed the course of the present road for some distance east of Picklescott, but the section running past Smethcott Pool appears to date only from the inclosure of the Common, the former route having followed what is now a green way to join the Smethcott portway at Branmills.[72] The roads running west from Picklescott towards the Thresholds and northwards towards Wilderley were probably in origin no more than outracks to common land on Picklescott and Wilderley Hills. Wildreck Farm, deriving its name from the outrack of Wilderley manor, seems to have lain on an ancient road which ran round the southern edge of Smethcott Common. This is recorded in 1340 when it ran from Smethcott Pool to Hollicot Cross[73]—probably the road junction at Pease Lane. Although no other ancient roads are recorded on the Common, it is likely that the straight roads laid out here in 1798 follow approximately the line of former roads.[74]

[48] Wolryche-Whitmore MSS., Dudmaston, inclosure award, Smethcott Common, 1798.
[49] Ibid. leases, 1676–92.
[50] Ibid. lease, 1755.
[51] Ibid. inclosure award, Smethcott Common, 1798.
[52] Ibid. ct. r. 1601–99 *passim*; S.R.O. 883/95.
[53] S.P.L., Haughmond Cart. f. 132ᵛ.
[54] Wolryche-Whitmore MSS., Dudmaston, lease, 1652.
[55] S.P.L., Deeds 6579.
[56] Ibid.
[57] Ex inf. Mr. J. Shakeshaft, Underhill Hall.
[58] Description of common fields based on Lich. Dioc. Regy., glebe terrier, 1612; Wolryche-Whitmore MSS., Dudmaston, ct. r. 1496–1618; ibid. deed, 1617; ibid. leases, 1653, 1692; Apley Park estate office, survey, 1675.
[59] Wolryche-Whitmore MSS., Dudmaston, grant, n.d.
[60] Lich. Dioc. Regy., glebe terrier, 1612.
[61] C 142/533/79.
[62] Apley Park estate office, survey, 1675.
[63] Description of Picklescott common fields based on

S.P.L., Haughmond Cart. f. 164ᵛ; Wolryche-Whitmore MSS., Dudmaston, deed, 1601; S.R.O. 665 uncat., ct. r. of manor of Boveria, 1507–38.
[64] S.R.O. 665 uncat., ct. r. of manor of Boveria, 1507–38.
[65] Par. rec., tithe appt.
[66] Local inf.
[67] S.P.L., Deeds 3451. Field-names cited below are taken from S.R.O. 650/2 (sale partics. 1877).
[68] Apley Park estate office, map, 1777; Lich. Dioc. Regy., glebe terrier, 1767.
[69] Wolryche-Whitmore MSS., Dudmaston, lease, 1651. The name was preserved in adjacent fields north of Smethcott in 1777; Apley Park estate office, map, 1777.
[70] S.P.L., Haughmond Cart. f. 164ᵛ.
[71] Ibid.
[72] Apley Park estate office, map, 1777.
[73] Wolryche-Whitmore MSS., Dudmaston, partition of woodland, 1340.
[74] Apley Park estate office, map, 1777.

Of the ancient hamlets in the parish Smethcott has moved away from its original site near the church[75] and has shrunk with the development of isolated farms to the north, Betchcott had probably dwindled to its present size by the end of the Middle Ages, and Picklescott alone still retains the lineaments of a medieval village.

Smethcott church, though rebuilt in 1850, contains some original features and has stood on its present site since at least the 12th century.[76] To the west of the church is the mound of a motte-and-bailey castle, clearly designed to command the road in the valley below. The original village probably lay along this road, north-eastward from Branmills. The latter is a small stone house, probably built in the 18th century, but was originally known as Brand (i.e. burnt) Mill[77] and is presumably the site of the medieval mill. Roads from Picklescott and Betchcott formerly met the road to Shrewsbury at this point. The old rectory, first recorded on its present site in 1612,[78] stands on higher ground to the south of the road, but a timber-framed tithe-barn stood by the roadside, opposite the sunken way leading up to the church, until its demolition in 1960.[79] The only other buildings near the original site of the village are the new rectory, now Rectory Farm, built in 1839,[80] and the school, built in 1867.[81] It is probable that the focus of the village had already moved eastwards by the early 13th century, for in 1235 it was said that Smethcott Wood had been wasted near the village and that huts had been erected there.[82] The castle ceased to be the residence of the lord of the manor after c. 1272, when it passed to the Burnells of Acton Burnell,[83] and by 1315 no manorial buildings remained.[84] The top of the motte was removed c. 1764, when the underlying gravel was used for road repairs.[85] Excavation on the site in 1956 and 1957 produced early 13th-century pottery in the ditch surrounding the castle.[86] The foundations of a horseshoe-shaped stone structure were then found outside the ditch.[87]

On its new site, close to the eastern edge of Smethcott Common, the village seems to have continued little changed in size until the 18th century. There were probably 8 farm-houses here in 1675,[88] but by 1777, when there were 3 large farms and a blacksmith's shop,[89] the village was already much as it is today. Of the 3 farms, Smethcott Farm and Red House Farm then belonged to freeholders, who also held on lease the sites of 3 former farmsteads.[90] The third farm of 1777, on the road to Smethcott Pool,[91] has since been demolished. Smethcott Farm consists of an early-17th-century timber-framed house of two bays with a central chimney stack, now cased in stone and rough-cast,

to which a kitchen was later added, while Red House Farm, rebuilt in brick in the 19th century, retains one bay of the former timber-framed house. The Bynords, some 300 yards north of Red House along the former road to Shrewsbury, is the only survivor of the 3 farmhouses which had gone out of use by 1777.[92] Now carefully restored, its plan resembles that of Smethcott Farm. Lawley View is a modern house on the site of another of the former farm-houses. The smithy stood opposite Corner House in 1777, when it was occupied by Benjamin Partridge, who gave his name to Ben's Pool nearby.[93] It was said to be nearly down in 1808,[94] and had gone by 1844, when the smithy stood immediately north of Red House Farm.[95]

Since the early 18th century Betchcott has consisted of 3 farms,[96] but, as it possessed a set of common fields, a hamlet clearly existed here in the Middle Ages. In 1538 there seem to have been several tenants-at-will here, in addition to the occupiers of the 3 principal farms.[97] A fourth farm, known as Waring's tenement, had been broken up by 1717.[98] Middle Betchcott Farm, standing on sand and gravel alongside the portway to Picklescott, probably occupies the site of the medieval manor-house.[99] Among the farm buildings is a 5-bay barn, containing 3 cruck trusses, which may have been a tithe barn, while a smaller building adjoining the present farm-house contains two closed cruck trusses at each gable and may once have been a house. A chapel, still in use in the early 16th century,[1] was said c. 1830 to have stood to the west of this farm, where gravestones had been discovered.[2] The 3 existing farm-houses all date from the early 17th century. Upper and Middle Betchcott Farms have identical ground-plans—two rooms on each side of a central chimney stack with a service wing at the west end. Both are cased in brick and have small 19th-century additions. Betchcott Hall (formerly Lower Betchcott Farm) was originally similar in scale and plan, but has been considerably enlarged since the 19th century. It contains an elaborate 17th-century staircase, but this is thought to have come from elsewhere.[3]

Picklescott has changed little in size since the Middle Ages. The village stands on Picklescott Brook at the junction of roads leading to Betchcott, Smethcott, Wilderley, and The Thresholds. At the cross-roads in the valley bottom is a group of cottages most of which were formerly occupied by tradesmen. The Gate House, a wheelwright's shop in the later 19th century,[4] is said to have been an alehouse, known as 'The Gate Hangs Well',[5] and is probably the alehouse first recorded in 1616.[6] This closed c. 1800[7] and its place was taken by 'The Bottle and

[75] See plate facing p. 97.
[76] See p. 157.
[77] Apley Park estate office, map, 1777.
[78] Lich. Dioc. Regy., glebe terrier, 1612.
[79] Ex inf. Mr. W. G. Middleton, Old Rectory Farm.
[80] Par. rec., mortgage for erection of parsonage, 1839.
[81] Ed. 7/103/218.
[82] Eyton, vi. 340.
[83] B.M. Harl. MS. 1982, f. 63ᵛ; Eyton, vi. 253.
[84] C 134/48/9.
[85] W.S.L. 350/40/3.
[86] *Medieval Arch.* i. 157; ibid. ii. 195.
[87] Ibid.
[88] Apley Park estate office, survey, 1675.
[89] Ibid. survey and map, 1777.
[90] Ibid.

[91] Ibid. [92] Ibid. [93] Ibid.
[94] Wolryche-Whitmore MSS., Dudmaston, survey, c. 1808.
[95] Par. rec., tithe appt.
[96] Q. Sess., reg. papists' estates, 1717.
[97] S.C. 6/Hen. VIII/3009 mm. 32–33.
[98] Q. Sess., reg. papists' estates, 1717.
[99] cf. S.C. 6/Hen. VIII/3009 m. 33d.; S.C. 6/967/1.
[1] S.C. 6/Hen. VIII/3009 m. 33d.
[2] W.S.L. 350/40/3.
[3] Ex inf. Mrs. J. A. Bovill, Betchcott Hall.
[4] Ex inf. Mr. V. W. E. Chidley, 'The Bottle and Glass', Picklescott.
[5] Ibid.
[6] Q. Sess., alehouse reg.
[7] Ibid.

Glass', the present inn, which was originally a farm-house and was first licensed as an alehouse in 1837.[8] The farm-houses all stand on higher ground around the edge of the village. Two of them, The Vandells and Standish Cottage (formerly Top House Farm), are now private residences and a third, which stood opposite Standish Cottage, has been demolished.

Apart from 2 19th-century cottages at the cross-roads and 2 bungalows to the north of Standish Cottage, all the existing houses in Picklescott seem to have been originally timber-framed and to date from the early 17th century. With the exception of Standish Cottage, however, they have all been cased in brick or stone. The largest is Hall Farm, identical in plan with the Betchcott farm-houses, but larger in scale. The Vandells, which had ceased to be a farm-house by 1844,[9] is a small L-shaped house. The south wall of the projecting west wing is of coursed rubble and has ashlar quoins and mullioned windows. A datestone under the eaves reads 'I.C. . . . 16 . . . 9', perhaps referring to Joseph Charlton, who occupied a one-hearth house in the village in 1662.[10] The ground-plan of Standish Cottage resembles that of The Vandells, but the plan of Bank Farm and 'The Bottle and Glass' consists of a continuous range of building, of four and five bays respectively.

New Hall Farm, Bank Farm, and Coppice Farm, whose lands still extended in 1777 over the greater part of the land in the north of the parish then lying outside Smethcott Common,[11] probably represent the earliest settlement outside the confines of the ancient hamlets. Although New Hall Farm is not recorded before 1583, when it was described as a capital messuage,[12] it seems likely on analogy with Moat Farm, Stapleton[13] and Castle Hill, Wool-staston,[14] that it stands on the site of a late medieval manor-house, built on a more accessible and more fertile site than that of the castle near the church. The house was occupied by the Phillips family, lords of part of Smethcott manor, between 1583 and 1662, when it contained 6 hearths,[15] but since that date has been no more than a farm-house. The present house, timber-framed and cased in brick, is probably only part of the original. Closely spaced vertical studs are visible along part of the north wall, and inside the house, at first-floor level on the adjoining part of the original west wall is a small scroll-shaped bracket, similar to those at Netley Old Hall—another Phillips house[16]—which was probably intended to support an oriel window. The history of Bank Farm, which derives its name from the large rectangular earthwork, of unknown age, some 350 yards to the north-east,[17] cannot be traced earlier than 1777, when it was known as the Upper House.[18]

It is a brick-cased timber-framed house of 3 bays, with an original chimney stack on the north gable, to which a west wing was later added. Another house to the south-east, called Lower House in 1777,[19] has since been demolished. Coppice Farm, still externally timber-framed, is first recorded in 1585,[20] and was occupied until 1619 by the lessee of Trentham's Wood.[21] A large room at the south-east of the present house, containing a chimney stack on one gable, probably dates from this period, but the plan has been complicated by the addition of two small timber-framed wings to the north and a stone kitchen to the south-west. Greenfields, an 18th-century stone cottage north-east of Coppice Farm, probably stands on the site of a cottage first recorded in 1625, when its tenant was given charge of the adjacent rabbit-warren.[22]

Squatter settlement in the south-east of the parish, near Walkmills, seems to have taken place in the first quarter of the 17th century. Two fulling mills, then known as Upper Mills (later as the Dyehouse and now as nos. 5–6 Holdings, Walkmills), are first recorded in 1620.[23] The course of the mill-leet can still be seen to the north of the house, but the mill had closed by the early 19th century.[24] The house incorporates a two-bay building with a central chimney stack, but was considerably enlarged in the early 19th century. Pillar House and no. 29, Walk-mills, on the road to Leebotwood to the north of the mill, are both brick-cased timber-framed houses of early 17th-century date. The Fields, an isolated house to the north of the road, is probably the cottage at Pluntnall Coppice recorded in 1625.[25]

To the north, 2 houses stood on the road from Walkmills to Parkhead in 1777,[26] but they had been demolished by 1844, when the site of the larger of them was marked by the field-name Old House Piece.[27] These can probably be connected with encroachments at the Linacre presented at the manor court in 1681.[28] In 1777 there were 3 cottages near the parish boundary, to the west and north of Longnor Park Farm,[29] of which one is still standing. Two squatters are recorded here in 1681,[30] one of whom, Thomas Gwynne, was a member of a family resident in Smethcott Wood by 1615.[31] Cottagers in this part of the parish seem to have found employment in Longnor Park, for Gwynne's neighbour William Teckoe helped to erect hedges there when it was disparked c. 1686,[32] while a cottager near Pluntnall Coppice had been huntsman to Sir Uvedale Corbett.[33] A house had been erected at Parkhead by 1619,[34] and there were 2 houses here in 1777[35] and 1844.[36] The surviving cottage here is brick-built and can probably be associated with a chicory factory set up nearby shortly before 1845.[37]

8 Q. Sess., *Return of Licensed Houses* (1896), 55.
9 Par. rec., tithe appt.
10 E 179/255/35 m. 76d.
11 Apley Park estate office, map, 1777.
12 Wolryche-Whitmore MSS., Dudmaston, lease, 1583.
13 See p. 163.
14 See p. 171.
15 Wolryche-Whitmore MSS., Dudmaston, leases, 1583–1627; ibid. deeds, 1618, 1660; E 179/255/35 m. 77d.
16 See p. 163.
17 *V.C.H. Salop.* i. 380–1.
18 Apley Park estate office, survey, 1777.
19 Ibid.
20 Wolryche-Whitmore MSS., Dudmaston, deed, 1585.
21 Ibid. deeds, 1615–22; Sta. Cha. 8/74/14.
22 Wolryche-Whitmore MSS Dudmaston, lease, 1625.
23 Ibid. ct. r. 1620.
24 See p. 156.
25 Wolryche-Whitmore MSS., Dudmaston, ct. r. 1625.
26 Apley Park estate office, survey and map, 1777.
27 Par. rec., tithe appt.
28 Wolryche-Whitmore MSS., Dudmaston, ct. r. 1681.
29 Apley Park estate office, survey and map, 1777.
30 Wolryche-Whitmore MSS., Dudmaston, ct. r. 1681.
31 *S.P.R. Lich.* i (2), 132.
32 S.R.O. 567 uncat., depositions, Uvedale Corbett v. Roger Pope, 1688.
33 Ibid.
34 Wolryche-Whitmore MSS., Dudmaston, ct. r. 1619.
35 Apley Park estate office, survey and map, 1777.
36 Par. rec., tithe appt.
37 Hope-Edwardes MSS., Linley Hall, sale partics. 1845.

Three of the 4 houses still standing within the bounds of the former Smethcott Common—New House Farm, Pool House, and the Slad—are timber-framed houses of 17th-century date.[38] The two former are cased in stone, but the Slad, a derelict cottage on the eastern edge of the Picklescott common fields, still has the greater part of its timber-framed walls exposed. Two houses stood on the site of the Parish Cottages, in the centre of the common, when they were granted to the parish in 1741.[39] The present cottages—a low range of buildings with a thatched roof—probably date from the later 18th century.

Of the existing houses in the upland areas to the south of Coppice Farm, Underhill Hall is the only one likely to have been built before the 18th century. A cottage had, however, been erected at Smethcott Bank, then called Hollicot Bach, by 1585,[40] and at least 3 families were living here in the early 17th century.[41] The name Hollicot, though no longer given to the stream which flows past Smethcott Bank, is preserved in the names of fields running westwards towards Pease Lane. In the earlier Middle Ages the lords of Smethcott manor had demesne lands in this unlikely spot, said in 1340 to have been formerly in cultivation.[42] Small deposits of sand and gravel are to be found nearby and it is likely that this is the site of a deserted hamlet.

Underhill Hall still possesses timber-framed farm buildings and was itself originally of similar construction. Its original ground-plan consisted of two rooms on each side of a central chimney stack, with an unheated service room to the east. An oak newel stair against the south wall has simple floral designs carved in low relief on its newels and probably dates from the early 17th century, but the oak panelling lining the walls of two ground-floor rooms is likely to be a later insertion. The house was enlarged and remodelled internally, probably at the end of the 17th century. The roof was raised, enabling an attic story to be added, and the house now has an impressive brick north front, with 6 bays of casement windows and a small central porch. In 1722 the house passed, with Wilderley manor, to the Powys family of Berwick[43] who, like later owners of the estate, seem to have used it as a hunting lodge. By 1755 Henry Powys had laid out a small park around the house and had stocked two nearby pools with fish.[44]

No visible trace of timber-framing is to be found in the other small stone houses in this area. Park Gate and the two houses at Pease Lane are, or were

originally, of two bays with chimney stacks on one gable, and the two existing houses at Smethcott Bank have a similar plan. Wildreck Farm, where cottages are first recorded in the 1720s,[45] and Pogan Hall have a more symmetrical ground-plan, with chimney stacks on each gable and a central staircase. They probably date from the late 18th century.

There were said to be 178 adults in the parish in 1676.[46] Its population rose from 338 in 1801 to 371 in 1841[47] but, with the abandonment of isolated cottages in the north of the parish, it has since fallen steadily. There were 283 inhabitants in 1881,[48] 261 in 1921,[49] and 198 in 1961.[50]

MANOR. Roger, Earl of Shrewsbury, was overlord of *SMETHCOTT* manor in 1086 and Edmund its mesne lord,[51] but the manor presumably passed to the Honor of Montgomery after 1102[52] and in 1254 was held by Prince Edward, as guardian of the heir of William Cauntelow.[53] After the death of George Cauntelow in 1273[54] the overlordship passed to his daughter Millicent and her husband Eudes la Zouche[55] and thereafter continued in the Zouche family. Their estate here was, however, described as a mesne tenure under the Mortimers, Earls of March, between 1360 and 1424,[56] probably owing to confusion with Meole Brace, where the Cauntelows and Zouches had been mesne tenants of the Mortimer family since the early 13th century,[57] and in the early 17th century the manor was said to be held of the Crown in chief.[58] The overlordship is last recorded in 1635.[59]

Eldred, the tenant of Smethcott manor in 1086,[60] can probably be identified with the Eldred who then held the manor of Acton Scott,[61] since both manors were held by representatives of the same family during the 12th and 13th centuries.[62] One William, tenant of Smethcott manor in the later 12th century,[63] was dead by 1203, when the manor was claimed by his daughters Christine, wife of John le Poer, Maud, wife of Richard de Linley, and Margery, wife of Baldwin Fitz Robert.[64] It subsequently remained in divided ownership among their descendants.

Christine, with her second husband Philip de Hulega,[65] and her third husband Stephen de Patinton,[66] appears as one of the co-parceners of Smethcott manor in the first quarter of the 13th century, and seems to have been succeeded by Miles Pichard,[67] whose son[68] Roger Pichard was lord between 1254 and 1272.[69] Shortly after this Roger sold his portion of the manor to Hugh Burnell

[38] New House Farm was probably built in 1677: dated inscription on bedroom door.
[39] *24th Rep. Com. Char.*, H.C. 231, p. 389 (1831), xi.
[40] Wolryche-Whitmore MSS., Dudmaston, deed, 1585.
[41] *S.P.R. Lich.* i (2), 109, 111, 132.
[42] Wolryche-Whitmore MSS., Dudmaston, partition of woodland, 1340.
[43] See p. 153.
[44] S.P.L., Deeds 3515.
[45] S.R.O. 883/95.
[46] *T.S.A.S.* 2nd ser. i. 82.
[47] *Census*, 1801–41.
[48] Ibid. 1881.
[49] Ibid. 1921.
[50] Ibid. 1961.
[51] *V.C.H. Salop.* i. 342.
[52] Eyton, xi. 120.
[53] *Rot. Hund.* (Rec. Com.), ii. 62.

[54] *Cal. Inq. p.m.* ii, pp. 16–17.
[55] *Cal. Fine R.* 1272–1307, 18; *Cal. Close*, 1272–9, 294.
[56] *Cal. Inq. p.m.* xiv, p. 350; *Cal. Close*, 1360–4, 159; ibid. 1396–9, 457, 460; C 139/19/32.
[57] Eyton, vi. 351–7.
[58] C 142/293/66; C 142/505/112.
[59] C 142/505/112.
[60] *V.C.H. Salop.* i. 342.
[61] Ibid. 343.
[62] Eyton, xi. 375–80.
[63] Ibid. vi. 250.
[64] Ibid.
[65] S.P.L., Haughmond Cart. f. 163ᵛ.
[66] Ibid. f. 134.
[67] Ibid.
[68] Bodl. MS. Blakeway 2, f. 142.
[69] *Rot. Hund.* (Rec. Com.), ii. 62; E 32/145 m. 1; Eyton, vi. 251–2.

of Langley,[70] first recorded as lord in 1284.[71] Hugh's son Philip Burnell held lands in Smethcott at his death in 1294[72] and this third of the manor followed the descent of Acton Burnell until the 16th century.[73] Part of the estate was sold shortly after 1541 by Sir John Dudley to Sir Robert Acton of Ribbesford (Worcs.), together with the adjoining manor of Woolstaston.[74] This was conveyed to Roger Pope in 1544,[75] subsequently following the descent of Woolstaston manor.[76] The remainder seems to have been sold to Sir Thomas Lacon, who held lands in Smethcott of Sir John Dudley at his death in 1536.[77] This property, first described as a portion of the manor of Smethcott in 1589,[78] passed from father to son in the Lacon family until 1611, when Francis Lacon sold it to Thomas Phillips.[79] Following the bankruptcy of the latter's son Richard, the estate was purchased by Roger Pope in 1667.[80]

Maud, wife of Richard de Linley, was dead by 1227, when her husband appears as one of the lords of Smethcott manor.[81] The latter had been succeeded before 1235 by his son Richard,[82] whose daughter Alice probably married Thomas Purcel, one of the lords of Smethcott in 1253[83] and 1255.[84] By 1284 this portion of the manor had passed to Reynold Scott,[85] who had been succeeded by his son Walter before 1320.[86] In 1322 the latter granted to Richard Tristram half of his estate here[87] and this subsequently followed a separate descent as a sixth part of the manor. The part retained by Scott passed by descent in the family of Acton of Acton Scott.[88] On the death of Richard Acton in 1590 it passed to his son Edward,[89] who had no male issue, his only child being a daughter Frances who married Walter Acton of Aldenham.[90] The Actons of Aldenham are not known to have had any property in Smethcott at this period and the subsequent history of this portion of the manor is not known.

Richard Tristram settled his share of the manor on his son Richard in 1339.[91] The estate had passed by 1392 to William Bronington and his wife Isabel,[92] but its descent during the 15th century cannot be established. It can, however, be identified with the sixth part of the manor held by the Trentham family in 1550,[93] since this included Trentham's Coppice—an area of woodland assigned to John

Scott and Richard Tristram in 1340.[94] This estate was sold by Thomas Trentham to Richard Prince in 1585[95] and on the latter's death in 1598 passed to his son Francis, then a minor.[96] The estate was mortgaged in 1615[97] and in 1625 was sold by Richard Prince and John Bradley to Roger Pope.[98]

The third portion of the manor, claimed in 1203 by Margery, wife of Baldwin Fitz Robert, remained in her hands for many years after her husband's death in 1233,[99] for she was still living in 1252.[1] Although her son Stephen was described as lord of Smethcott[2] and his son Roger had some interest in the manor,[3] Margery's grandson[4] Philip appears as lord of this portion of the manor between 1255 and 1283.[5] The estate passed to his son Roger de Smethcott, lord between 1290 and 1320,[6] and to Roger's son William, recorded between 1327 and 1355.[7] One or more members of the Smethcott family, each named William, held this portion of the manor between 1393 and 1463.[8] Its subsequent descent is not clear, but it probably passed into divided ownership. The sixth part of Smethcott manor held by John, son of Edmund Braddock, in 1595[9] probably represents part of the lands once held by the Smethcott family, since it included woodland in the east of the parish assigned to William de Smethcott in 1340.[10] This was sold in 1605 to Robert Barnfield,[11] who sold it to Charles Scriven in the following year,[12] the latter conveying it to Roger Pope in 1607.[13] The descent of the other moiety of this portion is unknown, but it may have passed to the Phillips family, who already had a freehold estate at Picklescott in the 15th century,[14] since the assigns of William Phillips held a share of the advowson in 1563.[15] If so, it presumably passed in 1667,[16] with the rest of the Phillips estate in Smethcott, to Roger Pope, who had thus reunited the manor of Smethcott under one ownership. The manor subsequently followed the descent of Woolstaston until the sale of the Wolryche-Whitmore estate in 1919.[17]

OTHER ESTATES. Most of the east and north of the parish lay in the Smethcott manorial estate until the 19th century. On the higher land to the west, Betchcott and part of Picklescott were members

[70] B.M. Harl. MS. 1982, f. 63^v.
[71] Feud. Aids, iv. 215.
[72] Cal. Inq. p.m. iii, p. 122.
[73] See p. 7.
[74] Wolryche-Whitmore MSS., Dudmaston, deed, 1544; ibid. inspeximus of depositions, 1580.
[75] Ibid.
[76] See pp. 172–3.
[77] C 142/58/60.
[78] C.P. 25(2)/261/31 Eliz. I/East.
[79] C.P. 25(2)/343/9 Jas. I/East.
[80] Wolryche-Whitmore MSS., Dudmaston, deeds, 1667–9.
[81] S.P.L., Haughmond Cart. f. 134.
[82] Ibid. f. 163^v.; Eyton, vi. 255.
[83] Eyton, vi. 251.
[84] Rot. Hund. (Rec. Com.), ii. 62.
[85] Feud. Aids, iv. 215.
[86] Eyton, vi. 253–4.
[87] Wolryche-Whitmore MSS., Dudmaston, deed, 1322.
[88] Eyton, vi. 257; Wolryche-Whitmore MSS., Dudmaston, ct. r. 1496, 1532; C 142/60/55.
[89] C 142/228/7.
[90] Visit. Salop. 1623 (Harl. Soc. xxviii), i. 10.
[91] Wolryche-Whitmore MSS., Dudmaston, deed, 1339.
[92] Eyton, vi. 257.
[93] Cal. Pat. 1550–3, 10.
[94] Wolryche-Whitmore MSS., Dudmaston, partition of woodland, 1340.
[95] Ibid. deed, 1585.
[96] C 142/252/41.
[97] Wolryche-Whitmore MSS., Dudmaston, deed, 1615.
[98] Ibid. deed, 1625.
[99] Eyton, vi. 252.
[1] Ibid.
[2] Ibid.; Wolryche-Whitmore MSS., Dudmaston, deed, n.d.
[3] Ibid.
[4] Eyton, vi. 252.
[5] Rot. Hund. (Rec. Com.), ii. 62; Cal. Close, 1272–9, 294; Abbrev. Plac. (Rec. Com.), 198; Eyton, vi. 254.
[6] Eyton, vi. 254.
[7] Ibid. 254, 257; T.S.A.S., 2nd ser. xi. 366.
[8] Eyton, vi. 254, 257; Bodl. MS. Blakeway 15, f. 74; C 145/263/10; Salop. Peace Roll, 1400–14, 63.
[9] S.P.L., Deeds 7085.
[10] Wolryche-Whitmore MSS., Dudmaston, partition of woodland, 1340.
[11] Ibid. deed, 1605.
[12] Ibid. 1606.
[13] Ibid. 1607; Req. 2/307/10.
[14] Wolryche-Whitmore MSS., Dudmaston, deed, 1448.
[15] Bodl. MS. Blakeway 15, f. 74.
[16] Wolryche-Whitmore MSS., Dudmaston, deeds, 1667–9.
[17] See p. 173.

of Haughmond Abbey's manor of Boveria during the Middle Ages, while the manor of Wilderley extended deep into the parish, between Picklescott and Pease Lane. Like Betchcott, Wilderley manor was held by Haughmond Abbey during the Middle Ages and its later descent is given elsewhere.[18] The estate was not broken up until the death of Mary Walker in 1957, when Underhill Hall, Coppice Farm, and other smaller farms were purchased by their tenants.[19]

Land at Betchcott, together with pasture there formerly held by Bletherus the hermit, both at that time within the royal manor of Condover,[20] were granted by Henry II to Haughmond Abbey shortly before 1170.[21] By 1235 half of Picklescott, previously granted to the Abbey of Strata Marcella by Robert Fitz Madoc[22] and exchanged by that Abbey with Thomas Corbet,[23] was granted by the latter to Haughmond Abbey in exchange for lands at Edderton, near Wentnor.[24] In the course of the 13th century the Abbey acquired a little over one virgate from 4 free tenants at Picklescott.[25] The Abbey's estate included Betchcott and 4 messuages at Picklescott in 1538.[26] In 1545 the Betchcott portion of the estate was granted to Thomas Ireland[27] and remained in the Ireland family[28] until it was sold to Thomas Powys, the owner of the Wilderley estate, in 1722.[29] Like Wilderley, Betchcott followed the descent of Stapleton manor until 1877, when the 3 farms there were purchased by William Groves.[30] The estate passed to T. S. Walker in 1905, but was broken up in 1925.[31]

Haughmond Abbey's properties in Picklescott were granted, with the manor of Wilderley, to Edward Fiennes, Lord Clinton and Saye, in 1551.[32] They are not recorded in descriptions of the Wilderley estate after 1597[33] and were probably sold shortly after this date, thus accounting for several of the small freehold estates found at Picklescott from the 17th century onwards.

ECONOMIC HISTORY. In 1086, when the manor of Smethcott was assessed at one hide and was valued at 4s.,[34] it probably extended over the whole parish, with the exception of Betchcott. The latter was not recorded in 1086, but lay within the royal forest of Botwood and was uninhabited, save for a hermit, when granted to Haughmond Abbey c. 1170.[35] The complex history of landownership in the parish is due to the partition of Smethcott manor at the end of the 12th century and to the growth and subsequent divisions of the estate of Haughmond Abbey in Betchcott, Picklescott, and Wilderley.

The manor of Smethcott was assessed at only half a hide in 1255,[36] the remainder of the Domesday assessment being accounted for by the estate at Picklescott granted to Haughmond Abbey before 1235.[37] In 1340 woodland in the north of the parish was divided among the lords of the 3 portions of the manor.[38] An area to the east of Smethcott Dingle was allotted to William de Smethcott and woodland in the north-west of the parish, roughly corresponding with the present Coppice Farm, was allotted to John Scott and Richard Tristram, while the remaining central portion was the share of Aline Burnell. The deed of partition[39] refers to tenanted lands at Smethcott as having already been divided and although it is not clear on what principle this division was made, it is likely that each lord's share of cultivated land adjoined his share of woodland and that the manorial estate was thus divided, north and south, into three roughly equal areas. Thus half of the field called the Criftin, north-east of the church, and Pluntnall, near Walkmills in the east of the parish, were held by William de Smethcott in the 13th century,[40] while half of Frogpool (now Smethcott Pool), lying near the boundary between Smethcott and Picklescott on the west, belonged to John Scott in 1320.[41] The site of the castle lay in the Burnell portion in 1428,[42] but the rent of the mill was then shared by all 4 lords.[43]

There is little reliable evidence for the size of the various portions of the manor before they were reunited in the 17th century. In the portion descending from Christine[44] rents produced 45s. 9½d. a year in 1294 and 39s. in 1428.[45] Part of this estate passed in the 16th century to the Lacon family, who were said to hold 410 a. in Smethcott in 1609.[46] In 1653 Richard Phillips, to whom the Lacon property had descended, held 7 messuages and lands in the parish.[47] The area held by the Pope family before the purchases of Roger Pope in the early 17th century is not known. The eastern portion of the manor, held by the successors of Margery, seems to have included most of the houses in Smethcott township after the desertion of its original site near the church. When sold to Roger Pope in 1607 it included half the Hall of Smethcott (New Hall Farm), Braddocks Coppice on the Leebotwood boundary, and the lands of 11 other tenants.[48] The history of Maud's portion is least well documented. There is no indication of the size of the Acton estate in Smethcott, but in the later 16th century Richard Prince held Trentham's Wood and adjoining lands near Pease Lane.[49]

Prince's estate thus included the area known as

[18] See pp. 134–5.
[19] Underhill Hall title-deeds, *penes* Lloyds Bank, Shrewsbury.
[20] *Bk. of Fees*, 146.
[21] S.P.L., Haughmond Cart. f. 132.
[22] Ibid. f. 163ᵛ.
[23] Ibid. ff. 163ᵛ–164.
[24] Ibid.
[25] Ibid. ff. 164–164ᵛ.
[26] S.C. 6/Hen. VIII/3009 mm. 32–33.
[27] *L. & P. Hen. VIII*, xx (1), p. 222.
[28] C 142/104/83; C 142/259/40; C 142/345/122; Q. Sess. reg., papists' estates, 1717.
[29] S.P.L., Deeds 3276, 3387, 3451.
[30] Betchcott Hall title-deeds *penes* Messrs. G. H. Morgan & Sons, solicitors, Shrewsbury.
[31] Ibid.
[32] *Cal. Pat.* 1550–3, 206.

[33] S.P.L., Deeds 3463, 3515.
[34] *V.C.H. Salop.* i. 342.
[35] S.P.L., Haughmond Cart. f. 132.
[36] *Rot. Hund.* (Rec. Com.), ii. 62.
[37] S.P.L., Haughmond Cart. ff. 163ᵛ–164.
[38] Wolryche-Whitmore MSS., Dudmaston, partition of woodland, 1340.
[39] Ibid.
[40] Ibid. deed, n.d.
[41] S.R.O. 322, deeds, no. 86.
[42] Ibid. 1011 uncat., bailiff's acct. 1428–9.
[43] Ibid.   [44] See p. 151.
[45] *Cal. Inq. p.m.* iii, p. 122; S.R.O. 1011 uncat., bailiff's acct. 1428–9.
[46] C 142/312/147.
[47] Wolryche-Whitmore MSS., Dudmaston, deed, 1668.
[48] Ibid. deed 1607.
[49] Ibid. deed 1585.

Hollicot, said in 1340 to be part of the demesne lands of the manor.[50] This, together with any other demesne which there may have been nearer to Smethcott village, presumably ceased to be kept in hand after the manor passed into divided ownership. There were no demesne lands or buildings in the portion of Edward Burnell in 1315, although this included the castle site.[51] Roger Pope had constructed a rabbit-warren in Trentham's Wood by 1625,[52] but the Popes held no land in hand in the parish in 1675[53] and the lord of the manor held only 9 a. of woodland in 1777.[54] Thomas Phillips and his son Richard—Smethcott's only resident lords of the manor since medieval times—seem to have lived at New Hall between 1583 and 1662,[55] but the greater part of their estate lay in the adjoining township of Netley.[56]

The Pope family bought out the lords of the remaining portions of the manor between 1607 and 1667[57] and between 1601 and 1624 Roger Pope acquired 2 small freehold estates in Smethcott and a freehold of some 72 a. in Picklescott.[58] By 1675, when the manor had been reunited, it comprised 668 a.[59] and it had been enlarged to 746 a. by 1777.[60] A further 342 a. were added at the inclosure of Smethcott Common in 1798[61] and in 1807 the manorial estate contained 1,141 a.[62] In the following year, however, 622 a. were put up for sale, comprising New Hall, Bank, Coppice, and Branmill Farms and the scattered holding of William Heighway in Picklescott.[63] The estate had been reduced to 506 a. by 1844[64] and continued unchanged until it was broken up in 1919.[65]

There is little evidence before the 18th century for the acreage of the various freehold properties in the west of the parish, which derived from the medieval estate of Haughmond Abbey. A description of its bounds in 1253[66] indicates that the whole township of Betchcott lay within the estate granted to Haughmond Abbey c. 1170.[67] After the Dissolution the Betchcott estate remained unchanged in size[68] until the early years of the present century, when properties in Picklescott were acquired by the Walker family.[69] One carucate at Betchcott lay in demesne in 1291, when stock there was valued at £1 8s. 8d.,[70] but by 1446 the demesne lands and meadows here had been leased to the tenant of the manor-house[71] and no land was kept in hand by

subsequent owners of the estate until the later 19th century.[72]

That part of Wilderley manor which extended into Smethcott, on the eastern slopes of Cothercott Hill, was presumably woodland in the Middle Ages. Until the inclosure of Smethcott Common its eastern boundary lay near the road across the common, running from Picklescott, towards Netley. It thus included Underhill Hall, Park Gate, Smethcott Bank, and Wildreck,[73] but after 1798 it was restricted to the area west of Hollicot Brook.[74] At the inclosure of the common 62 a. were allotted to H. W. Powys as lord of Wilderley[75] and he acquired Coppice Farm c. 1809.[76] This estate amounted to 461 a. in 1844, when Powys, who also held 626 a. at Betchcott, was the largest landowner in the parish.[77] Henry Powys seems to have lived at Underhill Hall in 1755, when he had lands worth £31 10s. a year in hand,[78] but the Hall had been leased by the early 19th century[79] and the owner had no land in hand here in 1844.[80]

Small freeholds have always been numerous in the parish. Three 13th-century grants to free tenants[81] suggest that the lords of Smethcott manor were using this device to encourage assarting. In 1315 there were said to be 15 free tenants in the portion of the manor held by Edward Burnell,[82] but this probably represents the total number of freeholds in the whole manor. Of the 2 Smethcott freeholds bought into the manorial estate in the early 17th century, one seems to have been in origin copyhold land, held by the Rogers family in the later 15th century,[83] to which Roger Parkes was admitted in 1532,[84] and was sold to Roger Pope by William Parkes in 1624.[85] The other, known as Wilcock's Lye, which had also belonged to the Parkes family, passed by marriage in 1521[86] to David Gyles, whose grandson sold it to Pope in 1617.[87] A third freehold, held by the Phillips family since 1448,[88] was probably later merged with the Phillips portion of the manor, thus passing to the Popes in 1667.[89] Four freeholds remained in Smethcott in 1675.[90] These continued unchanged in size until the pattern of landownership was complicated by the inclosure of the common and the sale of part of the manorial estate in the early 19th century.

Lawley View was occupied in the early 17th

---

[50] Wolryche-Whitmore MSS., Dudmaston, partition of woodland, 1340.
[51] C 134/48/9.
[52] Wolryche-Whitmore MSS., Dudmaston, lease, 1625.
[53] Apley Park estate office, survey, 1675.
[54] Ibid. survey, 1777.
[55] Wolryche-Whitmore MSS., Dudmaston, leases, 1583–1627; ibid. deeds, 1618, 1660; E 179/255/35 m. 77d.
[56] See p. 165.   [57] See p. 152.
[58] Wolryche-Whitmore MSS., Dudmaston, deeds, 1601–24.
[59] Apley Park estate office, survey, 1675.
[60] Ibid. survey, 1777.
[61] Wolryche-Whitmore MSS., Dudmaston, inclosure award, Smethcott Common, 1798.
[62] Ibid. survey, 1807.
[63] Ibid. sale partics. 1808.
[64] Par. rec., tithe appt.
[65] S.C.C. title-deeds, SH 12 (survey, 1917).
[66] S.P.L., Haughmond Cart. f. 132ᵛ.
[67] Ibid. f. 132.
[68] Q. Sess., reg. papists' estates, 1717; par. rec., tithe appt.; S.R.O. 650/2.
[69] Betchcott Hall title-deeds.

[70] Tax. Eccl. (Rec. Com.), 260.
[71] S.C. 6/967/1.
[72] S.R.O. 650/2.
[73] Wolryche-Whitmore MSS., Dudmaston, inclosure award, Smethcott Common, 1798.
[74] Par. rec., tithe appt.
[75] Wolryche-Whitmore MSS., Dudmaston, inclosure award, Smethcott Common, 1798.
[76] Ibid. sale partics. 1808.
[77] Par. rec., tithe appt.
[78] S.P.L., Deeds 3515.
[79] W.S.L. 350/40/3.
[80] Par. rec., tithe appt.
[81] Wolryche-Whitmore MSS., Dudmaston, grants, n.d.
[82] C 134/48/3.
[83] Wolryche-Whitmore MSS., Dudmaston, deeds, 1486, 1498; ibid. ct. r. 1496.
[84] Ibid. ct. r. 1532.
[85] Ibid. deed, 1624.
[86] S.P.L., Deeds 1891.
[87] Wolryche-Whitmore MSS., Dudmaston, deed, 1617.
[88] Ibid. deed, 1448.
[89] Ibid. deeds, 1667–9.
[90] Apley Park estate office, survey, 1675.

century by Robert Parkes, who had a freehold of some 30 a. at his death in 1634.[91] This estate had passed by 1675 to William Rogers,[92] whose descendants held it until 1820.[93] The Partridge family, who first appear in Betchcott in the 14th century[94] and who were the wealthiest family in Smethcott township in 1544,[95] occupied a house on the site of Red House Farm. John Partridge held 30 a. in Smethcott at his death in 1633[96] and by 1675, when it had passed to Edward Higgs, it contained 52 a.[97] It was held by William Beaumont in 1777[98] and by Eleanor Beaumont in 1798, when she received a 30-acre allotment on the common and 11 a. by exchange with the lord of the manor.[99] By 1844 the farm was part of Richard Bromley's estate in Smethcott and Picklescott.[1] A small freehold of some 10 a. at Branmills was held by the Townsend family between 1675 and 1793 and was sold to Samuel Groves in 1802.[2]

In 1844 Panton Corbett of Longnor held 73 a. in the east of the parish, adjoining Longnor Park.[3] The bulk of this was bought from the manorial estate in 1821,[4] but since 1691 the Corbetts had owned a strip of land along the edge of the Park, allotted to Sir Uvedale Corbett in lieu of common rights in Smethcott Wood.[5]

The remaining 19th-century freeholds in Smethcott dated from the sale of part of the manorial estate in 1808.[6] New Hall and Bank Farms (338 a.) were then bought by Charles Guest,[7] who sold them to J. T. Hope c. 1849,[8] since which date they have formed part of the Netley estate. Coppice Farm passed to the Wilderley estate[9] and land near Branmills, including the site of the castle, was sold to Samuel Groves.[10]

Since the early 19th century the whole of Picklescott township has been in the hands of a number of small freeholders. During the Middle Ages half the township was held by Haughmond Abbey,[11] while the remainder, which lay within Smethcott manor,[12] seems to have been entirely in the possession of free tenants. Top House Farm, the only part of Picklescott within the manorial estate in the 18th century,[13] was a freehold in the possession of William Wilcox in the 15th century.[14] It was purchased by Roger Pope in 1601[15] and when put up for sale in 1808 still consisted of small scattered fields—the fossilized remains of an open-field

holding.[16] Hall Farm, in the early 17th century the property of the Phillips family,[17] had been purchased before 1685 by Richard Corfield, whose descendants held it until 1772, when it was sold to John Rogers.[18] By 1796 it had been acquired by William Smith, who then held 100 a. in Picklescott[19] and who was allotted 54 a. at the inclosure of Smethcott Common.[20] The estate was sold in 1809 to Richard Bromley,[21] said c. 1830 to be the largest landowner in the township,[22] but in 1839 the farm was settled on Bromley's daughter Mary and her husband Edward Chidley,[23] who in 1844 owned 236 a. in Picklescott and Smethcott.[24] The history of the remaining farms in Picklescott cannot be traced earlier than c. 1750; it is likely that they derive from the medieval estate of Haughmond Abbey.

In 1796 7 Picklescott freeholders held 271 a. in the township[25] and 6 of them received allotments totalling 137 a. at the inclosure of the Common.[26] By 1844 the 7 freeholders had increased their total holdings to 588 a., but this included Red House Farm in Smethcott.[27] Edward Chidley, the largest of the freeholders, was a newcomer to the parish, having begun his career as a farm-servant of Richard Bromley,[28] and only the Bromley family could claim a long association with the village. Two members of this family were resident in Picklescott in 1544[29] and Bromleys were tenants on the neighbouring manor of Wilderley in 1446.[30] Over the parish as a whole the number of small freeholders remained constant at about 18 during the later 19th century.[31]

Thus until the 19th century about two-thirds of the parish lay in three large estates—Smethcott manor, Betchcott, and Wilderley—and of the remaining third about half was held by small freeholders in Smethcott and Picklescott, while the remainder was common land. Evidence for the tenurial history of the larger estates is scanty before the 18th century. The only recorded tenants at Smethcott in 1086 were 2 radmen and a bordar, who together held one plough.[32] With the division of the manor at the end of the 12th century it becomes impossible to calculate the number of tenants or the size of their holdings until the estate was reunited in the 17th century. The lease for 3 lives was commonly employed until c. 1730,[33] but had been replaced by short-term leases by 1755.[34]

[91] C 142/533/79.
[92] C 3/436/55; Apley Park estate office, survey, 1675.
[93] Title-deeds penes Mr. F. S. Ross, Castle Hill, Woolstaston.
[94] Cal. Pat. 1340–3, 498; ibid. 1348–50, 257.
[95] E 179/166/168.
[96] C 142/532/17.
[97] Apley Park estate office, survey, 1675.
[98] Ibid. survey, 1777.
[99] Wolryche-Whitmore MSS., Dudmaston, inclosure award, Smethcott Common, 1798.
[1] Par. rec., tithe appt.
[2] Apley Park estate office, survey, 1675; Pool House title-deeds penes Midland Bank, Shrewsbury.
[3] Par. rec., tithe appt.
[4] Wolryche-Whitmore MSS., Dudmaston, deed, 1821.
[5] Ibid. deed, 1691.
[6] Ibid. sale partics. 1808.
[7] S.R.O. 1359 uncat., deed, 1826.
[8] Hope-Edwardes MSS., Linley Hall, sale partics. 1845, and related papers.
[9] Par. rec., tithe appt.   [10] Ibid.
[11] S.C. 6/Hen. VIII/3009 mm. 32–33.
[12] Wolryche-Whitmore MSS., Dudmaston, deeds, 1322, 1339.

[13] Apley Park estate office, survey, 1777.
[14] S.P.L., Haughmond Cart. f. 164v.
[15] Wolryche-Whitmore MSS., Dudmaston, deed, 1601.
[16] Ibid. sale partics. 1808.
[17] S.P.L., Deeds 10345–6.   [18] Ibid.
[19] Wolryche-Whitmore MSS., Dudmaston, survey, c. 1796.
[20] Ibid. inclosure award, Smethcott Common, 1798.
[21] Hall Farm title-deeds penes Messrs. J. C. H. Bowdler & Sons, solicitors, Shrewsbury.
[22] W.S.L. 350/40/3.
[23] Hall Farm title-deeds.
[24] Par. rec., tithe appt.
[25] Wolryche-Whitmore MSS., Dudmaston, survey, c. 1796.
[26] Ibid. inclosure award, Smethcott Common, 1798.
[27] Par. rec., tithe appt.
[28] Hall Farm title-deeds.
[29] E 179/166/168.
[30] S.C. 6/967/1.
[31] Par. rec., poor rate, 1870; S.R.O. 1168/1/107.
[32] V.C.H. Salop. i. 342.
[33] Wolryche-Whitmore MSS., Dudmaston, leases, 1583–1730.
[34] Ibid. leases, 1755–1809.

In addition to heriot and suit of court, 17th-century lessees of the Pope family were required to perform one, two, or four days work at harvest and occasionally to carry timber.[35] The annual rental rose from £103 in 1665[36] to £191 by 1740[37] and to £353 by 1780.[38] There were 43 tenants in the manorial estate in 1675, of whom only one held more than 100 a., while 35 holdings were less than 25 a.[39] By 1777 the number of tenants had been reduced to 25 and nearly 500 a. lay in two large farms, but there were only 3 other farms of more than 25 a.[40] Some of the farms then extended into neighbouring parishes. Subsequent changes in farm sizes in the estate as a whole are discussed under Leebotwood.[41]

Assized rents produced 6s. 5d. a year on Haughmond Abbey's estate at Betchcott and Picklescott in 1291.[42] At Betchcott 3 farms were held on long leases in 1538 and annual rents totalling 19s. were then paid by tenants-at-will.[43] Nearly all of the abbey's Picklescott estate was held on long leases by two tenants,[44] one of whom, Roger Heighway, was a member of a family who had been tenants of the abbey here since at least 1395.[45] The Picklescott estate seems to have passed to small freeholders soon after 1597,[46] but at Betchcott the farms have remained unchanged in size until the present day, save for the disappearance of one small farm in the early 18th century.[47]

The small farm remained as characteristic a feature in Smethcott in the mid-19th century as it had been before the inclosure of the Common, and smallholders appear to have become more numerous in the later 19th century. In 1844 there were in the parish as a whole 11 farms of over 100 a. and 25 holdings of 1–25 a. By 1905, when the number of persons holding over 1 a. had increased from 47 to 51, there were 12 large farms and 31 holdings of less than 25 a.[48]

There is little evidence for land-use in the parish before the 19th century. During the Middle Ages Betchcott was part of the composite manor of Boveria, which seems to have centred on a sheepwalk near the Thresholds,[49] and from its sheltered situation it may be inferred that Betchcott was used for winter pasturage. Half a sack of wool, valued at 5 marks, was taken from John Partridge of Betchcott for the use of the Crown in 1341.[50] There were only 425 a. of arable in the parish in 1801, when wheat was the chief crop,[51] but a considerable acreage of pasture was said to have been ploughed

up in response to the high corn prices of 1808 and 1810.[52] Since the small farmers could not afford to return this newly formed arable to pasture after 1815,[53] the parish maintained a high level of arable land during the earlier 19th century. In 1844 1,313 a., or about half the total area of the parish, was still under the plough.[54] Although there was a good deal of arable land in the east of the parish in 1964, milk production was then the basis of the economy of the small farms to the west.[55] On the larger farms at Betchcott the sheep still retained its ancient predominance, coupled with the production of beef cattle.[56]

Smethcott mill is first recorded in the 13th century[57] and in 1428 was leased to John Sankey.[58] This presumably stood on Walkmill Brook, near Branmills, but is not known to have been in use after the 15th century. Two fulling mills had been set up, downstream from Branmills in the south-east corner of the parish, by the early 17th century, when they were known as the Upper Mills.[59] Occupied by the Owen family from at least 1620,[60] they were leased in 1692 to Hannah Rogers,[61] whose descendants held the mills throughout the 18th century. Thomas Owen, the tenant in 1676, was a dyer[62] and by 1777 the mill was known as the Dyehouse.[63] Welsh cloth and flannel were being dyed here at the end of the 18th century,[64] but it seems to have been no more than a smallholding by 1844.[65] Two other fullers were said to be resident in Smethcott in the early 17th century,[66] and the field-name Tainter Yard, south of New Hall Farm,[67] suggests that a fulling mill may once have stood there. Betchcott had a mill in the early 13th century,[68] but no mill is recorded at Picklescott. Coal was mined for a short period, c. 1740, at the Haines, to the east of Bank Farm,[69] and the field-name Brick-kiln Leasow found in adjoining fields[70] suggests that the coal was used for the manufacture of bricks on the spot.

A smith and a carpenter, who were resident in Smethcott in the early 14th century,[71] had their counterparts in the 19th-century village. The smithy, near Red House Farm, and a wheelwright at the Bynords were in business in 1844.[72] The former closed soon after this date,[73] but the wheelwright continued until c. 1930.[74] No tradesmen are recorded at Picklescott before the later 18th century. A smithy was erected at Always Cottage by John Partridge c. 1773[75] and continued in business until c. 1922.[76] There appears to have been a second

[35] Wolryche-Whitmore MSS. Dudmaston, leases, 1613–85.
[36] Apley Park estate office, accts. 1665–1730.
[37] Ibid. accts. 1732–48.
[38] Ibid. accts. 1748–80.
[39] Ibid. survey, 1675.
[40] Ibid. survey, 1777.
[41] See p. 103.
[42] Tax. Eccl. (Rec. Com.), 260.
[43] S.C. 6/Hen. VIII/3009 mm. 32–33.
[44] Ibid.
[45] S.P.L., Haughmond Cart. f. 164ᵛ.
[46] See p. 153.
[47] Q. Sess., reg. papists' estates, 1717; par. rec., tithe appt.
[48] Par. rec., tithe appt.; S.R.O. 1168/1/107.
[49] S.C. 6/967/1.
[50] Cal. Pat. 1340–3, 498.
[51] H.O. 67/14/237.
[52] S.P.L., MS. 4471.   [53] Ibid.
[54] Par. rec., tithe appt.
[55] Local inf.
[56] Ex inf. Mr. N. F. V. Carter, Middle Farm, Betchcott.

[57] Wolryche-Whitmore MSS., Dudmaston, grant, n.d.
[58] S.R.O. 1011 uncat., bailiff's acct. 1428–9.
[59] Wolryche-Whitmore MSS., Dudmaston, ct. r. 1620, 1632; ibid. lease, 1676.
[60] Ibid.
[61] Ibid. lease, 1692.
[62] Ibid. lease, 1676.
[63] Apley Park estate office, survey, 1777.
[64] A. Aikin, Jnl. of a Tour through North Wales (1797), 81.
[65] Par. rec., tithe appt.
[66] Wolryche-Whitmore MSS., Dudmaston, ct. r. 1620.
[67] Apley Park estate office, survey and map, 1777.
[68] S.P.L., Haughmond Cart. f. 164.
[69] S.R.O. 567 uncat., lease, 1738.
[70] Par. rec., tithe appt.
[71] T.S.A.S. 2nd ser. xi. 366; E 179/166/2 m. 5.
[72] Par. rec., tithe appt.
[73] Bagshaw's Dir. Salop. (1851).
[74] Ex inf. Mr. T. W. Davies, The Bynords, Smethcott.
[75] Wolryche-Whitmore MSS., Dudmaston, ct. r. 1773.
[76] Ex inf. Mr. V. W. E. Chidley, 'The Bottle and Glass', Picklescott.

blacksmith in the village between 1851 and 1870[77] and wheelwright's shops at Brook House and the Gate House are said to have closed at about the same time as the smithy at Always Cottage.[78] During the 17th and 18th centuries a number of spinners and weavers lived on the Common,[79] where there was also a tailor, 1606–50,[80] and a baker, 1670–1709.[81] A glover, recorded in 1620 and 1634,[82] and a shoemaker, 1704–71,[83] may also have lived there. The most notable of these craftsmen was the wood-carver William Hill, whose cottage, now demolished, stood near Smethcott Bank. He was in business between 1850 and the 1880s and had a considerable local reputation.[84] Examples of his work are to be seen in Smethcott church, Woolstaston church and rectory, and Netley Hall.

LOCAL GOVERNMENT. Separate manor courts appear to have been held by the lords of each portion of Smethcott manor. For the portion held by the Pope family there are court rolls, 1601–34, 1681–93, and presentments, 1747–74.[85] Leases by the Lacon and Phillips families between 1585 and 1663[86] specified suit of court and there are copyhold admissions at the court of the Acton family, 1496 and 1532.[87] During the Middle Ages Betchcott and Picklescott lay within the jurisdiction of the composite manor of Boveria, for which there are court rolls, 1507–38.[88] Betchcott tenants owed suit at Cothercott in the early 19th century[89] and after the Dissolution tenants in Picklescott attended the Wilderley manor court. There are court rolls for the latter, 1547–51 and 1718–45.[90] No officers appear to have been appointed at these courts and their jurisdiction did not include the assize of bread and ale. From the 17th century onwards most of their business concerned encroachments and other offences on the commons.

The parish records include churchwardens' accounts, 1862–99, and overseers' accounts, 1810–37. In the 19th century there were two churchwardens, one for the Upper and one for the Lower division of the parish. Each accounted separately until 1890 and before economies were introduced in 1869 each received a salary of 8s. a year. Church rates were replaced by voluntary contributions in 1869. Like the churchwardens, the two overseers each acted for one of the two divisions of the parish and accounted separately until 1832. Poor rates had

risen from some £5 a year in the 1690s[91] to about £40 a year in the later 18th century[92] and to £89 a year by 1803.[93] Annual expenditure on poor relief rose to a peak of £232 in 1818 and fluctuated between £100 and £198 in the 1820s. Two cottages and 2½ a. land on Smethcott Common, conveyed to the parish officers in trust for the poor in 1741,[94] were in use as poor-houses by 1776.[95] The 3 inmates were evicted in 1828, when there were 4 cottages on the site, and subsequently 2 cottages were occupied by paupers and the other 2 were let, their rents being applied to the poor rate.[96] In 1783 a Woolstaston farmer contracted to maintain and employ all the poor in the parish for one year for £27.[97] There is no evidence that this experiment was repeated.

CHURCH. Although the church is not mentioned before 1341,[98] Roger *clericus* who, was a resident of Smethcott in 1262[99] may have been the rector and the church, though largely rebuilt in 1850, still contains some 12th-century features.[1] There is no evidence to support Eyton's assumption[2] that it was, like Betchcott, originally a chapelry of Condover. The living is a rectory and has been united with Woolstaston since 1929.[3] It has, however, been served by the rector of Pulverbatch since 1955.[4]

Since the consent of the three portioners of Condover was obtained at its appropriation to Haughmond Abbey shortly before 1183,[5] the former chapel of Betchcott must at that time have been accounted a chapelry of Condover. The chapel was still in existence in 1536,[6] but was apparently allowed to fall into ruin after the Dissolution.[7] The parochial status of Betchcott remained uncertain until the mid-19th century. In the earlier 18th century it was stated to be a chapelry of Leebotwood on the grounds that its inhabitants had two pews in the church there and had repaired a section of the churchyard wall in 1746.[8] The parish clerk of Smethcott alleged in 1842 that Betchcott people had only been allowed to bury at Smethcott in comparatively recent times,[9] but the Smethcott parish registers contain a number of entries of Betchcott burials from the early 17th century onwards.[10] The inhabitants of Betchcott always paid poor rates to Smethcott, but paid no church rates until 1830.[11]

Until the 17th century the advowson of Smethcott followed the descent of the manor, the lords of

[77] *Bagshaw's Dir. Salop.* (1851); *Kelly's Dir. Salop.* (1870).

[78] Ex inf. Mr. V. W. E. Chidley, 'The Bottle and Glass'.

[79] Wolryche-Whitmore MSS., Dudmaston, leases, 1606–1701; ibid. ct. r. 1620–34; *S.P.R. Lich.* i (2), 110–93.

[80] Wolryche-Whitmore MSS., Dudmaston, leases, 1606, 1650.

[81] *S.P.R. Lich.* i (2), 119, 129, 135.

[82] Wolryche-Whitmore MSS., Dudmaston, ct. r. 1620, 1634.

[83] *S.P.R. Lich.* i (2), 133, 193.

[84] *Kelly's Dir. Salop.* (1863–85); *S.P.R. Lich.* i (2), 190–1; *Salop. Shreds & Patches*, iv. 44; Woolstaston par. rec., notebooks of the Revd. E. D. Carr.

[85] Wolryche-Whitmore MSS., Dudmaston, ct. r. 1601–1774.

[86] Ibid. leases, 1585–1663.

[87] Ibid. ct. r. 1496, 1532.

[88] S.R.O. 665 uncat., ct. r. 1507–38.

[89] W.S.L. 350/40/3.

[90] S.C. 2/197/154; S.R.O. 883/95.

[91] Bodl. MS. Blakeway 8, f. 478.

[92] *Rep. Cttee. on Overseers' Returns, 1777*, p. 442, H.C.

(1st ser. ix, reprinted 1803); *Rep. Cttee. on State of Poor, 1787*, p. 658, H.C. (1st ser. ix, reprinted 1803).

[93] *Poor Law Abstract, 1803*, H.C. 175, pp. 416–17 (1803–4), xiii.

[94] *24th Rep. Com. Char.*, H.C. 231, p. 389 (1831), xi.

[95] *Rep. Cttee. on Overseers' Returns, 1777*, p. 442.

[96] *24th Rep. Com. Char.* 389; par. rec., overseers' accts. 1810–37, and bills, 1828.

[97] Par. rec., contract for maintenance of poor, 1783.

[98] *Inq. Non.* (Rec. Com.), 191.

[99] E 32/145 m. 1.

[1] *S.P.R. Lich.* i (2), 190–1.

[2] Eyton, vi. 256.

[3] *Lond. Gaz.* 1927, pp. 8238–9.

[4] Ex inf. the Rector of Pulverbatch.

[5] S.P.L., Haughmond Cart. f. 133.

[6] S.C. 6/Hen. VIII/3009 m. 33d.

[7] See p. 160.

[8] Lich. Dioc. Regy., Leebotwood glebe terriers, 1730–87.

[9] S.P.L., MS. 4471.

[10] *S.P.R. Lich.* i (2), 109–96 *passim*.

[11] W.S.L. 350/40/3; S.P.L., MS. 4471.

each portion of the manor presenting in rotation.[12] Although the share of the advowson held by Richard Phillips was conveyed, with his sixth part of the manor, to Roger Pope in 1667,[13] Phillips's grandson Richard Beddow of Shrewsbury successfully claimed the advowson against Catherine Pope in 1749.[14] Beddow was patron in 1763,[15] but by 1784 the advowson had passed to Ruth, widow of James Lacy of Twickenham (Mdx.).[16] It was held by Mr. Langley in 1799[17] and had been purchased by Henry Fletcher, rector of Smethcott, by 1823.[18] On Fletcher's death in 1830 the Bishop presented by lapse[19] and since 1837 the trustees of William Hulme have been patrons of the living.[20]

The church was worth 33s. 4d. in 1341[21] and its gross value was said to be £4 13s. 4d. in 1535.[22] The glebe and tithes were valued at £34 a year in 1655[23] and the living was worth about the same amount in the early 18th century.[24] Its annual gross value had risen to £200 by 1799[25] and to £360 by 1823,[26] but in 1835 the rector's average annual income was only £276.[27]

A tenement, and a messuage and a half virgate in Smethcott, granted to the rector in 1343[28] and 1350[29] respectively, may represent the greater part of the later glebe, which included a messuage in Picklescott and scattered strips in the common fields of Smethcott in 1612.[30] It had been inclosed by 1675,[31] but has never been consolidated. It was said to contain some 30 a. in the 18th century,[32] but a further 10½ a. near Smethcott Pool were allotted to the rector at the inclosure of the Common.[33] The glebe was said to be worth £8 a year in 1655.[34] The greater part was leased after c. 1793,[35] but the rector kept 18 a. in hand in 1884.[36]

The tithes were said to be worth £26 a year in 1655.[37] A modus on hay tithes in Picklescott had been introduced by 1698[38] and a modus on barren cows, calves, and colts by 1752.[39] The owner of Longnor Park was said in 1752 to provide the rector each year with a side of venison in lieu of tithes on land in the east of the parish which had been taken into the Park in 1691.[40] This custom was last recorded in 1841.[41] No modus on corn tithes was in use,[42] but it was said in 1842 that tithes had never been collected in kind in living memory.[43] During the later 18th century the inhabitants compounded for their tithes for some £250 a year and by 1793 the tithes were leased to the tenant of the glebe.[44] The rent paid for them, then £200 a year, had risen to £347 a year by 1813, but fell to £236 a year by 1817.[45] They were leased for £282 a year in 1841.[46] In the following year the rector made an attempt to raise the annual rent of the tithes by 20 per cent.[47] and in 1844 they were commuted for a rent-charge of £310 a year.[48] The tithes of Betchcott, granted with the chapel to Thomas Ireland in 1545,[49] were subsequently vested in the owner of the Betchcott estate. They were worth £5 a year in 1655[50] and about the same amount in 1717.[51] A customary payment of 6s. 8d. a year by the inhabitants of Betchcott to the rector of Smethcott is first recorded in 1718[52] and was still being paid in 1884.[53] Three small pieces of land, said to be worth 4d. a year in 1547[54] and given to provide Easter candles in the church, were sold by the Crown in 1549.[55]

John Beddow (rector 1663–1708)[56] and his son Thomas (rector 1708–46)[57] were the only rectors to combine a lengthy tenure of the living with residence in the parish. They were relatives of the patron of the living,[58] while Roger de Smethcott (rector 1312–38)[59] and Richard Phillips (rector c. 1653–8)[60] were relatives of one of the lords of the manor. One of the 15th-century incumbents was a graduate,[61] but the appointment of graduate rectors does not seem to have been normal before the 18th century.[62] Roger de Smethcott had leave of absence in 1314 and 1319, in the first instance for study,[63] and James atte Venne (rector 1381–92)[64] had leave to be absent in the service of Elizabeth, lady of Lutrell, in 1384.[65] Richard Wolley (rector 1612–53),[66] who was also rector of Leighton,[67] appears to have been continuously non-resident, employing as curate, c. 1624–39, Rowland Jaundrell,[68] who was presented for wearing unseemly apparel in 1639.[69] Richard Phillips and Roger Ellis, the 2 known incumbents

[12] Eyton, vi. 257; Bodl. MS. Blakeway 15, f. 14.
[13] Wolryche-Whitmore MSS., Dudmaston, deeds, 1667–9.
[14] S.P.R. Lich. i (2), 152–3.
[15] Lich. Dioc. Regy., glebe terriers, 1763.
[16] T.S.A.S. 4th ser. vi. 298.
[17] Visit. Archd. Salop. 1799.
[18] Ibid. 1823.
[19] S.P.L., MS. 4471.
[20] Ibid; Crockford (1961–2).
[21] Inq. Non. (Rec. Com.), 191.
[22] Valor Eccl. (Rec. Com.), iii. 183.
[23] T.S.A.S. xlvii. 27.
[24] Lich. Dioc. Regy., glebe terrier, 1705.
[25] Visit. Archd. Salop. 1799.
[26] Ibid. 1823.
[27] Rep. Com. Eccl. Revenues [67], pp. 498–9, H.C. (1835), xxii.
[28] Wolryche-Whitmore MSS., Dudmaston, deed, 1343.
[29] S.P.L., Deeds 164.
[30] Lich. Dioc. Regy., glebe terrier, 1612.
[31] Apley Park estate office, survey, 1675.
[32] Lich. Dioc. Regy., glebe terriers, 1698–1767.
[33] Wolryche-Whitmore MSS., Dudmaston, inclosure award, Smethcott Common, 1798.
[34] T.S.A.S. xlvii. 27.
[35] S.P.L., MS. 4471.
[36] Par. rec., terrier, 1884.
[37] T.S.A.S. xlvii. 27.
[38] Lich. Dioc. Regy., glebe terrier, 1698.
[39] Ibid. 1752–1841; par. rec., tithe appt.

[40] Lich. Dioc. Regy., glebe terrier, 1752.
[41] Ibid. 1841.
[42] Par. rec., tithe appt.
[43] S.P.L., MS. 4471.
[44] Ibid.
[45] Ibid.
[46] Ibid.
[47] Ibid.
[48] Par. rec., tithe appt.
[49] L. & P. Hen. VIII, xx (1), p. 222.
[50] T.S.A.S. xlvii. 27.
[51] Q. Sess., reg. papists' estates, 1717.
[52] Lich. Dioc. Regy., glebe terrier, 1718.
[53] Par. rec., terrier, 1884.
[54] T.S.A.S. 3rd ser. x. 374.
[55] Cal. Pat. 1549–51, 15.
[56] T.S.A.S. 3rd ser. v. 372; S.P.R. Lich. i (2), 118.
[57] T.S.A.S. 4th ser. v. 188, 200.
[58] See above.
[59] Eyton, vi. 257.
[60] S.P.R. Lich. i (2), 115–16; T.S.A.S. xlvii. 27.
[61] Bodl. MS. Blakeway 15, f. 74.
[62] Richard Phillips (c. 1653–8) was a graduate: S.P.R. Lich. i (2), intro. p. iv.
[63] Eyton, vi. 257.
[64] Ibid.
[65] S.H.C. NS x (2), 87.
[66] S.P.R. Lich. i (2), 115.
[67] Lich. Dioc. Regy., B/v 1/62.
[68] S.P.R. Lich. i (2), 123–6.
[69] Lich. Dioc. Regy., B/v 1/65.

during the Interregnum,[70] were resident, as were their successors, John and Thomas Beddow, but the living was held by 4 non-resident rectors between 1750 and 1842. David Rice (rector 1750–84)[71] lived at Longnor and employed curates only during his old age.[72] His successor Henry Fletcher (rector 1784–1830),[73] who held the living longer than any other known incumbent, lived at Twickenham (Mdx.)[74] and employed a succession of curates at Smethcott. W. C. Curtis, who lived at Condover, was curate 1779–1817,[75] and Henry Male, the curate of Woolstaston,[76] was appointed curate here in 1824 at a salary of £60 a year.[77] Subsequent curates normally received £100 a year and lived at the parsonage.[78] Rectors were normally resident after the building of the new parsonage in 1839, but curates were occasionally employed during the illnesses of R. J. Buddicom (rector 1842–62).[79] The Old Rectory, now a smallholding, is a two-bay house with a chimney-stack at the west gable. Its walls are externally of stone, but their thickness suggests that this is probably a casing over the original timber frame. The house was of the same size in 1612,[80] but a third bay, containing farm buildings, had been erected by 1718,[81] and by 1763 it had outshuts alongside the north and south walls.[82] In 1799 the house was described as small and mean, but in good repair[83] and in 1823 it was occupied by a poor family.[84] The New Rectory, built in 1839,[85] is a larger brick house with a pleasing view across the valley of Walkmill Brook to the south. It was sold in 1953.[86]

Communion was still administered only 4 times a year in 1847, when there were 21 communicants.[87] David Rice, who held 3 other livings, had a morning service at Smethcott, normally at 11 a.m., between 1769 and 1774.[88] By 1799 there were two services on Sundays in the summer and one in winter,[89] but again only one service in 1823.[90] Two Sunday services were normally held from 1842 until the union with Woolstaston in 1929.[91] The church seems to have had a choir in the early 19th century, its members receiving a fee of £1 a year, which was discontinued in 1869.[92] Accompaniment was provided by a bassviol, played by William Hill the carver until the 1880s.[93]

The church of ST. MICHAEL[94] now consists of a chancel and nave, with a south porch and a small wooden bell-turret at the west end. Although it was rebuilt in 1849–50, with the exception of part of the

west wall, the side walls of the porch, and a small part of the adjacent south wall, surviving original features indicate that the church dates from the 12th century. The semicircular tympanum of the north door, which bears traces of carving, was replaced in 1850, as was the smaller tympanum of the priest's door in the south wall of the chancel. A larger tympanum of similar type above the south door was broken during the rebuilding and was not replaced. A small round-headed window in the north wall of the chancel has been preserved and four fragments of 12th-century masonry, with nail-head ornament, are built into the north and south walls of the chancel.

The south and west walls of the church were said to have been rebuilt in 1699,[95] when a round-headed window was probably inserted in the south wall of the nave. A large brick bell-turret was erected at the west end in 1724[96] and a brick porch was built outside the south door c. 1764.[97] The east end was said to have been rebuilt in 1800.[98]

Although the church was said to be in good repair in 1799,[99] its dilapidated condition was used as the excuse for its rebuilding in 1849–50. This operation, which cost £650, was directed by the architect J. P. Harrison and apart from the east widow, which was made at Shrewsbury, the work was performed by local masons. The walls were constructed from the materials of the original church, supplemented by stone from a nearby quarry. Hoar Edge sandstone was used for quoins and the framing of doors and windows and Grinshill stone for window tracery. The hammer-beam roof was the work of William Hill, who made use of the timbers of the original roof.[1]

The interior contains no ancient fittings, apart from the font—a large, roughly shaped oval one, with a wooden lid—but the pews, probably reconstructed in 1850, incorporate pieces of 17th-century oak panelling. Before 1850 the church had a small gallery at the west end, first recorded in 1823.[2] The altar rails appear to be the work of William Hill, but the pulpit and reading desk are of more recent date. The sanctuary was panelled in oak in 1952.

The church had two bells in 1552.[3] These were recast by John Rudhall in 1789,[4] but by 1823 one of them was cracked[5] and was recast by C. & R. Mears in 1850.[6] The silver chalice which was in use in 1552[7] is still in the church. The bowl and lid date from c. 1500. There are traces of gilding inside the

[70] S.P.R. Lich. i (2), 115–16; T.S.A.S. xlvii. 27; E 179/255/35 m. 77d.
[71] T.S.A.S. 4th ser. v. 201; ibid. vi. 298.
[72] S.P.R. Lich. i (2), intro. p. iv; Lich. Dioc. Regy., glebe terrier, 1779; ibid. bishop's transcripts.
[73] T.S.A.S. 4th ser. vi. 298; 24th Rep. Com. Char. 389.
[74] Visit. Archd. Salop. 1799.
[75] S.P.R. Lich. i (2), intro. p. iv; Lich. Dioc. Regy., bishop's transcripts.
[76] See p. 176.
[77] Par. rec., curate's licence, 1824.
[78] Ibid. 1831–60.
[79] Ibid.
[80] Lich. Dioc. Regy., glebe terrier, 1612.
[81] Ibid. 1718.
[82] Ibid. 1763.
[83] Visit. Archd. Salop. 1799.
[84] Ibid. 1823.
[85] Par. rec., mortgage for erection of parsonage, 1839.
[86] Ex inf. Mr. T. W. Davies, The Bynords, Smethcott.
[87] Visit. Archd. Salop. 1823.
[88] N.L.W., MS. 18454B.

[89] Visit. Archd. Salop. 1799.
[90] Ibid. 1823.
[91] Ibid. 1843; local inf.
[92] Par. rec., churchwardens' accts. 1862–99.
[93] Ex inf. Mrs. T. W. Davies, The Bynords, Smethcott.
[94] Description of church based, except where otherwise stated, on S.P.L., MS. 372, vol. i, p. 41; acct. of rebuilding, 1850, in S.P.R. Lich. i (2), 190–1; Cranage, vi. 508.
[95] Memo. by William Hill in par. rec., par. reg. 1747–1812.
[96] Ibid.
[97] W.S.L. 350/40/3.
[98] Par. rec., par. reg. 1747–1812.
[99] Visit. Archd. Salop. 1799.
[1] Par. rec., par. reg. 1747–1812.
[2] Visit. Archd. Salop. 1823.
[3] T.S.A.S. 2nd ser. xii. 100.
[4] Par. rec., churchwardens' bill, 1789; Walters, Ch. Bells Salop. 223.
[5] Visit. Archd. Salop. 1823.
[6] Walters, Ch. Bells Salop. 223.
[7] T.S.A.S. 2nd ser. xii. 100.

bowl and the remains of its hexagonal medieval stem can still be seen. A circular stem was attached to the bowl, c. 1630.[8] The rest of the plate comprises a pewter chalice, paten, and flagon, which were in use in the early 19th century, a silver-plated paten and flagon, probably acquired after the rebuilding of the church, and a silver paten given by J. B. Walker of Betchcott Hall in 1911.[9] The registers begin in 1612.[10]

Betchcott chapel, first recorded c. 1183,[11] may have been in origin the oratory of the hermit Bletherus.[12] Although the chalice, plate, sanctus bell, and other church goods were in the hands of a lay lessee shortly after 1510,[13] one John Tonge was chaplain here in 1538.[14] The chapel was still standing when the estate was granted to Thomas Ireland in 1545[15] and is last recorded in 1614,[16] but it had probably been destroyed by this date.

NONCONFORMITY. Two families were said to be Anabaptists in the later 17th century[17] and there were 4 dissenters in the parish in 1676.[18] No dissenters remained by 1799[19] and there is no subsequent evidence of nonconformity.

SCHOOLS. A Sunday School, established by 1822,[20] was attended by 30 children in the following year.[21] This closed soon afterwards, but was re-opened in 1832[22] and is last recorded in 1847.[23]

A day school kept by Thomas Hill at Picklescott is first recorded in 1799,[24] when it was supported by the rector, the curate, and the lord of the manor,[25] but it seems to have closed after Hill's death in 1809.[26] There were 2 private schools in the parish in 1818,[27] but apparently none in 1823.[28] Part of the income from the charity established by the Revd. Henry Fletcher in 1810 was to be applied to the education of 6 poor children[29] and in 1833 the teacher of one of the 3 schools in the parish received £5 a year from this source.[30] The fees of 30 other children then attending school in Smethcott were paid by their parents.[31] The curate was then commended for his exertions in the promotion of education, including the establishment of a lending library, but 'till lately' the inspectors reported 'the inhabitants of the parish have been suffered to remain in the greatest ignorance, the elders being for the most part unable to read.'[32] In 1843 25 children, including some from Woolstaston and Church Stretton, attended the day school and there were 12 at the infant school.[33] There were 24 children at the school in 1846[34] and 30 in the following year.[35]

A new school was built in 1867 on a site provided by the lord of the manor and was united with the National Society in 1866.[36] The school was supported by Fletcher's Charity and other parish charities, which produced about a third of its income in 1868, and by voluntary contributions and school-pence.[37] The latter had been abolished by 1893, when the school was in receipt of a government grant.[38] It became a Controlled school in 1954.[39] Average attendance rose from 40 in 1868[40] to between 50 and 60, 1900–13.[41] Only 16 children attended in 1963[42] and the school was closed in 1964, when the children were transferred to Longnor school.[43]

CHARITIES. In 1741[44] the lords of Smethcott and Wilderley manors each granted a cottage on Smethcott Common to the parish officers for the use of the poor. The endowment of this charity, known as the Poor's Land, consisted by 1844 of 4 cottages and 2½ a. land.[45] Two of the cottages were occupied by paupers rent-free, c. 1830, when rents from the land and the two other cottages produced £11 a year. The net income had always been expended by the overseers in poor relief.[46] A recommendation by the Charity Commissioners that it should be given away as a charity was not adopted, since surplus income was transferred to the Board of Guardians until 1867. Under a scheme of that year, the Rector and parish officers were appointed trustees of the Poor's Land, half the income of which was to be given to the poor and half to the school. Since 1862 the charity has had an annual income of some £8,[47] which was distributed in accordance with the Scheme of 1867 until the closure of the school in 1964.

In 1810 the Revd. Henry Fletcher transferred £200 stock to the Rector and curate of Smethcott in trust for the poor, directing that half the income of this charity was to be applied to the education of 6 poor children and half to the relief of 6 widows. The income was distributed by the curate until 1817[48] and thereafter by the rector and church-

8 Arkwright and Bourne, Ch. Plate Ludlow Archd. 35.
9 Ibid.
10 Printed to 1812 in S.P.R. Lich. i (2), 109–96.
11 S.P.L., Haughmond Cart. f. 133; B.M. Harl. MS. 3868, f. 10ᵛ.
12 S.P.L., Haughmond Cart. f. 132.
13 Salop. N. & Q. i (1885), 176.
14 S.C. 6/Hen. VIII/3009 m. 33d.
15 L. & P. Hen. VIII, xx (1), p. 222.
16 C 142/345/122.
17 Lich. Dioc. Regy., B/v 1/72, 74, 81, 87.
18 T.S.A.S. 2nd ser. i. 82.
19 Visit. Archd. Salop. 1799.
20 Par. rec., overseers' accts. 1810–37.
21 Visit. Archd. Salop. 1823.
22 Educ. Enquiry Abstract, H.C. 62, p. 784 (1835), xlii.
23 Visit. Archd. Salop. 1847.
24 Ibid. 1799.
25 Ibid.
26 S.P.R. Lich. i (2), 188.
27 Digest of Returns to Cttee. on Educ. of Poor, H.C. 224, p. 761 (1819), ix (2).
28 Visit. Archd. Salop. 1823.
29 24th Rep. Com. Char. 389.

30 Educ. Enquiry Abstract, p. 784.
31 Ibid.
32 Ibid.
33 Visit. Archd. Salop. 1843.
34 Nat. Soc. Ch. School Returns, 1846–7.
35 Visit. Archd. Salop. 1847.
36 Ed. 7/103/218; par. rec., conveyance of site, 1863.
37 Ed. 7/103/218.
38 Return of Schs. 1893 [C. 7529], p. 512, H.C. (1894), lxv.
39 Ex inf. S.C.C. Educ. Dept.
40 Ed. 7/103/218.
41 Voluntary Schs. Returns, H.C. 178–XXIV, p. 25 (1906), lxxxviii; Kelly's Dir. Salop. (1900–13).
42 Ex inf. S.C.C. Educ. Dept.
43 Ibid.
44 Except where otherwise stated, account of charities based on 24th Rep. Com. Char., H.C. 231, p. 389 (1831), xi; Char. Com. files.
45 Par. rec., tithe appt.
46 Ibid. overseers' accts. 1810–37.
47 Digest of Endowed Char. 1862–3, H.C. 433, pp. 206–7 (1867–8), lii.
48 S.P.R. Lich. i (2), intro. p. iv; Lich. Dioc. Regy., bishop's transcripts.

wardens. The charity yielded an income of £10 a year c. 1830, £6 of which was given to 7 poor widows and the remainder applied to educating poor children. Its annual income had fallen to £6 6s. by 1862.[49] In 1905 half of the endowment was transferred to a separate account, styled the Fletcher Educational Foundation. The remainder, which produced an annual income of £5 4s. 8d. in 1963, has been given to poor widows since 1905.

STAPLETON

THE parish of Stapleton lies on rising ground between the Cound valley on the east and the foothills of the Long Mynd on the west. It contains 2,554 a.[1] and comprises the townships of Stapleton and Netley. The latter, lying in the south-east of the parish, contained 642 a. in 1843.[2] The parish is bounded by the River Cound on the north-east and on the south and south-west the boundary follows for short distances tributaries of the Cound, but the whole of the western boundary passes through former woodland and does not make use of natural features. The boundary with Wilderley manor on the south-west was fixed by agreement in 1227.[3] Farther north the manorial boundaries of Stapleton, Longden, and Pulverbatch were determined in 1385,[4] but the boundary with Pulverbatch was again in dispute in the later 16th century[5] and was not settled until 1610, when an area known as 'the Challenge Land', west of Moat Farm, was transferred to Pulverbatch.[6] The present course of the north-western boundary, adjoining Exfordsgreen, dates only from the inclosure of Stapleton Common, c. 1807.[7]

In the north-east, where the village of Stapleton stands, the land is flat and lies between 300 and 350 feet. It rises, however, to 375 feet on the glacial moraine which forms the northern boundary with Chatford in Condover and to 450 feet at Hurst Bank, an outlier of Lyth Hill, in the north-west. In this valley several streams, which run north-eastwards across the parish, unite to flow into the River Cound near Wayford bridge. Over the remainder of the parish the land rises gently towards the south-west, reaching 500 feet at the boundary with Smethcott. The streams are flanked by belts of alluvial soil and associated river-gravels, which are broadest at the village and in the south-east around Netley Hall. There are extensive deposits of sand and gravel north-east of the village, on either side of the Shrewsbury road, and at Signal Bank in the south of the parish. Apart from the area around Corfield's Coppice, west of Dorrington, boulder clay is restricted to the south-west and north-west quarters of the parish.

Although well-endowed with light soils, the greater part of the parish above the 350-foot contour was woodland or waste during the Middle Ages. In the western half of the parish lay Steplewood, which extended into Longden and Pulverbatch, while Shadymoor, partly woodland and partly ill-drained moorland, occupied a wide belt of land running from the boundary with Wilderley in the south-west to that with Dorrington in the east, thus forming a barrier between the townships of Stapleton and Netley. Steplewood was a bailiwick of the Long Forest, but was removed from its jurisdiction in 1250, when it was quit of waste and regard.[8] A number of small assarts, made by the men of Stapleton and Netley, are recorded in 1209[9] and in 1235 Steplewood was said to have been much wasted in the past.[10] Shadymoor is first so named in the 17th century.[11] It was known as Stanleymoor in the 14th century[12] and as Shadwell moor in 1547.[13] There were said to be 514 a. of woodland in Stapleton manor in 1443,[14] but only 65 a. remained by 1651.[15] The latter, then known as Stapleton Wood,[16] is probably represented by the present Corfield's Coppice and Big and Little Shadymoor Coppices. There were 50 a. of woodland in the whole parish in the 1830s,[17] but a further 20 a. had been planted in the Stapleton estate by 1877.[18]

Of the two medieval parks in the parish, the larger, known as the Great Park, seems to have occupied most of Shadymoor in medieval times. This would account for the 'Park' field-names found in the area to the west of Lower Shadymoor Farm.[19] The nucleus of this park was a small inclosure, known as Alsemore, said in 1284 to have been cleared and held by the lord of the manor from time out of mind.[20] A grant of free warren was obtained in 1290[21] and a park had been formed on Stanleymoor by 1311.[22] This was worth 40s. a year in 1327,[23] when the manorial demesne also included a rabbit-warren,[24] on the gravel ridge near Wayford

---

[49] Digest of Endowed Char. 1862–3, pp. 206–7.
[1] O.S. Area Bk. (1883). The following topographical description is based, except where otherwise stated, on O.S. Map 1″, sheet lxi (1st edn.); O.S. Maps 6″ Salop. 41, 49 (1st and later edns.); O.S. Map 1/25,000, SJ 40 (1957); Rocque, Map of Salop. (1752); Baugh, Map of Salop. (1808); B.M. O.S. 2″ orig. drawings, sheet 207 (1817); Geol. Survey Map (drift), sheet 152 (1932); S.R.O. 883/64 (Stapleton tithe appt. 1838 and map, 1839); ibid. 883/65 (Netley tithe appt. 1843 and map, 1844). This article was written in 1963 and revised in 1965. Thanks are due to Miss M. J. Haseler of Bayston Hill for her helpful criticism.   [2] S.R.O. 883/65.
[3] S.P.L., Haughmond Cart. f. 229.
[4] Cal. Inq. Misc. iv, p. 177.
[5] C 3/7/22; S.P.L., Deeds 6848B, depositions, c. 1595.
[6] S.P.L., Deeds 6873.
[7] The date of its inclosure is not known, but adjoining commons in Condover and Longden were inclosed in 1807 and 1806 respectively: see pp. 30, 248.

[8] Eyton, vi. 340.
[9] E 32/144 m. 1.
[10] Eyton, vi. 340.
[11] S.R.O. 883/4.
[12] Cal. Pat. 1307–13, 385.
[13] S.C. 2/197/54. A name probably derived from a well known as 'Sad well' on the boundary with Pulverbatch: S.P.L., Haughmond Cart. f. 229.
[14] C.P. 25(1)/195/22/26.
[15] N.L.W., Chirk Castle 6970.
[16] Ibid.
[17] S.R.O. 883/65; Hope-Edwardes MSS., Linley Hall, valuation of Netley estate, 1835.
[18] S.R.O. 1192 uncat., sale partics. 1877.
[19] Ibid. 883/65.
[20] C 143/7/17.
[21] Cal. Chart. R. ii. 342.
[22] Cal. Pat. 1307–13, 385.
[23] C.P. 40/283 m. 487 d.
[24] Ibid.

bridge,[25] and a sparrow-hawk eyrie.[26] A second park, called the Little Park, was formed within Steplewood and can probably be associated with Moat Farm, first recorded in the mid-14th century, when it was occupied by a son of the lord of the manor.[27] In 1578 the western boundary of this park followed the parish boundary with Pulverbatch[28] and its extent can be deduced from the 'park' field-names to the north of Moat Farm.[29] Both parks seem to have been leased to the tenants by 1453.[30]

To the north of Little Park lay an area of common land, part of Steplewood in 1385[31] and later known as Hurst Common,[32] which extended into Pontesbury and Condover parishes. Its bounds were uncertain in 1612,[33] but the Stapleton portion was said to comprise 200 a. in 1651.[34] Pastures called the Vinnals, to the north-east of Vinnals Farm, seem to have been inclosed by 1453[35] and further considerable encroachments at the Hurst are recorded in the later 17th century.[36] The remainder was inclosed c. 1807.[37]

The little evidence available suggests that the common fields of Stapleton were restricted to the sand and gravel soils in the north-east of the parish.[38] Conigree Field lay near Wayford bridge, Spanyate Field or Vinnals Field to the north of the village, and Hall Field to the south of the village. The last came to be known as Half Field after inclosure and may account for the names Hay Field and Home Field found here in 1839. The common fields were still in existence in 1612, but had probably been inclosed by 1651.[39]

At Netley the common fields had probably already ceased to exist by 1086, when the manor was said to be waste.[40] Hetheshall Field and Hurst Field, recorded in 1453,[41] when they were apparently pasture, may once have been common fields. The amount of rent paid for them, 53s. 4d. and 56s. 4d. respectively, suggests that they were large and the former was held jointly by the tenants of Dorrington.[42] The third field may have been called Dudmill Field, the name given to a field on the boundary with Dorrington in 1612.[43]

The road from Shrewsbury to Ludlow runs across the eastern edge of the parish and all the remaining roads are now little more than country lanes. This section of the Shrewsbury–Ludlow road was probably of little importance before it was turnpiked in 1756.[44] It probably replaced, as the route to Shrewsbury, the road running through the village from Wayford bridge. At the north-west of the village,[45]

where it skirts the former Hurst Common, the last-mentioned road was known as Spanyate Lane. It seems formerly to have continued northwards from Exfordsgreen and to have joined a road running from Shrewsbury to the top of Lyth Hill.[46] It is joined at or near the village by three other roads, of which the most important was the group of roads from Wilderley, Pulverbatch, and Wrentnall, which unite at Moat Farm and run north-eastwards past Bridge Farm to Stapleton. This road was diverted westwards in 1826,[47] when the new parsonage was built,[48] but formerly crossed Stapleton brook by Long Bridge[49] and met Spanyate Lane near the church, opposite another ancient road leading past Chatford to Condover. A road which leaves the village street near Olde Farm and cuts across the present Shrewsbury road, runs by Gonsal to join the Radmore ridgeway at Great Ryton. Isolated farms at Netley and Shadymoor are approached from Dorrington on a road which was formerly the main route from the Long Mynd towards Shrewsbury.[50]

Stapleton village thus stands at a river crossing and a road junction. Its name is probably derived from the adjoining forest of Steplewood, but it is not recorded in Domesday Book and is first named in the mid-12th century.[51] Eyton's identification of the two Domesday manors of Hundeslit (i.e. 'Huni's lyth') with the later manor of Stapleton[52] is probably correct. If, as was the case elsewhere in the county, each Domesday manor represented a distinct hamlet, one of these may have been at Wayford. Sybil de Wayford occurs in 1353,[53] and there was a smithy at Wayford by 1356.[54] Only 3 tenants are recorded in manors of Hundeslit in 1086,[55] but the scale and unusual construction of the church, built in the 13th century,[56] suggest that Stapleton was a considerable settlement by that time. The manor contained no fewer than 55 tenants in 1327,[57] only a few of whom can have lived at Netley or on other isolated holdings.

The village, however, stands on the northern edge of the flood-plain of Stapleton Brook. Houses, like the old parsonage, which stood too near the brook, were still liable to be flooded in the 19th century.[58] As the former woodland was cleared, settlement increasingly took the form of isolated farms on the higher land to the south and west. The mound to the east of the church, which, if it is a castle motte,[59] was clearly sited to control the road junction at this point, had by the 14th century ceased to be the site of the residence of the lord of the manor.[60] Of the

[25] cf. S.R.O. 883/65.
[26] C.P. 40/283 m. 487d.
[27] Hope-Edwardes MSS., Linley Hall, deed, c. 1343–53.
[28] S.R.O. 665 uncat., deed, 1578.
[29] Ibid. 883/65.
[30] Ibid. 956/1.
[31] Cal. Inq. Misc. iv, p. 177.
[32] S.R.O. 883/65.
[33] Lich. Dioc. Regy., glebe terrier, 1612.
[34] N.L.W., Chirk Castle 6970.
[35] S.R.O. 956/1. Inclosures by the lady of the manor at 'Vinnals waste' are again recorded in 1534: S.P.L., MS. 393.
[36] S.R.O. 883/94–5.
[37] See p. 161 n. 7 above.
[38] Description of common fields based on Lich. Dioc. Regy., glebe terriers, 1612–1718; S.R.O. 883/65; Loton Hall MSS., ct. r. 1579.
[39] N.L.W., Chirk Castle 6970.
[40] V.C.H. Salop. i. 343.
[41] S.R.O. 956/1.

[42] Ibid.
[43] Lich. Dioc. Regy., glebe terrier, 1612.
[44] Shrewsbury–Church Stretton road Act, 29 Geo. II, c. 61 (priv. act).
[45] S.R.O. 883/95.
[46] See p. 31.
[47] Q. Sess. Orders, iii. 260; Q. Sess. rolls, Mich. 1826.
[48] See p. 168.
[49] S.R.O. 883/95.
[50] See p. 148.
[51] Eyton, vi. 108.   [52] Ibid.
[53] S.P.L., Deeds 2791.
[54] Loton Hall MSS., ct. r. 1356–7. cf. S.P.L., Deeds 2797.
[55] V.C.H. Salop. i. 324, 342.
[56] See pp. 168–9.
[57] C.P. 40/283 m. 487d.
[58] Visit. Archd. Salop. 1823, and ex inf. Miss M. J. Haseler, Bayston Hill.
[59] V.C.H. Salop. i. 387; T. Wright, Uriconium, 46–47.
[60] See p. 163.

three farm-houses in the village, Manor Farm and Olde Farm are cased in brick. The exterior of Bridge Farm is rough-cast, but all three were originally timber-framed. The parsonage to the west of the church, sold in 1960 and now known as Cambrian House, was built in 1827.[61] Its predecessor, now Rectory Cottages, stands near the brook, south-west of Olde Farm, on the cobbled lane which may formerly have continued across the brook by a ford, leading to one of the common fields. The house was rebuilt between 1635 and 1655 after the former parsonage had been burnt down c. 1624.[62] It is an L-shaped timber-framed structure of 3 bays, with a chimney-stack on the south gable. A brick north wing was added in the 19th century. After the new rectory was built, the house was occupied for some years by a small-holder,[63] but it had been converted into cottages by 1877.[64] With the development of isolated farms conversion of ancient farm-houses in the village into cottages was already taking place in the later 17th century.[65] A timber-framed house east of Olde Farm had been converted into 3 cottages by 1838[66] and was derelict in 1963. Another old house, perhaps the 17th-century mill,[67] which stood on the brook opposite Bridge Farm, was occupied as 3 cottages in 1838[68] and has since been demolished. An alehouse, first recorded in 1590,[69] was closed in 1760.[70] The former smithy, a small brick house at the cross-roads north-west of the church, occupied this site by 1678.[71] The only additions to the village since the early 19th century have been the school (1874),[72] several houses at the east end of the village, built in the present century, and 7 bungalows to the west of the smithy, built in 1962.

The manor of Netley was said to be waste in 1086,[73] but stone axe-heads found in the 19th century,[74] and the field-name Old Town, which is found in the adjacent parts of Dorrington and Longnor,[75] may be evidence that a hamlet once existed on or near the site of Netley Hall. During the Middle Ages Netley was a member of Stapleton manor and subsequent settlement here seems always to have taken the form of scattered farms, three of which stand close together around Signal Bank. The large areas of pasture held by 5 tenants in Netley in 1453,[76] including what appears to be one of the former common fields, probably represent the existing 5 farms—an arrangement which has been preserved by the fragmentation of the Netley estate after 1470.[77] With the exception of Netley Hall the farm-houses are timber-framed and all of early-17th-century date. The finest is Netley Old Hall, probably built by Thomas Phillips,[78] which is an L-shaped house, containing 8 hearths in 1662.[79] In

the south wing, which has a jettied upper floor, one room contains a Jacobean fireplace with some 17th-century wainscot and originally had a plaster ceiling. Upper and Lower Netley Farms both have central chimney-stacks, and Side Netley, though rebuilt in the early 19th century, contains on the ground floor a single 17th-century room, four feet above the level of the remainder of the house.

Netley Hall, rebuilt by Edward Haycock, 1854–8,[80] is a brick house of five bays in the Classical style, with stone quoins, bands, and window-dressings. A central stone porch on the north-east front is flanked by pairs of Tuscan columns and the house is surmounted by an open stone balustrade. The east lodge, on the main road to Shrewsbury in Condover parish, is a two-storied house in the Gothic style, built in 1826,[81] and its design was copied in the north lodge in 1936.[82]

The remaining isolated farms in the parish all stand in areas cleared from the forest in medieval or later times. The oldest is Moat Farm, first recorded c. 1350[83] and occupied by the lord of the manor or his relatives in the 14th and 16th centuries.[84] The house stands at one corner of a medieval moated site, the moat being bounded by a stone retaining wall on the inner face. As it now stands the house consists of a timber-framed service wing and, at right angles to it, a brick-cased house of two bays. The latter has a central-stack plan and probably dates from the early 17th century, but it contains moulded ceiling beams of earlier date. A timber-framed gatehouse, to the east of the service wing, was demolished in the 1930s.[85] An impressive quadrangle of early-18th-century farm buildings stands to the north of the house. On the road to Wilderley, south-west of Moat Farm, is Upper Moat farm, whose brick exterior may encase an earlier timber frame. Two cottages stood in Stapleton wood, west of Moat Farm, in 1600[86] and there were said to be 8 cottages in the wood by 1651,[87] but none of the existing cottages near Moat Farm is older than the later 18th century. The cottages near Upper Moat Farm are associated with late-18th-century coal workings.[88]

Richard de Stanleye, who occurs in 1327[89] and 1332,[90] may have lived at Shadymoor, part of which was then known as Stanleymoor.[91] Isolated houses in this part of the parish, which are first recorded in the later 17th century,[92] were then described as cottages.[93] It is likely that Lower and Middle Shadymoor Farms were originally of this type. The former is cased in brick and has 19th-century additions to the north, but was originally a small timber-framed house with a chimney-stack on the

[61] Visit. Archd. Salop. 1823.
[62] Lich. Dioc. Regy., B/v 1/48, 53, 55; T.S.A.S. xlvii. 27.
[63] S.R.O. 883/64.
[64] Ibid. 1192 uncat., sale partics. 1877.
[65] Ibid. 883/95.
[66] Ibid. 883/64.
[67] Ibid. 883/4.
[68] Ibid. 883/64.
[69] N.L.W., Pitchford Hall uncat., alehouse recognisances, 1590.
[70] Q. Sess., alehouse reg.
[71] S.R.O. 883/4.
[72] Ed. 7/103/224.
[73] V.C.H. Salop. i. 343.
[74] Bagshaw's Dir. Salop. (1851).
[75] See p. 35.
[76] S.R.O. 956/1.

[77] See p. 165.
[78] Ibid.
[79] E 179/255/35 m. 76.
[80] Pevsner, Shropshire, 216.
[81] Datestone.
[82] Ibid.
[83] Hope-Edwardes MSS., Linley Hall, deed, c. 1343–53.
[84] See p. 164.
[85] S.R.O. 1192 uncat., photograph, 1938.
[86] S.P.L., Deeds 6848B, plan of Steplewood, 1600.
[87] N.L.W., Chirk Castle 6970.
[88] See p. 167.
[89] T.S.A.S. 2nd ser. xi. 361.
[90] E 179/166/2 m. 5.
[91] See p. 161.
[92] S.R.O. 883/94.
[93] Ibid.

west gable. Middle Shadymoor Farm, which retains its timber-framed exterior and is thatched, now contains 3 bays and has a central chimney-stack. The western bay, however, appears to have been built at a later date[94], so that originally this house also was of 2 bays with a western gable chimney-stack. Upper Shadymoor Farm was rebuilt in 1916.[95]

Wet Reans Farm, north-west of Stapleton village, was burnt down after 1903[96] and The Vinnals is the only surviving old house within the area of the former Hurst Common. A house is recorded at the Vinnals in 1569[97] and it is possible that the western bay of the existing house is of 16th-century date, for its roof level has been raised to correspond with the rest of the house, which was built in the early 17th century. Little Vinnals, north-east of The Vinnals, is a brick house, built between 1817 and 1839.[98] In 1817 the only cottages on the road to Exfordsgreen were the 3 parish poor-houses,[99] but two more cottages had been built here by 1839.[1]

Only 9 of the 55 tenants of Stapleton manor recorded in 1327[2] appear on a tax-list of the same year.[3] The parish had 175 adult inhabitants in 1676[4] and a population of 228 in 1801.[5] The population had risen to 281 by 1861,[6] but has since fallen. It stood at 245 in 1891, 213 in 1911, and 191 in 1961.[7]

MANORS. The manor of *STAPLETON*, first recorded in the mid-12th century, was plausibly identified by Eyton with the two Domesday manors of Hundeslit.[8] In 1086 both these manors were held of Roger, Earl of Shrewsbury.[9] The estate of William Cauntelow, overlord of Stapleton manor in 1242,[10] passed in 1276 to Eudes la Zouche in right of his wife Millicent.[11] The overlordship remained in the Zouche family until 1399, when it was granted to Eleanor, widow of Roger Mortimer.[12] Her son, Edmund, Earl of March, was overlord in 1425,[13] but the overlordship had reverted to the Zouche family when last recorded in 1600.[14]

One of the two manors of Hundeslit, held by the freeman Huning before 1066,[15] had passed by 1086 to Ranulf, who held it of Roger Corbet, the mesne lord.[16] The other manor was held by Alric before 1066[17] and by Alward in 1086.[18] No later record has been found of the manors of Hundeslit, or of their tenants. By Stephen's reign both manors, together with the Domesday manor of Netley, were probably held, under the name of Stapleton manor, by Baldwin de Stapleton,[19] who was still living in 1165.[20] By 1188 Baldwin had been succeeded by his son Philip,[21] who died c. 1231,[22] and the manor remained in the Stapleton family until the 15th century, the following being lords: Robert, c. 1231–1243;[23] John, 1243–c. 1267;[24] Robert, c. 1267–1327;[25] Robert (probably grandson of the preceding lord),[26] 1327–56;[27] Robert, 1356–75.[28] Moat Farm, 120 a. of demesne, and rents of some 19 tenants were settled on the latter between 1343 and 1353, before his father's death.[29] Robert de Stapleton was succeeded in 1375 by his son John, then a minor.[30] John was still living in 1408[31] and was succeeded by his son John, on whom the manor was settled for life in 1442.[32] The reversion of the manor was then settled on the latter's son Leonard,[33] wrongly said to have been lord of Stapleton in 1431.[34] John de Stapleton was still living in 1446,[35] but both he and his son Leonard were dead by 1450, when the manor was held by the husbands or descendants of the five daughters of John de Stapleton.[36] The Stapleton inheritance was divided in 1470, when the greater part of the township of Stapleton was assigned to John Leighton, son of Elizabeth Stapleton.[37] This estate, under the name of Stapleton manor, passed from father to son in the Leighton family[38] until 1613, the following being lords: John, 1450–96; Thomas, 1496–1519; John, 1519–32;[39] Edward, 1536–93;[40] Thomas, 1594–1600;[41] Robert, 1600–13.[42] Robert Leighton then sold the manor to Sir John Egerton,[43] later Earl of Bridgewater,[44] who sold it to Peter Langley in 1646.[45] The latter died in 1651,[46] when the manor passed to his brother John Langley and descended from father to son until 1701, the following being lords: John, 1651–64; John, 1664–71; Henry, 1671–88; Jonathan, 1688–1701.[47] The last-named devised his estates to his friend Edward Baldwyn,[48] on whose death in 1735[49] the manor passed to Baldwyn's sister Bridget, wife

94 The horizontal timbers are at a different level.
95 Datestone.
96 O.S. Map 6″ Salop. 41 (2nd edn.).
97 C 3/7/22. cf. S.P.L., MS. 393 (Longden ct. r. 1568).
98 B.M. O.S. 2″ orig. drawings, sheet 207 (1817); S.R.O. 883/64.
99 B.M. O.S. 2″ orig. drawings, sheet 207 (1817).
1 S.R.O. 883/64.
2 C.P. 40/283 m. 587d.
3 T.S.A.S. 2nd ser. xi. 361.
4 Ibid. i. 82.
5 Census, 1801.
6 Ibid. 1861.
7 Ibid. 1891–1961.
8 Eyton, vi. 108.
9 V.C.H. Salop. i. 324, 342.
10 Bk. of Fees, 966.
11 Cal. Close, 1272–9, 294.
12 Ibid. 1396–9, 457.
13 C 139/19/32.
14 S.R.O. 1060/464.
15 V.C.H. Salop. i. 324.
16 Ibid.
17 Ibid. 342.
18 Ibid.
19 Eyton, vi. 109.
20 Ibid.
21 Ibid. xi. 358.
22 Ibid. vi. 112.

23 Ibid.; Bk. of Fees, 966.
24 Rot. Hund. (Rec. Com.), ii. 62; Eyton, xi. 360–1.
25 Cal. Close, 1272–9, 294; C.P. 40/273 m. 74; C.P. 40/283 m. 487d.; S.P.L., Deeds 2784.
26 Eyton, vi. 115.
27 C.P. 40/273 m. 74; S.P.L., Deeds 2792.
28 S.P.L., Deeds 2792–4; Cal. Inq. p.m. xiv, p. 280.
29 Hope-Edwardes MSS., Linley Hall, deed, c. 1343–53.
30 Cal. Inq. p.m. xiv, p. 280.
31 S.P.L., Deeds 2800.
32 Ibid. 2803–4; C.P. 25(1)/195/22/26.
33 Ibid.
34 Feud. Aids, iv. 264.
35 Hope-Edwardes MSS., Linley Hall, deed, 1446.
36 S.P.L., Deeds 2838; Eyton, vi. 118.
37 T.S.A.S. 4th ser. vi. 221–2.
38 For pedigree see S.P.L., MS. 2789, pp. 96–97.
39 C 142/53/2.
40 Ibid.; C 142/239/109.
41 C 142/239/109; C 142/261/25.
42 C 142/261/25.
43 C.P. 43/124 rot. 59.
44 Complete Peerage, ii. 311.
45 C.P. 25(2)/478/22 Chas. I East.
46 For pedigree see Owen and Blakeway, Hist. Shrewsbury, ii. 137.
47 Ibid.
48 S.R.O. 1058 uncat., abstract of title, 1726–1802.
49 Ibid.

of Thomas Powys.[50] It was afterwards held by their son, Henry Powys, 1743–74,[51] Henry's nephew, Thomas Jelf Powys, 1774–1805,[52] and the latter's son H. W. Powys, 1805–75.[53] Rudolph, Earl of Denbigh, great-nephew of H. W. Powys, then succeeded to the estate, but sold it to R. L. Purcell Llewelyn in 1878.[54] The latter's sister-in-law, Annie E. Purcell, sold it to Eric, Alywn, and Nellie Good-behere in 1937[55] and the estate was sold to the tenants in 1960.[56]

The manor of *NETLEY* was held by the freeman Elmar before 1066[57] and in 1086, when it was said to be waste, Roger, Earl of Shrewsbury, was over-lord.[58] It was probably annexed to Stapleton manor in the course of the 12th century, but in 1470 the township of Netley was assigned to four of the heirs of John de Stapleton.[59] Side Netley, assigned to John Leighton in 1470,[60] followed the descent of Stapleton manor until 1802.[61] Of the other three portions, that of Robert Cresset continued in his family[62] until 1611, when it was sold to Thomas Corbett of Longnor,[63] who conveyed it to Thomas Phillips of Smethcott in 1612.[64] That of Thomas Walwen passed by descent in his family[65] until 1586, when it was sold to Anthony Kyrle.[66] The latter's daughter Sarah married William Scuda-more,[67] who sold the property to Thomas Phillips in 1616.[68] The remaining portion was assigned to Thomas Horde in 1470[69] and was sold by his descendants[70] to William Jenks of Dorrington in 1594.[71] Sir Roger Owen of Condover purchased this estate in 1603,[72] but in 1619 the greater part was sold to Thomas Phillips,[73] who had thus acquired the whole township, with the exception of Side Netley. His son Richard Phillips, however, sold Higher Netley, Lower Netley, and Netley Old Hall to John Haynes in 1658[74] and the farm on the site of Netley Hall to Richard Nash in 1664.[75] The latter was sold to Thomas Browne in 1671[76] and passed by descent to the following: John Longslow (son-in-law), 1697–c. 1721; John Longslow (son), c. 1721–1761; Edward Atkis (son-in-law), 1761–80; Samuel Sneade (son-in-law), 1780–88.[77] It was then sold to Jonathan Scott,[78] who purchased Side Netley in 1802[79] and conveyed both properties to J. T. Hope in 1812.[80] The remainder of the Phillips estate, sold in 1658 to John Haynes, descended in 1676 to his daughter Mary, wife of Thomas Edwardes,[81] and remained in the Edwardes family[82] until 1790, when it passed by marriage to John Thomas Hope.[83] After 1812 Hope held the whole township of Netley and at his death in 1854 the estate passed to his son Thomas Henry Hope, who then assumed the name of Hope-Edwardes.[84] He died in 1871 and the estate was then held succes-sively by the following brothers and sisters of T. H. Hope-Edwardes: St. Leger Frederick, 1871–99; Herbert Jasper, 1899–1917; Ellen, 1919; Julia, 1919–27.[85] In 1927 it passed to Miss Clare Coldwell, great-neice of the last named, who married Mr. Jasper More of Linley Hall in 1944 and is the present owner.[86]

ECONOMIC HISTORY. Of the two Domesday manors of Hundeslit one was said to contain $1\frac{1}{2}$ virgate and the other half a virgate.[87] The former had fallen in value from 16s. to 12s. between 1066 and 1086, while the latter was worth 3s. before 1066 and 4s. in 1086.[88] The manor of Netley, assessed at one hide in 1086, was then waste and worth 12s.[89] In the 12th century these three manors were probably combined to form the manor of Stapleton, assessed at $1\frac{1}{2}$ hide in 1255[90] and said to be worth £56 14s. 9d. in 1327.[91]

Apart from 3 free tenants recorded in 1327, whose rents totalled 24s. 9d.,[92] no other freehold estates are known to have existed in the parish before the partition of the manor in 1470. The whole of Stapleton, with one of the Netley farms, was then assigned to John Leighton[93] and, as the manor of Stapleton, remained little changed in size until the later 19th century. Land on the north-eastern boundary, including Old Mills, comprising 23 a. in 1839,[94] was sold to Sir Roger Owen in 1603[95] and was subsequently part of the Condover manorial estate. Side Netley (157 a.) was sold in 1802.[96] The manorial estate amounted to 1,757 a. in 1651[97] and 1,771 a. in 1877,[98] when 681 a. was sold to St. Leger Hope-Edwardes of Netley.[99] The remainder of Netley township continued in divided ownership, until briefly united by Thomas Phillips in the early 17th century, and after 1658 again lay in two separate

50 Ibid.
51 Ibid.   52 Ibid.
53 S.R.O. 1192 uncat., abstract of title, 1801–78.
54 Ibid. abstract of title, 1872–1905.
55 Ibid. abstract of title, 1905–37.
56 Ex inf. Mr. H. T. Tudor, Olde Farm, Stapleton.
57 *V.C.H. Salop.* i. 343.
58 Ibid.
59 *T.S.A.S.* 4th ser. v. 221–2.
60 Ibid.
61 S.R.O. 1058 uncat., deed, 1802.
62 Eyton, vi. 118; S.P.L., Haughmond Cart. f. 136; C.P. 25(2)/342/3 Jas. I Mich.
63 S.R.O. 567 uncat., deed, 1611.
64 Ibid. deed, 1612.
65 Eyton, vi. 118; S.P.L., Deeds 3293.
66 C 142/230/49.
67 *Duncombe's Hist. Herefs.* ed. W. H. Cooke, iii. 185.
68 Hope-Edwardes MSS., Linley Hall, schedule of deeds 1887.
69 *T.S.A.S.* 4th ser. v. 221–2.
70 Eyton, vi. 118. For pedigree see S.P.L., MS. 4645, p. 392.
71 C.P. 25(2)/203/36 Eliz. I Mich.
72 C.P. 25(2)/342/1 Jas. I Trin.
73 Hope-Edwardes MSS., Linley Hall, schedule of deeds, 1887.

74 S.R.O. 1058 uncat., abstract of title, 1658–1702.
75 Ibid. abstract of title, 1663–1802.
76 Ibid.
77 Ibid. Bracketed entries indicate relationship to pre-ceding owner.
78 S.R.O. 1058 uncat., deed, 1788.
79 Ibid. deed, 1802.
80 Ibid. deed, 1812.
81 For pedigree see S.P.L., MS. 2789, p. 48.
82 Ibid.
83 Burke, *Land. Gent.* (1952), p. 1820.
84 Ibid.
85 Ibid.
86 Ibid.
87 *V.C.H. Salop.* i. 324, 342.
88 Ibid.
89 Ibid. 343.
90 *Rot. Hund.* (Rec. Com.), ii. 62.
91 C.P. 40/283 m. 487d.
92 Ibid.
93 *T.S.A.S.* 4th ser. v. 221–2.
94 S.R.O. 883/64.
95 C.P. 25(2)/342/1 Jas. I Trin.
96 S.R.O. 1058 uncat., deed, 1802.
97 N.L.W., Chirk Castle 6970.
98 S.R.O. 1192 uncat., sale partics. 1877.
99 Ibid. 883/66.

estates. The larger of these, held by the Edwardes family in the 18th century, contained 394 a. in 1770.[1] J. T. Hope owned the whole of Netley township after 1812 and held 642 a. in the parish in 1843.[2] The acreage of that part of the Netley estate which lay within the parish was doubled by the purchase of part of Stapleton manor in 1877[3] and by 1858 a further 713 a. had been acquired in Dorrington, Leebotwood, and Smethcott.[4]

The smaller of the two manors of Hundeslit was said in 1086 to have land for half a plough in demesne.[5] The area of demesne land had, however, been considerably extended by 1327, when it comprised 3 carucates of arable, 24 a. meadow, and 165 a. pasture.[6] It is probable that the Little Park, as well as the Great Park, was already in existence at this date and that the manor house, then valued at 13s. 4d.,[7] stood on the site of Moat Farm, not on the motte in the village. Before 1353 this house, along with 120 a. demesne, was settled on the son of the lord of the manor,[8] who was still resident there in the 1370s[9] after succeeding his father as lord. The demesne and the two parks were kept in hand in 1356[10] but appear to have been leased by 1453.[11] Joyce Leighton, a relative of the lord of the manor, lived at Moat Farm in the later 16th century.[12] By 1620 the house had been let to Richard Holbeck,[13] the tenant of Longnor Forge,[14] who was succeeded here, as at the forge, by Roger Blakeway in 1624.[15] Only woodland was subsequently kept in hand by the lord of the manor.[16]

A radman and two villeins were the only tenants on the two manors of Hundeslit in 1086,[17] but by 1327 the manor of Stapleton had 32 customary tenants and 20 cottars.[18] The labour services of the customary tenants were then worth only 26s. 8d.[19] and they appear to have held their lands on lease in the later 14th century.[20] In 1453 24 tenants in Stapleton paid assized rents of £9 3s. 4d. and herbage rents of £4 5s. 8d., while Netley was held by 5 tenants who paid herbage rents totalling £11.[21] Rents in Stapleton manor produced £162 a year in 1651, when 22 tenants held 1,595 a. on long leases and 14 tenants-at-will held 258 a.[22] Moat Farm, always large, then contained 326 a. and there were 4 other farms of over 100 a., but 22 holdings were smaller than 50 a.[23] Large farms predominated in Stapleton

in 1838, when there were 9 farms of over 100 a., one of 71 a., and 10 holdings of under 25 a.[24] There has been little subsequent change in farm-sizes here.

On the freehold estates in Netley the three-life lease had been replaced by short-term leases by 1740,[25] but the sizes of the farms seem to have remained little changed since the 15th century.[26] In 1812 over half the township was let as a 345-acre farm for £880 a year, but post-war depression brought this experiment to an end.[27] Although farm-sizes here were subject to considerable temporary fluctuations in the earlier 19th century,[28] farms remained small. Only 2 of the 5 farms contained more than 100 a. in 1843.[29] A rental of £1,231 a year in 1821,[30] no doubt created by war-time inflation, was reduced to £820 in 1824[31] and to £668 by 1843.[32] Drainage and improvements to farm buildings in the 1840s and 1850s[33] had enabled the landlord to increase the rental to £770 by 1863.[34] Although J. T. Hope kept 117 a. in hand in 1843,[35] most of this was let soon afterwards[36] and only a small acreage seems to have been kept in hand with Netley Hall in the later 19th century.[37] In 1954 the Hall, together with 23 a. in Netley, and Grove Farm, Dorrington (184 a.), was leased to Kenneth Beeston,[38] and has since served as the headquarters of Kenneth Beeston Farms Ltd., a group of farms specializing in cattle-breeding.

There were said to be 539 a. arable in the parish in 1801, when the chief crop was wheat.[39] The proportion of arable increased in the early 19th century. By 1838 Stapleton township contained 1,306 a. arable and only 460 a. grassland.[40] Netley township contained 380 a. arable and 239 a. pasture in 1843.[41]

A grant of a market and fair was probably obtained by the lord of the manor in 1258,[42] but no subsequent reference to either has been found. A mill is first recorded in 1327, when it was worth 100s.[43] By 1453 there were two mills on the River Cound in the north-east corner of the parish.[44] These were then known as Clee mills,[45] probably deriving their name from the gravel ridge which runs along the eastern boundary of the parish at this point. After 1603 they lay in the Condover manorial estate[46] and were occupied by the Blakeway family for most of the 17th century.[47] Another mill, held by the

[1] Hope-Edwardes MSS., Linley Hall, survey, 1770.
[2] S.R.O. 883/65.
[3] Ibid. 883/66.
[4] Hope-Edwardes MSS., Linley Hall, survey, 1770.
[5] V.C.H. Salop. i. 342.
[6] C.P. 40/283 m. 487d.
[7] Ibid.
[8] Hope-Edwardes MSS., Linley Hall, deed, c. 1343-53.
[9] S.H.C. N.S. viii. 65.
[10] Loton Hall MSS., ct. r. 1356-7.
[11] S.R.O. 956/1.
[12] C 142/239/109.
[13] Lich. Dioc. Regy., B/v 1/39; Staffs. R.O., D 239/M 3033.
[14] See p. 112.
[15] Staffs. R.O., D 239/M 3033.
[16] S.R.O. 883/64.
[17] V.C.H. Salop. i. 324, 342.
[18] C.P. 40/283 m. 487d.
[19] Ibid.
[20] S.P.L., Deeds 2793, 2797-8.
[21] S.R.O. 956/1.
[22] N.L.W., Chirk Castle 6970.
[23] Ibid.
[24] S.R.O. 883/64.
[25] Hope-Edwardes MSS., Linley Hall, rental, 1740.

[26] Ibid. rentals, 1740, 1796; ibid. survey, 1770; ibid. accts. 1821-43; S.R.O. 956/1; ibid. 1058 uncat., abstracts of title to Netley estate, 1658-1702, 1663-1802.
[27] Hope-Edwardes MSS., Linley Hall, lease, 1812.
[28] Ibid. accts. 1821-54.
[29] S.R.O. 883/65.
[30] Hope-Edwardes MSS., Linley Hall, accts. 1821-43.
[31] Ibid. [32] Ibid.
[33] Ibid. accts. 1844-63; ibid. jnls. of T. H. Hope, 1843-62.
[34] Ibid.
[35] S.R.O. 883/65.
[36] Ibid.; Hope-Edwardes MSS., Linley Hall, jnls. of T. H. Hope, 1843-62.
[37] Ibid.
[38] Ex inf. Messrs. Burd and Evans, land agents, Shrewsbury.
[39] H.O. 67/14/245.
[40] S.R.O. 883/64.
[41] Ibid. 883/65.
[42] Eyton, vi. 112.
[43] C.P. 40/283 m. 487d.
[44] S.R.O. 956/1.
[45] Ibid.
[46] C.P. 25(2)/342/1 Jas. I Trin.
[47] Lich. Dioc. Regy., glebe terrier, 1612; S.R.O. 883/4.

Crockett family in 1599 and 1678,[48] probably stood in the village. One William le Walker was a tenant of Stapleton manor in 1353[49] and William Walker, who held a field called 'Teynter Mede' in 1453,[50] was probably a fuller.

The field known as Old Coalpit Field on the boundary with Pulverbatch, near Upper Moat Cottages,[51] marks the site of a colliery known to have been in operation c. 1764–82.[52] A brick-works had been established nearby before 1877.[53] Coal was also mined to the west of Stapleton village, near Wet Reans Farm, in the early 19th century.[54] Sand had been dug commercially from a pit north-east of Stapleton village by 1882,[55] but the deep bed of sand and gravel to the north of Wayford bridge was not worked until c. 1926.[56]

Village tradesmen included a blacksmith, a wheelwright, a joiner, and a shoemaker in the later 19th century.[57] Only the blacksmith and wheelwright remained in business after 1900 and these went out of business c. 1934 and c. 1926 respectively.[58]

LOCAL GOVERNMENT. There are manor court rolls for Stapleton manor, 1356–7, 1579–84,[59] 1674–82, and 1718–45.[60] The jurisdiction of the manor court, which included view of frankpledge, extended over the whole parish.

The parish records include vestry minutes, 1866–1949, churchwardens' accounts, 1670–1708 and 1736–1865, and overseers' accounts 1670–1823.[61] The parish had the normal complement of two churchwardens and two overseers, appointed in rotation from among the holders of ancient tenements. In the 17th and early 18th centuries the churchwardens of one year served as sidesmen in the next year and as overseers in the following year. A rector's and a people's warden were appointed after 1759, but this does not appear to have affected the former rotation of offices.

The overseers normally rendered a combined account for their year of office until 1800; thereafter each overseer accounted for half the year. Annual expenditure on poor relief, which ranged from £5 to £10 in the later 17th century, rarely exceeded £50 a year before 1780. It rose rapidly after 1792, reaching £404 a year in 1802 and £562, its highest level, in 1818. A poor-house was being rented from the lord of the manor in 1678[62] and by 1781 three houses on Stapleton Common were in use for this purpose.[63] Paupers in the poor-houses were let to contractors in 1737[64] and between 1782 and 1786.[65]

In 1820 the maintenance of all the poor was let to John Barney, who was, however, discharged in 1823 after producing unsatisfactory accounts.[66] In addition to the normal provision for the poor—payment of rents, repair of houses, and free coal—the overseers made some attempt to counter hardship caused by rising food prices during the Napoleonic Wars. Seed potatoes were supplied to the poor in 1790 and 1795 and annually from 1800 to 1820. In 1801 wheat and barley were purchased and sold to the poor at reduced prices.

The parish had three highway surveyors in 1678,[67] representing Stapleton, Netley, and the outlying farms (the 'Outside'). Their expenditure was met by the overseers, so that no separate highway rate was levied. The Long Bridge at Stapleton was a collective responsibility, each tenant being responsible for a measured portion of it in 1678.[68] The two constables, still appointed at the manor court in 1718, served in rotation like the churchwardens and overseers.[69]

CHURCH. Stapleton church is first recorded in 1291.[70] It was originally a chapelry of Condover,[71] but seems to have acquired rights of burial as the result of a petition to the Pope in 1399.[72] By 1535 the only record of its dependent status was a pension of 10s. a year paid to Shrewsbury Abbey, appropriators of Condover church.[73]

The advowson followed the descent of the manor until 1450, when it passed to the heirs of John de Stapleton.[74] The latter's representatives presented jointly until at least 1536,[75] but in 1626 the three patrons—the Earl of Bridgewater, Sir William Owen, and Thomas Phillips—agreed to present by turns.[76] The lord of Stapleton manor acquired the shares of two of the patrons c. 1680[77] and in 1739.[78] Thereafter the advowson again followed the descent of the manor until 1878, when the Earl of Denbigh retained the advowson at the sale of the manorial estate.[79] It was purchased c. 1900 by R. W. Preston,[80] who subsequently sold it to John Haseler. It was held by the latter's brother, Rowland Haseler, Rector of Stapleton, 1915–40, and has since been vested in Rowland's executors.[81]

The living is a rectory and has been held in plurality with Dorrington since 1952.[82] It was said to be worth £4 in 1291,[83] £7 in 1535,[84] and £54 in 1655.[85] By 1799 its gross annual value had risen to £400[86] and in 1835 its average net income was £581 a year.[87] The tithes, which were worth

[48] N.L.W., Chirk Castle 6970; S.R.O. 883/4.
[49] S.P.L., Deeds 2791.
[50] S.R.O. 956/1.
[51] Ibid. 883/64.
[52] Ibid. 883/294, 310–4.
[53] S.R.O. 1192 uncat., sale partics. 1877.
[54] R. I. Murchison, *The Silurian System* (1839), 94.
[55] O.S. Map 25" Salop. 41/14.
[56] Ex inf. Mrs. E. A. Hone, Chessington, Surr.
[57] *Bagshaw's Dir. Salop.* (1851); *Kelly's Dir. Salop.* (1870–1900).
[58] *Kelly's Dir. Salop.* (1900–34).
[59] Loton Hall MSS., ct. r. 1356–7, 1579–84.
[60] S.R.O. 883/95.
[61] Ibid. 883/4–5, 24–28, 53.
[62] Ibid. 883/4.
[63] Ibid. 883/27.
[64] Ibid. 883/26.
[65] Ibid. 883/27.
[66] Ibid. 883/28.
[67] Ibid. 883/4.
[68] Ibid.

[69] Ibid. 883/95.
[70] *Tax. Eccl.* (Rec. Com.), 244.
[71] *Cal. Papal Regs.* v. 320.
[72] Ibid.
[73] *Valor Eccl.* (Rec. Com.), iii. 184.
[74] Eyton, vi. 118.
[75] S.P.L., MS. 4374.
[76] S.R.O. 883/527.
[77] Ibid.   [78] Ibid.
[79] *Kelly's Dir. Salop.* (1879–1900).
[80] Ibid. (1905).
[81] Heref. Dioc. Regy., reg. 1902–19, p. 608, and ex inf. Revd. D. B. Haseler.
[82] Heref. Dioc. Regy., reg. 1938–53, p. 558; ibid. reg. 1953–date, p. 150.
[83] *Tax. Eccl.* (Rec. Com.), 244.
[84] *Valor Eccl.* (Rec. Com.), iii. 184.
[85] *T.S.A.S.* xlvii. 27.
[86] Visit. Archd. Salop. 1799.
[87] *Rep. Com. Eccl. Revenues* [67], pp. 500–1, H.C. (1835), xxii.

£2 13s. 4d. in 1341,[88] were taken in kind until commutation, with the exception of a modus on Old Mills Farm.[89] The tithes of Stapleton township were commuted for a rent-charge of £464 in 1838[90] and those of Netley for a rent-charge of £165 in 1843.[91] The glebe consisted of scattered strips in the common fields in 1612,[92] but by 1681 it had been inclosed and partially consolidated.[93] It comprised 18 a. in 1718[94] but in 1827 this was exchanged for a compact holding of 11 a. near the church.[95] The glebe was leased for £5 10s. a year in 1681[96] and was said to be worth £24 a year in 1805.[97]

The parsonage, first recorded in 1612,[98] was burnt down c. 1624[99] and rebuilt, presumably on the same site, between 1635 and 1655.[1] It was said to be in decent repair in 1799,[2] but, since it was small, low-lying, and subject to flooding, a new parsonage was built to the east of the church in 1827,[3] with the aid of a grant of £1,200 from Queen Anne's Bounty.[4] It was sold in 1960.[5]

Only one of the medieval rectors is likely to have been a relative of the lord of the manor.[6] Thomas Royston (rector, 1680–1738)[7] was the son of one of the joint patrons of the living[8] and for much of the 19th century the living was held by 3 close relatives of the lord of the manor—Edward Powys (rector 1790–1819),[9] E. R. B. Feilding (rector 1824–54),[10] and C. W. A. Feilding (rector 1863–94).[11] Of 11 rectors, 1580–1894, only two served for less than 20 years, the longest incumbencies being those of Roland Harris (rector 1580–1624)[12] and Thomas Royston. A curate was employed by Roger Barber rector 1625–c. 1655)[13] and curates were continuously employed from at least 1730 until 1824.[14] The inadequacy of the parsonage was partly responsible for the non-residence of 18th-century incumbents.[15] After the building of the new parsonage in 1827 the rectors were normally resident and took a close interest in parish affairs. C. W. A. Feilding, who was a High Churchman, permitted members of the Societas Sancti Spiritus, a short-lived religious community, to take services at Stapleton on several occasions between 1873 and 1875.[16] In the winter of 1881–2 he employed as curate Richard Morgan, who styled himself Archbishop of Caerleon-on-Usk.[17] Feilding subscribed largely towards the restoration of the church in 1867[18] and towards the building of the school in 1874.[19] In 1867 he opposed the appropriation of pews in the restored church as 'illegal and proving a hindrance to the spiritual welfare of the parish and an injustice to the poor' but was overruled by the vestry.[20] The pews were made free in 1877 after intervention by the Archdeacon and the Bishop of Lichfield.[21]

Communion was administered between 3 and 5 times a year in the later 17th century and during the 18th century.[22] In 1799 it was administered 5 times a year[23] and 6 times a year by 1847.[24] Weekly communions had been introduced by C. W. A. Feilding before 1871.[25] The average number of communicants was 30 in 1823[26] and 40 in 1843.[27] Two services were held on Sundays between 1799 and 1851.[28] In 1851 60 adults attended the morning service and 36 in the afternoon.[29] Psalm-singers are recorded between 1772 and 1856[30] and a flute was used for accompaniment in 1845.[31] The organ, formerly at Longnor Hall, was not acquired until 1944.[32]

The church of *ST. JOHN THE BAPTIST*[33] consists of a nave and chancel, to which a tower and vestry were added in the 19th century. The nave and chancel, built in the 13th century, were originally of two stories. A piscina high on the south wall of the chancel confirms that the church was originally on the upper floor, the ground floor presumably forming an undercroft. On the ground floor the walls are 4 feet thick and are constructed of millstone grit. The walls of the upper story, 3 feet thick, are of friable cream sandstone to window level and mostly of red sandstone above.

Dressings are of red sandstone for the most part. In the undercroft were 4 unglazed slit windows on the north wall and one on the south. The upper floor had an east window of 3 graded lancets and a west window consisting of one or two lancets. It had 4 lancet windows on the north wall and 3 on the south. The undercroft was entered by a wide round-headed doorway at the west end of the south wall, above which was the south door of the church. The latter has a pointed arch and faces a smaller pointed doorway on the north wall. Access to the doors of the upper floor of the church, which are 6½ feet above the present ground level, was presumably by external wooden stairs. The two floors

88 Inq. Non. (Rec. Com.), 192.
89 Lich. Dioc. Regy., glebe terriers, 1718–1832; S.R.O. 883/64.
90 S.R.O. 883/64.
91 Ibid. 883/65.
92 Lich. Dioc. Regy., glebe terrier, 1612.
93 Ibid. 1681.
94 Ibid. 1718.
95 Ibid. 1828.
96 Ibid. 1681.
97 Ibid. 1805.
98 Ibid. 1612.
99 Ibid. B/v 1/48.
1 Ibid. B/v 1/55; T.S.A.S. xlvii. 27.
2 Visit. Archd. Salop. 1799.
3 Lich. Dioc. Regy., glebe terrier, 1828.
4 Ibid. 1845.
5 Ex inf. Mrs. C. G. Llewellyn, Cambrian House, Stapleton.
6 Reginald de Stepulton, 1408: Eyton, vi. 118.
7 S.R.O. 883/97; T.S.A.S. 4th ser. v. 197.
8 S.R.O. 883/527.
9 Ibid. 883/97.
10 S.P.R. Lich. i (3), 196.
11 Ibid.
12 Ibid. 5; T.S.A.S. 3rd ser. i. 260.

13 T.S.A.S. 3rd ser. i. 263; ibid. xlvii, 27; Lich. Dioc. Regy., B/v 1/48.
14 Lich. Dioc. Regy., B/v 1/96; S.P.R. Lich. i (3), 44, 47, 49.
15 S.R.O. 883/106.
16 Ibid. 883/55.
17 Ibid. 883/107.
18 Ibid. 883/53.
19 Ibid.
20 Ibid.
21 Ibid.
22 Ibid. 883/4–5
23 Visit. Archd. Salop. 1799.
24 Ibid. 1843.
25 S.R.O. 883/55.
26 Visit. Archd. Salop. 1823.
27 Ibid. 1843.
28 Ibid. 1799, 1823, 1843; H.O. 129/359/1/20.
29 Ibid.
30 S.R.O. 883/5, 24.   31 Ibid.
32 Heref. Dioc. Regy., reg. 1938–53, p. 227.
33 Except where otherwise stated, description of church based on S.P.L., MS. 372, vol. i, p. 3; S.P.L., T. F. Dukes watercolours (churches), no. 149; S.P.L., J. H. Smith collect. no. 193; Visit. Archd. Salop. 1799, 1823, 1843; S.R.O. 883/53; Cranage, vi. 509–13.

were thrown into one at some time during the later Middle Ages, when a pointed priest's door was inserted in the south wall of the chancel mid-way between the upper and lower floors. The obstruction of the undercroft windows on the south side has presumably been caused by the rising level of the churchyard since burial rights were granted after 1399.[34] Until 1867 the church had a trussed-rafter roof with a wall-plate carved with shields and a continuous billet-moulding.

By 1786 one of the more westerly lancets in the south wall of the nave had been replaced by a square casement window and, when the church was repaired with the aid of a church brief in 1789, a similar window was inserted within the frame of the south door. Both these windows were renewed in the Decorated style during the incumbency of E. R. B. Feilding and again at the restoration of 1867. The tower at the west end, in a simple Classical style, was added in 1832[35] to replace a wooden bell-turret at the west end of the nave and at about the same time a brick vestry was built to the north of the chancel. In 1786 the church was entered through the south door of the undercroft, where a timber-framed porch then stood, but by 1808 a door had been inserted in the west end. The church is now entered through the west door of the tower.

The church was restored under the direction of H. Carpenter in 1867, when the chancel was extended eastwards and a new vestry was built in the Early English style on the north wall of the chancel. A few medieval tiles were discovered and traces of wall-painting were revealed when the walls were stripped of their plaster, but armorial glass, recorded in 1823, appears to have been destroyed. The eaves level was raised and the medieval roof, then covered by a plaster ceiling, was replaced by a trussed-rafter roof in the chancel and a collar-braced roof in the nave.

New pews and a semicircular altar and communion rails, installed in the 1790s,[36] were replaced by the existing pews and chancel furniture in 1867. The altar is made of pieces of 17th-century oak panelling and the free-standing wooden candle-sticks in the sanctuary are said to be German work of c. 1500. A gallery at the west end, erected before 1782,[37] was removed in 1857.[38] The present octagonal font was brought from Uppington church in 1887, replacing a marble bowl on an iron stand,

which had been in use since at least 1823. An earlier round stone font was discovered in the church in 1867.

There were 2 bells in 1552[39] and 3 in 1752.[40] Two of the latter were cast in 1722 and 1736 by Abraham and Abel Rudhall respectively.[41] The church still had three bells in 1906,[42] but there are now 6, two of which were acquired in 1948.[43] A clock is first recorded in 1672[44] and was converted into a pendulum clock in 1697,[45] but this had been removed by 1823.[46] The plate consisted of a silver and gilt chalice and paten in 1552[47] and a silver chalice, with pewter paten and flagon, in 1679.[48] The present paten dates from 1802[49] but its matching chalice was melted down and remade in 1867.[50] The registers are complete from 1635.[51] An earlier register, beginning in 1558, was missing by 1831.[52]

NONCONFORMITY. There were said to be some Methodists in the parish in 1799[53] and a meeting house was licensed in 1807,[54] but there were no nonconformists here by 1823.[55]

SCHOOLS. Although the curate was licensed to teach in 1626[56] and there was a schoolmaster resident in the parish between 1699 and 1718,[57] there is no other evidence of a day school in Stapleton before the 19th century. In 1818 a school, attended by 15–20 children, was maintained by subscription and school-pence.[58] The school was held in the church in 1846, when there were 33 pupils,[59] but it had closed by 1870, when the vestry considered it 'advisable' to establish a school by voluntary subscription.[60] A school was built in 1874 on land provided by the lord of the manor, its cost being met largely by subscriptions and a voluntary rate.[61] This school was supported by private subscription and by school-pence until the latter were abolished in 1891.[62] It was also in receipt of a government grant after 1875.[63] The school was constantly in debt until 1884[64] and in 1879 there were fears that a School Board might be established.[65] Sixteen children attended on the school's opening in 1874[66] and 39 in 1887,[67] but it had fallen to 34 by 1906[68] and by 1921 there were only 14 children on the books.[69] The school was closed in 1922,[70] when the children were transferred to Dorrington school.[71]

CHARITIES. None known.

[34] Cal. Papal Regs. v. 320.
[35] W.S.L. 350/40/3.
[36] S.R.O. 883/52, 115–17.
[37] Ibid. 883/5.
[38] Ibid. 883/24.
[39] T.S.A.S. 2nd ser. xii. 102, 318.
[40] Walters, Ch. Bells Salop. 223.
[41] Ibid.
[42] Ibid.
[43] S.R.O. 883/230; Heref. Dioc. Regy., reg. 1938–53, p. 376.
[44] S.R.O. 883/4.
[45] Ibid.
[46] Visit. Archd. Salop. 1823.
[47] T.S.A.S. 2nd ser. xii. 102, 318.
[48] S.R.O. 883/4.
[49] Arkwright and Bourne, Ch. Plate Ludlow Archd. 56.
[50] S.R.O. 883/53.
[51] Printed to 1812 in S.P.R. Lich. i (3), 197–250.
[52] Ibid. intro. p. i.

[53] Visit. Archd. Salop. 1799.
[54] Q. Sess. Orders, iii. 141.
[55] Visit. Archd. Salop. 1823.
[56] Lich. Dioc. Regy., B/v 1/48.
[57] Ibid. B/v 1/90, 93, 95.
[58] Digest of Returns to Cttee. on Educ. of Poor, H.C. 224, p. 761 (1819), ix (2).
[59] Nat. Soc. Ch. School Returns, 1846–7.
[60] S.R.O. 883/53.
[61] Ibid. 883/54; Ed. 7/103/224.
[62] S.R.O. 883/93.
[63] Ibid.
[64] Ibid.
[65] Ibid. 883/71.
[66] Ibid. 883/92.
[67] Ibid. 883/71.
[68] Voluntary Schs. Returns, H.C. 178–XXIV, p. 25 (1906), lxxxviii.
[69] S.R.O. 883/74.
[70] Ibid.   [71] Ibid.

WOOLSTASTON

THE small parish of Woolstaston, on the northern foothills of the Long Mynd, contains 841 a.[1] It is bounded on three sides by the steep, wooded valleys of tributaries of the River Cound—Betchcott Brook on the west, Walkmill Brook on the north, and Broad Brook on the south. The eastern boundary with Leebotwood runs in part along a glacial moraine, which was once the western boundary of Woolstaston Wood, and was fixed in the early 13th century.[2] On the south-west the boundary seems originally to have followed the upper reaches of Betchcott Brook and Broad Brook as far as Duckley Nap and the Hoarstone which stood nearby, thus including a narrow strip of common land on the Long Mynd. This was said to be the boundary c. 1695,[3] but it has followed its present course since c. 1743, when the parish lost its common rights on the Long Mynd.[4]

The land rises from 500 feet in the east to some 900 feet in the west, but Lazar Hill, on the south-western boundary, rises to 1,000 feet. Glacial moraines, composed of stony drift, are responsible for the undulating landscape of the parish. The largest of these makes up the rising ground to the west on which the village stands, while three narrow ridges run from north to south across the lower eastern half of the parish. There are a number of isolated deposits of sand and gravel, chiefly along Betchcott Brook and Walkmill Brook, but much of the land between the ridges is boulder clay, which, until the 19th century, was dotted with pools[5] or, like Catmore to the north of Yew Tree Cottage, was in a permanently waterlogged condition owing to impeded drainage.

Although the manor was said to contain wood for only 12 swine in 1086,[6] about half of the parish was woodland until the later 17th century. Woolstaston Wood, which covered the lower ground in the east, contained 321 a. in 1674, when its western boundary ran roughly north and south from Yew Tree Cottage. Woodland still covers the valleys of Betch-cott Brook and Walkmill Brook in the north-west of the parish and once extended along Broad Brook in the south. Field-names like Birches (i.e. Breaches), north of the village, and Brandmoor, south-west of Yew Tree Cottage, indicate that these woods originally covered a wider area in the west of the parish. Castle Hill, the earliest recorded assart, was made by the lady of the manor in the early 13th

century,[7] but her successors played no direct part in clearance until the 17th century. Medieval free tenancies appear to have been created to encourage the clearance of woodland. Such land made up the greater part of the estate of the Bowdler family[8]—the largest and longest-lived of the free tenants here—and much of the land belonging to free tenants whose properties were bought back into the manorial estate in the early 17th century consisted of assarts.[9] One of these tenants held fields called the Parks (19 a.).[10] There is no other evidence for a medieval park in the parish, but a grant of free warren was obtained in 1281.[11] Woodland still bulked large in the life of the parish in the 16th and 17th centuries, when encroachments and other offences in the woods accounted for nearly all the business of the manor court.[12] Five tenants had inclosed 31 a. in the wood in 1578,[13] but nearly all the squatter settlement at this period was confined to Walkmill Brook. In 1634 a thousand cords of wood were sold to the tenants of Longnor Forge[14] and in 1674 132 a. of Woolstaston Wood were inclosed and felled.[15] Further inclosures took place c. 1690 and c. 1715.[16] By 1777 all that remained of the wood was a 24-acre common, between Castle Hill and the road to Leebotwood, which had been cleared of timber and was held with one of the farms. Some 30 a. of woodland, most of it in Spring Coppice and Black-pool Coppice, were then kept in hand, while woodland called Dickens Coppy lay along Betchcott Brook. It has changed little in distribution or extent since that date.

During the 17th century the inhabitants of Woolstaston enjoyed common rights in that part of the Long Mynd which was later claimed as part of the parish. Such rights are not recorded before 1634,[17] but the boundary as described c. 1695, running to the Hoarstone near Duckley Nap,[18] has the marks of antiquity and resembles those of other parishes adjoining the Long Mynd. The parish appears to have lost its common rights in 1743, following a lawsuit with the inhabitants of Church Stretton. Among other evidence brought by Church Stretton was the failure of Woolstaston to bury a man found dead in this part of the Long Mynd; this probably accounts for the name Deadmans Bach, given to the upper reaches of Broad Brook.[19]

The former common fields[20] all lay in the west of the parish, on the stony drift and small deposits of

[1] O.S. *Area Bk.* (1883). The following topographical description is based, except where otherwise stated, on O.S. Map 1″, sheet lxi (1st edn.); O.S. Maps 6″ Salop. 48, 49 (1st and later edns.); O.S. Maps 1/25,000, SO 49 (1956); Rocque, *Map of Salop.* (1752); Baugh, *Map of Salop.* (1808); B.M. O.S. 2″ orig. drawings, sheet 207 (1817); Geol. Survey Map (drift), sheet 152 (1932); par. rec., tithe appt. and map, 1840; Apley Park estate office, survey, 1675; ibid. survey and map, 1777; Wolryche-Whitmore MSS., Dudmaston, map of Woolstaston Wood, 1674. This article was written in 1963 and revised in 1965. Thanks are due to Mr. A. M. Bown, Woolstaston Hall, for his helpful criticism.
[2] S.P.L., Haughmond Cart. ff. 134–5.
[3] S.P.L., Deeds 6583.
[4] Ibid.
[5] e.g. Fish Pool, north of the village, and Seething Well, in the Wood.
[6] *V.C.H. Salop.* i. 326.

[7] E 32/144 m. 3; S.P.L., Haughmond Cart. ff. 134–5.
[8] See p. 174.
[9] Wolryche-Whitmore MSS., Dudmaston, deeds, 1608–17.
[10] Ibid. deed, 1616.
[11] *Cal. Chart. R.* 1257–1300, 249.
[12] Wolryche-Whitmore MSS., Dudmaston, ct. r. 1556–1699.
[13] C 2/Eliz. I/H 11/57.
[14] Wolryche-Whitmore MSS., Dudmaston, deed, 1634.
[15] Ibid. map of Woolstaston Wood, 1674.
[16] S.P.L., Deeds 6583.
[17] Heref. Dioc. Regy., glebe terrier, 1634.
[18] S.P.L., Deeds 6583. [19] Ibid.
[20] Description of common fields based on Heref. Dioc. Regy., glebe terriers, c. 1589–1634; Wolryche-Whitmore MSS., Dudmaston, deed, 1667; ibid. ct. r. 1601; Apley Park estate office, survey, 1675; ibid. survey and map, 1777; par. rec., tithe appt.

sand and gravel which surround the village. Beech Field lay to the west, Stankless (or Stankley) Field to the south, and Lower Field ran towards Walkmill Brook on the north. The glebe had been completely inclosed by 1634[21] and, although common-field lands were still in existence in the 1660s,[22] none remained by 1675.[23]

The village stands at the junction of roads running down the northern slopes of the Long Mynd with the road to Leebotwood. Of the former that leaving the parish at Colliersley was once known as Stankleys Lane[24] and was the highway to Church Stretton in the 17th century,[25] while the road to Duckley Nap was described as the road to Bishop's Castle in 1743.[26] It is probable that a road, now closed, running northwards to Branmills and on to Smethcott,[27] was originally the principal route from Woolstaston towards Shrewsbury. The present approach is from Leebotwood, but this road is not likely to have been of any importance before the clearance of Woolstaston Wood. The early-13th century description of the bounds of Leebotwood and Woolstaston[28] describes as a high road a now vanished road running across the south-east corner of the parish towards Lower Wood and records Leebotwood churchyard, but makes no mention of the existing road. It was still scarcely ever used for wheeled traffic when E. D. Carr came to Woolstaston as curate in 1855 and was then in a very bad state of repair.[29]

The village stands at 800 feet, commanding fine views across the Cound valley to the east and the Church Stretton gap to the south. With a soil largely unsuitable for arable farming[30] and an inadequate water-supply[31] it has always been a very small community. In 1675 the parish contained only 20 houses and at least 9 of these were in or near Woolstaston Wood.[32] Castle Bank, to the west of Rectory Farm, is the site of a motte-and-bailey castle,[33] standing at the junction of the roads running down from the Long Mynd with the former road running northwards towards Smethcott. The site had been deserted by the end of the 13th century,[34] its place having probably been taken by Castle Hill on the eastern boundary of the parish, where the lady of the manor had built a house nearly a century before.[35] The Hall, first recorded c. 1589,[36] stood to the south of Castle Bank. All that now remains is the west wing, built in the 1670s.[37] The church, in the centre of the village, faces a small village green, planted with trees, which was laid out by E. D. Carr in 1865 on the site of a dung-heap.[38] Carr also

built the Village Hall[39] and was responsible for the enlargement of the rectory—a notable early example of the half-timber revival.[40]

Apart from the Hall and the rectory, no house in 17th-century Woolstaston contained more than one hearth[41] and most were described as 'low and mean' in 1685.[42] Such a description would not, however, fit nos. 38 and 39, Woolstaston. Now two cottages, this was originally the home of the Bowdler family. It comprises a two-bay cruck hall of late medieval date, and a two-storied cross-wing. The later has a trussed rafter roof, with crown posts, and is probably contemporary with the hall, but its black-and-white exterior is merely plaster, and dates from c. 1878, when the house was occupied by the rector's coachman.[43] A chimney-stack and an upper floor with elaborately chamfered ceiling-beams were inserted in the cruck hall in the 16th century and a stone-built smithy was added at the south end of the hall in the later 19th century. Upper House Farm and Rectory Farm are timber-framed and probably of early-17th-century date. The former was enlarged in the present century by the addition of a brick south wing, while the south end of Rectory Farm is constructed of reused timber, which may have come from the older part of the Hall when it was demolished in the later 18th century.[44] The house contains some 17th-century oak wainscot, perhaps also from the Hall.

Castle Hill, a large natural mound in the north-east corner of the parish,[45] is probably the site of the house which Amilia de Woolstaston had erected in a clearing on the borders of Woolstaston and Leebotwood before 1209[46] and is the only known instance of medieval settlement in Woolstaston Wood. Castle Hill Farm, to the east of the mound, is a timber-framed house, not built before the 17th century and remodelled in the early 19th century, when a brick central chimney stack was built and a front door inserted in the middle of the east wall. The principal area of squatter settlement was along Walkmill Brook, where a group of fulling mills was already flourishing in the early 16th century.[47] Two of these mills lay in Woolstaston, but they are not recorded before the 17th century.[48] The first known fulling mill in the parish was on Broad Brook, to the south of the wood, and belonged to the Sankey family, millers of Leebotwood, in the 1530s.[49] A house was still standing in this part of the parish in 1777, by the side of the former road from Leebotwood to Lower Wood,[50] but it had gone by 1840.[51] The fulling mill at Mill Farm on Walkmill Brook is

21 Heref. Dioc. Regy., glebe terrier, 1634.
22 Wolryche-Whitmore MSS., Dudmaston, deed, 1667.
23 Apley Park estate office, survey, 1675.
24 Ibid. survey and map, 1777.
25 Wolryche-Whitmore MSS., Dudmaston, deed, 1667.
26 S.P.L., Deeds 6583.
27 Apley Park estate office, survey and map, 1777.
28 S.P.L., Haughmond Cart. ff. 134–5.
29 Par. rec., notebks. of E. D. Carr.
30 See p. 174.
31 For an account of the methods adopted to supply water to the parsonage in the later 19th century, see par. rec., notebks. of E. D. Carr.
32 Apley Park estate office, survey, 1675; Wolryche-Whitmore MSS., Dudmaston, map of Woolstaston Wood, 1674.   33 V.C.H. Salop. i. 402.
34 C 133/63/32. No pottery later than the early 14th century was found when a section of the ditch was excavated in 1965: ex inf. Mr. R. T. Rowley.

35 E 32/144 m. 3; S.P.L., Haughmond Cart. ff. 134–5.
36 Heref. Dioc. Regy., glebe terrier, c. 1589.
37 See p. 173.
38 Par. rec., notebks. of E. D. Carr.
39 Ibid.
40 See p. 176.
41 E 179/255/35 m. 77; Hearth Tax, 1672, 128.
42 Heref. Dioc. Regy., visitation papers, box 22, letter from rector, 1685.
43 Par. rec., notebks. of E. D. Carr. Quarter-round moulding on the central hall truss suggests a date of c. 1380.
44 See p. 173.
45 V.C.H. Salop. i. 388–9.
46 E 32/144 m. 3; S.P.L., Haughmond Cart. ff. 134–5.
47 See p. 103.
48 See p. 175.
49 See pp. 174–5.
50 Apley Park estate office, survey and map, 1777.
51 Par. rec., tithe appt.

first recorded in 1604.[52] It continued as a corn mill throughout the 19th century and is still used to generate electricity. The house was enlarged in stone in the 18th century, but was originally a timber-framed house of two bays with a stone chimney-stack on the east gable. Its upper floor has probably been inserted and the roof has been raised. Another 17th-century mill to the east of Mill Farm has been demolished since 1840.[53] Besides the houses already mentioned, there were 4 other cottages near Walkmill Brook in 1777.[54] Only one of these now survives. This is no. 33A, Woolstaston, a timber-framed house south-east of Mill Farm, occupied in the later 18th century by John Edwards,[55] who is said to have been a highwayman.[56]

Four cottages stood near Barn House, in the middle of the wood, in 1674.[57] More cottages seem to have been built here in the later 17th century, for there were said to be 5 cottages in the wood in 1681,[58] 7 in 1690,[59] and 9 in 1699.[60] All trace of settlement here had, however, disappeared by 1777[61] and the existing houses in this part of the parish are all modern. Three other isolated houses date from the 18th century—Colliersley, a stone-built house first recorded in 1743[62] but perhaps in origin a wood-collier's cottage, Meadow Place, built after 1777 on the site of the pound,[63] and Yew Tree Cottage, originally thatched and built of stone,[64] but rebuilt c. 1960. A few cottages near Upper House Farm and on the road to Colliersley were built in the later 19th century.

The parish contained 20 houses in 1675[65] and was said to have an adult population of 48 in the following year.[66] There were 101 inhabitants in 1801,[67] but numbers declined steadily to 64 by 1861.[68] A marked rise in population to 97 in 1881[69] coincides with the incumbency of E. D. Carr, and it has fluctuated between 84 and 96 from 1891 until 1951.[70] There were 75 inhabitants in 1961.[71]

MANOR. In 1086 Robert Fitz Corbet held of Earl Roger the manor of *WOOLSTASTON*, which before 1066 had been held as two manors by the freemen Chetel and Alvric.[72] Robert's estate here passed by marriage to the Boterell family[73] and

Aubrey, widow of William Boterell, was overlord between 1216 and 1242.[74] She was dead by 1255, when the manor was said to be held of William Boterell.[75] The overlordship of the Boterells is again recorded in 1294[76] and 1301,[77] but in 1315 the manor was held of the Crown in chief.[78] Roger Groby was said to be overlord when this is last recorded in 1455[79] and 1465.[80]

The first known tenant of the manor was William de Wytenton,[81] who settled it on his daughter Amilia on her marriage with Roger le Engleys.[82] The latter appears as an under-tenant of William Boterell in the later 12th century,[83] but was dead by 1209, when Amilia was holding the manor.[84] Her lands were forfeited to the Crown in 1216,[85] but were restored to her in the following year.[86] By 1242 Amilia had conveyed the manor to one Roger le Engleys,[87] whose relationship to her is not known, and against whom Amilia's grand-daughter Joan brought an action for recovery of the manor in 1251.[88] In 1253 Roger acknowledged her title to the estate and in return he and his wife were granted one third of the manor for their lives.[89] Joan le Engleys held the manor in 1254,[90] but had been succeeded by her son Giles de Berkeley before 1272, when John, nephew of Roger le Engleys, was claiming the manor.[91] Soon afterwards it was acquired by Robert Burnell, and was granted by him to his nephew Hugh Burnell, who was dead by 1279,[92] when it had reverted to Robert.[93] Giles de Berkeley, however, appears as mesne lord in 1292.[94]

The manor followed the descent of Acton Burnell until 1316, when it was assigned in dower to Aline, widow of Edward Burnell.[95] After her death in 1363[96] it again followed the descent of Acton Burnell until 1533, when Thomas, Duke of Norfolk, conveyed it to Sir John Dudley.[97] Shortly after 1541[98] Dudley sold the manor to Sir Robert Acton of Ribbesford,[99] who in 1544 sold it to Richard Andrews of Hailes (Glos.).[1] Andrews in the same year sold it to Roger Pope.[2] In 1556, however, the manor was held by Thomas Montgomery,[3] who was said to have held it in right of his wife Elizabeth and later to have conveyed it to Roger Pope.[4]

On the death of Roger Pope in 1573[5] the manor

52 Wolryche-Whitmore MSS., Dudmaston, ct. r. 1604.
53 Par. rec., tithe appt.
54 Apley Park estate office, survey and map, 1777.
55 Ibid.
56 Par. rec., notebks. of E. D. Carr.
57 Wolryche-Whitmore MSS., Dudmaston, map of Woolstaston Wood, 1674.
58 Ibid. ct. r. 1681.
59 Ibid. 1690.
60 Ibid. 1699.
61 Apley Park estate office, survey and map, 1777.
62 S.P.L., Deeds 6583.
63 Apley Park estate office, survey and map, 1777.
64 Ex inf. Mr. J. E. Jarrett.
65 Wolryche-Whitmore MSS., Dudmaston, map of Woolstaston Wood, 1674; Apley Park estate office, survey, 1675.
66 T.S.A.S. 2nd ser. i. 88.
67 Census, 1801.
68 Ibid. 1811–61.
69 Ibid. 1871–81.
70 Ibid. 1891–1951.
71 Ibid. 1961.
72 V.C.H. Salop. i. 326.
73 Eyton, vi. 152.
74 Rot. Litt. Claus. (Rec. Com.), i. 280; Bk. of Fees, 966.
75 Rot. Hund. (Rec. Com.), ii. 62. Rectius Reginald Boterell: Eyton, vi. 155.

76 Cal. Inq. p.m. iii, p. 122.
77 Ibid. p. 443.
78 Ibid. v, p. 393.
79 C 139/158/28.
80 C 140/13/27.
81 Eyton, vi. 154.
82 Ibid.   83 Ibid. ii. 6.
84 E 32/144 m. 3.
85 Rot. Litt. Claus. (Rec. Com.), i. 280.
86 Ibid. 373.
87 Bk. of Fees, 966.
88 Eyton, vi. 154.
89 Ibid. 154–5.
90 Rot. Hund. (Rec. Com.), ii. 62.
91 Eyton, vi. 155.
92 Cal. Close, 1272–9, 521.
93 Ibid.
94 Cal. Inq. p.m. iii, p. 50.
95 Cal. Close, 1313–8, 264.
96 Cal. Inq. p.m. xi, p. 373.
97 C.P. 40/1079, Carte, no. 1.
98 L. & P. Hen. VIII, xvi, p. 240; C.P. 25(2)/35/234.
99 Wolryche-Whitmore MSS., Dudmaston, depositions, 1580.
1 Ibid. deed, 1544.   2 Ibid.
3 Ibid. ct. r. 1556.
4 C 2/Eliz. I/H 11/57.
5 C 142/293/66.

passed to Lucy, widow of Roger's son Thomas,[6] on whom it had been settled in 1555.[7] She, with her second husband Thomas Charlton,[8] held the manor until her death in 1606,[9] when she was succeeded by Roger Pope, her son by her first husband.[10] The manor passed from father to son in the Pope family[11] during the 17th century, the following being lords: Roger, 1606–28;[12] Richard, 1628–36;[13] Roger, 1636 –47;[14] Roger, 1647–1710.[15] It subsequently followed the descent of Leebotwood manor. Manorial rights lapsed after the sale of the estate in 1920,[16] but the Hall and Hall Farm, comprising much of the southern half of the parish, have been owned by T. S. Luce, 1920–1, J. N. Parker, 1921–42, J. L. Craddock, 1942–3, and Mr. A. M. Bown since 1943.[17]

Castle Bank is probably the site of the medieval manor-house which was no longer standing in 1292.[18] Although the existing portion of Woolstaston Hall was not built until the 1670s, there is evidence for an earlier manor-house. A member of the Bowdler family lived at a house known as the Hall c. 1589[19] and in 1620.[20] Thomas Colebarne, steward of the Pope family, occupied a house of 13 hearths here in 1662.[21] Work was in progress at the Hall in 1671,[22] and these extensions may have been financed by the sale of timber from Woolstaston Wood, which was inclosed shortly after 1674.[23] Three brick-kilns which in 1674 stood in the west of the wood,[24] presumably supplied bricks for the Hall. Roger Pope was resident in 1672, when the house had 14 hearths,[25] but it was said in 1685 to have been uninhabited for many years.[26] The house was originally H-shaped and comprised a central block with two projecting wings. A balustrade ran round the top of the house, and in front was a stone gateway, surmounted by lions.[27] It contained 37 rooms in 1754, when, on the death of Catherine Pope, it ceased to be the residence of the lord of the manor.[28] The furniture was sold in 1772[29] and, although an estimate for repairs was obtained from Jonathan Scoltock in 1774,[30] most of the house was demolished c. 1784.[31] Much of the panelling was then taken to Apley Park,[32] but some of it was used to panel a room at The Farm, Leebotwood.[33] Two large tapestries from the Hall were given to the Revd. E. D. Carr by the tenant of The Farm, and hung in the rectory in the later 19th century.[34]

All that now remains of the Hall is the south wing. This is a two-story building, with attics and basement, of 7 bays with a hipped roof, and is brick-built with stone quoins. A brick string course runs round the house at first-floor level, but on the east and north walls—which formed part of the front of the original house—the string course is of stone. The sandstone central doorway on the south front is surmounted by a pediment between two urns and its lintel and pilasters are carved with grotesque heads and floral swags, now much decayed. The interior, which on the ground floor originally comprised two rooms, retains much of its late-17th-century oak panelling and cornices. Chimney-stacks on the north wall and west gable are part of the original structure. The former has a staircase, concealed by panelling, beside it. The combined entrance and staircase hall in the centre of the wing was evidently constructed after the main part of the house had been demolished. The staircase is of reused wood and the 17th-century wainscot came from Church Stretton church.[35] The sash windows were probably inserted in the 19th century, when a brick kitchen-wing was added on the north side.

ECONOMIC HISTORY. The manor was assessed at two hides in 1086, when its value had fallen from 40s. to 12s. since before the Conquest.[36] It was valued at 116s. 2d. in 1294[37] and at 101s. in 1316.[38]

In 1086 there was one plough on the demesne,[39] which included half a carucate of arable land in 1292,[40] 53 a. in 1294,[41] and 30 a. in 1315.[42] It was held on lease by William Tipping in 1429.[43] Roger Pope presumably kept some land in hand in the later 16th century, when he had a flock of sheep in the manor,[44] but the basis of the later manorial estate seems to have been the small freeholds purchased by the lord of the manor in the early 17th century. In 1675 151 a. were kept in hand,[45] and in 1754 the home farm was still fully stocked.[46] Sir Thomas Whitmore continued direct farming for some years after he acquired the manor—he had 32 cattle and 264 sheep here in 1760[47]—but this was discontinued about 1761[48] and in the later 18th century the lord's only income, other than rents, was derived from timber-sales and the manufacture

[6] Ibid.
[7] Wolryche-Whitmore MSS., Dudmaston, marriage settlement, 1555.
[8] C 142/293/66.   [9] Ibid.
[10] Ibid.; Wolryche-Whitmore MSS., Dudmaston, livery of seisin, 1606.
[11] For particulars of the family, see *T.S.A.S.* l. 37–48.
[12] C 142/452/46.   [13] Ibid.; C 142/555/92.
[14] A minor, wardship granted to Sir Thomas Middleton, 1637; Wolryche-Whitmore MSS., Dudmaston.
[15] *T.S.A.S.* l. 46–47.
[16] Ex inf. Capt. G. C. Wolryche-Whitmore.
[17] Title-deeds *penes* Mr. A. M. Bown, Woolstaston Hall.
[18] C 133/63/32; Bodl. MS. Blakeway, f. 278ᵛ.
[19] Heref. Dioc. Regy., glebe terrier, c. 1589.
[20] Wolryche-Whitmore MSS., Dudmaston, ct. r. 1620.
[21] E 179/255/35 m. 77.
[22] Apley Park estate office, accts. 1665–78.
[23] See p. 170.
[24] Wolryche-Whitmore MSS., Dudmaston, map of Woolstaston Wood, 1674.
[25] *Hearth Tax, 1672*, 128.
[26] Heref. Dioc. Regy., visitation papers, box 22, letter from rector, 1685.

[27] Par. rec., notebks. of E. D. Carr.
[28] Apley Park estate office, inventory of Catherine Pope, 1754.
[29] Ibid. accts. 1750–95.
[30] Ibid.
[31] Ibid.; W.S.L., 350/40/3.
[32] Apley Park estate office, accts. 1750–95.
[33] Par. rec., notebks. of E. D. Carr.
[34] Ibid.
[35] Ex inf. Mrs. A. M. Bown.
[36] *V.C.H. Salop.* i. 326.
[37] C 133/68/10; *Cal. Inq. Misc.* i, p. 470.
[38] *Cal. Close, 1313–18*, 264.
[39] *V.C.H. Salop.* i. 326.
[40] C 133/63/32.
[41] C 133/68/10.
[42] C 134/48/9.
[43] S.R.O. 1011 uncat., bailiff's acct. 1428–9.
[44] Wolryche-Whitmore MSS., Dudmaston, acct. of sheep at Woolstaston and Smethcott, 1590–1612.
[45] Apley Park estate office, survey, 1675.
[46] Ibid. inventory of Catherine Pope, 1754.
[47] Ibid. accts. 1750–95.
[48] Ibid.

of bricks.[49] The 30 a. kept in hand in 1777[50] consisted wholly of woodland, which was still in hand in 1840.[51]

Three free tenants are recorded in the 13th century.[52] Rents of free tenants produced 32s. in 1294,[53] and there were 6 of them in the manor in 1315.[54] Lands in the south-east of the parish, held by the Sankey family in the early 16th century,[55] were conveyed to Roger Pope in 1608[56] and between 1613 and his death in 1628, he had purchased the estates of four other freeholders.[57] The only considerable freehold in the parish, however, was that held by the Bowdler family. This is first recorded in 1310, when the lord of the manor confirmed William Bowdler in possession of lands in the parish, apparently including the site of the castle, which he had formerly held of Robert Burnell (d. 1292).[58] In the following year William was granted a further 6 a. in Woolstaston Wood.[59] Roger Bowdler was a tenant here in 1420[60] and in 1517 Thomas Bowdler was said to have inclosed 14 a. of arable land.[61] At least 5 members of the family held land in the parish c. 1589, when one of them lived at the Hall,[62] and 4 Bowdlers were suitors at the manor court in 1620.[63] William Bowdler, who died in 1649, left goods valued at £1,000[64] and in 1672 the only resident member of the family was William Bowdler, described as a gentleman.[65] He was allotted 23 a. at the inclosure of Woolstaston Wood in 1674[66] and in the following year held 71 a. in the parish.[67] After the death of George Bowdler in 1737 the family ceased to live at Woolstaston.[68] Their estate, then comprising 69 a., was purchased by the lord of the manor in 1782,[69] but 41 a. which had formerly belonged to the Bowdlers was in the hands of 3 small freeholders in 1840.[70]

In 1086 7 villeins had between them 1½ plough and there was said to be room for 3 more ploughs.[71] Customary tenants performed a day's reaping service each year in 1294, when their rents totalled 74s.[72] Copyhold tenure had ceased by the early 17th century, when the normal form of tenure was the 99-year lease.[73] This had been replaced by the 21-year lease before 1744.[74] There were 15 tenants in 1665[75] and of the 16 tenants in 1675 none held over 100 a. and only two had farms of over 50 a.[76] After this date the larger farms tended increasingly

to include lands in Leebotwood and Smethcott. The growth of farm-sizes can thus only be considered in relation to the estate as a whole and is discussed elsewhere.[77] The farms in the village, however, remained little changed in size in the 19th century and were tenanted by the same families for unusually long periods. Thus the Everalls were continuously tenants of Hall Farm, and the Clee family were tenants of Castle Hill Farm, between 1777 and 1920, while the Heighway family occupied Rectory Farm for most of the 19th century.[78] All three families had been resident in the parish since the early 17th century.[79] The annual rental rose from £118 in 1665[80] to £162 by 1733,[81] and to £335 by 1780,[82] but there were normally heavy arrears until after 1740. Since the sale of the manorial estate most of the farms have been owner-occupied.

Until the parish lost its common rights on the Long Mynd in the 18th century,[83] sheep formed the basis of its economy. The demesne arable was said to be of poor quality in 1292[84] and in 1341 the major part of the rector's income was derived from small tithes.[85] The Popes, who were originally Shrewsbury drapers, seem to have concentrated on sheep-farming while they held the manor. They kept about 100 sheep here in the 1590s[86] and had a flock of nearly 700 on the Long Mynd in the later 17th century.[87] Catherine Pope had 369 sheep at her death in 1754.[88] Deponents in 1743 gave estimates, ranging from 1,300 to 2,300, of the total number of sheep once kept by Woolstaston farmers on the Long Mynd, the largest flocks being those of Thomas Colebarne (600–700 sheep) and Mr. Harrington (400–500 sheep).[89] In 1801, when there were 228 a. of arable in the parish, it was said that 25 years before there had only been one third as much arable land.[90] Wheat was the chief crop in 1801, but the large acreage of turnips (32 a.)[91] may indicate that stock-rearing was still important. The arable acreage had risen to 437 a. by 1840,[92] but there is no evidence as to how long this high proportion was maintained. Stock-rearing is now the predominant type of farming in the parish.

A mill is first recorded here in 1292, when it was worth 12s.[93] Its site is not known, but it may have stood on Walkmill Brook, north-west of the village, near Branmill (formerly Brand Mill) in Smethcott

[49] Apley Park estate office, accts. 1750–95.
[50] Ibid. survey, 1777.
[51] Par. rec., tithe appt.
[52] Eyton, vi. 154–6.
[53] C 133/68/10.
[54] C 134/48/9.
[55] See p. 175.
[56] Wolryche-Whitmore MSS., Dudmaston, deed, 1608.
[57] Ibid. deeds, 1613–17; C 142/555/92.
[58] Bodl. MS. Blakeway 3, f. 278v.
[59] Eyton, vi. 156.
[60] S.C. 6/1117/14.
[61] C 47/7/2/3 m. 34d.
[62] Heref. Dioc. Regy., glebe terrier, c. 1589.
[63] Wolryche-Whitmore MSS., Dudmaston, ct. r. 1620.
[64] C 3/434/104.
[65] Hearth Tax, 1672, 128.
[66] Wolryche-Whitmore MSS., Dudmaston, deed, 1674.
[67] Apley Park estate office, survey, 1675.
[68] Wolryche-Whitmore MSS., Dudmaston, Bowdler title-deeds, 1722–1805.
[69] Ibid.
[70] Par. rec., tithe appt.
[71] V.C.H. Salop. i. 326.
[72] C 133/68/10.

[73] Wolryche-Whitmore, MSS., Dudmaston, leases passim.
[74] Ibid.
[75] Apley Park estate office, accts. 1665–78.
[76] Ibid. survey, 1675.
[77] See p. 103.
[78] Apley Park estate office, survey, 1777; Wolryche-Whitmore MSS., Dudmaston, surveys, 1769, 1807, 1817; par. rec., tithe appt.; Kelly's Dir. Salop. (1856–1917).
[79] S.P.R. Heref. i (5), 245–74 passim.
[80] Apley Park estate office, accts. 1665–78.
[81] Ibid. 1732–48.
[82] Ibid. 1749–80.
[83] See p. 170.
[84] C 133/63/32.
[85] Inq. Non. (Rec. Com.), 193.
[86] Wolryche-Whitmore MSS., Dudmaston, acct. of sheep at Woolstaston and Smethcott, 1590–1612.
[87] S.P.L., Deeds 6583.
[88] Apley Park estate office, inventory of Catherine Pope, 1754.
[89] S.P.L., Deeds 6583.
[90] H.O. 67/12/250.
[91] Ibid.
[92] Par. rec., tithe appt.
[93] C 133/63/32.

parish, for adjoining fields in Woolstaston were called Brand Mill in 1777.[94] In the early 16th century the Sankey family owned a fulling mill in Woolstaston.[95] It probably stood in the south-east corner of the parish, on Broad Brook,[96] and was thus not far from Leebotwood mill, also held by the Sankeys at this time.[97] This mill had been rebuilt by 1539, when it had passed to Thomas Walker, whose son William sold it to Oliver Harris c. 1570. There were two fulling mills on this site in 1579, but they seem to have gone out of use by 1608, when the property was sold to the lord of the manor.[98]

The mill at Mill Farm, on Walkmill Brook, is not recorded before the 17th century. It was occupied as a corn mill and a fulling mill by the Bartlam family between 1604 and 1675.[99] Although it belonged to Richard Phillips of Netley in 1654,[1] the mill was in the manorial estate by 1675[2] and, under the name Tanner's mill, was leased to Thomas Parsons in 1681.[3] It was probably enlarged by James Davies, to whom it was leased in 1787.[4] The mill ceased to be used for grinding corn in the 1920s,[5] but has been restored by the present owner of Mill Farm and is now used to generate electricity. Another fulling mill, some 300 yards east of Mill Farm, was occupied by Samuel Parks in 1675[6] and by Francis Wilding in 1757,[7] but had gone out of use by 1777.[8]

An unusual diversity of occupations is found in the parish in the early 17th century. Eight tradesmen appear among the suitors at the manor court in 1620,[9] and 12 tradesmen in a similar list of 1632.[10] The latter comprised 3 fullers, 3 weavers, 2 glovers, a dyer, a draper, a tailor, and a carpenter, most of whom were squatters on the fringes of Woolstaston Wood. No reference has been found to tradesmen in the parish in the 18th century and scarcely any remained in the later 19th century. A shoemaker was in business between 1851 and 1905,[11] but the smithy is not recorded before 1900[12] and closed soon after 1919.[13]

LOCAL GOVERNMENT. There are manor court rolls for occasional years between 1556 and 1699.[14]

The court normally met once a year, in the spring, in the early 17th century. Its jurisdiction did not include the assize of bread and ale and in the 17th century it was almost exclusively concerned with encroachments and other offences in Woolstaston Wood.

The parish records include a parish book, containing accounts of churchwardens and overseers, 1719–55. At this time there was one churchwarden and one overseer.[15] Their income was derived mainly from lewns, which had not by 1755 been replaced by a pound rate, but the churchwardens also took pew rents after 1735. Poor rates fluctuated between 13s. 9d. and £10 a year in the early 18th century, but were seldom more than £4 a year. They had risen to £21 by 1776,[16] and to £39 by 1803.[17] They reached a peak of £90 a year in 1819,[18] but fell from £55 in 1821[19] to £21 in 1834.[20] No workhouse or poor-house is recorded.

CHURCH. The church is first mentioned 1272.[21] The living is a rectory and has been united with Smethcott since 1929.[22] Since 1952, however, it has been served for short periods by the incumbents of various neighbouring parishes.[23] The advowson has always followed the descent of the manor, with the exception of the years 1316–63, when it followed the descent of Acton Burnell manor during the widowhood of Aline Burnell.[24] Captain G. C. Wolryche-Whitmore was joint patron of the living in 1963.[25]

The church was said to be worth 40s. in 1294[26] and 1426,[27] and 53s. 4d. in 1536.[28] The rector had an average annual gross income of £165 in 1835.[29] The glebe, which was said to comprise 4 a. in the early 17th century[30] and 7 a. since 1675,[31] was worth £4 a year in 1655.[32] Originally a scattered holding in the common fields, it was inclosed and partly consolidated between 1614 and 1634.[33] It was further consolidated c. 1808[34] and in 1840 most of the glebe lay in a compact block north and east of the rectory.[35] The greater part was sold, together with the rectory, in 1963.[36] A timber-framed tithe-barn which stood by the east wall of the church-yard was demolished

[94] Apley Park estate office, survey and map, 1777.
[95] History of this mill based on C 3/118/42; Wolryche-Whitmore MSS., Dudmaston, inspeximus, 1581, of proceedings in Council of Marches, 1579–81; ibid. exemplification, 1585, of judgement in Ct. of Common Pleas, 1581.
[96] Widows Field, or Woodhouse Field, adjoining the mill, lay in this part of the parish: Wolryche-Whitmore MSS., Dudmaston, map of Woolstaston Wood, 1674; ibid. deed, 1675; ibid. lease, 1674.
[97] See p. 103.
[98] Wolryche-Whitmore MSS., Dudmaston, deed, 1608.
[99] Ibid. ct. r. 1604–32; Apley Park estate office, survey, 1675.
[1] Wolryche-Whitmore MSS., Dudmaston, lease, 1681.
[2] Apley Park estate office, survey, 1675.
[3] Wolryche-Whitmore MSS., Dudmaston, lease, 1681.
[4] Ibid. lease, 1787.
[5] Kelly's Dir. Salop. (1917–26).
[6] Apley Park estate office, survey, 1675.
[7] S.R.O. 567 uncat., plan of mills on Walkmill Brook, c. 1757.
[8] Apley Park estate office, survey, 1777.
[9] Wolryche-Whitmore MSS., Dudmaston, ct. r. 1620.
[10] Ibid. 1632.
[11] Bagshaw's Dir. Salop. (1851); Kelly's Dir. Salop. (1856–1905).
[12] Kelly's Dir. Salop. (1900–13).
[13] S.C.C. title-deeds, SH 12 (sale partics. 1919).
[14] Wolryche-Whitmore MSS., Dudmaston, ct. r. 1556–1699.

[15] The parish also had a single churchwarden in the 17th century: Heref. Dioc. Regy., visitation papers, box 3, letter from rector, 1679.
[16] Rep. Cttee. on Overseers' Returns, 1777, p. 442, H.C. (1st ser. ix, reprinted 1803).
[17] Poor Law Abstract, 1803, H.C. 175, pp. 416–17 (1803–4), xiii.
[18] Rep. Cttee. on Poor Rate Returns, 1822, Suppl. App. H.C. 556, p. 141 (1822), v.   [19] Ibid.
[20] Acct. of Money Expended on Poor, 1830–4, H.C. 444, p. 344 (1835), xlvii.
[21] Eyton, vi. 157.
[22] Lond. Gaz. 1927, pp. 8338–9.
[23] Local inf.
[24] Eyton, vi. 157; C.P. 25(1)/194/7/39; C.P. 25(1)/194/12/54.
[25] Crockford (1961–62).
[26] C 133/68/10.
[27] Reg. T. Spofford (C. & Y.S.), 94.
[28] Reg. C. Bothe (C. & Y.S.), 368.
[29] Rep. Com. Eccl. Revenues [67], pp. 456–7, H.C. (1835), xxii.
[30] Heref. Dioc. Regy., glebe terriers, c. 1589–1634.
[31] Apley Park estate office, survey, 1675; ibid. survey, 1777; par. rec., tithe appt.
[32] T.S.A.S. xlvii. 27.
[33] Heref. Dioc. Regy., glebe terriers, 1614, 1634.
[34] Par. rec., notebks. of E. D. Carr.
[35] Ibid., tithe appt.
[36] Ex inf. Miss E. Adair, Woolstaston Rectory.

in 1865.[37] The tithes were worth £11 a year in 1655[38] and in the later 18th century they were let to the tenants for £70 a year.[39] They were commuted for a rent-charge of £143 in 1840.[40] Income from this source had risen to £168 a year by 1860, but had fallen to £99 a year by 1898.[41]

Lady Meadow (4 a.) is first recorded in 1620, when it was said to have been held by the church-wardens time out of mind, its income being employed for church repairs.[42] Although later thought to have been given by the Pope family,[43] its name indicates that it was in origin a medieval endowment. Liability for the rent-charge has now been transferred to an adjoining field.[44] A rent of 16d., issuing from a nearby field called Condovers Leys, which was being paid to the churchwardens in 1620[45] and in the early 18th century,[46] had by 1840 been exchanged for a small field called Church Patch.[47] In the early 18th century £1 4s. a year was derived from these endowments[48] and the two fields have been let for between £1 and £2 a year since the early 19th century.[49]

Of the 11 rectors of Woolstaston, c. 1590–1900,[50] all died while holding the living and 6 served for more than 30 years. Two early-14th-century rectors were employed in the service of the patron of the living.[51] John Wall (rector 1808–17), Edmund Carr (rector 1817–64), and Edmund Donald Carr (rector 1865–1900) were relatives of the lord of the manor. Most of the rectors have been graduates since 1625, the first recorded being William Colebarne (rector 1625–55), who is also the only rector likely to have come from a Woolstaston family. With few exceptions, the rectors were resident until the early 19th century, many of them being buried in the parish. John Robbins (rector 1709–28) and Lewis Williams (rector 1780–1808) also served Leebotwood and Longnor and assistant curates were employed in the 1770s.[52] John Wall and Edmund Carr were rectors of Quatt, where they lived, while the living was served by a succession of assistant curates, 1809–64. Henry Male, curate from 1823 until 1854, received an annual stipend of £80 in 1835,[53] and was followed by Edmund Donald Carr, who succeeded his father as rector in 1865.

The parsonage was burnt down in the early 17th century,[54] but the rectors were resident until at least 1672, when the house contained two hearths.[55] It was rebuilt by John Robbins shortly before 1716[56] and until 1858 was a three-bay brick house of two stories with attics. It faced south and on the ground floor consisted of two rooms on each side of a small central hall. There were two chimney-stacks on the north wall, with a kitchen beyond.[57] The house is said to have been improved by Lewis Williams[58] and sash windows were inserted by John Wall.[59] It was described as 'comfortable and convenient' c. 1830,[60] but E. D. Carr considered it 'a mere cottage' on his arrival in 1855.[61] Between 1858 and 1885 he enlarged the house by the addition of a new wing on the south side and so remodelled the remainder that scarcely any trace of the 18th-century parsonage can now be seen.[62] The alterations were directed by William Hill, a Smethcott wood-carver, who then had a considerable local reputation, and all the external walls were faced in half-timbered style, using wood from the former tithe-barn and from a barn in Smethcott.[63] Early-17th-century wainscot in the hall came from Church Stretton church, but wood carving elsewhere was the work of William Hill, whose most notable contribution was a fireplace in Jacobean style in the drawing room, erected in 1879.[64]

Communion was usually administered 4 times a year in the early 18th century[65] and 6 times a year in 1793.[66] Services were held once on Sundays between 1716[67] and 1855.[68] At the latter date only five or six people attended and no attempt was made at singing. [69] A second Sunday serivce was then introduced by E. D. Carr.[70]

The church of *ST. MICHAEL*,[71] built in the later 12th or early 13th century, consists of a chancel, nave, and western bell-turret, to which a vestry and small south transept were added in 1865.[72] Its walls are of rubble, but the upper part of the east wall has been re-faced in ashlar. The 5 existing lancet windows are original, as is the two-light pointed window in the west wall, but they were lengthened when the church was restored. The 3 lancets of the east window were originally of the same height, but the central lancet was raised in 1858, when a stained-glass memorial window to William Wolryche-Whitmore was inserted. The

37 Par. rec., notebks. of E. D. Carr.
38 *T.S.A.S.* xlvii. 27.
39 B.M. Add. MS. 21018, f. 218ᵛ.
40 Par. rec., tithe appt.
41 Par. rec., rector's accts. 1859–98.
42 *S.P.R. Lich.* vi (1), 204–5; *24th Rep. Com. Char.*, H.C. 231, p. 390 (1831), xi.
43 *24th Rep. Com. Char.* p. 390.
44 Ex inf. Mr. A. M. Bown.
45 *S.P.R. Lich.* vi (1), 204–5.
46 Par. rec., churchwardens' accts. 1719–54.
47 Ibid., tithe appt.
48 Ibid. churchwardens' accts. 1719–54.
49 *24th Rep. Com. Char.* p. 390; Char. Com. files; *Bagshaw's Dir. Salop.* (1851); *Kelly's Dir. Salop.* (1895–1941).
50 This paragraph is based on *Instit. Dioc. Heref. passim*; *S.P.R. Heref.* i (5), Woolstaston intro. pp. iv–v, and pp. 246–74 passim; *T.S.A.S.* xlvi. 44; B.M. Add. MS. 21018, f. 218ᵛ.
51 Eyton, vi. 157; *Cal. Pat.* 1338–40, 302.
52 Heref. Dioc. Regy., reg. 1755–71, f. 193; ibid. 1772–1802, f. 61.
53 *Rep. Com. Eccl. Revenues* [67], pp. 456–7, H.C. (1835), xxii.
54 Heref. Dioc. Regy., glebe terrier, c. 1606–28.

55 *Hearth Tax, 1672*, 128.
56 Heref. Dioc. Regy., visitation papers, box 69, churchwardens' presentment, 1716; W.S.L. 350/40/3.
57 Copy of drawing, 1855, at Rectory.
58 B.M. Add. MS. 21018, f. 218ᵛ.
59 *S.P.R. Heref.* i (5), Woolstaston intro. p. v.
60 W.S.L. 350/40/3.
61 Par. rec., notebks. of E. D. Carr.
62 Ibid.
63 Ibid.
64 Ibid.
65 Heref. Dioc. Regy., visitation papers, box 69, churchwardens' presentment, 1716; ibid. box 65, churchwardens' presentment, 1719.
66 B.M. Add. MS. 21018, f. 218ᵛ.
67 Ibid.; Heref. Dioc. Regy., visitation papers, box 69, churchwardens' presentment, 1716; ibid. box 65, churchwardens' presentment, 1719.
68 Par. rec., notebks. of E. D. Carr.
69 Ibid.   70 Ibid.
71 So styled by E. D. Carr, on the evidence of the parish wake, formerly held in late September: par. rec., notebks. of E. D. Carr.
72 Description of church based, except where otherwise stated, on S.P.L., MS. 372, vol. i, p. 42; par. rec., notebks. of E. D. Carr; Cranage, vi. 514–15.

lintel of the round-headed priest's door in the south wall consists of a single stone; the chamfer on the jambs has spur stops and continues on the lintel. The south door has a pointed arch, with a plain chamfer and a depressed segmental rear-arch. The lintel of the north door is slightly curved and has plain chamfered jambs. There is a piscina with a pointed arch in the south wall of the chancel and a round-headed aumbry opposite in the north wall.

Most of the lancet windows were blocked, probably in the 17th century, when 2 large mullioned and transomed windows, rising above the level of the eaves, were inserted in the north and south walls of the nave. Another large square-headed window was inserted in the south wall, at the junction of chancel and nave. The priest's door and the north door were blocked and the open timber-framed south porch was replaced by a brick one between 1787 and 1855. Inside the church the roof was ceiled and a plaster partition was erected at the west end to form a vestry under the bell-turret.[73]

A careful restoration of the church was undertaken by E. D. Carr in 1864–5, under the supervision of William Hill of Smethcott. The vestry on the north wall of the nave and the south transept were added, the brick south porch was replaced by a timber-framed one, and a new bell-turret was erected at the west end. The priest's door and the north door were unblocked, the latter becoming the entrance to the vestry. The surviving blocked lancet windows were opened and two-light windows were inserted in the south wall of the nave and the north wall of the chancel. A small round window was set above the window in the west wall, matching the arrangement of windows in the new south transept.

The nave and chancel had a continuous roof until 1865. A hammer-beam roof was then erected at a lower level over the chancel, but the medieval trussed-rafter roof of the nave was reconstructed in its original form and the stone tiles which formerly covered the church were replaced.

Two stones, thought to be remains of the medieval altar, which were found under the chancel floor during the restoration, have been built into the wall of the south transept. The font, which stood at the west end of the church in the 17th century,[74] had been moved to the north door by 1855 but was returned to its original position in 1865. It consists of two bowls, both probably of 12th-century date, placed one on top of the other. The upper bowl is circular, with a simple square moulded band near the top. The lower bowl, also circular but much larger in diameter, has two rounded mouldings. One of the fonts is thought to have come from the

former chapel of Womerton. Wall-paintings found during the restoration could not be preserved, but some of their designs were copied in the new wooden fittings in the chancel.

The nave had no proper flooring before the present tiles were laid in 1865. Box pews were installed in the 18th century, probably in 1735, when pew-rents were introduced. The pews occupied by the rector and the tenant of the Hall had boarded floors, but the remainder stood on the bare ground, with a covering of straw. At the restoration panelling from the old pews was used to construct the new ones. The communion table is an oak chest on legs of c. 1700. The richly carved pulpit, reading desk, lectern, and altar rails are the work of William Hill, and were paid for by the proceeds of a booklet written by the rector describing his experiences when lost on the Long Mynd during a snow-storm in January 1865.[75] The stained glass in the west window is by David Evans of Shrewsbury. That in the east window was installed in 1906 in memory of E. D. Carr, but the brass plate recording the glass of 1858 was not then removed.

There are no monuments in the church, but members of the Pope family were buried in the chancel in the 17th century.[76] The Pope crest, built into the wall of the vestry, was found on one of the farms[77] and probably came from the Hall. This absence of monuments, like the scarcity of old tombstones in the churchyard, may be explained by the practice, current in the parish in the early 19th century, of removing tombstones for building purposes.[78]

The two bells, which have been in the church since 1552,[79] were recast by Abraham Rudhall in 1722.[80] The church had a silver chalice and paten in 1552.[81] The present chalice was made c. 1620–30, but its bowl is older than its stem.[82] A silver paten and flagon were given by Mrs. Mercy Pope in 1720 and a silver paten was presented to the parish in memory of the Revd. W. T. Burgess in 1912.[83] The registers are complete from 1601.[84]

NONCONFORMITY. The Everall family were said to be Anabaptists in 1668[85] and there was one dissenter in the parish in 1676,[86] but there is no later record of nonconformity.

SCHOOLS. There has never been a school in the parish, the children having always attended schools at Leebotwood and Smethcott.[87]

CHARITIES. None known.

[73] Heref. Dioc. Regy., visitation papers, box 3, letter from rector, 1679.   [74] Ibid.
[75] E. D. Carr, *A Night in the Snow* (London, 1865).
[76] Heref. Dioc. Regy., visitation papers, box 3, letter from rector, 1679.
[77] Par. rec., notebks. of E. D. Carr.
[78] Ibid.
[79] *T.S.A.S.* 2nd ser. xii. 99, 319.
[80] Walters, *Ch. Bells Salop.* 101; par. rec., churchwardens' accts. 1719–54.

[81] *T.S.A.S.* 2nd ser. xii. 99, 319.
[82] Arkwright and Bourne, *Ch. Plate Ludlow Archd.* 64.
[83] Ibid.
[84] Printed to 1812 in *S.P.R. Heref.* i (5), 245–74.
[85] Heref. Dioc. Regy., visitation papers, box 18, churchwardens' presentment, 1668.
[86] *T.S.A.S.* 2nd ser. i. 88.
[87] *Returns relating to Elem. Educ.*, H.C. 201, p. 332 (1871), lv; *Kelly's Dir. Salop.* (1885–1917); local inf.

FORD HUNDRED

FORD Hundred has the River Severn as its northern boundary and extends westwards from Shrewsbury to the Welsh border. The countryside here is in general relatively flat. To the west, however, the hundred takes in some part of the Breiddens and the Long Mountain and to the south, where the hundred boundary runs across the northern foothills of the Stiperstones and the Long Mynd, Pontesford Hill forms an impressive feature in the landscape south of Pontesbury village. The Rea valley is the most densely settled part of the hundred and has probably always been the most prosperous. It is bounded on the north by a broad expanse of ill-drained boulder clay which once made up a continuous belt of heathland between Shrewsbury and the Long Mountain. The hundred contains a number of castle-sites, most of which were designed to control roads leading to Shrewsbury from Welshpool and Montgomery. Great changes have taken place in the pattern of settlement in the hundred since the earlier Middle Ages; out of some 70 former hamlets 9 have been deserted and 33 have shrunk to single farms. This process has been most marked in Alberbury-with-Cardeston, where only 5 of the original 24 settlements still survive as recognizable hamlets. Pontesbury and Minsterley are now the only large villages and the district is almost wholly agricultural. There is evidence of specialization in cattle-rearing in the Rea valley from the Middle Ages but mixed farming is now general. Much of the hundred lies in the Hanwood coalfield and coal-mining is recorded in Alberbury, Pontesbury, and Westbury from the early 17th century onwards. The Snailbeach lead mine was the most productive in the West Shropshire lead-mining district during the 19th century.

The Hundred of Ford was represented in 1086 by Ruesset Hundred, then held by the lord of Alberbury manor.[1] Its former name contains the suffix 'saetan' ('inhabitants')[2] and the first element probably refers to the outcrop of breccia south-west of Alberbury village. Woodland here was known as Rew Wood during the Middle Ages[3] and the neighbouring hamlet of Rowton appears to have derived its name from the same root.[4] The hundred was renamed in the earlier 12th century, when Ford replaced Alberbury as its *caput* and it became a royal hundred.[5] The townships of Preston Montford and Dinthill (in Shrewsbury St. Alkmund parish), Horton, Woodcote, and part of Onslow (in Shrewsbury St. Chad parish), Little Hanwood (in Pontesbury parish), and the parish of Great Hanwood were accounted members of Ford Hundred in the 13th century,[6] but had been annexed to the Liberties of Shrewsbury by 1515.[7] Preston Montford and Dinthill appear to have withdrawn their suit from the hundred court in the earlier 13th century.[8] Bausley manor was recorded under Ruesset Hundred in 1086, but was not assessed to geld at this time and was occupied by two Welsh tenants.[9] It was not accounted part of Ford Hundred at any later date and has been a member of Deythur Hundred, Montgomeryshire, since the Act of Union, 1536.[10] Perendon in Westbury and a number of townships in the west of Alberbury parish were taken into Welshry in

---

[1] *V.C.H. Salop.* i. 316.
[2] Ibid. 283.
[3] See p. 184.
[4] See p. 190.
[5] Eyton, i. 23; ibid. iv. 242; ibid. vii. 1.

[6] *Rot. Hund.* (Rec. Com.), ii. 66; J.I. 1/734 m. 29d.
[7] *T.S.A.S.* 2nd ser. ii. 73.
[8] *Rot. Hund.* (Rec. Com.), ii. 66; J.I. 1/739 m. 70d.
[9] *V.C.H. Salop.* i. 324.
[10] Eyton, vii. 98.

OSWESTRY HUNDRED

PIMHILL HUNDRED

WALES

National Boundary

Haywood

River Severn →

LIBERTIES OF SHREWSBURY

FORD

A L B E R B U R Y

National Boundary

Great

Wollaston

Wattlesborough

CARDESTON

W E S T B U R Y

P O N T E S B U R Y

Lt. Hanwood etc.

CHIRBURY
HUNDRED

Minsterley

Habberley Office

Longden

Oaks

CHIRBURY
HUNDRED
det.

C O N D O V E R

Grimmer

HABBERLEY

HUNDRED

W O R T H E N

Upper and

Nether Heath

N

Stitt

Gatten

RATLINGHOPE

N

THE HUNDRED OF
FORD c.1840

0   1 miles 2   3

the 13th century[11] and were said to be wholly outside the county in 1292.[12] This district formed part of the Nether Gorther, a liberty of the barons of Caus during the later Middle Ages.[13] The English townships in the Nether Gorther resumed their suit at Ford hundred court after 1539.[14]

The townships of Gatten (in Ratlinghope parish), Upper and Nether Heath (near Hope in Worthen parish), and Habberley Office (now Eastridge Wood in Worthen parish) which, as members of the Domesday manor of Worthen, presumably lay in Purslow Hundred during the Middle Ages, had unaccountably been annexed to Ford Hundred by the 16th century.[15] Gatten, which first appeared in Ford Hundred for taxation purposes in 1571,[16] no longer did suit at the hundred court by 1698.[17] Suit was performed by Upper and Nether Heath between 1698 and 1838,[18] but Habberley Office had ceased to send representatives to the hundred court by 1778.[19]

The hundred remained in the hands of the Crown until the 17th century and was administered by hundred bailiffs,[20] who seem to have been appointed by the sheriff until the early 16th century.[21] Richard ap Reynold, bailiff in 1584,[22] is said to have been appointed by the Crown[23] and in 1589 William Thomas was appointed bailiff for life.[24] The hundred was conveyed to George and Thomas Whitmore in 1612[25] and in 1615 George Whitmore sold it to Sir Roger Owen of Condover.[26] It subsequently followed the descent of the manors of Condover and Westbury.[27]

The large manor of Ford, which was making a separate presentment at the eyre by 1221,[28] was quit of suit at the hundred court in 1230[29] and was styled a liberty in the later 13th century.[30] Although the barons of Caus were deemed to owe suit at the hundred court in 1255,[31] Peter Corbet claimed jurisdiction over felonies in 1274[32] and alleged in 1292 that his manors of Caus, Vennington, and Wallop had been quit of suit time out of mind.[33] These three manors, with Ree and Westley in Westbury parish and Coton and Leigh in Worthen, were styled the 'Hundred of Caus' in 1353.[34] This franchise seems to have lapsed after the Middle Ages, for Vennington and Winsley did suit at the hundred court in and after 1698.[35] Peter Corbet also claimed in 1292 to hold view of frankpledge in Minsterley manor and to hear all pleas normally dealt with at the sheriff's tourn.[36] Although Minsterley Park owed suit at the hundred court until the early 19th century[37] there is no evidence that suitors from Minsterley were at any time obliged to attend. Wattlesborough and Cardeston no longer did suit in the 16th century[38] and suitors from Alberbury, who had previously presented breaches of the peace at the hundred court, did not appear at the court after c. 1574.[39] Presentments from Pontesbury were made in 1569,[40] but these had been discontinued by 1698, when Habberley, Rowton, and several townships in Westbury parish had also ceased to attend sessions of the court.[41]

[11] See pp. 202, 325.
[12] *Plac. de Quo Warr.* (Rec. Com.), 686.
[13] See p. 325. [14] Ibid.
[15] Eyton, vi. 165; ibid. vii. 1; ibid. xi. 190. The history of these townships is reserved for treatment in a later volume.
[16] E 179/167/46.
[17] S.P.L., Deeds 6042.
[18] Ibid.; S.R.O. 1011 (Smythe Owen) uncat., hundred ct. r. 1778–1838. [19] Ibid.
[20] *Rot. Hund.* (Rec. Com.), ii. 66, 96; J.I. 1/734 m. 32; J.I. 1/736 m. 24; J.I. 1/739 mm. 46, 71.
[21] C 1/1309/34.
[22] E 134/26 Eliz. I East./12.
[23] Loton Hall MSS., bill of Roger Owen v. Sir Edward Leighton, c. 1706.
[24] T. F. Dukes, *Antiquities of Shropshire* (Shrewsbury, 1844), 99.
[25] S.P.L., Deeds 15757.
[26] Ibid. 15756.
[27] See pp. 38–39.
[28] J.I. 1/733(a) m. 10d.
[29] *Cal. Close,* 1227–31, 424.
[30] J.I. 1/739 mm. 46, 83.
[31] *Rot. Hund.* (Rec. Com.), ii. 66. [32] Ibid. 96.
[33] *Plac. de Quo Warr.* (Rec. Com.), 686.
[34] Longleat MSS., unbound 3670.
[35] S.P.L., Deeds 6042; S.R.O. 1011 (Smythe Owen) uncat., hundred ct. r. 1778–1838.
[36] *Plac. de Quo Warr.* (Rec. Com.), 677.
[37] S.R.O. 1011 (Smythe Owen) uncat., hundred ct. r. 1778–1838.
[38] E 134/26 Eliz. I East./12.
[39] Ibid.; E 134/Misc./2474.
[40] Loton Hall MSS., hundred ct. r. 1569.
[41] S.P.L., Deeds 6042.

The bailiff of the hundred was paying 6½ marks a year to the sheriff in 1255,[42] but the value of the hundred had fallen to 5 marks by 1274[43] and to 4 marks by 1292.[44] It was sold for only £100 to Sir Roger Owen in 1615.[45]

There are hundred court rolls 1569,[46] 1698–1705,[47] and 1778–1838.[48] The court, which met twice a year after 1698, seems to have been held at different places within the hundred in the later 16th century,[49] but probably met regularly at Westbury after the hundred was acquired by the lord of that manor. By 1776 a combined court was held for Westbury manor and Ford Hundred.[50] During the period covered by its surviving records the court concerned itself almost exclusively with encroachments on the waste and breaches of the assize of bread and ale.

ALBERBURY-WITH-CARDESTON

THE parish of Alberbury,[1] part of which lay in Wales, formerly included the following townships or hamlets in England: Alberbury, Amaston, Berley, Benthall, Braggington, Little Bretchell, Bronrotpol, Bulthey, Eyton, Hargrave, Hayes, Loton, Rowton, Little Shrawardine, Trefnant, Whitfield, Winnington, Great Wollaston, and Little Wollaston. Braggington, with two small areas to the south, comprising in all 371 a., formed a detached part of Alberbury within Cardeston parish.[2] The townships of Bausley, Criggion, Middletown, and Uppington, all now civil parishes, have lain in Montgomeryshire since the Act of Union and are not included in this account of the parish.

The chapelry of Great Wollaston was maintaining its own poor by the 18th century[3] and has since been accounted a separate civil parish. It includes the townships of Bulthey, Trefnant, Winnington, and Great Wollaston, and the former hamlets of Berley, Bronrotpol, Hargrave, and Whitfield.

Alberbury, with Great Wollaston chapelry, contained 8,838 a. in 1882,[4] but in 1886 the civil parish of Alberbury was united with that of Cardeston (2,410 a.).[5] The latter included, in addition to Cardeston township, the greater part of the townships of Wattlesborough and Great Bretchell and some 458 a. near Haywood in the loop of the Severn north of Hayes. Since the history of these two parishes is closely related in most respects they are here treated together.

The parish boundary of Alberbury-with-Cardeston and Great Wollaston follows the course of the River Severn to the north, but on the east and south it makes little use of natural features. In the south-west, however, where the boundary runs along the upper slopes of the Long Mountain, it follows the road from Westbury to Welshpool. The eastern boundary, which is also the boundary with Wales, follows the course of County Brook across the valley between the Long Mountain and the Brieddens, then runs northwards between Middletown and Bulthey Hills. From Bulthey to the Severn the boundary takes an irregular course to the south of Bausley Hill, following a tributary of Braggington Brook north of Lower Braggington but turning southwards to exclude the area once occupied by Pecknall Wood.

Most of the anomalies in the boundaries of Alberbury and Cardeston were removed by the union of the two parishes in 1886. The only major boundary change, that with Ford to the east, is discussed elsewhere.[6] Although no changes are known to have been made in the ill-defined southern boundary near Wattlesborough Heath, some sections of it were the subject of disputes with Westbury parish in the 17th and 18th centuries. Hargrave Wood, which lay in the eastward projection of the parish boundary west of the hamlet of Marsh, was said to be 'in controversy' in 1602[7] and Hayford Farm, to the east, was a member of Westbury manor from the 12th century onwards.[8] Westbury claimed in the later 18th century that its northern boundary on Wattlesborough Heath ran to the north of the main road from Shrewsbury to Welshpool, to include the whole of the squatter settlements of Halfway House and Wattlesborough Heath.[9] A detached part of

---

[42] *Rot. Hund.* (Rec. Com.), ii. 66.   [43] Ibid. 96.
[44] J.I. 1/739 m. 70d.
[45] S.P.L., Deeds 15756.
[46] Loton Hall MSS.
[47] S.P.L., Deeds 6042.
[48] S.R.O. 1011 (Smythe Owen) uncat.
[49] E 134/26 Eliz. I East./12.
[50] S.R.O. 1011 (Smythe Owen) uncat., suit roll, 1776.
[1] Except where otherwise stated, the following topographical description is based on O.S. Maps 1″, sheets lx, lxi (1st edn.); O.S. Maps 6″ Salop. 26, 27, 32, 33, 39, 40 (1st and later edns.); O.S. Maps 1/25,000, SJ 31 (1956), SJ 20, 30, 41 (1957), SJ 21 (1959); Rocque, *Map of Salop.* (1752); Baugh, *Map of Salop.* (1808); B.M. O.S. 2″ orig. drawings, sheets 199 (1816), 320 (1827); Geol. Survey Map (drift), sheet 152 (1932); R. W. Pocock and others, *Geol. Shrews. District* (1938) *passim*; Alberbury par. rec.,

Alberbury tithe appt., 1843, and map, 1842, Great Wollaston tithe appt. 1848, and map, 1842, tithe appts. and maps of Bulthey, 1840, Rowton and Amaston, 1848, Trefnant, 1843, Winnington, 1843; Cardeston par. rec., tithe appt and map, 1846. This article was written in 1965. It is in part based on material supplied by Mr. L. C. Lloyd of Cardeston, to whom thanks are also due for much useful advice.
[2] See map on p. 188.
[3] *Rep. Cttee. on Overseers' Returns, 1777*, p. 658, H.C (1st ser. ix, reprinted 1803).
[4] O.S. *Area Bks.* (1882–3).
[5] Ibid. (1882); *Census*, 1891.
[6] See p. 223.
[7] All Souls mun., Horedon maps, Alberbury 1.
[8] See p. 207.
[9] S.R.O. 665 uncat., plans of Wattlesborough Heath, 1792.

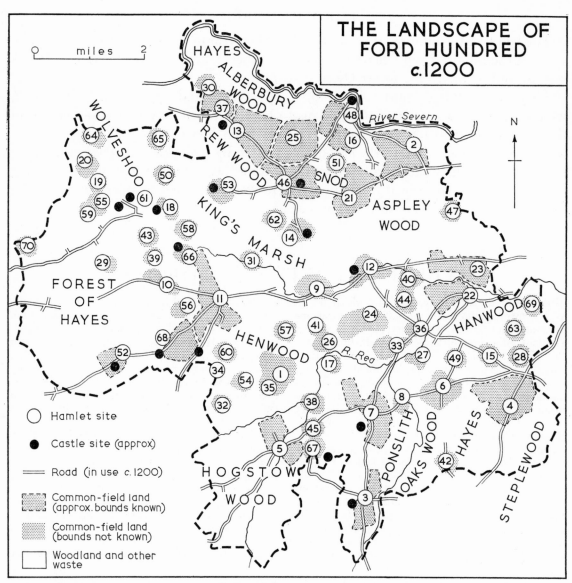

THE LANDSCAPE OF FORD HUNDRED c.1200

HAYES
ALBERBURY WOOD
River Severn
WOLVESHOO
REW WOOD
SNOD
ASPLEY WOOD
KING'S MARSH
FOREST OF HAYES
HENWOOD
HANWOOD
PONSLITH
OAKS WOOD
HAYES
STEPLEWOOD
HOGSTOW WOOD

N

○ Hamlet site
● Castle site (approx)
═ Road (in use c.1200)
▨ Common-field land (approx. bounds known)
░ Common-field land (bounds not known)
☐ Woodland and other waste

miles

See note below map on p. 4

KEY TO HAMLETS

A. SURVIVING HAMLETS

1. Asterley	4. Longden
2. Ford	5. Minsterley
3. Habberley	6. Plealey

7. Pontesbury	10. Vennington
8. Pontesford	11. Westbury
9. Stoney Stretton	12. Yockleton

B. HAMLETS SHRUNKEN AFTER c. 1200

13. Alberbury	26. Farley	39. Marsh	52. Wallop
14. Amaston	27. Halston	40. Newnham	53. Wattlesborough
15. Arscott	28. Hanwood, Little	41. Newton, Lower	54. Westley
16. Benthall	29. Hargrave	42. Oaks	55. Whitfield
17. Boycott	30. Hayes	43. 'Perendon'	56. Whitton
18. Bretchell, Great	31. Hayford	44. Polmere	57. Wigley
19. 'Bronrotpol'	32. Hem	45. Poulton	58. Wigmore
20. Bulthey	33. Hinton	46. Rowton	59. Winnington
21. Cardeston	34. Hurst	47. Sascott	60. Winsley
22. Cruckmeole	35. Lake	48. Shrawardine, Little	61. Wollaston, Great
23. Cruckton	36. Lea	49. Sibberscott	62. Wollaston, Little
24. Edge	37. Loton	50. Stanford, Upper	63. Woodhall
25. Eyton	38. Malehurst	51. 'Stokes'	

C. HAMLETS DESERTED AFTER c. 1200

64. 'Berley'	66. 'Brerelawe'	68. Caus	70. Trefnant
65. Braggington	67. Callow	69. Panson	

NOTE. The sites of 'Vachrige' in Alberbury parish, Marton in Pontesbury, and Ree in Westbury are not marked. Evidence is insufficient to establish whether Little Bretchell, Glyn, and Lower Stanford in Alberbury parish were originally hamlets. The site of Winnington is uncertain and the site of Wigmore, shown here as at Upper Wigmore, may have been at Lower Wigmore (not marked).

Winnington township (102 a.) on the western slopes of the Long Mountain, east of Monksfields, was transferred to Westbury parish in 1934.[10] Upper Stanford (65 a.), formerly a detached part of Bausley civil parish, was transferred to Alberbury in 1886.[11]

The most significant feature in the geography of Alberbury-with-Cardeston is an outcrop of breccia which forms a crescent-shaped ridge, about 3 miles in length, running south-eastwards from Loton Park past Rowton to Cardeston.[12] The outcrop rises to some 500 feet in Loton Deer Park and to the north-west of Rowton is about ½ mile wide. To the east of Rowton, where a fault occurs, the outcrop is about half this width. The land north and east of the ridge rises gently from some 190 feet along the Severn to 300 feet near the hamlets of Alberbury, Rowton, and Cardeston. The alluvial flood-plain of the Severn and its river-terraces occupy a large area to the north, particularly in the loop of the river north of Hayes. Over the remainder of these northern lowlands Triassic sandstones and pebble-beds are largely covered by boulder clay drift.

To the south and west of the breccia outcrop is the area formerly known as Wattlesborough Heath— a broad, flat expanse of poorly drained, stiff, and somewhat stoney boulder clay, most of it lying between 400 and 425 feet. The former hamlet of Wattlesborough stood on a slight rise (some 450 feet) in the centre of the Heath and similar relatively elevated sites were occupied by the former hamlets of Amaston and Little Wollaston on its eastern edge and by Upper Stanford and Great Bretchell to the west.

Differences in geography and in geological structure account for some of the many contrasts between the history of Cardeston and the eastern portion of Alberbury parish on the one hand, and of that part of Alberbury parish lying to the west of the Heath on the other. The latter area, which corresponds with the present civil parish of Great Wollaston, was formerly known for administrative purposes as the Upper Division. This term has been used in subsequent references to the area.

Wattlesborough Heath forms a watershed. Streams to the north and east, notably Cardeston, Bragging-ton, and Loton Brooks, flow northwards to the Severn. Wollaston Brook to the west, formerly known as King's Brook,[13] rises on the Heath and is fed by tributaries from the hills to the north and south. Under the name Trewern Brook it flows westwards to join the Severn near Welshpool. The Silurian rocks, which make up most of the high ground in the Upper Division, outcrop above the Keele beds and Coed-yr-Allt sandstones under-lying Wattlesborough Heath along a line running roughly north and south from Great Wollaston hamlet. Most of the former hamlets in the Upper Division stood below the 500-foot contour in the valley of Wollaston Brook, where the subsoil is mainly boulder clay. To the south of the valley the steep slopes of the Long Mountain rise to about 1,100 feet in the south-west of the parish. Bulthey Hill, to the north of the valley, rises to 1,000 feet and is capped with volcanic conglomerate.

Evidence for the evolution of the landscape, scanty enough for the northern lowlands, becomes progressively less adequate as one moves westwards across the parish and is generally unsatisfactory for most townships in the Upper Division. There were three main areas of woodland or waste during the Middle Ages—the lower land alongside the Severn in the north, Wattlesborough Heath and the adjacent Rew Wood in the centre, and virtually the whole of the Upper Division outside the small common fields of its hamlets.

Woodland on the south bank of the Severn ex-tended as far south as the 200-foot contour and was most extensive north of Hayes. The latter area prob-ably represents the 'haye' recorded in Loton manor in 1086,[14] which was accounted a demesne wood of the lords of Caus in 1272.[15] Peter Corbet of Caus retained his right to hunt this woodland when he granted the hamlet of Hayes to the lord of Wattlesborough manor in 1278, but the latter was then given licence to make assarts in it.[16] Assarts called 'Hugynslye' and 'Hondelegh' are recorded in 1379,[17] the latter being represented by fields called Great and Little Hoggins on the bank of the Severn south-west of Haywood. 'Fynchestocking', also recorded in 1379,[18] can probably be identified with adjoining fields called Stockings and Stocking Bank. This low-lying tract, cleared of timber by the 16th century, has subsequently been used for cattle-rearing.[19] A 'day-house' at the Hayes is recorded in 1651.[20]

Alberbury Wood, separated from the Hayes in the Middle Ages by demesne meadows along Loton Brook,[21] ran eastwards as far as White Abbey.[22] Its southern boundary followed a line east and west of Lower Wood Farm.[23] A strip of woodland on the bank of the Severn to the west of White Abbey was granted to Alberbury Priory c. 1226[24] and was known as the Abbey Park in the 16th century.[25] Fields to the south of the road from Lower Wood Farm to White Abbey, known as 'The Haugh' and 'Birches' in the 16th century,[26] were assarted in the course of the Middle Ages, as was a field called 'Vernylie',[27] which is probably represented by Ferny Bank, on the western edge of the wood. Alberbury Wood, which was restricted to the area north-west of Lower Wood Farm by the mid-16th century,[28] was being inclosed in 1579.[29] Cleared land here was leased piecemeal to the tenants of Alberbury between 1585 and 1594.[30]

Eyton Wood extended as far south as the

[10] County Review Order, 1934.
[11] Census, 1891.
[12] I. D. Mercer, 'The Geography of the Alberbury Breccia', Field Studies, i (1), 102–15.
[13] B.M. Eg. Roll 2197; Loton Hall MSS., depositions, Roger Owen v. Robert and Edward Leighton, c. 1685.
[14] V.C.H. Salop. i. 325.
[15] Rot. Hund. (Rec. Com.), ii. 96.
[16] Eyton, vii. 110.
[17] S.P.L., Deeds 6172.
[18] Ibid.
[19] Sta. Cha. 2/26/105; Loton Hall MSS., lease, 1599.

[20] Loton Hall MSS., lease, 1651.
[21] Ibid., Wattleborough reeve's accts. 1374–8; ibid., lease, 1585.
[22] All Souls mun., Horedon maps, Alberbury 2, 3.
[23] Ibid.
[24] T.S.A.S. 4th ser. xi. 292.
[25] S.R.O. 1123/3.
[26] All Souls mun., Horedon maps, Alberbury 2, 3.
[27] Loton Hall MSS., exchange, 1500.
[28] All Souls mun., Horedon maps, Alberbury 2, 3.
[29] C 2/Eliz. I/A 8/58.
[30] Loton Hall MSS., leases, 1585–94.

field-road, now disused, running towards Little Shrawardine from the lane between Eyton and White Abbey.[31] Woodmoors, on the bank of the Severn on the township boundary with Little Shrawardine, was among the lands granted to Alberbury Priory in the course of the 13th century and was being cleared of timber at this time.[32] The remainder of the wood had been divided into two parts by the mid-16th century. Eyton's Leyes (or Eyton's Hayes) to the north, probably in origin a demesne wood, was inclosed c. 1549 and divided into fields c. 1567,[33] but the present Eyton Gorse may be a surviving remnant of medieval woodland. It can be identified with 'ley gors', recorded in the 13th century.[34] The southern part of Eyton Wood, on ill-drained boulder clay above the 200-foot contour, had been common to the inhabitants of Eyton during the Middle Ages.[35] It had probably been cleared of timber by 1579, when it was known as Eyton Common.[36]

There is some evidence for the survival into the later Middle Ages of a second belt of woodland in the northern lowlands, lying close to the road from Alberbury to Benthall Cross. The only surviving woodland in this area is Snod Coppice, north-west of Rowton. This is now a soft-wood plantation, but it stands in an area of ancient woodland which bore the same name in the early 14th century.[37] Medieval lords of Rowton manor appear to have had a park in the area of the present Rowton Lawn, to the east of Snod Coppice. Park Furlong lay in Snod Field[38] and an assart called 'Park Lee' seems to have been in demesne in 1375.[39] The field-names 'Shirteley' (later The Chircles) and Hockley[40] are evidence that this woodland once extended into the north of Cardeston township. A wood at The Chircles still contained 26 a. in 1622.[41] The common fields of Eyton and Alberbury lay on both sides of the road to Benthall Cross, but 'the great pasture' of Eyton, which adjoined the road in the 13th century,[42] was probably a clearing in this belt of woodland. Westmoor, in the south of Little Shrawardine township,[43] was probably so named since it lay on the western boundary of the manor of Ford.

Loton Deer Park, to the south of the present road from Alberbury to Coedway, corresponds roughly with the area occupied by Rew Wood in the Middle Ages—running for the most part along the breccia outcrop. Small fields near Sunny Bank mark the south-eastern end of the wood and it was bounded on the west and south-west by Loton Brook.[44] The Deer Park and the Park to the north

of the road were probably formed shortly after the Leighton family moved from Wattlesborough to Loton Hall in the early 18th century.

To the south of the breccia outcrop the badly drained tract stretching from Ford Heath on the east to Great Wollaston on the west was, until the 16th century, largely made up of woodland and moor, broken only by the tiny common fields of hamlets sited on patches of higher ground. Areas of waste in the townships of Cardeston and Amaston were known as Cardeston Wood[45] and Amaston Wood[46] respectively during the later Middle Ages. Wattlesborough Heath, also known as 'King's Marsh' and 'Rhos y Drevrythe',[47] lay for the most part in Wattlesborough township, where its northern boundary seems to have followed Braggington Brook, taking in Wattlesborough Lawn and fields to the south and south-east of Wattlesborough Hall called Cunneries and Fegg.[48] To the south, where the present parish boundary appears to have been fixed by the end of the 16th century,[49] the Heath adjoined Stretton Heath and other wastes in Westbury parish. It also extended westwards into the manors of Great Wollaston and Bronrotpol.[50] A group of 'moor' and 'coppice' field-names along the valley south-west of Great Wollaston may represent the moor called 'Alphyn Moor' or 'Gornellfyn', recorded c. 1540.[51] To the east the Heath formerly covered part of the townships of Rowton and Little Wollaston. In 1634 it was said to adjoin the eastern edge of the hamlet of Rowton[52] and there are numerous 'wood' field-names in the area between Orchard Farm and Grange Farm.

The inhabitants of adjoining hamlets had common rights in Wattlesborough Heath at all times of a year.[53] Drifts were regularly held in the 16th and 17th centuries.[54] It was said c. 1685 that livestock was commonly driven on these occasions to Wattlesborough Lawn, a 'better part of the waste whereto the cattle most come'.[55] Rights of jurisdiction over the Heath were in dispute in 1272, when the lord of Alberbury manor claimed common rights there.[56] Following a lawsuit in the 1580s between the lord of Wattlesborough and the lessee of Ford Hundred,[57] the former, whose claim to jurisdiction over one third of the Heath was confirmed, took a lease of the remainder from the lord of the hundred.[58] Attempts by the lords of Wattlesborough to exercise jurisdiction over the whole of the Heath led to further lawsuits c. 1685 and c. 1706.[59]

Assarting in Cardeston, Amaston, and Wattlesborough Heaths was well advanced by 1379, when woodland clearings formed part of many holdings

---

[31] All Souls mun., Horedon maps, Alberbury 2.
[32] Ibid., Alberbury deeds 47, 104.
[33] Ibid. 168.
[34] Ibid. 46.
[35] Ibid. 170(e); S.R.O. 1123/1.
[36] All Souls mun., Alberbury deeds 168.
[37] S.P.L., MS. 75, deed, 1303; Cal. Inq. p.m. vi, pp. 8, 101.
[38] S.P.L., MS. 75, deed, 1321.
[39] Loton Hall MSS., Rowton reeve's acct. 1375.
[40] S.P.L., Deeds 6172; Loton Hall mun., Cardeston survey, 1713; ibid., lease, 1767.
[41] Loton Hall MSS., lease, 1622.
[42] All Souls mun., Alberbury deeds 52.
[43] Ibid. 55.
[44] Ibid. Horedon maps, Alberbury 1, 3, 4; Loton Hall mun., Alberbury ct. r. 1652, 1659–64.
[45] Loton Hall MSS., Cardeston ct. r. 1451.

[46] S.P.L., Deeds 6172.
[47] E 134/26 Eliz. I East./12.
[48] Ibid.; E 134/Misc. 2473–4; Loton Hall MSS., depositions, Roger Owen v. Robert and Edward Leighton, c. 1685; ibid. answer of Edward Leighton, 1708.
[49] All Souls mun., Horedon maps, Alberbury 1.
[50] S.R.O. 665 uncat., survey of Wattleborough Heath, c. 1780; E 134/26 Eliz. I East./12.
[51] C 1/822/4–5.
[52] S.R.O. 1123/7.
[53] E 134/26 Eliz. I East./12; E 134/Misc. 2473–4.
[54] Ibid.; Loton Hall MSS., legal papers, 1685–1708.
[55] Loton Hall MSS., depositions, Roger Owen v. Robert and Edward Leighton, c. 1685.
[56] Eyton, vii. 105.
[57] E 134/26 Eliz. I East./12; E 134/Misc. 2473–4.
[58] Loton Hall MSS., legal papers, 1685–1708.
[59] Ibid.

there, and in some cases the land so cleared had been added to the common fields.[60] The waste of Cardeston manor, known in the 15th century as Cardeston Wood, seems to have occupied the whole of the township south of Cardeston Brook. In 1379 3 tenants here held assarts at 'Rowley', west of Heath Farm, Cardeston.[61] Cardeston Park, lying in a westward projection of the township boundary between two tributaries of Cardeston Brook, had been formed before 1374.[62] Its medieval bounds are preserved in those of the present Cardeston Park Farm. By 1713 only 11 a. of woodland remained in Cardeston township.[63] The name Amaston Heath appears to have been applied to the waste lying between Heath Farm, Amaston, and the township boundary with Cardeston. The clearing known as 'Ambaslyegh' in 1379, when it was held by 3 tenants for a rent of 6s. 8d.,[64] can be identified with fields called Hamsleys, immediately north-east of Wood End Farm.

Numerous 14th-century assarts in Wattlesborough manor, most of which cannot be identified, included 'Pyndelye'.[65] This survived in the field-name Pant Lees, applied to fields on Loton Brook, north of Wattlesborough Hall. On the eastern edge of the Heath, fields called 'Badlees' had been cleared before 1537.[66] The lord of Rowton manor was felling timber in this area in the 1630s[67] and in 1691 woodland at the Burrows, north of Grange Farm, and at Crow Wood and The Feg to the south was sold to provide cordwood for local ironmasters.[68] Inclosure of the central part of the Heath, in the south of Wattlesborough township, seems to have been the work of squatters who, according to late-16th-century deponents, first appeared here c. 1540.[69] By 1584 about a quarter of this part of the Heath had been inclosed in this way,[70] but there were still 339 a. of uninclosed common within Wattlesborough manor in 1715.[71] The area of the Heath in Wattlesborough, Rowton, and Great Wollaston manors had been reduced to some 225 a. by c. 1780, when this remaining portion was inclosed.[72]

The 9 hamlets of the Upper Division were no more than small clearings in a continuous expanse of woodland in the earlier Middle Ages. In Bulthey township 'wood' field-names occur as far south as the Welshpool road and eastwards to Bank Farm. This was probably the wood known in 1278 as 'Wlveshoo', when it extended from King's Brook (Wollaston Brook) to the bounds of Bausley on the north.[73] Bulthey Common, the bounds of which were described c. 1685,[74] seems to have lain on the southern slopes of Bulthey Hill. Hargrave Hill and the northern slopes of the Long Mountain formed

part of the Forest of Hayes during the Middle Ages and, apart from the common fields of Hargrave, woodland probably covered the whole of the area to the south of the old Welshpool road at this time. In the centre of the Upper Division the clay-capped Glyn plateau running south-west from Winnington Green formed a third area of woodland. A wood called The Coppice still stood near Winnington Green in 1765, but by this date the area had been inclosed with the exception of Glyn Common, on the steep slope above County Brook south of Glyn Farm.[75]

Common rights in these three areas do not appear to have been restricted to the inhabitants of particular hamlets. In 1590 the tenant of Hargrave Farm enjoyed common rights on the Breiddens as well as in Hargrave Wood and on the Long Mountain[76] and in 1779 the inhabitants of Glyn and Great Wollaston were claiming common rights on the Long Mountain.[77]

Much of the Upper Division woodland lay on land possessing relatively good natural drainage and it seems likely that the greater part had been cleared by the end of the 16th century. In 1345 the tenant of Bronrotpol manor had been given licence to make inclosures[78] and Trefnant Park, first recorded in 1465,[79] seems to have lain on the southern slopes of the Glyn plateau. Reynold Williams, the most substantial freeholder in the Upper Division during the 16th century, inclosed some 140 a. of waste by agreement with other landowners in the 1580s.[80] This probably included the fields called 'Stepless' (Steep Lees), on the lower slopes of Hargrave Hill and near Lane Farm, which were described as pasture in 1599.[81] Another part of Hargrave Wood had been converted into a rabbit-warren by 1623.[82] Common land on the top of the Long Mountain, including 96 a. in Trefnant township, was inclosed shortly before 1807.[83] A common at Winnington Green had also been inclosed by this date,[84] but Bulthey and Glyn Commons were not inclosed until c. 1811.[85] By the 1840s, when Alberbury and Cardeston contained a total of 394 a. woodland, only 98 a. lay in the Upper Division.[86]

The common fields of all townships in the Upper Division appear to have been inclosed during the Middle Ages, but in the east the common fields of Alberbury, Cardeston, Eyton, Rowton, and Little Shrawardine seem to have survived, if only in fragmentary form, until the earlier 17th century. Evidence for the names, location, and date of inclosure of the common fields is set out below.

Alberbury.[87] Rew Field lay on the lower slopes of the breccia outcrop, south of the road to Benthall Cross. Cross Field, with another field the name of

[60] S.P.L., Deeds 6172.
[61] Ibid.
[62] Loton Hall MSS., Cardeston ct. r. 1374.
[63] Ibid. Cardeston survey, 1713.
[64] S.P.L., Deeds 6172.
[65] Ibid.
[66] Ibid. MS. 69, deed, 1537.
[67] Ibid. Deeds 17048.
[68] Ibid. 17005.
[69] E 134/26 Eliz. I East./12; E 134/Misc. 2473-4.
[70] Ibid.
[71] Loton Hall MSS., Wattlesborough survey, 1715.
[72] S.R.O. 665 uncat., survey of Wattlesborough Heath, c. 1780.
[73] B.M. Eg. Roll 2197.
[74] Loton Hall MSS., depositions, Roger Owen v. Robert and Edward Leighton, c. 1685.

[75] S.R.O. 552 uncat., survey of Wolley estate, 1765.
[76] S.P.L., Deeds 2899.
[77] Ibid. 3019.
[78] C.P. 40/344 rot. 559.
[79] B.M. Eg. Roll 2196.
[80] C 3/255/91.
[81] S.R.O. 166 uncat., marriage settlement of Reynold Williams, 1599.
[82] S.P.L., Deeds 2903.
[83] S.R.O. 552 uncat., survey of Wolley estate, 1807; Alberbury par. rec., Trefnant tithe appt. 1843.
[84] S.R.O. 552 uncat., survey of Wolley estate, 1807.
[85] Ibid. 1123/25, letter, 1810.
[86] Alberbury par. rec., tithe appts.
[87] Description based on All Souls mun., Horedon maps, Alberbury 3; Loton Hall MSS., Alberbury ct. r. 1652, 1664; ibid. exchange, 1500.

which is not recorded, ran northwards from this road towards Alberbury Wood, north and east of the village. The common fields were still intact in 1593 and appear to have been functioning as late as 1664.

Amaston. Names and location not known. In 1379 two tenants held selions called 'Stocket Land',[88] suggesting that assarted lands were being added to the common fields in the latter Middle Ages. Three 'great pastures', said to contain 400 a. and formerly held in common by the freeholders of Amaston, were inclosed by agreement c. 1545.[89] It is probable that these were the Amaston common fields, rather than an area of cleared woodland.

Benthall. The common fields presumably lay to the west of Benthall Farm, since Benthall Common lay immediately to the east.[90] The field-name Towns Field occurs west of the house in 1842.[91] Shirtley Furlong, recorded in 1646,[92] probably lay to the south-west of the house.

Braggington. The ridge and furrow which surrounds the site of the deserted hamlet of Braggington is also visible to the south of Bragginton Hall.

Bulthey. The field-name 'Kruns', which occurs in fields to the north-east of Great Wollaston vicarage, represents the common field known as The Crimes, where a Great and Little Furlong are recorded in 1629.[93] Open-field lands were recorded at the same date in Cae Croyes (Cross Field).[94] Fields called Cae Hair, Cae Hill, and Cae Bella ('Kar r Berllan', 1629),[95] immediately south of the more westerly of the two farms now called Bulthey Farm, may also have formed part of the Bulthey common fields.

Cardeston.[96] Whiston Field, north of the village, adjoined the common fields of Ford on the east, Cardeston Brook on the south, and The Chircles on the north-west. Edge Field lay on the breccia outcrop, west and north-west of the village, and adjoined Cardeston Park. The field-name Brook Furlong, south of Cardeston Brook to the east of the village, may indicate the position of the third field, but there is some evidence that this was made up of lands assarted from Cardeston Heath in the later Middle Ages. Black Furlong, which was common-field land in the early 17th century, can be identified with fields called The Furlongs on the southern boundary of the township. Assarts at 'Rowley' and in three other parts of the Heath were described as butts or selions in 1379. The common fields were still in part uninclosed in 1636.

Eyton.[97] Common fields here were more extensive than those of the two other shrunken hamlets in the northern lowlands (Benthall and Little Shrawardine), extending from Eyton Wood to the southern boundary of the township. Evidence for their location

is not clear, but suggests that Cross Field adjoined the common fields of Alberbury to the west of Eyton and that the two other fields lay respectively north-east and south-east of the hamlet. Partial inclosure had taken place by 1596.

Hargrave. Ridge and furrow can be seen in Hargrave Field, in the relatively flat area east of Hargrave Farm. This field had been inclosed and converted to pasture by 1599.[98]

Loton and Hayes. Nothing is known of the common fields of Hayes. Lower Spone Field in Loton, bounded on the east by the common fields of Alberbury and on the west by a road to Hayes, seems to have lain in what is now the northern part of Loton Park.[99] Another field, presumably called Upper Spone Field, lay to the west of Loton Brook. Its name is preserved in Spawns House and in field-names to the north. The Loton common fields were still in use in 1442,[1] but were probably converted to pasture for cattle rearing in the early 16th century.[2]

Rowton.[3] Two of the common fields lay on the northern slopes of the breccia outcrop, probably divided by the road from Rowton to Alberbury. Snod Field presumably lay in the area now occupied by Rowton Park and Bean Field to the west of the road. 'Galud acre', the name of a furlong in the latter field, is preserved in the field-name Gallants Piece. Ridge and furrow is visible in fields called Peplows, once part of this common field. The third field, known as Quere Field in the 15th century, ran towards Cardeston Brook, south of the hamlet. Inclosure took place here in the early 17th century, when 'the field grounds being over-worn with tillage', they were converted to pasture.[4]

Little Shrawardine. The common fields were called Little Field, Cross Field, and Barrett Field,[5] of which the latter lay to the south of Little Shrawardine Farm, in Benthall township.[6] They were inclosed by means of exchanges made c. 1636.[7]

Wattlesborough. Moor Field, in which 18 tenants held parcels of land in 1379,[8] was probably one of the common fields. Another, which was said to adjoin Rowton Marsh,[9] presumably lay to the south-east of Wattlesborough Hall. Ridge and furrow can be seen in fields to the south and south-west of the Hall.

Little Wollaston. A common field called Espe Field is recorded in 1634.[10] Ridge and furrow is visible in Calves Yard, north of Grange Farm.

Two major roads run from east to west across Alberbury-with-Cardeston, the road from Shrewsbury to Welshpool and that running past Alberbury towards Llanfyllin. The present isolated position of the castle and former hamlet of Wattlesborough suggests that in the earlier Middle Ages the route towards Welshpool may have skirted the northern

[88] S.P.L., Deeds 6172.
[89] C 2/Eliz. I/S 5/42; C 3/161/2; C 3/158/39; C 3/163/52.
[90] Alberbury par. rec., tithe appt.
[91] Ibid.
[92] S.P.L., Deeds 157.
[93] S.R.O. 227/19.
[94] Ibid.   [95] Ibid.
[96] Description based on Heref. Dioc. Regy., glebe terriers, c. 1600, 1636; S.P.L., Deeds 6172.
[97] Description based on All Souls mun., Alberbury deeds 51–52, 55, 57–58; S.R.O. 1123/2.
[98] S.R.O. 166 uncat., marriage settlement of Reynold Williams, 1599.

[99] Loton Hall MSS., lease, 1599.
[1] Heref. City Libr. 9133/33.
[2] Sta. Cha. 2/26/105.
[3] Description based on S.P.L., MS. 75, deeds c. 1300, 1303, 1321, 1341, 1497.
[4] All Souls mun., Alberbury deeds 215; S.P.L., deeds 17048.
[5] S.P.L., Deeds 81, 152, 155, 157.
[6] Alberbury par. rec., tithe appt.
[7] S.P.L., Deeds 152.
[8] Ibid. 6172.
[9] Loton Hall MSS., lease, 1354.
[10] S.R.O. 1123/7.

edge of Wattlesborough Heath at this point. The lane running northwards from Ivyend Farm, now the only means of access to Wattlesborough Hall, has been constructed since 1846, when the Hall was approached by a road running westwards from Spring Cottage on the Welshpool road.[11] The field-road running north-westwards from the Hall towards Windmill Farm was not shown as a road in the early 19th century.[12]

By the end of the 16th century the Welshpool road followed its present course as far west as Halfway House. It then ran south-westwards past Lane Farm and Winnington Hall towards Buttington, around the lower slopes of the Long Mountain.[13] The road was turnpiked in 1758.[14] The section of the present Welshpool road which runs along the foot of Middletown Hill, west of Great Wollaston, became a turnpike in 1801.[15] Although the Buttington route was still accounted a turnpike road in the mid-19th century,[16] it had apparently been superseded by the Middletown road before 1822.[17] Small diversions of the Welshpool road were made at Cardeston in 1734[18] and at Rowton in 1836.[19]

The road past Alberbury to Llanfyllin had been turnpiked by 1780[20] and there was a toll-gate in Alberbury village by 1783.[21] The section of the road running across the breccia outcrop to the south of the village, between the road leading to Rowton and that to Hayes, is the result of a diversion made c. 1780. The road had formerly skirted the higher ground, following the alignment of the road from Rowton around the north side of Alberbury church.[22] A plaque on the roadside by the side of Prince's Oak, on the Welsh border, commemorates the visit made to Wales by George, Prince of Wales, in 1806.[23] The tree, which was standing at this time, was enclosed with iron railings in 1813.[24]

Roads from Ford and Rowton, both now disused, formerly ran northwards to a ford across the Severn at Little Shrawardine. That from Little Shrawardine to Rowton formerly continued to the south of the Welshpool road along what is now a footpath to join the roads to Grange Farm (Little Wollaston) and Heath Farm (Amaston).[25] The course of these latter roads further south has not been established.

Several other minor roads in the parish have become disused following the shrinkage of hamlets along their course. The only remaining public road in the northern lowlands is that from Alberbury to White Abbey, which was one of three alternative routes to Alberbury Priory during the Middle Ages.[26] The disused road from Eyton to White Abbey was still being maintained as a public road in 1786.[27] In the Upper Division the lane from Plas-y-Court to Winnington Green, which formerly continued southwards to join the old Welshpool road,[28] was described as a portway in the later 17th century.[29] Farther west, the track running northwards from Trefnant Farm (or Lower Trefnant) to Glyn Common was known at this time as Pull Cough Lane ('pwll coch', red pool).[30]

Estimates of the population of Alberbury before 1801 make no distinction between the English and Welsh parts of the parish. The whole parish was said to contain 923 adults in 1676,[31] when there were 71 adults in Cardeston parish.[32] The population of Alberbury parish was put at 1,776 in 1777.[33] Statistics derived from the parish registers of Alberbury, Cardeston, and Ford, 1661–1810,[34] suggest that the population of these 3 parishes was comparatively stationary until the second decade of the 18th century and that it rose rapidly after 1760. While the death-rate remained constant throughout the period, the marriage-rate rose after 1740 and is clearly connected with a marked rise in the number of baptisms in the later 18th century. The average annual natural increase (excess of baptisms over burials) was rarely more than 10 per cent. before 1760, but was consistently over 30 per cent. in the period 1760–1810.

Cardeston and the English part of Alberbury contained 1,349 inhabitants in 1811[35]—the corresponding figure of 881 for 1801 is clearly an error.[36] The population of the two parishes reached a peak of 1,437 in 1841[37] and has steadily declined since that date. There were 1,084 inhabitants in 1901[38] and 939 in 1961.[39]

A Friendly Society had been established at Alberbury by 1803, when it had 62 members.[40] The Halfway House and Great Wollaston Friendly Society had been formed by 1821 and a female Friendly Society, covering both parishes, by 1834.[41] Worthies include the puritan divine Thomas Ball (1590–1659) and the astronomer Charles Pritchard (1808–93), both of whom were born in the parish.[42]

DEVELOPMENT OF SETTLEMENT. The only evidence which may indicate prehistoric settlement within the parish is a Bronze Age inhumation burial in a wedge-shaped cist, discovered in 1942 beneath a ploughed-down round barrow near the road to Alberbury, south-west of Eyton.[43] The

[11] Cardeston par. rec., tithe appt.
[12] B.M. O.S. 2″ orig. drawings, sheet 320 (1827).
[13] All Souls mun., Horedon maps, Alberbury 1.
[14] Shrewsbury road Act, 31 Geo. II, c. 67 (priv. act).
[15] Ibid. 41 Geo. III, c. 88 (priv. act).
[16] Q. Sess., dep. plans 186.
[17] Shrewsbury District road Act, 3 Geo. IV, c. 42 (priv. act.).
[18] Q. Sess. Orders, ii. 84; S.R.O. 1123/25, letter, 1796.
[19] Q. Sess. Orders, iii. 309.
[20] T.S.A.S. 3rd ser. viii, map facing p. 63.
[21] Q. Sess. Rolls, 73.
[22] All Souls mun., Horedon maps, Alberbury 3.
[23] Salop. N. & Q. n.s. iv. 77–78.
[24] S.R.O. 1123/25, letter, 1813.
[25] B.M. O.S. 2″ orig. drawings, sheet 320 (1827).
[26] All Souls mun., Horedon maps, Alberbury 3; ibid. Alberbury deeds 165, 168, 170 (e); S.R.O. 1123/1.
[27] Q. Sess. Rolls, 82, 86.
[28] B.M. O.S. 2″ orig. drawings, sheet 199 (1816).

[29] S.P.L., Deeds 3012.
[30] Ibid. 2860, 2862; S.R.O. 166 uncat., deed, 1709; ibid. 523/16.
[31] T.S.A.S. 2nd ser. i. 87.   [32] Ibid. 88.
[33] B.M. Add. MS. 21018, f. 278ᵛ.
[34] What follows is based on information supplied by Mr. L. C. Lloyd. The three parishes cannot be considered separately since most burials took place at Alberbury.
[35] Census, 1811.
[36] Ibid. 1801.
[37] Ibid. 1841.
[38] Ibid. 1901.
[39] Ibid. 1961.
[40] Poor Law Abstract, 1803, H.C. 175, pp. 416–17 (1803–4), xiii.
[41] Q. Sess. Orders, iii. 238, 285; Q. Sess., index to Friendly Soc. rules.
[42] D.N.B.
[43] O.S. Nat. Grid SJ 369138. For preliminary report see T.S.A.S. li. 139–45.

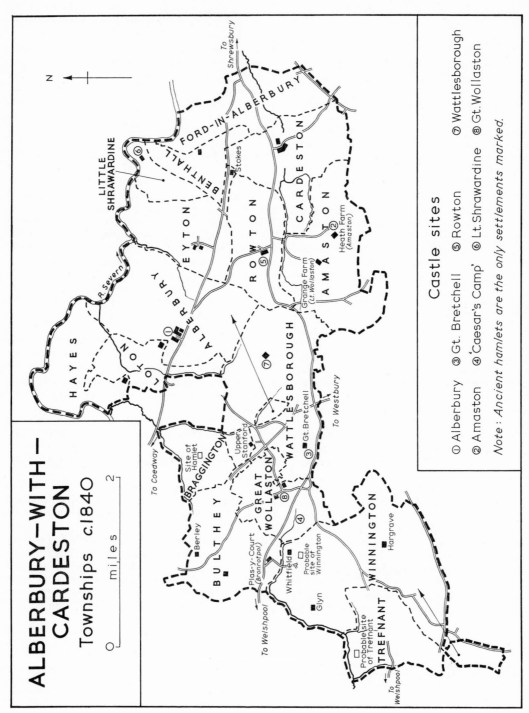

ALBERBURY—WITH—
CARDESTON

Townships c.1840

miles
0   1   2

N

R. Severn

To Shrewsbury

HAYES

LITTLE SHRAWARDINE

BENTHALL

FORD-IN-ALBERBURY

To Shrewsbury

EYTON

Stokes

CARDESTON

ROWTON

Grange Farm
(Lt. Wollaston)

AMASTON

Heath Farm
(Amaston)

ALBERBURY

LOTON

To Coedway

Site of
Hamlet

BRAGGINGTON

Berley

Upper
Stanford

WATTLESBOROUGH

Gt. Bretchell

To Westbury

BULTHEY

Plas-y-Court
(Bronrotpol)

GREAT
WOLLASTON

Whitfield

To Welshpool

Glyn

Probable
site of Winnington

WINNINGTON

Hargrave

Probable site
of Trefnant

TREFNANT

To
Welshpool

Castle sites

① Alberbury   ③ Gt. Bretchell   ⑤ Rowton   ⑦ Wattlesborough
② Amaston   ④ 'Caesar's Camp' ⑥ Lt. Shrawardine ⑧ Gt. Wollaston

Note: Ancient hamlets are the only settlements marked.

Based on tithe apportionments and maps, 1840–8

188

'Waetelleburne' which occurs among lands granted to Peterborough Abbey in a forged charter purporting to date from 664 has been somewhat doubtfully identified with Wattlesborough.[44] Shifnal, the Lizard, and Cosford, also named in the charter, lie on the eastern borders of Shropshire, and 'Waetelleburne' is more likely to refer to a vill in the same area.

A number of castle-sites, presumably of 12th-century date, indicate the part played by the parish in the pattern of defence against the Welsh in the country west of Shrewsbury. Most of them were clearly designed to control roads from Wales. Alberbury Castle,[45] on the northern slopes of the breccia outcrop, originally stood above and to the south of the road from Llanfyllin. Wattlesborough Castle,[46] the motte at Great Bretchell,[47] and the motte and bailey at Great Wollaston[48] mark the sites of castles controlling movement up the valley between the Breiddens and the Long Mountain. There is a ring-motte known as 'Caesar's Camp' by the side of Wollaston Brook, south-west of Great Wollaston,[49] and a 'moat' said in the later 19th century to be visible immediately east of Upper Stanford Farm[50] may also have been a ring-motte. The element 'moat' which occurs in several field-names immediately east of Dingle Mill, Trefnant,[51] is perhaps evidence for a further castle-site at the western end of the Breidden–Long Mountain gap.

In addition to the motte and bailey at Little Shrawardine,[52] the north-south route in the east of the parish was controlled by Rowton Castle, standing at its junction with the Welshpool road. Although no masonry remains of this castle have survived, it is known to have stood on the site of the present house.[53] A well-defined ring-motte and bailey stands to the east of Heath Farm, Amaston,[54] on the former road south of Rowton.

There are extensive structural remains of the stone castles of Alberbury and Wattlesborough, which were occupied as manor-houses until the 14th and 18th centuries respectively. Rowton Castle was rebuilt c. 1700[55] and it is possible that the sites at Great Wollaston and Trefnant were occupied during the later Middle Ages, but the remaining castle-sites appear to have gone out of use by the later 13th century.

All the ancient hamlets in Alberbury-with-Cardeston have shrunk since the earlier Middle Ages; 17 are now represented by single farms. The process of shrinkage had in many cases been completed before the close of the Middle Ages, particularly in the Upper Division, but Alberbury, Cardeston, Eyton, and probably Rowton also, were reduced to their present size as a result of estate improvement in the 18th century. A smaller number of medieval houses have survived than is customary in this part of Shropshire. There are several timber-framed houses in the Upper Division, where smaller freeholds were numerous. On the Leighton and Lyster estates, which made up the greater part of the east of Alberbury-with-Cardeston, a great deal of rebuilding took place in the later 18th and early 19th centuries, the normal building material being breccia from estate quarries.

Alberbury, Cardeston, and Rowton, always the largest of the hamlets in the northern lowlands, all stand on the edge of the breccia outcrop. In each case the original plan of these hamlets has been disguised by road diversions, and at Alberbury, by a deliberate re-planning of settlement.

There is no evidence for the size of Alberbury during the Middle Ages, but there were said to be 11 'principal messuages' here in 1588.[56] There were at least 31 houses in Alberbury township in 1662,[57] most of which stood in the hamlet. The former road through Alberbury ran north-westwards on the alignment of the present road from Rowton, passing immediately north of the farm-house at Upper Farm, then forking to enclose a small oval area north-east of the churchyard. The short section of road running eastwards from the churchyard and past the Old Post Office and Green Dragon House is part of the more southerly of these two roads. The other road, the course of which cannot now be traced on the ground, ran north-westwards from Upper Farm and past the southern edge of the farm buildings at Lower Farm. Crossing what later became the gardens of Loton Hall, it passed about 100 yards to the south of the Hall and rejoined the present road to Llanfyllin at Prince's Oak—thus following the line of the Welsh border from Prince's Oak to Loton Brook. The present road running northwards past the castle and the church as far as Lower Farm existed in 1593, but then continued northwards as one of 3 roads from Alberbury to Alberbury Priory. The area north-east of the church, thus bounded by roads on three sides, was presumably a village green. Two houses stood within this enclosure in 1593 but most of the houses then appear to have stood by the roadside to the south and east. The vicarage and the smithy, however, stood to the south of the road north-west of the church, and by 1780 a shop and a workhouse had been built to the north of the churchyard. The hamlet had included 2 alehouses since at least 1539,[58] both of which had 2 hearths in 1662.[59] Richard Parton, publican here between 1662 and 1719,[60] probably occupied an alehouse on the site of the Old Post Office.

The plan of Alberbury was radically changed by Sir Charlton Leighton between 1780 and 1783,[61] when the main road was diverted southwards. The 3 farm-houses then remaining in the hamlet—Upper Farm, Lower Farm, and Genner's Farm—were leased in 1781 to William Flavel, the tenant of Upper Farm.[62] The cottages in the hamlet were

[44] F. M. Stenton, 'Medehamstede and its colonies', *Hist. Essays in honour of James Tait* (Manchester, 1933), 314.
[45] See p. 196.
[46] See pp. 197–8.
[47] *T.S.A.S.* liii. 88.
[48] Ibid.; *V.C.H. Salop.* i. 401–2.
[49] *T.S.A.S.* liii. 85; *V.C.H. Salop.* i. 382.
[50] S.P.L., MS. 240, p. 52.
[51] Alberbury par. rec., Trefnant tithe appt.
[52] *V.C.H. Salop.* i. 390.
[53] All Souls mun., Horedon maps, Alberbury 1; S.R.O. 49/476.

[54] *T.S.A.S.* liii. 84. See plate facing p. 133.
[55] S.R.O. 49/476.
[56] Loton Hall MSS., lease, 1588. Except where otherwise stated, description of Alberbury based on All Souls mun., Horedon maps, Alberbury 3; *T.S.A.S.* 3rd ser. viii, map facing p. 63; Alberbury par. rec., tithe appt.
[57] E 179/255/35 m. 83d.
[58] Loton Hall MSS., Alberbury ct. r. 1539.
[59] E 179/255/35 m. 83d.
[60] Loton Hall MSS., Alberbury ct. r. 1662–1719.
[61] B.M. Add. MS. 21018, f. 278ᵛ; W.S.L. 350/40/3.
[62] Loton Hall MSS., lease, 1781.

demolished, most of their occupants being provided with new cottages on Wattlesborough Heath.[63] New and more conveniently sited cottages in the hamlet were, however, provided for the schoolmaster and the Loton gardener.[64] The smithy was moved to the junction of the Shrewsbury and Rowton roads :[65] it has since been demolished. Both alehouses appear to have been closed in 1779–80.[66] That on the site of the Old Post Office became a shop in 1780[67] and the adjoining Green Dragon House seems to have become an alehouse at the same time, continuing in business until the 1890s.[68] The vicarage alone remained on its ancient site until 1867, when a new house was built on an isolated site south-east of the church.[69]

No timber-framed houses remain in the hamlet. The Old Post Office and Green Dragon House, which are brick-built with string courses at first-floor level, date from the earlier 18th century. The Old Post Office has a brick modillion cornice. Apart from the vicarage and a group of Council houses to the east of the hamlet the remaining houses are built of breccia and appear to date from the earlier 19th century. The school was rebuilt in 1845[70] and a cottage to the north of the churchyard is dated 1843. Thus, while the plan of the existing hamlet dates from c. 1780, its houses are for the most part the product of a somewhat later period of building activity, contemporary with the remodelling of Loton Hall and the erection of the Loton and Alberbury Lodges.[71]

The road from Ford Heath, which joins the Welshpool road at Cardeston, now turns northwards west of Cardeston church, but formerly continued westwards past Church Farm, joining the Welshpool road by the group of cottages some 600 yards north-west of the hamlet.[72] The houses in Cardeston originally seem to have stood on both sides of this former road, between the church and the pound, west of Church Farm.[73] There were 20 tenants here in the 14th century[74] and the inhabitants included 2 alesellers and a butcher in 1451.[75] Although some of the 21 Cardeston tenants recorded in 1713[76] lived outside the hamlet, shrinkage does not appear to have taken place here until c. 1785. Church Farm was then rebuilt on the site of 2 former houses[77] and has since been the only farm-house in the hamlet. Its buildings were erected in 1786 on the line of the former road.[78] Of the remaining houses 3 have been built since the Second World War, while Cardeston Manor, The Old School House, and the pair of cottages north of the church all date from the 19th century. A cottage adjoining the west end of

the churchyard and another near Cardeston Brook south of the church have been demolished since 1846.[79]

Rowton, which appears as 'Rutune' in 1086,[80] presumably takes its name from the adjacent Rew Wood. The Domesday manor was said to have replaced 4 pre-Conquest manors[81]—possibly an indication that there were originally 3 other hamlets, since deserted, in the township. Rowton manor had 11 tenants in 1379.[82] There were at least 8 houses in the township in 1662, apart from the manor-house, but none of them contained more than a single hearth.[83] The smithy, closed since c. 1937,[84] has occupied its site at the junction of the Welshpool road with those from Alberbury and Little Shrawardine since at least 1634.[85] In 1602 the hamlet lay to the north of the smithy, along the former road to Little Shrawardine.[86] The pound stood at the junction of this road with that to Alberbury, marking the northern end of the hamlet.[87] By 1848 Rowton consisted only of the smithy and two farms, both the latter being occupied by a single tenant.[88] These 3 houses are all constructed of breccia and date from the early 19th century, but a barn at Home Farm contains much reused timber. Two cottages were built to the west of Home Farm in the later 19th century. Six Council houses on the Alberbury road, Rowton Castle Cottage, and other houses occupied by the staff of the Blind School at Rowton Castle, have been built since 1945. There was an alehouse in the hamlet in 1453,[89] but later references to an alehouse in Rowton[90] probably refer to The Windmill Inn, some 750 yards to the west.

Of the remaining hamlets in the northern lowlands, Loton, Hayes, Benthall, and Little Shrawardine have shrunk to single farms, while Eyton consists of 2 farms and 2 cottages. Loton was a manor in 1086 when its only recorded inhabitant was a single serf.[91] Hayes, deriving its name from the 'haye' or enclosed woodland of the Domesday manor of Loton,[92] is first recorded as a hamlet by this name in 1278[93] and may thus be a relatively late woodland settlement. There is, however, some evidence to suggest that this hamlet was known as Hope (i.e. 'valley settlement') in the earlier 13th century. A tenement in 'la Hope' was then said to lie in the Field of Loton[94] and a path from Hope to Bausley passed through Loton township and adjoined Loton Brook.[95] Richard de Hope appears in 1303 as a witness to a Rowton deed.[96]

Loton and Hayes were both large hamlets in the later Middle Ages. In 1379, when the standard holding in both townships was a single noke

63 B.M. Add. MS. 21018, f. 278[v].
64 Loton Hall MSS., leases, 1780–1.
65 Ibid. 1783; Alberbury par. rec., tithe appt.
66 Q. Sess., alehouse reg.
67 Loton Hall MSS., lease, 1780; Alberbury par. rec., tithe appt.
68 Q. Sess., alehouse reg.; Kelly's Dir. Salop. (1856–91).
69 Alberbury par. rec., churchwardens' accts. 1843–1928.
70 Ed. 7/102/5.
71 The Lodges were built in 1832 and 1849 respectively: datestones.
72 Cardeston par. rec., tithe appt.
73 Ibid.; All Souls mun., Horedon maps, Alberbury 1.
74 C 133/98/30; S.P.L., Deeds 6172.
75 Heref. City Libr. 9133/31.
76 Loton Hall MSS., Cardeston survey, 1713.
77 Ibid. building contract, 1785.
78 Ibid. 1786.

79 Cardeston par. rec., tithe appt.
80 V.C.H. Salop. i. 342.
81 Ibid.
82 S.P.L., Deeds 6172.
83 E 179/255/35 m. 83d.
84 Kelly's Dir. Salop. (1937–41).
85 S.R.O. 1123/7.
86 All Souls mun., Horedon maps, Alberbury 1.
87 Ibid.
88 Alberbury par. rec., Rowton and Amaston tithe appt.
89 Heref. City Libr. 9133/18.
90 Q. Sess., alehouse reg.
91 V.C.H. Salop. i. 325.
92 Ibid.
93 Eyton, vii. 110.
94 All Souls mun., Alberbury deeds 96.
95 Ibid. 97.
96 S.P.L., MS. 75, deed, 1303.

($\frac{1}{4}$ virgate), the 18 tenants of Loton held between them 6 messuages and 7 cottages, while there were 21 tenants at Hayes, holding 17 messuages and 6 cottages.[97] Two alesellers and a butcher lived at Loton in 1451.[98] Some shrinkage probably took place during the 15th century, for in 1442 9 nokes in Loton were said to have been held by a single tenant.[99] The two hamlets, which still contained 18 households in the early 16th century,[1] were depopulated between 1516 and 1532, when both townships were leased to 4 Shrewsbury butchers who were said to have expelled all the tenants and converted the land from tillage to pasture.[2] In 1599 a messuage at Loton and the greater part of its former common fields were leased to a Shrewsbury draper.[3]

There can be little doubt that the site of the medieval hamlet of Hayes is that now occupied by Lower Hayes Farm, west of Loton Brook on rising ground which puts it out of reach of the Severn floods common in this part of the parish. The house, which contained 4 hearths in 1672,[4] is timber-framed but the roof level was raised in the 19th century when its walls were cased in breccia. It is T-shaped, consisting on the ground floor of a hall and kitchen with a central stack and a cross-wing to the south.

The site of medieval Loton is less easy to determine. The hamlet's common fields lay in the centre of the township, between Alberbury village and Upper Hayes Farm.[5] The low-lying area north of Loton brook was known in the 13th century as Loton Moor,[6] while the area contained in the southward projection of the township boundary, along the western edge of the breccia outcrop,[7] was presumably in origin common woodland. The hamlet may have stood on the site of Upper Hayes Farm, on the north-western edge of the common fields, but the present house, built of breccia, dates from c. 1800 and neither the house nor the farm buildings contain any fragments of earlier timber-framed buildings. Loton Hall is a more likely site, although it stands only a few yards from Alberbury village. A substantial house stood here before the Hall became the principal residence of the Leighton family in the early 18th century[8] and the existence of an alehouse at Loton in 1615[9] suggests that the hamlet stood near a main road, as did Loton Hall until the 1780s.

There is no evidence for the size of Eyton during the Middle Ages, but there were at least 12 houses in the township in 1662, 4 of which contained more than one hearth.[10] There were only two large farms at Eyton by 1753,[11] but there were still 4 cottages

in the hamlet in 1842.[12] Three cottages had been built before 1593 by the side of the road to Alberbury Priory, north of Eyton,[13] two of which were still standing in 1842.[14] Trinity chapel, Eyton, which is marked on a map of 1593,[15] but is not otherwise recorded, stood to the west of Lower Eyton Farm in a field called Chapel Bank in 1842.[16]

Upper Eyton Farm and the two surviving cottages at Eyton are of early-19th-century date, but Lower Eyton Farm is a timber-framed house, much altered and cased in brick. A range of buildings to the east of the house contains a quantity of reused timber, including ovolo-moulded ceiling beams, and the barn at the east end of this range has roof-trusses constructed with portions of smoke-blackened cruck blades.

One of the two medieval manors of Eyton, which was said in 1086 to have been held as two manors before the Conquest,[17] was sometimes given the distinctive name Eyton Stokes during the 13th century.[18] There can be little doubt that the two pre-Conquest manors represented two separate settlements—Eyton itself and a hamlet on the site of Stocksfield, a 17th-century timber-framed cottage to the south of the Alberbury road near the North Lodge of Rowton Park. Stocks Field and the adjoining Smithy Field lay within this manor in the later Middle Ages.[19] A path from Eyton to 'le Stockes' is recorded in the 13th century,[20] when William and Thomas de Stockes witnessed a Rowton deed.[21] The same surname was borne by at least two Rowton families in the early 14th century.[22] No house is recorded at Stocks Field until 1516,[23] but there appear to have been about 4 houses here in the early 17th century.[24]

Benthall and Little Shrawardine contained 13 and 12 tenants respectively in 1308,[25] but a few of these held lands in both hamlets or in adjoining settlements and about half the tenants in each hamlet were merely cottars.[26] The hamlets shrank with the growth of large copyhold estates in Ford manor in the later Middle Ages and in 1601 6 tenants held the 12 messuages which still remained in the two hamlets.[27] In 1659 both townships were merged in the copyhold estate of Thomas Griffiths,[28] who built Benthall Farm in the following year.[29] There seems to have been at least one other house at Benthall in 1672[30] and there were still two cottages, in addition to the farmhouse, at Little Shrawardine in 1842.[31]

Benthall Farm[32] is a brick house on a sandstone plinth and is of 3 stories, with string courses at floor levels. The original house was L-shaped and

[97] S.P.L. Deeds 6172.
[98] Heref. City Libr. 9133/31.
[99] Ibid. 9133/33.
[1] Sta. Cha. 2/26/105.
[2] Ibid.
[3] Loton Hall MSS., lease, 1599.
[4] *Hearth Tax, 1672,* 154–5.
[5] See p. 186.
[6] All Souls mun., Alberbury deeds 96.
[7] Alberbury par. rec., tithe appt.
[8] See p. 199.
[9] Q. Sess., alehouse reg.
[10] E. 179/255/35 m. 83d.
[11] S.R.O. 112 uncat., deed, 1753.
[12] Alberbury par. rec., tithe appt.
[13] All Souls mun., Horedon maps, Alberbury 2.
[14] Alberbury par. rec., tithe appt.
[15] All Souls mun., Horedon maps, Alberbury 1, 3.

[16] Alberbury par. rec., tithe appt.
[17] *V.C.H. Salop.* i. 342.
[18] Eyton, vii. 122.
[19] S.P.L., Deeds 337, 12522.
[20] All Souls mun., Alberbury deeds 51.
[21] S.P.L., MS. 75, deed, c. 1300.
[22] Ibid. deeds, 1321, 1341.
[23] S.P.L., Deeds 12522.
[24] All Souls mun., Horedon maps, Alberbury 1; *S.P.R. Heref.* vi. 36, 46, 56.
[25] C 134/5/4.
[26] Ibid.
[27] S.P.L., Deeds 12706.
[28] S.R.O. 169/1.
[29] Datestone.
[30] *Hearth Tax, 1672,* 159.
[31] Alberbury par. rec., tithe appt.
[32] For some description see *T.S.A.S.* 4th ser. vi. 283–5.

was entered by a door in the middle of the south-east wall, but another door was inserted in the west wall *c.* 1700, when a new wing was built to the south-west, externally in the same style as the original house. Although many of the windows have been blocked, several early-18th-century sash windows remain. There is a heavy oak newel stair and panelling of late Jacobean type in one of the bedrooms, but the bolection-moulded panelling, doors, and fireplaces elsewhere in the house date from *c.* 1700. Little Shrawardine Farm is a brick house of early-19th-century date.

The 7 former hamlets on the boulder clay plateau south and west of the breccia outcrop have all shrunk to single farms. Wattlesborough, the largest of these hamlets during the Middle Ages, contained 20 tenants in 1300[33] and 29 in 1379.[34] The 5 Wattlesborough tax-payers of 1542[35] probably all lived in the hamlet, since squatter settlement on the Heath was only beginning at this time, but it is not possible to distinguish residents of the hamlet from squatters in later sources. Wattlesborough Castle, which seems to have been continuously occupied by the lord of the manor until the early 18th century,[36] was the only house on the site of the former hamlet by 1715, when virtually the whole of the medieval common-field area was kept in hand as demesne.[37]

There is some evidence that shrinkage at Amaston and Little Wollaston occurred in the 14th century. Seven tenants were recorded on Amaston manor in 1086[38] and there were at least 8 families in the two hamlets in 1327.[39] In 1379 Amaston manor contained only 4 tenants. Grange Farm, which occupies the site of Little Wollaston, was originally a 4-bay house of cruck construction in which an upper floor and central chimney-stack were inserted *c.* 1600. This must have been the home of a substantial peasant, perhaps Thomas Thornes, who was building up an estate here, 1516–35.[40] It is thus likely that Little Wollaston had shrunk to its present size by the mid-16th century. At Amaston, however, there were several small freeholds in the 16th and 17th centuries and a recognizable hamlet may have survived until the 1690s, when the last of the freeholds was bought into the Rowton estate.[41] Heath Farm, Amaston, on the site of the former hamlet, is built of a mixture of breccia, purplish sandstone, and brick. It dates from *c.* 1800 and contains no internal features from an earlier house.

Although Hayford Farm probably represents a former hamlet, there is no record of anything more than a mill and a single farm on this site since 1281, when Hayford is first recorded.[42] The house, which is brick-built, was probably erected in 1856 as were the farm-buildings.[43] The last fragments of the

mill, to the north of the house, were removed within living memory.[44]

Among the hamlets on the western edge of Wattlesborough Heath only Braggington appears to have been anything more than a single farm by the close of the Middle Ages. First recorded in 1255,[45] it had 16 tenants in 1300 all of whom had Welsh names.[46] In 1471 Braggington was said to be worth only 6*s.* since it had been 'almost wasted by the spoliation of thieves and other malefactors'.[47] Nearly a dozen families were described as resident at Braggington in the earlier 17th century.[48] Some of these may have lived at Lower Braggington and after 1651 no families were recorded here other than the residents of Braggington Hall. The site of the former hamlet appears to have been a D-shaped earthwork, surrounded by a ditch and inner rampart, some 400 yards north-east of the Hall.[49] Evidence found when the site was excavated in 1963 also suggests a final desertion at about 1650. The principal building was a rectangular late-medieval house with a partition at the west end. The house contained the remains of a clay oven with the iron nozzle of a pair of large bellows still in place, and a quanitity of iron slag was found in another part of the site. Pottery finds ranged in date from the 13th to the 17th century.[50]

Although there were 8 tenants at Great Bretchell in 1379,[51] it was normally leased as a pasture to a single tenant in the 15th century[52] and was known as Bretchell Farm by 1515.[53] The present stone-built house dates from the 19th century, but some of the buildings may have been built in 1786.[54] Little Bretchell was a member of Great Wollaston manor when first recorded in 1301.[55] A single house stood there in 1597[56] and there is no evidence that it was ever a hamlet. Upper Stanford (now Stanford Farm), until 1886 a detached part of Bausley township and thus in Wales,[57] was the homestead of the Asterley family from the 17th to the 19th century[58] and, like Great Bretchell, presumably shrank to a single farm in the later Middle Ages. This 17th-century timber-framed house was later cased in stone. Lower Stanford (now The Hole) is first recorded, as a single farm, in 1575.[59]

In spite of the precedent set by the foundation of Alberbury Priory in the early 13th century[60] very few isolated farms were established on cleared woodland in the northern lowlands. Lower Wood Farm and Red Abbey, on the road from Alberbury to the Priory, both stand on the southern edge of the former Alberbury Wood. The former is built of breccia and is dated 1836, while the latter is a brick house of *c.* 1800. No house stood on either site in the 1590s,[61] but a house had been built in the Wood

[33] C 133/98/30.
[34] S.P.L., Deeds 6172.
[35] E 179/166/169.
[36] See p. 198.
[37] Loton Hall MSS., Wattlesborough survey, 1715.
[38] *V.C.H. Salop.* i. 342.
[39] *T.S.A.S.* 2nd ser. x. 124.
[40] See p. 207.
[41] See pp. 205–7.
[42] C.P. 25(1)/193/5/59.
[43] Datestone.
[44] Ex inf. Mr. J. S. Jones, Hayford Farm.
[45] *Cal. Pat.* 1247–58, 507.
[46] C 133/98/30.
[47] C 140/39/61.
[48] *S.P.R. Heref.* vi. 19–26, 34–158 *passim.*

[49] O.S. Nat. Grid SJ 336140.
[50] *Medieval Arch.* viii. 286, 288.
[51] S.P.L., Deeds 6172.
[52] Ibid. 6173; Heref. City Libr. 9133/33; C 1/44/243.
[53] Loton Hall MSS., lease, 1515.
[54] Ibid. building contract, 1786.
[55] *Cal. Inq. p.m.* iii, p. 506.
[56] S.R.O. 166 uncat., marriage settlement of Thomas Williams, 1597.
[57] *Census,* 1891.
[58] *S.P.R. Heref.* vi. *passim;* title-deeds *penes* Mr. R. C. Edwards, Stanford Farm.
[59] Loton Hall MSS., lease, 1575.
[60] Alberbury Priory is reserved for treatment in *V.C.H. Salop.* vol. ii. See also *T.S.A.S.* 4th ser. xi. 257–303.
[61] All Souls mun., Horedon maps, Alberbury, 2, 3.

by 1611[62] and Lower Wood Farm is recorded in 1714.[63] Farm buildings at Lower Wood Farm were rebuilt in 1787.[64] A demolished cottage at Haywood, close to the Severn and north of Hayes, occupied a site known to have been inhabited in 1610.[65]

Isolated farms are rather more numerous on the former heathlands south and south-west of Cardeston. Cardeston Park Farm presumably occupies a medieval site, but the present large T-shaped farmhouse was built in breccia in 1842[66] and the buildings are dated 1843–71.[67] Wood End Farm, Lower Farm, and Upper Farm (now known as Heath Farm, Cardeston) are also of 19th-century date and no evidence has been found to indicate when these isolated sites were first occupied. Orchard Farm, west of Little Wollaston, probably stands on the site of a house built near 'Badlees' in the 1530s.[68]

The first cottages were said to have been built on Wattlesborough Heath c. 1544.[69] There were about 8 cottages here by 1584[70] and roughly the same number in the earlier 17th century,[71] but by 1711 there were at least 32 cottages in that part of the Heath lying within Wattlesborough manor.[72] The scattered cottages and smallholdings on the eastern fringes of the Heath, near the road running southwards past Orchard Farm towards Stretton Heath, reflect the 17th-century pattern of settlement. The more compact settlement along the Welshpool road to the west is probably the result of rebuilding and re-siting following the inclosure of the Heath c. 1780. Cottagers from Alberbury are said to have been provided with new homes here[73] and the proportion of squatters depending for a livelihood upon their smallholdings seems also to have fallen at this time. Of 16 persons to whom cottages on the Heath were leased, 1782–3, 11 were craftsmen or limeworkers.[74] Brickworks established at Bretchell, Halfway House, and Wattlesborough Heath[75] provided employment when the demand for labour at the lime-works declined in the earlier 19th century.

Alehouses known as The Nag's Head and Marston's House stood on the Heath in the 17th century.[76] The former, which stood near Wattlesborough Lawns, had been demolished by 1708.[77] Marston's House stood on the western edge of the Wattlesborough common fields[78] and is presumably the house on the road from Halfway House to Stanford which was known as Barley Mow House in the 1840s.[79]

Spring Cottage and two houses on the road towards Stretton Heath appear to be the only surviving

17th-century timber-framed squatter cottages on the Heath. Nearly all the remaining houses have been built in breccia by the Leightons of Loton Hall. A few may date from the later 18th century, but from the evidence of the dated houses the main period of building activity appears to have been the years 1830–50. A group of cottages to the west of the lane to Lower Wigmore, most of them brick-built, stand on land belonging in the 19th century to small freeholders.[80] Primitive Methodist chapels dated 1853 and 1893 also stand in this area.

The Upper Division contained 9 hamlets in the Middle Ages. Of these Great Wollaston alone survives as something more than a single farm. Six of these hamlets appear to have stood in the valley to the west of Great Wollaston and 3 on the higher ground to the north and south. Of the latter, Bulthey was probably the hamlet described as 'Bronrotpol secunda' in 1289[81] but no evidence for its size during the Middle Ages has been found. Its site seems to have been one of the two farms, both now called Bulthey Farm, standing at 600 feet and 700 feet respectively on the southern slopes of Bulthey Hill. Both houses are brick-built and of 19th-century date, but the location of Bulthey's common fields suggests that the higher and more westerly of the two farms is the more likely site. The few scattered cottages now known as Bulthey at the north-eastern end of Bulthey Hill, which are constructed of brick or stone, are the product of squatter settlement. Three such cottages on Bulthey Common are recorded in 1685.[82]

A few yards to the east of these cottages the field-name Beverley, at the south-western end of Kempster's Hill,[83] points to the site of the hamlet known as 'Berley' during the Middle Ages.[84] At least 3 families lived at Beverley in the early 17th century[85] and 3 or 4 houses still stood here in 1685.[86] The last survivor of this hamlet is an empty cottage to the south of the lane skirting the foot of Kempster's Hill, which has timber-framed walls and stone gables.

Hargrave, standing at 675 feet on the northern slopes of the Long Mountain, contained 8 tenants in 1353,[87] but had probably shrunk to a single farm by 1540, when the whole township lay in the freehold estate of Reynold Williams of Great Wollaston.[88] There were at least 3 other houses in the township in the early 17th century,[89] but these appear to have been the homesteads of isolated farms on higher ground to the south. Hargrave Farm was probably built by Richard Bagot shortly after 1623,

62 S.P.R. Heref. vi. 41.
63 Ibid. 339.
64 Loton Hall MSS., building contract, 1787.
65 S.P.R. Heref. vi. 40, 55; Loton Hall MSS., lease, 1635.
66 Datestone.
67 Datestones.
68 S.P.L., MS. 69, deeds, 1537, 1539.
69 E 134/Misc. 2474.
70 E 134/26 Eliz. I East./12; E 134/Misc. 2473–4.
71 Loton Hall MSS., depositions, Roger Owen v. Robert and Edward Leighton, c. 1685.
72 Ibid. Wattlesborough ct. r. 1711.
73 B.M. Add. MS. 21018, f. 278v; W.S.L. 350/40/3.
74 Loton Hall MSS., leases, 1782–3.
75 See p. 211.
76 Loton Hall MSS., depositions, Roger Owen v. Robert and Edward Leighton, c. 1685.
77 Ibid. depositions, Edward Leighton v. Roger Owen, 1708.

78 Ibid. depositions, Roger Owen v. Robert and Edward Leighton, c. 1685.
79 Cardeston par. rec., tithe appt.
80 Ibid.
81 Reg. R. Swinfield (C. & Y.S.), 221.
82 Loton Hall MSS., depositions, Roger Owen v. Robert and Edward Leighton, c. 1685.
83 Alberbury par. rec., Bulthey tithe appt.
84 B.M. Eg. Roll 2197; Reg. R. Swinfield (C. & Y.S.), 221; C.P. 25(1)/194/8/26; All Souls mun., Alberbury deeds 24; Bodl. MS. Gough Salop. 4, f. 119v.
85 S.R.O. 166 uncat., marriage settlement of Thomas Williams, 1597; S.P.R. Heref. vi. 36–157 passim.
86 Loton Hall MSS., depositions, Roger Owen v. Robert and Edward Leighton, c. 1685.
87 T.S.A.S. liv. 330.
88 Ibid. 327.
89 S.R.O. 166 uncat., marriage settlement of Thomas Williams, 1597; S.P.L., Deeds 4199.

when he purchased this portion of the Williams estate.[90] It is an L-shaped timber-framed house, now rough-cast, containing on the ground floor a hall with a parlour wing to the east and a chimney stack at the junction of hall and parlour. The hall is jettied and a door on the south front has a timber-framed porch. A kitchen wing was later added to the north.

Clearance of woodland on the slopes of the Long Mountain and on the Glyn plateau in the 15th and 16th centuries led to a radical change in the pattern of settlement in the rest of the Upper Division. It is possible to establish the sites of only 4 of the 6 medieval lowland hamlets. Great Wollaston contained at least 6 houses in the early 17th century,[91] one of which was then an alehouse.[92] The hamlet had probably been reduced to its present size by 1779, when the principal estate here comprised 2 large farms, a smallholding, and a smithy.[93] The two existing farm-houses, to the north and south of the chapel, are brick-built and of 19th-century date, as is the group of stone cottages to the east. The Mount, a brick-cased timber-framed house to the south of the castle motte, was known as 'The Study' in 1670[94] and as 'Mott House' in the 18th century.[95]

Bronrotpol, which stood on the site of Plas-y-Court Farm, contained at least 6 tenants in 1353[96] and at least 3 in 1540.[97] There were 3 cottages here, in addition to the farm-house, in the early 17th century.[98] The name Plas-y-Court first occurs in 1563 in the form 'le place court'.[99] It was perhaps the meeting-place either of the manor court of the Nether Gorther or of that for the manors of Bronrotpol, Trefnant, and Great Wollaston, which were at this time united in the hands of the Williams family.[1] When the farm-house[2] was rebuilt in the earlier 19th century an oak newel stair and a cast iron fireback dated 1678 were retained from an earlier house. The stair has been removed since 1915. Its newels had tall carved finials and fleurs-de-lis carved in low relief on the sides.

Whitfield Farm, 500 yards south-south-west of Plas-y-Court, occupies the site of the medieval hamlet of Whitfield. There were 6 tenants here in 1353,[3] but it has probably been no more than a single farm since 1543.[4] The present brick farm-house dates only from the 19th century; a former house on the same site was said to be 'down' in 1765.[5]

Trefnant—the name means 'brook settlement'—probably stood near the junction of County Brook and Wollaston Brook. Its site is indicated by the 'moat' field-names immediately east of Dingle Mill

(formerly called Trefnant Mill).[6] Trefnant manor contained 9 tenants in 1465,[7] but it is likely that some of these already lived outside the hamlet.

Although Winnington was probably the largest of these western hamlets—it contained 18 tenants in 1353[8]—its site is uncertain. It may be represented by the more northerly of the two farms at Winnington Green, now known as The Green Farm. This is the only house in the Upper Division likely to be of medieval date. It is now a 3-bay house of cruck construction, but may originally have been larger. A chimney stack and upper floor were inserted c. 1600. The mantel above the hall fireplace is carved in low relief with a complex sequence of motifs, including dragons, human figures, and a pierced heart.[9] The other farm at Winnington Green, some 200 yards south of The Green Farm, is a brick-cased timber-framed house of 17th-century date. Both farms, however, were surrounded in the 19th century by small irregularly shaped fields, most of which bore names indicating that they were assarts from the woodland of the Glyn plateau to the west.[10] The Green Farm may thus be an early example of the isolated farm in cleared woodland. Medieval Winnington may, alternatively, have stood nearer to the old Welshpool road, in the vicinity of Winnington Hall or Lower Winnington Farm.

A hamlet known as 'Baghret' in 1292[11] and as 'Vachrige' in the 16th and 17th centuries,[12] seems also to have stood near the old Welshpool road.[13] Glyn is not recorded before the 17th century[14] and Glyn Farm is unlikely to represent a shrunken hamlet. The brick farm-house here is of 19th-century date, but it replaces an earlier house already standing in 1653[15] and containing 3 hearths in 1662.[16]

Most of the remaining farms in the Upper Division stand on or near the old Welshpool road. Lower Winnington, Lane Farm, Trefnant Farm (formerly Hungerhill Farm), and Upper Trefnant (formerly County Brook House) appear to have been rebuilt in brick in the 18th and 19th centuries, but Winnington Hall, Hall Mill, and Trefnant Hall (or Lower Trefnant) are timber-framed. The three latter houses all lay in the Williams estate in the later 16th century.[17] Winnington Hall was first so called in 1614,[18] but a house on this site appears to have been occupied by the Williams family since at least 1543.[19] It passed out of this family in 1668, but was occupied by substantial freeholders until the 1730s.[20] The present house[21] dates from the early 17th century, but it had been partly rebuilt or

[90] S.P.L., Deeds 2903.
[91] S.R.O. 166 uncat., marriage settlement of Thomas Williams, 1597.
[92] Q. Sess., alehouse reg.
[93] S.P.L., Deeds 3019.
[94] S.R.O. 166 uncat., lease, 1670.
[95] Ibid. 552 uncat., survey of Wolley estate, 1765.
[96] T.S.A.S. liv. 330.
[97] Ibid. 327.
[98] S.P.L., Deeds 15753.
[99] Ibid. 2495.
[1] See p. 203.
[2] For description see T.S.A.S. 4th ser. v. 334–5.
[3] Ibid. liv. 330.
[4] S.R.O. 166 uncat., marriage settlement of Robert Williams, 1543.
[5] Ibid. 552 uncat., survey of Wolley estate, 1765.
[6] Alberbury par. rec., Trefnant tithe appt.
[7] B.M. Eg. Roll 2196.

[8] T.S.A.S. liv. 330.
[9] See plate facing p. 216.
[10] Alberbury par. rec., Winnington tithe appt.
[11] B.M. Eg. Roll 2197; Plac. de Quo Warr. (Rec. Com.), 681.
[12] S.P.L., Deeds 2809; S.R.O. 166 uncat., marriage settlement of Thomas Williams, 1597; ibid. marriage settlement of John Williams, 1642.
[13] S.R.O. 166 uncat., deeds, 1666, 1668.
[14] Ibid. deed, 1653.
[15] Ibid.
[16] E 179/255/35 m. 83.
[17] S.R.O. 166 uncat., marriage settlement of Thomas Williams, 1597.
[18] Ibid. marriage settlement of Thomas Williams, 1614.
[19] Ibid. marriage settlement of Robert Williams, 1543.
[20] See p. 208.
[21] For some description see T.S.A.S. 4th ser. iv. 261, 264.

enlarged in brick before 1765.[22] The remaining timber-framed walls were rebuilt in brick in 1849,[23] when a new low-pitched roof was erected. The wall-posts of the former house still remain and a blocked early-17th-century casement window in the south wall retains its original wooden frame. An oak newel stair against the south wall has carved finials and fleurs-de-lis in low relief; another of slightly different design at the north end of the house appears to have been introduced from elsewhere. Finely moulded ceiling-beams, joists, and wall-timbers from the original house have been reused in a nearby barn. A circular brick dovecote, north-west of the house, was built shortly before 1765,[24] but was demolished after 1914.[25] Hall Mill, not recorded before 1670,[26] was probably built not long before this date. The original house, of 2 stories with attics, consisted of 2 timber-framed bays (now brick-cased) with a lateral stack on the north wall. A brick bay has since been added to the east and a kitchen and other outbuildings to the north.

Trefnant Hall,[27] known in the 17th century as the New House, was first so named in 1597, when it was occupied by a tenant of the Williams family.[28] It had been sold by 1653 to Thomas Breeze,[29] whose family were resident until 1705.[30] As originally built in the later 16th century, the Hall was a T-shaped house of 2 stories and its roof was of butt-purlin construction. The ground floor contained a hall and a small buttery, with a lateral stack on the east wall, and two parlours in an unheated south wing. The house was remodelled soon after its purchase by Thomas Breeze. A new east wall, enclosing the lateral stack in the hall, produced the existing L-shaped plan and a heavy oak stair was inserted in the larger of the two parlours. An increase in the assessment of the house from 4 to 8 hearths between 1662 and 1672[31] dates these alterations and suggests that the chimney stack on the south wall, serving fireplaces in the parlours and bedrooms over, was also erected at this time. The two fireplaces on the first floor have bolection mouldings. Some of the external brickwork may date from the 17th century, but the house was extensively repaired by its tenant shortly before 1817.[32]

The former Rose and Crown alehouse, on the old Welshpool road north-east of Hall Mill, was known by the same name in 1767[33] and can probably be identified with the alehouse kept by Ralph Slater of Hargrave, 1613–17.[34] It was still open in 1856, when it was occupied by the Winnington blacksmith,[35] but had closed by 1870.[36]

At least two of the small farmsteads on the upper slopes of the Long Mountain had been established by the close of the 16th century. Mountain Farm, known to have existed in 1602,[37] may stand on the site of a cottage erected by Reynold Williams on Hargrave Common c. 1510[38] and Winnington Lodge Farm appears as 'The Lodge' in 1602.[39] Both these houses are stone-built and probably date from the 18th century, as do most of the isolated farms in the Westbury portion of the Long Mountain.[40]

Settlement on Glyn Common was also a 16th-century development. Old Parr's Cottage, home of the celebrated Thomas Parr, who died in 1635, it is said at the age of 152,[41] is first recorded in 1588.[42] It was burnt down in 1959. Glyn Common Farm, constructed for the most part from reused timber, is a small 2-bay house with a gable stack, but the two remaining houses on the Common are of more recent date.

MANORS. The manor of *ALBERBURY* was held by King Edward before the Conquest and by Roger Fitz Corbet of Roger, Earl of Shrewsbury, in 1086.[43] The Corbets of Caus and their successors were subsequently its overlords. The manor was held as 1 knight's fee in 1242[44] and in 1248 the tenant, Fulk Fitz Warin, acknowledged that his service to his overlord, Thomas Corbet, included suit at the court of Caus every 3 weeks and the provision of a knight or two serjeants for castle-guard at Caus for 40 days during wars with the Welsh.[45] In the course of a dispute shortly before 1255, when Thomas Corbet called Fulk's father a traitor, Fulk rendered back his homage and refused to hold land of Corbet again.[46] On this pretext Corbet attempted to eject Fulk from the manor and the resulting lawsuit was still in progress in 1260.[47] In and after 1468 the manor was said to be held of the Crown as of the barony of Caus.[48]

Ralph the fat, the first recorded tenant of the manor, granted Alberbury church to Shrewsbury Abbey between 1141 and 1155.[49] Fulk Fitz Warin (I), who held estates in the county by 1158,[50] may have succeeded Ralph at Alberbury. His son Fulk Fitz Warin (II) was presumably in possession of the manor c. 1180, when he was involved in a dispute with Shrewsbury Abbey concerning the church.[51] Fulk probably died in 1197.[52] Part of his estates passed to his widow Hawise, who was still living in 1226,[53] but Alberbury was in the hands of his son Fulk Fitz Warin (III) when the latter's estates escheated to the Crown during his rebellion, 1201–3.[54] Fulk, who was styled Fulk de Alberbury c.

[22] S.R.O. 552 uncat., survey of Wolley estate, 1765.
[23] Datestone.
[24] S.R.O. 552 uncat., survey of Wolley estate, 1765.
[25] *T.S.A.S.* 4th ser. iv. 261, 264.
[26] S.R.O. 166 uncat., lease, 1670.
[27] For some description see *T.S.A.S.* 4th ser. iv. 260–1.
[28] S.R.O. 166 uncat., marriage settlement of Thomas Williams, 1597.
[29] Ibid. deed, 1653.
[30] Ibid. deed, 1705.
[31] E 179/255/35 m. 83; *Hearth Tax, 1672,* 154.
[32] S.R.O. 552 uncat., letter, Richard Broughall to J. Probert, 1817.
[33] *S.P.R. Heref.* vi. 449.
[34] Q. Sess., alehouse reg.
[35] *Kelly's Dir. Salop.* (1856).
[36] Ibid. (1870).
[37] All Souls mun., Horedon maps, Alberbury 1.

[38] Loton Hall MSS., copy order of Council of the Marches, c. 1510.
[39] All Souls mun., Horedon maps, Alberbury 1.
[40] See p. 307.
[41] *D.N.B.*; *Salop. Shreds & Patches,* i. 92–97, 154–5.
[42] S.P.L., Deeds 2809.
[43] *V.C.H. Salop.* i. 316.
[44] *Bk. of Fees,* 964, 971.
[45] Eyton, vii. 78–79.
[46] Ibid. 80–81.
[47] Ibid. 80–82.
[48] *Cal. Pat.* 1467–77, 134; C 142/53/2; C 142/426/104.
[49] Eyton, vii. 67.
[50] Ibid. 68.
[51] Ibid. 69.
[52] Ibid. 71.
[53] Ibid.
[54] Ibid. 72; All Souls mun., Alberbury deeds 5.

1220,[55] was lord of the manor in 1242[56] and 1248[57] He appears to have been alive in 1256,[58] but was dead by 1260.[59] He is said to have been blind for the last 7 years of his life[60] and appears to have transferred the manor to his son Fulk Fitz Warin (IV) before 1252.[61] Shortly before his death in 1264[62] Fulk (IV) granted the manor, except the Welshry, to his younger brother, also named Fulk.[63] This was intended as a temporary endowment, pending the provision of lands of equivalent value elsewhere. The younger Fulk, later known as Fulk Glas,[64] remained in possession of the manor, refusing to accept other lands in exchange in spite of lawsuits brought against him by Constance, widow of Fulk Fitz Warin (IV), in 1267[65] and by the latter's son Fulk Fitz Warin (V) of Whittington between 1292 and 1307.[66] Fulk Glas was dead by 1311, when the manor was settled on his son Fulk Glas (II) and his wife Agnes,[67] and in 1320 Fulk Fitz Warin (VI) of Whittington released his claims on the manor.[68]

Fulk Glas (II), who was apparently resident at Alberbury in 1327 and 1332,[69] is known to have been lord of the manor until 1347,[70] but the descent of the manor in the later 14th century is obscure. It appears to have been held in 1375 by Richard de Pontesbury,[71] whose daughter Katherine, then said to have been ravished by evildoers,[72] may be the Katherine, wife of James de la Mare, who held two thirds of the manor in 1415.[73] A reversionary interest in the estate was then vested in Hugh Burgh,[74] but by 1428 the portion of Katherine de la Mare had been acquired by Sir John Talbot, later Viscount Lisle.[75] The latter, who held the manor at his death in 1453,[76] probably had only a life interest, for the manor passed, not to his son Thomas, Viscount Lisle,[77] but to his elder brother John, Earl of Shrewsbury (d. 1460).[78] The latter's son John, Earl of Shrewsbury, obtained livery of the manor in 1468[79] and at his death in 1473[80] Alberbury passed to his son George, Earl of Shrewsbury.[81] George was then a minor, but was granted an annuity of £8 from the manor in 1484[82] and obtained livery while still under age in 1486.[83]

In 1500 George, Earl of Shrewsbury, conveyed the manor to Stephen Kemsey, who immediately exchanged it with Sir Thomas Leighton for other estates in the county.[84] The manor has since descended in the Leighton family and with two exceptions has always passed from father to son. The following members of the family[85] have been lords of the manor: Thomas, 1500–19; John, 1519–32;[86] Joyce, widow of Sir John Leighton, and her second husband Richard Lee, during the minority of John's son Edward, 1532–48;[87] Edward, 1548–93;[88] Thomas, 1593–1600;[89] Robert, 1600–26;[90] Edward, 1626–32;[91] Robert, 1632–89;[92] Edward, 1689–1711;[93] Edward, 1711–56; Charlton, 1756–80; Charlton, 1780–4; Robert (brother), 1784–1819; Baldwin (cousin), 1819–28; Baldwin, 1828–71; Baldwyn, 1871–97; Bryan Baldwin, 1897–1919; Richard Tihel, 1919–57; Michael John, since 1957.

One third of the manor of Alberbury was held in 1415 by Alice, wife of John de Eyton.[94] It had presumably descended to her from her father Roger Marsh,[95] tenant of one of the adjoining manors of Eyton, but he is not known to have had any interest in Alberbury manor. This portion seems to have passed to William Acton of Acton Scott (d. 1463) at his marriage to Margaret, daughter of John de Eyton,[96] and it was held by Thomas Acton at his death in 1537.[97] It passed from father to son in the Acton family during the 16th century and is last recorded as a manor in 1598.[98]

Alberbury Castle was probably built by Fulk Fitz Warin (III) in the early 13th century. Its remains include a rectangular keep, which probably originally contained a first-floor hall, and a curtain wall enclosing an area of about $\frac{1}{4}$ acre. All dressed stone from the interior walls, doorways, and window-openings in the keep has been robbed apart from a fragment of the head of a chamfered sandstone plinth on the west wall and two stones forming part of the splayed reveals of a window on the south wall. The curtain wall may be contemporary with the keep, but it is not possible to identify any original openings. The tympanum of a round-headed doorway to the south-east is dated 1646, but the east and west doorways are 19th-century insertions.

The manor of *WATTLESBOROUGH*, held by Edric before the Conquest, was also in the estate

[55] Eyton, ii. 14.
[56] *Bk. of Fees*, 964, 971.
[57] Eyton, vii. 78–79.
[58] Ibid. 80–81.
[59] Ibid. 82.
[60] Ibid. 78.
[61] Ibid. 79–81.
[62] Ibid. 83.
[63] Ibid. 85.
[64] First so-called in 1292: ibid. 84–85.
[65] Ibid. 84.
[66] Ibid. 84–85; *Abbrev. Rot. Orig.* (Rec. Com.), i. 159.
[67] C.P. 25(1)/194/8/28.
[68] Eyton, vii. 86; Loton Hall MSS., deed, 1320.
[69] *T.S.A.S.* 2nd ser. x. 128; E 179/166/2 m. 5d.
[70] *Feud. Aids*, iv. 241; *Cal. Inq. p.m.* ix, pp. 34–35; *Cal. Close*, 1346–9, 331.
[71] *Cal. Pat.* 1374–7, 226.
[72] Ibid.
[73] C.P. 25(1)/195/21/2–3.
[74] Ibid.
[75] *Feud. Aids*, iv. 255, 261; *Complete Peerage*, viii. 55–58; *Cal. Pat.* 1467–77, 79.
[76] C 139/181/62.
[77] *Complete Peerage*, vii. 58.
[78] Ibid. xi. 704–5; *Cal. Pat.* 1467–77, 133–4.
[79] *Cal. Pat.* 1467–77, 133–4.

[80] *Complete Peerage*, xi. 706.
[81] *Cal. Pat.* 1467–77, 402.
[82] Ibid. 1476–85, 503.
[83] *Complete Peerage*, xi. 706–7.
[84] Loton Hall MSS., deeds, 1500.
[85] For pedigree see S.P.L., MS. 4646, p. 18; ibid. MS. 2789, pp. 86–103; Burke, *Peerage* (1959), 1346–7. For biographical notices see *T.S.A.S.* 4th ser. 25, 29–31, 39, 158; ibid. xii. 6, 36, 42, 217, 223, 239; *Montg. Collect.* v. 431–3; Blakeway, *Sheriffs of Salop.* 16, 24, 74, 80–81, 91, 151, 189, 221–2.
[86] C 142/53/2.
[87] Ibid.; Loton Hall MSS., lease, 1545; C.P. 25(2)/62/496/2 Edw. VI East.
[88] C.P. 25(2)/62/496/2 Edw. VI East.; C 142/239/109.
[89] C 142/239/109; C 142/261/25.
[90] C 142/261/25; C 142/426/104.
[91] C 142/426/104.
[92] A minor in 1632. Wardship granted to William Stevens in 1639; Loton Hall MSS., grant, 1639.
[93] Created a baronet in 1693: Burke, *Peerage* (1959), 1346.
[94] C.P. 25(1)/195/21/2–3.
[95] *Visit. Salop. 1623* (Harl. Soc. xxix), ii. 8.
[96] Ibid.; S.P.L., MS. 2790, pp. 329–30.
[97] C 142/30/55.
[98] C.P. 25(2)/203/40 Eliz. I Mich.

of Roger Fitz Corbet by 1086[99] and was subsequently held as 1 knight's fee under the successors of Roger Fitz Corbet as lords of Caus.[1]

In the course of the 12th century the manor was granted to a member of the family of Corbet of Wattlesborough, whose relationship to the Corbets of Caus is not known.[2] Richard Corbet, who was living c. 1179,[3] was a tenant of Robert Corbet of Caus in the early 13th century.[4] He had been succeeded before 1225 by his son Richard,[5] who held Wattlesborough manor in 1242.[6] Richard's son Robert Corbet of Moreton Corbet, who held the manor in 1255,[7] died in 1300, when it passed to his son Thomas.[8] Before his death in 1310 Thomas settled the manor jointly on himself and his son Robert, who was then a minor.[9] Robert was said to be lord of the manor in 1316[10] and Fulk le Strange, who had possession of the manor in 1322,[11] was probably acting only as Robert's guardian.[12] In 1366 the manor was settled on Robert Corbet and his wife Elizabeth, with remainder to their son Fulk.[13] Robert died in 1375[14] and his widow Elizabeth was probably dead by 1379, when Wattlesborough was among the estates of Fulk Corbet.[15] The latter died in 1382[16] and the wardship and marriage of his daughter and heir Elizabeth were granted to the Queen in 1385.[17] Elizabeth married John Mawddy, who possessed no estate in the manor at his death in 1403.[18] Wattlesborough had probably already been settled on their son Fulk, at whose death in 1414[19] it passed to his sister Elizabeth wife of Hugh Burgh.[20] Fulk's widow Isabel, however, held a third of the manor in dower until her death in 1429, when this passed to Hugh's son John Burgh.[21] John obtained the remainder of the manor at his father's death in the following year.[22] Sir John Burgh died in 1471, leaving as heirs Thomas Leighton (son of his daughter Ancoret), John Newport (son of his daughter Elizabeth), and his daughters Isabel, wife of John Lingen, and Elizabeth, wife of Thomas Mytton.[23] Following a lawsuit brought by Joan, widow of Sir John Burgh, in 1472,[24] Sir John's heirs granted her a life estate in the manor in 1474.[25] Joan was dead by 1501, when the estates of Sir John Burgh were divided among his heirs.[26] The manor of Wattlesborough, with its members, was then allotted to Sir Thomas Leighton[27] and has since followed the descent of Alberbury manor.

The older buildings at Wattlesborough Hall consist of a square tower or keep, a low wing to the north-east of it, and an 18th-century farmhouse built against its south-east wall, probably on the site of an earlier structure.[28] The tower is thought to date from the late 12th century and several of its surviving features support this view.[29] There are no signs that stone curtain walls were attached to it, nor has evidence been found to support the tradition that there were originally four such towers; it is probable that any additional defences consisted of wooden palisades.[30]

All the buildings are of stone, the walls of the tower being faced with fine ashlar masonry and having two flat buttresses at each angle. The tower has three stories and is about 25 feet square externally, the walls being 6 feet thick at the base.[31] There are indications that there was originally a pitched roof covering the two lower floors and that above this the top story consisted of some form of platform behind a defensive parapet.[32] The parapet formerly extended several feet above the heads of the buttresses and contained two loops on each face.[33] There is no trace of a 12th-century entrance on the ground floor, but at first-floor level there is a blocked round-headed opening in the south-east wall, perhaps originally approached by external steps which are now missing. A stone newel stair rises from the first floor upwards in the thickness of the wall at the east angle. At the same level in the north angle there is access to a garderobe, the remains of which, supported on corbels, are visible externally. Spouts to carry away water from the internal roof project through the north-east and south-west walls. Two windows of 12th-century character have survived at first-floor level; elsewhere the windows are evidently of later date.

On the ground floor, below the round-headed opening, is a large pointed doorway, now blocked. This may have been inserted in the late 13th or 14th century, either as an external door or as access to some structure on the site of the present farmhouse. Probably later still, in the 14th or 15th century, the roof was raised to the top of the parapet, giving an extra room on the second floor. This had a small ogee-headed window facing north-east and a more elaborate 15th-century window with two cusped lights in the south-east wall: the latter is now partly obscured by the farm-house roof.

[99] V.C.H. Salop. i. 325.
[1] Bk. of Fees, 964, 971; Rot. Hund. (Rec. Com.), ii. 66; Cal. Inq. p.m. iii, p. 504.
[2] Eyton, vii. 100–1.
[3] Ibid. 102.
[4] Ibid.
[5] Ibid.
[6] Bk. of Fees, 964, 971.
[7] Rot. Hund. (Rec. Com.), ii. 66; Cal. Pat. 1247–58, 507.
[8] Cal. Inq. p.m. iii, p. 504.
[9] Ibid. v, pp. 96–97; Cal. Close, 1307–13, 215.
[10] Feud. Aids, iv. 235.
[11] Cal. Pat. 1321–4, 50.
[12] cf. Cal. Inq. p.m. v, pp. 96–97.
[13] C.P. 25(1)/195/17/9.
[14] Cal. Inq. p.m. xiv, pp. 110–11.
[15] S.P.L., Deeds 6172; Cal. Close, 1381–5, 20.
[16] Cal. Fine R. 1377–83, 373.
[17] Cal. Pat. 1381–5, 545.
[18] C 137/44/34.
[19] C 138/8/34.
[20] Ibid.
[21] C 139/49/32.
[22] C 139/50/47. The manor was in the hands of the Crown during John's minority in 1431: Feud. Aids, iv. 261.
[23] C 140/39/61.
[24] C 1/44/243.
[25] Cal. Close, 1468–76, 359.
[26] T.S.A.S. 4th ser. v. 214–18.
[27] Ibid.
[28] See plate facing p. 217.
[29] It may be noted, however, that there are similarities in layout between Wattlesborough Hall and a number of partly fortified manor houses elsewhere which date from considerably later periods. In these a medieval hall is found in conjunction with a defensive tower wing containing the principal 'chambers' of the house. E.g. Clifton Castle (Westmld.), Branthwaite (Cumb.), Longthorpe (Northants.).
[30] P. A. Barker, article on Wattlesborough Hall in Salop. Mag. April 1963, 26.
[31] E. Blore, 'Wattlesborough Tower', Arch. Jnl. xxv, no. 98 (1868), plans facing p. 98.
[32] Eyton, vii. 108.
[33] Arch. Jnl. xxv. no. 98, plate facing p. 100 (view of c. 1819).

Windows in the rooms below appear to have been inserted or enlarged at the same time.[34] Both upper rooms now have stone fireplaces, probably of 16th-century date.

The north-east wing has been so much altered at various times that its original form and function remain obscure. It contains several slightly pointed single-light windows and this has led to the suggestion that it was built in the 13th century.[35] At some period it had a higher roof-line and an upper story which contained a fireplace and was entered from the first floor of the tower. Possibly this upper story was a timber-framed structure.

Between 1562 and 1567 the Welsh genealogist Griffith Hiraethog visited Wattlesborough and recorded the arms displayed in the glass of the windows and elsewhere.[36] His account gives some idea of the principal rooms in use at that date. The 'hall', which had at least three windows, was probably the first-floor room of the tower; alternatively it may have occupied the farm-house site. A 'stone upper room' may be identified with the second floor room in the tower; this had armorial glass in one window and '13 coats above the chimney'. There was also a 'small standing place above the head of the parlour', which contained both a window and a fireplace. The parlour itself was evidently a large room with 'front windows' and a 'great window'; its walls bore inscriptions as well as shields of arms, some of them 'in the border'. This suggests that the parlour was lined with panelling, surmounted by a carved frieze. Clearly there was no place in the tower for such a room, which may have been situated on the demolished upper floor of the north-east wing or in some structure on the farm-house site.

Wattlesborough remained the chief residence of the Leighton family until c. 1711, when Sir Edward Leighton moved to Loton Hall.[37] It was probably soon after this that the farm-house was built. It is a two-storied building of five bays, one end abutting on the tower, the other having a parapeted gable. The central doorway on the north-east front has a projecting keystone and voussoirs, the window-heads being similarly treated. At about the same period the upper part of the tower seems to have been altered, although it is unlikely that its lower rooms were then in use. In the early 19th century it still had a hipped roof with dormer windows and was crowned by a lantern or turret standing on a square central platform.[38] By the middle of the century the walls had been lowered by several feet and a new roof built.[39] In 1962 uninhabited parts of Wattlesborough Hall were scheduled as an Ancient Monument and soon afterwards the walls were repaired at the joint expense of Sir Michael Leighton, the Ministry of Public Building and Works, and the Shropshire County Council.[40] The large rectangular moated inclosure to the south-west of the house appears to be the 'moat' recorded in 1379.[41]

During the later Middle Ages Wattlesborough manor included Braggington, Great Bretchell, Cardeston, Hayes, and Loton. Braggington was held by Robert Corbet of Wattlesborough when first recorded in 1255[42] and his estate here was confirmed by Peter Corbet of Caus in 1278.[43] Great Bretchell appears to have been a member of one of the two Domesday manors of Marsh in Westbury parish[44] and is first named in 1220, when lands here formed part of the estate claimed by Margaret, widow, of Guy de Marsh, from the heirs of Guy's brother Hugh.[45] It was held by Roger de Marsh in 1242,[46] but the greater part of the hamlet seems to have been acquired before 1270 by Robert Corbet of Wattlesborough.[47] The Eyton family, as successors of Roger de Marsh, appear as mesne lords of Great Bretchell between 1300 and 1430.[48] They may have retained some lands here, for lands at Great Bretchell were accounted part of the manor of Eyton when it was sold to Thomas Hill in 1753.[49] Robert Corbet of Wattlesborough was said in 1301 to hold 11 a. and a meadow in Bretchell of Howell Pigot, lord of Great Wollaston manor.[50] This estate is not again recorded in Wattlesborough manor and was probably at Little Bretchell, a member of Great Wollaston manor at a later period.[51]

CARDESTON manor was held by the freeman Levenot before the Conquest and by one Gilbert as under-tenant of Roger Fitz Corbet by 1086.[52] It was a member of Wattlesborough manor by 1255.[53]

The manor of LOTON was held by Edric before the Conquest and by Roger Fitz Corbet in 1086.[54] It may have passed to Roger's brother Robert, who granted lands called 'Locheton' to Shrewsbury Abbey between 1108 and 1121.[55] This grant, however, is more likely to refer to Loughton in Chetton parish, which was later a possession of the abbey. Like Cardeston Loton was a member of Wattlesborough manor by 1255,[56] but the greater part appears to have been occupied by Eynon ap Griffith as under-tenant of Robert Corbet in the later 13th century.[57] Corbet had, however, obtained possession of Eynon's estate before 1300.[58] Cadogan de Lugton, who was fined for a forest offence in 1184,[59] and Cadogan ap Howel and Cadogan ap Griffith who granted lands at Loton to Alberbury Priory in the earlier 13th century,[60] had perhaps preceded Eynon ap Griffith as under-tenants here.

Hayes can probably be identified with the 'haye' recorded on the Domesday manor of Loton.[61] This

[34] Arch. Jnl. xxv, no. 98, plate facing p. 101. Blore considered that some of the windows were of mid-14th-century date. [35] Ibid.
[36] T.S.A.S. 4th ser. v. 222–4.
[37] Arch. Jnl. xxv, no. 98, 100. Blore's informant was Sir Baldwin Leighton's daughter.
[38] Ibid. plate facing p. 100.
[39] Eyton, vii, plate facing p. 108.
[40] Ex inf. Min. Public Building and Works.
[41] S.P.L., Deeds 6172.
[42] Cal. Pat. 1247–58, 507.
[43] Eyton, vii. 110.
[44] See pp. 315–6.
[45] Eyton, vii. 123–4; Cur. Reg. R. ix. 315.
[46] T.S.A.S. 4th ser. vi. 179–80.
[47] Eyton, vii. 104.

[48] Cal. Inq. p.m. iii, p. 504; C 136/107/46; C 137/44/34; C 139/50/47.
[49] S.R.O. 112 uncat., deed, 1753.
[50] Cal. Inq. p.m. iii, pp. 505–6.
[51] B.M. Add. Ch. 37623.
[52] V.C.H. Salop. i. 325.
[53] Rot. Hund. (Rec. Com.), ii. 66.
[54] V.C.H. Salop. i. 325.
[55] Eyton, vii. 109.
[56] Rot. Hund. (Rec. Com.), ii. 66.
[57] Cal. Inq. p.m. iii, pp. 505–6.
[58] Ibid.
[59] Pipe R. 1185 (P.R.S. xxxiv), 129; ibid. 1193 (P.R.S. N.S. iii), 112.
[60] All Souls mun., Alberbury deeds 37–40.
[61] V.C.H. Salop. i. 325.

seems to have been held in demesne by Roger Fitz Corbet's successors as lords of Caus, for Thomas Corbet was said to hold a free 'haye' at Loton in 1272.[62] In 1278 Peter, son of Thomas Corbet, granted the haye of Loton to Robert Corbet of Wattlesborough.[63]

The Wattlesborough estate remained thus constituted until the earlier 17th century. The manor of *BRAGGINGTON* was settled on Robert Owen at his marriage to Mary, daughter of Sir Thomas Leighton, in 1614[64] and passed from father to son until 1685, the following being owners: Robert Owen, 1614–29; Leighton Owen, 1629–57; Thomas Owen, 1657–85.[65] The last devised a life interest in the estate to his mother Elizabeth,[66] after whose death in 1702[67] it appears to have been held by Thomas's sister Martha, wife of Edward Griffiths, during the infancy of her son Leighton Owen Griffiths.[68] It was held by the following members of the Griffiths family until the early 19th century: Leighton Owen, c. 1717–1748; Samuel (son), 1748–67; Joseph (brother), 1767–72; Leighton Delamere (son), 1772–c. 1828.[69] Braggington was then purchased by Thomas Parr,[70] who held 262 a. here in 1843.[71] It was bought back into the Loton estate by Sir Baldwin Leighton in 1849,[72] but was sold in 1962.[73]

Braggington Hall,[74] built by Thomas Owen in 1675, is a C-shaped 3-story house of brick with sandstone dressings. There are moulded string courses on the north front, which consists of a gabled central block of 3 bays, with projecting gabled wings, each of 2 bays. The mullioned and transomed windows, several of which are now blocked, have splay mouldings and there are two small oval windows in the south wall. The north door is flanked by plain heavy columns. The bases of the columns and the entablature and datestone above are badly weathered. In plan the Hall consists on the ground floor of a large central hall, with a lateral stack on the north wall, a parlour wing to the east, and a kitchen to the west. A finely carved stair in the parlour wing, with raking balusters and tall finials on its newels, was removed shortly before 1913; only its strings and treads now remain. There is a second stair of simpler construction at the west end of the hall. The fireplaces have projecting moulded cornices, that in the hall being ornamented with strapwork.

Hayes was still a member of Wattlesborough manor in 1635,[75] but Sir Thomas Thynne held lands in Hayes, Wattlesborough, and Alberbury at his death in 1642.[76] A pasture at Hayes called Maes Issa was held by Thomas Hunt in 1655[77] and both

Maes Issa and Hayes were the property of Rowland Hunt by 1689.[78] Hayes was owned by the Jenkins family in the 18th century,[79] by John Morris in 1802,[80] and by John Lloyd in 1843.[81] Some part was bought back into the Loton estate in 1860.[82]

A substantial house may have stood on the site of Loton Hall by 1643, when Robert Leighton, a relative of the lord of the manor, lived at Loton.[83] This may be the 5-hearth house which was occupied by Nathaniel Stone in 1662.[84] The oldest part of the present house dates from about 1670–80. It appears originally to have been a two-storied brick building with stone dressings and a hipped roof.[85] On the entrance front, which faces south, the central block is flanked by projecting side wings. In spite of later alterations the 17th-century stone doorway, with its fluted Ionic pilasters, is still in existence. The window above it has Corinthian columns supporting a steep pediment, crowned by a shield of arms with an ornate crest. The hall occupies the whole of the central block and the principal staircase (now altered) is in the east wing. There are indications that the side wings originally projected to the north, giving the house an H-shaped plan.[86]

In the early 18th century a large addition, also of brick with stone dressings, was built along the north side of the house, masking the wings and apparently incorporating them in its structure.[87] The new range, which was both longer and taller than the original building, has three stories and a basement. Its impressive north front is of nine bays and is surmounted by a parapet with balustraded panels. The former central doorway, at one time approached by steps, has been converted into a window; it is flanked by Tuscan pilasters and has a segmental pediment.

Between 1825 and 1839 additions were made at both east and west ends of the house and the exterior of the 17th-century portion was remodelled.[88] This work was all carried out in the then fashionable 'Elizabethan' style. The windows were surmounted by hood moulds and the chimneys given tall clustered shafts. Gables replaced the hipped roofs on the front wings and a small central gable was added. The space between the wings was filled with an arcaded porch of three bays with columns below and a balustrade above. In the same style two detached blocks of stables and outbuildings were erected, flanking the semicircular gravel sweep in front of the house; these apparently replaced earlier buildings in the same position.[89] At this period also a balustraded terrace was constructed along the north front.[90] The last addition to Loton Hall took place in the 1870s, when a large wing in

[62] *Rot. Hund.* (Rec. Com.) ii. 96.
[63] Eyton, vii. 110.
[64] C.P. 25(2)/343/11 Jas. I Hil.; *T.S.A.S.* 4th ser. v. 317.
[65] For pedigree see *T.S.A.S.* 4th ser. v. 316–20.
[66] Ibid. 319–20.
[67] Ibid. 320.
[68] Ibid. 320–1.
[69] For pedigree see ibid. 321, 322–3; S.R.O. 1011 (Griffiths) uncat., abstract of title, 1752–1828; S.P.L., Deeds 6253.
[70] S.R.O. 1011 (Griffiths) uncat., abstract of title, 1752–1828.
[71] Alberbury par. rec., tithe appt.
[72] F. C. Childe, *Extracts from Letters & Speeches, &c., of Sir Baldwin Leighton, Bt.* (Shrewsbury, 1875), 7.
[73] Local inf.
[74] For some description see *T.S.A.S.* 4th ser. v. 313–16.

[75] C.P. 25(2)/477/11 Chas. I East.; Loton Hall MSS., lease, 1622.
[76] C 142/765/47.
[77] S.P.L., Deeds 17447.
[78] S.R.O. 366/148.
[79] S.R.O. 836/73–74; S.P.L., Deeds 3228.
[80] S.P.L., Deeds 17975.
[81] Alberbury par. rec., tithe appt.; Cardeston par. rec., tithe appt.
[82] S.R.O. 1011 uncat., deed, 1796.
[83] Loton Hall MSS., lease, 1643.
[84] E 179/255/35 m. 83d.
[85] Pevsner, *Shropshire*, 175.   [86] Ibid.
[87] The base of the east wing is visible in the cellars.
[88] S.R.O. 1060/46.
[89] *T.S.A.S.* 3rd ser. viii, map facing p. 63.
[90] S.R.O. 1060/46.

the Tudor style was built at an oblique angle at its south-east corner;[91] this contains a lofty ballroom.

In the main building there is 17th-century oak panelling and an open fireplace in the hall. The 18th-century range contains some fine panelled rooms with moulded cornices and fluted pilasters.

Of the two manors of *EYTON* recorded in 1086 the manor later known as Eyton Stokes[92] was held before the Conquest as two manors by Siward and Ulvric.[93] In 1086 it was held as a single manor by Alric of Roger, Earl of Shrewsbury.[94] Alric, who may be identical with a man of the same name who held Stapleton manor before the Conquest,[95] may have been replaced here, as at Stapleton, by Alward Fitz Elmund shortly after 1086, for both manors seem to have formed part of the barony of Montgomery from the time of its creation by Henry I.[96] Eyton was held of William Cauntelow in 1242.[97] On the death of George Cauntelow in 1272 the overlordship passed to Eudes la Zouche in right of his wife Millicent.[98] By 1361, however, the Zouches of Haringworth were accounted mesne lords under the Earl of March.[99]

Roger de Aston, who held this manor of Eyton in 1242,[1] was still in possession *c.* 1251,[2] but by 1255 the manor had passed to Roger Fitz Matthew.[3] Roger de Aston, however, retained some interest here, presumably as mesne lord, for his nephew John le Knight of Aston was said to owe 3s. rent for a moiety of Eyton in 1274.[4] By 1284, when Roger Fitz Matthew is last recorded as lord of this manor,[5] part was said to be held by Roger, son of William de Horton.[6] The latter first occurs at Eyton in 1262.[7] Members of 3 other families had acquired some interest in this manor by the later 13th century, when the Mansells, the Hords, and Roger son of Robert Parfrey of Eyton granted portions of its desmesne and waste lands to Alberbury Priory.[8]

The portion of this manor held by Roger de Horton in 1284 seems to have been acquired by Roger Kynaston of Walford in the later 15th century, for among property acquired by him in 1496 was a chief rent of 3s. formerly held by Thomas Horton.[9] The Kynaston estate in Eyton passed by marriage before 1562 to Robert Corbet of Stanwardine.[10] It was said to comprise a messuage and 32 a. in 1615[11] and is last recorded in the hands of the Corbet family in 1634.[12]

The messuage and virgate in Eyton held by Roger

de la Halle *c.* 1300[13] probably represents another fragment of this manor. John de la Halle was the most highly assessed of the inhabitants of Eyton in 1327 and 1332.[14] This property followed the descent of Oaks manor in Pontesbury until the later 16th century.[15] It was held by the Skirmston family in the 15th century[16] and was described as a manor in 1573, when Margaret Newport appointed a bailiff here.[17] No later evidence for the descent of this estate has been found.

The other Domesday manor of Eyton was held by Elmar before 1066 and by Roger Fitz Corbet in 1086.[18] The latter's successors were subsequently accounted its overlords.[19] Hugh de Marsh, who held lands at Eyton in the time of Henry II,[20] is the first known tenant of this manor. He died before 1210,[21] when his estate passed to his son Robert.[22] In 1220 Margaret, widow of Hugh's eldest son Guy, who had died before his father, unsuccessfully sued Hugh's 9 daughters for dower at Eyton.[23] On Robert's death, before 1221,[24] the manor passed to William de Marsh, who appears to have been Robert's brother.[25] William's son Roger, who held the manor in 1242,[26] was succeeded by his son Roger in the 1270s[27] and the latter's son William de Eyton was lord by 1301.[28] The manor was held by the Eyton family during the 14th century, but had passed by marriage before 1431[29] to William Acton of Acton Scott. It remained in the hands of the Acton family until 1753, when Sir Richard Acton sold it to Thomas Hill of Tern.[30] In 1857 Richard, Lord Berwick, sold the manor to Frederick Lloyd Jones,[31] whose descendants held it until 1948.[32] Upper Eyton Farm was then purchased by Mr. J. A. Davies senior and Lower Eyton Farm by Mr. J. A. Davies junior.[33]

The manor of *ROWTON* was held as 4 manors by 4 thegns before the Conquest, when *AMASTON* manor was held by the freeman Elmund.[34] The two manors had for practical purposes been united by 1086, when Rowton was held by Elmund's son Alward and Amaston by Elmund and Alward jointly.[35] As on Alric's Domesday manor of Eyton these estates presumably became members of the barony of Montgomery early in the 12th century. Robert de Bollers, baron of Montgomery, granted lands at Rowton to Shrewsbury Abbey *c.* 1200[36] and William Cauntelow was overlord in 1251.[37] The overlordship subsequently followed the

[91] Pevsner, *Shropshire*, 175.
[92] Eyton, vii. 122.
[93] *V.C.H. Salop.* i. 342. [94] Ibid.
[95] See p. 164.
[96] Eyton, vi. 109; ibid. vii. 120.
[97] *Bk. of Fees*, 966.
[98] *Cal. Inq. p.m.* iii, p. 19; *Cal. Fine R. 1272–1307*, 15, 18; *Cal. Close, 1272–9*, 68.
[99] *Cal. Inq. p.m.* xiv, p. 350.
[1] *Bk. of Fees*, 966.
[2] Eyton, vii. 121.
[3] *Rot. Hund.* (Rec. Com.), ii. 66.
[4] Eyton, vii. 122; ibid. xi. 107.
[5] *Feud. Aids*, iv. 216.
[6] Ibid.
[7] All Souls mun., Alberbury deeds 103.
[8] Ibid. 25–106 *passim*.
[9] S.P.L., Deeds 103, 107, 126–7.
[10] C.P. 25(2)/200/4 Eliz. I Mich.; *Visit. Salop. 1623* (Harl. Soc. xxviii–xxix), i. 137; ii. 294.
[11] C 142/352/140.
[12] C.P. 25(2)/477/10 Chas. I Mich.
[13] Loton Hall MSS., deed, *c.* 1300.

[14] *T.S.A.S.* 2nd ser. x. 142; E 179/166/2 m. 5d.
[15] See p. 266.
[16] S.R.O. 166 uncat., deeds, 1411, 1451.
[17] Ibid. 1573.
[18] *V.C.H. Salop.* i. 325.
[19] *Bk. of Fees*, 964, 971; *Rot. Hund.* (Rec. Com.), ii. 66; C 136/76/27; C 136/107/46; C 138/180/59.
[20] Eyton, vii. 124.
[21] *Cur. Reg. R.* ix. 315.
[22] Ibid.
[23] Ibid. 169, 315; Eyton, vii. 123–4.
[24] Eyton, vii. 124.
[25] Not his son as suggested by Eyton: ibid., vii. 124–5.
[26] *Bk. of Fees*, 964, 971.
[27] Eyton, vii. 128–9.
[28] All Souls mun., Alberbury deeds 56.
[29] *Feud. Aids*, iv. 261.
[30] S.R.O. 112 uncat., deed, 1753.
[31] Lower Eyton Farm title-deeds *penes* Mr. J. A. Davies.
[32] Ibid. [33] Ibid.
[34] *V.C.H. Salop.* i. 342. [35] Ibid.
[36] *Rot. Hund.* (Rec. Com.), ii. 66.
[37] Eyton, vii. 174.

descent of that of Alric's manor of Eyton. The manor of Rowton and Amaston was held as 1 knight's fee in 1272[38] and in 1284 the moiety of the manor held by John le Poer owed the service of 2 footmen for 40 days in time of war.[39]

Roger de Say was presumably tenant of the manor of Rowton and Amaston by 1208, when he was defendant in a lawsuit concerning 2 virgates in Amaston.[40] He had been succeeded before 1235 by his daughters Amice and Lucy.[41] By 1250 Amice was married to John le Poer and Lucy to Nicholas Meverell,[42] each of whom was said to hold one hide in Rowton and Amaston c. 1251.[43] One virgate had been granted before 1255 to William de Bicton[44] and the tenants of both moieties were involved in a number of lawsuits with other free tenants between 1256 and 1272.[45] Nicholas Meverell was dead by 1272, when his widow Lucy and her second husband Walter de Aylesbury granted a carucate in Rowton to Henry de Bray.[46] This transaction may have been merely a mortgage, for Walter de Aylesbury was still accounted responsible in 1280 for a share of the service due to the overlord.[47] Walter granted all his lands in Eyton and Amaston to Philip son of Hugh Burnell c. 1290.[48] The latter's uncle Robert Burnell held the manor of Rowton in chief at his death in 1292,[49] but Philip himself, who was Robert's heir, was said in 1294 to hold a messuage and land at Rowton as under-tenant of John le Poer, the tenant of the other moiety of the manor.[50] The Burnells appear to have acquired all the lands held here by Walter de Aylesbury, but the descendants of John le Poer retained some estate in the manor during the 14th century. John's son Nicholas le Poer settled a messuage and half-virgate in Amaston on his daughter Amice and her husband Philip de Binweston[51] and in 1318 he settled 2 messuages and one virgate in Rowton on himself and his wife Maud.[52] Nicholas appears, however, to have conveyed the greater part of his estate between 1303 and 1317 to Roger de Ford,[53] whose nephew John de Ford held a capital messuage at Rowton at his death in 1319.[54] The Poer estate is last recorded in 1368, when Gillian, widow of John Poer, released her interest in a messuage, a carucate of land, and rents in Rowton to her son John Poer, Archdeacon of Bath.[55]

The manor of Rowton and Amaston followed the descent of Acton Burnell manor until 1463,[56] but Robert Corbet, tenant of the adjoining manor of Wattlesborough, had become under-tenant here by 1356[57] and at his death in 1375 was said to hold the manor of Nicholas Burnell for £9 a year.[58] Robert's son Fulk, who was under-tenant of the manor in 1379,[59] was succeeded in 1382 by his brother Roger,[60] whose widow Margaret held the manor of Hugh Burnell for the same rent at her death in 1395.[61] Roger's son Robert Corbet came of age in 1405,[62] but no later reference to this under-tenancy had been found.

In 1463 John, Lord Lovell, sold the manor of Rowton and Amaston to the Shrewsbury merchant William Lyster.[63] The manor passed from father to son in the Lyster family[64] until 1698, the following being lords: William, living 1482; Richard, c. 1496–1521; John, c. 1544–58;[65] Richard, c. 1581;[66] Michael, c. 1588–1598;[67] Richard, 1598–1635;[68] Thomas, 1635–56;[69] Richard, 1656–98. Richard Lyster devised the Rowton estate to his grandson Richard,[70] who died in 1766. The estate was then held by the last Richard's widow Anne until her death in 1781, when it passed to Richard's nephew Richard Lyster. It again passed from father to son in this branch of the family[71] until 1863, the following being lords: Richard, 1781–95; Richard, 1795–1807; Richard, 1807–19; Henry, 1819–63. Henry's widow, Lady Charlotte Lyster, made the estate over in 1880 to her nephew Sir Montagu W. Lowry Corry, who was created Baron Rowton in the same year. The latter, who died in 1903, was succeeded by his nephew Major (afterwards Brigadier General) Noel A. Lowry Corry,[72] who sold most of the Rowton estate to Major A. E. Lees shortly before 1922.[73] The estate was purchased by Messrs. Silcocks Ltd. in 1941.[74]

By will dated 1696 Richard Lyster instructed his executors to spend £1,000 in building a house at Rowton 'upon the bank where the old castle stands, or near thereunto'.[75] The provisions of the will appear to have been carried out within the next few years, but no trace can now be found of any structure which might have formed part of the medieval castle. The rectangular brick building which constitutes the core of the present house dates therefore from c. 1700. Its exterior has been largely masked by later alterations but it was originally of two stories

[38] Rot. Hund. (Rec. Com.), ii. 89.
[39] Feud. Aids, iv. 216.
[40] T.S.A.S. 2nd ser. x. 323.
[41] Eyton, vii. 174.
[42] Ibid.
[43] Ibid.
[44] Rot. Hund. (Rec. Com.), ii. 66.
[45] Eyton, vii. 175, 177.
[46] Ibid. 177.
[47] Abbrev. Plac. (Rec. Com.), 198.
[48] Eyton, vii. 176.
[49] Cal. Inq. p.m. iii, p. 50.
[50] Ibid. p. 122.
[51] S.P.L., MS. 75, deed, c. 1300.
[52] Ibid. deed, 1318.
[53] Ibid. deed, 1303; S.P.L., MS. 69, deed, 1315; Cal. Inq. p.m. vi, p. 86.
[54] Cal. Inq. p.m. vi, p. 101.
[55] S.P.L., MS. 75, deed, 1368.
[56] Cal. Inq. p.m. viii, p. 496; C 137/50/39; C 138/54/116; C 139/158/28. See also p. 7.
[57] Cal. Chart. R. 1341–1417, 148.
[58] Cal. Inq. p.m. xiv, pp. 110–11.
[59] S.P.L., Deeds 6172.

[60] Cal. Close, 1381–6, 166.
[61] C 136/86/12; C 137/50/39.
[62] C 137/50/39.
[63] C.P. 25(1)/195/23/3.
[64] For pedigree see S.P.L., MS. 2793, pp. 80, 83; Visit. Salop. 1623 (Harl. Soc. xxix), ii. 328–9. For biographical notices see Owen and Blakeway, Hist. Shrewsbury, i. 277–8, 405, 423, 455; Blakeway, Sheriffs of Salop. 144–5, 239; T.S.A.S. 3rd ser, iv. 261–2; ibid. 4th ser. xii. 16–17, 228–9, 248; Montg. Collect. xxx, 236–41.
[65] E 179/166/165; S.P.L., MS. 69, settlement by Katherine Lyster, 1558.
[66] C.P. 25(2)/201/23 Eliz. I Mich.
[67] C2/Jas. I/W 1/57.
[68] C 142/559/136.
[69] Ibid.
[70] S.R.O. 49/476.
[71] For pedigree see S.P.L., MS. 2793, p. 83; H. L. L. Denny, Memorials of an Ancient House (Edinburgh, 1913), 304–5.
[72] Denny, op. cit. 305; Burke, Peerage (1959), 202.
[73] Kelly's Dir. Salop. (1917, 1922).
[74] Ex inf. Mr. P. W. Powell, Home Farm, Rowton.
[75] S.R.O. 49/476.

with cellars below and attics, lit by dormer windows in the hipped roof, above. The entrance front, facing south-east, probably had a central doorway and five windows across the upper floor. Internally the house was three rooms long by two rooms wide. Two of those at the front retain oak panelling of 1704, restored in 1907,[76] but other original fittings have disappeared.

The first major alterations took place between 1809 and 1812 to the designs of George Wyatt.[77] A three-storied wing was added at the north end of the house and the whole of the north-west front was remodelled. Wyatt used Classical details internally, where an impressive saloon in this style occupies the ground floor of the new wing. The medieval associations of the site evidently suggested a more romantic treatment for the exterior. Hood moulds to the windows and embattled parapets were introduced, as well as a north porch of three Tudor arches. An undated drawing at Rowton Castle shows the north-west front at this stage. The inclusion of one of the square angle turrets belonging to the low-level wing to the west suggests that this addition may also have been of 1809–12. The transformation of the plain house of c. 1700 into the present picturesque group of buildings was completed between 1824 and 1828 by Henry Lyster and his wife, formerly Lady Charlotte Ashley Cooper.[78] They appear to have been responsible for the gabled extension southwards of Wyatt's wing, for the stone facing and Tudor features along the south-east front, and for the massive circular tower at the west corner of the house. The walled courtyard on the lower ground to the west, with its square towers, gatehouse, and embattled outbuildings, dates from 1828.[79] Gen. N. A. Lowry Corry is said to have transferred the principal entrance to the north side of the house.[80] After its acquisition by the Royal Normal College for the Blind in 1941 several temporary and permanent buildings were erected in the grounds and a brick stable block was adapted for use as classrooms. The alleged siege of Rowton Castle during the Civil War is a late-19th-century fabrication which first appeared in print in 1899.[81]

A small estate at LITTLE WOLLASTON, which was not subsequently described as a manor, was held before the Conquest by the freeman Ulviet.[82] This was held by Roger Fitz Corbet in 1086, when it was assessed at ½ hide,[83] and Thomas Corbet of Caus was overlord in 1255.[84] Robert Meriloun, the first recorded tenant, was involved in a lawsuit over a half-virgate at Little Wollaston in 1203.[85] The estate was held in 1255 by Robert

Meriloun[86] and by 1267 it seems to have passed to Robert's brother Richard, whose nephew William then made an unsuccessful attempt to obtain possession.[87] The later history of this property cannot be established. It is presumably represented by one or more of the freehold estates recorded at Little Wollaston in the later Middle Ages, all of which had been acquired by the Lyster family of Rowton before the end of the 17th century.

The hamlets of 'Baghret', Berley, Bronrotpol, Bulthey, Hargrave, Trefnant, Whitfield, and Winnington formed part of the district known since the 13th century as the NETHER GORTHER.[88] Evidence for the earlier history of the Nether Gorther is scanty, but it was probably at one time a member of the Domesday manor of Alreton. Great Wollaston manor, which was not hidated in 1255,[89] was probably in origin also a member of the Nether Gorther, but was granted to a military tenant of Caus barony in the course of the 12th century. The tenants of the lord of Great Wollaston were said to have been drawn into the Welshry of Caus by Thomas Corbet c. 1242[90] and in 1272 they were in the hands of Llewelyn, Prince of Wales.[91] Since there is no indication that the inhabitants of Great Wollaston itself ever held their lands by Welsh tenures, the above probably refers to the tenantry of the Nether Gorther as a whole and suggests that the latter were under the jurisdiction of Great Wollaston manor before 1242. Peter Corbet of Caus was thus simply restoring the Nether Gorther to its earlier condition when, having regained possession of these hamlets from the Welsh, he granted them to the lord of Great Wollaston in 1278, to hold in Welshry by military service only.[92] The arrangement of 1278 does not, however, appear to have been a lasting one. Quo Warranto proceedings were instituted against Peter Corbet in 1292 for having placed these hamlets in Welshry[93] and the Nether Gorther was accounted part of the barony of Caus throughout the later Middle Ages.[94] In 1572 Edward, Lord Stafford, conveyed the reputed manor of Nether Gorther to Richard Hussey,[95] who was succeeded by his son Edward in 1574.[96] The latter leased it for 21 years to Reynold Williams, lord of Great Wollaston manor, in 1580.[97] The manor of Nether Gorther was still in the hands of the Hussey family in 1641[98] and was the property of Philip Eyton in 1704.[99]

In and after 1242 the manor of GREAT WOLLASTON was held as one knight's fee of the barony of Caus.[1] Robert Fitz Rufus, who granted lands at Bronrotpol to Strata Marcella Abbey some

[76] Inscription on panelling.
[77] H. M. Colvin, *Biog. Dict. of Eng. Archit.* 722; Pevsner, *Shropshire*, 236.
[78] Pevsner, *Shropshire*, 236.
[79] Date on buildings. See also plate facing p. 236.
[80] *Salop. Mag.* Feb. 1954, 18.
[81] The first known reference to the siege is in G. W. Fisher, *Annals of Shrewsbury School* (1899), 153 n. A possible foundation for the legend may be the allegation made in 1650 that Sir Thomas Lyster had sent his wife with money for the garrison at Ludlow after the capture of Shrewsbury by the Parliamentary forces: *Cal. Cttee. for Money*, iii. 1185. These references were supplied by Mr. L. C. Lloyd.
[82] *V.C.H. Salop.* i. 324.
[83] Ibid.
[84] *Rot. Hund.* (Rec. Com.), ii. 66.
[85] *T.S.A.S.* 2nd ser. xi. 250; Eyton, vii. 114.
[86] *Rot. Hund.* (Rec. Com.), ii. 66.

[87] Eyton, vii. 115.
[88] i.e. 'Gorddwr', or 'land beyond the water': J. E. Lloyd, *Hist. of Wales*, ii. 734.
[89] *Rot. Hund.* (Rec. Com.), ii. 66.
[90] Ibid. 96.
[91] Ibid. See also C. J. Spurgeon, 'Gwyddgrug Castle', *Montg. Collect.* lvii. 129–36.
[92] B.M. Eg. Roll 2197.
[93] *Plac. de Quo Warr.* (Rec. Com.), 681.
[94] *Cal. Pat.* 1301–7, 55–56, 355; ibid. 1307–13, 586; B.M. Eg. Roll 2196; ibid. Add. Ch. 54409; *T.S.A.S.* liv. 327–30.
[95] C.P. 25(2)/200/14 Eliz. I Hil.
[96] C 142/167/75.
[97] C 3/225/91.
[98] C 142/702/40.
[99] *Q. Sess. Orders*, i. 216.
[1] *Bk. of Fees*, 964, 971; *Rot. Hund.* (Rec. Com.), ii. 66; *Feud. Aids*, iv. 241.

time before 1255, was described as lord of Wollaston.[2] Unless this is merely an alternative name for Robert Pigot, he is likely to have been tenant of the manor during the later 12th century. Robert Pigot, the tenant in 1242,[3] was presumably preceded by his father William, who held lands at Great Wollaston in the early 13th century.[4] Ralph Fitz William, who claimed lands in Wollaston ('Wilagescot') and Aston Pigott in 1221,[5] was probably an earlier member of the Pigot family and may be the Ralph Fitz Pigot who was among the tenants of the barony of Caus in 1180.[6] Robert Pigot, who was last recorded as lord of Great Wollaston in 1278,[7] had been succeeded before 1292 by Howel Pigot.[8] The latter was still living in 1316,[9] but was dead by 1332.[10] In 1311 he had settled part of his estate on his sons Howel, Griffith, and Robert, reserving a life interest to himself.[11] The manor appears to have passed to Peter Pigot, presumably the eldest son of Howel Pigot the elder. Peter, who was resident in Great Wollaston in 1332,[12] died before 1346,[13] leaving as heirs his daughters Parnel and Joan.[14]

Joan's husband, John Corbet of Wollaston, was said to be lord of Great Wollaston in 1346,[15] but probably held only a moiety of the manor as did his descendant Thomas Corbet in 1428 and 1431.[16] The subsequent history of this moiety is not clear, but it presumably passed successively to the latter's son and grandson, William and Thomas Corbet.[17] On the death of the last named his estate passed to his daughters Joan, wife of John Hopton, and Catherine, wife of John Blount.[18] Hopton was disputing the title of the lord of the other moiety of the manor to lands in Great Wollaston c. 1535.[19]

Parnel, daughter of Peter Pigot, married Hugh de Paunton.[20] Griffith ap Rerith, who held the other moiety of the manor in 1428 and 1431,[21] appears to have been the husband of her grand-daughter Margaret Fairford.[22] Griffith's son and heir, David ap Griffith,[23] succeeded to the estate settled in 1311 on Howel Pigot at the death of the latter's granddaughter Parnel.[24] He is said to have held this moiety of the manor for 70 years and was succeeded by his son William, who held it for 60 years.[25] By 1510 the latter's son Reynold Williams was in possession of the estate,[26] which was described as the manor of Great Wollaston in 1539.[27] Reynold Williams settled an estate at Winnington on his younger son Robert in 1543.[28] He was still alive in 1544,[29] but his son Thomas appears to have been in possession of the Wollaston estate by 1550.[30] The latter was succeeded at his death in 1594[31] by his son Reynold under the terms of a settlement of 1574.[32] The Williams estate included by this date the manors of Trefnant and Bronrotpol in addition to that of Great Wollaston and the greater part of the remainder of the Upper Division.[33] After Reynold's death in 1612,[34] however, his son Thomas, who was said to be 'an unthrift and wilful spender and waster',[35] alienated a great part of the property.[36] The remainder, including Winnington Hall, passed to John Williams of Winnington, great-nephew of Thomas, who sold it in 1668 to John Thomas of Shrewsbury.[37] The subsequent history of this estate, which was not styled a manor after 1612, is discussed elsewhere.[38] The Sparrow family were styled lords of Great Wollaston manor early in the present century.[39]

Within the Nether Gorther the estates of the Paunton family at Trefnant and of Strata Marcella Abbey at Bronrotpol were accounted manors in the later Middle Ages. The manor of *TREFNANT* is first recorded in 1315, when it was settled by Hugh de Paunton on himself and his wife Joan, with remainders to his sons Hugh and William.[40] Hugh de Paunton was resident in 1327,[41] but by 1332 the manor had passed to John de Paunton,[42] whose son John obtained livery in 1394.[43] In 1405 John's widow Joan obtained possession of a third of the manor in dower.[44] The Paunton family is last recorded in 1465, when the manor of Trefnant was in the hands of the lord of Caus as overlord during the minority of John son of William Paunton.[45] By 1574 the manor had been purchased by Thomas Williams from one John Pole.[46] It is last described as a manor in 1612.[47]

Robert Fitz Rufus, lord of Great Wollaston, granted lands at Bronrotpol to Strata Marcella Abbey, probably in the later 12th century.[48] Although this estate was said to amount to a mere half-virgate in 1255,[49] it was styled the manor of

[2] *Cal. Chart. R.* 1300–26, 441; *Rot. Hund.* (Rec. Com.), ii. 66.
[3] *Bk. of Fees*, 964, 971.
[4] All Souls mun., Alberbury deeds 9, 12, 13.
[5] Eyton, xi. 105.
[6] Ibid. vii. 118; ibid. xi. 105–6.
[7] B.M. Eg. Roll 2197.
[8] Eyton, vii. 114; *Cal. Inq. p.m.* iii, pp. 505–6.
[9] *Feud. Aids*, iv. 235.
[10] E 179/166/2 m. 5d.
[11] C.P. 25(2)/194/8/26–27, 37.
[12] E 179/166/2 m. 5d.
[13] *Feud. Aids*, iv. 241.
[14] S.P.L., MS. 2788, p. 73; ibid. MS. 2792, p. 301.
[15] *Feud. Aids*, iv. 241.
[16] Ibid. 255, 261.
[17] S.P.L., MS. 2788, p. 73; *Visit. Salop. 1623* (Harl. Soc. xxviii), i. 134–5.
[18] Ibid.
[19] C 1/822/4–5.
[20] S.P.L., MS. 2792, p. 301; *Visit. Salop. 1623* (Harl. Soc. xxix), ii. 506.
[21] *Feud. Aids*, iv. 255, 261.
[22] S.P.L., MS. 2792, p. 301; *Visit. Salop. 1623* (Harl. Soc. xxix), ii. 506.
[23] Ibid.
[24] C 1/822/4–5.   [25] Ibid.
[26] Loton Hall MSS., copy order of Council of the Marches, c. 1510.

[27] C.P. 40/1103 rot. 100. For pedigree of Williams family see S.P.L., MS. 2792, pp. 301–4; *Visit. Salop. 1623* (Harl. Soc. xxix), ii. 505–7.
[28] S.R.O. 166 uncat., marriage settlement of Robert Williams, 1543.
[29] E 179/166/165.
[30] S.R.O. 1123/3.
[31] C 142/293/60.
[32] Ibid.; C.P. 25(2)/200/16 Eliz. I Trin.
[33] Ibid.; C.P. 25(2)/203/37 Eliz. I Trin.; S.R.O. 166 uncat., marriage settlement of Thomas Williams, 1597.
[34] C 142/332/141.
[35] C 3/468/35.
[36] C.P. 25(2)/343/17 Jas. I Trin.; S.P.L., Deeds 2776, 2903, 3131, 4199; S.R.O. 166 uncat., deed, 1625.
[37] S.R.O. 166 uncat., deed, 1668.
[38] See p. 208.
[39] *Kelly's Dir. Salop.* (1909–29).
[40] C.P. 25(1)/194/9/13.
[41] *T.S.A.S.* 2nd ser. x. 144.
[42] E 179/166/2 m. 5d.
[43] *Cal. Close*, 1392–6, 219; B.M. Add. Ch. 46338.
[44] C.P. 40/576 rot. 435.
[45] B.M. Eg. Roll 2196.
[46] C 3/188/25; C.P. 25(2)/200/16 Eliz. I Trin.
[47] C 142/332/141.
[48] *Cal. Chart. R.* 1300–26, 441; *Rot. Hund.* (Rec. Com.), ii. 66.
[49] *Rot. Hund.* (Rec. Com.), ii. 66.

BRONROTPOL in 1342, when it was leased for life to William Banaster.[50] The latter obtained a further and more favourable lease of the manor in 1345, when he successfully defended his estate here in a lawsuit brought by the abbot, who alleged that the leases had been made without the consent of the chapter.[51] The manor was still in the hands of William's descendants in 1498, when John Banaster of Hadnall held it of the abbey in socage.[52] By 1595, when it was coming to be known as Plas-y-Court, the estate had been acquired by Reynold Williams,[53] whose son Thomas conveyed it to Edward Donne of Shrewsbury in 1619.[54] After Edwards' death in 1629[55] the manor was held in dower by his widow Margaret until her death in 1642,[56] when it passed to Edward's grandson Edward.[57] On the death of the latter's grandson, the Revd. Edward Donne, in 1745, Plas-y-Court passed to his sister and heir Josina, wife of Thomas Gardner of Sansaw.[58] It remained in the Gardner family until *c.* 1917.[59]

ECONOMIC HISTORY. Ten manors in Alberbury and Cardeston are recorded in Domesday Book.[60] Most of the Upper Division seems to have lain in 1086 in the vast manor of Alreton, from which it cannot be distinguished. Welsh devastation probably accounts for the evident poverty of these 10 manors in 1086. Little Wollaston and one of the 2 manors at Eyton were then said to be waste, while Wattlesborough and Rowton had been waste before the Conquest. Wattlesborough and Alberbury were the only manors whose values had risen since 1066 —both were worth 20*s.* in 1086—while the value of 4 other manors had fallen. On 7 of the 10 manors there was said to be land available for a total of some 15 more ploughs, while only 10½ ploughs are recorded on the lands of lords and tenants of all the manors in the two parishes. All the manors were small. Amaston, Rowton, and Wattlesborough were assessed at 2 hides each, but 6 others were of one hide or less and the total assessment of all the manors was only 13 hides. Demesnes, which were recorded only on 4 manors, were correspondingly small. Wattlesborough contained demesne land for 3 ploughs, but land for only one plough was recorded at Alberbury, Cardeston, and Loton. Ten serfs in all were employed on the demesnes of the 4 manors.

In addition to military considerations the small size and relative poverty of the estates here may have been a reason for their consolidation in fewer hands after the Conquest. There appear to have been 13 landowners here before 1066, the smallest estates being those of the 4 thegns who held Rowton as 4 manors and those of Siward and Ulvric, who held as 2 manors the 3 virgates of the manor of Eyton

Stokes. Some consolidation had already taken place before the Conquest, for Edric held Wattlesborough and Loton and Elmar held Benthall and the other manor of Eyton. Only 3 men held the 10 manors of 1086. Six manors formed part of the estates of Roger Fitz Corbet, of which only Cardeston had yet been granted to an undertenant. Elmund and his son Alward held the manors of Rowton, Amaston, and Benthall. Alric, who held the manor of Eyton Stokes, was perhaps succeeded by Alward soon after 1086.[61]

This simple pattern of landownership was modified as a result of the creation of under-tenancies on the estates of the Corbets of Caus in the course of the 12th century. Alberbury manor followed a separate descent until 1500 and Little Wollaston seems to have been broken up into freeholds in the later 13th century, but Cardeston, Loton, and Wattlesborough, granted to the Corbets of Wattlesborough in the 12th century, subsequently remained united. The manors of Rowton and Amaston continued as a single estate until the present century, but Benthall, with Little Shrawardine, was merged in the manor of Ford soon after 1086.[62] The two Domesday manors of Eyton followed separate descents during the Middle Ages.

Scarcely anything is known of the administration of Alberbury manor during the Middle Ages. The manor increased in size from 1 hide to 2 hides between 1086 and 1255[63] and its demesne was apparently still in hand in 1272, when 9 oxen were among property taken by the overlord from the lord of the manor.[64]

The manors of Cardeston, Loton, and Wattlesborough also included the hamlets of Hayes, Braggington, and Great Bretchell. The estate was assessed at 3 hides in 1255[65] and was said to be worth £20 14*s.* 11*d.* in 1300.[66] At the latter date the demesne at Wattlesborough included 240 a. arable.[67] There is no evidence that demesne arable was kept in hand during the later Middle Ages, except at Wattlesborough, where none is explicitly recorded in the hands of the tenants in 1379.[68] By 1414, however, the Wattlesborough demesne yielded only herbage dues.[69] The demesne arable at Cardeston had been leased to the tenants before 1379, when they paid a joint rent of 3 quarters of wheat, 3 quarters of rye, and 6 quarters of oats.[70] A 'noris-hous' and kitchen at Cardeston, from which materials were being removed in 1375,[71] may have been part of a manor-house. Cardeston Park, first recorded in 1374,[72] may have replaced an earlier inclosure, described as the 'Old Park' in 1379.[73] At this time underwood seems to have been the sole produce of the park,[74] but it was fenced in 1415[75] and in 1418 was stocked with the lord's beasts.[76] Meadow land

[50] C.P. 40/344 rot. 559.
[51] Ibid.
[52] *Cal. Inq. p.m. Hen. VII*, ii, pp. 149–50.
[53] C.P. 25(2)/203/37 Eliz. I Trin.
[54] C.P. 25(2)/343/17 Jas. I Trin.
[55] *T.S.A.S.* 4th ser. v. 335.
[56] S.P.L., Deeds 15753; C 142/702/40.
[57] For pedigree of Donne family see *T.S.A.S.* 4th ser. v. 335–7.
[58] S.P.L., MS. 2792, p. 554.
[59] *Kelly's Dir. Salop.* (1885–1917).
[60] *V.C.H. Salop.* i. 316, 324, 325, 342.
[61] See p. 200.
[62] Eyton, vii. 179.

[63] *V.C.H. Salop.* i. 316; *Rot. Hund.* (Rec. Com.), ii. 66.
[64] *Rot. Hund.* (Rec. Com.), ii. 96.
[65] Ibid. ii. 66.
[66] C 132/98/30.
[67] Ibid.
[68] S.P.L., Deeds 6172.
[69] Ibid. 6173.
[70] Ibid. 6172.
[71] Loton Hall MSS., Cardeston ct. r. 1375.
[72] Ibid. 1374.
[73] S.P.L., Deeds 6172.
[74] Loton Hall MSS., Cardeston reeve's acct. 1375.
[75] Heref. City Libr. 9133/37.
[76] S.R.O. 800 uncat., Cardeston reeve's acct. 1418.

in most townships within the estate was still kept in hand in the earlier 15th century,[77] the largest areas being in Loton and Hayes. In 1375 20s. was paid for mowing Hay Meadow at Hayes and a barn was built there for hay. The tenants of Loton and Hayes were required to work for 2 days making hay in the lord's meadows there, 1437–46. A small income was also derived from the sale of underwood in Haywood. This produced 40s. in 1374 and the wood was in hand in 1453.

Alberbury manor was acquired in 1500 by Sir Thomas Leighton, who inherited the Wattlesborough estate in the following year. Both estates have since been held by his descendants. The manorial estate was created for the most part by the conversion of customary tenures into leaseholds—a process already far advanced on the Wattlesborough estate in the 14th century.[78] Minor adjustments in boundaries at Alberbury were made by means of exchanges with the tenants in 1500,[79] and in 1652 the lands of the Leighton, Acton, and All Souls estates in Alberbury township were defined.[80] A portion of the former Park of Alberbury Priory had been acquired before 1542[81] and the estate was further enlarged following the clearance of Alberbury Wood in the later 16th century. Hayes and Maes Issa, alienated before 1639,[82] and Braggington (326 a.), settled on Robert Owen in 1614,[83] were for the most part bought back into the manorial estate in the 19th century. Apart from Lower Stanford Farm, bought in 1836,[84] no other additions to the estate by purchase are known.

The Leighton estate included 770 a. in Cardeston township in 1713,[85] 864 a. in Wattlesborough in 1715,[86] and 1,461 a. in Alberbury parish in 1802.[87] It amounted to 3,788 a. as a whole in the 1840s.[88] Demesne lands at Wattlesborough, valued at £80 in 1599,[89] comprised 406 a. in 1715.[90] Cardeston Park, which was enlarged in the early 16th century,[91] was stocked with 20 cows when leased in 1544.[92] It was valued at £20 a year in 1599, but at £60 in the following year.[93] It was leased by 1713, when it contained 173 a.[94] No lands appear to have been kept in hand in Alberbury township until the early 18th century, when the Leighton family moved from Wattlesborough to Loton Hall. Hayes Farm and other lands bordering the Severn were kept in hand in 1754.[95] Loton Park, which had probably been formed by this date, was disparked shortly before 1776[96] and had been leased to a farmer by 1793.[97]

In 1802, when Loton Park (306 a.) was occupied by William Jellicoe, 93 a. elsewhere was kept in hand.[98] Since 1826 the Park has again been kept in hand.[99] It contained 227 a. in 1842, when a further 60 a. were occupied by the lord.[1]

The manors of Rowton and Amaston had been reduced in size from 4 to 2 hides between 1086 and 1255.[2] At the latter date Shrewsbury Abbey and William de Bicton each held a virgate here[3] and several other free tenancies had been created before the mid-13th century.[4] The moiety of the manor held by Philip Burnell included 114 a. demesne arable in 1294,[5] but the manor-house and demesne of the moiety held by Nicholas le Poer seems to have been granted shortly after 1303 to the free tenant Roger de Ford.[6] Although the lord received nothing more than rents in 1346,[7] the location of the former demesne was still known in the later 14th century. In 1379 6½ nokes of demesne were held by 6 of the Rowton tenants.[8]

The principal freeholds in Rowton, Amaston, and Little Wollaston were gradually bought into the Rowton manorial estate in the 2 centuries following the purchase of the manor by William Lyster in 1463. A messuage in Rowton was acquired from Robert ap Eynon in 1466[9] and a larger property in all 3 townships was purchased from the Sturry family in 1545.[10] It was alleged in 1638 that Thomas Lyster had recently purchased and inclosed the greater part of the Rowton common fields[11] and in 1694 Richard Lyster bought an estate at Little Wollaston from Rowland Hunt and others.[12] In 1783 an allotment of 50 a. was made to Richard Lyster following the inclosure of Wattlesborough Heath.[13] The estate amounted to 1,333 a. in 1848, when it included the whole of the townships of Rowton, Amaston, and Little Wollaston, with the exception of Hayford Farm (104 a.), some 91 a. on Wattlesborough Heath, and 2 smallholdings (10 a.).[14] The Lysters had 339 a. in hand in 1802[15] and were said to have enlarged their demesne c. 1810,[16] but only 168 a. were kept in hand in 1848.[17]

The manor of Eyton Stokes was broken up into a number of freeholds in the later 13th century. Its lands appear to have been held by 3 free tenants in the later 16th century.[18] The other manor of Eyton, which was merged with a third of Alberbury manor, probably in the later 14th century, was said to contain 7 messuages in 1607.[19] The portion of the estate lying in Alberbury township had been sold,

[77] What follows is based on Loton Hall MSS., reeve's accts. 1374–8; S.P.L., Deeds 6173; S.R.O. 800 uncat., reeve's accts. 1418; Heref. City Libr. 9133/33.
[78] S.P.L., Deeds 6172.
[79] Loton Hall MSS., exchange, 1500.
[80] Ibid. Alberbury ct. r. 1652.
[81] All Souls mun., Alberbury deeds 144.
[82] See p. 199.
[83] Ibid.
[84] S.R.O. 1060/46.
[85] Loton Hall MSS., Cardeston survey, 1713.
[86] Ibid. Wattlesborough survey, 1715.
[87] S.P.L., Deeds 17975.
[88] Alberbury par. rec., tithe appts.; Cardeston par. rec., tithe appt.
[89] Longleat MSS., unbound 4308.
[90] Loton Hall MSS., Wattlesborough survey, 1715.
[91] Trans. R.H.S. N.S. viii. 322.
[92] Loton Hall MSS., lease, 1544.
[93] Longleat MSS., unbound 4308.
[94] Loton Hall MSS., Cardeston survey, 1713.
[95] Ibid. rental, 1754.

[96] Ibid. 1776.
[97] B.M. Add. MS. 21018, f. 279.
[98] S.P.L., Deeds 17975.
[99] S.R.O. 1060/46; Kelly's Dir. Salop (1856–1941).
[1] Alberbury par. rec., tithe appt.
[2] V.C.H. Salop. i. 342; Rot. Hund. (Rec. Com.), ii. 66.
[3] Rot. Hund. (Rec. Com.), ii. 66.
[4] Eyton, vii. 175, 177.
[5] Cal. Inq. p.m. iii, p. 122.
[6] Ibid. vi, p. 101.
[7] Ibid. viii, p. 496.
[8] S.P.L., Deeds 6172.
[9] S.P.L., MS. 75, deed, 1466.
[10] Ibid. MS. 69, deed, 1545.
[11] S.P.L., Deeds 17048.
[12] S.P.L., MS. 69, deed, 1694.
[13] Loton Hall MSS., allotment, 1783.
[14] Alberbury par. rec., Rowton and Amaston tithe appt.
[15] S.R.O. 515 uncat., V. Vickers surveys, iv. 368–9.
[16] Ibid. 1123/25, letter, 1810.
[17] Alberbury par. rec., Rowton and Amaston tithe appt.
[18] S.R.O. 1123/1.
[19] C 2/Jas. I/O 3/49.

presumably to the Leighton family, before 1806.[20] In 1843, when the Revd. Richard Noel Hill held 573 a. in the parish, his estate here included virtually the whole of Eyton township and no lands outside.[21]

The most prominent of the comparatively small number of ancient freeholds in the eastern part of Alberbury parish was the estate of Alberbury Priory. Following an abortive grant of the site to Lilleshall Abbey c. 1221–6,[22] Fulk Fitz Warin (III) granted it to the Grandmontine order shortly before 1232.[23] The priory's original estate included, in addition to the site of the conventual buildings, Broad Meadow on the boundary of Alberbury and Eyton townships, the township of Pecknall, a fishery on the Severn, and extensive common rights in Alberbury Wood.[24] A further 24 a. were given at the death of Fulk's wife.[25] A substantial part of one of the manors of Eyton passed to the priory in the later 13th century[26] and small areas of land were acquired in Loton[27] and Great Wollaston.[28] In 1291 the estate was said to include 2 carucates in Pecknall and 3 nokes at Eyton.[29] After having been administered by a succession of royal keepers from 1386, the estate was granted in 1441 to All Souls College, Oxford, its present owners.[30] In the 1840s the College estate amounted to 333 a., of which 224 a. lay in Pecknall.[31]

The greater part of the priory estate was kept in hand until the later 14th century. It was stocked with 6 cows and 60 sheep in 1291[32] and with 8 plough-oxen and a small number of other cattle in 1342, when there were 61½ a. arable.[33] The estate was said to be leased in 1365,[34] and in 1373 Pecknall was let to a group of 4 peasants.[35] Rents at Eyton and Great Wollaston produced 13s. 8d. a year in 1291[36] and the prior was said to receive 41s. 2d. a year in rents in 1345.[37] The rent of £13 6s. 8d. required by the Crown in 1386[38] was probably excessive, since the keeper was imprisoned for arrears in 1396,[39] but the rent was set at £26 13s. 4d. a year after 1414[40] and the estate was leased at the same rent by All Souls until 1475.[41] The rent fluctuated between £21 and £36 a year in the earlier 16th century, but was set at £24 in 1576 and remained unchanged until the early 19th century.[42] After 1441 the estate, together with the great tithes, was let to a single tenant—to various local gentry until 1555, and to members of the Wood family, 1566–1717.[43] The Woods resided

at the Priory and presumably kept some part of the estate in hand, but other College tenants leased the whole estate to under-tenants. In 1550 the College tenant received only £4 2s. 8d. in rents, but the rectory and the great tithes of the English part of the parish alone were then worth £63 11s. 8d.[44] Rents yielded £52 5s. a year in 1708.[45]

A large copyhold estate associated with Benthall Farm was created as a result of piecemeal accumulation by the Griffiths family between the 15th and later 17th centuries. William Hughes, the first-known member of this family, held only a messuage and half a virgate in Benthall in 1437,[46] but his descendant Richard Griffin held 4 messuages and 2 virgates in Benthall and Little Shrawardine by 1490.[47] By 1646 the estate had grown to 3 messuages and 18½ nokes in these two townships.[48] Thomas Griffiths and his son Henry, who acquired a further 6½ nokes in Little Shrawardine from the Dyos family in 1659,[49] built Benthall Farm in the following year.[50] Some 329 a. in Ford parish were added to the estate between 1659 and 1695.[51] The estate was held by Henry Griffiths, 1660–c. 1678; Henry Biggs (I), a kinsman, c. 1678–1688; Henry Biggs (II), 1688–1706; Lucy, widow of Henry Biggs (II), 1706–58.[52] On Lucy's death the estate passed to her son-in-law George Smythe of Nibley (Glos.)[53] and was bought in 1774 by John Ashby,[54] who sold the Ford portion in 1775[55] and sold the remainder (612 a.) to the Severne family in 1788.[56] The estate amounted to some 520 a. during the 19th century[57] and part, including Benthall Farm, is still in the hands of the Severne family.[58]

The two principal freeholds created in the later 13th century by the fragmentation of Rowton and Amaston manors did not survive beyond the 14th century. The Ford family, who held a substantial estate in Ford manor by 1246,[59] had acquired land at Rowton before 1272.[60] Roger de Ford, to whom Nicholas le Poer granted Snod Wood in 1303,[61] also held 6 nokes in Rowton at his death in 1317.[62] Roger's nephew John also held the manor-house and some 2½ virgates in the manor in 1319[63] and further lands were acquired, 1321–41.[64] Ralph de Ford, a free tenant in Rowton in 1379,[65] is the last recorded member of the family. Richard Hord, who held half a virgate in Rowton in the later 13th century,[66] conveyed his estate to Philip Hord in 1332.[67] The

20 S.R.O. 515 uncat., V. Vickers surveys, iv. 238.
21 Alberbury par. rec., tithe appt.
22 T.S.A.S. 4th ser. xi. 291–2.
23 Ibid. 292–3.
24 Ibid.
25 Ibid. 292.
26 All Souls mun., Alberbury deeds passim.
27 Ibid. 96–100.
28 Ibid. 6–15.
29 Tax. Eccl. (Rec. Com.), 163.
30 T.S.A.S. 4th ser. xi. 275–8; Cal. Pat. 1436–41, 563.
31 Alberbury par. rec., tithe appts.
32 Tax. Eccl. (Rec. Com.), 163.
33 C 145/147/13.
34 Cal. Pat. 1364–7, 202.
35 All Souls mun., Alberbury deeds 24.
36 Tax. Eccl. (Rec. Com.), 163.
37 Cal. Close, 1343–6, 563.
38 Cal. Fine R. 1383–91, 136.
39 T.S.A.S. 4th ser. xi. 276.
40 Ibid. 277.
41 All Souls mun., Alberbury leases passim.
42 Ibid.
43 Ibid.
44 S.R.O. 1123/3.

45 Loton Hall MSS., bill of complaint of Peter Wood, c. 1720.
46 S.P.L., Deeds 86.
47 Ibid. 144.
48 Ibid. 157.
49 S.R.O. 169/1.
50 See p. 191.
51 S.R.O. 169/1.
52 For pedigree see ibid. 169/1–3; T.S.A.S. 4th ser. vi. 282–3.
53 S.R.O. 169/3.
54 Ibid.
55 Ibid.
56 Ibid. 248/1.
57 S.P.L., Deeds 17975; Alberbury par. rec., tithe appt.
58 Local inf.
59 See p. 230.
60 Eyton, vii. 177.
61 S.P.L., MS. 75, deed, 1303.
62 Cal. Inq. p.m. vi, p. 86.
63 Ibid. p. 101.
64 S.P.L., MS. 75, deeds, 1321, 1341.
65 S.P.L., Deeds 6172.
66 S.P.L., MS. 75, deed, late 13th cent.
67 Ibid. deed, 1332.

latter, described as of Marton,[68] is perhaps the same as the Philip of Binweston who obtained lands in Rowton and Amaston at his marriage to Amice, daughter of Nicolas le Poer, c. 1300.[69] The Hord family are not found at Rowton after 1334[70] and the small freehold which they held in the adjoining manor of Little Wollaston passed to Adam de Bicton in 1315.[71]

A few other small freeholds in Rowton, Amaston, and Little Wollaston survived until the 17th century, but the descent of only one of them can be traced through the later Middle Ages. The Willaston family of Little Wollaston, who are first recorded in 1271,[72] retained their freehold here until 1516, when William Willaston sold it to Thomas Thornes.[73] The latter acquired further lands in 1529 and 1535[74] and in 1539 settled his estate on his daughter Joyce and her husband Edward Slegge.[75] The estate was sold in 1582 to Edward Davies of Trewern.[76] The Higgons family, who held a freehold in Little Wollaston in 1392,[77] seem to have retained the estate until 1623, when it passed by marriage to George Browne of Edge.[78] It included 2 messuages in Little Wollaston and Amaston when acquired in 1657 by Rowland Hunt[79] and was bought into the Rowton estate in 1694.[80]

Hayford Farm normally followed the descent of Westbury manor, but in 1281 Odo de Hodnet settled the reversion of this estate on his son Richard.[81] The latter's title was in dispute in 1292.[82] Thomas de Hodnet, who held Hayford in 1348,[83] conveyed it in 1374 to John de Ludlow, lord of Westbury manor, in exchange for Henley manor, near Ludlow,[84] and the estate subsequently followed the descent of Westbury manor. It was said to comprise 1 carucate during the Middle Ages[85] and amounted to 112 a. in 1848.[86]

In 1834 an observer remarked that in the eastern or 'level' part of Alberbury the landowners were few 'and persons of property'. In the upper Division or 'hilly parts' of the parish, however, the land was 'very much divided' and belonged 'generally to persons of small property'.[87] The eastern part of Alberbury-with-Cardeston—a total of 6,917 a.— belonged to 19 landowners in the 1840s. Ten of these held fewer than 5 a. apiece and 6,115 a. lay on the 4 large estates of Leighton, Lyster, Hill, and Severne. By contrast 23 proprietors owned the 3,350 a. of the Upper Division at this time. The largest estates were those of the Revd. Laurence Gardner at Bulthey and Winnington (837 a.) and Sir Richard Jenkins at Winnington and Great Wollaston (725 a.); there were 7 other estates of 100–400 a. and 10 of 5–100 a.[88]

The 19th-century freeholds of the Upper Division have a complex history, only part of which can be reconstructed from existing evidence. With the exception of Great Wollaston manor and the reputed manors of Trefnant and Bronrotpol, the Upper Division lay within the Nether Gorther during the Middle Ages and it is evident from the names of tenants in these townships that they were predominantly Welsh until the later 16th century.

Little is known of the size of the manors of Great Wollaston, Trefnant, and Bronrotpol and still less of the manner in which they were administered. Great Wollaston was assessed at 2 hides in 1255[89] and its lord settled a total of 4 messuages and 7 virgates on his 3 younger sons in 1311.[90] Demesne lands at 'Wonnechnohebret', recorded in 1278,[91] can be identified with the so-called manor of Winchnerchbrook, an appurtenance of Great Wollaston manor in the later 16th century.[92] The manor of Trefnant had 8 tenants in 1465, whose rents totalled £4 11s. 6d.;[93] the demesne was then held by 3 tenants for a rent of 18s.[94] By 1343 Strata Marcella Abbey had established a grange at Bronrotpol.[95] Their estate here, then leased to William Banaster, included tenements in Whitfield and common rights in Berley, Bronrotpol, Little Bretchell, and Great Wollaston,[96] but by 1498 it was described as a single messuage.[97]

Until their enfranchisement in 1435[98] the remaining inhabitants of the Nether Gorther were Welsh bond-tenants of the lords of Caus. There were 38 such tenants in Bronrotpol, Hargrave, Whitfield, and Winnington in 1353, each of whom performed 3 days labour services in the autumn.[99] In 1517 the tenants of the Nether Gorther paid only nominal money rents,[1] but in 1590 Reynold Williams did not deny an allegation that he had seized the lands of a number of villeins regardant and had sold them for £600.[2]

Concentration of holdings in fewer hands was evidently a consequence of enfranchisement. By 1540, when there were only 11 free tenants in the 4 English townships of the Nether Gorther, Reynold Williams had by far the largest estate. He owed 14s. 10½d. of the total reserved rent of 39s. 10d. and occupied holdings in all 4 townships, including the whole of Hargrave. Another substantial tenant was William Lingen, with 5 holdings in Winnington, and 3 other tenants held lands in 2 or more townships.[3]

[68] Ibid.
[69] Ibid. deed, c. 1300.
[70] Ibid. deed, 1334.
[71] S.P.L., MS. 69, deed, 1315.
[72] Eyton, vii. 115.
[73] S.P.L., MS. 69, deed, 1516.
[74] Ibid. deeds, 1529, 1535.
[75] Ibid. deed, 1539.
[76] Ibid. deed, 1582.
[77] Ibid. deed, 1392.
[78] Ibid. deed, 1623.
[79] Ibid. deeds, 1655–7.
[80] Ibid. deed, 1694.
[81] C.P. 25(1)/193/5/59; Eyton, ix. 334.
[82] Eyton, vii. 58.
[83] Cal. Inq. Misc. iii, p. 8.
[84] Cal. Pat. 1370–4, 462.
[85] C.P. 25(1)/193/5/59; Eyton, vii. 58; Cal. Close, 1399–1402, 52.

[86] Alberbury par. rec., Rowton and Amaston tithe appt.
[87] Rep. Com. Poor Laws, App. (B 1), Pt. 5, H.C. 44, p. 385 (1834), xxxiv.
[88] Alberbury and Cardeston par. rec., tithe appts.
[89] Rot. Hund. (Rec. Com.), ii. 66.
[90] C.P. 25(1)/198/8/26–27, 37.
[91] B.M. Eg. Roll 2197.
[92] C.P. 25(2)/200/16 Eliz. I Trin.
[93] B.M. Eg. Roll 2196.
[94] Ibid.
[95] C.P. 40/344 rot. 559.
[96] Ibid.
[97] Cal. Inq. p.m. Hen. VII, ii, pp. 149–50.
[98] B.M. Add. Ch. 54409.
[99] T.S.A.S. liv. 330.
[1] B.M. Add. Ch. 54409.
[2] C 3/225/91.
[3] T.S.A.S. liv. 327–30.

By the end of the 16th century nearly the whole of the Upper Division seems to have been in the possession of the Williams family. In 1597 Reynold Williams owned the manors of Great Wollaston, Trefnant, and Bronrotpol and 33 messuages in 8 hamlets.[4] Only one other substantial freehold estate is known at this period. The Porter family were already freeholders at Bronrotpol in 1540[5] and in 1600 Hugh Porter owned 7 messuages and 92 a. land in Bronrotpol, Bulthey, and Winnington.[6]

Most of the 19th-century freeholds thus represent portions of the Williams estate, the greater part of which was sold by Thomas Williams and his son John between 1619 and 1653.[7] The nucleus of the Gardner estate in Bulthey and Winnington was the manor of Bronrotpol, sold to Edward Donne in 1619,[8] but the other freeholds were created somewhat later. The Jenkins estate in Great Wollaston and Winnington was formed as a result of purchases by Richard Jenkins between 1684 and 1700.[9] These included Hargrave House, sold by Thomas Williams to Richard Bagot in 1623, and 3 other fragments of the Williams estate. It amounted to 412 a. by 1779[10] and a further 300 a. had been added by the 1840s.[11]

The remainder of the Williams estate—Winnington Hall and lands in Winnington, Whitfield, Hargrave, and 'Vachrige'—was purchased in 1668 by John Thomas of Shrewsbury.[12] Thomas had already bought most of the former Williams property sold to Sir Thomas Harries of Boreatton c. 1624[13] and he added another small property at Winnington in 1675.[14] In 1681, when the Thomas estate amounted to 678 a., it lay mainly in Great Wollaston and Trefnant,[15] but most of the Great Wollaston property was sold to Richard Jenkins in 1695.[16] The estate passed under the will of John Thomas (d. 1737) to his cousin Mary, wife of Thomas Wolley.[17] Wolley had in the previous year bought the New House, Trefnant, and Old Parr's Cottage.[18] In 1765 the Wolley estate contained 469 a. and included Winnington Hall, Hall Mill, and Trefnant Hall.[19] It had grown to 681 a. by the 1840s but was then in divided ownership.[20]

Most of the Porter freehold was purchased in 1682 by Henry Biggs [21] and followed the descent of Benthall Farm[22] until 1762, when it was sold to John Ambler of Ford.[23] In 1813, when the greater part was sold, it amounted to 239 a.[24] Only 38 a. remained in the possession of Ambler's successor George Tomline in 1843[25] and this was sold in 1855.[26]

Only 30 tenants—9 villeins, 17 bordars, and 4 radmen—are recorded in the 10 Alberbury manors of 1086.[27] By 1300 there were 40 tenants in the manors of Cardeston, Loton, and Wattlesborough and a total of 92 tenants are recorded in 1379 in the 5 manors then administered with Wattlesborough. In 1300 the 24 villeins of Wattlesborough and Cardeston each held half a virgate, but at Loton the noke ($\frac{1}{4}$ virgate) was the standard holding and at Braggington, which was held under Welsh tenure, only 2 of the 16 tenants held as much as 20 a. Smallholdings were numerous in the Wattlesborough group of manors in 1379. Thirty tenants then held half a virgate or more—in most cases the standard half virgate of 1300—and 62 occupied holdings of smaller size. Most of the latter lay in Wattlesborough and in Loton and Hayes. In many cases, however, standard holdings were augmented by assarts and portions of demesne, the area of which is not given. There is scarcely any evidence for the size of holdings in the Wattlesborough group in the 15th century. Of 7 holdings recorded in Cardeston court rolls, 1451-3, 4 were of half a virgate and 2 of one noke.[28] Six of 7 holdings recorded at Loton at this time consisted of single nokes as in the 14th century, but John Salter held 9 nokes here before 1442.[29] The township of Great Bretchell, which had 8 tenants in 1379,[30] was being leased as a single farm by 1515.[31]

Rents of customary tenants in Cardeston, Loton, and Wattlesborough produced £6 13s. 4d. in 1300, when a further £1 10s. 8d. was received in tallage.[32] The 22 free tenants of Braggington and Wattlesborough then paid rents of 18s. 10d.[33] The rents of customary and leasehold tenants in the Wattlesborough group totalled £25 17s. 5d. in 1379[34] and £28 10s. 7d. in 1442.[35] In 1300 labour services of 5 days a year were due from the standard half-virgate holdings in Cardeston and Wattlesborough and the same services were owed by holders of nokes in Loton.[36] Somewhat heavier services were due in 1379, when customary tenants in Cardeston, Hayes, and Loton owed from 8 to 10 days a year.[37] Wattlesborough tenants were paying 'worksilver' by 1374[38] and there is no evidence that the services recorded in 1379 were in fact performed.

In 1379 41 of the 92 tenants in the Wattlesborough group were tenants-at-will and a further 25, the nature of whose tenure is not given, were probably of the same status. The remainder included one free tenant and 25 leaseholders. One of the latter held on a 10-year lease, but the remainder had

[4] S.R.O. 166 uncat., marriage settlement of Thomas Williams, 1597.
[5] T.S.A.S. liv. 327.
[6] C 142/298/60.
[7] S.P.L., Deeds 2903, 3008, 3131; C.P. 25(2)/343/17 Jas. I Trin.
[8] C.P. 25(2)/343/17 Jas. I Trin.
[9] S.P.L., Deeds 3014, 3017, 3045, 4200, 4203.
[10] Ibid. 3019.
[11] Alberbury par. rec., Winnington and Great Wollaston tithe appts.
[12] S.R.O. 166 uncat., deed, 1668.
[13] Ibid. deeds, 1624, 1625, 1665; S.P.L., Deeds 3131.
[14] S.R.O. 166 uncat., deed, 1675.
[15] Ibid. 552 uncat., survey of Thomas estate, 1681.
[16] S.P.L., Deeds 3017.
[17] S.R.O. 166 uncat., will of John Thomas, 1727.
[18] Ibid. deed, 1736.
[19] Ibid. 552 uncat., survey and map of Wolley estate, 1765.

[20] Alberbury par. rec., Trefnant and Winnington tithe appts.
[21] S.P.L., Deeds 2880.
[22] Ibid.   [23] Ibid.
[24] S.R.O. 529/10.
[25] Alberbury par. rec., Winnington tithe appt.
[26] S.R.O. 529/58.
[27] Except where otherwise stated, this paragraph is based on V.C.H. Salop. i. 316, 324, 325, 342; C 133/98/30; S.P.L., Deeds 6172.
[28] Heref. City Libr. 9133/17, 18, 31.
[29] Ibid. 17, 18, 31, 33.
[30] S.P.L., Deeds 6172.
[31] Loton Hall MSS., lease, 1515.
[32] C 133/98/30.   [33] Ibid.
[34] S.P.L., Deeds 6172.
[35] Heref. City Libr. 9133/33.
[36] C 133/98/30.
[37] S.P.L., Deeds 6172.
[38] Loton Hall MSS., Wattlesborough ct. r. 1374.

life-leases, most of which were granted between 1355 and 1377.[39]

Rents of customary tenants produced £4 7s. 2d. on Robert Burnell's manor of Rowton in 1292.[40] They also owed 10s. in tallage and their labour services were valued at 4s. 3d.[41] During the greater part of the 14th century Rowton and Amaston were administered with Wattlesborough and in 1379 forms of tenure on both estates were very similar. Five of the tenants were tenants-at-will and 5 had life-leases.[42] There is scarcely any evidence for the medieval tenurial history of other manors in the eastern part of Alberbury-with-Cardeston (or the Lower Division) and what is known of conditions in the Upper Division has been discussed above.

By 1599 the number of tenants in the Wattlesborough group had been reduced to 29.[43] There were then 23 tenants in Alberbury manor.[44] Consolidation of holdings presumably took place shortly after the Alberbury and Wattlesborough estates were united in 1501. The only evidence for this development occurs at Loton and Hayes, which were leased as a single unit to 4 butchers c. 1530.[45] The increase in the number of tenants on the Leighton estate in the 17th and 18th centuries can be accounted for by the proliferation of squatter settlement on Wattlesborough Heath. The 62 tenants of Wattlesborough and Cardeston, 1713–15, included only 2 farms of over 100 a. and 8 of 50–100 a. The remaining tenants held fewer than 25 a. and the 35 such holdings in Wattlesborough were described as 'inclosures'.[46] There were 83 tenants in the whole Leighton estate in 1754[47] and 108 in 1776.[48] A reduction to 99 by 1788[49] was probably a consequence of the inclosure of Wattlesborough Heath and the replanning of Alberbury village c. 1780, when the 3 farms in the village were leased to William Flavel.[50] Large farms were a feature of the estate by 1802, when the portion in Alberbury parish comprised 5 farms of over 100 a. and 40 holdings of under 25 a.[51]

Leasehold, if it had not already become the main form of tenure here, quickly replaced copyhold after the estate passed to Sir Thomas Leighton; no copyholds remained by the 1540s.[52] Too small a proportion of leases for the Leighton estate[53] have survived to establish any general trends. A mixture of 21-year leases and leases for longer terms appear to have been employed until the end of the 18th century. The three-life lease, which was never the predominant type on this estate, remained in use until the 1780s; Flavel's lease of 1781 being the last known three-life lease of a farm. Leases of cottages and smallholdings on Wattlesborough Heath and

in Alberbury village, 1780–3, were all for one or more lives. In addition to covenants for the payment of heriot and suit of court, two tenants were required to perform military service in the later 16th century. Tack-hogs and wood-hens were required, 1592–1622, and small labour services required during this period, were still being specified in cottage leases in the later 18th century.

Rents from the whole Leighton estate totalled £612 in 1599.[54] Only £45 was then paid by the 37 tenants of Alberbury and Cardeston manors,[55] but rack-rents seem to have been introduced shortly afterwards, raising the total rental to £1,047.[56] Rents rose from £1,930 to £2,624 between 1754 and 1776.[57] They averaged £3,768 a year in the decade 1819–28[58] and had risen to £4,641 by the 1860s.[59]

Large farms had been established on the Rowton and Eyton estates by 1802.[60] On the former 339 a. was in hand, 901 a. in 4 farms of over 100 a., and 98 a. in 20 smaller holdings. All but 18 a. of the Eyton estate then lay in 2 large farms. No general evidence for land tenure on the freehold estates of the Upper Division is available until the mid-19th century. John Thomas kept 65 a. in hand in 1681,[61] but no part of the Jenkins, Wolley, or Ambler estates was occupied by their owners in the later 18th century.[62] As on the Leighton estate the three-life lease was still in use on these freeholds at this date.[63] In 1765 424 a. of the 496-acre Wolley estate lay in 3 farms of over 100 a.[64] and a slightly smaller proportion of the Jenkins estate lay in 2 large farms in 1779.[65] The whole Ambler estate was let as a single farm in 1813.[66]

In spite of the contrast in landownership between the Upper and Lower Divisions, there was little, if any, difference in the general size of farms in Alberbury and Cardeston as a whole in the 1840s.[67] About 70 per cent. of the total area lay in 38 farms of over 100 a. but, whereas there were 7 farms of over 300 a. in the Lower Division, only one such farm was to be found in the Upper Division. Eight persons occupied farms of 25–100 a. and about 108 persons occupied smallholdings of 1–25 a., most of the latter being found on Wattlesborough Heath. The small owner-occupier then played a very insignificant role. There were only 6 such persons in Cardeston and the Lower Division, none of whom occupied more than 3 a., but they were somewhat more important in the Upper Division, where 2 of the 7 of them had estates of over 100 a.

Wattlesborough Heath and the western hills provided a large area of common land and as late as 1793 the greater part of the parish was said to be used for grazing.[68] In 1782, when 48 inhabitants of

[39] S.P.L., Deeds 6172.
[40] C 133/63/32.
[41] Ibid.
[42] S.P.L., Deeds 6172.
[43] Longleat MSS., unbound 4308.
[44] Ibid.
[45] Sta. Cha. 2/26/105.
[46] Loton Hall MSS., Cardeston survey, 1713; ibid. Wattlesborough survey, 1715.
[47] Ibid. rental, 1754.
[48] Ibid. 1776.
[49] Ibid. 1788.
[50] Ibid. lease, 1781.
[51] S.P.L., Deeds 17975.
[52] Loton Hall MSS., Alberbury ct. r. 1539–42.
[53] What follows is based on ibid. leases, 1515–1783.
[54] Longleat MSS., unbound 4308.

[55] Ibid.
[56] Ibid.
[57] Loton Hall MSS., rentals, 1754, 1776.
[58] S.R.O. 1060/46.
[59] Ibid.
[60] S.P.L., Deeds 17975.
[61] S.R.O. 552 uncat., survey of Thomas estate, 1681.
[62] Ibid. survey of Wolley estate, 1765; ibid. 529/10; S.P.L., Deeds 3019.
[63] S.R.O. 552 uncat., leases, 1700–92; S.P.L., Deeds, 3004–5.
[64] S.R.O. 552 uncat., survey of Wolley estate, 1765.
[65] S.P.L., Deeds 3019.
[66] S.R.O. 529/10.
[67] This paragraph is based on Alberbury and Cardeston par. rec., tithe appts.
[68] B.M. Add. MS. 21018, f. 279.

the English portion of Alberbury parish paid small tithes on a total of 440 cows and 378 calves, 5 farms had over 20 cows and 14 had 10–19 cows.[69] There appears to have been no significant change in the number of cattle in the parish between 1782 and 1827.[70] Even in the more hilly Upper Division, however, quite a high proportion of the land appears to have been under the plough in the later 18th century. Approximately half (224 a.) of the Wolley estate in Trefnant, Winnington, and Whitfield was arable in 1765.[71] In 1801 crops were grown on 2,690 a. in Alberbury and on 519 a. in Cardeston[72] —a little over a third of the total acreage. Wheat was then the chief crop in both parishes.[73] In the 1840s, when the same area contained approximately equal proportions of arable (4,770 a.) and pasture (4,779 a.), the proportion of arable to pasture was slightly higher in the Upper Division than elsewhere.[74]

The earliest recorded mill in the parish is that at Alberbury Priory. When the site of the priory was granted to them in the 1220s, the monks of Grandmont were given licence to construct mills and mill-pools wherever they wished and to cut whatever leets were necessary to supply water.[75] The mill, which stood to the south of the priory, was fed by means of leets from Alberbury and Eyton Brooks.[76] It was worth only 2s. a year in 1370[77] and presumably fell into decay soon after this date. The site, however, was still known in 1579.[78] Hayford Mill is first recorded in 1281.[79] The two mills there were said to be very decayed in 1607, when the tenant was provided with timber to repair them,[80] and the mill was no longer in use in 1848.[81]

Other water-mills are recorded at Whitfield in 1278,[82] and at Alberbury,[83] Benthall,[84] Cardeston,[85] Wattlesborough,[86] and Great Wollaston[87] during the 14th century. A mill at Hayes, in existence by 1379,[88] was out of repair in 1437[89] and was said in 1446 to have been swept away in a tempest.[90] Dingle Mill, Trefnant, was the only water-mill in the parish still in use in the 19th century.[91] It is first recorded in 1465, when it was leased for 25s. a year,[92] and in 1597, when there were 2 mills on the site, it lay in the Williams estate.[93] Dingle Mill was still working in 1941[94] but has since closed. Hall Mill, Winnington, probably built by a member of the Williams family in the early 17th century, is first recorded in 1670.[95] It was in use in 1733[96] but had probably closed by 1766.[97]

The lack of adequate streams in the area of Wattlesborough Heath probably accounts for the early appearance of windmills along the breccia outcrop between Alberbury and Cardeston. Alberbury windmill, at the southern end of Rew Wood, had been built by 1379.[98] In 1774, when this area formed part of Loton Deer Park, the mill was rebuilt on a new site at Sunny Bank.[99] Part of the stone-built body of the mill is still standing. Rowton windmill, which stood on the site of the Windmill Inn in 1593[1] but is not later recorded, may have been constructed before 1332, when one William the miller was a resident of Rowton.[2] A windmill at Windmill Farm, north-east of Wattlesborough Hall, was known by the nickname 'Many Fingers' in 1579.[3] It was still in use in 1669[4] but was disused by 1767.[5] A fourth windmill, at Cardeston, stood in 1602 on a knoll some 600 yards north-west of the village.[6]

A fishery on the Severn formed part of the original endowment of Alberbury Priory[7] and a fishery and weir at Little Shrawardine, held by the Dyos family in the later 16th and early 17th centuries,[8] is last recorded in 1738.[9] Another weir on the Severn, north-west of Hayes, was said to be disused in 1754.[10]

The breccia outcrop, which is the only exposed rock suitable for building purposes in the drift-covered eastern part of Alberbury-with-Cardeston, was evidently quarried from an early period. It was used in the Bronze Age cist-burial at Eyton[11] and, during the Middle Ages, in the construction of Alberbury Castle and the tower at Alberbury church. The Leighton estate included a 'millstone quarry' worth £100 a year in 1599.[12] The breccia was not, however, extensively used for building purposes until the later 18th century, when it became the principal material used in the rebuilding of farm-houses and cottages on the Leighton and Lyster estates.[13] The latest dated example of its use is in extensions at Wattlesborough school of 1904.

At an earlier period the highly calcareous breccia was more important as a source of lime. Numerous quarries formerly associated with lime-kilns are to be found along the north-eastern boundary of Loton Deer Park, near Rock Plantation at the southern edge of the Park, and alongside the road from Rowton to Cardeston. In 1643 the tenant of a

---

[69] Alberbury par. rec., vicar's accts. of small tithes, 1782.
[70] Ibid. 1782–1827.
[71] S.R.O. 552 uncat., survey of Wolley estate, 1765.
[72] H.O. 67/12/2, 57.
[73] Ibid.
[74] Alberbury and Cardeston par. rec., tithe appts.
[75] T.S.A.S. 4th ser. xi. 292–3.
[76] Ibid. map facing p. 260.
[77] All Souls mun., Alberbury deeds 190.
[78] T.S.A.S. 4th ser. xi, map facing p. 260.
[79] C.P. 25(1)/193/5/59.
[80] S.R.O. 665 uncat., lease, 1607.
[81] Alberbury par. rec., tithe appt.
[82] B.M. Eg. Roll 2197.
[83] Abbrev. Rot. Orig. (Rec. Com.), i. 159.
[84] T.S.A.S. 2nd ser. x. 117.
[85] S.P.L., Deeds 6172.
[86] C 133/98/30.
[87] C.P. 25(1)/198/8/26–7, 37.
[88] S.P.L., Deeds 6172.
[89] Ibid. 6173.
[90] Ibid.
[91] Bagshaw's Dir. Salop (1851).

[92] B.M. Eg. Roll 2196.
[93] S.R.O. 166 uncat., marriage settlement of Thomas Williams, 1597.
[94] Kelly's Dir. Salop. (1941).
[95] S.R.O. 166 uncat., lease, 1670.
[96] Ibid. 552 uncat., lease, 1733.
[97] Ibid. lease, 1766.
[98] S.P.L., Deeds 6172.
[99] Loton Hall MSS., agreement, 1774.
[1] All Souls mun., Horedon maps, Alberbury 3.
[2] E 179/166/2 m. 5d.
[3] T.S.A.S. 4th ser. xi, map facing p. 260.
[4] Loton Hall MSS., lease, 1669.
[5] Ibid. 1767.
[6] All Souls mun., Horedon maps, Alberbury 1.
[7] T.S.A.S. 4th ser. xi. 292.
[8] Hist. MSS. Com. 10th Rep. App. IV, 443; C 2/Jas. I/ D 9/1.
[9] S.R.O. 303/88.
[10] Loton Hall MSS., rental, 1754.
[11] T.S.A.S. li. 142.
[12] Longleat MSS., unbound 4308.
[13] Field Studies, i (1), 102–15.

messuage in Loton was given licence to take stone for lime-burning out of the quarry there,[14] and in 1720 lime-kilns at Rew Wood and Windmill (now Sunny) Bank, were leased to Thomas Smith, a Wrentnall coalminer.[15] By 1754, when the Loton works were said to be worth £20 a year, they were occupied by Peter Rogers.[16] Kilns had been set up near Rock Plantation by 1767.[17] The Cardeston lime-works had been established by 1660, when Cardeston lime was used at Alberbury church.[18] All lime-kilns on the Leighton estate were taken in hand in 1762, but they were apparently leased by 1776.[19] The Loton lime-works were let at £530 a year in 1809 and in 1817 the Cardeston lime-works were closed. Five master-limemen were employed at Loton in 1834, when there were 28 kilns there, and the Loton lime-works were still working in 1869. Royalties of £200 a year were paid on lime burnt in 1754, and of £303 10s. in 1757, when 910 kilns (3,640 tons) were burnt. The works appear to have been most productive c. 1760–90. In 1763 1,395 kilns of lime were burnt and royalties, which produced £600 a year in 1776 and £500 in 1788, had fallen to £116 by 1802. Lime-rock was being burnt at the rate of some 5,000 tons annually in 1825–7, some 4,000 tons annually in 1828–42, and normally less than 2,000 tons annually in 1846–69. Lime-kilns had been established on the Lyster estate at Rowton by 1802, when they were let to the tenant of Little Wollaston Farm.[20] These were reopened in 1841 but closed a year later.[21]

In the area between Halfway House and Braggington, at the north-western end of the Hanwood Coalfield, somewhat desultory coal-mining took place during the 18th and early 19th centuries. A 'mine pit' recorded near Bulthey Hill c. 1685 is the first-known of these workings.[22] In 1700 John Thomas was preparing to establish a coal-work on his Great Wollaston estate.[23] Chapel Field, Great Wollaston, was said to be 'destroyed by coal pits' in 1779[24] and there were pits in Wollaston Piece, east of the hamlet, in the following year.[25] A colliery still existed at Great Wollaston in 1793,[26] but in 1839 all workings here were said to have been abandoned long before.[27] Another colliery had been established at Great Bretchell Farm by 1780, when it was supplying coal for the Leighton lime-works,[28] but it seems to have closed soon afterwards. Another attempt to find coal at Bretchell in 1840 was un-

successful,[29] but a mine here was in use c. 1855–65.[30] The site of the Braggington Colliery, established by 1784,[31] lay north-west of Braggington Hall.[32] The colliery occupied 12 a. in 1802[33] and, although it was said to have closed by 1839,[34] pits at Braggington were still in use in 1853.[35] Trials for coal were made at Cardeston in the 1760s.[36]

Clay suitable for brick manufacture is found at and near Halfway House and has been used for this purpose since the 16th century. Sir Edward Leighton was said to have dug clay in Wattlesborough Heath to make bricks c. 1584[37] and Robert Leighton built two brick-kilns on the Heath c. 1665.[38] During the 19th century at least 3 brick-yards were set up along the Welshpool road. The Red Heart brickyard, at the cross-roads to the east of Halfway House, was leased in 1828 to Thomas Phillips,[39] who was still its tenant in 1848.[40] In addition to quarry- and drainage-tiles 90,000 bricks were produced here in 1828.[41] The yard was closed in 1862, when the clay was nearly worked out.[42] Another brick-yard, immediately east of Wattlesborough school, was occupied by John Lamb in 1848,[43] and the Bretchell Colliery Co. were making brick from clay in Maule Meadow, west of Bretchell, in the 1860s.[44] Both the last-mentioned brick-yards seem to have closed by 1870.[45]

Lead, barytes, and other minerals occurring in faults on Bulthey Hill, along the western parish boundary, were extracted by means of 2 shafts to the north of the Welshpool road and an adit level driven northwards from the valley to the south of the road.[46] The adit had been cut before 1836, when lead and barytes on the hill were leased by the Revd. Laurence Gardner.[47] The mine was again leased in 1871[48] but no production figures are recorded before 1879. Between 1879 and 1914 5,691 tons of barytes were raised but only one ton of lead is recorded.[49] A further 2,700 tons of barytes were raised when the mine was reopened during the First World War.[50]

A weekly market on Tuesdays and a 3-day fair on 24–26 July were established at Wattlesborough in 1272.[51] No later evidence of a market has been found, but the fair was held annually until 1857 in a field called Market Piece, south-east of Wattlesborough Hall.[52] In 1719 the 18 recorded transactions at the fair all concerned horses,[53] but sheep-sales predominated in 1803, when the fair was held on

[14] Loton Hall MSS., lease, 1643.
[15] Ibid. 1720.
[16] Ibid. rental, 1754.
[17] Ibid. lease of Windmill Farm, 1767.
[18] Alberbury par. rec., churchwardens' accts. 1658–79.
[19] What follows is based on S.R.O. 1060/46.
[20] S.P.L., Deeds 17975.
[21] S.R.O. 1060/46.
[22] Loton Hall MSS., depositions, Roger Owen v. Robert and Edward Leighton, c. 1685.
[23] S.R.O. 552 uncat., lease, 1700.
[24] S.P.L., Deeds 3019.
[25] Loton Hall MSS., lease, 1780.
[26] B.M. Add. MS. 21018, f. 279.
[27] Murchison, Silurian System (1839), 82–83.
[28] Loton Hall MSS., lease, 1780.
[29] S.R.O. 1060/46.
[30] R. W. Pocock and others, Geol. Shrews. District (1938), 137, 142; S.R.O. 1011 uncat., papers re Bretchell Brickworks, 1855–66.
[31] Alberbury par. rec., churchwardens' accts. 1773–1809.
[32] O.S. 1" (1st edn.), sheet lx.

[33] S.P.L., Deeds 17975.
[34] Murchison, Silurian System (1839), 62–63.
[35] Geol. Shrews. District, 137.
[36] S.P.L., Deeds 17956–7.
[37] E 134/26 Eliz. I East./12.
[38] Loton Hall MSS., depositions, Roger Owen v. Robert and Edward Leighton, c. 1685.
[39] S.R.O. 1060/46.
[40] Cardeston par. rec., tithe appt.
[41] S.R.O. 1060/46.
[42] Ibid.
[43] Cardeston par. rec., tithe appt.
[44] S.R.O. 1011 uncat., papers re Bretchell Brickworks, 1855–66.
[45] Kelly's Dir. Salop. (1870).
[46] Bull. Geol. Survey, xiv. 41–42.
[47] S.R.O. 261/1.
[48] Ibid. 1011 (Gardner) uncat., lease, 1871.
[49] Bull. Geol. Survey, xiv. 41–42.
[50] Ibid.
[51] Cal. Chart. R. 1256–1300, 184.
[52] Byegones (1878–9), 270.
[53] Loton Hall MSS., toll bk. 1719.

5 August.[54] A few colts were then sold and there were stalls for the sale of cloth and pedlars' ware.[55] In 1284 the lord of the manor obtained licence to establish at Alberbury a weekly market and two annual fairs, in June and September,[56] but there is no evidence that these were in fact established. In 1851 Alberbury was said to have a fair on 8 August, but this probably refers to Wattlesborough Fair.[57]

Alberbury and Cardeston maintained a relatively high proportion of tradesmen until the later 19th century. There were 19 tradesmen among the 97 householders in the two parishes assessed to the poll tax of 1379, including 5 tailors and 2 carpenters.[58] During the 16th and 17th centuries blacksmiths are recorded at Rowton (from 1625), Winnington (from 1661), and Great Wollaston (from 1597), shoemakers at Alberbury, Cardeston, and Great Wollaston, and a butcher at Alberbury.[59] During the first decade of the 18th century Alberbury parish contained at least 28 tradesmen, among them 7 blacksmiths, 4 wheelwrights, 4 tailors, and 3 shoemakers.[60] In spite of extensive squatter settlement, weavers do not seem to have been numerous—only two are recorded in the 17th and early 18th centuries.[61]

A great increase in the number of tradesmen appears to have followed the inclosure of Wattlesborough Heath. In 1851, when there were 259 inhabited houses in Alberbury parish, about 80 persons did not earn their livelihood from agriculture.[62] The lime-kilns and coal mines then required scarcely any full-time labour—only one lime-burner and 4 colliers are recorded—but there were 9 tailors, 6 dressmakers, and 7 shoemakers and 24 persons were engaged in building or allied occupations.[63] The number of tradesmen recorded in the parish fell from 15 in 1870 to 11 by 1900 and to 7 by 1941, when nearly all of them lived at Halfway House.[64] The tradesmen of 1941 included the blacksmith at Alberbury, the Rowton smithy having closed by 1937 and those at Great Wollaston and Winnington by 1891.[65]

LOCAL GOVERNMENT. There are court rolls for Alberbury manor, 1542, 1652, 1659–77, 1711–20, and 1819–32, and for the manor of Wattlesborough and Cardeston 1374–5, 1377, 1539–42, 1574, 1613–16, 1639, 1659–64, 1712–20, and 1819–32.[66] No court rolls are known for the manor of Rowton and Amaston. Inhabitants of the Nether Gorther owed suit at the court of the Welshry of Caus in the later Middle Ages.[67] The lord of Great Wollaston manor held a court until c. 1605[68] and a manor court was held by the lord of Bulthey manor in the later 18th century,[69] but there is no evidence that such courts were held in other townships of the Upper Division. The jurisdiction of the manor courts of Alberbury, Wattlesborough, and Cardeston included view of

frankpledge—the lord of Wattlesborough obtained a confirmation of this privilege in 1356[70]—and the assize of bread and ale. Constables were being appointed at both courts in the 16th and 17th centuries. Two great courts were held annually at Alberbury in the mid-17th century. The three-weekly court baron was still meeting to hear pleas between parties in 1677, but appears to have ceased by 1711, when great courts alone are recorded. By the later 18th century the court's business was restricted to the presentment of a formalized list of encroachments and the appointment of a petty constable for Alberbury township. The Wattlesborough manor court was concerned only with encroachments after 1711.

By 1659 Alberbury parish had been divided for administrative purposes into two Divisions.[71] The Lower Division comprised the hamlets of Alberbury, Amaston, Benthall, Braggington, Eyton, Hayes, Loton, Rowton, Little Shrawardine, and Lower Stanford, with those parts of the townships of Cardeston and Ford which lay within Alberbury parish. The Upper Division contained Bulthey, Trefnant, Winnington, Great Wollaston, and the Welsh townships, but the 4 English townships, under the name Wollaston Quarter, were accounted a separate unit for purposes of poor relief by the early 18th century.

The Alberbury parish records include churchwardens' accounts, 1658–1704 and 1757–1928 (which contain occasional vestry minutes after 1809), and accounts of 'use money', 1766–1847. No overseers' accounts are known to survive, but there is a quantity of settlement and other papers, 1663–1810. Although a select vestry, consisting of representatives from the 6 principal townships, was established in 1679, no such formal arrangement seems to have been in use in the 18th century and the vestry was an open one in the 19th century. The two churchwardens rendered a combined account in 1658, but thereafter a separate account was rendered by the churchwarden of each Division. Following the creation of the perpetual curacies of Great Wollaston and Criggion in the 18th century the range of disbursements by the churchwarden of the Upper Division was gradually restricted. In the 1840s he merely paid his quotas of visitation expenses, the cost of bread and wine, and the schoolmaster's salary. A single account was rendered by both churchwardens after 1850. Church rates, assessed on a pound rate after 1782, were regularly levied until 1850 and were used on occasion in the 1850s in face of mounting opposition. A rate was last levied in 1860 to pay for a new burial ground and after 1872 church expenses were met by quarterly collections.

The parish clerk was entitled to a portion of the corn tithes, known as the Bell Sheaf. These were

[54] Plymley, *Agric. Salop.* 338.
[55] Ibid.
[56] *Cal. Chart. R.* 1256–1300, 275.
[57] *Bagshaw's Dir. Salop.* (1851).
[58] E 179/242/33.
[59] *S.P.R. Heref.* vi, *passim*; Loton Hall MSS., leases, 1661, 1685; S.P.L., Deeds 3009; S.R.O. 1123/7; ibid. 166 uncat., deeds, 1685; S.P.L., Deeds 1597, 1691; ibid. 552 uncat., survey of Thomas estate, 1681.
[60] *S.P.R. Heref.* vi. 295–320.
[61] S.R.O. 1093 uncat., lease, 1661; ibid. 552 uncat. lease, 1654.

[62] H.O. 107/1991/4.
[63] Ibid.
[64] *Kelly's Dir. Salop.* (1870–1941).
[65] Ibid.
[66] Heref. City Libr. 9133/17, 18, 31; Loton Hall MSS.; Bodl. MS. Gough Salop. 4, ff. 119v–120.
[67] See p. 325.
[68] Loton Hall MSS., depositions, Roger Owen *v.* Robert and Edward Leighton, c. 1685.
[69] S.R.O. 1011 (Dukes) uncat., ct. r. 1783.
[70] *Cal. Chart. R.* 1341–1417, 148.
[71] Alberbury par. rec., churchwardens' accts. 1658–79.

commuted for a rent charge of £7 8s. 6d. in the 1840s.[72] John Mitchell (vicar 1866–86) adopted the practice of appointing his non-resident friends to this office and by 1887 the rent charge was being applied towards the organist's salary. The number of highway surveyors appointed rose steadily from 2 in 1658 to 7 after 1691,[73] but no records of their activities have survived.

Although a poor rate for the Upper Division was entered in the churchwardens' accounts in 1675, overseers do not figure among the lists of officers appointed at Easter vestries until 1692. It is possible that, until the end of the 17th century, the expenses of poor relief were met by the proceeds of the parish stock. The parish had 7 overseers by 1789, 2 of whom acted for Alberbury township,[74] and an assistant overseer was being employed by 1834.[75] Poor rates in the Lower Division, which produced a little over £300 a year between 1776 and 1785,[76] had risen to £612 by 1803.[77] They reached a peak of some £835 a year between 1816 and 1819,[78] but were rarely more than £550 a year during the 1820s.[79] No payments of regular weekly relief were being made in 1834, but allowances for coal and rent were sometimes made.[80] There appears to have been a workhouse in Alberbury township by 1766,[81] but it was said in 1793 to have proved a failure.[82]

There are overseers' accounts for Wollaston Quarter, 1725–35 and 1770–1836, together with a quantity of 18th-century settlement and other papers.[83] John Thomas, who was apparently overseer of this Quarter, 1708–36, also levied rates for the maintenance of Wollaston chapel and the payment of its minister.[84] In the later 18th century, when the single overseer of Wollaston Quarter served only for one year at a time, the upkeep of the chapel was still in part a charge on the poor rate. The Quarter had its own vestry meetings by the 1770s. This had become a select vestry ('the committee') by 1817 and a salaried vestry clerk was being employed by 1826. Annual expenditure on poor relief rose from £70 in 1770 to £220 in 1795. It was normally a little more than £300 in the period 1800–15, but reached a peak of £603 in 1817, dropping to c. £250 in the 1820s. No workhouse is recorded, but a cottage was leased as a poor-house in 1776 and another was bought by the overseers in 1826.

The Cardeston parish records include churchwardens' accounts, 1715–1821, and overseers' accounts, 1782–1837. One man held the offices of churchwarden and overseer annually, 1715–30, when a single church and poor rate was levied, and thereafter the parish had one overseer and one churchwarden. In the 18th century the church-

wardens were appointed sidesmen in the year following their term of office. A salaried assistant overseer was employed, 1825–35. Church rates were levied annually and lewns were replaced by a pound rate at the rebuilding of Cardeston Church in 1748, continuing in use thereafter. Disbursements on poor relief rose from £20 in 1726 to £102 by 1784. They were normally a little more than £200 between 1795 and 1815, but rose to £364 in 1817. A workhouse was leased from the lord of the manor throughout the period covered by the accounts. Flax and hemp were spun and woven by the inmates in 1786 and 1794, but it seems normally to have been no more than a poor-house.

CHURCHES. Alberbury church is first recorded in the mid-12th century,[85] but it was served by 4 priests until the 13th century[86] and is clearly a pre-Conquest 'minster' church, like those of Pontesbury and Westbury. It has been argued that Alberbury, under the Welsh name Llanfihangel-yng-Nghentyn (St. Michael's in the Lowlands), was originally a dependency of Meifod (Montg.),[87] but claims to the tithes of certain hamlets in the west of Alberbury made by 13th-century incumbents of Meifod probably reflect nothing more than the uncertain status of the Upper and Nether Gorther at this time. The boundary between the dioceses of Hereford and St. Asaph at this point had been in dispute since at least 1236[88] and in 1265 many hamlets in the Gorther were said to pay half their tithes to the church of Meifod.[89] The dispute was settled in 1288, substantially in Hereford's favour, when this part of the diocesan boundary was adjudged to follow the course of the River Severn,[90] and in the following year a claim by the Rector of Welshpool to tithes in 13 hamlets in the Nether Gorther was quashed.[91]

Great Wollaston, a chapelry of Alberbury parish first recorded in 1289,[92] included the townships of Great Wollaston, Bulthey, Winnington, and Trefnant in Shropshire and Middletown and Uppington in Montgomeryshire. It became for practical purposes an independent benefice in the earlier 18th century[93] and was constituted an ecclesiastical parish in 1864.[94] Inhabitants of Ford and Cardeston paid tithes and church rates to Alberbury until the 19th century,[95] but such payments were made in respect of land in these townships which lay in Alberbury parish and are not evidence of an original dependence on Alberbury.

Ralph the fat, lord of Alberbury manor, granted the church to Shrewsbury Abbey between 1141 and 1155.[96] Before 1186 the abbey had surrendered it to Ralph's successor Fulk Fitz Warin (II), who at

72 Ibid. tithe appts.
73 Ibid. churchwardens' accts. 1658–1704.
74 S.P.L., MS. 372, vol. i, f. 77ᵛ.
75 Rep. Com. Poor Laws, App. (B 1). pt. 2, H.C. 44, p. 385 (1834), xxxi.
76 Rep. Cttee. on Overseers' Returns, 1777, p. 442, H.C. (1st ser. ix, reprinted 1803); Rep. Cttee. on State of Poor, 1787, p. 658, H.C. (1st ser. ix, reprinted 1803).
77 Poor Law Abstract, 1803, H.C. 175, pp. 416–17 (1803–4), xiii.
78 Rep. Cttee. on Poor Rate Returns, 1822, Suppl. App., H.C. 556, p. 141 (1822), v.
79 Ibid. 1825, H.C. 334, p. 177 (1825), iv; Acct. of Money Expended on Poor, 1825–9, H.C. 83, p. 391 (1830–1), xi.
80 Rep. Com. Poor Laws, App. (B 1), pt. 2, p. 385.
81 S.P.R. Heref. vi. 448.

82 B.M. Add. MS. 21018, f. 279.
83 In custody of Great Wollaston Parish Council, 1965.
84 S.R.O. 552 uncat., accts. of John Thomas, 1677–1736.
85 N.L.W., Shrews. Cart. no. 36.
86 T.S.A.S. 4th ser. xi. 294.
87 D. R. Thomas, History of the Diocese of St. Asaph (Oswestry, 1908), i. 7, 44; ii. 136.
88 Cal. Papal Regs. i. 151.
89 Thomas, op. cit. i. 44.
90 Reg. R. Swinfield (C. & Y.S.), 185–212.
91 Ibid. 221–6.
92 Ibid. 217.   93 See p. 219.
94 Lond. Gaz. 1864, p. 3048.
95 Alberbury par. rec., churchwardens' accts. 1658–1928; Ford par. rec., tithe appt.
96 N.L.W., Shrews. Cart. no. 36.

about this time granted lands at Tadlow (Cambs.) to the abbey in settlement of disputes respecting the advowson of Alberbury.[97] In 1201-3, when the estates of Fulk Fitz Warin (III) were held in escheat by his overlord Robert Corbet of Caus, the latter granted the advowson of two of the four portions of Alberbury to William and Hugh Corbet.[98] Although Alberbury Priory did not obtain any interest in the advowson at its foundation c. 1226,[99] it was said to be patron in 1259, when the church was appropriated to the priory.[1] By this date the priory already held one of the four portions. Another was surrendered in the same year by one Guichard, a priest in the diocese of Lyons,[2] and Thomas Corbet released his interest in the remaining two portions in 1262.[3] The living has been a vicarage since 1289.[4] It was united with Cardeston in 1929[5] but has been served by the Rector of Ford since 1965.

The Crown presented to the living in 1337,[6] during a temporary seizure of the priory's estate, and in 1344, when the rectory was restored to the priory, the advowson was retained by the Crown.[7] The priory made two attempts to present to the living in 1349,[8] but the Crown recovered the advowson in 1356.[9] The Fitz Warins of Whittington, descendants of the founder of the priory, seem to have been claiming the advowson at this time. When releasing his right to Alberbury manor to Fulk Glas in 1320 Fulk Fitz Warin reserved to himself the advowson of the priory and the church[10] and in 1357 the Crown claimed to hold the advowson as guardian of the heir of Fulk Fitz Warin.[11] The advowson was held by the Crown until the later 16th century and did not pass, with Alberbury Priory, to All Souls in 1441. The Crown presented in 1444[12] and 1579,[13] but the bishop presented by lapse on two occasions in the early 16th century.[14] By 1616, however, the advowson was held by All Souls,[15] who presented to the living until 1921, when the advowson was transferred to the Bishop of Hereford.[16]

The rectory, restored to Alberbury Priory in 1344, passed in 1441 to All Souls,[17] whose title was confirmed in 1461[18] and who are the present rectors. A new instrument of appropriation, obtained in 1521,[19] was probably made necessary to combat claims on the former priory estate by Sir Thomas Leighton.[20]

At its appropriation in 1259 half of the profits of the rectory were directed to be paid to Alberbury Priory and half to the mother-house of Grandmont.[21] Grandmont received no income until 1287, when the priory agreed to pay £6 13s. 4d. a year to the mother-house.[22] The rectory was said to be worth 15 marks in 1284,[23] 20 marks in 1345,[24] and 40 marks in the following year.[25] These are, however, valuations of the priory's whole estate in Alberbury, in addition to the tithes and glebe belonging to the church. The rectory was leased to the lord of Caus for £26 13s. 4d. in 1378.[26] Between 1386 and 1441 it was held, with the rest of the priory estate, by a succession of Crown lessees[27] and the practice of leasing the two elements of the estate to a single tenant was continued by All Souls.[28] The rectory was valued at £224 in 1655,[29] but this too is clearly an estimate of the total value of the estate. Lessees of the priory estate undertook extensive repairs to the chancel of the parish church in the 1420s.[30] Repairs to the chancel were on occasion expressly excepted in 15th- and 16th-century leases,[31] but were always the responsibility of the tenant after 1589.[32]

In 1289 all the great tithes, apart from tithes of hay in Great Wollaston, were assigned to the priory.[33] The rectorial tithes were said to be worth £13 6s. 8d. in 1343.[34] At this period they may have been collected by the vicar, together with the small tithes, for in 1338 the chaplain of Alberbury undertook to hand over to the priory 30 quarters of wheat and oats arising from the tithes of Trefnant.[35] In 1472, when the great tithes produced £24 4s. 6d., tithes of wool and lamb were collected in kind, but the remainder were leased to the more prosperous peasants in each township.[36] Tenants of All Souls in and after the 16th century normally underlet all the great tithes in this way. In 1550, when the tithes of the English part of the parish produced £35 11s. 6d. a year, they were leased to 9 persons;[37] in the early 19th century the practice was to lease them to a farmer in each township.[38] Corn tithes were being collected in kind in the later 16th century.[39] Inhabitants of Alberbury were complaining at this time of rack-renting of tithes and the great tithes[40] of the English part of the parish had risen in value to £114 by 1655.[41] They were worth £405 a year in 1707[42] and were set for £496 in 1777, but rose from £655 in 1793 to £1,500 by

[97] N.L.W., Shrews. Cart. no. 286.
[98] All Souls mun., Alberbury deeds 5.
[99] *T.S.A.S.* 4th ser. xi. 292-3.
[1] Ibid. 293-5.
[2] Ibid. 294-5.
[3] All Souls mun., Alberbury deeds 5.
[4] *Reg. R. Swinfield* (C. & Y.S.), 217-18.
[5] Heref. Dioc. Regy., reg. 1926-38, p. 216.
[6] *Cal. Pat.* 1334-8, 557.
[7] *Cal. Close*, 1343-6, 408.
[8] *Reg. J. Trillek* (C. & Y.S.), 379, 380.
[9] Ibid. 46.
[10] Loton Hall MSS., deed, 1320.
[11] *Cal. Pat.* 1354-8, 547-8.
[12] Ibid. 1441-6, 251.
[13] *Instit. Dioc. Heref.* 26.
[14] Ibid. 1; *Reg. R. Mayew* (C. & Y.S.), 284.
[15] *Instit. Dioc. Heref.* 28.
[16] Heref. Dioc. Regy., reg. 1919-26, p. 140.
[17] *Cal. Pat.* 1436-41, 563.
[18] Ibid. 1461-7, 148.
[19] *Reg. C. Bothe* (C. & Y.S.), i. 96-98.
[20] *T.S.A.S.* 4th ser. xi. 283-4.

[21] Ibid. 294-5.
[22] Ibid. 264-5.
[23] *Reg. R. Swinfield* (C. & Y.S.), 524.
[24] *Cal. Close*, 1343-6, 563.
[25] *Reg. J. Trillek* (C. & Y.S.), 288.
[26] Longleat MSS., unbound 3741.
[27] *T.S.A.S.* 4th ser. xi. 275-7.
[28] All Souls mun., Alberbury leases *passim*.
[29] *T.S.A.S.* xlvii. 25.
[30] S.C. 6/965/16.
[31] All Souls mun., Alberbury leases 4, 6, 10, 12.
[32] Ibid. 20-30; ibid. Leiger Bk. 1684-1707, ff. 246-7; S.R.O. 1123/11-18.
[33] *Reg. R. Swinfield* (C. & Y.S.), 217-18.
[34] *T.S.A.S.* 4th ser. xi. 271.
[35] All Souls mun., Alberbury deeds 121.
[36] Ibid. 192.
[37] S.R.O. 1123/10.
[38] Ibid. 1123/25.
[39] All Souls mun., Alberbury deeds 167(g).
[40] Ibid. 160.
[41] *T.S.A.S.* xlvii. 25.
[42] All Souls mun., Alberbury deeds 222.

1813.[43] Between 1840 and 1850 the rectorial tithes were commuted for rent-charges totalling £1,395, of which £988 was derived from the English part of the parish.[44]

The origin of a pension of £1 6s. 8d. payable to the Rector of Diddlebury is not known. It is first recorded in 1291[45] and was thereafter paid to the Dean and Chapter of Hereford, to whom Diddlebury rectory had been assigned in 1283.[46] This pension was among the payments reserved in the renewed appropriation of 1521,[47] but by the early 17th century the chapter claimed a portion of the corn and hay tithes in Rowton and Amaston townships. Following a dispute with All Souls, the chapter were allotted two-thirds of the corn and hay tithes of certain lands in Amaston in 1634.[48] These were commuted for a rent charge of £40 in 1848.[49]

No formal provision had been made for a vicar in 1259 and in 1284 the bishop expressed an intention to review the vicar's portion.[50] Negotiations with the priory were opened in 1286[51] and in 1289 the vicar's income was defined. He was allotted the hay tithes of Great Wollaston, all the small tithes, and all other altar-dues except 'living mortuaries'. The cost of chancel repairs, clerical taxes, and the provision of service-books, vestments, vessels, and other ornaments were to be borne equally by the vicar and the priory. The vicar was to provide lights for the chancel, collect Peter's Pence, pay procurations and synodals, and pay 6s. 8d. a year to the priory as a token of subjection.[52]

The vicarage appears to have declined in value during the later Middle Ages. It was valued at £6 13s. 4d. in 1291[53] and at only £5 in 1535.[54] The vicar complained of his inadequate endowment in 1368,[55] but at the investigation which followed this claim seems to have been countered by an allegation that he had been admitted by simony.[56] An annual fee of 15s. was being paid to the vicar by All Souls in 1459,[57] but when monks from Grandmont attempted to regain possession of the priory in 1473 the vicar, Richard Wilde, was prominent among their local supporters.[58] In a lease of the priory estate in 1550 All Souls stipulated that their tenant should pay £5 a year to the vicar.[59] This sum, which represented the stipend of the former priest of St. Stephen's chantry chapel,[60] was assigned as a permanent augmentation in 1552 for the provision of a curate.[61] Between 1580 and 1623 vicars were obliged to enter into a bond not to seek to augment the value of the living.[62]

The vicarage was said to be worth £40 a year in 1655[63] and a detailed valuation of the vicarage c. 1700 put its gross profits at £51 15s. 6d.[64] Thomas Hotchkiss (vicar 1678–1714),[65] who was said in 1704 to have been complaining of the poverty of the living 'ever since he was vicar',[66] proposed in 1706 that the lessee of the rectory should take the profits of the vicarage, paying him £60 a year.[67] In 1727 the value of the living was augmented by a grant of £400, half of which was granted by Queen Anne's Bounty to meet a benefaction of £100 from the Revd. James Smith and £100 raised by subscription.[68] Some time before 1850 further grants totalling £905 were made by All Souls[69] and in 1835 the annual value of the vicarage was said to be £187.[70] A tithe rent-charge of £100 was granted by All Souls to the vicarage in 1858.[71]

Since the greater part of the income of the vicarage was derived from small tithes until the 18th century, incumbents not surprisingly went to some pains in their collection. The inhabitants of Great Wollaston and Winnington complained in 1595 that the vicar had doubled the value of the small tithes in these townships and was tithing servants' wages at more than the customary rate.[72] In the early 17th century the All Souls tenant alleged that the vicar was claiming tithes on inclosures recently made on the commons and on the Abbey demesnes.[73] In 1700 the small tithes and herbage dues produced £26 11s. 4d. and a further £16 3s. was derived from Easter duties.[74] Income from these two sources had not risen significantly by the 1780s. In 1782 the small tithes and Easter dues produced about £45 a year. Herbage dues were subject to fluctuation, but produced on average some £15 a year between 1784 and 1787; a further £12 a year was normally obtained in this period from tithes on clover sown.[75] No small tithes were collected in kind in the later 18th century, when moduses were in use for cows, colts, and beehives.[76] In addition a small number of parishioners paid moduses for unspecified purposes. In 1792 19 of the 187 persons from whom tithes were due paid such additional moduses, most of them being residents of Bausley and Criggion.[77] The small tithes were commuted between 1840 and 1850 for a rent charge of £149 7s. 10d., £94 17s. 10d. of which was charged on the English part of the parish.[78]

No reference has been found to the vicarial glebe before 1793, when it was said to amount to 6½ a. recently acquired by exchange with the lord of the manor.[79] This presumably refers to the glebe in Alberbury township, which amounted to 9 a. in

---

43 S.R.O. 1123/24–25.
44 Alberbury par. rec., tithe appts.
45 Tax. Eccl. (Rec. Com.), 167.
46 Eyton, v. 174.
47 Reg. C. Bothe (C. & Y.S.), i. 96–98.
48 S.R.O. 1123/4, 7.
49 Alberbury par. rec., Rowton and Amaston tithe appt.
50 Reg. R. Swinfield (C. & Y.S.), 524.
51 Ibid. 216.
52 Ibid. 217–18.
53 Tax. Eccl. (Rec. Com.), 167.
54 Valor Eccl. (Rec. Com.), iii. 214.
55 Reg. L. Charlton (C. & Y.S.), 48.
56 Ibid. 52.
57 All Souls mun., accts. 1459–60.
58 T.S.A.S. 4th ser. xi. 280–1.
59 S.R.O. 1123/3.
60 See p. 216.
61 T.S.A.S. 4th ser. xi. 285–6.
62 All Souls mun., Alberbury deeds 166, 174, 186, 215.
63 T.S.A.S. xlvii. 25.
64 All Souls mun., Alberbury deeds 195.
65 Instit. Dioc. Heref. 41, 65.
66 All Souls mun., Alberbury deeds 221.
67 Ibid. 223.
68 C. Hodgson, Queen Anne's Bounty (1845), 142, 289.
69 Heref. Dioc. Regy., diocese bk. c. 1850.
70 Rep. Com. Eccl. Revenues [67], pp. 428–9, H.C. (1835). xxii.
71 Heref. Dioc. Regy., reg. 1857–69, p. 84.
72 All Souls mun., Alberbury deeds 183.
73 Ibid. 215.
74 Ibid. 195.
75 Alberbury par. rec., vicar's accts. of small tithes, 1782–7.
76 Ibid. 1782–1824.
77 Ibid. 1792–3.
78 Ibid. tithe appts.
79 B.M. Add. MS. 21018, f. 279v.

1843, when it lay close to the vicarage.[80] By this date, however, the vicar also held 31 a. glebe in Bausley township, most of which lay near Pecknall[81] and was probably a comparatively recent gift from All Souls. In 1860 14 a. of the Bausley glebe was conveyed to All Souls in exchange for a tithe rent charge of £24 on lands in Eyton township.[82]

Following charges by the vicar and parishioners that All Souls had neglected to provide services at Alberbury Priory for the souls of founders and benefactors, a chantry was established in the priory chapel of St. Stephen shortly after 1475.[83] The chantry priest's stipend of £5 was paid by All Souls[84] and in 1535 it was derived from the proceeds of the great tithes.[85] Although the chaplain of St. Stephen's seems also to have served as curate in the parish church,[86] St. Stephen's chapel was much frequented in the early 16th century, when it was a pilgrimage centre.[87] All Souls was discharged from this payment in 1552, when the stipend was remitted to the College's tenant on condition that he fought any action which might be brought by the parishioners to recover it.[88] The parishioners stated later in the 16th century that until 1569 the stipend of £5 had been paid by the tenant to the churchwardens for the use of a school.[89] A second chantry, said in 1547 to be endowed with a stock of cattle worth 62s.,[90] was presumably in the parish church.

None of the 23 recorded vicars of Alberbury before 1540 is known to have been a graduate and, presumably on account of the low value of the benefice, few held the living for more than a few years. Of the 14 vicars in this period whose dates of incumbency are known, only 2 held the living for more than 20 years and 7 remained for no more than two years. Although the living remained a comparatively poor one until the 19th century, a higher proportion of post-Reformation incumbents were resident and they tended to hold the living for long periods. Of 16 vicars 1540–1900 7 served for more than 20 years, the longest incumbencies being those of Thomas Clark (1623–59)[91] and William Thornes (1778–1828).[92] Apart from the four vicars who also served at Cardeston, pluralism seems to have been uncommon. Henry Jones (vicar c. 1588–1614)[93] was master of Oswestry Grammar School;[94] in 1595 Reynold Williams of Great Wollaston alleged that he ate at other mens' tables and kept no hospitality.[95] Seven of the 12 vicars who held the living between 1614 and 1900 were continuously resident. Of the remainder Thomas Clark was still living in Alberbury in 1642[96] but was buried at Fitz, where he had become rector in 1616.[97] Bryan Faussett (vicar 1747–65)[98] and his successor Charles Grainger (vicar 1765–78)[99] were each resident only for the first 4 years of their incumbencies[1] and R. W. Huntley (vicar 1829–57)[2] ceased to reside in 1839.[3] All vicars have been resident since 1857.

Provision was made in 1289 for a priest and a deacon, in addition to the vicar.[4] The office of assistant priest or sacristan was filled by William le Mareschal (alias William the sacristan) in the later 13th century[5] and probably by Nicholas le Mareschal in 1338.[6] The provision of a sacristan, or sexton, was said in 1397 to be the joint responsibility of the rector and vicar, the rector's share of his stipend being 8s. 4d.[7] A sexton or 'vicar's priest'[8] seems to have been regularly employed until the Reformation. As a local man he fulfilled an essential function, since he would be able to communicate with the Welsh-speaking inhabitants of the Upper Division. In a petition to All Souls in the later 16th century the parishioners alleged that past vicars 'had always one priest which was called the vicar's priest . . . which had or did understand both the languages, forasmuch as part of the said parish are of the Welshry and cannot understand the English tongue'.[9]

Although late-16th-century vicars continued to employ curates,[10] there appears to have been a deterioration in pastoral standards. The parishioners complained at this time that it had frequently been necessary to call in clergy from neighbouring parishes to conduct baptisms and burials and that they had received no sermon for 20 years.[11] Edward Wall, curate here by 1642,[12] himself employed no curate after he succeeded Thomas Clark as vicar in 1659.[13] David Price (curate 1750–56)[14] and R. Roberts (curate 1757–65)[15] served the living during the non-residence of Bryan Faussett and 3 curates were employed by Charles Grainger between 1766 and 1778.[16] The last of these was William Thornes, appointed curate in 1773,[17] who succeeded Grainger as vicar in 1778. Thornes rarely employed curates, but his non-resident successor R. W. Huntley employed them continuously.[18]

The parsonage, which contained 2 hearths in the later 17th century,[19] was rebuilt by William Thornes at his own expense[20] and altered in 1839.[21] The

[80] Alberbury par. rec., tithe appt.
[81] Ibid. Bausley tithe appt.
[82] Ibid. exchange, 1860.
[83] T.S.A.S. 4th ser. xi. 280, 282.
[84] Ibid.; ibid. 3rd ser. x. 359; Valor Eccl. (Rec. Com.) iii. 214.
[85] Valor Eccl. (Rec. Com.), iii. 214.
[86] T.S.A.S. 4th ser. xi. 286.
[87] All Souls mun., Alberbury deeds 168.
[88] Ibid. 151, 154.
[89] Ibid. 167 (i).
[90] T.S.A.S. 3rd ser. x. 381.
[91] Instit. Dioc. Heref. 29; S.P.R. Lich. iv (1), 24.
[92] Instit. Dioc. Heref. 110, 149.
[93] All Souls mun., Alberbury deeds 183; S.P.R. Heref. vi. 53.
[94] All Souls mun., Alberbury deeds 183.
[95] Ibid.
[96] S.P.R. Heref. vi. 29.
[97] T.S.A.S. 3rd ser. i. 263.
[98] Instit. Dioc. Heref. 86, 98.
[99] Ibid. 98, 110.

[1] S.P.R. Heref. vi. 406–9, 614.
[2] Instit. Dioc. Heref. 149, 172.
[3] Alberbury par. rec., churchwardens' accts. 1809–44.
[4] Reg. R. Swinfield (C. & Y.S.), 217–18.
[5] All Souls mun., Alberbury deeds 3, 56, 97.
[6] Ibid. 121.
[7] E.H.R. xlv. 462.
[8] All Souls mun., Alberbury deeds 167(g).
[9] Ibid.
[10] Ibid. 183; T.S.A.S. xlvi. 42; S.P.R. Heref. vi. 15.
[11] All Souls mun., Alberbury deeds 167(g).
[12] S.P.R. Heref. vi. 29.
[13] Alberbury par. rec., churchwardens' accts. 1658–79.
[14] S.P.R. Heref. vi. 410.
[15] Ibid. 436–46.
[16] Ibid. 517–623.
[17] Heref. Dioc. Regy., reg. 1772–1802, f. 27.
[18] Ibid. 1822–42, pp. 407, 575; ibid. 1847–56, pp. 267, 313.
[19] E 179/255/35 m. 83d.; Hearth Tax, 1672, 159.
[20] B.M. Add. MS. 21018, f. 279ᵛ.
[21] Heref. Dioc. Regy., reg. 1822–42, p. 415.

WESTBURY: north gable of Upper Lake Farm showing cruck construction

ALBERBURY-WITH-CARDESTON: symbolic carving on fireplace lintel, The Green Farm, Winnington

LONGNOR: corbel head on wall-post at The Moat House

ALBERBURY-WITH-CARDESTON: Alberbury Church from the north-east

ALBERBURY-WITH-CARDESTON: the keep at Wattlesborough Hall from the north, c. 1868

FORD CHURCH: the nave roof

house was said to be unfit for habitation in 1867,[22] when its site was conveyed to Sir Baldwin Leighton.[23] A new parsonage, to designs by S. Poultney Smith, was completed in 1868.[24] Datestones inscribed 'T.H. 1631' and 'T. Grainger 1708' and a mantel from the library were among fragments preserved from the former parsonage.[25]

During the later 17th century communion was normally administered at Christmas, Easter, and Michaelmas, 3 communion services apparently being held during Easter Week.[26] Monthly communions had been introduced by 1793, but were thinly attended; there were about 180 Easter communicants but only one or two dozen communicants at the monthly celebrations.[27] At this time morning and evening services were provided on Sundays, with 2 sermons in summer and one in winter.[28] The return to the Ecclesiastical Census of 1851 has not survived. A body of psalm-singers was formed in 1788, when one Mr. Michenor was employed 'to improve and instruct any young people that were willing to sing psalms'.[29] An organ given by the curate in 1843[30] was removed in 1858[31] and music was provided by a harmonium until 1877, when a new organ was bought.[32] This was rebuilt in 1903[33] and replaced by the present organ in 1964.

The church of *ST. MICHAEL*[34] consists of nave, chancel, south aisle, and north-eastern tower. The south aisle, commonly known as the Loton Chapel, and the east end of the nave are built of sandstone and date from the earlier 14th century. The chamfers of the pointed chancel arch are not continued on the imposts and the greater part of the east wall of the nave appears to be contemporary with that of the south aisle. Corbels to the north and south of the chancel arch presumably mark the position of a rood-beam. The south aisle is divided from the nave by an arcade of 3 pointed arches. The piers, which are of quatrefoil section, consist of 4 filleted members with spur-shafts between them and have scroll capitals. There is a small and finely moulded south door. The very tall and wide east window was already blocked in 1789; above it is a cusped image-niche. The smaller west window is a convex-sided triangle and has geometrical tracery as does the more easterly of the two windows in the south wall. The remaining window in the south wall is of 3 lights, with plain intersecting tracery, and may be a slightly later insertion. The sloping heads of the buttresses have triangular cusped panels containing carved heads; similar panels occur on the gable parapets. Within the aisle there is a trefoil-headed piscina and a cusped round-arched tomb-recess in the south wall.

The tower may date from the later 12th century, but was modified when the nave and south aisle were built in the early 14th century. Like the Norman tower of the former church at Pontesbury it stands at the north-east end of the nave. It is of 4 stages

and has a steep saddleback roof. Unlike the rest of the church it is built of breccia, but its clasping buttresses, the pilaster buttress in the centre of the north wall, and other dressings are of sandstone. String courses run round the two lower stages. Apart from the buttresses, surviving late-12th-century features include narrow lancets with wide-splayed rear-arches on the north and west walls and the gable windows of the roof. The latter are slightly pointed and consist of 2 large pointed lights divided by a round forked mullion. The lower portion of the south wall is of sandstone and a small pointed door, giving access to the nave at this point, is now blocked. The windows of the third and fourth stages of the tower, cusped lancets and cusped two-light windows respectively, were inserted in the early 14th century. The saddleback roof seems also to have been added at this time. On the north its stone-coped parapet has small triangular panels resembling those of the south aisle. Squinches at the base of the roof were probably intended for a spire or parapet. The trussed-rafter roof of the tower, which includes some reused timber, was, however, rebuilt or extensively repaired in 1662.[35]

The remainder of the church was rebuilt in the 1840s. Virtually the only surviving original feature is a flying buttress at the south-west end of the nave and little is known of the former appearance of the western half of the nave from documentary sources. It had two lancets and a door in the north wall in the early 19th century. A string course and corbels on the west wall of the south aisle probably mark the position of a roof over the former porch outside the south door.

The western half of the nave was rebuilt in the Decorated style in 1846–7, when a 5-light west window with intersecting tracery and a new south door were constructed.[36] When the chancel was rebuilt in 1846[37] some attempt seems to have been made to reproduce the appearance of the former east end, for in 1789 this had 2 pointed lancets divided by a central buttress, above which was a small round window. The south wall then contained 3 lancets and 2 later square-headed windows of 2 lights, and there appear to have been 2 larger lancets on the north wall. All were replaced by tall lancets in 1846, when a small vestry was built on the north wall.

The fine nave roof is of arch-braced collar-beam construction with moulded arch-braces and cusped members above the collars. There are 5 rows of moulded side-purlins, each supported by pairs of cusped double windbraces, forming quatrefoils in each roof panel. The two westernmost bays have only 3 rows of side-purlins and are without windbraces, while the truss at the west end is of hammer-beam construction. There was a scissor-truss at the eastern gable of the nave in 1789.[38] The roof was restored in 1903,[39] when a ceiling inserted in 1783[40]

[22] Alberbury par. rec., churchwardens' accts. 1843–1928.
[23] Ibid. conveyance, 1867.
[24] Ibid. churchwardens' accts. 1843–1928.
[25] Ibid.
[26] Ibid. 1658–1704.
[27] B.M. Add. MS. 21018, f. 279ᵛ.
[28] Ibid.
[29] Alberbury par. rec., churchwardens' accts. 1773–1810.
[30] Ibid. 1809–44.
[31] Ibid. 1843–1928.
[32] Ibid.
[33] *Kelly's Dir. Salop.* (1905).

[34] Except where otherwise stated, description of church based on S.P.L., MS. 372, vol. i, p. 77; S.P.L., T. F. Dukes watercolours (churches), nos. 5, 10; S.P.L., J. H. Smith collect., no. 3; Cranage, vi. 517–23; Pevsner, *Shropshire*, 53–54. See also plate on facing page.
[35] Par. rec., churchwardens' accts. 1658–79.
[36] Ibid. 1843–1928; datestone.
[37] Datestone.
[38] S.P.L., MS. 372, vol. i, p. 77.
[39] *Kelly's Dir. Salop.* (1905).
[40] Alberbury par. rec., churchwardens' accts. 1757–1809.

was removed. The south aisle has a simple arch-braced collar-beam roof with 2 rows of side-purlins and single windbraces. The tie-beams to which old carving has been applied, were inserted in the 19th century. The hammer-beam roof of the chancel dates from 1846 and is panelled to resemble the cusped windbraces of the nave roof.

The church was repewed shortly after 1617[41] and, although again repewed in 1785[42] and 1871,[43] the existing pews in the nave retain a quantity of Jacobean panelling. Further panelling of this period was used in 1930 to construct the screen of the choir vestry at the west end.[44] A gallery was erected in 1660[45] and another in 1785,[46] but their position is not known. The Gothic pews of the south aisle are dated 1840 and those of the chancel presumably date from 1846. Apart from a 17th-century oak parish chest the remaining church fittings are of 19th-century date. A pulpit purchased in 1759[47] was removed in 1847.[48] The present stone pulpit was presented by Lady Charlotte Lyster in 1883[49] and the hexagonal font is probably of the same date.

Apart from a few fragments of medieval stained glass in one of the windows in the south aisle, the numerous stained-glass memorial windows are all of 19th-century date. The memorial to Sir Baldwin Leighton (d. 1897) in the south aisle is a notable example of Art Nouveau glass.[50] The south aisle also contains wall monuments to members of the Leighton family, 1688–1919, and on the north wall of the nave, adjoining the tower, is a group of monuments to the Lyster family and their successors at Rowton, 1691–1916. That of Sir Richard Lyster (d. 1691) was removed from Old St. Chad's, Shrewsbury, and that of Sir Richard Lyster (d. 1766) is signed by T. F. Pritchard.

The church contained 3 bells in 1552.[51] Another was cast in 1659 by Thomas Cleobury of Wellington,[52] who presumably also cast the 'great bell' in 1668.[53] There were 4 bells in the early 18th century, but in 1759 these were replaced by 5 bells, cast by Abel Rudhall of Gloucester.[54] One of the bells was recast in 1821.[55] Rhyming rules for the ringers, dated 1759, are on a board in the belfry. The church clock, which is first recorded in 1651,[56] was set in the tower in 1670.[57]

An inventory of service books, vestments, and ornaments delivered to the vicar by All Souls in 1445 included a cross containing a relic of the True Cross. This cross, which probably came from the priory, had been removed to All Souls College by 1448.[58]

The church had a silver chalice in 1552.[59] The present plate[60] is made up as follows: a silver plate, dated 1661, given by Sir Richard Lyster in 1719; 2 chalices, 2 patens, 2 flagons, and a plate, all of silver and dated 1759–64, given by Mrs. Lucy Biggs; a silver chalice and paten of 1900; a pewter flagon, perhaps that which was purchased in 1669.[61] The registers are complete from 1564.[62]

The stepped base and chamfered stem of a medieval cross stand in the churchyard to the south of the church, its cross having been replaced by a sundial. Before the diversion of the village street, c. 1780, the churchyard was entered through a stone lych-gate, with a gabled roof, to the north-east of the church.[63] A new burial ground, south-east of the church, was acquired in 1862.[64]

Great Wollaston chapel is first recorded in 1289,[65] but its status during the later Middle Ages is obscure and it was regarded in the 16th century as the private chapel of the lord of Great Wollaston manor. The inhabitants alleged in 1570 that the chapel was 'firstly erected' by one of the predecessors of Thomas Williams 'for the private ease of his own house'.[66] Williams was said in 1578 to have proved that the chapel was intended for his private use and that others worshipped there by his permission[67] and in 1597 the chapel was accounted part of the manorial estate.[68] By 1578, however, the inhabitants of Great Wollaston were making some contribution towards the maintenance of the chapel[69] and it was no longer regarded as a private chapel in the later 17th century.

The hay tithes of Great Wollaston, reserved to the Vicar of Alberbury in 1289,[70] may have been intended as an endowment for the chapel. These tithes seem to have been paid to All Souls as rector in 1473.[71] They were certainly part of the rectorial estate in the early 17th century, when the vicar made an unsuccessful attempt to recover them,[72] but in 1655 part of the stipend of the Curate of Great Wollaston was said to be 'a tithe hay' worth £2 6s. 8d. a year.[73]

Until the mid-16th century the chapel was normally served by the Vicar of Alberbury, or his curate, who took morning services there, 'receiving some popish pence and his dinner for his pains'.[74] Thomas Williams, whose family appear to have held a lease of the great tithes of the Upper Division until c. 1566,[75] apparently maintained the fabric of the chapel at his own expense. It was alleged in 1570 that no curate had been provided by the vicar since c. 1540 and that Williams, who had been obliged to employ a curate at his own expense, was threatening to close the chapel.[76] The Vicar of Alberbury was ordered to continue the service of Great Wollaston

[41] Heref. Dioc. Regy., reg. 1627–37, f. 4ᵛ.
[42] Alberbury par. rec., churchwardens' accts. 1757–1809.
[43] Heref. Dioc. Regy., reg. 1869–83, p. 128.
[44] Ibid. 1926–38, p. 258.
[45] Alberbury par. rec., churchwardens' accts. 1658–79.
[46] Ibid. 1757–1809.
[47] Ibid.   [48] Ibid. 1809–44.
[49] Plaque on pulpit.
[50] Pevsner, Shropshire, 54.
[51] T.S.A.S. 2nd ser. xii. 337.
[52] Alberbury par. rec., churchwardens' accts. 1658–79.
[53] Ibid.
[54] Walters, Ch. Bells Salop. 201–2.
[55] Ibid.
[56] S.P.R. Heref. vi. 26.
[57] Alberbury par. rec., churchwardens' accts. 1658–79.
[58] T.S.A.S. 4th ser. xi. 279.
[59] Ibid. 2nd ser. xii. 337.

[60] Arkwright and Bourne, Ch. Plate Ludlow Archd. 2–3.
[61] Alberbury par. rec., churchwardens' accts. 1658–79.
[62] Printed to 1812 in S.P.R. Heref. vi.
[63] T.S.A.S. 3rd ser. viii, sketch of c. 1777 facing p. 70.
[64] Heref. Dioc. Regy., reg. 1857–69, p. 307.
[65] Reg. R. Swinfield (C. & Y.S.), 217.
[66] All Souls mun., Alberbury deeds 160.
[67] Ibid. 164.
[68] S.R.O. 166 uncat., marriage settlement of Thomas Williams, 1597.
[69] All Souls mun., Alberbury deeds 164.
[70] Reg. R. Swinfield (C. & Y.S.), 217.
[71] All Souls mun., Alberbury deeds 192.
[72] Ibid. 215.
[73] T.S.A.S. xlvii. 25–26.
[74] All Souls mun., Alberbury deeds 164.
[75] Ibid. 160, 213; S.R.O. 1123/3.
[76] All Souls mun., Alberbury deeds 160, 213.

by the Council of the Marches in 1578,[77] but later in the same year agreed to discharge this obligation by an annual payment of £4.[78] The object of this transaction was evidently to endow a resident curate, who would take evening services on Sundays and Holy Days and during Lent.[79] Although the Curate of Alberbury was serving the chapel in 1587[80] and the vicar was still taking Sunday morning services here in 1793,[81] Great Wollaston had its own curate from the early 18th century.[82]

The curate's stipend was said to amount to some £8 a year in 1578, half of which was raised by contributions from the inhabitants,[83] and the chapelry was said to be worth £6 a year in 1587.[84] In 1655 the curate still received £4 a year from the vicar, part of which was said to be in respect of tithe hay; contributions from the inhabitants were then uncertain in amount.[85] In the early 18th century 'Reading Money', as the contributory part of the curate's stipend was called, was collected by means of a rate of 1d. in the pound and the curate was also receiving small tithes from all townships in the chapelry except Bulthey.[86] Mr. Linehill, curate in 1713, received £2 8s. 'Reading Money', Samuel Jones was paid £6 15s. for a year's service in 1726, and between 1727 and 1734 Thomas Lyster was paid at the rate of 6s. a week.[87]

John Thomas (d. 1737) left a rent charge of £200, arising from lands at Whitfield, for the maintenance of a curate.[88] This bequest was met by an equivalent grant from Queen Anne's Bounty, who gave a further £600 between 1773 and 1810, and in 1824 the chapelry obtained a Parliamentary grant of £1,400.[89] The living thus became a perpetual curacy, the Vicar of Alberbury being accounted the patron, and institutions are recorded in the bishops' registers from 1781.[90] In 1835 the curate had an average annual income of £95.[91] By 1851 part of the endowment had been laid out in the purchase of some 20 a. glebe, then worth £38 a year, while £55 a year was paid by Queen Anne's Bounty and £2 11s. was derived from other sources.[92]

Although John Thomas had assigned a house at Great Wollaston for use as a parsonage,[93] all perpetual curates appear to have been non-resident until 1869, when the present parsonage was built on the Welshpool road, midway between Great Wollaston and Middletown.[94]

In the later 16th century Reynold Williams claimed that congregations of 200–300 people

frequently attended Great Wollaston chapel.[95] It seems to have been used by those living outside the bounds of the chapelry, for residents of Marsh, Braggington, and Stanford contributed to the cost of a north gallery in 1684.[96] Average congregations of 50 at morning services were reported in 1851, but only 2 persons then attended afternoon services.[97]

The church of ST. JOHN, Great Wollaston,[98] was built in 1787–8,[99] replacing a former chapel on the same site. It consists of a nave and chancel under one roof, with a western porch and gabled bell-cote. It appears to reproduce the dimensions of the former chapel, which also consisted of a nave and chancel in one and was 68 feet long by 16 feet wide.[1] The chapel was said to be very much decayed in 1672, when direction was given to provide new pews.[2] Stone rubble from the former chapel was reused in 1787–8 as a cheaper alternative to brick, but dressings and the moulded cornice are of Pecknall stone.[3] The 3 windows in the north wall were round-headed, with projecting stone surrounds and keystones, and there was a west door with a semicircular window above it in the same style. Simple tracery was added to the south windows in 1885, when the west porch was added and an east window of 3 graded round-headed lights was inserted. The gabled bell-cote replaced a hexagonal bell-turret in 1911.[4] Most of the simple church fittings date from the restoration of 1885; the only relic of the former chapel is an 18th-century brass commemorating 'Old Parr'.[5]

Great Wollaston chapel had 2 bells in 1552[6] and now has a single bell, cast in 1678 by Thomas Roberts of Shrewsbury.[7] There was a silver chalice here in 1552.[8] The plate now consists of a silver chalice, dated 1640 and given by Richard Wolley, and a silver paten and flagon of 1866.[9] The registers begin in 1849.

Cardeston church is first recorded in 1276,[10] but the church contains a single-12th century feature. There is no evidence that it was originally a dependency of Alberbury, but the distribution of the 3 detached portions of Cardeston parish suggests that this was so. In 1341 small tithes in Cardeston, worth 12s., were said to be paid to the mother church.[11] This clearly refers to Alberbury, but these tithes were in fact paid only by that part of Cardeston township which lay in Alberbury parish. The latter were worth about £2 a year in 1655.[12]

Although it was described as a rectory in 1276,[13]

77 Ibid. 183.
78 Ibid.
79 Ibid.
80 T.S.A.S. xlvi. 42.
81 B.M. Add. MS. 21018, f. 279v.
82 S.R.O. 552 uncat., accts of John Thomas, 1677–1736.
83 All Souls mun., Alberbury deeds 164.
84 T.S.A.S. xlvi. 42.
85 Ibid. xlvii. 25–26.
86 S.R.O. 552 uncat., accts of John Thomas, 1677–1736.
87 Ibid.
88 Ibid. 166 uncat., will of John Thomas, 1727.
89 C. Hodgson, Queen Anne's Bounty (1845), 290.
90 Instit. Dioc. Heref. 113–211 passim.
91 Rep. Com. Eccl. Revenues, pp. 456–7.
92 H.O. 129/359/4/4; Bagshaw's Dir. Salop. (1851).
93 S.R.O. 166 uncat., will of John Thomas, 1727.
94 Ibid. 1011 (Gardner) uncat., conveyance of site, 1869.
95 All Souls mun., Alberbury deeds 183.
96 S.P.L., Deeds 3042.
97 H.O. 129/359/4/4.
98 Dedication first recorded in 1595: All Souls mun.,

Alberbury deeds 183. Except where otherwise stated, description of church based on S.P.L., J. H. Smith collect. no. 219; S.P.L., T. F. Dukes watercolours (churches), no. 168; Cranage, vi. 538–9.
99 Great Wollaston par. rec., overseers' accts. 1770–1802.
1 Birmingham Univ. Libr., Mytton's Ch. Notes, vol. i, f. 63a.
2 Heref. Dioc. Regy., reg. 1672–82, f. 9.
3 Great Wollaston par. rec., overseers' accts. 1770–1802.
4 Plaque in church.
5 See p. 195.
6 T.S.A.S. 2nd ser. xii. 337.
7 Alberbury par. rec., churchwardens' accts. 1658–79. Walters, Ch. Bells Salop. 210.
8 T.S.A.S. 2nd ser. xii. 337.
9 Arkwright and Bourne, Ch. Plate Ludlow Archd. 63–64.
10 Reg. T. Cantilupe (C. & Y.S.), 36.
11 Inq. Non. (Rec. Com.), 186.
12 T.S.A.S. xlvii. 26.
13 Reg. T. Cantilupe (C. & Y.S.), 36.

Cardeston was accounted a parochial chapelry during the Middle Ages.[14] In 1547, when Cardeston church was treated as a chantry, it was wrongly said to lie in Alberbury parish and to have been founded by Sir John Burgh in the earlier 15th century.[15] Incumbents of Cardeston have been styled rectors since 1535.[16] The living was united with Alberbury in 1929,[17] but has been served by the Rector of Pontesbury since 1965.

The lords of Cardeston manor have been patrons of the living since the later 13th century, but by 1276 the right of presentation was vested in Wigmore Abbey,[18] which is last known to have exercised this right in 1471.[19] An annual pension of 8s. payable to the abbey is not recorded before 1535.[20] Since the Crown presented to the living in 1547,[21] this payment presumably represents a composition made before 1276, in return for which the abbey made over the patronage to the lord of the manor, rather than a more recent commutation of the abbey's right of presentation. A fee-farm rent, which had been increased to 8s. 10d. by the mid-19th century,[22] is still paid by the incumbent.[23]

The glebe and tithes were said to be worth 28s. in 1341[24] and 66s. 8d. in 1535.[25] In 1547, when the gross value of the living was put at 74s. 8d., the incumbent was said to receive a 'stipend' of 52s. 1d.[26] The value of the living had risen to £27 by 1655[27] and in 1835 the rector had a gross annual income of £321.[28] The net income of the living seems to have been about £200 in the later 19th century.[29]

The glebe appears to have remained unchanged in size, though not in composition, since the early 17th century, when it included a 14-acre close called Black Furlongs on the southern boundary of Cardeston township and about 11 a. in two of the Cardeston common fields.[30] The latter, which had been partially consolidated by 1636,[31] were exchanged in 1786 for closes called Lady Crofts, north of the church, which the rector then took on a 99-year lease.[32] The glebe amounted to 30 a. in 1846, when the greater part was leased,[33] and it was said to be worth £40 in 1851.[34] Medieval incumbents of Cardeston also leased lands in Wattlesborough[35]

and in 1713 the rector held 83 a. in Cardeston of the lord of the manor.[36]

The tithes were worth £150 a year in 1793[37] and in 1846, when moduses were being paid on cows and calves, they were commuted for a rent charge of £267.[38] Tithes arising from 704 a., apparently comprising Cardeston Park and demesne lands at Wattlesborough, had been acquired by the lord of the manor before the end of the 16th century.[39] These were valued at £10 in 1599[40] and at £150 in 1793.[41] They were commuted for a rent charge of £120 in 1846, when further rent charges totalling £1 1s. 6d. were apportioned to 7 small freeholders on Wattlesborough Heath.[42]

William de Cardeston, instituted to the living in 1276,[43] can probably be identified with the William Pecche, parson of Cardeston, who was killed by John de Stockes c. 1293.[44] The dates of incumbency of most of the rectors is unknown before the later 17th century. Five of 11 rectors, 1661–1904, served for more than 20 years. The 5 rectors who held the living between 1661 and 1775 were all resident and all died in office.[45] Fulk Corbet (instituted in 1304),[46] Edward Leighton (rector 1775–1804),[47] and Francis Leighton (rector 1828–71)[48] were close relatives of the lord of the manor, while Thomas Lyster (rector 1457–71)[49] may have been a member of the Lyster family of Rowton. Four rectors before 1929 held the living in plurality with Alberbury.[50]

Curates were continuously employed at a stipend of £40 a year between 1775 and 1828,[51] when the rectors were non-resident, probably owing to the inadequacy of the parsonage. This house, which stood to the north of the church, was maintained in good condition by the tenant in 1793,[52] but was described as unfit for residence in 1835.[53] It was later converted into two cottages.[54] Francis Leighton having served as curate of Cardeston 1826–8,[55] built a new parsonage between 1832 and 1837, with some financial assistance from the patron.[56] This large house, now known as Cardeston Manor, is built of breccia in the Tudor style.

Communion was administered 4 times a year throughout the 18th century.[57] A single Sunday service was held in 1793,[58] but there were morning

[14] Tax. Eccl. (Rec. Com.), 167, 175; Reg. J. Trillek (C. & Y.S.), 381; Cal. Pat. 1408–13, 24.
[15] T.S.A.S. 3rd ser. x. 331.
[16] Valor Eccl. (Rec. Com.), iii. 213.
[17] Heref. Dioc. Regy. reg. 1926–38, p. 216.
[18] Reg. T. Cantilupe (C. & Y.S.), 36.
[19] Reg. J. Stanbury (C. & Y.S.), 187.
[20] Valor Eccl. (Rec. Com.), iii. 213.
[21] Instit. Dioc. Heref. 6.
[22] Eyton, vii. 111.
[23] Ex inf. the Rector of Pontesbury.
[24] Inq. Non. (Rec. Com.), 186.
[25] Valor Eccl. (Rec. Com.), iii. 213.
[26] T.S.A.S. 3rd ser. x. 331. [27] Ibid. xlvii. 26.
[28] Rep. Com. Eccl. Revenues, pp. 434–5.
[29] Kelly's Dir. Salop. (1870–1900).
[30] Heref. Dioc. Regy., glebe terrier, c. 1600.
[31] Ibid. 1636.
[32] Loton Hall MSS., exchange, 1786.
[33] Cardeston par. rec., tithe appt.
[34] H.O. 129/359/4/1.
[35] Loton Hall MSS., lease, 1354; Heref. City Libr. 9133/33.
[36] Loton Hall MSS., Cardeston survey, 1713.
[37] B.M. Add. MS. 21018, f. 285ᵛ.
[38] Cardeston par. rec. tithe appt.
[39] Longleat MSS., unbound 4308.
[40] Ibid.

[41] B.M. Add. MS. 21018, f. 285ᵛ.
[42] Cardeston par. rec., tithe appt.
[43] Reg. T. Cantilupe (C. & Y.S.), 36.
[44] Cal. Pat. 1292–1301, 6.
[45] Instit. Dioc. Heref. 32–106.
[46] Reg. R. Swinfield (C. & Y.S.), 536.
[47] Instit. Dioc. Heref. 131; S.P.R. Heref. vi, p. v.
[48] Instit. Dioc. Heref. 148, 183.
[49] Reg. J. Stanbury (C. & Y.S.), 175, 187.
[50] John de Roden, inst. 1349, vicar of Alberbury 1356–7: Reg. J. Trillek (C. & Y.S.), 381; Cal. Pat. 1354–8, 344, 585. Richard Wilde, rector 1471–92, vicar of Alberbury c. 1473–4: Reg. J. Stanbury (C. & Y.S.), 187; Reg. T. Mylling (C. & Y.S.), 201; T.S.A.S. 4th ser. xi. 280. James Edwards, inst. 1570, vicar of Alberbury by 1563: Instit. Dioc. Heref. 20; T.S.A.S. 4th ser. xi. 200. William Thornes, rector 1804–28, vicar of Alberbury 1778–1829: Instit. Dioc. Heref. 110, 131, 148, 149.
[51] S.P.R. Heref. v (5), 29–34; Heref. Dioc. Regy., reg. 1772–1802, ff. 58, 138, 150, 182; ibid. 1791–1821, f. 128ᵛ.; ibid. 1822–42, pp. 28, 73; B.M. Add. MS. 21018, f. 285ᵛ.
[52] B.M. Add. MS. 21018, f. 285ᵛ.
[53] Rep. Com. Eccl. Revenues, pp. 434–5.
[54] S.P.R. Heref. v (5), Cardeston intro. p. iv.
[55] Heref. Dioc. Regy., reg. 1822–42, p. 73.
[56] S.R.O. 1060/46; B.M. Add. MS. 21018, f. 285ᵛ.
[57] Cardeston par. rec., churchwardens' accts. 1715–1821.
[58] B.M. Add. MS. 21018, f. 285ᵛ.

and evening services here in 1851, when average congregations of 70 were reported at the morning service.[59] Instruction was being given to a female psalm-singer in 1767[60] and a body of psalm-singers, established in 1779, was given 2 guineas a year between 1797 and 1820.[61] A barrel-organ, by the London maker T. C. Bates, was acquired in the mid-19th century and was last used *c.* 1879.[62] It was moved from the tower to its present position at the west end of the nave in 1935.[63]

The church of *ST. MICHAEL*, Cardeston,[64] is built of breccia and consists of nave, chancel, and western tower. The fabric of the nave and chancel dates from 1749, when the church was rebuilt, 'being so very much decayed in the walls and roof',[65] but probably preserved the dimensions and ground-plan of the former church. In the early 18th century the latter consisted of a nave (45 feet long and 14 feet wide) and chancel (13 feet long and 11 feet wide), with a wooden bell-turret.[66] The discovery during restoration in 1905 of the round rear-arch of a late-12th century window in the south wall of the chancel[67] suggests that this part of the church was not rebuilt in 1749. The former church probably also possessed a gallery, for the beam supporting the present western gallery is dated 1678.[68]

The expenses of rebuilding the church in 1749 were in part met by the proceeds of church rates, but a proportion was derived from private bene-factions.[69] Four round-headed windows with sand-stone surrounds and keystones were inserted in the south wall of the nave. The west door with semi-circular window above and the single window in the south wall of the chancel were in the same style. A wooden bell-turret was set at the west end of the nave, but the appearance of the east end of 1749 is not known.

The round chancel arch is the only surviving architectural feature of the 18th-century church. The western tower was added in 1844 in a restoration largely financed by Sir Baldwin and Lady Leighton.[70] It is linked by a short passage-way to the west end of the nave and is of two stages, the lower being square and the upper stage becoming octagonal above angle broaches. At the same time the 4 windows in the nave were remodelled in the Perpendicular style, an east window of similar design was inserted, and the south window of the chancel was replaced by a priest's door. A vestry was added to the north of the chancel in 1905.[71]

The nave ceiling of 1749 was removed in 1905, when the roofs of the nave and chancel were lined with boarding.[72] The tiled floor of the church was laid in 1879.[73]

The nave is largely of 19th-century date, but incorporates king posts of the 1749 church. The late-medieval octagonal font was moved into the tower in 1905.[74] The only other fittings of earlier date than 1749 are the Jacobean oak communion table, the parish chest of 1703, and the gallery beam. The pews—there were 19 in 1793[75]—were replaced by open benches in 1879, when pitch-pine choir stalls were provided.[76] The latter were renewed in 1905[77] and replaced by oak ones in 1935.[78] The altar-rails and lectern date from 1879[79] and the pulpit from 1905, when the chancel screen was erected.[80] The lych-gate and stained glass in the east window date from 1912.[81]

Cardeston church possessed a single bell in 1552.[82] The present bell, dated 1700, was probably made by a Wellington bell-founder.[83] No church plate was recorded here in 1552.[84] The plate now includes a silver paten of 1594, an early-17th-century silver chalice, a silver paten given by Elizabeth Turner in 1733, a silver flagon of 1875, and a silver paten given by the rector in 1905.[85] The registers are complete from 1706.[86]

Wattlesborough school was licensed for services in 1928.[87] The brick mission chapel of St. Margaret, Wattlesborough Heath, was dedicated in 1931.[88]

NONCONFORMITY. No papists or dissenters are recorded at Cardeston in 1676,[89] when there were 4 papists and 11 dissenters in Alberbury parish.[90] It seems likely that the latter were associated with Leighton Owen of Braggington Hall, a prominent Anabaptist[91] whose widow Elizabeth licensed the Hall as a dissenting meeting-house in 1691.[92] There is no later evidence of organized nonconformity in the English part of Alberbury parish. A Methodist chapel, managed by Robert Maddox of Winnington Lodge Farm, reported an average congregation of 40 persons in 1851,[93] but this may have stood at Middletown, where a Wesleyan Methodist chapel was built in 1886.[94] A Primitive Methodist chapel at Wattlesborough Heath was built in 1853[95] and was superseded in 1893 by the present chapel on the Welshpool road.[96]

SCHOOLS. Following a petition from the parishioners of Alberbury, who were 'of mind to erect a

---

[59] H.O. 129/359/4/1.
[60] Cardeston par. rec., churchwardens' accts. 1715–81.
[61] Ibid. 1715–1821.
[62] Cranage, vi. 524; *Salop. Mag.* Oct. 1956, p. 27.
[63] Heref. Dioc. Regy., reg. 1926–38, p. 453.
[64] Except where otherwise stated, description of church based on S.P.L., MS. 372, vol. 2, p. 16; S.P.L., J. H. Smith collect. no. 42; Cranage, vi. 524.
[65] Cardeston par. rec., churchwardens' accts. 1715–81.
[66] Birm. Univ. Libr., Mytton's Ch. Notes, vol. 2, f. 2.
[67] *Kelly's Dir. Salop.* (1929); Pevsner, *Shropshire*, 93.
[68] *S.P.R. Heref.* v (5), Cardeston intro. p. iii.
[69] Cardeston par. rec., churchwardens' accts. 1715–81; inscription on west gable of nave.
[70] S.R.O. 1060/46; *S.P.R. Heref.* v (2), Cardeston intro. p. iii.
[71] Heref. Dioc. Regy., reg. 1902–19, pp. 148–50.
[72] Ibid.
[73] *Salop. Shreds & Patches*, iii. 220.
[74] Heref. Dioc. Regy., reg. 1902–19, pp. 148–50.
[75] B.M. Add MS. 21018, f. 285ᵛ.
[76] *Salop. Shreds & Patches*, iii. 220.

[77] Heref. Dioc. Regy., reg. 1902–19, pp. 148–50.
[78] Ibid. 1926–38, p. 453.
[79] *Salop. Shreds & Patches*, iii. 220.
[80] Heref. Dioc. Regy., reg. 1902–19, pp. 148–50.
[81] Ibid. 520.
[82] *T.S.A.S.* 2nd ser. xii. 337.
[83] Walters, *Ch. Bells Salop*, 202.
[84] *T.S.A.S.* 2nd ser. xii. 337.
[85] Arkwright and Bourne, *Ch. Plate Ludlow Archd.* 15.
[86] Printed to 1812, with bishops' transcripts, 1663–1706, in *S.P.R. Heref.* v (2), 327–74.
[87] Heref. Dioc. Regy., reg. 1926–38, p. 114.
[88] Ibid. p. 333.
[89] *T.S.A.S.* 2nd ser. i. 88.
[90] Ibid. 87.
[91] Ibid. 4th ser. v. 317–19.
[92] *Q. Sess. Orders*, i. 130.
[93] H.O. 129/359/4/5.
[94] *Kelly's Dir. Salop.* (1885, 1900).
[95] Datestone.
[96] Datestone; *Kelly's Dir. Salop.* (1909).

grammar school',[97] the sum of 5 marks formerly paid by All Souls College to the chantry of St. Stephen was applied in 1580 to the salary of a schoolmaster at Alberbury.[98] The Warden of All Souls was then made responsible for the appointment of graduate masters[99] and such masters were appointed in 1591 and 1622.[1] All Souls were still paying £3 6s. 8d. annually to the school in the latter 19th century, but in 1624 the parish undertook to pay a portion of the master's stipend[2] and from the later 17th century a further £3 6s. 8d. was paid annually to the master by the churchwardens.[3] Responsibility for the appointment of masters seems to have passed in the course of the 17th century to the vicar, who also nominated foundation scholars.[4]

The parish clerk appears to have been master, 1649–58,[5] but the vicar, Edward Wall, was master, 1664–77,[6] as was his successor Thomas Hotchkiss, 1681–3.[7] Although the curate, David Price, was master in the 1750s,[8] all other known masters after 1683 have been laymen.[9]

During the 18th century, when 8 foundation scholars attended free of charge, other fee-paying pupils were also taken.[10] In the 1750s David Price, who took boarders, taught Classics himself and employed an assistant to teach reading, writing, and arithmetic.[11] The school, which stood in the churchyard,[12] was enlarged in 1778[13] and rebuilt on the same site in 1794.[14] In 1845, when a new school was built on the glebe, the old school became the master's house.[15] The new school was affiliated to the National Society and was placed under the management of All Souls College, the Archdeacon of Salop, and the Vicar of Alberbury.[16] It was enlarged in 1868 and 1870.[17]

In 1818 the school had no income other than its endowment of £6 13s. 4d.,[18] but by 1833 this was being supplemented by school pence and by subscriptions from local gentry.[19] The latter produced £48 a year in 1850, when £31 was derived from school pence and £6 from church collections, and the school was thereafter in receipt of a government grant.[20] By 1878 the school was £58 in debt, but

this was reduced by voluntary contributions in the following year.[21] In 1893, when school pence had been abolished, £67 was derived from a government grant and £38 from subscriptions.[22]

About 60 children attended the school in 1793,[23] but there were apparently no pupils other than foundation scholars in 1818, when it was reported that 'the poor have not the means of education, but are desirous of possessing them'.[24] Between 60 and 70 children normally attended the school later in the 19th century[25] and by 1846 the staff included a master and mistress.[26] The school, which became Controlled in 1954,[27] was closed in 1965, when most of the children were transferred to Ford school.[28]

The Perpetual Curate of Great Wollaston was required to 'teach school constantly' under the terms of the will of John Thomas, 1727,[29] but no school was established in the chapelry until 1819.[30] This school appears to have been held at the curate's house[31] until 1874, when the present school, on the Welshpool road, was built.[32] In 1893, when the school received a government grant of £59, £47 was derived from subscriptions and £5 from an endowment.[33] Thirteen children attended at their parents' expense in 1833.[34] Numbers rose to 27 by 1847[35] and to 31 by 1871,[36] and increased further after the erection of the new school. There were 59 pupils in 1893[37] and 42 in 1906.[38] The school became Controlled in 1954.[39]

Edward Lockley of Cardeston, schoolmaster, who was buried in 1767,[40] may have taught at a school in this village. In 1818 7 or 8 children attended a private school in Cardeston.[41] A school built by Sir Baldwin Leighton c. 1828[42] was attended by 14 pupils in 1833,[43] but had closed by 1846.[44]

Wattlesborough school was built by Sir Baldwin Leighton between 1835 and 1837[45] and was enlarged in 1871, 1893, and 1904.[46] School pence were being collected in 1846,[47] but the school was otherwise supported by the Leighton family until 1871, after which date it was in receipt of a government grant.[48] In 1893 £62 was received in government grant and £25 from voluntary contributions.[49] The

97 All Souls mun., Alberbury deeds 167(g), 167(i).
98 Ibid. 167(j), 217.
99 Ibid.
1 Ibid. 167(e), 216.
2 Ibid. 218.
3 Alberbury par. rec., churchwardens' accts. 1658–1928.
4 B.M. Add. MS. 21018, f. 279.
5 S.P.R. Heref. vi. 126, 154, 169, 178.
6 Alberbury par. rec., churchwardens' accts. 1658–79.
7 Ibid. 1679–1704.
8 Salop. Shreds & Patches, i. 122.
9 Alberbury par. rec., churchwardens' accts. 1679–1928; Heref. Dioc. Regy., reg. 1682–1709, f. 133.
10 B.M. Add. MS. 21018, f. 279; Alberbury par. rec., acct. of 'Offering Money', 1766–1847.
11 Salop. Shreds & Patches, i. 122.
12 B.M. Add. MS. 21018, f. 279.
13 Alberbury par. rec., churchwardens' accts. 1757–84.
14 Ibid. 1773–1809.
15 Ibid. conveyance of site, 1845; Ed. 7/102/5.
16 Ibid.
17 Kelly's Dir. Salop. (1885).
18 Digest of Returns to Cttee. on Educ. of Poor, H.C. 224, p. 745 (1819), ix (2).
19 Educ. Enquiry Abstract, H.C. 62, p. 768 (1835), xlii.
20 Ed. 7/102/5.
21 Alberbury par. rec., churchwardens' accts. 1843–1928.
22 Return of Schs. 1893 [C. 7529], p. 502, H.C. (1894), lxv.
23 B.M. Add. MS. 21018, f. 279.
24 Digest of Returns to Cttee. on Educ. of Poor, p. 745.
25 Educ. Enquiry Abstract, p. 768; Ed. 7/102/5; Kelly's Dir. Salop. (1885–1913); Returns relating to Elem. Educ. H.C. 201, p. 334 (1871), lv.
26 Nat. Soc. Ch. School Returns, 1846–7.
27 Ex inf. S.C.C. Educ. Dept.
28 Ibid.
29 S.R.O. 166 uncat., will of John Thomas, 1727.
30 Digest of Returns to Cttee. on Educ. of Poor, p. 768.
31 Nat. Soc. Ch. School Returns, 1846–7.
32 Ed. 7/102/104.
33 Return of Schs., 1893, p. 506.
34 Educ. Enquiry Abstract, p. 768.
35 Nat. Soc. Ch. School Returns, 1846–7.
36 Returns relating to Elem. Educ., p. 334.
37 Return of Schs., 1893, p. 506.
38 Voluntary Schs. Returns, H.C. 178–XXIV, p. 21 (1906), lxxxviii.
39 Ex inf. S.C.C. Educ. Dept.
40 S.P.R. Heref. vi. 450.
41 Digest of Returns to Cttee. on Educ. of Poor, p. 748.
42 F. C. Childe, Extracts from Letters & Speeches, &c., o Sir Baldwin Leighton, Bt. (Shrewsbury, 1875), 6.
43 Educ. Enquiry Abstract, p. 771.
44 Nat. Soc. Ch. School Returns, 1846–7.
45 S.R.O. 1060/46.
46 Kelly's Dir. Salop. (1885, 1895); datestones.
47 Nat. Soc. Ch. School Returns, 1846–7.
48 Ed. 7/102/6.
49 Return of Schs., 1893, p. 502.

school became Controlled in 1953.[50] Attendance rose from 29 in 1846[51] to 45 in 1871,[52] and between 70 and 80 children attended between 1885 and 1913.[53]

CHARITIES. A number of small bequests to the poor, combined to form a parish stock, had been administered by the Alberbury churchwardens since the mid-17th century.[54] The stock, which amounted to £52 in 1660, and to £59 10s. in 1691, was lent on bond and the interest was distributed among the poor.[55] The sum of £2 14s. was distributed in 1670 and £3 11s. 3d. in 1691.[56] By 1776, when the annual income had risen to £13, distribution took place at Christmas.[57] The parish stock, which amounted to £169 by the end of the 18th century, then represented bequests by 12 donors. The sum of £165 from this source was lent to build a workhouse at Bausley in 1779 and £8 5s. interest was being paid annually by the overseers c. 1830. The loan was redeemed in 1834, when £150 was invested in stock, but in 1840 the stock was sold and the capital invested in the Welshpool Turnpike. In the early 19th century 20s. a year, representing a 17th-century bequest by Richard Haines,[58] was distributed in bread at Christmas and the remainder of the income from the parish stock was distributed in money at the same time. The income had fallen to £6 by 1861 and was at that time distributed by the vicar in food, clothing, and coal. The capital appears to have been lost c. 1874 when the Welshpool Turnpike came to an end.

A bequest of £100 made at an unknown date by Richard Lyster had been lent to the Shrewsbury House of Industry by 1830, when the annual interest of £5 was being distributed in money at Christmas among the poor of Alberbury parish. The capital was invested in the Watling Street Turnpike in 1840 and was probably lost, like the parish stock, c. 1874.

During his lifetime John Asterley of Stanford gave £10 to the poor of Wattlesborough township. Until at least 1861 the annual interest of 10s. was distributed by his descendants on Good Friday,

most of it being applied to the poor of Bausley c. 1830, but it has since been lost.

By will made before 1786 John Morgan left £10 to provide bread for the poor of Alberbury parish and a similar sum for the poor of Cardeston. The annual interest of £1, divided equally between the two parishes, was treated as a rent-charge on a farm at Melverley. In 1830 Alberbury's share was being distributed in bread by the owner of the farm on Good Friday. By 1861 responsibility for distribution in Alberbury had passed to the vicar, but Alberbury's share of the charity was withheld by the tenant in 1876 and it has since been lost. Until 1833 the annual interest of 10s. received by Cardeston was distributed in money by the churchwardens. The rector, who then assumed responsibility, was still distributing the charity in 1900.

Owen George left £50 to the chapelry of Great Wollaston. From the annual interest of £3, 40s. was to be paid to the minister of the chapel for preaching 6 sermons and 20s. was to be distributed in bread among such poor as came to hear the sermons. By the early 19th century this bequest had been converted into a rent-charge on Plas-y-Court Farm. The minister then received only 30s. a year and 20s. was distributed by the overseer of Wollaston Quarter. The income remained unchanged until 1950, when the rent-charge was redeemed for £100, which was then invested in stock. Recipients of bread were being chosen by the tenant of Plas-y-Court in 1872, but by 1902 the charity was administered by the vicar and churchwardens of Great Wollaston.

A bequest of £10 to the poor of Great Wollaston made by Elizabeth, wife of Collins Woolridge, was applied towards the cost of building a vestry here c. 1819 and 10s. was paid annually by the overseer in respect of this charity until 1836. The charity was said to be lost c. 1861, but it was revived in 1866 when £10, paid by Col. Harries of Cruckton, was invested in stock. The George and Woolridge charities have been jointly administered during the present century. Distributions in bread had ceased by 1935 and in 1964 30s. was paid annually to the vicar and 30s. given in money to the poor.

FORD

THE boundaries of the modern civil parish of Ford do not correspond with those of the ancient township. That township, which was said to contain 1,773 a. in 1847,[1] included some 570 a. to the west of the village in the parish of Alberbury.[2] Tithes from this latter area were paid to Ford after 1701[3] and it was treated for civil purposes as part of Ford parish in the 18th century.[4] Although the tithe rent-charge due from Ford-in-Alberbury (as the area was called)

continued to be paid to Ford after commutation in 1847,[5] the western boundary of the parish was re-defined in 1846 and thereafter the civil parish no longer included that part of the township which lay in Alberbury.[6] The area treated in this article is the township, not the more restricted civil parish.

The boundary with Pontesbury on the south, formerly in dispute, was fixed in 1846, when 22 a. lying in Cruckton and claimed as a detached part

[50] Ex inf. S.C.C. Educ. Dept.
[51] Nat. Soc. *Ch. Sch. Returns*, 1846–7.
[52] *Returns relating to Elem. Educ.*, p. 334.
[53] *Kelly's Dir. Salop.* (1885–1913).
[54] Alberbury par. rec., churchwardens' accts., 1658–1704. Except where otherwise stated, account of charities based on *24th Rep. Com. Char.*, H.C. 231, pp. 390–1 (1831), xi; *Digest of Endowed Char., 1862–3*, H.C. 433, pp. 158–9, 168–9 (1867–8), lii; Char. Com. files.
[55] Alberbury par. rec., churchwardens' accts. 1658–1704.
[56] Ibid.

[57] Ibid. 1757–84; ibid. accts. of 'Offering Money', 1766–1847.
[58] Heref. Dioc. Regy., visitation papers, box 44, churchwardens' presentment, 1672.
[1] Par. rec., tithe appt. 1847. This article was written in 1964 and revised in 1965. Thanks are particularly due to the Revd. J. E. G. Cartlidge, formerly Vicar of Ford, for much good advice.
[2] Ibid.
[3] S.R.O. 1123/8.
[4] Par. rec., overseers' accts. 1774–1820.
[5] Ibid. tithe appt.
[6] Ibid. boundary award, 1846.

of Ford parish, were adjudged to be in the parish of Pontesbury.[7] A further 5 a. in Cruckton, however, remained a detached part of Ford parish until transferred to Pontesbury in 1884.[8] Since 1884 the civil parish has contained 1,202 a.[9]

The parish boundary, like that of the township, follows the River Severn to the north but elsewhere makes use of no natural features.[10] On the west the present parish boundary appears to follow, to the north of the Welshpool road, the boundary between the former common fields of Ford and Benthall Common. The township boundary, some 700 yards to the west, ran along the western edge of Benthall Common and came to within a few yards of Cardeston village, taking in Benthall Stone Farm, Whiston Priory, Whiston Farm, Coppy House, Dodlee, and Far Broadway Farm. It met the present parish boundary at the cross-roads on Ford Heath, where the Primitive Methodist chapel stands. The boundary with Pontesbury and Bicton on the south and east does not appear to have been materially affected by the award of 1846, and presumably corresponds with that of the township.

The northern half of the township is drained by Cardeston Brook, a tributary of the Severn which was known in the 17th century as Longmoor Brook.[11] This stream flows north-eastwards from Cardeston and passes through the village. The land here, relatively flat apart from the low hills formed by deposits of sand and gravel around the village and by an outcrop of sandstone to the west of Cross Gates Inn, rises from 200 feet along the Severn to some 300 feet to the south of Cardeston Brook. In the north-west and on Ford Heath to the south of the brook, where the land rises to a plateau at some 350 feet, the subsoil is boulder clay.

During the early Middle Ages cultivation was restricted to the area north of the Welshpool road. Ford's common fields were flanked by Benthall Common on the west and Onslow Common on the east, while oak forest covered most of the land to the south of the road. The little that is known of Benthall Common suggests that the greater part had been inclosed by the 16th century. A field in the Common known as Quankhams, north-west of Benthall Stone Farm, is first recorded, in the form 'Quonkerne', in 1575.[12] Novers Rough, on the banks of the Severn to the north, and Hogmoor at the southern end of the Common had been inclosed by the 1660s.[13] An outrack, or drift-way, leading to the common is recorded in 1681, when it was leased to the tenant of Cross Gates Inn.[14] Several small rectangular fields to the north of Benthall Stone Farm were, however, called 'common land' in 1847[15] and may be the product of formal inclosure

in the later 18th century. The southern end of Benthall Common, adjoining Cardeston Brook, was known as Whiston. This name was perhaps derived from a stone, like that at Benthall Cross, at a cross-roads on the Welshpool road, for Whiston Cross is recorded in 1688.[16]

When inclosed in 1771[17] Onslow Common did not extend into Ford, but the adjacent site of the squatter settlement at Chavel was waste land c. 1775[18] and field-names in the north-east of the parish—Miry Wicket, Hell Wicket, and Brandart[19]—indicate that assarting had taken place here.

A line drawn from Shoot Hill past Moor House and Coppy House to Dodlee would mark approximately the southern limits of assarting in medieval Ford. The area cleared of forest thus comprised the clays to the north of the Ford Heath plateau, which slope gently northwards towards Cardeston Brook and thus possess adequate natural drainage. The lord of the manor was concerning himself directly with assarting in the mid-13th century for between 1246 and 1254 James de Audley permitted Richard Pride of Shrewsbury to fell 1,000 oaks in the manor,[20] and had cleared a small wood called 'Serthul'.[21] The latter presumably lay in the area now known as Shoothill where a patchwork of small and irregularly shaped fields, typical of medieval assarting, survived until the 19th century.[22] The principal wood was known in the 13th century as Aspley Wood[23] of which Gough's Coppice, to the west of Shoothill, is a surviving remnant. Some time before 1272 the tenants of Ford manor obtained a grant of the soil of this wood and of the Heath to the south, as far as the boundary of Newnham in Pontesbury.[24] Subsequent clearance thus ceased to be of direct interest to the lord of the manor and its progress is consequently ill-documented. The grant reserved to the free tenant Geoffrey de Ford a moor below Aspley Wood,[25] the location of which is preserved in 'moor' field-names to the north of Gough's Coppice.[26] Many other fields in this part of the parish by their names and shape betray their origin as medieval assarts. Fields called Breeches lie to the north of Moor House and one called Pell Beggar to the south. Other such field-names hereabout include Dukes Camp (adjoining Coppy House), Wigwall, and the adjacent Alderman Croft (near Dodlee).[27]

Two other smaller woods survived the Middle Ages. Birchley Coppice, first recorded before 1272,[28] stood to the north of Coppy House and appears to have been cleared c. 1769, when it contained 30 a.,[29] while Burd's Coppice, north-east of Dodlee, is probably the wood known as Dodlee in the 16th and 17th centuries[30] but takes its name from a 19th-

[7] Par. rec., boundary award, 1846.
[8] O.S. *Area Bk.* (1882); Local Government Bd. Order 17485.
[9] Ibid.
[10] The following topographical description is based, except where otherwise stated, on O.S. Map 1″, sheet lxi (1st edn.); O.S. Map 6″ Salop. 33 (1st and later edns.); O.S. Maps 1/25,000, SJ 41 (1957), SJ 31 (1959); Rocque, *Map of Salop.* (1752); Baugh, *Map of Salop* (1808); B.M. O.S. 2″ orig. drawings, sheets 199 (1816), 320 (1827); Geol. Survey map (drift), sheet 152 (1932); par. rec., tithe appt. and map, 1847.
[11] S.R.O. 169/1.
[12] S.P.L., Deeds 68.
[13] S.R.O. 169/1.
[14] Ibid.
[15] Par. rec., tithe appt.

[16] S.R.O. 169/1.
[17] Inclosure award, 1771, in Q. Sess., reg. papists' deeds, p. 155.
[18] S.P.L., Deeds 1707.
[19] Par. rec., tithe appt.
[20] *Rot. Hund.* (Rec. Com.), ii. 66.
[21] Ibid.
[22] Par. rec., tithe appt.
[23] B.M. Add. Ch. 73106.
[24] Ibid.
[25] Ibid.
[26] Gough's Coppice was known as Moor Coppice in the 19th century: par. rec., tithe appt.
[27] Par. rec., tithe appt.; S.R.O. 169/1.
[28] B.M. Add. Ch. 73106.
[29] E 126/29/Hil. 1769 no. 23.
[30] B.M. Add. Ch. 73108; S.R.O. 49/481; ibid. 169/1.

century owner of Whiston Priory.[31] Only 23 a. of woodland remained in the parish by 1847.[32]

The line of small fields running along the south-western boundary of the township, between Dodlee and Broadway Farm, are presumably ancient assarts and contrast with the larger fields, rectangular in shape, found over the greater part of the Ford Heath plateau. The latter are the result of a formal inclosure which took place between 1735 and 1750, when parts of the Heath were allotted to the tenants.[33]

The township's common fields were known as Beanshill Field (or Deepdale), Whiston Field, and Lower Field (or Old Field), but the available evidence provides only a general indication as to where each of them lay.[34] Beanshill Field, to the north-west of the village, ran from Cardeston Brook to Beanshill on the eastern edge of Benthall Common and was bounded on the north by meadows along-side the Severn. Whiston Field lay to the south of Beanshill Field and ran from the village south-westwards towards Whiston Common. Lower Field, which presumably lay to the east of the village, is once recorded in 1575 and still existed in 1604. It must, however, have been inclosed soon after this date, for after 1650 the township possessed only two common fields. Open-field strips are recorded until 1703, but inclosure seems to have taken place piecemeal in the later 17th century. There are several references to newly inclosed open-field lands between 1668 and 1673 and this process was no doubt connected with the consolidation by exchange of the larger copyhold estates in the township, which was taking place between 1660 and 1680.

The road from Shrewsbury to Welshpool, turn-piked in 1758,[35] runs through the centre of the parish. This crossed Cardeston Brook at Welshman's Ford, where a footbridge was replaced by a stone bridge in 1792 when the road between it and Cross Gates Inn was widened.[36] The only other major road in the parish is that from Alberbury, which meets the Welshpool road to the west of Cross Gates Inn and was turnpiked by 1780.[37] Near Benthall Stone Farm this road crosses Sandy Lane, a green lane running northwards from Ford Heath to Little Shrawardine. The sandstone base of a cross, at this road junction, was formerly known as Maiden Cross and now called Benthall Cross.[38]

Ford may derive its name, like the adjacent hamlet of Montford, from its proximity to one or more fords across the Severn. The village stands at the junction of two roads running northwards from Ford Heath, of which that from Cruckton, through Shoothill, was probably the more important.[39] The section of the latter road north of the Welshpool road was formerly known as the Portway.[40] North of the village roads once ran towards Little Shrawar-dine and Preston Montford. Their course was still

known in the early 19th century,[41] but both have long fallen out of public use. A number of other roads in the north of the parish have been closed since the early 19th century,[42] including Marsh Lane which once ran from Ford village to Chavel and is last recorded in 1745.[43]

The existing public roads on the Heath, which are straight and have wide verges, were presumably laid out at its inclosure in the mid-18th century. They followed their present course in 1752.[44] Two earlier roads leading to the Heath are no longer public roads: Kittyoak Lane (Kittahoe in the 17th century),[45] running southwards from Cross Gates Inn, and Birchley Lane,[46] a southern continuation of Sandy Lane.

The Shropshire and Montgomeryshire Railway, which ran north-eastwards across the parish and had a station at Cross Gates, was opened in 1866.[47] The line was closed in 1880, but was reopened in 1911 as The Shropshire and Montgomeryshire Light Railway. The latter closed in 1933.[48]

Apart from the large Council estate to the south, which now links Ford to the Welshpool road, the present distribution of houses in the village appears to preserve the ancient pattern of settlement. They are grouped in two distinct areas, separated by the brook, over which a stone bridge was built in 1856.[49] One group of houses stands near the church and along the former road to Little Shrawardine and the other, to the east of the brook, stands on New Street (the former road to Preston Montford) and the Portway.

The church, occupying the highest spot in the village on the top of the ridge of sand and gravel known as Catshill, includes some 12th-century features, but the churchyard was not inclosed until 1861.[50] Adjoining it stand Ford House and Ford Mansion, former residences respectively of the Ambler and Waring families. Ford House, to the east of the church, contains 2 stories with attics and was built in the early 18th century.[51] It is of brick with stone dressings and has a modillion cornice. The principal east and west fronts are of 5 bays. The roof is double-gabled, the valley being masked at the ends by a straight parapet, with angle vases on the east façade. The central doorway on the east front is flanked by Tuscan pilasters against a rusticated surround and has a pediment above, while that on the west front has a Tuscan porch. The dining room and bedroom above, occupying two bays to the south of the house, contain good panelling. The staircase in a central staircase hall to the east has 3 balusters to each tread, one fluted, one turned, and one spiral, resembling the stair of Whitton Hall, built c. 1730.[52] The brick dovecote, coach-house, and barn to the north of the house are also of 18th-century date. The Ambler family lived here until 1793,[53] after which date the house was occupied as a gentleman's

[31] See p. 232.
[32] Par. rec., tithe appt.
[33] S.R.O. 169/2–3.
[34] Description of common fields based in S.P.L., Deeds 68, 83, 112, 146, 11047, 12706; S.R.O. 169/1–2.
[35] Shrewsbury road Act, 31 Geo. II, c. 67 (priv. act).
[36] Q. Sess., dep. plans 198.
[37] See p. 187.
[38] S.R.O. 169/2–3; Salop. N. & Q. N.S. iv (2), 11, 19–20, 32, 45.
[39] Q. Sess. Orders, ii. 168.
[40] S.R.O. 169/2; par. rec., tithe appt.

[41] B.M. O.S. 2″ orig. drawings, sheets 199 (1816), 320 (1827); S.R.O. 529/10.
[42] Ibid.
[43] S.R.O. 169/2.
[44] Rocque, Map of Salop. (1752).
[45] S.R.O. 169/1.　　　　　　　　　　　　[46] Ibid.
[47] Ex inf. Brit. Trans. Rec.　　　　　　[48] Ibid.
[49] Par. rec., subscription list for bridge, 1856.
[50] Heref. Dioc. Regy., reg. 1857–69, p. 197.
[51] For some account, see T.S.A.S. 4th ser. vi. 288–92.
[52] See p. 314.
[53] Par. rec., overseers' accts., 1774–1820.

residence by a succession of tenants until 1839, when it was bought by the Revd. R. Lingen-Burton,[54] whose family were the principal land-owners in Ford during the later 19th century. Brook House, timber-framed and of early-17th-century date, which stands to the south of Ford House, was originally L-shaped, but its east wing was later demolished.[55] The tradition that this was the original house of the Ambler family, who occupied a 6-hearth house in the village in 1662,[56] may be correct. It was the farm-house of the Wall family during the later 18th century, but its ownership cannot be traced earlier than 1734.[57]

Ford Mansion stands to the west of the church. It comprises an early-17th-century timber-framed house, now brick-cased, of which all original features apart from the fireplace and stair are now concealed, and an east range, added in 1779.[58] The latter, which is of 2 stories, is brick-built and has a stone string-course at first-floor level and a stone cornice with a brick parapet above. The three central bays on the east façade are set forward a little and are surmounted by a brick pediment with a blank shield and swags. The stone central doorway is flanked by columns, supporting a fluted frieze and pediment, and the window above also has a stone surround. The house ceased to be occupied by its builder, Francis Waring, after 1785 and has been no more than a farm-house since that time.[59]

The remaining houses in the west of the village are of stone or brick. None appears to have been built before the later 18th century apart from a timber-framed house, adjoining Brook Cottage, demolished since 1950.[60] Most of them, however, appear to occupy ancient sites, for houses stood there in 1813, before the dispersal of the larger copyhold estates and the consequent increase in the number of cottages and smallholdings in the village.[61] Only two of them are known to have been built on virgin sites in the early 19th century—Clifton House, a Georgian house of 3 bays, built c. 1822 by Thomas Davies[62] (formerly the tenant of Ford Mansion),[63] and the smallholding to the east, built between 1835 and 1847.[64]

A house on the site of Ford Hall, which contained a hall, parlour, and kitchen on the ground floor in 1705[65] and had 3 hearths in 1662,[66] was described as a capital messuage in 1665.[67] This house then belonged to Griffith Davies,[68] who sold it to John Calcott in 1669.[69] The present house was built by George Calcott in 1729.[70] A brick house on a stone plinth, of 2 stories with attics, it has a hipped roof and was at first U-shaped. The south front may originally have been of 5 bays, but now has only 3 windows on each story. Some original window-

openings with keystones and segmental heads, survive in the east and west walls. Inside is an oak staircase with turned balusters and square newels and there are some original oak doors and door-frames. One room on the ground floor contains moulded ceiling beams and cornice. A single-story kitchen wing was built to the north somewhat later in the 18th century. Sash windows on the south front and elsewhere date from c. 1800, when a new central south door, with a fanlight, was inserted. Later in the 19th century further outbuildings were added to the north, bay windows were set against the east and west walls, and attic windows were inserted. The latest addition is a front porch; the pedimented doorcase of c. 1800 was then moved to the rear of the house.

The 3 larger houses in the village were thus built by wealthy copyholders and none of them is likely to stand on the site of the medieval manor-house. The latter seems to have passed to a free tenant by 1317[71] and was occupied by his descendants under the name of the Hall of Ford in 1601.[72] It may have stood within the semicircular embankment east of the brook, to which Bank Farm owes its name. Wall Hill, the name of the hillock to the south-east of Bank Farm,[73] may refer to the manor-house, or to a yet earlier site. The present farm-house is the most substantial of the surviving early-17th-century houses in the village, but its ownership cannot be traced earlier than the 19th century.[74] Now L-shaped, its original ground plan seems to have been of two rooms with a central chimney stack. The heavy ceiling beams and mantels have well-cut chamfers and stops. In 1746,[75] when the house was cased in brick, a stone-built south wing was added, incorporating the parlour of the original house.

New Street, besides leading to Preston Montford, was probably also once the route to the mill, whose site is marked by the field-name Mill Leasow, near the junction of Cardeston Brook and the River Severn. On this road stands Oak Cottage, the only surviving medieval house in the village. This comprises a 2-bay cruck hall and storied solar wing at the east end. The latter, which is partly close-studded, may have been added in the 16th century. A chimney stack, placed axially at the junction of hall and solar, and the first floor in the hall were probably inserted c. 1600. Ownership of the house cannot be traced earlier than 1813, when it had already been reduced to cottage status.[76] Two other houses in this part of the village are of 17th-century date. Old School House, standing on a road from Street to Ford House which was closed in 1841,[77] was occupied as a farm-house until 1843[78] and was subsequently used for some 30 years as the village

---

[54] Par. rec., overseers' accts., 1774–1820; S.R.O. 529/18–36; ibid. 955 uncat., conveyance 1842.
[55] Ex inf. Mr. S. Morley Tonkin.
[56] E 179/255/35 m. 82.
[57] S.R.O. 169/2–3; ibid. 248/1–2.
[58] For some account, see *T.S.A.S.* 4th ser. vi. 292. See also plate facing p. 236.
[59] Par. rec., overseers' accts. 1774–1820; ibid. tithe appt.
[60] Local inf.
[61] S.R.O. 529/10.
[62] Ibid. 169/11–14.
[63] Par. rec., overseers' accts. 1774–1820.
[64] S.R.O. 169/11–14; par. rec., tithe appt.
[65] S.R.O. 49/497; *S.P.R. Heref.* vi. 310.
[66] E 179/255/35 m. 82.

[67] S.R.O. 169/1.
[68] Ibid.
[69] Ibid.
[70] Datestone. For some description, see *T.S.A.S.* 4th ser. vi. 285–7, where the house is wrongly said to have been the residence of the Crosse family.
[71] See p. 230.
[72] S.P.L., Deeds 12706.
[73] Par. rec., tithe appt.
[74] Ibid.; S.R.O. 169/11–15; ibid. 248/2; par. rec., overseers' accts. 1774–1820.
[75] Datestone.
[76] S.R.O. 529/10.
[77] Q. Sess. rolls, Hil. 1841.
[78] S.R.O. 169/13.

school.[79] The original house was L-shaped, containing two rooms with a central stack and an unheated north wing. It was encased in brick in the later 17th century and brick cottages were added to the east and west in the early 19th century. Lower Farm, still externally timber-framed, was largely demolished in 1964. Apart from Five Acres, built by the village shopkeeper between 1814 and 1847,[80] and the vicarage, built in 1870,[81] the remaining houses in the east of the village all occupy ancient sites,[82] but the only one likely to have been built before 1750 is The Cottage, opposite the vicarage. This is a stone house of two bays with a chimney stack in the north gable, its single internal wall being timber-framed. Occupied by the Fox family from the 17th to the 19th century,[83] it is known to have been standing in 1745[84] and may be the one-hearth house held by Richard Fox in 1662.[85]

The earliest recorded houses on the line of the Welshpool road were the two inns, known since the 17th century as Pavement Gates and Cross Gates.[86] Both were probably in use as inns by the early 17th century, for 3 alehouses were recorded in the parish, 1613–18.[87] Cross Gates Inn, first named in 1643,[88] belonged until 1671 to the Morris family, who also had a smithy nearby.[89] It was bought in 1712 by Thomas Wilde, whose descendants were its owners, but not its occupiers, until the later 19th century.[90] The inn seems originally to have consisted of two structurally separate houses, for in 1665 the property was described as 2 messuages.[91] One of these was a two-bay house with a central stack, set back from and at right angles to the main road, while the other, of two bays with a chimney stack on the west gable, lay alongside the road. The latter was presumably the original inn—the stone cellar beneath is recorded in 1671.[92] The house owes its present external appearance to Thomas Wilde, who in 1724[93] linked the two houses, added wings to the north and west, and cased or rebuilt the timber-framed east front in brick. The hipped roof may have been raised at a later date. Pavement Gates Inn, recorded by name from 1660,[94] was smaller than Cross Gates. It contained 3 hearths in 1662[95] and survived as a modest timber-framed house with a thatched roof until c. 1930, when a new inn was built on its site.[96]

The squatter settlement of Chavel developed alongside the Welshpool road on waste land at the south-western end of Onslow Common, where a cottage is first recorded in 1672,[97] and is first named, in the form Chaville, in 1776.[98] There were 8 houses

here in 1847.[99] The oldest of the existing houses at Chavel is no. 1, Chavel, set back from the main road on the line of Marsh Lane. This is stone-built with a central stack and was standing c. 1775.[1] Other stone houses here are Burton Cottage, standing on Marsh Lane like no. 1, Chavel, which it resembles in plan, and no. 8, Chavel, to the south of the main road, which was occupied by a blacksmith in the 19th century.[2] Nos. 5–7, Chavel, a somewhat more pretentious house than the others, possesses a coach-house and is said to bave been built for an early-19th-century incumbent of Ford.[3]

The only other house on the Welshpool road, between Chavel and Cross Gates Inn, likely to have been built before the 19th century is Brookfield— a small stone house to the north of the road near Welshman's Ford. This was formerly the smithy[4] and is similar in plan to the older cottages at Chavel. The stone-built house opposite, a wheelwright's shop until c. 1934,[5] probably dates from the early 19th century. Two cottages had been built by 1847 at Buttlane Head[6]—the junction of the Welshpool road with that from Cruckton to Ford. The Methodist chapel was built here in 1850,[7] followed by a manse in 1867[8] and the school in 1873.[9] Eight Council houses were built to the west of the school in 1921[10] and a further 70 Council houses have been built since 1945,[11] linking settlement at Buttlane Head with the village.

Settlement on the former Benthall Common and at Whiston dates in the main from the second quarter of the 19th century, but Novers Tenement, on the green lane north of Benthall Stone Farm, was standing by 1775.[12] Several of the houses here, like Benthall Stone Farm and Whiston Villa, were in origin smallholdings created after the break-up of the estates of the Ambler and Waring families.[13] The largest of them is Whiston Priory, a stone house built between 1834 and 1842 by Timotheus Burd, a Shrewsbury surveyor who acquired an estate of some 125 a. in the parish by piecemeal purchases between 1834 and 1851.[14] Fairfield House, The Elms, and Whiston Farm have been built since 1847.[15]

Settlement on the northern slopes of Ford Heath, first recorded in the later 16th century, consists of scattered farms and cottages, the greatest concentration being at Shoothill. Although woodland at Shoothill was already being cleared in the 13th century,[16] no houses are recorded here before the later 17th century[17] and few of those now standing were built before 1800. Several, like Cruckfield,

[79] See p. 237.
[80] S.R.O. 169/11–14; par. rec., tithe appt.
[81] Heref. Dioc. Regy., reg. 1869–83, pp. 34, 136; par. rec., plans of parsonage, 1870.
[82] S.R.O. 529/10; B.M. O.S. 2″ orig. drawings, sheet 320 (1827).
[83] S.R.O. 169/1–3, 11–13; ibid. 248/1–2; par. rec., tithe appt.
[84] S.R.O. 169/2.
[85] E 179/255/35 m. 82.
[86] S.R.O. 169/1.
[87] Q. Sess., alehouse reg.
[88] S.P.L., Deeds 11050.
[89] S.R.O. 169/1.
[90] Ibid. 169/1–3, 11–18; ibid. 248/1–2.
[91] Ibid. 169/1.
[92] Ibid.
[93] Datestone.
[94] S.R.O. 169/1.
[95] E 179/255/35 m. 82.

[96] Local inf.
[97] S.R.O. 169/1.
[98] Ibid. 169/3.
[99] Par. rec., tithe appt.
[1] S.P.L., Deeds 1707.
[2] Par. rec., tithe appt.
[3] Ex inf. Mr. W. Parry.
[4] Par. rec., tithe appt.
[5] Ibid.; Kelly's Dir. Salop. (1856–1934).
[6] Par. rec., tithe appt.
[7] Datestone.   [8] Ibid.
[9] Ed. 7/102/101.
[10] Datestone.
[11] Ex inf. Atcham R.D.C.
[12] S.R.O. 169/3.
[13] Ibid. 169/11–15; ibid. 248/2; par. rec., tithe appt.
[14] Ibid.
[15] Par. rec., tithe appt.
[16] Rot. Hund. (Rec. Com.), ii. 66.
[17] S.R.O. 169/1

Dinthill Cottage, and Newhouse, were the homesteads of smallholdings created in the early 19th century.[18] Cruckfield, however, was originally a timber-framed house of early-17th-century date and Dinthill Cottage is a brick-cased timber-framed house. Shoothill Farm, the only large farm here, was built c. 1850 by William Hudson, who acquired his land at the Waring sale in 1844.[19] Ford Villa, a large brick house of the later 19th century, stands on the site of the homestead of the Morris family, smallholders at Shoothill by 1730.[20]

Coppy House and Moor House, first recorded in 1699[21] and 1672[22] respectively, are both brick-cased timber-framed houses with central chimney stacks, typical of the earlier 17th century. The latter, which belonged, like Ford Hall, to the Calcott family,[23] has a Georgian north wing. The first clear reference to a house at Dodlee is found in the 1670s, when it was a 6-acre smallholding.[24] The present 2-bay house is stone-built, with a central stack, and probably dates from the early 18th century. Far Broadway Farm, also of stone, has a similar ground-plan and is presumably of the same date as Dodlee.

Although 4 cottages appear to have stood on the Ford Heath plateau, in the south of the parish, by 1718,[25] none of the existing houses precedes in date the inclosure of the Heath in the mid-18th century. The oldest is Tithe House Farm, a brick house dated 1755,[26] built by Thomas Ambler, the impropriator of the tithes of Ford, and subsequently occupied by his tithe-collector.[27] A tithe-barn, formerly timber-framed, stands to the east of the house. Apart from the Primitive Methodist chapel (1867)[28] and manse (1865)[29] and a few houses built since 1945 the remaining houses on the Heath are stone-built and of early-19th-century date.

There were said to be 88 adults in the parish in 1676.[30] There were 193 inhabitants in 1793,[31] and the population grew steadily until 1881, when it stood at 373.[32] It had fallen to 321 by 1911 but, with the erection of Council houses, it has again risen since 1921.[33] There were 641 inhabitants in 1961.[34]

MANOR. The manor of FORD has always been considerably more extensive than the parish. It was said to contain 14 berewicks in 1086,[35] which would include Ford itself and Arscott, Cruckmeole, Cruckton, Edge, Lea, Marton, Newnham, Plealey, Pontesford, Sascott, and Sibberscott, all in Pontesbury parish.[36] The manors of Benthall, in Alberbury parish, and Polmere, in Pontesbury parish, appear to have been merged with that of Ford shortly after 1102[37] and the hamlet of Little Shrawardine was a member of the manor by 1308.[38]

The manor was held by Edwin, Earl of Mercia, before the Conquest,[39] but was granted to Roger, Earl of Shrewsbury, presumably at the creation of the earldom of Shrewsbury in 1071.[40] Roger himself held the manor in 1086,[41] but it was forfeited after the rebellion of Robert of Bellême in 1102[42] and remained in the hands of the Crown until 1155, when it was granted to Reynold, Earl of Cornwall.[43] It reverted to the Crown on the latter's death in 1175[44] and remained a royal manor until 1230. A grant of lands in Ford to John le Strange in 1197 appears to have been abortive,[45] but the manor may have been held by Thomas de Erdington, c. 1216–18, in exchange for the honour of Montgomery.[46] In 1230 it was granted to Henry de Audley,[47] who was succeeded in 1246 by his son James.[48] The latter died in 1272[49] and his son James in the following year,[50] when the manor passed successively to the latter's three brothers, Henry, 1273–6,[51] William, 1276–82,[52] and Nicholas, 1282–99.[53] Ela, widow of James the elder, however, held a third of the manor in dower from 1272 until her death in 1299[54] and Maud, widow of his son James, to whom the remainder of the manor was assigned in dower in 1274,[55] was allotted a further third of the manor in 1275,[56] but she died in the following year.[57] Lucy, widow of Henry de Audley, was assigned part of the manor in dower in 1278.[58] She was still living in 1303,[59] but seems no longer to have had any estate here by 1283.[60]

On the death of Nicholas de Audley in 1299 the manor passed to his son Thomas, then a minor,[61] wardship being granted to Amadeus, Count of Savoy, in 1301[62] and to Piers Gaveston before 1308.[63] Thomas died while still under age in 1308[64] and was succeeded by his brother Nicholas, who obtained livery of the manor in 1314.[65] Dower was assigned in 1308 to Thomas's widow Eve,[66] who still held a life interest in the manor in 1335,[67] but had

[18] S.R.O. 169/11–14; ibid. 248/2; par. rec., tithe appt.
[19] S.R.O. 169/14.
[20] Ibid. 169/2–3, 11–14; ibid. 248/1–2; par. rec., tithe appt.
[21] S.R.O 169/1.
[22] Ibid.
[23] Ibid. 169/1–3, 11–14; ibid. 248/1–2.
[24] Ibid. 169/1.
[25] Q. Sess., reg. papists' estates, 1718.
[26] Datestone.
[27] Par. rec., overseers' accts. 1774–1820; ibid. tithe appt.; S.R.O. 529/7–41; S.P.L., Deeds 11024.
[28] Datestone.
[29] Ibid.
[30] T.S.A.S. 2nd ser. i. 88.
[31] B.M. Add. MS. 21018, f. 295.
[32] Census, 1801–81.
[33] Ibid. 1891–1931.
[34] Ibid. 1961.
[35] V.C.H. Salop. i. 316.
[36] Eyton, vii. 180.
[37] Ibid. 179–80.
[38] Ibid. 192.
[39] V.C.H. Salop. i. 316.
[40] Complete Peerage, xi. app. pp. 155–8.
[41] V.C.H. Salop. i. 316.
[42] Complete Peerage, xi. 692–3; Rot. Hund. (Rec. Com.), ii. 87.
[43] Eyton, vii. 180–2; Red Bk. Exch. (Rolls Ser.), 692.

[44] Pipe R. 1175 (P.R.S. xxii), 37; Eyton, vii. 182.
[45] Pipe R. 1197 (P.R.S. N.S. viii), 156.
[46] Cal. Inq. p.m. i, p. 287; Eyton, xi. 130–1.
[47] Cal. Chart. R. 1226–57, 124; Close R. 1227–31, 424; Pipe R. 1230 (P.R.S. N.S. iv), 229.
[48] Ex. e Rot. Fin. (Rec. Com.), ii. 2.
[49] Close R. 1268–72, 582.
[50] Cal. Inq. p.m. ii, p. 68.
[51] Ibid. pp. 68, 122.
[52] Ibid. pp. 122, 287.
[53] Ibid. p. 287; ibid. iii, p. 409.
[54] Ibid. pp. 68, 122, 287; ibid. iii, p. 409; Cal. Fine R. 1272–1307, 419.
[55] Cal. Inq. p.m. ii, p. 68.
[56] Cal. Close, 1272–9, 234.
[57] Cal. Inq. p.m. ii, p. 122.
[58] Ibid. p. 62.
[59] S.H.C. vii. 114.
[60] Cal. Inq. p.m. ii, p. 287.
[61] Ibid. iii, p. 409.
[62] Cal. Close, 1296–1302, 442.
[63] Cal. Inq. p.m. v, p. 31.
[64] Ibid. p. 29.
[65] Cal. Close, 1313–18, 44.
[66] Cal. Inq. p.m. v, p. 31.
[67] Cal. Pat. 1334–8, 181.

surrendered this before her death in 1369.[68] Nicholas de Audley died in 1316.[69] Wardship of his infant son James was committed in 1317 to John de Charlton,[70] who was succeeded as guardian by Ralph de Camoys in 1324[71] and by Roger Mortimer in 1327.[72] Joan, widow of Nicholas de Audley, was assigned a third of the manor in dower in 1317,[73] but she was dead by 1322.[74]

James, Lord Audley, obtained seisin while still a minor in 1329[75] and held the manor until his death in 1386.[76] It then passed to his son Nicholas, who already had some interest in the manor under his marriage settlement of 1341.[77] The latter died without issue in 1391,[78] when the manor passed, under a settlement of 1390,[79] to his widow Elizabeth,[80] who died in 1400.[81] The manor then fell into divided ownership, one moiety passing to John Tuchet, nephew of Nicholas, Lord Audley, and the other moiety to Nicholas's sister Margaret, wife of Roger Hilary.[82]

John Tuchet, who had assumed the title of Lord Audley by 1405,[83] obtained seisin of his moiety of the manor in 1401.[84] He was succeeded at his death in 1408[85] by his son James, who was then a minor,[86] wardship being granted to William, Lord Ros of Hamlake.[87] James, Lord Audley, was killed at the battle of Blore Heath (1459),[88] when his son John obtained special livery of his estates.[89] At the latter's death in 1490[90] this moiety passed to his son James, on whom it had been settled in 1487.[91] James, Lord Audley, was executed in 1497 for his part in the Cornish rising of that year[92] and his estates passed by attainder to the Crown.[93] His moiety of Ford manor, however, was recovered by his widow Joan, who appointed Thomas Leighton as her steward there in 1510,[94] but she became lunatic shortly after her husband's death[95] and remained so until her death in 1532.[96] Robert Brograve, who was

appointed her guardian in 1515,[97] leased his interest in the manor in 1523 to Sir John Talbot, lord of the other moiety,[98] following a dispute with John Leighton, Joan Audley's steward.[99] Joan's son John Audley obtained livery of his mother's estates in 1534,[1] but was dead by 1542, when title to this moiety of the manor was in dispute between John Audley's brother and heir James and John Seyntlow, who had married John's widow Margaret.[2] James Audley and his son Richard sold the moiety in 1550 to Alan Hord,[3] whose son Thomas Hord sold it in 1587 to Sir John Talbot of Grafton,[4] the lord of the other moiety of the manor.

Margaret, wife of Roger Hilary, to whom the other moiety descended in 1400,[5] died in 1411[6] when, apparently under the terms of a settlement of 1404,[7] it passed to the lawyer Sir Hugh Huls.[8] On the latter's death in 1415[9] this moiety passed to his son Thomas,[10] who died in 1420,[11] leaving as heir a daughter Margaret, then aged two.[12] Margaret's wardship was granted to William Troutbeck,[13] whose son John she had married by the time she came of age in 1433,[14] and at her death in 1456[15] the moiety passed to her husband under a settlement of 1445.[16] John Troutbeck died in 1458[17] and his son and heir William[18] was killed, like the lord of the other moiety, at the battle of Blore Heath in 1459,[19] when William's widow Margaret obtained wardship of his son William.[20] The latter died in 1510,[21] when this moiety passed to his niece Margaret, wife of Sir John Talbot.[22] Under the terms of a settlement of 1521[23] it descended, on John's death in 1550,[24] to his son Sir John Talbot of Grafton,[25] who died in 1555.[26] The latter's estates passed to his son John,[27] but Ford was among the lands held in dower by Sir John's widow Frances.[28]

Sir John Talbot, who purchased the other moiety of the manor in 1587,[29] died in 1611[30] and was

[68] Cal. Inq. p.m. xiii, p. 72; cf. Complete Peerage, i. 339; ibid. ii. 115.
[69] Cal. Inq. p.m. vi, p. 41.
[70] Cal. Fine R. 1307–19, 317; Abbrev. Rot. Orig. (Rec. Com.), i. 237; Cal. Pat. 1313–17, 677.
[71] Cal. Fine R. 1319–27, 275; Abbrev. Rot. Orig. (Rec. Com.), i. 278.
[72] Cal. Close, 1330–3, 387–8.
[73] Ibid. 1313–18, 390, 393, 548–9; Abbrev. Rot. Orig. (Rec. Com.), i. 239.
[74] Cal. Fine R. 1319–27, 89; Abbrev. Rot. Orig. (Rec. Com.), i. 262.
[75] Cal. Close, 1327–30, 498; Cal. Pat. 1327–30, 531.
[76] C 136/38/1.
[77] Cal. Close, 1364–8, 237–9; Cal. Pat. 1340–3, 422. For other settlements see Cal. Pat. 1334–8, 181; ibid. 1370–4, 456; Abbrev. Rot. Orig. (Rec. Com.), ii. 334; C.P. 25(1)/195/17/54.
[78] C 136/69/1.
[79] Cal. Pat. 1388–92, 316; Cal. Close, 1389–92, 397.
[80] C.P. 25(1)/289/56/225.
[81] C 137/26/56.
[82] C 136/69/1; C.P. 25(1)/289/56/255; C 137/26/56.
[83] Complete Peerage, i. 340–1.
[84] Cal. Fine R. 1399–1405, 112.
[85] C 137/73/47.
[86] Ibid.
[87] Cal. Pat. 1408–13, 173.
[88] Ibid. 1452–61, 582.
[89] Ibid. 539.
[90] Cal. Inq. p.m. Hen. VII, i, pp. 247–8.
[91] Ibid.
[92] C 142/78/121; Cal. Pat. 1494–1509, 115.
[93] Rot. Parl. (Rec. Com.), vi. 544–8.
[94] S.P.L., MS. 2789, app. p. 8.
[95] C 142/78/121.
[96] Complete Peerage, i. 342.

[97] L. & P. Hen. VIII, ii (1), p. 154; ibid. ii (2), p. 926.
[98] B.M. Add. Ch. 73098.
[99] Sta. Cha. 2/6, ff. 121–3; Sta. Cha. 3/8/34.
[1] L. & P. Hen. VIII, p. 175. Not to be confused with John, Lord Audley (1483–c. 1558), son of James, Lord Audley, by his first wife Margaret: Complete Peerage, i. 342.
[2] C 1/935/35–37.
[3] B.M. Add. Ch. 73100–1; C.P. 25(2)/62/497.
[4] B.M. Add. Ch. 73107–8, 73110, 73112.
[5] C 136/69/1; C.P. 25(1)/289/56/225; C 137/26/56.
[6] C 137/84/36.
[7] C 138/13/14.
[8] He may already have been in possession by 1410: Cal. Pat. 1408–13, 173.
[9] C 138/13/14.
[10] Ibid.; Cal. Fine R. 1413–22, 117–18.
[11] C 138/50/91.   [12] Ibid.
[13] B.M. Add. Roll 74180.   [14] Ibid.
[15] C 139/163/8.
[16] Cal. Pat. 1441–6, 331; C.P. 25(1)/293/70/298.
[17] C 139/172/21.
[18] Ibid.
[19] Cal. Pat. 1452–61, 582; C 139/177/47.
[20] Ibid.
[21] C 142/26/90.
[22] Ibid.
[23] L. & P. Hen. VIII, iii (2), p. 675; C.P. 25(2)/51/363; C.P. 40/1033 rot. 100.
[24] S.P.L., MS. 2791, p. 30.
[25] Visit. Salop. 1623 (Harl. Soc. xxix), ii. 452.
[26] Eng. Topog. (Gent. Mag.), x. 22.
[27] V.C.H. Worcs. iii. 126.
[28] B.M. Add. Ch. 73104.
[29] Ibid. 73107–8, 73110, 73112.
[30] C 142/345/146. cf. V.C.H. Worcs. iii. 126–7; Complete Peerage, xi. 717.

succeeded by his son George,[31] who in 1618 became Earl of Shrewsbury, on the death of his fourth cousin Edward, Earl of Shrewsbury.[32] The manor was held by the Earls of Shrewsbury until 1824, the following being lords:[33] George, 1611–30;[34] John (nephew), 1630–54;[35] Francis (son), 1654–67; Charles (son), 1667–1718;[36] George (cousin), 1718–33;[37] George (son), 1733–87;[38] Charles (nephew), 1787–1824. Charles, Earl of Shrewsbury, sold the manor to Henry Wakeman in 1824[39] and it passed from father to son in the Wakeman family until c. 1875, the following being lords: Henry, 1824–31; Offley Penbury, 1831–58; Offley, 1858–c. 1875.[40] By 1877 the manor had been purchased by Henry de Grey Warter,[41] at those death in 1884[42] it passed to his daughter Mary Eliza Tatham Warter.[43] Her son Henry de Gray Warter Tatham Warter, who succeeded in 1897,[44] sold the manor in 1923 to Arthur Gill.[45] The latter died later in the same year and the last known owners of the manor were his daughters Emily Gill and Elizabeth Alder.[46]

ECONOMIC HISTORY. The manor was assessed at 15 hides in 1086, when its annual value was said to have risen from £9 to £34 since the Conquest.[47] It was held for £5 13s. 4d. a year by the Crown's tenant in the mid-12th century[48] and rendered £30 a year to the sheriff in the early 13th century.[49] The annual fee-farm rent of £12 reserved to the Crown when the manor was granted to Henry de Audley in 1230[50] is last recorded in 1785.[51] The manor was said in 1273 to be worth £66 8s. a year,[52] probably an under-estimate, for in the following year two-thirds of the manor were valued at £56 8s. 7d.[53] In 1308, however, the whole manor was worth only a little over £70 a year[54] and by 1317 its value had fallen to £57 13s.[55] Rents produced £76 a year in 1497[56] and £71 in 1601,[57] and in the 18th century the manor was valued at £66 16s. 6d. a year.[58]

The extensive demesne of 1086, when it contained land for 16 ploughs and had a labour-force of 20 serfs and 6 bondwomen,[59] was still in hand in the early 13th century, for 40 oxen were bought in 1209 for the 10 ploughs on the demesne, as well as 68 cows

and 40 sows.[60] The demesne was leased to the tenant shortly after 1230[61] and none is recorded in later-13th-century surveys of the manor. There was said to be no manor-house or demesne in 1317,[62] but part of the demesne had again been taken in hand by 1420, when the moiety of the manor held by Thomas Huls was said to include a ruinous manor-house, 100 a. arable, and 40 a. meadow.[63] This resumption of demesne is likely to have been one of the causes of unrest among the tenants at this time.

When the manor was reunited under one lord in 1587 an attempt seems to have been made to identify the former demesne lands. The location of much of the demesne arable had long been forgotten and the resulting survey[64] recorded for the most part only scattered meadows and parcels of waste. It included the sites of Lea and Ford mills, meadows in Cruckmeole, Cruckton, Lea, and Plealey, and waste land on Pontesford Hill, Ford Heath, and at Benthall and Little Shrawardine. Meadows at Cruckton and the mill-site at Lea were then held on lease, but the remainder had become merged with the holdings of the copyhold tenants.[65] Some 34 a. in Arscott, Cruckton, and Pontesford, accounted demesne land in 1797,[66] were sold in 1824.[67] Three cottages on Pontesford Hill were allotted to the lord of the manor at its inclosure in 1828,[68] but these were sold in 1830.[69]

That part of the manor which lay in the township of Ford included a single freehold estate, first recorded in the mid-13th century.[70] It seems likely that this originally comprised the manor-house and a portion of the demesne, for its house was described as a capital messuage in 1317[71] and as the Hall of Ford in 1601,[72] but the estate was enlarged before 1272, when Geoffrey de Ford was granted lands in the waste near Aspley Wood.[73] The property had passed by 1308 to Roger de Ford, who then held a carucate of land,[74] said to contain 60 a. in 1317,[75] but 120 a. in 1319.[76] Roger was succeeded at his death in 1317 by his nephew John, but in 1319 it reverted to Roger's son Hugh,[77] who was still living in 1327.[78] No member of this family was

[31] Complete Peerage, xi. 717.
[32] Ibid., xi. 716–17.
[33] For pedigree see ibid., xi. 717–25. Bracketed entries after names indicate relationship to preceding lord.
[34] C 142/506/159.
[35] Ibid.; S.P.L., MS. 2791, p. 40.
[36] For date of death see S.P.L., MS. 2791, p. 41.
[37] Self-styled Earl of Shrewsbury, on whom the family estates were settled: S.P.L., MS. 2791, p. 18. George's brother Gilbert (d. 1743), de jure Earl of Shrewsbury, was a Roman Catholic priest: Complete Peerage, xi. 724.
[38] Succeeded to earldom on the death of his uncle Gilbert in 1743: Complete Peerage, xi. 724–5.
[39] S.R.O. 938 uncat., abstract of title, 1856.
[40] Burke, Peerage (1959), 2300; S.R.O. 169/11–14.
[41] S.R.O. 169/17.
[42] Burke, Land. Gent. (1952), 2651.
[43] Ibid.   [44] Ibid.
[45] Ex inf. Messrs. Sprott, Stokes, and Turnbull, solicitors, Shrewsbury.
[46] Ibid.
[47] V.C.H. Salop. i. 316.
[48] Red Bk. Exch. (Rolls Ser.), ii. 692; Pipe R. 1161–75 (P.R.S. iv–xxii), passim.
[49] Pipe R. 1214 (P.R.S. N.S. xxxv), 119–20; Rot. Hund. (Rec. Com.), ii. 66.
[50] Cal. Chart. R. 1226–57, 124.
[51] S.R.O. 123/1.

[52] Rot. Hund. (Rec. Com.), ii. 96.
[53] C 133/8/6.
[54] C 134/5/9.
[55] C 134/56/3; Cal. Close, 1313–18, 390.
[56] S.C. 11/828.
[57] S.P.L., Deeds 12706.
[58] Q. Sess., reg. papists' estates, 1718, 1741, 1787.
[59] V.C.H. Salop. i. 316.
[60] Pipe R. 1209 (P.R.S. N.S. xxiv), 146. cf. Pipe R. 1202 (P.R.S. N.S. xv), 47.
[61] Rot. Hund. (Rec. Com.), ii. 66.
[62] C 134/56/3.
[63] C 138/50/91.
[64] B.M. Add. MS. 73108.
[65] S.P.L., Deeds 12706.
[66] S.P.L., MS. 2364.
[67] S.R.O. 437 uncat., deed, 1824.
[68] Ibid. 785/157.
[69] Ibid. 437 uncat., deed, 1830.
[70] B.M. Add. Ch. 73106.
[71] Cal. Inq. p.m. vi, p. 86.
[72] S.P.L., Deeds 12706.
[73] B.M. Add. Ch. 73106. cf. Rot. Hund. (Rec. Com.), ii. 87.
[74] C 134/5/4.
[75] Cal. Inq. p.m. vi, p. 86.
[76] Ibid. p. 101.
[77] Ibid. pp. 86, 101.
[78] T.S.A.S. 2nd ser. x. 116.

resident in the manor in 1379[79] and when last recorded in 1601 the estate was held by the daughters of William Phillips of Cruckmeole.[80] It may later have been merged with the large copyhold estate of the Ambler family, which included at least 17 a. of freehold land in 1842.[81]

The tenants of Ford manor in 1086 comprised 50 villeins and 14 bordars, who had between them 29 ploughs.[82] There is no evidence for forms of tenure here while the manor was in the hands of the Crown.[83] Shortly after 1230 Henry de Audley leased the manor to the tenants for £10 a year[84] and his son James granted them Aspley Wood and adjacent heathland, with licence to take beasts of warren throughout the manor in return for a down-payment of £30 and a rent of 10s. a year.[85] The Audleys took advantage of the licence to levy tallage whenever the king tallaged his demesne, contained in the grant of 1230,[86] and raised 89 marks by this means between 1230 and 1254.[87]

Since the main roads from Welshpool and Montgomery passed through the manor, its inhabitants, must frequently have suffered from Welsh incursions. In 1214 the annual rent of £30 due to the Crown was remitted on account of burning by the Welsh[88] and in 1260, during a foray carried out by a band of Welshmen, with the connivance of the lords of neighbouring manors, the vill of Ford was burnt down, 28 men were killed, wounded, or taken prisoner, and 260 oxen and cows, 80 sheep, and 57 horses were carried off as booty.[89] In common with the rest of Ford Hundred the manor was exempted from lay and clerical taxation in the early 15th century on account of damage inflicted during Owen Glendower's revolt.[90]

Rents of customary tenants totalled £65 in 1308[91] and had thus continued virtually unchanged since the early 13th century. The township of Ford then contained 37 tenants, 19 of whom had holdings of a half-virgate (30 a.) or more, and only 5 held less than a half-noke (7½ a.). The half-virgate, held by 15 tenants, was then the typical holding.[92] The tenants had shaken off the last vestiges of bond tenure by 1317, when they were described as sokemen,[93] but in the later 14th century the lords of the manor seem to have attempted to depress their status. Exemplifications of the Domesday entry relating to the manor were obtained by the tenants in 1385[94] and again in 1444,[95] and in 1386[96] and 1410[97] they were said to have banded together to refuse services due to the lord. On the moiety of the manor held by Thomas Huls in 1420 only 4 marks were derived from assized rents, while there were 20 tenants-at-

will.[98] Lawsuits between the lord of the manor and various tenants, between 1588 and 1593,[99] were nominally concerned with the proper custody of the manor court rolls—the tenants alleging that they were the responsibility of an elected customary bailiff—but in fact expressed the tenants' resistance to an attempt by the lord to raise their rents and exact higher entry fines.[1]

In 1608 Talbot accepted a composition of £1,880 13s. from the tenants in return for a confirmation of their ancient customs, which were then embodied in a Chancery decree.[2] This provided that copyholds should descend to the youngest son, that entry fines should be limited to one year's rent, and that wardship of minors should be entrusted to their mother or next of kin. Tenants were not to be subject to forfeiture for waste, business concerning boundaries, roads, and water-courses was to be dealt with by the copyholders themselves at the manor court, and a scale of fees was laid down.[3]

The decree in effect limited the lord's control over the copyholders to the collection of chief rents, although he continued to lease what remained of the demesne and derived some income from the rents of cottages on the Heath.[4] Rents received from Ford township remained virtually unchanged during the 17th century—£12 9s. 11d. in 1601[5] and £12 14s. 7d. in 1712[6]—and their increase to £15 18s. 9d. by 1785[7] was a result of the inclosure of Ford Heath c. 1750.[8] The number of tenants in the township, 37 in 1308,[9] had fallen to 20 by 1601,[10] but most holdings were still of moderate size. Only three tenants held more than one virgate (60 a.), while 11 tenants held 2 nokes (30 a.) or less.[11]

None of the tenant families found in Ford in the 14th century still held land there in 1601,[12] but, owing in part to the strict rules of inheritance embodied in the decree of 1608, holdings thereafter tended to remain in the hands of the same families. Of the 13 families holding land in Ford in 1601, the Ambler, Waring, Griffiths, Wall, and Dax families retained their copyholds until the early 19th century. The Calcott family, later Calcott-Gough, who first acquired land in Ford in 1669, survived until 1836. The concentration of land in the hands of an ever-smaller number of copyholders during the period 1601–c. 1800—there were 20 tenants in 1601, 15 in 1712, and only 11 in 1785—was due, not so much to purchases, as to the amalgamation of holdings of different branches of the same family in the hands of that branch which continued to produce heirs.

The Amblers and Warings, who between them

[79] E 179/166/23.
[80] S.P.L., Deeds 12706.
[81] S.R.O. 955 uncat., conveyance, 1842.
[82] V.C.H. Salop. i. 316.
[83] For tallages see table in Eyton, vi. 11.
[84] Rot. Hund. (Rec. Com.), ii. 66.
[85] B.M. Add. Ch. 73106, cf. Cal. Chart. R. 1226–57, 409.
[86] Cal. Chart. R. 1226–57, 124.
[87] Rot. Hund. (Rec. Com.), ii. 66. Payment of tallage is last recorded in 1313: Cal. Close, 1307–13, 519.
[88] Pipe R. 1214 (P.R.S. N.S. xxxv), 119–20.
[89] Close R. 1259–61, 180.
[90] E 179/166/37; E 179/166/55; Reg. R. Mascall (C. & Y.S.), 21, 120.
[91] C 134/5/4, 19.
[92] Ibid.
[93] C 134/56/3.
[94] Cal. Pat. 1385–9, 54.
[95] Ibid. 1441–6, 276.

[96] Ibid. 1385–9, 171, 178.
[97] Ibid. 1408–13, 173.
[98] C 138/50/91.
[99] Req. 2/87/27; B.M. Add. MS. 46458, ff. 66, 67, 69–70, 158–64; B.M. Add. Ch. 73114.
[1] Cf. S.P.L., Deeds 11287.
[2] Ibid. Deeds 12538. Abstract in T.S.A.S. 4th ser. vi. 341–50.
[3] Ibid.
[4] Q. Sess., reg. papists' estates, 1718, 1741, 1787.
[5] S.P.L., Deeds 12706.
[6] S.R.O. 123/1.
[7] Ibid.
[8] See p. 225.
[9] C 134/5/4.
[10] S.P.L., Deeds 12706.   [11] Ibid.
[12] What follows is based on E 179/166/23; S.P.L., Deeds 12706; S.R.O. 123/1; S.R.O. 169/1–3, 11–14; ibid. 248/1–2.

held well over half the parish in the later 18th century, had both established themselves in Ford by 1545, when out of 7 recorded tax-payers one was an Ambler and 4 were Warings.[13] By 1601 6 members of the Ambler family held a total of 16 nokes here, nearly a third of the total arable area at this time.[14] Four branches of the family were still resident in Ford in the later 17th century, chief of them being Thomas Ambler (1622–72) and his son John (1665–99),[15] but after the death of George Ambler of Shrewsbury in 1754 the only representatives to hold land in Ford were John Ambler (1717–86) of Ford House and his brother Thomas (1728–93), the perpetual curate of Ford. The size of John Ambler's ancestral estate is not known, but in 1775 he greatly enlarged it by the purchase of 9 messuages and 316 a. from the Griffiths family. Thomas Ambler, who had inherited 3 messuages and a virgate from George Ambler in 1754, succeeded to most of his brother's lands in 1787. He was holding some 550 a. at his death in 1793, when the estate was again divided between his daughter Frances Fowler and his grand-daughter Frances. The latter acquired her aunt's portion in 1810 and in the following year married W. E. Tomline. In 1814 Tomline sold some 300 a.,[16] and a further 188 a. were sold by his son George in 1839 and 1843, after which date only Tithe House Farm remained in the estate.[17]

Although 4 branches of the Waring family held land in Ford in 1545[18] and 3 in 1601,[19] when their combined holdings amounted to 15 nokes, only one branch remained by 1692.[20] The estate was still relatively small in 1716, when it comprised 3 messuages and lands,[21] but was enlarged by a number of small purchases between 1719 and 1814, the largest being Dodlee, bought in 1778.[22] The estate comprised 370 a. when it was dispersed by sale in 1844.[23] The estate of the Calcott family, who first appeared in the parish in 1669, when John Calcott bought Ford Hall,[24] passed by marriage to the Gough family in 1749.[25] It seems to have comprised some 185 a. by 1775, but after a number of small sales between 1776 and 1818, the remaining 111 a., including the Hall, were sold in 1837.[26]

The largest estate in the parish in the earlier 18th century was that of the Biggs family of Benthall Farm in Alberbury.[27] Before 1659 this estate had been restricted to the townships of Benthall and Little Shrawardine, but between 1659 and 1673 Thomas Griffiths and his son Henry purchased 7 messuages and lands in Ford, and a further 4 messuages here were bought by the latter's kinsman and heir, Henry Biggs, between 1678 and 1695. The estate included 10 messuages in Ford in 1735, but on the death of Lucy Biggs in 1758 it passed to her daughters Lucy and Sarah and in 1775 9 messuages and 329 a. in Ford were sold, the principal purchaser being John Ambler. The remainder of the estate, which passed to the Severne family,[28] included 108 a. in Ford in 1847.[29]

The pattern of landownership in the parish was radically altered as a result of the sale and dispersal of the Ambler, Waring, and Gough estates between 1814 and 1844, when over 1,000 a. changed hands,[30] and Ford has subsequently been a community of small landowners. The process was virtually complete by 1847, when there were no fewer than 48 proprietors here, 37 of whom possessed less than 50 a., and only 8 properties belonged to families who had held land in the parish before 1814.[31] There were then only 4 estates of over 100 a.,[32] the only one of a size comparable with the large 18th-century copyholds being that of the Revd. R. Lingen Burton, who had acquired 426 a., including Ford House and Ford Mansion, between 1843 and 1846.[33] Ford House was later sold, but the Lingen Burton estate remained substantially intact until the Second World War. Some 50 a. were then sold to the War Office, and the remainder—Mansion House Farm and Lower Farm—were sold in 1951 and 1957 respectively.[34] A more modest estate was built up in similar fashion by the surveyor Timotheus Burd of Whiston Priory,[35] but the two other holdings of over 100 a. in 1847 were merely outlying portions of the long-established estates of the Harries family of Cruckton and the Severne family of Benthall.[36] Copyhold tenure continued in Ford until 1922, but most of the larger estates were enfranchised between 1857 and 1872.[37]

It is not possible to establish how many of the copyholders were owner-occupiers before the 19th century. Although the lord's licence was required to lease copyholds, only a small proportion of such licences appear to have been entered in the court books after 1700.[38] The greater part of the Ambler and Waring estates were occupied by leasehold tenants in the early 19th century[39] and a number of other copyholders at this time are known to have been non-resident. In 1847 19 of the 48 landowners occupied all or most of their lands, while 23 were non-resident. The parish then contained 93 occupiers, of whom about half were cottagers, holding less than an acre apiece. There were only 4 occupiers of farms larger than 100 a. and 26 of them held less than 25 a.[40]

Open-field strips appear to have been largely consolidated by c. 1650[41] and the numerous exchanges which took place in the later 17th century[42] were presumably intended to rationalise the boundaries of individual copyhold estates, but the

[13] E 179/166/189.
[14] S.P.L., Deeds 12706.
[15] What follows is based on S.R.O. 169/1–3, 11–15; ibid. 248/1–2. For pedigrees see T.S.A.S. 4th ser. vi. 288–91.
[16] S.R.O. 529/10.
[17] Ibid. 529/47; ibid. 169/13.
[18] E 179/166/189. For pedigree see T.S.A.S. 4th ser. vi. 293–4.
[19] S.P.L., Deeds 12706.
[20] S.R.O. 169/1.
[21] Ibid. 169/2.
[22] Ibid. 169/2–3; ibid. 248/1–2; S.P.L., Deeds 1707.
[23] S.R.O. 169/14.
[24] Ibid. 169/1.
[25] Ibid. 169/3.
[26] Ibid. 169/3, 11–13; ibid. 248/1–2.

[27] What follows is based on ibid. 169/1–3, 11; ibid. 248/1–2. For pedigree see T.S.A.S. 4th ser. vi. 282–3.
[28] See p. 206.
[29] Par. rec., tithe appt.
[30] S.R.O. 169/11–14.
[31] Par. rec., tithe appt.
[32] Ibid.
[33] Ibid.; S.R.O. 169/14.
[34] Ex inf. Mr. D. Salt.
[35] S.R.O. 169/12–15.
[36] Par. rec., tithe appt.
[37] S.R.O. 169/14–18.
[38] Ibid. 169/1–3; ibid. 248/1–2.
[39] Ibid. 529/7; par. rec., tithe appt.
[40] Par. rec., tithe appt.
[41] See p. 225.
[42] S.R.O. 169/1.

larger copyholds still consisted of widely scattered fields in the early 19th century[43] and many of them included distant allotments on Ford Heath as well as lands nearer the village.[44] The smaller estates created by the sales of the early 19th century, however, normally consisted of one or two compact groups of fields.[45] The parish was said to be chiefly arable in 1793,[46] but only 356 a. were said to be under the plough in 1801, when the chief crops were wheat and barley.[47] The arable acreage had risen more than three-fold by 1847, when it amounted to 1,100 a.[48]

The mill, which rendered an annual rent of 3 ores in 1086,[49] was worth 13s. 4d. a year in 1299[50] and 1308[51] and 10s. in 1317.[52] It was ruinous by 1420[53] and was never rebuilt.[54] A fishery, worth 2s. a year in 1086[55] and 3s. a year in 1308,[56] is not again recorded until 1588.[57] Montford weir, probably representing the fishery of 1086, was said to be decayed in 1601,[58] but the weir at Little Shrawardine was then being leased for 13s. 4d. a year,[59] and for a guinea a year in the 18th century.[60]

There are few references to tradesmen in the parish before the 19th century, when their number increased to keep pace with an expanding population. A smithy at Cross Gates Inn, in business in the later 17th century,[61] appears to have been moved to Welshman's Ford in the 18th century,[62] where it was joined by a wheelwright's shop. The latter closed shortly after 1934, but the smithy continued until after 1941.[63] Another smithy had been established at Chavel by 1847[64] and the village shop opened c. 1814.[65] In 1851 the parish contained, in addition to the above, 4 shoemakers, 2 shop-keepers, a tailor, and a carpenter.[66] A butcher's shop had been opened by 1856.[67] The tailor and carpenter had gone by 1885, but a butcher and a shoemaker were still in business in 1941.[68] The garage at Pavement Gates was opened shortly before 1926.[69]

LOCAL GOVERNMENT. There are court books for the manor of Ford, 1653–1922, and minutes of presentments, 1824–78.[70] The manor was quit of suit at county and hundred courts in 1230,[71] but cases of interference by the sheriff's officers were reported in 1274.[72] The gallows then recorded[73] probably stood in a small detached part of Ford parish near Cruckton, where there was in 1587 a field called Hangman's Pleck.[74] A building known as the Prison House seems to have stood in Ford

village.[75] The manorial officers included a steward, an improver, and a customary bailiff. Held by the Leighton family between 1497 and 1524,[76] the office of steward was filled by a Shrewsbury attorney after 1653.[77] The improver, whose functions presumably lapsed after the decree of 1608 had standardized the rents and fines of copyholders, is not recorded by name after 1588.[78] All copyholders, except women and clergymen, were liable to serve as customary bailiff for a year, and the duty passed in rotation among the townships within the manor, Ford itself being liable for service every third year.[79]

View of frankpledge was held at Easter and Michaelmas until 1877, while courts baron were held as occasion demanded. The court met about 6 times a year in the later 17th century, but seldom more than 4 times a year after c. 1750. All courts met at Ford, 1653–74, and at Newnham, 1674–1728. After this date view of frankpledge continued to be held at Newnham until 1766, at an alehouse in Nox, 1766–1811, and at a Cruckton alehouse, 1812–75, but sessions of the court baron were held in different townships of the manor convenient for the business in hand until 1849. After 1849 the business of the court baron was transacted at the office of the steward and it is unlikely that any formal sessions of the manor court took place after 1877. Business recorded in the court books relates entirely to the transfer of copyhold lands. Registers of presentments, in which other proceedings at the view of frankpledge were recorded, have not survived for the period before 1824 and thereafter contain only elections of constables and the presentment of a formal list of encroachments at Pontesford.

The parish records include vestry minutes, 1858–76, churchwardens' accounts, 1846–1935, and overseers' accounts, 1774–1820. Memoranda of vestry meetings in the overseers' accounts show that the vestry normally met 4 times a year in the later 18th century and that about 6 persons attended. John Ambler and his brother Thomas appear normally to have taken the chair. Vestry meetings continued to be held 3 or 4 times a year until the 1870s, but attendances never rose above 4 except when contentious issues were in prospect.

The parish had 2 churchwardens and one overseer of the poor. The former drew the whole of their income from church rates, which were abolished in 1869, and replaced by church-collections in 1872. 'Lewns' for the poor were replaced by a pound rate in 1798. Some £20 a year was expended on poor

43 Ibid. 169/11–15; ibid. 248/1–2; ibid. 529/10.
44 Ibid.
45 Par. rec., tithe appt.
46 B.M. Add. MS. 21018, f. 295.
47 H.O. 67/12/88.
48 Par. rec., tithe appt.
49 V.C.H. Salop. i. 316.
50 C 135/89/7.
51 C 134/5/4.
52 C 134/56/3.
53 C 138/50/91.
54 B.M. Add. Ch. 73108; S.P.L., Deeds 12706.
55 V.C.H. Salop. i. 316.
56 C 134/5/4.
57 C.P. 25(2)/202/30 Eliz. I Hil.
58 S.P.L., Deeds 12706.
59 Ibid.
60 Q. Sess., reg. papists' estates, 1741, 1787.
61 S.R.O. 169/1.
62 See p. 227.

63 Kelly's Dir. Salop. (1856–1941).
64 Par. rec., tithe appt.
65 Ibid.; S.R.O. 169/11.
66 Bagshaw's Dir. Salop. (1851).
67 Kelly's Dir. Salop. (1856).
68 Ibid. (1885–1941).
69 Ibid. (1926).
70 S.R.O. 169/1–3, 11–18; ibid. 248/1–2. Court records before 1653 were already missing in 1824; ibid. 1011 uncat., schedule of ct. bks. 1824.
71 Cal. Chart. R. 1226–57, 124.
72 Rot. Hund. (Rec. Com.), ii. 87.
73 Ibid. 96.
74 B.M. Add. Ch. 73108.
75 Ibid.
76 S.C. 11/828; Sta. Cha. 2/6, f. 121.
77 S.R.O. 169/1–3, 11–18; ibid. 248/1–2.
78 B.M. Add. MS. 46458, ff. 158–64.
79 Copy of a decree . . . between the lord and tenants of the Manor of Ford (Shrewsbury, 1775), 35.

relief until 1775 and disbursements averaged £40 a year in the period 1775–95. Expenditure rose to £57 in 1795 and to £84 in 1796, but exceeded £100 a year only in the period 1808–19 and was usually about £70 a year in the 1820s.[80] This relatively small rise in the cost of poor relief was probably due in some measure to the existence of three Friendly Societies in the parish, of which 96 persons were members in 1803.[81] Rice and corn seem to have been supplied to the poor at reduced prices in 1800 and in the following year a quantity of potatoes was bought for their use. No reference has been found to a workhouse or poor-house in the parish.

CHURCH. The church is first recorded in 1221.[82] It was then said to be in the gift of the Crown and to be a chapel dependent on the chapel of St. Michael in Shrewsbury castle[83]—an arrangement likely to date from the period 1071–1102, when the manor was held in demesne by the Earls of Shrewsbury.[84] Not alienated when the manor was granted to Henry de Audley in 1230, Ford chapel continued in Crown patronage as a dependency of St. Michael's in the Castle until 1410[85] and, as a member of the royal peculiar of St. Michael's, it was exempt from the jurisdiction of the Bishop of Hereford.[86]

The chapel of St. Michael in the Castle was granted by the Crown in 1410 as part of the endowment of Battlefield College,[87] this appropriation becoming effective on the resignation of the chaplain in 1416.[88] Ford chapel was held by Battlefield College until the dissolution of the college in 1548,[89] when it again passed into the hands of the Crown and was subsequently styled a church.[90] The church and tithes had been leased for life before 1548 to Henry Wynne,[91] who appears as perpetual curate of Ford between 1553 and 1563,[92] and in 1576 William Harries obtained a 21-year lease of the church and tithes, to begin in 1583.[93] The revenues of the church were styled a rectory in 1590, when the Crown sold them to John Wynne.[94] The latter sold the rectory to William Phillips of Cruckton, at whose death in 1592 it passed to his daughter Margery, wife of Richard Lake of Boycott,[95] who sold it to John Garbett in 1609.[96] Garbett conveyed the rectory in 1612 to John Reynolds of Ford,[97] whose widow Katherine was impropriator in 1655.[98] At her death in 1660[99] the rectory passed, under a settlement of 1612,[1] to Thomas Ambler, great-nephew of her first husband William Ambler,[2] and was held by his descendants until the early 19th century.[3] John Ambler (d. 1786) devised it to his brother, the Revd. Thomas Ambler, at whose death in 1793 it passed to his grand-daughter Frances, who married W. E. Tomline in 1811.[4] Responsibility for chancel repairs passed in 1842 to the Revd. R. Lingen Burton[5] and W. E. Tomline's son George sold the rectory in 1856 to John Naylor.[6] The last, and his son J. M. Naylor, disposed of their impropriate tithes in Ford between 1869 and 1921,[7] but retained the advowson until 1927, when J. M. Naylor transferred it to the Bishop of Hereford.[8]

The annual value of the chapel rose from one mark in 1221[9] to 100s. by 1254.[10] It was valued at £10 in 1291[11] and 1331,[12] but was said to be worth only £6 13s. 4d. in 1536.[13] After its appropriation to Battlefield College, the chapel's income was derived solely from tithes, for it possessed no glebe until the later 18th century, even its right to the churchyard being in doubt until 1861.[14] The tithes were held on lease for £3 6s. 8d. a year in 1535[15] and were let for the same amount until 1590,[16] but by 1655 their annual value had risen to £20.[17] They were said to be worth £550 a year in 1810,[18] probably an inflated value owing to war-time conditions, for they were valued at only £334 in 1817[19] and at £234 in 1822.[20] They produced about £290 a year between 1826 and 1829, but only a little more than £200 a year in the 1830s.[21] Tithes of hay, wool, lambs, pigs, and geese were said still to be collected in kind in 1833,[22] and moduses only on cows and calves were recorded in 1847.[23] Between 1817 and 1846, however, only a small proportion of the tithes was in fact collected in kind.[24]

Attempts made between 1339 and 1345 by the chaplain of Ford to acquire the tithes of Arscott, Cruckmeole, Cruckton, Lea, and Sibberscott, all members of the manor of Ford but in the parish of Pontesbury, appear to have been unsuccessful.[25] Following disputes with All Souls College, impropriators of Alberbury, the tithes of Ford-in-Alberbury were demised in 1701 by the College's tenant, Basil Wood of the White Abbey, to Elizabeth Ambler and her son John, impropriators of Ford, for an

[80] Rep. Cttee. on Poor Rate Returns, 1822, Suppl. App., H.C. 556, p. 141 (1822), v; ibid. 1825, H.C. 334, p. 177 (1825), iv; Acct. of Money Expended on Poor, 1825–9, H.C. 83, p. 391 (1830–1), xi.
[81] Poor Law Abstract, 1803, H.C. 175, pp. 406–7 (1803–4), xiii.
[82] Bk. of Fees, 1342.
[83] Ibid.
[84] See p. 228.
[85] Rot. Hund. (Rec. Com.), ii. 66.
[86] Cal. Pat. 1374–7, 154.
[87] T.S.A.S. 3rd ser. iii. 187–90.
[88] Ibid. 197; Cal. Close, 1413–19, 384.
[89] T.S.A.S. 3rd ser. iii. 242–3.
[90] Ibid. 243–6.
[91] Ibid.
[92] Ibid. 2nd ser. xii. 318; ibid. 4th ser. xi. 200.
[93] Bodl. MS. Blakeway 2, f. 270v.
[94] Ibid.
[95] Ibid.
[96] Ibid.; C.P. 25(2)/342/6 Jas. I Hil.
[97] Cal. Cttee. for Compounding, 2537.
[98] T.S.A.S. xlvii. 26.
[99] Ibid. 4th ser. vi. 288.
[1] Cal. Cttee. for Compounding, 2537.

[2] T.S.A.S. 4th ser. vi. 288–90; C.P. 25(2)/713/18 Chas. II East.
[3] Par. rec., abstract of title to rectory, 1856.
[4] Ibid.
[5] S.R.O. 955 uncat., conveyance, 1842.
[6] Par. rec., conveyance, 1856.
[7] Ibid. 1869, 1875, 1921.
[8] Lond. Gaz. 1927, p. 4558.
[9] Bk. of Fees, 1342.
[10] Rot. Hund. (Rec. Com.), ii. 66.
[11] Tax. Eccl. (Rec. Com.), 167.
[12] Reg. T. Charlton (C. & Y.S.), 47.
[13] Reg. C. Bothe (C. & Y.S.), 369.
[14] See p. 237.
[15] Valor Eccl. (Rec. Com.), iii. 195.
[16] T.S.A.S. 3rd ser. iii. 243–6; Bodl. MS. Blakeway 2, f. 270v.
[17] T.S.A.S. xlvii. 26.
[18] S.R.O. 529/7.
[19] Ibid. 529/18.
[20] Ibid. 529/19.
[21] Ibid. 529/20–33.
[22] S.P.L., Deeds 11024.
[23] Par. rec., tithe appt.
[24] S.R.O. 529/18–41.
[25] Cal. Pat. 1338–40, 360, 481; ibid. 1314–15, 280; Owen and Blakeway, Hist. Shrewsbury, ii. 423.

annual rent of £11.[26] This rent was no longer paid after 1815, the College not asserting its rights presumably because of the doubtful legality of the demise of 1701,[27] and George Tomline's rights to tithes of corn, hay, wool, wood, and lambs in this area were confirmed in 1847.[28]

In 1847 George Tomline, as impropriator, was entitled to tithes arising from 1,263 a. in the township of Ford. The tithes of the remaining 510 a. belonged to 15 other landowners.[29] The most considerable of these was the Revd. R. Lingen Burton, to whom Tomline had conveyed the tithes of some 168 a. in 1842,[30] and the others presumably acquired their tithes during the sales of the Tomline estate, 1839–42.[31] The tithes were commuted for a rent-charge of £307 16s. 6d. in 1847, £229 5s. being apportioned to George Tomline, £7 1s. to the vicar of Alberbury in lieu of small tithes of Ford-in-Alberbury, and £71 10s. 6d. to the other tithe-owners.[32]

The living was a perpetual curacy from the 16th century until 1870. As a former member of the royal peculiar of St. Michael in the Castle, it was treated as a donative. The curate received an annual stipend of £5 from the impropriator c. 1590[33] and in 1655.[34] This had been raised to £8 a year by c. 1705, when the curacy had also been endowed by a Captain Jones with an estate worth £10 a year.[35] Captain Jones's endowment is not again recorded, but the annual stipend of £8 was paid by the impropriator until 1842,[36] when responsibility for its payment passed to the Revd. R. Lingen Burton,[37] whose descendant E. R. L. Burton Lingen redeemed it in 1949.[38] The curate's income was augmented by grants totalling £400 made by Queen Anne's Bounty in 1726 and 1779 to meet equivalent benefactions by the Revd. J. Millington and the Revd. Humphrey Gwynne in 1726 and by the Revd. Mr. Waring in 1778.[39] The £800 thus obtained was invested between 1773 and 1821 in the purchase of some 63 a. glebe in Melverley, Brockton in Worthen, and Leighton (Montg.),[40] which were worth £80 a year in 1839 and 1851,[41] bringing the total annual income of the curacy to about £90 in the earlier 19th century.[42] The glebe was let for £104 a year in 1858.[43] Glebe at Leighton was conveyed to John Naylor, the impropriator, in 1875, in exchange for a rent-charge of £38 arising from tithes in Ford,[44] and the remainder of the glebe was sold in 1918.[45]

The living was styled a vicarage after 1869 and in 1870 the benefice was endowed with £1,275 by the Ecclesiastical Commissioners for the erection of a parsonage,[46] part of this endowment being derived from a tithe rent-charge of £60 conveyed by Naylor in 1869.[47] The living had a net income of some £150 a year between 1870 and 1900.[48]

Until 1417 the church was served by the chaplains of St. Michael in the Castle. At least one is known to have been a graduate,[49] but none of them had any close association with the parish, nor are any known to have been related to the lord of the manor. After the resignation of John de Repingdon, chaplain of St. Michael's in 1416,[50] the parish appears to have been without a priest for many years. The Bishop of Bath and Wells, a relative of the lord of the manor, found it necessary to urge that Battlefield College should provide a priest, c. 1440.[51] The chaplains of Battlefield were instructed in the will (1444) of Roger Ive, Master of the College, to say mass weekly on Mondays at Ford,[52] but the church had been leased to a curate by 1548[53] and was probably held on the same terms in 1535.[54]

Perpetual curates were not regularly instituted by the Bishop of Hereford until after 1764[55] and the dates of their incumbencies cannot be established before the later 17th century, but the available evidence suggests that incumbencies of curates in the 16th and 17th centuries were as short as those of their successors in the early 19th century. Of 25 incumbents whose dates are known between 1548 and 1910, only 4 held the living for more than 20 years.[56] Thomas Ambler, assistant curate, 1755–64,[57] and perpetual curate, 1764–93,[58] was a younger brother of the impropriator, and R. Lingen Burton (curate 1839–48)[59] built up a large estate in the parish during his incumbency. Apart from B. F. Leighton of Loton Park, Alberbury, who was assistant curate, 1828–34, and perpetual curate, 1834–39,[60] none of the other perpetual curates is known to have had any local connexions. Significant changes in the status of the living and in the church itself—the erection of a parsonage (1870) and the restoration of the church (1875)—took place during the short incumbency of Thomas Auden, 1869–79.[61]

The absence of a parsonage, coupled with the low

[26] S.R.O. 1123/8.
[27] Par. rec., abstract of title to rectory, 1856.
[28] Ibid. tithe appt.
[29] Ibid.
[30] S.R.O. 955 uncat., conveyance, 1842.
[31] S.R.O. 529/36.
[32] Par. rec., tithe appt.
[33] T.S.A.S. xlvi. 42.
[34] Ibid. xlvii. 26.
[35] Heref. Dioc. Regy., visitation papers, box 44.
[36] Par. rec., abstract of title to rectory, 1856; S.R.O. 529/18–35.
[37] S.R.O. 955 uncat., conveyance, 1842.
[38] Par. rec., correspondence re stipend, 1945–9.
[39] C. Hodgson, Queen Anne's Bounty (1845), 290.
[40] Par. rec., maps of glebe, 1785–8; ibid. correspondence re sale of glebe, 1918–19.
[41] Heref. Dioc. Regy., reg. 1822–42, p. 426; H.O. 129/359/4/3.
[42] Rep. Com. Eccl. Revenues [67], pp. 438–9, H.C. (1835), xxii.
[43] Par. rec., vestry minutes, 1858–76.
[44] Ibid. exchange, 1875.
[45] Ibid. correspondence re sale of glebe, 1918–19.

[46] Lond. Gaz. 1870, p. 1033; Heref. Dioc. Regy., reg. 1869–83, p. 34.
[47] Par. rec., conveyance, 1869.
[48] Kelly's Dir. Salop. (1870–1900).
[49] Master Adam de Dysiaco alias Saverne, recorded 1291–2; Owen and Blakeway, Hist. Shrewsbury, i. 422; Eyton, vii. 193.
[50] Cal. Close, 1413–19, 354.
[51] T.S.A.S. 3rd ser. iii. 200–1.
[52] Ibid. 206–7.
[53] Ibid. 244.
[54] Valor Eccl. (Rec. Com.), iii. 195.
[55] Instit. Dioc. Heref. 97.
[56] Ralph Ridgeway, c. 1678–1700: S.P.R. Heref. i (2), 81; ibid. xii. 234. Humphrey Gwynne, 1700–39: ibid. i (2), 85. Thomas Ambler, 1764–93: Instit. Dioc. Heref. 97, 122. John Lewis, 1879–1910: ibid. 193; Kelly's Dir. Salop. (1917).
[57] S.P.R. Heref. i (2), 92, 109.
[58] Instit. Dioc. Heref. 97, 122.
[59] Ibid. 164; S.P.R. Heref. i (2), p. iv.
[60] S.P.R. Heref. i (2), p. iv; Instit. Dioc. Heref. 153; B.M. Add. MS. 21018, f. 295ᵛ.
[61] Instit. Dioc. Heref. 181, 193.

value of the living, was clearly responsible for the short incumbencies of Ford curates until the later 19th century. The curate was said to be resident c. 1587,[62] perhaps living at the tenement in Ford which was sold, with the church, in 1590.[63] It is not known how many of the 17th-century curates were resident, but Nathaniel Plott, who was probably curate shortly before 1678, kept a school at Myddle and presumably lived there.[64] Thomas Ambler may have lived at Ford Mansion, the home of his wife's family, the Warings,[65] and occupied Ford House after his brother's death in 1786.[66] He employed assistant curates during his old age,[67] the most regular being James Matthews, a master at Shrewsbury School,[68] who received an annual stipend of £32 in 1801,[69] and officiated at Ford between 1790 and 1804.[70] Assistant curates were normally employed from 1811 until 1834, at a stipend of £50 a year.[71] After this date perpetual curates served the living in person, but until 1870 usually lived outside the parish.[72] R. Lingen Burton and J. J. Wason (curate 1848–52), however, lived at Ford House.[73]

Lands worth 2d. a year were said in 1548 to have been given to endow lights in the church.[74] A body of singers received an annual fee of £2 between 1846 and 1857 but was evidently disbanded after 1860.[75] In 1851 the curate reported average attendances of 60 at Sunday morning services and 48 in the afternoon during the summer, winter attendances averaging 48 in the morning and 20 in the afternoon.[76] Church attendance had thus declined considerably since c. 1705, when 200 persons were said to resort to church.[77]

The church of *ST. MICHAEL*[78] consists of a nave and chancel under one roof, to which a north aisle was added in 1875. Though largely rebuilt in the 19th century, the nave and chancel reproduce the dimensions of the former church, which, on the evidence of the few surviving original features, was built in the late 12th or early 13th century. The priest's door in the south wall of the chancel has a pointed arch, and the south doorway of the nave a round arch with half-round moulding. No trace remains of the north door of the nave, blocked by the early 19th century. The only surviving original window is a small lancet, set in a splayed, round-headed, rear arch. Until 1875 this window was set in the south wall near the junction of nave and chancel, but it was then moved to its present position, immediately east of the south door. Two large round-headed windows were inserted in the north and south walls of the nave c. 1717,[79] but the chancel retained its original triple-lancet east window until 1832,[80] when this was replaced by a

rectangular mullioned window of 3 lights. There are 2 pairs of diagonal buttresses, of uncertain date, against the east wall and 2 later buttresses on the south wall, giving abutment to hammer-beam trusses.

A squat wooden bell-turret at the west end of the nave was replaced by a more slender one in the mid-19th century and at the same time a stone porch outside the south door was removed and the south door blocked. A new entrance to the church was made in the west wall and against this was erected a large stone porch, which may also have served as a vestry.

The nave roof, which was probably erected in the 15th century, consists of 4 trusses, alternately of hammer-beam and collar-and-tie-beam construction. The trusses are connected by two rows of side-purlins, the two eastern bays of the nave having two rows of elaborately carved double-wind-braces, forming cusped circles in each roof panel, with a row of single wind-braces of the same type above the upper purlins.[81] By the mid-19th century the collar-and-tie-beam truss at the junction of nave and chancel had been filled and plastered over; this may have been an original feature, intended to form a chancel arch.

The chancel, described as dilapidated in 1827,[82] was rebuilt in 1832.[83] In 1875 the north aisle was built, divided from the nave by an arcade supported on 3 piers. A vestry and a small aisle for the use of the children, now containing the organ, was built to the north of the chancel. The original entrance through the south door was then restored and a new stone porch was erected. The west porch was opened to the nave and the west door was blocked, a 2-light window being inserted above. The bell-turret was replaced by a stone bell-cote containing 2 bells and the ceiling which then concealed the roof of the church was removed. Three windows in Decorated style were inserted in the south wall and a 3-light east window replaced the mullioned window of 1832.

The chancel screen and the reredos were virtually the only fittings to survive the restoration of 1875. The latter, given by R. N. Pemberton (perpetual curate 1817–19),[84] consists of an assemblage of Jacobean carved panels with, as a centre-piece, a set of five panels with human figures, said to be the work of an Antwerp wood-carver of c. 1530.[85] The chancel screen dates, like the roof, from the 15th century, but its northern half was largely restored in 1875. The lower part of the screen, now open, originally contained carved woodwork, which was removed in 1717 and used in the gallery then erected at the west end.[86] Box pews were set up in

62 *T.S.A.S.* xlvi. 42.
63 Par. rec., abstract of title to rectory, 1856.
64 Gough, *Hist. of Myddle* (1875), 162.
65 *T.S.A.S.* 4th ser. vi. 291.
66 B.M. Add. MS. 21018, f. 295.
67 *S.P.R. Heref.* i (2), 109.
68 B.M. Add. MS. 33124, ff. 59–68.   69 Ibid.
70 *S.P.R. Heref.* i (2), 112.
71 Ibid. pp. iv, 113; B.M. Add. MS. 21018, f. 295ᵛ; Heref. Dioc. Regy., reg. 1791–1821, p. 128; ibid. 1822–42, pp. 28, 88; *Rep. Com. Eccl. Revenues* [67], pp. 438–9, H.C. (1835), xxii.
72 Heref. Dioc. Regy., reg. 1857–69, p. 238.
73 Ibid. 1822–42, p. 426; par. rec., tithe appt.; H.O. 129/359/4/3.
74 *T.S.A.S.* 3rd ser. x. 374.

75 Par. rec., churchwardens' accts. 1846–1935.
76 H.O. 129/359/4/3.
77 Heref. Dioc. Regy., visitation papers, box 44.
78 The following architectural description is based, except where otherwise stated, on S.P.L., MS. 372, vol. ii, p. 13; S.P.L., J. H. Smith collect. no. 87; photographs of church, c. 1870, in vestry; W.S.L. 350/40/3; par. rec., faculty for church restoration, 1875; *Salop. Shreds & Patches,* i. 178–9; Cranage, vi. 526–7.
79 Heref. Dioc. Regy., reg. 1710–23, ff. 59–60ᵛ.
80 S.R.O. 529/27.
81 See plate facing p. 217.
82 S.R.O. 529/23.   83 Ibid. 529/27.
84 *Instit. Dioc. Heref.* 141, 143.
85 Pevsner, *Shropshire,* 131.
86 Heref. Dioc. Regy., reg. 1710–23, ff. 59–60ᵛ.

ALBERBURY-WITH-CARDESTON: ROWTON CASTLE FROM THE SOUTH-WEST

Showing, behind the Gothic additions of 1809–28, the hipped roof of the plain 18th-century house

FORD: FORD MANSION FROM THE EAST

WESTBURY: SNAILBEACH LEAD-MINE FROM THE EAST

HABBERLEY FROM THE SOUTH-WEST
Showing the ridge-and-furrow of one of the former common fields

the nave and chancel at the same time,[87] but were replaced by the existing open pews of pitch-pine in 1875, when the gallery was removed. Choir-stalls were installed in the chancel in 1937. Before 1875 the pulpit, reading desk, and slender pedestal font stood in the north-east corner of the nave. These were not retained at the restoration, when the present oak pulpit was set up in the south-east corner of the nave, and a new font at the west end. Three tablets commemorating members of the Ambler family, 1786–90, are the only notable monuments. All three were originally in the chancel, but two were moved to the south wall of the nave in 1875.

The church has had 2 bells since the 16th century.[88] One of them has no inscription, but was probably cast c. 1300, while the other is stamped with rosettes and dragons and may date from the 15th century.[89] The silver chalice and paten possessed by the church in 1553[90] have not survived, the oldest of the existing plate being a silver chalice of 1640, purchased in 1642. A silver chalice cover was acquired in 1693 and a pewter flagon and alms-dish probably in the same year, since all three carry the same initials. The latter were replaced by a silver flagon and alms-dish, given by members of the Waring family in 1766 and 1774 respectively, and a silver paten was given by Mrs. E. G. King in 1910.[91] The registers are complete from 1589.[92]

Although traces of early burials have been found in the churchyard,[93] it had gone out of use by the 17th century.[94] Burials took place either within the church or at Alberbury[95] until 1861, when the churchyard was fenced and consecrated as a burial ground.[96] Stone for the churchyard wall and the impressive pair of cast iron gates, were given by Sir Baldwin Leighton of Loton Park, on condition that inhabitants of Cardeston and of Ford-in-Alberbury might be buried there.[97] Although these terms were accepted by the vestry in 1861,[98] they were revoked in 1876.[99]

NONCONFORMITY. There were said to be no dissenters in the parish in 1676[1] or in 1767[2] and the earlier of the two Methodist chapels owes its foundation to a dispute between members of the vestry and the perpetual curate in 1860. Thomas Hudson, the chairman of the vestry, provided a site for a Metho-dist chapel in that year, and before its erection meetings were held at the house of Edward Bufton, another member of the vestry.[3] By 1864 this chapel had been affiliated to the United Methodist Free Church and was served by the minister of Albert St. chapel, Shrewsbury.[4] The Primitive Methodist chapel on Ford Heath was erected in 1867 and enlarged in 1891.[5] Both chapels were in use in 1964.

SCHOOLS. A Sunday School, supported by subscription, had been established by 1817.[6] Attendances of 40 children are recorded then and in the following year[7] and 30 children attended in 1833.[8] It may have been discontinued after 1838, when subscriptions from the impropriator of the living, apparently to this school, ceased to be paid,[9] but the parish again had a Sunday School in 1846.[10]

A schoolmaster was resident in the parish in 1831,[11] and in 1833 20 children attended a day school at their parents' expense.[12] In 1846 31 children attended on Sundays, but only 3 during the week.[13] This was, however, considered sufficient for the needs of the parish.[14] This school, which was held in what is now known as the Old School House,[15] continued until replaced by the National School in 1873 and had 30 pupils in 1871.[16]

A National School was erected in 1873[17] on land given by R. Lingen Burton.[18] It then had an annual income of £46, derived in equal proportions from school pence, voluntary contributions, and a government grant.[19] School pence had been abolished by 1893, when £55 was received from a government grant and £42 from voluntary contributions.[20] The school was filled to capacity in the later 19th century, average attendances rising from 50 in 1885[21] to about 80 in the period 1891–1913.[22] It became a Controlled school in 1951[23] and 2 new classrooms were added in 1954.[24]

CHARITIES. By will, proved in 1728, Joseph Waring gave £10 to the parish officers to provide bread for the poor.[25] This benefaction produced an annual income of 10s. in 1786, when bread was distributed to the poor on St. Thomas's Day.[26] The capital was never invested, but was deemed to be due from the Waring estate generally and was lost after the sale of the estate in 1844.[27]

[87] Ibid.
[88] T.S.A.S. 2nd ser. xii. 318.
[89] Walters, Ch. Bells Salop. 202–3.
[90] T.S.A.S. 2nd ser. xii. 318.
[91] Arkwright and Bourne, Ch. Plate Ludlow Archd. 29.
[92] Printed to 1812 in S.P.R. Heref. i (2), 63–113.
[93] Ibid. 108.
[94] Heref. Dioc. Regy., visitation papers, box 44.
[95] S.P.R. Heref. i (2), 108.
[96] Heref. Dioc. Regy., reg. 1857–69, p. 197.
[97] Par. rec., vestry minutes, 1858–76.
[98] Ibid.   [99] Ibid.
[1] T.S.A.S. 2nd ser. i. 88.
[2] Heref. Dioc. Regy., return of papists, 1767.
[3] Par. rec., vestry minutes, 1858–76; Shrewsbury Methodist circuit records, conveyance of site, 1860.
[4] Shrewsbury Methodist circuit records, trust deeds, 1864–1939; W. E. Morris, History of Methodism in Shrewsbury and District (Shrewsbury, 1960), 44–45.
[5] Morris, op. cit. 45–46.
[6] B.M. Add. MS. 21018, f. 295; Educ. Enquiry Abstract, H.C. 62, p. 774 (1835), xlii.
[7] B.M. Add. MS. 21018, f. 295; Digest of Returns to Cttee. on Educ. of Poor, H.C. 224, p. 751 (1819), ix (2).

[8] Educ. Enquiry Abstract, p. 774.
[9] S.R.O. 529/18–32.
[10] Nat. Soc. Ch. School Returns, 1846–7.
[11] S.R.O. 169/12.
[12] Educ. Enquiry Abstract, p. 774.
[13] Nat. Soc. Ch. School Returns, 1846–7.
[14] Ibid.
[15] Ex inf. Mr. W. Parry.
[16] Returns relating to Elem. Educ., H.C. 201, p. 334 (1871), lv.
[17] Ed. 7/102/101.
[18] Par. rec., conveyance, 1872.
[19] Ed. 7/102/101.
[20] Return of Schs., 1893 [C. 7529], p. 506, H.C. (1894), lxv.
[21] Kelly's Dir. Salop. (1885).
[22] Ibid. (1891–1913); Return of Schs., 1893, p. 506; Voluntary Schs. Returns, H.C. 178–XXIV, p. 21 (1906), lxxxviii.
[23] Ex inf. S.C.C. Educ. Dept.
[24] Ibid.
[25] 24th Rep. Com. Char., H.C. 231, p. 391 (1831), xi.
[26] Ibid.
[27] Char. Com. files.

HABBERLEY

HABBERLEY is not recorded by name in Domesday Book, when it seems to have been a member of the vast manor of Worthen. It probably became an independent parish in the course of the 12th century.[1] The parish contains 804 a.[2] and lies in the valley between Pontesford Hill, Lawn Hill, and Huglith on the east, and the northern extremity of the Stiperstones on the west.

On the east the parish boundary follows Habberley Brook and on the north-east skirts the lower slopes of Earls Hill. The western boundary follows roughly the 700-foot contour along the edge of Eastridge Wood. The latter was formerly part of Hogstow Forest and lies in an area known since the later Middle Ages as Habberley Office. Prestley Farm, to the east of Habberley Brook and in Pulverbatch parish, has lain in the manor of Habberley since at least 1382.[3]

The parish lies on gently sloping ground, which rises from 475 feet in the north to 750 feet above Marsley Farm in the south. In addition to Habberley Brook the southern half of the parish is drained by one of its tributaries, known as Black Sitch in the early 17th century.[4] This tributary rises on Lordshill and flows northwards towards Habberley Hall, then turns eastwards, flowing to the south of the village street and joining Habberley Brook near the mill.

Over the greater part of the parish the subsoil is boulder clay. A narrow belt of alluvial soil and flood gravels adjoins Habberley Brook and there is a small sandy ridge to the north-west of the village. Marsley Farm stands on a glacial moraine, formerly called the Audley,[5] and Callow Hill, to the north-east of the village, is composed of Cambrian quartzite like Pontesford Hill, of which it is an outlier.

Although there is very little documentary evidence for the historical geography of the parish, it is possible to deduce the outlines of its medieval landscape. The sandy ridge to the north-west of the village impeded the natural drainage of the higher ground to the west, producing an area of moorland west of the Pontesbury road, which was known as 'Stodefallemore' in the Middle Ages.[6] Leas Coppice in the north-west corner of the parish is a remnant of the woodland which once covered the remainder of this area. The field-name element 'lye', given to several assarts here in 1382,[7] still figured (in the form 'Lees') in the names of a number of fields north-west of the village in the 18th century.[8] Another late-14th-century assart in this area had the significant name 'le Byrches'.[9]

Much of the well-drained clay soils to the south of the village lay within the common fields, but along the western boundary the higher ground on the slopes of Eastridge Wood was probably at one time common pasture land. In the later 16th century the rector had common rights at Hartbeach[10]—the name given to the valley, to the north of the Audley, cut by Black Sitch as it enters the parish. The Audley was presumably also in origin an area of rough pasture, like the similar glacial moraine north of Stapleton village. It had been inclosed by the later 16th century and Hartbeach before 1607.[11] Until the later 16th century the tenants of Habberley also had rights of common for pigs in Habberley Office,[12] which may explain the relatively early disappearance of common lands within the parish.

Of the common fields[13] Pitchill Field lay to the north of the village and is first recorded in the form 'Pedeshull'. Cross Field and Marsley Field lay to the south of the village, to the east and west of the road to Westcott respectively, extending as far south as the foot of the Marsley moraine. The common fields were inclosed at some date between 1624 and 1767.[14]

Two roads, neither of which is now of more than local importance, traverse the parish. One, which leaves the road from Shrewsbury to Bishop's Castle near Cothercott Hill, runs past Westcott and up the Habberley valley towards Pontesbury and the other, from Pulverbatch to Minsterley, runs from east to west across the parish. The first of these roads was, however, a major route from south-west Shropshire to Pontesbury before the present road from Pontesbury to Bishop's Castle, by way of Minsterley and the Hope valley, was laid out in the 1830s.[15] The second was probably the route taken by the Bishop of Hereford in his journey from Church Stretton to Pontesbury in 1290.[16] Habberley Hall, which stands at the junction of the roads to Pontesbury and Minsterley, appears to occupy the site of small castle, probably a ringwork, designed to control these roads. Such would be a reasonable explanation of the low but distinct mound on which the house stands.

The church stands at the junction of the roads from Westcott and Pulverbatch and most of the houses in the small straggling village stand alongside the Pulverbatch road to the east. In addition to the parsonage, Hall Farm and Middle Farm were originally timber-framed houses, but both have been enlarged and cased in brick. Another timber-framed house to the east of Middle Farm was

---

[1] See p. 242. This article was written in 1964 and revised in 1965.
[2] O.S. *Area Bk.* (1883). The following topographical description is based, except where otherwise stated, on O.S. Map 1″, sheet lxi (1st edn.); O.S. Maps 6″ Salop 48 (1st and later edns.); O.S. Maps 1/25,000, SJ 30, 40 (1957); Rocque, *Map of Salop.* (1752); Baugh, *Map of Salop.* (1808); B.M. O.S. 2″ orig. drawings, sheet 199 (1816); Geol. Survey Map (drift), sheet 152 (1932); Heref. Dioc. Regy., tithe appt. 1849, and map, 1839; Staffs. R.O., D 590/367 (map of Habberley manor, *c.* 1760).
[3] S.P.L., Deeds 6172.
[4] Heref. Dioc. Regy., glebe terriers, 1607–24.
[5] Ibid.
[6] S.P.L., Deeds 6172.

[7] Ibid.
[8] Staffs. R.O., D 590/367.
[9] S.P.L., Deeds 6172.
[10] Heref. Dioc. Regy., glebe terriers, 1607–24.
[11] Ibid.
[12] S.P.L., Deeds 2495.
[13] Description of common fields based on S.P.L., Deeds 6171–2; Heref. Dioc. Regy., glebe terriers, 1607–24. See plate facing p. 237.
[14] Heref. Dioc. Regy., glebe terrier, 1624; S.P.L., MS. 2505.
[15] See p. 301.
[16] *Household Roll of Ric. de Swinfield* (Camd. Soc. 1st ser. lxii), cxci; J. R. H. Moorman, *Church Life in England in the 13th century* (Camb. 1946), 187–91.

demolished in 1964. The only house, apart from the Hall, on the Pontesbury road north of the church is the pair of cottages now known as nos. 1–2, Habberley Road. This was originally a timber-framed farmhouse, but had been reduced to cottage status by the later 18th century.[17] Settlement at the eastern end of the village is a more recent development. The mill occupies a medieval site, but was largely rebuilt in 1839.[18] The pair of cottages nearest the brook consists of a single-bay cottage of flimsy timber-framed construction, to which a further bay was later added in stone, but the remaining brick cottages here were built in the early 19th century on the small freehold estate of the Bromley family.[19] Lower Farm, to the north of these cottages, is also of brick. It does not appear to contain any concealed timber-framing and probably dates from the 18th century.

There was an alehouse in the village in 1616.[20] There were 2 in 1754,[21] but they had both closed by 1765.[22] Two alehouses which had been opened shortly before 1839, no doubt encouraged by the Beer Act of 1830, were then closed by the squire's agent.[23] One of these alehouses was among the group of cottages at the east end of the village.[24] The other, adjoining the churchyard,[25] was subsequently reopened and was known by its present name, 'The Mytton Arms', by 1856.[26] This was originally a timber-framed house, but its exterior was cased in brick and its roof raised in the 19th century. The small stone building opposite 'The Mytton Arms' was, until c. 1900, the village smithy.[27] A field to the south of Black Sitch on the east side of the Westcott road was known as Forge Meadow in 1839.[28] It is likely that the small timber-framed house by the brook to the north of this field is the site of an earlier smithy.

The small proportion of ancient woodland in the parish, coupled with the relatively large area occupied by the common fields, precluded the development of isolated farms here. The only example is Marsley Farm, a rough-cast, timber-framed house of 3 bays with a chimney-stack on its south gable, which was probably built in the early 17th century, shortly after the common at the Audley had been inclosed. The house may, however, stand on the site of a Saxon royal hunting-lodge, known as 'Marsetelie' in 1086.[29] The only other isolated dwellings in the parish formed part of the extensive squatter settlement at the foot of Pontesford Hill, most of which lies in Pontesbury parish.

Five of these cottages stood in Habberley parish in 1839,[30] but only one of them was still standing in 1964.

The village was considerably more populous in the earlier 14th century, when the manor contained 37 messuages,[31] than it was in 1801, when there were only 19 houses in the parish as a whole.[32] Habberley was said to have an adult population of 50 in 1676.[33] The population rose from 104 in 1801 to 151 by 1821.[34] A decline to 112 in 1861 was said to be due in part to the migration of young people from the parish and there were only 86 inhabitants in 1891, but the parish normally had a population of some 130 persons in the later 19th century.[35] Since 1901, however, the population has steadily declined; there were only 66 inhabitants in 1961.[36]

A parish wake was still being held in the churchyard in the early 19th century[37] and the custom of firing a concealed gun at weddings was still observed in 1964.[38]

MANOR.   When first recorded in 1240 the manor of *HABBERLEY* was held of the barony of Thomas Corbet of Caus.[39] Eyton's suggestion[40] that it was a member of Minsterley manor in 1086 is improbable. It is more likely to have been one of the 13 berewicks of Worthen manor then held by Roger Corbet.[41] The manor continued to be held of the lords of Caus until the end of feudal tenures.[42]

Adam de Arundel, tenant of the manor in 1242,[43] had been succeeded before 1274 by John de Arundel,[44] who settled the reversion of two-thirds of the manor on Robert Corbet of Moreton Corbet and his wife Maud in 1297.[45] The latter, who can probably be identified with the Maud de Arundel recorded in 1272,[46] may have been the mother of John de Arundel, for she and Robert Corbet already held a third of the manor by 1297,[47] probably in dower. The whole manor passed to Maud some time after Robert's death in 1300.[48] At her death in 1309[49] she was succeeded by her son Thomas Corbet, who died in the following year, leaving as heir his son Robert, then a minor.[50] Robert's wardship was entrusted to the overlord, Peter Corbet of Caus, who was still his guardian in 1316.[51] A settlement made by Robert Corbet before 1347, under which the manor was to pass at his death to his son John,[52] was frustrated by John's death in that year.[53] The latter's widow released her interest in the manor to Robert,[54] who then settled it on his son Fulk.[55] Fulk succeeded to the manor

[17] Staffs. R.O., D 590/367.
[18] Ibid. D 590/746, letter, G. Robinson to Mrs. Mytton, 7 Aug. 1839.
[19] Heref. Dioc. Regy., tithe appt.
[20] Q. Sess., alehouse reg.
[21] Ibid.
[22] Ibid.
[23] Staffs. R.O., D 590/746, letter, 7 Aug. 1839.
[24] Heref. Dioc. Regy., tithe appt.
[25] Ibid.
[26] *Kelly's Dir. Salop.* (1856).
[27] Ibid. (1863–1900); Heref. Dioc. Regy., tithe appt.
[28] Heref. Dioc. Regy., tithe appt.
[29] *V.C.H. Salop.* i. 309.
[30] Heref. Dioc. Regy., tithe appt.
[31] S.P.L., Deeds 6172.
[32] *Census*, 1801.
[33] *T.S.A.S.* 2nd ser. i. 88.
[34] *Census*, 1801–21.
[35] Ibid. 1861–1901.
[36] Ibid. 1901–61.

[37] Par. rec., churchwardens' accts. 1702–1809.
[38] Ex inf. Dr. L. W. Hamp, Habberley Hall. cf. *Eddowes's Jnl.* 5 July 1848.
[39] *Bk. of Fees*, 964.
[40] Eyton, vii. 47.
[41] *V.C.H. Salop.* i. 325.
[42] *Feud. Aids*, iv. 241; *Cal. Inq. p.m.* v, pp. 46, 96; ibid. xiv, p. 110; C 138/8/34; C 139/50/47; C 140/39/61; C 142/152/60; C 142/200/64.
[43] *Bk. of Fees*, 964.
[44] C 133/7/8.
[45] Eyton, iv. 354–5.
[46] Ibid. vii. 48 n.
[47] Ibid. 48.
[48] *Cal. Inq. p.m.* iv, p. 505.
[49] Ibid. v, p. 46.
[50] Ibid. p. 96.
[51] *Feud. Aids*, iv. 234.
[52] S.P.L., MS. 269, f. 16.
[53] Ibid.   [54] Ibid.
[55] C 135/243/7.

on Robert's death in 1375[56] and on his death in 1382 it passed to his widow Elizabeth for life, under the terms of the settlement.[57] Elizabeth, daughter and heir of Fulk Corbet, married John Mawddy and their son Fulk, who was lord of the manor at his death in 1414,[58] had probably obtained possession before his father's death in 1403.[59] Fulk's widow Isabel held a third of the manor in dower until 1430,[60] but the remainder passed in 1414 to his sister Elizabeth, wife of Hugh Burgh.[61] The manor followed the descent of Wattlesborough manor in Cardeston until 1501[62] when, on the partition of the estates of Sir John Burgh, it was allotted to Thomas Mytton, husband of Sir John's daughter Elizabeth.[63]

Until 1583 the manor descended from father to son in the Mytton family,[64] the following being lords: Thomas, 1501–4; William, 1504–14; Richard, 1514–53;[65] Edward, 1553–68;[66] Edward, 1568–83.[67] It was then held until 1615[68] by Anne, widow of Edward Mytton, who subsequently married William Leighton. After 1615 it again descended in the Mytton family until 1846, the following being lords: Richard, 1615–c. 1640;[69] Thomas, c. 1640–1656; Richard, 1656–69;[70] Richard, 1669–1718;[71] Richard, 1718–31; John (brother), 1731–56; John, 1756–83; John, 1783–98; John, 1798–1834; John Fox Fitz-Giffard, 1834–46. The last, who came of age in 1844,[72] sold the manor in 1846 to William Hanbury Sparrow, who died in 1867, having settled the estate for life on his son Frederick Turton Sparrow. The latter died in 1888 and in 1898 the estate was purchased from the Sparrow trustees by Heighway Jones of Earlsdale, Pontesbury. On the death of Heighway Jones in 1915, his estate passed to his sister Mary Jane Jones. She assigned her life interest in 1919 to Col. Frederick Caton Jones, who in the same year acquired the reversionary interest of Redmond Jones in the family estates in Habberley and Pulverbatch. Col. Frederick Caton Jones died in 1944, when the manor passed to his nephew Dr. John Chitty, the lord in 1964.

There seems to have been a manor-house at Habberley in 1380, when Elizabeth Corbet had licence for a private oratory here.[73] This manor-house would presumably have occupied the site of Habberley Hall, for the low mound on which the house stands is likely to be a castle-site. The older timber-framed portion of the Hall was built by William Leighton in 1593,[74] but the central bay is unusually wide and the spine-beam of its clumsily contrived ceiling has cracked from its excessive load. It is thus possible that the work undertaken in 1593 was the adaptation of a medieval open hall,

rather than the erection of a new house. The present roof is of collar-and-tie-beam construction and is clearly no older than 1593. As built or reconstructed in 1593 the Hall appears to have been a rectangular house, consisting on the ground floor of a central hall, flanked by pairs of smaller rooms to the north and south. The upper floor was originally jettied on all sides. A door on the east wall opens on the lower end of the hall and is probably the original entrance. Over the door is a replica of the original inscription—'This hous builded as you see A.D. 1593 by W.L.'[75] On the west wall of the hall is a lateral stone chimney-stack. Two gabled wings, added to the east of the house in the early 17th century, have close vertical studding on the ground floor, similar to that in the original house, and diagonal braces above. The first-floor windows on the gables of these projecting wings have moulded sills and supporting brackets. The principal rooms in the older part of the house retain some original fittings and are panelled in plain oak, with a fluted frieze, augmented on the ground floor by a few 17th-century carved panels brought from elsewhere in the present century.

The Hall was normally occupied by tenant-farmers after the mid-17th century,[76] but the antiquary William Mytton lived there for a short period before his death in 1746.[77] A brick south wing was added in the later 19th century by William Hanbury Sparrow, who lived here after purchasing the manorial estate in 1846.[78] Buildings were demolished to make way for this wing,[79] but, since it stands at a lower level than the rest of the house, these are unlikely to have formed part of the original house. Sparrow also laid out the garden and formed a 22-acre park in the fields to the west of the Hall.[80] Since his death the Hall has not been occupied by the lord of the manor.

ECONOMIC HISTORY. Virtually the only information about the administration of the manor in medieval times is provided by an extent of 1382.[81] Rents totalling £7 17s. 6½d. were then due from the tenants.[82] The value of the manor was put at £5 9s. 4¾d. in 1426[83] and at £8 8s. 3½d. in 1443.[84] The demesne, which had by 1382 been leased piecemeal to the tenants, included 'Stodefallemore' and Prestley moor.[85] Like the mill these two areas were leased as a portion of the demesne throughout the 15th century.[86]

At least one freehold estate was created by John de Arundel, lord of the manor in the later 13th century.[87] This comprised a messuage and one

[56] C 135/243/7.
[57] C 136/25/7.
[58] C 138/8/34.
[59] C 137/44/34.
[60] Cal. Fine R. 1413–22, 74; C 139/49/32.
[61] Ibid.
[62] See p. 197.
[63] T.S.A.S. 4th ser. v. 217.
[64] For pedigree see S.P.L., MS. 2791, pp. 526–31; ibid. MS. 4080, p. 2002.
[65] C 142/152/60.
[66] Ibid.
[67] C 142/200/64.
[68] S.P.R. Heref. v (4), 10.
[69] S.P.L., Deeds 4008.
[70] P.C.C. 25 Penn.
[71] T.S.A.S. 4th ser. xii. 222.
[72] Account of descent of manor after 1846 based on

Heighway Jones title-deeds, penes Messrs. Sprott, Stokes, and Turnbull, solicitors, Shrewsbury.
[73] Reg. J. Gilbert (C. & Y.S.), 19.
[74] T.S.A.S. 1st ser. viii. 197.
[75] Ibid.
[76] E 179/255/35 m. 8od.; Hearth Tax, 1672, 157.
[77] Par. rec., overseers' accts. 1741–85.
[78] Kelly's Dir. Salop. (1856–85).
[79] T.S.A.S. 1st ser. viii. 196–7.
[80] Heighway Jones title-deeds, sale partics. 1898.
[81] S.P.L., Deeds 6172.
[82] Ibid.
[83] Heref. City Libr. 9133/39.
[84] Ibid. 9133/33.
[85] S.P.L., Deeds 6172.
[86] Heref. City Libr. 9133/33, 37, 39; S.R.O. 840 uncat., bailiff's acct. 1419–20.
[87] Eyton, vii. 49.

noke ($\frac{1}{4}$ virgate) and was subsequently conveyed by the son of the Rector of Habberley to William Fitz-Madoc of Pontesford.[88] It may have been this estate which was held in 1382 by Hugh Hodgkins and William Taillour under a grant made by John de Arundel.[89] In 1382 there were 10 other freeholders in the manor,[90] who held a total of 14 nokes, together with portions of the former demesne. Two of them held their lands under grants of 1364 and 1370. John Corbet, who then held a composite estate consisting of freehold and leasehold land,[91] is recorded as a free tenant here between 1368 and 1412.[92] He may have been the ancestor of Joan Browne *alias* Corbet, who owned a 70-acre freehold in the parish in 1607.[93] Three other freeholds were held in the early 17th century by Thomas Hinton,[94] John Phillips of Marsley,[95] and John Bradley.[96] A small freehold was purchased by the lord of the manor from Richard Williams in 1681[97] and a larger estate from the Symonds family in 1767.[98] After this date the manorial estate included the whole parish, with the exception of 5 cottages belonging to the Bromley and Medlicott families.[99] William Hanbury Sparrow purchased Huglith Farm, Pulverbatch, in 1864 and Lawn Farm, Pulverbatch, was acquired by Heighway Jones in 1910.[1] Between 1898 and 1945 the manor formed part of the Earlsdale estate, which amounted to over 2,200 a. in 1928, but most of the Habberley manorial estate was sold in 1945. Only 284 a. in the parish was owned by the lord of the manor by 1947.[2]

Some land was presumably kept in hand when the lord was resident at the Hall in the later 16th and early 17th centuries. Richard Mytton acquired a portion of the glebe adjoining the Hall in order to consolidate his home farm some time before 1637.[3] John Mytton kept two large farms in hand in the 1750s,[4] but after the later 18th century the lord only retained a small area of woodland, amounting to 22 a. in 1849.[5] Timber sales produced £838 in 1836[6] and in 1839 the woodland in the manor was replanted.[7]

The 24 holdings of those described in the extent of 1382[8] as tenants-at-will amounted to 28 nokes, or roughly two-thirds of the ancient cultivated area, the remainder being held by free tenants. Eight of these tenants also held assarts and portions of former demesne and the lands of 2 tenants (3 nokes) were then in the lord's hands. Eight of the so-called tenants-at-will in fact held their lands on leases for 2 or 3 lives granted by the lord of the manor between 1366 and 1373.[9] In addition to John Corbet two other tenants held both free and unfree land. Hugh de Pontesford, who held 3 nokes of freehold land, a half virgate by lease, and half of 'Stodefallemore', and whose son John held a further 4 nokes by lease, was the most substantial of the Habberley tenants at this time. The noke had clearly once been the normal holding of customary tenants here. Fourteen of the 22 tenants-at-will who possessed no lands under another form of tenure held a single noke apiece, 4 held 2 nokes each, and the remainder were cottagers.[10]

There are no more surveys of the manorial estate until the later 18th century, when it consisted of 5 farms, three of which were of over 100 a., the mill, and 6 smaller properties.[11] Hall Farm, the largest of the farms, had by 1809 been combined with Middle Farm to produce a holding of 363 a.,[12] but they had been separated by 1849, when the 5 large farms were all of over 100 a.[13] The estate also included at this date 5 holdings of under 6 a. and 8 cottagers.[14] In 1898 the Habberley portion of the Sparrow estate included 4 farms of over 100 a., 2 of some 70 a., and 4 smallholdings.[15] The annual rental rose from £423 in 1783[16] to a little over £800 in the later 1820s, when there were usually some £200 of arrears.[17] The area of arable land in the parish rose from 271 a. in 1801, when wheat was the chief crop,[18] to 485 a. by 1849.[19]

The absence of a resident parson and squire may have been in part responsible for the unusually depressed condition of the Habberley cottagers in the earlier 19th century. They were said to be badly off in 1793, when their diet of bread, cheese, and potatoes was supplemented by a weak broth, known locally as 'jupping', given by farmers to their labourers.[20] In 1839 the agent reported that the cottagers were still 'in a wretched state', and that the unsavoury character of the village was heightened by the rough behaviour of colliers and lead-smelters, who frequented the 2 alehouses there.[21]

The mill is first recorded in 1370, when its rent of 16s. a year was assigned to the free tenant John Corbet,[22] but it is clearly of more ancient date. The only form of service due from the tenants in 1382 was the carriage of mill-stones to the mill whenever necessary.[23] This suggests that the mill may once have served an area larger than Habberley village and is perhaps a survival from the period when Habberley was a member of Worthen manor. The mill was held on a life-lease in 1370, but this had been replaced by short-term leases by the earlier 15th century.[24] It remained in use until at least

[88] Ibid.
[89] S.P.L., Deeds 6172.
[90] Ibid.
[91] Ibid.
[92] S.R.O. 567 uncat., deeds, 1368–1412.
[93] C 2/Jas. I/B 29/20.
[94] C 142/298/100.
[95] Wolryche-Whitmore MSS., Dudmaston, deed, 1614.
[96] C 142/469/170.
[97] S.P.L., MS 2505.
[98] Ibid.
[99] Heref. Dioc. Regy., tithe appt. The Medlicott freehold was purchased by the lord of the manor in 1861: Heighway Jones title-deeds.
[1] Heighway Jones title-deeds.
[2] Ibid.
[3] *S.P.R. Lich.* vi (1), 192–3.
[4] Par. rec., overseers' accts. 1741–85.
[5] Heref. Dioc. Regy., tithe appt.
[6] Staffs. R.O., D 590/746, timber accts. 1836.

[7] Ibid. letter, 7 Aug. 1839.
[8] S.P.L., Deeds 6172.
[9] Ibid.
[10] Ibid.
[11] S.P.L., MS. 2498; Heighway Jones title-deeds, abstract of title, 1846.
[12] S.R.O. 515/7.
[13] Heref. Dioc. Regy., tithe appt.
[14] Ibid.
[15] Heighway Jones title-deeds, sale partics. 1898.
[16] S.P.L., MS. 2498.
[17] S.R.O. 840 uncat., accts. 1826–30.
[18] H.O. 67/12/98.
[19] Heref. Dioc. Regy., tithe appt.
[20] B.M. Add. MS. 21018, f. 299.
[21] Staffs. R.O., D 590/746, letter, 7 Aug. 1839.
[22] S.R.O. 567 uncat., lease, 1370.
[23] S.P.L., Deeds 6172.
[24] S.R.O. 567 uncat., lease, 1370; Heref. City Libr. 9133/33, 39.

1909,[25] having been reconstructed in 1839.[26] A field adjoining Black Sitch, to the west of the Hall, was known as Tainter Yard in the 18th century[27] and probably marks the site of a fulling mill. One David le Walker was among the tenants in 1382,[28] but no such mill is recorded then or later. The small population of the village provided little scope for other tradesmen. There were 2 blacksmiths in 1851,[29] but after 1863 only one, who was also the miller.[30] The smithy closed c. 1900, but a wheelwright remained in business until shortly before the Second World War.[31] The village also had a shop between 1895[32] and 1964.

LOCAL GOVERNMENT. There are manor court rolls, 1451[33] and 1453.[34] The court was held twice a year in the later Middle Ages and its jurisdiction included view of frankpledge and the assize of bread and ale.[35] It was still meeting in the early 19th century.[36]

The parish records include churchwardens' accounts, 1702–1809, and overseers' accounts, 1741–85. During this period the parish had two churchwardens and a single overseer. The latter also served as surveyor of the highways and rendered a single account for both these functions. Lewns had been replaced by pound rates by the time the accounts begin. Statute-labour was still in use on the roads in 1761, when most of the expenses incurred were in the maintenance of small bridges over streams in the village.

Expenditure on poor relief fluctuated between £6 and £20 a year, 1743–80. Poor rates had risen to £38 by 1803[37] and reached a peak of £77 in 1818,[38] but during the 1820s never rose above £54 a year.[39] A poor-house was being rented from the lord of the manor by 1776.[40]

CHURCH. A priest is first recorded at Habberley in the later 13th century,[41] but the church contains some 12th-century features. The living has been styled a rectory since at least 1536,[42] but was described as a chapelry in the 14th century.[43] This probably reflects an original dependence on Worthen church. There is no evidence for Eyton's suggestion[44] that Minsterley or Westbury was the mother church.

Since 1949 the living has been served by the Rector of Minsterley.[45] The advowson has always followed the descent of the manor.[46]

The church was said to be worth £4 0s. 2d. in 1536[47] and £10 in 1655.[48] The rector had an average annual gross income of £172 in 1835.[49] The glebe amounted to some 35 a. in the early 17th century,[50] but had been reduced to 25 a. by 1839.[51] This was probably the result of an exchange made with the lord of the manor shortly before 1637. The latter then obtained 6½ a. of glebe land near the Hall, but his successors demanded rent for the land given to the rector in exchange.[52] By 1607 an allotment of 16 a. at the Audley had been made to the rector in lieu of common rights there,[53] but the remainder of the glebe was still unenclosed in 1624.[54] By the later 18th century it consisted of two compact groups of fields in the south of the parish.[55] The glebe has probably been continuously leased since the early 18th century and in 1839 was occupied by the tenants of several adjacent holdings.[56] It was let for £26 3s. a year in 1851,[57] and for £24 in 1898.[58] There is no evidence for the value or mode of collection of tithes in the parish before 1849, when they were commuted for a rent-charge of £138.[59]

Until the 19th century none of the rectors was a relative of the lord of the manor. Walter Pride, instituted in 1341,[60] obtained leave of absence in 1348 as a member of the household of Lionel, Duke of Clarence.[61] Between 1524 and c. 1624 the living was held successively by Roger Hyncks and Thomas Hyncks.[62] They may have been father and son, as were John and Thomas Cooper, rectors from c. 1654 until 1736.[63] After the latter's death most rectors employed assistant curates and were probably non-resident. Thomas Mills (rector 1758–97),[64] who had been assistant curate here for two years before his institution,[65] lived at Pulverbatch, where he was curate, and employed an assistant curate at Habberley at a salary of £30 a year.[66] John Pigott (rector 1802–45),[67] who was a cousin of the patron,[68] held the living in plurality with Edgmond, where he lived.[69] He normally employed the assistant curates of Minsterley as his assistant curates at Habberley, paying them £40 a year until 1834, when the annual

[25] Kelly's Dir. Salop. (1909).
[26] Staffs. R.O., D 590/746, letter, 7 Aug. 1839.
[27] Ibid. D 590/367.   [28] S.P.L., Deeds 6172.
[29] Bagshaw's Dir. Salop. (1851).
[30] Kelly's Dir. Salop. (1863–1900).
[31] Ibid. (1900–41).   [32] Ibid. (1895).
[33] Heref. City Libr. 9133/18
[34] S.P.L., Deeds 6171.
[35] Cal. Pat. 1381–5, 29.
[36] W.S.L. 350/40/3.
[37] Poor Law Abstract, 1803, H.C. 175, pp. 416–17 (1803–4), xiii.
[38] Rep. Cttee. on Poor Rate Returns, 1822, Suppl. App., H.C. 556, p. 141 (1822), v.
[39] Ibid. 1825, H.C. 334, p. 177 (1825), iv; Acct. of Money expended on Poor, 1825–9, H.C. 83, p. 391 (1830–1), xi.
[40] Rep. Cttee. on Overseers' Returns, 1777, p. 442, H.C. (1st ser. ix, reprinted 1803); par. rec., overseers' accts. 1741–85.
[41] Eyton, vii. 50.
[42] Valor Eccl. (Rec. Com.), iii. 213.
[43] Reg. J. Trillek (C. & Y.S.), 383; Reg. J. Gilbert (C. & Y.S.), 19.
[44] Eyton, vii. 49.
[45] Q. Sess., reg. of electors, 1948, 1949; local inf.
[46] In 1350, however, Joan, wife of Robert Harley, the sister of the patron, presented to the living: Reg. J. Trillek (C. & Y.S.), 383.

[47] Valor Eccl. (Rec. Com.), iii. 213.
[48] T.S.A.S. xlvii. 25.
[49] Rep. Com. Eccl. Revenues [67], pp. 438–9, H.C. (1835), xxii.
[50] Heref. Dioc. Regy., glebe terriers, 1607–24.
[51] Ibid. tithe appt.
[52] S.P.R. Lich. vi (1), 192–3.
[53] Heref. Dioc. Regy., glebe terrier, 1607.
[54] Ibid. 1624.
[55] Staffs. R.O., D 590/367.
[56] Heref. Dioc. Regy., tithe appt.
[57] H.O. 129/359/2/20.
[58] Heighway Jones title-deeds, sale partics. 1898.
[59] Heref. Dioc. Regy., tithe appt.
[60] Cal. Pat. 1340–3, 275.
[61] Reg. J. Trillek (C. & Y.S.), 395.
[62] Reg. C. Bothe (C. & Y.S.), ii. 337; T.S.A.S. 1st ser. viii. 195; S.P.R. Heref. v (4), intro. p. v; Heref. Dioc. Regy., glebe terrier, 1624.
[63] S.P.R. Heref. v (4), intro. p. v; ibid. 12; Instit. Dioc. Heref. 41, 79.
[64] Instit. Dioc. Heref. 93, 127.
[65] S.P.R. Heref. v (4), intro. p. v.
[66] Heref. Dioc. Regy., reg. 1772–1802, ff. 116, 185. See also p. 139.
[67] Instit. Dioc. Heref. 130, 161.
[68] S.P.R. Heref. v (4), intro. p. v.
[69] Rep. Com. Eccl. Revenues [67], pp. 438–9.

stipend was raised to £50.[70] In answer to complaints by John Mytton's agent in 1839, who was voicing the unpopularity of this arrangement among the villagers,[71] the rector claimed that it had received the sanction of the bishop in view of the low value of both livings.[72] Pigott's successor, Charles Kenyon (rector 1845–51),[73] employed Richard White as assistant curate at a salary of £80 a year.[74] Perhaps in deference to local feeling, White was obliged to reside by the terms of his appointment[75] and continued to do so after he succeeded Kenyon as rector in 1851.[76]

The parsonage, which has occupied its present site since at least 1624,[77] was probably built by Thomas Hyncks (rector c. 1573–c. 1624).[78] It is an L-shaped timber-framed house with a central chimney-stack heating the two rooms in the projecting west wing. Since the house still had a structurally separate kitchen in the early 17th century,[79] one of the heated ground-floor rooms may have been intended as a study. A timber-framed barn to the east of the house was presumably once a tithe-barn. Although the rectors ceased to live at the parsonage after 1736, it was occasionally occupied by their assistant curates,[80] and was said to comprise a parlour, kitchen, and 5 bedrooms in 1793.[81] In 1839 Mytton's agent reported that the outbuildings were 'a complete heap of ruins' and that the house itself was 'let to a huckster and most of the windows . . . bricked up'.[82] A brick south wing was added by Richard White, probably in the 1850s. The parsonage was sold in 1949.[83]

Communion was administered 2 or 3 times a year in the earlier 18th century,[84] and 4 times a year in 1793, when there was an average of 8–10 communicants.[85] Services were then held once on Sundays and drew congregations of 40–60 persons.[86] In 1839, when only an evening service was held, the parishioners complained that the attendance of the curate was so irregular that 'we don't know to an hour when church begins'.[87] Richard White had re-introduced morning and evening services by 1851, but had average congregations of only 23 in the morning and 32 in the evening.[88] A body of psalm-singers are first recorded in 1793[89] and in 1809 a pitch-pipe was bought for their use.[90] The date of installation of the present small two-manual American organ is not known. Since the early 17th century the inhabitants of Habberley Office seem to have attended services at Habberley church, where their baptisms and burials were frequently registered.[91] A suggestion made in 1655[92] that this area should be annexed to Habberley parish was not adopted.

The church, which is said to be dedicated to *ST. MARY* or *ST. JAMES*,[93] consists of a nave and chancel under one roof, the latter having an aisle to the north and the former a western bell-cote. Its walls are for the most part of coarse local grit-stone and the only surviving original features are the late-12th-century north and south doorways. The latter has a plain and much-restored semicircular tympanum with a chamfered edge and there is a similar but smaller tympanum above the north door. The heavy diagonal buttress on the south-west corner is dated 1648[94] and the crude south-eastern buttress of the chancel was probably built c. 1678, when the 'end' of the church was said to be in decay.[95] There are no original windows, the earliest now surviving being the 3-light square-headed window on the south wall of the chancel, which dates from the later 16th century. An east window with 4 transomed lights, probably dating from the same period, was in 1845 replaced by a window of 3 graded lights in the Early English style.[96] In 1864, when this in its turn was replaced by the present 3-light window in the Decorated style, a similar window was inserted at the west end and the remaining windows were remodelled in the same style.[97] The east and west windows contain stained glass dated 1868 and 1883 respectively.

A gallery bearing the royal arms and lighted by a southern dormer was erected at the west end by Richard Padland in 1575.[98] This was removed in 1864, when the weather-boarded bell-turret was replaced by a stone gabled bell-cote containing two bells. The north aisle of the chancel, converted into a vestry in 1864, probably dates from the same period as the former western gallery and the south window of the chancel and may have been intended as the Mytton family pew. It is divided from the chancel by a moulded supporting beam. The roof of the nave and chancel, erected in 1864, is supported by alternating arch-braced collar-beam and king-post trusses.

Although most of the church fittings were renewed in 1864, the pulpit dates from the early 19th century and there is much reused woodwork, including the balusters of the communion rails (c. 1700) and late-17th-century oak panelling in the pews and along the nave walls below window-level. There is an early-17th-century oak chair in the chancel and an 18th-century table on claw feet in the vestry. The small round font may date from the 12th century, but it is said to have been recut in 1766[99] and its pedestal was probably made in 1864. The only monument of note is the slate slab of William

---

[70] Heref. Dioc. Regy., reg. 1822–42, pp. 131, 238.
[71] Staffs. R.O., D 590/746, letter, 7 Aug. 1839.
[72] Ibid. letter, J. D. Pigott to G. Robinson, 16 Sept. 1839.
[73] *Instit. Dioc. Heref.* 161, 166.
[74] Heref. Dioc. Regy., reg. 1847–56, pp. 103, 147, 198.
[75] Ibid. p. 147.
[76] *Bagshaw's Dir. Salop.* (1851).
[77] Heref. Dioc. Regy., glebe terrier, 1624.
[78] Ibid.; *S.P.R. Heref.* v (4), intro. p. vi.
[79] Heref. Dioc. Regy., glebe terrier, 1624.
[80] Ibid. reg. 1791–1821, f. 136.
[81] B.M. Add. MS. 21018, f. 299ᵛ.
[82] Staffs. R.O., D 590/746, letter, 7 Aug. 1839.
[83] Q. Sess., reg. of electors, 1948, 1949; local inf.
[84] Par. rec., churchwardens' accts. 1702–1809.
[85] B.M. Add. MS. 21018, f. 299ᵛ.   [86] Ibid.
[87] Staffs. R.O., D 590/746, letter, 7 Aug. 1839.

[88] H.O. 129/359/2/20.
[89] Par. rec., churchwardens' accts. 1702–1809.
[90] Ibid.
[91] *S.P.R. Heref.* v (4), 285–326 *passim*.
[92] *T.S.A.S.* xlvii. 25.
[93] Ibid. 1st ser. viii. 191. The following description is based, except where otherwise stated, in S.P.L. MS. 372, vol. ii, p. 8; S.P.L., T. F. Dukes watercolours (churches), no. 84; S.P.L. J. H. Smith collect. no. 90; Cranage, vi. 528–9.
[94] Datestone.
[95] Heref. Dioc. Regy., visitation papers, box 18, churchwardens' presentment, 1678.
[96] *Bagshaw's Dir. Salop.* (1851).
[97] *S.P.R. Heref.* v (4), intro. p. iv.
[98] Birmingham Univ. Libr., Mytton's Ch. Notes, vol. iv, f. 1a.
[99] Par. rec., churchwardens' accts. 1702–1809.

Mytton, the antiquary (d. 1746), which lies under the altar.

The church still retains the two bells it had in 1552.[1] One of them is of 13th-century date, but the other was probably recast in 1754.[2] A clock is recorded between 1703 and 1730.[3] The church had a silver chalice and paten in 1552.[4] The present plate consists of a chalice given by the lord of the manor in 1774, and a chalice and 3 patens given in 1923.[5] The registers are complete from 1598, but some entries survive from an earlier register, beginning in 1573.[6]

NONCONFORMITY. None known.[7]

SCHOOLS. A dame school was being held in a rent-free cottage in the village in 1793[8] and a day-school, perhaps a direct descendant of this establishment, continued with ever-dwindling attendances during the earlier 19th century. It had 35 pupils in 1818,[9] 11 in 1833,[10] and only 8 in 1846, when the older children attended Pontesbury school.[11]

Although an elementary school was said to be in course of erection in 1871,[12] there is no subsequent record of a school in the parish. The children attended Pontesbury school in 1964.

CHARITIES. By will of 1654 Edward Corbet left to the poor an annual rent-charge of 6s. arising from a messuage and lands in Pontesbury, to be distributed on Good Friday by the rector and parish officers.[13] The rent-charge was being paid by the owner of Hill Farm, Pontesbury, c. 1831, when it was distributed by the curate. Hill Farm later passed to the Heighway Jones family, who made an unsuccessful attempt to redeem the rent-charge in 1900. No payment has been made since the death of Col. Caton Jones in 1942.

John Gittins (d. 1808) left £20 to the poor and a further £20 was added by his widow Elizabeth (d. 1819). By c. 1831 these sums had been invested and the interest was being distributed at Christmas in bread and doles by the curate. The principal was used in 1925 to purchase £53 stock and 18s. 6d. was distributed half yearly among the poor in 1931. In 1964 £1 was distributed among a few poor persons.[14]

PONTESBURY

THE large parish of Pontesbury now contains 10,701 a.[1] and includes the townships of Arscott, Asterley, Boycott, Cruckmeole, Cruckton, Edge, Farley, Halston, Little Hanwood, Hinton, Lea, Longden, Malehurst, Newnham, Oaks, Plealey, Polmere, Pontesbury, Pontesford, Sascott, and Sibberscott.[2] The hamlet of Marton was deserted at an early period, its lands being later merged in the adjacent townships of Newnham and Lea.[3] The lands of the shrunken hamlet of Polmere were also accounted part of these two townships by the 19th century. The shrunken hamlets of Woodhall and Panson were members of Little Hanwood township by that time. The parish crossed hundredal boundaries, for Oaks lay in Condover Hundred and Little Hanwood was a member of the Liberties of Shrewsbury.

In 1884 small detached portions of Great Hanwood (19 a.), Meole Brace (9 a.), and Ford (5 a.)

parishes, lying in Cruckmeole township, were transferred to Pontesbury parish.[4] Ford had claimed a further 22 a. at Cruckmeole in the earlier 19th century, but this area was adjudged to be part of Pontesbury parish in 1846.[5] The remaining anomalies in the north-eastern boundary were removed in the present century. Until 1934, when this area was transferred to Bicton,[6] the parish included a portion of the township of Onslow and its northern boundary ran through the middle of Onslow Hall. The history of Onslow township is reserved for treatment under the Liberties of Shrewsbury. Some 50 a., including Hanwood brickworks, Paper Mill Coppice, and some house property in Great Hanwood village, were transferred from Pontesbury to Great Hanwood parish in 1947.[7] The only boundary change elsewhere in the parish has been the addition of Earl's Hill Farm (141 a.), formerly a detached part of Worthen parish, in 1884.[8]

[1] T.S.A.S. 2nd ser. xii. 337.
[2] Walters, Ch. Bells Salop. 203; par. rec., churchwardens' accts. 1702–1809.
[3] Par. rec., churchwardens' accts. 1702–1809.
[4] T.S.A.S. 2nd ser. xii. 318.
[5] Arkwright and Bourne, Ch. Plate Ludlow Archd. 31.
[6] Printed to 1812 in S.P.R. Heref. v (4), 285–326.
[7] A Quaker meeting-house, said to have been licensed at Habberley in 1713, was in fact situated at Westcott in Ratlinghope parish: Q. Sess. order bk. July 1713; R. F. Skinner, Nonconformity in Shropshire (Shrewsbury, 1964), 30.
[8] B.M. Add. MS. 21018, f. 299.
[9] Digest of Returns to Cttee. on Educ. of Poor, H.C. 224, p. 751 (1819), ix (2).
[10] Educ. Enquiry Abstract, H.C. 62, p. 775 (1835), xlii.
[11] Nat. Soc. Ch. School Returns, 1846–7.
[12] Returns relating to Elem. Educ., H.C. 201, p. 334 (1871), lv.
[13] Account of charities based on 24th Rep. Com. Char., H.C. 231, pp. 391–2 (1831), xi; Char. Com. files.
[14] Ex inf. the Rector.
[1] Census, 1961. The following topographical description is based, except where otherwise stated, on O.S. Maps 1″ sheets lx, lxi (1st edn.); O.S. Maps 6″ Salop. 33, 34, 40, 41

(1st and later edns.); O.S. Maps 1/25,000, SJ 30, 40, 41 (1957); Rocque, Map of Salop. (1752); Baugh, Map of Salop. (1808); Greenwood, Map of Salop. (1827); B.M. O.S. 2″ orig. drawings, sheets 199 (1816), 207 (1817), 320 (1827); Geol. Survey Map (drift), sheet 152 (1931); R. W. Pocock and others, Geol. Shrews. District (1938) passim; S.R.O. 437/4, 5 (tithe appts., Pontesbury first portion, 1842, and second portion, 1837); ibid. 785/181–2 (tithe maps, first portion, 1842, and second portion, 1840); Heref. Dioc. Regy., Longden tithe appt. 1841, and map, 1838; S.P.L., Plans 16 (map of Harries estate, 1754); S.R.O. 665 uncat., survey and map of Pontesbury manorial estate, c. 1769; Hope-Edwardes MSS., Linley Hall, survey and map of Edwardes estate, 1770. This article was written in 1965. Among many others who have assisted in its preparation, thanks are particularly due to Miss L. F. Chitty, O.B.E., M.A., F.S.A., and Mr. P. T. Bradley of Pontesbury, and to Mrs. A. N. Fielden of Longden.
[2] See map on p. 245.
[3] S.R.O. 169/1.
[4] Census, 1891; O.S. Area Bk. (1882).
[5] Ford par. rec., boundary award, 1846.
[6] S.C.C., County Review Order, 1934.
[7] S.R.O. 785/387.
[8] Census, 1891.

The parish boundary, of little general significance in so large a parish, makes very little use of natural features. To the south of Pontesbury village it projects southwards to take in Pontesbury and Pontesford Hills. It follows Asterley Brook in the west, Walleybourne Brook below Oaks and Longden to the south-east, and Welbatch Brook past Annscroft

the 300-foot contour on adjoining river terraces. The land here falls gently from some 300 feet in the west to some 250 feet at Cruckmeole and the wide valley of the Rea was much subject to flooding, especially when its tributaries, the faster-flowing Pontesford and Pontesbury Brooks, were in spate. Some attempt was made by landowners in Hinton,

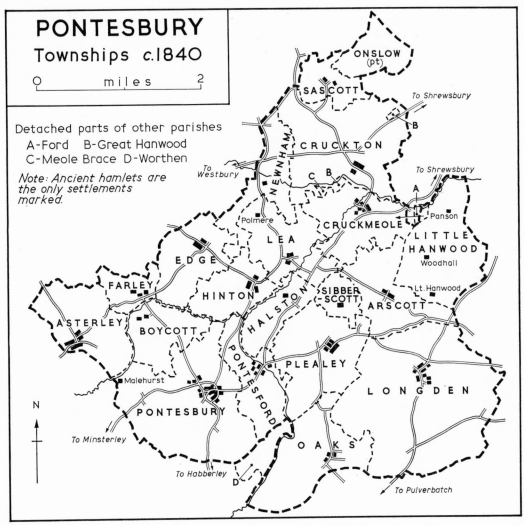

Based on tithe apportionments and maps, 1837-42

in the east. The boundary with Ford on the north-east was laid out in 1846[9] and that between Longden, Condover, and Stapleton in the east was probably defined at the inclosure of Longden Common in 1806.[10] Rea Brook, flowing north-eastwards through the centre of the parish, was employed as a boundary in most of the townships to the west of Cruckmeole, and a similar function was served by the range of hills running north-eastwards from Pontesford Hill, which divided Pontesford and Plealey from Oaks and Longden.

Rea Brook takes a meandering course through the centre of the parish from Malehurst to Great Hanwood. Its valley formed a focus for settlement—12 of the hamlets in the parish stand on or near

Farley, and Boycott to improve the course of the Rea in the mid-18th century,[11] but flooding was not effectively controlled until after 1909, when the Westbury, Minsterley, and Pontesbury Drainage Board was formed.[12] Alluvial soils are most extensive between Newnham and Great Hanwood, near the confluence of Rea Brook and Yockleton Brook.

To the north of the Rea the land rises gently to some 350 feet along the northern boundary. Outside the flood-plain it consists for the most part of boulder clay, but a sandstone outcrop at Edge rises to 400 feet and there are other outcrops of sandstone at Farley and Asterley. There are extensive deposits of sand and gravel to the north and south of Yockleton Brook and at Sascott in the far north of the parish.

[9] Ford par. rec., boundary award, 1846.
[10] Copy Longden Common inclosure award, 1806, *penes* Mrs. A. N. Fielden, Longden Manor.

[11] S.P.L., Deeds 10671-2. cf. Plymley, *Agric. Salop.* 180, 238-40.
[12] Ex inf. Mr. A. E. Hadley, Clerk to the Rea Internal Drainage Board. See also S.P.L., Deeds 13902.

The landscape to the south of the Rea is dominated by the hills along the southern boundary of the parish. The largest of these is Earl's Hill, more commonly known by the name of its northern portion, Pontesford Hill. Its summit is crowned by a large hill-fort and there is a smaller earthwork at 600 feet on Pontesford Hill itself.[13] The hill is composed of volcanic Uriconian rocks, of which there are smaller outcrops at Radlith and Broom-patch to the north-east. Pontesbury and Nills Hills to the south of Pontesbury village rise to 600 feet. They are outliers of the Stiperstones and consist of Ordovician rocks, but sandstone occurs on the lower slopes of Pontesbury Hill, to the west of the village. Pontesford Hill is flanked by Sheinton shales to the west and by Pontesford shales to the east, but the shales which make up the high ground to the east of Pontesford Brook are derived not from the Stiperstones but from the Long Mynd.[14] These rise to 825 feet to the west of Oaks village and to 900 feet at Church Hill, and extend as far north as Plealey village. An expanse of boulder clay covers the east of the parish, broken only by a belt of alluvium and river gravels along Longden Brook, and rises gently from some 350 feet along the eastern boundary to some 550 feet at its junction with the steeper slopes of the hill-country around Oaks. To the north of Longden a boulder clay plateau, on which stand Little Hanwood, Panson, and Moat Hall, forms a capping over Keele Beds sandstone which outcrops south of Great Hanwood and at Arscott Coppice. This is matched in the west of the parish by the low-lying tract of boulder clay between Pontesbury Brook and Rea Brook, north-west of Pontesbury village. Sand and gravel occurs in significant quantities only near Halston and Sibberscott.

There appear to have been three major areas of woodland and waste within the parish during the Middle Ages. The most extensive lay on the hills and higher ground along the southern boundary, the second formed a triangle between Arsott, Cruck-meole, and Great Hanwood, and the third lay on the southern slopes of Ford Heath, to the north of Cruckton and Newnham. The original extent of the southern woodland and the story of its clearance is not well documented except in Longden manor. On the slopes of Pontesbury and Pontesford Hills moorland and waste were probably more extensive than woodland, except on the boulder clays south of Malehurst. Woodhouse Farm, first recorded in the early 16th century,[15] presumably stood on the northern edge of woodland here. The wood probably extended to Pontesbury Brook, on the south-western edge of Pontesbury village, since no common-field land lay in this area.[16] The house

known as Bridgeleys takes its name from adjacent fields, and the lane leading past it is probably that described as the outrack, or driftway, to Woodhouse in 1557.[17] Wolpyttes (or Wolf-pits) Lane, recorded in the early 16th century,[18] seems to have been the name then given to the road from Pontesbury to Gully Green. There is little evidence of woodland on the steep north-western slopes of Pontesford Hill, most of which lay above the timber-line. The common fields of Pontesbury reached the lower slopes of the hill, Ditchers Furlong extending almost to the road round its foot.[19] To the north-east, however, woodland on the high ground between the hill and Pontesford Brook seems originally to have extended as far north as the road from Pontesford to Pontesbury. The field-name Breeches occurs to the north of Hill Farm,[20] and the area around Earls-dale was known as 'Pontesford waste' in the later 16th century.[21]

No assarting is known to have taken place on the slopes of Pontesbury and Pontesford Hills before the 16th century. 'Cadoganslyes', first recorded c. 1540,[22] probably lay near Bridgeleys, and pastures called 'Balls Lye' and 'Older Lye', near Pontesford Hill, are recorded in 1589.[23] Although the Pontesbury tenants denied an allegation made by the lord of the manor in 1601 that they had inclosed 'sundry great wastes' at Ponslith (Pontesford Hill) and the Nills,[24] there are signs of a quickening in the pace of assarting at this time. Two encroachments on the hills were presented at the manor court in 1602, 5 in 1604, and 8 in 1607.[25] In 1622 a bye-law forbidding the felling of timber on Ponslith was issued.[26] The Corbets of Nills Farm seem to have been the most active of the tenants in this respect. Their holding included two assarts to the west of Pontesford Hill c. 1600,[27] and Thomas Corbet was presented for encroachments at the Nills in 1623.[28]

In Pontesford township inclosures on the waste had been made before 1587,[29] and in 1601 3 tenants paid rents for lands on the hill.[30] By 1769 61 a. common land remained on Pontesbury Hill and the Nills.[31] Extensive squatting at Gully Green and the Nills had reduced the commons to only 35 a. at their inclosure in 1848.[32] The commons on Pontesford Hill were less seriously affected by industrial squatting. The portion of the hill lying in Pontesbury manor contained 50 a. common land c. 1769,[33] and that in Pontesford township amounted to 33 a. in 1813.[34] The latter, then containing 27 a., was inclosed in 1828,[35] and the Pontesbury portion (50 a.) in 1848.[36]

The woodland around Earlsdale formerly continued to the east of Pontesford Brook. Radlith Wood is all that now remains of a wood which seems originally to have extended to Rea Brook at

[13] For plans and descriptions see *V.C.H. Salop.* i. 368–9; *T.S.A.S.* 3rd ser. vii. 166–72; *Arch. Jnl.* cxix. 66–91.
[14] For a select bibliography on the geology of Pontesford Hill and its vicinity see *Geol. Mag.* xcviii (5), p. 376.
[15] S.R.O. 665 uncat., Pontesbury ct. r. 1548, 1557; S.P.L., MS. 300 (ct. r. *c.* 1548).
[16] See pp. 249–50.
[17] S.R.O. 665 uncat., Pontesbury ct. r. 1557.
[18] S.P.L., MS. 300 (ct. r. *c.* 1548).
[19] See pp. 249–50.
[20] S.R.O. 169/1 (Ford ct. r. 1671).
[21] B.M. Add. Ch. 73108.
[22] S.P.L., MS. 300 (ct. r. *c.* 1540).
[23] S.P.L., Deeds 6819.
[24] C 2/Eliz. I/L 8/15.

[25] S.P.L., M.S. 300.
[26] Ibid.
[27] C 2/Eliz. 1/C 15/4.
[28] S.P.L., MS. 300.
[29] B.M. Add. Ch. 73108.
[30] S.P.L., Deeds 12706.
[31] S.R.O. 665 uncat., survey of Pontesbury manorial estate, *c.* 1769.
[32] Ibid. 785/180.
[33] Ibid. 665 uncat., survey of Pontesbury manorial estate, *c.* 1769.
[34] Ibid. 1011 uncat., map of encroachments on Pontesford Hill, 1813.
[35] S.R.O. 785/157.
[36] Ibid. 785/180.

New Mills.[37] A group of fields called Chirhayes ('Churcheys' in the 17th century) occupy the area between Radlith Wood and the 450-foot contour in the south-west of Plealey township. Fields called Dunsdale, between Chirhayes and Plealey village, were described as common pasture in 1593,[38] and 'coppice' field-names occur near the south bank of the Rea, west of Halston Farm. Radlith was separated by a belt of moorland, still used as common pasture in the later 17th century, from another woodland area now represented by Lingcroft Coppice and Broompatch. The outcrops of Longmyndian shales on which these woods lay formed a natural boundary between the large manor of Ford and the manors of Oaks and Longden to the south. Between Broompatch and Plealey Villa, however, the boundary seems to have run through an area cleared of timber at an earlier period and was here marked by a boundary ditch, known as the 'Mereditch'.[39]

As its name suggests, the greater part of Oaks township was covered with forest in the early Middle Ages. Its tiny set of common fields lay on the clay slopes to the south and east of the hamlet.[40] In the 12th century, however, the manor passed into the hands of a community of free tenants, who seem to have cleared virtually all the woodland in the manor by the end of the 13th century apart from that on the steep slope above Pontesford Brook, still occupied by Oaks Wood. The demesne wood was described as 'Edgeheld' in 1305,[41] indicating that it was then restricted to these slopes. Fields called Armsley, to the west of the hamlet, can be identified with the clearing called 'Knerrisleye' c. 1300,[42] which was said in 1401 to be permanently inclosed.[43] Later in the 15th century, however, when lands near Church Hill were described as 'lord's pastures', Armsley was styled 'the lord's waste',[44] and it may be the area known as Oaks Common in the later 17th century.[45] The acreage of woodland in the township seems to have reached its lowest level in the 18th century. The manor contained 105 a. wood c. 1769, but only 68 a. were thickly planted.[46] A small fir plantation had been set at the southern end of Oaks Wood by 1842, when there were 81 a. wood in the township,[47] and by the end of the 19th century Oaks Wood amounted to 145 a.[48] It was dedicated for forestry purposes in 1952.[49]

In Longden field-names provide abundant evidence of the former extent of woodland which, in the earlier Middle Ages, covered the boulder clays to the south of the township, extending to within a few yards of the village.[50] The lord of the manor obtained a grant of free warren in 1282[51] and in the following year the manorial wood was said to be bounded on the east by the road from Longden to Pulverbatch, on the south by the present parish boundary, and on the west by the common fields of Oaks.[52] Known as The Hayes during the later Middle Ages, this wood is now represented by Hayes Coppice, near the southern boundary, and Longden Coppice, east of Longden Manor. The numerous fields containing the elements 'ley' and 'stocking' found between these two coppices are the product of forest clearance which was in full swing in the later 15th century and which had probably been completed by the end of the 16th century. In 1429 the free tenant John Adams obtained a grant of several pasture in The Hayes during the winter months, and no fewer than 37 persons were presented for trespasses there in 1472. Assarted lands formed a regular feature in all holdings described in the court rolls after the 1460s, and in 1582 12 field-roads were laid out to connect distant assarts with homesteads in the village. The inhabitants of Oaks were clearing woodland on the western edge of The Hayes in the later 16th century. In 1576 the lord of Oaks manor was said to have moved the manorial boundary here out of its right course, while his tenants occupied assarts called 'Caldrons Hays' and 'Cow Hays'. A group of fields called 'Dews Ley', to the west of the present Hayes Coppice, were accounted part of Oaks township in 1842.[53] Hayes Coppice has contained some 26 a. since 1838. Longden Coppice amounted to 57 a. in 1797,[54] but part was cleared after the sale of the manorial estate in 1827.[55] By 1838 it had been reduced to 12 a. and it has not since changed in size. Longden Park, which contained some 260 a. at the end of the 19th century, when it extended from Longden Manor to Woodhouse Farm,[56] included most of the lands inclosed from The Hayes in the later Middle Ages. It was formed by Henry de Grey Warter after 1858.[57]

The woodland to the east of the road to Pulverbatch was accounted part of Steplewood Forest in 1283, when it was held in common by the tenants of Longden, Stapleton, and Pulverbatch.[58] The Longden portion, later known as Longden Wood, remained a common wood. Drainage of this area was impeded by the ridge of shales on the eastern boundary of the township, between Hurst Bank and Exfordsgreen, and most of it remained uninclosed until the early 19th century. Apart from a cockshoot, recorded in 1475, no activity is recorded in Longden Wood until the later 16th century, when encroachments began to be made along its eastern edge. Two tenants were said to have made inclosures at Hurst Bank in 1558, and by the end of the century the small fields near Exfordsgreen called Eggmoor, the Lees, Eastons Low, and Broomy Stile, had been inclosed from the waste. Woodland to the west was apparently cleared in the early 17th century. In 1615

[37] Except where otherwise stated, this paragraph is based on S.R.O. 169/1–3; ibid. 437/4, 5; ibid. 785/181–2.
[38] B.M. Add. Ch. 73114.
[39] S.P.L., MS. 393 (Longden ct. r. 1548, 1568).
[40] See p. 249.
[41] S.P.L., Deeds 10600.
[42] Ibid. 10598.
[43] Ibid. 10606.
[44] Ibid. 2600.
[45] S.R.O. 665 uncat., Oaks lease, 1660.
[46] Ibid. survey of Pontesbury manorial estate, c. 1769.
[47] Ibid. 437/5; ibid. 785/181.
[48] Sale partics. Longden manor, c. 1890, penes Mrs. A. N. Fielden, Longden Manor.

[49] Ex inf. Forestry Com.
[50] Description of Longden woodland based, except where otherwise stated, on S.P.L., MS. 392–3 (Longden ct. r., 1292–1851); Heref. Dioc. Regy., Longden tithe appt.
[51] Cal. Chart. R. 1257–1300, 262.
[52] Cal. Inq. Misc. i, pp. 373–4.
[53] S.R.O. 437/5; ibid. 785/181.
[54] S.P.L., MS. 2364.
[55] Title-deeds penes Mrs. A. N. Fielden, Longden Manor.
[56] Sale partics. Longden Manor, c. 1890, penes Mrs. A. N. Fielden.
[57] See p. 270.
[58] Cal. Inq. Misc. i, pp. 373–4.

15 persons were presented at the manor court for taking wood here, and one tenant for not filling in saw-pits. By 1630 Londgen Wood could be described as 'common pasture', and it was subsequently known as Longden Common. Encroachments, associated with isolated settlement at Exfordsgreen, Hurst Bank, and in the Common itself, were regularly presented at the manor court between 1651 and 1752. Ten such offenders were presented in 1651, 15 in 1667, and 21 by 1670. The common comprised 202 a. in 1797[59] and was inclosed in 1806, when the straight road across it, running eastwards from Woodhouse Farm, was presumably laid out.[60]

A number of coppices are still standing on the slopes to the south of Rea Brook, between Arscott and Cruckmeole. Several of them were replanted when they formed part of the estate of the Harries family of Cruckton, notably by Edward Harries in the later 18th century,[61] but they stand in an area of ancient woodland, which presumably gave its name to Great and Little Hanwood. Panson and Woodhall seem to have stood along the eastern edge of this wood,[62] and 'ley' field-names indicate that it once extended as far west as Shorthill. That part of Cruckmeole township which lay to the south of Rea Brook was known as 'Meoles Heath' in 1587.[63] The outcrop of sandstone north of Arscott, which was called 'The Knorr' in the 16th century when it was used as rough pasture,[64] marked the southern limits of this triangle of woodland.

Ford Heath, known until the 16th century as 'Aspley Wood',[65] was said in the 13th century to extend as far south as the common fields of Newnham.[66] The small fields in Newnham township immediately north of Yockleton Brook[67] appear to have been assarts in origin. Further east the southern boundary of the heath seems to have followed roughly the course of the road from Shrewsbury to Westbury, for common-field lands occupied the area between this road and the brook in the west of Cruckton township.[68] The road leading from Newnham past Nox to Ford was described as an outrack, or driftway, to the heath in the 17th century,[69] and the small fields north-west of Nox, on the well-drained southern slopes of the heath,[70] are probably the result of medieval assarting. The numerous tiny fields on the Ford Heath plateau in the north of Newnham and Cruckton townships[71] are not, however, as ancient as their size might suggest. They occupy a part of the heath which was not inclosed until the mid-18th century, and were produced by the sub-division of larger fields formed at the inclosure.[72] The only extensive survivor of former woodland on the southern slopes of the heath is Long Coppice, north-west of Cruckton. The remaining woods—Horton Lane, Moves, Jenkin's

and Bucks Coppices—lie in the wide flat belt of boulder clay extending north-westwards from Cruckton towards Horton and Woodcote. These areas of ancient woodland have probably survived, like those to the south of Cruckmeole, owing to the interest in forestry shown by the Harries family. Sascott lay on the eastern edge of the heath. Its common fields were still surrounded on three sides by woodland and waste in the later 16th century— Fernhill to the north, High Lee Wood to the south-east, and Longmoor Coppice (near Coppice House) to the south-west[73]—but no woodland remained there by 1842.[74]

Among isolated areas of woodland on the clays in the Rea valley the largest seems to have been Moorwood. This wood presumably lay to the north of Pontesbury, on each side of the road to Boycott, since it was granted to Henry Haynes in 1633[75] and can be identified with the lands in this area held by his descendant Thomas Edwardes in 1770.[76] Part of the Pontesbury manorial demesne in the Middle Ages, it was said to contain 50 a. in 1586,[77] but the greater part had probably been cleared long before. Moorwood was described as pasture land in 1425[78] and the lord of the manor was rearing cattle here in the early 17th century.[79] A small area of woodland to the west of the road, however, was still standing in 1770, when it was known as Boycott Coppice.[80] This was flanked to the south by fields called Moorhead and to the east by The Hurst and Burnt Gates,[81] indicating that the wood originally extended from the Rea to Malehurst Brook. The landscape around the sandstone outcrop at Edge seems to have resembled that of the Woodhall plateau. Woods at Edge called Great Wood, Bowers Wood, and Round Turnor Wood[82] probably lay on the high ground north-west of the hamlet. Moorland called Ransmoors occupied the valley between Edge and Polmere, to the south of Marton Pool,[83] and 'assart' field-names to the west of Hinton[84] follow the lower slopes of the Edge sandstone ridge.

Only in Pontesbury and Longden townships is there sufficient evidence to reconstruct the extent of the former common fields. Those of Boycott, Farley, Malehurst, and Woodhall had been inclosed before the end of the Middle Ages, and those of most of the townships in Ford manor were no longer in existence when adequate records begin after 1650. The common fields of Cruckton and Cruckmeole appear to have been inclosed by agreement in 1579 and 1631 respectively. In Polmere, Plealey, and Pontesbury, however, fragments of common-field land survived until the mid-18th century. The available evidence for the location of the common fields in most of the townships in the parish is summarized below.

[59] S.P.L., MS. 2364.
[60] Copy Longden Common inclosure award, 1806, penes Mrs. A. N. Fielden.
[61] S.P.L., Deeds 12837.
[62] T.S.A.S. 3rd ser. vi. 169.
[63] B.M. Add. Ch. 73108.
[64] Ibid.; S.P.L., Deeds 11026, 12575, 12706.
[65] B.M. Add. Ch. 73106; C 133/15/3; S.P.L., Deeds 11116.
[66] B.M. Add. Ch. 73106.
[67] S.R.O. 437/5; ibid. 785/181
[68] See p. 249.
[69] S.R.O. 169/1 (Ford ct. r. 1667).
[70] Ibid. 437/5; ibid. 785/181.   [71] Ibid.
[72] S.P.L., Plans 16.
[73] B.M. Add. Ch. 73108; S.P.L., Deeds 11000, 12517, 12706.
[74] S.R.O. 437/5; ibid. 785/181.
[75] S.P.L., Deeds 6840.
[76] Hope-Edwardes MSS., Linley Hall, survey, 1770.
[77] S.P.L., Deeds 6785.
[78] S.R.O. 665 uncat., Pontesbury ct. r. 1425.
[79] Ibid. accts. 1603–4.
[80] Hope-Edwardes MSS., Linley Hall, survey, 1770.
[81] Ibid.
[82] S.R.O. 169/1–2 (Ford ct. r. 1672, 1699, 1719).
[83] S.P.L., Plans 16; S.R.O. 437/5; ibid. 785/181.
[84] Ibid.

Arscott. Air photographs show ridge-and-furrow at The Pumps, south-east of the cross-roads near Arscott House, and to the south of Arscott Coppice.[85] The field-name 'Aukmeadow Furlong' occurs in 1670, but the common fields had been inclosed by 1650.[86]

Asterley. Not known. They presumably included the fields to the west of the road from Asterley to Hinwood called Upper and Lower Botts in 1842.[87]

Cruckmeole. The field-name Furlongs is found to the east of the mill in 1754,[88] but the principal area of common-field land seems to have been the ridge of sand and gravel running towards Newnham, to the south of Yockleton Brook. Great and Little Furlongs occur here in 1840,[89] and New Leasow is presumably the New Inclosure recorded in 1696.[90] Robert Phillips was in 1631 given licence to inclose common-field lands in Cruckmeole by exchange with 5 other tenants,[91] and there is no later record of common fields in the township.

Cruckton. Two of the common fields were known as Dresses Field and Little Field.[92] The former is now represented by fields called Dressells,[93] south of Holly Bank Farm, where ridge-and-furrow is visible. The field-names Wheat Furlong and Two Pit Furlong, which occur on the slopes of Ford Heath to the west of Holly Bank Farm,[94] probably lay in Little Field. The third field seems to have lain to the east of the hamlet, near Cruckton Mill, where an adjoining field was called Mill Furlong in 1754.[95] John Harries exchanged 12 pastures in the 3 common fields with 3 other tenants in 1579.[96]

Edge. The field-names Farley Field and Newton Field on the western slopes of the Edge plateau, and Hinton Field to the south-east of the hamlet,[97] may preserve the names and location of the former common fields. One of the Edge fields adjoined those of Farley in 1425.[98] They had ceased to exist by 1650.

Farley. In 1425 the 3 common fields were leased to 5 tenants, to be held in severalty.[99]

Halston. Air photographs show ridge-and-furrow alongside the Shrewsbury road, south-west of Halston Farm.[1]

Hinton. The common fields were still functioning in 1550.[2] One of them, called Over Field in 1568,[3] probably lay on the higher ground north of the hamlet. Air photographs show ridge-and-furrow in 3 isolated fields to the west and south-west of the hamlet.[4]

Lea. The common fields had been inclosed by 1650. Air photographs show ridge-and-furrow in Cow Pasture, immediately south of the hamlet.[5]

Longden. The common fields[6] were restricted to the area immediately north and sough of Longden Brook. Little High Field, which lay on the north of the brook, west of the village, extended as far as the township boundary with Plealey. Withen Furlong, recorded in this field in 1528, has its name preserved in adjoining fields in Plealey, known as Withenall. Hay Field, also called Brome Hill Field, ran southwestwards towards Longden Hay, and Folkeys Field lay alongside the brook to the east of the village. Folkeys Field included Mill Furlong and Ash Acres—the latter being corrupted to Hare Shakers by the early 19th century. A by-law of 1505 that none should mow meadows or reans in the common fields suggests that 'green reans' were in use here in the later Middle Ages. Common fields are last recorded, under the name Town Field, in 1636, but had probably been consolidated by exchange and inclosed continuously since the 15th century.

Newnham. Common field land was restricted to the sandy ridge to the south of Yockleton Brook, and had been inclosed by 1650. A field in this area called Hanging Furlong is, however, listed among assarts in the township in 1601.[7]

Polmere. Although only 3 tenants held land in Polmere by 1601,[8] the common fields appear to have survived until the early 18th century and open-field strips are last recorded in 1754.[9] The remaining common-field lands were described as Polmere Town Field in 1719.[10] The latter lay to the south of Polmere Farm, where the field-name Polmere Field occurs in 1842.[11]

Oaks. Air photographs show extensive ridge-and-furrow on the slopes to the south and east of the hamlet.[12] A common field to the east of Oaks, then adjoining Longden Hay, was called 'Wassheres Field' in 1374,[13] but the names of the other fields are not recorded. They were still functioning when last mentioned in 1556.[14]

Plealey.[15] Bine Field lay to the north of the village and Pontesford Field, which included Densdale Furlong, to the south-west. Common fields called Little and Upper Field are recorded in the early 18th century. They presumably survived until this period since the number of small copyhold estates in the township made inclosure a complex process. Numerous transfers of small areas of land in the period 1730–50 suggest that consolidation and inclosure was taking place at this time.

Pontesbury.[16] The Field towards Ponslith, known since the 16th century as Woodhouse, Woodhall, or

[85] Air photographs, penes Preston Montford Field Centre.
[86] S.R.O. 169/1.
[87] Ibid. 437/5; ibid. 785/181.
[88] S.P.L., Plans 16.
[89] S.R.O. 437/4; ibid. 785/182.
[90] Ibid. 169/1.
[91] S.P.L., Deeds 11046.
[92] Ibid. 11108.
[93] S.R.O. 437/5; ibid. 785/181.
[94] Ibid.
[95] S.P.L., Plans 16.
[96] S.P.L., Deeds 11108.
[97] S.R.O. 437/5; ibid. 785/181.
[98] Ibid. 665 uncat., Pontesbury ct. r. 1425.
[99] Ibid.
[1] Air photographs, penes Preston Montford Field Centre.
[2] S.R.O. 665 uncat., Pontesbury ct. r. 1550.
[3] Ibid. ct. r. 1568.

[4] Air photographs, penes Preston Montford Field Centre.
[5] Ibid.
[6] Description of Longden common fields based on S.P.L., MS. 393.
[7] S.P.L., Deeds 12706.
[8] Ibid.
[9] S.R.O. 169/1–3.
[10] Ibid. 169/2.
[11] Ibid. 437/5; ibid. 785/181.
[12] Air photographs, penes Preston Montford Field Centre.
[13] S.P.L., Deeds 10605.
[14] S.R.O. 665 uncat., lease, 1556.
[15] Description of Plealey common fields based on S.R.O. 169/1–3.
[16] Description of Pontesbury common fields based on S.P.L., Deeds 6794, 6833, 6842, 10666; S.P.L., MS. 300; S.R.O. 437/5; ibid. 785/181; ibid. 665 uncat., Pontesbury ct. r. 1548; C 3/235/49.

Whitwell Field, lay to the south of the village. It was bounded on the west by Gully Green and by the northern slopes of Pontesford Hill to the east. The Field towards Boycott, or North Field, lay south of Moorwood, and Hollings Field ran north-eastwards to the township boundary with Pontesford. Open-field strips in Whitwell Field are recorded as late as 1735.[17]

Pontesford.[18] One or more of the common fields lay alongside Pontesford Brook, south of the hamlet, and another lay to the east of the brook where ridge-and-furrow is visible. One of three long narrow fields adjoining the brook was called Long Furlong in 1842. A common field called Southorne Field occurs in 1675 and open-field strips are last recorded in 1691, when they were said to lie in the Town Field.

Sascott. 'Aldefeld', recorded in 1513,[19] lay on the sand and gravel north-east of the hamlet, since it included Sascott Pool, and 'furlong' field-names occur south-west of Sascott.[20] The common fields had been inclosed by 1650.

Sibberscott. Apart from Lee Field, recorded in 1493,[21] nothing is known of the common fields here.

Woodhall. A pasture called Nine Ridges, which in 1576 lay to the east of Woodhall,[22] and the field-names Gylden Furlong (1610)[23] and Haugh Furlong (1640)[24] are evidence that this shrunken hamlet once possessed a set of common fields.

Meadow land played an important part in the economy of most townships in the parish, in particular at Cruckmeole, where Yockleton Brook falls into the Rea. Dole-meadows called Moor Meadow, Roberts Meadow, and Lake Meadow are found in this township,[25] and the small detached portions of Ford, Great Hanwood, and Meole Brace parishes at Cruckmeole consisted for the most part of meadowland.[26] Similar common meadows were still in use in the 16th and 17th centuries along the Rea and its tributaries in the following townships: Arscott (Town Meadow),[27] Asterley (Hacknell, Bridge Meadow),[28] Boycott (The Feg),[29] Cruckton (Cruckhey Meadow),[30] Edge, Lea and Newnham (Hinton Meadow on Yockleton Brook),[31] Longden (Fowkey and Swatters Meadow),[32] Plealey (Marsh Meadow),[33] Pontesbury (Thirty Meadows, on Malhurst Brook, corrupted by the early 17th century to Turdie Meadow),[34] and Pontesford (Over Moor).[35] Meadows called Wallymore, Rolles Meadow, Nemors, Stocky Meadow, and Lady Meadow, on the south bank of the Rea between Moorwood

and New Mills, lay in the Pontesbury manorial demesne.[36]

Early evidence on roads in the parish is scanty, but such as there is suggests that the road pattern is still much the same as it was in the Middle Ages. Main roads from Shrewsbury to Westbury, Minsterley, and (via Longden) to Bishop's Castle pass through the parish. The section of the Westbury road running due west to the north of Cruckton follows the alignment of a Roman road. This originally continued eastwards along a green lane, known since at least the 18th century as Thieves' Lane,[37] but with the replacement of Uriconium by Shrewsbury as the centre of communications, a new road—Horton Lane—was constructed across the boulder clay plain to the north. Bequests for the maintenance of Horton Lane are frequently met with in medieval wills locally,[38] and the northern townships as far west as Asterley were still held responsible for maintaining the lane in the early 17th century.[39] The Westbury road was turnpiked in 1758.[40] The road from Shrewsbury to Minsterley, which runs through the middle of the parish, was turnpiked in the same year.[41] Between Great Hanwood and Pontesford this runs close to Rea Brook and was probably subject to flooding until the course of the Rea was improved. No reference has been found to this section of the road during the Middle Ages, and it is not clearly shown on county maps before 1752.[42] It may have replaced, as the main route from Pontesbury to Shrewsbury, roads on higher ground passing through Plealey and Sibberscott to the south of the Rea, and through Hinton, Lea, and Cruckmeole to the north, of which only parts are still public roads. By 1754, however, the main road followed its present course to the north of Lea Cross,[43] where isolated settlement is first recorded in the mid-17th century.[44] Pontesford Bridge was rebuilt in 1795–6[45] and extensively repaired in 1809[46] and 1831.[47] The bridge was widened in 1961.[48] The field-name Butterbridge, occurring on both sides of Pontesford Brook a short distance north-east of the present bridge,[49] may mark the original site of the bridge. It is thought that the main road once ran a little to the north-west of its present alignment at this point, passing close by Pontesford House,[50] but it has followed its present course since at least 1816.[51]

The road to Bishop's Castle, through Longden, was described as *via regia* in 1560.[52] The section to the north of Longden village was turnpiked in

[17] Heighway Jones title-deeds, *penes* Messrs. Sprott, Stokes, and Turnbull, solicitors, Shrewsbury.
[18] Description of Pontesford common fields based on S.R.O. 169/1; ibid. 437/5; ibid. 785/181.
[19] S.P.L., Deeds 11114.
[20] S.R.O. 437/5; ibid. 785/181.
[21] Ibid. 665 uncat., lease, 1493.
[22] Ibid. 171 uncat., deed, 1576.
[23] Ibid. deed, 1610.
[24] Ibid. marriage settlement of Thomas Wolley, 1640.
[25] Ibid. 169/1.
[26] S.P.L., Plans 16.
[27] S.R.O. 169/1 (Ford ct. r. 1674).
[28] S.P.L., Deeds 14094.   [29] Ibid. 14052.
[30] Ibid. 12511, 12827.
[31] S.R.O. 169/1 (Ford ct. r. 1690).
[32] S.P.L., MS. 393.
[33] S.R.O. 169/2 (Ford ct. r. 1712, 1740).
[35] S.P.L., MS. 300; Heref. Dioc. Regy., glebe terrier, 1640.

[35] S.R.O. 169/1 (Ford ct. r. 1691).
[36] Ibid. 665 uncat., Pontesbury ct. r. 1425; ibid. Condover accts., 1603–4; S.P.L., MS. 300; S.P.L., Deeds 6784.
[37] S.P.L., Plans 16.
[38] Ex inf. Mr. J. B. Lawson, Pulverbatch.
[39] S.P.L., Deeds 11011.
[40] Shrewsbury road Act, 31 Geo. II, c. 67 (priv. act).
[41] Ibid.
[42] See Morden, *Map of Salop* (1695); Bowen, *Map of Salop.* (1751); Rocque, *Map of Salop* (1752).
[43] S.P.L., Plans 16.
[44] See p. 257.
[45] *Q. Sess. Orders*, iii. 74, 77.
[46] Ibid. 158.
[47] Q. Sess., bridge bks. 1831.
[48] Ex inf. Mr. P. T. Bradley, Pontesbury.
[49] S.R.O. 169/1; ibid. 437/5; ibid. 785/181.
[50] Ex inf. Miss L. F. Chitty, Pontesbury.
[51] B.M. O.S. 2″ orig. drawings, sheet 199 (1816).
[52] S.P.L., MS. 393.

1756[53] and that to the south in 1768.[54] At Stoneford, where the road crosses Welbatch Brook, a bridge had been erected by 1576,[55] but the road crossed Longden Brook, in the centre of the village, by a ford until Longden Bridge was built in 1805.[56]

A road running north-westwards across the parish, from Exfordsgreen through Arscott and Lea, is a cross-country route from Condover and is probably a Roman road. It passes close by the site of a Roman villa at Lea and north-west of this hamlet it probably followed the line of the present footpath to Yockleton,[57] skirting the former woodland of the Edge plateau to the west. It crossed the Rea at a ford near Lea Cross. A footbridge had been constructed here before 1884,[58] when a cast iron bridge was erected and short sections of the road on each side of the bridge were straightened.[59] With the development of settlement at Pontesbury, however, this road presumably declined in importance, its place being taken by the road from Exfordsgreen past Longden and Plealey to Pontesford. Except at Exfordsgreen, both roads pass through a part of the parish which was cleared of woodland at a relatively early period.

The only other bridge across the Rea before the 19th century was that at Boycott, where a small wooden bridge was built by Richard Lake in the early 17th century for his private use, with timber supplied by the lord of the manor.[60] Cruckton Bridge, replacing a ford on the road from Cruckton to Cruckmeole, was erected by Thomas Harries in 1839[61] and rebuilt in 1929.[62] Bridges at New Mills and Malehurst also date from the 19th century.[63]

Relatively few minor roads in the parish have gone out of use, the largest group being the roads linking shrunken settlements on the Woodhall plateau. A road which formerly ran north of the Rea, between Cruckton and Great Hanwood, left the present road from Cruckton to Cruckmeole near Hanwoodgate Pool.[64] In Longden a public road which formerly ran westwards from the village through Longden Coppice to Oaks Hall was deemed only a bridle-way in 1864.[65] In 1904 this bridle-way, and another from Oaks Hall towards Hayes Coppice, were diverted to follow the northern and southern boundaries of Longden Park respectively.[66] Former roads from Oaks to Habberley and to Skin Mill Cottage, accounted bridle-ways c. 1834,[67] are now footpaths.

The railway from Great Hanwood to Minsterley, which runs from east to west across the parish, was opened in 1861.[68] Stations at Plealey Road and Pontesbury, opened in that year, were closed in 1951.[69]

The parish was said to contain an adult population of 721 in 1676.[70] There were 2,053 inhabitants in 1801,[71] when the influence of mining and lead-smelting was already being felt, and the population rose steadily, by about 300 each decade, until 1861, when there were 3,466 inhabitants.[72] Analysis of the 1851 census[73] shows that very few of the miners and lead-smelters then living in the parish had migrated there over great distances. Of those in the townships of Pontesbury and Pontesford only 24 were born outside a 5-mile radius of Pontesbury, of whom 18 came from Wales. With the decline of coal mining the population fell during the later 19th century, reaching 2,542 by 1901,[74] but it has since risen once more. There were 3,039 inhabitants in 1961.[75]

A Friendly Society was meeting at the 'Seven Stars', Pontesbury, in 1794.[76] Two similar societies are recorded at Pontesbury, two at Pontesford, and two at Longden in the early 19th century.[77] A local custom of searching for a golden arrow on Pontesford Hill on Palm Sunday was said to be 'not wholly fallen into desuetude' in the 1850s[78] and was observed until the First World War.[79] The puritan divine Edward Corbet (d. 1658) and the Latin poet Owen Corbet (1646–71) were born in the parish.[80]

DEVELOPMENT OF SETTLEMENT. Pontesbury, now the only large village in the parish, stands on gently sloping ground on the north-east bank of Pontesbury Brook and at the foot of Pontesford and Pontesbury Hills.[81] Although the tradition that it was the site of the Battle of Posentesbyrig (661) is no longer generally accepted,[82] the name and the unusual plan of the village suggest that it was already a settlement of some importance in the Anglo-Saxon period. The name, which appears in the form 'Pantesberie' in 1086,[83] probably contains as its first element the Welsh 'pant', a hollow, and would thus mean 'the burh in the valley'. An oval ring-road, now known as Hall Bank to the north, Chapel Street to the east, and Brookside to the south-west, surrounds most of the older houses in the village. As no significant changes have been made in the alignment of roads here since at least 1769,[84] this ring-road may follow the line of a defensive earthwork. The church stands at the highest point in the village, roughly in the centre of the area bounded by this road. It now contains few features earlier than the 13th century, but was until c. 1825 very largely a 12th-century building.[85] Four roads running inwards from the ring-road converge at the two islands to the south of the church, occupied by the former school and the

[53] Shrewsbury road Act, 29 Geo. II, c. 61 (priv. act).
[54] Bishop's Castle road Act, 8 Geo. III, c. 51 (priv. act).
[55] S.P.L., MS. 393.
[56] Q. Sess. Orders, iii. 127.
[57] Ex inf. Dr. A. W. J. Houghton, Oakwood, Pulverbatch.
[58] Q. Sess., dep. plans, bridges, 84; T.S.A.S. lvi. 119.
[59] Ibid.
[60] S.P.L., MS. 300 (ct. r. 1649).
[61] S.P.L., Watton press-cuttings, iii. 331.
[62] Plaque on bridge.
[63] Par. rec., commonplace bk. of Chas. Drury.
[64] S.P.L., Plans 16.
[65] Pontesbury par. rec., vestry minutes, 1839–1964.
[66] Longden Manor title-deeds, penes Messrs. Eland, Hore, Patersons, solicitors, Lincoln's Inn Fields.
[67] Declaration re roads through Oaks Wood, c. 1834, penes Mrs. A. N. Fielden, Longden Manor.
[68] Ex inf. Brit. Trans. Rec.   [69] Ibid.

[70] T.S.A.S. 2nd ser. i. 87.
[71] Census, 1801.   [72] Ibid. 1811–61.
[73] H.O. 107/1991/5.
[74] Census, 1861–1901.   [75] Ibid. 1961.
[76] Q. Sess., index of Friendly Soc. rules.
[77] Ibid.
[78] Par. rec, commonplace bk. of Chas. Drury, where the arrow is said to have been a silver one. See also C. S. Burne, Shropshire Folklore (1883), 330–3.
[79] Ex inf. Miss L. F. Chitty and Mrs. A. N. Fielden.
[80] D.N.B.
[81] See plate facing p. 252.
[82] Anglo-Saxon Chronicle, ed. Dorothy Whitelock (1961), 21.
[83] V.C.H. Salop. i. 325.
[84] S.R.O. 665 uncat., survey of Pontesbury manorial estate, c. 1769.
[85] See p. 288.

Britannia Inn, both of which were demolished in 1965. These two islands probably mark the site of the village green, for the short road to the east of the school was formerly known as Stanniel Market[86]—markets were still being held here c. 1900[87]—and the former Bridge House, which stood south-west of the Britannia Inn until its demolition in 1965, seems to have been the house known in the 18th century as Maypole House Farm.[88] It was a timber-framed house, much altered internally and cased in brick and stone c. 1804.[89]

Pontesbury occupied an important strategic position in the defence of the country west of Shrewsbury during the Norman period. It stood on the principal route from Wales up the Rea valley, at the point where this is joined by the road from Habberley (Chapel Street), then a major route from the hill-country to the south. A castle, constructed to the east of the church, at the junction of these two roads, has been shown to be a ring-work as the result of excavations, 1961–4. On the eastern edge of the ring-work the rubble foundations of a massive square keep were uncovered in 1964. The archaeological evidence suggests that the ring-work was constructed during the 12th century, that the tower was added c. 1200, and that the castle was destroyed by fire c. 1300 and not re-occupied.[90] There were said to be no buildings here in 1353.[91] Leland, however, saw 'great tokens of stones fallen down of a great manor place or castle' when he visited Pontesbury c. 1540.[92] Portions of the reddish sandstone walls of the castle were still visible in the mid-19th century[93] and quantities of late-19th-century pottery, which could clearly be associated with the robbing of building-stone from the site, were discovered when the keep was excavated. The present alignment of Chapel Street, Castle Meadow, and Main Road, enclosing the ring-work, suggests that there was a large outer bailey. The latter appears to have had a stone wall, for the name Stanniel, given in the early 19th century to the section of Main Road north of the castle-site (Stanniel Street),[94] to Castle Meadow on the south (Stanniel Road),[95] as well as to the market on the west, first occurs c. 1540 in the form 'Stanwall' (i.e. stone wall).[96] Stanniel Street ran past the south wall of the churchyard. This stood some 8 feet above the level of the road until the latter was raised early in the present century.[97] It is, however, of rubble and is unlikely to be older than the 19th century. The section of Main Road west of the church, running towards The Railway Inn, was known as Pavement Street in the early 19th century[98] and may be the 'Castle Pavement' recorded by Leland.[99] It runs through low-lying land and was presumably a medieval paved causeway. It crossed Pontesbury Brook by a ford until a culvert was constructed in 1869.[1]

The development of isolated farms and of squatter cottages on Pontesford and Pontesbury Hills was already in progress in the mid-16th century and may account for the relatively low density of houses within the ancient nucleus of the village. The distribution of surviving timber-framed buildings suggests that medieval settlement was concentrated in two somewhat restricted areas—on the banks of Pontesbury Brook to the south-west and on the ring-road east of the church. The only timber-framed building in the village outside these two areas is South View, the group of cottages south-east of the church.

Pontesbury Mill, known to have been in use between 1086 and 1286,[2] presumably stood in the first of these areas, and four of the five known ale-houses in the village—The Railway Inn, The Plough Inn, and the former Brittania and White Horse Inns—were also concentrated here. The Britannia Inn on the former green was built of brick and stone and probably dated from the early 19th century, but the other three are considerably older. The Railway Inn, at the junction of Main Road with the roads to Farley and Minsterley, was formerly known as The Seven Stars[3] and was well established by the end of the 18th century, when it was the meeting-place of a village Friendly Society.[4] The former White Horse Inn, which stands on the north-east bank of the brook, near the short lane linking Brookside with Main Road, is a stone-cased timber-framed house of the earlier 17th century, while The Plough Inn, at the south end of Brookside, where the brook still crosses the road by a ford, is the only surviving medieval house in the village. It is a four- or five-bay house of cruck construction, to which two further box-framed bays were added in the course of the 17th century. Three other buildings of cruck construction are known in the area adjoining the brook. The use of portions of cruck blades in the 18th-century tithe barn of the Old Rectory indicates that this house, formerly the parsonage of the rector of the third portion,[5] occupies its medieval site. Birch Row, a group of cottages which stood opposite the Old Rectory until their demolition in 1958,[6] was another cruck house similar in scale to the Plough Inn.[7] A 3-bay barn standing between the White Horse Inn and Main Road dates from a late period in the development of cruck construction and is unlikely ever to have been a house. There are at least three other timber-framed houses near the brook—Brook House, Crescent House, and Chetwynd—of which only the first-named is uncased.

In the second area of early settlement, east of the church, are the parsonages of the two more wealthy portioners of Pontesbury.[8] Neither now contains anything earlier than the later 17th century, but both are known to occupy their ancient sites and

[86] Plan of Laurence estate, 1831, in Heighway Jones title-deeds, penes Messrs. Sprott, Stokes, and Turnbull, solicitors, Shrewsbury.

[87] Ex inf. Mr. R. J. Pugh, Pontesbury Hill.

[88] Hope-Edwardes MSS., Linley Hall, survey, 1770; ibid. sale partics. 1800; S.P.L., ED v.f. (transcript of title-deeds of Maypole House Farm, 1711–1804); par. rec., poor rates, 1810–30; S.R.O. 437/5; ibid. 785/181.

[89] S.P.L., ED v.f. (transcript of title-deeds, 1711–1804).

[90] Description based on excavation report by Mr. P. A. Barker in T.S.A.S. lvii (3), 206–23.

[91] C 135/124/9.

[92] Leland, Itin. (ed. Toulmin Smith), ii. 26.

[93] Par. rec., commonplace bk. of Chas. Drury.

[94] Plan of Laurence estate, 1831, in Heighway Jones title-deeds.   [95] Ibid.

[96] S.P.L., MS. 300.

[97] Ex inf. Mr. R. J. Pugh, Pontesbury Hill.

[98] Plan of Laurence estate, 1831, in Heighway Jones title-deeds.

[99] Leland, Itin. (ed. Toulmin Smith), ii. 26.

[1] Plaque on culvert.

[2] V.C.H. Salop. i. 325; C 133/45/2.

[3] Q. Sess., alehouse reg.; S.R.O. 437/5; ibid. 785/181.

[4] Q. Sess., index of Friendly Soc. rules.

[5] See p. 287.   [6] Local inf.

[7] Pevsner, Shropshire, 230, where it is wrongly named the Old Rectory.   [8] For description see p. 287.

The church from the north-east in 1788, showing the Norman tower which later collapsed

The village from the south in 1967. The stone keep of the Norman castle stood within the small circular inclosure towards the right of the picture and the line of its inner and outer baileys has dictated the course of roads surrounding the site. An outer ring road, which continues to the north of the church, probably represents the boundary of the pre-Conquest 'burh'

PONTESBURY

CRESSAGE: CHRISTCHURCH FROM THE WEST
Built in 1841

WEST FRONT OF MINSTERLEY CHURCH
Built in 1688–9

there are reused cruck blades in the former tithe barn of the second portion. The Red Lion Inn, formerly The Angel,[9] was originally timber-framed, but was considerably enlarged in the 19th century, and Manor Cottages, north of the inn, is a T-shaped timber-framed house of 2 stories with attics, dating from the later 17th century and cased in brick in the early 19th century. White Hall, to the east of the road, was known as Hall Farm in 1770.[10] It is a Georgian house externally, but incorporates an earlier timber-framed house.

Coal was being mined in the neighbourhood of Pontesbury from the early 17th century[11] and indications that the village was changing from a purely agricultural into a semi-industrial community were already apparent by the end of that century. Six cottages in the village were reported in 1691 to have been converted from ancient farmsteads.[12] Squatter settlement along the outer edge of the castle in Chapel Street probably began in the early 18th century. Nos. 6 and 7, Habberley Road, opposite the Baptist chapel, is a brick-cased timber-framed house with a typologically late form of roof construction, also found in the timber-framed cottage adjoining the north wall of the chapel. The latter is first recorded in 1770, when it was held with a 7-acre smallholding and was occupied by Charles Barber,[13] manager of the parish workhouse.[14] The smithy, now demolished, which stood to the east of the junction of Chapel Street and the Shrewsbury road, had been built by 1770.[15] Nos. 1 and 2, Main Road, to the west of the junction, appear to be brick-built, but stand on the site of a cottage occupied in the 1770s by Miles Field, who was then presented at the manor court for erecting a cottage on the road to Shrewsbury and enclosing part of the Castle Ring.[16] The former primary school in the centre of the village stood on the site of a grammar school erected c. 1765[17] and the Britannia Inn was built soon afterwards, thus destroying the village green. Two cottages near the churchyard were presented as encroachments in the 1790s.[18]

Only a small number of houses were built within the bounds of the ancient village in its brief period of industrial prosperity in the earlier 19th century, among them Manchester House, Oaklands, and Bennetts' Stores on Main Road, and the row of cottages on Station Road opposite the Railway Inn. The owners and managers of the mines and lead-smelting works, notably the Heighway family of Pontesford and John Laurence, manager of the White Grit Company, tended to live outside the village. Laurence built and lived at Further Croft on the Minsterley road.[19] This is a brick-built two-story house of 4 bays, with an ornamental wrought iron east porch. The stone barn to the west of the house and an adjoining building, now a house, were originally part of Laurence's smelting works.[20] On Linley Terrace (formerly Boogy Lane), south-

east of the village, one of the 3 mid-19th-century brick houses known as Linley Terrace may have been the home of the manager of the Boogy Lane Colliery. While most of the workers lived in squatter cottages on the surrounding hills, their influence led to the erection of the Baptist and Congregational chapels in 1828 and 1839 respectively, the enlargement of the village alehouses, and an increase in the number of small tradesmen. There were at least 24 tradesmen in the village by 1851.[21]

Little building took place in the village for many years after the closure of the mines and lead-smelting works c. 1860. The school was rebuilt and the schoolmaster's house erected in 1875.[22] Brookmoors, on the Habberley road south of The Plough Inn, is a range of terrace houses built by the Rector of Pontesbury in the 1920s for the use of church-goers only, and was consequently nicknamed 'Holy Row'.[23] Since the 1930s, however, Pontesbury has developed rapidly as a dormitory settlement. Private houses were built along the main roads east and west of the village before the Second World War, and since 1945 private housing estates have been built at Ashford Drive in the west, on Main Road to the east, and along Habberley Road to the south. By 1962 48 Council houses and 24 flats had been built,[24] principally to the south-east of the village, near the new Secondary Modern and Primary schools.

With the exception of Hill Farm, a 3-bay house, partly timber-framed and partly stone, at the foot of Pontesford Hill, the isolated farms to the south of Pontesbury village are brick-built and appear to be no older than the early 19th century. Nills Farm, The Poplars, Mount Farm, and Newhouse Farm are T-shaped in plan with 3-bay fronts. Nills Farm, which retains a timber-framed barn, occupies an older site, since the Corbets of the Nills were resident here in the later 16th century.[25] Woodhouse is a cottage built c. 1825 on the site of an earlier farm-house destroyed by fire.[26]

While essentially a relic of Pontesbury's short era as an industrial village, the large squatter settlement on Pontesbury Hill can trace its ancestry back to the early 17th century. The first recorded house here was 'Eyckyns house on the hill', named in 1615[27] and probably the same as 'Lickys house on Pontesbury Hill' of 1687.[28] An increasing number of persons were being amerced for inhabiting cottages on 'Pontesbury waste' in the later 17th century— 11 by 1673 and 20 by 1692[29]—but this is more likely to refer to settlement on Pontesford Hill. Meadow Place, near the foot of Pontesbury Hill, is timber-framed, but all other surviving older cottages here are of stone and are unlikely to have been built before the later 18th century. A parish work-house, which survives in much-altered form as 4 cottages, was built in 1732[30] and gave the name Workhouse Bank to the lower slopes of the hill.

[9] Hope-Edwardes MSS., Linley Hall, rental, 1838; ibid. accts. 1821–43; S.R.O. 437/5; ibid. 785/181.
[10] Hope-Edwardes MSS., Linley Hall, survey, 1770.
[11] See p. 279.
[12] S.P.L., MS. 300.
[13] Hope-Edwardes MSS., Linley Hall, survey, 1770.
[14] See p. 283.
[15] Hope-Edwardes MSS., Linley Hall, survey, 1770.
[16] S.R.O. 1011 uncat., presentments, 1774–1844.
[17] See pp. 292–3.
[18] S.R.O. 1011 uncat., presentments, 1774–1844.

[19] Plan of Laurence estate, 1831, in Heighway Jones title-deeds.   [20] Ibid.
[21] Bagshaw's Dir. Salop. (1851).
[22] See p. 293.
[23] Ex inf. Mrs. I. E. Madeley, Brookmoors.
[24] Ex inf. Atcham R.D.C.
[25] C 2/Eliz. I/L8/15.
[26] Hope-Edwardes MSS., Linley Hall, cottage plans, c. 1825.
[27] S.P.L., Deeds 6845.   [28] S.R.O. 49/135.
[29] S.P.L., MS. 300.   [30] See p. 283.

There appear to have been no more than 3 cottages and a smithy on the hill c. 1769.[31] The initiator of extensive settlement here was John Laurence, who from c. 1785 encouraged his colliers to erect cottages on the commons, supplying them with building materials.[32] Some evidence of the pace of subsequent settlement is provided by the manor court rolls, which record 12 cottages in 1793, 17 in 1799, and 26 by 1810, but some of these were erected elsewhere than on the hill.[33]

There were about a hundred cottages on Pontesbury Hill by 1842,[34] but many more were erected between 1843, when an agreement was made to inclose the hill, and 1848, when the inclosure award was completed.[35] Most of the cottages erected between 1785 and 1848 were originally hastily contrived turf huts—2 such are recorded in 1793.[36] In 1836 a vestry resolution refers to 'huts . . . wherein several men, women, and children are all living together in one room, whereby the morals of many children are corrupted and vice and immorality encouraged to a great extent'.[37] Nearly all of these huts had been replaced by stone cottages before 1857.[38] The common house-type on the hill in the later 19th century was a single-story stone cottage of 2 or 3 bays.[39] Very few of these now remain, at least 30 having been demolished in the present century.[40]

In contrast to Pontesbury Hill, squatter settlement on Pontesford Hill was virtually complete before the beginning of the mining period. It is a spring-line settlement, and is first recorded in 1637, when Roger Poyner was presented for erecting a cottage 'on the waste called Ponslith',[41] and was most extensive on the western slopes of the hill, within the manor of Pontesbury, where there were already 19 cottages c. 1769.[42] Only about 9 cottages were built to the west of the hill between 1769 and 1842,[43] and about half of the cottages standing here in 1842 have since been demolished. By 1813 there were 14 cottages on the north-eastern slopes of the hill, in the manor of Ford and in Pontesford township.[44] Four more were built in the course of the 19th century, but 7 cottages to the south of Earlsdale Cottages were demolished after 1842.[45] As on Pontesbury Hill, a number of cottages were hastily erected to the west of Pontesford Hill during the 1840s. Six such cottages were presented at the manor court in 1840 and 14 in 1844.[46] In 1858 the 10 Pontesford Hill cottages within the Pontesbury

manorial estate included 3 mud huts and a clod cottage.[47] All existing houses on the hill have either been enlarged or rebuilt since the later 19th century.

Of the remaining hamlets in the valley to the south of Rea Brook, Pontesford and Plealey are still of moderate size, while Arscott has shrunk to two farms, and Sibberscott and Halston to one each. Eleven tenants of Ford manor lived at Pontesford in 1308,[48] and there were 10 messuages here, held by 6 tenants, in 1601.[49] The number of copyholders at Pontesford remained virtually unchanged until the end of the 18th century, after which date a great part of the hamlet was acquired by Samuel Heighway and his descendants.[50] Later developments have not materially affected the medieval settlement pattern here, for most of the houses stand near the banks of Pontesford Brook. Upper and Lower Mills, to the south and north of the main road respectively, had both been established by 1593,[51] and one of them occupies the site of the mill first recorded in 1299.[52] Both mills were acquired in 1799 by William Heighway,[53] who rebuilt them shortly afterwards. The mill building at Upper Mill is dated 1804[54] and the house 1882.[55] The tan-house from which the Heighway family derived its initial fortunes stood on the east bank of the brook, immediately south of the main road.[56] It is first recorded in 1599[57] and was demolished c. 1925.[58] Cottages adjoining the tan-house were demolished at the same time.[59] The original house of the Heighway family, now Bridge Cottages, was partly destroyed in a flood in 1811.[60] Its place was taken by Pontesford House and Earlsdale, both of which were normally occupied by members of the Heighway family and their Jones descendants until the 1930s. Pontesford House, on the north of the road to Pontesbury, was probably built in the 1830s,[61] but its Tudor-style windows and the elongated dormers on the south-east wall were probably added later in the 19th century. Earlsdale, an isolated house on the high ground north-east of Pontesford Hill, incorporates the L-shaped stone farmstead of the Davies family, who already occupied a house on this site by 1671.[62] The property was purchased by Samuel Heighway in 1777[63] but was still occupied by a tenant in 1810.[64] Pool Place, as the house was then called,[65] seems to have become William Heighway's residence after the former Heighway house had been damaged by the flood of 1811. It was occupied by him in the 1820s[66] but was leased in 1833.[67] William's sisters and heirs,

31 S.R.O. 665 uncat., survey of Pontesbury manorial estate, c. 1769.
32 Par. rec., commonplace bk. of Chas Drury.
33 S.R.O. 1011 uncat., presentments, 1774–1844.
34 Ibid. 437/5; ibid. 785/181.
35 Ibid. 785/180; par. rec., commonplace bk. of Chas. Drury.
36 S.R.O. 1011 uncat., presentments, 1774–1844.
37 N.L.W., J. R. Hughes (1962), 4 (Pontesbury vestry minutes, 1816–39).
38 Par. rec., commonplace bk. of Chas. Drury.
39 Ex inf. Mrs. E. A. Evans, New House, Pontesbury Hill.
40 Ibid.
41 S.P.L., MS. 300. John Ponslyth (b. 1548), was presumably born on Pontesford Hill: S.P.R. Heref. xii (1), 9.
42 S.R.O. 665 uncat., survey of Pontesbury manorial estate, c. 1769.
43 Ibid.; ibid. 437/5; ibid. 785/181.
44 Ibid. 1011 uncat., map of Pontesford Hill, 1813.
45 Ibid. 437/5; ibid. 785/157, 181; O.S. 6″ Salop. 40 (2nd edn.).

46 S.R.O. 1011 uncat., presentments, 1774–1844.
47 Ibid. 802 uncat., rental, 1858.
48 C 134/5/1.
49 S.P.L., Deeds 12706.
50 S.R.O. 169/1–3, 11–15; ibid. 248/1–2.
51 C 142/267/68.
52 C 133/87/9.
53 S.R.O. 248/2 (Ford ct. r. 1799).
54 Date on collar-beam.   55 Datestone.
56 Ex inf. Mr. T. Hamer, Upper Mill.
57 S.P.L., Deeds 16038.
58 Ex inf. Mr. T. Hamer, Upper Mill.
59 Ex inf. Miss L. F. Chitty.
60 C. Hulbert, Hist. Shrewsbury (1837), i. 275.
61 Ibid. ii. 195. The house was complete by 1842: S.R.O. 437/5; ibid. 785/181.
62 S.R.O. 169/1 (Ford ct. r. 1671).
63 Ibid. 169/3 (ibid. 1777).
64 Ibid. 248/2 (ibid. 1810).
65 Ibid. 169/11–12; ibid. 248/2.
66 Ibid. 169/11–12.
67 Ibid. 437/13, lease, 1833.

Elizabeth and Mary Heighway, were living at Pontesford House in 1842,[68] but Pool Place, known in the later 19th century as Earlsdale, again became the family home after Heighway Jones returned from Australia shortly before 1860.[69] One reason for the choice of this site may have been to avoid a repetition of the flood; another was clearly to exploit the fine view which the house commanded across the Rea valley to the north. William Heighway encased the north and west walls of the house in a Gothic façade, with 2-light pointed windows set in rectangular hood-moulds, an embattled central porch, and embattled parapet. There are no original Gothic features inside the house, the only notable internal feature being a doorcase with a broken pediment in the principal room on the ground floor. A studio, in the form of a low tower, was erected on second-floor level to the south of the house c. 1920.

Apart from Bridge Cottages, surviving timber-framed houses in Pontesford include the Malthouse (a barn reroofed in the early 19th century), Brook-side (formerly the home of the Bowyer family),[70] and one of the group of gothicized estate cottages south-west of Pontesford House. Another timber-framed farm-house, brick-cased and rough-cast, stands at the junction of the main road with the road to Pontesford Hill in the area formerly known as The Green.[71] Two large barns on either side of the latter road are all that now remain of the Pontesford lead-smelting houses.[72] That to the west of the road belonged to the Snailbeach Company and was erected soon after 1784.[73] The White Grit smelt-house, east of the road, was erected between 1828 and 1842.[74] Their tall chimneys, raised in the 1850s after proceedings had been brought against the owners by the rectors of Pontesbury,[75] were demolished c. 1919.[76] Pit-mounds, and the ivy-clad ruins of an engine-house north of the main road at this point, mark the site of the Nag's Head Colliery. The latter took its name from The Nag's Head Inn, a stone-built house on the main road midway between Pontesford and Pontesbury. This was already an alehouse in 1753,[77] but its round-headed Gothic windows probably date from the early 19th century.

The pattern of settlement at Plealey, where there were 27 tenants in 1308[78] and 14 tenants holding 20 messuages between them in 1601,[79] has probably changed less than in any other hamlet in the parish since the early 17th century. This is largely because the hamlet has always been a community of small copyholders. The six farm-houses (one of them now a private house) are grouped round a square ring-road, while the cottages of tradesmen and farm workers stand on the three roads radiating from this centre. The 3 surviving buildings of cruck construction—Brookgate Farm, a barn at Galliers

Farm, and fragmentary remains in a building at Plealey Farm—all stand in the north-east of the hamlet, along the brook, and may be evidence for its original site. Brookgate Farm consists of a cruck hall and service bay, to which a cross-wing (on the north-west) and a kitchen wing (at the south-east end) were added in the early 17th century. A portion of the elaborately cusped spere truss is visible to the east of the inserted fireplace at the lower end of the hall. A cast iron fireback dated 1638 and bearing the initials 'R.P.E.', which now forms the base of a fireplace in the kitchen wing, probably dates the early-17th-century alterations to the house and iden-tifies those responsible as Richard and Elinor Peers.[80]

The remaining Plealey farm-houses are notable for their Georgian fronts, but the only one of them dating as a whole from the early 19th century is Red House. This has a north front of 3 bays and a pedimented doorcase. The hipped roof dates from 1952; before this date the house was of 3 stories.[81] In the central staircase hall is a 'flying' staircase with cast iron balusters. Elsewhere Georgian work is no more than a casing or addition to earlier timber-framed houses. Plealey House, the least affected by later alterations, consists of a hall with a cross-wing at the north-east end, to which a timber-framed wing at the south-west end was added at a slightly later date. Plealey Farm, Galliers Farm, and Spencer Lodge have been so thoroughly remodelled that their original plans are difficult to establish. Plealey Farm, which has a central porch on its north front, supported by Tuscan columns, was probably enlarged and cased in brick in 1815.[82] It retains on the south wall an oak door of early-17th-century date. Galliers Farm was occupied as a summer residence by Edward Waring, Lucasian professor of mathematics at Cambridge, c. 1788–98,[83] but its 3-bay north front was probably added by his successor Richard France,[84] who also built the small brick chapel to the north-east of the house.[85] In the course of the 17th century secondary settlement appears to have developed south-west of the village, near the junction of the road from Oaks to Halston with that from Plealey to Pontesford. A cottage at 'the cross' is recorded in 1626,[86] and several of the cottages now standing here are timber-framed. The smithy, which was established shortly before 1698,[87] has been occupied since the later 18th century by the Bromley family.[88] An alehouse, recorded at Plealey, 1753–72,[89] may have stood in this part of the village.

Two farm-houses—Arscott House and Arscott Hall—and a private house are all that now remains of the former hamlet of Arscott. This was a large settlement in 1308, when there were 21 tenants here,[90] but by 1601 it contained only 6 messuages, held by 4 tenants.[91] The final stage in the shrinkage, in the later 18th century, is associated with the growth of the estate of the Harries family of Cruckton.

[68] Ibid. 437/5; ibid. 785/181.
[69] Ibid. 437/13, deeds passim.
[70] Ibid. 437/5; ibid. 785/181.
[71] Ibid. 785/157.
[72] Ibid. 437/5; ibid. 785/181.   [73] See p. 280.
[74] S.R.O. 785/157, 181; ibid. 437/5.
[75] Par. rec., commonplace bk. of Chas. Drury.
[76] Ex inf. Mr. T. Hamer, Upper Mill.
[77] Q. Sess., alehouse reg.
[78] C 134/5/1.   [79] S.P.L., Deeds 12706.
[80] S.P.R. Heref. xii (1), 100–26; S.R.O. 169/1; ibid. 437/4; ibid. 785/182.

[81] Ex inf. Mr. W. E. Willner, Red House, Plealey.
[82] Date on fireplace.
[83] S.R.O. 248/1–2; D.N.B.
[84] S.R.O. 169/11–13; ibid. 248/2; ibid. 437/4; ibid. 785/182.
[85] See p. 292.
[86] S.P.L., Deeds 11045.
[87] S.R.O. 169/1 (Ford ct. r. 1698).
[88] S.P.L., MS. 2364; S.R.O. 437/4; ibid. 785/182.
[89] Q. Sess., alehouse reg.
[90] C 134/5/1.
[91] S.P.L., Deeds 12706.

The latter, who had possessed 2 houses and a copyhold estate of some 100 a. at Arscott since the 16th century,[92] bought out the other 3 copyholders between 1777 and 1822,[93] and by 1840 the hamlet had been reduced to its present size.[94] Arscott House, which is timber-framed, dates from the earlier 17th century and was then occupied by the Applebury family.[95] It consists of a 2-bay hall and kitchen, of central-stack plan, with a jettied cross-wing at the north end. Although the cross-wing has a lower roof than the rest of the house, there is no internal evidence that it is of a different date. Arscott Hall, to the east of Arscott House, is a large brick house of late-18th-century date. There was no house on this site in the mid-18th-century[96] and it may have been built for Edward Harries, who was living at Arscott in 1802.[97] The cross-roads west of these two houses is the result of a minor diversion carried out between 1765 and 1816.[98] The road to Lea, a supposed Roman road, formerly ran a little to the south of its present course here and the roads to Cruckmeole and Plealey joined it at two different points.[99]

Sibberscott Manor,[1] which dates from the later 16th century, is timber-framed with closely spaced vertical studs, but is now largely cased in brick. It consists of a hall and service bay with a cross-wing at the south-east and a chimney stack set axially at the junction of the hall and cross-wing. The cross-wing was probably built at a slightly later date. There is a door on the north wall at the lower end of the hall, beneath a jettied porch which has a bargeboard carved with vine ornament and quatrefoils incised on the bressumer and framing below. Both cross-wing and hall were originally jettied at first-floor level. The roof is of collar-and-tie-beam construction, with butt-purlins, and ceiling beams on the ground floor all have wide chamfers. The builder of the house cannot be identified. Before 1660 it was held by Thomas Barret in right of his wife Rebecca.[2] Most of the Barret estate, including the Manor, was sold piecemeal to Henry Warter between 1738 and 1749.[3] Henry's son Dr. Joseph Warter lived at Sibberscott,[4] but after his death in 1812[5] the Manor became a farm-house.[6] Four tenants held lands at Sibberscott in 1276[7] and in 1601,[8] and there appear to have been two houses here during the 17th century.[9] The second house may have been the 3-bay cruck barn standing to the north of the Manor.

As at Sibberscott the final stage of shrinkage at Halston took place in the 17th century and was due to the growth of the estate of the Corbets of Halston. Richard Corbet, admitted to 2 messuages at Halston

on his father's death in 1602,[10] acquired 2 more messuages in the township later in the same year.[11] He was said to hold 3 messuages here in 1604[12] and at his death in 1622,[13] and there were said to be 4 other tenants at Halston in 1615.[14] Halston Farm appears to have been the only house remaining by the end of the 17th century.[15] This is a brick-cased timber-framed house with a somewhat complex plan which may have been produced by the combination of two originally separate houses. In 1749 Halston Farm was described as two messuages now united.[16] The oldest part of the house is the south wing. This was originally a two-bay house of $1\frac{1}{2}$ story with a central stack, but the roof was later raised to 2-story height. To the north are two parallel and adjoining wings of 2 stories with attics, both of which are timber-framed. The west wing is probably the earlier of the two. It retains its original roof and one of the bedrooms contains early-17th-century oak wainscot. The east wing has an oak newel stair of c. 1650, but its roof was renewed in the 19th century. Both wings had probably been added by 1662, when the house contained 4 hearths.[17] It was described as a capital messuage in 1684,[18] but has been no more than a farm-house since the death of Abigail Corbet in 1695.[19]

The development of isolated farms and squatter cottages east of Pontesford Brook, between Rea Brook and the southern hills, was less extensive than that to the south of Pontesbury and Pontesford. New Mills, erected before 1464[20] at the confluence of Pontesford Brook and the Rea in the Pontesbury manorial demesne, is the earliest isolated site here. The farm-house was largely rebuilt in stone c. 1800, as was the mill. Surviving earlier features, however, suggest that it was formerly a 2-bay timber-framed house with a lateral chimney stack on the east wall. Shorthill Farm, near Lea Cross church, is first recorded in 1641 by the name Shorthill House,[21] and belonged to the Wolley family of Woodhall until the early 19th century.[22] Another house had been built here by 1761,[23] but the existing houses near Shorthill Farm are of 19th-century date. Two of the houses at Little Plealey, by the roadside midway between Pontesford and Plealey, have been cottages since at least 1840,[24] but the older of them, which is timber-framed, is probably the homestead of a small farm created by the Archer family in 1691, partly from the waste and partly from land newly inclosed from the Pontesford common fields.[25] The remaining isolated farm in this area is Plealey Villa, which occupies the site of a house first recorded in 1713[26] and held from 1738 until 1820 by the Gowen

[92] S.P.L., Deeds 10998, 11109, 12706.
[93] S.R.O. 248/1–2; ibid. 169/1.
[94] Ibid. 437/4; ibid. 785/182.
[95] S.P.L., Deeds 12706; S.R.O. 169/1.
[96] S.P.L., Plans 16; ibid. Deeds 11499.
[97] S.R.O. 248/2.
[98] S.P.L., Deeds 11499; B.M. O.S. 2″ orig. drawings, sheet 199 (1816).
[99] Ibid.
[1] Description of house based on survey by Mr. J. W. Tonkin, Wigmore, Herefs.
[2] S.R.O. 169/1 (Ford ct. r. 1660).
[3] Ibid. 169/2–3.
[4] Ibid. 169/3; ibid. 248/1–2.
[5] Ibid. 248/2.
[6] Ibid. 437/4; ibid. 785/182.
[7] C 133/15/3.
[8] S.P.L., Deeds 12706.
[9] S.R.O. 169/1.

[10] S.P.L., MS. 300.
[11] Ibid.
[12] Ibid.
[13] Ibid.
[14] Ibid.
[15] E 134/10 and 11 Wm. III Hil./29.
[16] S.P.L., Deeds 10660.
[17] E 179/255/35 m. 80d.
[18] S.P.L., Deeds 10621.
[19] E 134/10 and 11 Wm. III Hil./29; S.P.L., Deeds 10621–73 passim.
[20] S.P.L., Deeds 6784.
[21] S.R.O. 171 uncat., deed, 1641.
[22] Ibid. deeds 1641–1724; S.P.L., MS. 2364.
[23] S.R.O. 169/3 (Ford ct. r. 1761).
[24] Ibid. 437/4; ibid. 785/182.
[25] Ibid. 169/1 (Ford ct. r. 1691).
[26] Ibid. 169/2 (ibid. 1713).

family of Panson.[27] Wholly rebuilt in the early 19th century, this is a square brick house of 2 stories with a hipped roof. It has a north front of 3 bays and a central porch supported by slender columns.

The earliest squatter settlement in this part of the Rea valley was at the road junction at Lea Cross. Its nucleus was an alehouse and 'shop', first recorded in 1671.[28] The alehouse, known in 1671 and 1842[29] as Lea Cross House, is a timber-framed house of two bays with a chimney stack on the north gable. It probably dates from the mid-17th century, but was enlarged, cased in brick, and re-roofed in the 19th century. The 'shop' of 1671[30] was presumably the smithy, which stood to the north of the road until it was demolished for road-widening purposes in 1938.[31] A few other houses, built since the 19th century, stand on the main road nearby. Lea Cross school was built in 1822,[32] the church in 1888,[33] and the parsonage and church hall before 1927.[34] A similar development is found during the 17th century at Gadbridge Lane, on the former parish boundary east of Cruckmeole, where the road to Shrewsbury crosses Rea Brook and is joined by a now-disused road from Arscott. There were 5 cottages and a smithy here in 1840.[35] The latter is first recorded in 1668,[36] but had been rebuilt by 1825[37] and had closed before 1885.[38] One of the cottages had been an alehouse known as 'The Pigeon' open between 1753 and 1772,[39] but closed before 1825.[40]

Little Halston, on the main road 500 yards north of Pontesford Bridge, was a 5-acre smallholding in 1842.[41] It is a T-shaped 2-story brick house, not recorded before 1816.[42] Small groups of cottages at Tags Gutter, Shorthill, and to the north of Arscott are not recorded before the early 19th century,[43] and are for the most part associated with collieries in the Arscott district. Twelve Council houses and five bungalows have been built to the north-west of the former Plealey Road station since the 1930s, and since 1945 a number of private houses and bungalows have been built along the road from Pontesford to Annscroft.

Of the 12 former hamlets to the north of the Rea, 7 are no more than small groups of houses and 4 have shrunk to single farms. Only Asterley has survived as a village of moderate size. Until the 19th century the township was divided among a number of small freeholders, many of whom were non-resident.[44] In the 19th century a large estate was built up here by the Gardners of Asterley Hall Farm. This coincided with the development of coal-mining to the north and east of the village, and the farmsteads of former freeholders were rebuilt or remodelled to serve as

colliers' cottages, several of which were derelict in 1965. There were 58 occupied houses in Asterley township in 1841.[45] A barn at Upper Farm is a 5-bay building of cruck construction. Its roof timbers are partially smoke-blackened and other constructional features indicate that it was originally a house. The only other house in the village which is now externally timber-framed is nos. 8 and 9, Asterley. This is dated 1675[46] and was originally a 3-bay house of 2 stories with a central chimney stack. An original newel stair against the stack has fretted balusters, but most of the external walls were cased in brick and a new roof, of lower pitch, was constructed in the 19th century. The 2-bay south wing of Brook House Farm, now cased in brick, is a fragment of a larger timber-framed house, and the use of butt-purlins in its collar-and-tie-beam roof suggests a relatively early date. For the rest Asterley bears the stamp of its brief period as a prosperous industrial village. The remaining houses are externally of brick or stone, and examination of derelict examples suggests that most of them were completely rebuilt in the 19th century, although roof timbers and ceiling beams of earlier houses were occasionally reused.

A small group of 'service' buildings stood in the centre of Asterley village, at the junction of the village street with the road past Hinwood to Westbury. There were 2 alehouses here from the 18th century until 1900,[47] of which the Windmill Inn, to the south of the village street, is still open. The second alehouse, now derelict, is one of a group of cottages to the north of this road.[48] The Primitive Methodist chapel, built in 1834,[49] stands at the road junction and is a 2-bay stone building with large round-headed windows. A smithy, now demolished, adjoined the house to the east of the chapel.[50] A brick Anglican mission church was erected in 1869 on the road to Farley to the north.[51] A small number of isolated cottages and other buildings had been built by 1842 near the coal pits north of the village, among them a tower windmill on the Westbury road,[52] the body of which was still standing in 1965. The squatter settlement at Hinwood, on the parish boundary with Westbury, now includes no houses earlier than the 19th century, but is likely to be a product of 18th-century mining activity. The Westbury road was much used by coal-wagons in this period; it was described as the road 'to the coal pits' in 1729,[53] and was said to be deeply rutted and impassable in 1781.[54] The settlement was already in existence by 1816[55] and numbered about a dozen cottages in 1842.[56] Four smallholdings on the road to Farley were built shortly after 1935.[57]

27 Ibid. 169/2–3, 11; ibid. 248/1–2.
28 Ibid. 169/1 (Ford ct. r. 1671).
29 Ibid. 437/5; ibid. 785/181.
30 Ibid. 169/1 (Ford ct. r. 1671).
31 Ex inf. Mr. J. T. Armstrong, Mangerton, Lea Cross. cf. S.C.C. Minutes, 1932–3, p. 211.
32 See p. 293.
33 See p. 290.
34 See p. 284.
35 S.R.O. 437/4; ibid. 785/182.
36 Ibid. 169/1 (Ford ct. r. 1668).
37 Ibid. 169/12 (Ford ct. r. 1825).
38 Kelly's Dir. Salop. (1856–85).
39 Q. Sess., alehouse reg.
40 S.R.O. 169/12 (Ford ct. r. 1825).
41 Ibid. 437/4; ibid. 785/182.
42 B.M. O.S. 2″ orig. drawings, sheet 199 (1816).

43 Ibid; ibid. sheet 320 (1827); S.R.O. 169/11; ibid. 248/2.
44 See pp. 267–8.
45 Census, 1841.
46 Datestone.
47 Q. Sess., alehouse reg.; Kelly's Dir. Salop. (1856–1900).
48 S.R.O. 437/5; ibid. 785/181.
49 Datestone.
50 S.R.O. 437/5; ibid. 785/181.
51 See p. 290.
52 S.R.O. 437/5; ibid. 785/181.
53 Q. Sess. rolls, Trin. 1729.
54 Ibid. East. 1781.
55 B.M. O.S. 2″ orig. drawings, sheet 199 (1816).
56 S.R.O. 437/5; ibid. 785/181.
57 S.C.C. Minutes, 1935–6, pp. 51, 119.

Although its common fields had been leased to a group of 5 tenants from neighbouring villages in 1425,[58] Farley appears to have survived as a community until at least the early 17th century, for 9 inhabitants owed suit at Pontesbury manor court in 1619.[59] Of the 3 farms which make up the present hamlet Farley House incorporates a rough-cast timber-framed house of 2 bays and has two timber-framed farm buildings, but the west front of the house dates from the 19th century. Farley Grange and The Firs are brick-built and of 19th century-date.

There appear to have been 8 houses at Edge until the later 17th century.[60] There were 8 tenants here in 1276[61] and 1308,[62] and the 6 tenants of 1601 held 8 messuages between them.[63] Only 3 farms—the present Red House, Edgegrove, and Lower Farm—remained by 1712, the sites of the other messuages having passed, with their lands, to copyholders in Lea, Newnham, and Polmere at the end of the 17th century.[64] The farm-lands here were consolidated by means of exchanges in the early 19th century,[65] and by 1842 all 3 farms were of over 100 a.[66] Their timber-framed farm-houses are still standing, but only Edgegrove is now occupied. Red House Farm and Lower Farm have now been merged and a new farm-house has been built. Edgegrove, the exterior of which is rough-cast, seems originally to have been an L-shaped house of 3 bays and 2 stories, with a central stack. A cross-wing at the west end, however, has a separate and lower roof and was originally of close-studded timber-framed construction. It is probably a fragment of an earlier house. In the early 19th century the roof of the rest of the house was raised to provide attics and a further bay was added to the north-east. The house thus became T-shaped, with a 3-bay Georgian east front, which has a central porch supported by pairs of Tuscan columns. The former farm-house at Lower Farm is a timber-framed house, cased in brick and rough-cast, probably dating from the mid-17th century. One room on the ground floor has finely moulded ceiling beams and oak panelling. The Red House comprises 1½ bay of a timber-framed house of early-17th-century date, the remainder of which was demolished c. 1800, when a new brick house, of 3 bays and 2 stories with attics, was built to the west at an oblique angle. The timber-framed portion, which is of close-studded construction, has a jettied gable with a carved bressumer and the console and sill of an oriel window.

A few cottages have been built at Edge since the 18th century. Cobbler's Patch, a small field north of Lower Farm, marks the site of a shoemaker's cottage first recorded c. 1764[67] and demolished by 1842.[68] The Villa, east of Edgegrove, is a T-shaped brick house of the earlier 19th century, while the modern farm-house of the smallholding on the Farley road occupies the site of 4 cottages erected by Hamlet Harrison shortly after 1812.[69]

Hinton, like Edge, contained about 8 households in the earlier 17th century,[70] and it possessed an alehouse in 1604.[71] The 11 houses recorded here in 1662[72] probably included a few outside the hamlet. The Ward family, who owned the greater part of Hinton by the later 17th century,[73] then lived in a house on the site of Hinton Hall. Reused timbers in the cellar of the present house include a fragment of wall-plate derived from a house of close-studded timber-frame construction. The house was rebuilt in brick in 1749[74] by Richard Ward Offley, shortly after he had succeeded his mother in possession of the estate. It faces south and is of 2 stories, consisting of a central block of 3 bays, flanked by 2 projecting wings. It has a low-pitched roof with broad eaves, and the gables of the wings have wooden mouldings to resemble pediments. A central colonnade, and a classical portico on the service bay at the east end were added in 1923.[75] The interior of the house was extensively damaged by fire in 1950.[76] The small brick lodge to the east of the Hall, by the side of the road to Lea, may have been built in 1749. It has two large round-headed windows on the south wall and two smaller square windows with ogee-headed relieving arches on the north. Hinton Farm was originally timber-framed, consisting of a 2-bay house with a northern cross-wing projecting to the east. The central truss in the house is a form of upper open cruck truss, probably intended to enable the roof-space to be used as an attic. There is early-17th-century wainscot in a party-wall on the ground floor of the cross-wing and in one of the bedrooms. The plan was complicated in the early 19th century, when the house was cased in brick, the interior was remodelled, a south wing added, and additions made on the west wall. Of the remaining houses Hinton Grange is a brick-cased timber-framed house, and Bytake Farm may also have been timber-framed originally. An isolated smallholding north of Hinton, on the road to Edge, was already there in 1842.[77]

Lea seems to have shrunk to something approaching its present size in the course of the Middle Ages. There were 16 tenants here in 1276[78] and only 8 by 1601.[79] In 1842 the hamlet consisted of one large farm, a smallholding, and 9 cottages.[80] One group of cottages was rebuilt as a Tudor-style farm-house in the later 19th century and is now known as Lea Hall. Two others have been demolished, one of them being replaced by the pair of modern cottages near Lea Hall.[81] Lea Farm, now externally of brick, incorporates an L-shaped timber-framed house. The west wing may once have been of cruck construction.[82] Two further gabled wings were added to

[58] S.R.O. 665 uncat., Pontesbury ct. r. 1425.
[59] S.P.L., MS. 300.
[60] S.R.O. 169/1.
[61] C 133/15/3.
[62] C 134/5/1.
[63] S.P.L., Deeds 12706.
[64] S.R.O. 169/1–2.
[65] Ibid. 169/11; ibid. 248/2.
[66] Ibid. 437/5; ibid. 785/181.
[67] Ibid. 169/3 (Ford ct. r. 1764).
[68] Ibid. 437/5; ibid. 785/181.
[69] Ibid.; ibid. 248/2 (Ford ct. r. 1812).
[70] S.P.L., MS. 300.

[71] Ibid.
[72] E 179/255/35 m. 8od.
[73] See p. 275.
[74] Datestone.
[75] Ex inf. Mrs. A. M. Head, Hinton Hall.
[76] Ibid.
[77] S.R.O. 437/5; ibid. 785/181.
[78] C 133/15/3.
[79] S.P.L., Deeds 12706.
[80] S.R.O. 437/5; ibid. 785/181.
[81] Ex inf. Mr. O. D. Wakeman, Lea Hall.
[82] A curved 'tree' is said to have been found during repairs to the house: ex inf. Miss E. Savage, Lea Farm.

the south of the house in the 19th century, when a new low-pitched roof was constructed over the remainder. Lea stands on a supposed Roman road and a Roman villa was discovered in 1793 in the field known as Causeway Meadow, to the east of the road between the hamlet and Rea Brook.[83] A tessellated pavement[84] found at this time was not preserved. An unsuccessful attempt was made to establish the plan of the villa in 1956–7, when late-2nd-century pottery was found here.[85]

There were 28 tenants at Cruckmeole in 1308,[86] but by 1601 the settlement contained only 11 messuages.[87] The later reduction in the number of copyholders here, from 10 in 1601 to 4 by 1785,[88] was a result of the growth of the estates of the Phillips (later Harries) and Warter families. The distribution of surviving old houses indicates that the medieval village stood on Rea Brook, at the point where this is crossed by a former road from Lea towards Great Hanwood. Middle House, Cruckmeole Farm, and the school, which stand to the east of this group, on or near the present road to Pontesbury, have all been built since the later 18th century.

Cruckmeole House, the former residence of the Warter family,[89] has been considerably enlarged since the later 18th century. It incorporates an L-shaped timber-framed house of 2 stories, with a chimney stack set axially at the junction of hall and cross-wing. The roof timbers of the former house are still for the most part intact and the timber-framing of the projecting bay of the cross-wing is exposed internally to the north-west of the present house. An elaborately carved Jacobean stair newel, now forming the lintel of a cellar window, suggests that the former house was of early-17th-century date, but the ribbed moulding on the wooden lintel and jambs of the original fireplace may be of earlier date. The house was extended in brick to the south and east in the later 18th century. Still of 2 stories, it has an east front of 5 bays, with a hipped roof and low stone parapet, in which the 3 central bays are set forward beneath a pedimented gable. The central door has a pedimented doorcase with fanlight, and a wrought iron porch runs the length of the 3 central bays. Flat-roofed single-story wings to the north and south were among additions made to the house by Henry de Grey Warter in the 1850s.[90]

Cruckmeole Old Hall, on a low-lying site to the west of Rea Brook, was originally the home of the Phillips family.[91] It ceased to be occupied by this family after 1767, when their estate passed to Thomas Harries of Cruckton,[92] and was in divided occupation by 1840, part being a cottage and the remainder the homestead of a 23-acre smallholding.[93] It has now been occupied for many years as 4 cottages. The oldest part of the house is the west wing, which consists on the ground floor of two

rooms (a hall and a parlour) divided by a cross-passage. This probably dates from the later 16th century. One of the fireplaces—probably associated with the ashlar chimney-stack on the west wall—is said to have been dated 1588.[94] The east wing seems to have been added as a service wing c. 1625, when a jettied porch of 2 stories was built in the centre of the south wall. A block of sandstone bearing the date '1676' is now set in the garden wall to the south of the house.

The three remaining houses in this part of the hamlet—Hall Farm, Mill House, and Cruckmeole Cottage—are all timber-framed but have been enlarged and cased in brick and stone. The mill, now known as Mill Farm, stands on a mill-race some 250 yards south-west of Old Hall. The site is known to have been occupied since 1308.[95] In the centre of the present house is a single bay of a former timber-framed house, but the remainder dates, like the mill, from c. 1800.

Cruckton Hall, Home Farm, the pair of cottages to the east, and the former mill on Yockleton Brook to the south make up all that now remains of the hamlet of Cruckton. The number of tenants here fell from 17 in 1308[96] to 5 in 1601.[97] There were still 9 houses in Cruckton in 1601,[98] but the hamlet had shrunk to its present size by the mid-18th century[99] as a consequence of the growth of the estate of the Harries family of Cruckton Hall. The Hall, which stands on the site of an earlier timber-framed house, has been a County Council nursery school since 1947.[1] It is said to have been 'almost new built' in brick by Edward Harries in the 1770s.[2] His house, of 3 stories, consisted of a central block of 5 bays, in which the 3 central bays are set forward under a pediment, flanked by wings which project northwards. The sash windows on the north wall have segmental heads. There is a brick string course at first-floor level and a moulded stone one at second-floor level. The west wing, which is not symmetrical, contains early-17th-century ceiling beams on the ground floor and is a remnant of the former house. The latter, which comprised a hall, parlour, kitchen, and service wing in 1684,[3] was of 2 stories with lofts over[4] and must have been similar in scale to Cruckmeole Old Hall. A little later in the 18th century a kitchen wing was added to the west, together with a dining room with a splayed end and a new staircase on the south side of the house. A tall block at the east end of the south front, containing a lofty drawing room with a bedroom over, probably dates from c. 1812, when Edward Harries' son Thomas succeeded to the estate.[5] A billiard room to the north-east, and probably the north porch also, were built c. 1900. The stable block north-west of the Hall, which has a clock-tower, and the octagonal brick dovecote to the north, were probably built by

[83] V.C.H. Salop. i. 358.
[84] Ibid. plate facing p. 360.
[85] T.S.A.S. lvi. 26–27.
[86] C 134/5/1.
[87] S.P.L., Deeds 12706.
[88] S.R.O. 123/1.
[89] Ibid. 437/4; ibid. 785/182.
[90] Letter, Henry de Grey Warter to Edward Haycock, 1863, penes Mrs. A. N. Fielden, Longden Manor.
[91] S.R.O. 437/4; ibid. 785/182; ibid. 169/1–3; ibid. 248/1–2.
[92] See p. 274.
[93] S.R.O. 437/4; ibid. 785/182.

[94] Shrewsbury Chronicle 13, 20 June 1913. Date '1588, and initials 'W.P.' then recorded by H. E. Forrest, were not visible in 1965.
[95] C 134/5/1.
[96] Ibid.
[97] S.P.L., Deeds 12706.
[98] Ibid.
[99] Ibid., Plans 16.
[1] S.C.C. Minutes, 1947–8, pp. 10, 316.
[2] Arthur Young, Tours in England and Wales (reprint, 1932), 160–1.
[3] S.P.L., Deeds 12740.
[4] Ibid.   [5] See p. 274.

Edward Harries; the farmery to the north-east is of somewhat later date.

Home Farm, a brick-cased timber-framed house, is T-shaped and of 2 stories with attics. It consists on the ground floor of a large hall, recently divided into smaller rooms, and an eastern cross-wing containing a kitchen and service bay. A 2-story porch on the south wall, at the junction of cross-wing and hall, has had its doorway blocked, but the original oak door is now set at the west end of the south wall of the hall. The roof timbers cannot now be seen, but there are indications that the hall was once an open hall. It is unusually wide and the transverse ceiling beams are supported by props on the first floor. Apart from an inserted corner fireplace near the former porch, the only other fireplace in the hall is an external stack at the west end of the north wall. The cottages to the east of Home Farm were occupied by a blacksmith and a carpenter in 1842[6] but, like the mill, they appear to be of 19th-century date. Cruckton chapel, at the junction of the road to Cruckmeole with the former road to Hanwood, was erected in 1839–40.[7] Six County Council smallholdings were formed to the east and north of Cruckton after 1930,[8] and a group of Council houses was built to the north of the road, west of the church, in 1949.[9] A Roman villa was then found on the green in front of these houses and was later partially excavated.[10]

The five remaining hamlets to the north of Rea Brook are more severely shrunken. Malehurst has consisted of a single farm and Boycott of two farms since the later Middle Ages, while Newnham and Polmere have shrunk to single farms since the 17th century. Malehurst was a reputed manor in the Middle Ages[11] and the house was described as 'Malehurst Hall' in 1529,[12] but it was occupied as a tenant-farm after 1655.[13] A fish pool in Mill Leasow, east of the house, is recorded in 1685,[14] when the tenant was given licence to repair the house and rebuild the farm buildings.[15] The present house, which is of brick, was largely rebuilt in the earlier 19th century, but includes reused timbers and some early-17th-century panelling in doors.

Boycott Hall Farm, formerly surrounded by a moat,[16] was originally an open hall. The screen dividing the lower end of the hall from the screens passage is still in position, and several of the roof-trusses are smoke-blackened, although they are now of butt-purlin collar-and-tie-beam construction. The house was probably built by the Lake family, first recorded as prosperous copyholders in Boycott in 1539.[17] Upper floors and the chimney-stack at the west (upper) end of the hall were probably inserted shortly after 1621, when the house was purchased

by Thomas Nicholls.[18] The service bay at the east end was rebuilt at this time and contained a parlour and drawing room in 1692.[19] The exterior may have been cased in brick in the later 17th century, when the house passed to William Boycott, but Richard Lake of Boycott was buying quantities of brick from the lord of Pontesbury manor as early as 1604.[20] A bolection-moulded fireplace on the first floor above the hall is one of the very few alterations to the house made by the Boycott family. Boycott Farm, to the west of the Hall, occupies an ancient site,[21] but was rebuilt in brick c. 1796.[22]

There were 12 tenants at Newnham in 1276,[23] when there was also a mill here,[24] and 6 tenants in 1601.[25] The township contained 7 messuages at the latter date,[26] and 11 houses are recorded in 1662,[27] but these would include the squatter settlement at Nox and perhaps a few isolated houses on Ford Heath. Although it is not normally possible to distinguish houses in Newnham hamlet from those elsewhere in the township until the later 18th century, it seems likely that the Higgons and Niccolls families, the principal Newnham copyholders in the later 17th century, both lived in the hamlet. Richard Niccolls acquired 3 messuages in Newnham in 1683[28] and the Higgons house was described as a capital messuage in 1682[29] and 1730.[30] The latter probably stood on the site of Newnham Hall, since it was already occupied by John Niccolls when he acquired it from the representatives of Richard Higgons in 1735.[31] The Hall was built by John Niccolls in 1723[32] and contains no fragments of the earlier house apart from reused timbers in the cellar and in the square brick dovecote to the north. It was then an L-shaped brick house, probably of two stories with attics, and has string courses at first and second floor levels. A stable block east of the house is dated 1780,[33] but subsequent alterations to the house are likely to have taken place in the early 19th century. These included the addition of a bay at the south-east, the raising of the roof to 3-story height, and the insertion of sash windows, notably on the stuccoed north front, which has a central porch supported by pairs of Tuscan columns.

Polmere seems to have comprised some half-dozen houses during the Middle Ages.[34] Only two appear to have remained by 1601,[35] and it has consisted of a single farm since the early 18th century.[36] Polmere Farm, facing south, dates from the early 19th century and is a 3-bay brick house of 2 stories with attics, with a single-story kitchen to the north. The central south door has a pedimented doorcase and fanlight, and the large ground-floor windows on the south front have segmental heads.

Sascott has never been more than a tiny hamlet.

[6] S.R.O. 437/5; ibid. 785/181.
[7] See p. 290.
[8] S.C.C. Minutes, 1929–30, pp. 110, 316–17.
[9] Ex inf. Atcham R.D.C.
[10] No excavation report has yet been published. For brief reports see Proc. Caradoc and Severn Valley Field Club, xiii. 42; J.R.S. xli. 130.
[11] See p. 268.
[12] C 1/656/26.
[13] See p. 268.
[14] S.P.L., Deeds 14313.
[15] Ibid.
[16] Ex inf. Mr. J. D. Pryce, Boycott Hall.
[17] See p. 268.
[18] S.P.L., Deeds 14055–6.
[19] Ibid. 14036.

[20] Ibid. 7025.
[21] Hope-Edwardes MSS., Linley Hall, survey, 1770.
[22] Ibid. accts. 1796.
[23] C 133/15/3.
[24] Ibid.
[25] S.P.L., Deeds 12706.
[26] Ibid.
[27] E 179/255/35 m. 81.
[28] S.R.O. 169/1 (Ford ct. r. 1683).
[29] Ibid. (ibid. 1682).
[30] Ibid. 169/2 (ibid. 1730).
[31] Ibid. (ibid. 1735).
[32] Datestone. For some account of the house, see T.S.A.S. 4th ser. ix. 233–7.
[33] Datestone.
[34] C 133/15/3; C 134/5/1.
[35] S.P.L., Deeds 12706.
[36] S.R.O. 169/1–3.

There were only 4 tenants here in the early 14th century[37] and in 1601,[38] and the settlement seems to have shrunk to the two existing farms by the beginning of the 18th century.[39] Sascott Farm, owned in the 18th century by the Oswell family,[40] was formerly a timber-framed house of 2 bays with a chimney-stack on the east gable. It was cased in brick, the roof raised, and a further bay added to the east, probably in 1814,[41] when the farm was purchased by Thomas Harries of Cruckton. The brick north wing is dated 1868.[42] The Beeches, part of the Harries estate since the mid-18th century,[43] appears to have been rebuilt in the mid-19th century.

The only isolated large farms in that part of the parish lying to the north of Rea Brook are Holly Bank and Horton Lodge, on the road from Shrewsbury to Yockleton, north of Cruckton. The former, first recorded in 1797,[44] is a 3-bay brick house of 3 stories, built at about this time. Horton Lodge, of similar date, is of 3 stories and on its 3-bay south front has a central porch supported by slender columns.

The earliest squatter settlement on the southern fringe of Ford Heath occurs at Nox. This road junction was known in the earlier 17th century as 'the Cross Gate under Newnham',[45] and by 1653 an alehouse had been built here by Richard Nock,[46] from whom the settlement takes its name. The alehouse, which stood to the south of the road, was known as the 'Star and Ball',[47] and was the regular meeting-place of the Ford manor court, 1674–1811.[48] It had closed by the 1820s[49] and was a butcher's shop in the later 19th century.[50] Known as Nox House, it is now a private house. It was formerly an L-shaped timber-framed house, but was cased in brick and its roof was raised to 3-story height in the early 19th century, when a stable was built to the west and a stone barn to the east. The smithy, which was erected by John Nock opposite the alehouse c. 1668,[51] is still in business. The 'Hare and Hounds', on the Shrewsbury road north of Cruckton, is first recorded in 1753.[52] It was occupied by the Ward family, 1777–1841,[53] and succeeded the 'Star and Ball' as the meeting place of the Ford manor court from 1812 until formal sessions of the court ceased in 1875.[54]

Nearly all the other old houses on the Heath are, and have always been, smallholdings. Bank House and Coppice House are known to have been standing in 1754[55] and are both brick-cased timber-framed houses. The windows on the south front of Bank House have ogee-headed relieving arches. The smallholdings immediately north and west of Bucks Coppice had also been established by 1754;[56] one of them is presumably the 'Bucks Gate House' first

named in 1681.[57] School House, on the parish boundary with Ford, appears to be a brick-cased timber-framed house. Upper and Lower House probably stand on the sites of the two houses known as 'Heath House' in the later 18th century. One of these had been built by 1690[58] but was rebuilt shortly before 1787,[59] and the other was described as lately erected in 1784.[60] New House was probably built shortly before 1806.[61]

Longden stands on the road from Shrewsbury to Pulverbatch on either side of Longden Brook, the 'long valley' of which gave the village its name.[62] The Shrewsbury road is crossed, north of the village, by the road from Condover to Pontesbury, but this had little effect on settlement here until the present century. The only old house near the road junction is Cross House, first recorded in the 15th century. With the exception of Middle Farm, all the farm-houses stood to the south of the brook in the earlier 19th century,[63] and this was probably the area occupied by the medieval village. Although the chapel stands north of the brook, it contains no features earlier than the 16th century. It seems to have been in origin a private manorial chapel[64] and probably replaced a medieval building south of the brook, near the manor-house. The manor-house, which was granted to the Adams family before 1463,[65] stood on the site of Longden Hall Farm. Among other reused timbers in the roof of the present house are portions of cruck blades, probably derived from the 15th-century Adams house. The Hall appears to have been rebuilt in 1602,[66] but it preserves in some respects a medieval ground-plan. It has a cross-passage, in which is a newel stair having flat balusters with raked mouldings. A room to the west of the passage has a lateral stack on the south wall and classical mouldings on its ceiling beams; its early-17th-century oak wainscot was removed c. 1912.[67] The room to the west of this appears, on the evidence of the external brickwork, to have been added in the later 17th century. Its ceiling beams, however, have plain 6-inch chamfers and a stair similar to that in the cross-passage is set against the south wall. The 3 bays to the east of the cross-passage appear to have been unheated in 1602, since the lateral stack in the south wall, now serving the kitchen, is clearly a later insertion. The house was cased in brick in the later 17th century, when the west wing was probably added. There is a moulded stone string course at first floor level on the north front. This runs midway along the gable walls and is continued in brick at the rear. The central north door originally had a moulded brick pediment. Some mullioned and transomed windows remain on the north and east walls. Others were

37 C 134/5/1; *T.S.A.S.* 2nd ser. x. 122.
38 S.P.L., Deeds 12706.
39 S.R.O. 169/1–3.
40 Ibid.; ibid. 248/1–2.
41 Ibid. 169/11 (Ford ct. r. 1814).
42 Datestone.
43 S.P.L., Plans 16.
44 S.R.O. 248/2 (Ford ct. r. 1797).
45 S.P.L., Deeds 11055.
46 Ibid.
47 S.R.O. 248/1 (Ford ct. r. 1788).
48 Ibid. 169/1–3; ibid. 248/1–2.
49 Not recorded in Q. Sess., alehouse reg. 1822–8.
50 Ex inf. Mr. C. F. Greenwood, Nox House.
51 S.R.O. 169/1 (Ford ct. r. 1668).
52 Q. Sess., alehouse reg.

53 Ibid.; S.R.O. 169/11–13; ibid. 248/2.
54 S.R.O. 169/11–16; ibid. 248/2.
55 S.P.L., Plans 16.
56 Ibid.
57 S.P.L., Deeds 996.
58 S.R.O. 169/1 (Ford ct. r. 1690).
59 Ibid. 248/1 (ibid. 1787).
60 Ibid. (ibid. 1784).
61 Ibid. 248/2 (ibid. 1806).
62 *Eng. Place-Name Elements* (E.P.N.S. xxv–xxvi), i. 138; ibid. ii. 15.
63 S.R.O. 802 uncat., map of Longden manor, 1812.
64 See p. 290.
65 See p. 270.
66 Bodl. MS. Gough Salop. 11, p. 74.
67 Ex inf. Mrs. A. N. Fielden, Longden Manor.

replaced by sash windows in the early 19th century, when the roof was hipped.

The remaining farms to the south of the brook—Hall Farm, Longden, Lower Farm, and the Poplars—were reconstructed in the early 19th century, but all contain portions of earlier timber-framed houses. A service wing at Hall Farm contains an upper open cruck truss, and a building to the east of the farm-house, demolished c. 1960, is said to have been of cruck construction.[68] The farm buildings, of 19th-century date, include a dovehouse set above the granary, and there is a brick gazebo, known locally as 'the summer-house', by the roadside in the garden. The Poplars, first recorded under its earlier name 'Lye House' in 1596,[69] appears to have been a 2-bay house with a chimney stack on the west gable until a 3-bay north wing of 2 stories with attics was added c. 1800. Lower Farm was probably once a 3-bay house with a central stack. A smithy, which stood by the brook to the east of the road, is first recorded in 1593,[70] but has been demolished since 1941.[71] A mill, recorded in 1315,[72] but apparently disused by 1346,[73] presumably also stood in this part of the village.

Most of the houses to the north of the brook have been built since the early 19th century. Middle Farm, which formerly stood on a small green south of the chapel,[74] is a 3-bay house with a central stack, cased in brick and re-roofed in the 19th century. Cottages to the north of Middle Farm, known as Church Row, were demolished in 1938,[75] and the row of brick cottages immediately south of the chapel incorporate a timber-framed house. Cross House is the largest surviving timber-framed house in the north of the village. A house on its site was held by Alice del Cross in 1430[76] and the property was occupied by her descendants until 1750.[77] It consists of a hall and a jettied northern cross-wing, with a chimney-stack set axially at their junction, and dates from the early 17th century. The ceiling beams of the principal ground-floor room of the cross-wing have ovolo-moulded chamfers.

Four Longden alehouses were licensed in 1613,[78] but 2 of them were suppressed in 1615.[79] The village had two ale houses after 1753.[80] One stood immediately north-east of The Tankerville Arms,[81] but the latter, then described as newly built, had replaced it by 1811,[82] and the former inn had been converted into 6 cottages before 1841.[83] Four early-19th-century cottages, adjoining the Primitive Methodist chapel, are the oldest of the isolated houses along the Shrewsbury road to the north of the village.

Arscott Villa, standing west of this road, was built in 1867,[84] but probably occupies the site of a small-holding first recorded in 1712.[85] Since the erection of the Primitive Methodist chapel in 1870[86] the cross-roads near Cross House has developed as a new focus of settlement. The school was built here in 1873[87] and the Village Hall in 1923.[88] The parsonage, built in 1915,[89] stands a short distance west of the cross-roads, and a number of private houses and bungalows, together with a group of Council houses, have been built here since 1945.

Oaks was a community of small freeholders in the 13th and 14th centuries, but by the 15th century most of the hamlet was held by the Jennings family of Walleybourne.[90] A consolidated manorial estate was established here in the later 16th century, when the lord of the manor was briefly resident at Oaks Hall, but no later owners of the estate lived there.[91] The hamlet shrank during the 18th century from about six houses in 1700[92] to 4 by c. 1769[93] and to 3 by 1795.[94] Lower Farm, the only one of these still used as a farm-house, consists of a 2-bay house of cruck construction, to which a western cross-wing was added c. 1600 and a stone-built east wing in 1783.[95] Upper Farm has been built since 1842,[96] the sites of the two other 18th-century farm-houses being now occupied by cottages.[97] A pair of cottages at the south end of the hamlet are of late-19th-century date.

The earlier history of Little Hanwood, Woodhall, Panson, and Moat Hall is obscure. Panson is now a deserted site and the others are single farms, but all, apart from Moat Hall, appear to have been hamlets in the early Middle Ages. There is no evidence that Little Hanwood possessed a set of common fields and the hamlet, if such it was, was being treated as a single freehold estate in the later 12th century.[98] There were, however, two farms here in 1717.[99] Little Hanwood was a single farm in 1840,[1] and now consists of no more than the kennels of the South Shropshire Hunt. Common-field names are recorded at Woodhall, 1576–1640,[2] and lands here were assessed in terms of virgates in the 12th and 13th centuries.[3] It has been no more than a single farm since the 15th century.[4] The present house[5] dates substantially from the early 18th century, but a T-shaped timber-framed south wing, containing a kitchen, dairy, and parlour in 1765,[6] has since been rebuilt in brick. Fragments of the earlier house remain: a piece of timber in the attic is inscribed 'June. Wilm. Woley. 1616', there are reused wall-timbers in the cellar, and parts of the

[68] Ex inf. Mr. H. H. Jones, Longden Hall Farm.
[69] S.P.L., MS. 393.
[70] Ibid.
[71] *Kelly's Dir. Salop.* (1941).
[72] C 134/48/9.
[73] C 135/82/1.
[74] Heref. Dioc. Regy., Longden tithe appt.
[75] Ex inf. Mrs. A. N. Fielden, Longden Manor.
[76] S.P.L., MS. 393.
[77] Ibid. MS. 392–3.
[78] Q. Sess., alehouse reg.
[79] Ibid.
[80] Ibid.
[81] S.P.L., MS. 392.
[82] Ibid.
[83] Heref. Dioc. Regy., Longden tithe appt.
[84] Datestone.
[85] S.R.O. 169/2 (Ford ct. r. 1712).
[86] Worship Reg.
[87] See p. 294.

[88] Datestone.
[89] See p. 291.
[90] See p. 277.
[91] See pp. 266–7.
[92] S.P.L., Deeds 13462.
[93] S.R.O. 665 uncat., survey of Oaks estate, c. 1769.
[94] Oaks title-deeds, *penes* Mrs. A. N. Fielden, Longden Manor.
[95] Datestone.
[96] S.R.O. 437/5; ibid. 785/181.
[97] Ibid.
[98] See p. 269.
[99] Q. Sess., reg. papists' estates, 1717.
[1] S.R.O. 437/4; ibid. 785/182.
[2] See p. 250.
[3] Eyton, vii. 135–7.
[4] See p. 269.
[5] For some account of the house, see *T.S.A.S.* 4th ser. iv. 258–60.
[6] S.R.O. 552 uncat., survey of Wolley estate, 1765.

west and south walls of the north wing contain timber-framing. The north wing is brick-built and of 2 stories and attics, with a hipped roof largely concealed by a tall brick parapet on 3 sides. It retains most of its original sash windows, with thick glazing bars, notably on the first floor of the north front. The staircase in the central hall rises to attic level. It has 3 balusters to each tread and has parquet floors on landings. The room to the east of the hall contains plain oak panelling.

No record has been found of Panson before the 15th century, when it was a reputed manor,[7] but the original form of its name—'Painston'[8]—is evidence that it was once a hamlet. The settlement is now marked by a circular moated inclosure and it presumably shrank to a single house quite early in the Middle Ages. A former house here, which had been a farm on the Moat Hall estate since 1621,[9] was replaced by a group of 3 cottages in the early 19th century.[10] These were demolished in 1964.

Moat Hall takes its name from a circular moat formerly surrounding the house. It is a timber-framed house[11] of early-17th-century date and was probably built by Roger Berrington. It is now cased in brick at ground-floor level and rough-cast above. It is L-shaped, consisting on the ground floor of a hall and parlour with a small service bay to the south-west. The latter was subsequently extended westwards under a slightly lower roof. There is a gable stack at the north end of the hall, and an axial stack between the parlour and service bay, near which is the original newel stair and cellar-entrance. The east front was originally jettied and has an original door opening into the hall and an open timber porch. The latter, and the lateral ceiling beam of the hall, have ovolo-moulded chamfers. To the west of the hall the roof has been extended to cover a later outshot. The portion of the original west wall thus preserved is constructed with closely spaced studding and includes an original ground-floor window and the brackets of an oriel window on the first floor. The bedroom over the hall has a fine plaster ceiling ornamented in relief with a central Tudor rose, bay trees, oak trees, vines, and fleurs-de-lis. Panelling in the bedroom and four elaborate Jacobean fireplaces, three of which bore the arms of the Berrington family, were removed from the house and sold before 1945.[12]

Isolated settlement in the southern woodland, in the townships of Plealey, Oaks, and Longden, is first recorded in the later 16th century. The earliest isolated house is Oaks Hall, probably built before 1570.[13] At about the same time the lord of Oaks manor erected a fulling mill on Pontesford Brook,

in the deep valley between Oaks Wood and Pontesford Hill.[14] A short-lived corn mill nearby seems to have been in use between 1573 and 1601, when its materials were given to the tenant of the fulling mill.[15] The latter, later converted into a leather mill,[16] was known as Skin Mill Cottage in the 19th century.[17] It ceased to be occupied c. 1905,[18] and only the rubble foundations of buildings now remain on the site. Cottages at Radlith are recorded from 1712 onwards.[19] In 1840 a 9-acre smallholding and a cottage stood near Pontesford Brook[20] and a wheelwright's shop, built c. 1827,[21] stood on the roadside between Oaks Hall and Plealey.[22] The homestead of the smallholding is stone-built, but two late-19th-century brick cottages stand on the site of the adjoining cottage. Four cottages at Broompatch, built shortly before 1829,[23] and the 3 cottages known as Cherryhayes belonged in 1840 to Thomas Wilkinson of Plealey Farm.[24]

Longden Manor,[25] on a former road from Longden to Oaks Hall, was built between 1863 and 1866.[26] It occupies the site of an isolated farm, known as Coppice House, which is first named in 1719[27] and was the homestead of a 204-acre farm in 1859.[28] The Manor was designed by its owner, Henry de Grey Warter, with some assistance from the architect Edward Haycock. It was a large, square, stone house, with dressings of Grinshill stone, in Tudor style, and was of 3 stories. The house had a large stone porch on the east front and its most striking internal feature was the central staircase hall, rising the full height of the house. There was a clock tower at the north-east corner and a range of buildings adjoined the north wall. Internal alterations were made by William Swire, c. 1905–10. The Manor was demolished in 1954[29] and a smaller house has since been erected on its site. Three lodges—Oaks Hall Lodge to the west, Longden Lodge to the east, and Hayes Lodge to the south—were constructed between 1860 and 1910.[30]

Most of the remaining isolated farms and squatter cottages in Longden township stand on the fringes of the former Longden Common—on the road to Pulverbatch (its western boundary), and along the parish boundary to the south and east. By 1610 there were already 4 cottages in those parts of the squatter settlements of Exfordsgreen and Hurst Bank which lay within the parish,[31] and there were in addition 5 cottages in Longden Wood by 1615.[32] The cottagers adjoining the Common were ordered in 1654 not to keep dogs to frighten sheep there.[33] Of the three isolated farms in the area of the Common only Roundhouse Farm near Exfordsgreen now contains any features earlier than the 18th century.

[7] S.P.L., MS. 393 (ct. r. 1478).
[8] Ibid.
[9] Bodl. MS. Gough Salop. 13, p. 9.
[10] S.R.O. 437/4; ibid. 785/182.
[11] For some account of the house, describing fittings no longer there, see H. E. Forrest, *Some Old Shropshire Houses* (Shrewsbury, 1924), 181–3.
[12] Ex inf. Mr. G. T. Davies, Moat Hall.
[13] See p. 267.
[14] S.R.O. 665 uncat., leases, 1570, 1589.
[15] Ibid. leases, 1573, 1601.
[16] Ibid. lease, 1699.
[17] O.S. Map 6″ Salop. 40 (2nd edn.).
[18] Local inf.
[19] S.R.O. 169/2–3; ibid. 248/1–2.
[20] Ibid. 437/4; ibid. 785/182.
[21] Ibid. 169/12 (Ford ct. r. 1827).

[22] Ibid. 437/4; ibid. 785/182.
[23] Ibid. 169/12 (Ford ct. r. 1829).
[24] Ibid. 437/4; ibid. 785/182.
[25] Description of house, except where otherwise stated, based on plans and specifications, 1863, and plans 1905–10, *penes* Mrs. A. N. Fielden, Longden Manor.
[26] *Kelly's Dir. Salop.* (1885).
[27] Longden manor title-deeds, *penes* Mrs. A. N. Fielden, Longden Manor.
[28] Ibid.
[29] Ex inf. Mrs. A. N. Fielden.
[30] Datestones and plans, *penes* Mrs. A. N. Fielden. Oaks Hall Lodge, now Oaks Hall Cottage, incorporates an earlier house.
[31] S.P.L., MS. 393.
[32] Ibid.
[33] Ibid.

Woodhouse Farm was enlarged in 1870[34] and an older wing to the west has since been demolished.[35] Wood Farm probably dates from the later 18th century. The squatter settlements at Stapleton Common, Hurst Bank, and Exfordsgreen extend into Stapleton and Condover parishes. Most of the existing houses in the Longden portion had been built by 1812.[36] Several were smallholdings in 1838[37] and clearly date from the earliest stages of squatter settlement. Only 'Tin Tops' east of Hall Farm, Longden, and a smallholding near Roundhouse Farm are still externally timber-framed, the remainder having been rebuilt or enlarged. The oldest of the cottages on Longden Common Lane, along the southern edge of the Common, seem to have been built in the later 18th century to house miners from nearby coal-pits in Longden and Pulverbatch. Most of them were still occupied by miners in the early years of the present century,[38] when local mines had long since closed. The cottages were originally of stone, but nearly all have been enlarged or rebuilt in brick. The Red Lion Inn, on the main road at the head of this lane, dates from the early 19th century, as does the 'Royal Oak', a former ale-house opposite, which closed c. 1939.[39] The only notable additions to settlement south of Longden during the 19th century were the Congregational chapel on the Pulverbatch road, built in 1837,[40] and the Primitive Methodist chapel at Hurst Bank, built in 1831.[41] A small number of houses have been built since 1945, principally at Stapleton Common and on Longden Common Lane.

MANORS. The townships of Arscott, Cruckmeole, Cruckton, Edge, Lea, Newnham, Plealey, Pontesford, Sascott, and Sibberscott lay within the manor of *FORD*, the descent of which is given under that parish.[42] The township of Polmere, which may be represented by the manor of 'Pole' recorded in 1086,[43] became part of Ford manor soon after this date.[44]

The manor of *PONTESBURY* was held in 1086 by Roger Fitz Corbet as mesne lord under Roger, Earl of Shrewsbury.[45] The Earl's overlordship is not later recorded, and presumably lapsed after 1102,[46] but the manor continued to be held of Roger Fitz

Corbet's successors as lords of Caus until the 14th century. Following a lawsuit between the tenant and Thomas Corbet of Caus,[47] the service due from the manor was fixed in 1237 at ½ knight's fee,[48] but in 1242 the tenant was contesting Corbet's demand for suit every 3 weeks at his court of Caus,[49] and a further lawsuit between Corbet and his tenant, which began in 1249,[50] was still unsettled in 1272.[51] The overlordship of the lords of Caus appears to have been extinguished when the manor was acquired by the Crown c. 1307 for, although said to be held of Caus in 1346,[52] it was always reckoned to be held in chief after 1353.[53]

The freeman Ernui, who had held the manor before 1066,[54] was still its tenant in 1086.[55] By 1200 the manor was in the hands of Herbert Fitz Herbert,[56] who had probably become under-tenant of the Corbets here in the reign of Henry II.[57] He had been succeeded before 1204[58] by his son Peter Fitz Herbert, who died in 1235.[59] One third of the manor was then assigned in dower to Peter's widow Isabel,[60] and the remainder passed to his son Herbert Fitz Peter.[61] On the latter's death in 1248,[62] he was succeeded by his brother Reynold,[63] who died in 1286.[64] The manor then passed to Reynold's son John,[65] who sold it to Rhys ap Howell in 1305.[66] It passed to the Crown in 1309, in exchange for the manor of Talgarth (Brecknock),[67] and was then granted to John de Charlton, lord of Powys.[68] The latter, however, was already in possession of the manor by 1307, when he was granted free warren in his demesne at Pontesbury.[69] Agnes, widow of John Fitz Reynold, sued Charlton for dower in the manor in 1312,[70] and a similar plea was made by Eleanor, widow of John's son Herbert in 1328.[71] John de Charlton died in 1353[72] and the manor passed from father to son in the Charlton family[73] until 1401, the following being lords: John (II), 1353–60;[74] John (III), 1360–74;[75] John (IV), 1374–1401.[76] Joan, widow of John de Charlton (III), was assigned a third of the manor in dower in 1374[77] and held it until her death in 1397.[78] On the death of John de Charlton (IV) the manor passed to his brother Edward,[79] who died in 1421.[80] Edward's estates were divided between his two daughters, Pontesbury falling to Joan, widow of Sir John

³⁴ Datestone.
³⁵ Ex inf. Mrs. A. N. Fielden.
³⁶ S.R.O. 802 uncat., map of Longden manor, 1812.
³⁷ Heref. Dioc. Regy., Longden tithe appt.
³⁸ Ex inf. Mr. A. E. Mapp, Longden Common Lane.
³⁹ Ibid.
⁴⁰ See p. 292.
⁴¹ Ibid.
⁴² See pp. 228–30.
⁴³ *V.C.H. Salop.* i. 342.
⁴⁴ Eyton, vii. 180.
⁴⁵ *V.C.H. Salop.* i. 325.
⁴⁶ Eyton, vii. 209–10, 220–2.
⁴⁷ Ibid. vii. 131–2; *Bracton's Note Bk.* ed. Maitland, ii. 500.
⁴⁸ *T.S.A.S.* 4th ser. i. 396.
⁴⁹ Eyton, vii. 132.
⁵⁰ Ibid.; J.I. 1/177 m. 3d.
⁵¹ Eyton, vii. 132–3.
⁵² *Feud. Aids*, iv. 241.
⁵³ *Cal. Inq. p.m.* x, p. 111.
⁵⁴ *V.C.H. Salop.* i. 325.
⁵⁵ Ibid.
⁵⁶ Eyton, vii. 131; ibid. vi. 110; *Rot. Cur. Reg.* (Rec. Com.), ii. 166, 187; *T.S.A.S.* 2nd ser. xi. 246.
⁵⁷ Eyton, vii. 131. He was living c. 1165–1203: ibid. 50–2.

⁵⁸ Ibid. 153.
⁵⁹ *Close R.* 1234–7, 101.
⁶⁰ Ibid. 101–2.
⁶¹ *Bk. of Fees*, i. 540; ibid. ii. 972.
⁶² *Close R.* 1247–51, 66.
⁶³ Ibid.
⁶⁴ *Cal. Inq. p.m.* ii, p. 364.
⁶⁵ Ibid.
⁶⁶ C.P. 25(1)/194/7/147.
⁶⁷ *Cal. Chart. R.* 1300–26, 125; *Cal. Close*, 1307–13, 139; *Cal. Fine R.* 1307–19, 37, 38; *Cal. Inq. p.m.* v, p. 107.
⁶⁸ *Cal. Chart. R.* 1300–26, 127.
⁶⁹ Ibid. 107.
⁷⁰ *Select Cases in King's Bench* (Selden Soc. lvii), p. cxxx; *Cal. Close*, 1307–13, 488.
⁷¹ C.P. 40/275 m. 291d.
⁷² *Cal. Inq. p.m.* x, p. 111.
⁷³ For pedigree see *Complete Peerage*, iii. 160–2.
⁷⁴ Ibid.; ibid. x. 498.
⁷⁵ Ibid. x. 498; ibid. xiv. 21.
⁷⁶ Ibid. xiv. 21; C 137/33/40. Wardship of John de Charlton (IV) was granted to Sir Richard Arundel in 1375: *Cal. Fine R.* 1369–77, 286.
⁷⁷ *Cal. Inq. p.m.* xiv, p. 22; *Cal. Close*, 1374–5, 124.
⁷⁸ *Cal. Close*, 1396–9, 151; C 136/98/13.
⁷⁹ *Cal. Fine R.* 1399–1405, 146.
⁸⁰ C 138/59/53.

Grey.[81] She died in 1425[82] and was succeeded by her son Henry, then a minor[83] who obtained livery of the manor in 1441[84] and died in 1450.[85] The manor then passed from father to son in the family of Grey, lords of Powys, until 1551,[86] the following being lords: Richard, 1450–66;[87] John (I), 1466–94;[88] John (II), 1494–1504;[89] Edward, 1504–51.[90] Sir Edward Grey, whose wardship was granted to Edward Knyvett in 1514,[91] obtained livery of his estates in 1525.[92] By will of 1544[93] he devised the manor for life to his mistress Jane Orwell, with remainder to his illegitimate son Edward Grey. Sir Edward Grey died in 1551[94] and for the next half-century title to his estates was in dispute between his former mistress, her husband John Herbert, and his son Edward on the one hand, and George and Thomas Vernon, with their descendants, on the other. The Vernons laid claim to the estates of Sir Edward Grey, as well as the barony of Powys, by descent from Elizabeth, alleged daughter of Margaret Tuchet by her first husband Sir Richard Grey (d. 1466).[95]

The manor seems to have been in the possession of the Vernons in the 1550s,[96] but in 1559 Jane and John Herbert and Edward Grey brought an action for recovery of the manor[97] and in the following year it was committed to Edward Grey until judgement had been given.[98] Jane and her husband held courts at Pontesbury in 1564 and 1568[99] but, although she was still living in 1596,[1] Jane appears to have relinquished her estate to her son Edward when he came of age in 1568.[2] Possession of the manor was again in dispute between 1569 and 1576,[3] and Henry and John Vernon were requiring the tenants to attorn to them in 1579.[4] In 1581, when the latter divided the Grey estates between them, Pontesbury was assigned to Henry Vernon of Stokesay,[5] who held courts there between 1589 and 1597.[6] William Leighton of Stretton, who married Joan, daughter of Edward Grey,[7] purchased the manor from Henry

Vernon in 1599,[8] and Grey released his claims in the manor to Leighton in the following year.[9] In 1602 Leighton conveyed the manor to Sir Roger Owen,[10] and it subsequently followed the descent of Condover manor.[11]

Roger, Earl of Shrewsbury, was overlord of *LONGDEN* manor in 1086,[12] but this suzerainty presumably came to an end in 1102.[13] In the 12th century the manor became *caput* of the barony of Boterell and in and after 1254 it was said to be held in chief.[14] Although rated at $\frac{1}{2}$ knight's fee in 1254,[15] it was held by serjeantry in 1274, when the tenant provided 2 serjeants, one armed with a lance and one with arrows, for war in Wales.[16] The same service is recorded until 1294[17] but in 1315 it was again stated that the manor, then rated at $\frac{1}{4}$ knight's fee, was held by knight service in chief as of the honor of Montgomery.[18]

The manor was held by the freeman Leofric before 1066,[19] but had passed to Robert Fitz Corbet by 1086.[20] The latter was still living in 1121[21] and at his death Longden passed to his daughter Alice, who married William Boterell (I) some time after 1140.[22] The manor passed in 1175 to his son William Boterell (II), who was dead by 1212.[23] The latter's son William Boterell (III) was then a minor[24] and Longden was presumably held by Aubrey, widow of William Boterell (II),[25] but her son probably took possession of the manor in 1220, when he had livery of his Cornish lands.[26] William Boterell (III) was certainly lord by 1236[27] and at his death in 1243[28] was succeeded by his brother Reynold.[29] The latter died in 1274,[30] having settled the manor on his son William in the preceding year.[31] William Boterell conveyed the manor to Robert Burnell *c.* 1282[32] and it followed the descent of Acton Burnell manor[33] until 1541, when it was purchased by Alan Hord.[34] Hord died in 1554[35] and his son Thomas sold the manor to Richard Prince in 1562.[36] It remained in the possession of

---

[81] *Cal. Fine R.* 1413–22, 399, 442.
[82] C 139/24/36.
[83] Ibid.
[84] *Cal. Close,* 1441–7, 11–12.
[85] C 139/140/30.
[86] For pedigree see *Complete Peerage,* vi. 137–43.
[87] C 139/140/30; C 140/21/35. Came of age 1458: C 139/170/42.
[88] C 140/21/35; *Cal. Inq. p.m.* Hen. VII. i, pp. 420–1. Obtained livery 1481: *Cal. Pat.* 1476–85, 233.
[89] *Cal. Inq. p.m.* Hen. VII, i, pp. 420–1; ibid. ii, pp. 484–5. Died while still a minor. Wardship was granted in 1494 to Edward Sutton, Lord Dudley, whose daughter he married: *Cal. Pat.* 1494–1509, 11; *Complete Peerage,* vi. 141.
[90] *Cal. Inq. p.m.* Hen. VII, ii, pp. 484–5; C 142/94/28.
[91] *L. & P. Hen. VIII,* i (2), p. 1400.
[92] Ibid. iv (1), p. 609.
[93] Text in M. C. Jones, *The Feudal Barons of Powys* (1868), 90.
[94] C 142/94/28.
[95] The Vernon claim is most fully discussed in M. C. Jones, op. cit. 104–13. See also *Complete Peerage,* vi. 697–9.
[96] C 1/1356/44–5; C 3/134/61; *T.S.A.S.* 2nd ser. v. 237.
[97] C 3/91/4.
[98] *Cal. Pat.* 1558–60, 366.
[99] S.P.L., Deeds 6781, 9433.
[1] *Complete Peerage,* x. 642.
[2] Ibid.
[3] S.P.L., Deeds 6782, 7086; E 132/5 f. 196.
[4] S.P.L., Deeds 9150.
[5] Ibid. 6852.
[6] Ibid. 6794, 6819; S.R.O. 665 uncat., ct. r. 1597–1600.

[7] S.P.L., Deeds 6939; *Visit. Salop. 1623* (Harl. Soc. xxix), ii. 325.
[8] S.P.L., Deeds 6786–90.
[9] Ibid. 1989, 6806–11, 6939.
[10] Ibid. 6791.
[11] See pp. 38–39.
[12] *V.C.H. Salop.* i. 326.
[13] Eyton, vii. 209–10, 220–2.
[14] *Rot. Hund.* (Rec. Com.), ii. 66.
[15] Ibid.
[16] *Cal. Inq. p.m.* ii, p. 35.
[17] *Rot. Hund.* (Rec. Com.), ii. 96; *Feud. Aids,* iv. 216; *Cal. Inq. p.m.* iii, p. 121.
[18] *Cal. Inq. p.m.* v, p. 392. cf. ibid. viii, p. 495. The serjeantry is again recorded in 1383: ibid. xv, p. 289.
[19] *V.C.H. Salop.* i. 326.
[20] Ibid.
[21] Eyton, vii. 9–10.
[22] Ibid. 157.
[23] Ibid. 160–6; *Bk. of Fees,* i. 144.
[24] Eyton, vii. 166.
[25] Ibid. 166–7.
[26] Ibid. 166.
[27] *Bk. of Fees,* i. 539–40.
[28] *Ex. e Rot. Fin.* (Rec. Com.), i. 400.
[29] Ibid.; Eyton, vii. 166.
[30] *Cal. Inq. p.m.* ii, p. 35.
[31] Ibid.
[32] *Cal. Inq. Misc.* i, p. 436; cf. *Cal. Chart. R.* 1257–1300, 262; Eyton, vii. 169.
[33] See p. 7.
[34] C.P. 40/1109 m. 10.
[35] C 142/104/109.
[36] C.P. 25(2)/200/8 Eliz. I Mich. Prince held his first court at Longden in 1562: S.P.L., MS. 393.

the Prince family[37] until 1703, the following being lords: Richard, 1562–98;[38] Francis (son), 1598–1616;[39] Mary, widow of Francis Prince and her second husband John Andrews, 1616–29;[40] Richard, brother of Francis Prince, 1629–65;[41] Philip (son), 1665–90;[42] Francis (nephew), 1690–2;[43] William (brother), 1692–1703.[44] On the death of William Prince the manor passed to Mary, daughter of his brother Francis.[45] She married John Astley, who died in 1771,[46] when the manor passed to Charles, Earl of Tankerville, son of Astley's daughter Alicia.[47] He was succeeded in 1822 by his son Charles Augustus, Earl of Tankerville,[48] who sold the manorial estate in 1825.[49] Manorial rights, which were not included in the sale, passed during the Earl's lifetime to his son Charles, Lord Ossulston, who enfranchised the sole surviving copyholder in 1852.[50] The manor court met for the last time in 1851[51] and manorial rights appear to have lapsed soon after this date. The development of the Longden Manor estate, built up after 1859 by Henry de Grey Warter, is discussed elsewhere.[52]

The manor of *OAKS* was held before the Conquest by the freeman Ernuit,[53] probably to be identified with Ernui, who then held the neighbouring manors of Wrentnall[54] and Pontesbury.[55] It had been acquired before 1086 by Robert Fitz Corbet[56] and probably descended, like Longden manor, to William Boterell (I), husband of Robert's daughter Alice. Although the tenant of Oaks manor is associated with William Boterell as a witness to a charter in the time of Henry II,[57] the Boterell overlordship is not explicitly recorded and had probably lapsed by the end of the 12th century. Some time before 1191 the manor was granted to Robert de Girros,[58] whose heir was said to be overlord in 1254.[59] Its overlordship is not again recorded until 1484 when, without any apparent justification, the manor was said to be held of Sir John Boteler, lord of Pulverbatch manor.[60]

William de Bicton, who acquired a hide in Oaks in 1199,[61] probably held the manor under Robert de Girros before 1191.[62] He was living between 1174 and 1209[63] and was probably succeeded by one Thomas de Bicton.[64] William, son of Thomas de Bicton, who is described as lord of Oaks *c.* 1250,[65] is recorded between 1247 and 1252,[66] but was dead by 1254,[67] when the manor was held by his daughters Isabel and Margery.[68] They still held the manor in 1272,[69] and the lord of Bicton was said to be overlord in 1377,[70] but by 1305 the manor had passed to Richard Burnell of Langley.[71] The latter had acquired a virgate in Oaks in 1293,[72] and his ancestor William Burnell already held lands there before 1248.[73] The manor followed the descent of Langley manor until 1377[74] when, on the death of Edward Burnell,[75] it passed to his daughter Katherine, wife of John de Stapleton, who appears as lord in 1383.[76] It presumably followed the descent of Stapleton manor in the earlier 15th century[77] but, unlike Stapleton, did not pass after 1450 to one of the descendants of the 5 daughters of John de Stapleton, for Hugh de Stapleton held the manor at his death in 1484.[78] By 1498, however, it was in the hands of Sir Thomas Leighton, lord of Stapleton manor,[79] who exchanged Oaks and other manors for that of Alberbury with Stephen Kemsey in 1500.[80] On the death of Stephen Kemsey in 1540[81] the manor passed to his son Robert,[82] who sold it to his brother Simon Kemsey in 1559.[83] The manor was purchased shortly after 1573 by Thomas Marriott.[84] The latter sold it in 1576 to Thomas Sherer,[85] whose son[86] Gerard sold it to Sir Francis Newport in 1600.[87] Newport was still lord in 1612,[88] but had sold the manor by 1617 to Sir Roger Owen.[89] It followed the descent of Condover manor[90] until 1794, when it was purchased by Henry, John, and Joseph Warter, the three sons of Henry Warter of Cruckmeole.[91] John Warter, who died in 1821, was succeeded by his son Henry Diggory Warter, who acquired Joseph's portion from the latter's grandson Henry Warter Meredith in 1831.[92] The Revd.

[37] For pedigree see S.P.L., MS. 2792, pp. 487–9; Owen and Blakeway, *Hist. Shrewsbury*, ii. 140; *T.S.A.S.* 4th ser. viii. 122–32.
[38] C 142/252/41.
[39] Ibid.; C 142/374/79.
[40] Said to be lords in 1629: S.R.O. 665 uncat., Longden ct. r. 1629.
[41] C 142/374/79; S.P.L., MS. 2792, p. 488.
[42] S.P.L., MS. 392 (ct. r. 1668).
[43] Ibid. (ct. r. 1690–1); Owen and Blakeway, *Hist. Shrewsbury*, ii. 140.
[44] S.P.L., MS. 2792, p. 489.
[45] Ibid. MS. 392 (ct. r. 1704).
[46] Ibid. MS. 2794, p. 131.
[47] Ibid.; *Complete Peerage*, xii (1), 634–5; *T.S.A.S.* 4th ser. viii. 131.
[48] *Complete Peerage*, xii (1), 635.
[49] Longden manor title-deeds, *penes* Mrs. A. N. Fielden.
[50] Ibid.
[51] S.P.L., MS. 392.
[52] See p. 271.
[53] *V.C.H. Salop.* i. 326.
[54] Ibid. 341.
[55] Ibid. 325.
[56] Ibid. 326.
[57] Eyton, vi. 50.
[58] Ibid. 78.
[59] *Rot. Hund.* (Rec. Com.), ii. 62.
[60] C 141/2/17; C 142/63/41.
[61] *T.S.A.S.* 2nd ser. x. 311.
[62] He was probably farmer of the manor in 1194, when it was still in the hands of the Crown after the death of Robert de Girros: *Pipe R.* 1194 (P.R.S. N.S. v), 5.

[63] Eyton, ii. 66 n.; ibid. vi. 74, 106, 172; ibid. x. 164.
[64] S.P.L., Deeds 10597.
[65] Ibid. 10597, 10599.
[66] Eyton, x. 164–5.
[67] *Rot. Hund.* (Rec. Com.), ii. 62.
[68] Ibid.; Eyton, vi. 168.
[69] Eyton, vi. 168.
[70] *Cal. Inq. p.m.* xiv, p. 304.
[71] S.P.L., Deeds 10600.
[72] Eyton, vi. 168.
[73] S.P.L., Deeds 10599.
[74] See p. 143.
[75] *Cal. Inq. p.m.* xiv, p. 305.
[76] S.P.L., Deeds 10609.
[77] See p. 164.
[78] D 141/2/17; S.R.O. 665 uncat., deeds, 1478–84.
[79] S.P.L., Deeds 2600.
[80] Loton Hall MSS., exchange, 1500.
[81] C 142/63/41.
[82] Ibid.
[83] S.P.L., Deeds 10613–14, 10651 C.P. 25(2)/200/Eliz. I Hil.
[84] S.P.L., Deeds 10615–16, 10652–4.
[85] Ibid. 10616; C.P. 25(2)/200/18 Eliz. I Mich.
[86] *T.S.A.S.* liv. 35.
[87] C.P. 25(2)/203/42 & 43 Eliz. I Mich.
[88] S.P.L., Deeds 10617.
[89] C 142/374/86.
[90] See p. 38.
[91] Oaks manor title-deeds, *penes* Mrs. A. N. Fielden, Longden Manor. For pedigree see S.P.L., MS. 4647, p. 57; Burke, *Land. Gent.* (1952), pp. 2649–51.
[92] Oaks manor title-deeds.

John Wood Warter, brother of Henry Diggory Warter, acquired his great-uncle Henry's share of the estate *c.* 1834, but conveyed it in 1854 to his nephew Henry de Grey Warter, son of Henry Diggory Warter, who had thus reunited the manor.[93] Henry de Grey Warter died in 1884, having devised Oaks manor, with his Longden estate, for life to his daughter Mary Eliza Tatham, who assumed the name of Warter in the following year.[94] On her death in 1897 the estate passed to her son Henry de Grey Warter Tatham Warter,[95] who sold Longden and Oaks to William Swire in 1905.[96] Swire died in 1942 and in 1953 his widow Mrs. J. L. E. Swire sold the estate to the National Provincial Bank, who sold it to the Church Commissioners in 1956.[97] It has since been dispersed by sale.

Oaks Hall[98] was sold in 1658 by the lord of the manor to Thomas Pagett, who conveyed it to John Wood in 1682. The latter's descendant Abigail, wife of William Smith, sold the Hall in 1773 to Dr. Pryce Owen. Thomas Jones sold it in 1818 to John Whitehurst, whose family were owners until it was reunited with the manorial estate in 1911. The Hall, an isolated house some 1,050 yards north of the hamlet of Oaks, was probably built shortly before 1570 by Simon Kemsey.[99] The house has not been occupied by the lord of the manor since 1600.[1] It was no more than a farm-house in the 19th century[2] and is now occupied as two cottages. It is an H-shaped house of 2 stories. Its walls are rough-cast and it now contains few original features. In 1600 it comprised, on the ground floor, a hall, parlour, kitchen, and study.[3] Mention of a gallery[4] suggests that the house may then have had a screens passage at the lower end of the hall, probably on the line of the present door on the south-west front. The hall and parlour contained panelling in 1600, as did the chambers over,[5] but this is said to have been removed in the later 19th century.[6]

OTHER ESTATES. The 2 hides in Asterley which were held of Pontesbury church in 1254[7] can probably be identified with the 1½ hide in Pontesbury manor said to be quit of geld in 1086.[8] The pattern of landownership in this township was already complex in 1254, when half the estate was held by Robert Wyscart and the other half by 10 freeholders.[9] There appear to have been some 6 freeholders here in the later Middle Ages. Two of these small freeholds passed in the 17th century into the Boycott estate of the Nicholls family, and a third passed to the

Olivers of Polmere in the 18th century, but they normally formed outlying portions of the estates of non-resident owners.

William de Lake, one of the 3 freeholders recorded in Asterley in the later 13th century,[10] conveyed a half virgate here to William de Acton in 1278.[11] This property may have passed to William Banaster by marriage with Joan de Acton,[12] for his descendant William Banaster was said to be lord of Asterley in 1316.[13] Haughmond Abbey, which appears to have obtained some interest in the Banaster estate from Richard Banaster, quitclaimed it to his son John in 1426.[14] By 1441 it had passed to Robert Banaster, who then settled it on himself and his wife Alice, with remainder to his son Thomas.[15] The latter can probably be identified with the Thomas Banaster *alias* Lingen, on whom the estate was settled in 1457.[16] His widow Isette, who later married Thomas Longford, was confirmed in possession in 1480,[17] and was still living in the early 16th century, when she conveyed her interest to William Lingen.[18] The Banaster estate was, however, by this date in the possession of Richard Nicholls and John Mansell, who claimed to have acquired it from William Lingen's father John.[19] They presumably sold it to John Tibby, who was associated with them in the lawsuit which they brought to disprove William Lingen's title.[20] John Tibby was still a landowner here in 1546,[21] but the descent of his freehold, not to be confused with that of his kinsmen and contemporary Thomas Tibby, is obscure. It is probably represented by the half messuage, late of Richard Tibby, settled on Richard Ridge at his marriage to Eleanor Weaver in 1647,[22] and sold by Ridge to Thomas Nicholls of Boycott in 1658.[23]

An estate at Asterley held by the Corbets of Leigh is first recorded in 1381, at the death of Sir Roger Corbet.[24] This was held by William Corbet in 1562,[25] and in 1627 by his great-grandson, Pelham Corbet,[26] who appears to have sold it to Richard Nicholls of Asterley in 1656.[27] Richard, son of Richard Nicholls, sold the estate to Rowland Nicholls in 1675[28] and, like the Banaster freehold, it was subsequently part of the Boycott estate.

A small estate held at Asterley by Haughmond Abbey at the Dissolution[29] appears to have been acquired from the Skirmston family under the terms of a settlement of 1397.[30] In 1544 this was granted by the Crown to John Warner,[31] who immediately sold it to Thomas Kerry.[32] The latter acquired

93 Ibid.
94 Ibid.
95 Burke, *Land. Gent.* (1952), p. 2650.
96 Longden manor title-deeds, *penes* Messrs. Eland, Hore, Patersons, solicitors, Lincoln's Inn Fields.
97 Ibid.
98 Descent based in Bodl. MS. Blakeway 3, f. 104, and notes *penes* Mrs. A. N. Fielden, Longden Manor.
99 S.R.O. 665 uncat., lease, 1570.
1 Ibid. lease, 1600.
2 Ibid. 437/5; ibid. 785/181.
3 Ibid. 665 uncat., lease, 1600.
4 Ibid.
5 Ibid.
6 Local inf.
7 *Rot. Hund.* (Rec. Com.), ii. 66.
8 *V.C.H. Salop.* i. 325.
9 *Rot. Hund.* (Rec. Com.), ii. 66.
10 Eyton, vii. 143.
11 Ibid.
12 S.P.L., MS. 2789, p. 150.

13 *Feud. Aids*, iv. 235.
14 S.P.L., Haughmond Cart. f. 24.
15 Ibid. ff. 24–24ᵛ.
16 Req. 2/4/62.
17 Ibid.
18 Ibid.
19 Ibid.
20 Ibid.; E 179/166/132.
21 E 179/166/189.
22 S.P.L., Deeds 14074.
23 Ibid. 14080–1.
24 C 136/78/16.
25 C.P. 25(2)/200/4 Eliz. I Hil.
26 S.R.O. 322 uncat., rental, 1627.
27 S.P.L., Deeds 14079.
28 Ibid. 14089.
29 S.C. 6/Hen. VIII/3009 m. 49d.
30 S.P.L., Haughmond Cart. f. 23ᵛ. The abbey was in possession by 1412: ibid. f. 24.
31 *L. & P. Hen. VIII*, xix (1), p. 618.
32 Ibid. p. 639.

another Asterley freehold, held since the later 15th century by the Saintpierre family, c. 1566.[33] The descent of this estate cannot be traced after the death of George Kerry in 1613.[34]

Thomas Tibby, who held lands in Asterley in 1546,[35] was said at his death in 1594 to hold one bovate of land here of the heirs of Richard de Horton.[36] Henry Smith of Yockleton, the overlord of this freehold in 1606,[37] sold his interest to the lord of Pontesbury manor in 1609.[38] Thomas, son of Thomas Tibby, held 30 a. in Asterley at his death in 1611,[39] but after the death of his son Thomas while still a minor in 1613 the freehold passed to the latter's three sisters[40] and its subsequent history is not known.

William Burley, who owned a messuage in Asterley in 1723,[41] was a member of a family long resident in the village,[42] but his ancestors appear to have been leaseholders under the Corbets of Leigh.[43] His property was acquired by John Oliver in 1756[44] and was held by a Mrs. Oliver in 1797, when it comprised 125 a.[45]

The largest freehold estate in Asterley during the 19th century was that of the Gardner family, who also owned coal mines in the township.[46] This had grown from 53 a. in 1797[47] to 183 a. in 1842,[48] and amounted to 336 a. when dispersed by sale in 1912.[49]

Philip de Stapleton acquired a freehold estate at Boycott in the later 12th century, in right of his wife Emma,[50] for a lawsuit concerning it was brought by Emma against the lord of Pontesbury manor, 1200–3.[51] The estate was presumably held by the descendants of Philip de Stapleton during the 13th century, for the whole vill of Boycott was in the hands of Robert de Stapleton in 1321,[52] but by 1374 it had been merged with the manor of Pontesbury.[53] Although held on a life-lease by Richard Wystanton in 1421,[54] the estate later seems to have been accounted part of the copyhold lands of the manor. Richard Lake, whose ancestors had been resident in the neighbouring hamlet of Asterley since the early 14th century[55] and are first recorded at Boycott in 1539,[56] was among the copyholders of Pontesbury manor who, in 1615, were granted their lands in socage.[57] His property at Boycott,

which then amounted to 110 a.,[58] was purchased in 1621 by Thomas Nicholls,[59] who added Malehurst to the estate in 1655.[60] Orlando, grandson of Thomas Nicholls,[61] sold Boycott and Malehurst c. 1693 to William Boycott,[62] whose descendants[63] retained the estate until 1921, the following being owners: William, c. 1693–1707; Francis (son), 1707–43;[64] William (brother), 1743–62; William (nephew), 1762–5;[65] Thomas (brother), 1765–98; Thomas (son), 1798–1856; Emma (daughter), 1856–86; Cathcart Wight-Boycott (nephew), 1886–91; Thomas (son), 1891–1916; Anne (widow) 1916–21. The estate, which also included Poulton and Winsley in Westbury parish, amounted to 631 a. in 1799,[66] but some 300 a. were then sold,[67] and Thomas Boycott owned only 240 a. in the parish in 1842.[68] The remainder was sold in 1921.[69]

The reputed manor of Malehurst, in origin an under-tenancy of Pontesbury manor[70] probably created in the 12th century, was held by Richard Corbet of Malehurst in 1254, when it was assessed at half a hide.[71] Soon after this date it appears to have passed to a family who took their name from the hamlet. Isabel de Malehurst was the highest assessed of the inhabitants of Pontesbury in the taxation of 1327,[72] and in 1374 Thomas de Malehurst held a carucate of land here.[73] The estate is first described as a manor in 1406, when Thomas's widow Margaret recovered it against one William Malehurst.[74] The family is last recorded in the early 16th century, when Thomas Malehurst, probably great-grandson of the above Thomas, claimed the title-deeds of Malehurst Hall,[75] but the estate seems to have passed by 1450 to the Burley family.[76] Hugh Burley obtained a lease of the adjacent Monkhalst Meadow in Minsterley in 1535,[77] and in 1567 Malehurst was settled on Thomas Burley, grandson of Hugh.[78] Thomas died in 1603[79] and his son Thomas in 1614,[80] when the estate passed to the latter's son Roger, then a minor.[81] On Roger's death in 1636[82] it descended to his infant daughter Abigail, who sold it to Thomas Nicholls of Boycott in 1655.[83]

Ancient freeholds at Little Hanwood, Moat Hall, Panson, and Woodhall probably developed from

[33] C 1/679/34; C 3/157/22; C 3/173/2; Req. 2/74/38; Req. 2/210/62.
[34] C 142/337/97.
[35] E 179/166/189; S.P.L., Deeds 3653.
[36] C 142/242/37(1); C 142/263/62.
[37] C 142/291/18.
[38] S.P.L., Deeds 6812.
[39] C 142/320/55.
[40] C 142/338/66.
[41] S.P.L., Deeds 14544.
[42] E 179/166/132.
[43] S.R.O. 322 uncat., rental, 1627.
[44] S.P.L., Deeds 14544.
[45] S.P.L., MS. 2364.
[46] See p. 280.
[47] S.P.L., MS. 2364.
[48] S.R.O. 437/5; ibid. 785/181.
[49] Title-deeds of Church Farm, Asterley, penes Messrs. J. C. H. Bowdler and Son, solicitors, Shrewsbury.
[50] Eyton, vi. 109–10; Rot. Cur. Reg. (Rec. Com.), ii. 166.
[51] Ibid.; T.S.A.S. 2nd ser. xi. 246.
[52] Cat. Anct. D. v, A13599.
[53] C 135/237/1.
[54] C 138/59/53.
[55] T.S.A.S. 2nd ser. x. 137. For pedigree see B. Botfield, Stemmata Botevilliana (1858), 141.
[56] S.R.O. 665 uncat., Pontesbury ct. r. 1539.
[57] S.P.L., Deeds 6838, 14050.
[58] Ibid.
[59] Ibid. 14055–6.
[60] Ibid. 14309.
[61] S.P.L., C 57 v.f. (pedigree by the Revd. D. Maclean, 1952).
[62] S.P.L., Deeds 14316, 14534.
[63] For pedigree see S.P.L., MS. 2794, pp. 344–7; Burke, Land. Gent. (1952), p. 243.
[64] S.P.L., Deeds 13809.
[65] Ibid. 14547.
[66] Ibid. 13778.
[67] Ibid.
[68] S.R.O. 437/5; ibid. 785/181.
[69] Boycott Hall title-deeds, penes Midland Bank, Bishop's Castle.
[70] Rot. Hund. (Rec. Com.), ii. 66.
[71] Ibid.
[72] T.S.A.S. 2nd ser. x. 138.
[73] C 135/237/1.
[74] Bodl. MS. Blakeway 3, f. 104.
[75] C 1/656/26.
[76] S.P.L., MS. 2788, p. 376.
[77] S.P.L., Deeds 13785.
[78] C.P. 25(2)/200/9 Eliz. I Mich.
[79] S.P.L., MS. 2788, p. 376.
[80] C 142/344/118.
[81] Ibid.
[82] S.P.L., MS. 2788, p. 376.
[83] S.P.L., Deeds 14309.

12th-century under-tenancies of the barony of Longden, for their owners owed suit at Longden manor court in the 15th and 16th centuries.[84] In the later 12th century Reynold de Pontesbury granted Little Hanwood to his brother Adam,[85] whose father Elmund de Tucfor had held a half virgate at Woodhouse.[86] Distil de Hanwood, to whom a rent of 12d. was reserved in the grant of Little Hanwood,[87] may have been the original tenant, both of Little Hanwood and Woodhouse, under the Boterells of Longden. Distil's son Matthew granted Elmund's estate at Woodhouse to the latter's son Adam.[88] Adam, son of Elmund, subsequently granted a half virgate at Woodhouse to Parnel, daughter of Hugh de Marsh,[89] but must have held other lands here, for a virgate at Woodhouse passed to Robert Fitz Sewel on his marriage with Adam's daughter Emma.[90]

The later Moat Hall, Woodhall, and Woodhouse estates appear to be in origin portions of the Woodhouse estate of Robert Fitz Sewel, which was broken up in the earlier 13th century. A quarter virgate assigned to David, son of Henry de Woodhouse, in 1221,[91] passed soon afterwards to Thomas de Leton,[92] then to the latter's sister Gillian,[93] who granted it to William de Stapleton.[94] Some time after 1256 William de Stapleton acquired a further quarter virgate, previously held by John de Arundel[95] and presumably another part of the Fitz Sewel estate. He was dead by 1292, when his widow Isabel was sued for dower by the widow of John, son of John de Arundel.[96] The Stapletons are not recorded here after this date and their estate appears to have passed to the Berrington family. Richard de Berrington already held land in Longden manor in 1292,[97] but the family's association with the estate which afterwards became known as Moat Hall[98] cannot be traced earlier than 1367, when lands at Woodhouse were acquired by Thomas de Berrington from Thomas le Skinner of Longden.[99] Thomas settled the estate in 1398 on his son William,[1] who was still living in 1417[2] but had been succeeded by Robert Berrington before 1429.[3] Robert's widow Joan held the estate in dower between 1461 and 1472,[4] and their son Thomas between 1475 and 1483.[5] By 1492 it had passed to the latter's son John,[6] who may have enlarged the

property by his marriage to Elizabeth, one of the daughters and heirs of William Skirmston of Woodhouse.[7] The estate passed from father to son in the Berrington family[8] until 1811, the following being owners: John, recorded 1492–9; Thomas, c. 1527–55; Roger c. 1557–96; Thomas, 1596–1640; William, 1640–66;[9] Thomas, 1666–1719; William, 1719–66; Thomas, 1766–80; William, 1780–90; Thomas, 1790–1811. On the death of Thomas Berrington in 1811[10] the estate passed to his uncle Philip Berrington of Stock (Essex), who died in 1818,[11] having devised the Moat Hall estate to John Berington of Winsley (Worcs.), a distant relative by marriage.[12] Until 1945 it was held by the following members of this family:[13] John, 1818–52; John (son) 1852–92; Charles Michael (cousin), 1892–7; William (son), 1897–1940; Mr. W. J. C. Berington (son), 1940–5. In 1945 Moat Hall Farm was sold to the tenant Mr. J. W. Davies.[14] The latter's brother Mr. G. T. Davies, who then purchased Panson Farm, has owned both farms since 1955.[15]

A further portion of the estate of Robert Fitz Sewel is probably represented by the quarter virgate at Woodhouse held by Thomas le Hore in right of his wife Alice.[16] In 1286 this was granted to Richard de la Halle.[17] Though not later recorded here, the de la Halle family appear in the neighbouring manor of Oaks, where Richard's widow Isabel and his son John acquired small freeholds between 1314 and 1323.[18] These properties were held in 1372 by John de Wodehalle,[19] probably grandson of John de la Halle, but had passed to Thomas Skirmston by 1401.[20] The latter appears as a free tenant in Longden manor, in respect of his estate at Woodhall, between 1429 and 1461,[21] and had been succeeded before 1480 by William Skirmston,[22] at whose death in 1484[23] his estate passed to his daughters Elizabeth and Margaret.[24] The former married John Berrington of Moat Hall,[25] but the greater part of the Skirmston estate at Oaks and Woodhall fell to Margaret Skirmston of Hill House, otherwise Woodhouse,[26] who was a suitor at Longden manor court between 1495 and 1527.[27] Margaret seems to have married Thomas Bromley, whose daughter Margaret had carried Woodhall and Hill House to her husband Richard Newport by 1562.[28] The latter died in 1570,[29] and the estate was held in

[84] S.P.L., MS. 393.
[85] Bodl. MS. Gough Salop. 13, p. 9; Eyton, vii. 135.
[86] Bodl. MS. Gough Salop. 13, p. 7; Eyton, vii. 136.
[87] Bodl. MS. Gough Salop. 13, p. 9.
[88] Ibid. p. 7.
[89] Ibid.
[90] Eyton, vii. 136; T.S.A.S. 3rd ser. vi. 169.
[91] T.S.A.S. 3rd ser. vi. 169.
[92] Bodl. MS. Gough Salop. 13, p. 8.
[93] Eyton, vii. 136.
[94] Ibid.
[95] Ibid.; Bodl. MS. Gough Salop. 13, p. 7.
[96] Eyton, iv. 354; ibid. vii. 137.
[97] S.P.L., MS. 393.
[98] Known as the manor of Woodhouse, 1594: C.P. 25(2)/203/36 Eliz. I East. Known as Moat Hall since 1600: C.P. 25(2)/203/42 Eliz. I East.
[99] Cal. Close, 1364–8, 366–7.
[1] Bodl. MS. Gough Salop. 13, p. 8.
[2] S.P.L., Deeds 2490.
[3] S.P.L., MS. 393.
[4] Ibid.
[5] Ibid.
[6] Ibid.
[7] S.P.L., Deeds 2600.
[8] For pedigree see S.P.L., MS. 2794, pp. 463–8; H. E.

Forrest, Some Old Shropshire Houses (Shrewsbury, 1924), 183–6.
[9] His estate was sequestered in 1647: Cal. Cttee. for Compounding, iv. 2538.
[10] H. E. Forrest, op. cit. 185.
[11] Ibid.
[12] Burke, Land. Gent. (1952), p. 164.
[13] For pedigree see ibid. 163–4; Moat Hall title-deeds, penes The Agricultural Mortgage Corporation.
[14] Moat Hall title-deeds.
[15] Ibid.
[16] Eyton, vii. 137.
[17] Ibid.
[18] S.P.L., Deeds 10601–3.
[19] Ibid. 10604.
[20] Ibid. 2600.
[21] S.P.L., MS. 393.
[22] Ibid.
[23] S.P.L., Deeds 2600.
[24] Ibid.
[25] Ibid.
[26] S.P.L., MS. 393 (ct. r. 1526); S.R.O. 171 uncat., deeds, 1576, 1612.
[27] S.P.L., MS. 393.
[28] Ibid.; ibid., MS. 2791, p. 406.
[29] Ibid., MS. 2791, p. 406.

dower by his widow until her death in 1598,[30] when it passed to their son Francis, who sold it to William Wolley in 1612.[31] The estate, enlarged by the purchase of Shorthill in 1641,[32] was held by the descendants of William Wolley until 1824,[33] the following being owners: William, 1612–28; Thomas (grandson), 1628–65; Thomas (son), 1665–1725; Thomas (son), 1725–31; Richard (son), 1731–63; Thomas (son), 1763–99. It was then held by Judith, widow of the last, until her death in 1824. Following lawsuits in 1825 and 1826[34] to determine who was next of kin, the estate passed to Mary, wife of Edward Oldnall, the devisee of Thomas Wolley's second cousin, Frances Wolley.[35] In the later 19th century Woodhall was owned by Clive Phillipps-Wolley,[36] whose executors conveyed the estate to Samuel Atherton in 1917.[37] The latter sold it to the present owner, Mr. W. Savage, in 1950.[38]

Although the moat at Panson suggests that this was already the homestead of a freehold estate in the 12th or early 13th century, it is not recorded before the 15th century, when it was a reputed manor.[39] It was held by Hugh Wytheford in 1429,[40] by John Wytheford from 1461 until his death in 1478,[41] and by Thomas Wytheford between 1492 and 1502.[42] In 1520 it was conveyed by John Wytheford to John Packington,[43] who appears to have sold it in 1527.[44] It was acquired in 1537 by Thomas Hosier,[45] whose son Edward settled it on his mother Alice for life in 1546.[46] Edward Hosier held the estate in 1562,[47] but by 1576 it had passed to John Draycott.[48] In 1621 it was purchased by Thomas Berrington,[49] and was subsequently part of the Moat Hall estate.

In 1299 Vivian de Rossall granted a carucate at Woodhouse to Nicholas Dod.[50] This estate cannot be traced at a later date, but John Dod of Woodhouse, whose bullocks were stolen by Welshmen in 1411,[51] may have been a descendant of Nicholas. Sir Richard Mytton, probably a Mytton of Shipton,[52] held rents at Woodhouse at his death in 1437,[53] and in 1621 Thomas Pigott held a 30-acre freehold in Little Hanwood of Edward Onslow.[54] The latter's ancestors appear as free tenants of Longden manor in the 15th and 16th centuries, but this was in respect of 4 virgates at Onslow.[55]

The only other considerable freehold estate within Longden manor was that of the Adams family. The family is thought to have originated in Kent,[56] the first member recorded in Longden being John Adams, who in 1429 obtained a lease of the lord's enclosed wood there.[57] The nucleus of the Adams estate was the manor-house and a portion of the demesne granted to John Adams in 1463[58] and previously held by his father William.[59] John Adams was surveyor-general to Francis, Lord Lovell, the lord of Longden manor, in 1482.[60] His grandson Thomas owed an annual rent of £3 6s. 8d. for his freehold estate at his death in 1527,[61] when he also held 5 messuages and lands by copyhold tenure.[62] His copyhold estate descended to his younger son Richard,[63] but had passed by 1548 to Peter Adams,[64] whose son John claimed 16 nokes ($\frac{1}{4}$ virgates) of copyhold land in 1563,[65] and it remained with Peter's descendants until 1724, when it was acquired by the lord of the manor.[66] The freehold passed in 1527 to Thomas Adams's elder son William,[67] and descended from father to son in this branch of the family[68] until 1728. On the death of Richard Adams in 1728, the estate passed to his sister Elizabeth and her husband William Ashwood[69] and was held successively by William Ashwood, 1728–39, John Ashwood (son), 1739–54, and Thomas Ashwood (son), 1754–67.[70] Dorothy, sister and heir of Thomas Ashwood, married Sir Henry Hawley in 1771,[71] and the estate passed from father to son[72] until 1859, the following being owners: Henry Hawley, 1771–1826; Henry Hawley, 1826–31, Joseph Henry Hawley, 1831–59. It was bought in 1859 by Henry de Grey Warter and has subsequently followed the descent of Oaks manor. The estate, which does not appear to have been significantly enlarged in the 18th and early 19th centuries, included in 1593 3 houses in Longden in addition to the manor-house, the 2 mills at Pontesford, and 5 copyhold messuages and lands in Pontesbury manor.[73] The Pontesbury copyholds were enfranchised in 1615,[74] and in 1659 William Adams held 7 messuages in Longden and 6 in Pontesbury at his marriage to Judith Boycott.[75] The estate amounted to 511 a. in 1797, of which some 450 a. lay in Longden township.[76] The Hawleys did not take advantage of the opportunity offered by the sale of the manorial estate in 1826 of enlarging their Longden property, apart from buying back Longden Coppice—part of the ancient Adams free-

[30] S.P.L., MS. 2791, p. 406; S.R.O. 171 uncat., deed, 1579.
[31] S.R.O. 171 uncat., deed, 1612.
[32] Ibid. deed, 1641.
[33] For pedigree see *T.S.A.S.* 4th ser. iv. 252–7, 262–3.
[34] Ibid. 255–7.
[35] Ibid.   [36] Ibid.
[37] Ex inf. Mr. W. Savage, Woodhall.
[38] Woodhall title-deeds, *penes* National Provincial Bank, Shrewsbury.
[39] S.P.L., MS. 393 (ct. r. 1478).
[40] Ibid. (ct. r. 1429).
[41] Ibid. (ct. r. 1461–8).
[42] Ibid. (ct. r. 1492–1502).
[43] C.P. 25(2)/35/232/12 Hen. VIII Trin.
[44] C.P. 25(2)/35/232/18 Hen. VIII Hil.
[45] C.P. 25(2)/35/233/29 Hen. VIII Mich.
[46] Bodl. MS. Gough Salop. 13, p. 11.
[47] S.P.L., MS. 393.
[48] S.R.O. 171 uncat., deed, 1576.
[49] Bodl. MS. Gough Salop. 13, p. 9.
[50] Eyton, vii. 137.
[51] *Salop. Peace Roll, 1404–14,* 104.
[52] S.P.L., MS. 2791, pp. 501–2.
[53] C 139/80/29.

[54] C 142/388/1.
[55] S.P.L., MS. 393.
[56] Ibid. MS. 2794, p. 105.
[57] Ibid. MS. 393 (ct. r. 1429).
[58] Ibid. (ct. r. 1534).
[59] Ibid.
[60] Ibid. (ct. r. 1482).
[61] Ibid. (ct. r. 1527).
[62] Ibid.
[63] Ibid.
[64] Ibid. (ct. r. 1548).
[65] Ibid. (ct. r. 1563).
[66] Ibid. MS. 392 (ct. r. 1667, 1690, 1720, 1724).
[67] Ibid. MS. 393 (ct. r. 1527).
[68] For pedigree see ibid. MS. 2794, pp. 105–7.
[69] Ibid.; N.L.W., Ness Strange 163.
[70] S.P.L., MS. 4645, p. 181.
[71] Ibid.; S.R.O. 437/13, deed, 1799.
[72] For pedigree see S.P.L., MS. 4645, p. 181; Burke, *Peerage* (1959), p. 1097; Longden manor title-deeds, *penes* Mrs. A. N. Fielden, Longden Manor.
[73] C 142/267/68; C 142/432/132.
[74] S.P.L., Deeds 6824.
[75] Ibid. 14477–8.
[76] S.P.L., MS. 2364.

hold which had been sold in 1719.[77] Joseph Hawley held 600 a. in Longden in 1841, including Longden Hall, Woodhouse Farm, and Coppice Farm.[78]

The Hawley estate, with Oaks Manor, formed the basis of the large estate built up in the two decades after 1859 by Henry de Grey Warter. Members of the Warter family were already resident in the parish in 1308, when Adam le Wartoner held a half virgate in Cruckmeole[79]—a property which seems to have remained in the possession of the family until the present century.[80] For centuries the Warters remained small copyholders in Ford manor. In 1601 John Warter held a virgate at Cruckmeole and Thomas Warter 3 nokes at Newnham,[81] but in the later 17th century they began the slow accumulation of additional lands, which had by 1797 turned the family into one of the larger landowners in the parish. A messuage and lands at Lea and Sibberscott were bought in 1697 by John Warter,[82] whose son Henry bought the 5-noke Rutter copyhold at Cruckmeole in 1723[83] and acquired some 100 a. in Lea, Plealey, and Sibberscott from the Barrett family between 1731 and 1749.[84] Henry Warter died in 1763,[85] having settled the ancestral holding at Cruckmeole on his widow Mary,[86] who was succeeded at her death in 1790 by his youngest son John.[87] The estates at Lea and Sibberscott were divided between Henry's two elder sons Henry and Joseph in 1764,[88] but the latter acquired his brother's moiety in 1802.[89] On Joseph's death in 1812 this part of the estate passed to his grandson Henry Warter,[90] who assumed the additional name of Meredith in 1823.[91] The latter owned 167 a. at Lea and Sibberscott in 1842.[92] The Cruckmeole estate, amounting to 215 a. in 1840,[93] was then held by Henry Diggory Warter,[94] son of John Warter (d. 1821),[95] and at his death in 1853 passed to his youngest son, the Revd. Edward Warter.[96]

Henry de Grey Warter, second son of Henry Diggory Warter, thus inherited no part of the family's copyhold estate in Ford manor from his father in 1853. He had, however, inherited a part of Oaks manor from his grandfather in 1821[97] and was in sole possession of this estate in 1842, when it contained 563 a.[98] In addition to the Hawley estate he purchased some 350 a. in Longden, formerly in the manorial estate, between 1863 and 1874, and bought in two small copyholds in 1867 and 1872.[99] He built Longden Manor between 1863 and 1866[1] and at his death in 1884 was in possession of 2,292 a. in Longden, Oaks, Plealey, and Halston.[2] He had inherited the ancestral family holding at Cruckmeole on the death of his uncle the Revd. Edward Warter in 1878,[3] but in 1884 this passed to Henry's nephew Lt. Col. Henry de Grey Warter and was not subsequently held with the Longden Manor estate.[4] The latter followed the descent of Oaks Manor after 1884.[5] Outlying portions of the estate were sold c. 1890,[6] and it amounted to 1,618 a. when purchased by William Swire in 1905.[7] The Swire family acquired Oaks Hall in 1911,[8] and Cross House, Longden, in 1936.[9]

ECONOMIC HISTORY. The greater part of the parish lay within the manors of Pontesbury, Ford, Longden, and Oaks. Recorded demesnes were small, except in Pontesbury manor, and by the 15th century at least tenure was by copyhold of inheritance. An agreement of 1608 ended a long period of disputes over forms of tenure between the tenants of Ford manor and their lords and thereafter copyholders here enjoyed most of the attributes of freehold tenure.[10] The copyholders of Pontesbury manor were all enfranchised in 1615.[11] By contrast, the lords of Longden and Oaks were buying in numbers of copyholds and freeholds in the course of the 16th century. The extensive manorial estates thus created survived until the 19th century. The principal ancient freeholds originated as 12th-century fiefs of the manors of Pontesbury and Longden and continued with little change in size until the present century.

The manor of Pontesbury was assessed at $4\frac{1}{2}$ hides in 1086, when its value was said to have fallen from £8 to £6 since before the Conquest.[12] A further $1\frac{1}{2}$ hide, then exempt from geld,[13] can probably be identified with the estate at Asterley held by the church of Pontesbury in 1254.[14] The manor seems to have included lands outside the parish in 1086, since the reduction in its assessment to 2 hides in 1254[15] cannot be otherwise accounted for. The manor of Malehurst, assessed at a $\frac{1}{2}$ hide in 1254,[16] was detached from Pontesbury manor in the course of the 12th century,[17] but Farley manor, assessed at one hide in 1086,[18] was later merged with that of Pontesbury. In the later Middle Ages Pontesbury manor included the townships of Pontesbury, Boycott, Farley, Halston, and Hinton,[19] thus forming a compact territorial unit in the valley of the Rea. It was valued at £18 14s. 8d. in 1286[20] and at only £3 12s.

[77] Longden manor title-deeds.
[78] Heref. Dioc. Regy., Longden tithe appt.
[79] C 134/5/1.
[80] Burke, Land. Gent. (1952), pp. 2649–51.
[81] S.P.L., Deeds 12706.
[82] S.R.O. 169/1 (Ford ct. r. 1697).
[83] Ibid. 169/2 (ibid. 1723).
[84] Ibid. 169/2–3.
[85] S.P.L., MS. 4647, p. 57.
[86] S.R.O. 169/3 (Ford ct. r. 1763).
[87] Ibid. 248/1 (ibid. 1790).
[88] Ibid. 169/3 (ibid. 1764).
[89] Ibid. 248/2 (ibid. 1803).
[90] Ibid. (ibid. 1812); S.P.L., MS. 4647, p. 57.
[91] S.P.L., MS. 4647, p. 57.
[92] S.R.O. 437/4–5; ibid. 785/181–2.
[93] Ibid. 437/4; ibid. 785/182.
[94] Ibid.
[95] Burke, Land. Gent. (1952), p. 2650.
[96] Ibid.
[97] See p. 266.
[98] S.R.O. 437/5; ibid. 785/181.

[99] Longden manor title-deeds.
[1] See p. 263.
[2] Sale partics., Longden Manor c. 1890, penes Mrs. A. N. Fielden, Longden Manor.
[3] Burke, Land. Gent. (1952), p. 2650.
[4] Ibid.
[5] See p. 267.
[6] Sale partics., Longden Manor c. 1890.
[7] Longden Manor title-deeds, penes Messrs. Eland, Hore, Patersons, solicitors, Lincoln's Inn Fields.
[8] Ibid. penes Mrs. A. N. Fielden.
[9] Ibid.
[10] See p. 231.
[11] S.P.L., Deeds 6821–48, 10646–7.
[12] V.C.H. Salop. i. 325.
[13] Ibid.
[14] Rot. Hund. (Rec. Com.), ii. 66.
[15] Ibid.   [16] Ibid.
[17] See p. 268.
[18] V.C.H. Salop. i. 325.
[19] S.P.L., Deeds 6784.
[20] C 133/45/2.

in 1353.[21] The latter was clearly an under-estimate. A similar low valuation of £4 18s. 8d. was returned in 1374,[22] but this was raised to £11 18s. in the light of a revised survey made in the following year.[23]

The reduction in the value of the manor after 1286 may be accounted for by the abandonment of Pontesbury castle[24] and the consequent decline in the size and value of the demesne. The demesne was already large in 1086, when it amounted to 4 hides, on which 4 serfs were employed.[25] In 1286 it comprised 6 carucates of arable, 5 a. meadow, and 3 a. moor,[26] but by 1353 the arable area had been reduced to a single carucate of infertile land.[27] The whole had been leased by 1401[28] and in 1425 it was held on short-term leases by several tenants.[29] The greater part of the demesne arable, which presumably lay in Pontesbury township, was thus the first to be leased, and there is no evidence for its location. The remainder, however, preserved its identity in the later Middle Ages, distinct from the copyhold lands of the manor.[30] Its unusual distribution suggests that the lords of Pontesbury manor specialized in cattle-rearing in the 12th and 13th centuries. It comprised meadows called Wallymore, Stocky Meadow, and Rolles Meadow, on the banks of the Rea to the north of Pontesbury village, rough pasture at Moorwood, and an upland demesne farm at Pollardine, some miles to the south in Ratlinghope parish.[31] The township of Farley—another riverside area—was leased to 6 tenants in 1425, on terms similar to those in other demesne leases made in the same year.[32] This would suggest that the whole township was taken in hand by the lord of Pontesbury manor when he acquired Farley manor. This manor seems to have consisted largely of demesne land in 1086, when there were 3 serfs and one plough on the demesne and the only tenants were 3 bordars with one plough.[33] In 1411 24 oxen and cows were stolen by Welshmen from the tenant of Moorwood.[34] In leases of the demesne meadows in 1425, common rights of other copyholders were explicitly excluded, and Stocky Meadow was leased to the tenants of Pontesbury as a whole.[35] A group of 4 tenants, to whom two of the Farley common fields were then leased, were given licence to erect a pound there large enough to contain 40 beasts.[36] This marked emphasis on cattle-rearing among the early-15th-century tenants of the demesne probably represents a continuation of earlier practices, and was reverted to by the lord when, for a brief period in the early 17th century, he again held part of the medieval demesne in hand. In 1603 and 1604 Sir Roger Owen was rearing fatstock at Moorwood and was producing malting barley, butter, and cheese at Boycott for consumption at Condover Hall.[37]

Small purchases made by Sir Roger Owen in Pontesbury between 1604 and 1610[38] seem to have been no more than resumptions of portions of the demesne. The manorial estate, representing that part of the demesne not alienated before 1353, survived unchanged until the later 18th century, but no part was kept in hand after 1617.[39] Apart from cottages on commons at Pontesford Hill, Pontesbury Hill, and the Nills, it comprised a 125-acre farm and 7 houses in the village in 1794.[40] The farm and some of the houses were sold in 1795[41] and by 1797 the lord retained only the site of the castle, 4 houses in Pontesbury, and his rights as lord of the soil of the commons.[42]

In 1086 the 16 recorded tenants of Pontesbury manor, who included 10 villeins, held between them 5 ploughs.[43] There is little evidence for forms of tenure here before the 15th century, but it seems probable that the Pontesbury copyholders, like those of Ford manor, enjoyed a privileged position after the lords of the manor ceased to be resident in the later 13th century. Assized rents were said to produce a modest £4 5s. 4d. in 1286[44] and in surveys of the manor after 1353 the tenants are all described as free tenants.[45] A rise in rents from £8 6s. 8d. in 1375[46] to £40 in 1401[47] can be accounted for by increased income from demesne leases. A custumal drawn up at the request of the lord of the manor in 1464[48] failed to define his rights in regard to entry fines, but in other respects gave the customary tenants complete freedom to manage their own affairs in the manor court. All copyholds were of inheritance, descent to the youngest son being in use in the townships of Hinton, Halston, and Farley, and primogeniture in Pontesbury, Malehurst, and Boycott. The demesne lands were specified and all other lands were not to be liable to forfeiture by the lord, unless surrendered voluntarily by a tenant during the minority of his heir. Court procedure in matters of inheritance, surrenders, and lawsuits over copyholds was prescribed, the tenants claimed the right 'to make and ordain customs for the wealth of the lordship at all times needful'.

The decision to enfranchise the Pontesbury copyholders in 1615 brought to an end a half-century of disputes between lords of the manor and the tenants. An attempt to depress the status of the copyholders seems to have been made by the Vernons in the 1570s. A transcript of the Domesday entry for Pontesbury was obtained in 1577[49] and a transcript of the custumal of 1464 in 1579.[50] In the latter year the tenants brought an action in Chancery against the lords of the manor, alleging that they had required the tenants to attorn to them and had granted leases to make their copyhold estates void.[51]

21 C 135/124/9.
22 C 135/237/1.
23 Ibid.; *Cal. Pat.* 1374–7, 148.
24 See p. 252.
25 *V.C.H. Salop.* i. 325.
26 C 133/45/2.
27 C 135/124/9.
28 C 137/33/40.
29 S.R.O. 665 uncat., ct. r. 1425.
30 Ibid.; S.P.L., Deeds 6784.
31 Ibid.; S.R.O. 437/5; ibid. 785/181; S.P.L., Deeds 6791.
32 S.R.O. 665 uncat., ct. r. 1425.
33 *V.C.H. Salop.* i. 325.
34 *Salop. Peace Roll, 1404–14*, 104.
35 S.R.O. 665 uncat., ct. r. 1425.

36 Ibid.
37 Ibid., Condover accts. 1603; S.P.L., Deeds 7025.
38 S.P.L., MS. 300 (ct. r. 1604); S.P.L., Deeds 6813–4, 9486; S.R.O. 665 uncat., deed, 1610.
39 S.P.L., Deeds 6791; S.R.O. 665 uncat., survey of manorial estate, c. 1769.
40 S.R.O. 1011 uncat., sale partics. 1794.
41 Ibid. acct. of sales, 1795.
42 S.P.L., MS. 2364.
43 *V.C.H. Salop.* i. 325.
44 C 133/45/2.
45 C 135/114/9; C 135/237/1; *Cal. Inq. p.m.* x, p. 498.
46 C 135/237/1.
47 C 137/33/40.
48 S.P.L., Deeds 6784.
49 Ibid. 6803–4.
50 Ibid. 6784.
51 Ibid. 9150.

In 1601 William Leighton took issue with the 7 principal tenants, alleging that they held the manor court rolls, were adding portions of the demesne to their own lands, and inclosing common lands.[52] The tenants paid £200 in 1607 for licence to continue to pay the customary entry fines.[53]

There were in 1603 30 tenants in the manor, both copyhold and leasehold, whose rents produced £18 15s. 2d. a year.[54] A more thorough analysis of the tenantry made in 1614, on the eve of enfranchisement, classed 27 as 'free tenants' (i.e. copyholders), 10 as leaseholders, and 56 as inhabitants or other sub-tenants.[55] Some 1,100 a. of copyhold land were converted into socage in 1615 at the rate of 15s. an acre.[56] This covered all but one of the copyhold estates and, since only 19 persons then obtained freehold estates, some amalgamation of holdings must have taken place at this time. Only two of the freeholds thus established were of over 100 a., Richard Corbet's estate of some 300 a. in Halston and Farley being by far the largest. Seven of the estates were of one virgate (60 a.) or more, 4 were of 30–60 a., 2 of 15–30 a., and 4 of less than 15 a. The single remaining copyhold, consisting of lands at Boycott and Farley, was held by Henry Haynes,[57] the bailiff of the lord of the manor and lessee of the demesne,[58] who acquired the freehold of this estate and of part of the demesne lands in 1633 in exchange for his copyhold lands in Condover manor.[59]

Changes in the value and in the administration of Ford manor during the Middle Ages, and the subsequent history of its demesne, are discussed elsewhere.[60] As in Ford township, the half-virgate (30 a.) was in 1308 the typical holding in the Pontesbury portion of Ford manor.[61] There were then 166 tenants here, of whom at least 87 possessed holdings of this size. Only 5 holdings were larger than one virgate, but 38 were smaller than one noke.[62] In addition to the estate of Roger de Ford the manor included in 1308 a carucate of freehold land, held by one Nicholas for 21s. 8d. a year.[63] This can probably be identified with the yardland of freehold land at Cruckton held by George Hosier in 1601.[64]

The sporadic attempts made by the lords of the manor from the 14th century onwards to bring the tenants of Ford under closer control, culminating in the decree of 1608, are described elsewhere.[65] They had little effect on the development of copyhold estates, and a survey of 1601[66] shows the result of the operation, during the later Middle Ages, of a free market in land. The total number of tenants in the Pontesbury portion of the manor had fallen from 166 in 1308 to 47 by 1601, a decline in the number of tenants being particularly marked in Arscott, Cruckton, and Newnham. Ten tenants held lands in more than one township and 32 holdings

were larger than one virgate (60 a.), only 4 tenants having less than a half virgate.

From 1608 the copyholders of Ford manor held their lands, for all practical purposes, on the same terms as did the freeholders of Pontesbury manor after 1615. The estates of five persons already lay partly in Ford and partly in Pontesbury manor at this time.[67] Consequently the two classes of landowner are combined in the discussion which follows. This does not, however, include the ancient freehold estates, or Longden and Oaks manors.

By 1615 there were 62 landholders in Ford and Pontesbury manors,[68] of whom 16 possessed estates of over 100 a. (including 4 estates of over 200 a.), while a further 37 persons owned between 25 a. and 100 a. apiece. Only 9 persons appear to have owned less than 25 a. each. In 1797[69] ten estates were of over 200 a., 7 of 100–200 a., and only 13 of 25–100 a. An increase to 35 in the number of holdings of under 25 a. can be largely accounted for by the sale of the Pontesbury manorial estate in 1794 and by the industrialization of the western part of the parish. The pattern of landownership had not radically altered by 1842,[70] when there were again 17 estates of over 100 a. but only 5 persons then owned estates of 50–100 a. and the number of smaller properties had risen to 62. The area covered by estates of over 200 a. increased fourfold between the early 17th and mid-19th centuries—some 1,000 a. in 1615, 3,716 a. in 1797, and 4,678 a. in 1842.

The subsequent history of the larger early-17th-century freeholds shows a continuity of tenure similar to that found in Ford parish. The history of the estate at Boycott granted in 1615 to Richard Lake has already been discussed.[71] Enlarged in 1655 by the purchase of Malehurst, it was held by the Boycott family from c. 1693 until 1921.[72] Of the remaining estates in Ford and Pontesbury manors the four largest in 1797[73]—Harries of Cruckton (1,494 a.), Warter of Cruckmeole (732 a.), Offley of Hinton (253 a.), and Hope of Pontesbury (565 a.) —were still then held by the descendants of their early-17th-century owners.[74] The Harries and Warter estates had a continuous history stretching back to medieval times. The Warters,[75] who are first recorded among the tenants of Ford manor in 1308, are the only landowning family known to have been continuously resident in the parish from the early 14th to the early 20th century. They possessed only a modest property in Cruckmeole, Lea, and Sibberscott until three Warter brothers purchased the manor of Oaks in 1795. The greater part of Longden township was added after 1859 by Henry de Grey Warter, the builder of Longden Manor.

The Harries family,[76] by far the largest land-

[52] C 2/Eliz. I/L8/15.
[53] S.P.L., MS. 300 (ct. r. 1607).
[54] S.R.O. 665 uncat., Condover accts. 1603; S.P.L., Deeds 7025.
[55] S.P.L., MS. 300 (ct. r. 1614).
[56] S.P.L., Deeds 6821–48, 10646–7, on which what follows is based.
[57] Ibid. 6716.
[58] S.R.O. 665 uncat., deed, 1610.
[59] S.P.L., Deeds 6716, 6840.
[60] See pp. 230–1.
[61] C 134/5/1.
[62] Ibid.
[63] Ibid.
[64] S.P.L., Deeds 12706.

[65] See p. 231.
[66] S.P.L., Deeds 12706.
[67] Ibid. 6821–48, 10646–7, 12706.
[68] Ibid.
[69] S.P.L., MS. 2364.
[70] S.R.O. 437/4–5; ibid. 785/181–2.
[71] See p. 268.
[72] Ibid.
[73] S.P.L., MS. 2364.
[74] S.P.L., Deeds 12706.
[75] See p. 271.
[76] Except where otherwise stated, genealogical information on Harries family is drawn from S.P.L., Deeds 15261; S.P.L., MS. 2792, pp. 440–3; Burke, Land. Gent. (1879), p. 743; ibid. (1925), p. 989.

owners in the parish in the 18th and early 19th centuries, are first recorded as copyholders in Ford manor in the 15th century,[77] but the husbandmen Richard Her' and Stephen Heirs, recorded in the manor in 1379,[78] may have been their ancestors. In 1489 Hugh Harries possessed half a virgate in Cruckton,[79] presumably the ancestral family holding, but John Harries had acquired 3½ nokes (c. 53 a.) in Arscott by 1463.[80] John's grandson John, who was among the highest assessed to the taxation of 1542,[81] is found buying meadow land in Cruckton and a fishpool in Sascott in the following year.[82] In 1579, in what appears to have been a general consolidation of the Cruckton copyholds, John Harries was allotted Dresses Field and Little Field among other lands.[83] By 1601, when he held some 330 a. in Cruckton, Arscott, Sibberscott, and Sascott, John Harries was already owner of the largest copyhold estate in Ford manor.[84] His son Richard, who procured the enfranchisement of the estate for £204 in 1607,[85] married in 1609 into the gentle family of Smallman of Wilderhope.[86]

By the end of the 17th century some 170 a. of copyhold land had been added to the estate, principally by the purchase of the holdings of the Onslow and Polmer families in Cruckton in 1642 and 1670 respectively.[87] On the death of Thomas Harries in 1694 the estate passed to his sister Mary, then wife of Sir Fleetwood Dormer of Arle (Glos.). She died in 1697, having devised her freehold property to her kinsman Thomas Harries of Prescott and her copyhold estates to his son John.[88] On John's death in 1746 his son Thomas succeeded to the copyhold estate and held the freeholds jointly with his mother Sarah (d. 1772).[89] Part of the estate seems to have been settled on Thomas's son the Revd. Edward Harries (1743–1812), who held 473 a. in Pontesbury parish in 1797.[90] He lived at Cruckton Hall from 1773 until 1782 when, having become a Unitarian, he resigned his preferment in the Church and moved to Great Hanwood.[91] The principal copyhold acquisition in the 18th century was the 300-acre estate of Robert Phillips in Cruckmeole, Newnham, and Sascott.[92] This comprised the modest copyholds held by two branches of the Phillips family in the 17th century,[93] which were combined in 1702[94] and which passed to Thomas Harries in 1767 in right of his wife Mary, daughter of Robert Phillips.[95] In addition 159 a. in Arscott were purchased in 1777[96] and 131 a., mainly in Cruckmeole, were bought between 1772 and 1791.[97]

On the death of Thomas Harries in 1798, Edward settled the copyhold portion of the estate on his son Thomas, who had possession of the whole estate after his father's death in 1812.[98] Minor purchases were made at the dispersal of ancient copyhold estates in Ford, Sascott, and Arscott between 1814 and 1822,[99] the largest being 105 a. at Sascott acquired from the Oswell family.[1] The estate amounted to 2,037 a. in Pontesbury and Ford parishes in 1842.[2] It passed in 1848 to Francis Harries, nephew of Thomas, who enfranchised the copyhold portion of the estate in 1856[3] and purchased the Horton Lodge estate in 1860.[4] On the death of Francis the property passed to his brother Col. Thomas Harries, who was succeeded in 1879 by his cousin Major-General Charles V. Jenkins, to whom the reversion had been devised under the will of Francis Harries. The estate passed, on the death of General Jenkins in 1892, to his grandson Major Charles Jenkins, who sold the greater part in 1929.[5]

The estate of Henry Haynes at Boycott, Farley, and Pontesbury, which was enfranchised in 1633,[6] seems to have been enlarged in the course of the 17th century by the purchase of several Pontesbury freeholds.[7] It passed, with the Haynes estate at Netley in Stapleton parish, to Thomas Edwardes at his marriage with Mary, daughter and heir of Thomas Haynes in 1689,[8] and followed the descent of the Netley estate[9] until the later 19th century. It amounted to 614 a. in 1770, when it included Hall Farm, Maypole Farm, Nills Farm, and Woodhouse Farm in Pontesbury, in addition to farms at Boycott and Farley.[10] In 1800, when it comprised 639 a., the greater part of the estate was sold[11] and T. H. Hope owned only 195 a. in the parish in 1842.[12]

The largest of the freeholds in Pontesbury manor created by the enfranchisement of 1615, that of Richard Corbet at Halston and Farley,[13] seems to have continued without subsequent enlargement until the 19th century. It remained in the Corbet family until 1696 when, on the death of Abigail, widow of John Corbet, it passed to Nicholas Lechmere in right of his wife Judith, John Corbet's daughter.[14] In 1700, however, it was acquired by John Teeton, a mortgagee,[15] after whose death in 1739 half the estate passed to his widow Susan and half to his son John.[16] The Teeton family are not recorded as owners after 1749[17] and by 1797 the estate, then comprising 252 a., had been acquired by

---

[77] S.P.L., Deeds 10998.
[78] E 179/166/23.
[79] S.P.L., Deeds 11111.
[80] Ibid. 10998.
[81] E 179/166/169.
[82] S.P.L., Deeds 11105.
[83] Ibid. 11108.
[84] Ibid. 12706.
[85] Ibid. 11026, 12532.
[86] Ibid. 12575.
[87] Ibid. 12507, 12837; S.R.O. 169/1.
[88] S.R.O. 169/1; S.P.L., Deeds 11126.
[89] S.R.O. 169/3 (Ford ct. r. 1746–8).
[90] S.P.L., MS. 2364.
[91] S.P.L., Deeds 15279.
[92] S.R.O. 248/2 (Ford ct. r. 1797).
[93] S.P.L., Deeds 12706; S.R.O. 169/1.
[94] S.R.O. 169/1 (Ford ct. r. 1702).
[95] Ibid. 169/2 (ibid. 1767).
[96] Ibid. (ibid. 1777); S.P.L., Deeds 11499.
[97] S.R.O. 248/2 (Ford ct. r. 1797).

[98] Ibid. (ibid. 1797, 1810).
[99] Ibid. 169/11.
[1] Ibid. (Ford ct. r. 1814).
[2] Ibid. 437/4–5; ibid. 785/181–2; Ford par. rec., tithe appt.
[3] S.R.O. 938 uncat., enfranchisement papers, 1856–7.
[4] Par. rec., commonplace bk. of Chas. Drury.
[5] S.C.C., SH. 37 (sale partics. 1929).
[6] S.P.L., Deeds 6716, 6840.
[7] S.P.L., E.D. v.f. (transcript of title-deeds of Maypole House Farm, 1711–1804); S.P.L., MS. 300 (ct. r. 1637).
[8] S.P.L., MS. 2789, p. 48; C.P. 25(2)/794/4 Jas. II Mich.; C.P. 25(2)/867/1 Wm. and Mary Trin.
[9] See p. 165.
[10] Hope-Edwardes MSS., Linley Hall, survey, 1770.
[11] Ibid. sale partics. 1800.
[12] S.R.O. 437/5; ibid. 785/181.
[13] S.P.L., Deeds 6822.
[14] Ibid. 10621–2; E 134/10 & 11 Wm. III/Hil. 29.
[15] S.P.L., Deeds 10648–50, 10657.
[16] Ibid. 10662.   [17] Ibid. 10660.

Robert Pemberton,[18] whose descendant was owner in 1842.[19]

The Ward family of Hinton[20] were one of the few to hold lands both of Ford and Pontesbury manors in the early 17th century, when Arthur Ward held some 130 a. in Lea[21] and some 80 a. in Hinton,[22] which were enfranchised in 1607[23] and 1615[24] respectively. The family acquired further copyhold lands in Lea in 1661.[25] The estate seems to have increased in size after this date and amounted to 524 a. in 1842.[26] On the death of Arthur, grandson of Arthur Ward, in 1685 it passed to his daughter Elizabeth, wife of Robert Offley.[27] It was held by the Offley family until 1818 when, on the death of Sarah, widow of Richard Ward Offley, it passed to her daughter Sarah, wife of Henry Wakeman, and subsequently followed the descent of Ford manor until 1923.[28]

Six out of the seven larger estates in Ford and Pontesbury manors thus remained in the same family, or passed only by marriage to another, between the early 16th and later 19th centuries. Such continuity of tenure was by no means typical here in estates of more modest proportions. Only one other property—that of the Phillips family of Plealey—was held by the same family between 1601 and 1874.[29] Analysis of changes in landownership within Ford manor[30] shows that the holdings of 18 of the 47 tenants of 1601 had already passed to other families by 1660. A further 7 changed hands between 1678 and 1700, 12 in the period 1700–50, and 5 between 1750 and 1800. Only 5 copyholders in 1842 were thus descendants of the tenants of 1601. Excluding the large estates of the Harries, Warter, Boycott, and Offley families, there were in 1785 28 copyholders in Ford manor. The history of 3 of these cannot be traced, but of the remaining 25 copyholders, 10 had acquired their estates since 1750 and 9 in the period 1700–50. Representatives of 10 of the copyholders of 1785 still held their lands in 1842; 7 of the estates had been sold between 1785 and 1815, and 8 between 1815 and 1839.

Five of 28 copyholds of 1785 were of over 200 a.[31] and had been built up, normally in a piecemeal fashion, since the later 17th century by the ancestors of the owner in 1785.[32] The oldest was that of the Niccolls family of Newnham,[33] the nucleus of which

was a 10-noke holding purchased from the representatives of the Dennis family in 1683.[34] Further purchases in Lea and Newnham between 1787 and 1839[35] had increased the size of the estate to 294 a. by 1842.[36] It was held by the Niccolls family until 1922.[37] The neighbouring estate of the Olivers at Lea and Polmere was more short-lived. John Oliver bought a messuage at Polmere in 1763[38] and his son Bold Oliver, who bought 4½ nokes at Lea and Marton in 1788,[39] held 220 a. in 1797.[40] In 1810 the estate passed to Bold Oliver's daughters Elizabeth and Jemina, and was sold in 1812 and 1825.[41] Two substantial copyholds at Plealey were carved out of the Phillips family's estate there in the 18th century. The Cambridge mathematician Dr. Edward Waring[42] owned 215 a. in that township in 1797.[43] This had been acquired by his ancestor John Waring in 1718.[44] It descended to Edward's sister Alicia Harper in 1808 and passed out of the family in 1820.[45] The other estate, amounting to 204 a. in 1797,[46] was acquired by Francis Tipton in 1771,[47] and was still held by one of his daughters in 1840.[48]

The most recent, and by the mid-19th century the largest, of these latter-day copyholds was that of the Heighway family. William Heighway of Longville, who acquired a lease of the tanhouse at Pontesford in 1710,[49] is the first member of the family known to have been resident in the parish. Presumably with the profits derived from the tannery, his descendant Samuel Heighway purchased the tanhouse, with other cottages and land at Pontesford, in 1772[50] and acquired 3 other small properties in the township between 1777 and 1786.[51] From 1784 the family were indirectly concerned in mining and lead-smelting locally,[52] and profits from royalties clearly helped to finance their piecemeal purchases in Pontesford, Pontesbury, and Plealey between 1797 and the 1890s.[53] The estate comprised 234 a. in 1797,[54] 291 a. in 1842,[55] and 902 a. by 1928.[56] The greater part was sold in 1952.[57]

The history of landownership in the manors of Longden and Oaks is markedly different from that of the remainder of the parish. The manor of Longden was assessed at 3 hides in 1086, when its value was said to have fallen from £4 to 40s. since before the Conquest.[58] A reduction in its hidage to two hides

[18] S.P.L., MS. 2364.
[19] S.R.O. 437/5; ibid. 785/181.
[20] For pedigree of the Ward, Offley, and Wakeman familes, see S.P.L., MS. 2791, p. 147.
[21] S.P.L., Deeds 12706.
[22] Ibid. 6834.
[23] Ibid. 11026.
[24] Ibid. 6834.
[25] S.R.O. 169/1 (Ford ct. r. 1661).
[26] Ibid. 437/5; ibid. 785/181.
[27] Ibid. 169/1 (Ford ct. r. 1685, 1690).
[28] Sale partics. 1923, penes Mr. E. R. Griffiths, Hinton Farm.
[29] S.P.L., Deeds 12706; S.R.O. 169/1.
[30] What follows is based on S.P.L., Deeds 12706. S.R.O. 123/1; ibid. 169/1–3, 11–15; ibid. 248/102.
[31] S.R.O. 123/1; S.P.L., MS. 2364.
[32] S.R.O. 169/1–3; ibid. 248/1.
[33] For pedigree, see T.S.A.S. 4th ser. ix. 236–7; Salop. N. & Q. 3rd ser. iii. 39–40, 53–55.
[34] S.R.O. 169/1 (Ford ct. r. 1683).
[35] Ibid. 248/1–2 (ibid. 1787, 1812); ibid. 169/13 (ibid. 1839).
[36] Ibid. 437/5; ibid. 785/181.
[37] T.S.A.S. 4th ser. ix. 237.

[38] S.R.O. 169/3 (Ford ct. r. 1763).
[39] Ibid. 248/1 (ibid. 1788).
[40] S.P.L., MS. 2364.
[41] S.R.O. 248/2 (Ford ct. r. 1810, 1812); ibid. 169/12 (ibid. 1825).
[42] D.N.B.
[43] S.P.L., MS. 2364.
[44] S.R.O. 169/2 (Ford ct. r. 1718).
[45] Ibid. 248/2 (ibid. 1808); ibid. 169/11 (ibid. 1819, 1820).
[46] S.P.L., MS. 2364.
[47] S.R.O. 169/3 (Ford ct. r. 1771).
[48] Ibid. 248/2 (ibid. 1800); ibid. 437/4; ibid. 785/182.
[49] Notes from Heighway title-deeds, penes Miss L. F. Chitty.
[50] S.R.O. 169/3 (Ford ct. r. 1772).
[51] Ibid. (ibid. 1777); ibid. 248/1 (ibid. 1780, 1786).
[52] See pp. 279–80.
[53] S.R.O. 169/11–18; ibid. 248/2; ibid. 437/13 passim.
[54] S.P.L., MS. 2364.
[55] Ibid. 437/5; ibid. 785/181.
[56] Heighway Jones title-deeds, penes Messrs. Sprott, Stokes, and Turnbull, solicitors, Shrewsbury.
[57] Ibid.
[58] V.C.H. Salop. i. 326.

by 1254[59] can be accounted for by the early-12th-century enfeoffments discussed above.[60] The area of demesne appears to have changed little between 1086 and the mid-14th century. It contained land sufficient for 2 ploughs in 1086, when there were 4 serfs in the manor.[61] There were, in addition to small areas of meadow and pasture, 80 a. demesne arable in 1294,[62] 70 a. in 1315,[63] and 60 a. in 1346.[64] A manor-house is recorded in 1294[65] and 1315[66] but had probably been leased by 1346.[67] It was among the property granted to the free tenant John Adams in 1463, when it was said to have been formerly occupied by his father.[68] The demesne arable had been leased piecemeal before 1430.[69] Although a bailiff of Steplewood and The Hayes continued to be responsible for the administration of the demesne woodland throughout the later Middle Ages,[70] manorial woodland at 'Ashull' had been leased to the tenants by 1292[71] and pasture rights in The Hayes, leased in 1429 to John Adams in return for half the amercements,[72] remained in the possession of his descendants.[73]

Richard Prince, who purchased 8 messuages and lands from 4 tenants between 1566 and 1587,[74] began the process of buying up copyholds which was to transform the manorial estate into the largest property in the township by the early 19th century. John Astley bought Longden Coppice (57 a.) from Richard Adams in 1719,[75] inherited the copyhold of another branch of the Adams family in 1724,[76] and purchased the Benyon family's copyhold in 1762.[77] By 1797 the manorial estate comprised 920 a.[78] and a further 119 a. were added at the inclosure of Longden Common in 1806.[79] The whole estate appears to have been sold in 1826,[80] for the Earl of Tankerville no longer owned any property in the township by 1841.[81]

Rents of 59s. 2d. a year were paid by free tenants in 1294[82] and some 30s. in the earlier 14th century.[83] These however, merely represented payments by tenants of fiefs of the barony of Longden.[84] Apart from the Adams family, members of the Cross, Cooper, and Higgins families held small freeholds in Longden in the later 15th century,[85] but these seem to have become merged with their copyhold estates.

The 19 recorded tenants in 1086 included a villein, 3 radmen, 9 bordars, and 6 cottars, who held only 2 ploughs between them.[86] Rents of customary tenants, which produced 58s. 2d. a year in 1294,[87] had risen to £8 6s. 6d. by 1315, when there appear

to have been 20 such tenants.[88] Analysis of the court rolls[89] shows that there were about a dozen copyholders in the manor in the later 15th century, 7 of whom had holdings of a half virgate (30 a.) or less. As in the manors of Ford and Pontesbury inheritance was by the youngest son[90] and until the 1550s the tenants seem to have enjoyed the same measure of independence in ordering their affairs. Most holdings included assarted lands, which were treated as part of the copyhold, and there is evidence for a general consolidation of open-field holdings by means of exchange in the later 15th and early 16th centuries. By the 1560s 5 tenants held copyhold estates of more than one virgate, the largest being the 15 nokes held by the Adams family and the 12 nokes held by the Corbets.

An attempt was made to bring the copyholders under control after the manor was bought by Alan Hord in 1541. Orders were given in 1550 for a survey of exchanges between tenants to be made for the steward,[91] and in the following year the tenants appear to have compounded for such exchanges by a fine.[92] In the later 16th century one of the tenants alleged, in a lawsuit against the lord of the manor, that the lord had tried to force him to accept a lease of his copyhold.[93] As a result of the expansion of the manorial estate, copyhold tenure had virtually disappeared by the early 19th century, when of the 4 copyhold estates the 73 a. held by the Hesketh family of Cross House was the only one consisting of anything more than cottage property.[94]

The manor of Oaks was assessed at 2 hides in 1086, when it included a small demesne sufficient for half a plough, with 2 serfs.[95] A radman, a villein, and a bordar had only one plough between them.[96] Four ploughlands appear to have gone out of cultivation here since before the Conquest and the value of the manor had fallen from 40s. to 8s. in the same period.[97] It was perhaps in an effort to increase the value of the manor by the encouragement of assarting that both the demesne and the lands of the customary tenants were granted to free tenants some time in the 12th century. The earliest-recorded of these was William Fitz Geoffrey, who was confirmed in possession of the messuage and virgate formerly held by his father in 1199.[98] It is likely that this property included the manor-house, for the residence of William's descendant was described as a capital messuage in 1305.[99] There appear to have been about half a dozen free tenants at Oaks in the 13th century,[1] but during the later

[59] *Rot. Hund.* (Rec. Com.), ii. 66.
[60] See p. 269.
[61] *V.C.H. Salop.* i. 326.
[62] C 133/68/10.
[63] C 134/48/9.
[64] C 135/82/1.
[65] C 133/68/10.
[66] C 134/48/9.
[67] C 135/82/1.
[68] S.P.L., MS. 393 (ct. r. 1463).
[69] Ibid. (ct. r. 1430).
[70] Ibid. (ct. r. 1509, 1515).
[71] Ibid. (ct. r. 1292).
[72] Ibid. (ct. r. 1429).
[73] See pp. 270–1.
[74] S.P.L., MS. 393 (ct. r. 1566, 1568, 1587).
[75] Longden manor title-deeds, *penes* Mrs. A. N. Fielden.
[76] S.P.L., MS. 392 (ct. r. 1720, 1724).
[77] Ibid. (ct. r. 1762). [78] Ibid. 2364.
[79] Copy Longden Common inclosure award, *penes* Mrs. A. N. Fielden.

[80] Longden manor title-deeds, *penes* Mrs. A. N. Fielden.
[81] Heref. Dioc. Regy., Longden tithe appt.
[82] C 133/68/10.
[83] C 134/48/9; C 135/82/1.
[84] See p. 282.
[85] S.P.L., MS. 393 (ct. r. 1467, 1472, 1533).
[86] *V.C.H. Salop.* i. 326.
[87] C 133/68/10.
[88] C 134/48/9.
[89] What follows is based on S.P.L., MS. 393.
[90] Ibid. (ct. r. 1527).
[91] Ibid. (ct. r. 1550).
[92] Ibid. (ct. r. 1551).
[93] C 3/32/107.
[94] S.P.L., MS. 392 (ct. r. 1808–20); ibid. 2364.
[95] *V.C.H. Salop.* i. 326.
[96] Ibid.
[97] Ibid.
[98] *T.S.A.S.* 2nd ser. x. 311.
[99] S.P.L., Deeds 10600.
[1] Ibid. 10597–10601; *Close R.* 1268–72, 575.

Middle Ages the greater part of the former manorial estate was held by the de la Halle family of Woodhall and the Jennings family of Walleybourne. By 1314 the former held a half virgate in Oaks,[2] which descended with the Woodhall estate to the Skirmston and Newport families.[3] Margaret Newport held 1½ virgate in Oaks in 1563.[4] The more extensive property of the Jennings family comprised 4 messuages and 2½ virgates in 1563.[5] Part was probably inherited from the Walleybourne family, who held lands in Oaks in 1372,[6] but Thomas Jennings was buying other freeholds here in the 1470s.[7] By the early 17th century all the former freeholds were in the hands of the lord of the manor, but the stages by which this was accomplished are not entirely clear. The lord already owned at least one virgate here before 1500[8] and further lands had been acquired by the 1550s.[9] The Newport freehold was presumably merged in the manorial estate when Sir Francis Newport bought the manor in 1600, and the Jennings freehold estate here was conveyed in 1604, with Walleybourne, to Sir Roger Owen,[10] who soon afterwards became lord of the manor. With the exception of Oaks Hall the whole township of Oaks subsequently lay within the manorial estate.[11]

Information on the size of farms and forms of tenure in the parish as a whole is not available until the end of the 18th century. The portion of the Pontesbury manorial estate remaining in the hands of the lord of the manor after 1615 was too small to justify a reorganization of farms. From the early 17th century until most of it was sold in 1794 the estate consisted of a single farm of some 125 a. and a few cottages.[12] As lords of the soil of commons on Pontesbury and Pontesford Hills, however, the Owen family continued to derive some income from the quit-rents of squatter cottages.[13] Nearly 60 such cottages still owed these rents in 1868.[14]

At Oaks 21-year leases were employed by Robert Kemsey and his successors in the later 16th century[15] and, although 3-life leases were introduced by Sir Francis Newport in 1600,[16] these had been replaced by 21-year leases as early as 1699.[17] The number of tenants fell from 7 in 1700[18] to 5 in 1794, when two of the farms were of over 100 a.[19] Farm-sizes had not changed by 1842, when there were still 5 tenants,[20] but after the formation of the Longden Manor estate the whole township, apart from Upper and Lower Oaks Farms, was part of Longden Park.[21] There is no evidence for farm-sizes on the Longden manorial estate before 1797,

when 729 a. of the 920 a. owned by Lord Tankerville lay in 4 farms of over 100 a.[22]

So far as geographical and social factors permitted, the large farm had clearly become predominant in the parish by 1797, alike on manorial estates, ancient freeholds, and the larger estates in Ford and Pontesbury manors.[23] Of the 16 estates of over 200 a. in the parish ten belonged to absentee landlords and only one, the Heighway estate at Pontesford, was largely occupied by its owner. There were in addition, however, 12 owner-occupied farms of over 50 a., most of them in Ford manor. Both in 1797 and 1842 about one-third of all farms of over 50 a. were wholly or largely owner-occupied. The 73 holdings of over 1 a. recorded on the 16 larger estates included 22 farms of over 100 a., 4 estates consisting only of a single large farm. The most striking example of consolidation occurred on the Boycott estate. There were 7 tenants here in 1773, when the estate included two farms of over 100 a. and two smaller holdings,[24] but by 1797 the whole estate (433 a.) was occupied on a two-life lease as a single farm, and it was still held in the same manner in 1842. Less dramatic changes on the Edwardes estate at Pontesbury reduced the number of tenants from 18 in 1728 to 13 by 1796, and increased the annual rental from £160 to £503 in the same period.[25] In 1770 one of the farms was of over 100 a., and 4 others of 50–100 a.;[26] no significant changes in farm-size stook place before the greater part of the estate was sold in 1800.[27] On the Harries estate the transition to larger farms seems to have taken place in the early 19th century, for it contained only 2 farms of over 100 a. in 1797 but 6 such farms in 1842. The division of the estate between Thomas Harries and his son Edward in the later 18th century[28] was probably the reason for this delay, for in other respects this family seem always to have taken a close interest in agricultural improvements.

Cattle-breeding, which may have been practised on a large scale by the lords of Pontesbury manor in the earlier Middle Ages,[29] seems always to have been an important factor in the agriculture of the parish. In addition to stealing 24 oxen and cows from the lessee of the Pontesbury demesne pastures at Moorwood in 1411,[30] Welsh cattle-thieves in the same year took 38 bullocks and heifers from John Dod of Woodhouse[31]—probably the Woodhouse near Longden.[32] Geographical factors were largely responsible for this emphasis on cattle-breeding, for much

[2] S.P.L., Deeds 10601.
[3] See pp. 269–70.
[4] S.P.L., Deeds 2600.
[5] Ibid.
[6] Ibid. 10604; see also p. 135.
[7] S.P.L., Deeds 10612, 12866.
[8] Loton Hall MSS., lease, 1501.
[9] S.R.O. 665 uncat., leases, 1556–7.
[10] C.P. 25(2)/342/2 Jas. I Mich.
[11] S.P.L., Deeds 13462; S.R.O. 665 uncat., survey of manorial estate, c. 1769; S.P.L., MS. 2364.
[12] Ibid.; S.R.O. 1011 (Smythe Owen) uncat., sale partics. 1794; ibid. 665 uncat., leases, 1602–1733; S.P.L., Deeds 7038, 9378, 13433.
[13] S.R.O. 1011 (Smythe Owen) uncat., rentals, 1803–68.
[14] Ibid.
[15] Ibid. 665 uncat., leases, 1556–99; S.P.L., Deeds 7073.
[16] S.R.O. 665 uncat., leases, 1600–60; S.P.L., Deeds 5342, 13465.
[17] S.R.O. 665 uncat., lease, 1699; S.P.L., Deeds 5343.

[18] S.P.L., Deeds 13462.
[19] S.R.O. 1011 (Smythe Owen) uncat., sale partics., 1794.
[20] S.R.O. 437/4; ibid. 784/181.
[21] Sale partics., Longden Manor, c. 1890, penes Mrs. A. N. Fielden, Longden Manor.
[22] S.P.L., MS. 2364.
[23] The following paragraph is based, except where otherwise stated, on S.P.L., MS. 2364; S.R.O. 437/4–5; ibid. 785/181–2; Heref. Dioc. Regy., Longden tithe appt.
[24] S.P.L., Deeds 14341; S.P.L., MS. 2534.
[25] Hope-Edwardes MSS., Linley Hall, accts. 1728–60, 1796–99.
[26] Ibid. survey, 1770.
[27] Ibid. sale partics. 1800.
[28] See p. 274.
[29] See p. 272.
[30] Salop. Peace Roll 1404–14, 103.
[31] Ibid. 104.
[32] See p. 270.

of the parish lies in the valley of the Rea. The low-lying lands on the banks of the Rea were liable to flooding and were probably too damp for use as sheep pasture. An early reference to underground drainage occurs in 1675, when an Asterley tenant on the Boycott estate was given licence to make such drains.[33]

The Harries family, who always kept a great part of their estate in hand—$2\frac{3}{4}$ virgates in 1609,[34] 298 a. in 1797,[35] and 284 a. in 1842[36]—appear to have been managing water-meadows at Cruckton as early as 1698. All the landowners in the township then paid to have the Rea scoured to draw water off Cruckton Meadow and in 1701 floodgates were erected in the meadow.[37] By 1776 the practice was in general use throughout the district. In a report on local farming methods the Revd. Edward Harries stated that 'all the farmers take every opportunity of throwing the water over their lands whenever they can', and went on to describe his own methods of watering meadows at Cruckton, which had resulted in the doubling of his hay-crop.[38] Although he kept only a small herd of cows for domestic supplies of dairy produce, Edward Harries reared many oxen, but sold them as store-cattle.[39] He was an authority on forestry[40] like his father Thomas Harries, who planted 22 a. of oaks and 7 a. of fir and other softwoods in the estate between 1750 and 1767.[41]

Two alternative forms of 7-course rotation were in use in the district in the later 18th century. Both included 2-year clover leys, but no sainfoin was grown.[42] Roughly one-third of the parish was under the plough in 1801, when there were 3,173 a. arable.[43] Wheat was the principal crop, closely followed by barley.[44] An appreciable quantity of turnips (51 a.) are then recorded,[45] but these were probably grown only as a fallow crop on dry soils.[46] The returns of 1801 are, however, not likely to be reliable, since they were based on the rectors' tithe accounts and not on direct returns from farmers.[47] The parish contained 6,373 a. arable c. 1842, when Longden township had the unusually high proportion of 1,207 a. arable and only 348 a. pasture.[48] On the estate of J. T. Hope in 1800 Boycott, Farley, Woodhouse, and Nills Farms had roughly equal acreages of arable and pasture.[49] Land-use figures

for the Boycott family's farm at Boycott (c. 240 a.) show an increase in the arable area from some 85 a. in 1793[50] to 151 a. by 1817[51] but it had fallen to 123 a. by 1839.[52]

Fourteen mills are known to have existed in the parish, 8 of them on Rea Brook and 4 on Pontesford Brook. The site of the mill recorded in Pontesbury manor in 1086[53] is not known, but it presumably stood on Pontesbury brook near the village. It was still in use in 1286, when it was valued at 20s.[54] By 1464 another mill, later known as New Mills, had been erected on the demesne at the junction of Rea and Pontesford Brooks.[55] There were two mills on this site when it passed to the Corbet family of Halston in 1603.[56] They became a small owner-occupied freehold after the dispersal of the Corbet estate in the mid-18th century.[57] In the later 19th century, when New Mills formed part of the Longden Manor estate, one of the mills was used for corn and the other for clover,[58] but they went out of use soon after 1891.[59]

A mill which stood at Cruckmeole by 1308[60] was later rebuilt or moved to another site, for the two water-mills here were described as 'New Mills' in 1561.[61] The mill belonged to the Onslow family in the later 16th century,[62] but passed to Jane Downes (d. 1644), sister of John Onslow,[63] whose heir William Rocke sold it to Thomas Orton in 1670.[64] It was acquired in 1676 by Robert Phillips of Cruckmeole[65] and passed, with the rest of the Phillips estate, to Thomas Harries in 1767.[66] The mill went out of use c. 1909.[67] Cruckton Mill probably occupied its present site by 1345,[68] but was said to be decayed in 1601.[69] It is next recorded in 1797,[70] but had closed by 1885.[71] Arthur Ward of Hinton erected a mill shortly before 1601.[72] This is last recorded in 1692, when it appears to have stood upstream from New Mills.[73] Other short-lived mills on Rea Brook are recorded at Lea in 1308[74] and at Malehurst, 1633–55.[75]

A mill worth 10s. a year is recorded at Pontesford in 1299.[76] A second mill had been erected by 1593[77] and they have subsequently been known as Upper and Lower Mills. They belonged to the Adams family of Longden and their descendants[78] from 1593 until 1799, when they were added to the Heighway estate.[79] Both mills were working until

[33] S.P.L., Deeds 14091.
[34] Ibid. 12575.
[35] S.P.L., MS. 2364.
[36] S.R.O. 437/5; ibid. 785/181.
[37] S.P.L., Deeds 12827.
[38] A. Young, *Tours in England and Wales* (reprint, 1932), 160.
[39] Ibid. 155–6.
[40] *T.S.A.S.* 2nd ser. iv. 84–95.
[41] S.P.L., Deeds 12837.
[42] A. Young, op. cit. 154–5.
[43] H.O. 67/12/190–2.
[44] Ibid.
[45] Ibid.
[46] Plymley, *Agric. Salop.* 162.
[47] H.O. 67/12/190.
[48] S.R.O. 437/4–5; ibid. 785/181–2; Heref. Dioc. Regy., Longden tithe appt.
[49] Hope-Edwardes MSS., Linley Hall, sale partics. 1800.
[50] S.P.L., Deeds 13915.
[51] Ibid. 13779.
[52] Ibid.
[53] *V.C.H. Salop.* i. 325.
[54] C 133/45/2.
[55] S.P.L., Deeds 6784.

[56] S.P.L., MS. 300 (Pontesbury ct. r. 1603).
[57] Ibid. MS. 2364.
[58] Sale partics., Longden Manor, c. 1890, *penes* Mrs. A. N. Fielden, Longden Manor.
[59] *Kelly's Dir. Salop.* (1891).
[60] C 134/5/1.
[61] S.R.O. 665 uncat., letter of attorney, 1561; S.P.L., Deeds 11034.
[62] Ibid.; S.P.L., Deeds 12706.
[63] S.P.L., Deeds 11044.
[64] S.R.O. 169/1 (Ford ct. r. 1670).
[65] Ibid. (ct. r. 1676).
[66] Ibid. (ibid. 1767).
[67] *Kelly's Dir. Salop.* (1909).
[68] Owen and Blakeway, *Hist. Shrewsbury*, ii. 423.
[69] S.P.L., Deeds 12706.
[70] S.P.L., MS. 2364.
[71] *Kelly's Dir. Salop.* (1870–85).
[72] C 2/Eliz. I/L8/15.
[73] S.P.L., MS. 300 (Pontesbury ct. r. 1692).
[74] C 134/5/1.
[75] S.P.L., Deeds 14301, 14309.
[76] C 133/87/7.
[77] C 142/267/68.
[78] See p. 270.
[79] S.R.O. 437/13, deed, 1799.

the 1920s[80] and Lower Mill remained in use until the 1950s.[81] Skin Mill Cottage, upstream from Pontesford Mills, stood on the site of 2 fulling-mills erected by the lord of Oaks manor shortly before 1570 and then leased to Humphrey Pitts, dyer.[82] A pair of corn-mills, built nearby, were leased to Richard Swatman in 1573,[83] but were probably dismantled c. 1601, when Pitts obtained a lease of both mill-sites and was given licence to rebuild the corn-mill nearer to his own house.[84] The building was converted in 1699 into a leather-mill,[85] which was still in use in 1797[86] but had closed by 1842.[87] A water-mill at Longden, recorded in 1315,[88] appears to have gone out of use by 1346.[89]

Richard Lake of Boycott was in 1609 granted fishing rights in that part of Rea Brook which lay in Pontesbury manor,[90] and had erected a weir at Hacknell Meadow by 1612, when this involved him in a dispute with Thomas Burley of Malehurst.[91] The Harries family had a fishery at Cruckmeole in the 1760s.[92]

Although coal-mining is recorded in the parish from the early 17th-century onwards, it remained a small-scale enterprise until c. 1780, when the development of the Snailbeach and other lead-mines on the Stiperstones created a large local demand for coal. Subsequent mining development was, until c. 1850, largely restricted to the townships of Pontesbury and Pontesford, most of it being carried out by the agents of the Snailbeach and White Grit mines. These collieries had, however, all closed by 1860 and in the later 19th century the Asterley, Arscott, and Shorthill collieries were producing coal mainly for domestic use, small coal and slack being used at brickworks on the mine-sites.

Two Pontesbury tenants were presented at the manor court for digging coal in 1604.[93] In the same year a Pontesbury blacksmith was given leave to get coal in the manor[94] and by 1617 coal from Pontesbury was being used at Condover Hall.[95] During the 17th century mining in Pontesbury township seems to have been restricted to shallow pits to the south of the village,[96] but by 1770 it had been mined west of the village, to the north of the Minsterley road.[97] At Malehurst, to the north of this road, where the field-name Coalpit Leasow is found in 1606,[98] Orlando Nicholls was said to have found coal c. 1680.[99] Minerals were reserved in a lease of Malehurst Hall in 1685,[1] but there is no other record of

mining on the Boycott estate at Malehurst and Boycott until the 1770s, when Boycott colliery was leased to William Howell.[2] Mines had been opened at Asterley by 1710.[3] Charles Gibbon leased 26 a. north of Asterley village to 3 coalmasters in 1741,[4] but this mine appears to have closed in 1743[5] and there is no later reference to mining in the township until the mid-19th century. The extraction of coal in the east of the parish seems to have been an 18th-century development. In 1757 mineral rights were leased in lands to the north of Longden township, near Arscott Villa,[6] and a colliery had been established near Arscott Coppice by 1767.[7] Mines to the south of Longden Common may have been opened, like the adjoining mines in Pulverbatch parish,[8] in the later 18th century.

The earliest lead-smelting-house in the parish was that at Malehurst, erected by Jonathan Scott and Richard Jeffries. In 1778 they obtained a 50-year lease of all mines on the Boycott estates in Pontesbury and Westbury and took over William Howell's colliery at Boycott.[9] In the same year they purchased a Boulton and Watt engine.[10] The smelting plant was let to Francis Lloyd and others in 1783,[11] and in 1790 to John Laurence, agent for the White Grit Company.[12] The colliery at Boycott closed in 1795, when Laurence began using coal from his own mines in Pontesbury.[13] He had bought 8 a. here for mining purposes at the sale of the manorial estate in 1794,[14] and in the following year was extracting coal from some 25 a. west of the Malehurst smelt-house, held on lease from J. T. Hope.[15] Sales of 5,133 tons of thin coal and of 3,904 tons of yard coal are recorded at this mine between July 1808 and July 1811, when 2,715 tons were consumed by the engine.[16] By 1831 the Malehurst smelt-house had gone out of use, for Laurence had by this date built another smelt-house near the Horseshoe Inn, Pontesbury.[17] By 1842 the White Grit Company had erected yet another smelt-house at Pontesford,[18] but this was no longer held by the Company in 1844.[19]

Mining operations by the Snailbeach Company were concentrated in the area north and east of Pontesbury village. In 1784 their agent Thomas Lovett obtained from Samuel Heighway a lease of several fields adjoining the road from Pontesford to Pontesbury, between the Nag's Head Inn and Pontesford Brook.[20] This was later known as the

[80] *Kelly's Dir. Salop.* (1922–6).
[81] Ex inf. Mr. T. D. Morgan, Lower Mill.
[82] S.R.O. 665 uncat., lease, 1570.
[83] Ibid. lease, 1573.
[84] Ibid. 1601; S.P.L., Deeds 7073.
[85] S.R.O. 665 uncat., lease, 1699.
[86] S.P.L., MS. 2364.
[87] S.R.O. 437/5; ibid. 785/181.
[88] C 134/48/9.
[89] C 135/82/1.
[90] S.P.L., Deeds 7038.
[91] Sta. Cha. 8/203/3.
[92] S.R.O. 169/3 (ct. r. 1767).
[93] S.P.L., MS. 300 (ct. r. 1604).
[94] S.P.L., Deeds 7025.
[95] S.R.O. 665 uncat., household accts. 1617.
[96] S.P.L., MS. 300 (ct. r. 1663, 1667).
[97] Hope-Edwardes MSS., Linley Hall, survey, 1770; S.R.O. 1011 (Dukes) uncat., Pontesbury presentments, 1785–91; S.P.L., Deeds 9994.
[98] S.P.L., MS. 300 (ct. r. 1606).
[99] Longleat MSS., Thynne papers, xxi, f. 20.
[1] S.P.L., Deeds 14313.

[2] Ibid. 14338, 14340.
[3] S.R.O. 837/78.
[4] S.P.L., MS. 2737.
[5] Ibid.
[6] Ibid. MS. 392 (ct. r. 1757).
[7] S.P.L., Deeds 12837.
[8] See p. 137.
[9] S.P.L., Deeds 13913, 14338.
[10] H. W. Dickinson and R. Jenkins, *James Watt and the Steam Engine* (Oxford, 1927), 138.
[11] S.P.L., Deeds 11786.
[12] Ibid. 13914.
[13] Ibid.
[14] S.R.O. 1011 (Smythe Owen) uncat., sale partics. 1794.
[15] Hope-Edwardes MSS., Linley Hall, accts. 1796–9; ibid. sale partics. 1800.
[16] S.R.O. 1222/48.
[17] Plan of Laurence estate, 1831, in Heighway Jones title-deeds, *penes* Messrs. Sprott, Stokes, and Turnbull, solicitors, Shrewsbury.
[18] S.R.O. 437/5; ibid. 785/181.
[19] Ibid. 437/13, lease, 1844.
[20] Ibid. lease, 1784.

Nag's Head Colliery and after 1802 its area of operation was extended to the east of Pontesford Brook,[21] where a tall stone engine-house is still standing. A smelt-house was built at Pontesford shortly after 1784.[22] The Snailbeach Company also acquired mining rights in 1792 on the glebe lands of the third portion of Pontesbury to the north of Pontesbury village,[23] and Lovett bought 17 a. at the sale of the manorial estate in 1794.[24] The Nag's Head Colliery closed in 1857,[25] having produced 27,652 tons of coal in the preceding decade,[26] and coal-mining in Pontesbury township had ceased by 1859.[27] The Pontesford smelt-houses, however, remained in use until c. 1873.[28] There were said to be 127 colliers in the parish in 1831[29] and in 1851 the two smelting-houses at Pontesford employed 90 men and 35 boys.[30]

There is no documentary evidence for coal-mining at Asterley during the later 18th and early 19th centuries. In 1842, however, Henry Gardner owned the pits later known as Brick Kiln Pits, north-east of the village, and the adjacent brickyard.[31] The Marsh Hill and Windmill Pits, to the north of the village, and the Bacon Pits to the east were opened later in the 19th century;[32] they had all closed by 1896.[33] The Boycott Colliery, south of Boycott Farm, had been opened before 1842, when it was occupied by William Cross and Company.[34] It was closed in 1893.[35] A short-lived colliery to the north of the road from Farley to Asterley appears to have opened c. 1876.[36] Closed in 1883, it was reopened and again abandoned in 1896.[37]

Arscott Colliery, and the earlier of the two groups of coal pits known in the mid-19th century as the Shorthill Pits, appear to have been established under an 81-acre mining lease granted by Thomas Harries of Cruckton to Isaac Thompson, Mark Baugh, and Ralph Steadman in 1838.[38] The lease stipulated that coal in an area extending north-westwards from Gipsy Coppice, Arscott, was to be exhausted before work began on a second area, on the south bank of Rea Brook, north-east of Lea Cross.[39] The Arscott Colliery, which in the later 19th century worked 3 shafts north of the village, also had a brickworks north-east of Arscott Hall.[40]

The colliery was held by William Cotton in 1856[41] and belonged to the Proctor family by 1870 and until 1885,[42] when it passed to Elizabeth Smallshaw, whose descendants have since owned the mines.[43] The pit at Gipsy Coppice was closed in 1904.[44] A new pit was opened at Little Hanwood in 1910, but the colliery closed in 1919.[45]

The two collieries known in 1851 as Shorthill[46] probably worked the Clanbrook and other pits in the area north-east of Lea Cross specified in the lease of 1838.[47] The later Shorthill Colliery, south-west of Cruckmeole, belonged in 1873 to Samuel Atherton, who also owned Hanwood Colliery 850 yards to the east.[48] By the end of the 19th century the Shorthill shaft was used only for pumping purposes.[49] The Hanwood Colliery worked the Thin Coal over a considerable area, extending about a mile to the north,[50] and was producing some 25,000 tons of coal a year in the two decades before the Second World War.[51] To ease the problem of drainage an area of unworked coal separated their workings from those of the Arscott Colliery.[52]

Two shafts to the north of Moat Hall had been opened by 1851, when they were held by Messrs. Crapper and Proctor.[53] The Moat Hall Colliery, linked by a tramway to the Shrewsbury road at Annscroft,[54] was held by the Shorthouse family and their partners from c. 1856 until c. 1919.[55] It was then acquired by Mr. A. N. Fielden,[56] who purchased Hanwood Colliery c. 1921.[57] Mr. Fielden subsequently closed the Moat Hall shaft, but continued to mine the underlying coal from the Hanwood shaft.[58] The number of men employed below ground at the colliery fell from 248 in 1921 to 159 in 1931 and to 50 by 1941.[59] The colliery closed in 1942.[60]

Any mining which may once have been carried on in the north of Longden township had long ceased by 1839.[61] A colliery on Longden Common, near Sydnall Cottage, is recorded in the 1840s[62] and a pit here was re-opened for a short period by one Fowles shortly before the First World War.[63] Mining operations here, as in the adjoining pits in Pulverbatch and Stapleton parishes, were rendered uneconomic by drainage difficulties.[64]

[21] S.R.O. 437/13, lease, 1802.
[22] Ibid. 1784.
[23] S.P.L., Deeds 11509.
[24] S.R.O. 1011 (Smythe Owen) uncat., sale partics. 1794.
[25] Par. rec., commonplace bk. of Chas. Drury.
[26] S.R.O. 437/13, memorandum, 1858.
[27] Par. rec., commonplace bk. of Chas. Drury.
[28] S.R.O. 437/13, lease, 1873.
[29] Census, 1831.
[30] H.O. 107/1990/359/2.
[31] S.R.O. 437/4; ibid. 785/182.
[32] R. W. Pocock and others, Geol. Shrews. District (1938), 139–40, 143.
[33] Ibid., and ex inf. Mr. I. J. Brown, Dinnington, Sheffield.
[34] S.R.O. 437/5; ibid. 785/181.
[35] Geol. Shrews. District. 139.
[36] Report of Inspectors of Mines, 1876 [C. 1734], p. 41, H.C. (1877), xxiii.
[37] Geol. Shrews. District. 139.
[38] S.P.L., Deeds 11220; cf. Murchison, Silurian System (1839), 90.
[39] S.P.L., Deeds 11220.
[40] Geol. Shrews. District. 145–6.
[41] Kelly's Dir. Salop. (1856).
[42] Ibid. (1870); Report of Inspectors of Mines, 1873 [C. 1056], pp. 78–79, H.C. (1874), xiii; ibid. 1883 [C.4058], pp. 140–1, H.C. (1884), xix.

[43] Kelly's Dir. Salop. (1885–1917); and ex inf. Mr. I. J. Brown.
[44] Geol. Shrews. District, 139; and ex inf. Mr. A. N. Fielden, Longden Manor.
[45] Ibid.
[46] Bagshaw's Dir. Salop. (1851).
[47] S.P.L., Deeds 11220.
[48] Report of Inspectors of Mines, 1873 [C. 1056], pp. 78–79, H.C. (1874), xiii.
[49] Ex inf. Mr. A. N. Fielden.
[50] Ibid.; Geol. Shrews. District, 145.
[51] Ex inf. Mr. I. J. Brown.
[52] Geol. Shrews. District, 145.
[53] Bagshaw's Dir. Salop. (1851). Earlier workings here are noted in Murchison, Silurian System (1839), 90.
[54] O.S. Map 6" Salop. 41 (2nd edn.).
[55] Kelly's Dir. Salop. (1856–1900); and ex inf. Mr. A. N. Fielden.
[56] Ex inf. Mr. A. N. Fielden.
[57] Ibid.
[58] Ibid.
[59] Ex inf. Mr. I. J. Brown.
[60] Ex inf. Mr. A. N. Fielden.
[61] Murchison, Silurian System, 90; Heref. Dioc. Regy., Longden tithe appt.
[62] Geol. Shrews. District, 149.
[63] Local inf.
[64] Ibid.

A barytes-processing plant, linked by an aerial ropeway to the Huglith mine, was established at Malehurst Mill *c.* 1910[65] and was in use until 1949, when the ropeway was taken down.[66] The buildings were purchased by Mr. H. P. Davies in 1956 and are now in use for the preparation of animal foodstuffs.[67]

A stone quarry on Pontesbury Hill is recorded in 1827.[68] Two quarries were reserved for the use of the parish highway surveyors when the hill was inclosed in 1848,[69] and roadstone appears to have been quarried here continuously since that date. Messrs. Hayward's quarry on Pontesbury Hill was leased after 1894 to the County Council,[70] who purchased it in 1954.[71]

In Pontesbury, and to a lesser extent in Pontesford, Plealey, and Longden, a substantial class of small tradesmen grew up in the earlier 19th century as those villages became industrialized.[72] Before 1800 Pontesbury contained only the tradesmen to be expected in an agricultural village. A tailor and a smith are recorded in 1379[73] and 2 shops and 2 blacksmiths in the 1790s.[74] By 1851, when mining activity had already passed its peak, there were 24 tradesmen in the village, excluding alehouses. Some reduction in the number may have followed the closure of the Pontesbury mines in 1859, for only 17 tradesmen are recorded in 1870. Since 1885 there have normally been some 25 tradesmen in the village. Although Directories record an increase in the number of tradesmen from 23 to 33 between 1891 and 1900, the population of the parish as a whole declined during this decade. Until 1900 over half of the tradesmen were engaged in the provision of food and clothing. There were 4 coal-merchants in 1851, 2 between 1870 and 1900, and one thereafter. A watchmaker first appears in 1885, a florist in 1900, and a hairdresser in 1909. A newsagent, a garage, and 2 banks had been opened by 1922.

The Pontesford tanhouse, associated with the Upper Mill, is first recorded in 1599[75] and was occupied until the later 17th century by the Tipton family.[76] William Heighway and his son Samuel were tanners by trade, but the tanhouse probably ceased to be used for this purpose in the early years of the 19th century. A tailor is recorded at Pontesford in 1671[77] and a shoemaker in 1772.[78] The village has never had a smithy, but there was a wheelwright here in 1870. There was a shop at Pontesford in the later 19th century and other tradesmen then recorded include a shoemaker 1870–91, a decorator 1870–1929, and a carpenter 1885–1929.

The smithy at Plealey has stood on its present site since at least 1698[79] and since 1797 has been occupied by the Bromley family.[80] A wheelwright's shop, established *c.* 1827,[81] remained in business until shortly after 1917 and there was a shoemaker in the village, 1829–63.[82] A shop had been opened by 1885 and there were 2 shops here, 1926–41. A garage had been opened by 1934.

A field known as the Forge Yard, recorded at Longden in 1513,[83] probably marked the site of the smithy, which is first named in 1593.[84] The village had two blacksmiths 1797–1863,[85] and 3 of them 1870–85, but only one since 1909. In addition to 39 colliers, there were 18 other tradesmen in Longden in 1851, including 4 bricklayers, 2 shopkeepers, and 2 wheelwrights.[86] There were normally 3 shops between 1863 and 1941, but no wheelwright after 1870. At least 10 tradesmen still lived in the village in 1941.

Mining activity in the later 19th century provided scope for a moderate number of tradesmen at Asterley, Arscott, and Cruckmeole. A smithy at Asterley, first recorded in 1797,[87] and a shop, in existence by 1842,[88] remained in business until *c.* 1937. There was also a wheelwright in the village, 1881–85, and a saddler at Hinwood, 1917–41. There were two shops at Cruckmeole by 1840,[89] one of which survived until 1941, and a butcher is recorded between 1885 and 1909. At Arscott no tradesmen are recorded other than a shopkeeper, who was in business between 1840[90] and 1941.

Elsewhere in the parish the only notable craftsmen were the blacksmiths who had set up in business, in association with alehouses, at cross-road sites at Lea Cross, Gadbridge Lane, and Nox before the middle of the 17th century.[91] There is little evidence for tradesmen in the remaining hamlets. A carpenter and a blacksmith at Cruckton, first recorded in 1842,[92] had both gone out of business by the end of the 19th century. A tailor and shoemaker occupied a cottage at Edge in the later 18th century[93] and a barn at Panson was somewhat improbably described as a shop in 1840.[94]

LOCAL GOVERNMENT. Pontesbury, with Malehurst, was accounted a member of the barony of Caus during the Middle Ages, but there is no evidence that this involved anything more than the personal attendance of the lord of the manor at the honorial court.[95] There are a few court rolls for Pontesbury manor, 1425–1600,[96] most of them dating from the later 16th century, a modern transcript

[65] *Bull. Geol. Survey*, xiv. 38.
[66] Ex inf. Mr. E. Davies, Malehurst Mill.
[67] Ex inf. Mr. H. P. Davies, Mount Edgebold, Shrewsbury.
[68] S.R.O. 1011 (Smythe Owen) uncat., rent accts. 1803–40.
[69] Ibid. 785/180.
[70] *S.C.C. Minutes*, 1894–7, p. 5.
[71] Ibid. 1953–4, p. 176.
[72] The following account of trades in the parish is based, except where otherwise stated, on *Bagshaw's Dir. Salop.* (1851) and *Kelly's Dir. Salop.* (1856–1941).
[73] E 179/166/23.
[74] S.P.L., MS. 2364; S.R.O. 1011 (Smythe Owen) uncat., sale partics. 1794; Hope-Edwardes MSS., Linley Hall, sale partics. 1800.
[75] S.P.L., Deeds 16038.
[76] Ibid. 12706; S.R.O. 169/1 (Ford ct. r. 1668, 1678).
[77] S.R.O. 169/1 (ibid. 1671).
[78] Ibid. 169/3 (ibid. 1772).

[79] Ibid. 169/1 (ibid. 1698).
[80] S.P.L., MS. 2364; S.R.O. 437/4; ibid. 785/182.
[81] S.R.O. 169/12 (Ford ct. r. 1827).
[82] Ibid. (ibid. 1829).
[83] S.P.L., MS. 393 (ct. r. 1513).
[84] Ibid. (ibid. 1593).
[85] Ibid. MS. 2364; Heref. Dioc. Regy., Longden tithe appt.
[86] H.O. 107/1990/359/2.
[87] S.P.L., MS. 2364.
[88] S.R.O. 437/5; ibid. 785/181.
[89] Ibid. 437/4; ibid. 785/182.
[90] Ibid.
[91] See pp. 257, 261.
[92] S.R.O. 437/5; ibid. 785/181.
[93] Ibid. 169/3 (Ford ct. r. 1764).
[94] Ibid. 437/4; ibid. 785/182.
[95] See p. 264.
[96] S.R.O. 665 uncat.; S.P.L., Deeds 6781, 6793–4, 6819, 9433, 9485.

of court rolls, 1601–1705,[97] and presentments, 1774–1844.[98] Great courts were held in spring and autumn. Small courts, concerned with pleas between parties, apparently continued to be held at three-weekly intervals until 1613, after which date only great courts were held—a change which coincides with the enfranchisement of most of the copyholders in 1615. The jurisdiction of the court, which included the assize of bread and ale, covered the townships of Boycott, Farley, Halston, Hinton, and Pontesbury, for which constables were elected. After 1699 the court's business was restricted to the presentment of encroachments on the commons and the election of constables. No manor courts were held after the inclosure of Pontesbury Hill in 1848.[99]

A few medieval court rolls of Longden manor, the earliest being dated 1292, survive in an early-17th-century transcript.[1] This also contains a tolerably complete series of copy court rolls, 1472–1643, and original minutes of business, 1651–1851. Vestiges of the jurisdiction formerly enjoyed by the honorial court of Longden barony survived until the earlier 17th century in that suit of court was owed by free tenants at Brerelawe, Marsh, and Wigmore in Westbury parish, at Panson and Moat Hall in Pontesbury, and at Onslow, all of them in origin fiefs of Longden barony. In the 17th century, and perhaps as early as the later 15th century, the court met at irregular intervals as occasion demanded. Its sessions were held at Longden chapel in 1629, at a building known as the Court House after 1783, and at The Tankerville Arms after 1813. Its jurisdiction did not include the assize of bread and ale and no constables or other officers were appointed at the court.

Extracts from the court rolls of the manor of Oaks, 1420–1522,[2] are too meagre to provide information on its jurisdiction. The greater part of the parish lay within Ford manor, the surviving records and jurisdiction of which court are discussed elsewhere.[3] A body known as the 'Corporation of Pontesbury' which was meeting in the village in 1776, when Baldwin Leighton was mayor,[4] seems to have been of a similar character to that existing at Acton Burnell at the same period,[5] though with less historical justification.

The parish records include vestry minutes from 1793, churchwardens' accounts for Pontesbury, 1840–79, and for Cruckton chapel, 1845–87, and a complex but incomplete set of overseers' accounts, 1787–1835.[6] The four Quarters into which the parish was divided for administrative purposes did not follow ecclesiastical or manorial boundaries, but probably represent an arrangement more ancient than the later 18th century, when they are first recorded. The Quarters and their constituent townships were as follows: Cruckton Quarter (Cruckmeole, Cruckton, Newnham and Nox, Sascott, Sibberscott, and the Hamlets), Edge Quarter (Edge, Farley, Halston, Hinton, Lea, Plealey, and Polmere), Longden Quarter (Arscott, Longden, and

Oaks), Pontesbury Quarter (Asterley, Boycott, Malehurst, Pontesbury, and Pontesford). Though an independent chapelry, Longden was assessed to church and poor rates with the remainder of the parish, but levied its own highway rates.[7]

A body known as 'The Eight Men', recorded in 1647,[8] were still at least in theory acting as a vestry in 1770, when they appointed a vestry clerk.[9] A select vestry, known as 'The Committee of Directors of the Poor', was introduced in 1793. This normally consisted of the overseers and one representative from each Quarter. Meetings were held fortnightly, and took place after 1803 at Pontesbury school. The schoolmaster, John Stretch, was appointed vestry clerk in 1803 and retained the office until his death in 1833. Although its business was restricted in the 1790s to the supervision of poor relief, the operation of a workhouse test, and the organization of supplementary relief in times of stress, the Committee of Directors soon assumed control of all aspects of parish business. It seems to have become an open vestry after 1839.

Until 1852 the two churchwardens rendered separate accounts, each collecting and disbursing rates from two of the Quarters, but thereafter a single account was rendered. Church rates were levied annually until 1868. They were then replaced by collections but, in spite of opposition from the vestry, voluntary church rates were introduced in 1870 and remained in use until 1882.

Each Quarter had a single overseer of the poor, who occasionally served by deputy. The overseers rendered separate accounts, of which the following incomplete sets have survived: Cruckton, 1801–19; Edge, 1760–1817 and 1824–35; Longden, 1765–1818; Pontesbury, 1757–80 and 1827–32. Until 1789 copies of these were entered by the parish clerk in an engrossed account for the whole parish. Printed registers of weekly relief payments, of which only a few specimens survive, were introduced in 1806. The vestry clerk was appointed assistant overseer at a salary of 50 guineas a year in 1813. This experiment had been abandoned by 1814, but was tried again with more success in 1821. William Nicholls, then appointed acting overseer, remained in office until his death and was succeeded by his son in 1835.

Expenditure on poor relief, a modest £169 a year in 1770, had risen to £401 by 1775. It reached £780 in 1782, but was normally between £500 and £600 a year in the 1780s. Reliable expenditure figures are not available for the parish as a whole after 1788. In Edge and Longden Quarters, where some £130 was spent on the poor in 1788, expenditure rose to over £250 a year in the crisis years 1795–6, but was normally less than £200 a year in that decade. A marked rise in expenditure occurred after 1800 in the three Quarters for which accounts have survived, and in 1803 the parish was said to be spending £1,642 a year on poor relief.[10] This had risen to £2,272 by 1816[11] and reached a peak of £2,631 in

[97] S.P.L., MS. 300.
[98] S.R.O. 1011 (Dukes) uncat.
[99] Ibid. (Smythe Owen), case for opinion, 1867.
[1] S.P.L., MS. 392–3, and S.R.O. 665 uncat., ct. r. 1629.
[2] S.P.L., Deeds 2600.
[3] See p. 233.
[4] Salop. N. & Q. 1st ser. i. 48.
[5] See p. 10.

[6] In parish chest, with exception of N.L.W., J. R. Hughes (1962), 3, 4 (vestry minutes, 1803–39).
[7] Par. rec., commonplace bk. of Chas. Drury.
[8] S.P.R. Heref. xii (1), 144.   [9] Ibid. 336, 383.
[10] Poor Law Abstract, 1803, H.C. 175, pp. 416–17 (1803–4), xiii.
[11] Rep. Cttee. on Poor Rate Returns, 1822, Suppl. App., H.C. 556, p. 141 (1822), v.

1818,[12] but was well below £2,000 a year after 1821.[13]

By 1760 and until 1774 the poor were let to a contractor, Charles Barber, who administered the workhouse and paid regular outdoor relief. The overseers themselves made weekly relief payments, 1774–86, when each Quarter was responsible for supplying provisions for the workhouse for 3 months each year, but Barber seems to have been retained as workhouse manager. Between 1788 and 1798 all aspects of poor relief, other than the collection of rates, were administered by a contractor, under the supervision of the Committee of Directors. The overseers resumed responsibility for outdoor relief in 1798, and until 1835 the workhouse alone was let to a contractor. The office of workhouse manager was filled by Richard Cooper from 1803 until 1815, when the workhouse was placed in the charge of a committee of 24 'respectable' inhabitants, two of whom were to be responsible each month for the purchase of provisions and clothing, and for setting the inmates to work. This experiment seems to have been a failure. In spite of a purge of its inmates carried out in 1817, the workhouse was said to be ruinous and excessively expensive and in the following year was again let to Richard Cooper, who was still manager in 1824. A final expedient was adopted in 1835, whereby all the poor were let to William Croft, a local publican, for £1,000 a year, under the supervision of a parochial Board of Guardians. This was probably intended as a preliminary to the adoption of the provisions of the Poor Law Amendment Act. Contracts for medical attendance were made with William Blakeway, 1807–8, Thomas Williams, 1811–17, and Mr. Skrymsher, 1823.

The workhouse, at Workhouse Bank, Pontesbury, was established in 1732,[14] its site being held on a long lease.[15] It had 20 inmates in 1776[16] and 24 in 1803.[17] A workhouse register, 1803–27, shows that there were seldom more than 20 inmates at any one time during this period. Between 1793 and 1804 the inmates were employed in linen-weaving and in the 1790s the cloth produced was distributed among the outdoor poor as clothing.

Noteworthy expedients were adopted by the parish to provide supplementary relief in the crisis years 1795 and 1800 and during the post-war depression. An increase in the proportion of relief paid in kind was already apparent in 1794. In January 1795 a special rate was levied to supply the poor with cheap flour and in May of that year a fund of £108 was raised for the same purpose. More sophisticated methods were adopted in 1800. In January the vestry instituted the compulsory purchase of corn from farmers in the parish at 2s. a bushel below the market price and in November all farmers were required to supply specified

quantities at a shilling a 'strike' ($\frac{1}{12}$ bushel). Out of a total of £728 disbursed by the overseer of Cruckton Quarter in 1800, £137 was spent on potatoes, flour, corn, and cheese for the poor. In 1813 the vestry resolved to put troublesome pauper children to work at the Hanwood factory of Messrs. Marshall, Hutton & Co., where children aged from 9 to 12 were to receive between 2s. 9d. and 4s. a week, and those aged from 12 to 14 5s. to 6s. a week. Steps were taken in 1816 to ascertain the number of unemployed coal-miners and lead-smelters in the parish, and committees were established in each Quarter to find work during the winter of 1816–17. The unemployed were engaged on road repairs in Edge and Longden Quarters in 1817.

CHURCHES. The church is first named in 1254[18] and Reynold, parson of Pontesbury, recorded in the early 13th century,[19] is the first known incumbent. Since, however, Pontesbury church was a 'minster', served by 3 portioners until 1909, it is likely to be a pre-Conquest foundation. An estate of 1½ hide, apparently held by the church quit of geld in 1086,[20] had been alienated before 1254.[21] From the later Middle Ages Longden and Pulverbatch were accounted chapelries of Pontesbury,[22] but it is unlikely that they were originally dependent.

The first, second, and third portions were known during the Middle Ages as the David, Nicholas, and Ratford portions respectively, from the names of their incumbents in 1291;[23] by 1374 the second and third portions were also known as Childhall and Coldhall respectively,[24] no doubt from the residences of their rectors. These names were last used in 1640.[25] The first portioner appears to have enjoyed a vague precedence in the later Middle Ages. He was styled Dean of Pontesbury between 1394 and 1540[26] and the parsonage of the first portion is still known as the Deanery. The rector of the third portion was, however, styled dean in 1277.[27]

Until 1840 the rector of the first portion was responsible for the service of the church for 26 weeks in each year and the second and third portioners for 13 weeks each.[28] This arrangement does not appear to have led to friction between the portioners until the early 19th century. All three portioners were involved in proceedings in the consistory court in 1277–8,[29] but this appears to have been due to a feud between the lord of the manor and the rector of the third portion. A clash of personalities between the reforming Charles Drury (rector of the second portion, 1824–69)[30] and the conservative Hamlet Harrison (rector of the first portion, 1809–43),[31] came to a head over the former's proposal in 1837 to erect a chapel of ease for the second portion at Cruckton, to serve hamlets in the east of the parish, whose inhabitants were unable to attend the parish

[12] Ibid.
[13] Ibid. *1825*, H.C. 334, p. 177 (1825), iv; *Acct. of Money Expended on Poor, 1825–9*, H.C. 83, p. 391 (1830–1), xi; ibid. *1830–4*, H.C. 444, p. 344 (1835), xlvii.
[14] *24th Rep. Com. Char.*, H.C. 231, p. 393 (1831), xi.
[15] Ibid.
[16] *Rep. Cttee. on Overseers' Returns, 1777*, p. 442, H.C. (1st ser. ix, reprinted 1803).
[17] *Poor Law Abstract*, 1803, pp. 416–17.
[18] *Rot. Hund.* (Rec. Com.), ii. 66.
[19] Eyton, vi. 202.
[20] *V.C.H. Salop.* i. 325; Eyton, vii. 143.

[21] *Rot. Hund.* (Rec. Com.), ii. 66.
[22] See pp. 138, 290.
[23] *Tax. Eccl.* (Rec. Com.), 167.
[24] *Cal. Inq. p.m.* xiv, p. 22.
[25] Heref. Dioc. Regy., glebe terrier, 1640.
[26] S.P.L., Deeds 429, 6796; Leland, *Itin.* (ed. Toulmin-Smith), ii. 26.
[27] *Reg. T. Cantilupe* (C. & Y.S.), 153.
[28] Par. rec., commonplace bk. of Chas. Drury.
[29] *Reg. T. Cantilupe* (C. & Y.S.), 143–93 *passim*.
[30] *Instit. Dioc. Heref.* 146, 182.
[31] Ibid. 135, 160.

church.[32] Harrison refused his consent to the scheme and the rector of the third portion felt obliged to respect the wishes of his patron, E. W. Smythe Owen, who opposed anything likely to alter the value of his advowson.[33] Cruckton chapel was consecrated in 1840[34] and the primary object of a decree issued by the Bishop of Hereford in that year,[35] apportioning spiritual duties within the parish, was to regularize the chapel's position. Responsibility for spiritual duties in the following areas was assigned to each portioner: the first portioner, Pontesbury, Malehurst, Boycott, and that part of Pontesford township lying to the west of Pontesford Brook (some 1,850 a.); the second portioner, Arscott, Cruckmeole, Cruckton, Horton, Nox, Sascott, Shorthill, Sibberscott, the Hamlets (that is, Little Hanwood, Moat Hall, Onslow, Panson, and Woodhall), and parts of Newnham and Plealey (3,680 a.); the third portioner, Asterley, Edge, Farley, Halston, Hinton, Lea, Oaks, Polmere, part of Newnham and Pontesford, and Radlith in Plealey (3,000 a.).[36] Sunday services at the parish church were to continue as before, the rector of the first portion taking them for two Sundays in each lunar month, and the other portioners 13 weeks each.[37] Longden, which possessed its own curate, was a benefice without cure of souls and the decree made the rectors of the second and third portions each responsible for spiritiual duties there for six months in the year.[38]

Objections to the decree made by Hamlet Harrison were overruled,[39] but it was the principal reason for almost continual friction between the portioners in the later 19th and early 20th centuries. Negotiations to convert Longden into a living with cure of souls came to an end in 1857, when the patron of the third portion refused his consent to the scheme.[40] A more elaborate scheme on the same lines was put forward by Henry de Grey Warter, impropriator of Longden chapel, in 1866.[41] He proposed that Longden should become an ecclesiastical district, to include Oaks township, and offered to contribute towards the endowment of the living. Like Warter's suggestion, rival schemes submitted to the Ecclesiastical Commissioners in 1872 by the rectors of Pontesbury and the parishioners came to nothing. The rectors then proposed that the rector of the third portion should serve Asterley and Longden.[42] The parishioners objected that the two villages were 5 miles distant from each other and that the income of the third portioner was inadequate to cover double services, describing the scheme as 'most unnatural, unreasonable, and objectionable'.[43] They suggested that Asterley should be held with Cruckton by the second portioner, leaving Longden alone to the rector of the third portion.[44]

The debate was further complicated by S. J. Hawkes, Drury's successor as rector of the second portion, who in 1888 built a chapel at Lea Cross.[45] Intended as a memorial to his mother, this building is a proprietary chapel.[46] A licence for worship granted in 1904[47] was revoked in 1925,[48] but renewed in 1927.[49] On the death of S. J. Hawkes the chapel passed to his sister Mary (d. 1927), who built a parsonage and a church hall.[50] In 1941, when management of the chapel and parsonage was vested in the Hereford Diocesan Board of Patronage, the chapel had an endowment fund represented by £9,421 stock.[51] Hawkes wished Lea Cross to take the place of Cruckton chapel, since he did not consider the latter well sited to serve his portion.[52] Lea Cross chapel in fact stood on ground assigned to the third portion in 1840, and its anomalous position prompted yet more proposals to adjust the territories of the three portions.[53]

The area of disagreement was somewhat reduced after the merger of the first and second portions in 1909,[54] but the problem of reapportioning spiritual duties in the parish was under continuous discussion until 1935,[55] when an order to this effect was issued.[56] Under the order that part of the territory of the third portion which lay to the south of the railway from Shrewsbury to Welshpool and west of Rea Brook was transferred to the rector of the first and second portions. The rector of the third portion retained only Halston, Oaks, and Radlith of the area assigned to him in 1840, but was also to be responsible for the service of Longden chapel.[57]

Until 1794 the advowson of the three portions normally followed the descent of the manor of Pontesbury. Negotiations to appropriate the church to Haughmond Abbey in 1317 were abortive.[58] On the death of John de Charlton in 1374 the advowson of the first portion was assigned in dower to his widow Joan,[59] but reverted to the lord of the manor at her death in 1397.[60] The three advowsons followed separate descents during the 15th century, after the partition of the estates of Edward Charlton in 1421.[61] The advowson of the first portion was then assigned to his daughter Joyce,[62] but had been reunited with the manor by 1446.[63] That of the second portion passed to Edward's widow Elizabeth and her second husband John Sutton, Lord Dudley.[64] On Elizabeth's death in 1477[65] it appears to have passed to John Grey, lord of the manor, who presented in 1490.[66] The advowson of the third portion was presumably assigned to Joyce, daughter of Edward Charlton in or after 1421, for it was held

[32] Par. rec., acct. of building Cruckton chapel, 1837–47.
[33] Ibid.
[34] Heref. Dioc. Regy., reg. 1822–42, pp. 482–5.
[35] Ibid. pp. 506–15.
[36] Ibid.
[37] Ibid.
[38] Ibid.
[39] Par. rec., commonplace bk. of Chas. Drury.
[40] Ibid.
[41] S.R.O. 437/8.
[42] Ibid. 1011 uncat., memorial to Eccl. Com., c. 1872; par. rec., vestry minutes, 1839–1964.
[43] Ibid.
[44] Ibid.
[45] See p. 290.
[46] Char. Com. files.
[47] Heref. Dioc. Regy., reg. 1902–19, p. 84.
[48] Ibid. reg. 1919–26, pp. 398–9.
[49] Ibid. reg. 1926–38, p. 30.
[50] Char. Com. files.   [51] Ibid.
[52] S.R.O. 437/9.
[53] Par. rec., draft memorial to Queen's College, c. 1889.
[54] See p. 285.
[55] S.R.O. 677 passim.
[56] Heref. Dioc. Regy., reg. 1926–38, pp. 450–2.
[57] Ibid.
[58] Cal. Pat. 1313–17, 618.
[59] Cal. Close, 1374–7, 124.
[60] Ibid. 1396–9, 151.
[61] C 138/61/80.   [62] Ibid.
[63] Reg. T. Spofford (C. & Y.S.), 367.
[64] Ibid. 364; Reg. R. Boulers (C. & Y.S.), 22.
[65] C 140/69/19.
[66] Reg. T. Mylling (C. & Y.S.), 198.

by her son John, Earl of Worcester, at his execution in 1470.[67] It then passed to John's sister Joan, wife of Edmund Ingoldsthorp, who died in 1495,[68] but had been reunited with the manor by 1519.[69]

Like the manor, the advowsons were claimed in the later 16th century by the Vernons, who presented in 1575[70] and 1576,[71] but all three passed in 1602 to Sir Roger Owen.[72] His descendants were patrons until the end of the 18th century, but frequently sold the right of presentation.[73]

In 1794, when the advowsons of the first and second portions were sold,[74] the former was purchased by John Hand of Whitchurch,[75] who sold it to Joseph Harrison in 1809.[76] It later passed to Hamlet Harrison, rector of the first portion, whose trustees presented in 1844.[77] Thomas Harrison, a farmer of West Derby (Lancs.), who was patron by 1847,[78] sold the advowson to William Harrison, rector of this portion, in 1858[79] and Miss A. Harrison was patron in 1905.[80] Mrs. Frances Seddon, patron by 1910,[81] transferred the advowson to R. T. Seddon in 1915.[82] It passed to Mrs. Eubank in 1923[83] and in 1933 to St. Chad's Hall (later College), Durham, the present patrons.[84] Mrs. Congreve, who purchased the advowson of the second portion in 1794,[85] sold it in 1804 to the Michel Visitors of Queen's College, Oxford,[86] who were its patrons until 1908, when the advowson passed to Mrs. Frances Seddon.[87] The first and second portions were merged in 1910.[88] The advowson of the third portion, retained by the Owen family in 1794, had passed by 1882 to Henry de Grey Warter.[89] The executors of Major J. de Grey Tatham Warter were patrons in 1965.[90]

The combined annual value of the three portions was said to be £26 13s. 4d. in 1291,[91] £27 2s. 4d. in 1341,[92] and £42 17s. in 1535.[93] During the Middle Ages the first and second portions were normally assigned the same value, the third portion being worth about half as much,[94] but a somewhat different grading is found in a valuation of the manor of 1374.[95] The respective values of the portions were here given as £10, £13 6s. 8d., and £3 6s. 8d.,[96] suggesting that the second portion was already the most valuable. Their respective values were said to be £70, £80, and £55 in 1655,[97] and in 1794 the annual income of the first portion was £300, and that of the second portion £500.[98] In 1835 the net annual income of the three portions was £800, £825, and £483[99] respectively, the relatively high valuation of the first portion being attributed to the high rate at which its tithes were let.[1] No reliable information on the values of all three portions in the later 19th century is available, but the second portion had a net income of only £540 c. 1857[2] and the third portion a net income of £470 in 1872.[3]

The glebe of the three portions all lay within Pontesbury township, that of the first portion to the south-east, that of the second portion to the north, and that of the third portion to the west of the village.[4] No attempt seems to have been made to consolidate it between the early 17th century[5] and 1842, when the rector of each portion held 22 a., 59 a., and 61 a. respectively.[6] The glebe of each portion was said in 1640 to be worth £9, £22, and £23 respectively,[7] but no comprehensive later valuations are known. In 1797 the rector of the second portion kept his glebe in hand, and the glebe of the first portioner was occupied by his curate, but the whole of the third portion glebe was held on lease.[8] The latter was normally leased in the 19th century,[9] as was the greater part of the second portion glebe.[10] During this period the rectors of the first and third portions enhanced the value of their glebes by mining leases, first recorded (on the third portion) in 1792.[11] At his death in 1901 William Harrison, rector of the first portion, devised £700 to Queen Anne's Bounty as compensation for the royalties he had received for unauthorized working of the glebe minerals.[12] Some 23 a. of the glebe of the united first and second portions has been sold since 1918, and some 18 a. of third portion glebe have been sold since 1906.[13]

A claim made in the mid-14th century by the chaplain of St. Michael's in the Castle, Shrewsbury, as perpetual curate of Ford, to tithes in those townships which lay in Ford manor was apparently

[67] *Cal. Pat.* 1467–77, 277–8; C 140/34/53, where it is wrongly said to be the Childhall portion.
[68] *Cal. Inq. p.m. Hen. VII*, i, pp. 463–4, 473.
[69] *L. & P. Hen. VIII*, iii (1), p. 146.
[70] *Instit. Dioc. Heref.* 23.
[71] Ibid. 24.
[72] S.P.L., Deeds 6791.
[73] Ibid. 6799; N.L.W., Ottley Papers 1299; *Instit. Dioc. Heref.* 45, 46, 60, 62, 97.
[74] S.R.O. 665 uncat., acct. of sales, 1795.
[75] Ibid.
[76] S.P.L., Deeds 12375.
[77] *Instit. Dioc. Heref.* 160.
[78] Ibid. 163.
[79] Par. rec., commonplace bk. of Chas. Drury.
[80] *Kelly's Dir. Salop.* (1905); ex inf. Miss L. F. Chitty.
[81] Heref. Dioc. Regy., reg. 1902–19, p. 396.
[82] Ibid. p. 602.
[83] Ibid. 1919–26, p. 294.
[84] Ibid. 1926–38, p. 394.
[85] S.R.O. 665 uncat., acct. of sales, 1795.
[86] Par. rec., commonplace bk. of Chas. Drury.
[87] Heref. Dioc. Regy., reg. 1902–19, p. 294.
[88] Ibid. 1902–19, p. 396.
[89] Ibid. 1869–83, p. 689.
[90] *Crockford* (1963–4).
[91] *Tax. Eccl.* (Rec. Com.), 167.
[92] *Inq. Non.* (Rec. Com.), 185.

[93] *Valor Eccl.* (Rec. Com.), iii. 213. A slightly higher valuation is given in the following year: *Reg. C. Bothe* (C. & Y.S.), 368.
[94] *Tax. Eccl.* (Rec. Com.), 167; *Valor Eccl.* (Rec. Com.), iii. 213.
[95] C 135/237/1.
[96] Ibid.
[97] *T.S.A.S.* xlvii. 23–24.
[98] S.R.O. 665 uncat., sale partics. 1794.
[99] *Rep. Com. Eccl. Revenues* [67], pp. 448–9, H.C. (1835), xxii.
[1] Par. rec., acct. of building Cruckton chapel, 1837–47.
[2] Ibid. commonplace bk. of Chas. Drury.
[3] S.R.O. 1011 uncat., correspondence *re* sale of advowson, 1872.
[4] S.R.O. 437/5; ibid. 785/181.
[5] Heref. Dioc. Regy., glebe terrier, 1640.
[6] S.R.O. 437/5; ibid. 785/181.
[7] Heref. Dioc. Regy., glebe terrier, 1640.
[8] S.P.L., MS. 2364.
[9] S.R.O. 437/5; ibid. 785/181; ibid. 1011 (Smythe Owen) uncat., valuation of third portion, 1872.
[10] S.R.O. 437/5; ibid. 785/181; par. rec., commonplace bk. of Chas. Drury (valuations of second portion, 1857, 1861).
[11] S.P.L., Deeds 11509; S.R.O. 437/13, lease, 1849.
[12] Par. rec., letter *re* income of first and second portions, 1923.
[13] Ex inf. Church Com.

unsuccessful,[14] but may account for the tithes in Cruckton and Lea, then worth £9 a year, which were held by the impropriator of Ford in 1655.[15] The tithes of the second portion, normally leased since the later 17th century, yielded £760 a year in 1824 and £822 when re-let in the following year.[16] Those of the first portion were valued at £757 net in 1809.[17] Little is otherwise known of the mode of collection of tithes in the parish before 1842, when moduses were in use for milch cows, calves, and colts.[18] The complex pattern of tithing revealed by the tithe apportionments of 1840 and 1842[19] may be summarized as follows: the rector of the first portion claimed tithes from 3,013 a. in 11 townships, and portions of tithes in 4 others, the rector of the second portion claimed tithes from some 2,940 a. in 14 townships and half the tithes of Asterley, and the rector of the third portion claimed tithes from 865 a. in 4 townships, two-thirds of the tithes of Farley, and a modus of £1 on 53 a. in Asterley. These tithes were then commuted for rent-charges of £780, £658, and £205 respectively.[20] In addition, a rent-charge of £120 15s. was allotted to Hamlet Harrison, rector of the first portion, for impropriate tithes over 644 a. in Cruckmeole, Cruckton, and Lea, and £7 to George Tomline, impropriator of Ford, for 36 a. in Cruckton, then claimed as a detached part of Ford parish.[21] Tithes arising from the Harries estate in Cruckton and Newnham were held to be merged in the freehold.[22]

Of 53 known portioners of Pontesbury, 1277–1540, only 7 seem to have held their livings for more than 20 years, four of these being rectors of the first portion. A high proportion of medieval rectors were graduates and in the 15th century these included Thomas Bradshaw, clerk of the Duke of Bedford,[23] and William London, agent for Thomas Beckington at the Papal court.[24] David and Walter Fitz Reynold, who held the first and second portions in 1278,[25] were relatives of the lord of the manor, as was Philip ap Howell (rector of the first portion, 1308–52).[26] Humphrey, Griffin, Lewis, and William, sons of John de Charlton, held the first and second portions during the years 1339–84, frequently exchanging them among themselves.[27]

Incumbencies tended to be longer after the Reformation. In the period 1536–1900 24 out of 46 rectors held their livings for more than 20 years, and 33 died in office.[28] Long incumbencies occurred notably in the 19th century, when the first portion was held by two rectors in the period 1809–1901, and the second portion by three rectors, 1804–1909. The third portion, less wealthy and without an adequate parsonage, was held by 5 rectors in this period. During the later 17th and 18th centuries 5 rectors were close relatives of the lord of the manor or of the individual to whom the right of presentation had been granted. All rectors of the first portion, 1809–1931, were relatives of the patron. Three rectors held at different times more than one portion in the early 17th century, but the device of combining two portions under one rector was only employed once before 1910. Henry Baldwin, rector of the third portion, 1707–37,[29] was also rector of the first portion from 1710.[30]

The little evidence available suggests that rectors were normally resident in the 13th and 14th centuries. Chaplains, occasionally mentioned between 1277 and 1453,[31] were probably merely assistant clergy. In the later 15th century, however, all three rectors appear to have been non-resident, 3 different groups of curates being recorded in 1475,[32] 1479,[33] and 1482.[34] John Cole (rector of the first portion, 1520–36)[35] was a sub-dean of the King's chapel,[36] but was probably resident at Pontesbury, since he was said to have gone to great expense to improve his parsonage.[37] His successor John ap Rhys ap Griffin (rector of the first portion, 1536–75)[38] had formerly been a Cistercian monk[39] and appears in 1538 in a list of clergy living in fornication and avowtry for money.[40] All three portioners were said to be resident in 1567[41] and 1587,[42] but in the 1570s their duties appear to have been performed by a single curate, Lancelot Lake, who received an annual salary of £6.[43] Richard Sutton, curate in 1552,[44] may have been employed in a similar capacity.

Most later rectors of the first portion have always been resident, but they employed assistant curates between 1761 and 1866.[45] The salary of the curate of the first portion rose from only £30 in 1828[46] to £100 by 1846.[47] Rectors of the second portion are known to have been resident from 1540 until 1614,[48] and between 1639 and 1662,[49] but were non-resident from 1672[50] until 1770, when the parsonage of this portion was rebuilt by Edward Leighton.[51] They subsequently lived at Pontesbury until the merger of the two portions in 1910. Assistant curates

---

[14] See p. 234.
[15] *T.S.A.S.* xlvii. 23–24.
[16] S.R.O. 665 uncat., lease, 1660; ibid. 775 uncat., leases, 1714; par. rec., commonplace bk. of Chas. Drury.
[17] S.P.L., Deeds 12375.
[18] S.R.O. 437/4–5; ibid. 785/181–2.
[19] Ibid.   [20] Ibid.
[21] Ibid.   [22] Ibid.
[23] *Reg. E. Lacy* (C. & Y.S.), 113; *Reg. T. Spofford* (C. & Y.S.), 367.
[24] *Reg. T. Spofford* (C. & Y.S.), 364; *Reg. R. Boulers* (C. & Y.S.), 22.
[25] *Reg. T. Cantilupe* (C. & Y.S.), 143–93 *passim*.
[26] Eyton, vii. 140; *Reg. J. Trillek* (C. & Y.S.), 386.
[27] *Reg. J. Trillek* (C. & Y.S.), 373, 386, 389, 391, 408; *Reg. W. Courtenay* (C. & Y.S.), 13, 118; *Cal. Papal Pets.* i. 280.
[28] This paragraph is based on *Instit. Dioc. Heref. passim.*
[29] Ibid. 60, 80.
[30] Ibid. 62.
[31] *Reg. T. Cantilupe* (C. & Y.S.), 143, 153; *Reg. J. Gilbert* (C. & Y.S.), 66; *Reg. J. Stanbury* (C. & Y.S.), 192; S.P.L., Deeds 6795.

[32] *Reg. T. Mylling* (C. & Y.S.), 12.
[33] Ibid. 140.
[34] Ibid. 77.
[35] *Reg. C. Bothe* (C. & Y.S.), 333, 377.
[36] Leland, *Itin.* (ed. Toulmin Smith), ii. 26.
[37] Ibid.
[38] *Reg. C. Bothe* (C. & Y.S.), 377; E 123/5 f. 196.
[39] Ibid.
[40] *L. & P. Hen. VIII*, xiii, p. 507.
[41] *T.S.A.S.* 4th ser. xii. 100.
[42] Ibid. xlvi. 40.
[43] E 123/5 ff. 92, 196.
[44] *T.S.A.S.* 2nd ser. xii. 319.
[45] *S.P.R. Heref.* xii (1), 365–95, 497–518; Heref. Dioc. Regy., reg. 1822–42, pp. 92, 667; ibid. 1842–6, p. 335; ibid. 1857–69, pp. 404, 420, 477, 511.
[46] Heref. Dioc. Regy., reg. 1822–42, p. 92.
[47] Ibid. 1842–6, p. 335.
[48] *T.S.A.S.* 4th ser. xii. 100; ibid. xlvi. 40; *S.P.R. Heref.* xii. 3–98 *passim.*
[49] *S.P.R. Heref.* xii. 149, 151; E 179/255/35 m. 81d.
[50] *Hearth Tax, 1672,* 151–2.
[51] Heref. Dioc. Regy., reg. 1755–71, f. 207ᵛ.

were employed between 1733 and 1773,[52] and after 1840 a curate was appointed to take charge of Cruckton chapel.[53] Rectors of the third portion were normally non-resident, for lack of a suitable parsonage, after the death of Ralph Morhall in 1681.[54] The parsonage was occupied by the curate of the third portion in 1797[55] and 1824,[56] and by the curate of the first portion in 1846,[57] but was no more than a cottage by 1872.[58] Rectors of the third portion in the 19th century normally found suitable accommodation elsewhere. The rector lived at Hinton, 1847–55,[59] at Yockleton, 1885,[60] at Hinton Hall, 1891,[61] and at Cruckmeole, 1909–13.[62]

The parsonage of the first portion, which stood to the east of the church, was demolished in 1965. A former parsonage, said to have been extensively altered by John Cole in the earlier 16th century,[63] contained 7 hearths in the later 17th century.[64] This had been demolished by 1712, when it was said to have been 'old and much decayed'.[65] A faculty was then obtained for the erection of a brick parsonage on or near this site.[66] This probably related to the west wing of the recently demolished house, although its appearance, both internally and externally, suggests a date much later in the 18th century. The house contained 4 rooms on each floor, as stipulated in the faculty, and its dimensions (42×32 feet) roughly corresponded with those laid down in 1712 (41×35 feet).[67] It had a west front of 5 bays and was of 3 stories with string courses at first- and second-floor levels, and its low-pitched gabled roof had stone-coped gables. The boxing of the sash windows on the west front was not set back from the wall but, where they remained, the glazing bars were of the thin, later-18th-century type. The west door, opening on a staircase-hall, was framed by flat pilasters; a wooden porch was added in the 19th century. The two-story brick kitchen wing to the rear of the house, with wide fireplaces and a high timbered ceiling, may well have dated from 1712.

The parsonage of the second portion stands to the north-east of the church. It ceased to be occupied by the rector after 1910 and is now known as the Manor House. The house was much altered c. 1825,[68] but the main structure, built in 1770,[69] incorporates on the east side two bays of the parsonage built by William Owen in 1661.[70] Owen's parsonage, originally timber-framed, was probably of 3 bays, for it contained 3 hearths in 1662[71] and included a hall, parlour, and kitchen on the ground floor in 1770.[72] This older portion of the house no longer retains its original roof, but of the two projecting lateral chimney-stacks on the east wall, one is of 17th-century brick and the other, serving the kitchen, is stone-built. The parsonage was described as ruinous and beyond repair in 1770, when the rector obtained a faculty to build two parlours, with bedrooms and attics over and a cellar beneath.[73] He constructed a square brick house of 3 stories, containing 3 bays on the north front, with a low-pitched hipped roof. Virtually the only architectural features of this house still visible are two blocked windows on the north wall. One of these, at first-floor level, has a keystone and plain brick voussoirs. Nearly all the remaining windows and doorways, in addition to such internal features as staircases, fireplaces, and moulded ceilings, date from the earlier 19th century, when the house was remodelled in the Tudor style by Charles Drury, who also added a north porch, flanked by gabled single-story wings.[74] The datestone of the parsonage of 1661, set in a corner fireplace on the first floor in the older part of the house, is not in its original position. The panelling in this and the adjoining room is of 17th-century date and has been in the house since at least 1920.[75] In the 1930s the parsonage was used as a school to prepare candidates for admission to St. Chad's College, Durham.[76] It was sold in 1964.[77] A 5-bay tithe barn to the north of the house is of box-frame construction, but the tie-beams of its 4 internal trusses have been made from cruck blades, presumably from an earlier barn on the same site.

Now known as the Old Rectory, the former parsonage of the third portion stands some distance from the church, to the west of Pontesbury Brook. It is a small timber-framed house, which was cased in stone in 1767.[78] It was originally L-shaped, but the west bay of the southern cross-wing has been removed, and additions were made to the west of the house in the 19th century. The 3-bay tithe barn to the east of the house, which was rebuilt shortly before 1712,[79] contains portions of reused cruck blades in its roof-trusses.

A guild of St. Anne in Pontesbury church occurs in 1540[80] and a chantry of Our Lady, endowed with lands worth 4s. a year and served by a chantry priest, is recorded in 1548.[81] The endowment of this chantry was acquired by Rowland Harries of Shrewsbury in the following year.[82] Stocks of cattle, appraised at £8 15s. and £6, were said in 1548 to have been given towards the maintenance of a priest,[83] and a rent-charge of 5s. a year from Asterley to find lights in the church.[84]

Arrangements for services at Pontesbury church

[52] Ibid. 1772–1802, f. 27; *S.P.R. Heref.* xii (1), 302, 497–9.
[53] Heref. Dioc. Regy., reg. 1822–42, p. 503; ibid. 1847–56, p. 300; ibid. 1857–69, p. 629; par. rec., commonplace bk. of Chas. Drury.
[54] *S.P.R. Heref.* xii (1), 203.
[55] S.P.L., MS. 2364.
[56] Heref. Dioc. Regy., reg. 1822–42, p. 42.
[57] Ibid. 1842–6, p. 335.
[58] S.R.O. 1011 (Smythe Owen) uncat., memorial to Eccl. Com. c. 1872.
[59] Heref. Dioc. Regy., reg. 1847–56, pp. 1, 582.
[60] *Kelly's Dir. Salop.* (1885).
[61] Ibid. (1891).
[62] Ibid. (1909–13).
[63] Leland, *Itin.* (ed. Toulmin Smith), ii. 26.
[64] E 179/255/35 m. 81d.
[65] Heref Dioc. Regy., reg. 1710–23, f. 17.

[66] Ibid.
[67] Ibid.
[68] Par. rec., commonplace bk. of Chas. Drury.
[69] Heref. Dioc. Regy., reg. 1755–71, f. 207ᵛ.
[70] Datestone, now on fireplace on first floor.
[71] E 179/255/35 m. 81d.
[72] Heref. Dioc. Regy., reg. 1755–71, f. 207ᵛ.
[73] Ibid.
[74] Par. rec., commonplace bk. of Chas. Drury.
[75] Ex inf. Mrs. A. N. Fielden.
[76] Ex inf. The Principal, St. Chad's College.
[77] Ibid.
[78] Datestone.
[79] Heref. Dioc. Regy., reg. 1710–23, f. 17ᵛ.
[80] *T.S.A.S.* liv. 61.
[81] Ibid. 3rd ser. x. 358.
[82] *Cal. Pat.* 1549–51, 15; Bodl. MS. Blakeway 2, f. 271.
[83] *T.S.A.S.* 3rd ser. x. 380–1.   [84] Ibid. 373.

before the 19th century are not known. A body of psalm-singers, recorded in 1793,[85] received an annual fee of 5 guineas until 1856.[86] Musical accompaniment was provided by a violoncello in the 1840s.[87] An organ, formerly at Harrow School, was presented by Henry de Grey Warter in 1861.[88] This stands in the former singing gallery at the west end of the nave, but is no longer in use, having been replaced by a smaller organ given by Heighway Jones in 1907.[89] Monthly communion was said to have been 'recently' introduced c. 1850, when 70–80 persons took Easter communion.[90] The church then had average congregations of 250–300 on Sundays,[91] but as many as a thousand might attend on Whit Monday, the Club anniversary.[92] At Cruckton chapel services in 1840 were held on Sunday mornings at 11 a.m., together with an afternoon service in the winter months and evensong in the summer.[93] Communion was then celebrated 5 times a year.[94] Average congregations of 230 attended morning services at the chapel in 1840 and 1841,[95] and it continued to be well attended until the later years of the incumbency of S. J. Hawkes.[96] A body of singers, who received £3 10s. a year until 1869, were at first accompanied by a violoncello and clarionet[97] and by a harmonium after 1857.[98]

Before 1825 the church of *ST. GEORGE*, Pontesbury,[99] consisted of a chancel, nave, north and south aisles, and a northern tower. The tower, and probably the nave also, were built in the 12th century. The former was a fine example of Norman work. Originally separate from the church, it was built of reddish sandstone and was of 3 stages, divided by string courses. On each of 3 sides of the upper stage was a round-headed window consisting of two small round-headed lights, divided by a shaft with an enriched capital. The two lower stages contained very small round-headed lights. It had flat pilaster buttresses at its corners, that on the north-east being enlarged to house a spiral stair. An embattled parapet, probably of Grinshill stone, and a pyramidal roof were added later, but the parapet was supported on a corbel-table of 12th-century date. The chancel, which has survived substantially unaltered, was built in reddish stone c. 1300 and was divided from the nave by a pointed chancel arch. It has a pointed east window of 5 lights with intersecting tracery, interrupted to form a quatrefoil at the apex. Above this is a small lancet window, and there are 3 pointed 2-light windows with forking tracery set in wide-splayed rear-arches in the north and south walls. The priest's door on the south wall has a drop-arch. The trussed-rafter roof is contemporary and its cornice is decorated with quatrefoils.

Of the two aisles that on the north was probably constructed in the earlier 13th century. It was under the same roof as the nave, from which it was divided by an arcade of 3 round-headed arches, supported by clustered columns, each capital being differently carved, and its pointed north door appears to have been decorated with billet-moulding. The south aisle, which probably had a separate roof, contained a Lady Chapel, recorded in 1652,[1] and was added in the early 14th century. It had large pointed windows on the east and west, and a 3-light window with cusped intersecting tracery on the south wall. At about the same time, or a little later, another 3-light window was inserted above the west door. Most of the buttresses were probably contemporary with the structures they supported, but two larger buttresses at the west end and one on the south wall were added in 1772, when the church was said to be slipping westwards.[2]

Apart from a timber-framed porch outside the south door no significant alterations to the fabric seem to have been made until the 18th century, when mullioned windows were inserted in the south and north walls and a dormer window was set in the nave roof, above the level of the roof of the south aisle. The lower part of the east window had been bricked up by 1788, when a door had been inserted in the east wall of the tower and a large, low, round-headed window in the east wall of the north aisle.

Concern for the stability of the church was felt as early as 1772,[3] and in 1810–11 local architects, including Mr. Haycock and Mr. Carline, were called in to examine the fabric.[4] Soon after this the tower collapsed and in 1825 what remained of the nave and aisles were taken down.[5] A substantial body of parishioners wished to take advantage of this and, by erecting 3 smaller churches in the parish, to bring to an end the anomalous system of serving the living.[6] This was opposed by the rector of the first portion, who seems to have been responsible for the choice of design for the new nave and aisles,[7] which was produced by John Turner of Whitchurch.[8] The rector of the second portion favoured a plan for a cruciform church, with a central tower, put forward by Carline of Shrewsbury.[9] In the end a single new church was built at a cost of £5,000, most of which was raised by loans and mortgages, and was opened in 1829.[10] Turner died before its completion and was succeeded as architect by Samuel Smith of Madeley.[11] It was built in the Early English style and contained, like the former church, a nave with north and south aisles and a porch on the south wall, but the tower was set

85 Par. rec., minutes of Directors of the Poor, 1793–1802.
86 Ibid. churchwardens' accts. 1840–79.
87 Ibid.
88 Ibid. vestry minutes, 1839–1964; *Kelly's Dir. Salop.* (1885).
89 *Kelly's Dir. Salop.* (1909).
90 B.M. Add. MS. 21018, f. 318.
91 H.O. 129/359/2/6.
92 B.M. Add. MS. 21018, f. 318.
93 Par. rec., acct. of building Cruckton chapel, 1837–47.
94 Ibid.   95 Ibid.
96 H.O. 129/359/2/4; par. rec., memorial to Queen's College, c. 1889.
97 Par. rec., Cruckton chapelwardens' accts. 1845–87.
98 Ibid. commonplace bk. of Chas. Drury.
99 So styled in 1254: *Rot. Hund.* (Rec. Com.), ii. 66. The following architectural description is based, except where

otherwise stated, on S.P.L., MS. 372, vol. i, p. 69; ibid. vol. iii, p. 102; S.P.L., T. F. Dukes watercolours (churches), no. 119; *Gent. Mag.* (1827), plate facing p. 297; *Eng. Topog.* (Gent. Mag.), x. 113; par. rec., commonplace bk. of Chas. Drury; Cranage, vi. 533–5. See also plate facing p. 252.
1 S.P.L., Deeds 14078.
2 B.M. Add. MS. 21018, f. 318.   3 Ibid.
4 N.L.W., J. R. Hughes (1962), 3.
5 Par. rec., commonplace bk. of Chas. Drury; *Q. Sess. Orders*, iii. 250; *Eng. Topog.* (Gent. Mag.), x. 113.
6 Par. rec., commonplace bk. of Chas. Drury.
7 Ibid.
8 Ibid.; Pevsner, *Shropshire*, 230.
9 Par. rec., commonplace bk. of Chas. Drury.
10 Ibid.
11 Ibid.; ibid. churchwardens' accts. 1840–79.

against the south-west end of the nave. The red sandstone of the former church was reused in some parts of the fabric, which was elsewhere built of yellowish stone rubble with dressings of Grinshill stone. There are 4 pairs of lancets on the north and south walls and clerestory windows to the nave. The tower is of four stages, the belfry stage being exceptionally high, with pairs of corner buttresses. The aisles are divided from the nave by arcades of 5 pointed arches, supported by piers of quatrefoil section resting on tall bases. Much of the stone of the arches and piers came from the former arcade, but appears to have been recut. The chancel arch was rebuilt, but no other alterations were made to the fabric of the chancel.

No significant structural changes have since been made in the church. In 1897 plaster was removed from the walls of the nave, colouring formerly applied to the arcades was stripped, and the brick window arches were cased in cement.[12] Minor alterations were made to the fabric of the chancel in 1904, when its roof was restored.[13] Improvements to the west end of the nave were proposed at the same time,[14] but were not put into effect. The panelled wooden ceilings of the nave and aisles, however, appear to date from 1904.[15]

Little is known of the internal appearance of the former church. The pulpit and reading desk stood at the east end of the nave, close to the arcade of the north aisle.[16] Pews at the east end of the north and south aisles were set cross-wise, to face the pulpit, and were described as 'the aisle leading to the belfry' and the 'cross aisle' respectively.[17] A gallery in Classical style was erected at the west end in 1754[18] and the church was repewed in 1781–2.[19]

When the nave and aisles were rebuilt all their former fittings were deemed the property of the builders.[20] The font, however, which was then broken, was bought by Charles Drury and was restored to the church in 1857.[21] This is of 12th-century date and is a plain round one, with deep scolloping beneath the bowl. Drury also saved the upper part of the south door, which he placed in the porch of his parsonage.[22] Jacobean panelling used in the box-pews set up in the nave in 1829[23] probably came from the former church, but these were replaced by the existing open benches in 1897.[24] Some of this panelling may have been used in the construction of the screen below the organ gallery. A large 3-decker pulpit was set up at the south-east end of the nave in 1829[25] and remained in use until 1904, when a smaller pulpit was erected at the north-east end.[26]

The chancel owes its present internal appearance to the restoration of 1904, commemorated in the stained glass east window, when the screen and choir stalls were inserted.[27] Early-17th-century oak panelling round the walls was set up shortly before 1917.[28] A piscina in the south wall has a trefoil arch and is presumably contemporary with the main structure. The aumbry in the north wall has a door dated 1652. A Jacobean communion table stands in the sanctuary but has long been out of use. A marble-topped table with a Classical reredos, installed shortly before 1788,[29] was in use until 1866, when a new communion table and reredos, by G. E. Street, was installed by the rector of the first portion.[30] Six medieval tiles, set in the south wall of the chancel, came from the former church.[31] The church contains two parish chests, one of the early 17th century and the other dated 1700. An iron-bound chest with painted panels dates from the early 17th century but is of continental origin.

Most of the notable monuments in the nave and aisles appear to have survived the rebuilding.[32] They include 18th-century tablets commemorating members of the Boycott, Oliver, and Phillips families. In the chancel is an elaborate wall-monument to Thomas Davies, a London merchant (d. 1674). It was erected by his nephew in the mid-18th century and has two small standing figures, with a sailing ship below. A painting of Thomas Ottley (d. 1636), formerly against the north wall of the chancel,[33] is said to have been removed from the church by the Revd. R. T. Seddon.[34] Other persons commemorated by tablets include Owen Davies (d. 1614) and Henry Baldwin (d. 1737), Rectors of Pontesbury. There are 19th-century tablets and stained glass windows in the chancel and aisles to members of the Harrison and Heighway families.

There were 3 great bells and a sanctus bell in the church in 1552[35] and 5 bells were cast by Thomas Roberts of Shrewsbury in 1681.[36] These were recast into 6 bells in 1830,[37] but one of the latter was again recast in 1869.[38] A set of 8 tubular bells was acquired in 1893.[39] A curfew bell was being rung here from 5 November until Christmas in the early 19th century,[40] and the unusual custom of tolling 13 times at a man's funeral and 12 for a woman's was still observed c. 1900.[41] There was a clock in the tower in 1788.[42] The present one was bought in 1858.[43]

The church possessed 2 silver chalices and a paten in 1552,[44] but the oldest of the existing plate[45] is a silver paten, presented in 1718. A silver communion cup, paten, flagon, and 2 platters were acquired in

[12] Par. rec., vestry minutes, 1839–1964; ibid. acct. of restoration, 1886–97; *Kelly's Dir. Salop.* (1900).
[13] Par. rec., vestry minutes, 1839–1964; *Kelly's Dir. Salop.* (1905).
[14] Par. rec., vestry minutes, 1839–1964.
[15] Ibid.
[16] *S.P.R. Heref.* xii (1), 144–5, 376.
[17] Ibid. 144–5, 410–14.
[18] Heref. Dioc. Regy., reg. 1723–54, f. 153ᵛ; B.M. Add. MS. 21018, f. 318.
[19] Heref. Dioc. Regy., reg. 1772–1802, f. 114ᵛ; *S.P.R. Heref.* xii (1), 410–14.
[20] Par. rec., commonplace bk. of Chas. Drury.
[21] Ibid.   [22] Ibid.
[23] Cranage, vi. 534.
[24] Par. rec., vestry minutes, 1839–1964.
[25] Cranage, vi. 534.
[26] Par. rec., vestry minutes, 1839–1964.
[27] Ibid.; Heref. Dioc. Regy., reg. 1902–19, pp. 144–5; *Kelly's Dir. Salop.* (1905).

[28] *Kelly's Dir. Salop.* (1917).
[29] S.P.L., MS. 372, vol. i, p. 69.
[30] Par. rec., commonplace bk. of Chas. Drury.
[31] Ex inf. Miss L. F. Chitty.
[32] Monuments existing in 1827 are listed in *Eng. Topog.* (Gent. Mag.), x. 113–15.
[33] Ibid. 113–14; ex inf. Miss L. F. Chitty.
[34] Ex inf. Miss L. F. Chitty.
[35] *T.S.A.S.* 2nd ser. xii. 319, 336.
[36] Walters, *Ch. Bells Salop.* 205–6.
[37] N.L.W., J. R. Hughes (1962), 4.
[38] Walters, *Ch. Bells Salop.* 205–6.
[39] *Kelly's Dir. Salop.* (1895).
[40] Par. rec., commonplace bk. of Chas. Drury.
[41] Walters, *Ch. Bells Salop.* 206.
[42] S.P.L., MS. 372, vol. i, p. 69.
[43] Par. rec., vestry minutes, 1839–1964.
[44] *T.S.A.S.* 2nd ser. xii. 319.
[45] Description of plate based on Arkwright and Bourne, *Ch. Plate Ludlow Archd.* 50.

1784, and 2 further chalices and patens were given in 1910 and 1944. There is also a secular silver cup of 1880 and a private communion set of 1938. The registers are complete from 1538.[46]

The churchyard was enlarged in 1856, in which year burials within the church were prohibited,[47] but it was already proving inadequate in 1875, when a proposal was made to convert Lea Cross School into a cemetery chapel.[48] Burials in the churchyard were discontinued in 1902,[49] when land for a new cemetery in the village was provided by the rector of the first portion.[50]

The chapel of *ST. THOMAS*, Cruckton,[51] was erected on a site given in 1838 by Thomas Harries of Cruckton,[52] who stipulated that he should be the first to be buried there.[53] The architect, Edward Haycock, gave his services freely and the Alberbury breccia of which the chapel is constructed was provided free of royalties from the Rowton quarries. The cost of erection, totalling £949, was wholly met by subscriptions. Opened in 1840, the chapel is a simple building in the Early English style, consisting of a nave and a small chancel with a vestry on the south wall, a west porch, and a bell-cote containing a single small bell at the west end. All its windows are broad lancets.

The chapel retains its original open benches and a western gallery, supported on cast iron pillars, but most of the other fittings appear to have been renewed in the early 20th century, after a period of disuse, c. 1887–1909.[54] A pulpit and reading desk were given by Thomas Harries in 1840, but these were removed in the 1880s and there is now a plain wooden desk and a stone pulpit with marble shafts. The slender octagonal font is probably of the same date as the pulpit. The chancel was remodelled c. 1929, when early-17th-century oak panelling was set on the north and south walls. The base of the communion table is a framed table with baluster legs, of mid-17th-century date. The plate comprises a silver chalice of 1769, formerly used for sick-visiting in Pontesbury, and a silver chalice and paten given by the Mothers' Union in 1953.[55]

The small brick mission chapel at Asterley was built by the rector of the third portion in 1869.[56] It has a single bell, presumably installed at this time,[57] and an undated silver-plate chalice and paten.[58] A burial ground at Asterley was consecrated in 1899.[59]

The proprietary church of *ST. ANNE*, Lea Cross, was built in 1888 at the expense of S. J. Hawkes, rector of the second portion, on a site given by Col. Meredith-Warter to designs by J. L. Randall of Shrewsbury.[60] It is of red brick and consists of a chancel, nave, and a large central tower with a pyramidal roof. The tower is flanked by short transepts with lean-to roofs, set between its buttresses, that on the north containing an organ, installed in 1906.[61] At the west end, divided from the nave by an arcade of stone arches supported on marble pillars, is a low baptistery, with a porch to the north and a vestry to the south. There is a 5-light east window, a large circular west window, 3-light windows in the upper stage of the tower, and groups of lancets in the nave. The nave has an arch-braced collar-beam roof and the chancel a panelled wooden ceiling. The chancel is dominated by the large altar-tomb of Mrs. Anne Hawkes (d. 1882), the mother of the builder. There is an elaborate marble pulpit. The font, also of marble, stands in a small apse in the baptistery. The church has 8 tubular bells, installed in 1893,[62] and an undated silver chalice and paten in medieval style.[63]

Longden chapel was described as a chapel-of-ease when first recorded in 1548.[64] It was presumably in origin the private chapel of the barons of Longden and was still accounted a donative, without cure of souls, in the 19th century.[65] The advowson followed the descent of the manor until 1827 when, on the dispersal of the Tankerville estate, it was purchased by John Homfrey.[66] John Breeze, who was patron when instituted perpetual curate here in 1857,[67] had sold the advowson by 1866 to Henry de Grey Warter,[68] and since 1882 the advowsons of Longden and of the third portion of Pontesbury have been in the hands of the same patron.

The annual stipend of 2s 10d. received by the curate of Longden in 1548[69] perhaps represents the annual value of his glebe. This seems then to have comprised two fields, which were sold by the Crown as chantry lands in 1549.[70] Between 1746 and 1832 the value of the living was augmented by grants totalling £800 from Queen Anne's Bounty.[71] In 1786 18 a. glebe were purchased at Bausley in Alberbury parish[72] and a further 2 a. were added at the inclosure of Longden Common in 1806.[73] The glebe was let for some £25 a year in 1851[74] and the Bausley portion was sold in 1916.[75] The living was said to be worth £78 a year in 1866.[76]

Since spiritual duties in the township were the responsibility of the rectors of the second and third portions of Pontesbury until 1935,[77] earlier curates of Longden were non-resident and held it with

[46] Printed to 1812 in *S.P.R. Heref.* xii (1).
[47] Par. rec., regulations for churchyard, 1856.
[48] Ibid. vestry minutes, 1839–1964.
[49] Ibid. Order in Council, 1902.
[50] Heref. Dioc. Regy., reg. 1902–19, pp. 15, 38; par. rec., vestry minutes, 1839–1964.
[51] Description of church based on par. rec., acct. of building Cruckton chapel, 1837–47; ibid. commonplace bk. of Chas. Drury; ibid. Cruckton chapelwardens' accts. 1845–87; S.P.L., Watton press-cuttings, iii. 331–5; Cranage, vi. 525.
[52] Heref. Dioc. Regy., reg. 1822–42, p. 478.
[53] Par. rec., commonplace bk. of Chas. Drury.
[54] Ibid. Cruckton chapelwardens' accts. 1845–87; Cranage, vi. 525.
[55] Arkwright and Bourne, *Ch. Plate Ludlow Archd.* 25–26.
[56] Heref. Dioc. Regy., reg. 1869–83, p. 23.
[57] Walters, *Ch. Bells Salop.* 206.
[58] Arkwright and Bourne, *Ch. Plate Ludlow Archd.* 5.
[59] Heref. Dioc. Regy., reg. 1883–1901, pp. 681–3.

[60] *Salop. Shreds & Patches*, viii. 188.
[61] *Kelly's Dir. Salop.* (1909).
[62] Walters, *Ch. Bells Salop.* 206.
[63] Arkwright and Bourne, *Ch. Plate Ludlow Archd.* 36.
[64] *T.S.A.S.* 3rd ser. x. 358.
[65] Heref. Dioc. Regy., reg. 1822–42, pp. 506–15; S.R.O. 437/8.
[66] B.M. Add. MS. 21018, f. 305; Heref. Dioc. Regy., reg. 1822–42, p. 86.
[67] *Kelly's Dir. Salop.* (1863).
[68] S.R.O. 437/8.
[69] *T.S.A.S.* 3rd ser. x. 358.
[70] *Cal. Pat.* 1549–51, 15.
[71] Hodgson, *Queen Anne's Bounty* (1845), 290.
[72] Ex inf. Church Com.
[73] Copy Longden Common inclosure award, *penes* Mrs. A. N. Fielden, Longden Manor.
[74] H.O. 129/359/2/5.
[75] Ex inf. Church Com.
[76] S.R.O. 437/8.
[77] See p. 284.

another living. Thomas Mills, curate in 1767,[78] was curate of Church Pulverbatch[79] and his successor Lewis Williams (curate 1781–1808)[80] was Rector of Woolstaston.[81] William Vaughan (curate 1823–27)[82] and Edward Homfrey (curate 1827–56)[83] were also assistant curates of Ford.[84] After 1880, however, the rectors of Pontesbury third portion were also instituted perpetual curates of Longden[85] and the two livings were united in 1935.[86] The living has been held in plurality with Annscroft since 1954.[87] A parsonage was built on a site provided by William Swire in 1915.[88]

Before 1827 services were held once in three weeks and communion twice a year for those unable to attend Pontesbury church.[89] Edward Homfrey, however, introduced regular Sunday evening services and celebrated communion 5 times a year.[90] Since the church was said to be unconsecrated, it was the practice in the earlier 19th century to move the communion table into the aisle, the congregation receiving communion in their pews.[91] Burials took place at Pontesbury until the chapel yard was licensed as a burial ground in 1842.[92]

The chapel of *ST. RUTHEN*,[93] Longden, consists of a nave, a shallow apsidal chancel, a western porch and vestry, and has a wooden bell-turret at the west end. Although it contains no features earlier than the 16th century, the north and south walls of the nave may be medieval. The chapel yard is first recorded in 1569[94] and the manor court met at the chapel in 1629.[95] The south door of the nave, now blocked, has a depressed four-centred arch and probably dates from the later 16th century, as does the roof of the nave. The latter is supported by 3 collar-and-tie-beam trusses, the tie-beams having chamfers and stops, but only the central truss survives unaltered. The chapel was repaired in the later 18th century by the lord of the manor and a member of the Ashwood family,[96] who probably added an apsidal chancel of brick with stone dressings, inserted square-headed mullioned and transomed windows in the nave, and rebuilt the west wall in brick. The principal internal alteration at this time was the erection of a western gallery, entered through a door, now blocked, at the west end. The south door was probably blocked in 1877, when the chapel was restored by the patron. He added a porch and vestry at the west end, inserted pointed 2-light windows in the nave, and probably rebuilt the chancel, which contains a 3-light east

window in the Decorated style.[97] Small windows were inserted in the north and south walls of the chancel in 1938.[98] Pews were replaced by the present open benches in 1877, and the gallery was presumably removed at this time. The only fitting earlier than the 19th century is the pulpit, which is of panelled oak and dates from the later 17th century. The font, which has a baluster stem and marble bowl, was set in the new nave of Pontesbury church in 1829, but was transferred to Longden in 1864.[99] A cast iron fireback, which previously formed the base of a stove in the chapel, is now in the church porch. This is dated 1647 and probably came from Longden Hall Farm.[1] The chapel's single bell is probably medieval.[2] The plate includes a silver chalice and paten of 1703, a silver flagon of 1781, and 2 silver chalices of 1800.[3] The registers begin in 1843.

NONCONFORMITY. A small number of Roman Catholics was resident in the parish in the later 17th century, principally members of the Berrington family of Moat Hall. In addition to Thomas Berrington and his wife, the wives of 3 other inhabitants were presented as recusants in 1668[4] and in 1676 there were said to be 8 Roman Catholics in the parish.[5]

The parish contained only 6 dissenters in 1676[6] and, apart from a family of Quakers recorded *c.* 1750,[7] there is no other evidence of nonconformity here before the 19th century. Dissenting meeting-houses, whose precise location cannot be established, were licensed in Pontesbury in 1802,[8] 1807,[9] and 1821.[10] With one exception all existing nonconformist chapels in the parish were founded between 1821 and 1851, and at the latter date upwards of 800 persons attended services at nonconformist places of worship.[11] The rector of the second portion, in an analysis of the religious affiliations of his parishioners *c.* 1857,[12] stated that all the gentry resident in the parish were members of the Established Church and that only 9 of the 62 larger farmers were nonconformist; the smaller farmers were generally Anglicans. He estimated that about one third of all the parish tradesmen were nonconformists and attributed this to the influence of colliery managers and agents, most of whom came from Wales or Cornwall and who, he alleged, frequently had a private interest in the shops patronized by their workmen.

The Baptist chapel, Pontesbury, was built in

[78] Heref. Dioc. Regy., return of papists, 1767.
[79] See p. 139.
[80] Heref. Dioc. Regy., reg. 1772–1802, f. 109; ibid. reg. 1791–1821, p. 71.
[81] See p. 176.
[82] Heref. Dioc. Regy., reg. 1822–42, pp. 28, 86.
[83] Ibid. 86; ibid. reg. 1847–56, p. 33.
[84] Ibid. reg. 1822–42, p. 28; B.M. Add. MS. 21018, f. 295ᵛ.
[85] Heref. Dioc. Regy., reg. 1869–83, p. 575.
[86] See p. 284.
[87] Heref. Dioc. Regy., reg. 1953–date, p. 44.
[88] Ibid. 1902–19, p. 610.
[89] B.M. Add. MS. 21018, f. 305.
[90] Ibid.   [91] Ibid.
[92] *S.P.R. Heref.* xii (1) *passim*; Heref. Dioc. Regy., reg. 1842–6, p. 21.
[93] Dedication to this non-existent saint first recorded in the later 19th century: *Kelly's Dir. Salop.* (1895); *T.S.A.S.* 2nd ser. iv. 180, n. 12. The field-name 'Swithins Door', which occurs south-west of Church Hill in Oaks township, may preserve the original dedication: S.R.O.

437/5; ibid. 785/181. Architectural description based, except where otherwise stated, on S.P.L., MS. 372, vol. 2, p. 80; S.P.L., J. H. Smith collect., no. 128; Cranage, vi. 530.
[94] S.P.L., MS. 393.   [95] Ibid.
[96] B.M. Add. MS. 21018, f. 305.
[97] *Kelly's Dir. Salop.* (1885); Cranage, vi. 530.
[98] Heref. Dioc. Regy., reg. 1938–53, p. 19.
[99] Pontesbury par. rec., vestry minutes, 1839–1964.
[1] Date '1647' and initials 'A.A. A.A.' on fireback.
[2] Walters, *Ch. Bells Salop.* 204.
[3] Arkwright and Bourne, *Ch. Plate Ludlow Archd.* 38–39.
[4] Heref. Dioc. Regy. visitation papers, box 43, church-wardens' presentment, 1668.
[5] *T.S.A.S.* 2nd ser. i. 87.
[6] Ibid.
[7] *S.P.R. Heref.* xii (1), 340, 369.
[8] *Q. Sess. Orders*, iii. 112.
[9] Ibid. 141.   [10] Ibid. 222.
[11] H.O. 129/359/2/7–19.
[12] Par. rec., commonplace bk. of Chas. Drury.

1828, when it was known as Mr. Goff's School.[13] It was flourishing in 1851, when an average of 240 persons attended evening services and there were 60 Sunday school children.[14] In 1963 the church had 44 members.[15] A second Baptist congregation existed in Pontesbury in 1851.[16] This then met at a private house and had some 30 members,[17] but is not later recorded. At Plealey the houses of Richard France and Edward Owen were licensed as dissenting meeting-houses in 1824 and 1825 respectively.[18] The latter appears to have ceased soon afterwards, but in 1828 France built a chapel in the village.[19] This was originally a Congregational chapel, but it was the private property of Richard France and was never vested in trustees.[20] When he changed his views on baptism in the 1830s it became a Baptist chapel,[21] and by 1851 it had, for similar reasons, become a Wesleyan Methodist chapel[22] and has subsequently remained one.[23] Fifty persons attended morning services here in 1851.[24] Those who had formerly attended the Congregational chapel at Plealey, together with Congregationalists at Pontesbury who had previously attended Minsterley chapel,[25] built a Congregational chapel at Pontesbury in 1839.[26] The chapel was renovated and enlarged in 1871.[27] This has always been served by the minister of Minsterley.[28] A congregation of 86 attended afternoon services at the chapel in 1851, when there were 45 Sunday school children,[29] and in 1959 the chapel had 74 members and 85 children.[30] In the later 19th century a mission station was established at Pontesford, where fortnightly prayer meetings were held.[31]

Salem Congregational chapel, Longden Common, was built in 1837,[32] taking the place of a meeting at a private house, licensed in 1834.[33] The chapel closed after the departure of its first minister,[34] but had re-opened by 1851, when it had an evening congregation of 61 and 50 Sunday school children.[35] The chapel is now served by the minister of Dorrington chapel.[36]

The Methodists, who established more chapels in the parish than any other denomination, took a characteristic interest in settlements of industrial squatters, like Pontesbury Hill, and in ancient hamlets like Arscott and Asterley, which had developed into mining villages. Apart from Plealey chapel the only Wesleyan Methodist chapel in the

parish is that on Pontesbury Hill. The Old Chapel was built in 1834[37] and was replaced by a new chapel in 1897.[38] Only 30 persons attended afternoon services here in 1851.[39] Hurst Bank chapel, near Exfordsgreen, was the first Primitive Methodist chapel to be built in the parish. Meetings at a private house were licensed in 1821[40] and the chapel was erected in 1831.[41] Some 60 persons attended morning services here in 1851[42] and it was enlarged in 1863,[43] but it is now closed and has been converted into a private house. Asterley Primitive Methodist chapel, built in 1834,[44] had an average congregation of 70 in 1851, when there were 85 Sunday school children.[45] Zion Primitive Methodist chapel, Pontesbury Hill, built in 1845, reported an average congregation of 70 in 1851.[46] The Primitive Methodist chapel at Longden, the last nonconformist chapel to be established in the parish, was built in 1870.[47] House-meetings of Primitive Methodists are recorded at Arscott, Pontesford, and Pontesford Hill in 1851, when they had a combined attendance of some 120 persons,[48] but in no case did these lead to the erection of a chapel.

A small and presumably short-lived congregation of Latter Day Saints was meeting at a house in Asterley in 1851,[49] and the Salvation Army had a barracks at Pontesbury, c. 1888–94.[50] The Apostolic Church, Pontesbury Hill, was built in 1926.[51]

SCHOOLS. A school was in existence in Pontesbury in the later 16th century, for burials of the schoolmasters are recorded between 1574 and 1634[52] and a building known as the 'school house' lay in the manorial estate in 1593.[53] Shortly before 1765 a school was erected by subscription and was placed under the management of the 33 principal subscribers and their heirs.[54] By vestry resolution of 1765 the sum of £4 a year was to be paid to the master for the education of 8 poor children.[55] The wording of the resolution is ambiguous, but the intention seems to have been that the sum should be paid out of the poor rates and that it represented the interest of £100, part of the Hem Charity endowment which had been lost by the parish in the earlier 18th century.[56] This sum was paid to the master by the overseers from 1765 until the application of poor rates to this purpose was made illegal

[13] Q. Sess. Orders, iii. 268; Char. Com. files.
[14] H.O. 129/359/2/15.
[15] Baptist Handbk. (1963).
[16] H.O. 129/359/2/13.   [17] Ibid.
[18] Q. Sess. Orders, iii. 242, 250.
[19] Ibid. 271.
[20] E. Elliot, A History of Congregationalism in Shropshire (Oswestry, 1898), 140.
[21] Ibid.
[22] Ibid.; H.O. 129/359/2/7.
[23] Worship Reg.
[24] H.O. 129/359/2/7.
[25] Elliot, op. cit. 140.
[26] Heref. Dioc. Regy., reg. 1822–42, p. 433.
[27] Elliot, op. cit. 140.
[28] Ibid.; Congreg. Yearbk. (1959).
[29] H.O. 129/359/2/14.
[30] Congreg. Yearbk. (1959).
[31] Elliot, op. cit. 140.
[32] Heref. Dioc. Regy., reg. 1822–42, p. 320; Elliot, op. cit. 249–50.
[33] Q. Sess. Orders, iii. 300.
[34] Elliot, op. cit. 249–50.
[35] H.O. 129/359/2/9.

[36] Congreg. Yearbk. (1959).
[37] H.O. 129/359/2/16.
[38] Worship Reg.; Char. Com. files.
[39] H.O. 129/359/2/16.
[40] Worship Reg.
[41] Heref. Dioc. Regy., reg. 1822–42, 174.
[42] H.O. 129/359/2/10.
[43] W. E. Morris, History of Methodism in Shrewsbury and District (Shrewsbury, 1960), 43.
[44] Datestone.
[45] H.O. 129/359/2/19.
[46] H.O. 129/359/2/17; Q. Sess. Orders, iv. 59.
[47] Worship Reg.; Morris, op. cit. 49.
[48] H.O. 129/359/2/8, 11, 12.
[49] H.O. 129/359/2/18.
[50] Worship Reg.
[51] Ex inf. Mr. P. T. Bradley.
[52] S.P.R. Heref. xii (1), 39, 46, 127.
[53] S.P.L., Deeds 6786.
[54] K. W. Berry, Pontesbury National (C. of E.) School (Much Wenlock, 1961), 2, 23.
[55] Ibid. 2.
[56] Ibid. 2–3; 24th Rep. Com. Char., H.C. 231, p. 392 (1831), xi.

by the Poor Law Amendment Act, 1834.[57] In 1840 one of the 8 annual pensions of £3 paid to poor widows from the Hem Charity was applied to the school[58] and was still being paid in 1877.[59]

Until 1849 doubt seems to have existed whether management of the school was vested in the descendants of the original subscribers or in the vestry,[60] and this may account for the independent attitude of several masters after 1833. John Vaughan, the first master, died in 1791[61] and the school is said to have flourished under his successor Bayley, who taught grammar, geography, mensuration, and surveying.[62] It seems to have declined under John Stretch, the vestry clerk, who was master c. 1803–33,[63] for in 1818 he taught only the 8 foundation scholars and 12 other children,[64] but attendance had risen to 40 by 1833.[65] John Reynolds was appointed master on Stretch's death in 1833, but the latter's grandson James Cross refused to vacate the school premises.[66] Reynolds got possession in 1834,[67] but when dismissed later in the same year for having married a Baptist, he too refused to give up the school[68] and was not ejected until 1837.[69] The next master, John Bayley, made an undertaking in writing to vacate the the school if removed from office,[70] but in 1840, when he was dismissed for incompetence, having lost all his pupils,[71] Forester Cross took possession of the school and refused to leave until threatened with formal eviction in 1846.[72]

Steps were then taken to regularize the management of the school, which had been placed in union with the National Society in 1821.[73] By a trust deed of 1849, when the school was formally conveyed by the Board of Guardians to the rectors and churchwardens, management was vested in a committee consisting of the rectors and 6 resident subscribers, all of them Churchmen.[74]

An average of 100 children attended the school between 1847 and 1856,[75] but the existing buildings were too small and were described by the rector of the first portion in 1854 as damp, low, ill-ventilated, and ready to fall to the ground.[76] A new school to accommodate 200 children[77] was built in 1855 at a cost of some £900,[78] most of which was derived from subscriptions and government grant.[79] The

old school then became the master's house, but was demolished in 1875, when an infant department was added to the new school.[80]

In 1855 the school's income, apart from £3 from the Hem charity, was derived from subscriptions (£45) and school pence, levied on a graduated scale (£30).[81] It was in receipt of a government grant after this date,[82] but in the later 19th century the greater part of its income came from subscriptions, which amounted to £88 a year in 1893,[83] when school pence had been abolished.[84] Attendance rose from 144 in 1871[85] to about 200 in the early years of the present century.[86] The school was managed under the terms of the trust deed of 1849 until it became a Controlled school in 1958.[87] It was used as a primary school between 1957 and 1961. A new primary school was then opened in Linley Avenue, Pontesbury, and the National School was demolished in 1965.

Negotiations to establish a Senior School at Pontesbury began in 1937[88] and tenders were invited in 1939,[89] but further progress was interrupted by the Second World War. A 15-acre site was purchased in 1944[90] and in 1949 senior pupils from the National School were taught in H.O.R.S.A. huts erected here.[91] A Secondary Modern School was built on this site in 1957.[92]

Lea Cross School was built in 1822 on a site given by Henry Warter, at a cost of some £360, most of which was raised by subscription, but which included a grant from the National Society.[93] Although Thomas Harries and H. D. Warter became trustees in 1823,[94] the school was said to have no management committee in 1852,[95] and in 1872 it was managed by the rectors of the second and third portions.[96] A Charity Commission Scheme of 1899, whereby the rector of the second portion, his curate, and 3 other trustees were appointed managers,[97] remained in force until the school became Controlled in 1956.[98] In 1833 the school was financed by subscriptions and school pence.[99] The latter were, however, returned to the children in the form of clothing.[1] Subscriptions produced £55 and school pence £12 in 1852.[2] Although the school was thereafter in receipt of a government grant,[3]

[57] Par. rec., overseers' accts. 1765–1834.
[58] Ibid. commonplace bk. of Chas. Drury.
[59] Char. Com. files.
[60] N.L.W., J. R. Hughes (1962), 4 sub anno 1835.
[61] Berry, op. cit. 2; S.P.R. Heref. xii (1), 436; Heref. Dioc. Regy., reg. 1772–1802, f. 56.
[62] Par. rec., commonplace bk. of Chas. Drury.
[63] N.L.W., J. R. Hughes (1962), 3, 4.
[64] Digest of Returns to Cttee on Educ. of Poor, H.C. 224, p. 758 (1819), ix (2).
[65] Educ. Enquiry Abstract, H.C. 62, p. 780 (1835), xlii.
[66] Berry, op. cit. 4.
[67] Ibid.
[68] Ibid.
[69] N.L.W., J. R. Hughes (1962), 4.
[70] Berry, op. cit. 26.
[71] Ibid. 4.
[72] Ibid.; par. rec., churchwardens' accts., 1840–79 sub anno 1846.
[73] Nat. Soc., school files.
[74] Par. rec., trust deed, 1849.
[75] Ibid., commonplace bk. of Chas. Drury; Ed. 7/102/190; Nat. Soc., school files.
[76] Berry, op. cit. 6; Nat. Soc., school files.
[77] Kelly's Dir. Salop. (1856).
[78] Berry, op. cit. 6–7; par. rec., commonplace bk. of Chas. Drury.
[79] Berry, op. cit. 6.

[80] Ibid. 7.
[81] Ed. 7/102/190.
[82] Ibid.
[83] Return of Schs., 1893 [C. 7529], p. 510, H.C. (1894), lxv.
[84] Ibid.
[85] Returns relating to Elem. Educ., H.C. 201, p. 334 (1871), lv.
[86] Kelly's Dir. Salop. (1900–13); Voluntary Schs. Returns, H.C. 178–XXIV, p. 24 (1906), lxxxviii.
[87] Ex inf. S.C.C. Educ. Dept.
[88] S.C.C. Minutes (Educ.), 1937–8, p. 272.
[89] Ibid. 1939–40, p. 100.
[90] Ibid. 1944–5, p. 198.
[91] Berry, op. cit. 7.
[92] For plans see The Architect and Building News, 24 Dec. 1958, pp. 426–30.
[93] Ed. 7/102/193; Nat. Soc., school files; par. rec., commonplace bk. of Chas. Drury.
[94] Ed. 7/102/193.
[95] Ibid.
[96] Ibid.
[97] Char. Com. files.
[98] Ex inf. S.C.C. Educ. Dept.
[99] Educ. Enquiry Abstract, p. 780.
[1] Ibid.
[2] Ed. 7/102/193.
[3] Ibid.

voluntary contributions, apparently paid solely by the rector of the second portion,[4] made up the greater part of its income until the end of the 19th century.[5] The school was built to accommodate 150 children[6] and was at first attended by children from Pontesbury, Pontesford, Longden, and Hanwood, as well as those in its immediate vicinity,[7] but their numbers are said to have fallen off soon afterwards[8] and in 1833 part of the school's equipment, together with its master, were transferred to Pontesbury National school.[9] By 1857 part of the school had been converted into a schoolmaster's house.[10] Recorded attendance figures, however, do not suggest any marked decline in the earlier 19th century. Ninety children attended in 1833,[11] 92 in 1852,[12] and 106 in the following year.[13] Numbers fell after 1870, and in 1893 the average attendance was only 30,[14] but it seems to have improved after 1899, for there were 51 pupils in 1906.[15]

Three other National schools were established in the parish between 1871 and 1873, presumably to forestall the formation of a School Board—a matter which was the subject of heated debate here in 1871.[16] Asterley school, built in 1871 on a site provided by Henry Gardner,[17] was intended for the children of this part of the third portion. Its income included a permanent endowment of £16 a year and was supplemented in 1893 by a government grant of £39 and voluntary contributions of £9.[18] About 50 children attended between 1885 and 1913.[19] The school became Controlled in 1956 but was closed in 1964.[20]

Longden Church of England school was built in 1873 to the same designs as Asterley school for the use of children in Longden, Oaks, Plealey, and Sibberscott.[21] Management was then vested in a committee including the rectors of the second and third portions and the curate of Longden.[22] It became an Aided school in 1952.[23] Attendance here rose from 38 in 1873[24] to over 80 in the early 20th century.[25]

Cruckmeole school was built in 1873 on a site provided by Francis Harries of Cruckton[26] and was intended for the children living in the northeast of the parish,[27] between 70 and 80 of whom attended between 1885 and 1913.[28] The rector of the second portion and 11 others were constituted managers in 1873,[29] and the school became Controlled in 1956.[30]

Sunday Schools at Pontesbury and Longden were

attended by 100 pupils in 1818[31] and that at Pontesbury was flourishing in the 1840s owing to the unsatisfactory state of the day school there.[32] A Baptist Sunday school had been established in Pontesbury by 1833, when 45 children attended at their parents' expense,[33] and the Longden Congregational chapel was being used as a school during the week in 1851.[34] A number of dame schools existed in Pontesbury in the earlier 19th century;[35] there was still at least one in the village in 1895.[36] A Middle Class school recorded in 1874, when it was held in the schoolroom of the Congregational chapel,[37] seems to have been a short-lived product of the debates over the establishment of a School Board two years earlier.

CHARITIES. Thomas Davies (d. 1574)[38] left £200 for the use of the poor, and a further £30 was left to the same use by John Peers of Marsh in Westbury (d. 1626), his widow Eleanor Peers (d. 1635), and Thomas Higgons, rector of the third portion (d. 1635). In 1716, when these sums were used to purchase a messuage and 22 a. land at the Hem in Westbury parish, the vestry directed that the income should be applied to the support of 12 decayed householders. The charity has since been known as the Hem Charity. The annual income of the charity fell from £25, c. 1830, to £16 by 1897 and unsuccessful attempts were made to sell the estate in 1921 and 1928, but its income had risen to £30 by 1962. In the earlier 19th century 8 poor widows received life-pensions from the charity, amounting to £3–£4 a year apiece. In 1840, however, one of the pensions was applied to Pontesbury school. This was intended to replace an annual payment of £4 formerly paid by the overseers out of the poor rates, which was then supposed to have represented the interest of part of the Owen and Phillips charities, lost by the parish in the 18th century. Payments to the school were discontinued after the scheme of 1897 required that the proceeds of the Hem Charity should be applied to the general benefit of the poor. In 1962 annual pensions of £3 were being paid to 8 widows.

At an unknown date Ellen Owen left £100 for the poor, but £63 10s. of the principal was lost on bad security. The remainder of this legacy (£30), together with £10 left by Mary Phillips (d. 1729), appears to have been invested in the Minsterley turnpike road, the interest being distributed with

[4] Kelly's Dir. Salop. (1885, 1891).
[5] Ed. 7/102/193; Return of Schs., 1893, p. 510.
[6] Par. rec., commonplace bk. of Chas. Drury.
[7] Ibid.
[8] Ibid.
[9] Berry, op. cit. 4.
[10] Par. rec., commonplace bk. of Chas. Drury.
[11] Educ. Enquiry Abstract, p. 780.
[12] Ed. 7/102/193.
[13] Ibid.
[14] Kelly's Dir. Salop. (1885–91); Returns relating to Elem. Educ., p. 334; Return of Schs., 1893, p. 510.
[15] Voluntary Schs. Returns, p. 24.
[16] Nat. Soc., school files; Berry, op. cit. 17–19.
[17] Ed. 7/102/191; par. rec., conveyance of site, 1871.
[18] Return of Schs., 1893, p. 510.
[19] Ibid.; Kelly's Dir. Salop. (1885–1913); Voluntary Schs. Returns, p. 24.
[20] Ex inf. S.C.C. Educ. Dept.
[21] Ed. 7/102/194.
[22] Ibid.
[23] Ex inf. S.C.C. Educ. Dept.

[24] Ed. 7/102/194.
[25] Kelly's Dir. Salop. (1905–13); Voluntary Schs. Returns, p. 24.
[26] Par. rec., conveyance of site, 1873.
[27] Ibid.
[28] Kelly's Dir. Salop. (1885–1913); Return of Schs., 1893, p. 510; Voluntary Schs. Returns, p. 24.
[29] Par. rec., conveyance of site, 1873.
[30] Ex inf. S.C.C. Educ. Dept.
[31] Digest of Returns to Cttee. on Educ. of Poor, p. 758.
[32] Nat. Soc., Ch. School Returns, 1846–7; par. rec., commonplace bk. of Chas. Drury.
[33] Educ. Enquiry Abstract, p. 780.
[34] H.O. 129/359/2/9; Bagshaw's Dir. Salop. (1851).
[35] Digest of Returns to Cttee. on Educ. of Poor, p. 758; Educ. Enquiry Abstract, p. 780; par. rec., commonplace bk. of Chas. Drury.
[36] Berry, op. cit. 8.   [37] Ibid.
[38] Account of charities based, except where otherwise stated, on 24th Rep. Com. Char., H.C. 231, pp. 392–3 (1831), xi; Digest of Endowed Charities, 1862–3, H.C. 433, pp. 194–5 (1867–8), lii; Char. Com. files.

the Hem Charity. This produced an annual income of £1 12s. in 1862 but had been lost by 1893.

A legacy of £50, left to the poor by John Davies (d. 1723), was misappropriated towards the expenses of erection of the workhouse in 1732. By codicil of 1801 John Jones gave the parish officers a rent-charge of 20s., arising from lands in the parish, to be distributed in bread to the poor. His son distributed the charity in bread until the estate was sold in 1820, but the new owner failed to continue the payments.

By will proved in 1833 Barbara Harries left £200, the interest of which was to be distributed to the poor at Christmas. The principal had been invested in stock by 1856, when the charity had an annual income of £5 13s. 8d., £2 of which was used to purchase flannel and the remainder was distributed among local clothing clubs.

By will proved in 1879 Ann Pitt left £110 stock to the rector of the first portion for the repair of the Phillips family tomb in the churchyard and directed that any surplus should be given to the poor of

Pontesbury village. Although the Charity Commissioners declared void the principal purpose of this bequest in 1893 and 1921, £2 arising from this charity was being applied towards the upkeep of the churchyard in 1931. In 1963 the annual interest of £3 was all distributed to the poor.

The Pontesford Jubilee Trust was established by Derwas Owen Jones in 1887, when he vested £1,080 stock in trustees. The interest was to be distributed in the form of goods by the rector of the first portion to 8 poor persons living within 1½ mile of Pontesbury church. Recipients were to be nominated by the founder during his lifetime and thereafter by his right heirs. A further £1,950 stock was added to the fund between 1893 and 1906, when 16 persons were in receipt of weekly payments. In 1955 interest on stock to the value of £3,414 was being distributed as a private charity by Mrs. A. Caton-Jones, but since the latter's death in 1964 this charity has been vested in the Rector of Pontesbury.[39]

WESTBURY

THE large parish of Westbury, which contains 11,504 a.,[1] comprises the townships of Caus, Forest, Lake, Marsh, Minsterley, Newton, Stoney Stretton, Vennington, Wallop, Westbury, Westley, Whitton, Winsley, and Yockleton. Also within the parish are the sites of the deserted hamlets of Brerelawe, Ree, and Callow, and single farms representing the shrunken hamlets of Perendon, Wigley, and Poulton. The Forest of Hayes, only part of which lies in Westbury parish, was a chase in the Middle Ages, but scattered settlement is recorded here from the 16th century and the Westbury portion was accounted a township by 1659.[2] The township of Minsterley (2,773 a.), which maintained its own poor after 1766,[3] was subsequently accounted a separate civil parish. It became an ecclesiastical parish in 1910.[4]

To the north the parish boundary runs for the most part through the former heathland which forms the watershed between Yockleton Brook to the south and Cardeston Brook to the north. Near Hayford Farm it follows Yockleton Brook for a short distance and to the west of the squatter settlement at Wattlesborough Heath it follows roughly the course of the road from Shrewsbury to Welshpool. In the east, to the south of Yockleton and Stoney Stretton, the boundary passes through a former woodland area until, west of Hinwood, Crook-a-Moor Brook[5] forms the boundary with Pontesbury

parish. Between Callow Hill and Snailbeach the south-eastern boundary runs along the foot of the Stiperstones and its outliers, on a somewhat erratic course which probably represents the northern boundary of Stiperstones Forest, granted to Robert Corbet in 1190.[6] The south-western boundary with Worthen runs in part along Minsterley Brook, Rea Brook, and its tributary Hogstow Brook and near Westley follows the line of the Hem drain. At Hurst Farm the boundary turns westwards and, after running along the crest of Aston Hill, takes in the eastern slopes of the Long Mountain. An ancient road running northwards from Rowley forms part of the western boundary here, while on the north the boundary follows, between Monksfields and Vron Gate, the course of the ancient ridgeway over the Long Mountain. From Vron Gate the boundary runs northwards, past Hargrave Bank, to meet the Shrewsbury–Welshpool road west of Halfway House. Part of Wattlesborough Heath was transferred to Cardeston parish c. 1792[7] and that part of the squatter settlement of Snailbeach which lay in Westbury parish was transferred to Worthen parish in 1934.[8] Rea Brook formed the township boundary between Minsterley and the remainder of the parish, but scarcely any of the other township boundaries appear to have followed natural features.

In its landscape the parish falls into three main divisions—the valley of Yockleton Brook to the

39 Ex inf. the Rector.
1 Acreage includes that of Minsterley, now a separate civil parish: O.S. Area Bk. (1883); Census, 1961. The following topographical description is based, except where otherwise stated, on O.S. Maps 1", sheets lx, lxi (1st edn.); O.S. Maps 6" Salop. 32, 33, 39, 40 (1st and later edns.); O.S. Maps 1/25,000, SJ 31 (1956), SJ 20, 30, 40, 41 (1957); Rocque, Map of Salop. (1752); Baugh, Map of Salop. (1808); B.M. O.S. 2" orig. drawings, sheet 199 (1816); Geol. Survey Map (drift), sheet 152 (1932); R. W. Pocock and others, Geol. Shrews. District (1938), passim; S.R.O. 1361/102 (Minsterley tithe appt. 1841, and map, 1838); ibid. 1361/103 (Westbury tithe appt. 1841, and map, 1839); ibid. 1361/104 (Caus, Forest, and Wallop tithe appt. and map, 1841); ibid. 1361/105 (Westley, Winsley, Lake, and Hem tithe appt. 1841, and map, undated); ibid.

1361/106 (Marsh, Vennington, Whitton, and Wigmore tithe appt. 1841, and map, undated); Heref. Dioc. Regy., Stoney Stretton tithe appt. 1843, and map, undated; ibid. Yockleton tithe appt. 1840, and map, undated; S.R.O. 152/1 (survey and map of Minsterley manorial estate, 1766); S.P.L., Deeds 13642 (survey and map of Westbury manorial estate, 1768). This article was written in 1965. Thanks are particularly due to Miss L. F. Chitty, Ingleside, Pontesbury, for criticism and advice.
2 S.R.O. 1361/1.   3 Ibid. 1361/68.
4 Heref. Dioc. Regy., reg. 1902–19, p. 436.
5 S.P.L., Deeds 14588.
6 Eyton, vii. 12.
7 S.R.O. 665 uncat., survey of Wattlesborough Heath, c. 1792.
8 S.C.C., County Review Order, 1934.

north, that of Rea Brook to the south, and the eastern slopes of the Long Mountain to the west. The Long Mountain, which rises to about 1,150 feet on the western boundary of the parish, provides a relatively fertile soil on its more gentle upland slopes. The Silurian shales of which it is composed[9] have been quarried for building purposes at Harbeach Dingle,

on smaller outcrops of sandstone near Stoney Stretton and Lower Newton Farm.[11] 'Bell' pit-mounds in Quarry Woods are evidence of the coal-mining carried out in the area south-east of Westbury village since the later 17th century.[12]

Yockleton Brook, which rises near Hargrave Farm in Alberbury, flows across the north of the parish

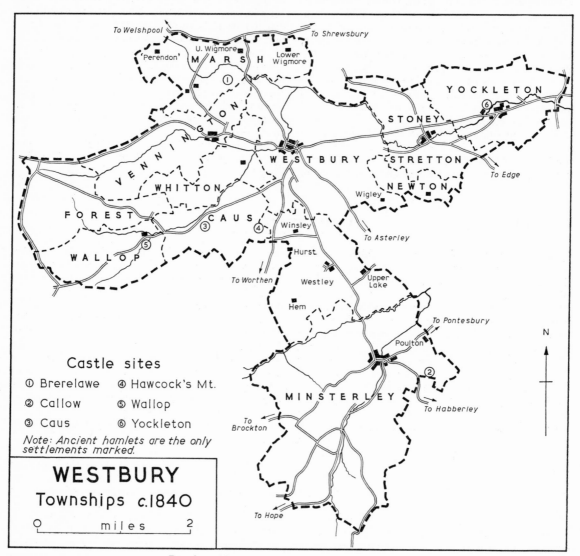

Castle sites

① Brerelawe   ④ Hawcock's Mt.

② Callow   ⑤ Wallop

③ Caus   ⑥ Yockleton

Note: Ancient hamlets are the only settlements marked.

WESTBURY

Townships c.1840

0   miles   2

Based on tithe apportionments and maps, 1838–43

Broomhill Wood, and Oakley Wood. The last was producing stone roofing slates in the earlier 18th century[10] and is probably the quarry from which slates were obtained for work at Caus Castle in the later Middle Ages. Whitton and Vennington Brooks, which rise near Haywood Farm and Nant-y-Myssels respectively, have cut deep valleys in their course down the mountain. They unite near Whitton Hall and join Yockleton Brook to the north of Westbury village.

The sandstone ridge to the south-east of Westbury village, known as Broxtons Wood and Quarry Woods, reaches a height of 500 feet and forms a watershed between Yockleton and Rea Brooks. In the later 18th century quarries were in use here and

through relatively level country, most of which lies between the 300- and 400-foot contours. Extensive deposits of sand and gravel at the foot of the Long Mountain probably account for the relatively dense settlement found during the earlier Middle Ages in the district north-west of Westbury village. Apart from the shrunken hamlets of Marsh, Perendon, and Wigmore, the district also includes the site of the deserted hamlet of Brerelawe.[13] Flood gravels occur along the south bank of Yockleton Brook and peat is found to the north of Stoney Stretton. The subsoil elsewhere to the north of the parish is boulder clay.

To the south Rea Brook flows sluggishly through a wide valley. It is fed by numerous tributaries from

[9] *Proc. Geol. Assoc.* lxiii (2), 168.
[10] S.R.O. 279/210; ibid. 1251/9.

[11] *Geol. Shrews. District*, 220.
[12] Ibid. 142.

[13] See p. 305.

the Long Mountain and from the Stiperstones to the south, the largest of which is Minsterley Brook. The broad expanse of flat boulder clay known as the Hem, to the north of the Rea between Minsterley and Hurst, remained ill-drained until the 19th century.[14] Two differing types of rock underlie the higher ground along the southern boundary. Silurian shales outcrop around Etsell, where they were quarried in the 18th century,[15] but between Snailbeach and Callow Hill these are superseded by Ordovician Mytton flags and shales. Intrusive dolerite, found at Callow Hill, has been quarried for roadstone since the beginning of the present century,[16] but more important in the economic history of the parish have been the lead and other minerals found in a fault in the Mytton flags at Snailbeach, which has been mined intermittently since Roman times.[17]

The principal areas of woodland during the Middle Ages were the Forest of Hayes, which lay on the Long Mountain, and Hogstow Forest on the rising ground to the south of Minsterley village. A smaller belt of woodland lay on the sandstone ridge south-east of Westbury village and a small part of the former woodland area later known as Cardeston, Stretton, and Wattlesborough Heaths lay to the north of the parish. An area of moorland extended southwards from Stretton Heath towards Minsterley, cutting across the centre of the parish.

The Forest of Hayes, only a small part of which lies in the parish, was probably one of the 'hayes' recorded in the Domesday manor of Worthen.[18] It was known by the Welsh as 'Ffridd Cefn Digoll' during the Middle Ages,[19] taking its name from an Iron Age hill-fort, now known as Beacon Ring, standing in that part of the Long Mountain which is now in Wales. The eastern boundary of the Forest ran from Haywood Farm along Rookery Dingle to Wallop Hall and then northwards along the edge of Oakley Wood and across Diptree Hills to the western edge of Blackmore.[20] Although it belonged to the manor of Caus, it was probably not included in Thomas Corbet's grant of free warren there in 1246,[21] for in 1293 it was alleged that 'le Haye' was a free chase by immemorial usage.[22] Thomas Corbet was alleged to have extended the bounds of the forest before his death in 1274,[23] but the extension clearly did not affect Westbury parish. During the later Middle Ages the herbage of the forest was normally let and pigs were pastured there by adjacent townships.[24] No isolated settlements are recorded here before the 16th century, when the Act of Union and the activities of the Council of the

Marches had created relatively peaceful conditions in this part of the Welsh border. The Forest was divided into walks c. 1546,[25] of which Baldhill Okeley, Harbache, Wynstons Field, Llarecoyd, and Nant-y-Musco walks, recorded in 1564,[26] can still be identified from field- and place-names. By 1581 it was said to be 'all mountain ground, the wood thereof spoiled, saving that it is set thinly with shrubs, hazel, and a few old oaks',[27] and by this date the main woods were probably already confined to the escarpment, as they were in the 19th century.[28] Other woods adjoined the Forest of Hayes to the south and east. The common lands of Wallop, south of Haywood Farm, included woods known in the 16th century as Longlyth and Rowlyth,[29] and now as Langley Wood and Rowley Hill. The tenants of the Wallop freeholder William Lingen of the Hurst were prosecuted for felling timber in Langley Wood in 1542,[30] John Lingen was alleged to have committed waste here c. 1574,[31] and encroachments by cottagers are first recorded in 1564.[32] Little timber remained on these hills by 1581, when they were described as 'high mountain ground and apt for sheep and other cattle.'[33] During the 17th century woodland seems to have been confined to the steeper slopes at Oakley and Broomhill and the northern slopes of Langley Hill. From the latter, now known as Tiled House Wood, 6,000 cords of wood were sold to the ironmaster Philip Foley in 1674.[34] A partial inclosure of Rowley and Langley Hills seems to have taken place in 1677;[35] the remaining 311 a. were inclosed between 1694[36] and 1696.[37]

South of Wallop woodland formerly covered Aston Hill and the ridge to the east on which Caus Castle stood. The castle park, probably established in 1246 when a grant of free warren was obtained[38] and described as woodland in 1300,[39] lay to the south-west of the castle. Assarts are recorded in 1362 at Wintle Field,[40] part of the Caus demesne lands on the edge of Caus Beach. The park comprised some 250 a. at its prime.[41] During the Middle Ages its herbage was normally let,[42] a practice which was continued in the 16th century[43] until the Thynnes, lords of the manor, resumed direct farming of the demesne.[44] It was probably disparked after the destruction of the castle in 1645[45] and had been divided among the tenants by 1679.[46] Cordwood in Caus Beach was sold to Francis Wolfe of Coalbrookdale Furnace in 1680[47] and by 1841 the only woodland here, apart from roughs at Caus Castle and Caus Beach, was 17 a. in Park Wood on the western edge of the ancient park.[48]

The part of the Long Mountain now known as

[14] See pp. 299–300.
[15] S.R.O. 152/1.
[16] See p. 322.
[17] Ibid.
[18] V.C.H. Salop. i. 324.
[19] W.S.L. 1721/1/1, f. 134ᵛ.
[20] S.R.O. 1361/104.
[21] Cal. Chart. R. 1226–57, 294.
[22] Plac. de Quo Warr. (Rec. Com.), 718.
[23] Rot. Hund. (Rec. Com.), ii. 213.
[24] Longleat MSS., unbound 4010–11; B.M. Eg. Roll 2196.
[25] W.S.L. 1721/1/1, f. 113.
[26] Staffs. R.O., D 641/1/2/243.
[27] Longleat MSS., unbound 4030.
[28] S.R.O. 1361/104.
[29] Longleat MSS., unbound 4030.
[30] Heref. City Libr., MS. 23628, f. 28.

[31] C 3/213/23.
[32] Staffs. R.O., D 641/1/2/243.
[33] Longleat MSS., unbound 4030.
[34] Ibid. 4133.
[35] Longleat MSS., Thynne Papers, vol. xx, f. 339.
[36] S.R.O. 279/331.
[37] Ibid. 279/332.
[38] Cal. Chart. R. 1226–57, 294.
[39] C 133/94/6.
[40] Longleat MSS., unbound 3982.
[41] Ibid. 3992.
[42] Ibid. acct. r. of Caus manor, passim.
[43] Heref. City Libr., MS. 23628, f. 39; E 36/150, f. 58.
[44] See p. 318.
[45] See p. 309.
[46] Longleat MSS., unbound 3392.
[47] Longleat MSS., Thynne Papers, vol. xxi, ff. 156, 210.
[48] S.R.O. 1361/104.

Caus Mountain and Blackmore was formerly common land in the townships of Whitton and Vennington. It was described as waste in 1581[49] and in 1600 the slopes near Vron Gate were thickly set with underwood, consisting of oak, ash, maple, hazel, thorn, and blackthorn,[50] which were probably indigenous over a wide area. There is no evidence for medieval assarting here, but 200 a. near The Vron appear to have been inclosed *c.* 1600.[51] Later inclosure was preceded by squatting. This was already extensive in 1677[52] and numerous encroachments on Blackmore are recorded in the later 18th century.[53] Diptree Hills and adjacent lands in Vennington Common had been inclosed before 1770,[54] when inclosure took place at The Shrives (some 50 a.), which made up the greater part of Whitton Common.[55]

By 1841 215 a. of woodland remained in the townships of Caus, Forest, and Wallop,[56] nearly all of it along the steep southern slopes of the Long Mountain, and only 37 a. in Whitton and Vennington townships.[57] In the later 19th century the Severne family made new plantations at Cottage Dingle, Diptree Hills, Gorsty Covert near the Forest, and on Wallop Hill and enlarged the Quabbs on Blackmore.[58] Wallop Hill has since been cleared.

The manor of Minsterley included two leagues of woodland in 1086.[59] This forest, known as Hogstow,[60] extended from Minsterley village south-westwards into Worthen parish, south-eastwards to Habberley Office (Eastridge Wood), and northwards to Rea Brook. By 1352 Hogstow had been divided into four bailiwicks[61] and was under the supervision of a hereditary master-forester.[62] A deer-leap was constructed at Snailbeach in 1352[63] and in 1370 deer were so plentiful in the forest that in the neighbouring village of Hope the hilly ground was said to be uncultivated because of their depredations.[64] Peter Corbet in 1299,[65] and Ralph, Earl of Stafford, in 1357,[66] had special commissions to investigate large-scale poaching of deer in the forest. Hogstow Forest was said to contain 600 fallow deer in 1521[67] and they were still common in 1562,[68] but disappeared as the pace of forest clearance increased in the 17th century. Leland noted, *c.* 1540, that Hogstow Forest 'hath deer and is large and one way cometh almost to Caus castle'.[69]

Two parks—Minsterley Park and Lower Hogstow—were formed in Hogstow Forest during the Middle Ages. Minsterley Park, which lay on both sides of Rea Brook south-west of Minsterley village, is first recorded in 1274.[70] It was said to contain 300 a. in 1300[71] and probably included the site of the deserted hamlet of Ree, to the north of the brook, which had been absorbed into the demesne lands of Thomas Corbet in 1251.[72] The park was being used as a stud-farm between 1371[73] and 1402[74] and as pasture in the 15th century.[75] By the later 16th century the part lying north of the brook was known as the Over Park and that to the south as the Nether Park.[76] The latter was still 'well-furnished with timber trees' in 1581, but timber in the Over Park was then said to be 'spoiled'.[77] Minsterley Park Farm, containing 240 a. in 1841,[78] preserves the ancient boundaries of the park. Lower Hogstow, described as a free 'haye' in 1300 when it was said to contain 200 a.,[79] lay on the south bank of the Rea to the west of Minsterley Park, where Lower Hogstow Farm now stands. Like Minsterley Park it was paled[80] and was normally used for the lord's horses in the later 14th century.[81] Many deer were carried off from Lower Hogstow by poachers in 1357.[82] It was still 'well replenished with oaks' in 1581; recent improvements to the pasture then recorded seem to have entailed nothing more than the grubbing up of underwood and the clearance of alder thickets in the low-lying land adjoining the brook.[83]

The hamlets of Callow, Lake, Minsterley, Poulton, and Westley shared common rights in Minsterley Wood and the inhabitants of Habberley, Hope, and Malehurst enjoyed rights of pannage there.[84] Like Hogstow Wood it was originally a part of the vast Stiperstones Forest and extended as far northwards as the present Rea Brook Farm and New House Farm. Minsterley freeholders, notably the descendants of Richard de Hope and Robert de Clough, had extensive common rights in the wood during the Middle Ages. The former, who was quit of pannage in Hogstow Wood, was granted common pasture for all his tenants in Minsterley, Malehurst, and Poulton *c.* 1274,[85] and in 1320 Robert de Clough was granted pannage for 30 pigs and common pasture for all animals except goats in an area between Wagbeach and Hope.[86] Little assarting is recorded in Minsterley Wood before *c.* 1533, when Lord Stafford inclosed a large area east of Minsterley Brook and south of New House Farm.[87] Some 160 a. to the north of New House Farm, later known as Freeholders' Wood, was then allotted to the freeholders as compensation for loss of common rights.[88] Although the timber in Freeholders' Wood was reserved to the lord, it was said in 1581 to have been 'almost spoiled by the tenants'[89] and unlicensed

49 Longleat MSS., unbound 4030.
50 S.R.O. 103 uncat., lease, 1600.
51 C 142/261/151; T. F. Dukes, *Antiquities of Shropshire* (Shrewsbury, 1844), p. lxxvii.
52 S.R.O. 279/155.
53 Ibid. 279/251–85; ibid. 1011 uncat., Ford Hund. presentments, 1778–1805.
54 Ibid. 279/333–5.
55 Ibid.; ibid. 1011 uncat., case papers *re* Vennington Common, 1799.
56 S.R.O. 1361/104.
57 Ibid. 1361/106.
58 Ibid. 1361/80.
59 *V.C.H. Salop.* i. 316.
60 Longleat MSS., unbound 4180.
61 Ibid. 3705.
62 Heref. City Libr. MS. 23628, f. 20.
63 Longleat MSS., unbound 3705.
64 *Cal. Inq. p.m.* xiii, p. 17.
65 *Cal. Pat.* 1292–1301, 476.
66 Ibid. 1354–8, 616.
67 E 36/150 f. 58.
68 S.P.L., Deeds 2494.
69 Leland, *Itin.* ed. Toulmin Smith, ii. 27.
70 C 133/7/8.
71 C 133/94/6.
72 *Rot. Hund.* (Rec. Com.), ii. 66. See also p. 306.
73 Longleat MSS., unbound 4114.
74 Ibid. 3997.
75 Ibid. 4010.
76 Ibid. 4030; S.R.O. 837/50.
77 Longleat MSS., unbound 4030.
78 S.R.O. 1361/102.
79 C 133/94/6.
80 Longleat MSS., unbound 3996.
81 Ibid.
82 *Cal. Pat.* 1354–8, 616.
83 Longleat MSS., unbound 4030.
84 S.P.L., Deeds 2495.
85 Longleat MSS., unbound 4180.
86 Heref. City Libr., MS. 23628, ff. 22v–23.
87 Longleat MSS., unbound 4301.
88 Heref. City Libr., MS. 23628, ff. 33–34v.
89 Longleat MSS., unbound 4030.

felling of timber continued in the 17th century.[90] Only 160 a. of Minsterley Wood remained uninclosed by 1581, when it was 'well-replenished with great timber trees of oak, and with old hazel, thorn, elm, birch, and withy'.[91] In 1673 that part of the wood lying west of Minsterley Brook together with the surviving portions of Hogstow Forest, amounted to 571 a.[92] The whole area, still densely wooded in parts, had probably been inclosed by 1676[93] and seems to have been cleared in the 1680s, when there were large sales of timber and cordwood.[94] Minsterley township contained only 92 a. of woodland in 1766, nearly all of which lay in Lady Oak Coppice (now called Spring Coppice) and College Coppice,[95] and 89 a. in 1841.[96] Apart from a plantation north of Minsterley Park, planted by 1881 but felled before 1949,[97] there has been no subsequent change.

Field-names show that woodland formerly ran south-eastwards from Westbury village as far as Hinwood, Wigley, and Newton.[98] Hinwood takes its name from a neighbouring wood known as Henwood in the 17th century,[99] and it seems likely that this was the name by which the whole area of woodland here was known during the Middle Ages. It may be identified with the 100-acre wood called 'Pelhemyny' recorded in 1267.[1] Only 3 small coppices survived in the mid-18th century; Broxtons Wood near Westbury village, Lady Field Wood (10 a.) near Hinwood, and a 10-acre coppice near Wigley Farm.[2] Broxtons Wood, formerly known as Foxholes Wood, derives its present name from Roger Broxon, its tenant c. 1630.[3] The coppices near Hinwood and Wigley had been cleared by 1841, when Broxtons Wood contained only 9 a.[4] Quarry Woods, to the south of Broxtons Wood, have been planted since 1841[5] to conceal the numerous pitmounds in this area.

This belt of woodland extended eastwards across the southern portion of the townships of Stoney Stretton and Yockleton. Newton Wood Coppice is a remnant of Newton Wood, still large in 1584,[6] whose original extent can be deduced from adjacent field-names. Assarts at Bores Butts, recorded in 1382,[7] can be related to the field of the same name in 1841 on the boundary between Stoney Stretton and Edge[8] and the field-name Brandstyles occurs south of Yockleton.[9]

The principal area of woodland in Stoney Stretton and Yockleton, however, lay on the heathland to the north of those hamlets, which was known as Kings

Marsh in 1584.[10] The two manors were said to contain woodland for 100 swine in 1086.[11] Thomas Corbet, who procured a grant of free warren here in 1246,[12] had formed a park to the west of Yockleton hamlet by 1274.[13] This contained 70 a. in 1300[14] and its centre was presumably Yockleton Park Farm. 'Hay' field-names are widespread in the area west of Park Farm[15] and there were still 20 a. of woodland north of Lynches Farm (or 'The Lynches') to the east of Yockleton township, in the 18th century.[16] Some progress appears to have been made during the later Middle Ages in the clearance of that part of the heath which possessed good natural drainage. Assarts called 'Bruch Heth' and 'the Penyacre near Newnham' occur in Yockleton manor in 1382,[17] while 'Ganelith Green' in Stoney Stretton was probably also a heathland clearing.[18] By 1763 scarcely any of the relatively small portion of heathland in Yockleton township remained uninclosed,[19] but 81 a. of open common on Stretton Heath were not inclosed until 1808.[20] Surviving timber on Yockleton Heath was felled and sold to local ironmasters in 1691[21] and 23 a. woodland in the Yockleton manorial estate was cleared and converted to arable in the later 18th century.[22]

Inadequate natural drainage on the flat land at the foot of the Long Mountain produced an area of moorland, or meadow-land at its best, running from north to south across the parish between Minsterley and Halfway House. To the north these conditions account for the place-names Marsh and Wigmore, while Ledmoor and The Hams in Vennington and Oxmoor and Sarn in Wigmore indicate the marshy nature of the land here.[23] Commons known as Nethermoor and Deepmoor lay alongside Yockleton Brook to the north-east of Westbury village, near Hayford Farm and Siteley respectively.[24] Both had been inclosed by 1631,[25] but Nethermoor was still waterlogged in 1768, when it was known as Westbury Bad Ground,[26] and in the 19th century the field-names Birchmore, Rhossy Piece, and Rushy Meadow were found in the area of Deepmoor.[27] Similar conditions occurred at the foot of the Edge plateau, south of Yockleton, where the field-name 'Halywellsmor' is recorded in 1382.[28] The Hem, to the north of Rea Brook between Minsterley and Hurst, was the largest of these areas of moor and meadowland. This was common to the tenants of Westley and Lake until its inclosure in 1610.[29] Demesne meadows called

[90] S.R.O. 279/136.
[91] Longleat MSS., unbound 4030.
[92] Ibid. 4061.
[93] Longleat MSS., Thynne Papers, vol. xx, f. 34.
[94] Ibid. vols. xxi–xxiii, letters of Thos. Hawkes and Sam. Peers, *passim*.
[95] S.R.O. 152/1.
[96] Ibid. 1361/102.
[97] O.S. Map 6″ Salop. 40 (1st edn.); O.S. Map 1/25,000, SJ 30 (1957).
[98] S.P.L., Deeds 13642.
[99] S.R.O. 665 uncat., lease, 1630.
[1] J.I. 1/177 m. 3d.
[2] S.P.L., Deeds 13642.
[3] S.R.O. 665 uncat., lease, 1630.
[4] Ibid. 1361/103.
[5] Ibid.
[6] T. F. Dukes, *Antiquities of Shropshire* (Shrewsbury, 1844), p. lxxvii; Longleat MSS., unbound 4211.
[7] S.P.L., Deeds 6172.
[8] Heref. Dioc. Regy., Stoney Stretton tithe appt.
[9] Ibid.

[10] E 134/26 Eliz. I/12.
[11] *V.C.H. Salop.* i. 325.
[12] *Cal. Chart. R.* i. 294.
[13] C 133/7/8.
[14] C 133/94/6.
[15] Heref. Dioc. Regy., Yockleton tithe appt.
[16] Map, 1763, in Lynches Farm title-deeds, *penes* Mr. T. B. Bromley.
[17] S.P.L., Deeds 6172.
[18] Ibid.
[19] Map, 1763, in Lynches Farm title-deeds.
[20] Ibid. inclosure maps, 1808.
[21] S.P.L., Deeds 17005.
[22] Map, 1787, in Onslow Hall title-deeds *penes* Mr. C. J. Wingfield.
[23] S.R.O. 1361/106.
[24] Heref. Dioc. Regy., glebe terrier, n.d.
[25] S.R.O. 665 uncat., lease, 1631.
[26] S.P.L., Deeds 13642.
[27] S.R.O. 1361/103.
[28] S.P.L., Deeds 6172.
[29] Ibid. 6765–6, 6768, 6771, 6775, 6777.

'Noltmore' and 'Dodkyssemeadow'[30] lay to the south of the Rea, near Minsterley Park Farm, while to the east of Minsterley village, at the confluence of Rea and Minsterley Brooks, lay the meadows known as Monks Hays, held in the Middle Ages by Buildwas Abbey.[31] A medieval fishpond near Hurst, known as Tydwals Pool,[32] had been drained by 1581.[33] The Hem Drain (or Hurst Ditch) which forms the parish boundary with Worthen at this point, is recorded in 1766[34] and Monks Hays were drained in the later 18th century.[35] Further improvements to the drainage of the Rea Valley west of Horsebridge were undertaken under an Act of 1799;[36] by 1804 the Hem drain had been improved and a new drain made at Lower Hogstow.[37]

In the larger hamlets in the parish the common fields appear to have survived until the 17th century. Those of Westbury and Wallop were uninclosed in 1613[38] and 1634[39] respectively and those of Vennington were inclosed c. 1681.[40] The Minsterley common fields were the last to go, owing to the number of small freeholders in the township. The agent of the lord of the manor considered that there was little hope of bringing about inclosure here in 1681,[41] but the process was complete by 1766.[42] There is no evidence for the date of inclosure at Stoney Stretton, Westley, and Yockleton. The common fields of the remaining townships, all of them containing shrunken hamlets, presumably disappeared during the Middle Ages. The whole township of Wigmore was let as pasture in 1483.[43]

Evidence for the names and location of the common fields in those townships where this is available is set out below.

Caus. The common fields lay to the east of the castle and included Wintle Field, above Caus Beach, and Old Caus Field (later corrupted to Hawcocks Field), near Hawcocks Mount. They formed part of the demesne lands of Caus until the 14th century.[44]

Minsterley. Lye Field, Horsebridge Field, and Coppice Greve Field are recorded in 1546.[45] The two former lay to the north of the village on each side of the road to Horsebridge and the latter to the south-east, along the Habberley Road.

Stoney Stretton. Field-names show common-field land on the gravels to the south of Yockleton Brook and on the higher ground north of the village.[46] Ridge-and-furrow is visible in Hall Meadow, immediately north of Stretton Hall.[47]

Wallop. Oakley Field lay to the north of the village, Middle Field to the west, and Langley Field on the northern slopes of Langley Wood, where ridge-and-furrow can still be seen.[48]

Westbury. Wintle Field, to the south-west of the village, between Westbury Brook and the Worthen road, adjoined a common field of the same name in Caus township. Wood Field lay on each side of the road to Westley and Wigmore Hill Field on each side of that to Westbury station.[49]

During the early Middle Ages the natural route systems of the Rea valley and the Long Mountain were of considerable strategic importance in the defence of the Welsh march west of Shrewsbury. The principal route to Shrewsbury ran up the Camlad valley from Chirbury towards Worthen, then along each side of the Rea to Westbury and Pontesbury. At Westbury this valley route is joined by a ridgeway running over the Long Mountain, and a 'burh' was presumably established at this important road junction in Saxon times. Frontier guards are said to have been killed at Westbury in 1053.[50] Westbury's strategic importance was somewhat diminished after the Norman Conquest, when Montgomery Castle was constructed as a first line of defence, but four castles, perhaps forming part of a coherent system of defence in depth between Montgomery and Shrewsbury, lay within the parish.[51] At Yockleton a motte controlled a ford across Yockleton Brook and stood near the junction of the road from Shrewsbury to Westbury with a supposed Roman road, now a footpath, running northwards from Lea.[52] A ring-work at Hawcocks Mount, later superseded by Caus Castle, commanded a wide view across the Rea valley and the Long Mountain.[53] The latter was complemented, to the south of Rea Brook, by a castle on Callow Hill, near Minsterley.[54]

The present road from Shrewsbury to Westbury, west of Cruckton, is thought to follow the alignment of a Roman road from Wroxeter to forts at Forden Gaer and Caersws.[55] Although it stands a little to the south, Stoney Stretton presumably takes its name from this road. Between Yockleton and Westbury the road runs through marshy ground at the two points where it crosses Yockleton Brook; at The Moors in Yockleton and at Stedford Bridge Meadow, west of the Elephant and Castle Inn. It was probably for this reason that this part of the road was abandoned during the Middle Ages in favour of an alternative route to the south of the brook. This rejoined the Roman road near Siteley Farm. Both roads were in existence in 1512, when one is described as via regia and the other, presumably the Roman road, as the 'stony causeway'.[56] The line of the Roman road was turnpiked in 1758[57] and the medieval route west of Stoney Stretton then fell into disuse apart from the section which served as a means of access to Wigley and Lower Newton

[30] Longleat MSS., unbound 3836, 3996.
[31] T.S.A.S. 4th ser. vi. 180–1; S.P.L., Deeds 14295.
[32] N.L.W., MS. 7851D, f. 421.
[33] Longleat MSS., unbound 4030.
[34] Q. Sess. rolls, Trin. 1766.
[35] S.P.L., Deeds, 14471.
[36] Ibid. 13902; Worthen inclosure Act, 39 & 40 Geo. III, c. 92 (local and personal act).
[37] Q. Sess., dep. plans, A 5.
[38] Heref. Dioc. Regy., glebe terrier, 1613.
[39] Longleat MSS., unbound 3632.
[40] Longleat MSS., Thynne Papers, vol. xxi, f. 236.
[41] Ibid. f. 228.
[42] S.R.O. 152/1.
[43] Ibid. 840 uncat., lease, 1483.
[44] Longleat MSS., unbound 3841, 3982, 3992; S.R.O. 1361/104.

[45] Longleat MSS., unbound 3544.
[46] Heref. Dioc. Regy., Stoney Stretton tithe appt.
[47] S.P.L., air photographs of Roman road, Meole Brace to Yockleton.
[48] Longleat MSS., unbound 3632, 3680, 3685, 3794.
[49] Heref. Dioc. Regy., glebe terriers, n.d., 1604–13.
[50] Anglo-Saxon Chron. ed. Dorothy Whitelock (1961), 128. Whether this is the Salop. or Glos. Westbury is not clear.
[51] T.S.A.S. liii. 83–84.
[52] Ex inf. Dr. A. W. J. Houghton, The Oakwood, Pulverbatch.
[53] See p. 303.
[54] See p. 306.
[55] V.C.H. Salop. i. 271–2.
[56] S.R.O. 665 uncat., deed, 1512.
[57] Shrewsbury road Act, 31 Geo. II, c. 67 (priv. act).

Farms. Of the three bridges over Yockleton Brook on the turnpike road between Westbury and Nox, New Bridge (west of Stoney Stretton) dates from 1767[58] and the bridge to the east of Yockleton from 1789.[59] The bridge to the west of Yockleton, which was built in 1784,[60] was rebuilt above flood-level in 1853.[61] South-west of Westbury the Roman road to Forden formerly followed what is now merely a footpath past Hawcocks Mount and Mondaytown towards Aston Rogers, west of the present road.[62] The existing line of this road, in use by 1768,[63] may be the result of a medieval diversion, since it formed the boundary of the demesne lands of Caus.[64]

Of the other roads which converge at Westbury that to Caus formerly left the village street east of Beeches Farm and ran along the crest of Whitton Hill, joining the present road near Caus Castle.[65] This road was still in use in 1768,[66] but had been diverted to its present course by 1816.[67] The road to Asterley was in origin a field-road to the common wood of Hinwood, but became of some importance in the 18th century, when it was used by coal-wagons from the Asterley mines. It was being used for this purpose in 1729[68] and, though disused in 1768,[69] was repaired c. 1781.[70] A footpath from Hinwood to Winsley, also used by coal-wagons in 1736,[71] would have provided a short-cut for west-bound traffic. In the Middle Ages the road from Westbury past Vennington and along the crest of the Long Mountain appears to have been the main road to Newtown[72] and it was still being used as an alternative route to Welshpool in 1822.[73]

The most important of the roads passing through Minsterley, the other main road-junction in the parish, was the road from Pontesbury, which passed through the village to join the Westbury–Montgomery road at Brockton. The section east of Minsterley was turnpiked in 1758[74] and that to the west in 1768.[75] This road, and that from Minsterley to Habberley, was controlled by the castle at Callow Hill. The road to Hope formerly left the village street west of the smithy and, after briefly following the alignment of the present road at Plox Green, followed the lane known as Drury Lane towards Hope Farm.[76] The road to Snailbeach, which meets this road at Plox Green, went no further than the Snailbeach mine in 1766,[77] but had been extended as far as the Pennerley and Bog mines by 1808.[78]

The volume of traffic on the Hope road increased in the later 18th century with the development of lead-mining on the Stiperstones. Hope Lane was out of repair in 1804[79] and Minsterley bridge, seriously damaged in the flood of 1811,[80] required repair in 1820[81] and 1827.[82] A new turnpike road running along Minsterley Brook and up the Hope valley was constructed between 1834 and 1838.[83] This did not cross Minsterley bridge, but, following the line of an old field-road to Freeholders' Wood, ran to the east of the brook as far as Plox bridge.

The Shrewsbury and Welshpool Railway, which runs across the north of the parish, was opened in 1862, providing stations at Yockleton and north of Westbury village.[84] Both stations were closed in 1960.[85] Of more importance to the lead-mining region to the south was the spur from Great Hanwood to Minsterley, opened in 1861.[86] Minsterley station closed for passenger traffic in 1951.[87] The narrow-gauge Snailbeach District Railway, constructed in 1877, linked the Snailbeach mine directly with the spur at Pontesbury.[88] Other lead mines continued to carry their products by road to Minsterley station; steam traction engines were used for this purpose in the early years of the present century.[89] Schemes to extend the Snailbeach Railway southwards[90] and to construct a light railway from Minsterley to Chirbury[91] were mooted in the 1890s but came to nothing. Some relief was, however, provided by an aerial ropeway from the Bog mine to the Malehurst barytes mill, constructed in 1918.[92]

The parish was said to have an adult population of 817 in 1676[93] and contained 1,991 inhabitants in 1801.[94] The township of Minsterley was separately enumerated after 1811, when it had a population of 705.[95] This had risen to 988 by 1851, but thereafter fell slowly to 798 by 1891 and 744 by 1931.[96] An apparent decline to 656 in 1951[97] is accounted for by the transfer of part of Snailbeach to Worthen parish in 1934[98] and by 1961 the population of Minsterley township had risen to 909.[99] The remainder of the parish displayed similar demographic tendencies during the 19th century. Its population rose from 1,490 in 1811 to 1,655 by 1861 but had fallen to 1,130 by 1901 and has continued to fall in the present century; there were 1,070 inhabitants in 1951 and only 957 in 1961.[1]

[58] Q. Sess., dep. plans 201.
[59] Ibid.
[60] Ibid.
[61] Ibid. 211.
[62] Course of road traced by Mr. W. G. Putnam, Newtown (Montg.). See *Archaeology in Wales, 1964* (Newsletter of C.B.A. Group 2), no. 4, p. 15.
[63] S.P.L., Deeds 13642.
[64] S.R.O. 1361/104.
[65] S.P.L., Deeds 13642.
[66] Ibid.
[67] B.M. O.S. 2″ orig. drawings, sheet 199 (1816).
[68] Q. Sess. rolls, Trin. 1729.
[69] S.P.L., Deeds 13642.
[70] Q. Sess. rolls, East. 1781.
[71] S.P.L., Deeds 14588.
[72] W.S.L. 1721/1/1, f. 185.
[73] *Q. Sess. Orders,* iii. 227.
[74] Shrewsbury road Act, 31 Geo. II, c. 67 (priv. act).
[75] Bishop's Castle road Act, 8 Geo. III, c. 51 (priv. act).
[76] S.R.O. 152/1.
[77] Ibid.
[78] Baugh, *Map of Salop.* (1808).
[79] Q. Sess. rolls, East. 1804.

[80] *Q. Sess. Rolls,* 204; *Q. Sess. Orders,* iii. 181.
[81] Q. Sess., dep. plans 112.
[82] Ibid.
[83] Ibid. 242; S.R.O. 1361/102.
[84] Ex inf. Brit. Trans. Rec.
[85] Ibid.
[86] Ibid.
[87] Ibid.
[88] E. S. Tonks, *The Snailbeach District Railway* (Birmingham, 1950), 15.
[89] Longleat MSS., unbound, Rack E, agent's letters, 1916–18.
[90] E. S. Tonks, op. cit. 7, 17.
[91] Q. Sess., dep. plans 521.
[92] Longleat MSS., unbound, Rack E, agent's letters, 1916–18.
[93] *T.S.A.S.* 2nd ser. i. 88.
[94] *Census,* 1801.
[95] Ibid. 1811.
[96] Ibid. 1811–1931.
[97] Ibid. 1951.
[98] S.C.C., County Review Order, 1934.
[99] *Census,* 1961.
[1] Ibid. 1811–1961.

Friendly Societies were established at Westbury in 1795[2] and at Minsterley by 1822.[3] The lutenist John Maynard (fl. 1611) was at one time a member of the Thynne household at Caus and the Syriac scholar the Revd. William Cureton (1808–64) was born at Westbury.[4]

DEVELOPMENT OF SETTLEMENT. Although the small D-shaped inclosure in the centre of West-bury village, within which stand the church, the parsonage, and the former smithy, may have been produced fortuitously by the course of roads which converge there, it may alternatively represent the earthwork surrounding the Saxon 'burh', which seems to have given the village its name. All the farm-houses stand on the outer edge of this central inclosure—a pattern which has persisted since at least 1768.[5] Grange Farm is a timber-framed house, later cased in brick. Although none of the remaining houses in the village appears from its brick or stone exterior to have been built before the later 18th century, extended investigation of interiors would probably reveal other examples of cased timber-framing. The former smithy and the Lion Inn stand to the south of the central inclosure, at its junction with roads to the south and east. The smithy, a whitewashed stone cottage east of the rectory, closed in 1946,[6] but probably occupies the site of the smithy first recorded in 1601.[7] The inn, which formerly stood at the junction of the Worthen and Asterley roads, was demolished in 1965, when a new inn was opened on an adjoining site. The former inn was a brick-cased timber-framed house with a round tower in the south-west corner. The village had 4 alehouses throughout the 17th century,[8] and 3 in the later 18th century.[9] In 1841 the Salopian Stores, on the corner of the Vennington road, was described as a beerhouse,[10] but the Lion has been the only alehouse here since the 1870s.[11] A stone-built toll-house at the junction of the Worthen road with that to Minsterley, south-west of the village, has ogee-headed windows. It closely resembles a toll-house at Minsterley[12] and both were presum-ably built c. 1768, when the road was turnpiked. The parish workhouse, built in 1761,[13] stood on the Shrewsbury road east of the village. It was let as a cottage after c. 1800,[14] and has since been demolished. The Hermitage, a Georgian brick house to the north of the church, was formerly a charity school, built in 1728[15] and enlarged in 1736.[16] It was sold in 1850 when the present school was built on the road to Hayford Mill.[17] By 1768 seven squatter cottages had been built on the Vennington road, west of the village, in an area known as The Common Plock.[18] Most of them are still standing. Two pairs of estate cottages were built to the north of the churchyard in the mid-19th century, one of which is dated 1858, and a further group of estate cottages was erected on the Vennington road in 1901.[19] Ten Council houses were built on the Shrewsbury road before 1939, and 8 houses and 8 flats have been built on the Asterley road since 1945.[20]

More timber-framed houses appear to have survived in Minsterley, the only other village in the parish which may be termed large by local standards. The centre of the village is the road junction known as The Square, east of Minsterley bridge. All three surviving alehouses stand here. The Bridge Inn (formerly the Miners' Arms)[21] and the Bath Arms (formerly the Angel)[22] have been in use for this purpose since the mid-18th century,[23] but the present houses date only from the 19th century. The Crown and Sceptre, formerly the homestead of a freeholder,[24] became an alehouse in 1846.[25] It is a four-bay house of cruck construction, in which an upper floor was inserted in the earlier 17th century. The exterior is now roughcast over brick. Several other timber-framed houses stand to the south of the Crown and Sceptre, alongside the brook. They include Chapel House, a house of 1½ story with a central stack. This was the meeting-house of the local Independent congregation until the Congre-gational Chapel—a simple building in Classical style—was built next to The Crown and Sceptre in 1833.[26] Cobblestones and Yew Tree Cottage are of similar plan, as is no. 4 Callow Crescent to the north of the Habberley Road.

Despite its name there is no evidence that Minsterley possessed a church before the present chapel was built to the west of the brook in 1689.[27] Other timber-framed houses west of the brook include Minsterley Hall, built in 1653 but con-taining fragments of earlier work possibly derived from Caus Castle,[28] and Hall Farm. The mill, last recorded in 1679,[29] probably stood near the Hall, for the mill-pond now forms part of the Hall garden.

There is little evidence of timber-framing in other parts of the village. Upper House Farm, to the north of the Brockton road, was rebuilt c. 1900, but incorporates a portion of a timber-framed house of central-stack plan. One of the houses to the north of the chapel has exposed timbers in the rear gable. Acacia House is a four-bay brick house of early-19th-century date and the smithy opposite dates from the same period, but the remaining houses on this road were built later in the 19th century. Settlement along the Shrewsbury road, near the Minsterley Creamery and Rea Valley Foods Ltd., dates for the most part from the early 20th century.

[2] Q. Sess. Orders, iii. 71.
[3] Ibid. iii. 227.
[4] D.N.B.
[5] S.P.L., Deeds 13642.
[6] Ex inf. Mr. H. Passant, Vennington.
[7] S.P.L., Deeds 6867.
[8] Q. Sess., alehouse reg.
[9] Ibid.
[10] S.R.O. 1361/103.
[11] Kelly's Dir. Salop. (1870–1941).
[12] See plate facing p. 83.
[13] S.R.O. 1361/67.
[14] Ibid. 1011 (Smythe-Owen) uncat., accts. 1803–7, 1815–40.
[15] Par. rec., school minutes and accts. 1728–1848.

[16] Ibid.; S.R.O. 1011 (Smythe-Owen) uncat., convey-ance of site, 1736.
[17] Ed. 7/103/249.
[18] S.P.L., Deeds 13642.
[19] Datestones.
[20] Ex inf. Atcham R.D.C.
[21] Kelly's Dir. Salop. (1934).
[22] Ibid. (1870).
[23] Q. Sess., alehouse reg.
[24] S.R.O. 152/1.
[25] Ibid. 83 uncat., Minsterley poor rate, 1846.
[26] Datestone.
[27] See p. 329.
[28] See pp. 311–12.
[29] Longleat MSS., unbound 3966.

There was, however, a single house at Little Minsterley in 1766[30] and three houses by 1838.[31] A Primitive Methodist chapel was built in 1850 in the cul-de-sac north of the village known as The Grove.[32] The row of brick cottages adjoining it date from c. 1862.[33] Several houses have been built since the later 19th century on the Westley road, linking The Grove with the rest of the village, and the chapel was rebuilt on a new site in 1926.[34] The school was built in 1845[35] on the road to Plox Green, but few other houses were erected in this part of the village until the 1920s. There has since been ribbon development along this road, including 8 Council houses, built since 1932,[36] and many private bungalows, built since 1950. A large Council housing estate, numbering 70 houses and 8 flats, has been built since 1945 to the east of the village.[37]

The township of Caus, first named in 1165,[38] was thought by Eyton to be the Domesday manor of 'Alretone'.[39] The latter, however, can be identified with Trewern (Montg.), which was known by its Saxon name, 'Halreton', 'Allereton', or 'Olreton', until the end of the 13th century.[40] Caus Castle, which takes it name from the Pays de Caux in Normandy,[41] probably lay within one of the 13 unnamed berewicks of the Domesday manor of Worthen.[42] There is some evidence that the castle superseded a nearby pre-Conquest settlement, as well as an earlier ring-work, at Hawcocks Mount.[43] The latter stands ¾ mile east of Caus Castle, in a field known in 1361 as 'Aldecausefield' (Old Caus Field),[44] subsequently corrupted to Hawcocks Field.[45] Hawcocks Mount formerly stood on the main road from Westbury to Montgomery and the ridge-and-furrow still visible in the field in which the ring-work stands can plausibly be associated with a deserted hamlet. The castle and borough of Caus are discussed elsewhere.[46]

The former hamlet of Wallop stood in the valley west of Caus Castle. It is now represented by Lower Wallop Farm, but contained at least 3 farm-houses in 1634.[47] Four cottages recorded at this date may have been encroachments in Langley Wood.[48] In 1381 Wallop included a moated capital messuage with a dovecote;[49] the 'castle ditch' recorded c. 1350[50] probably refers to this building. A memory of its site seems to be preserved in the field-name Moat Bank[51] (Moat Meadow in 1634)[52] in an unlikely spot south of the road to Rowley, 500 yards south-west of Lower Wallop Farm.[53] The latter, a substantial house of brick and stone, incorporates part of an earlier timber-framed house to the north

and was probably enlarged shortly after 1810.[54] A smithy, rebuilt in the 19th century,[55] stands at a road junction ¼ mile east of Lower Wallop Farm and nearby are 2 Council houses built since 1945.[56]

In the north of the parish hamlets of moderate size have contrived to survive only at Vennington and on well-drained sites at Yockleton and Stoney Stretton. At Marsh and Wigmore settlement has become dispersed, while Perendon has shrunk to a single farm and the hamlet of Brerelawe is deserted.

Vennington, which stands on the ridgeway leading from Westbury over the Long Mountain, was called 'Feniton' when first recorded in 1256.[57] The name presumably refers to the marshy nature of the ground hereabouts, as is the case in the neighbouring hamlets of Marsh and Wigmore. Vennington lay within the manor of Whitton and a 'hall place' here, recorded in 1378,[58] may have been the residence of one of the lords of that manor. A 3-hearth house at Vennington, held by the lord of Whitton in 1662,[59] was rebuilt by his son Lingen Topp c. 1675 and was later known as New or White House.[60] Its site has not been established. Porch House to the north of the road in the centre of the village is a timber-framed house of central-stack plan with a two-storied porch, now blocked, in the centre of its south wall. It bears the date 1664, which, although set on the house in recent times, is said to have been taken from a dated beam inside the house.[61] Lower Farm, at right angles to the village street, consists of a two-bay timber-framed house to which a brick and stone north wing was added c. 1800. The latter probably replaced a portion of the former house, since a jettied porch, now blocked, adjoins it on the east wall. The Old Shop, at the west end of the village, has an exposed timber-framed east gable. Vennington Farm and Top Farm appear to have been rebuilt since the later 18th century. A watermill on the stream south of the village is first recorded in 1310[62] and was in use until c. 1913, being powered by a steam engine in its later years.[63] The brick and stone body of a tower windmill stands to the west of the village.

Yockleton, recorded in the form 'Ioclehuile' in 1086,[64] and as 'Lokelthulle' and 'Yokethul' later in the Middle Ages,[65] did not acquire the suffix '-ton' until after 1300.[66] The village now stands on a former Roman road, but its original site may have been on the banks of Yockleton Brook, a little to the north of the road. The site of a medieval chapel, still standing in 1655,[67] appears to have been the field north of the brook and east of the present village called Chapel

[30] S.R.O. 152/1.
[31] Ibid. 1361/102.
[32] H.O. 129/359/3/5.
[33] S.R.O. 83 uncat., Minsterley poor rate, 1862.
[34] Datestone.
[35] Ibid.
[36] Ibid.
[37] Ex inf. Atcham R.D.C.
[38] Eyton, vii. 11.
[39] Ibid. 5–7.
[40] Cal. Close, 1261–4, 265; Reg. R. Swinfield (C. & Y.S.), 221; All Souls mun., Alberbury Deeds, no. 113; Bull. Bd. of Celtic Studies, xi (1), 51; Salop. Newsletter, no. 28.
[41] Eyton, vii. 6.
[42] V.C.H. Salop. i. 325.
[43] Ibid. 388–9; T.S.A.S. liii. 89.
[44] Longleat MSS., unbound 3841.
[45] Ibid. 3992, 4004; S.R.O. 1361/104.
[46] See pp. 308–10.
[47] Longleat MSS., unbound 3632.

[48] Ibid.
[49] Ibid. 3724.
[50] N.L.W., Wynnstay 117, ff. 101, 101ᵛ.
[51] Longleat MSS., unbound 3632.
[52] S.R.O. 1361/104.
[53] O.S. Nat. Grid 322072.
[54] S.R.O. 279/61.
[55] Ex inf. Mr. K. Roberts, Lower Wallop Farm.
[56] Ex inf. Atcham R.D.C.
[57] Eyton, vii. 26.
[58] Longleat MSS., unbound 3965.
[59] E 179/255/35 m. 82.
[60] S.R.O. 1361/1 (poor rate, 1675).
[61] Ex inf. Mr. H. Passant, Vennington.
[62] S.P.L., MS. 2, f. 422ᵛ.
[63] Kelly's Dir. Salop. (1885–1913).
[64] V.C.H. Salop. i. 325.
[65] Eyton, vii. 51–52.
[66] Feud. Aids, iv. 235.
[67] T.S.A.S. xlvii. 25.

Field in 1763.[68] A motte was constructed on the low ridge some distance west of the village, probably in the 12th century.[69] Bank House, Upper House Farm, Yockleton Villa, Yockleton Hall, and nos. 6 and 7, The Cop (formerly Cop Farm) occupy the sites of ancient farmsteads, but only the first three are still farm-houses. Bank Farm, originally a small timber-framed house with a stack on the south gable, was cased in brick and extended westwards in the 19th century. To the east of the house, alongside the road, is a five-bay barn of cruck construction, possibly the medieval tithe-barn of Shrewsbury Abbey.[70] Upper House Farm, formerly the freehold of the Meredith Family,[71] is a brick-cased timber-framed house, originally of 3 bays. A small section of curved timber in the south wall of the hall may be a portion of a cruck blade. Yockleton Villa, at the east end of the village, is a brick house of c. 1800 with a pedimented doorcase and fanlight. The Hall was probably rebuilt by the surgeon William Blakeway, who became its tenant in 1804.[72] It is a brick house of 3 stories with a stuccoed east front and central porch. The house was a gentleman's residence during the 19th century[73] and had become a preparatory school by 1885,[74] when a classroom and dormitory were built to the north. The former Cop Farm, now two cottages, is a timber-framed house of the earlier 17th century. Its farm buildings, adjoining the road, had been converted into a garage by 1922.[75] Adjoining the garage is the village shop, another timber-framed house, as is Wingfield House to the south of the road. The latter was an alehouse in the later 19th century,[76] but in 1839 the only alehouse in the village stood to the north of the road.[77] Yockleton possessed a mill in 1086[78] and had two by 1349.[79] The Lower Mill is a brick-and-stone house to the east of the village and was in use until c. 1937.[80] The Upper Mill, near the motte west of the village, was converted into a fulling mill in 1654.[81] Known as the Clover Mill in 1839,[82] it was disused by 1881.[83] A stone cottage west of Bank House Farm was a smithy throughout the 19th century.[84] The church and parsonage, built in 1861,[85] and the school, built in 1864,[86] all stand on the gravel ridge to the west of the village near the motte. Two pairs of estate cottages were built in the village c. 1850 on the sites of earlier houses and a single Council house was erected in 1936.[87] Several bungalows have been built on vacant sites in and near the village since 1945 and a large private housing estate to the east of the village was in course of erection in 1965.

Stoney Stretton presumably derives its name from the Roman road to the north which was known as 'Stoney Causeway' in the early 16th century.[88] It was a community of relatively prosperous freeholders and copyholders in the later Middle Ages[89] and in 1672 4 out of 12 houses had 2 hearths or more.[90] Stretton Hall is the only large house in the hamlet. The south wing, which has a blocked doorway on the east wall framed by Ionic pilasters and a broken pediment, appears to be a fragment of a late-17th-century house. Facing this doorway is a wide newel stair with turned balusters rising to attic level, but in all other respects the south wing was remodelled by John Parry shortly after 1813,[91] when the rest of the earlier house was replaced by a new north wing. This is of stuccoed brick and is of 3 stories. It has a north front of 3 bays and a central porch. Stretton Manor Farm, which probably dates from the later 15th century, consists of a 2-bay hall and a service bay of cruck construction, with a solar wing at the west end.[92] This wing and the service bay have always had upper floors, but the fireplace and upper floor over the hall, and the stair at the north end of the screens passage were inserted c. 1600. Home Farm, by the roadside east of the Hall, occupies the site of another medieval freehold. It was held by the Oakley family from the mid-17th century[93] and was known as Oakley House in 1842,[94] but appears to have been rebuilt in brick in the 19th century. Lower House Farm is an enlarged timber-framed house. A smithy, which stood in 1842 on the south bank of Yockleton Brook at the ford near Manor Farm,[95] has since been demolished. One of the timber-framed cottages, now derelict, to the north of Manor Farm, was a beerhouse in 1842[96] and may be the alehouse recorded in Stretton between 1613[97] and 1796.[98] The nearest inn is now The Elephant and Castle, on the Westbury road north-west of the hamlet, which opened shortly before 1851.[99] A brick-and-stone cottage on Old Lane, west of Stretton, is now a smallholding and an adjoining timber-framed cottage has been converted into a farm building.

The hamlet of Marsh appears to have been dispersed into scattered farms by 1086, for it then contained two manors, one of which was said to have been occupied as 3 manors before the Conquest.[1] Marche Manor and Marche Farm appear to have been the residences of the lords of each moiety of the manor after it was divided between the heirs of John de Eyton in the early 15th century.[2] In 1665 the lord of one moiety lived at Marsh Farm, then called Lower Marsh.[3] Marche Manor was known as Upper Marsh in 1765[4] and as Marsh Hall in

[68] Map, 1763, in Lynches Farm title-deeds.
[69] V.C.H. Salop. i. 388–9.
[70] See p. 330.
[71] Map, 1763, in Lynches Farm title-deeds.
[72] Ibid. lease, 1804.
[73] Heref. Dioc. Regy., Yockleton tithe appt.; Kelly's Dir. Salop. (1856–85).
[74] Kelly's Dir. Salop. (1885).
[75] Ibid. (1922). [76] Ibid. (1856–1900).
[77] Heref. Dioc. Regy., Yockleton tithe appt.
[78] V.C.H. Salop. i. 325.
[79] C 135/96/14.
[80] Ex inf. Mr. T. B. Bromley, Lynches Farm.
[81] S.P.L., Deeds 1670.
[82] Heref. Dioc. Regy., Yockleton tithe appt.
[83] Kelly's Dir. Salop. (1881).
[84] Ibid. (1856–1941); Heref. Dioc. Regy., Yockleton tithe appt.

[85] Heref. Dioc. Regy., reg. 1857–69, pp. 109, 206.
[86] Ed. 7/103/251.
[87] Datestone.
[88] S.R.O. 665 uncat., deed, 1512.
[89] S.P.L., Deeds 6172.
[90] Hearth Tax, 1672, 154.
[91] Par. rec., churchwardens' accts. 1807–48 (rates).
[92] Solar and hall are contemporary.
[93] S.R.O. 90/19.
[94] Heref. Dioc. Regy., Stoney Stretton tithe appt.
[95] Ibid. [96] Ibid.
[97] Q. Sess., alehouse reg.
[98] Ibid.
[99] Bagshaw's Dir. Salop. (1851).
[1] V.C.H. Salop. i. 325, 326.
[2] See p. 315.
[3] S.R.O. 1361/1 (poor rate, 1665).
[4] S.P.L., Deeds 3226.

1801.[5] It was occupied as a farm-house after 1705,[6] but was converted into cottages in the 19th century[7] until it was extensively restored by F. W. Wateridge *c.* 1892.[8] The latter lived at Marche Hall. This house includes fragments of an earlier timber-framed house, but was largely rebuilt in brick by the Wood family in the early 19th century. Before 1891 it was a T-shaped house of 2 stories and had a north front of 3 bays with a central free-stone porch. Another porch on the west wall was supported by Tuscan columns.[9] Alterations carried out by Wateridge between 1891 and 1922 included the panelling of the interior in Jacobean style, the insertion of bay windows on the east front, the erection of a parapet and balustrade to conceal the roof, and extensive additions at the rear.[10] A ball-room has been added to the south since 1922.[11] There appear to have been 3 houses in 1594 on the site now occupied by Marsh Farm.[12] One of these, occupied by the lord of the manor in 1665,[13] had 4 hearths in 1662[14] and 5 hearths in 1672.[15] The present farm-house probably contains part of this large house. As it now stands, it is a brick-cased timber-framed house of 2 bays with an original chimney-stack on the west gable. A stream runs through the semi-basement under the east bay. A further bay was added to the west and a wing on the north wall *c.* 1863,[16] when cast iron window frames of Gothic design were inserted in most of the windows. Two timber-framed farm buildings are largely constructed with reused timbers. Marche Manor Farm, near the Manor, has been built since 1922.[17]

The hamlet of Wigmore, now represented by two isolated farms known as Upper and Lower Wigmore, had probably shrunk to its present size by the later Middle Ages. By 1483 the township had been divided into two large pastures,[18] and in 1503 the tenant of one of these was required to make a 'sufficient and able moat',[19] which suggests the establishment of a new farm outside the original hamlet. By the mid-17th century Wigmore consisted of 3 farms,[20] each of which had a single hearth in 1672.[21] Red Hart Farm, which stood between Upper and Lower Wigmore, was still occupied in 1738,[22] but seems to have been demolished before 1772.[23] The two remaining farm-houses are both timber-framed houses dating from the earlier 17th century, later enlarged and cased in brick.

The site of Brerelawe, east of Marche Hall, is marked by a small ring-work.[24] During the 13th century it was the residence of a family known as Muneton or Brerelawe.[25] Later it was held with Wigmore[26] or Marsh,[27] but the date of its desertion cannot be established. A mill on Yockleton Brook, to the north of Brerelawe, is recorded in 1267[28] and 5 fields adjoining the ring-work were called Brierleys in 1840.[29] Perendon lay partly in Marsh Manor and partly in the Welshry of Caus known as Nether Gorther.[30] The township had been divided between Westbury and Alberbury parishes by the 13th century.[31] A single farm, known as Little Parton, stood on the site of the hamlet by 1624.[32] This has been known as Parton Wood since the 18th century[33] and has been converted into cottages since 1840.[34]

Of the 8 remaining hamlets in the centre of the parish, Ree, Poulton, and Callow are deserted, Wigley and Winsley have shrunk to single farms, and Newton and Lake to two farms each. Only Westley is still recognizably a hamlet. The evidence that Wigley was once a hamlet is slender but conclusive—the presence of ridge-and-furrow near Wigley Farm. One Reynold de Wigley was among those assessed to the taxation of 1327,[35] but Wigley is not again recorded until 1516.[36] Wigley Farm is a timber-framed house, cased in brick and stone, of 2 bays with a stack on the north-east gable. Lower Newton Farm, presumably on the site of the former hamlet of Newton, is surrounded by a square moat[37] and was in a derelict condition in 1965. It is a large timber-framed house of 2 stories, later cased in brick and stone, and consists on the ground floor of a hall and northern cross-wing.[38] A modern datestone over a door on the east wall of the hall reads 'V.C. 1555'. This refers to Vincent Corbet, who held Newton in the mid-17th century,[39] and is clearly an error for 1655. The cross-wing, which originally projected further to the east than it does now, is considerably older than 1655, for it contains 2 ogee-headed doors and a central newel stair, probably of 15th-century date. The lateral chimney-stack at the east end of the north wall is presumably a later insertion. The hall is divided on the ground floor into 2 rooms with a thin panelled partition and has 2 lateral chimney stacks, one of brick and the other of stone, on the west wall. It preserves the dimensions of the medieval open hall which must once have stood here, but the upper floor and the roof are of 17th-century date. Upper Newton Farm, 900 yards north-west of Lower Newton, is a brick-cased timber-framed house of 3 bays with a stack on the west gable.

Westley, which stands on a lane leading to former

[5] Marche Manor title-deeds *penes* Mrs. R. H. Hazan.
[6] S.R.O. 1187/19.
[7] *T.S.A.S.* 4th ser. v. 180.
[8] Ibid. For some description of the house see ibid. 180–4.
[9] Photograph *penes* Mr. A. A. Peake, Marche Hall.
[10] Ibid. sale partics., 1922.
[11] Ibid.
[12] C 142/247/83.
[13] S.R.O. 1361/1 (poor rate, 1665).
[14] E 179/255/35 m. 83.
[15] *Hearth Tax, 1672*, 156.
[16] Dated brick.
[17] Sale partics. 1922, in Marche Manor title-deeds.
[18] S.R.O. 840 uncat., lease, 1483.
[19] Ibid.
[20] Ibid. leases, 1647, 1649, 1669; ibid. accts. 1685–6.
[21] *Hearth Tax, 1672*, 156.
[22] S.R.O. 840 uncat., estate map, 1738.

[23] Ibid. lease, 1772.
[24] *V.C.H. Salop.* i. 382.
[25] Eyton, xi. 79.
[26] S.R.O. 840 uncat., Wigmore title-deeds, 1317–1605.
[27] S.P.L., MS. 593.
[28] Eyton, vii. 171.
[29] S.R.O. 1361/106.
[30] *Plac. de Quo Warr.* (Rec. Com.), 686; *T.S.A.S.* liv. 327, 331.
[31] S.P.L., Deeds 2903.
[32] Ibid.
[33] Ibid. 3229.
[34] S.R.O. 1361/106.
[35] *T.S.A.S.* 2nd ser. x. 143.
[36] S.R.O. 665 uncat., Westbury bailiff's acct. 1516.
[37] *V.C.H. Salop.* i. 405. It is said to have been known as Broughcastle: C. Hulbert, *Manual of Salop.* (1839), 78.
[38] For some description see *T.S.A.S.* 4th ser. ix. 237.
[39] S.P.L., MS. 2788, p. 128.

common land at the Hem, contained at least 8 houses in 1445[40] and 1540.[41] It was still of this size in 1783,[42] when one of the farm-houses had become cottages. In 1844 it contained 4 farms and 2 cottages,[43] all of which are still standing. Middle Farm is a timber-framed house of 3 bays with a central stack. Lower Farm, also timber-framed and now derelict, consists of a hall with a stack on the south gable and to the north a 2-bay cross-wing. Home Farm was rebuilt in brick and stone c. 1800, making use of some earlier timbers, and Westley Hall Farm, part of the same freehold,[44] was rebuilt in brick at about the same date.

Winsley Hall, built in 1805,[45] stands on the site of the former hamlet of Winsley. There were only two farms here by 1699;[46] a cottage is also recorded in 1736.[47] The single farm remaining in 1799 was demolished when the Hall was built.[48] A home farm, built to the south of the road between 1841 and 1863,[49] has since been demolished. Hurst Farm, to the south of Winsley, was a member of the township of Coton and Hurst, the greater part of which lay within Worthen parish.

The hamlet of Lake presumably stood near Upper Lake Farm, on the west bank of Crook-a-moor Brook and only a few yards from Asterley in Pontesbury parish. It contained at least 5 tenants in 1384,[50] 3 tenants c. 1540,[51] and 3 houses in 1783.[52] Upper Lake Farm originally comprised a 2-bay hall and service bay of cruck construction and a southern solar wing. Only the two northern bays of the cruck house still survive, the southern bay and the solar wing having been replaced by a timber-framed house of 2 stories in the earlier 17th century.[53] It was a medieval freehold and was held by the Treves family between 1540 and 1681.[54] Lower Lake Farm, in the fields to the south of Upper Lake, was derelict in 1965. It is a small brick-cased timber-framed house of 2 bays with a chimney-stack on the south gable. Two groups of cottages built at Upper Lake by 1841[55] probably housed workers from the Asterley coal-pits. They had been demolished by 1965. In 1841 a single cottage stood at Horsebridge,[56] on the road to Minsterley south-west of Lake. Further cottages built here in the mid-19th century were occupied by small tradesmen.[57]

The precise site of the deserted hamlet of Ree, a Domesday manor[58] absorbed into the demesne of Caus in 1251,[59] cannot be established. It clearly stood on the banks of Rea Brook and is known to have been near Westley.[60] Its site may have been the large circular ditched enclosure south-west of Lower Hem Farm.[61]

The Corbets of Caus[62] constructed a castle on the site of an Iron Age hill-fort[63] on Callow Hill. This castle, probably of stone, was disused by c. 1274,[64] but its remains were observed by Leland c. 1540.[65] Stone taken in 1688 from Callow Hill for the foundations of Minsterley chapel[66] may have come from the castle. Two hamlets formerly stood at the foot of the hill. The site of Callow hamlet is not known. At least two cottages are recorded there in 1541[67] and in 1635 it still contained two houses, one of which was known as Callow Hill House.[68] Of two cottages recorded in 1766 one stood on the hill to the east of the site of the castle and the other at the foot of the hill to the west.[69] The hamlet of Poulton, granted to a free tenant c. 1274,[70] contained at least 2 tenants in 1384[71] and 1430,[72] but had shrunk to a single farm, described as a capital messuage, by 1636.[73] Poulton Farm, built in the early 19th century, is a T-shaped brick house with a west front of 3 bays and a central porch.

Virtually the only isolated settlement in the parish during the Middle Ages was that associated with the parks of Minsterley and Yockleton. The 'marehouse' in Minsterley Park recorded in 1371[74] seems to have been converted into a 'day-house' by 1568.[75] By the later 16th century there were probably farm-houses in both parts of the Park, north and south of Rea Brook,[76] and these were still occupied in 1795.[77] Lower Park Farm, north of the brook, had been demolished by 1831.[78] Minsterley Park Farm, south of the brook, was almost entirely rebuilt c. 1795, when only the service wing of the former house was preserved,[79] and it was again reconstructed as a 3-story house in the early 19th century. The house, however, contains reused ceiling beams from the original house and part of an original staircase. Yockleton Park Farm seems to have been established by the later 16th century.[80] The oldest part of the present house was probably built in the earlier 17th century. The whole is now cased in brick and additions have been made to the east and west. The only other isolated site likely to have been occupied during the Middle Ages is that of Broomhill Farm, a 19th-century house near Caus Castle. A shepherd's hut is recorded here in 1445[81]

40 Longleat MSS., unbound 4010.
41 *T.S.A.S.* liv. 57.
42 S.R.O. 807/231.
43 Ibid. 1361/105.
44 Ibid.
45 See pp. 314–15.
46 S.P.L., Deeds 14217.
47 Ibid. 14588.
48 Ibid. 14589; S.R.O. 515/3, pp. 339–40.
49 S.R.O. 1361/105; ibid. 279/113.
50 Longleat MSS., unbound 3513.
51 Ibid. 4051.
52 S.R.O. 807/231.
53 See plate facing p. 216.
54 Longleat MSS., unbound 4051; S.P.L., Deeds 9301.
55 S.R.O. 1361/105.
56 Ibid.
57 *Kelly's Dir. Salop.* (1879–1909).
58 *V.C.H. Salop.* i. 324; Eyton, vii. 116–17.
59 *Rot. Hund.* (Rec. Com.), ii. 66.
60 Eyton, vii. 117.
61 Site located from the air by Dr. J. K. St. Joseph and partially excavated by Mr. P. C. Ozanne in 1958: *Proc.*

Prehist. Soc. N.S. xxv (1959), 276. Pottery finds included some medieval sherds: ex inf. Mr. P. A. Barker, Church House, Annscroft.
62 Longleat MSS., unbound 4180.
63 *V.C.H. Salop.* i. 366.
64 Longleat MSS., unbound 4180.
65 Leland, *Itin.* ed. Toulmin Smith, ii. 26.
66 Longleat MSS., Thynne Papers, vol. xxiii, f. 338.
67 *T.S.A.S.* liv. 55.
68 Longleat MSS., unbound 4190.
69 S.R.O. 152/1.
70 Longleat MSS., unbound 4180.
71 Ibid. 3513.
72 Ibid. 4183.
73 Ibid. 4188.
74 Ibid. 4114.
75 S.R.O. 837/50.
76 Longleat MSS., unbound 4030.
77 S.R.O. 665 uncat., farm-house plans, c. 1795.
78 Ibid. 1361/101.
79 Ibid. 665 uncat., farm-house plans, c. 1795.
80 S.P.L., Deeds 12523.
81 Longleat MSS., unbound 4010.

and in 1466 the site contained a house and barn, each of 4 bays, as well as a sheep-cote.[82]

Green Farm, Wood Farm, and Snailbeach Farm were probably established in the area formerly covered by Hogstow Forest shortly after its inclosure; all of them dated from the earlier 17th century. Green Farm, formerly known as Plox Green Farm, stands on the edge of the former common fields of Minsterley. It is timber-framed and had an original ground-plan of 2 bays with a gable stack. Wood Farm is of similar plan, and Snailbeach Farm, timber-framed in 1861,[83] has since been rebuilt in brick.

A corn-mill and fulling mill had been established at Hogstow Mill by 1581.[84] The mill was burnt down in 1814[85] and rebuilt in the following year, but the timber-framed house is still standing. This was originally of 3 bays with a central stack, but it is now cased in brick and additions have been made along the north wall.

Only two isolated farms were established in the former woodland south-east of Westbury village. Woodhouse Farm is a two-bay timber-framed house of central-stack plan, to which a north bay and an eastern dairy have been added since the 18th century.[86] Siteley Farm, which may have been built after 1768,[87] had a single room on each floor c. 1795[88] and was rebuilt in brick in the 19th century. A small-holding at Lysons Coppice, south of Quarry Woods, is recorded in 1768[89] and cottages had been built for colliers in Quarry Woods by 1841,[90] but these had been demolished by the end of the 19th century.

Lynches Farm (or 'The Lynches') standing on the southern slopes of Ford Heath, on the eastern boundary of the parish and adjoining the squatter settlement of Nox in Pontesbury parish, is first named in 1612 when it was occupied by John Harries.[91] The house was said to contain 8 hearths in 1662[92] and 9 hearths in 1672.[93] It was occupied by the lords of Yockleton manor during the 18th century.[94] It is a timber-framed house, built in the second quarter of the 17th century and cased in brick in 1735, when pilaster buttresses were set against the corners and the roof was hipped.[95] Its unusual ground-plan comprises a projecting central hall, a parlour to the south, and a kitchen to the north. Chimney stacks in the kitchen and parlour are of sandstone and the parlour contains an elaborate Jacobean fireplace. There are ovolo-moulded ceiling beams and contemporary oak wainscot in the hall and parlour and a newel stair with flat fretted balusters on the east wall between these two rooms.

Although a house is recorded at the Hem in 1658,[96] both existing farms here—Hem Farm and Lower Hem Farm—appear to date from the 19th century.

The uplands of the Long Mountain, which might otherwise have proved attractive to medieval settlers, were wild and lawless during the Middle Ages. Peaceful conditions were only established in the 16th century, when there is evidence of settlement in valleys and on slopes sheltered from the prevailing westerly winds. All the houses in this area were originally timber-framed,[97] but after c. 1690 the local mudstone became the principal building material[98] until replaced by brick in the mid-19th century.

In 1541 a cottage was built at Wynstons Green,[99] near Forest Farm. Forest Farm itself, formerly known as Latha-coed, is first recorded in 1564.[1] The oldest part of the present house is of stone. It has a ground-plan of two bays with a chimney-stack on the east gable and is not likely to be older than c. 1700. A National school was built to the north of the farm-house in 1864.[2] The cottages in Harbache Dingle and Nant-y-Myssels Farm, where pastures are named in 1564,[3] probably represent mid-16th century habitation sites, but the latter is now of similar plan and date to Forest Farm. Wallop Hall, on the southern boundary of the Forest of Hayes, appears to have been newly built by John Severne between 1664 and 1671[4] but was demolished in 1953.[5] Haywood Farm is first recorded in 1629[6] but was rebuilt in stone in the early 19th century. Hazells Farm, on the former Wallop Common, was probably in origin one of a group of squatter cottages first recorded in 1564.[7] A group of nearby cottages, built before 1694,[8] has since been demolished. The Knapps, rebuilt in the 19th century, occupies the site of another cottage first recorded in 1564.[9] Whitton Grange, which retains early-17th-century ceiling-beams, was probably rebuilt in brick and stone c. 1770.[10]

Squatter settlement on Whitton and Vennington Commons, on the eastern slopes of the Long Mountain, seems to have begun in the early 17th century.[11] A farm is recorded near Vron Gate in 1609[12] and there were at least 10 cottages on Vennington Common by 1677.[13] The Seven Stars, Vron Gate, which is first so named in 1777,[14] has been an alehouse since at least 1754.[15] The two decades between 1780 and 1800 seem to have been the most active period for squatting here, particularly on Caus Mountain and Blackmore, and nearly all the cottages and smallholdings—of stone, with gable chimney stacks—probably date from these

[82] B.M. Eg. Roll 2196.
[83] Longleat MSS., unbound, Rack E, survey, 1816.
[84] Ibid. 4030.
[85] Ibid. Rack E, acct. 1814.
[86] S.R.O. 665 uncat., farm-house plans, c. 1795.
[87] S.P.L., Deeds 13642.
[88] S.R.O. 665 uncat., farm-house plans, c. 1795.
[89] S.P.L., Deeds 13642.
[90] S.R.O. 1361/103.
[91] N.L.W., Wynnstay (1952), box X/63.
[92] E 179/255/35 m. 84.
[93] Hearth Tax, 1672, 159.
[94] Lynches Farm title-deeds.
[95] For some description see T.S.A.S. 4th ser. vi. 281.
[96] S.P.L., Deeds 6779.
[97] S.R.O. 279/331–2.
[98] Ibid. 837/74, 76, 80.

[99] T.S.A.S. liv. 335; S.R.O. 1361/104.
[1] Staffs. R.O., D 641/1/2/243; S.R.O. 837/58; ibid. 1361/54 (church rate, 1807).
[2] Ed. 7/103/250.
[3] Staffs. R.O., D 641/1/2/243.
[4] S.R.O. 1361/1 (poor rates, 1664–71).
[5] Ex inf. Mr. K. Roberts, Lower Wallop Farm.
[6] S.R.O. 837/54.
[7] Staffs. R.O., D 641/1/2/243.
[8] S.R.O. 279/331–2.
[9] Staffs. R.O., D 641/1/2/243.
[10] S.R.O. 665 uncat., letter, J. Topp to E. Kilvert, 13 Apr. 1771.
[11] Inclosures are recorded in 1600: C 142/261/151.
[12] S.P.L., Deeds 17351.   [13] S.R.O. 279/157.
[14] Longleat MSS., unbound, Rack E, accts. 1777.
[15] Q. Sess., alehouse reg.

years.[16] In 1841 there were 7 cottages on Caus Mountain Lane, 9 on or near Blackmore, and 9 near Vron Gate.[17]

Squatting on the heathlands along the northern boundary of the parish is first recorded in the later 16th century.[18] There were 6 cottages on Yockleton Heath by 1763,[19] and 9 by 1839,[20] but such cottages were more numerous on the larger Stretton Heath. Fifteen cottages already stood here by 1699[21] and there were 19, most of them along the southern edge of the heath, in 1787.[22] By 1843 a number of other cottages had been built on land allotted to the lord of the manor at the inclosure of the heath in 1808.[23] The few cottages now remaining on Stretton Heath appear to be all of 19th-century date.

Cottages had already been erected in Hogstow Forest by 1562, when cottagers were admonished to be of 'good aberinge' to the lord's wood and game,[24] and several cottages are recorded in Minsterley Common Wood in 1581.[25] Several of the existing cottages in this area are timber-framed, notably Pottery Cottage (near Rea Brook Farm), a small 2-bay cottage on the former main road near Plox Green, a ruined cottage at Bank House, near Etsell, and Oakfields, a 2-bay cottage west of Hogstow Mill. Oakfields was known as Little Hogstow in 1766[26] and 1841.[27] In 1766, when there was only one cottage at Plox Green (now no. 13, Plox Green, a one-room cottage with a gable chimney-stack), one cottage had been built at Wagbeach, 3 at the Waterwheel, and 6 at the Lady Oak and along Drury Lane.[28] Settlement at the Waterwheel, formerly known as The Brook, is associated with a fulling mill, established there by 1581[29] and in use until 1695.[30] From 1863[31] until c. 1926[32] its site was occupied by a barytes mill. The Lady Oak takes its name from an oak tree which stood at the cross-roads until 1757.[33] An alehouse is recorded there between 1776 and 1796.[34] Most of the cottages at Plox Green and in the area to the south, however, were built in the 1830s,[35] following the construction of the new turnpike road to Bishop's Castle. There were 11 cottages at Plox Green and the same number at Wagbeach by 1837 and a similar expansion along Drury Lane took place at this time.[36]

The only large squatter settlement in the parish is at Snailbeach, south-east of Minsterley, where lead was mined continuously from 1782 until 1913.[37] The settlement, which takes its name from the valley in which the mine lies, stands at some 800 feet on the northern slopes of the Stiperstones and is partly in

Westbury and partly in the ancient parish of Worthen. Its bizarre landscape of derelict engine-houses and winding gear, vast grey spoil and tailing-heaps, and the drab squatter settlement which grew up near the mine, are evidence of the most prosperous and productive lead mine of the South Shropshire mining district.[38] There were no houses here in 1766, when the only buildings were those in the immediate neighbourhood of the mine.[39] By 1837, however, there were 16 cottages in the Westbury portion of Snailbeach[40] and there were 27 such cottages by 1854.[41] Snailbeach had reached its present size by 1872,[42] when all the cottages at the mine and along the road to Pennerley past Crows Nest belonged to Lord Bath. The cottages are almost without exception built of the greyish-brown local stone and are of two stories with gable chimney stacks. The only evidence of planned cottages is a terrace near the Lower Works, built before 1872.[43] The low standard of these cottages was alleged to have been the cause of typhoid and scarlet fever epidemics, which were said to have been 'most frequent . . . for many years past' in 1870.[44]

THE CASTLE AND BOROUGH OF CAUS. The ruins of Caus Castle[45] stand at 700 feet on an isolated spur of the Long Mountain, a mile south-west of Westbury village, and command a wide prospect over the Rea valley to the east and south and over the Long Mountain to the west. It has been suggested that the site may have been that of an Iron-Age hill-fort,[46] but the evidence is inconclusive. The original castle, which was probably built by Roger Fitz Corbet in the late 11th or early 12th century, as the *caput* of his barony, consisted of a motte and bailey aligned from north-east to south-west on the top of the ridge, with the motte at the south-west end. The defences consisted of a single ditch to the the east, where the ground falls sharply away, and a double ditch on the west and north. The motte now stands 55 feet above the bottom of the castle ditch, which has itself been cut some 12 feet into the rock below. To the north and west of the castle-site is a large area, enclosed within a single rampart, in which the borough of Caus formerly stood.

The castle was garrisoned by the Crown in 1165[47] and Robert Corbet had a Crown grant for work at the castle in 1198.[48] This period of building activity probably represents the transition from a timber to a stone castle. On the top of the motte there are remains of a tower with sandstone dressings and there is a well in the ditch to the west of the motte.

[16] S.R.O. 279/259–80.
[17] Ibid. 1361/106.
[18] E 134/26 Eliz. I/12; Loton Hall MSS., Ford Hund. ct. r. 1569.
[19] Map, 1763, in Lynches Farm title-deeds.
[20] Heref. Dioc. Regy., Yockleton tithe appt.
[21] S.P.L., Deeds 6042.
[22] Map, 1787, in Onslow Hall title-deeds.
[23] Leases, 1808, in Lynches Farm title-deeds; Heref. Dioc. Regy., Stoney Stretton tithe appt.
[24] S.P.L., Deeds 2495.
[25] Longleat MSS., unbound 4030.
[26] S.R.O. 152/1.
[27] Ibid. 1361/102.
[28] Ibid. 152/1.
[29] Longleat MSS., unbound 4030.
[30] Ibid. 4202.
[31] S.R.O. 83 uncat., Minsterley poor rate, 1863.
[32] Kelly's Dir. Salop (1926).
[33] Montgom. Collect. xviii. 383.
[34] Q. Sess., alehouse reg.
[35] S.R.O. 1361/100, 101; ibid. 83 uncat., Minsterley poor rates, 1837–62.
[36] Ibid. 83 uncat., Minsterley poor rate, 1837.
[37] See pp. 322–4.
[38] See plate facing p. 237.
[39] S.R.O. 152/1.
[40] Ibid. 1361/102.
[41] Ibid.
[42] Q. Sess., dep. plans 474.
[43] Ibid.
[44] S.R.O. 800 uncat., box 25, Mine Manager's report, Jan. 1870.
[45] Account of earthwork and physical remains based on V.C.H. Salop. i. 399–400, and observations by Miss L. F. Chitty, Mr. P. A. Barker, and Mr. F. Noble. See also T.S.A.S. 3rd ser. vi, plate facing p. 106.
[46] Ex inf. Miss L. F. Chitty, Pontesbury. See also Arch. Camb. civ. 199.
[47] Pipe R. 1165 (P.R.S. viii), 98.
[48] Ibid. 1198 (P.R.S. n.s. ix), 108.

The upper part of the well-shaft is corbelled and has a square head. To the south-east of the bailey are the foundations of a rectangular building, some 75 feet long and 25 feet wide, which was probably the great hall. At the north-eastern gateway of the bailey part of the walls of one of the D-shaped towers is still standing. All visible masonry is of local mudstone, probably that quarried from the ditches, apart from the red sandstone used in the tower on the motte. The sandstone may have come from Wattlesborough where stone was being obtained in 1444.[49] The castle had an inner and an outer bailey in 1400, when the latter contained the kennels and stables.[50] There were also inner and outer gates, one of which was called the Great Gate in 1458.[51] The outer gate, in which there was a prison,[52] was separated from the castle ditch by the barbican,[53] in which there were at least two chambers.[54] There appear to have been houses below the barbican.[55] A 'new' tower, recorded in 1379,[56] and Grymbald's Tower, repaired in 1395,[57] cannot be located, but a postern called Wolvesgate, recorded in 1379,[58] probably gave access to the borough.[59] The chapel of St. Nicholas appears to have been opposite the inner gate.[60] There were extensive new works between 1367 and 1379,[61] but their exact nature has not been established.

The castle seems to have been continuously occupied by the Corbet family until the death of Beatrice Corbet in 1347,[62] but after 1400 the Staffords appear to have made only rare visits to it. The castle was garrisoned during Glendower's rising[63] and during the rebellion of Sir Griffith Vaughan in 1444,[64] but there is no evidence that it played any part in military operations on the Welsh March before the death of Humphrey, Duke of Buckingham, in 1460. During the 15th century the castle was normally used only as an administrative centre. The courts of Over and Nether Gorther (the Welshry of Caus) were held there, and a checker or counting house was recorded in 1458.[65] The constable and gaoler were probably the only permanent residents.

At this period the castle appears to have been kept in moderate repair, but when it came into the hands of the Crown after the execution of Edward, Duke of Buckingham, in 1521, it was said to be 'in great ruin and decay'.[66] Henry Stafford, Lord Stafford, regained possession of part of his estates, including the castle, in 1522,[67] and extensive repairs and alterations were in progress in 1541.[68] The

outer gate was then remodelled and a court-house was constructed in the barbican.[69] A room over the court-house, known as the gallery, had probably been built by 1556,[70] when a number of carvers were at work in the castle. In this year a 'new house' was built and chimneys and fireplaces were being inserted.[71] A brick building below the castle, known as the 'walk', was also erected in 1556.[72] A pair of virginals was among its furniture in 1605.[73] It was known as the White Walk in 1612[74] and may have been the Long Walk, near the castle bridge, recorded in 1630.[75] In 1581 the castle was said to contain an 'innermost gatehouse and a chapel covered with lead, and kitchens, larders and other rooms covered with slate, but all very ruinous and in great decay'; the hall, great chamber, butteries, cellars, pantry and other houses of office, were also said to be in decay at this time.[76]

Lord Stafford, who sold the castle to Sir Rowland Hayward in 1573,[77] refused to give possession to Hayward's son-in-law John Thynne, and expelled Thynne's tenants in 1578.[78] Thynne subsequently gained possession at law, but Lord Stafford would not give up the castle, despite commands to appear before the Privy Council and the Council of the Marches.[79] In 1590 Thynne, with the assistance of the sheriff, attacked the castle during the absence of Lord Stafford, and after a short defence by Lady Stafford, gained possession.[80] The Thynnes came into residence shortly afterwards and inventories taken at the deaths of Sir John Thynne in 1604[81] and of his widow Joan in 1612[82] indicate either that the castle was not so ruinous as the survey of 1581 would suggest, or that they had completely renovated it. The whole castle was then occupied and well furnished. After the death of Joan Thynne her son Thomas does not appear to have been frequently resident,[83] but in 1630 extensive alterations were made, involving the complete rebuilding of the domestic offices,[84] and it was alleged c. 1640 that he had spent over £800 on repairs to the castle.[85] In 1645 the castle was garrisoned for the king, but it surrendered after a short siege[86] and was demolished soon afterwards.[87] Some of the fittings appear to have been reused in Minsterley Hall,[88] built after the destruction of the castle as the Thynne family's Shropshire residence. The castle was used as a quarry for road-stone in the 18th and early 19th centuries, but a considerable quantity of masonry is said to have been still standing c. 1830.[89]

[49] Longleat MSS., unbound 4010.
[50] S.R.O. 279/131; *T.S.A.S.* 3rd ser. vi. 108–13.
[51] Longleat MSS., unbound 3847.
[52] Ibid. 4030.
[53] Ibid. 4010.
[54] B.M. Add. Roll 54409.
[55] Longleat MSS., unbound 4010.
[56] Ibid. 3742.
[57] Ibid. 3984.
[58] Ibid. 3742.
[59] Ibid. 4010.
[60] Ibid. 3792.
[61] Ibid. 3716, 3730, 3738, 3750.
[62] *Cal. Inq. p.m.* ix, pp. 34–35.
[63] S.R.O. 279/131.
[64] Longleat MSS., unbound 4010.
[65] Ibid. 3847.
[66] E 36/150 f. 58; *L. & P. Hen. VIII*, ii (1), p. 509.
[67] *L. & P. Hen. VIII*, iii (2), p. 1084.
[68] *T.S.A.S.* liv. 334–5.
[69] Ibid. 335.

[70] Longleat MSS., unbound 3952.
[71] Ibid.
[72] Ibid.
[73] Ibid. 3848.
[74] Ibid. 3952.
[75] Ibid. 4026.
[76] Ibid. 4030.
[77] Ibid. 3489.
[78] Ibid. 3858; *Acts of P.C.* 1577–8, 206.
[79] P. Williams, *The Council of the Marches of Wales under Elizabeth I* (1958), 308–9.
[80] *T.S.A.S.* 1st ser. iii. 320.
[81] Longleat MSS., unbound 3848.
[82] Ibid. 3952.
[83] Ibid. 4026.　　　　　　　　　　　　[84] Ibid.
[85] Ibid. 3804.
[86] Mrs. Stackhouse Acton, *The Garrisons of Shropshire, 1642–8* (1867), 41–42.
[87] Longleat MSS., Thynne Papers, vol. xxxiii, f. 109.
[88] See pp. 311–12.
[89] W.S.L. 350/40/3.

The borough of Caus, which stood within the outer ramparts of the castle, is first recorded by name in 1272, when Thomas Corbet endowed the chapel of St. Margaret which he had founded there.[90] It was probably in existence by 1200, when Robert Corbet obtained a grant of a weekly market at Caus.[91] By 1300 the borough had been encircled with a wall.[92] Its two gates, the East Gate to the north-east of the castle, where there is a breach in the rampart, and Wallop Gate, south-west of the castle, where there are remains of a massive stone gate-house, are first recorded in 1371.[93] Streets known as Castle Street and St. Margaret Street are recorded in 1447[94] and the course of the road from Wallop Gate to the East Gate, in use as a field-road in 1816,[95] is still visible. The entire street-plan could still be made out in the early 19th century.[96] The borough contained 28 burgage-tenements in 1274,[97] 34 in 1300,[98] and 58 c. 1349,[99] but went into decay after the Black Death. By 1361 many of the houses were without tenants[1] and they continued untenanted for the remainder of the 14th century.[2] In 1444 8 burgages were burnt during the rebellion of Sir Griffith Vaughan[3] and only 20 burgages remained in occupation by 1455.[4] By 1541, when 10 burgages are recorded, there were only two tenants and both gate-houses were untenanted for lack of repairs.[5] In 1581 the borough contained 4 cottages of which 3 were ruinous[6] and the fourth newly built by one of the lessees of the castle demesne.[7] In 1614 a freeholder rebuilt a house 'in the place where the last house was burnt', probably near the East Gate,[8] but no house is subsequently mentioned.

Caus Castle Farm, standing immediately north of the site of the borough, appears to have been rebuilt shortly after 1810 when Lord Bath sold his Caus estate,[9] but it contains some reused timbers and its north wall is timber-framed. It is of brick and stone, now rough-cast, and has a 5-bay north-east front with 3 projecting gables. A fine timber-framed barn of 5 bays stands to the west of the house.

The free chapel of St. Nicholas in Caus Castle was probably a 12th-century foundation.[10] Its incumbents were styled rectors and the advowson followed the descent of Caus manor until 1547, when the chapel passed to the Crown as a chantry.[11] The chapel had been endowed with the tithes of Caus demesne by 1277.[12] These tithes were later said to be derived from lands in the townships of Caus,

Forest, Minsterley, Poulton, and Callow within the parish, and in Munlyn, probably Lower Munlyn in Forden (Montg.).[13] In 1570 the chapel and its tithes were granted to William Jones and John Grey, who sold them to Robert Clough of Minsterley in 1571.[14] Clough's descendants held them until the later 18th century, when tithes in Caus and Forest were sold to John Severne[15] and those in Minsterley, Poulton, and Callow to Thomas Lovett.[16] The tithes were said to be worth 26s. 8d. in 1547[17] and £30 in 1655.[18] They were commuted for a total rent-charge of £368 in 1841.[19] The presentation of rectors is rarely recorded.[20] In 1397 the chapel was said to have been leased without permission from the bishop[21] and it was leased before 1521 to William Powdertoft,[22] who still held it in 1547.[23] The chapel was still standing in 1612[24] and, as it was then furnished, it was probably used as a domestic chapel until the destruction of Caus Castle in 1645.

The chapel of St. Margaret in the borough of Caus was founded by Thomas Corbet and his wife Isabel in 1272.[25] Two chaplains were then endowed with 120 a. land in the demesne of Caus, a meadow, and common pasture for 16 bullocks, 6 cows, 100 ewes, 2 horses or mares, and 50 pigs.[26] The foundation was to be without prejudice to Westbury church, to which a yearly payment of 2 lb. wax was to be made. Retired chaplains were to receive a pension, with diet in the lord's household.[27] No presentations to the chapel are recorded, but John Woderton was probably chaplain in 1447, when the chapel is last recorded.[28]

MANORS. The barony of *CAUS*, created in the early 12th century,[29] included the manors of Caus, Marsh, Minsterley, Ree, Westbury, Whitton, Winsley, and Yockleton in Westbury parish, in addition to manors elsewhere, all of which had been held of Roger, Earl of Shrewsbury, by Roger Fitz Corbet in 1086.[30] Apart from the manors of Caus, Minsterley, and Yockleton, these were all granted to under-tenants by Roger's heirs in the course of the 12th century.

By 1086 the earl of Shrewsbury had succeeded King Edward as overlord of *MINSTERLEY* manor,[31] and Edric as overlord of that of *YOCKLE-TON*.[32] The earl's overlordship lapsed after 1102[33] and these manors were subsequently held in chief.[34]

90 *Reg. R. Swinfield* (C. & Y.S.), 162–4.
91 B.M. Cott. Ch. xi. 72.
92 C 133/94/6.
93 Longleat MSS., unbound 4114.
94 Heref. City Libr., MS. 23628, f. 24ᵛ.
95 B.M. O.S. 2″ orig. drawings, sheet 199 (1816).
96 S.P.L., Deeds 15383.
97 C 133/7/8.
98 C 133/94/6.
99 Longleat MSS., unbound 3846.
1 Ibid. 3841.
2 Ibid. 2845, 3679, 3697, 3799, 4012.
3 Ibid. 3988; *Welsh D.N.B.*
4 Longleat MSS., unbound 3846.
5 *T.S.A.S.* liv. 46.
6 Longleat MSS., unbound 4030.
7 Ibid. 4004.
8 Longleat MSS., Thynne Papers, vol. vii, f. 190.
9 S.R.O. 279/61.
10 Ibid. 279/57.
11 *Reg. T. Cantilupe* (C. & Y.S.), 45; *T.S.A.S.* 3rd ser. x. 358.
12 *Reg. T. Cantilupe* (C. & Y.S.), 45.
13 S.R.O. 279/57.

14 Ibid. 279/56; S.P.L., Deeds 92.
15 S.R.O. 279/58, 59; C 78/1885 no. 9; S.R.O. 1187/19, pp. 7–8.
16 S.R.O. 1187/19, pp. 7–8.
17 *T.S.A.S.* 3rd ser. x. 358.
18 Ibid. xlvii. 25.
19 S.R.O. 1361/102, 104.
20 *Reg. J. Trillek* (C. & Y.S.), 373.
21 *E.H.R.* xlv. 461.
22 Heref. City Libr., MS. 23628, f. 2.
23 *T.S.A.S.* 3rd ser. x. 358.
24 Longleat MSS., unbound 3952; Longleat MSS., Thynne Papers, vol. xxxiii, f. 109.
25 *Reg. R. Swinfield* (C. & Y.S.), 162–4.
26 Ibid.
27 Ibid.
28 Longleat MSS., unbound 4010; Heref. City Libr., MS. 23628, f. 24ᵛ.
29 I. J. Sanders, *English Baronies* (Oxford, 1960), 29.
30 *V.C.H. Salop.* i. 316, 324–5.
31 Ibid.
32 Ibid.
33 Eyton, i. 245.
34 C 133/7/8; *Cal. Inq. p.m.* ix, p. 186; C 142/478/132; C 142/535/47.

Roger Fitz Corbet presumably succeeded his father Corbet shortly before 1086, for the latter seems to have been alive in 1081.[35] Roger may have been living c. 1136,[36] but the date of his death is not known and the descent of his estates in the mid-12th century is not clear. Roger's eldest son William appears to have died without issue[37] and to have been succeeded by his brother Ebrard.[38] The estate then passed to Simon Corbet, either son or brother of Ebrard, who was dead by 1155,[39] when his son Roger was in possession.[40] Roger was presumably dead by 1165, when Caus castle was garrisoned by the Crown,[41] and had been succeeded before 1176 by Robert, son of his brother Simon Corbet.[42] Robert held the barony until his death in 1222,[43] apart from a few months in 1217 when Caus castle was seized by the Crown because of the rebellion of his son Thomas.[44] The barony passed from father to son until 1322, the following being lords: Thomas Corbet, 1222–74;[45] Peter (I), 1274–1300;[46] Peter (II), 1300–22.[47] Alice, widow of Peter Corbet (I), was granted dower in 1305[48] and Beatrice, wife of Peter Corbet (II), was jointly seised of the barony at the latter's death.[49] She obtained livery in 1322[50] and died without direct heirs in 1347,[51] when the barony was divided. Caus Castle, with the manors of Caus and Minsterley, passed to Ralph, Earl of Stafford, great-grandson of Alice, daughter of Thomas Corbet,[52] and Yockleton manor passed to Robert de Harley in right of his wife Margaret, another descendant of Thomas Corbet.[53]

On the death of Ralph, Earl of Stafford, in 1372,[54] Caus and Minsterley manors passed to his son Hugh, who died in 1386.[55] The latter's son Thomas came of age in 1390,[56] but died without issue in 1392, when he was succeeded by his brother William who died while still a minor in 1395. Edmund, brother of the last-named, to whom the manor then passed, came of age in 1400,[57] but was killed at the Battle of Shrewsbury (1403). He had married Anne, widow of his elder brother Thomas, to whom a third of the estate was assigned in dower.[58] Custody of two-thirds of the issues of Caus were granted to the Queen in 1404,[59] when the marriage of Edmund's infant son Humphrey was granted to her.[60] Humphrey, who obtained livery of the

estate in 1423,[61] married Anne Neville, to whom the estate passed at his death in 1460.[62] At her death in 1480 Anne was succeeded by her son Henry, Duke of Buckingham. The latter's estates were forfeited to the Crown on his attainder in 1483, but were restored to his son Edward, who held them until he in his turn was attainted in 1521. Caus and Minsterley were restored in the following year to Edward's son Henry Stafford,[63] who was succeeded in 1563[64] by his son Henry. On the latter's death in 1566, the manors passed to his brother Edward Stafford, who sold them to Sir Rowland Hayward in 1573.[65]

Hayward settled the manors of Caus and Minsterley in 1576 on his daughter Joan and her husband Sir John Thynne[66] and after the latter's death in 1604[67] Joan held them until 1612,[68] when she was succeeded by her son Thomas Thynne.[69] Under the terms of a settlement of 1639[70] the manors passed, on the death of Thomas Thynne in 1642, to his eldest surviving son by his second marriage, Sir Henry Frederick Thynne. The latter died in 1680 and was succeeded by his son Thomas, who was created Viscount Weymouth in 1682. Thomas Thynne, great-nephew of the last-named, inherited the estate in 1714, and it passed from father to son until 1920, the following being lords: Thomas, 1714–51; Thomas (created Marquess of Bath in 1789), 1751–96; Thomas, 1796–1837; Henry Frederick, 1837; John Alexander, 1837–96; Thomas Henry, 1896–1920.

The manor of Caus, which had been sold to Thomas Hawley in 1810,[71] passed successively, by sale, to Owen Thomas, 1838–45;[72] John Phillips, 1845–63,[73] and Robert Miller, 1863–68.[74] Miller sold Caus manor in 1868 to J. E. Severne,[75] in whose family it remained until the sale of the Severne estate in 1920.[76] The manor of Minsterley was sold in the same year,[77] since which date manorial rights in both manors appear to have lapsed.

Minsterley Hall, which was built by Sir Henry Frederick Thynne in 1653[78] after the destruction of Caus Castle, incorporates part of an earlier house, probably the 'handsome new house' built by the freeholder Robert Clough c. 1581[79] which was acquired by Sir Thomas Thynne in 1634.[80] The

[35] Eyton, vii. 8.
[36] Ibid. 10.
[37] Ibid.
[38] Ibid.
[39] Ibid. 10–11.
[40] Ibid. 11.
[41] *Pipe R.* 1165 (P.R.S. viii), 98.
[42] Ibid. 1176 (P.R.S. xxv), 58.
[43] *Ex. e Rot. Fin.* (Rec. Com.), i. 94–95.
[44] *Pat. R.* 1216–25, 120.
[45] *Cal. Inq. p.m.* ii, p. 62.
[46] Ibid. pp. 451–2.
[47] Ibid. vi, p. 183.
[48] *Cal. Pat.* 1301–7, 353.
[49] *Cal. Inq. p.m.* vi, p. 183.
[50] *Cal. Close,* 1318–23, 158.
[51] *Cal. Inq. p.m.* ix, pp. 34–35.
[52] Ibid.; *Cal. Fine R.* 1347–56, 52–53.
[53] Ibid.
[54] C 135/79/62.
[55] Except where otherwise stated, descent of the manor, 1372–1573, based in *Complete Peerage,* ii. 388–91; ibid. xii (1), 174–85.
[56] *Cal. Close,* 1389–92, 231.
[57] Ibid. 1399–1402, 229.
[58] *Cal. Pat.* 1401–5, 347.

[59] Ibid.
[60] Ibid. 378.
[61] *Cal. Close,* 1422–29, 89.
[62] Heref. City Libr., MS. 23628, f. 15ᵛ.
[63] *L. & P. Hen. VIII,* iii (2), p. 1084.
[64] *S.P.R. Heref.* xii. 22.
[65] Longleat MSS., unbound 3489.
[66] Ibid. 3912.
[67] B. Botfield, *Stemmata Botevilliana* (1858), 59.
[68] Longleat MSS., unbound 3952.
[69] Except where otherwise stated, descent of manor since 1573 based on Burke, *Peerage* (1959), p. 168; *Complete Peerage,* ii. 24–27; ibid. xii (2), 585–9.
[70] Longleat MSS., Thynne Papers, xxxiii, f. 167.
[71] S.R.O. 279/61.
[72] Ibid. 279/95, 104.
[73] Ibid. 279/104, 114.
[74] Ibid. 279/114.
[75] Winsley Hall title-deeds *penes* Messrs. Salt and Sons, solicitors, Shrewsbury.
[76] S.R.O. 1361/80.
[77] S.C.C. title-deeds, RB 18/1.
[78] Birmingham Univ. Libr., Mytton's Ch. Notes, vol. iv, f. 151a.
[79] Longleat MSS., unbound 4030.
[80] Ibid. 3928.

Hall, which faces west, is a timber-framed house of two stories with attics. It has a slightly jettied first floor and transverse gables at each end. Two dormer windows light the attics on each front. The earlier part of the house is the transverse wing at the north end, which has a slightly lower roof. This has two lateral chimney stacks on the north wall, one of which has been rebuilt. Between them is a two-story porch, which may have contained the original staircase. There are two newel stairs in the later portion of the house, one of which has fretted balusters with raked mouldings and may be of late-16th-century date, but neither of them occupies an original position. A carved oak screen at the upper end of the hall is an amalgam of 16th- and 17th-century woodwork, the earlier portions of which may have come from Caus Castle. The house was restored in 1872,[81] when the ground floor on the east front was rebuilt in brick.

Robert de Harley and his wife Margaret, to whom Yockleton manor was assigned in 1347,[82] both died in 1349.[83] Their son Robert, who held the manor jointly with his wife Joan, daughter of Robert Corbet of Moreton Corbet, settled it in 1364 on Joan's brother Fulk Corbet for life with remainder to Joan's right heirs.[84] A further settlement of 1367, under which the remainder was granted to Fulk's brother Roger,[85] was held to be invalid on the death of Fulk Corbet in 1382[86] and the manor then passed to Fulk's daughter Elizabeth.[87] Elizabeth, who married John Mawddy, came of age in 1390.[88] Her title to the manor was confirmed in 1391[89] and she died in 1395.[90] Her husband John Mawddy, who died in 1403,[91] was succeeded by his son Fulk, wardship of whom was granted to the Queen in the same year.[92] He came of age in 1412[93] and died in 1414.[94] Fulk's widow Isabel, who was then assigned a third of the manor in dower,[95] held it until her death in 1429.[96] The remainder passed to Fulk's sister Elizabeth, wife of Hugh Burgh.[97] On Hugh's death in 1430 he was succeeded by his son John,[98] wardship of whom was granted to Joan, widow of William Clopton,[99] whose daughter he subsequently married.[1] John received livery in 1435[2] and on his death in 1471 title to the manor was disputed between his widow Joan and his heirs John Newport, Thomas Leighton, Isabel, wife of John Lingen, and Elizabeth, wife of Thomas

Mytton.[3] The manor was assigned in dower to Joan Burgh in 1474[4] and had reverted to John Burgh's heirs by 1501, when his estates were divided between them.[5]

Yockleton manor was then awarded to Isabel, wife of John Lingen (I),[6] who was succeeded by her son John (II) at her death in 1523.[7] The manor passed from father to son in the Lingen family until 1554, the following being lords: John (II), 1523–30;[8] John (III), 1530–47;[9] John (IV), 1547–54.[10] Jane, daughter of John Lingen (IV), married William Shelley of Michelgrove (Suss.),[11] a recusant whose estates were in the hands of the Crown in 1587.[12] Jane had regained possession of Yockleton before her death in 1610, when she was succeeded by her cousin William Lingen.[13] William's son Henry, to whom the manor passed in 1636,[14] sold it to Walter Waring in 1641.[15] Edmund Waring, who purchased the manor in 1665,[16] was succeeded at his death in 1683 by his daughter Hannah, wife of George Ashby of Quenby (Leics.).[17] The manor was held by the male line of the Ashby family until 1785, the following being lords: George, 1683–1728; John (son), 1728–56; John (son), 1756–79; Edmund (brother), 1779–85. On Edmund's death the manor passed to his daughters Elizabeth, wife of Robert Hall, and Hannah, wife of John Maddock, who sold it to Rowland Wingfield of Onslow in 1789.[18] It was subsequently held by the following members of the Wingfield family:[19] Rowland, 1789–1818; John (son), 1818–62; Charles George (nephew), 1862–91; Col. Charles Ralph, 1891–1923. The estate was sold shortly after the death of Col. C. R. B. Wingfield in 1923.[20]

The manor of *WESTBURY*, held by Ernui before 1066, was held by Roger Fitz Corbet under Roger, Earl of Shrewsbury, in 1086.[21] After the lapse of the suzerainty of the Earls of Shrewsbury in 1102,[22] the manor was held of the barony of Caus until the end of feudal tenures.[23]

Odo de Hodnet, the first known tenant of the manor, died in 1201,[24] when it escheated to the overlord, Robert Corbet, since Odo's son Baldwin was an outlaw.[25] Baldwin, who was pardoned in 1203[26] when his estates were restored to him,[27] died in 1225.[28] Wardship of his son Odo was granted to William de Hodnet, probably his uncle.[29] Odo, who obtained livery of the manor in 1228,[30] was

[81] *Kelly's Dir. Salop.* (1885).
[82] *Cal. Fine R.* 1347–56, 52–53; *Cal. Inq. p.m.* ix, p. 186.
[83] *Cal. Inq. p.m.* ix, p. 186.
[84] *Cal. Inq. Misc.* iv, pp. 136–8.
[85] Ibid.
[86] Ibid.
[87] Ibid.
[88] *Cal. Close*, 1389–92, 123.
[89] Ibid. 202, 256.
[90] *Cal. Fine R.* 1391–9, 154.
[91] C 137/44/34.
[92] *Cal. Pat.* 1401–5, 332.
[93] *Cal. Close*, 1409–13, 375.
[94] C 138/8/30.
[95] C 139/49/32.
[96] Ibid.
[97] C 138/8/34.
[98] C 139/50/47.
[99] *Cal. Fine R.* 1430–7, 21–22.
[1] *Visit. Salop. 1623* (Harl. Soc. xxviii), i. 60.
[2] *Cal. Close*, 1429–35, 337.
[3] C 140/39/61.
[4] *Cal. Close*, 1468–74, 359–60.
[5] *T.S.A.S.* 4th ser. v. 215.
[6] Ibid.

[7] C 142/38/31.
[8] C 142/51/65.
[9] S.P.L., MS. 2791, p. 321.
[10] Ibid. p. 320.
[11] Ibid.
[12] S.C. 12/32/26.
[13] C 142/332/163.
[14] C 142/478/132.
[15] N.L.W., Wynnstay (1952), box Y/43.
[16] Deed, 1665, in Lynches Farm title-deeds.
[17] Descent of manor, 1683–1789, based on *T.S.A.S.* 4th ser. vi. 27–29.
[18] Lynches Farm title-deeds.
[19] Descent of manor after 1798 based on Burke, *Land. Gent.* (1925), p. 1914.
[20] Ex inf. Mr. C. J. Wingfield, Onslow Hall.
[21] *V.C.H. Salop.* i. 325.
[22] Eyton, i. 245.
[23] C 133/7/8; C 142/374/86.
[24] Eyton, vii. 54.
[25] Ibid.   [26] Ibid.
[27] Ibid. 54–55.
[28] *Ex. e Rot. Fin.* (Rec. Com.), i. 124–5.
[29] Ibid. 133; Eyton, vii. 56.
[30] *Close R.* 1227–31, 17.

succeeded at his death in 1284 by his son William de Hodnet.[31] In 1301 William settled the reversion of the manor on his daughter Maud and her husband William de Ludlow.[32] The latter was in possession at his death in 1316[33] and the manor remained in the hands of his widow Maud.[34] Maud died in 1347,[35] when the manor was seized by the Crown on account of the outlawry of Laurence de Ludlow.[36] The latter, who was pardoned in 1348,[37] died in 1353,[38] when the manor passed to his widow Hawise.[39] She was succeeded by her son John de Ludlow, at whose death in 1382[40] a third of the manor was assigned in dower to his widow Joan.[41] The remainder passed to his son Richard, who was succeeded by his brother John in 1391.[42] The manor was held jointly by the latter and his wife Isabel, who remained in possession after John's death in 1398.[43] She later married Fulk Pembruge[44] and was succeeded by her son William de Ludlow at her death in 1447.[45] The manor passed in 1474 to William's son Richard,[46] who died in 1499[47] leaving as heirs his two daughters Anne and Alice, wives respectively of the brothers Thomas and Humphrey Vernon, and in 1520 the manor was divided between them.[48]

The moiety of Anne Vernon passed in 1562 to Henry, grandson of Thomas Vernon.[49] Humphrey, husband of Alice Vernon, was succeeded at his death in 1542 by his son George,[50] who died in 1553.[51] This moiety was then held successively by George Vernon's sons Richard (d. 1560)[52] and John (d. 1591).[53] The latter purchased the other moiety of the manor from his cousin Henry Vernon in 1581[54] and his son Robert sold Westbury manor to Sir Roger Owen in 1601.[55] The manor followed the descent of Condover manor until 1891, when it was purchased by John Whitaker,[56] and has since followed the descent of Winsley manor.

The manor of *WHITTON* was held by the freeman Levenot, Leimer, and Ulchetil before the Conquest.[57] Like Westbury manor it was held in 1086 by Roger Fitz Corbet of Roger, Earl of Shrewsbury, and had the same overlords during the Middle Ages.[58] After 1521, however, the manor was held in chief.[59]

In 1242 the manor was held by Robert and Roger de Whitton,[60] who were not related. Robert, who probably succeeded Richard[61] and Simon de Whitton,[62] recorded in the early 13th century, was still alive in 1274.[63] The descent of his moiety of the manor is obscure until the 15th century. He had been succeeded before 1292 by Simon de Whitton,[64] the lord of this moiety in 1316.[65] The latter's son Simon was lord in 1333[66] and his grandson William by 1346.[67] John son of William de Whitton, Sheriff of Shropshire in 1362,[68] was still living in 1399.[69] John Lingen was accounted lord of this moiety in 1428[70] and William Whitton in 1431,[71] but by 1450 the moiety had passed to William Lingen, in right of his wife, who was a daughter of John de Whitton.[72] It descended from father to son in the Lingen family until c. 1600,[73] when, on the death of Thomas Lingen, it passed to Alexander Topp, husband of Thomas's daughter and heir Elizabeth.[74] It descended from father to son in the Topp family until 1778,[75] the following being lords: Alexander, c. 1600–1663; Lingen, 1663–88; Alexander, 1688–1722; John, 1722–36; John, 1736–78. On the death of John Topp the manor, by this date reunited, passed to his nephew Richard Lloyd, who then assumed the name of Topp. He was succeeded in 1829 by his son John, after whose death in 1836 the manor was held successively by John's mother Anne Topp, 1836–54, and by his widow Mary, 1854–75.

In 1877 Agatha and Isabella, daughters of John Topp, sold Whitton to Dr. J. E. Severne.[76] The estate was held successively by the latter's brothers E. C. Severne, 1899–1909, and E. W. Severne, 1909–14,[77] and manorial rights lapsed at the sale of the Severne estate in 1920.[78]

Roger de Whitton, the other tenant of Whitton manor in 1242,[79] was more commonly known as Roger Burnell.[80] He was son of Simon Burnell[81] and is first recorded c. 1210–20.[82] He was still living in 1274[83] and his son Hugh,[84] who held this moiety in 1316,[85] was still alive in 1333.[86] Hugh's son John, who was lord in 1346,[87] was dead by 1398,[88] when his estate was in the hands of his nephews Sir John Burley and William Spenser and of Phillip de Callaughton in right of his wife Isabel.[89] William

31 *Cal. Inq. p.m.* ii, p. 321.
32 C.P. 25(1)/194/7/42.
33 *Cal. Inq. p.m.* vi, p. 33.
34 *Cal. Close, 1313–18*, 381.
35 *Cal. Inq. p.m.* ix, pp. 2–3.
36 *Cal. Pat. 1348–50*, 85.
37 Ibid. 90.
38 *Cal. Inq. p.m.* x, pp. 102–3.
39 *Cal. Close, 1349–54*, 579.
40 C 136/19/16.
41 Ibid.
42 C 136/67/1.
43 C 136/103/29; *Cal. Close, 1396–9*, 334–5.
44 C 139/125/9.   45 Ibid.
46 *Cal. Fine R. 1471–85*, 82.
47 Ibid. *1485–1509*, 271.
48 *Cat. Anct. D.* vi, C 7569.
49 C 142/132/15.
50 C 142/66/70.
51 C 142/104/70.
52 S.P.L., MS. 362, p. 474.
53 C 142/233/103.
54 S.R.O. 665 uncat., deed, 1581.
55 S.P.L., Deeds 6867.
56 Winsley Hall title-deeds.
57 *V.C.H. Salop.* i. 325.
58 Ibid.; *Bk. of Fees*, 964.
59 C 142/112/154; C 142/212/49; C 142/374/86.
60 Longleat MSS., unbound 4211; *Bk. of Fees*, 964.

61 Eyton, vii. 65.   62 Ibid. 18.
63 Ibid. 60.   64 Ibid.
65 *Feud. Aids*, iv. 235.
66 S.P.L., Deeds 9332; S.P.L., MS. 2, f. 422ᵛ.
67 S.P.L., MS. 2, f. 422ᵛ; *Feud. Aids*, iv. 241.
68 Blakeway, *Sheriffs of Salop.* 12.
69 C 136/107/46.
70 *Feud. Aids*, iv. 255.
71 Ibid. 261.
72 S.P.L., MS. 2, f. 423.
73 Ibid. MS. 2791, p. 327.
74 Ibid. MS. 2793, p. 63.
75 Except where otherwise stated, descent of manor c. 1600–1875, based on S.P.L., MS. 2793, pp. 63–65.
76 S.R.O. 1361/80.
77 Burke, *Land. Gent.* (1925), p. 1586.
78 Whitton Hall title-deeds *penes* Mr. F. W. Halliday.
79 *Bk. of Fees*, 964.
80 Eyton, vii. 65.
81 S.P.L., MS. 2, f. 423; Longleat MSS., unbound 4211 (16th-century pedigree of Topp Family).
82 Eyton, vii. 65–66.
83 Ibid. 66
84 S.P.L., Deeds 9332–3.
85 *Feud. Aids*, iv, 235.
86 S.P.L., MS. 2, f. 422ᵛ.
87 *Feud. Aids*, iv. 241.
88 S.P.L., MS. 2, f. 422ᵛ.
89 Ibid.

Spenser seems later to have acquired the whole of this moiety, which passed successively to his son and grandson, both named William Spenser.[90] The last-named died in 1556,[91] and in 1576 Richard, son of William Spenser, granted the estate to his brother Thomas.[92] William Spenser, who succeeded his father Thomas in 1587,[93] sold this moiety in 1613 to Sir Roger Owen,[94] whose brother Sir William Owen sold it to Alexander Topp, lord of the other moiety, in 1623.[95]

A third portion of Whitton manor, held by Geoffrey le Taillour in 1347,[96] appears to have passed by 1428 to Peter de Callaughton.[97] In 1431 this was held by John ap Griffith, ancestor of the Gough family of Marsh.[98] This small estate can probably be identified with the lands in Vennington held by John Gough of Marsh in 1619.[99]

Two datestones of 1727 and 1731, formerly in the garden wall of Whitton Hall, bear the initials 'I.T.U.'[1] and indicate that the Hall was built by John Topp and his wife Ursula. The Hall, which faces south, is a well-built brick house of 2 stories with attics, consisting of a central block of 3 bays, flanked by gabled projecting wings. The datestones probably came from the south front, where stone dressings have been rebuilt in brick since c. 1830.[2] The central block has a stone pediment on the south front and on the north, which has a parapet and balustrade, its central bay is set forward to form a porch. There are brick string courses at first- and second-floor levels. An east wing, built since 1920 in the same style as the remainder of the house, contains an apsidal drawing room which rises to second-floor level.[3]

On the ground floor the central hall contains painted oak and pine panelling and has a mid-18th-century hob grate with marble surround. The study, also panelled in pine, contains a fireplace flanked by fluted pilasters, with a mantel carved with an intricate arabesque and fretwork frieze. The staircase in the porch on the north has three balusters to each tread, one twisted, one fluted, and one turned, and there is a rather less elaborate but contemporary stair in the east wing. Two bedrooms contain inserted 17th-century oak panelling, including panels inscribed 'I.N.R.I.', 'S.P.E.', and 'T.S.M.'. The last set of initials suggest that part of this panelling may have come from the manor-house of the Spenser family. Most of the remaining bedrooms have pine-panelled mantels and late-18th-century cast iron grates with marble surrounds. A roof truss in the attic, in the centre of the central block, con-

tains curved principal rafters, consisting of two jointed members.

Buildings to the south-west of the house include a round dovecote contemporary with the house and a stable-block with a cupola and a weather vane dated 1756. There are two 18th-century summer-houses, one in the garden with a lattice front and pagoda roof, bearing the Topp crest as a finial, and the other, on the hill south of the house, which is octagonal and has ogee-headed windows.

The manor of *WINSLEY* was held by Seward before the Conquest[4] and its overlordship followed the same descent as Whitton in and after 1086. Some time between 1121 and 1136 Roger Fitz Corbet granted the manor to Shrewsbury Abbey,[5] who retained it until the Dissolution. It was granted by the Crown in 1544 to John Warner,[6] who immediately sold it to Thomas Kerry.[7] The manor passed to Humphrey, brother of Thomas Kerry, who was succeeded in 1555 by his son Thomas.[8] In 1581, when the manor was held for life by William Wele of Shrewsbury, the reversion was vested in Thomas's younger brother George Kerry.[9] Nicholas Gibbons of Shrewsbury, lord of Winsley manor by 1628, then settled it on his younger son Francis,[10] who mortgaged it to Timothy Tourneur of Shrewsbury in 1637.[11] Tourneur had acquired the freehold of the manor by 1648, when he settled it on his daughter Mary at her marriage with Samuel Lloyd,[12] and in 1654 Elizabeth, widow of Francis Gibbons, and her children released to them any interest they may have retained in the estate.[13]

The manor was divided between Lloyd's two daughters, Mary, wife of Kenrick Eyton, and Abigail, wife of Gibson St. Leger, in 1699,[14] when Mary Eyton conveyed her share to Francis, Earl of Bradford.[15] In the following year Gibson and Abigail St. Leger sold their moiety of the manor to Richard Boycott,[16] who purchased Lord Bradford's moiety in 1706.[17] The manor followed the descent of Malehurst and Boycott in Pontesbury parish until 1804,[18] when Thomas Boycott sold it to Samuel Snead.[19] It passed in 1819 to Snead's daughter Harriet, wife of John Blakeway Tipton,[20] who sold it to John Phillips in 1839.[21] The latter conveyed Winsley in 1863 to Robert Miller,[22] who sold it to John Whitaker in 1868.[23] Whitaker was succeeded in 1899 by his son James, whose daughter, Mrs. F. R. Kaye, is the present owner of the estate.[24]

There is no evidence for a manor-house at Winsley before the Hall was built by Samuel Snead in 1805.[25] The house is of brick and consists of a central block

[90] Longleat MSS., unbound 4211.
[91] C 142/112/154.
[92] C 142/212/49.
[93] Ibid.
[94] C.P. 25(2)/343/9 Jas. I Hil.
[95] S.R.O. 1011 uncat., case-papers *re* Vennington Common, 1799.
[96] *Cal. Inq. p.m.* ix, pp. 34–35.
[97] *Feud. Aids*, iv. 255.
[98] Ibid. 261; *Visit. Salop. 1623* (Harl. Soc. xxviii), i. 202.
[99] C 142/502/19.
[1] For a description of the house, see *T.S.A.S.* 4th ser. v. 173–5.
[2] S.P.L., T. F. Dukes watercolours (houses), no. 41.
[3] Whitton Hall title-deeds.
[4] *V.C.H. Salop.* i. 324.
[5] N.L.W., MS. 7851D, f. 271; Eyton, vii. 10.
[6] *L. & P. Hen. VIII*, xix, p. 618.
[7] Ibid. p. 639.

[8] *Visit. Salop. 1623* (Harl. Soc. xxix), ii. 286; C 142/108/107.
[9] Longleat MSS., unbound 4030.
[10] C 142/458/147.
[11] S.P.L., Deeds 14183.
[12] Ibid.
[13] Ibid. 14203.
[14] Ibid. 14211.
[15] Ibid. 14220.
[16] Ibid. 14221.
[17] Ibid. 14185.
[18] See p. 268.
[19] Winsley Hall title-deeds.
[20] Ibid.
[21] Ibid.
[22] Ibid.
[23] Ibid.
[24] Burke, *Land. Gent.* (1965), i, p. 718.
[25] Datestone.

of 3 bays, with a hipped roof, a service wing at the west end, probably of the same date, and an east wing added in 1898.[26] The central bay on the south front, which is slightly set forward, has a pedimented porch supported by Tuscan columns. An apsidal drawing room on the south front[27] was replaced *c.* 1926 by a square central bay.[28] At the same time the ground-floor rooms were extended to north and south and a balcony was constructed at first-floor level.[29] Most of the plaster ceilings on the ground floor were renewed *c.* 1926.[30]

The manor of *REE*,[31] probably the small unnamed manor held by Earl Morcar before the Conquest and by Roger Fitz Corbet of Roger, Earl of Shrewsbury in 1086,[32] was later a member of the barony of Caus. William de Aqua, recorded in 1198,[33] may have been its tenant, and in 1242 the manor was held by Ralph de Ree.[34] In 1251 the latter granted it to Thomas Corbet in exchange for lands in Minsterley[35] and it is last recorded as a manor in 1346.[36]

Of the two manors named *MARSH* in 1086, the larger, which was then said to contain 2 hides, appears to have comprised the township of Marsh and half of the shrunken hamlet of Perendon.[37] It was held by Alvric before 1066 and in 1086 was held of Roger, Earl of Shrewsbury, by Robert Fitz Corbet.[38] The overlordship seems to have passed *c.* 1141 to William Boterell in right of his wife Alice, daughter of Robert Fitz Corbet.[39] The manor was said in 1255 to be held of the Boterell family as of the manor of Longden.[40] The lords of Longden manor continued overlords of Marsh manor until the end of feudal tenures.[41]

Hugh de Marsh, who died in 1209,[42] is the first known tenant of the manor and may have been in possession by 1189.[43] He was probably succeeded by his youngest son Robert Fitz Hugh, also known as Robert de Eyton, who granted lands at Marsh to Haughmond Abbey shortly before his death *c.* 1221,[44] when the manor seems to have passed to his nephew Roger, who confirmed this grant.[45] Roger, who was lord in 1242,[46] was dead by 1270.[47] His son Roger, living in 1280,[48] was dead by 1292, when the manor was held by his son William de Eyton,[49] who was still alive in 1318.[50] One William de Eyton was lord in 1356[51] and John de Eyton and

William de Eyton were residents of Marsh in 1401[52] and 1402[53] respectively.

On the death of William de Eyton the manor was divided between his sisters.[54] One moiety passed to Joan, wife of Roger Clayton,[55] and was held in 1431[56] by John Gough, son of John ap Griffith and Joan's daughter Eleanor.[57] John, who was dead by 1493,[58] was succeeded by his son Roger, perhaps the same as the Roger Gough who died *c.* 1560.[59] This moiety descended from father to son in the Gough family until 1705, the following being lords: John, *c.* 1560–1576;[60] Thomas, 1576–1614;[61] Thomas, 1614–29;[62] Roger, 1629–80;[63] Thomas, 1680–1702;[64] Roger, 1702–5. The last named, who was required to sell the manor under the terms of his father's will,[65] conveyed it to Thomas Jenkins in 1705.[66] Jenkins, who acquired the other moiety of the manor in 1730,[67] died later in the same year and the manor was held by the following members of the Jenkins family[68] until 1801: Richard (son), 1730–43; Richard (son), 1743–58; John (brother), 1758–71; Richard (son), 1771–97; Richard (son), 1797–1801. The trustees of Richard Jenkins, then an infant, sold the greater part of the estate, including Marsh Hall (the present Marche Manor), to John Wood of Hanwood in 1801,[69] but appear to have retained the manorial rights. Marsh Hall passed from father to son in the Wood family until 1891, the following being owners: John, 1801–13; John Clavering, 1813–35; John, 1835–89; John Clavering, 1889–91.[70] John Brown, who purchased the estate in 1891,[71] sold it in the following year to F. W. Wateridge.[72] The estate was dispersed in 1924, when the manorhouse was purchased by A. A. Montgomery, whose widow sold it in 1958 to Mrs. R. H. Hazan, the owner in 1965.[73]

The other moiety of Marsh manor passed in the early 15th century to Eleanor, daughter of John de Eyton,[74] who married into the Purslow family. It was held by Robert Purslow (d. 1571)[75] and his son John, 1571–94,[76] whose son Robert sold it to John Peers in 1611.[77] The latter's descendants, who were living at Lower Marsh (now Marche Farm) in the mid-17th century,[78] held this moiety until 1730, when it was sold to Thomas Jenkins.[79]

The smaller of the two Domesday manors of

26 Ibid.
27 S.R.O. 279/113.
28 Ex inf. Mrs. F. R. Kaye, Winsley Hall.
29 Ibid.
30 Ibid.
31 Eyton, vii. 116.
32 *V.C.H. Salop.* i. 324.
33 Eyton, vii. 116.
34 *Bk. of Fees*, 972.
35 *Rot. Hund.* (Rec. Com.), ii. 66.
36 *Feud. Aids*, iv. 241.
37 *V.C.H. Salop.* i. 326; *Cal. Inq. Misc.* i, p. 353.
38 *V.C.H. Salop.* i. 326.
39 Eyton, vii. 145.
40 *Rot. Hund.* (Rec. Com.), ii. 66, 67.
41 *Cal. Inq. Misc.* i, p. 353; S.P.L., MS. 593; C 142/457/118.
42 Eyton, vii. 123.
43 Ibid.
44 Ibid. 124; S.P.L., Haughmond Cart. f. 141ᵛ.
45 S.P.L., Haughmond Cart. f. 142.
46 *Bk. of Fees*, 971.
47 *Cal. Inq. Misc.* i, p. 353.
48 S.P.L., MS. 4077, p. 562.
49 Ibid.
50 S.R.O. 840 uncat., deed, 1318.
51 *T.S.A.S.* 3rd ser. iii. 71.

52 *Salop. Peace Roll, 1404–14*, 59.
53 Ibid. 69.
54 *T.S.A.S.* 3rd ser. iii. 71.
55 *Visit. Salop. 1623* (Harl. Soc. xxviii), i. 202.
56 S.P.L., MS. 593 (Longden ct. r. 1431).
57 *Visit. Salop. 1623* (Harl. Soc. xxviii), i. 202.
58 S.P.L., MS. 593 (Longden ct. r. 1493).
59 *T.S.A.S.* 4th ser. v. 176.
60 Ibid.
61 Ibid.
62 C 142/457/118.
63 *T.S.A.S.* 4th ser. v. 178.
64 Ibid.
65 Ibid. 179.
66 S.R.O. 1187/19, schedule of deeds, p. 14.
67 S.P.L., Deeds 3153.
68 For pedigree see S.P.L., MS. 2325, pp. 154–5.
69 Marche Manor title-deeds.
70 Ibid.   71 Ibid.
72 Ibid.   73 Ibid.
74 *Visit. Salop. 1623* (Harl. Soc. xxix), ii. 414–16.
75 C 142/162/176.
76 C 142/247/83.
77 C.P. 25(2)/343/9 Jas. I Mich.
78 *Cal. Cttee. for Compounding*, 123; S.R.O. 1361/1 (poor rate, 1665).
79 S.P.L., Deeds 3153.

MARSH—it was said to contain only 3 virgates in 1086—had been held as 3 manors before the Conquest by the freemen Leviet, Dainz and Weniet.[80] It appears to have included the remainder of Perendon and some part of the shrunken hamlet of Great Bretchell in Cardeston parish. It was held in 1086 by Roger Fitz Corbet of Roger, Earl of Shrewsbury,[81] but its identity was lost soon afterwards. Half of Perendon, held by Roger Pigot of Peter Corbet of Caus in 1278,[82] was held by his descendant Reynold Williams, lord of Great Wollaston manor in Alberbury, when it next appears in 1541.[83]

Like the larger of the two Marsh manors the manor of *WIGMORE* was held by Alvric before the Conquest, and by Robert Fitz Corbet in 1086.[84] The lords of Longden manor were likewise its overlords throughout the Middle Ages. Adam de Brerelawe, who may have held Wigmore manor in 1221,[85] seems to have been preceded here by his father Philip.[86] Adam, who held the manor in 1255,[87] was still alive in 1274.[88] He appears to have been succeeded by Adam Hager of Leigh,[89] whose son Thomas conveyed Wigmore to Thomas Colle in 1317.[90] The manor descended in the Colle family[91] until 1604, when John Colle sold it to William Jones of Shrewsbury.[92] It was held by the following members of the Jones family[93] until 1782: William 1605–12; Edward (son), 1612–48; William (son), 1648–62; Thomas (brother), 1662–92; William (son), 1692–4; Thomas (son), 1694–1715; Thomas (uncle), 1715–37; Thomas (son), 1737–45; Edward (cousin), 1745–53; Thomas (son), 1753–82. The manor then passed to Thomas Tyrrwhit, cousin of Sir Thomas Jones, who then assumed the name Tyrrwhit-Jones. It was sold in 1824[94] and was held by Richard Hilhouse in 1841.[95]

OTHER ESTATES. Newton, apparently an undertenancy of Yocklton manor,[96] was held by John Burnell, one of the lords of Whitton manor, in 1349.[97] At the partition of Burnell's estates in 1398 a moiety of Newton was assigned to William Spenser and the other to Sir John Burley.[98] While the former followed the descent of the Spenser estate at Whitton until last recorded in 1632,[99] Burley's moiety was divided before 1499 between the Trussell and Littleton families, co-heirs of his son William.[1] Property at Newton acquired by John, Earl of Oxford, before 1562, was then sold to Thomas Grosvenor,[2] whose descendant William Grosvenor

was still in possession in 1641.[3] The greater part of the township, however, was held in 1587 by Henry Corbet of Newton,[4] whose descendants lived at Lower Newton Farm and remained in possession of the estate until 1849.[5] It then passed to Robert Jones, nephew of John Corbet,[6] and belonged to Robert Corbet Jones in 1895,[7] but had been sold to James Whitaker of Winsley Hall before 1900.[8]

ECONOMIC HISTORY. The nine manors which lay within Westbury parish in 1086 were assessed at a total of 22¼ hides.[9] King Edward and Edric, the chief landowners here before the Conquest, each held 6 hides (Minsterley and Yocklton),[10] while a further 3 hides (Marsh and Wigmore) were held by Alvric.[11] Four of the 5 remaining manors were small estates of free men. By 1086 the whole parish formed part of the demesne lands of Roger Fitz Corbet,[12] apart from an estate of 3 hides at Marsh and Wigmore held by his brother Robert.[13] The practice of enfeoffing military tenants, which had already been adopted by 1086 in other parts of Roger Fitz Corbet's Shropshire estates,[14] was applied to his Westbury properties at a slightly later date. In the course of the early 12th century all the Domesday manors in Westbury were granted to such tenants, with the exception of Minsterley, Yocklton, and the demesne of Caus. The pattern of landownership thus established, complicated by the fragmentation of Domesday manors and the development of smaller free tenancies, persisted with remarkably little change until the 19th century.

Until the end of the 13th century Welsh incursions probably retarded economic development here. Thomas Corbet of Caus was engaged in constant warfare with his relative Griffith ap Gwenwynwyn in the mid-13th century.[15] In 1267 it was said that the inhabitants of Winsley fled to the woods for fear of the Welsh.[16] Perendon was occupied by the Welsh c. 1265[17] and in 1272 Thomas Corbet obtained 400 marks compensation from the Crown for his losses.[18] Minsterley,[19] Whitton,[20] and the borough of Caus[21] were burnt during the rebellion of Owen Glendower and the townships of Caus, Marsh, Vennington, Westbury, and Yocklton were excused from taxation in 1405–6.[22] Some of the houses thus destroyed in Minsterley had not been rebuilt by 1445[23] and the rebellion was said to be the reason for the lapse of labour-services in this manor,[24] but the burning of Caus merely hastened

80 *V.C.H. Salop.* i. 325.
81 Ibid.
82 B.M. Eg. Roll 2197.
83 *T.S.A.S.* liv. 327.
84 *V.C.H. Salop.* i. 326.
85 Eyton, vii. 171.
86 Ibid. xi. 78.
87 *Rot. Hund.* (Rec. Com.), ii. 66.
88 C 133/7/8.
89 Eyton, xi. 113.
90 S.R.O. 840 uncat., deed, 1317.
91 S.P.L., MS. 4077, p. 323; ibid. MS. 4085, pp. 4479–80.
92 S.R.O. 840 uncat., deed, 1604.
93 For pedigree see *T.S.A.S.* 3rd ser. iv. 309–15; S.P.L., MS. 2792, pp. 475–7.
94 S.R.O. 840 uncat., sale partics. 1824.
95 S.R.O. 1361/106.
96 S.P.L., Deeds 6172.
97 Ibid. 9336.
98 S.P.L., MS. 2, f. 422ᵛ.
99 C 142/529/120.
1 *Cal. Close,* 1447–54, 482; C 142/20/46; C 142/22/78.
2 C.P. 25(2)/200/4 Eliz. I Hil.
3 C 142/610/98.
4 S.C. 12/32/26.
5 S.P.L., MS. 2788, p. 128.
6 Ibid.
7 *Kelly's Dir. Salop.* (1895).
8 Ibid. (1900).
9 *V.C.H. Salop.* i. 316, 324–5.
10 Ibid. 316, 325.
11 Ibid. 326.
12 Ibid. 316, 324–5.
13 Ibid. 326.
14 Ibid. 316, 324–5.
15 *Montg. Collect.* i. 26–32.
16 Eyton, vii. 64.
17 *Cal. Inq. Misc.* i, p. 353.
18 *Cal. Pat.* 1266–72, 622.
19 E 179/166/55.
20 Longleat MSS., unbound 4211.
21 Ibid.
22 E 179/166/37; E 179/166/48.
23 Longleat MSS., unbound 4010.
24 Ibid.

a process of decay which had begun in the mid-14th century.[25] Part of Caus borough was again burnt during the rebellion of Sir Griffith Vaughan in 1444[26] and in 1466 the Earl of Shrewsbury came to Caus with 200 men 'for the good rule of the lordship'.[27]

The uplands to the west of the parish were unsettled and used for little besides rough pasture until the later 16th century.[28] During the Middle Ages they were subject to the depredations of Welsh cattle-thieves. Pastures on the Long Mountain were unlet for this reason in the early 16th century.[29] A due known as 'porthnant bagell', paid by the tenants of Winnington in Alberbury parish to the north of the Long Mountain, was said in 1537 to be used to provide a hayward to guard the cattle on the mountain 'for that the country was then wild and many outlaws and thieves haunting amongst them, by whom their cattle were daily stolen and conveyed away off the mountains'.[30] A 'watching place' at Mulsop and a 'swearing ford' are recorded in a description of the bounds of the Forest of Hayes in 1546.[31] At the latter, it was said, 'it hath been used to swear the tracks of stolen cattle'.[32]

Of the Domesday manors of Roger Fitz Corbet only Caus, Minsterley, and Yockleton remained in the hands of the barons of Caus after the early 12th-century alienations. Yockleton manor became a separate estate after 1347[33] but Caus and Minsterley survived, with some later adjustments, as the largest property in the parish until the 19th century. Caus Castle and its adjoining demesne did not exist in 1086, when Minsterley manor was assessed at 6 hides and was said to be worth 65s.[34] The latter was valued at £30 13s. 9d.[35] in 1300. A few alterations to the boundaries of the estate took place in the 13th century: the manor of Ree was acquired by exchange for lands in Minsterley in 1251,[36] the deserted hamlet of Coton was merged in the demesne of Caus in 1252,[37] and the manor of Hope in Worthen parish was added, 1274–8, in exchange for the hamlet of Poulton.[38]

The whole demesne of Caus, which included common-field lands in Wallop, was kept in hand until the later 14th century. It amounted to 4 carucates in 1274[39] but had been reduced to 3 carucates by 1300,[40] perhaps as a result of the alienation

of Poulton.[41] Surviving ministers' accounts cover only the closing years of demesne farming here. The staff of manorial servants numbered 4 ploughholders, 4 plough-drivers, 3 shepherds, and a cowherd in 1374.[42] The demesne included 113 a. arable in 1377[43] and 123 a. in the following year;[44] wheat and oats were then the only crops sown. In 1374 39 oxen were employed on the demesne,[45] but their number had fallen to 16 by 1382,[46] and these were all leased with the demesne arable in the following year.[47] Stock-rearing was, however, the basis of demesne farming here. There were 879 sheep at Caus and Wallop in 1374, 352 of which later died of murrain,[48] but the number of sheep had fallen to 529 by 1390[49] and to 439 when the flock is last recorded in 1402.[50] The demesne also included small dairy-farms at Wallop and at Capsall in Worthen parish.[51] The 8 cows at Wallop were set at farm in 1375[52] and cows last occur in the accounts in 1379.[53] The demesne arable was leased to the tenants in 1383 at a rent of the third sheaf.[54] In 1388 two-thirds of the arable was set on 9-year leases to 5 tenants[55] and in the following year the remaining third was set on 12-year leases to 3 others.[56] Rents then reserved totalled £3 6s. 8d. a year[57] and the demesne arable was leased at similar rents until 1542.[58]

Land sufficient for 2 ploughs lay in the demesne of Minsterley manor in 1086, when there was land available for 2 more ploughs.[59] The demesne included 2 carucates of arable in 1274[60] and 3 carucates (360 a.) in 1300.[61] Although there was no demesne arable in 1350,[62] the lords of Caus kept meadow land and the 2 parks at Minsterley in hand throughout the 14th century. The demesne meadows which included 'Noltmoor' in Westley township,[63] were said to comprise 20 a. in 1274[64] and 24 a. in 1300.[65] They were used to provide hay for the lord's stud-farm in Minsterley Park during the 14th century,[66] but had been leased by 1445[67] and yielded an annual rent of 15s. between 1453[68] and 1564.[69] Minsterley Park, said to be worth 13s. 4d. in 1274[70] and £6 in 1300, when it contained 300 a.,[71] included a stud-farm between 1359[72] and 1402.[73] It had been leased by 1424, the tenant providing pasture for 6 mares and foals,[74] but was still occupied by the lord's horses in 1453.[75] A dairy-farm in the

25 See p. 310.
26 Longleat MSS., unbound 4010.
27 B.M. Add. Ch. 22644.
28 See p. 297.
29 B.M. Eg. Roll 2198.
30 W.S.L. 1721/1/1, f. 202.
31 N.L.W., Wynnstay 118, f. 113.
32 Ibid.
33 Cal. Fine R. 1347–56, 52–53.
34 V.C.H. Salop. i. 316.
35 C 133/94/6.
36 Rot. Hund. (Rec. Com.), ii. 66.
37 Ibid.
38 Longleat MSS., unbound 4180.
39 C 133/7/8.
40 C 133/94/6.
41 In 1570 it was said that Poulton had once formed part of the demesne of Caus: S.P.L., Deeds 92.
42 Longleat MSS., unbound 3834.
43 Ibid. 3685.
44 Ibid. 3664.
45 Ibid. 3834.
46 Ibid. 3801.
47 Ibid. 3661.
48 Ibid. 3834.
49 Ibid. 3788.

50 Ibid. 4139.
51 Ibid. 3713.
52 Ibid. 3799.
53 Ibid. 3724.
54 Ibid. 3661.
55 Ibid. 3788.
56 Ibid.
57 Ibid.
58 Ibid. 3990, 4010, 4011, 4301; T.S.A.S. liv. 46–47.
59 V.C.H. Salop. i. 316.
60 C 133/7/8.
61 C 133/94/6.
62 Longleat MSS., unbound 3977.
63 Ibid. 3996.
64 C 133/7/8.
65 C 133/94/6.
66 Longleat MSS., unbound 3728, 3739.
67 Ibid. 4010.
68 Ibid. 4011.
69 Staffs. R.O., D 641/1/2/224.
70 C 133/7/8.
71 C 133/94/6.
72 Longleat MSS., unbound 3552.
73 Ibid. 4139.
74 Ibid. 3531.
75 Ibid. 4011.

Park was held on lease in 1564.[76] Lower Hogstow Park, probably the 200-acre 'haye' recorded in 1300,[77] had been leased before 1424.[78]

Nine tenants at Minsterley were described as bondmen in 1274, when they each performed 2 days week-work,[79] and they were probably descendants of the 4 *bovarii* recorded here in 1086.[80] The ten bondmen of 1300 each held a half-virgate at a rent of 2s.,[81] but their labour-services had probably been commuted by 1348, when the 4 bondmen paid rents of 10s. each for holdings of the same size.[82] In 1086 8 villeins and 4 bordars here had 8 ploughs between them.[83] There were said to be no customary tenants at Minsterley in 1274, when the 14 virgates formerly held by them were waste.[84] They reappear, however, in 1300, when 26 tenants were described as tenants-at-will and 'penimen'.[85] Twenty of them held half-virgates, while 5 held a noke ($\frac{1}{4}$ virgate) apiece, and their rents totalled £6 6s. 6d.[86] By 1348 there were 32 tenants of half virgates and at least 12 cottars.[87] The Black Death carried off the 4 bondmen,[88] who do not reappear,[89] and killed 7 half-virgaters and 8 cottars.[90] Small labour-services were due from all tenants here in 1359[91] and all but 6 of the tenants performed such services in 1372.[92] Nine of them were allowed to commute their services for lack of plough-beasts in 1376[93] and all labour-services had been commuted by 1388.[94] Rents in Minsterley, Westley, and Callow brought in £15 16s. 2d. in 1384[95] and the rental continued at about this level until the early 16th century.[96] A few tenants in advowry, who paid 4d. or 8d. a year for licence to reside in the manor, are found in Caus and Minsterley from the later 14th century until the mid-15th century.[97] Five tenants from Wilderley were received in advowry in 1428[98] and 5s. 2d. was derived from such rents in 1445.[99]

Newly inclosed lands in Hogstow Forest produced rents of £6 12s. 4d. a year in 1533[1] and 571 a. in the western part of Hogstow Wood were cleared and added to the Minsterley manorial estate in 1676.[2] Four freeholds in Minsterley were acquired by Sir Thomas Thynne in the 1630s.[3] Enlargement of the estate by purchase and forest clearance was balanced by the sale of the Forest of Hayes in 1572[4] and of Westley township in 1603.[5] The Caus demesne

amounted to 552 a. in 1679 and the estate as a whole contained 1,049 a. at its sale in 1810.[6] In 1838 Lord Bath held 2,233 a. in Minsterley township.[7]

The demesne lands of Caus were leased for £20 a year in 1542.[8] The dairy farm at Broomhill, leased in 1536,[9] was taken in hand in 1540.[10] Lands adjoining the castle, let on a 99-year lease in 1573,[11] were taken in hand after 1581[12] and until 1620 were used mainly for the production of corn for the market.[13] After 1620 most of the demesne was let on yearly tenancies,[14] but a little land remained in hand until the destruction of the castle.[15] Between 1620 and 1639 the Thynnes were using demesne pastures at Caus to accommodate cattle and sheep purchased locally and awaiting transit to their estates at Kempsford (Glos.) and Longleat (Wilts.).[16]

Sales of timber and cordwood were an important source of revenue in the later 17th century. Phillip Foley, who purchased 6,000 cords at Caus and Wallop for 5s. 6d. a cord in 1674,[17] assigned the contract to Francis Wolfe of Coalbrookdale in the following year.[18] Wolfe secured a larger contract in 1680 at the high rate of 5s. 9d. a cord,[19] which Thynne's agent had gained by bargaining with other ironmasters.[20] Wolfe was released from his contract owing to financial difficulties in 1687,[21] when the agent reported that the other ironmasters, enraged by Thynne's sharp practice in 1680, 'will not deal with your lordship until necessity compel them'.[22] After 1768 receipts from timber-sales normally averaged £100 a year and sales producing £3,900 between 1771 and 1775, £1,278 between 1792 and 1794, and £1,514 between 1823 and 1827 indicate that the woodlands on the estate were being carefully managed.[23]

In 1527 Henry, Earl of Stafford, issued instructions that his Shropshire estates, whether copyhold or otherwise, were to be relet 'by indenture or bill'.[24] Although the 3-life lease was in general use on the Minsterley estate by 1581, when all but one of the 19 tenants held by this form of tenure,[25] these changes had little effect here on the size of farms or on the level of rents. In 1541 16 of the 20 Minsterley tenants held half-virgates.[26] Their rents, then producing some £8 a year,[27] had risen only to £12 by 1581, when the half virgate was still the predominant

[76] Staffs. R.O., D 641/1/2/243.
[77] C 133/94/6.
[78] Longleat MSS., unbound 3531.
[79] C 133/7/8.
[80] *V.C.H. Salop.* i. 316.
[81] C 133/94/6.
[82] Longleat MSS., unbound 3660.
[83] *V.C.H. Salop.* i. 316.
[84] C 133/7/8.
[85] C 133/94/6.
[86] Ibid.
[87] Longleat MSS., unbound 3660.
[88] Ibid. 3977.
[89] Ibid. 3728.
[90] Ibid. 3977.
[91] Ibid. 3552.
[92] Ibid. 3505.
[93] Ibid. 3728.
[94] Ibid. 3514.
[95] Ibid. 3798.
[96] Ibid. 3846, 3847, 3988, 4010, 4011, 4301; *T.S.A.S.* liv. 55–57.
[97] Longleat MSS., unbound 3531, 3728, 3831.
[98] Ibid. 3531.
[99] Ibid. 4010.
[1] Ibid. 4301.
[2] Ibid. 4061.

[3] Ibid. 3546, 3879, 3928, 4188.
[4] S.R.O. 837/52.
[5] S.P.L., Deeds 6756.
[6] Longleat MSS., unbound 4026; S.R.O. 279/61.
[7] S.R.O. 1361/102.
[8] Heref. City Libr., MS. 23628, f. 39.
[9] W.S.L. 1721/1/1, f. 209.
[10] Ibid.
[11] Longleat MSS., unbound 4004.
[12] Ibid. 4030.
[13] Longleat MSS., Thynne Papers, box 57, book 16; ibid. MSS., unbound 4026.
[14] Longleat MSS., unbound 4026.
[15] Ibid.   [16] Ibid.
[17] Ibid. 4133.
[18] Longleat MSS., Thynne Papers, vol. xx, f. 244.
[19] Ibid. vol. xxi, f. 118.
[20] Ibid. vol. xxi, letters of Thomas Hawkes, 1680–1 *passim.*
[21] Ibid. vol. xxiii, f. 132.
[22] Ibid. f. 140.
[23] Ibid. MSS., unbound, Rack E, accts. 1734–1840 *passim.*
[24] B.M. Add. MS. 36542, f. 27.
[25] Longleat MSS., unbound 4030.
[26] *T.S.A.S.* liv. 56–57.
[27] Longleat MSS., unbound 4030.

farm size.[28] Income from rents rose with the conversion to tenure-at-will in the earlier 17th century. Only one such tenant appears in 1581,[29] but by 1640 there were 14 of them.[30] By 1651 two-thirds of the tenants held on rack-rents, producing £136 10s. a year and the remaining 9 leaseholders paid only £7 10s.[31] Although there was already one farm of 262 a. at Caus in 1679,[32] the transition to large farms was the result of a reorganization of the estate carried out by the trustees of Thomas, Lord Weymouth, c. 1751.[33] By 1766 most of the Minsterley estate (1,188 a.) lay in 7 farms of over 100 acres.[34] The 8 farms existing at Caus in 1679[35] had been reduced to 3 by 1774[36] and in 1810 nearly all the Caus estate lay in one large farm.[37] On the Minsterley estate the rental rose from £293 in 1734[38] to £453 by 1771.[39] It reached £1,000 in 1808 and remained at this level until the mid-19th century, though with large arrears.[40]

By the later 13th century the Minsterley manorial estate had been reduced in size by the alienation of lands in Minsterley, Callow, Lake, Poulton, and Westley to free tenants.[41] Similar developments were responsible for the shrinkage of 3 other Domesday manors in the parish. Yockleton manor was assessed at 6 hides in 1086,[42] but Newton township had become a separate estate by the mid-14th century,[43] and between 1382[44] and 1665[45] Yockleton Park and the whole of Stoney Stretton township were granted to free tenants. In 1787 the manorial estate contained only 430 a.[46] The townships of Coton and Hurst appear to have been detached before 1126 from the manor of Winsley.[47] This manor was assessed at 2 hides in 1086[48] but amounted to only 146 a. in 1736.[49] Although the manor of Whitton grew from 1½ hide to 2 hides between 1086[50] and 1255,[51] probably as a result of the addition of part of Vennington township,[52] a substantial part of the former manorial estate was in the hands of freeholders in the later Middle Ages.[53] Wigmore manor, which was assessed at 1 hide in 1086,[54] seems also to have continued unaltered in size; it contained 265 a. in 1737.[55]

An early example of the deliberate enlargment of a manorial estate occurs at Whitton, where William Spenser, taking advantage of the destruction of the hamlet during the rising of Owen Glendower, 'did compass by purchase sundry of those freeholders and converted them into demesne' in the early 15th century.[56] The two moieties of Whitton manor were united in the hands of Alexander Topp in 1623.[57] Additional lands were acquired at the inclosure of common lands at the Vron c. 1600[58] and at the inclosure of Caus Mountain in 1774.[59] Three freeholds obtained by purchase and inheritance between 1722 and 1777[60] were sold in 1786[61] and by 1841 the Whitton estate amounted to 547 a.[62]

Sir Roger Owen, who bought Westbury manor in 1601,[63] purchased Minsterley Park and the township of Westley in 1603[64] and the Topp freehold at Westbury and Westley in 1623.[65] He also initiated the inclosure of the Hem in 1610,[66] and of Henwood[67] and the commons of Westbury, made before 1631.[68] Westley was sold in the later 17th century[69] and the Westbury estate (including Hayford in Alberbury) amounted to 1,731 a., c. 1768.[70] The Owen estate here had been reduced to 1,191 a. by 1841,[71] as a result of the sale of Minsterley Park in 1794[72] and of 236 a. in Westbury in 1802,[73] but the latter was later bought back into the estate. It comprised 1,347 a. in 1891.[74]

The Winsley manorial estate, still amounting to only 146 a. in 1799,[75] was a creation of the 19th century. It had grown to 205 a. by 1841[76] and in 1845 Hurst, Caus Castle, and Hawcocks Farms were added;[77] it amounted to 869 a. by 1863.[78] Caus Castle and Hawcocks Farms were sold in 1868,[79] but the latter was again purchased in 1924.[80] John Whitaker bought the Westbury manorial estate in 1891[81] and in 1965 his descendant owned some 1,650 a. in the parish.[82] The manor of Marsh, formerly in divided ownership,[83] was reunited by Thomas Jenkins in 1730,[84] when it contained c. 560 a.,[85] but 337 a. were sold, with Marsh Hall, in 1801.[86]

[28] Ibid.
[29] Ibid.
[30] Ibid. 4023.
[31] Longleat MSS., Thynne Papers, vol. xxxiii, f. 105.
[32] Longleat MSS., unbound 4026.
[33] Ibid. Rack E, acct. c. 1751.
[34] S.R.O. 152/1.
[35] Longleat MSS., unbound 4026.
[36] Ibid. Rack E, acct. 1774.
[37] S.R.O. 279/61.
[38] Longleat MSS., unbound, Rack E, acct. 1734.
[39] Ibid. 1771.
[40] Ibid. 1808–40.
[41] See p. 320.
[42] V.C.H. Salop. i. 325.
[43] See p. 316.
[44] S.P.L., Deeds 6172.
[45] Deed, 1665, in Lynches Farm title-deeds.
[46] Map, 1787, in Onslow Hall title-deeds.
[47] Eyton, vii. 10.
[48] V.C.H. Salop. i. 324.
[49] S.P.L., Deeds 14588.
[50] V.C.H. Salop. i. 325.
[51] Rot. Hund. (Rec. Com.), ii. 66.
[52] Eyton, vii. 66.
[53] See pp. 320–1.
[54] V.C.H. Salop. i. 326.
[55] S.R.O. 840 uncat., survey, 1737.
[56] Longleat MSS., unbound 4211.
[57] S.R.O. 1011 uncat., case papers re Vennington Common, 1799.

[58] C 142/261/151; S.R.O. 103 uncat., contract for sale of underwood at Vron Gate, 1600.
[59] S.R.O. 1011 (Parr) uncat., abstract of title, 1716–86.
[60] Ibid.
[61] Ibid. abstract of title, 1786–1830.
[62] Ibid. 1361/106.
[63] S.P.L., Deeds 6867.
[64] Ibid. 6756.
[65] Ibid. 9351.
[66] Ibid. 6765–6, 6768, 6771, 6775, 6777.
[67] S.R.O. 665 uncat., lease 1630.
[68] Ibid. lease, 1631.
[69] Date of sale not known, but before 1736: S.P.L., Deeds 14588.
[70] Ibid. 13642.
[71] S.R.O. 1361/103.
[72] Ibid. 665 uncat., sale partics. 1794.
[73] Ibid.
[74] Winsley Hall title-deeds.
[75] S.R.O. 515/3.
[76] Ibid. 1361/105.
[77] Ibid. 279/54, 104.
[78] Ibid. 279/114.
[79] Winsley Hall title-deeds.
[80] Ibid.   [81] Ibid.
[82] Ex inf. Major S. P. L. Groves, Fairford, Glos.
[83] See pp. 315–16.
[84] Ibid.
[85] Deed, 1801, in Marche Manor title-deeds; S.R.O. 1361/106.
[86] Deed, 1801, in Marche Manor title-deeds.

Yockleton manor, which was held with Caus and Minsterley until 1347,[87] possessed a large demesne until the mid-14th century. There was demesne here sufficient for 3 ploughs in 1086, when the tenantry included 8 serfs.[88] The area of demesne arable fell from 4 carucates in 1274[89] to 3 carucates (360 a.) in 1300,[90] but it then included a 70-acre park and a fish-pond.[91] In 1349 the 2 carucates remaining in demesne were said to have fallen in value from 40s. to 6s. 8d. on account of the Black Death[92] and by 1382 all the demesne, then reckoned at 283 a. had been leased to the tenants.[93] Westbury manor, where there was demesne sufficient for one plough in 1086,[94] included 180 a. demesne arable in 1316.[95] There is virtually no evidence, after 1086, for the size or management of demesne on the remaining manors outside the estate of the Corbets of Caus.

Freeholds formed an important element on the manors of Minsterley and Yockleton during the Middle Ages. Most of these freeholds were established before the end of the 13th century, apparently with the object of creating a hereditary class of minor baronial officials. The Minsterley freeholders paid nominal rents in kind,[96] and those of Yockleton held by military service.[97] In 1274 the 33 freeholders in Minsterley township each held a half virgate.[98] A larger freehold was formed shortly afterwards, when Richard de Hope obtained 2 virgates in Minsterley and a carucate in Poulton and Callow,[99] and two early-14th-century feoffments are recorded —the 60 a. granted to Hugh Baret in 1311[1] and the virgate granted to Robert de Clough in 1320.[2] The Hope[3] and Clough[4] freeholds, and that of the Corbet family, one of the freeholds of 1274,[5] were bought back into the manorial estate in the 1630s,[6] but the Baret estate passed to the Tipton family,[7] who were still freeholders at Minsterley in the later 18th century.[8] Three other ancient freeholds survived at Minsterley in 1766[9] and two of them, amounting to 152 a., still remained in 1838.[10] A freehold estate at Westley, held by Robert le Proude in 1274,[11] had passed to the lord of Whitton manor by 1384[12] and became part of the Westbury manorial estate in 1623,[13] but two other estates here, owned by the

Betton and Botfield families in 1783,[14] presumably represent medieval freeholds. The descendants of Roger and Robert de Lake, free tenants at Lake in 1274,[15] were resident there throughout the Middle Ages.[16] Only one branch of the Lake family is recorded here c. 1540, when they held Lower Lake.[17] Upper Lake was at that time the property of the Treves family,[18] from whom it passed to Richard Clough in 1681.[19] The whole township consisted of 3 small freehold estates c. 1540[20] and in 1783,[21] but had been acquired by the Warter family of Cruckmeole before 1844.[22]

There were 4 free tenants at Yockleton in 1274,[23] 5 in 1382,[24] and 6 in 1587.[25] Only one of these estates, the 1½ virgate held by Roger Burnell in 1274,[26] lay in Yockleton township. This was held by Hugh Harris in 1587[27] and passed by marriage in 1655 to Rowland Hunt of Boreatton.[28] It was bought by William Meredith in 1694,[29] when it included Yockleton Park, and it amounted to some 380 a. in 1787,[30] but had been broken up into 3 smaller freeholds by 1841.[31] The remaining freeholds lay in Stoney Stretton. Their descent is obscure, but the farms held in 1843 by John Oakley (102 a.) and John Griffiths (45 a.)[32] may have descended from freeholders of the same name in 1587.[33] The largest freehold in the township in 1843 was the 398 a. owned by John Parry of Stretton Hall.[34] Acquired by John's father John Parry in 1791[35] this estate had been held in the early 18th century by John Harries.[36] It contained 611 a. when dispersed by sale in 1946.[37]

Vennington was a community of small freeholders until the 19th century. The Corbets of Leigh, who held a half virgate in Whitton and Vennington, are recorded here between 1398 and 1627[38] and a junior branch of the Burnell family were resident in Vennington throughout the 14th century.[39] The largest freehold during the 17th and 18th centuries seems to have been that purchased by Edward Davies of Trewern from Edward Slegge in 1582.[40] This was said to comprise 2 messuages and 40 a. in 1590[41] and 3 messuages in 1600.[42] It passed by marriage in 1655 to Rowland Hunt of Boreatton,[43] whose descendant

87 See pp. 310–12.
88 V.C.H. Salop. i. 325.
89 C 133/7/8.
90 C 133/94/6.
91 Ibid.
92 C 135/96/14.
93 S.P.L. Deeds 6172.
94 V.C.H. Salop. i. 325.
95 C 134/55/6.
96 Longleat MSS., unbound 3728; ibid. Minsterley acct. r. passim.
97 S.P.L., Deeds 6172.
98 C 133/7/8.
99 Longleat MSS., unbound 4180.
1 Heref. City Libr., MS. 23628, f. 40v.
2 Ibid. f. 22v.
3 Longleat MSS., unbound 3773, 4186; C 142/344/18.
4 Longleat MSS., unbound 3728, 4010, 4030; T.S.A.S. liv. 56.
5 C 133/7/8; Longleat MSS., unbound 3827, 4030.
6 Longleat MSS., unbound 3879, 3928, 4188.
7 Ibid. 3728, 4010, 4030.
8 S.R.O. 93/300.
9 Ibid. 152/1.
10 Ibid. 1361/102.
11 C 133/7/8.
12 Longleat MSS., unbound 3798.
13 S.P.L., Deeds 9351.
14 S.R.O. 807/231.
15 C 133/7/8.

16 Longleat MSS., unbound 3660, 3798.
17 Ibid. 4051.   18 Ibid.
19 S.P.L., Deeds 9301.
20 Longleat MSS., unbound 4051.
21 S.R.O. 807/231.
22 Ibid. 1361/105.
23 C 133/7/8.
24 S.P.L., Deeds 6172.
25 S.C. 12/32/26.
26 C 133/7/8.
27 S.C. 12/32/26.
28 S.P.L., Deeds 17447.
29 Ibid. 17349.
30 Map, 1787, in Onslow Hall title-deeds; S.R.O. 515/6, pp. 318–19; Heref. Dioc. Regy., Yockleton tithe appt.
31 Heref. Dioc. Regy., Yockleton tithe appt.
32 Ibid.
33 S.C. 12/32/26.
34 Heref. Dioc. Regy., Stoney Stretton tithe appt.
35 Stoney Stretton Hall title-deeds penes Messrs. H. W. Hughes & Son, solicitors, Shrewsbury.
36 S.R.O. 90/19.
37 Sale partics., 1946, in Stoney Stretton Hall title-deeds.
38 C 136/87/3; C 142/283/92; S.P.L., Deeds 5901; S.R.O. 322 uncat., rental of Corbet of Leigh, 1627.
39 S.P.L., Deeds 9333; C 136/87/3.
40 S.P.L., MS. 69.
41 C 142/228/43.
42 C 142/261/151.
43 S.P.L., Deeds 17447.

sold it to John Topp of Whitton in 1770.[44] In 1770 Topp also purchased from the Gittoes family[45] a freehold formerly held by the Gough family.[46] These two freeholds passed in 1830 to Thomas Parr,[47] who in 1832 purchased another Vennington freehold belonging to another branch of the Davies family of Trewern.[48] Parr owned 480 a. in Vennington in 1841, when there were only two other freeholds there consisting of anything more than house property.[49] One of these, the 25 a. owned by Thomas Burley, probably represents the half-messuage held by Thomas Burley at his death in 1621.[50]

By far the largest of the freehold estates created in the parish since the end of the Middle Ages was that of the Severne family on the Long Mountain, which extended into Worthen parish and into Wales. The Forest of Hayes was purchased in 1572 by Richard Powell,[51] whose descendant Henry Powell sold it to John Severne in 1657.[52] A freehold in Wallop belonging to the Fox family was purchased between 1670 and 1758[53] and the Severne family obtained an allotment of 80 a. at the inclosure of Wallop Common in 1694–6.[54] The Westbury portion of the estate amounted to 1,062 a. in 1841[55] and was greatly extended in the later 19th century. In 1843 478 a. in Wallop, formerly part of the Caus manorial estate, was purchased by J. M. Severne and the Whitton manorial estate (547 a.) was bought in 1877.[56] At its sale in 1920 the Severne estate included 3,560 a. in Westbury and Worthen parishes.[57]

Evidence for tenurial history is slight outside the manors of Caus and Minsterley. In 1086 the 19 villeins and 6 bondmen on Yockleton manor had 8 ploughs between them.[58] There were 19 customary tenants there in 1274, all of whom were said to hold half virgates, and only 13 such tenants in 1300.[59] This regularity in the size of holdings had disappeared by 1382, when the 9 tenants at Stoney Stretton held lands ranging in size from one noke to 1½ virgate and the 6 Yockleton tenants held 182 a. demesne between them, in addition to the half-virgate customary holdings.[60] Light labour-services were recorded in 1382, but were clearly not exacted since all the demesne had been leased.[61] There were 16 leaseholders in 1587[62] whose rents produced £32 a year.

Copyhold tenure had disappeared in Westbury manor by 1601, when 6 tenants held on short-term leases and 8 on leases for 3 lives.[63] The 3-life lease probably went out of use here c. 1672 and by c. 1730 the whole manor was held on rack-rents then producing £551 a year.[64] Large farms had become normal on Westbury manor, as at Minsterley, by the mid-18th century. The 8 farms of over 100 a. comprised 1,191 a. in 1768, when only 105 a. of the manorial estate lay in smaller holdings.[65] Five large farms in 1841 and 4 in 1875 occupied a slightly larger proportion of the estate.[66] In Yockleton only one of the six farms in the manorial estate was of over 100 a. in 1787[67] and the transition to larger farms did not take place until after 1789, when the manor was purchased by Rowland Wingfield.[68] Nearly the whole estate lay in 3 large farms by 1840.[69] In the mid-19th century small farms were numerous only on Stretton Heath, Wattlesborough Heath, and the Long Mountain.[70] The 7 north-western townships (Caus, Forest, Marsh, Vennington, Wallop, Whitton, and Wigmore) included in 1841 13 farms of more than 100 a. and 30 holdings of 5–100 a.[71]

The parish as a whole contained 6,251 a. arable and 4,502 a. pasture c. 1840, when the acreage of pasture exceeded that of arable only in Minsterley township.[72] The Westbury manorial estate was, however, almost wholly converted to pasture by 1890,[73] and the Severne estate at Wallop and Whitton was mainly pasture in 1920.[74]

The only mill recorded in the parish in 1086 was that at Yockleton, which then rendered a load of malt annually.[75] It was said to be worth 20s. in 1274[76] and 10s. in 1300.[77] Another mill had been erected here before 1349, when both were worth nothing on account of the Black Death, but they normally rendered 10 quarters of corn.[78] The upper mill, west of the village, was held by Mariota le Walker in 1382 and was presumably then used as a fulling mill.[79] It was again converted into a fulling mill in 1654,[80] but was used as a corn mill in 1763[81] and is last recorded in 1840.[82] The lower mill, east of the village, contained 2 mills under one roof in 1653[83] and remained in use until 1937.[84]

Mills at Westbury, Vennington, Caus, and Brerelawe stood on tributaries of Yockleton Brook. Westbury mill, said to be in decay in 1274, was then worth 6s. 8d.[85] It had probably been repaired by 1316 when it was worth 13s. 4d.,[86] but it is not later recorded. A water mill was built at Vennington in 1310[87] and milling continued at this site until c. 1913.[88] The Vennington windmill is first recorded

[44] S.R.O. 1011 (Parr) uncat., abstract of title, 1680–1770.
[45] Ibid. abstract of title, 1698–1777.
[46] C 142/626/19.
[47] S.R.O. 1011 (Parr) uncat., abstract of title, 1786–1830.
[48] Ibid. 1187/19 (abstract of title, 1729–1831, section 27).
[49] Ibid. 1361/106.
[50] C 142/502/37.
[51] S.R.O. 837/52.
[52] Ibid. 837/65.
[53] Ibid. 1187/19, p. 11; ibid. 837/87.
[54] Ibid. 279/331–2.
[55] Ibid. 1361/104, 106.
[56] Ibid. 279/61; ibid. 1361/80.
[57] Ibid. 1361/80.
[58] V.C.H. Salop. i. 325.
[59] C 133/7/8; C 133/94/6.
[60] S.P.L., Deeds 6172.
[61] Ibid.
[62] S.C. 12/32/26.
[63] S.P.L., Deeds 6867.
[64] Ibid. 13633; S.R.O. 665 uncat., lease, 1672.
[65] S.P.L., Deeds 13642.
[66] S.R.O. 1361/103; ibid. 1011 (Smythe Owen) uncat., survey, 1875.

[67] Map, 1787, in Onslow Hall title-deeds.
[68] Lynches Farm title-deeds.
[69] Heref. Dioc. Regy., Yockleton tithe appt.
[70] S.R.O. 1361/103, 104, 106; Heref. Dioc. Regy., Stoney Stretton tithe appt.
[71] S.R.O. 1361/104, 106.
[72] Ibid. 1361/102–6.
[73] Ibid. 1011 (Smythe Owen) uncat., estate correspondence.
[74] Ibid. 1361/80.
[75] V.C.H. Salop. i. 325.
[76] C 133/7/8.
[77] C 133/94/6.
[78] C 135/96/14.
[79] S.P.L., Deeds 6172.
[80] Ibid. 1670.
[81] Map, 1763, in Lynches Farm title-deeds.
[82] Heref. Dioc. Regy., Yockleton tithe appt.
[83] N.L.W., Wynnstay (1952), box Z/30.
[84] Ex inf. Mr. T. B. Bromley, Lynches Farm.
[85] C 133/39/8.
[86] C 134/55/6.
[87] S.P.L., MS. 2, f. 422ᵛ.
[88] Kelly's Dir. Salop. (1913).

in 1808[89] but had closed by 1851.[90] The mill at Caus was worth 12s. 8d. in 1300.[91] The Park Mill at Caus, first recorded in 1374,[92] was taken down in 1622.[93] A reference to a mill at Brerelawe occurs in 1267.[94]

Minsterley mill, worth 13s. 4d. in 1274[95] and 30s. in 1300,[96] was let for 4 years at a corn-rent in 1352.[97] It was kept in hand between 1366 and 1376, but was again leased by 1382.[98] It was still in use in 1621[99] and is last recorded in 1679,[1] but had by this date been superseded by Hogstow Mill, erected upstream on Minsterley Brook before 1581.[2] Hogstow Mill continued in use until c. 1947.[3]

In addition to the upper mill at Yockleton fulling mills are recorded at Caus in the 1360s[4] and at Lower Hogstow between 1565 and 1695.[5] A disused fulling mill occurs at Minsterley in the later 18th century.[6]

Coal used at Caus Castle in 1556[7] may have come from Westbury, where pits are first recorded in 1598.[8] During the 17th century mining activity was restricted to shallow seams in the area now occupied by Broxtons and Quarry Woods, south-east of the village, where there are numerous 'bell' pit-mounds characteristic of the period.[9] Mines at Wigley Farm, opened in the earlier 18th century,[10] had been closed before 1768 for lack of efficient pumping equipment to permit the exploitation of the deeper seams.[11] Under the name of the Westbury Colliery this site was leased in 1781 to John Scott and Edward Jefferies,[12] who erected a Boulton and Watt pumping engine.[13] Their lease was renewed for 30 years in 1792[14] and is said to have been highly profitable, producing royalties of from £330 to £405 a year between 1803 and 1807.[15] Four shafts were in use in 1827[16] and another was sunk by Joseph Dickinson, lessee of the colliery, 1831–52.[17] The colliery was held by 3 partnerships for short periods in the 1850s and closed in 1862.[18]

Stone slates used for repairs at Caus Castle in 1445 and 1541 came from a quarry in the Castle Park.[19] Quarries at Broomhill Wood, Oakley Wood to the west of the castle, and at Shrives Common south-west of Vennington were producing slates until the mid-18th century.[20] A sandstone quarry in Quarry Woods, south-east of Westbury, was opened in 1771[21] and there were smaller quarries at Lower Newton and near Yockleton.[22] A road-stone quarry on Callow Hill was opened by Mr. S. J. Hayward in 1926.[23] This was leased in 1931 to the County Council, who purchased the quarry in 1956.[24] In 1964–5 it had an annual output of some 125,000 tons of asphalt and 52,000 tons of road-stone.[25]

Commercial brick manufacture is first recorded in the parish in 1831, when the lessees of Westbury Colliery were given licence to produce bricks for sale.[26] An estate brickyard to the north of the colliery, established in 1851, was taken over by the lessee of the colliery in 1854, but closed in the following year.[27] T. H. Kough established a brick and tile works by the side of the projected Shrewsbury and Welshpool Railway, near Westbury Station, in 1860.[28] A siding was constructed here in 1863 and a tramway to the clay-pits near Halfway House had been laid by 1886.[29] Known since at least 1904[30] as the Westbury Brick and Pipe Company, this concern had an average annual output of 3 million drainage pipes in 1964.[31]

The most important industrial activity in the parish has been the mining of lead at Snailbeach. The discovery here in 1796 of a pig of lead from the reign of the Emperor Hadrian suggests that the Romans mined lead in the vicinity.[32] Although there are general references to lead-mining on the estates of the Earls of Stafford during the Middle Ages,[33] there is nothing to suggest workings at Snailbeach until 1552 when one John Clifton held a mine in Hogstow Forest.[34] There were prospectors in Habberley Office in 1613.[35] In 1676 and 1688 contracts were made with some Derbyshire miners, reserving a royalty of the 7th dish on all ore mined or the 9th dish of smelted lead.[36] There is no further record of mining here until 1761, when Thomas Powys and his partners worked the mine for a brief period, possibly as a trial, for the same royalty.[37] The existence of a series of shafts along the line of the main vein in 1766[38] suggests systematic working and in the same year a new partnership took the mine and worked it until 1772.[39] After 1782, when the

[89] Baugh, *Map of Salop.* (1808).
[90] *Bagshaw's Dir. Salop.* (1851).
[91] C 133/94/6.
[92] Longleat MSS., unbound 3834.
[93] Ibid. 4028.
[94] Eyton, vii. 171.
[95] C 133/7/8.
[96] C 133/94/6.
[97] Longleat MSS., unbound 3776.
[98] Ibid. 3568, 3794, 3799.
[99] Ibid. 3625.
[1] Ibid. 3966.
[2] Ibid. 4030.
[3] Ex inf. Mrs. R. Pugh, Hogstow Mill.
[4] Longleat MSS., unbound 3700, 3794.
[5] Staffs. R.O., D 641/1/2/244; Longleat MSS., unbound 4202.
[6] S.R.O. 152/1.
[7] Longleat MSS., unbound 3944.
[8] S.R.O. 665 uncat., lease, 1598.
[9] *Geol. Shrews. District*, 142.
[10] S.P.L., Deeds 13633.
[11] Ibid. 13642; S.R.O. 665 uncat., petition for lease n.d.
[12] S.P.L., Deeds 13623.
[13] H. W. Dickinson and R. Jenkins, *James Watt and the Steam Engine* (Oxford, 1927), 138.
[14] S.P.L., Deeds 13625.
[15] Murchison, *Silurian System* (1839), 83; S.R.O. 1011 (Smythe-Owen) uncat., accts. 1803–7.

[16] *Eddowes Jnl.* 17 Oct. 1827.
[17] S.R.O. 1011 (Smythe-Owen) uncat., lease, 1831.
[18] Ibid. leases, 1852, 1855, 1859.
[19] Longleat MSS., unbound 4010; *T.S.A.S.* liv. 47.
[20] S.R.O. 279/210; ibid. 1251/9; ibid. 1011 uncat., case-papers re Vennington Common, 1799.
[21] Ibid. 665 uncat., letter J. Topp to E. Kilvert, 13 Apr. 1771.
[22] *Geol. Shrews. District*, 220.
[23] S.C.C. title-deeds, RB 18/2.
[24] Ibid.
[25] Ex inf. manager of quarry.
[26] S.R.O. 1011 (Smythe-Owen) uncat., lease, 1831.
[27] Ibid. leases, 1851–4, and dissolution of partnership, 1855; *Kelly's Dir. Salop.* (1856).
[28] Plaque in Shrewsbury Museum.
[29] S.P.L., Railway plans 24, 24A.
[30] *Kelly's Dir. Salop.* (1904).
[31] Ex inf. Mr. J. C. Gill, Westbury Brick & Pipe Co. Ltd.
[32] *V.C.H. Salop.* i. 265.
[33] Longleat MSS., unbound 3730, 3742.
[34] Bodl. MS. Blakeway 2, f. 225ᵛ.
[35] Longleat MSS., Thynne Papers, box 57, book 16.
[36] Ibid. vol. xx, f. 323; ibid. vol. xxiv, f. 7.
[37] Longleat MSS., unbound, Rack E, accts. 1734–1840.
[38] S.R.O. 152/1.
[39] Longleat MSS., unbound, Rack E, accts. 1734–1840.

Snailbeach Mining Company was formed by Thomas Lovett,[40] the same partnership worked the mine until the company was reconstituted by Act of Parliament in 1867.[41] The new company went into voluntary liquidation in 1885, when the lead market was depressed, but was immediately reformed and continued mining on a more limited scale until 1912.[42] The Halvans Company, who had some interest at Snailbeach by 1905,[43] obtained a lease of the mine in 1912.[44] This company was extracting barytes in shafts above the 112-yard level until 1924.[45] Small-scale workings in adits continued until 1948.[46]

Leases of the mine were normally made for 21 years,[47] and after 1887 the lessees had permission to work the spoil heaps.[48] The Snailbeach Company had explored the mine to a depth of 180 yards by 1797 and by 1820 had driven the Black Tom shaft with 6 levels on Lordshill, 3 on Resting Hill, and other levels at Callow Hill.[49] To drain the upper levels of the mine an adit-level, ¾ mile long, had been driven eastwards to the mine from the Waterwheel on Minsterley Brook.[50] A depth of 462 yards had been reached by 1872[51] and of 492 yards by 1884,[52] but no deeper levels were driven until after 1896.[53] During the later 19th century the company was under pressure from the royalty-owner, Lord Bath, to deepen the mine and to drive exploratory levels from Callow Hill to Snailbeach in an effort to locate new veins.[54] In 1896 Lord Bath waived his royalties for 3 years to enable the company to deepen the mine from 492 yards to 552 yards.[55] Ore-bearing ground under the Vessons, belonging to the Earl of Tankerville, was also worked by the company from 1782.[56]

Although a mining engineer described the mine as 'rich beyond most things that I have been acquainted with' in 1827,[57] expenditure on driving levels and exploration were extremely high—£41,042 between 1782 and 1820[58]—and much of it was unproductive, as at Callow Hill, where workings begun before 1820 were still being mined in 1827 and again c. 1867–78 without any recorded financial return.[59] The richest ore bodies were worked directly by the company, but where the yeild was

low 'tributers' were employed. These were paid a proportion of the value of the ore they raised[60] and became an important element in the labour force in the 1860s and 1870s, when the mine was becoming less productive.[61]

Until c. 1870 the mine manager was paid on a commission basis.[62] This was alleged to have retarded the development of the mine,[63] but under a new management the smelt-house was moved from Pontesford to Snailbeach in 1863[64] and the mine itself was modernized. The new smelt-house, to the north of the mine,[65] was remarkable for a chimney-flue extending several hundred yards from the works to a chimney on the slopes of Snailbeach Coppice.[66] It became derelict when smelting ceased in 1895[67] and was largely demolished in 1897.[68] A reservoir was constructed above the mine in 1872.[69] In the same year a new engine-shaft, called George's Shaft and containing cages for the men, was sunk to the 252-yard level.[70] A second engine-house was built in 1873[71] and a third in 1881 to house a compressor for the pneumatic equipment used below ground.[72] The workings above ground were linked by tramways to the smelt-house.[73]

The replacement of ladders by cages was said to have saved the company up to 1½ hour per man-shift for those working in the deeper levels,[74] but in 1895 7 men were killed when the cable failed and one of the cages fell to the bottom of the shaft.[75] Three 8-hour shifts were worked in 1872 and in 1878 the mine employed 130 men, of whom 29 were engaged in exploration.[76] Only 33 men were employed in 1921.[77]

The mine yielded 505 tons of lead ore between 1768 and 1772.[78] Production figures for the Snailbeach Company are not available before 1845, apart from the years 1782 and 1811, when 108 tons and 1,321 tons were produced respectively.[79] The high level of productivity during the early 19th century may, however, be gauged from the yield of royalties. These were fixed at $\frac{2}{15}$ of the annual value of ore until 1822, and at the same proportion of the value of pig lead thereafter.[80] Between 1782 and 1820 Lord Bath received £44,215 in royalties—always over £1,000 a year after 1805 and reaching a peak

[40] S.R.O. 800 uncat., box 25, Snailbeach Mining Co. papers.
[41] Ibid.
[42] Ibid.; *Bull. Geol. Survey*, xiv. 25.
[43] Snailbeach Mining accts. *penes* Shropshire Mining Club.
[44] Ex inf. Shropshire Mining Club; S.C.C. title-deeds, RB 18/2.
[45] Ex inf. Mr. I. J. Brown, Dinnington, Sheffield.
[46] Ibid.
[47] S.R.O. 800 uncat., box 25, leases and papers.
[48] Longleat MSS., unbound, Rack E, report to Marquis of Bath, Oct. 1887.
[49] S.R.O. 800 uncat., box 25, acct. of driving levels, 1782–1820.
[50] Ibid.; ibid. 328/3.
[51] Ibid. 800 uncat., box 25, Mine Manager's report, June 1872.
[52] Ibid. 328/2.
[53] Longleat MSS., unbound, Rack E, report to Marquis of Bath, 1896.
[54] Ibid. 1867–87.
[55] Ibid. lease, 1896.
[56] S.R.O. 800 uncat., box 25, articles, 1782; ibid. Mine Manager's reports, 1868–84.
[57] Ibid. letter, A. Francis to J. Jones, 17 Mar. 1827.
[58] Ibid. acct. of expenses of driving levels, 1782–1820.
[59] Ibid.; Longleat MSS., unbound, Rack E, reports to Marquis of Bath, 1867–87.
[60] Longleat MSS., unbound, Rack E, report to Marquis of Bath, 1867.
[61] S.R.O. 800 uncat., box 25, Mine Manager's report, Jan. 1870.
[62] Longleat MSS., unbound, Rack E, report to Marquis of Bath, 1872.
[63] Ibid.
[64] Ibid.; *Kelly's Dir. Salop.* (1863).
[65] *Kelly's Dir. Salop.* (1863).
[66] Q. Sess., dep. plans 474.
[67] *Kelly's Dir. Salop.* (1895).
[68] Ex inf. Shropshire Mining Club.
[69] S.R.O. 800 uncat., box 25, Mine Manager's report, June 1872.
[70] Ibid.; Longleat MSS., unbound, Rack E, report to Marquis of Bath, 1872.
[71] Datestone.
[72] Ibid.
[73] Q. Sess., dep. plans 474.
[74] Longleat MSS., unbound, Rack E, report to Marquis of Bath, 1872.
[75] *Shropshire Mag.* Apr. 1955.
[76] Longleat MSS., unbound, Rack E, report to Marquis of Bath, 1872, 1878.
[77] Ex inf. Mr. I. J. Brown.
[78] Longleat MSS., unbound, Rack E, estate accts., 1768–72.
[79] Ibid. 1782, 1811.
[80] Ibid. 1822–40.

of £3,165 in 1811.[81] The mine produced 131,913 tons of ore between 1845 and 1913.[82] Annual production fluctuated between 2,000 and 3,000 tons from 1845 until 1880 and, after a temporary decline to 200 tons in 1885, averaged 1,000 tons from 1885 until 1901.[83] After 1901 the yield declined greatly, only 13 tons of ore being extracted in 1913.[84]

As the output of lead declined in the later 19th century, the extraction of barytes from the upper levels of the mine became an important secondary activity and completely eclipsed lead production after 1910. In 1858 the output of barytes was only 30 tons, but after 1861 the demand was stimulated by improved rail transport on the Minsterley spur and later by the Snailbeach District Railway.[85] A total of 42,327 tons of barytes was extracted at the mine between 1865 and 1913, but during the First World War output rose to 5,000 tons a year.[86] Small quantities of witherite, zinc-blende, and fluorspar were also produced.[87] Pumping at the mine ceased in 1910 when water was allowed to reach adit-level.[88]

Since the mid-19th century Minsterley has attracted several manufacturing concerns, for whom a powerful incentive, apart from raw materials, was the existence of good railway facilities. In 1863 the Snailbeach Company leased a barytes mill at the Waterwheel to the Cliffdale Barytes Company,[89] who operated it until c. 1926.[90] Another barytes mill was built on Minsterley Brook, immediately south of the village, by Taylor, Gilbertson, and Co. in 1893.[91] This mill had closed by 1909.[92]

Minsterley Creamery,[93] established in 1906 by Wathes Bros., was owned by Messrs. Wathes, Cattell, and Gurden from 1916 until 1951, when it was sold to Independent Dairies Ltd. This firm was taken over by the Express Dairies Ltd. in 1961. The creamery originally supplied milk for the Birmingham market for short periods of the year, manufacturing cheese when milk was plentiful. It moved to its present site, near the railway, soon after 1916. The average daily intake of milk rose from 3,000 gallons in 1926 to 15,000 gallons by 1951. The creamery was considerably enlarged in the 1950s and it was handling an average of 40,000 galllons a day by 1961. Dairy products other than cheese have been made here since the 1930s. The creamery employed about 30 persons in 1926 and 231 in 1964. A bacon-curing factory—the Minsterley Ideal Food Factory—had been established by 1929.[94] It has been known since c. 1934 as Rea Valley Foods Ltd.[95] and is now a food-packaging concern.

The Snailbeach miners and the large scattered population in the south of the parish provided a livelihood for a number of small tradesmen in and near Minsterley village in the later 19th century. There were 23 tradesmen at Minsterley in 1851[96] and 3 omnibus proprietors by 1856.[97] Eleven tradesmen are recorded in Westbury village in 1851 and 7 at Stoney Stretton, but most of the latter probably lived on Stretton Heath.[98] Blacksmiths are recorded at Halfway House, 1775–c. 1922,[99] Stoney Stretton, 1716–1851,[1] Vennington, 1840–c. 1941,[2] Wallop, since 1841,[3] Westbury, 1601–c. 1941,[4] and Yockleton 1642–c. 1941.[5] In Minsterley township there were smithies at Etsell, c. 1856–70,[6] and at Plox Green, 1886–1922.[7] The smithy in Minsterley village and that at Wallop are the only ones still open.

A weekly market on Wednesdays was established in Caus borough in 1200[8] and a 3-day fair on 28–30 December was instituted here in 1248.[9] In 1270, however, Thomas Corbet of Caus established a weekly market on the same day at Worthen.[10] The latter market, better placed geographically, clearly replaced that at Caus. No reference to a market at Caus occurs in the Caus ministers' accounts, beginning in the later 14th century. Monthly cattle fairs and an autumn sheep sale were held at Minsterley between 1879 and 1905 and a yearly hiring fair is recorded here until 1937.[11]

LOCAL GOVERNMENT. The following court rolls and allied records are known to exist for the various manors in the parish: manor and hundred of Caus, court rolls, 1351–1648,[12] presentments, 1677–1827;[13] Minsterley manor, court rolls, 1352–1512[14] and 1562–3;[15] Westbury manor, presentments, 1776–1838;[16] Yockleton manor, court rolls, 1451–3,[17] and presentments, 1755–69.[18]

The service of 5½ knights fees was due to the Crown from the Barony of Caus in the 13th century.[19] By this date enfeoffments totalling 9¼ knights fees had been made within the barony, in addition to smaller feoffments also of military character.[20] Tenants by knight-service normally served in person in the Welsh wars, but the tenant of Pontesbury manor claimed to have paid scutage when distrained for service overseas in 1242.[21] Thomas

[81] Longleat MSS., unbound, Rack E, estate accts., 1782–1820.
[82] *Bull. Geol. Survey*, xiv. 24.
[83] *Mem. Geol. Survey, Special Mineral Reports*, xxiii, fig. 13.
[84] *Bull. Geol. Survey*, xiv. 24.
[85] Ibid.; S.R.O. 800 uncat., box 25, letter, J. R. Eddy to J. Williams, 16 Mar. 1863.
[86] *Bull. Geol. Survey*, xiv. 24.
[87] Ibid.; S.R.O. 800 uncat., box 25, Mine Manager's report, 1885.
[88] Ex inf. Mr. G. W. Hall, Gloucester.
[89] S.R.O. 83 uncat., Minsterley poor rate, 1837.
[90] *Kelly's Dir. Salop.* (1870–1926).
[91] Ibid. (1895).
[92] Ibid. (1905–9).
[93] Account of Creamery based on information supplied by Mr. A. W. Gurden, Stoney Stretton Hall.
[94] *Kelly's Dir. Salop.* (1929).   [95] Ibid. (1934)
[96] *Bagshaw's Dir. Salop.* (1851).
[97] *Kelly's Dir. Salop.* (1856).
[98] *Bagshaw's Dir. Salop.* (1851).
[99] S.R.O. 279/333; *Kelly's Dir. Salop.* (1922).
[1] S.R.O. 90/19; *Bagshaw's Dir. Salop.* (1851).

[2] S.R.O. 1361/106.
[3] Ibid. 1361/104.
[4] S.P.L., Deeds 6867, 13642; S.R.O. 665 uncat., leases, 1620, 1726; *Kelly's Dir. Salop.* (1941).
[5] Deed, 1642, in Lynches Farm title-deeds; S.R.O. 515/6, pp. 318–19; *Kelly's Dir. Salop.* (1941).
[6] *Kelly's Dir. Salop.* (1856–70).
[7] Ibid. (1886–1922).
[8] B.M. Cott. Ch. xi. 72.
[9] *Cal. Chart. R.* i. 330.
[10] Ibid. ii. 147.
[11] *Kelly's Dir. Salop.* (1879–1937).
[12] Longleat MSS., unbound *passim*; S.R.O. 279/132–3; S.P.L., Deeds 2495.
[13] S.R.O. 279/153–328.
[14] Longleat MSS., unbound *passim*.
[15] S.P.L., Deeds 2495.
[16] S.R.O. 1011 (Smythe-Owen) uncat., ct. r. for Westbury manor and Ford Hund. 1776–1838.
[17] Heref. City Libr. 9133/17, 18, 31.
[18] Lynches Farm title-deeds.
[19] *Rot. Hund.* (Rec. Com.), ii. 66.
[20] *Bk. of Fees*, 964; C 133/7/8; S.P.L., Deeds 6172.
[21] Eyton, vii. 132.

Corbet of Caus had a retinue of 25 persons in Wales in 1263,[22] at least 16 of whom held knights fees or free tenancies in the barony.[23] Free tenants also owed castle-guard; two of them were garrisoning Gwyddgrug castle at Nant Cribba in Over Gorther when it was surrendered to the Welsh in 1263.[24] Two ½ knights fees were said c. 1274 to have been formerly appurtenant to Callow castle, near Minsterley.[25]

The military relationship of the Corbets with their tenants remained strong until the end of the 13th century, when the threat from Wales subsided. It was also a personal relationship; nearly all surviving charters of the Corbets and their tenants in the 13th and early 14th centuries were witnessed by the Corbets or members of their retinue and it is likely that some of these charters were made in the honorial court of the barony.[26] This court, first recorded in 1242, was held every three weeks, and all the free tenants of the barony owed personal suit.[27] Suit at the honorial court continued to be demanded until the dissolution of the barony in the later 16th century, but free tenants rarely attended after the early 14th century.[28]

The Welshry of Caus originally included only townships held by Welsh tenure, all of which lay outside the parish, but Thomas Corbet is said to have taken the English township of Great Wollaston in Alberbury into Welshry c. 1250, and Griffith ap Gwenwynwyn withdrew Perendon and a group of townships in Alberbury parish from Ford Hundred into Welshry when he overran the lands of Thomas Corbet c. 1252.[29] These townships were later annexed to the 'manor' of Nether Gorther which, with Over Gorther, made up the Welshry of Caus in the later Middle Ages.[30] Courts of the Welshry were normally held, during the later Middle Ages, at Black Lake (now North Rowens Farm in Worthen parish).[31] Their jurisdiction extended to felonies, which were tried before the steward and the free tenants. Condemned felons were executed at Black Lake or at Caus castle, but could be redeemed on payment of a fine of £7.[32] The court's powers were curtailed at the Act of Union in 1536 and, following a test case brought before the Council of the Marches in 1539, it was ruled that the English townships in Nether Gorther should resume their suit at Ford Hundred court.[33]

The townships of Caus, Vennington, and Wallop were said in 1292 to have been a liberty from time out of mind.[34] They were quit of suit at hundred and county courts and at assizes and possessed a private jurisdiction which extended to felony.[35] This franchise, described as the 'Hundred of Caus' in 1353,[36] also included the townships of Coton and Leigh in Worthen parish, which had formerly been in Chirbury Hundred, and Ree and Winsley in Westbury.[37] A manorial gallows, recorded in 1274, may have stood in a field to the west of Winsley Hall known as Gallows Tree Leasow in 1844.[38] A prison at Caus Castle is recorded between 1273 and 1581.[39]

The townships of Callow, Lake, Minsterley, Poulton, and Westley owed suit at Minsterley manor court, whose jurisdiction included view of frankpledge and the assize of bread and ale.[40] Small courts met at 3-weekly intervals and two great courts were held annually, in spring and autumn.[41] The suit of Westley and Lake had been withdrawn by 1581[42] and there is no later record of manor courts here. Fulk Corbet was granted view of frankpledge and the assize of bread and ale in Yockleton manor for life in 1381.[43]

The Westbury parish records include churchwardens' accounts, 1763–1848,[44] and overseers' accounts, 1659–1715 and 1745–1835.[45] Scattered vestry minutes occur in these accounts,[46] and there are separate vestry minutes, 1746–65 and 1790–1822.[47] The parish had been divided for administrative purposes into 4 Quarters by the mid-17th century.[48] These were: Westbury Quarter (Vennington, Westbury, Whitton), Yockleton Quarter (Marsh, Stoney Stretton, Wigmore, Yockleton), Westley Quarter (Caus, Forest, Hurst, Lake, Westley, Winsley), and Minsterley Quarter. Minsterley became responsible for its own poor shortly before 1766, but the township continued to pay church rates to Westbury until 1848.[49] The parish had two churchwardens and 4 overseers (one serving for each Quarter).[50] A select vestry, consisting of the overseers and two representatives from each Quarter, was appointed in 1817.[51] This met fortnightly and was solely concerned with the administration of poor relief.

The overseers each accounted separately throughout the 18th century. Their duties were assumed by a salaried perpetual overseer, 1812–15 and 1817–21, and a deputy overseer with more limited powers was employed in 1832–3.[52] Between 1745 and 1754 all the poor were farmed to a succession of contractors for £70 a year and in 1758 they were farmed for the proceeds of a 7d. rate.[53] A workhouse was built in 1761 to ensure that the paupers were

[22] Cal. Pat. 1258–66, 287.
[23] Eyton, vii. 1–38 passim; ibid. xi. 95–116 passim.
[24] Welsh Assize Roll, 1277–84, ed. J. C. Davies, 31, 334. For this castle, see Montg. Collect. lvii. 125–36.
[25] Longleat MSS., unbound 4180.
[26] S.R.O. 840 uncat., deeds, late 13th cent.–1317; Heref. City Libr., MS. 23642 passim; All Souls mun., Alberbury Deeds, nos. 5–6, 8, 12–14, 27–28, 31, 33, 41, 44.
[27] Eyton, vii. 132; C 133/7/8; C 133/94/6.
[28] S.P.L., Deeds 2495; Longleat MSS., unbound, ct. r. passim.
[29] Rot. Hund. (Rec. Com.), ii. 96; Cal. Inq. Misc. i, p. 353.
[30] C 133/94/6. Gorther is 'gorddwr' or 'land beyond the water': J. E. Lloyd, Hist. of Wales, ii. 734.
[31] O.S. Nat. Grid. SJ 295076. T.S.A.S. liv. 333; Longleat MSS., unbound 4030; S.R.O. 837/66.
[32] B.M. Add. Ch. 22644; Longleat MSS., unbound 4030.
[33] Trans. Cymmrodorion Soc. (1937), 67; W.S.L. 1721/1/1, f. 208.
[34] Plac. de Quo Warr. (Rec. Com.), 686.

[35] Rot. Hund. (Rec. Com.), ii. 96.
[36] Longleat MSS., unbound 3670.
[37] Ibid.; Rot. Hund. (Rec. Com.), ii. 60, 96; Eyton, xi. 99.
[38] Rot. Hund. (Rec. Com.), ii. 96; S.R.O. 1361/105.
[39] Select Bills in Eyre (Selden Soc. xxx), 10; Longleat MSS., unbound 4030.
[40] Longleat MSS., unbound 3776.
[41] Ibid.
[42] Ibid. 4030.
[43] Cal. Pat. 1381–5, 29.
[44] S.R.O. 1361/54; par. rec., churchwardens' accts. 1807–48.
[45] S.R.O. 1361/1–6, 8, 55, 56, 67, 68, 70.
[46] Ibid. 1361/1–3, 68.
[47] Ibid. 1361/49, 57.
[48] Ibid. 1361/1.
[49] Ibid. 1361/68; par. rec., churchwarden's accts. 1807–48.
[50] S.R.O. 1361/1.
[51] Ibid. 1361/57.
[52] Ibid. 1361/7.
[53] Ibid. 1361/4, 5, 67.

accommodated 'in a proper manner upon the most easy terms'.[54] It was managed until 1766 by a Mr. Munslow, who seems to have employed the inmates in spinning and weaving, and in 1769 the poor in the workhouse were let to Charles Barber, manager of the Pontesbury workhouse.[55] The workhouse was reopened in 1791 with a woolcomber as master.[56] A variety of textiles was produced, including linsey, stockings, striped linen, table linen, and bed-covers.[57] There were never fewer than 20 paupers in the workhouse in 1797 but it was closed in 1801.[58] Pauper children were subsequently sent to 'the Factory', either the yarn-mill of Benyon and Bage at Shrewsbury or the mill at Great Hanwood.[59] A proposal to farm the poor was rejected in 1822.[60]

Contracts for medical attendance were made with Mytton Skrymsher of Minsterley, 1802–3 and 1805–7, William Blakeway of Yockleton, 1804–5 and 1808–11, and Mr. Williams, 1817–19.[61] Expenses of maintenance of bastard children were said in 1799 to be considerably more than those incurred for the aged and infirm poor and the vestry directed that offenders 'be dealt with according to the rigours of the law'.[62]

Poor rates rose from £31 in 1659 to £198 in 1759.[63] Minsterley levied its own poor rate after 1766; those in the remainder of the parish had risen to £344 by 1777 and stood at £985 in 1797.[64] They reached a peak of £2,318 in 1818 and were always in excess of £1,000 during the 1820s.[65] Minsterley's poor rates rose much less in proportion to its population. The rate stood at £42 in 1765,[66] £248 in 1803,[67] and £504 in 1818,[68] and during the 1820s was between £200 and £300 a year.[69]

CHURCHES. Westbury was said to have two priests when the church is first recorded in 1086.[70] The two portions, known as the Dextra and Sinistra, or first and second portions, were served by separate incumbents until 1862.[71] The second portion was then assigned to the newly created ecclesiastical parish of Yockleton,[72] but Westbury and Yockleton have been held in plurality since 1959.[73] A medieval chapel-of-ease at Yockleton was presumably served by Shrewsbury Abbey, who then held tithes there.[74] There is no evidence, apart from its name, that Minsterley was the site of a pre-Conquest 'minster' church. The present church there was consecrated as a chapel-of-ease to Westbury in 1692.[75] Minster-ley chapel was licensed for marriages in 1844,[76] and the township was created an ecclesiastical parish in 1910.[77] The chapels of Caus castle and borough are discussed elsewhere.[78]

The living of Westbury is a rectory and the advowson of both portions followed the descent of Westbury manor until the end of the 19th century. William de Wyne was patron in 1320, in right of his wife Maud, widow of William de Ludlow,[79] and the Crown presented in 1348, during the outlawry of Laurence de Ludlow.[80] During the 16th century, when the manor was in divided ownership, incumbents were sometimes presented singly and sometimes jointly by the patrons.[81] The advowson of both portions was retained by the lord of the manor after the creation of the ecclesiastical parish of Yockleton in 1862, but it appears to have been sold after the sale of the manorial estate in 1891. The Revd. F. Cooke was patron and rector of the first portion in 1894;[82] his heir the Revd. E. M. Cooke transferred the advowson to the Bishop of Hereford in 1961.[83] The Revd. E. G. Baker was patron and rector of the second portion in 1900.[84] The advowson of this portion was transferred to the Bishop of Hereford by Frances Baker in 1927.[85]

The combined value of both portions was said to be £20 in 1291.[86] The first portion, always the more wealthy of the two, had a gross annual value of £14 7s. in 1535, £80 in 1665, and £753 in 1835;[87] the second portion was worth £12 7s., £50, and £665 respectively at these dates.[88]

The tithes were worth £4 in 1341.[89] In the early 17th century they were divided equally between the two portioners, except in Westbury, where tithes of the demesne were held by the rector of the first portion.[90] At commutation moduses on cows and calves were in use in all townships except Minsterley, and moduses totalling £8 7s. 2d. were paid for hay tithes in Hurst, Lake, Stoney Stretton, Vennington, Westbury, Westley, Whitton, and Winsley.[91] Newton township paid a modus of £4 for all tithes.[92] Rent-charges of £601 12s. and £576 12s. were apportioned to the rectors of the first and second portions respectively when the tithes were commuted, 1840–3.[93] Impropriate tithes in Caus, Forest, Minsterley, and Yockleton, which had originally formed the endowment of medieval chapels at Caus and Yockleton, were then commuted for a total rent-charge of £404.[94]

54 S.R.O. 1361/67.
55 Ibid. 1361/54.
56 Ibid. 1361/57.
57 Ibid. 1361/65.
58 Ibid. 1361/6, 61.
59 Ibid. 1361/6, 57.
60 Ibid. 1361/57.
61 Ibid.   62 Ibid.
63 Ibid. 1361/1, 68.
64 Ibid. 1361/8.
65 Ibid. 1361/7, 56.
66 Ibid. 1361/67.
67 Poor Law Abstract, 1803, H.C. 175, pp. 416–17 (1803–4), xiii.
68 Rep. Cttee. on Poor Rate Returns, 1822, Suppl. App., H.C. 556, p. 141 (1822), v.
69 Ibid. 1825, H.C. 334, p. 177 (1825), iv; ibid. 1830, H.C. 83, p. 391 (1830–1), xi.
70 V.C.H. Salop. i. 325.
71 Heref. Dioc. Regy., reg. 1857–69, p. 268.
72 Ibid.
73 Ibid. 1953–date, p. 309.
74 See p. 330.
75 Heref. Dioc. Regy., reg. 1682–1709, ff. 138–55.

76 Ibid. 1842–6, p. 169.
77 Ibid. 1902–19, p. 436.
78 See p. 310.
79 Eyton, vii. 61.
80 Cal. Pat. 1348–50, 42.
81 Reg. R. Mayew (C. & Y.S.), 274, 282; Reg. C. Botha (C. & Y.S.), 344; Instit. Dioc. Heref. 19, 23, 24.
82 Instit. Dioc. Heref. 208.
83 Heref. Dioc. Regy., reg. 1953–date, pp. 364–5.
84 Instit. Dioc. Heref. 216.
85 Heref. Dioc. Regy., reg. 1926–38, pp. 49, 61.
86 Tax. Eccl. (Rec. Com.), 167.
87 Valor Eccl. (Rec. Com.), iii. 213; T.S.A.S. xlvii. 24; Rep. Com. Eccl. Revenues [67], pp. 454–5, H.C. (1835), xxii.   88 Ibid.
89 Inq. Non. (Rec. Com.), 185.
90 Heref. Dioc. Regy., glebe terriers, n.d., 1604–13.
91 S.R.O. 1361/103–6; Heref. Dioc. Regy., Stoney Stretton tithe appt.
92 Heref. Dioc. Regy., Stoney Stretton tithe appt.
93 S.R.O. 1361/102–6; Heref. Dioc. Regy., Stoney Stretton and Yockleton tithe appts.
94 S.R.O. 1361/102, 104; Heref. Dioc. Regy., Yockleton tithe appt.

The glebe, which was worth 40s. a year in 1341,[95] belonged entirely to the rector of the first portion.[96] It amounted to some 16 a. in the early 17th century, when it consisted of scattered commonfield lands and included rights of common for 8 beasts,[97] but by 1768 most of the glebe lay in a compact block north-west of Westbury village.[98] It comprised 35 a. in 1841, when part was leased.[99] In 1856 30 a. glebe north-west of the village was exchanged for house-property near the church and land on the road to Hayford, amounting in all to 17 a.[1] Most of the glebe was sold in 1957.[2]

Richard de Ludlow (rector of the first portion 1302–21, and of the second portion 1308–21)[3] is the only medieval rector known to have been a relative of the lord of the manor. He was deprived in 1321 for neglecting to proceed to major orders.[4] Edmund de Bath, rector of the first portion, had licenses to study canon law at Paris in 1276 and 1278[5] and John de Medersh, rector of the second portion, had license to study for one year in 1331.[6] Several examples of long incumbencies occur, notably in the more wealthy first portion. Between 1370 and 1498 the second portion was held successively by Nicholas de Burley (1370–1429)[7] and John Woderton (1430–98).[8] The latter also held one of the chapels at Caus.[9] John Kynaston (rector of the first portion 1530–69)[10] and John Corbet (rector of the second portion 1537–76)[11] held their livings throughout the Reformation period. The latter lived at Shrawardine, which he held in plurality with Westbury and Wistanstow.[12] Lengthy incumbencies of the first portion after the Reformation include those of Ambrose Phillips (1626–46, 1661–81)[13] and Thomas Lyster (1722–74).[14] The second portion was without a parsonage and few of its incumbents held the living for more than 20 years. John Eyton (rector of the second portion 1755–81)[15] was also rector of Pulverbatch[16] and Osborne Wight (rector of the second portion 1787–1800)[17] held the living in plurality with Pontesbury first portion and Condover, both of which belonged to the patron of Westbury.[18] John Smythe (rector of the second portion 1781–7 and of the first portion 1787–97),[19]

Charles Leicester (rector of the second portion 1820–58),[20] and G. A. Salusbury (rector of the first portion 1852–93)[21] were relatives of the patron.

There is some evidence that Westbury, like Pontesbury, originally had three portioners. A third incumbent, known as the sacristan, was presented by the patron on three occasions between 1277 and 1334,[22] but the sacristy was held by the rector of the first portion by 1348.[23]

Assistant curates were continuously employed during the 18th century, when one of them normally served at Minsterley.[24] The salary of the curate of the first portion rose from £35 in 1770[25] to £80 by 1843[26] and from £100 to £150 a year during the later 19th century.[27] Rather higher stipends were paid to curates of the second portion.[28] The rector of the first portion was paid £135 a year as curate of the second in 1853, but employed an assistant curate to serve both portions for £100 a year.[29]

The parsonage of the first portion has always occupied its present site, south of the church.[30] It is said to have been rebuilt in 1723,[31] but the present house is of early-19th-century date. The second portion possessed no parsonage until 1859, when a site at Yockleton was conveyed for this purpose.[32] The parsonage had been built by 1861.[33]

Of two chantries recorded in 1547, one was endowed with a stock of cattle appraised at £42 15s.[34] The other, founded by William Lingen of the Hurst after 1525,[35] was worth £6 a year and was endowed with leasehold lands at Pollardine in Worthen parish and with a stock of cattle.[36]

Psalm-singers are recorded continuously after 1776.[37] A small organ, purchased in 1807,[38] was sold in 1843 and replaced by a new organ in the following year.[39] The latter was rebuilt in 1926.[40] Richard Parry, organist in 1808, received a salary of 3 guineas and was the son of Richard Parry, leader of the psalm-singers in 1776.[41] Average congregations of 250 at morning services and of 80 in the afternoon were recorded in 1851.[42] A parish library established by G. A. Salusbury in 1851[43] contained some 150 books; these were regularly borrowed until 1880.[44]

[95] Inq. Non. (Rec. Com.), 185.
[96] Heref. Dioc. Regy., glebe terrier, n.d.
[97] Ibid. glebe terriers, n.d., 1604–13.
[98] S.P.L., Deeds 13642.
[99] S.R.O. 1361/103.
[1] Ibid. 107.
[2] Ex inf. Church Com.
[3] Eyton, vii. 61–62.
[4] Reg. A. Orleton (C. & Y.S.), 180, 184.
[5] Reg. T. Cantilupe (C. & Y.S.), 45, 157.
[6] Reg. T. Charlton (C. & Y.S.), 90.
[7] Reg. W. Courtenay (C. & Y.S.), 11; Reg. T. Spofford (C. & Y.S.), 356.
[8] Reg. T. Spofford (C. & Y.S.), 356; Reg. T. Mylling (C. & Y.S.), 198; Longleat MSS., unbound 4010; Heref. City Libr., MS. 23628, f. 16.
[9] See p. 310.
[10] Reg. R. Mayew (C. & Y.S.), 344; Instit. Dioc. Heref. 16.
[11] Reg. C. Bothe (C. & Y.S.), 378; Instit. Dioc. Heref. 24.
[12] T.S.A.S. 4th ser. xii. 100.
[13] Ibid. 3rd ser. v. 366; ibid. vii. 260, 295; Instit. Dioc. Heref. 44.
[14] Instit. Dioc. Heref. 69, 104.
[15] Ibid. 91, 114.
[16] Ibid. 113.
[17] S.P.R. Heref. xii (2), intro. p. iv.
[18] Ibid. xii (1), intro. p. ix.
[19] Instit. Dioc. Heref. 114, 118, 126.
[20] Ibid. 143, 173.

[21] Ibid. 167, 208.
[22] Reg. T. Cantilupe (C. & Y.S.), 300; Reg. R. Swinfield (C. & Y.S.), 527; Reg. T. Charlton (C. & Y.S.), 79, 80, 153.
[23] Cal. Pat. 1348–50, 34.
[24] S.P.R. Heref. xii (2), 270, 294, 369; S.R.O. 1118 uncat., petition for dismissal of curate, 1790; B.M. Add. MS. 21018, f. 310.
[25] Heref. Dioc. Regy., reg. 1755–71, f. 193.
[26] Ibid. 1842–6, p. 118.
[27] Ibid. 1857–69, p. 397; ibid. 1869–83, pp. 566, 714; ibid. 1883–1901, p. 262.
[28] Ibid. 1791–1821, f. 248ᵛ; ibid. 1822–42, pp. 47, 304; ibid. 1847–56, p. 104.
[29] Ibid. pp. 440, 447.
[30] Ibid. glebe terriers, n.d., 1604–13.
[31] W.S.L. 350/40/3.
[32] Heref. Dioc. Regy., reg. 1857–69, p. 109.
[33] Ibid. 206.
[34] T.S.A.S. 3rd ser. x. 380.
[35] E 310/23/123.
[36] T.S.A.S. 3rd ser. x. 378.
[37] S.R.O. 1361/54.
[38] Par. rec., pr. hist. of organ, 1926.
[39] Ibid.
[40] Ibid.
[41] Ibid. churchwardens' accts. 1807–48; S.R.O. 1361/54; B.M. Add. MS. 21018, f. 337.
[42] H.O. 129/359/3/7.
[43] Par. rec., borrowing book and pr. rules.
[44] Ibid.

The church of *ST. MARY*, Westbury,[45] consists of nave, chancel, north aisle, and western tower and is built of local sandstone, apart from the tower and the mouldings. It was restored by Richard and William Cureton, stonemasons, after the fall of the tower in 1753,[46] and by Oswell and Smith of Shrewsbury in 1887. The only surviving fragments of the medieval church are the nave roof, the 13th-century nave arcade, the east and west windows of the north aisle, the easternmost window of the nave, and parts of the walls of the nave and north aisle. In 1753, when a faculty was granted to demolish it, the chancel was 44½ feet long and was said to be a 'decayed and irregular building, much larger than is necessary and convenient'.[47] It probably contained at least 2 ogee-headed single-light windows, with stained glass bearing the raven crest of the Corbets of Caus.[48] The new chancel, described in the early 19th century as 'better suited for a nobleman's stable than a place of worship',[49] was 29 feet long and had a south door, a Venetian east window, and two square windows on the north and south sides.[50] In 1887, when its east wall was rebuilt, the chancel was remodelled in the Early English style; 3 graded lancets were inserted in the east window, 2 lancets were inserted in the south wall and one on the north, where a vestry was built. In 1790 there were 4 windows in the south wall of the nave and a dormer at the west end lighting a gallery. The easternmost window—a Decorated window of 3 lights—was adjoined by a smaller pointed window without tracery, while the remaining 2 windows, inserted in 1753,[51] were round-headed. The 3 westernmost windows were remodelled in the Decorated style in 1887. The 13th-century nave arcade has circular piers and capitals with a chamfer and roll moulding. The north aisle has a much-restored east window of *c.* 1300, containing 5 lights with intersecting tracery, and a two-light square-headed window of *c.* 1400 at the west end. A 2-light window and a small square window in the north wall were remodelled in the Decorated style in 1887, when a porch in the same style was added at the north door.

The fine nave roof consists of 9 arch-braced collar-beam trusses with cusped 'vee' struts above the collar and two rows of cusped wind-baces, the upper row forming quatrefoils. The north aisle has a boarded wagon-roof of uncertain date and the chancel a trussed-rafter roof dating from 1887.

The medieval tower, which probably had a wooden spire,[52] fell in 1753, destroying the south-west corner of the nave.[53] It was rebuilt in the Classical style and was untouched at the restoration of 1887. The west door has a rusticated surround and a large Venetian window above. The second story has circular windows with keystones and quoins on each face and the bell-stage has 4 round-headed openings. The parapet is swept up at the angles.

In 1753, when the interior of the church was plastered and whitewashed, a new pulpit and reading desk were made and the nave was repewed.[54] By 1781, when the nave was ceiled, there was a gallery at the west end.[55] All the fittings were renewed in 1887, when the ceiling and gallery were removed and the walls stripped and pointed. The chancel appears to have been left largely unfurnished when rebuilt in 1753, for in 1774 the parish agreed to buy 'whatever was wanting to adorn' it and an altar-piece was erected in the same year.[56] A font with a marble bowl and cast iron stand was given to the church in 1793.[57] The present octagonal font and stone pulpit, in the Perpendicular style, were both made in 1887. The bowl of the 18th-century font lies inside the present font.

Notable monuments by John Nelson of Shrewsbury include signed wall-tablets to John Ashby (1779), John and Thomas Severne (1779), and Vincent Corbet (1789). Nelson also executed the royal arms over the north door of the aisle (1781)[58] and the sundial-stand on the south side of the church (1792).[59] There is a group of monuments to the Topp family of Whitton in the north aisle, near their family vault, notably the heraldic slab to John Topp (1736). Hatchments formerly hanging in this aisle are now in the ringing-chamber of the tower.

The church plate consisted of two chalices and a silver pyx in 1553.[60] The existing plate includes a silver chalice and paten given by Dame Joan Thynne, dated 1609, a silver chalice and paten given by Reynold Pughe, dated 1630, and a paten given by Mrs. Sarah Swetman in 1705.[61] The church had 3 bells in 1553.[62] Five of the existing 6 bells were cast by Abraham Rudhall of Gloucester in 1722 and the sixth by Mears and Stainbank in 1926, when the bells were rehung.[63] A clock first recorded in 1764[64] was still working in 1849,[65] but was replaced by the present clock in 1920.[66] The registers are complete from 1637.[67]

The chapelry of Minsterley, an ecclesiastical parish since 1910,[68] was endowed by Thomas, Viscount Weymouth, in 1692 with a rent-charge of £60 a year derived from lands in Caus township.[69] The value of the living, formerly a perpetual curacy, was augmented by a grant of £800 from Queen Anne's Bounty in 1814.[70] The living had a gross annual income of £96 in 1835.[71] The advowson followed the descent of Minsterley manor until 1930, when Lord Bath transferred it to his son

[45] Description of church based, except where otherwise stated, on S.P.L., MS. 372, vol. ii, p. 5; S.P.L., T. F. Dukes watercolours (churches), nos. 164–7; S.P.L., J. H. Smith collect. no. 212; Heref. Dioc. Regy., reg. 1883–1901, p. 29; Pevsner, *Shropshire*, 311; Cranage, vi. 536–7.
[46] S.R.O. 1361/49.
[47] Heref. Dioc. Regy., reg. 1723–54, f. 146.
[48] Bodl. MS. Blakeway 2, f. 216.
[49] W.S.L. 350/40/3.
[50] Ibid.; Heref. Dioc. Regy., reg. 1723–54, f. 146.
[51] S.R.O. 1361/49.
[52] Ex inf. Mr. H. Passant, Vennington.
[53] S.R.O. 1361/49.
[54] Ibid.; S.P.L., Deeds 12666.
[55] S.R.O. 1361/54.
[56] Ibid.

[57] *S.P.R. Heref.* xii (2), 309.
[58] S.R.O. 1361/54.
[59] Ibid.
[60] *T.S.A.S.* 2nd ser. xii. 337.
[61] Arkwright and Bourne, *Ch. Plate Ludlow Archd.* 61.
[62] *T.S.A.S.* 2nd ser. xii. 337.
[63] Walters, *Ch. Bells Salop.* 208; par. rec., form of service at rededication of bells, 1926.
[64] S.R.O. 1361/54.
[65] Par. rec., churchwardens' accts. 1807–48.
[66] Heref. Dioc. Regy., reg. 1919–26, pp. 97–98.
[67] Printed to 1812 in *S.P.R. Heref.* xii (2).
[68] Heref. Dioc. Regy., reg. 1902–19, p. 436.
[69] Ibid. 1682–1709, ff. 138–55.
[70] C. Hodgson, *Queen Anne's Bounty* (1845), 290.
[71] *Rep. Com. Eccl. Revenues*, pp. 446–7.

Henry, Viscount Weymouth.[72] The latter transferred it to the Hereford Diocesan Board of Patronage in 1934.[73]

Only 3 of 14 curates of Minsterley, 1692–1891, held the living for more than 20 years and they appear to have been non-resident after the death of Benjamin Clemson (curate 1692–1718).[74] Their duties were undertaken by a resident assistant curate, normally one of the Westbury curates until 1800 and the curate of Habberley, 1800–39.[75] Isaac Davies, assistant curate in 1790, became so notorious for his immorality that the villagers successfully petitioned the curate for his dismissal.[76] A house at the west end of the church, built in 1692, was occupied by the curate of Minsterley or his assistant curate, but remained the property of the lord of the manor.[77] The present parsonage, west of the church, was built in 1872 on a site provided by the lord of the manor.[78]

Communion was administered 4 times a year in 1793, when the local farmers were said to be 'good attendants'.[79] Two services were held on Sundays in 1851, when 94 persons attended morning service and 53 in the evening.[80] An organ was bought in 1884.[81] The patron was responsible for repairs to the church until the early 19th century, but other expenses were met by the churchwardens of Westbury, to whom Minsterley continued to pay church rates.[82]

The church of *HOLY TRINITY*, Minsterley,[83] is a fine example of a late-17th-century country church, built in a mixture of Baroque and Classical styles. It consists of a nave and chancel under one roof, with a south porch and a western bell-turret. The church was built at the expense of Thomas, Viscount Weymouth, and its architect was William Taylor of London,[84] who was engaged at this time in extensive building operations at Longleat House.[85] The site was chosen in 1684[86] and its foundations were laid early in 1688.[87] Later in the same year contracts were made with Thomas Hudson of Shrewsbury for masonry and brickwork[88] and with Joseph Meatcham of Shrewsbury for structural woodwork and the gallery and pews.[89] The church had been completed by 1689[90] and it was consecrated in 1692.[91] The church has since undergone no structural change.

It is built of red brick, with dressings of Grinshill stone. Both the north and south walls have 7 buttresses with excessive batter for most of their height and between them on the north wall there are 6 tall round-arched windows with cherub-heads on the keystones. These are matched by 5 similar windows on the south wall, the place of the sixth being taken by the south porch, leading towards

Minsterley Hall. The porch has an eared rusticated doorcase and a segmental pediment. The west window is larger than those of the nave and has forked tracery. The west front is framed by two rusticated pilasters with egg-and-dart moulding on the capitals, above which is a segmental pediment. The west door, which is flanked by 2 small oblong windows, has ears and a keystone decorated with cherubs' heads. Above is a segmental arch and a frieze decorated with skull and cross-bones, hour-glass and swags, with volutes at each end. Above the door is an arched rusticated window flanked by two pilasters decorated with garlands, and two small oblong windows on either side light the gallery. The final stage of the west front is a square, eared, and ornamented frame containing the clock-face, above which is a pediment and shingled bell-turret. The latter has short bulging columns at its corners and is capped by 4 pediments.

The church is entered through the original panelled west door and under a western gallery, which forms a small ante-chapel. The gallery, supported by two wooden pillars, is divided into 3 bays by turned pillars and has a finely turned oak balustrade. The gallery and most of the fittings, including the panelling below window-level in the nave, are contemporary with the building of the church. The pulpit, which was originally on the north side, is similar to London work of the same date but provincial in execution. Like other work in the church it has raised and fielded panels with bolection moulding. There is a frieze along the top of the box and rising above it a hexagonal sounding-board with frieze and ogee dome. The plinth on which the pulpit stands was probably made in 1870, when the church was repewed and the pulpit moved to its present position on the south side.[92]

The chancel, which was probably raised to its present height above the nave in 1865,[93] is divided from the nave by a low panelled screen surmounted by a frieze and is entered through a pair of ramped gates with supporting ornaments. The chancel was probably occupied by the family pew until 1865, when the present choir-stalls were made from old materials. The turned communion rails are elegant late-17th-century work and the communion table is contemporary with them. On either side of the communion table are tall panelled tablets with segmental pediments reaching almost the full height of the church. The remainder of the chancel is panelled below window level.

The original round scolloped stone font stands on an octagonal baluster at the west end and hanging from the gallery are six 'maidens' garlands', dated 1736–94.[94] These were originally hung over pews on either side of the nave.[95]

[72] Heref. Dioc. Regy., reg. 1926–38, p. 227.
[73] Ibid. p. 408.
[74] *S.P.R. Heref.* xii (2), intro. p. v.
[75] Ibid. 270, 294, 369; ibid. v (4), intro. p. v; S.R.O. 1118 uncat., petition for dismissal of curate, 1790; B.M. Add. MS. 21018, f. 310; Heref. Dioc. Regy., reg. 1822–42, p. 135.
[76] S.R.O. 1118 uncat., petition for dismissal of curate, 1790.
[77] Longleat MSS., unbound 4202; W.S.L. 350/40/3.
[78] Heref. Dioc. Regy., reg. 1869–83, p. 148.
[79] B.M. Add. MS. 21018, f. 310.
[80] H.O. 129/359/3/1.
[81] *Kelly's Dir. Salop.* (1891).
[82] Longleat MSS., unbound, Rack E, accts. *passim*; S.R.O. 1361/54; par. rec., churchwardens' accts. 1807–48.

[83] Description of church based, except where otherwise stated, on S.P.L., MS. 372, vol. iii, p. 59; B.M. Add. MS. 21237, f. 342; Pevsner, *Shropshire*, 201–2; Cranage, vi. 531–2. See also plate facing p. 253.
[84] See Colvin, *Biog. Dict. of Eng. Archit.* 712.
[85] Longleat MSS., Thynne Papers, lxxvii, ff. 66–68, 99.
[86] Ibid. xxvi, f. 480; ibid. xxii, f. 146.
[87] Ibid. xxiii, f. 338; Longleat MSS., unbound 4036.
[88] Longleat MSS., unbound 4285.
[89] Ibid. 4162.
[90] B.M. Add. MS. 21237, f. 342.
[91] Heref. Dioc. Regy., reg. 1682–1709, ff. 138–55.
[92] *Kelly's Dir. Salop.* (1891).
[93] Ibid.
[94] B.M. Add. MS. 21013, f. 15.
[95] Ibid.

The plate includes two fine chalices with matching patens and a flagon, all dated 1691, given by Lady Thynne in 1692.[96] There are two other chalices and patens, one given to the church c. 1936 and the other in 1951.[97] The church had a single bell in 1740; a second bell was acquired in 1843.[98] Registration took place at Westbury until 1847,[99] but the banns register begins in 1844.

A chapel at Yockleton, to which there is no reference before the early 17th century,[1] was probably built by Shrewsbury Abbey, to whom the tithes of the demesne here were granted by Roger Corbet in 1094.[2] The chapel was said to be decayed but capable of repair in 1655.[3] There was no trace of it by 1763, when a field to the north of Yockleton Brook was known as Chapel Field.[4] In 1546 the demesne tithes were granted to William Acton of Aldenham,[5] who sold them to Robert Longe in the following year.[6] They passed on Longe's death to Henry Vynar, whose son Henry sold them to his sister Ann Danyell in 1586.[7] In 1661 Margaret Danyell conveyed them to Dame Vere Gaudy of Crowes Hall (Suff.),[8] who granted them to Margaret Danyell's servant Jane Snape in 1663.[9] They were purchased in 1704 by Elizabeth Ambler of Ford, who settled them on her son-in-law Richard Pryce in 1721.[10] The latter's daughter Mrs. Trevor conveyed the tithes to John Ashby in 1772 and they have since followed the descent of Yockleton manor.[11] The tithes were leased for 23s. 4d. in 1546,[12] £4 in 1582,[13] and £8 in 1655.[14] A rent-charge of £36 was apportioned to the impropriator at commutation in 1840 in lieu of a portion of these tithes, the remainder being deemed merged in the freehold.[15]

The church of HOLY TRINITY, Yockleton, was built in the Decorated style to designs by Edward Haycock the younger in 1861.[16] The main stone used was Alberbury breccia, but Cardeston and Grinshill sandstones of different colours were also used to give a decorative effect. The church consists of a nave, a south aisle with western tower and octagonal spire, and a chancel with a vestry to the north and an organ-chamber to the south. It has a 3-light east window and clerestory windows to the south of the nave. The chancel arch is supported by marble pilasters and there is a nave arcade of 3 arches. The nave has an arch-braced collar-beam roof and the chancel a trussed-rafter roof. All

fittings are contemporary with the building of the church, apart from the oak panelling in the sanctuary, inserted in 1914.[17] The single bell was cast by John Rudhall of Gloucester in 1787[18] and the plate includes a silver chalice and paten, given in 1946.[19]

The mission church of ST. LUKE, Snailbeach, built in the early English style in 1872[20] with local grey stone and red sandstone dressings, consists of nave, western vestry, and shallow apsidal chancel. The fittings include a panelled oak pulpit, dated 1705, and there is a single bell in the western bell-turret. A chalice and paten of silver plate were given c. 1930.[21]

NONCONFORMITY. The Fox family of the Hurst were recusants in 1646 and remained Roman Catholics as long as they held lands here, but were not always resident.[22] Mary, wife of Humphrey Ridge, was presented as a recusant in 1681.[23]

There was a 'schismatic' in the parish in 1668[24] and four dissenters in 1676.[25] A Quaker and two other dissenters were presented in 1681.[26] The farm-house of Samuel Hilditch at Lower Wigmore was licensed as a dissenting meeting-house in 1774[27] and his family may have been the family of 'sectaries' who were worshipping in their own house in 1793.[28] The Westbury colliers seldom attended church at this date,[29] but there is no early evidence of nonconformity among them. Caus Castle Farm, licensed as a dissenting meeting-house in 1795,[30] was probably the predecessor of the Primitive Methodist meeting at Vennington, which had an average congregation of 30 in 1851.[31] A Primitive Methodist chapel was built at Vron Gate in 1877.[32] A Baptist meeting at Stoney Stretton, under the leadership of the manager of Westbury Colliery, had an average congregation of 30 in 1851.[33]

Nonconformity was more widespread in Minsterley township. The Baptists first met at the Bridge Inn in 1794[34] and in the following year Chapel House was licensed as a dissenting meeting-house.[35] This was used by both Baptists and Independents until 1833, when the Congregational chapel was built.[36] By wills proved in 1839, 1840, and 1845 respectively, Sarah Nealor of Minsterley, Peter Parry of the Lady Oak, and Hannah Nealor of Hogstow Mill left a total of £290 for the support of the minister of the chapel.[37] The Congregational chapel had average congregations of 100 at morning

[96] Arkwright and Bourne, Ch. Plate Ludlow Archd. 45.
[97] Ibid.
[98] Walters, Ch. Bells Salop. 204–5.
[99] S.P.R. Heref. xii (2) passim.
[1] Heref. Dioc. Regy., glebe terriers, n.d., 1604–13.
[2] Eyton, vii. 9.
[3] T.S.A.S. xlvii. 25.
[4] Map, 1763, in Lynches Farm title-deeds.
[5] L. & P. Hen. VIII, xxi (1), p. 577.
[6] Deed, 1547, in Lynches Farm title-deeds.
[7] C 142/97/89; C 142/207/107; Lynches Farm title-deeds.
[8] Lynches Farm title-deeds.
[9] Ibid.
[10] Ibid.
[11] Ibid.
[12] S.C. 6/Hen. VIII/3010 m. 50.
[13] Lease, 1582, in Lynches Farm title-deeds.
[14] T.S.A.S. xlvii. 25.
[15] Heref. Dioc. Regy., Yockleton tithe appt.
[16] Pevsner, Shropshire, 331.
[17] Inscription on panelling.
[18] Walters, Ch. Bells Salop. 210.
[19] Arkwright and Bourne, Ch. Plate Ludlow Archd. 65.

[20] Kelly's Dir. Salop. (1891).
[21] Arkwright and Bourne, Ch. Plate Ludlow Archd. 55.
[22] Cal. Cttee. for Money, iii. 1221; Heref. Dioc. Regy., visitation papers, box 45, churchwardens' presentment, 1681; Q. Sess., reg. papists' estates, 1717–87.
[23] Heref. Dioc. Regy., visitation papers, box 45, churchwardens' presentment, 1681.
[24] Ibid. box 43, churchwardens' presentment, 1668.
[25] T.S.A.S. 2nd ser. i. 88.
[26] Heref. Dioc. Regy., visitation papers, box 45, churchwardens' presentment, 1681.
[27] Q. Sess., order bk. Trin. 1774; S.R.O. 840 uncat., accts. 1777.
[28] B.M. Add. MS. 21018, f. 337.
[29] Ibid.
[30] Q. Sess, order bk. East. 1795.
[31] H.O. 129/359/3/9.
[32] Datestone.
[33] H.O. 129/359/3/10.
[34] E. Elliot, A History of Congregationalism in Shropshire (Oswestry, 1898), 137.
[35] Q. Sess., order bk. East. 1795.
[36] Elliot, op. cit. 137; Q. Sess. Orders, iii. 299; datestone.
[37] Char. Com. files.

service and 40 Sunday school children in 1851.[38] An upper floor was inserted in the chapel to accommodate a schoolroom in the later 19th century.[39] The chapel had 68 members and 50 Sunday school children in 1959.[40] Houses licensed at Snailbeach in 1803[41] and at Snailbeach and Minsterley in 1812[42] were probably used by Methodists, who appear to have had a chapel adjoining the Bridge Inn in 1837.[43] A Primitive Methodist meeting, probably at the Lady Oak, was established in 1836[44] and had an average congregation of 20 in 1851.[45] The Grove Primitive Methodist chapel, built in 1850,[46] had a congregation of 69 at evening services in 1851.[47] The chapel was rebuilt on a new site in 1926.[48] A Calvinistic Methodist chapel, erected at the Lady Oak in 1851,[49] then had a congregation of 80 at afternoon services,[50] but was taken over by the Minsterley Congregational chapel in the later 19th century.[51]

SCHOOLS. A charity school at Westbury was endowed with a rent-charge of £30 a year by the Revd. John Earle in 1726.[52] Management of the school was vested in the rectors and churchwardens by Chancery decree of 1732, which directed that the school should contain 24 children, half of whom were to be chosen by the rectors and half by the churchwardens.[53] A salary of £10 a year was reserved for the master and the remainder of the income was to be applied to apprenticeships.[54] A school and master's house were built to the north of the church in 1728[55] and enlarged in 1736.[56] In addition to the 24 foundation scholars, 30 other children attended the school at their parents' expense in 1833.[57] Competition for places was so strong in 1835 that children were required to leave after they had been taught 'reading, writing, and the four first rules of arithmetic, with the proper method of working out a bill and receipt, which will sufficiently qualify them for an apprenticeship to any common trade'.[58] By 1846 the school contained only the 24 foundation scholars[59] and in 1850 it was merged with the new Westbury National school.[60]

A Sunday school, first recorded in 1818,[61] was attended by 40 girls in 1833.[62] There were then, in addition to the charity school, two day schools in the the village, attended by 31 and 18 children respectively.[63] These had been replaced before 1846 by a single school, attended by 90 children.[64] A National school was built in 1850 on a site provided by the rector of the first portion.[65] Its income was derived from the endowment of the former charity school, voluntary contributions, and school pence in 1851, but it was thereafter in receipt of a government grant.[66] Attendance fell from 150 in 1851[67] to 130 in 1871,[68] 88 in 1893,[69] and 62 in 1906,[70] as the result of the opening of other schools in the parish.

Yockleton National school was built in 1864 on a site adjoining the new church provided by the rector of the second portion and the churchwardens in 1859.[71] School pence were levied on a graduated scale in 1871, when any deficiency in income was made up by the rector.[72] Between 40 and 50 children attended the school, 1871–1906.[73] It became a Controlled school in 1951.[74]

The Forest National school was built on the estate of J. E. Severne in 1864 at his own expense.[75] Its income was derived from school pence and subscriptions from Severne in 1874.[76] About 30 children attended the school during the later 19th century.[77] It was purchased in 1923 by the Rector of Westbury, who conveyed it to the rector and churchwardens in 1925.[78] It was closed in 1957.[79]

In 1674 a schoolmaster at Minsterley received a salary from the lord of the manor.[80] A school is recorded here in 1822[81] and in 1833 78 children attended 5 day schools in the township.[82] By will dated 1819 Joshua Williams gave an unspecified sum for the support of a school at Minsterley and left the reversion of two annuities totalling £20 for the same purpose.[83] The first of these bequests was held to be void since no sum was stated in the will.[84] The annuities became available shortly before 1845, when Minsterley National school was built on a site provided by the lord of the manor.[85] Costs of erection were met by the lord of the manor, the Snailbeach Company, and by voluntary contributions.[86] It was enlarged in 1874,[87] 1896,[88] and 1958.[89] In 1851 £40 a year was being given to the school by the Snailbeach Company, who required their miners to

[38] H.O. 129/359/3/6.
[39] Elliot, op. cit. 140.
[40] *Congreg. Year Bk.* (1959).
[41] *Q. Sess. Orders,* iii. 119.
[42] Ibid. 175.
[43] S.R.O. 83 uncat., Minsterley poor rate, 1837.
[44] H.O. 129/359/3/3.
[45] Ibid.
[46] H.O. 129/359/3/5.
[47] Ibid.
[48] Datestone.
[49] H.O. 129/359/3/4.
[50] Ibid.
[51] Elliot, op. cit. 142.
[52] Par. rec., school minutes and accts. 1728–1848.
[53] Ibid.
[54] Ibid.
[55] Ibid.
[56] S.R.O. 1011 (Smythe-Owen) uncat., conveyance of site, 1736.
[57] *Educ. Enquiry Abstract,* H.C. 62, p. 786 (1835), xlii.
[58] Par. rec., school minutes and accts. 1728–1848.
[59] Nat. Soc. *Ch. Schools Returns,* 1846–7.
[60] Ed. 7/103/249.
[61] *Digest of Returns to Cttee. on Educ. of Poor,* H.C. 224, p. 763 (1819), ix (2).
[62] *Educ. Enquiry Abstract,* p. 786.
[63] Ibid.
[64] Nat. Soc. *Ch. Schools Returns,* 1846–7.

[65] Ed. 7/103/249.
[66] Ibid.
[67] Ibid.
[68] *Returns relating to Elem. Educ.,* H.C. 201, p. 334 (1871), lv.
[69] *Return of Schs., 1893* [C. 7529], p. 512, H.C. (1894), lxv.
[70] *Voluntary Schs. Returns,* H.C. 178–XXIV, p. 26 (1906), lxxxviii.
[71] Ed. 7/103/250.
[72] Ibid.
[73] Ibid.; *Return of Schs., 1893,* p. 512; *Voluntary Schs. Returns,* p. 26.
[74] Ex inf. S.C.C. Educ. Dept.
[75] Ed. 7/103/250.
[76] Ibid.
[77] Ibid.; *Return of Schs., 1893,* p. 512.
[78] Par. rec., rector's commonplace bk.
[79] Ex inf. S.C.C. Educ. Dept.
[80] Longleat MSS., unbound 3646.
[81] Westbury par. rec., churchwardens' accts. 1806–48.
[82] *Educ. Enquiry Abstract,* p. 786.
[83] Char. Com. files.
[84] Ibid.
[85] Ibid.; Ed. 7/102/152.
[86] Inscription over school entrance.
[87] *Kelly's Dir. Salop.* (1891).
[88] Ibid. (1922).
[89] Ex inf. S.C.C. Educ. Dept.

pay 6d. a quarter towards the education of their children.[90] The Williams bequest, augmented by subscriptions totalling £1,000, had been invested in stock by 1862, when it produced an annual income of £30.[91]

A graduated scale of school pence, in use by 1859, then produced £20 a year.[92] A sum of £24 was then derived from endowments and £26 from subscriptions.[93] The school was thereafter in receipt of a government grant, which covered half its expenses in 1893.[94] Attendances fell from 64 in 1859[95] to 37 by 1871,[96] but had risen to 90 by 1885[97] and to 140 by 1906.[98] The school was purchased by the County Council in 1933.[99]

There were 3 private schools at Minsterley in 1871, attended by 73 children, most of whom were girls.[1] One of these schools was affiliated to the Church of England and another to the Congregational chapel.[2] One of them was probably the ladies' boarding school recorded here between 1851 and 1870.[3]

CHARITIES. The sum of £83 13s. 4d. given to the poor by 10 persons before 1686, together with £30 given before 1711 by 5 other persons, was used in 1710 to purchase 17 a. lands called Mrs. Owen's Moors in Worthen parish, then worth some £9 a year.[4] The balance of the purchase price was made up with £40 given at about this time by 5 persons. The income from the Moors Charity was paid to the churchwardens during the 18th century. It produced £16 in 1769 and £23 12s. in 1793.[5] By 1807 the income, then nearly £36 a year, was being paid to the overseers and was disbursed with the poor rates,[6] but the churchwardens were still making charitable payments from their own funds c. 1830. Ten poor persons in Vennington then received 10s. on Candlemas Day, 5s. was given in bread to the poor of Minsterley, and 50s. was distributed in bread among the poor of the parish as a whole on Good Friday. On the recommendation of the Charity Commissioners, the vestry resolved at this time to apply a quarter of the rent to the provision of bread on Good Friday and to distribute the remainder in money, bread, or clothing on St. Thomas's Day. Rents of £52 were received in 1862, when £5 was distributed in bread and £47 in money.[7]

In 1845 £100 was given by Richard Hilhouse during his lifetime to the rector and the master of the charity school for the use of the aged poor. This was invested in stock in 1864, when the rector and churchwardens were appointed trustees. Some time before 1862 the Revd. Thomas Parr gave sums then represented by £217 and £326 stock to the use of the poor and of the National school respectively.[8] That part of Parr's Charity which was applied to the poor produced an annual income of £6 10s. 3d. in 1862.[9]

The Moors, Hilhouse, and Parr (Poor) Charities were amalgamated under a scheme of 1907 and have since been known as the United Charities. The combined income of the United Charities, then £23 3s., was to be applied to the general benefit of the poor and an amount not exceeding £10 could be distributed annually in money. The lands forming the endowment of the Moors Charity were sold in 1921 and 1927 for £715, subsequently invested in £981 stock. The United Charities had an annual income of £39 in 1963.

A rent-charge of £30 arising from lands in Vennington was vested in trustees for the use of Westbury charity school in 1716 and its management was regulated by Chancery decree of 1732. Responsibility for payment of the rent-charge was transferred to lands in Whitton in 1785. The rent-charge was redeemed, following a scheme of 1900, and was represented by £1,060 stock in 1954. The annual income of £26 10s. was distributed to schools at Westbury, Minsterley, and Yockleton in 1961. A bequest made to the school by one Betton, which produced £5 a year, was said to be paid by the Ironmongers' Company of London in 1861, but such payments had ceased by 1863.

By a codicil to her will, proved in 1887, Miss A. C. Topp left £3,500 to the Rector of Westbury and two other trustees, the interest of which was to be given to the poor of the parish in money, coal, blankets, or clothing. The bequest had been invested in £3,107 stock by 1900 and a further £105 stock had been added before 1917. Between 30 and 40 persons received grants under this charity, 1955–7, and in 1963 it had an annual income of £76.

By will proved in 1944 Mary Stone of Whitton Hall left £1,000 to the Rector and churchwardens of Westbury to provide coal, clothing, and other comforts for the aged poor at Christmas. This charity had an annual income of £50 in 1963, of which £45 was distributed among 18 persons.

[90] Bagshaw's Dir. Salop. (1851).
[91] Char. Com. files.
[92] Ed. 7/102/152.
[93] Ibid.
[94] Return of Schs., 1893, p. 508.
[95] Ed. 7/102/152.
[96] Returns relating to Elem. Educ., p. 334.
[97] Kelly's Dir. Salop. (1885).
[98] Voluntary Schs. Returns, p. 23.
[99] Ex inf. S.C.C. Educ. Dept.
[1] Returns relating to Elem. Educ., p. 334.

[2] Ibid.
[3] Bagshaw's Dir. Salop. (1851); Kelly's Dir. Salop. (1870).
[4] Account of charities based, except where otherwise stated, on 24th Rep. Com. Char., H.C. 231, pp. 393–7 (1831), xi and Char. Com. files.
[5] S.R.O. 1361/54.
[6] Ibid. 1361/6.
[7] Digest of Endowed Char. 1862–3, H.C. 433, pp. 212–3 (1867–8), lii.
[8] Ibid.
[9] Ibid.

INDEX